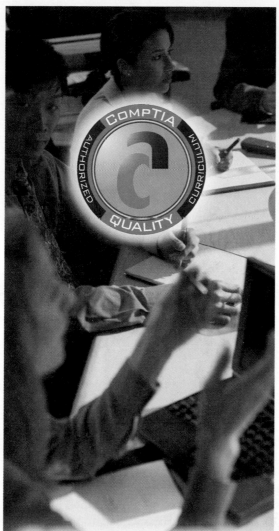

A+ CERTIFICATION CONCEPTS AND PRACTICE

Editor in Chief: Stephen Helba
Assistant Vice President and Publisher: Charles E. Stewart, Jr.
Production Editor: Alexandrina Benedicto Wolf
Design Coordinator: Diane Ernsberger
Cover art: Michael R. Hall
Production Manager: Matt Ottenweller
Marketing Manager: Ben Leonard

This book was set in Futura MD BT, Times New Roman, and Arial by Cathy J. Boulay, Marcraft International, Inc. It was printed and bound by Courier/Kendallville. The cover was printed by Phoenix Color Corp.

Written by Charles J. Brooks

Pearson Education Ltd.
Pearson Education Singapore Pte. Ltd.
Pearson Education Canada, Ltd.
Pearson Education—Japan

Pearson Education Australia Pty. Limited
Pearson Education North Asia Ltd.
Pearson Educación de Mexico, S.A. de C.V.
Pearson Education Malaysia Pte. Ltd.

10 9 8 7 6 5 4 3 2 1

ISBN 0-13-114772-2

Trademark Acknowledgments

All terms mentioned in this book that are known to be trademarks or service marks are listed below. Marcraft cannot attest to the accuracy of this information. Use of a term in this book should not be regarded as affecting the validity of any trademark or service mark.

IBM®, IBM-PC, PC/XT®, PC-AT, EGA, Micro Channel, OS/2, PS/2, and XGA are registered trademarks of International Business Machines Corporation.

CGA and VGA are trademarks of International Business Machines Corporation.

Microsoft®, MS-DOS®, MS-Windows, Windows 95, Windows 98, and Windows Me are registered trademarks of Microsoft Corporation.

Windows NT and Windows 2000 are a trademark of Microsoft Corporation.

Centronics is a registered trademark of Centronics Data Computer Corporation.

Freon and Mylar are registered trademarks of E. I. du Pont de Nemours and Co., Incorporated.

CompuServe is a registered trademark of CompuServe, Incorporated.

America Online is a registered trademark of America Online, Incorporated.

AMI is a registered trademark of American Megatrends, Incorporated.

Award Bios is a trademark of Award Software, Incorporated.

Panasonic is a registered trademark of Matsushita Communication Industrial Co., Ltd.

Intel, 386, 387, 386SX, 387SX, i486, 486, Pentium, Pentium II, Pentium III, Pentium Pro, and Pentium MMX are trademarks of Intel Corporation.

Cyrix is a registered trademark of the Cyrix Corporation.

NetWare, Novell, and UNIX are registered trademarks of Novell, Incorporated.

Microcom is a registered trademark of Microcom Systems, Incorporated.

Sound Blaster is a trademark of Creative Technology, Ltd.

Hayes is a registered trademark of Hayes Microcomputer Products, Incorporated.

Hewlett-Packard and LaserJet are registered trademarks of Hewlett-Packard Company.

PREFACE

THE DYNAMIC A+ TEST AND WHAT IT MEANS TO YOU!

Welcome to the fourth edition of the Marcraft/Prentice Hall *A+ Certification Concepts and Practices* course. This course has been designed to prepare its users to challenge the October 2003 version of the A+ Certification exams from the Computer Technology Industry Association. A+ Certification is a two-step process: You must pass a Core Hardware exam and a Microsoft Operating System Technologies exam. The Operating System Technologies exam must be passed within 90 days of the Core Hardware exam. For more information on CompTIA and the A+ exam, visit *http://www.comptia.org*.

The Marcraft/Prentice Hall *A+ Certification Concepts and Practice* training guide will provide you the knowledge and skills required to pass the A+ exam and become a certified computer service technician. A+ certification is recognized nationwide and is a hiring criterion used by companies such as AT&T, IBM, Lotus, Microsoft, and Digital. Therefore, becoming A + certified will enhance your job opportunities and career advancement potential.

CompTIA has changed its test delivery method for this and future versions of the exam. The previous version of the exam was initially delivered as fixed-length, linear tests derived from multiple test banks. The test items in the test banks were validated through rigorous psychometric review during a beta exam process. After the test items and pools had been validated, the exams were switched to an Adaptive delivery system that administered questions from the pool in reaction to how the test taker did on previous questions. The length of the exam was shortened to between 20 and 25 questions.

For the October 2003 version of the A+ exam, CompTIA has changed the format back to a fixed-length, linear format. However, the questions are no longer being validated through the beta test format. Instead, new test items were injected into the 2001 exam and administered as unscored questions prior to the release of the 2003 version. The psychometric evaluation of the questions is derived from these tests. When the new questions have been validated through this method, they will be injected into the live 2003 exam as scored questions.

From this point forward, CompTIA intends to routinely inject new questions into the exams as unscored items so that they can be validated. After validation, the questions will be returned to the question pools as scored items — thus creating a **dynamic test pool** that is continually being renewed.

DYNAMIC TEST TRACKING

To cope with this, Marcraft has established its **Dynamic Test Tracking** system that is available to everyone that purchases this product. Marcraft's Dynamic Test Tracking system is an online service that includes dynamic, interactive updates for each chapter and lab procedure in our course. These changes also include Test Tips and Curriculum Notes for any changes encountered in the A+ exams over the life of this exam version.

Thus, your courseware will never be out of date or incomplete.

MARCRAFT'S A+ CERTIFICATION COURSE

Many of you are aware that the Marcraft A+ course has been around since 1987 when it was an IC-level computer repair course. We're proud of the fact that we have been involved with the computer repair/information technology industry for so long and have had part in training so many people for dynamic professional careers.

Ten years ago an industry organization launched a vendor-neutral certification program for computer service technicians. The certification program was created in response to the industry's widespread needs for a performance standard for people working in the industry. The organization was the Computer Technology Industry Association (CompTIA) and the certification program was named the A+ certification program. CompTIA is still promoting this certification and has positioned it so that it is the logical entry point for anyone wanting to pursue any of the diverse career tracks that exist in the IT industry.

Early on, Marcraft saw the value provided by this certification and the CompTIA organization. It brought a well-honed list of real industry needs to technical training programs and removed the personal and local bias from these programs.

It also brought balance to the electronic/hardware vs. operating/software groups that have formed in the industry. That's why there are two parts to the exam — *Core Hardware* and *Operating System Technologies* — because in the past one or the other of these topics was often stressed at the expanse of the other.

While CompTIA set the standard for what to test for, Marcraft continues to deliver the best methods for preparing for both the A+ exam and the career it leads to. When preparing for the A+ exam you should always remember that it simply leads to a career — you still have to know what you're doing when you go to work.

In the last few years an educational concept known as "Blended Learning" has emerged. This concept has largely emerged since Computer-Based Training (CBT) and Web Based Training (WBT) have produced less than stellar results as stand-alone training methods. The Marcraft A+ course is designed primarily to work in an instructor-led, hands-on lab environment, with many built-in exam prep features supported by electronic presentation and assessment tools (i.e., blended learning).

1. As we have for many years, we bring you an outstanding theory and exam prep book designed to provide you with the information you need to pass the exam *and to do the job*.

2. We also include a full-featured, hands-on Lab Guide with 54 procedures that feature real computer service activities.

3. In the back of the book is a large electronic test bank of A+-related exam questions that allow the student to perform personal assessment of their exam readiness.

4. The Instructor's Guide is also full featured. It has all of the tools necessary to implement and manage a successful A+ certification/computer repair course.

Even though the course has been designed for the ILT environment, motivated individuals can use the pieces of the course for personal preparation. The theory book includes plenty of self-study pedagogy and, when combined with the ExamGear test engine and Marcraft's A+ test bank, provides a highly effective exam prep tool. The lab procedures can also be performed on standard equipment in a self-study environment.

October '03 Revisions

This version of the Marcraft *A+ Certification Concepts and Practice* theory guide is designed to cover both the Core Hardware and Operating System Technologies domains of the October 2003 A+ exam Upgrade. It has been updated to closely reflect the Domain and Objective structure published by CompTIA for the 220-301 and 220-302 certification exams posted on their website (*www.comptia.org*) in April of 2003.

New information has been added to this book to reflect the changes in the A+ Core Hardware test. The most noticeable changes occur in the area of networking technologies. There is considerable new emphasis on dial-up networking and Internet access technologies (i.e., DSL, cable modem, and wireless networking installations).

Other interesting changes include the addition of more extensive rewritable CD-ROM and DVD technologies. Also, advanced microprocessor cooling solutions, RAID structures, new SCSI technologies, fuel cell technologies, and touch screen technology have been added to the hardware exam.

Key Features

The pedagogical features of this book were carefully developed to provide readers with key content information, as well as review and testing opportunities. A complete A+ objectives map and Test Tip information boxes are included to help you key in on A+-specific materials. The locations of A+-specific materials are identified with Test Tip markers in the margin that help students focus on key content that they will be expected to know for the A+ certification exam. *Appendix A* provides a comprehensive listing of the A+ objectives.

Over 50 diagrams and screen dumps are included in each chapter to provide constant visual reinforcement of the concepts being discussed. Each chapter begins with a list of learning objectives that establishes a foundation and systematic preview of the chapter. Each chapter concludes with a chapter summary and a key-points review of its material.

Key terms are presented in bold type throughout the text. A comprehensive glossary of terms appears at the end of the text to provide quick, easy access to key term definitions that appear in each chapter. The key terms work in conjunction with the extensive Glossary at the end of the book. Key thoughts in the chapter are presented in special boxes to call special attention to them.

In this edition, we have added a new feature called Challenges to each chapter to challenge students to apply what they are learning to scenario-based situations that require more than a single word or sentence to evaluate. This feature has been very successful in our PassIT line of test prep products for IT professionals.

An abundance of test materials is available with this course. Each chapter contains a 10-question multiple-choice section and a 15-question section of open-ended review questions. Additional A+ test material can be found on the interactive CD-ROM that comes with the book. The 10 multiple-choice questions test knowledge of the basic concepts presented in the chapter, while the 15 open-ended review questions are designed to test critical thinking.

SUPPORT MATERIALS

In addition to the wealth of material in the theory manual, the Marcraft A+ course provides significant amounts of support materials. These include the following:

Interactive CD-ROM Test Engine

The *A+ Certification Concepts and Practice* book is accompanied by an additional comprehensive A+ test bank that is on a CD-ROM sealed on the back cover of the book. This CD testing material was developed to simulate the A+ Certification Exam testing process and materials and to allow students to complete practice tests, determine their weak points, and study more strategically.

The ExamGear test engine included on the accompanying CD provides three styles of testing:

- Study Mode – permits you to review questions and check the answers and references from within the test.

- Test Mode – simulates the actual fixed-length A+ exams.

- Adaptive Mode – permits you to take practice tests in the same adaptive mode that CompTIA eventually converts all of its exams into.

During the question review, the correct answer is presented on the screen along with the reference heading where the material can be found in the text. A single mouse click provides you with explanations of the correct answers.

The Lab Guide

Applying the concepts of the chapter to hands-on exercises is crucial to preparing for a successful career as a computer technician. The Lab Guide provides an excellent hands-on component to emphasize the theoretical materials. There are three types of Procedures included in the labs. First, introductory labs act as introductions to hardware and different types of software. A number of troubleshooting labs allow students to be tested under real problem situations. The instructor can insert software faults, simple hardware faults, or complex hardware faults into the system for the student to track down, isolate, and repair. A number of hardware/software installation labs are included as well. This allows students to install and set up hard drives, CD-ROM drives, modems, network cards, and more.

The Lab Procedures in the Marcraft Lab Guide do require certain hardware and software components to perform—it is after all a hands-on lab guide. However, these procedures are written around industry standard, commercially available hardware and software components. Therefore, they can be performed on standard PC compatible systems, using standard Microsoft operating systems and commercially available diagnostic and anti-virus software.

Marcraft does provide lab kits and trainers that make it convenient to deliver these labs. However, none of these products are required to be purchased from Marcraft to perform the procedures.

Teacher Support

An instructor's guide accompanies the course. Answers for all of the end-of-chapter quiz questions are included along with a reference point in the chapter where a particular item is covered. Sample schedules are included as guidelines for possible course implementations. Answers to all lab review questions and fill-in-the-blank steps are provided so that there is an indication of what the expected outcomes should be. Finally, descriptions of the numerous Marcraft software faults, hardware faults, and extended hardware faults are presented, along with suggested faults for particular labs as appropriate.

An electronic copy of the textbook is included on the CD-ROM disk at the back of the lab book.

Reference Shelf

In this edition of the *A+ Certification Concepts and Practice* book we have moved most of the fundamental "How Things Work" information to the CD-ROM that accompanies the theory manual. You will find a table of contents for the individual subjects on the CD under the Reference Shelf.

The reason for moving this information to the CD is that CompTIA does not require this type of knowledge for their certification. However, this information is important for students to have a full knowledge of how the elements of the computer do what they do. It provides a base that they can draw on as technology changes throughout their careers. We suggest that you incorporate information from these topics into your presentations as time allows.

The Reference Shelf contains additional information concerning:

1. How Microprocessors Work
2. How DMA Works
3. How Interrupts Work
4. Initiating I/O Transfers
5. Bits, Bytes, and Computer Words
6. Computer Buses
7. How a Parallel Printer Port Works
8. How a Serial Port Works
9. How Keyboards Work
10. How Magnetic Disks Work
11. How Video Displays Work
12. How Printers Work
13. How Modems Work
14. How Multimedia Works
15. How MACs Work
16. The Chips
17. Buses and Support Devices
18. The 8088 Microprocessor
19. Coprocessors
20. Soldering Techniques
21. The Parallel Port
22. Customer Satisfaction
23. Extended Glossary

As you can see from the Reference Shelf topics, we have included sections on the Apple Macintosh, multimedia, and customer satisfaction that may be of particular interest.

ORGANIZATION

In general, it is not necessary to move through this text in the same order that it is presented. Also, it is not necessary to teach any specific portion of the material to its extreme. Instead, the material can be adjusted to fit the length of your course. As a matter of fact, practicing IT professionals can use the material in the CD test banks to identify the areas where they need to brush up, and then use the text book to study that material directly.

Chapter 1 – *Basic PC Hardware* introduces microcomputer architecture and shows how those basic microcomputer structures come together to form an IBM PC-compatible personal computer system. The chapter charts the evolution of the PC from the days when small keyboard units were connected to a television set up to the powerful PCs available today.

Chapter 2 – *Advanced System Boards* deals with the system boards that form the heart of every microcomputer system. Micro-processors, microprocessor-support systems, and expansion buses are all covered in this chapter. The support systems include timing, DMA, interrupt, common memory structures, and different I/O bus schemes used to connect optional I/O devices to the system. The focus of the system board information in this chapter has shifted away from the ISA standards traditionally employed throughout the industry to the newer ATX standards now being used by most of the industry.

In addition, the chapter covers microprocessors from the Pentium, through the Pentium MMX, Pentium Pro, Pentium II, Pentium III, and Pentium 4. The operating characteristics of all these Intel microprocessors are presented in this chapter. Most of the new material in this chapter focuses on the Intel Pentium III models and the Cyrix and AMD Pentium-clone processors.

Chapter 2 also brings new system board–related technologies to the book. These include advanced microprocessors, newer cooling systems, additional expansion buses, and new CMOS setup options (i.e., Microprocessor Health and Security).

Chapter 3 – *Standard I/O Systems* begins by examining basic input/output structures used in PCs. The computer's fundamental I/O devices are covered, including the most common ports found in the PC compatible world—the parallel and serial I/O ports. However, there are a host of newer I/O systems being used in PCs these days. A good portion of the new information in this chapter is based on newer I/O bus designs including USB, Firewire, IrDA, and wireless communication specifications.

Chapter 3 has been upgraded to provide additional information concerning the latest versions of the newer I/O port specifications and I/O devices. These include touch pads, digital cameras, and PDAs.

The chapter concludes by investigating the operation of common input and output devices. In particular, keyboards, CRT monitors, mice, trackballs, joysticks, touch-sensitive screens, and scanners are covered.

Mass storage systems commonly used in microcomputers are presented in **Chapter 4** – *Mass Storage Systems*. These include floppy drives, hard drives, RAID systems, tape drives, and CD-ROM drives. System operation, installation, and configuration are presented for all of the mass storage systems mentioned.

The mass storage chapter has been expanded to include current IDE and SCSI interface specification, installation techniques and information, and advanced configuration information. It also includes additional information concerning rewritable CD and DVD drives.

Chapter 5 focuses on one of the hottest area of microcomputer growth: *Data Communications*. This chapter covers both local and wide area networks, along with the equipment and software required to operate them. The LAN material has been modified and expanded to include newer Ethernet specifications, cabling information, and newer networking technologies. Dial-up networking and modems are discussed here along with their application to the Internet.

The data communications chapter has been enhanced with expanded DSL, cable modem, wireless, and satellite networking information.

Printers are covered in **Chapter 6** from the workhorse dot-matrix printer to color ink-jet and high-speed laser printers. Theory, operation, and maintenance information is presented for all three types of printers. Specific troubleshooting information is also provided for each printer type in this chapter.

The new printers chapter includes up-to-date information on the newest interfaces commonly used with printers. It also includes three additional printer types referenced in the 2003 A+ Objectives—solid ink, thermal, and dye sublimation. The chapter also introduces material covering all of the advanced options being added to office printers (i.e., hard drives, memory, scanner, feeders, staplers, and collators).

In previous versions of the A+ exam, CompTIA specified a complete domain for *Portable Computer Systems*. **Chapter 7** focuses on the unique structures associated with this type of computer and how they are installed, configured, and maintained. It also describes the types of problems that are inherent with smaller computer systems.

The portable chapter has been expanded to include more information about installing, configuring, and repairing additional components associated with notebook computers. Information about fuel cells for portable computers has also been added.

The software side of the microcomputer system is covered in Chapters 8, 9, and 10. **Chapter 8** – *Operating System Fundamentals* provides a detailed examination of basic operating systems. In particular, it investigates the role of the system's BIOS and the Disk Operating System (DOS) in the operation of the system. The first half of the chapter covers topics associated with the ROM BIOS, including system bootup information, CMOS Setup routines, and Power On Self Test (POST) information.

The second half of the chapter is dedicated to command-line operations and uses MS-DOS commands to demonstrate this type of operation. While MS-DOS is no longer covered as an operating system in the A+ exam, this is no reason to believe that it has gone away. For the consumer, DOS has largely passed away. However, the technician must be able to use command-line utilities and commands to access and restore defective systems. Topics covered here include DOS disk structures, and drive-level, directory-level, and file-level command-line operations.

Chapter 9 – *Windows 9x* is an in-depth study of the Windows 9x operating systems. This chapter looks at installation, startup, structure, and operation of both Windows 95 and Windows 98 operating systems. Materials that apply to both versions are referred to as Windows 9x, whereas items specific to one version or the other are referred to as Windows 95 or Windows 98. In addition to installation, configuration, and operation information, the chapter also includes extensive information about handling application programs, printing, and wide and local area networking with Windows 9x.

Chapter 10 – *Windows NT/2000* is an in-depth study of the Windows NT 4.0 and Windows 2000 professional operating systems. This chapter follows the same paths for the Windows NT operating systems that Chapter 9 did for the Windows 9x systems. This is only natural since CompTIA lumped all of these operating systems into the same four domains: OS Fundamentals; Installation, Configuration, and Upgrading; Diagnosing and Troubleshooting; and Networking. Information that applies to both versions is referred to as Windows NT/2000, whereas items specific to one version or the other are referred to as Windows NT or Windows 2000. As with the Windows 9x chapter, this chapter also includes extensive information about handling application programs, printing, and wide and local area networking with Windows NT/2000.

One of the major additions to the A+ Operating System Technologies domain is the Windows XP Professional operating system. The Windows NT/2000 chapter has been upgraded to illustrate all of the A+-related facets of this new operating system, including its new user interfaces, tools and their locations, and administrative capabilities.

Chapter 11 – *Basic System Troubleshooting* addresses the fundamentals of troubleshooting microprocessor-based equipment. The chapter covers the use of diagnostic software to isolate system hardware problems. It also describes the Field-Replaceable Unit (FRU) method of hardware troubleshooting required for most field and bench repair work. The second half of the chapter deals with symptoms and troubleshooting procedures associated with the various hardware components typically associated with PCs. It also provides the first half of a comprehensive computer diagnosing and troubleshooting methodology.

Chapter 12 – *Operating System Troubleshooting* shifts the focus of troubleshooting to the software side of the system. It focuses on the three major categories of operating system-related problems: setup problems, startup problems, and operational problems. The chapter includes troubleshooting tools available with the different operating system versions and methods of using them. Important HDD support utilities, such as ScanDisk, backup, defragmentation, and anti-virus protection are highlighted here. This chapter also furnishes the second half of the complete computer troubleshooting methodology. Troubleshooting of application, printer, and networking problems related to operating systems is also covered here.

Windows XP material has also been added to the operating system troubleshooting chapter. Key additions in this area include new material on Driver Rollback functions, Restore points, and the System Restore feature.

Chapter 13 discusses important *Preventive Maintenance* procedures and safety considerations. The first section of the chapter investigates topics including cleaning, electrostatic discharges, power line problems, and Universal Power Supplies (UPS) along with other power line conditioning devices.

The chapter features preventive maintenance procedures for various system components. Suggested PM schedules are also presented. This chapter also covers safety issues commonly associated with computer systems. Although not an intrinsically unsafe environment, some areas of a computer system can be harmful if approached unawares.

Test Taking Tips

The A+ exam is an objective-based timed test. It covers the objectives listed in Appendix A of this book in a multiple-choice format. There are two general methods of preparing for the test. If you are an experienced technician using this material to obtain certification, use the testing features at the end of each chapter and on the accompanying CD to test each area of knowledge. Track your weak areas and spend the most time concentrating on them.

If you are a newcomer to the subject of serious computer repair, plan a systematic study of the materials, reserving the testing functions until each chapter has been completed.

In either case, after you complete the study materials, use the various testing functions available on the CD to practice taking the test. Use the Study and Exam modes to test yourself by chapter, or on a mixture of questions from all areas of the text. Practice until you are very certain that you are ready. The CD will provide you with explanations of questions and answers for your review.

- Answer the questions you know first. You can always go back later and work on questions you don't know.

- Don't leave any questions unanswered. They will be counted as incorrect.

- There are no trick questions. The correct answer is in there somewhere.

- Be aware of A+ questions that have more than one correct answer. Questions that have multiple correct answers can be identified by the special formatting applied to the letters of their possible answers. They are enclosed in a square box. When you encounter these questions, make sure to mark every answer that applies.

- Get plenty of hands-on practice before the test, using the time limit set for the test.

- Make certain to prepare for each test category listed above. The key is not to memorize, but to understand the topics.

- Take your watch. The A+ exam is a timed test. You will need to keep an eye on the time to make sure that you are getting to the items that you are most sure of.

- Get plenty of rest before taking the test.

ACKNOWLEDGMENTS

I would like to mention some of the people and groups who have been responsible for the success of this book. First I would like to thank Greg Michael, formerly of Howard W. Sams, for getting me involved in writing about microcomputer systems back in the early days of the IBM PC.

As always, I want to thank the staff here at Marcraft for making it easy to turn out a good product. Thanks to Paul Haven, Wanda Dawson, Gregory Ter-Oganov, Jason Ho, and Dan Smith from the Technical Services area for trying things out for me and giving me the latest updates for today's bus speeds and microprocessor ratings, as well as what's hot and not in the Windows OS world. Also, thanks to Mike Hall, Cathy Boulay, Yu-Wen Ho, Tony Tonda, and Stuart Palmer from the Product Development department for their excellent work in getting the text and lab books ready to go and looking good. Without these folks, there would be no timely delivery of the A+ product.

I also want to thank our new associates at Prentice Hall for all they bring to our projects: Charles Stewart, Alex Wolf, Karrie Converse-Jones, Bret Workman, and Matt Ottenweller for their excellent work in getting this book to you.

In addition, I would like to say thanks to Brian Alley of Boston University for his excellent guidance in bringing yet another version of this book up to speed.

As always, I want to thank my wife Robbie for all of her understanding, support, and help with these projects, as well as Robert, Jamaica, Michael, and now Joshua.

TABLE OF CONTENTS

CHAPTER 1 - BASIC PC HARDWARE

CHAPTER 2 - ADVANCED SYSTEM BOARDS

CHAPTER 3 - STANDARD I/O SYSTEMS

CHAPTER 4 - MASS STORAGE SYSTEMS

CHAPTER 5 - DATA COMMUNICATIONS

CHAPTER 6 - PRINTERS

CHAPTER 7 - PORTABLE SYSTEMS

CHAPTER 8 - OPERATING SYSTEM FUNDAMENTALS

CHAPTER 9 - WINDOWS 9X

CHAPTER 10 - WINDOWS NT/2000/XP

CHAPTER 11 - BASIC SYSTEM TROUBLESHOOTING

CHAPTER 12 - OPERATING SYSTEM TROUBLESHOOTING

CHAPTER 13 - PREVENTIVE MAINTENANCE

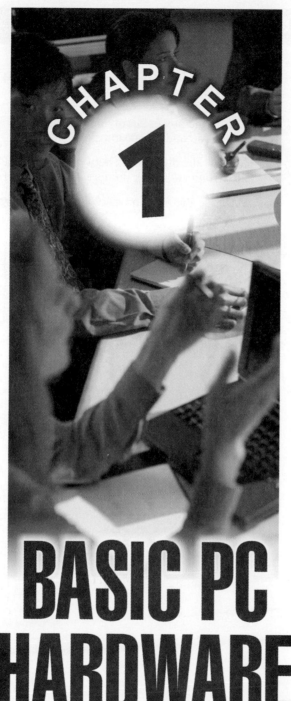

CHAPTER
1

BASIC PC HARDWARE

OBJECTIVES

OBJECTIVES

Upon completion of this chapter and its related lab procedures, you should be able to perform these tasks:

1. Locate the power supply unit, system board, system speaker, disk drive unit, and expansion slots.

2. Discuss the differences between different PC case styles and explain the strong and weak points associated with each.

3. Describe the function of typical PC power supplies.

4. Locate the system's RAM banks and use documentation to determine the amount of RAM installed.

5. Identify different types of RAM modules (DIP, SIP, SIMM, DIMM).

6. Identify common microprocessor IC package types.

7. Identify a Video Graphics Array (VGA) adapter card.

8. Recognize different disk drive types associated with PCs.

9. Describe typical external connections associated with purchase.

10. Define the functions of the computer's input/output units.

11. Explain the three classes of software used with computer systems.

12. Explain the function of the system ROM BIOS.

13. Describe the function and purpose of a disk operating system.

14. Describe the value of a graphical user interface.

15. Describe popular software application programs.

BASIC PC HARDWARE

INTRODUCTION

Every computer system consists of two parts: hardware devices that perform physical operations and software routines and programs that oversee and guide the actions of the hardware. Hardware consists of those parts of the computer that you can touch. Software is the logical, intangible parts of the computer. For this reason, the CompTIA (Computer Technology Industry Association) has established two distinct parts for their A+ Certification examination. The first part is the Core Hardware portion of the Certification. This makes sense because the hardware platform is the core of any computer system.

The first objective in the first domain of the A+ exam states that the technician should be able to identify basic terms, concepts, and functions of computer system modules, including how each module should work during normal operation. To this end, this first chapter is designed to introduce you to personal computer fundamentals.

As with any group or industry, the personal computer world has produced a peculiar vocabulary to describe its products and their functions. As this A+ objective indicates, the computer technician must be able to use that vocabulary to identify personal computer products and to understand how they work and what they do.

This chapter provides an introduction to common personal computer components, which includes a brief discussion of their theories of operation and the basic functions that each component supplies. This information also includes the standards that the industry has developed for these components.

The first portion of the chapter presents a short history of the personal computer. The remainder of the chapter deals with the hardware structures that make up typical PC-compatible computer systems. This serves as a foundation for presenting more advanced theory and troubleshooting materials in the following chapters.

PERSONAL COMPUTER EVOLUTION

In the early years of microcomputer history, the market was dominated by a group of small companies that produced computers intended mainly for playing video games. Serious computer applications were a secondary concern. Companies such as Commodore, Timex/Sinclair, Atari, and Tandy produced eight-bit machines for the emerging industry based on microprocessors from Intel, Motorola, Zilog, and Commodore.

In 1977 Apple Computers produced the Apple I. This was followed by a series of 8-bit microcomputers: the Apple II, Apple IIc, and Apple IIe. These units were single-board computers with built-in keyboards and a discrete monitor. With the IIe unit, Apple installed seven expansion connectors on its main board. They were included to allow the addition of adapter cards. Apple also produced a set of adapter cards that could be used with the IIe to provide additional capabilities. These units were very advanced for their time. In 1981, however, Apple introduced their powerful 16-bit **Macintosh (Mac)** system to the market. The features offered by the Mac represented a major shift in computing power. Departing from command-line operations, it offered a graphical operating environment. Using a small input device called a mouse, visual objects were selected from the display monitor to guide the operation of the system. This operating method found an eager audience of non-technical and public school system users.

Late in 1981, IBM entered the microcomputer market with the unveiling of their now famous IBM Personal Computer (PC). At the time of its introduction, the IBM PC was a drastic departure from the status quo of the microcomputer world. The original Apple Mac and IBM PC are depicted in Figure 1-1.

Macintosh (Mac)

APPLE MAC

IBM PC

Figure 1-1: Apple Mac and IBM PC

The IBM PC employed an Intel 8088 16/8-bit microprocessor (it processes data 16 bits at a time internally, but moves it around in 8-bit packages). Relatively speaking, the IBM PC was fast, powerful, flexible, and priced within the range of most individuals. The general public soon became aware of the tremendous possibilities of the personal computer, and the microcomputer quickly advanced from a simple game machine to an office tool with a seemingly endless range of advanced personal and business applications.

Extended Technology (XT)

Advanced Technology PC (PC-AT)

pseudo standards

Industry Standard Architecture (ISA)

In 1983, IBM added a small hard disk drive to the PC, and introduced its **Extended Technology (XT)** version. The success continued when, in 1984, IBM introduced the **Advanced Technology PC (PC-AT)**. The AT used a true 16-bit microprocessor (it processed 16 bits at a time internally and had a 16-bit external data bus) from Intel, called the 80286. The wider bus increased the speed of the computer's operation, because the 80286 was then able to transfer and process twice as much data as the 8088 could. The IBM PC-AT is depicted in Figure 1-2.

In addition to a more powerful microprocessor, the AT featured a higher capacity hard drive, a half-height floppy drive, and a 101-key keyboard.

The tremendous popularity of the original IBM PC-XT and AT systems created a set of **pseudo standards** for hardware and software compatibility. The AT architecture was so popular that it became known as the **Industry Standard Architecture (ISA)**. Even today, the majority of microcomputers are both hardware- and software-compatible with the original AT design.

Figure 1-2: IBM PC-AT

PC Compatibles

The openness of the PC architecture coupled with an abundance of PC-compatible hardware and software enticed several companies to develop PC-like computers of their own. These computers were referred to as **PC look-alikes**, **PC clones**, or more commonly as **PC-compatibles**. The cloning process was made possible by two events. First, the government-backed **Electronic Research and Service Organization (ERSO)** in Taiwan produced a non-copyright infringing version of the XT BIOS firmware that controlled the operation of the system. Second, IBM did not secure exclusive rights to the Microsoft Disk Operating System, which controlled the interaction between the system's hardware and application software.

Since the advent of PC-compatibles, the PC market has been fueled by the introduction of increasingly powerful microprocessors. Intel and other microprocessor manufacturers have introduced several improved microprocessors, such as the 80386, 80486, Pentium, Pentium Pro, Pentium MMX, Pentium II, Pentium III, and Pentium 4. All of these processors maintain backward compatibility with the original 8088 design. Intel resorted to using the Pentium name when clone microprocessor manufacturers used the 80x86 nomenclature. Intel dropped the numbering system and adopted the name strategy so that they could copyright it.

Many of the decisions made in designing the original PC-AT still influence the PC-compatible computer today. The AT architecture established industry standards for its:

- expansion bus

- system addressing

- peripheral addressing

- system resource allocations

Most microcomputers today are based on the AT design but incorporate newer microprocessors, expansion buses, and memory management structures. For this reason, every computer technician should possess a thorough understanding of the architecture developed in these systems. As you read through this book, you may notice that the majority of the discussion in it deals with PC-compatible designs. This is because that they occupy such a large portion of the personal computer market.

| PC look-alikes |
| PC clones |
| PC-compatibles |
| Electronic Research and Service Organization (ERSO) |

THE PC SYSTEM

A typical personal computer (PC) system, shown in Figure 1-3, is modular by design. It is called a system because it includes all of the components required to have a functional computer:

- **Input devices** — keyboard and mouse

- **Computer** — **system unit**

- **Output devices** — CRT monitor and a character printer

| Input devices |
| Computer |
| system unit |
| Output devices |

SPEAKER   MONITOR   SYSTEM UNIT   SPEAKER

PRINTER

MOUSE

KEYBOARD

Figure 1-3:
Typical Personal
Computer System

> The system unit is the main portion of the microcomputer system and is the basis of
> any PC system arrangement.

The components surrounding it vary from system to system, depending on what particular
functions the system is supposed to serve.

System Unit Cases

The system unit case is typically a metal chassis and removable cover that includes a plastic
front panel for aesthetic purposes. This box typically contains the basic parts of the computer
system. PCs have been packaged in a number of different case designs. These designs fall
into three basic styles: desktops, towers, and portables. Each design offers characteristics
that adapt the system for different environments. These characteristics for case design include mounting methods for the printed circuit boards, ventilation characteristics, total drive
capacity, footprint (the amount of desk space they take up), and portability.

Desktops

Some of the most familiar PC case styles are the desktop designs illustrated in Figure 1-4.
These units are designed to sit horizontally on a desk top (hence the name). The original
IBM-PC, XT, and AT designs use this case style. The PC and XT case styles measured 21"w
by 17"d by 5-1/2"h, whereas the AT case grew to 23"w by 17"d by 5-1/2"h.

| baby AT case |

A narrower desktop style, referred to as a **baby AT case**, was developed to take up less desk
space than the XT and AT. The reduced footprint was accomplished by using a half-height
power supply unit and limiting the number of disk drives. The disk drive cage did not reach
down to the floor of the system unit, allowing the system board to slide under the power supply and disk drive cage. The widths of baby AT cases varied from manufacturer to
manufacturer.

AT CASE STYLE

BABY AT CASE STYLE

PC AND XT CASE STYLE

LOW-PROFILE CASE STYLE

**Figure 1-4:
Desktop Case Designs**

A special variety of desktop cases, referred to as **low-profile desktops,** reduce the vertical height of the unit. A short bus-extender card, called a **back plane,** mounts in an expansion slot and allows adapter cards to be mounted in the unit horizontally. The case is thus enabled to be shorter. The horizontal mounting of the I/O cards in a low-profile case tends to create heat build-up problems. The heat rising from the system board flows around the I/O cards, adding to the heat they are generating. A standard back plane card is depicted in Figure 1-5. Low-profile power supplies and disk drives are also required to achieve the reduced height.

low-profile desktops

back plane

System **indicator lights** and **control buttons** are built into the front panel. Typical indicator lights include a power light, a hard drive activity light, and a turbo speed indicator light. Control buttons include a power switch, a turbo speed selection switch, and a *RESET* button. Older system units used an on/off flip switch that extended from the power supply at the right-rear edge of the case. Newer units place the on/off switch on the machine's front panel and use an internal

indicator lights

control buttons

Figure 1-5: Back Plane Card

power cable between the switch and the power supply unit. The power supply's external connections are made in the rear of the unit. The system's installed adapter cards are also accessed through the system's back panel. Figure 1-6 shows typical front panel controls and indicators.

FDD EJECT
FDD LED   BUTTON

POWER   HDD   RESET   POWER   DRIVE   CD-ROM   CD-ROM EJECT
LED   LED   BUTTON   BUTTON BAYS   LED   BUTTON

**Figure 1-6:
Typical Front Panel
Controls and Indicators**

The cover of the system unit slides (or lifts) off the base, as shown in Figure 1-7. The top of some designs slides forward after screws securing it to the back panel have been removed. In this style of case, the plastic front panel usually slides off with the metal top. In other designs, the top swings up from the rear and slides backwards to clear the case. The tops of these units are secured to the base by screws in the rear of the unit and screws or clips along the sides of the case. The plastic front panel is attached directly to the case.

Figure 1-7: Removing Cases from Desktop Units

The fit between the top and the case is very important in achieving FCC certification. A tight fit and electrical conductivity between the case and top are necessary to prevent unwanted radio interference from escaping the interior of the case. The inside face or the plastic front panel is coated with a conductive paint to limit the radio magnetic interference escaping from the case.

IC cooler fans

A fan in the power supply unit pulls in air through slots in the front of the case. The air flows over the system unit's internal components, into the power supply unit, and is exhausted through the back of the case. Heat build-up inside the system unit increases as more internal options are added to the system. To compensate for additional heat, it may be necessary to add additional fans to the case. Special **IC cooler fans** are often added to advanced microprocessors. These units are designed so that they can be attached directly to the IC and plug into one of the power supply's connectors.

Towers

Tower cases

Tower cases are designed to set vertically on the floor beneath a desk. Some AT users resorted to standing the computers on their sides under the desk to provide more usable workspace on the desktop. This prompted computer makers to develop cases that would naturally fit under the desk. IBM validated the tower design when they introduced their PS/2 models 60 and 80. Different tower case styles are depicted in Figure 1-8.

MINI TOWER   INVERTED DESKTOP   FULL TOWER   MID TOWER

Figure 1-8:
Tower Case Designs

Mini towers and mid towers are short towers designed to take up less vertical space. Internally, their design resembles a vertical desktop unit. They are considerably less expensive than the larger towers due to the reduced materials needed to produce them. Unlike their taller relatives, mini towers do not provide abundant space for internal add-ons or disk drives. However, they do possess the shortcomings of the full towers. Mini towers exist more as a function of marketing than as an application solution.

Many easy-access schemes have been developed to allow quick or convenient access to the inside of the system unit. Some towers use removable trays that the system board and I/O cards are plugged into before being slid into the unit. This allows all of the boards to be assembled outside the system unit. Other tower cases use hinged doors on the side of the case, allowing the system and I/O boards to swing away from the chassis.

The ventilation characteristics of most tower units tend to be poor. The reason is that the I/O cards are mounted horizontally. This permits the heat produced by lower boards to rise past the upper boards, adding to the cooling problem. To compensate for this deficiency, most tower units include a secondary case fan to help increase the airflow and dissipate the heat.

Portables

To free the computer user from the desk, an array of **portable PCs** have been developed. These units package the system unit, input units, and output unit into a single, light-weight package that can be carried by the user.

While early attempts at developing a portable PC produced smaller computers that could be carried by the user, they tended to be heavy and inconvenient to carry, and had short operating times between battery recharges. However, continued advancements in IC and peripheral component designs have provided truly portable, PC-compatible computers. A typical **notebook computer**, such as the one depicted in Figure 1-9, features a video display that is larger than those typically associated with PC-AT machines, hard drives that range into the tens of gigabytes, and CD-ROM/DVD drives. The capabilities of modern portable computers make them the equivalent of desktop or tower units in most respects.

Although portable systems operate like desktop and tower PCs, they have characteristics that are considerably different than the other PC designs. Therefore, they are covered in detail in Chapter 7 — *Portable Systems*.

**Figure 1-9:
A Typical Portable Computer**

The System Unit

The components inside the system unit can be divided into four distinct subunits: a switching power supply, the disk drives, the system board, and the adapter cards, as illustrated in Figure 1-10.

TEST TIP

Know the names of all the components of a typical PC system and be able to identify them by sight.

**Figure 1-10:
Components
Inside the
System Unit**

A typical desktop/tower system unit contains a single power supply unit that converts commercial power into the various levels required by the different devices in the system. The number and types of disk drives in the system vary according to the application the system is designed for. However, a single floppy-disk drive unit, a single hard-disk drive unit, and a single CD-ROM drive are typically installed to handle the system's mass storage requirements.

> The **system board** is the center of the system. It contains the portions of the system that define its computing power and speed. System boards are also referred to as **motherboards**, or **planar boards**. Any number of plug-in adapter cards may be installed to handle a wide array of PC peripheral equipment.

Typical adapter cards installed in a system include a **video adapter card** and some sort of **Input/Output (I/O) adapter card**. Peripheral devices such as printers and mice normally connect to the system through the rear of the system unit. These cards plug into **expansion slot connectors** on the back of the system board. In most desktop cases the keyboard also plugs into the back panel.

| system board |
| motherboards |
| planar boards |
| video adapter card |
| Input/Output (I/O) adapter card |
| expansion slot connectors |

In desktop cases, the system board is located in the floor of the unit, toward the left-rear corner. The power supply is located in the right-rear corner. Raised reinforcement rails in the floor of the system unit contain threaded holes and slip-in slots that the system board is anchored to. Small plastic feet are inserted into the system board and are set down in the slots. The system board is secured by sliding its feet into the narrow portion of the slot.

┌─ **TEST TIP** ─────────────┐
│ Memorize the different names the industry │
│ uses for system boards. │
└────────────────────────────┘

One or more brass standoffs are inserted into the threaded holes before installing the system board. After the system board has been anchored in place, a small machine screw is inserted through the system board opening and into the brass standoff. This arrangement provides electrical grounding between the system board and the case and helps to reduce **Electromagnetic Field Interference (EFI)** emitted from the board.

| Electromagnetic Field Interference (EFI) |

Every electrical conductor radiates a field of electromagnetic energy when an electrical current passes through it. Computer systems are made of hundreds of conductors. The intensity of these fields increases as the current is turned on and off.

Modern computers turn millions of digital switches in their ICs on and off each second, resulting in a substantial amount of energy radiating from the computer. The levels generated by the components of a typical system can easily surpass maximum-allowable radiation levels set by the **Federal Communications Commission (FCC)**. The fields generated can potentially interfere with reception of radio, television, and other communications signals under the FCC's jurisdiction. Therefore, computer manufacturers design grounding systems and case structures to limit the amount of EFI that can escape from the case. Basically, the FCC has established two certification levels for microcomputer systems:

| Federal Communications Commission (FCC) |

- Class A, for computers in business environments

- Class B, a stricter level directed at general consumers for the home environment

To be legal, FCC compliance stickers are required on computer units, along with certain information in their documentation. Looking inside a desktop system unit, as depicted in Figure 1-11, the arrangement of its major components can be seen.

Figure 1-11: Inside a Desktop Unit

full-height drive

half-height drives

The disk drive units are located in bays at the right-front corner of the system. XT-style units provided two side-by-side bays, each capable of handling a **full-height drive** (3.38" by 5.87" by 8") 5-1/4" unit. Newer desktops are designed to hold between three and five half-height 5-1/4" drives. Normally, a fixed drive bay capable of holding two or three **half-height drives** is built into the unit. Additional 5-1/4" or 3-1/2" removable drive bays may also be included. The removable bays are secured to the system unit with machine screws and provide easier access to the system board when removed.

Some cases require that the drive be attached to the case using machine screws, whereas AT-type cases have grooves in the drive bays that use slide-in mounting rails that are attached to the drive. The drives are held in place by the front panel of the slide-on case. The smaller 3-1/2" drives require special mounting brackets that adapt them to the 5-1/4" bays found in many desktop cases.

In tower units, the system board is mounted to the right side-panel of the case. The power supply unit is attached to the back panel. Indicator lights and control buttons are located toward the upper part of the front panel. The drive units are mounted in the disk drive bays located in the upper half of the front panel.

Although there is no real problem mounting hard and floppy drives on their side, as they were in the adapted PC-AT cases, older drives could lose tracking accuracy when mounted this way. Tower cases permit the disk drives to be mounted in a horizontal fashion. They also offer extended drive bay capabilities that make them especially useful in file server applications where many disk, CD-ROM, and tape drives are desired.

Portable computer manufacturers are typically concerned with two main objectives: minimize power consumption and minimize the size of the unit as far as practical. To accomplish the latter objective, the designers create proprietary designs that squeeze internal components into the smallest space possible. The result of these designs is that no two models are alike. Each one has a different, non-standard case and system board design.

Power Supplies

The system's **power supply unit** provides electrical power for every component inside the system unit. It converts commercial electrical power received from a 120 Vac, 60 Hz (or 220 Vac, 50 Hz outside the U.S.) outlet into other levels required by the components of the system. In desktop and tower PCs, the power supply is the shiny metal box located at the rear of the system unit. In older AT-style systems, it also passed the commercial alternating current (AC) through the on/off switch to the display monitor.

There are two basic types of power supplies to be aware of, **ATX power supplies** — designed according to newer ATX design specifications, and traditional **AT power supplies** — designed to support AT-compatible system boards. The ATX system board connector is a 20-pin connector. Figure 1-12 shows the wiring configuration diagram of an ATX system board power connector. Notice that it is keyed so that it cannot be installed incorrectly. This connection contains a signal line that the system board can use to turn off the power supply. This is a power saving feature referred to as a *soft switch*.

TEST TIP

Be aware that ATX power supplies can be shut off from the system itself.

POWER SUPPLY CONNECTOR PIN #

3.3 V	11	1	3.3 V
-12 V	12	2	3.3 V
COM	13	3	COM
PS-ON	14	4	5 V
COM	15	5	COM
COM	16	6	5 V
COM	17	7	COM
-5 V	18	8	PW-OK
5 V	19	9	5 VSB
5 V	20	10	12 V

**Figure 1-12:
The ATX System Board
Power Connector**

Several bundles of cable emerge from the power supply to provide power to the components of the system unit and to its peripherals. Typical desktop/tower power supplies produce four (or five) different levels of efficiently regulated dc voltage. These are; +5 V, −5 V, +12 V, and −12 V (the ATX design also provides a +3.3 V level to the system board). The power supply unit also provides the system's ground. The IC devices on the system board and adapter cards use the +5 V level. The +3.3 V level is used by the microprocessor.

The power supply delivers power to the system board, and its expansion slots, through the system board power connector displayed in the figure. The system board power connector provides the system board and the individual expansion slots with up to 1 ampere of current each. The basic four voltage levels are available for use through the system board's expansion slot connectors.

In AT-compatible power supplies, two six-wire bundles are typically marked P8 and P9. The physical construction of these power connectors is significantly different than that of the other bundles. They are designed so that they can be plugged into the system board's P1 and P2 power plugs, respectively, as depicted in Figure 1-13.

Figure 1-13:
P1/P2–P8/P9 Connection

WARNING

Don't switch the P8/P9 connectors! — Although they look alike, the voltage levels of the plugs are different. Reversing them can cause **severe damage**.

The P8/P9 connectors are normally keyed and numbered. However, their construction and appearance are identical. The voltage levels associated with the plugs are different and severe damage could result to the computer by reversing them. The power connector labeled P8 should be plugged into the circuit board connector nearest the rear of the unit, while connector P9 should be plugged into the connector next to it. A good rule of thumb to remember when attaching these two connectors to the system board is that the black wires in each bundle should be next to each other.

The other power supply bundles are used to supply power to optional systems, such as the disk drives, CD-ROM drives, and tape drives. These bundles provide a +5 and a +12 Vdc supply, as described in Figure 1-14. The larger connector is carried over from older PC/XT/AT designs, while the smaller connector has gained widespread usage with smaller form factor disk drives. The +5 V supply provides power for electronic components on the optional devices, while the +12 V level is used for disk drive motors and other devices that require a higher voltage. As the figure illustrates, these connectors are keyed, so they must be plugged in correctly.

In both AT and ATX units, the on/off switch is located on the front panel of the system unit and is connected to the power supply by a cable. In the ATX design, a special *Soft Switch* line is included between the system board and the power supply that enables the system to shut itself off under control of the system software. This enables power management components of the operating system software to manage the hardware's power usage. This concept is discussed further in Chapters 2 and 9. Figure 1-15 illustrates the typical power supply connections found in a desktop or tower unit.

Figure 1-14: Auxiliary Power Connectors

In AT-compatible units, the cooling fan pulls air through the case from the front and exhausts it out the rear of the power supply unit. Conversely, the ATX design pulls air in through the rear of the power supply unit and blows it directly onto the ATX system board.

Figure 1-15: System Power Supply Connections

In the United States, a grounded, three-prong power cord provides the ac input voltage to the power supply. The smaller vertical blade in the connector is considered the hot or phase side of the connector. A small slide switch on the back of the unit permits the power supply to be switched over to operate on 220 Vac input voltages found outside the United States. When the switch is set to the 220 position, the voltage supplied to the power supply's monitor outlet will also be 220. In this position, it is usually necessary to exchange the power cord for one that has a plug suited to the country the computer is being used in.

Power supply units come in a variety of shapes and power ratings. The major difference between the AT and the ATX power supply types is in their form factors. The ATX power supply is somewhat smaller in size than the AT-style power supply and the hole patterns of the two specifications are different. Figure 1-16 illustrates the relative physical differences of the two power supply specifications.

Figure 1-16: Desktop/Tower Power Supplies

Another point that differentiates power supplies is their power (or wattage) rating. Typical power ratings include 150-, 200-, and 250-watt versions.

System Boards

The system board is the center of the PC-compatible microcomputer system. It contains the circuitry that determines the computing power and speed of the entire system. In particular, it contains the microprocessor and control devices that form the brains of the system.

Major Components

read only memory (ROM)

random access memory (RAM)

cache memory

The major components of interest on a PC system board are the microprocessor; the system's primary **read only memory (ROM)**, **random access memory (RAM)**, and **cache memory** sections; expansion slot connectors; and microprocessor support ICs that coordinate the operation of the system. A typical system board layout is depicted in Figure 1-17.

POWER CONNECTOR

CPU AND FAN

MOUSE

KEYBOARD

I/O PORTS

GAME PORT

AUDIO

EXPANSION SLOTS

BATTERY

RAM SLOTS

DISK DRIVE CONNECTORS

FDD

HDD

FRONT PANEL CONNECTIONS

REAR

Figure 1-17:
Parts of a Typical
System Board

┌─ TEST TIP ─────────────────

Know the parts of a typical system board and make sure
that you can identify these components (and variations of
them) from a pictorial or photographic representation.

For orientation purposes, the end of the board where the keyboard connector, expansion slots, and power connectors are located is generally referred to as the rear of the board.

As mentioned earlier, the system board receives power from the power supply unit through special power connectors. These connectors are often located along the right-rear corner of the system board so that they are near the power supply unit. They are also keyed so that the power cord cannot be plugged in backward.

In AT-class computers the power connectors are typically labeled as P1 and P2 and are always located directly beside each other. However, they are identical and can be reversed. Therefore, AT system board power connectors should always be installed so that the black wires from each connector are together.

The system's keyboard connector is normally located along the back right edge of the board as well. In most AT-compatible systems, the keyboard connector is a round, five-pin DIN connector. ATX systems place a standard block of input/output connections along the back edge of the system board. This block contains two 6-pin mini-DIN connectors (also called PS/2 connectors) for the ATX keyboard and mouse.

The system board communicates with various optional input/output (I/O) and memory systems through adapter boards that plug into its expansion slots. These connectors are normally located along the left-rear portion of the system board so that the external devices they serve can access them through the rear case openings.

Microprocessors

The microprocessor is the major component of any system board. It can be thought of as the "brains" of the computer system, because it reads, interprets, and executes software instructions, and also carries out arithmetic and logical operations for the system.

For more in-depth information about how microprocessor systems actually work, refer to the Electronic Reference Shelf located on the CD that accompanies this book.

REFERENCE SHELF

The original PC and PC-XT computers were based on the 8/16-bit 8088 microprocessor from Intel. The IBM PC-AT system employed a 16-bit 80286 microprocessor. Since then, Intel has introduced several different microprocessors for the PC market. These include devices such as the 80386DX and SX, the 80486DX and SX, the Pentium (80586), the Pentium Pro (80686), and Pentium II/III/4 processors. Intel used the SX notation to define reduced function versions of existing microprocessors (e.g., the 80486SX was a version of the 80486DX that had some functionality removed). SX devices were normally created to produce price variations that kept the Intel product competitive with those of other manufacturers.

The popularity of the 80286-based IBM PC-AT introduced many standards that are still being addressed today. The 80286's internal register set was identical to the register set of the 8088. However, it possessed an extended instruction set and a 24-bit address bus. The address bus enabled it to directly access up to 16 MB of physical memory, and the extended instruction set provided two distinctly different addressing modes: **real mode** and **virtual-protected mode**.

real mode

virtual-protected mode

In real-mode operation, the microprocessor emulates an 8088/86 microprocessor, and can directly access only the first 1 MB of RAM addresses in segments of 64 kB. It can also only work on one task at a time. In this mode, the microprocessor produces addresses on its first 20 address pins only. If software increments the 80286's addresses past 0FFFFFh in this mode, the address will just roll over to 000000h and the four highest address bits will not be activated. This is the mode that Intel microprocessors default to on startup and reset.

protected mode

In **protected mode**, the microprocessor's upper address bits are enabled, and it can access physical memory addresses above the 1 MB limit (up to 16 MB for the 80286). If software increments the microprocessor's addresses past 0FFFFFh in protected mode, the address will increment to 100000h.

Protected mode can also be used to perform **virtual memory** operations. Virtual memory is RAM that doesn't physically exist. In these operations, the system treats an area of disk space as an extension of RAM memory. It uses this designated area to shift data from RAM memory to the disk (and vice versa) as required. This method enables the system to simulate large areas of RAM.

For mathematically intensive operations, some programs may shift portions of the work to special high-speed **math coprocessors**, if they are present in the system. These devices are specialized microprocessors that work in parallel with the main microprocessor and extend its instruction set to speed up math and logic operations. They basically add large register sets to the microprocessor, along with additional arithmetic processing instructions. The 8088, 80286, 80386SX/DX, and 80486SX microprocessors used external coprocessors. The 80486DX and Pentium processors have built-in coprocessors that are an integral part of the IC design.

Other IC manufacturers produce work-alike versions of the Intel processors that are referred to as **clones**. In response to clone microprocessor manufactures using the 80x86 nomenclature, Intel dropped their 80x86 numbering system after the 80486 and adopted the **Pentium** name so that they could copyright it.

All these microprocessors are backward compatible with the 8088 — that is, programs written specifically for the 8088 can be executed by any of the other processors.

Microprocessor Packages

Microprocessors have been produced in a number of different IC package styles depending on their vintage and manufacturer. The 8088 and 8086 microprocessors were 8/16-bit processors housed in a 40-pin **Dual In-line Package** (**DIP**). They featured a 20-bit address bus capable of accessing up to 1 MB of memory and were used on the original IBM PC and PC-XT units. Although some XTs used 8086-based system boards, the vast majority of PCs, XTs, and clones employed the 8088 processor.

The 80286 was manufactured in a variety of 68-pin IC types including a **Ceramic Leadless Chip Carrier** (**CLCC**), a **Plastic Leaded Chip Carrier** (**PLCC**), and a **Pin Grid Array** (**PGA**) package. CLCC devices are designed to set inside sockets. Contacts along the side and bottom of the device make connection with spring-loaded contacts embedded in the socket. PLCC ICs have small pins that gull-wing out from the sides of the chip and are soldered to the top of a PC board. PGA packages employ metal pins that protrude from the bottom of the chip. These pins are pressed into a corresponding flat socket that has been mounted on the PC board.

The 80286 processors were used in the IBM PC-AT and its compatibles. It featured a 24-bit address bus, a 16-bit data bus, and a 16-bit internal word size. The 24-bit address bus allowed it to directly access up to 16 MB of address space, even though DOS could only handle the 1 MB that it had been designed to handle with the 8088 systems. The full 16-bit internal and external word size gave it a 4X speed increase over 8088 systems running at the same clock speed. 80286s were produced in various speed ratings.

| virtual memory |

| math coprocessors |

| clones |

| Pentium |

| Dual In-line Package (DIP) |

| Ceramic Leadless Chip Carrier (CLCC) |

| Plastic Leaded Chip Carrier (PLCC) |

| Pin Grid Array (PGA) |

The 80386DX continued the evolution of the AT architecture and was produced in a 132-pin PGA package. A reduced-function 80386SX version was also produced in a 100-pin surface-mount IC package. These microprocessors were mainly used in AT clone systems. The DX version provided a 32-bit address bus, a 32-bit data bus, and a 32-bit internal word size. The 32-bit address bus provided up to 4 GB of memory addressing. The SX version featured a reduced 24-bit address bus and a 16-bit data bus. Both versions were produced in a variety of operating speeds and included advanced addressing modes.

The 80486DX and first-generation Pentium microprocessors returned to 168-pin and 273-pin PGA packages. Figure 1-18 depicts these microprocessor packages. The 80486 featured a 32-bit address bus, a 32-bit external data bus, and a 64-bit internal word size. The Pentium also features a 32-bit address bus. However, both the internal and external word size are 64-bits. Both units include on-board math coprocessors for intense numerical operations and special built-in memory areas, called cache memory, for high-speed data access to selected data. Like the 80386, these microprocessors are typically used in advanced AT clone computers.

Figure 1-18: Microprocessor Packages

sockets

Advanced Pentium processors use a variety of package and pin configurations that are discussed in Chapter 2 — *Advanced System Boards*.

PC manufacturers mount microprocessors in **sockets** so that they can be replaced easily. This allows a failed microprocessor to simply be exchanged for a working unit. It also enables the system board to be upgraded with improved processors when they are developed. With a socket, the existing microprocessor can be replaced with an improved compatible version to upgrade the speed or performance of the system.

The notches and dots on the various ICs are important keys when replacing a microprocessor. They specify the location of the IC's number 1 pin. This pin must be lined up with the **pin-1 notch** of the socket for proper insertion. In older systems, the microprocessors had to be forcibly removed from the socket using an IC extractor tool. As the typical microprocessor's pin count increased, special **Zero Insertion Force (ZIF)** sockets were implemented that allowed the microprocessor to be set in the socket without force and then clamped in place. An arm-activated clamping mechanism in the socket shifts to the side, locking the pins in place.

The writing on the IC package is also significant. It contains the number that identifies the type of device in the package and normally includes a speed rating for the device. All of the microprocessors discussed here are covered in greater detail in Chapter 2, along with their significant variations.

> **TEST TIP**
>
> Know how to locate pin-1 of a microprocessor and be aware that this is one of the most important aspects of replacing or updating a microprocessor.

Memory Units

All computers need a place to temporarily store information while other pieces of information are being processed. In digital computers, information storage is normally conducted at two different levels: **primary memory** (made up of semiconductor RAM and ROM chips) and **mass storage** (usually involving floppy- and hard-disk drives).

Most of the system's primary memory is located on the system board and typically exists in three forms:

- **Read Only Memory (ROM)** — which contains the computer's permanent startup programs

- **Random Access Memory (RAM)** — which is quick enough to operate directly with the microprocessor and can be read from and written to as often as desired

- **Cache memory** — a fast RAM system used to hold information that the microprocessor is likely to use

ROM devices store information permanently and are used to hold programs and data that do not change. RAM devices only retain the information stored in them as long as electrical power is applied to the IC. Any interruption of power will cause the contents of the memory to vanish. This is referred to as **volatile memory**. ROM, on the other hand, is **nonvolatile**.

> **TEST TIP**
>
> Be aware of which memory types are volatile and what this means.

Every system board contains one or two ROM ICs that hold the system's **Basic Input/Output System (BIOS)** program. The BIOS program contains the basic instructions for communications between the microprocessor and the various input and output devices in the system. Until recently, this information was stored permanently inside the ROM chips and could only be changed by replacing the chips.

Advancements in EEPROM technology have produced **flash ROM** devices that enable new BIOS information to be written (**downloaded**) into the ROM to update it. This can be done from an update disk, or it can be downloaded from another computer. Unlike RAM ICs, the contents of the flash ROM remain after the power has been removed from the chip. In either case, the upgraded BIOS must be compatible with the system board it is being used with and should be the latest version available.

The information in the BIOS represents all of the intelligence the computer has until it can load more information from another source, such as a hard or floppy disk. Taken together, the BIOS software (programming) and hardware (the ROM chip) are referred to as **firmware**. These ICs can be located anywhere on the system board and are usually easy to recognize due to their size and immediate proximity to each other.

In older PC designs — XT and AT — the system's RAM memory was composed of banks of discrete RAM ICs mounted in rows of **Dual In-line Pin (DIP)** sockets. Modern system board designs place groups of RAM ICs on small daughter board modules that plug into the system board vertically. This mounting method required less horizontal board space than individual sockets.

Older RAM module formats included plug-in **Single In-line Pin (SIP)** and snap-in **Single In-line Memory Modules (SIMMs)**. Current RAM modules used on Pentium-class system boards are supplied in the form of snap-in **Dual In-line Memory Modules (DIMMs)**. These modules use special snap-in sockets that support the module firmly. SIMMs and DIMMs are also keyed, so they cannot be plugged in backwards. SIMMs were historically available in 30- and 72-pin versions and serviced 80386 and 80486 processors. On the other hand, DIMMs are larger 168-pin boards designed to work efficiently with Pentium-class microprocessors.

SIMM and DIMM sockets are quite distinctive in that they are normally arranged side by side. However, they can be located anywhere on the system board. SIMMs are typically produced in 8- or 32- bit data storage configurations. The 8-bit modules must be arranged in **banks** to match the data bus size of the system's microprocessor. In order to work effectively with a 32-bit microprocessor, a bank of four 8-bit SIMMs would need to be used. Conversely, a single 32-bit SIMM could do the same job.

DIMMs, on the other hand, typically come in 32- and 64-bit widths to service more powerful microprocessors. Like the SIMMs, they must be arranged properly to fit the size of the system data bus. In both cases, the modules can be accessed in smaller 8- and 16-bit segments. SIMMs and DIMMs also come in 9-, 36-, and 72-bit versions that include parity checking bits for each byte of storage.

PCs are usually sold with less than their full RAM capacity. This enables users to purchase less expensive computers to fit their individual needs and yet retain the option to install more RAM if future applications call for it. SIMM and DIMM sizes are typically specified in an a-by-b format. For example, a 2-by-32 SIMM specification indicates that it is a dual, non-parity, 32-bit (4-byte) device. In this scheme, the capacity is derived by multiplying the two numbers and then dividing by eight (or nine for parity chips). DIP, SIP, SIMM, and DIMM modules are depicted in Figure 1-19.

Figure 1-19: DIP, SIP, SIMM, and DIMM Memory Modules

Chipsets

> Microprocessor manufacturers and third-party IC makers produce microprocessor-support chipsets that provide auxiliary services for each type of microprocessor.

The first digital computers were giants that took up entire rooms and required several technicians and engineers to operate. They were constructed with vacuum tubes and their computing power was very limited by comparison to modern computers. However, the advent of **integrated circuit (IC)** technology in 1964 launched a new era in compact electronic packaging. The much smaller, low-power transistor replaced the vacuum tube and the size of the computer began to shrink.

Current IC technology permits millions of circuit elements to be constructed on a single small piece of silicon. Some **very large-scale integration (VLSI)** devices (devices that exceed 100,000 integrated electronic elements) contain complete computer modules. These devices are commonly referred to as **application-specific integrated circuits (ASICs)**. By connecting a few ASIC devices together on a printed circuit board, computers that once inhabited an entire room have shrunk to fit on the top of an ordinary work desk, and now, into the palm of the hand. Figure 1-20 shows various integrated circuit package types.

For the IC manufacturer, PC compatibility means designing chipsets that use the same basic memory map that was employed in the IBM PC-AT (that is, the chipset's programmable registers, RAM, ROM, and other addresses had to be identical to those of the AT). Therefore, instructions and data in the program would be interpreted, processed, and distributed the same way in both systems. In doing so, the supporting chipset was decreased from eight major ICs and dozens of **Small Scale Integration (SSI)** devices to two or three VLSI chips and a handful of SSI devices.

In some highly integrated system boards, the only ICs that remain are the microprocessor, one or two ROM BIOS chips, a single chipset IC, and the system's memory modules. Figure 1-21 illustrates the relatively compact structure provided by a typical Pentium/PCI chipset. As the figure illustrates, the **chip** count on a typical Pentium-class system board only involves seven major ICs, including the microprocessor.

integrated circuit (IC)

very large-scale integration (VLSI)

application specific integrated circuits (ASICs)

Figure 1-20: Integrated Circuit Packages

Small-Scale Integration (SSI)

chip

Figure 1-21: Pentium Chipset

Configuration Settings

Each time the system is turned on, or reset, the BIOS program checks the system's **configuration settings** to determine what types of optional devices may be included in the system.

configuration settings

Depending on the model of the computer, the configuration information may be read from hardware jumper or switch settings, from battery-powered RAM, or, in some cases, a combination of jumper and software settings. The PC, PC-XT, and their clones used hardware switches for configuration purposes. The original PC-AT featured a battery-powered RAM area that held some of the system's advanced configuration information. This configuration storage area became known as **CMOS RAM**.

CMOS RAM

Real Time Clock (RTC)

Clone IC manufacturers quickly integrated the advanced software configuration function to their chipsets along with the system's **Real Time Clock (RTC)** function. The RTC function keeps track of time and date information for the system. Clone system board designers added a rechargeable Ni-Cad battery to their system boards to maintain the information when the system was turned off.

In newer systems, there are no rechargeable Ni-Cad batteries for the CMOS storage. Instead, the CMOS storage area and RTC functions have been integrated with a 10-year, non-replaceable lithium cell in an independent RTC module.

Since the configuration settings are the system's primary method of getting information about what options are installed, they must be set to accurately reflect the actual options being used with the system. If not, an error will occur. You should always suspect a configuration problem if a machine fails to operate immediately after a new component is installed. The CMOS configuration values can be accessed for change by pressing the CTRL and DEL keys (or some other key combination) simultaneously during the bootup procedure.

Plug-and-Play (PnP)

Plug-and-Play—Newer PCs possess the ability to automatically reconfigure themselves for new options that are installed. This feature is referred to as **Plug-and-Play (PnP)** capability.

In 1994, Microsoft and Intel teamed up to produce a set of system specifications that would enable options added to the system to automatically be configured for operation. Under this scenario, the user is not involved in setting hardware jumpers or CMOS entries. To accomplish this, the system's BIOS, expansion slots, and adapter cards are designed so that the system software can reconfigure them automatically.

During the startup process, the PnP BIOS examines the system for installed devices. Devices designed for Plug-and-Play compatibility can tell the BIOS what types of devices they are and how to communicate with them. This information is stored in an area of the CMOS memory so that the system can work with the device. Plug-and-Play information will be scattered throughout the remainder of the text as it applies to the topic being covered.

Connectors and Jumpers

System boards possess a number of jumpers and connectors that you must be aware of. PC-compatible system boards include **switches** and **jumper blocks** (called **BERG connectors** after the BERG connector company that developed them) to select operating options such as processor speed, installed RAM size, and so forth. You may be required to alter these settings if you change a component or install a new module in the system.

Figure 1-22 illustrates the operation of typical configuration jumpers and switches. A metal clip in the cap of the jumper creates an electrical short between the pins it is installed across. When the cap is removed, the electrical connection is also removed and an electrically open condition is created.

System boards and I/O cards may use **micro switches** for configuration purposes. These micro switches are normally integrated into a DIP package, as illustrated in the figure. The switches may use a rocker or slide switch mechanism to create the short or open condition. The switches are typically numbered sequentially and marked for on/off positioning. Since the switches are so small, they may simply be marked with an On or Off, or with a 1 or 0.

It is usually necessary to consult the PC board's installation guide to locate and properly set configuration jumpers and switches. The installation guide typically provides the locations of all the board's configuration jumpers and switches. It also defines the possible configuration settings, along with corresponding switch or jumper positions.

The system board is connected to the front panel's indicators and controls through BERG connectors. Over time, these connection points have become fairly standard between cases. The normal connections are the **power LED**, hard drive activity indicator, system **reset switch**, and **system speaker**. Older AT-style system boards also included **Turbo LED**, **Turbo switch**, and **keylock switch** connections to handle special high-speed operating modes and physical hardware—security locking devices.

Figure 1-22: Jumpers and Configuration Switches

switches

jumper blocks

BERG connectors

micro switches

power LED

reset switch

system speaker

Turbo LED

Turbo switch

keylock switch

Expansion Slots

It would be very expensive to design and build a computer that fits every conceivable user application. With this in mind, computer designers include standardized connectors that enable users to configure the system to their particular computing needs.

Most PCs use standardized expansion slot connectors that enable various types of peripheral devices to be attached to the system. Optional input/output devices, or their interface adapter boards, are plugged into these slots to connect the devices to the system's address, data, and control buses.

memory systems
expansion slots
PC-bus
AT-bus
Industry Standard Architecture (ISA)
Extended ISA (EISA)
Video Electronics Standards Association (VESA)
Peripheral Component Interconnect (PCI)
Accelerated Graphics Port (AGP)
Audio Modem Riser (AMR)
Communications and Networking Riser (CNR)

The system board communicates with various optional input/output (I/O) and **memory systems** through adapter boards that plug into its **expansion slots**. These connectors are normally located along the left-rear portion of the system board so that the external devices they serve can access them through openings at the rear of the case.

Several different types of expansion slots are in use today. A particular system board may contain only one type of slot, or it may have a few of each type of expansion slot. Be aware that adapter cards are compatible with particular types of slots, so it is important to know which type of slot is being used. The major expansion slot types are:

- 8-bit **PC-bus** slots

- 16-bit **AT-bus**, or **Industry Standard Architecture (ISA)** bus slots

- 32-bit **Extended ISA (EISA)** and Micro Channel Architecture (MCA) bus slots

- 32-bit **Video Electronics Standards Association (VESA)** and 32/64-bit **Peripheral Component Interconnect (PCI)** local bus slots

There are three additional slot technologies that have found their ways onto Pentium-class system boards. These specialized slots are:

- **Accelerated Graphics Port (AGP)** slots

- **Audio Modem Riser (AMR)** slots

- **Communications and Networking Riser (CNR)** slots

The PC-bus slot is the most famous example of an 8-bit expansion slot, while the AT-bus, or ISA bus, slot is the consummate 16-bit expansion bus. The 32-bit expansion buses include the MCA, EISA, VESA, and PCI buses.

The PC bus was included in the original PC, PC-XT, and XT clone computers. The expansion bus in the IBM PC-AT and its clones became the de facto Industry Standard Architecture for 16-bit computers. The EISA bus was used in 80386- and 80486-based AT clone computers. The MCA bus was featured in some models of IBM's Personal System 2 (PS/2) line of computers.

The 32-bit VESA and PCI buses are typically included on 80486- and Pentium-based computers along with traditional ISA slots.

The AGP slot is a 32-bit derivative of the PCI bus that was developed to provide a specialized interface for advanced video graphics adapters. The AMR and CNR slots were developed to handle specialized modems and sound cards that interact directly with the system.

These expansion slots are depicted in Figure 1-23 and are discussed in more detail in Chapter 2 — *Advanced System Boards*.

32-BIT ISA/VESA BUS SLOT

32-BIT EISA BUS SLOT

32-BIT PCI BUS SLOT

64-BIT PCI 2.2 V SLOT

16-BIT ISA BUS SLOT

32-BIT AGP SLOT

8-BIT PC-BUS SLOT

VESA CONNECTOR SLOT

Figure 1-23: Expansion Slot Connectors

Adapter Cards

The openness of the IBM PC XT and AT architectures, coupled with their overwhelming popularity, led companies to develop a wide assortment of expansion devices for them. Most of these devices communicate with the basic system through **adapter cards** that plug into the expansion slots of the computer's main board, as illustrated in Figure 1-24. They typically contain the interfacing and controller circuitry for the peripheral. However, in some cases the entire peripheral may be included on the adapter card.

This expansion approach enables a wide variety of peripheral devices to be added to the basic system to modify it for particular applications. For example, adapter cards allow less expensive devices to be used with an introductory system and yet still allow high-end, high-performance peripherals to be used with the same system for advanced applications.

There are three important characteristics associated with any adapter card:

- function

- expansion slot connector style

- size

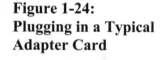

Figure 1-24: Plugging in a Typical Adapter Card

Many companies have developed expansion cards and devices for different types of computer applications. These include I/O controllers, disk drive controllers, video controllers, modems, and proprietary input/output devices, such as scanners.

The adapter cards in the original IBM PC were 13.2"l x 4.2"h. The PC normally came with a disk drive adapter card and a video card. These units were referred to as **full-size adapter cards**. These cards were so long that case manufacturers placed plastic guide rails at the front of the system unit to keep them from flexing due to system heating. A smaller (6.0"l x 4.2"h) printer adapter card was also made available for the PC. This size card is referred to as a **half-size card**. When the AT appeared the I/O cards became more powerful and taller (13.2"l x 4.8"h).

The AT cards became the standard against which later I/O cards have been measured. Like system boards, adapter cards have developed into smaller, more powerful units. Most current adapter cards are **2/3-size cards**, half-size cards, or smaller cards. In addition, the height of the cards has been significantly reduced. Many adapters are only half the height, or less, of the original AT cards. Therefore, they are referred to as **half-height cards**.

The only real requirements for adapter cards now are that they fit securely in the expansion slot, cover the slot opening in the rear of the system unit, and provide standard connectors for the types of devices they serve. Various adapter card designs are depicted in Figure 1-25. In this example, all of the cards employ an ISA edge connector. The same I/O functions and card sizes can be used to create cards for all of the other expansion slot types.

Figure 1-25:
Adapter Card
Designs

legacy cards

Most early adapter cards employed hardware jumpers, or configuration switches, that enabled them to be configured specifically for the system they were being used in. The user had to set up the card for operation and solve any interrupt or memory addressing conflicts that occurred. Such cards are referred to as **legacy cards**.

In newer PnP systems, adapter cards have the ability to identify themselves to the system during the startup process, along with supplying information about what type of device they are, how they are configured, and what resources they need access to. In addition, these cards must be able to be reconfigured by the system software if a conflict is detected between it and another system device.

video adapter card

Multi-I/O adapter card

Prior to the Pentium-based system boards, two types of adapter cards were traditionally supplied as standard equipment in most desktop and tower PC systems. These were a **video adapter card** and a **Multi-I/O adapter card**. However, in Pentium units, the Multi-I/O functions have been built into the system board. Similarly, both the video and I/O functions are an integral part of the system board in portable systems.

Video Adapter Cards

> The video adapter card provides the interface between the system board and the display monitor.

The original IBM PCs and XTs offered two types of display adapters, a **Monochrome (single color) Display Adapter** (**MDA**) and a **Color Graphic Adapter** (**CGA**). Both of these units also included the system's first parallel printer port connector.

These initial units have been followed by a number of improved and enhanced video adapters and monitors. The most common type of video adapter card currently in use is the **Video Graphics Array** (**VGA**) card, like the one depicted in Figure 1-26. The system uses it to control video output operations.

Unlike most other computer components, the VGA video standard uses analog signals and circuitry rather than digital signals. The main component of most video adapter cards is an ASIC device called the **Integrated Video Controller**. It is a microprocessor-like chip that oversees the operation of the entire adapter. It is capable of accessing RAM and ROM memory units on the card. The video RAM chips hold the information that is to be displayed on the screen. Their size determines the card's video and color capacities.

In addition to offering vastly improved color production capabilities, VGA provided superior resolution capabilities. Standard VGA resolution is defined as 720 x 400 pixels using 16 colors in text mode, and 640 x 480 pixels using 16 on-screen colors in graphics mode. However, improved-resolution VGA systems, referred to as **Super VGAs**, are now commonly available in formats of 1024 x 768 with 256 colors, 1024 x 768 with 16 colors, and 800 x 600 with 256 colors. The SVGA definition continues to expand, with video controller capabilities ranging up to 1280 x 1024 (with reduced color capabilities) currently available in the market.

IBM produced its own **Extended Graphics Array** standard, called the **XGA**. This standard was capable of both 800 x 600 and 1024 x 768 resolutions, but added a 132-column, 400-scan line resolution. Unfortunately, IBM based the original XGA on interlaced monitors, and therefore never received a large following.

The maximum resolution/color capabilities of a particular VGA adapter are ultimately dependent on the amount of on-board memory the adapter had installed. The standard 640 x 480 display format, using 16 colors, requires nearly 256 kB of video memory to operate (640 x 480 x 4/8 = 153,600 bytes). With 512 kB of video memory installed, the resolution can be improved to 1024 x 768, but only 16 colors are possible (1024 x 768 x 4/8 = 393,216 bytes). To achieve full 1024 x 768 resolution with 256 colors, the video memory has to be expanded to a full 1 MB (1024 x 768 x 8/8 = 786,432 bytes). Access to this memory is very flexible.

Monochrome Display Adapter (MDA)

Color Graphic Adapter (CGA)

Video Graphics Array (VGA)

Integrated Video Controller

VIDEO BIOS

VIDEO RAM

15-PIN VGA CONNECTOR

INTEGRATED VIDEO CONTROLLER

**Figure 1-26:
A Typical VGA Card**

Super VGA

Extended Graphics Array

XGA

Standard VGA monitors employ a 31.5 kHz horizontal scanning rate, while Super VGA monitors use frequencies between 35 and 48 kHz for their horizontal sync, depending on the **vertical refresh rate** of the adapter card. Standard VGA monitors repaint the screen (vertical refresh) at a frequency of 60 or 70 Hz, while Super VGA vertical scanning occurs at frequencies of 56, 60, and 72 Hz. A summary of the different video standards is presented in Table 1-1.

Table 1-1:
Video Standards

STANDARD	MODE	RESOLUTION (HXV PIXELS)	A/N DISPLAY	A/N CHARACTER	REFRESH RATE	HORIZONTAL SWEEP RATE	BUFFER ADDRESS
MDA (Monochrome Display Adapter)	Alphanumeric (A/N)	720 x 348 720 x 348	80 x 25	7 x 9 in 9 x 14	50/60	Non-interlaced	B0000–B7FFF B0000–B7FFF B0000–BFFFF
CGA (Color Graphics Adapter)	(A/N) Low-resolution Medium-resolution High-resolution (APA) All Points Addressable graphics	640 x 200 160 x 100 320 x 200 640 x 200	80 x 25	7 x 7 in 8 x 8	60	15 kHz	B8000–BBFFF
HGA (Hercules Graphics Adapter)	A/N Diag/Half/Full Graphics	720 x 348	80 x 25	7 x 9 in 9 x 14	50	18.1 kHz	B0000–BFFFF
EGA (Extended Graphics Adapter)	A/N Graphics	640 x 350 640 x 350	80 x 25 80 x 43	7 x 9 in 8 x 14	60 Hz	22.1 kHz	0A0000
VGA (Video Graphics Array Adapter)	Text Graphics	720 x 400 640 x 480	80 x 25 80 x 43	9 x 16	60 or 70 Hz	31.5 kHz	0A0000–0BFFFF
Super VGA (SVGA)	Text Graphics	1280 x 1024 1024 x 768 800 x 600	80 x 25 80 x 43	9 x 16	50, 60, or 72	35-48 kHz	0A0000–0BFFFF
XGA	Text Graphics	1024 x 768 800 x 600	132 x 25	9 x 16 8 x 16	44/70	35.5 kHz	0A0000–0BFFFF

The adapter also has a **video BIOS ROM** that is similar to the ROM BIOS on the system board. This BIOS acts as an extension of the system BIOS and is located between addresses C0000h and C7FFFh. It is used to store firmware routines that are specific only to video functions. This example supports 27 distinct modes of operation, as described in Table 1-2. These modes include various character-box sizes and resolution selections. It also includes two different methods of storing screen data in the video memory. The first method is the **A/N (Alphanumeric) mode**, which is used for text operations. The second method is an **All Points Addressable (APA) mode**, which is normally used for graphics applications.

Table 1-2:
Video BIOS Mode
Table

MODE (HEX)	T/G	COLOR	BOX SIZE	ALPHA SIZE	SCREEN SIZE	BUFFER START	PG	HSYNE (KHz)	VSYNE (Hz)	CRYSTAL (MHz)	RAM (kB)
0,1	A/N	16	8 x 8	40 x 25	320 x 200	B8000	8	31.5	70	25.175	256
2,3	A/N	16	8 x 8	80 x 25	640 x 200	B8000	8	31.5	70	25.175	256
0*,1*	A/N	16	8 x 14	40 x 25	320 x 350	B8000	8	31.5	70	25.175	256
2*,3*	A/N	16	8 x 14	80 x 25	640 x 350	B8000	8	31.5	70	25.175	256
0+,1+	A/N	16	9 x 16	40 x 25	360 x 400	B8000	8	31.5	70	28.322	256
2+,3+	A/N	16	9 x 16	80 x 25	720 x 400	B8000	8	31.5	70	38.322	256
4,5	APA	4	8 x 8	40 x 25	320 x 200	B8000	1	31.5	70	25.175	256
6	APA	2	8 x 8	80 x 25	640 x 200	B8000	1	31.5	70	25.175	256
7	A/N	-	9 x 14	80 x 25	720 x 350	B0000	8	31.5	70	28.322	256
7+	A/N	-	9 x 16	80 x 25	720 x 400	B0000	8	31.5	70	28.322	256
D	APA	16	8 x 8	40 x 25	320 x 200	A0000	8	31.5	70	25.175	256
E	APA	16	8 x 8	80 x 25	640 x 200	A0000	4	31.5	70	25.175	256
F	APA	-	8 x 14	80 x 25	640 x 350	A0000	2	31.5	70	25.175	256
10	APA	16	8 x 14	80 x 25	640 x 350	A0000	2	31.5	70	25.175	256
11	APA	2	8 x 16	80 x 30	640 x 480	A0000	1	31.5	60	25.175	256
12	APA	16	8 x 16	80 x 30	640 x 480	A0000	1	31.5	60	25.175	256
13	APA	256	8 x 8	40 x 25	320 x 200	A0000	1	31.5	70	25.175	256
18	A/N	16	9 x 16	80 x 30	720 x 480	B8000	1	31.5	60	28.322	256
19	A/N	16	9 x 8	80 x 43	720 x 473	B8000	1	31.5	70	28.322	256
1A	A/N	16	9 x 8	80 x 60	720 x 480	B8000	1	31.5	60	28.322	256
1B	A/N	16	9 x 16	132 x 25	1188 x 350	B8000	1	31.2	70	40.0	256
1C	A/N	16	9 x 16	132 x 30	1188 x 480	B8000	1	31.2	60	40.0	256
1D	A/N	16	9 x 8	132 x 43	1188 x 473	B8000	1	31.2	70	40.0	256
1E	A/N	16	9 x 8	132 x 60	1188 x 480	B8000	1	31.2	60	40.0	256
1F	APA	16	8 x 8	100 x 75	800 x 600	A0000	1	31.5	57	36	256
1F V	APA	16	8 x 8	100 x 75	800 x 600	A0000	1	48.0	70	50.35	256
20	APA	16	8 x 16	120 x 45	960 x 720	A0000	1	31.5	43 / 43	44.9	512
21	APA	16	8 x 16	128 x 48	1024 x 768	A0000	1	31.5	43 / 43	44.9	512
21 NI	APA	16	8 x 16	128 x 48	1024 x 768	A0000	1	48.5	60	65	512
21 V	APA	16	8 x 16	128 x 48	1024 x 768	A0000	1	56.5	70	75	512
22	APA	16	8 x 16	96 x 64	768 x 1024	A0000	1	38	35 / 35	44.9	512
23	APA	4	8 x 16	128 x 48	1024 x 768	A0000	1	35.5	43 / 43	44.9	512
24	APA	256	8 x 16	64 x 32	512 x 512	A0000	1	35.5	62	50.35	512
25	APA	256	8 x 14	80 x 25	640 x 400	A0000	1	31.5	70	50.35	512
26	APA	256	8 x 16	800 x 30	640 x 480	A0000	1	31.5	60	50.35	512
27	APA	256	8 x 8	100 x 75	800 x 600	A0000	1	35.5	57	36	512
27 V	APA	256	8 x 8	100 x 75	800 x 600	A0000	1	48.0	70	50.35	512

Note: NI:non-Interlaced mode. V:VESA mode

The video controller also contains the video **DAC (Digital-to-Analog Converter)** that converts digital data in the controller into the analog signal used to drive the display. The video output connector is a three-row DB-15 female connector used with analog VGA displays.

DAC
(Digital-to-Analog
Converter)

Other Adapter Cards

While the video display adapter card is typically the only adapter card required in the system, many other Input/Output (I/O) functions can be added to the system through adapter cards. Some of the most popular I/O cards in Pentium systems include:

- **Internal Modem cards** – These devices are used to carry on data communications through traditional telephone lines.

- **Local Area Network cards** – LAN cards are used to connect the local system to a group of other computers so they can share data and resources.

- **Sound cards** – Sound cards are used to provide high-quality audio output for the computer system.

Internal Modem cards

Local Area Network cards

Sound cards

Still other adapter cards can be added to the system to provide additional connectivity and functionality. Some of the newer adapters finding their way into PC systems include:

- *SCSI adapters* – Most PCs include a built-in IDE interface for peripherals. Many disk drive arrangements and peripherals are designed to use a Small Computer System Interface. For these devices to be used with the PC, a SCSI host adapter must be installed in one of the expansion slots to facilitate communications between the system and the device.

- *USB adapters* – Most new PCs include high-speed Universal Serial Bus (USB) connections. However, you can install additional USB connection points in the system by installing a USB adapter card in one of the expansion slots.

- *IEEE-1394 Firewire adapters* – While most newer PCs include a USB connection, they do not directly support IEEE-1384 Firewire connections commonly used with audio/video equipment. However, this bus specification can be supported by adding a Firewire adapter card to the system.

- *Wireless network adapters* – PCs don't directly support wireless networks or printers. However, these functions can be supported by adding a wireless networking adapter card to the system.

Figure 1-27 shows examples of these cards and their connections. While they represent most options added to computer systems, there are many other I/O devices that can be plugged into expansion slots to enhance the operation of the system.

Figure 1-27:
Typical I/O Cards

The System Speaker

The system's primary audio output device is a 2.25-inch, 8-ohm, ½-watt speaker, similar to the one depicted in Figure 1-28. This unit can be located behind the vertical vents in the front panel or under the power supply unit in a small plastic retainer. The system uses the speaker to prompt the user during certain events and to indicate certain errors in the system, such as video display failures, which can't be displayed on the screen. The user can also control the operation of the speaker through software. Its output frequency range extends through the complete audio range and, with proper programming, can be used to create arcade sounds and music.

EXTERNAL SPEAKERS

SYSTEM SPEAKER

SYSTEM BOARD

Figure 1-28:
System Speakers

As the figure illustrates, most consumer-oriented PCs now include a set of additional external speakers to provide a much higher quality audio output than the traditional system speaker is capable of. However, the system speaker remains because of its ability to produce beep-coded error messages and audible event indications even when major portions of the system may not be functioning.

Storage Devices

Programs and data disappear from the system's RAM when the computer is turned off. In addition, IC RAM devices tend to be too expensive to construct large memories that can hold multiple programs and large amounts of data. Therefore, storage systems that can be used for long-term data storage are desirable as a second level of memory.

With this in mind, a number of secondary memory technologies have been developed to extend the computer's memory capabilities and store data on a more permanent basis. These systems tend to be too slow to be used directly with the computer's microprocessor. The secondary memory unit holds the information and transfers it in batches to the computer's faster internal memory when requested.

From the beginning, most secondary memory systems have involved storing binary information in the form of magnetic charges on moving magnetic surfaces. However, optical storage methods such as CD-ROM and DVD have quickly moved to rival magnetic storage for popularity.

Magnetic storage has remained popular due to three factors:

- Low cost-per-bit of storage
- Intrinsically non-volatile nature
- It has successfully evolved upward in capacity

The major magnetic storage media are floppy disks, hard disks, and tape.

tracks

In magnetic disk systems, information is stored as magnetized spots arranged in concentric circles around the disk. These circles are referred to as **tracks** and are numbered, beginning with 0, from the outside edge inward. The number of tracks may range from 40 up to 2048, depending on the type of disk and drive being used.

cylinder

In hard-disk drives, multiple disks are stacked together on a common spindle. The corresponding tracks of each surface are logically arranged to form a **cylinder** (e.g., all of the track-0 tracks are taken together to form cylinder-0).

sectors

Since the tracks at the outer edge of the disk are longer than those at its center, each track is divided into an equal number of equal-sized blocks called **sectors**. This arrangement is used so that the logic circuitry for processing data going to, or coming from the disk can be as simple as possible. The number of sectors on a track may range from 8 to more than 60, depending on the disk and drive type, and the operating system software used to format it.

TEST TIP

Be able to describe the organization of PC-compatible disks (i.e., sectors, tracks, cylinders) and recognize examples of them associated with different disk types.

As an example, a typical IBM floppy disk will have 40 or 80 tracks per surface, with each track divided into 8, 9, or 18 sectors each. In a PC-compatible system, each sector holds 512 bytes of data. The organizational structure of a typical magnetic disk is illustrated in Figure 1-29.

**Figure 1-29:
The Organizational
Structure of a Magnetic
Disk**

REFERENCE
SHELF

For more in-depth information about how magnetic disk systems work, refer to the Electronic Reference Shelf located on the CD that accompanies this book.

In magnetic tape systems, data is stored in sequential tracks along the length of the tape, as depicted in Figure 1-30. Each track is divided into equal-sized blocks. The blocks are separated by small gaps of unrecorded space. **Multiple tracks** can be recorded across the width of the tape. Using multiple read/write heads, the tracks can be read simultaneously as the tape moves forward. The tracks can also be read in a **serpentine** manner, using a single read/write head.

While it is possible to directly access any of the sectors on a magnetic disk, the sections on the tape can only be accessed in a linear order. To access the information in block 32 of the tape, the previous 31 blocks must pass through the drive.

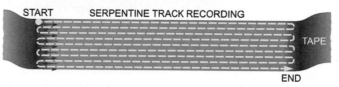

Tape generally represents a cheaper storage option, but its inherent slowness, due to its sequential nature, makes it less desirable than rotating magnetic disks. Disks offer much quicker access to large blocks of data, at a cost that is still affordable to most users.

**Figure 1-30:
Formats for
Storing Data on
Magnetic Tape**

Disk Drives

The system unit normally comes from the manufacturer with a **floppy-disk drive (FDD)**, a **hard-disk drive (HDD)**, and a **CD-ROM drive** installed, as illustrated in Figure 1-31.

**Figure 1-31:
The Disk Drives of
a Typical System**

The system's disk-drive capacity is not usually limited to the standard units installed. In most cases, the system cabinet is designed to hold additional disk drive units. These units can be an additional FDD, HDD, or CD-ROM unit, or a combination of these devices. Although three FDD units could physically be installed in most systems, the typical floppy-drive controller supports only two drives.

One or more HDD units can be installed in the system unit, along with the floppy drive(s). The system should normally be set up to recognize a single hard disk in the system as the **C: drive**. However, a single, physical hard-disk drive can be partitioned into two or more volumes that the system recognizes as **logical drives** C:, D:, and so on.

| C: drive |
| logical drives |

Floppy Drives

The most widely used data storage systems in personal computers are floppy-disk drive units. These units store information in the form of tiny, magnetized spots on small flexible disks that can be removed from the drive unit. Once the information has been written on the disk, it will remain there until the disk is magnetically erased or written over. The information remains on the disk even if it is removed from the disk drive or if power is removed from the system. Whenever the information is required by the system, it can be obtained by inserting the disk back into the drive and reading the data from the disk.

Floppy disks are relatively inexpensive and are easy to transport and store. In addition, they can easily be removed and replaced if they become full. Figure 1-32 depicts the major components of a typical floppy-disk drive unit.

In Pentium-class PCs, high-density, 3.5-inch floppy drives capable of holding 1.44 MB (1,474,560 bytes) are the norm. Older AT-class machines used high-density, 5.25-inch drives that could hold over 1,200,000 bytes (1.2 MB) of information. Older 8088-based machines employed 5.25-inch half-height and full-height drives that used disks capable of storing 368,640 bytes (referred to as 360 kB of information). The term **half-height** was used to describe drive units that were half as tall as the **full-height** drive units used with the original IBM PC. Smaller 3.5-inch half-height drives, capable of storing 720 kB (737,280 bytes) of information, were also used with 8088-based computers.

Figure 1-32: The Floppy-Disk Drive Unit

| half-height |
| full-height |

The typical floppy disk, depicted in Figure 1-33, is a flexible, 3.5-inch diameter mylar disk that has been coated with a ferromagnetic material. It is encased in a protective, hard plastic envelope that contains a low-friction liner that removes dust and contaminants from the disk as it turns within the envelope.

Figure 1-33: Floppy Disks

Typical floppy drives turn the disk at 300 or 360 RPM and the drive's R/W heads ride directly on the disk surface. Information is written to or read from the disk as it spins inside the envelope. The small LED on the front of the disk drive unit lights up whenever either of these operations is in progress.

The drive's read/write heads access the disk surface through a spring-loaded metal cover, which the drive unit moves out of the way. The drive spindle turns the disk by engaging a keyed metal wafer attached to the lower side of the disk. A small, sliding tab in the left-front corner of the envelope performs a write-protect function for the disk. If the tab covers the opening, the disk may be written to. If, however, the opening is clear, the disk is said to be "Write Protected," and the drive will not write information on the disk.

Current PC systems use a type of floppy disk referred to as Double-Sided, High-Density (DS-HD). This means that the disk can be used on both sides, and that advanced magnetic recording techniques may be used to effectively double or triple the storage capacity previously available using older recording techniques. These disks can hold 1.44 MB of information using Microsoft's FAT-based disk format.

This type of floppy-disk drive can also operate with an older type of floppy disk that is referred to as Double-Sided, Double-Density (DS-DD). This notation indicates that the disks are constructed so that they can be used on both sides, and that they can support recording techniques that double the storage capacity available with older recording techniques.

Hard Drives

The system's data storage potential is extended considerably by high-speed, high-capacity hard-disk drive units like the one shown in Figure 1-34. These units store much more information than floppy disks do. Modern hard drives typically have storage capacities ranging up to several gigabytes. Hard drives also differ from floppy drives in that they use rigid disks that are permanently sealed in the drive unit (non-removable).

The disks are aluminum platters coated with a nickel-cobalt or ferromagnetic material. Two or more platters are usually mounted on a common spindle, with spacers between them, to allow data to be recorded on both sides of each disk. The drive's read/write mechanism is sealed inside a dust-free compartment along with the disks.

Modern hard-disk drives come in sizes of 5.25-, 3.5-, and 2.5-inch diameters. Of these sizes, the 3.5-inch version is by far the most popular due to their association with personal and business desktop computers. Although popular for many years, 5.25-inch hard drives are quickly disappearing from the marketplace. Conversely, the popularity of the 2.5-inch drives is growing with the rising popularity of laptop and notebook-size computers. Hard drives ranging into gigabytes of storage are available for these machines.

Figure 1-34: Inside a Hard-Disk Drive

The hard-disk drives normally used with personal computers typically contain between 1 and 5 disks that are permanently mounted inside a sealed enclosure, along with the **Read/Write (R/W)** head mechanisms. There is one R/W head for each disk surface. The platters are typically turned at a speed between 5400 and 7200 RPM. This high rotational speed creates a thin cushion of air around the disk surface that causes the R/W heads to fly just above the disk.

The major differences between floppy- and hard-disk drives are storage capacity, data transfer rates, and cost. Another difference to note is the fact that hard-disk drives tend to be more delicate than floppy drives. Therefore, they require some special handling considerations to prevent both damage to the unit and loss of data. The disks in the HDD are not removable as floppy disks are. Therefore, it is possible to fill up a hard-disk drive. When this occurs, it will be necessary to delete information from the drive to make room for new information to be stored.

Conversely, floppy disks are prone to damage due to mishandling, static, temperature, and so on. In addition, they are easy to misplace and they provide limited storage of application software.

CD-ROM Drives

Soon after the **Compact Disc (CD)** — the term "disc" is used in place of disk to denote the fact that it is an optical disc instead of a magnetic disk — became popular for storing audio signals on optical material, the benefits of storing computer information in this manner became apparent. The typical CD can hold upwards of 600 MB of programs and data on a single, inexpensive, removable media. Originally, the information had to be placed on the CD by a disc manufacturer. Therefore, early discs used to hold digital data for computers were referred to as **CD-ROMs**.

The ROM designation refers to the fact that most of the original discs and drives were read-only in nature. While newer optical technologies have produced low-cost drives and discs that can be written and erased multiple times, the CD-ROM title is still commonly associated with this type of device. Figure 1-35 shows the components generally associated with a CD-ROM drive system.

Figure 1-35: Components of a CD-ROM System

Typical CD-ROM drives are constructed to fit in standard 5-1/4" half-height disk drive openings. They require a signal cable, typically IDE or SCSI, to communicate with the system, and a single options power connector. CD discs are inserted into the drive using an automatic sliding tray mechanism that positions the disc for use.

Drives that operate at the speed of a conventional audio CD player are called **single-speed (1X) drives**. Advanced drives that spin twice, and three times, as fast as the typical CD player are referred to as **double-speed (2X) drives**, **triple-speed (3X) drives**, and so forth. Single-speed drives transfer data at a rate of 150 kB per second, double-speed drive transfers occur at 300 kB per second, and so on. Most manufacturers are now focusing on 50X and 52X drives.

CD-ROM drives are capable of playing audio CDs. However, a CD player will not be able to produce any output from the CD-ROM disc. CDs are classified by a color-coding system that corresponds to their intended use. CDs that contain digital data intended for use in a computer are referred to as **Yellow Book** CDs. **Red Book** CDs refer to those formatted to contain digital music. **Orange Book** refers to the standard for CDs that are used in WORM drives. **Green Book** CDs are used with interactive CD systems, and **Blue Book** CDs are those associated with laser disc systems.

| single-speed (1x) drives |
| double-speed (2X) drives |
| triple-speed (3X) drives |
| **Yellow Book** |
| **Red Book** |
| **Orange Book** |
| **Green Book** |
| **Blue Book** |

Digital Versatile Discs

Newer compact disc technologies have produced a high-capacity disc, called a **digital versatile disc**, **digital video disc**, or **DVD** for short. These discs have capacities that range between 4.7 GB and 17 GB of data. Transfer rates associated with DVD drives range between 600 kBps and 1.3 MBps.

| digital versatile disc |
| digital video disc |
| **DVD** |

Like CDs, DVDs are available in DVD-ROM (write-once) and DVD-RAM (rewritable) formats. There are also DVD-Audio and DVD-Video specifications that can store up to 75 songs or an entire full-length movie. The DVD-Video standard employs the MPEG-2 compression standard to compress and decompress video data on the disc.

> For more information about MPEG, video data compression, and multimedia, refer to the *How Multimedia Works* section of the Electronic Reference Shelf on the CD that accompanies this book.

REFERENCE SHELF

Physically, the DVD drive looks and operates in the same manner as the traditional CD-ROM drive described earlier in this chapter. Newer manufacturing methods for the discs permit the minimum length of the pits and lands to be smaller. Therefore, they can be squeezed closer together on the disc. DVD drives also employ higher resolution lasers to decrease the track pitch (distance between adjacent tracks). Together, these two factors create the high data densities offered by DVD.

Tape Drives

Tape drive units are another popular type of information storage system. These systems can store large amounts of data on small, removable **tape cartridges**, similar to the one depicted in Figure 1-36.

Figure 1-36: A Tape Drive and Cartridge

Tapes tend to be more economic than other magnetic media when storing large amounts of data. However, access to information stored on tape tends to be very slow. This is caused by the fact that, unlike disks, tape operates in a linear fashion. The tape transport must run all of the tape past the drive's R/W heads to access data that is physically stored at the end of the tape.

Data backup has easily become the most widely used tape application. With the large amounts of information that can be stored on a hard-disk drive, a disk crash is a very serious problem. If the drive crashes, all of the information stored on the disk can be destroyed. This can easily add up to billions of pieces of information. Therefore, an inexpensive method of storing data away from the hard drive is desirable.

Therefore, tape drives are generally used to store large amounts of information that will not need to be accessed often, or quickly. Such information includes **backup copies** of programs and data. This type of data security is a necessity with records such as business transactions, payroll, artwork, etc.

Peripherals

Peripherals are devices and systems that are added to the basic system to extend its capabilities. These devices and systems can be divided into three general categories: **input systems**, **output systems**, and **memory systems**.

The standard peripherals associated with PCs are the alphanumeric **keyboard** and the **CRT monitor**. With the rapid growth of GUI-oriented software, the **mouse** has become a common input peripheral as well. The next most common peripheral is the **character printer**. These peripherals are used to produce hard-copy output on paper.

Many other types of peripheral equipment are routinely added to the basic system. Most peripheral devices interact with the basic system through adapter cards that plug into the system board's expansion slots. The peripheral devices connect to the adapter cards through expansion slot openings in back of the system unit. As long as there are open expansion slots, or other standard I/O connectors, it is possible to add compatible devices to the system.

External Connections and Devices

As we have already mentioned, the standard peripherals used with PCs are keyboards, CRT monitors, and mice. Figure 1-37 depicts a sample system with these devices. Most PCs use detachable keyboards that are connected to the system by a coiled cable. This cable may plug into a 5-pin DIN or 6-pin mini-DIN connector located on the rear of the system board. The connector is normally keyed so that it cannot be misaligned. The most widely used display device for current PCs is the **Video Graphics Array (VGA)** color monitor. The monitor's signal cable connects to a 15-pin D-shell connector at the back of the system unit. A mouse can be connected to a PC by attaching it to a 9-pin D-shell or 6-pin mini-DIN connector at the rear of the system.

Video Graphics Array (VGA)

Figure 1-37: Typical PC Peripherals

Figure 1-38: ATX Back Panel Connections

Figure 1-38 illustrates typical connectors found on the back of an ATX-style system. As you can see, most peripheral devices interact with the basic system through adapter cards that plug into the system board's expansion slots. The peripheral devices connect to the adapter cards through expansion slot openings in back of the system unit. As long as there are open expansion slots, or other standard I/O connectors, it is possible to add compatible devices to the system.

On the ATX back panel, many of the system board-related I/O functions have been grouped into a standardized block of connections as illustrated. The panel features two 6-pin PS/2 mini-DIN connectors. The lower connector is for the keyboard, while the upper connector is intended for use with a PS/2 serial mouse. Because these connectors are physically identical, it is relatively easy to confuse them. Just to the right of the keyboard and mouse ports are two USB connectors for attaching USB devices to the system. The master I/O block contains two DB-9M COM port connectors for use with serial devices and a DB-25F parallel-port connector for SPP, EPP, and ECP parallel devices. This board also features a game port and built-in audio connections. The DB-15F connector is the standard for the PC game port and is used to attach joysticks and other game-playing devices to. The audio block features standard RCA jacks for the microphone, audio-in, and speaker connections.

Network Interface Card (NIC)

Unshielded Twisted Pair (UTP)

British Naval Connector (BNC)

In the expansion slots to the right of the ATX I/O block, you will see a DB-15F VGA video connector, a 50-pin Centronics SCSI bus connector, two RJ-11 jacks for an internal modem (one is for the phone line while the other is used to attach a traditional telephone handset), and an RJ-45/BNC combination for making LAN connections with the system's **Network Interface Card (NIC)**. The DB-15F connector used with VGA video devices uses a three-row pin arrangement to differentiate it from the two-row DB-15F connector specified for the game port. This prevents them from being confused with each other. With the NIC card, the RJ-45 jack is used with **Unshielded Twisted Pair (UTP)** LAN cabling, while the **British Naval Connector (BNC)** is provided for coaxial cable connections. Network cabling is discussed in more detail in Chapter 5 — *Data Communications*.

Figure 1-39 illustrates external connections for a basic AT-style system configuration. The power supply unit provides three points of interest at the system's back panel. The first is the female power receptacle, which may be used to provide power to IBM PC-compatible monitors. Next to the monitor power receptacle is the power supply's input connector. The detachable power cord plugs into this socket. Beside the power connector is the power supply's fan vent. In a small opening near the power supply openings is the circular, five-pin DIN connector for connecting a keyboard to the system.

Figure 1-39: AT External Connections

Across the remainder of the back panel are eight expansion-slot openings. Typical interface connections found in a basic system include two RS-232C connectors, a parallel printer port connector, and a game adapter connector. In this illustration, the game-port connector is located above the parallel-port connector. On other systems, the locations of the various connectors may vary. The last connector on the back panel is the video adapter's monitor connector. This example features a VGA-compatible, 3-row, 15-pin RGB color-output port connector.

Keyboards

The keyboard type most widely used with desktop and tower units is a detachable, low-profile 101/102-key model depicted in Figure 1-40. These units are designed to provide the user with a high degree of mobility and functionality. The key tops are slightly concave to provide a comfortable feel to the typist. In addition, the key makes a noticeable tap when it bottoms out during a keystroke.

Figure 1-40: An Alphanumeric Keyboard

AT-style detachable keyboards use a round, 0.5", 5-pin DIN connector to plug into the PC's system board. The connection is most often made through a round opening in the rear of the system unit's case. In some case designs, a front-mounted 5-pin plug-in is included. The front-mounted connector is routed to the system board through an extension cable.

With the IBM PS/2 line, a smaller (0.25"), 6-pin mini-DIN connector was adopted. This connector type has been adopted in the ATX specification for both the mouse and keyboard. Other PC-compatibles use a modular, 6-pin AMP connector to interface the keyboard to the system. Figure 1-41 shows the various connection schemes used with detachable keyboards.

┌─ **TEST TIP** ─────────────────┐
│ Be aware that plugging non-hot swappable devices │
│ like the keyboard into the system while it is turned │
│ on can damage parts of the system. │
└────────────────────────────────┘

Figure 1-41: Connection Schemes for Detachable Keyboards

Video Displays

Desktop and tower units normally use a color **Cathode-Ray Tube (CRT)** display monitor, similar to the one shown in Figure 1-42, as standard video output equipment. The PC, PC/XT, and PC-AT often used monochrome (single-color) monitors. They could also use color monitors by simply adding a color video adapter card and monitor. The **color CRT monitor** is sometimes referred to as an **RGB monitor**, since the three primary colors that make a color CRT are red, green, and blue.

In an AT-compatible system, the monitor could be plugged into either a commercial power receptacle or the special receptacle provided by the power supply at the rear of the unit. This option depends on the type of power cable provided by the manufacturer. There is a special adapter cable available to match a standard 120 Vac plug to this power supply receptacle. ATX-style power supplies do not provide a pass-through power connection for the monitor. The monitor's **signal cable** (connected to the video adapter card) permits the monitor to be positioned away from the system unit if desired.

The display's normal external controls include:

- Brightness and contrast
- Horizontal and vertical sizing
- Horizontal and vertical position
- Skew (sides and top/bottom of picture drawn in)

Figure 1-42: The CRT Display Monitor

The controls for these functions are located in different positions on the monitor depending on its manufacturer. In addition, each function may be directly addressable or may be accessed through a menu system. There is also a power on/off switch on the monitor. Its location varies from model to model as well. If the monitor receives power through the system unit's power supply, the monitor's power switch can be set to On and the monitor will turn on and off along with the system.

Other Peripherals

Mice, joysticks, trackballs, and touch pads belong to a category of input devices called **pointing devices**. They are all small, handheld input devices that enable the user to interact with the system by moving a cursor or some other screen image around the display screen, and to choose options from an onscreen menu, instead of typing commands from a keyboard. Because pointing devices make it easier to interact with the computer than other types of input devices, they are, therefore, friendlier to the user.

The most widely used pointing device is the mouse. Mice are handheld devices that produce input data by being moved across a surface, such as a desktop. The mouse has become a standard input device for most systems because of the popularity of GUI-based software.

The **trackball mouse** detects positional changes through the movement of a rolling trackball that it rides on. As the mouse moves across a surface, the mouse circuitry detects the movement of the trackball and creates pulses that the system converts into positional information.

Mice may have one, two, or three buttons that can be pressed in different combinations to interact with software running in the system. When the cursor has been positioned onscreen, one or more of the mouse buttons can be "clicked" to execute an operation or select a variable from the screen. Specialized graphics software enables the user to operate the mouse as a drawing instrument.

A newer mouse design, referred to as a **wheel mouse**, includes a small thumb wheel built into the top of the mouse between the buttons. This wheel enables the user to efficiently scroll up and down the video screen without using scroll bars or arrows.

Some scrolling functions, such as click-and-drag text highlighting in a word processor, can be awkward when the text extends off the bottom of the screen. In faster computers, the automatic scroll functions in some software packages will take off at the bottom of the screen and scroll several pages before stopping. The wheel in the mouse is designed to control this type of action. Additional software drivers must be installed to handle the additional wheel functions for the mouse.

Joysticks are very popular input devices used primarily with computer video games. However, they can also provide a convenient computer/human interface for a number of other applications. These peripherals are X-Y positioning devices with a **gimbal** (handle) that can be moved forward, backward, left, right, or at any angular combination of these basic directions to move a cursor or other screen element across a video display. Buttons on the joystick can be used in the same manner as buttons on a mouse. Joysticks are normally connected to a 2-row, 15-pin female D-shell game-port connector on the back panel of the computer.

Touch pads (or touch panels) are pointing devices that supply X-Y positioning for cursors and other screen elements. The touch pad typically replaces the mouse in the system. The user controls the screen element by moving a finger across the pad surface. Clicking and double-clicking functions associated with mice can be accomplished by tapping a finger on the pad. Touch pads come as an integral part of many portable computers. However, they can be obtained as add-on devices that plug into standard serial ports.

Character printers are widely used peripheral devices. Most printers communicate with the system through a parallel interface. Parallel printers are connected to the 25-pin female D-shell connector at the rear of the system. However, many printers use serial interfacing so that they can be located further from the computer. Serial interface versions normally plug into a 9-pin or 25-pin male D-shell connector. Most often, the serial printer is connected to the 25-pin connector that has been set up as the system's second serial port. The first serial port is typically set up with the 9-pin connector and handles the mouse connection.

Newer printers may offer a standard parallel connection, a standard serial port connection interface, or both. It may also be able to handle newer high-speed Universal Serial Bus, Firewire, or direct network connections. These interfaces are covered in greater detail in Chapter 6 — *Printers*. Common PC peripheral connections are depicted in Figure 1-43.

POWER
INPUT

6-PIN DIN
PORTS

USB
PORTS

KEYBOARD
AND MOUSE
CONNECTORS

25-PIN
PRINTER
PORT

PRINTER
ADAPTER
CONNECTOR

GAME
ADAPTER
CONNECTOR

15-PIN
GAME
PORT

NETWORK
CONNECTOR

RJ-45
NETWORK
PORT

MONITOR
CONNECTOR

BACK OF
SYSTEM
UNIT

15-PIN
VIDEO
PORT

Figure 1-43: Typical Peripheral Connections

CHALLENGE #1

Your employer wants to build a computer for his home and has asked you to give him a list of parts to shop for. He wants the system to be able to:

- Play his favorite music from CDs
- Provide access to the Internet
- Play high-resolution video games
- Create paper copies of Internet documents

List the components that you would suggest that he purchase to build the computer system he wants.

SOFTWARE

software

system software

application software

games

learning software

Once the system's components are connected together and their power connectors have been plugged into a receptacle, the system is ready for operation. However, there is one thing still missing — the **software**. Without good software to oversee its operation, the most sophisticated computer hardware is worthless.

There are actually three general classes of software that can be discussed:

- **system software**
- **application software**
- **games** and **learning software**

The bulk of the software discussed in this book falls into the system software category. This is because this type of software requires more technical skills to manipulate and, therefore, most often involves the service person.

System Software

The system software category consists of special programs used by the system itself to control the computer's operation. Two classic examples of this type of software are the system's **Basic Input/Output System (BIOS)** program and the **Disk Operating System (DOS)**. These programs, described in Figure 1-44, control the operation of the other classes of software. The BIOS is located in a ROM IC device on the system board. Therefore, it is commonly referred to as **ROM BIOS**. The DOS software is normally located on a magnetic disk.

Basic Input/Output
System (BIOS)

Disk Operating
System (DOS)

ROM BIOS

**Figure 1-44:
System Software**

Basic Input/Output Systems

When a PC is turned on, the entire system is reset to a predetermined starting condition. From this state, it begins carrying out software instructions from its BIOS program. This small program is permanently stored in the ROM memory ICs located on the system board. The information stored in these chips represents all the inherent intelligence that the system has to begin with.

compatibility

A system's BIOS program is one of the keys to its **compatibility**. For example, to e IBM PC-compatible, the computer's BIOS must perform the same basic functions that the IBM PC's BIOS does. However, since the IBM BIOS software is copyrighted, the compatible's software must accomplish the same results that the original did in some different way.

POST (Power-On
Self-Tests)

initialization

Master Boot Record

booting up

cold boot

reset

warm boot

During the execution of the BIOS firmware routines, three major sets of operations are performed. First, the BIOS performs a series of diagnostic tests on the system, called **POST** or **Power-On Self-Tests**, to verify that it is operating correctly. If any of the system's basic components are malfunctioning, the tests will cause an error message or code to be displayed on the monitor screen, and/or an audio code to be output through the system's speaker.

The BIOS program also places starting values in the system's various programmable devices. These intelligent devices regulate the operation of different portions of the computer's hardware. This process is called **initialization**. As an example, when the system is first started, the BIOS moves the starting address and mode information into the DMA controller. Likewise, the locations of the computer's interrupt handler programs are written into the interrupt controller. This process is repeated for several of the microprocessor's support devices so that they have the information they need to begin operation.

Finally, the BIOS searches the system for a special program that it can use to load other programs into RAM. This program is called the **Master Boot Record (MBR)**. The boot record program contains information that allows the system to load a much more powerful control program, called the Disk Operating System, into RAM memory. Once the operating system has been loaded into the computer's memory, the BIOS gives it control over the system. From this point, the operating system will oversee the operation of the system.

This operation of transferring control of the system from the BIOS to the operating system is referred to as **booting up** the system. If the computer is started from the OFF condition, the process is referred to as a **cold boot**. If the system is restarted from the ON condition, the process is called a **reset**, or a **warm boot**.

The bootup process may take several seconds to perform depending on the configuration of the system. If a warm boot is performed, or if the POST has been disabled, the amount of time required for the system to get into operation is decreased. The three components of the bootup process are illustrated in Figures 1-45, 1-46, and 1-47.

**Figure 1-45:
The Steps of a Bootup:
Phase One - POST**

Figure 1-46:
The Steps of a Bootup:
Phase Two - Initialization

Figure 1-47:
The Steps of a Bootup:
Phase Three - Bootup

In the first phase of the operation, the BIOS tests the microprocessor (1) and the system's RAM memory (2). In the second phase, it furnishes starting information to the system's microprocessor support devices (1), video adapter card (2), and disk drive adapter card (3). Finally, the BIOS searches through the system in a predetermined sequence for a master boot record to turn over control of the computer to. In this case, it checks the floppy-disk drive first (1) and the hard-disk drive second (2). If a boot record is found in either location, the BIOS will move it onto the computer's RAM memory and turn over control to it (3).

CMOS Setup

During the initialization process, PCs check a battery-powered storage area on the system board called the **CMOS RAM** to determine what types of options were installed in the system. During bootup, the BIOS permits users to have access to this configuration information through its **CMOS Setup utility**.

When the computer is set up for the first time, or when new options are added to the system, it is necessary to run the CMOS Configuration Setup utility. The values input through the utility are stored in the system's CMOS Configuration registers. These registers are examined each time the system is booted up to tell the computer what types of devices are installed. Early in the startup process, the BIOS places a prompt on the display to tell the user that the CMOS Setup utility can be accessed by pressing a special key, or a given key combination. Typical keys and key combinations include: the DEL key, the ESC key, the F2 function key, the CTRL and ESC keys, and the CTRL-ALT-ESC key combination.

The keys, or key combinations, used to access the setup menus vary from one BIOS manufacturer to another. If the proper keys are not pressed within a predetermined amount of time, the BIOS program will continue with the bootup process. However, if the keys are pressed during this time interval, the bootup routine will be put on hold and the program will display a "CMOS Setup Selection" screen.

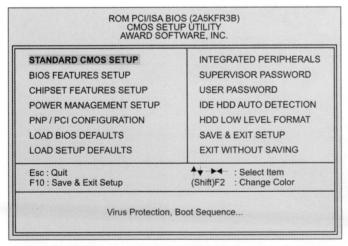

Every chipset variation has a specific BIOS designed for it. Therefore, there are functions specific to the design of system boards using that chipset. The example screen in the figure serves as the main menu for entering and exiting the CMOS Setup utility and for moving between its configuration pages.

A typical Configuration Setup screen is shown in Figure 1-48. Through this screen, the user enters the desired configuration values into the CMOS registers. The cursor on the screen can be moved from item to item using the keyboard's cursor control keys.

Figure 1-48: A CMOS Setup Selection Screen

Plug-and-Play

In most newer PCs, the BIOS, peripheral devices, and operating system employ **Plug-and-Play (PnP)** technology that enables the system to automatically determine what hardware devices are actually installed in the system and to allocate system resources to the devices to configure and manage them. This removes some of the responsibility for system configuration from the user or the technician. All three of the system components just mentioned must be PnP-compliant before automatic configuration can be carried out.

Plug-and-Play (PnP)

Basically, the PnP device communicates with the BIOS during the initialization phase of the startup to tell the system what type of device it is, where it is located in the system, and what its resource needs are. This information is stored on the device in the form of firmware. The BIOS stores the PnP information it collects from the devices in a special section of the CMOS RAM known as the **Extended System Configuration Data (ESCD)** area. This information is stored in the same manner as standard BIOS settings are stored. The BIOS and operating system both access the ESCD area each time the system is restarted to see if any information has changed. This enables the BIOS and operating system to work together in sorting out the needs of the installed devices and assigning them needed system resources. Figure 1-49 illustrates the basic PnP process.

Extended System Configuration Data (ESCD)

Figure 1-49: Plug-and-Play Operations

If no changes have occurred in the contents of the ESCD since the last bootup occurred, the BIOS will detect this and skip that portion of the boot process. When a PnP operating system checks the ESCD to see if any hardware changes have occurred, it will react accordingly and record any changes it finds in the hardware portion of its Registry. On some occasions, the system's PnP logic may not be able to resolve all of its resource needs and a configuration error will occur. In these cases, the technician, or the user, will have to manually resolve the configuration problem. The BIOS and operating system typically provide interfaces to the hardware configuration information so that users can manually override the system's Plug-and-Play resource assignments.

Operating Systems

Every portion of the system must be controlled and coordinated so that the millions of operations that occur every second are carried out correctly and on time. In addition, it is the job of the operating system to make the complexity of the personal computer as invisible as possible to the user.

Operating systems

Operating systems are programs designed to control the operation of a computer system. As a group, they are easily some of the most complex programs devised.

Likewise, the operating system acts as an intermediary between nearly as complex software applications, and the hardware they run on. Finally, the operating system accepts commands from the computer user, and carries them out to perform some desired operation.

Disk Operating System (DOS)

A **Disk Operating System (DOS)** is a collection of programs used to control overall computer operation in a disk-based system. These programs work in the background to allow the user of the computer to input characters from the keyboard, to define a file structure for storing records, or to output data to a monitor or printer. The disk operating system is responsible for finding and organizing your data and applications on the disk. The disk operating system can be divided into three distinct sections:

boot files

file management files

utility files

- **boot files** − take over control of the system from the ROM BIOS during startup

- **file management files** − enable the system to manage information within itself

- **utility files** − permit the user to manage system resources, troubleshoot the system, and configure the system

The operating system acts as a bridge between application programs and the computer, as described in Figure 1-50. These application programs allow the user to create files of data pertaining to certain applications such as word processing, remote data communications, business processing, and user programming languages.

Figure 1-50: The Position of DOS in the Computer System

Graphical User Interfaces

Another form of operating environment, referred to as a **Graphical User Interface (GUI)**, has gained widespread popularity in recent years. GUIs, like the Windows desktop depicted in Figure 1-51, employ a graphics display to represent procedures and programs that can be executed by the computer. These programs routinely use small pictures, called **icons**, to represent different programs. The advantage of using a GUI is that the user doesn't have to remember complicated commands to execute a program.

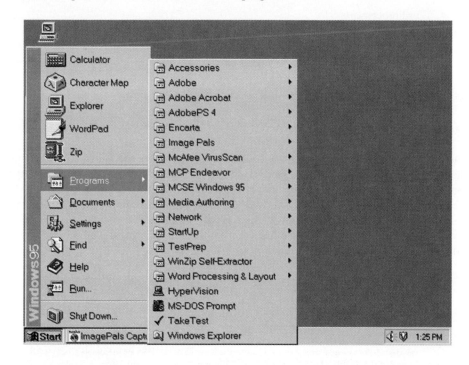

**Figure 1-51:
A Graphical User
Interface Screen**

APPLICATION SOFTWARE

The second major software category is application software. This category consists of programs that perform specialized tasks, such as word processing, accounting, and so forth. This category of software exists in two formats:

- Commercially available, user-oriented packages that may be purchased and used directly

- Programming language packages that developers can use to create user-oriented programs

Application software packages operate as extensions of the operating system. Depending on the type of operating system being used, an application program may directly control some system resources, such as printers and modems, while the operating system lends fundamental support in the background. In more advanced systems, the operating system supplies common input, output, and disk management functions for all applications in the system.

Commercial Application Packages

The openness of the personal computer market has generated a wide variety of different applications programs designed for use with them. Even a short discussion of all the software types available for the PC would take up more space than we can afford. However, a small group of these programs make up the vast majority of the software sold in this category. These programs are:

- Word processors

- Spreadsheets

- Graphic design packages

- Personal productivity tools

- Database Management Systems (DBMS)

Word processors are specialized software packages that can be used to create and edit alphanumeric texts, such as letters, memos, contracts, and other documents. These packages convert the computer into a super typewriter. Unlike typewriters, word processors enable the user to edit, check, and correct any errors before the document is committed to paper. Many word processors offer extended functions such as spelling checkers, as well as on-line dictionary and thesaurus functions that aid the writer in preparing the document. A typical word processor working page is depicted in Figure 1-52.

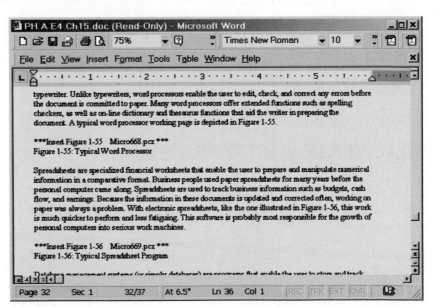

Figure 1-52: Typical Word Processor

Spreadsheets are specialized financial worksheets that enable the user to prepare and manipulate numerical information in a comparative format. Business people used paper spreadsheets for many years before the personal computer came along. Spreadsheets are used to track business information such as budgets, cash flow, and earnings. Because the information in these documents is updated and corrected often, working on paper was always a problem. With electronic spreadsheets, like the one illustrated in Figure 1-53, this work is much quicker to perform and less fatiguing. This software is probably most responsible for the growth of personal computers into serious work machines.

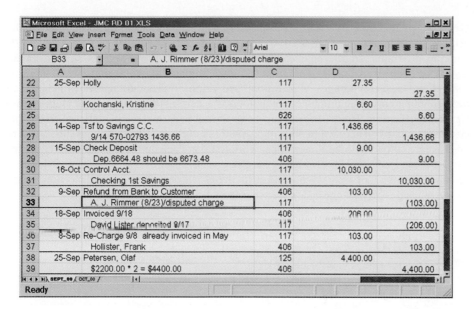

Figure 1-53: Typical Spreadsheet Program

Database management systems (or simply **databases**) are programs that enable the user to store and track vast amounts of related information about different subjects. Databases can be thought of as electronic boxes of note cards. You can keep several pieces of information related to a given subject on these electronic note cards.

For example, you might keep information on note cards for each of your relatives. The cards might contain their phone numbers, addresses, and birthdays. The database enables you to search and sort through the information in different ways. With a database program it would be no problem to sort out all of the relatives that have a birthday in a given month, or how many customers had purchased a given product from you in the last year. A typical database information page is depicted in Figure 1-54.

> Database management systems
>
> databases

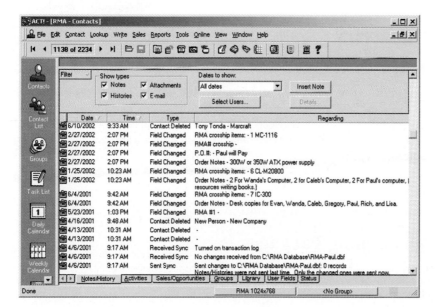

Figure 1-54: Typical Database Program

Graphics programs enable the user to create non-alphanumeric output from the computer. Simple graphics programs are used to create charts and graphs that represent data. More complex programs can be used to create artistic output in the form of lines, shapes, and images. Typically, graphic design programs produce graphics in two formats: as **bit-mapped images** and as **vector images**. With bit-mapped graphics, every dot (**pixel**) in the image is defined in memory. Vector images are defined as a starting point and a set of mathematical formulas in memory. Because vector images exist only as a set of mathematical models, their size can be scaled up or down easily without major distortions. Vector images can also be rotated easily, allowing three-dimensional work to take place on these images. On the other hand, bit-mapped graphics are tightly specified collections of spots across and down the screen. These types of images would be difficult to scale or rotate without distortion. A typical graphics design package is depicted in Figure 1-55.

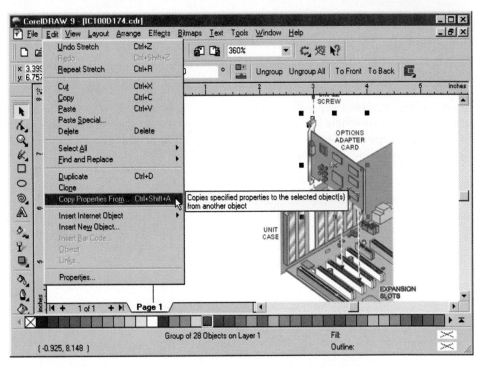

Figure 1-55: Typical Graphics Design Program

Personal productivity programs, also referred to as **desktop organizers**, encompass a variety of programs that simulate organizational tools found on typical business desks. They normally include items such as telephone directories, calculators, note pads, and calendar programs. Of course, many other types of application software are available for use with the PC. A meaningful discussion of all these software types is well beyond the scope of this book and certainly goes well beyond the scope of preparing for A+ testing.

Programming Packages

Because the only language that computers understand is their own machine language, and most humans don't relate well to machine languages, you'll need a piece of system software to convert whatever language you're programming into the machine's language. These conversion packages exist in two forms: **interpreters** and **compilers**. The distinction between the two is in how and when they convert the user language into machine language.

Interpreters convert the program as it is being **run** (executed). Compilers convert the entire user-language program into machine code before it is executed. Typically, compiled-language programs execute much faster than those written in interpretive languages. In addition, compiled languages typically provide the user with a much higher level of direct control over the computer's operation. In contrast, interpreted languages are usually slower, and less powerful, but their programs tend to be easier to write and use than those of compiled languages.

run

One of the most widely known programming environments is Microsoft's **Visual Basic** package. Unlike the previous command-line driven **BASIC** language versions, Visual Basic is a graphical programming tool that allows programmers to develop Windows applications on an artistic rather than a command-line basis. The programmer draws graphic elements and places them on the screen as desired. This tool is so powerful that it is used to produce large blocks of major applications, as well as finished Windows products. The finished product can be converted into an executable file using a Visual Basic utility. The only major drawback of Visual Basic is that major applications written in VB tend to run slowly, because it is an interpreted language.

Visual Basic

BASIC

Another alternative in programming exists for your computer — that is, to write programs in **Assembly language** (one step away from machine language) and run them through an **assembler** program. Assembly language is a human-readable form of machine language that uses short, symbolic instruction words, called **mnemonics**, to tell the computer what to do. Each line of an Assembly language program corresponds directly to one line of machine code. Writing programs in Assembly language enables the programmer to precisely control every aspect of the computer's operation during the execution of the program. This makes Assembly language the most powerful programming language you can use. To its detriment, Assembly language is complex, and requires the programmer to be extremely familiar with the internal operation of the system using the program.

Assembly language

assembler

mnemonics

A number of steps are required to create an Assembly language program:

1. You must create the program using an alphanumeric text editor.

2. The text file must be run through an **assembler program**, to convert the Assembly language into machine code.

3. Finally, the machine code must be run through a **linking program**, which puts the assembled machine code into the proper format to work with the operating system. In this final form, the program can be executed from DOS.

assembler program

linking program

For short and simple Assembly language programs, a DOS utility called **DEBUG** can be used to enter and run machine language and limited Assembly-language programs, without going through the various assembly steps. A sample DEBUG program is shown in Figure 1-56.

DEBUG

```
c:\>debug
-r

AX=0000  BX=0000  CX=0000  DX=0000  SP=FFEE  BP=0000  SI=0000  DI=0000
DS=20AB  ES=20AB  SS=20AB  IP=0100  NU UP EI PL NZ NA PO NC
20AB:100 0F      DB    0F

-d

20AB:0100 0F 00 B9 A8 FFF3 AE 47-61 03 IF 8B C3 48 12 B1    .......Ga.........H..
20AB:0110 04 8B C6 F7 0A 0A D0 D3-48 DA 2B D0 34 00 9A 20   ..........H.+.4.......
20AB:0120 00 DB D2 D3 E0 03 F0 8E-DA 8B C7 16 C2 B6 01 16   .....................
20AB:0130 C0 16 F8 8E C2 AC 8A D0-00 00 4E AD 8B C8 46 8A   ................N...F.
20AB:0140 C2 24 FE 3C B0 75 05 AC-F3 AA A0 0A EB 06 3C B2   ..$.<.U...........>.
20AB:0150 75 6D 6D 13 A8 01 50 14-74 B1 BE 32 01 8D 8B 1E   umm....P.+.2.......
20AB:0160 8E FC 12 A8 33 D2 29 E3-13 8B C2 03 C3 69 02 00   ......3.).......i.......
20AB:0170 0B F8 83 FF FF 74 11 26-01 1D E2 F3 81 00 94 FA   .......+.&.............
```

**Figure 1-56:
DEBUG Program**

Games and Educational Packages

Games and learning programs are among the leading titles in retail software sales. The games market has exploded as PC speeds have increased, and as output graphics have improved. However, on the technical side, there is generally not much call for repair associated with games software. Most games work with well-developed pointing devices, such as trackballs and joysticks, as the primary input devices. Although the housing designs of these products can be quite amazing, they tend to be simple and well-proven devices, requiring relatively little maintenance. Likewise, the software tends to be pretty straightforward from a user's point of view. It simply gets installed and runs.

**Computer-Aided
Instruction (CAI)**

**Computer-Based
Instruction (CBI)**

Computer-Aided Instruction (CAI) and **Computer-Based Instruction (CBI)** have become accepted means of delivering instructional materials. In CAI operations, the computer assists a human instructor in delivering information and tracking student responses. In CBI operations, the computer becomes the primary delivery vehicle for instructional materials.

As these teaching systems proliferate, more complex input, output, and processing devices are added to the system. A basic teaching system requires a minimum of a sound card, a fast hard drive, a CD-ROM drive, and a high-resolution video card. Beyond this, CAI and CBI systems may employ such wide-ranging peripherals as large LCD display panels, VGA-compatible overhead projectors, intelligent white boards, wireless mice and touch-sensitive screens as input devices, full-motion video capture cards, and a host of other multimedia-related equipment.

Version Numbers, Service Packs, and Patches

Software products never seem to get completely finished. They tend to be supplied in the form of a starting component and then undergo minor periodic changes until a major change in the product occurs. So that the user and the industry can keep track of where software products are within that cycle, the manufacturers assign software products **version numbers**.

Traditionally, when a programmer releases a software program for sale, a version number is assigned to it, such as Windows 3.11 or MS-DOS 6.22. The version number distinguishes the new release from prior releases of that same software. The larger the version number, the more recent the program and theoretically the more functions and features it has (and hopefully, the fewer problems and bugs it has).

When new features or capabilities are added to a program, it is given a new version number. Therefore, referring to a software package by its version number indicates its capabilities and operation. The number to the left of the decimal point is the major revision number, which usually changes when new features are added. The number(s) to the right of the decimal are minor revision numbers, which usually change when corrections are made to the program.

In 1995, Microsoft began a new method of referring to its software products. The initial product offering is given a name with the year of its origin appended to it (e.g., Windows 95, or Office 97). Major upgrades are delivered in a form known as Service Packs (collections of fixes and upgrades). Minor revisions are referred to as Updates. When software vintage needs to be discussed, such as when you are asking for technical assistance, the service pack installation is used (e.g., Windows 2000 Server — Service Pack 3 is running). Upgrades are typically assigned a number that no one remembers or speaks of after it has been installed on the machine. In both cases, Microsoft's preferred delivery method is through the Internet — no telephone/personnel cost, no media costs, and no mailing costs are incurred.

CHAPTER SUMMARY

This chapter has covered the fundamental hardware structures and components associated with PC-compatible personal computer systems. It has presented a mini-course on the basic organization and operation of the personal computer.

You should be able to identify the major components of a typical personal computer system and describe the function of each component. Finally, you should be able to describe the different levels of system software associated with a personal computer.

At this point, review the objectives listed at the beginning of the chapter to be certain that you understand and can perform each item listed there.

KEY POINTS REVIEW

This chapter has covered the fundamental hardware structures and components associated with PC-compatible personal computer systems. Review the following key points before moving into the Review and Exam Questions sections to make sure you are comfortable with each point. Afterward, answer the Review Questions that follow to verify your knowledge of the information.

- The tremendous popularity of the original IBM PC-XT and AT systems created a set of Pseudo Standards for hardware and software compatibility. The AT architecture became so popular that it has become the Industry Standard Architecture (ISA). The majority of microcomputers are both hardware- and software-compatible with the original AT design.

- The system unit is the main portion of the microcomputer system and is the basis of any PC system arrangement.

- The system board is the center of the system. It contains the portions of the system that define its computing power and speed.

- The system's power supply unit provides electrical power for every component inside the system unit, as well as supplying ac power to the video display monitor.

- The system board communicates with various optional Input/Output (I/O) and memory systems through adapter boards that plug into its expansion slots. These connectors are normally located along the left-rear portion of the system board so that the external devices they serve can access them through openings at the rear of the case.

- The microprocessor is the major component of any system board. It executes software instructions, and carries out arithmetic operations for the system.

- Microprocessor manufacturers always produce microprocessor-support chipsets that provide auxiliary services for the microprocessor.

- Each time the system is turned on, or reset, the BIOS program checks the system's Configuration Settings to determine what types of optional devices are included in the system.

- Newer microcomputers possess the capability to automatically reconfigure themselves for new options that are installed. This feature is referred to as Plug-and-Play (PnP) capability.

- The video adapter card provides the interface between the system board and the display monitor.

- The system unit normally comes from the manufacturer with a floppy-disk drive (FDD), a hard-disk drive (HDD), and a CD-ROM drive installed.

The following questions test your knowledge of the material presented in this chapter.

1. What are the major differences between AT and ATX power supplies (name three)?

2. List the four subunits typically found inside the system unit.

3. How can you avoid confusion between the DB-15F connectors for VGA and game port connections?

4. List three types of memory typically found on modern system boards.

5. Describe how data is stored on a magnetic disk.

6. List the devices normally found outside the system unit.

7. How are legacy cards different from PnP cards and how do they affect the system?

8. When connecting an AT power supply to a system board, what precaution should be taken?

9. What do the terms SIMM and DIMM stand for and what kind of devices are they?

10. What functions do microprocessors perform for the system?

11. Name a major drawback of tower cases.

12. Describe the organizational structure of a typical magnetic disk.

13. What is ESCD and how does it affect the operation of the system?

14. What is the data storage capacity of a typical CD-ROM?

15. List the three major sets of operations performed by the BIOS during startup.

1. What type of IC is the brain of the PC system?
   a. The ROM BIOS
   b. The ASIC device
   c. The memory controller
   d. The microprocessor

2. Name one weak feature of tower cases.
   a. Weak framework due to its vertical height
   b. Air flow through tower cases is generally not good
   c. High EFI radiation
   d. Requires excessive desk space in an office environment

3. Where is the system's BIOS program located?
   a. In ROM ICs located on the system board
   b. In the CMOS chip
   c. In the keyboard encoder
   d. In the microprocessor's L2 cache

4. What function does Plug and Play perform in the computer system?
   a. Enables system to automatically reconfigure itself
   b. Enables system to test itself
   c. Enables system to automatically load operating system files
   d. Enables system to automatically repair legacy configuration

5. Where is the MI/O function normally found in an ATX Pentium system?
   a. On the Multi-I/O card
   b. On the system board
   c. On the video card
   d. On the SCSI adapter card

6. In a PC-compatible system, _____.
   a. the BIOS must perform the same functions as the BIOS in an IBM PC
   b. the operating system must perform the same functions as the OS in an IBM PC
   c. the system must use the same ICs that the IBM PC used
   d. the system must use an IBM BIOS

7. Starting the computer from the power off condition is known as _____.
   a. warm boot
   b. cold boot
   c. Initialization
   d. Reset

8. Which of the following is not part of the bootup process?
   a. POST tests
   b. Initialization
   c. Loading MBR
   d. Executing utility files

9. The process of placing the starting values in a system's programmable devices is known as _____.
   a. POSTing
   b. initializing
   c. booting
   d. resetting

10. What is the main function of the MBR in a disk-based system?
    a. Test the basic system's hardware
    b. Load starting values into the system's intelligent devices
    c. Provide information to the system about loading the operating system
    d. Load the BIOS into RAM to start the system

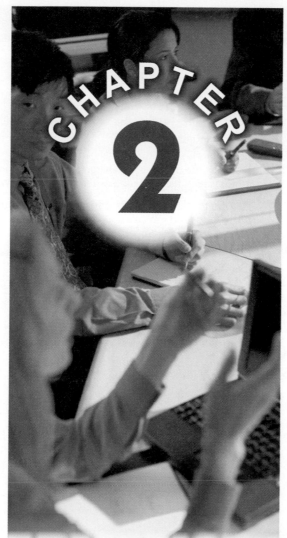

CHAPTER 2

ADVANCED SYSTEM BOARDS

OBJECTIVES

OBJECTIVES

Upon completion of this chapter and its related lab procedures, you will be prepared to:

1. Name popular Pentium class microprocessors and describe their basic characteristics, such as speeds, voltages, form-factors, and cache capabilities.

2. Differentiate between the characteristics of various types of RAM used in a PC system, including the different types of dynamic and static RAM.

3. Discuss typical memory organization schemes used with different system board types and, given a specific memory arrangement, identify the types of devices employed.

4. Identify the most popular types of motherboards, their components, and their architecture, including ATX as well as full and baby AT designs.

5. Identify typical system board components, including COMM ports, memory modules, and processor sockets.

6. Describe the characteristics of different expansion bus architectures, including ISA, PCI, AGP, USB, VESA, and PC Card specifications.

7. Discuss basic compatibility guidelines for different types of disk drive interfaces used with Pentium system boards, including the various types of IDE and SCSI devices.

8. State the purpose of CMOS RAM, what it typically contains, and how to change its basic parameters.

ADVANCED SYSTEM BOARDS

INTRODUCTION

The system board contains the components that form the basis of the computer system. Even though the system board's physical structure has changed over time, its logical structure has remained relatively constant. Since the original PC, the system board has contained the microprocessor, its support devices, the system's primary memory units, and the expansion-slot connectors. Figure 2-1 depicts a typical system board layout.

EXPANSION SLOT CONNECTORS   MICROPROCESSOR   KEYBOARD CONNECTOR

FRONT PANEL CONNECTIONS   CHIPSET   DIMM RAM   BATTERY   POWER CONNECTOR

Figure 2-1: A Typical System Board Layout

SYSTEM BOARD EVOLUTION

System boards fundamentally change for four reasons: new industry form-factors, new microprocessor designs, new expansion-slot types, and reduced chip counts. Reduced chip counts are typically the result of improved microprocessor support chipsets.

System Board Form Factors

form factor

It should be evident that all system boards are not alike. The term **form factor** is used to refer to the physical size and shape of a device. However, in the case of system boards, it also refers to their case style and power supply compatibility, as well as their I/O connection placement schemes. These factors come into play when assembling a new system from components, as well as in repair and upgrade situations where the system board is being replaced.

ATX System Boards

ATX form factor

ATX specification

The newest system board designation is the **ATX form factor** developed by Intel for Pentium-based systems. This specification is an evolution of the older baby AT form factor that moves the standard I/O functions to the system board.

> ┌─ **NOTE** ─────────────────────────────
>
> **The Changing Face of System Boards** — Chipset-based system boards and I/O cards tend to change often as IC manufacturers continue to integrate higher levels of circuitry into their devices.

The **ATX specification** basically rotates the baby AT form factor by 90 degrees, relocates the power supply connection, and moves the microprocessor and memory modules away from the expansion slots.

Figure 2-2 depicts a Pentium-based, ATX system board that directly supports the FDD, HDD, serial, and parallel ports. The board is 12" (305 mm) wide and 9.6" (244 mm) long. A revised, mini-ATX specification allows for 11.2"-by-8.2" system boards. The hole patterns for the ATX and mini-ATX system boards require a case that can accommodate the new boards. Although ATX shares most of its mounting-hole pattern with the baby-AT specification, it does not match exactly.

Figure 2-2: An ATX Pentium System Board

The power supply orientation enables a single fan to be used to cool the system. This provides reduced cost, reduced system noise, and improved reliability. The relocated microprocessor and memory modules allow full-length cards to be used in the expansion slots while providing easy upgrading of the microprocessor, RAM, and I/O cards.

The fully implemented ATX format also contains specifications for the power supply and I/O connector placements. In particular, the ATX specification for the power supply connection calls for a single, 20-pin power cord between the system board and the power supply unit rather than the typical P8/P9 cabling.

As illustrated in Figure 2-3, the new cable adds a +3.3 V (DC) supply to the traditional +/– 12 V (DC) and +/– 5 V (DC) supplies. A software-activated power switch can also be implemented through the ATX power connector specification. The PS-ON and 5VSB (5V Standby) signals can be controlled by the operating system to perform automatic system shutdowns.

┌─ **TEST TIP** ─────────────────┐
Know which type of system board can use a software power-off switch.
└────────────────────────────────┘

Figure 2-3:
An ATX Power Supply Connector

AT System Boards

The forerunner of the ATX system board was a derivative of the Industry Standard Architecture system board developed for the IBM PC-AT. The original **PC-AT system board** measured 30.5 x 33 centimeters.

PC-AT system board

PC

PC-XT system boards

baby AT system board

As the AT design became the de facto industry standard, printed-circuit-board manufacturers began to combine portions of the AT design into larger IC devices to reduce the size of their system boards. These chipset-based system boards were quickly reduced to match the original **PC** and **PC-XT system boards** (22 x 33 cm). This permitted the new 80286 boards to be installed in the smaller XT-style cases. This particular system board size, depicted in Figure 2-4, is referred to as a **baby AT system board**.

**Figure 2-4:
Baby AT
System Board**

System Board Compatibility

Obviously, the first consideration when installing or replacing a system board is whether it will physically fit and work with the other system components. In both of these situations, the following basic compatibility issues must be dealt with:

- The system board's form factor

- The case style

- The power supply connection type

System boards of different types have different mounting-hole patterns. Obviously the hole patterns of the replacement system board must match that of the case. If not, the replacement board cannot be installed or grounded properly.

Standard PC, PC-XT, and baby AT system boards share the same mounting hole patterns and can be exchanged with each other. However, the original PC-AT and ATX system boards have different hole pattern specifications. Most case manufacturers provide a variety of hole patterns in their designs to permit as many system board form factors as possible to be used with their cases.

Some clone system boards do not observe standard sizes (only compatible standoff spacing). If the case has a power supply that mounts in the floor of the unit, there may not be enough open width in the case to accommodate an extra-wide system board. The same can be said for a full-height disk drive bay. If the disk drive bay reaches from the floor of the case to its top, there will be no room for a wide system board to fit under it.

In addition to the mounting hole alignment issue, the case openings for expansion slots and port connections must be compatible with those of the system board. Various types of keyboard connectors have been used in different types of systems. Figure 1-43 (in Chapter 1) demonstrated the most common connectors used with PC keyboards: 6-pin mini DINs, 5-pin DINs, and RJ-11 plugs and jacks. PC-XT- and AT-compatible systems have historically used the 5-pin DIN connector. However, the 6-pin mini DIN is used with ATX systems. All three types of connectors have been used in non-compliant clone systems. If this is not taken into account when selecting a replacement board, additional expense may be incurred through the need to purchase an additional keyboard with the proper connector type.

┌─ TEST TIP ─┐
Remember which system board types use a 5-pin DIN connector.

Likewise, expansion-slot placement may vary somewhat between different form factors. The bad alignment created by this situation can make it difficult to install I/O cards in some systems. Similarly, I/O connectors mounted directly on the backs of some system boards may not line up with any openings in other case styles.

Expansion Slot Considerations

The types of adapter cards used in the system are another issue when replacing a system board. Make sure the new board has enough of the correct types of expansion slots to handle all the I/O cards that must be reinstalled. There is some upward compatibility between PC-bus, ISA, EISA, and VESA cards. Some PC-bus cards can be installed in ISA, EISA, and VESA slots—most cannot, however, because of a small skirt on the bottom of the card that is incompatible with the ISA extension portion of the slot. Both the EISA and VESA slots can accommodate ISA cards. Be aware that these relationships are not backward compatible. MCA and PCI are not compatible with the other bus types.

Some **low-profile (LTX)** cases are designed to be used with backplanes. In these units, the I/O cards are mounted horizontally on a backplane card that extends from an expansion slot on the motherboard. This arrangement produces a very low-profile desktop case style. The expansion slots in the back panel of the cases are horizontal as well. Therefore, standard system-board/adapter-card arrangements will not fit.

low-profile (LTX)

Power Supply Considerations

Power supply size, orientation, and connectors present another compatibility consideration. For example, an AT power supply cannot be installed in an ATX case. Because the AT bolt pattern is different than the ATX bolt pattern, it cannot be properly secured and grounded in the ATX case. Also, the single power connector from the ATX power supply will not connect to an AT system board's dual (P8/P9) power connector. Finally, ATX fans blow air into the case from the rear; AT power supplies pull it through the case from the front.

FRU Components

If system board FRU components, such as the microprocessor and/or RAM devices, are to be moved from the original system board to a replacement, they must be compatible with the new system board in terms of both physical characteristics and operating speed. Devices to be exchanged between system boards must physically fit in the sockets of the new board and be fast enough to work with the new system.

In the case of DRAM devices, a 30-pin SIMM from an older system cannot physically be used in a newer 72-pin SIMM slot. Even if the SIMM, or a 168-pin DIMM from the original board can be transferred, it must still have a sufficient speed rating to work in the new system. The same is true for cache memory upgrades. When moving a microprocessor to a new board, it must be socket compatible, voltage compatible, and speed compatible with the new board.

CHALLENGE #1

You have been called in as a computer consultant for the world's third largest banking organization. It wants to upgrade its existing computer systems to Pentium class systems. When you arrive, you discover that old Windows 3.11 operating systems are still running on 80386 computers. These systems use baby AT system boards, 2/3-size Multi-I/O cards, 9-pin serial mice, and 500 MB IDE hard drives. What should you advise the customer to do in order to upgrade the machines with the least cost and the most advantage?

Chipsets

chipset

IC manufacturers produce **chipset** packages that system board designers can use to support different microprocessors and standardized functions. While microprocessors have always had supporting chipsets supplied by their manufacturers, third-party chipsets began to appear when the AT architecture became the pseudo-standard for PC-compatible computers. Since then, IC manufacturers have tended to create chipsets for any complex circuitry that becomes a standard.

The original system board chipsets combined the major PC- and AT-compatible structures into larger integrated circuits. In particular, many IC makers produced single ICs that perform the AT interrupt, DMA, timer/counter, and real-time clock functions. These ICs also contained the address decoding and timing circuitry to support those functions.

half-size system board

Because chipset-based system boards require much fewer small- and medium-sized discrete devices to produce, printed-circuit-board manufacturers have been able to design much smaller PC boards.

HALF-SIZE AT SYSTEM BOARD

Figure 2-5: A Half-Size System Board

As VLSI technology improves, IC manufacturers continue to integrate higher levels of circuitry into their chips. All the functions of the four-chip chipset system board of Figure 2-4 are duplicated using the two-chip chipset system board depicted in Figure 2-5. The high level of circuit concentration in this chipset allows the size of the system board to be reduced even further. It is approximately half the length of a standard baby AT system board; therefore, this size system board is referred to as a **half-size system board**.

By combining larger blocks of circuitry into fewer ICs, a price reduction spiral is created. Having fewer ICs on the board reduces the manufacturing costs to produce the board. The material cost of the board is decreased due to its smaller physical size. The component cost is decreased because it is cheaper to buy a few VLSI chips than several SSI or MSI devices. Finally, the assembly cost is less because only a few items must be mounted on the board.

Reduced board costs create lower computer prices, which in turn create greater consumer demand for the computers. Increased demand for the computers, and therefore the chipsets, acts to further push down the prices of all the computer components.

It is normal to consider the ROM BIOS as an integral part of any chipset model because it is designed to support the register structure of a particular chipset. One of the major functions provided by the BIOS is the Chipset Features configuration screen in the CMOS Setup routine described later in this chapter. Technicians can use this tool to optimize the system settings to provide maximum internal performance. However, these settings tend to be very technical and require an extensive understanding of the specific system's component structure to configure. Therefore, replacing a ROM BIOS chip on a system board is not as simple as placing another ROM BIOS IC in the socket. The replacement BIOS must have correct information for the chipset being used on the system board.

Pentium Chipsets

Several IC manufacturers have developed chipsets to support the Pentium processor and its clones. Most of these designs feature a three-chip chipset that supports a combination PCI/ISA bus architecture. Figure 2-6 depicts a generic chipset arrangement for this type of system board.

**Figure 2-6:
Typical Pentium
Chipset**

The typical Pentium chipset consists of a Memory Controller (called the **North Bridge**), a PCI-to-ISA Host Bridge (referred to as the **South Bridge**), and an Enhanced I/O Controller. The Memory Controller provides the interface between the system's microprocessor, its various memory sections, and the PCI bus. In turn, the Host Bridge provides the interface between the PCI bus, the IDE bus, and the ISA bus. The Enhanced I/O Controller chip interfaces the standard PC peripherals (LPT, COM, and FDD interfaces) to the ISA bus.

This typical chipset arrangement may vary for a couple of reasons. The first reason is to include a specialized function, such as an AGP or USB interface. The second reason is to accommodate changes in bus specifications.

> North Bridge

> South Bridge

System Bus Speeds

Microprocessor and chipset manufacturers are continually developing products to speed up the operation of the system. One method of doing this is to speed up the movement of data across the system's data buses. Looking at the arrangement shown in Figure 2-6, you should note that the buses operating directly with the microprocessor and North Bridge are running at one speed, while the PCI bus is running at a different speed, and the ISA/MIO devices are running at still another speed. The chipset devices are responsible for coordinating the movement of signals and data between these different buses.

Front Side Bus (FSB)

Back Side Bus (BSB)

The bus between the microprocessor and the North Bridge is referred to as the **Front Side Bus (FSB)**. In advanced Pentium processors, a parallel bus called the **Back Side Bus (BSB)** connects the microprocessor with its internal L2 cache. Historically, the Pentium processors have operated at many speeds between 50 MHz and 1.1 GHz. At the same time the front side buses have been operating at 66 MHz, 100 MHz, and 133 MHz. Likewise, the PCI bus has operated at standard speeds of 33 MHz, 44 MHz, and 66 MHz. While the speeds of these buses have been improved, the speed of operation for the ISA bus has remained constant at 8 MHz.

Using an example of a current Pentium system board, the processor may run at 1.1 GHz internally, while the front side bus runs at 133 MHz, the PCI bus runs at 33 MHz, the IDE bus runs at 100 MHz, and the ISA bus runs at 8 MHz. The devices in the supporting chip set are responsible for coordinating data and control signal flow between the different buses. You can think of these buses as highways and streets where traffic travels at different speeds. The devices in the chipset act as on/off ramps and stoplights to effectively coordinate information movement across the buses.

TEST TIP

Know which processors can be used with which system board bus speeds.

Some settings on system boards are still enabled and configured through on-board jumpers or switches. Incorrectly setting processor-related system board jumpers causes a high number of failures for both new installations and upgrades. You should always refer to the system board's Installation Guide or User's Manual for definitions of these settings.

However, most newer system boards feature auto-detection functions as part of the PnP process that automatically detect different FRU components on the board (i.e., processors, fans, RAM modules, and adapter cards) and synchronize the different bus speed configurations. For example, the auto-detect feature will examine the installed microprocessor and the installed RAM modules to configure the front side bus for maximum microprocessor-memory operations. Similarly, the chipset may detect an advanced video adapter card in one of the expansion slots and adjust the expansion bus speed to maximize the performance of the video display. Likewise, the system will auto-detect the installed hard drives and CD-ROM drives and adjust the IDE bus speed to provide the best drive system performance based on what it finds.

Finally, the system evaluates the information it has acquired about its various components and buses and configures the north and south bridges so that they provide synchronization between their other buses and the PCI bus that connects them together. The PCI bus speed (and by default its AGP video slot derivative) does not change to accommodate different installed components. Its speed is established as a derivative of the microprocessor clock (not to be confused with the advertised speed rating of the microprocessor).

In some configurations, the microprocessor clock is set at a higher speed than the IC manufacturer suggests. This is referred to as **overclocking** the processor. Because the basic microprocessor is running faster than designed, both the front side bus and the PCI bus run faster than their stated values by a factor directly proportional to the amount that the microprocessor is overclocked.

Major Chipset Functions

The original IBM PC used a 7-chip chipset to support the 8088 microprocessor. These devices included the following intelligent support devices:

- An 8284 Clock Generator
- An 8288 Bus Controller
- An 8255 Parallel Peripheral Interface (PPI)
- An 8259 Programmable Interrupt Controller (PIC)
- An 8237 DMA Controller (DMAC)
- An 8253 Programmable Interval Timer (PIT)
- An 8042 Intelligent Keyboard Controller

The clock generator and bus controller ICs assisted the microprocessor with system clock and control bus functions. The PPI chip handled system configuration and on-board addressing functions for the system's intelligent devices.

The interrupt controller provided the system with eight channels of programmable interrupt capabilities. The 8237 DMA controller provided four channels of high-speed DMA data transfer service for the system. The 8253 was used to produce three programmable timer channel outputs to drive the system's time-of-day clock, DRAM refresh signal, and system speaker output signal. The PC/XT interrupt and DMA controller functions are shown in Figure 2-7.

Figure 2-7: PC/XT Interrupt and DMA Controller Functions

When the IBM PC-AT came to the market, it brought an upgraded chipset that expanded the capabilities of the system. IBM improved the basic 8284 and 8288 devices by upgrading them to 82284 and 82288 versions. Likewise, the keyboard controller and the three-channel timer/counter were updated in the AT.

The AT interrupt and DMA channel capabilities were both doubled by cascading two of each device together. Actually, the usable channel counts only rose to 15 and 7 respectively. In each case, one IC is the master device and the other is the slave device. One channel of each master device was used to accept input from the slave device. Therefore, that channel was not available for use by the system.

As an example, the output of the secondary interrupt controller is cascaded through the IRQ2 input of the master controller. In this way, the system sees all of the devices attached to the secondary controller as IRQ2. A priority resolver sorts out which interrupt from the slave controller is causing the interrupt. The PC-AT interrupt and DMA controller functions, shown in Figure 2-8, still form the basis for all PC-compatible architectures.

Figure 2-8: PC-AT Interrupt and DMA Controller Functions

Since the second interrupt controller is cascaded through the first controller, the system sees the priority of the IRQ lines as described in Table 2-1. The table also indicates the usage of each IRQ line.

Table 2-1:
IRQ's Priorities

AT PRIORITY	USE
IRQ0	System Board
IRQ1	System Board
IRQ2	System Board
IRQ8	System Board
IRQ9	I/O
IRQ10	I/O
IRQ11	I/O
IRQ12	I/O - System Board
IRQ13	System Board
IRQ14	I/O
IRQ15	I/O
IRQ3	I/O
IRQ4	I/O
IRQ5	I/O
IRQ6	I/O
IRQ7	I/O

Using the IRQ2 channel to front for the entire slave controller meant that the IRQ2 channel had to be removed from its position in the 8-bit PC-bus expansion slot that was used in the PC and PC-XT systems. Optional devices could no longer use this channel. Therefore, in the ISA bus that was introduced with the PC-AT (and is still used today), the IRQ position in the slot was replaced with IRQ9. These slots are described in the following sections.

Expansion Slots

The system's expansion slots provide the connecting point for most of its I/O devices. Interface cards communicate with the system through the extended microprocessor buses in these slots.

As mentioned in Chapter 1—*Basic PC Hardware*, expansion slots basically come in three formats: 8-bit, 16-bit, and 32-bit data buses. The PC-bus slot is the most famous example of an 8-bit expansion slot, while the ISA slot is the consummate 16-bit expansion bus. The 32-bit expansion buses include the MCA bus, the EISA bus, the VESA bus, and the PCI bus. Let's cover the 8-bit expansion slots first.

8-Bit Slots

The 8-bit expansion slots in the original PC, PC-XT, and their compatibles became the **de facto** industry connection standard for 8-bit systems. It was dubbed the **PC-bus standard**.

The PC-bus expansion slot connector, illustrated in Figure 2-9, featured an 8-bit, bi-directional data bus and 20 address lines for the I/O channel. It also provided six interrupt channels, control signals for memory and I/O read or write operations, clock and timing signals, and three channels of DMA control lines. In addition, the bus offered memory refresh timing signals, and an I/O channel check line for peripheral problems, as well as power and ground lines for the adapters that plug into the bus.

**Figure 2-9:
An 8-Bit PC-Bus
Expansion Slot**

16-Bit Slots

The overwhelming popularity of the IBM PC-AT established it as the 16-bit standard to which all other PC-compatible equipment is compared. Originally, this bus was called the **AT bus**. However, its widespread acceptance earned it the **Industry Standard Architecture (ISA)** title it now carries. As a matter of fact, the ISA slot is the most common expansion slot used with microcomputers. Even in units that have newer, faster 32-bit expansion slots, it is not uncommon to find one or more ISA slots.

This bus specification originally appeared on the 16-bit, 80286-based PC-AT system board. Its 16-bit data bus improved the performance of the system by enabling twice as much data to pass through the slot at a time. It also made transfers with 16-bit microprocessors a single-step operation. While the ISA bus ran at microprocessor-compatible speeds up to 10 or 12 MHz, incompatibility with slower I/O cards caused manufacturers to settle for running the bus at 8 or 8.33 MHz in newer designs.

Figure 2-10 shows an ISA-compatible expansion slot connector. These expansion slots actually exist in two parts: the slightly altered, 62-pin I/O connector, similar to the standard PC-bus connector, and a 36-pin auxiliary connector.

AT bus

Industry Standard Architecture (ISA)

TEST TIP

Remember that the ISA bus features a 16-bit data bus and runs at 8 or 8.33 MHz.

**Figure 2-10:
A 16-Bit ISA
Expansion Slot**

It provides twice as many interrupt and DMA channels as the PC bus specification. This made it possible to connect more peripheral devices to ISA systems. In order to maintain compatibility with older adapter cards, the transfer speed for the ISA bus was limited to the same speed as that of the older PC-bus.

32-Bit Architectures

As 32-bit microprocessors gained popularity, the shortcomings and restrictions of the 16-bit ISA bus became noticeable. Obviously, the ISA bus could not support the full, 32-bit capabilities of microprocessors such as the 80386DX, the 80486DX, and the Pentium. In addition, the physical organization of the signal lines in the ISA bus produced unacceptable levels of **Radio Frequency Interference (RFI)** as the bus speed increased. These factors caused designers to search for a new bus system to take advantage of the 32-bit bus and the faster operation of the processors.

Two legitimate 32-bit bus standards were developed to meet these challenges. These were the **Extended Industry Standard Architecture (EISA)** bus, which, as its name implies, was an extension of the existing ISA standard bus, and an IBM-sponsored proprietary bus standard called **Micro Channel Architecture (MCA)**.

Although both 32-bit designs were revolutionary and competed for the market, both have passed from the scene. In both cases, market demand did not support these designs and they were eventually replaced by other more acceptable standards.

Local Bus Designs

In order to speed up the operation of their systems, system board manufacturers began to add proprietary bus designs to their board to increase the speed and bandwidth for transfers between the microprocessor and a few selected peripherals. This was accomplished by creating special **local buses** between the devices that would enable the peripherals to operate at speeds close to that of the microprocessor.

When these designs began to appear, the peripherals that could be used in them were typically only available from the original system board manufacturer. The industry soon realized the benefits of such designs and the need for "standards." Currently, most Pentium system boards include a combination of ISA, AGP, and PCI expansion slots.

Initially, the **VL bus** offered the advantages of higher performance and lower costs than similar boards with PCI buses. In addition, the VL bus was typically implemented in such a way that 16-bit ISA cards could still use the traditional part of the expansion slot. However, improvements in the PCI standard have made it the bus of choice for most Pentium system boards.

Both local bus specifications include slot addressing capabilities and reserve memory space to allow for plug-and-play reconfiguration of each device installed in the system. Unfortunately, system boards that use these expansion slots normally have a few ISA-compatible slots also. This feature can seriously disrupt the plug-and-play concept since no identification or reconfiguration capabilities were designed into the ISA bus specification.

Radio Frequency Interference (RFI)

Extended Industry Standard Architecture (EISA)

Micro Channel Architecture (MCA)

local buses

VL bus

Due to industry moves away from anything related to ISA cards, the PCI bus has become the dominant force in system board designs. Each generation of PCI designs has provided fewer and fewer ISA buses. Current designs may include a single ISA connector for compatibility purposes or none at all.

PCI Local Bus

The **Peripheral Component Interconnect (PCI)** local bus was jointly developed by IBM, Intel, DEC, NCR, and Compaq. Its design incorporates three elements: a low-cost, high-performance local bus, the automatic configuration of installed expansion cards (plug-and-play), and the ability to expand with the introduction of new microprocessors and peripherals. The data transfer performance of the PCI local bus is 132 MBps using a 32-bit bus and 264 MBps using a 64-bit bus. This is accomplished even though the bus has a maximum clock frequency of 33 MHz.

Peripheral Component Interconnect (PCI)

The PCI peripheral device has 256 bytes of on-board memory to hold information as to what type of device it is. The peripheral device can be classified as a controller for a mass-storage device, a network interface, a display, or other hardware. The configuration space also contains control, status, and latency timer values. The latency timer register on the device determines the length of time that the device can control the bus for bus mastering operations.

Figure 2-11 illustrates the structure of a system based on PCI local bus chipset components.

Figure 2-11: PCI Bus Structure

The main component in the PCI-based system is the PCI bus controller, called the **host bridge**. This device monitors the microprocessor's address bus to determine whether addresses are intended for devices on the system board, in a PCI slot, or in one of the system board's other expansion slots.

host bridge

In PC-compatible systems, the PCI bus normally co-exists with an ISA bus. The PCI portion of the bus structure functions as a **mezzanine bus** between the ISA bus and the microprocessor's main bus system. The figure also depicts a **PCI-to-ISA bridge** that allows ISA adapters to be used in the PCI system. Other bridge devices can also accommodate either EISA or MCA adapters.

mezzanine bus

PCI-to-ISA bridge

The host bridge routes PCI data directly to the PCI expansion slots through the local bus. These transfers occur at speeds compatible with the microprocessor. However, it must route non-PCI data to the PCI-to-ISA bridge that converts it into a format compatible with the ISA expansion slot. In the case of ISA slots, the data is converted from the 64/32-bit to the 16-bit ISA format. These transfers occur at typical ISA bus speeds.

The original PCI bus employed 32-bit address and data buses. Its specification also defined a 64-bit multiplexed address and data bus variation for use with 64-bit processors, such as the Pentium. Its clock line was originally defined for a maximum frequency of 33 MHz and a 132 Mbps transfer rate. However, it can be used with microprocessors operating at higher clock frequencies (e.g., 66 MHz under the PCI 2.1 specification).

The PCI 2.2 and PCI 2.3 versions of the bus implemented two new slot structures to provide a true 64-bit data bus, as illustrated in Figure 2-12. The new PCI specification runs at 66 MHz to provide a 264 Mbps data throughput. The slot also features a reduced 3.3 Vdc power supply voltage to decrease signal interference levels generated by the 33 MHz operations. Adapters placed in the 32-bit section of the PCI 2.2 slot can operate with the 5 Vdc or 3.3 V supply levels. The back portion of the slot remains pin and signal compatible with the older 32-bit PCI slots. It retained its +5 Vdc operating voltage to remain compatible with older PCI 1.1 and 2.0 adapters.

An additional PCI bus improvement has been developed using a new slot layout for PCI 2.3. This slot is similar to the PCI 66-32/64 intermediate slot in size and appearance. However, it is keyed in such a manner that only adapter cards designed for this slot (or universal PCI cards) can be inserted. The slot also features a reduced 3.3 Vdc power supply voltage to decrease signal interference levels generated by the 66 MHz operations.

5.0 V 32-BIT 33 MHz

3.3 V 64-BIT 66 MHz

5.0 V 64-BIT 33 MHz

**Figure 2-12:
32-bit and 64-bit
PCI Slots**

PCI Configuration

The PCI standard is part of the plug-and-play hardware standard. As such, the system's BIOS and system software must support the PCI standard. Although the PCI function is

detection phase

self-configuring, many of its settings can be viewed and altered through the CMOS Setup utility. Figure 2-13 depicts the PCI PnP configuration information from a typical BIOS.

During a portion of the bootup known as the **detection phase**, the PnP-compatible BIOS checks the system for devices installed in the expansion slots to see what types they are, how they are configured, and which slots they are in. For PnP-compatible I/O cards, this information is held in a ROM device on the adapter card.

The BIOS reads the information from all of the cards and then assigns each adapter a **handle** (logical name) in the **PnP registry**. It then stores the configuration information for the various adapters in the registry as well. This process is shown in Figure 2-14. Next, the BIOS examines

```
                    ROM PCI/ISA BIOS (P155TVP4)
                        PNP AND PCI SETUP
                       AWARD SOFTWARE, INC.

Slot  1  (Right) IRQ   : Auto          DMA  1  Used By ISA    : No/ICU
Slot  2  IRQ           : Auto          DMA  3  Used By ISA    : No/ICU
Slot  3  IRQ           : Auto          DMA  5  Used By ISA    : No/ICU
Slot  4  IRQ           : Auto
PCI  Latency Timer     : 32 PCI Clock  ISA MEM Block BASE     : No/ICU

                                       NCR SCSI BIOS          : Auto
IRQ  3  Used By ISA  : No/ICU          USB Function           : Disabled
IRQ  4  Used By ISA  : No/ICU
IRQ  5  Used By ISA  : No/ICU
IRQ  6  Used By ISA  : No/ICU
IRQ  7  Used By ISA  : No/ICU
IRQ  8  Used By ISA  : No/ICU
IRQ  9  Used By ISA  : No/ICU
IRQ  10 Used By ISA  : No/ICU
IRQ  11 Used By ISA  : No/ICU
IRQ  12 Used By ISA  : No/ICU
IRQ  13 Used By ISA  : No/ICU          ESC  : Quit           ↑↓←→        : Select Item
IRQ  14 Used By ISA  : No/ICU          F1   : Help           PU/PD/+/-   : Modify
IRQ  15 Used By ISA  : No/ICU          F5   : Old Values     (Shift) F2  : Color
                                       F6   : Load BIOS Defaults
                                       F7   : Load Setup Defaults
```

Figure 2-13: PCI Configuration Settings

the adapter information against the system's basic configuration for **resource conflicts**. After evaluating the requirements of the cards and the system's resources, the PnP routine assigns system resources to the cards as required.

handle

PnP registry

resource conflicts

**Figure 2-14:
PCI Information
Acquisition**

TEST TIP

Know which system resources the PnP system must assign first and why.

Since the PnP process has no method for reconfiguring legacy devices during the resource assignment phase, it begins by assigning resources, such as IRQ assignments, to legacy devices before servicing the system's PnP devices.

TEST TIP

Know the process the PnP system employs to allocate resources to a new device in an existing system.

Likewise, if the BIOS detects the presence of a new device during the detection phase, it disables the resource settings for its existing cards, checks to see what resources are required and available, and then reallocates the system's resources as necessary.

Depending on the CMOS settings available with a particular PCI chipset, the startup procedure may be set up to configure and activate all of the PnP devices at startup. With other chipsets, it may also be possible to check all cards, but only enable those actually needed for startup. Some CMOS routines may contain several user-definable PCI configuration settings. Typically, these settings should be left in default positions. The rare occasion for changing a PCI setting occurs when directed to do so by a product's installation guide.

Systems may theoretically contain an unlimited number of PCI slots. However, a maximum of four slots are normally included on a system board due to signal loading considerations. The PCI bus includes four internal interrupt lines (INTa through INTd, or INT1 through INT4) that allow each PCI slot to activate up to four different interrupts. PCI interrupts should not be confused with the system's IRQ channels, although they can be associated with them if required by a particular device. In these cases, IRQ9 and IRQ10 are typically used.

AGP Slots

Accelerated Graphics Port (AGP)

Newer Pentium systems include an advanced **Accelerated Graphics Port (AGP)** interface for video graphics. The AGP interface is a variation of the PCI bus design that has been modified to handle the intense data throughput associated with three-dimensional graphics.

The AGP specification was introduced by Intel to provide a 32-bit video channel that runs at 66 MHz in basic 1X video mode. The standard also supports three high-speed modes that include a 2X (5.33 MBps), a 4X (1.07 GBps), and an 8X (2.1 GBps) mode.

TEST TIP

Know what type of device is plugged into an AGP slot.

The AGP standard provides for a direct channel between the AGP graphic controller and the system's main memory, instead of using the expansion buses for video data. This removes the video data traffic from the PCI buses. The speed provided by this direct link permits video data to be stored in system RAM instead of in special video memory. System boards designed for portable systems and single-board systems may incorporate the AGP function directly into the board without using a slot connector.

As illustrated in Figure 2-15, there have been three different types of slot connectors used to deliver the AGP function for system boards used in desktop and tower units. The system board typically features a single slot that is supported by a Pentium/AGP-compliant chipset. The original slot configuration had a key located toward the rear of the board. These slots were used with 3.3 V (2X) adapters. The second AGP slot version moved the key toward the front of the board so that it was not physically compatible with the older AGP adapters. These slots were used with 1.5 V (4X) adapters. The final revision of the AGP slot is the universal AGP slot that removes all keys so that it can accept any type of AGP card (including universal adapters). These slots can be used with 3.3 V, 1.5 V and 0.8 V (2X/4X/8X) adapters.

Figure 2-15:
AGP Slots

The newer 8X specification employs a lower supply voltage (0.8) than the 2X and 4 X speci-fications. When upgrading an AGP card or system board containing an AGP slot, you should always consult the system board and AGP adapter card's documentation to verify their com-patibility with each other. Usually the Chipset Features page of the CMOS Setup utility pro-vides user-configurable AGP slot parameters that can be used to manually configure the adapter's parameters.

The default setting for this option is *Autodetect*. In this mode, the PnP process will detect the card and assign the correct voltages and maximum speed settings for that type of card.

Audio Modem Risers

Intel has developed a new audio/modem standard for system board designs. This standard in-cludes an expansion slot connection, called the **Audio Modem Riser** (**AMR**), and a com-panion expansion card format, known as the **Mobile Daughter Card** (**MDC**). These components are depicted in Figure 2-16.

Figure 2-16:
Audio Modem Riser
Components

The design specification separates the analog and digital functions of audio (sound card) and modem devices. The analog portion of the function is placed on the MDC riser card while the digital functions are maintained on the system board. This permits the system board to be certified without passing through the extended FCC and international telecom certification process attached with modem certifications. Only the MDC needs to pass the FCC certifica-tion process.

**coder/decoder
(codec)**

The contents of the MDC basically consist of an analog audio **coder/decoder** (**codec**) or a modem circuit. The digital functions performed by the system board are a function of software instead of a hardware device such as a UART. The system microprocessor basically performs the UART functions under the control of the audio or modem software. This relationship makes the AMR device much less expensive, but places additional overhead on the operation of the microprocessor.

**Communications and
Networking Riser
(CNR)**

AMR slots are already being replaced in Pentium systems by a new design called the **Communications and Networking Riser** (**CNR**) card, depicted in Figure 2-17. This specification improves on the AMR specification by including support for advanced V.90 analog modems, multi-channel audio, telephone-based dial-up networking, and USB devices, as well as 10/100 Ethernet-based LAN adapters.

**Figure 2-17:
Communications and
Networking Riser Card**

PCMCIA Slots

As more and more desktop users began to adopt laptop and notebook computers for travel, they demanded that additional peripheral systems be included. With the limited space associated with portables, it became clear that a new method for installing options would need to be developed. At first, laptop and notebook manufacturers included proprietary expansion connectors for adding such devices as fax/modems, additional memory, and additional storage devices.

**Personal Computer
Memory Card
International
Association's
(PCMCIA)**

PC Card

In 1989, the **Personal Computer Memory Card International Association's** (**PCMCIA**) bus standard was introduced using a 68-pin JEIDA connector. A small form-factor expansion-card format, referred to as the **PC Card** format, was also adopted for use. This format was derived from earlier laptop/notebook memory card designs. The design of the bus specification enables the PC Card interface to be used for a wide variety of peripheral devices.

The PCMCIA slot connector is typically recessed in the portable's case. The credit card-sized PC cards slide into bays in the side of the case. They are normally pushed through a spring-loaded door on the side of the case and slide along guide rails molded into the sides of the bay. When fully inserted, the sockets built into the end of the cards engage the pins of the recessed connector. Peripheral devices are attached to the exposed end of the card through a small PC-Card connector, as illustrated in Figure 2-18.

Figure 2-18: PCMCIA Connections

Since PC Cards are primarily used with portable computer systems, they are discussed in detail in Chapter 7—*Portable Systems*.

Table 2-2 compares the capabilities of the various bus types commonly found in personal computers. It is quite apparent that the data transfer rates possible with each new version increase dramatically. The reason this is significant is that the expansion bus is a speed-limiting factor for many of the system's operations. Every peripheral access made through the expansion slots requires the entire computer to slow down to the operating speed of the bus.

Table 2-2: Expansion Bus Specifications

BUS TYPE	TRANSFER RATE	DATA BITS	ADDRESS BITS	DMA CHANNELS	INT CHANNELS
PC	1 MBps	8	20	4	6
ISA	8 MBps	16	24	8	11
EISA	32 MBps	32	32	8	11
MCA	20–40 MBps	32	32	None	11
VESA	150/275 MBps	32/64	32	None	1
PCI 2	132/264 MBps	32/64	32	None	3
PCI 2.1	264/528 MBps	32/64	32	None	3
AGP	266/533/1,070 MBps	32	32	None	3

I/O Connections

Pre-Pentium computers typically employed a Multi-I/O (MI/O) adapter card to provide standardized AT-compatible I/O connections. However, the chipsets used to construct Pentium-based system boards move these I/O functions to the system board by including the ports' interfaces and controllers in the chipset.

Pentium AT Ports

Figure 2-19: AT-Style Pentium System Board I/O Connections

The typical Pentium chipset integrates the circuitry for all the traditional MI/O functions, except the game port, into one or two VLSI chips. Figure 2-19 illustrates a sample arrangement for the AT-style Pentium system board's standard I/O connectors (ports).

The Pentium chipset normally provides a single, programmable parallel printer port, which allows a wide range of printers and other parallel devices to be connected to the system. Parallel I/O devices plug into a DB-25F connector located on an expansion-slot cover. This port is connected to the system board at the 26-pin BERG pin block PRT1.

Figure 2-20: AT-Style Serial-Port Connections

The last of the system board's I/O adapter functions are the RS-232C serial/asynchronous interface-port connections COM1 and COM2. These ports support serial communications for serial I/O devices, such as mice and modems. A ribbon cable connects the system board's COM1 connector to a DB-9M connector located on one of the unit's slot covers. This serial port is typically the system's first serial port and is normally the mouse connector.

Another ribbon cable connects the system board's COM2 connection to a DB-25F connector on one of the expansion-slot covers. This connector serves as the second logical serial port.

Separate hardware jumpers on the system board are typically used to configure the interrupt levels for the first and second serial ports (COM1 and COM2). Care should be taken when setting these jumpers because the two serial ports cannot share the same COM-port designation. Figure 2-20 illustrates the proper connection of the serial-port ribbon cables to the AT-style system board.

Pentium ATX Ports

On ATX-compliant system boards, the MI/O port connections have been moved to a vertical stack form factor located at the rear of the board. Figure 2-21 depicts the standard arrangement of the I/O port connections in an ATX system.

The ATX specification employs two 6-pin mini-DIN connectors for the mouse and keyboard. Of course, the fact that both connections use the same type of connector can lead to problems if they are reversed. The standard also provides for two USB port connections, a DB-25F D shell parallel printer port connector, two RS-232 serial COM ports implemented in a pair of DB-9M D-shell connectors, a DB-15F D-shell game port, and an RCA audio port. Unlike the AT-style integrated I/O connections, these port connections require no system board connecting cables that can become defective.

Figure 2-21: ATX System Board I/O Connections

┌─ **TEST TIP** ─────────────────────────────────┐

Be aware that the use of the 6-pin mini DIN in ATX systems can cause confusion between the keyboard and PS/2 mouse connections.

└──┘

On-Board Disk Drive Connections

Along with the I/O port connections, Pentium system boards moved the hard- and floppy-disk drive controller functions and interface connections to the system board, as illustrated in Figure 2-22. As is the case with most Pentium-based system boards, this example provides the system's IDE host adapter and floppy-disk drive controller interface connections.

The FDC portion of the chipset can control two floppy-disk drives whose signal cable connects to the system board at the 34-pin BERG block (labeled FD1 in Figure 2-22). As with any disk-drive connections, caution must be taken when connecting the floppy-disk drive signal cable to the system board; pin 1 of the connector must line up with the signal cable's indicator stripe.

Figure 2-22: Pentium Board Disk Drive Connections

IDE Connections

The IDE host adapter portion of the chipset is normally capable of controlling up to four hard-disk or CD-ROM drives. These adapters furnish two complete IDE channels—IDE1 and IDE2—that can handle one master and one slave device each. The hard drives and CD-ROM drives are connected to the system board's IDE connectors through 40-conductor ribbon cables at connectors ID1 or ID2.

The primary partition of the drive attached to the ID1 connector will be designated as a logical C: drive. If a second drive is attached to ID1 as a slave, its primary partition will be designated as a logical D: drive. If there is an additional *partition* on the first drive, it will be designated as the E: drive. The hierarchy of assigning logical drive designations in the IDE interface calls for primary partitions to be assigned sequentially from ID1 master, ID1 slave, ID2 master, to ID2 slave. This is followed by assigning *extended partitions* for each drive in the same order (drive partitions are logical divisions of hard-disk drives and are covered in detail in Chapters 4 and 8).

The hard drives are connected in much the same manner as the floppy drives. The first hard drive is connected to the end of the cable farthest away from the ID1 or ID2 connector. Observe the same cable orientation that was used for connecting the floppy-disk drives when connecting the cable to the FD1 connector for the hard drives. Figure 2-23 provides an example of the alignment of the FDD and HDD cables on the system board.

TEST TIP

You must be able to identify IDE system board connections from different ATX and AT system board drawings by their relative sizes and locations.

Figure 2-23: HDD and FDD System Board Connections

There are several versions of the IDE interface. Fortunately most of these versions are only concerned with the software and drivers that control the flow of information through the interface. With very minor exceptions the physical interface on the system board remains a 40-pin BERG connector.

System boards that used the original IDE specification provided one 40-pin connector on the board and offered a single IDE channel that could control two IDE devices (one master and one slave). Newer system boards feature two physical IDE connectors and implement one of the **Enhanced IDE**, or **EIDE** standards for communications. Each EIDE channel is capable of handling its own master and slave devices. Over time, the EIDE interface has been redefined to provide faster transfer rates, as well as to handle larger storage capacities. EIDE interfaces can also be used to control drive units such as a tape or CD-ROM. The EIDE interface is often described as an **ATAPI (AT Attachment Packet Interface)**, or a **Fast ATA (Fast AT Attachment)** interface.

You should be aware that two similar types of cables are used with EIDE devices. The newer EIDE enhancements provide higher data throughput using the standard 40-pin connector, by doubling the number of conductors in the cable to 80. In these cables, the IDE connector has remained compatible with the original 40-pin IDE standard, but each pin has been provided with its own ground conductor in the cable. When newer IDE devices are connected to the system using an older 40-conductor cable, they will operate at speeds compatible with the older IDE standards.

After the EIDE hardware has been installed, its operating mode must be configured correctly through the system's CMOS Setup utility. Newer system boards possess an auto-detect feature in the BIOS that communicates with the hard drives and automatically configures them for optimum use with the system. The CMOS Setup utility can be used to manually configure IDE channel parameters. Both IDE channels can be Enabled, Disabled, or placed in Auto-detect mode through CMOS settings. These settings are discussed under the "Chipset Features Screen" heading later in this chapter.

| Enhanced IDE |
| EIDE |
| ATAPI (AT Attachment Packet Interface) |
| Fast ATA (Fast AT Attachment) |

SCSI Connections

There are no industry-accepted equivalents for on-board SCSI adapters. Although a few such system board designs are available, they are not standard boards and have probably been created to fill the specific needs of a particular application. Therefore, SCSI devices require that a SCSI host adapter card be installed in most systems. SCSI host adapters are typically available for use with ISA, EISA, and PCI bus interfaces.

The built-in SCSI connector on the system board will normally be made through a 50-pin BERG header. Like the IDE drives, support for the on-board SCSI controller must be established through the CMOS Setup utility. The system BIOS provides support for the built-in SCSI controller through its CMOS Setup utility, whereas add-on adapter cards feature a BIOS extension on the card.

┌─ **TEST TIP** ─────────────┐
│ Be aware of the types of expansion slots that │
│ SCSI cards are typically available for. │
└────────────────────────────┘

Your colleague has faxed you the following drawing of an old, stripped system board he is planning to repopulate for use as a Linux mail server.

He is not sure about which components he must obtain to make it work again. From the drawing, what can you tell him about what he will need to get the board up and running again?

MICROPROCESSORS

The A+ Core objective 4.1 states that the test taker should be able to distinguish between popular CPU chips in terms of their basic characteristics.

Contents may include the following:

- Popular CPU chips (Pentium class compatible)

- Voltage

- Speeds (actual vs. advertised)

- Cache level I, II, III

- Sockets/Slots

- VRMs

INTEL PROCESSORS

When IBM was designing the first PC, it chose the Intel 8088 microprocessor and its supporting chipset as the standard CPU for its design. This was a natural decision since one of IBM's major competitors (Apple) was using the Motorola microprocessor for its designs. The choice to use the Intel microprocessor still impacts the design of PC-compatible systems. As a matter of fact, the microprocessors used in the vast majority of all PC-compatible microcomputers include the Intel 8088/86, 80286, 80386, 80486, and Pentium (80586 and 80686) devices.

The popularity of the original PCs, PC-XTs, and PC-ATs (and the software developed for them) has caused limitations to be built into the newer microprocessors to maintain compatibility with the microprocessors used in these systems. The popularity of these processors has been so high that it has produced a microprocessor clone market that designs processors to mimic the Intel design.

For the most part, the previous generations of microprocessors have disappeared from the marketplace, leaving the Pentium as the only processor type that needs to be discussed in detail. Therefore, the microprocessor material that follows builds on the earlier Intel models described in Chapter 1—*Basic PC Hardware*. We will first look at the Intel Pentium microprocessors that have set the trends in PC design and then explore the clone versions of these processors to see how they are different.

The Pentium Processor

The **Pentium processor** succeeded the 80486 microprocessor, and maintained compatibility with the other 80x86 microprocessors. When Intel introduced the Pentium, it discontinued the **80x86** naming convention it had previously used for its microprocessors. This was done so that Intel could copyright the name (numbers cannot be copyrighted) and prevent microprocessor clone manufacturers from using the same convention. Therefore, the 80586 became the Pentium.

The Pentium is a 32/64-bit microprocessor contained in a Ceramic Pin Grid Array package. The internal architecture of the Pentium is shown in Figure 2-24. The registers for the microprocessor and floating-point sections of the Pentium are identical to those of the 80486. It has a 64-bit data bus that allows it to handle **Quad Word** (or **Qword**) data transfers. The Pentium also contains two separate 8 kB caches, compared to only one in the 80486. One of the caches is used for instructions or code, and the other is used for data. The internal architecture of the Pentium resembles an 80486 in expanded form. The floating-point section operates up to five times faster than that of the FPU in the 80486.

The Pentium is referred to as a **superscalar** microprocessor because its architecture allows multiple instructions to be executed simultaneously. This is achieved through a **pipelining** process. Pipelining is a technique that uses multiple **stages** to speed up instruction execution. Each stage in the pipeline performs a part of the overall instruction execution, with all operations being completed at one stage before moving on to another stage. This technique allows streamlined circuitry to perform a specific function at each stage of the pipeline, thereby improving execution time. When an instruction moves from one stage to the next, a new instruction moves into the vacated stage. The Pentium contains two separate pipelines that can operate simultaneously. The first is called the **U-pipe** and the second the **V-pipe**.

| Pentium processor |
| 80x86 |

| Quad Word |
| Qword |

| superscalar |
| pipelining |
| stages |
| U-pipe |
| V-pipe |

**Figure 2-24:
Inside the Pentium
Microprocessor**

CPU cooling fan

P54Cs

Staggered Pin Grid
Array (SPGA)

The original Pentium processor architecture has appeared in three generations. The first-generation design, code named the P5, came in a 273-pin PGA package and operated at 60 or 66 MHz speeds. It used a single +5 Vdc operating voltage, which caused it to consume a large amount of power and generate a large amount of heat. The Pentium processor generated so much heat during normal operation that an additional **CPU cooling fan** was usually required.

The second-generation Pentiums, referred to as **P54Cs**, came in a 296-pin **Staggered Pin Grid Array (SPGA)** package and operated at 75, 90, 100, 120, 133, 150, and 166 MHz in different versions. For these devices, Intel reduced the power supply voltage level for the core of the processor to +3.3 Vdc to consume less power and provide faster operating speeds. Reducing the power supply level in effect moves the processor's high and low logic levels closer together, requiring less time to switch back and forth between them. The SPGA packaging made the second generation of Pentium devices incompatible with the first-generation system boards. The external interfaces of the processor continue to operate at +5 Vdc to be compatible with other system board components.

The second-generation devices also employed internal clock multipliers to increase performance. In this scenario, the system's buses run at the same speed as the clock signal introduced to the microprocessor. However, the internal clock multiplier causes the microprocessor to operate internally at some multiple of the external clock speed (i.e., a Pentium operating from a 50 MHz external clock and a 2x internal multiplier is actually running internally at 100 MHz).

Basically, all Pentium microprocessors use 50, 60, or 66 MHz external clock frequencies to generate their internal operating frequencies. The value of the internal multiplier is controlled by external hardware jumper settings on the system board.

The third-generation Pentiums, referred to as the **P55Cs**, use a 296-pin SPGA arrangement. This package adheres to the 321-pin Socket-7 specification designed by Intel. The P55C has been produced in versions that operate at 150, 166, 180, 200, and 233 MHz. This generation of Pentium devices operate at voltages below the +3.3 level established in the second generation of devices. The P55C is known as the **Pentium MMX (Multimedia Extension)** processor and is described in greater detail later in this chapter. A pin-out for the first-generation Pentium is shown in Figure 2-25.

Figure 2-25: The Pins of the Pentium Microprocessor

Advanced Pentium Architectures

Intel has continued to advance its Pentium line of microprocessors by introducing additional specifications including the Pentium MMX, Pentium Pro, Pentium II, Pentium III, XEON, Pentium 4, and Itanium processors.

At the same time, Intel's competitors have developed clone designs that equal or surpass the capabilities of the Intel versions. The following sections will look at the advancements Intel has produced and then focus on the clone processors that compete with them.

Pentium MMX

In the **Pentium MMX** processor, the multimedia and communications processing capabilities of the original Pentium device were extended by the addition of 57 multimedia-specific instructions to the instruction set.

Intel also increased the on-board L1 cache size to 32 kB. The cache has been divided into two separate 16 kB caches: the instruction cache and the data cache. The typical L2 cache used with the MMX was 256 kB or 512 kB.

The MMX added an additional multimedia-specific stage to the integer pipeline. This integrated stage handled MMX and integer instructions quickly. Improved branching prediction circuitry was also implemented to offer higher prediction accuracy and, thereby, provide higher processing speeds. The four Prefetch buffers in the MMX could hold up to four successive streams of code. The four write buffers were shared between the two pipelines to improve the memory write performance of the MMX.

The Pentium MMX processor was available in 166, 200, and 233 MHz versions and used a 321-pin, SPGA Socket-7 format. It required two separate operating voltages. One source was used to drive the Pentium processor core, while the other was used to power the processor's I/O pins. The pin-out of the Pentium MMX is shown in Figure 2-26.

Figure 2-26:
The Pins of the Pentium MMX Microprocessor

Compare Figures 2-25 and 2-26. Notice the staggered pin arrangement of the MMX device compared to the uniform row and column arrangement of the original Pentium devices. Also, notice the new signals added to the Pentium architecture for later versions. Some of these additional signals were used to implement the VRM and internal clock multiplier functions for the advanced Pentiums.

Pentium Pro

Intel departed from simply increasing the speed of its Pentium processor line by introducing the **Pentium Pro** processor. While compatible with all of the previous software written for the Intel processor line, the Pentium Pro is optimized to run 32-bit software.

However, it did not remain pin-compatible with the previous Pentium processors. Instead, Intel adopted a 2.46" x 2.66", 387-pin PGA configuration to house a Pentium Pro **processor core**, and an on-board 256 kB (or 512 kB) L2 cache. The L2 cache complements the 16 kB L1 cache in the Pentium core. This arrangement is illustrated in Figure 2-27. Notice that while they are on the same PGA device, the two components are not integrated into the same IC. The unit is covered by a gold-plated, copper/tungsten heat spreader.

The L2 on-board cache stores the most frequently used data not found in the processor's internal L1 cache, as close to the processor core as it can be without being integrated directly into the IC. A high-bandwidth cache bus (referred to as the backside bus) connects the processor and cache unit together. The bus (0.5 inches in length) allows the processor and external cache to communicate at a rate of 1.2 GB/second.

Figure 2-27: The Pentium Pro Microprocessor

The Pentium Pro is designed in a manner so that it can be used in typical, single-microprocessor applications or in multiple-processor environments, such as high-speed, high-volume file servers and workstations. Several dual-processor system boards have been designed for twin Pentium Pro processors. These boards, like the one shown in Figure 2-28, are created with two Pentium Pro sockets so that they can operate with either a single processor, or with dual processors. When dual processors are installed, logic circuitry in the Pentium Pro's core manages the requests for access to the system's memory and 64-bit buses.

Figure 2-28:
A Dual-Processor
System Board

Pentium II

Pentium II

Single Edge Contact
(SEC) cartridge

retention mechanism

Slot 1

Intel radically changed the form factor of the Pentium processors by housing the **Pentium II** processor in a new, **Single Edge Contact (SEC) cartridge**, depicted in Figure 2-29. This cartridge uses a special **retention mechanism** built into the system board to hold the device in place. The new proprietary socket design is referred to as the **Slot 1** specification and is designed to allow the microprocessor to eventually operate at bus speeds in excess of 300 MHz. This is the upper operating frequency limit for pin grid sockets.

TEST TIP

Remember which components Intel included in the SEC cartridge.

Figure 2-29: The
Pentium II Cartridge

Fan Heat Sink (FHS)

The cartridge also requires a special **Fan Heat Sink (FHS)** module and fan. Like the SEC cartridge, the FHS module requires special support mechanisms to hold it in place. The fan draws power from a special power connector on the system board, or from one of the system's optional power connectors.

Tag RAM

L2 Burst SRAM

Inside the cartridge, there is a substrate material on which the processor and related components are mounted. The components consist of the Pentium II processor core, a **Tag RAM**, and an **L2 Burst SRAM**. Tag RAM is used to track the attributes (read, modified, etc.) of data stored in the cache memory.

> **Pentium II**—The Pentium II includes all of the multimedia enhancements from the MMX processor, as well as retaining the power of the Pentium Pro's dynamic execution and 512 kB L2 cache features. The L1 cache is increased to 32 kB, while the L2 cache operates with a half-speed bus.

Figure 2-30 depicts the contents of the Pentium II cartridge.

Figure 2-30: Inside the Pentium II Cartridge

A second cartridge type, called the Single Edged Processor Package (SEPP), has been developed for use with the Slot 1 design. In this design, the boxed processor is not completely covered by the plastic housing as it is in the SEC design. Instead, the SEPP circuit board is accessible from the back side.

You can upload processor update information into the BIOS that has **Application Programming Interface (API)** capabilities built into it to modify the operation of Pentium Pro and Pentium II/III/4 processors. The microprocessor manufacturer places update information on its web site that can be downloaded by customers. The user transfers the update information from the update media to the system's BIOS via the API routine. If the updated data is relevant (as indicated by checking its processor stepping code), the API writes the updated microcode into the BIOS. This information will, in turn, be loaded into the processor each time the system is booted.

> **Application Programming Interface (API)**

Pentium III

Intel followed the Pentium II processor with a new Slot 1-compatible design it called the **Pentium III**. The original Pentium III processor (code-named Katmai) was designed around the Pentium II core, but increased the L2 cache size to 512 kB. It also increased the speed of the processor to 600 MHz including a 100 MHz front side bus speed.

> **Pentium III**

Intel followed the Pentium III design with a less expensive version that it named the Pentium **Celeron**. Unlike the original Pentium III, the Celeron version featured a 66 MHz bus speed and only 128 kB of L2 cache. Initially, the **Celeron Mendocino** was packaged in the SEC cartridge.

> ┌─ **TEST TIP** ─────────────────
> Be able to state the difference between Pentium II and Pentium III processors.

> **Celeron**

> **Celeron Mendocino**

Later versions of the Pentium III and Celeron processors were developed for the Intel **Socket 370** specification. This design returned to a 370-pin, ZIF socket/SPGA package arrangement, depicted in Figure 2-31.

Figure 2-31:
Socket 370/Celeron

The first pin grid array versions of the Pentium III and Celeron processors conformed to a standard called the **Plastic Pin Grid Array (PPGA)** 370 specification. Intel repackaged its processors into a PGA package to fit this specification. The PPGA design was introduced to produce inexpensive, moderate-performance Pentium systems. The design topped out at 533 MHz with a 66 MHz bus speed.

Intel upgraded the Socket 370 specification by introducing a variation called the **Flip Chip Pin Grid Array (FC-PGA)** 370 design. Intel made small modifications to the wiring of the socket to accommodate the Pentium III processor design. In addition, they employed a new 0.18 micron IC manufacturing technology to produce faster processor speeds (up to 1.12 GHz) and front-side bus speeds (100 MHz and 133 MHz). However, the new design only provides 256 kB of L2 cache.

Pentium III and Celeron processors designed with the 0.18 micron technology are referred to as **Coppermine** and **Coppermine 128** processors, respectively (the L2 cache in the Coppermine 128 is only 128 kB). Further developments of the Coppermine versions, referred to as **Tualatin**, employed 0.13 micron IC technology to achieve 1.4 GHz operating speeds with increased cache sizes (256 kB or 512 kB).

Xeon

Intel has produced three special versions of the Pentium III that they have collectively named the **Pentium Xeon**, as shown in Figure 2-32. These processors are designed to work with an edge-connector-based **Slot 2** specification that Intel has produced to extend their Slot 1/boxed-processor scheme to a 330-contact design. Each version features a different level of L2 cache (512 kB, 1 MB, 2 MB). The Xeon designs were produced to fill different, high-end server needs.

SCREWS

DUAL RETENTION
MECHANISM TOP

CLIPS

PROCESSOR

HEAT SINK

PROCESSOR
CONNECTOR

DUAL
RETENTION
MECHANISM

SYSTEM BOARD

SYSTEM BOARD

Figure 2-32: The Xeon Processor

The Xeon designs were produced to fill different, high-end server needs. The Xeon processor functions at speeds up to 866 MHz and is built upon the 0.18-micron process technology. The processor allows for highly scalable server solutions that support up to 32 processors. Benefits of the Xeon processor include:

- Scalability — Start small and add more processors later

- Faster I/O — Incorporates a I2O architecture and faster PCI

- Better Manageability — IPMI management allows cluster to be managed as one

- Flexibility — designed to industry-open physical and mechanical specifications

Pentium 4

Late in 2000, Intel released their newest Pentium version called the Williamette 423, or **Pentium 4** microprocessor. However, the Pentium 4 is not a continuation of the Pentium design. It is actually a new design (IA-32 NetBurst architecture) based on .18-micron IC construction technology. It employs a modified Socket 370 PGA design that uses 423 pins and boasts operating speeds up to 2.0 GHz. The system bus has been increased from 64 to 128 bits and operates at up to 400 MHz. The newer .13-micron versions are code named Northwood and operate at speeds up to 3.06 GHz. The newer Pentium 4 design employs an improved 478-pin version of the chip.

In addition to the new front side bus size, the Pentium 4 features new WPNI (Williamette Processor New Instructions) instructions in its instruction set. The L1 cache size has been reduced from 16 kB in the Pentium III to 8 kB for the Pentium 4. The L2 cache is 256 kB and can handle transfers on every clock cycle.

The operating voltage level for the Pentium 4 core is 1.7 Vdc. To dissipate the 55 watts of power (heat) that the microprocessor generates at 1.5 GHz, the case incorporates a metal cap that acts as a built-in heat sink. Firm contact must be maintained between the microprocessor's case and its built-in heat sink feature.

Pentium 4

Table 2-3 summarizes the characteristics of the Intel Pentium microprocessors.

Table 2-3: Characteristics of the Intel Pentium Microprocessors

TYPE	ADDRESS BUSWIDTH	SPACE	INTERNAL CLOCK SPEED (MHz)	DATA BUSWIDTH	MATH CO-PROCESSOR
Pentium	32	4 GB	50 - 100	64	On-board
Pentium MMX	32	4 GB	166 - 233	64	On-board
Pentium Pro	36	4 GB x 4	150 - 200	64	On-board
Pentium II	36	64 GB	233 - 450	64	On-board
Pentium III	36	64 GB	450 - 1 GHz	64	On-board
Celeron	36	64 GB	266 - 766	64	On-board
Pentium 4	36	64 GB	1.4 - 1.5 GHz	128	On-board

Itanium Processors

Itanium

Explicitly Parallel Instruction Computing (EPIC)

The Intel **Itanium** processor, depicted in Figure 2-33, provides a new architecture specifically for servers. It maximizes server performance through special processing techniques Intel refers to as **Explicitly Parallel Instruction Computing (EPIC)**. The Itanium architecture provides the following performance enhancements using the EPIC technology:

- *Predication* — the ability to identify a certain condition inline, rather than relying on inefficient test and branch algorithms. It uses branch prediction to work more efficiently with "if-then-else" statements. This eliminates or minimizes the number of memory accesses required to execute an instruction.

- *Speculation* — a function that improves the performance of the Itanium processor by allowing the compiler to schedule and store load instructions ahead of branches to reduce memory latency.

- *Parallelism* — delivers higher performance and scalability by enabling the compiler to provide more information to the processor, allowing it to execute multiple operations simultaneously on a sustained basis.

Figure 2-33: The Itanium Processor

The Itanium processor design features a new three-level, on-board cache system. The L1 cache size is 32 kB operating fully pipelined, while the L2 cache size is 96 kB and the new **L3 cache** is available in two sizes—2 MB or 4 MB. The cartridge's edge connector specification provides separate voltage levels for the processor and cache devices to improve signal integrity.

Because Itanium processors are designed to be available 100 percent of the time, they tend to be very expensive—often more expensive than the complete network operating system that it is running. However, the cost of the processor is nothing compared to the cost of most on-line businesses going down for just one hour.

Pentium Clones

As mentioned earlier in this chapter, Intel abandoned the 80x86 nomenclature in favor of names that could be copyrighted in an effort to distance themselves from the **clone microprocessor** manufacturers. When this occurred, the other manufacturers largely followed the 80x86 path, but eventually moved toward alternative numbering schemes as well.

AMD Processors

Advanced Micro Devices (AMD) offers several clone microprocessors: the 5x86 (X5), the 5x86 (K5), the K6, the K6PLUS-3D, and K7 microprocessors. The X5 offers operational and pin compatibility with the DX4. Its performance is equal to that of the Pentium and MMX processors. The K5 processor is compatible with the Pentium, and the K6 is compatible with the MMX. Both the K5 and K6 models are Socket-7 compatible, enabling them to be used in conventional Pentium and Pentium MMX system-board designs (with some small modifications). The K6 employs an extended 64 kB L1 cache that doubles the internal cache size of the Pentium II.

The K6PLUS-3D is operationally and performance compatible with the Pentium Pro, and the K7 is operationally and performance compatible with the Pentium II. However, neither of these units has a pin-out compatibility with another processor.

AMD continues to produce clone versions of Pentium processors. In some cases, the functions and performance of the AMD devices go beyond the Intel design they are cloning. Two notable AMD clone processors are the Athlon and the Duron.

The **Athlon** is a Pentium III clone processor. It is available in a Slot 1 cartridge clone, called the Slot A specification. Figure 2-34 depicts the cartridge version of the Athlon processor with a **Slot A** connector.

The Athlon is also available in a proprietary SPGA Socket A design that mimics the Intel Socket 370 specification. The **Socket A** specification employs a 462-pin ZIF socket and is only supported by two available chipsets.

BACK OF CARTRIDGE

SLOT A
CONNECTOR

FRONT OF CARTRIDGE

Figure 2-34: Slot A/Athlon Version

Three versions of the Athlon processor have been introduced so far. The first version was the K7 version that ran between 500 MHz and 700 MHz, provided a 128 kB L1 cache and a 512 kB L2 cache, and employed a 100 MHz system bus.

Subsequent Athlon versions have included the K75, Thunderbird, Thoroughbred, and Barton versions. Both versions are constructed using the 0.18-micron manufacturing technology. The K75 processor ran between 750 MHz and 1 GHz. Like the K7 version, it provided a 128 kB L1 cache and a 512 kB L2 cache, and employed a 100 MHz system bus. The Thunderbird version ran between 750 MHz and 1.2 GHz, provided a 128 kB L1 cache and a 256 kB L2 cache, and employed a 133 MHz system bus. The Thoroughbred featured 256 kB of L2 cache and the standard 64+64 kB L1 cache. It operated at speeds up to 2.8 GHz.

| Athlon XP |

The latest evolutions of the Athlon processor have been given the title of **Athlon XP**. These versions were based on the Thoroughbred and the newer Barton core versions. The Barton versions feature a 512 kB L2 cache, a slower clock speed, and a maximum processor speed of 3.0 GHz.

| Duron |

The **Duron** processor is a Celeron clone processor that conforms to the AMD Socket A specification. The Duron features processor speeds between 600 MHz and 800 MHz. It includes a 128 kB L1 cache and a 64 kB L2 cache. Like the newer Celerons, the Duron is constructed using 0.18-micron IC manufacturing technology.

In addition to the 80x86 numbering system, Intel used a Px identification up to the Pentium II. The Pentium II is identified as the Klamath processor. Subsequent improved versions have been dubbed: Deschutes, Covington, Mendocino, Katmai, Willamette, Northwood, Flagstaff (P7), Merced, and Tahoe.

Socket Specifications

| OverDrive processors |
| Socket 1 |
| Socket 3 |
| Socket 4 |
| Socket 6 |
| Socket 7 |
| Voltage Regulator Module (VRM) |
| Socket 5 |
| Socket 8 |

In addition to the clone processors, Intel has developed a line of upgrade microprocessors for their original units. These are referred to as **OverDrive** processors. An OverDrive unit may simply be the same type of microprocessor running at a higher clock speed, or it may be an advanced architecture microprocessor designed to operate from the same socket/pin configuration as the original. To accommodate this option, Intel has created specifications for eight socket designs, designated Socket 1 through Socket 8.

The specifications for **Socket 1** through **Socket 3** were developed for 80486SX, 80486DX, and 80486 OverDrive versions that use different pin numbers and power supply requirements. Likewise, the **Socket 4** through **Socket 6** specifications deal with various Pentium and OverDrive units that use different speeds and power supply requirements. The **Socket 7** design works with the fastest Pentium units and includes provision for a **Voltage Regulator Module (VRM)** to allow various power settings to be implemented through the socket. The Socket-7 specification corresponds to the second generation of Pentium devices that employ SPGA packaging. It is compatible with the **Socket 5**, straight-row PGA specification that the first-generation Pentium processors employed. Finally, the **Socket 8** specification is specific to the Pentium Pro processor.

Although the Intel Slot 1 design was originally developed for the Pentium II, it also serves its Celeron and Pentium III processor designs. Like Socket 7, the Slot 1 specification provides for variable processor core voltages (2.8 to 3.3) that permit faster operation and reduced power consumption. In addition, some suppliers have created daughter boards containing the Pentium Pro processor that can be plugged into the Slot 1 connector. This combination Socket 8/Slot 1 device is referred to as a slotket processor.

The **Slot 2** specification from Intel expands the Slot 1 SECC technology to a 330-contact cartridge (**SECC-2**) used with the Intel **Xeon** processor.

AMD produced a reversed version of the Slot 1 specification for its Athlon processor by turning the contacts of the Slot 1 design around. They titled the new design Slot A. While serving the same ends as the Slot 1 design, the Slot A and Slot 1 microprocessor cartridges are not compatible.

In a departure from its proprietary Slot connector development, Intel introduced a new ZIF socket standard, called Socket 370, for use with its Celeron processor. There are actually two versions of the Socket 370 specification. The first is the PPGA 370 variation intended for use with the Plastic Pin Grid Array (PPGA) version of the Celeron CPUs. The other is the Flip Chip Pin Grid Array (FC-PGA) version.

The term Flip Chip is used to describe a group of microprocessors that have provisions for attaching a heat sink directly to the microprocessor die. The processors in this category include the Cyrix III, Celeron, and Pentium III. Although the PPGA and FC-PGA processors will both plug into the 370 socket, that does not mean they will work in system boards designed for the other specification.

Likewise, AMD produced a 462-pin ZIF socket specification for the PGA versions of its Athlon and Duron processors. No other processors have been designed for this specification and only two chipsets have been produced to support it.

Table 2-4 summarizes the attributes of the various industry socket and slot specifications.

Slot 2
SECC-2
Xeon

Table 2-4: Intel Socket Specifications

NUMBER	PINS	VOLTAGES	MICROPROCESSORS
Socket 1	169 PGA	5	80486 SX/DXx, DX4 Overdrive
Socket 2	238 PGA	5	80486 SX/DXx, Pentium Overdrive
Socket 3	237 PGA	5/3.3	80486 SX/DXx, Pentium Overdrive
Socket 4	237 PGA	5	Pentium 60/66, 60/66 Overdrive
Socket 5	320 SPGA	3.3	Pentium 75-133, Pentium Overdrive
Socket 6	235 PGA	3.3	Never Implemented
Socket 7	321 SPGA	VRM (2.5 V-3.6 V)	Pentium 75-200, Pentium Overdrive
Socket 8	387 SPGA	VRM (2.2 V-3.5 V)	Pentium Pro
Slot 1	242 SECC/SEPP	VRM (1.5 V-2.5 V)	Celeron, Pentium II, Pentium III
Slot 2	330 SECC-2	VRM (1.5 V-2.5 V)	Xeon
Super Socket 7	321 SPGA	VRM (2.0 V-3.5 V)	AMD K6-2, K6-2+, K6-III, K6-III+, Pentium MMX, Pentium Pro
Socket 370	370 SPGA	VRM (1.1 V-2.5 V)	Cyrix III, Celeron, Pentium III
Slot A	242 Slot A	VRM (1.2 V-2.2 V)	AMD Athlon
Socket A	462 SPGA	VRM (12 V-2.2 V)	AMD Athlon, Duron

TEST TIP

Know which processors can be used with Slot 1 and Socket 370 connections. Also know which processors can be used in Slot A.

Your company does not want to replace all of its computers at this time. As a matter of fact, what it really wants to do is spend a little money to upgrade all its computers as much as it can now and wait as long as possible to replace them. As the Technical Service manager, they have asked you for a plan to upgrade the systems. You know that nearly all the systems in the company are Pentium II 350 MHz machines. What is the most current, fastest upgrade you can recommend to your board of directors?

MICROPROCESSOR CLOCK SPEEDS

In the Pentium processor, two speed settings can be established for the microprocessor—one speed for its internal core operations and a second speed for its external bus transfers. These two operational speeds are tied together through an internal clock multiplier system. The Socket-7 specification enabled system boards to be configured for different types of microprocessors using different operating speeds. In older systems, the operating speed of the microprocessor was configured through external settings.

Prior to Pentium II, all Pentium processors used 50, 60, or 66 MHz external clock frequencies to generate their internal operating frequencies. The value of the internal multiplier was controlled by external hardware jumper settings on the system board.

Pentium II processors moved to a 100 MHz external clock and front side bus. The Pentium III and all slot processors up to 1 GHz continued to use the 100 MHz clock and FSB. However, beginning with the Pentium III Coppermine, the external clock speed was increased to 133 MHz. At the same time, the Celeron processors retained the 66 MHz clock and bus speeds up to the 800 MHz Celeron versions.

The Pentium 4 processors use external clocks of 100 MHz and 133 MHz. From these clock inputs, the Pentium 4's internal clock multipliers generate core frequency of up to 3.06 GHz and front side bus frequencies of 400 MHz and 533 MHz. They have also used four different special memory buses with different memory types. In Pentium 4 systems, it is possible to set clock speeds for the memory and front side buses independently. The different memory bus configurations are designed to work with different types of RDRAM and run at speeds of 400 MHz, 600 MHz, and 800 MHz.

POWER-SUPPLY LEVELS

Beginning with the Pentium MMX, Intel adopted dual-voltage supply levels for the overall IC and for its core. Common Intel voltage supplies are +5/+5 for older units and +3.3/+3.3, +3.3/+2.8, +3.3/+1.8, and +3.3/1.45 for newer units.

Clone processors can use compatible voltages (especially if they are pin compatible) or completely different voltage levels. Common voltages for clone microprocessors include +5, +3.3, +2.5, and +2.2. The additional voltage levels are typically generated through special regulator circuits on the system board. In each case, the system board's user guide should be consulted any time the microprocessor is being replaced or upgraded.

From the Socket 7 processors until now, systems use a **Voltage Regulator Module (VRM)** to supply special voltage levels for different types of microprocessors that might be installed. The module may be designed as a plug-in module so that it can be replaced easily in case of component failure. This is a somewhat common occurrence with voltage regulator devices.

It also enables the system board to be upgraded when a new Pentium device is developed that requires a different voltage level, or a different voltage pairing.

Some multi-processor system boards have spaces for two or more VRM modules to be installed. The additional modules must be installed in VRM sockets, as illustrated in Figure 2-35, to support additional processors. VRMs can also be a source of server board failures. You should always check the processor voltages on a malfunctioning system board to verify that they are being supplied correctly. While VRMs rarely fail, you must be aware of them and know how they can affect the system's operation.

Figure 2-35: VRM Sockets

FANS, HEAT SINKS, AND COOLING SYSTEMS

The Pentium processor requires the presence of a heat-sinking device and a microprocessor fan unit for cooling purposes. As Figure 2-36 illustrates, these devices come in many forms including simple **passive heat sinks** and fan-cooled, **active heat sinks**.

Figure 2-36: Typical Microprocessor Cooling Systems

Passive heat sinks are finned metal slabs that can be clipped or glued with a heat-transmitting adhesive onto the top of the microprocessor. The fins increase the surface area of the heat sink, enabling it to dissipate heat more rapidly. Active heat sinks add a fan unit to move air across the heat sink. The fan moves the heat away from the heat sink and the microprocessor more rapidly.

ATX-style systems employ power supplies that use a reverse-flow fan that brings in cool air from the back of the unit and blows it directly onto the microprocessor. For this to work properly, the system board must adhere to the *ATX form factor* guidelines and place the microprocessor in the correct position on the system board. In theory, this design eliminates the need for special microprocessor cooling fans.

In newer Pentium systems, the BIOS interrogates the processor during startup and configures it appropriately. This prevents the user from subjecting the processor to potentially destructive conditions, such as overclocking. In addition, these systems can monitor the **health** of the processor while it is in operation and take steps to compensate for problems such as overheating. This normally involves speeding up or slowing down the processor fan to maintain a given operating temperature.

health

Advanced Cooling Systems

As system designers continue to push microprocessors for more speed, they also increase the amount of power that they dissipate. The latest microprocessor design techniques have created processors that generate over 80 watts of power that must be dissipated as heat. This is comparable to the heat generated by a heat lamp. It is beyond the capabilities of normal processor fans and heat sinks to effectively dissipate this much heat.

Simple air-cooling systems cannot create a large enough temperature differential to cool the processor. Therefore, system designers have begun to equip very high-speed systems with refrigerated cooling systems. Originally, the designers adopted water-based cooling systems that cooled and circulated water to carry heat away from the processor. Figure 2-37 depicts the components of a water-based cooling system typically used to cool processors that have been configured to run in overclocking conditions.

Figure 2-37: Water-Based Microprocessor Coolers

The water cooler system consists of:

- A water reservoir tank

- A water pump that circulates water throughout the cooling system

- A condenser coil radiator with fans that cool the water and exhaust heat into the outside atmosphere

- An **CPU cooling block** that connects directly to the microprocessor and extracts heat from it

The water pump operates from inside the reservoir tank and is used to force cooling water through the system. Most of the pumps for these systems are adaptations of home aquarium pumps and are designed for 120 Vac operation; therefore, they must have an external power cord.

The CPU cooling block consists of a copper-finned heat sink that mounts to a bracket installed around the microprocessor. Pentium 4 system boards have standard hole patterns already supplied to permit such devices to be attached to them. The heat sink is enclosed in a water jacket that permits cooling water to circulate around the fins. This enables heat to be removed from the processor faster than an air-cooled heat sink.

Heated water from the CPU cooler is pumped through the radiator. The radiator is composed of several coils of tubing to maximize the surface area that is used to dissipate heat. The additional fans push air across the coils and speed up the radiation process in the same manner as conventional CPU fans do for air-cooled heat sinks. The cooled water returns to the reservoir for recirculation.

More advanced liquid-based cooling systems have migrated to non-water coolants like those used in residential refrigerators or automobile air conditioners. Figure 2-38 shows the components associated with a refrigerated cooling system used with a PC system.

- An **evaporator** that mounts on top of the microprocessor

- A **condenser** with cooling fan that mounts to the case so that air can be exhausted to the outside of the case

- A **compressor** that places the cooling liquid under pressure so that it can perform refrigeration

- A **flow control/expansion device** – This component acts as a restriction in the lines of the system that causes the refrigerant to lose pressure and partially vaporize.

- Insulated tubing that connects the four major components in a closed-loop cooling circuit

As the figure illustrates, the components of the PC cooling system do not fit inside a typical desktop or tower unit. Instead, they must be used in cases that have been modified for them, or in cases that have been designed specifically for them.

Figure 2-38: PC Refrigerant Coolers

The four major components of the system are interconnected by a sealed piping system that holds a refrigerant liquid. The compressor is used to compress the refrigerant and pump it through the system. The high-pressure, high-temperature refrigerant first passes through the condenser unit where it exchanges heat with the surrounding air and cools somewhat.

Next, the refrigerant is forced through the flow control/expansion device, which restricts its flow and causes it to lose pressure as it passes through the device. The loss in pressure causes some of the refrigerant to change into a gas. In the process, the gaseous portion of the refrigerant extracts heat from the remaining liquid, and thereby cools it.

The refrigerant is then passed through the evaporator on the microprocessor in the form of a warm liquid. As air passes over the evaporator, heat is extracted from the processor body and passed to the cooler refrigerant. The remainder of the liquid refrigerant becomes a cool gas as it gathers heat from the evaporator, and is drawn back to the compressor where the process begins again.

As the air passes over the evaporator and cools, moisture can condense around the processor in the form of condensate. In order to protect the processor and printed circuit board around it, special insulating foam pads must be mounted around the microprocessor socket. In addition, special heating elements are typically mounted on the backside of the system board under the microprocessor socket position as illustrated in Figure 2-39.

**Figure 2-39:
Condensation
Prevention**

The BIOS controls the refrigerant cooling system through its Health Management system. This includes monitoring the actual temperature of the microprocessor and manipulating the cooling system to maintain a designated temperature level. It also controls the temperature of the heating pad under the printed circuit board.

This technology is not widely used in PCs. While the military has been using this type of cooling system for more than five years, it is just beginning to be used with commercial PCs. Because the liquid refrigerants used in these systems are considered hazardous to the environment, you must be aware that only individuals licensed to handle refrigerants can legally work on these units.

CONFIGURING MICROPROCESSORS

Most Pentium system boards are designed so that they can support a number of different microprocessor types and operating speeds. In older Pentium systems, the microprocessor's configuration settings were established largely through jumpers on the system board. These settings typically included such items as:

- *Microprocessor Type* — This setting tells the system what type of processor is installed. If this setting is incorrect, the system will assume that the installed processor is the one specified by the setting and try to interact with it on that basis. Depending on which microprocessor is indicated, the system POST might identify the processor incorrectly and still run—but not properly. In other cases, the processor might lock up during the POST or not run at all. In either case, the processor could be damaged.

- *Core-to-bus Speed Ratio* — Again, depending on the exact mismatch, the system might overclock the processor and run—but erratically. If the overclocking is less than 20%, the system might run without problems. However, the processor's life expectancy will be decreased. If the deviation is greater than 20%, the system might not come up at all and the processor might be damaged.

- *Bus Frequency Setting* — Configuring this setting incorrectly will cause the processor to run faster or slower. This is a common method employed by users to increase the operating speed of their older systems. If the variation is less than 20%, the system will probably work with a shortened processor life. Greater levels of overclocking the bus might cause the system to have random lockups.

- *Core Voltage Level* — This setting establishes the voltage level that the microprocessor core will operate at. The setting is linked to the processor's speed and power dissipation. Normally, the microprocessor will not operate at all if the voltage level is more than 20% too low. Conversely, if you operate a processor at a voltage level that is higher than its specified value, this can cause physical damage to it.

In these systems, the BIOS version must support the parameters of the microprocessor. If a microprocessor upgrade is performed and the BIOS code does not fully support the new processor, all the problems described earlier can occur. For example, if an 850 MHz Pentium III processor were installed in a system whose BIOS only supported processor speeds up to 600 MHz, the BIOS will only report a processor speed of 600 MHz during the POST portion of the startup. The system will actually be limited to running at 600 MHz. For this reason, the capabilities of the system BIOS should always be examined when performing microprocessor upgrades.

> **TEST TIP**
> Be aware of how older systems determine what type of microprocessor is installed and what its capabilities are.

> **TEST TIP**
> Know why a processor would show an incorrect speed rating.

Table 2-5: Microprocessor Characteristics

Table 2-5 summarizes the characteristics of the various microprocessors associated with the A+ exam.

MICROPROCESSOR	DIAMETER SIZE (mm)	VRM (VOLTS)	SPEED (MHz)	CACHE ON DIE (kB)	CACHE ON CARTRIDGE	CACHE ON BOARD (kB)	SOCKETS OR SLOT TYPES
Pentium	23.1x23.1	2.5–3.6	75–299	L1—8+8	-	L2—256/512	Socket 7
Pentium MMX AMD - K6-2:K6-3	25.4x25.4	2.0–3.5	166–550	L1—16+16 32+32	-	L2—255/1000	Socket Super 7
Pentium II/III Celeron (.25 micron)	25.4x25.4 18x62x140 Box	1.5–2.6	233–1000	L1—16+16	L2—256/512 128 kB	-	Slot 1
Xeon II/III (330) (.25 micron)	27.4x27.4 18x87x125 Box	1.5–2.6	500/550 700/900	L1—16+16	L2—512 kB 1 MB 2 M	-	Slot 2
Pentium III Celeron (.25 micron)	25.4x25.4 Slug 27.4x27.4 Opening	1.1–2.5	300–566	L1—16+16 L2—128/256	-	-	Socket 370 PPGA
Pentium III (Coppermine) Celeron (.18 micron)	9.3x11.3	1.1–2.5	566–1000	L1—16+16 L2—128/256	-	-	Socket 370 FC-PGA
Pentium III (Tualatin) Celeron (.13 micron)	31x31	1.1–2.5	800–1500	L1—16+16 L2— 128/256/512	-	-	FC-PGA2
Pentium IV (.18 micron)	31x31	1.75	1300–2000	L1—12+8 L2—256	-	-	Socket 423 FC-PGA
Pentium IV (.18 micron) (.13 micron)	31x31 33x33	1.75 1.50	1400–2000 1800–2200	L1—12+8 L2—512	-	-	FC-PGA2
Pentium Xeon (.18 micron)	31x31	1.4–1.8 1.7	1400–2000	L1—12+8 L2—256	-	-	Socket 603 FC-BGA
Pentium Xeon (.13 micron)	35x35	1.4–1.8 1.475	1800–2200	L1—12+8 L2—512	-	-	Socket 603 FC-BGA2
Itanium (.18 micron) (266 MHz)*	71.6x127.7	1.7	733/800	1—16+16 L2—512	L3—2 MB 4 MB	- -	PAC-418
Athlon Duron	9.1x13.1	1.75	800–1400	L1—64+64	L2—256 kB	-	Slot A 242 CPGA
Athlon Duron	11.1x11.6	1.75	733–1800	L1—64+64	L2—256	- -	Socket A 462 ORGA

*266 MHz system bus and 133 MHz address bus

CHALLENGE #4

Your company's board of directors approves your recommendation for upgrading their existing systems as outlined in challenge 3. When you upgrade the first system, you find that it is only running at 450 MHz. What should you do to get the system up to the speed you recommended to the board?

---

core voltage

> **TEST TIP**
>
> Be aware of how the system determines which type of microprocessor is installed and what its capabilities are.

It should be obvious that all of these variables must be configured correctly for the type of microprocessor actually installed in the system. If the **core voltage** level is set too high, then the microprocessor will probably overheat slowly, or burn out, depending on the amount of voltage applied. Conversely, if the voltage level is configured too low for the installed processor, then the system will most likely refuse to start. Likewise, setting the speed selection jumpers incorrectly can cause the system to think that a different processor is installed in the system.

RANDOM ACCESS MEMORY

The A+ Core objective 4.2 states that the test taker should be able to identify the types of RAM (Random Access Memory), form factors, and operational characteristics. Determine banking and speed requirements under given scenarios.

Content may include the following:

Types:

- EDO RAM (Extended Data Output RAM)
- DRAM (Dynamic Random Access Memory)
- SRAM (Static RAM)
- VRAM (Video RAM)
- WRAM (Windows Accelerator Card RAM)
- DDR (Double Data Rate)
- RAMBUS

Form Factors (including pin count)

- SIMM (Single In-line Memory Module)
- DIMM (Dual In-line Memory Module)
- SODIMM (Small Outline DIMM)
- RIMM (Rambus In-line Memory Module)

Operational characteristics:

- Memory chips (8-bit, 16-bit, and 32-bit)
- Parity chips versus non-parity chips
- ECC vs. non-ECC
- Single-sided vs. double-sided

Memory Systems

> As mentioned in Chapter 1 — *Basic PC Hardware*, there are normally three types of semiconductor memory found on a typical system board. These include the system's ROM BIOS ICs, the system's RAM memory, and the second-level cache memory unit.

A typical PC system board uses one or two 256 kB/128 kB x 8 ROM chips to hold the system's BIOS firmware. The system's memory map reserves memory locations from F0000 to FFFFF. These chips contain the firmware routines to handle startup of the system, the change-over to disk-based operations, video and printer output functions, as well as the Power-On Self-Test.

Two types of semiconductor RAM, **Static RAM (SRAM)** and **Dynamic RAM (DRAM)**, are used on system boards. Although they both perform the same types of functions, the methods they use are completely different. Static RAM stores bits in such a manner that they will remain as long as power to the chip is not interrupted. Dynamic RAM requires periodic refreshing to maintain data, even if electrical power is applied to the chip.

Dynamic RAM stores data bits on rows and columns of IC capacitors. Capacitors lose their charge over time. This is the reason that dynamic RAM devices require data refreshing operations. Static RAM uses IC transistors to store data and maintain it as long as power is supplied to the chip. Its transistor structure makes SRAM memory much faster than ordinary DRAM. However, it can only store about 25% as much data in a given size as a DRAM device. Therefore, it tends to be more expensive to create large memories with SRAM.

Whether the RAM is made up of static or dynamic RAM devices, all RAM systems have the disadvantage of being volatile. This means that any data stored in RAM will be lost if power to the computer is disrupted for any reason. On the other hand, both types of RAM have the advantage of being fast, with the ability to be written to and read from with equal ease.

Generally, static RAM is used in smaller memory systems, such as cache and video memories, where the added cost of refresh circuitry would increase the cost-per-bit of storage. Cache memory is a special memory structure that works directly with the microprocessor, whereas video memory is a specialized area that holds information to be displayed on the screen. On the other hand, DRAM is used in larger memory systems, such as the system's main memory, where the extra cost of refresh circuitry is distributed over a greater number of bits and is offset by the reduced operating cost associated with DRAM chips.

Advanced DRAM

Both types of RAM are brought together to create an improved DRAM, referred to as **Enhanced DRAM (EDRAM)**. By integrating an SRAM component into a DRAM device, a performance improvement of 40% can be gained. An independent write path allows the system to input new data without affecting the operation of the rest of the chip. These devices are used primarily in L2 cache memories.

Another modified DRAM type, referred to as **Synchronous DRAM (SDRAM)**, employs special internal registers and clock signals to organize data requests from memory. Unlike asynchronous memory modules, SDRAM devices operate in synchronicity with the system clock. Once an initial Read or Write access has been performed on the memory device, additional accesses can be conducted in a high-speed burst mode that operates at 1 access per clock cycle. This enables the microprocessor to perform other tasks while the data is being organized. Special internal configurations also speed up the operation of the SDRAM memory. The SDRAM device employs internal interleaving that permits one side of the memory to be accessed while the other half is completing an operation. Because there are two versions of SDRAM (2-clock and 4-clock) you must make certain that the SDRAM type you are using is supported by the system board's chipset.

Advanced SDRAM

Advanced versions of SDRAM include:

- **SDR-SDRAM** – Single Data Rate SDRAM. This version of SDRAM transfers data on one edge of the system clock signal.

- **SGRAM** – Synchronous Graphics RAM. This type of SDRAM is designed to handle high-performance graphics operations. It features dual-bank operations that permit two memory pages to be open at the same time.

- **ESDRAM** – Enhanced SDRAM. This advanced form of SDRAM employs small cache buffers to provide high data access rates. This type of SDRAM is used in L2 cache applications.

- **VCM-SDRAM** – Virtual Channel Memory SDRAM. This memory design has on-board cache buffers to improve multiple access times and to provide I/O transfers on each clock cycle. VCM SDRAM requires a special chipset to support it.

- **DDR-SDRAM** – Double Data Rate SDRAM. DDR is a form of SDR-SDRAM that can transfer data on both the leading and falling edges of each clock cycle. This capability doubles the data transfer rate of traditional SDR-DRAM. It is available in a number of standard formats including SODIMMs for portables.

- **EDDR-SDRAM** – Enhanced DDR SDRAM. EDDR is an advanced form of DDR SRAM that employs on-board cache registers to deliver improved performance.

Table 2-6 summarizes the characteristics and usage of various types of SDRAM.

**Table 2-6:
SDRAM Types**

	CONFIGURATION	VOLTAGE	DENSITY	FREQUENCY (MHz)	PACKAGE
RDRAM RIMM	32 x 16 32 x 18 64 x 16 64 x 18 128 x 16	2.5 V	64 MB 72 MB 96 MB 108 MB 128 MB 144 MB	300, 356, 400	184-pin RIMMs
DDR SRAM DIMMs (Unbuffered)	16 x 64 32 x 64	2.5 V	128 MB 256 MB	200, 266	184-pin DIMMs
DDR SRAM DIMMs (Registered)	32 x 72	2.5 V	256 MB	200, 266	184-pin DIMMs
SDRAM AIMM*	1 x 32	3.3 V	4 MB	166	66-pin AIMM
100-Pin DIMMs	1 x 32 2 x 32	3.3 V	4 MB 8 MB	100, 125	100-pin DIMMs
	2 x 32	3.3 V	8 MB	125	100-pin DIMM
	4 x 32 8 x 32	3.3 V	16 MB 32 MB	100, 125	100-pin DIMMs
	16 x 32	3.3 V	64 MB	100, 125	100-pin DIMM
	16 x 32 32 x 32	3.3 V	64 MB 128 MB	100, 125	100-pin DIMMs

* AIMM is a special memory card format used with AGP expansion slots.

Table 2-6: SDRAM Types (continued)

	CONFIGURATION	VOLTAGE	DENSITY	FREQUENCY (MHz)	PACKAGE
144-Pin SODIMMs	4 x 64	3.3 V	32 MB	100, 125, 133	144-pin SODIMM
	8 x 64	3.3 V	64 MB	66, 100	144-pin SODIMM
	8 x 64	3.3 V	64 MB	100, 133	144-pin SODIMM
	16 x 64	3.3 V	128 MB	66, 100	144-pin SODIMM
	32 x 64	3.3 V	256 MB	100, 133	144-pin SODIMM
168-Pin DIMMs	4 x 64 8 x 64 16 x 64	3.3 V	32 MB 64 MB 128 MB	66, 100, 133	168-pin SDRAM DIMMs
	8 x 64 16 x 64	3.3 V	64 MB 128 MB	66, 100, 133	168-pin DIMMs
	16 x 64 32 x 64	3.3 V	128 MB 256 MB	100, 133	168-pin DIMMs
	4 x 72 8 x 72 16 x 72	3.3 V	32 MB 64 MB 128 MB	66, 100, 133	168-pin DIMMs
	8 x 72 16 x 72	3.3 V	64 MB 128 MB	66, 100, 133	168-pin DIMMs
	8 x 72 16 x 72	3.3 V	64 MB 128 MB	100, 133	168-pin DIMMs
	16 x 72 32 x 72	3.3 V	128 MB 256 MB	100, 133	168-pin DIMM
	16 x 72 32 x 72 64 x 72	3.3 V	128 MB 256 MB 512 MB	100, 133	168-pin DIMM
	32 x 72 64 x 72	3.3 V	256 MB 512 MB	100, 133	168-pin DIMMs
	64 x 72	3.3 V	512 MB	100, 133	168-pin DIMMs
	64 x 72 128 x 72	3.3 V	512 MB 1 GB	100, 133	168-pin DIMMs
DRAM SIMMs	1 x 32 2 x 32	5 V	4 MB 8 MB	50 (EDO only), 60	72-pin SIMM
	4 x 32 8 x 32	5 V	16 MB 32 MB	50 (EDO only), 60	72-pin SIMM
	4 x 36 8 x 36	5 V	16 MB 32 MB	60	72-pin SIMMs
	4 x 36 8 x 36	5 V	16 MB 32 MB	50, 60	72-pin SIMMs

Table 2-6:
SDRAM Types
(continued)

	CONFIGURATION	VOLTAGE	DENSITY	SPEED (ns)	PACKAGE
EDO/FPM DRAM DIMMs/SODIMMs	1 x 32 2 x 32	3.3 V	4 MB 8 MB	50 (EDO only), 60	100-pin DIMM
	1 x 32 2 x 32 4 x 32	3.3 V	4 MB 8 MB 16 MB	50, 60	100-pin DIMMs
	4 x 32 8 x 32	3.3 V	16 MB 32 MB	50, 60	72-pin SODIMMs
	4 x 32 8 x 32	3.3 V	16 MB 32 MB	50, 60	144-pin SODIMMs
	4 x 64 8 x 64	3.3 V	32 MB 64 MB	50, 60	168-pin DIMMs
	4 x 64 8 x 64	3.3 V	32 MB 64 MB	50, 60	168-pin DIMMs
	8 x 64 16 x 64 32 x 64	3.3 V	64 MB 128 MB 256 MB	50, 60	168-pin DIMMs
	4 x 72	3.3 V	32 MB	50, 60	168-pin DIMMs
	4 x 72	3.3 V	32 MB	50, 60	168-pin DIMMs
	8 x 72 16 x 72 32 x 72	3.3 V	64 MB 128 MB 256 MB	50, 60	168-pin DIMMs
	8 x 72 16 x 72 32 x 72	3.3 V	64 MB 128 MB 256 MB	50, 60	168-pin DIMMs

Extended data out (EDO) memory increases the speed at which RAM operations are conducted by cutting out the 10-nanosecond wait time normally required between issuing memory addresses. This is accomplished by not disabling the data bus pins between bus cycles. EDO is an advanced type of fast page-mode DRAM, also referred to as hyper page-mode DRAM. The advantage of EDO DRAM is encountered when multiple sequential memory accesses are performed. By not turning off the data pin, each successive access after the first access is accomplished in two clock cycles rather than three.

Special memory devices have also been designed to optimize video memory-related activities. Among these are **Video RAM (VRAM)** and **Windows RAM (WRAM)**. In typical DRAM devices, access to the data stored inside is shared between the system microprocessor and the video controller. The microprocessor accesses the RAM to update the data in it and to keep it refreshed. The video controller moves data out of the memory to become screen information. Normally, both devices must access the data through the same data bus. VRAM employs a special dual-port access system to speed up video operations. WRAM, a special version of VRAM, is optimized to transfer blocks of data at a time. This enables it to operate at speeds of up to 150% of typical VRAM and costs up to 20% less.

Extended data out (EDO)

TEST TIP

Know the difference between EDO and fast page-mode DRAM.

Video RAM (VRAM)

Windows RAM (WRAM)

TEST TIP

Remember what type of application VRAM and WRAM are used in.

Rambus DRAM
(RDRAM)

Direct Rambus DRAM
(DRDRAM)

Rambus In-line
Memory Module
(RIMM)

heat spreader

A company named Rambus has designed a proprietary DRAM memory technology that promises very high data delivery speeds. The technology has been given a variety of different names that include **Rambus DRAM (RDRAM)**, **Direct Rambus DRAM (DRDRAM)**, and RIMM. The RIMM reference applies to a special 184-pin memory module that is designed to hold the Rambus devices. While these devices are often referred to as **Rambus In-line Memory Modules**, according to the Rambus company this is not actually the source for the acronym RIMM. Figure 2-40 shows that RIMMs look similar to DIMMS. However, their high-speed transfer modes generate considerably more heat than normal DIMMs. Therefore, RIMM modules include an aluminum heat shield, referred to as a **heat spreader**, to protect the chips from overheating.

The Rambus technology employs a special, internal 16-bit data channel that operates in conjunction with a 400 MHz clock. The 16-bit channel permits the device to operate at much higher speeds than more conventional 64-bit buses. While Intel had expressed some interest in exploring the technology for its future system board designs, the fact that it is a proprietary standard may hinder its acceptance in the market.

RIMMs look similar to DIMMs, but they have a different pin count. While RIMMs transfer data in 16-bit chunks, the faster access and transfer speed generates more heat.

Figure 2-40: RIMM Modules

SRAM

Like DRAM, SRAM is available in a number of different types. Many of the memory organization techniques described for DRAM are also implemented in SRAM.

Asynchronous
SRAM

Synchronous
SRAM

Pipeline SRAM

Burst-mode SRAM

- **Asynchronous SRAM** is standard SRAM that delivers data from the memory to the microprocessor and returns it to the cache in one clock cycle.

- **Synchronous SRAM** uses special clock signals and buffer storage to deliver data to the CPU in one clock cycle after the first cycle. The first address is stored and used to retrieve the data while the next address is on its way to the cache.

- **Pipeline SRAM** uses three clock cycles to fetch the first data and then accesses addresses within the selected page on each clock cycle.

- **Burst-mode SRAM** loads a number of consecutive data locations from the cache, over several clock cycles, based on a single address from the microprocessor.

In digital electronics terms, a buffer is a holding area for data shared by devices that operate at different speeds or have different priorities. These devices permit a memory module to operate without the delays that other devices impose. Some types of SDRAM memory modules contain buffer registers directly on the module. The buffer registers hold and retransmit the data signals through the memory chips.

The holding aspect permits the module to coordinate transfers with the outside system. The retransmission factor lowers the signal drain on the host system and enables the memory module to hold more memory chips. Registered and unbuffered memory modules cannot be mixed. The design of the chipset's memory controller dictates which types of memory the computer can use.

Memory Overhead

It has already been mentioned that DRAM devices, commonly used for the system's RAM, require periodic refreshing of their data. Some **refreshing** is performed simply by regular reading and writing of the memory by the system. However, additional circuitry must be used to ensure that every bit in the memory is refreshed within the allotted time frame. In addition to the circuitry, the reading and writing times used for refreshing must be taken into account when designing the system.

Another design factor associated with RAM is data **error detection**. A single incorrect bit can shut down the entire system instantly. With bits constantly moving in and out of RAM, it is crucial that all of the bits be transferred correctly. The most popular form of error detection in PC compatibles is **parity checking**. In this methodology, an extra bit is added to each word in RAM and checked each time it is used. Like refreshing, parity checking requires additional circuitry and memory overhead to operate.

refreshing

error detection

parity checking

DRAM Refresh

Dynamic RAM devices require that data stored in them be **refreshed**, or rewritten, periodically to keep it from fading away. As a matter of fact, each bit in the DRAM must be refreshed at least once every two milliseconds or the data will dissipate. Since it can't be assumed that each bit in the memory will be accessed during the normal operation of the system (within the time frame allotted), the need to constantly refresh the data in the DRAM requires special circuitry to perform this function.

refreshed

The extra circuitry and inconvenience associated with refreshing may initially make DRAM memory seem like a distant second choice behind static RAM. However, due to the simplicity of DRAM's internal structure, the bit-storage capacity of a DRAM chip is much greater than that of a similar static RAM chip, and it offers a much lower rate of power consumption. Both of these factors contribute to making DRAM memory the economical choice in certain RAM memory systems—even in light of the extra circuitry necessary for refreshing.

Error Checking and Correcting

Parity checking is a simple self-test used to detect RAM read-back errors. When a data byte is stored in memory, the occurrences of logic "1s" in the byte are added together by the parity generator/checker chip. This chip produces a parity bit that is added to, and stored along with, the data byte. Therefore, the data byte becomes a 9-bit word. Whenever the data word is read back from the memory, the parity bit is reapplied to the parity generator and recalculated.

> **TEST TIP**
>
> Know that parity is a method of checking stored data for errors by adding an additional bit to it when it is read from memory.

The recalculated parity value is then compared to the original parity value stored in memory. If the values do not match, a parity-error condition occurs and an error message is generated. Traditionally, there are two approaches to generating parity bits; the parity bit may be generated so that the total number of 1-bits equals an even number (**even parity**), or an odd number (**odd parity**).

To enable parity checking, an additional 9th bit is added to each byte stored in DRAM. On older systems, an extra memory chip was included with each bank of DRAM. In newer units, the extra storage is built into the SIMM and DIMM modules. Whether a particular system employs parity check or not depends on its chipset. Many newer chipsets have moved away from using parity checking altogether. In these cases, SIMMs and DIMMs with parity capability can be used, but the parity function will not function. In Pentium systems, the system board's user's guide or the BIOS' Extended CMOS Setup screen should be consulted to determine whether parity is supported. If so, the parity function can be enabled through this screen.

Figure 2-41 illustrates how the system's RAM and parity checking circuit work together.

Figure 2-41: How Parity Checking Works

TEST TIP

Be aware of the types of problems that can create NMI errors and what the consequences of these errors are.

When a parity error occurs, a **Non-Maskable Interrupt (NMI)** signal is co-generated in the system, causing the BIOS to execute its NMI handler routine. This routine will normally place a parity error message on the screen, along with an option to shut down the system, or continue.

In some applications, stability is of the utmost concern for the system design. In these systems, advanced RAM types that include **Error Checking and Correcting (ECC)** capabilities are used. ECC provides additional data integrity by detecting and often correcting errors in the information they process. However, the additional data manipulation that goes on inside the memory devices causes ECC RAM to provide lower performance than its non-ECC counterparts.

CHALLENGE #5

You are called on to check out a failing computer in the production department. When you arrive, you find that the system is continually locking up and rebooting when the operating system loads. What type of problem is the system likely to be having, and what should you do about it?

Advanced Memory Structures

As the operating speeds of microcomputers have continued to increase, it has become increasingly necessary to develop new memory strategies to keep pace with the other parts of the system. Some of these methods, such as developing faster DRAM chips, or including wait states in the memory-access cycles, are very fundamental in nature. However, these methods do not allow the entire system to operate at its full potential. Other, more elaborate memory management schemes have been employed on faster computers to maximize their overall performance.

Cache Memory

One method of increasing the memory-access speed of a computer is called **caching**. This memory management method assumes that most memory accesses are made within a limited block of addresses. Therefore, if the contents of these addresses are relocated into a special section of high-speed SRAM, then the microprocessor can access these locations without requiring any wait states.

caching

Cache memory is normally small to keep the cost of the system as low as possible. However, it is also very fast, even in comparison to fast DRAM devices.

Cache memory operations require a great deal of intelligent circuitry to operate and monitor the cache effectively. The cache controller circuitry must monitor the microprocessor's memory-access instructions to determine if the specified data is stored in the cache. If the information is in the cache, the control circuitry can present it to the microprocessor without incurring any wait states. This is referred to as a **hit**. If the information is not located in the cache, the access is passed on to the system's RAM and it is declared a **miss**.

hit

miss

The primary objective of the cache memory's control system is to maximize the ratio of hits to total accesses (hit rate), so that the majority of memory accesses are performed without wait states. One way to do this is to make the cache memory area as large as possible (thus raising the possibility of the desired information being in the cache). However, the relative cost, energy consumption, and physical size of SRAM devices work against this technique. Practical sizes for cache memories run between 16 kB–512 kB.

There are two basic methods of writing updated information into the cache. The first is to write data into the cache and the main memory at the same time. This is referred to as **Write-Thru Cache**. This method tends to be slow since the microprocessor has to wait for the slow DRAM access to be completed. The second method is known as **Write-Back Cache**. A write-back cache holds the data in the cache until the system has a quiet time and then writes it into the main memory.

The Intel 80486 and the original Pentium microprocessors (Pentium I and Pentium MMX) had a built-in first-level cache, referred to as **L1 cache,** that could be used for both instructions and data. The internal cache in these units was divided into four 2 kB blocks containing 128 sets of 16-byte lines each. Control of the internal cache is handled directly by the microprocessor. However, many system boards that supported these processors extended their caching capabilities by adding an external, second-level 256 kB/512 kB memory cache, referred to as an **L2 cache**.

With the Pentium Pro, Intel moved the 256 kB or 512 kB L2 cache from the system board to the processor package. This design technique continued through the Pentium II and III slot processors, so that the 256 kB /512 kB L2 cache resided in the microprocessor cartridge. In their Celeron and Coppermine devices, Intel moved the L2 cache (128 kB /256 kB and 256 kB/512 kB, respectively) onto the actual microprocessor dye. Moving the L2 cache onto the dye made the microprocessor directly responsible for managing the cache and enabled it to run at full speed with the microprocessor. In all of these systems, no cache existed on the system board.

When Intel designed the Itanium processor, they built in capabilities for managing an additional external level of cache in the microprocessor cartridge. This additional cache level was dubbed **L3 cache**. The Xeon processor has continued this design concept and improved it by moving a 1 MB or 2 MB L3 cache onto the microprocessor dye. Once again the external cache is able to run at full speed with the microprocessor.

The computer industry has taken a more liberal definition of L3 cache, sometimes referring to L3 cache as cache memory mounted on system boards with processors that possess on-board L1 and L2 cache. An external cache memory system is depicted in Figure 2-42.

Figure 2-42: An External Cache

Memory Paging and Interleaving

There are also other commonly used methods of organizing RAM memory so that it can be accessed more efficiently. Typically, memory accesses occur in two fashions, instruction fetches (which are generally sequential) and operand accesses (which tend to be random). **Paging** and **interleaving** memory schemes are designed to take advantage of the sequential nature of instruction fetches from memory.

The basic idea of page-mode DRAM operations is illustrated in Figure 2-43. Special memory devices called **page-mode** (or **static-column**) **RAM** are required for memory paging structures. In these memory devices, data is organized into groups of rows and columns called **pages**. Once a ROW access is made in the device, it is possible to access other column addresses within the same row without pre-charging its **Row Address Strobe (RAS)** line. This feature produces access times that are half that of normal DRAM memories. **Fast page-mode RAM** is a quicker version of page-mode RAM that has improved **Column Address Strobe (CAS)** access speed.

The operating principle behind memory interleaving is shown in Figure 2-44. Typical interleaving schemes divide the memory into two banks of RAM with one bank storing even addresses and the other storing odd addresses.

The RAS signals of the two banks overlap so that the time required to **pre-charge** one bank's RAS line is used for the active RAS time of the other bank. Therefore, there should never be a pre-charge time for either bank, as long as the accesses continue to be sequential. If a non-sequential access occurs, a miss is encountered and a wait state must be inserted in the timing. If the memory is organized into two banks, the operation is referred to as two-way interleaving. It is also common to organize the memory into four equal-sized banks. This organization effectively doubles the average 0-wait state hit space in the memory.

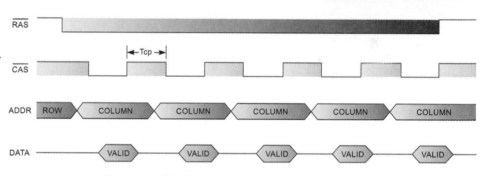

Figure 2-43: Page-Mode DRAM Operation

Figure 2-44: Memory Interleaving

SIMMs, DIMMs, and Banks

Older PC, PC-XT, and PC-AT system boards employed banks of discrete RAM ICs in Dual In-line Pin (DIP) sockets. Most of these system boards arranged nine pieces of 1 x 256 kb DRAM chips in the first two banks (0 and 1) and nine pieces of 1 x 64 kb chips in banks 2 and 3. The two banks of 256 kb chips provided a total of 512 kB of storage (the ninth chip of each bank supplied a parity bit for error checking).

Paging

interleaving

page-mode RAM

static-column RAM

pages

Row Address Strobe (RAS)

Fast page-mode RAM

Column Address Strobe (CAS)

pre-charge

The two banks of 64 kb chips extended the RAM memory capacity out to the full 640 kB. As with the 256 kb chips, the ninth bit was for parity.

Some system boards used two 4 x 256 kb chips with a 1 x 256 kb chip to create each of the first two banks. In any event, the system would typically run with one bank installed, two banks installed, or all of the banks installed. Bank 0 had to be filled first, followed by Bank 1, and then all four.

Early AT-clone system boards moved the system's RAM to 30-pin Single In-line Pin (SIP) modules, while further refinements produced snap-in Single In-line Memory Modules (SIMMs) and Dual In-line Memory Modules (DIMMs). Like the SIP, the SIMM and DIMM units mount vertically on the system board. However, instead of using a pin and socket arrangement, both use special snap-in sockets that support the module firmly. SIMMs and DIMMs are also keyed, so that they cannot be plugged in backwards. SIMMs are available in 30-pin and 72-pin versions, while DIMMs are larger 168-pin boards.

SIMM and DIMM sockets are quite distinctive in that they are normally arranged side by side. However, they can be located anywhere on the system board. SIMMs typically come in 8-bit or 32-bit bit data storage configurations. The 8-bit modules must be arranged in banks to match the data bus size of the system's microprocessor. In order to work effectively with a 32-bit microprocessor, a bank of four 8-bit SIMMs would need to be used. Conversely, a single 32-bit SIMM could do the same job.

DIMMs, on the other hand, typically come in 32-bit and 64-bit widths to service more powerful microprocessors. Like SIMMs, they must be arranged properly to fit the size of the system data bus. In both cases, the modules can be accessed in smaller 8- and 16-bit segments. SIMMs and DIMMs also come in 9-, 36-, and 72-bit versions that include parity-checking bits for each byte of storage (e.g., a 36-bit SIMM provides 32 data bits and 4 parity bits—one for each byte of data).

PCs are typically sold with less than their full RAM capacity. This allows users to purchase a less expensive computer to fit their individual needs and yet retain the option to install more RAM if future applications call for it. SIMM and DIMM sizes are typically specified in an a-by-b format. For example, a 2x32 SIMM specification indicates that it is a dual, non-parity, 32-bit (4-byte) device. In this scheme, the capacity is derived by multiplying the two numbers and then dividing by eight (or nine for parity chips). Figure 2-45 depicts typical upgrade strategies using SIMM and DIMM modules to increase the memory capabilities of a system board.

Figure 2-45: Plugging in SIMM and DIMM Memory Modules

CHALLENGE #6

You have been assigned to upgrade the memory in a number of your office's computers. When you open them, you discover that they have a three-slot DIMM arrangement. Also, you cannot locate a system board user manual for these computers. You install a 128 MB DIMM in each slot. When you start the computer, you see from the POST that the system only recognizes 256 MB of RAM. What happened to the other 128 MB of RAM, and how can you get the system to recognize it?

A special form factor DIMM, called the **Small Outline DIMM (SODIMM)** has been developed for use in notebook computers. The basic difference between SODIMMs and regular DIMMs is that the SODIMM is significantly smaller than the standard DIMM so that it takes up less space in notebook computers. Figure 2-46 depicts a 72-pin, a 144-pin, and a 200-pin SODIMM. The 72-pin SODIMM has a 32-bit data bus and the 144-pin version is 64 bits wide.

Figure 2-46: Small Outline DIMMs

A new small form factor memory module referred to as **MicroDIMM** has been introduced for the micro devices market (sub-notebook PCs) where size and performance are crucial. These units are nearly square 144-pin 32 Mb x 64 plug-in modules that are available with either SDRAM or DDR SDRAM components on board. Figure 2-47 shows a MicroDIMM module. They are approximately 1.54" (38.0 mm) by 1' (25.4 mm) high and unlike SODIMMs do not have any notches along their edge connector contacts. The height of MicroDIMM modules varies between different manufacturers.

MicroDIMM modules slide into a specialized spring-loaded socket. When the module is fully seated in the socket, two plastic clips snap into place to hold it securely. To release the module from the socket, simply spread the clips apart and the spring will shove the module out of the socket.

Figure 2-47: MicroDIMM

RAM Speeds

Another important factor to consider when dealing with RAM is its speed. Manufacturers mark RAM devices with speed information. DRAM modules are marked with a numbering system that indicates the number of clock cycles required for the initial Read operation, followed by information about the number of reads and cycles required to move a burst of data. As an example, a fast page-mode DRAM marked as 6-3-3-3 requires 6 cycles for the initial read and 3 cycles for each of three successive reads. This will move an entire 4-byte block of data. EDO and FPM can operate with bus speeds up to 66 MHz.

SDRAM devices are marked differently. Since they are designed to run synchronously with the system clock and use no wait states, a marking of 3:3:3 at 100 MHz on an SDRAM module specifies that:

- The CAS signal setup time is 3 bus cycles.

- The RAS to CAS change over time is 3 cycles.

- The RAS signal setup time is 3 clock cycles.

The bus speed is specified in MHz. These memory modules have been produced in the following specifications so far:

- PC66 (66 MHz or 15 nanoseconds)

- PC83 (83 MHz or 12 nanoseconds)

- PC100 (100 MHz or 10 nanoseconds)

- PC133 (133 MHz or 8 nanoseconds)

- PC150 (150 MHz or 4.5 nanoseconds)

- PC166 (166 MHz or 4 nanoseconds)

The PC66 and PC83 specifications were the first versions produced using this system. However, they never really gained widespread acceptance. On the other hand, the PC100 and PC133 versions did gain acceptance and are widely available today. The PC150 and PC166 versions are also common.

Continued advancements in memory module design have made the MHz and CAS setup time ratings obsolete. On-board buffering and advanced access strategies have made these measurements inconsequential. Instead, memory performance is now measured by total data **throughput** (also referred to as **bandwidth**) and in terms of gigabytes per second (GBps). As an example, some of the new standard specifications include:

- PC1600 (1.6 GBps/200 MHz/2:2:2)

- PC2100 (2.1 GBps/266 MHz/2:3:3)

- PC2600 (2.6 GBps/333 MHz/3:3:3)

- PC3200 (3.2 GBps/400 MHz/3:3:3)

The system board's documentation will provide information about the types of devices it can use and their speed ratings. It is important to install RAM that is compatible with the bus speed the system is running. Normally, installing RAM that is rated faster than the bus speed will not cause problems. However, installing slower RAM, or mixing RAM speed ratings in a system will cause the system to not start or to periodically lock up.

> **TEST TIP**
>
> Be aware of the consequences of mixing RAM with different speed ratings within a system.

CMOS RAM

The A+ Core objective 4.4 states that the test taker should be able to identify the purpose of CMOS (Complementary Metal-Oxide Semiconductor) memory, what it contains, and how and when to change its basic parameters. Given a scenario involving CMOS, choose the appropriate course of action.

CMOS settings:

- Default settings
- Printer parallel port — unidirectional, bi-directional, disable/enable, ECP, EPP
- COM/serial port — memory address, interrupt request, disable
- Hard drive — size and drive type
- Floppy drive — enable/disable drive or boot, speed, density
- Boot sequence
- Memory — speed, parity, non-parity
- Date/time
- Passwords
- Plug-and-Play BIOS
- Disabling on-board devices
- Disabling virus protection
- Power Management
- Security subsystem control
- Infrared

CMOS Setup Utilities

During the POST process, you can press the DEL key to access the CMOS Setup routines that modify the operation of some BIOS functions. In other BIOS types, the CTRL/ALT/ESC key combination can also be used to access the Setup utilities. The CMOS Setup utility's Main Menu screen, similar to the one depicted in Figure 2-48, appears whenever the CMOS Setup utility is engaged. This menu allows the user to select setup functions and exit choices. The most used entries include the Standard CMOS Setup, **BIOS Features Setup**, and **Chipset Features Setup** options. Selecting these, or any of the other Main Menu options, will lead into a corresponding submenu.

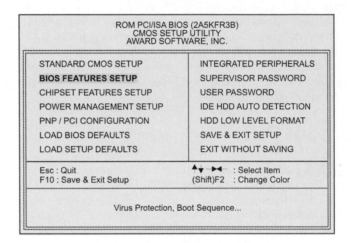

**Figure 2-48:
CMOS Main Menu
Screen**

Other typical menu items include **Power Management Setup, PnP/PCI Configuration, Integrated Peripherals**, and **Password Maintenance Services**. A given CMOS Setup utility may contain the same options as those listed in the sample, options that perform the same functions under a different name, or it may not contain some options at all. This example also offers two IDE HDD-related utilities, two options for starting with default system values, and two exit options.

BIOS designers have built two options (**Auto Configuration** and **Default Settings**) into newer versions to help users deal with the complexity of the advanced CMOS configuration. Newer system boards use an auto-configuration mode that takes over most of the setup decisions. This option works well in most cases, producing settings for an efficient, basic level of operation for standard devices in the system. However, it doesn't optimize the performance of the system. To do that, it's necessary to turn off the auto-configuration feature and insert the desired parameters into the configuration table. Two options typically exist for the auto-configuration function: **Auto Configure with Power-On Defaults** and **Auto Configure with BIOS Defaults**.

The auto-configuration power-on defaults provide the most conservative system options from the BIOS, and the most effective method of detecting BIOS-related system problems. These settings replace any user-entered configuration information in the CMOS Setup registers, disabling the turbo speed mode, turning off all memory caching, and setting all wait states to maximum, thus enabling the most basic part of the system for starting.

If these default values fail to boot the system, it indicates possible hardware problems such as incorrect jumper settings or bad components.

If you have entered an improper configuration setting and cannot determine which setting is causing the problem, using the auto-configuration with the BIOS defaults provides more flexibility than the power-on option. This selection also replaces the entered configuration settings with a new set of parameters from the BIOS, and gets you back into the CMOS Setup screen so that you can track down the problem. This is also the recommended starting point for optimizing the system's operation.

WARNING

Set values with caution—The settings in these menus enable the system to be configured and optimized for specific functions and devices. The **default values** are generally recommended for normal operation. Since incorrect Setup values can cause the system to fail, you should only change Setup values that really need to be changed. If changes are made that disable the system, pressing the Insert key on reset will override the settings and start the system with default values.

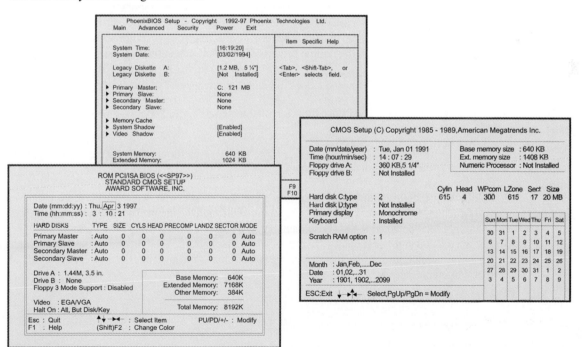

default values

The Standard CMOS Setup Screens

Standard CMOS Setup

Standard CMOS Setup screens from various manufacturers are depicted in Figure 2-49. They all provide the same basic information. They can be used to set the system clock/calendar, establish disk drive parameters and video display type, and specify which types of errors will halt the system during the POST.

The BIOS uses military time settings (i.e., 13:00:00 = 1 PM). The PgUp and PgDn keys are used to change the setting after it has been selected using the arrow keys. Some BIOS versions support Daylight Savings time by adding an hour when Daylight Savings time begins and subtracts it when standard time returns.

Figure 2-49: Standard CMOS Setup Screens

Current BIOS typically support 360 kB, 720 kB, 1.2 MB, 1.44 MB, and 2.88 MB floppy drive formats. The other area in this screen that may require some effort to set up is the HDD parameters section. All BIOS come with a list of hard drive types that they can support directly. However, they also provide an entry for user-definable drive settings. Historically, this entry has been referred to as the "Type 47", but may be located at any number in the list.

Auto Detection

Newer BIOS possess **Auto Detection** options to detect the type of hard drives installed in the system and automatically load their parameters into CMOS. Systems with Enhanced IDE capabilities support up to four IDE drives. However, the CMOS does not typically display information about CD-ROM drives or SCSI devices.

When the Auto Detect selection is chosen, the BIOS attempts to detect IDE devices in the system during the POST process and to determine the specifications and optimum operating mode for those devices. The drive specifications can also be selected from a built-in list of drive parameters, or they can be entered directly using the User option at the end of the list.

translation modes

Cyl/Hds/Sec (CHS)

Logical Block Addressing (LBA)

Four **translation modes** can be selected for each drive type; Auto, Normal, Large, and LBA. In Auto mode, the BIOS will establish the best operating mode for the drive. In Normal mode, the BIOS will support a maximum **Cyl/Hds/Sec (CHS)** setting of 1024/16/63. For larger drives (above 1024 cylinders), the Large and LBA modes are used. The Large option can be used with large drives that do not support **Logical Block Addressing (LBA)** techniques. For those drives that do, the LBA mode should be selected. In this mode, the IDE controller converts the sector/head/cylinder address into a physical block address that improves data throughput. Care should be taken when changing this BIOS setting since data loss may occur.

┌─ **TEST TIP** ─────────────────────┐
Know that the LBA mode for SCSI and IDE disk drives must be enabled in the CMOS to support hard drive sizes over 528 MB.
└──────────────────────────────────┘

Similarly, this BIOS supports standard EGA/VGA formats, as well as older 40- and 80-column CGA and monochrome formats. In the case of errors detected during the POST process, the BIOS can be set up to halt on different types of errors, or to ignore them and continue the bootup process. These settings include:

- *No Errors.* The POST does not stop for any errors.

- *All Errors.* The POST stops for all detected errors and prompts the user for corrective action.

- *A series of "All But" options.* The POST stops for all errors except those selected (i.e., all but disk or keyboard errors).

Finally, the screen displays the system's memory usage. The values displayed are derived from the POST process and cannot be changed through the menu. The BIOS displays the system's total detected RAM, Base memory, Extended memory, and Other memory (between the 640 kB and 1 MB marks). In most CMOS displays, the total memory does not equal the summation of the base and extended memory. This is because the BIOS reserves 384 kB for shadowing purposes.

┌─ **TEST TIP** ─────────────────────┐
Be aware that changing the translation mode setting for an existing drive may result in loss of all data.
└──────────────────────────────────┘

The BIOS Features Setup Screen

The *BIOS Features Setup* screen, shown in Figure 2-50, provides access to options that extend the standard ISA BIOS functions. This BIOS example includes a built-in virus warning utility that produces a warning message whenever a program tries to write to the boot sector of an HDD partition table. This function should be enabled for normal operations. However, it should be turned off when upgrading the operating system. The built-in virus warning utility checks the drive's boot sector for changes. The changes that the new operating system will attempt to make to the boot sector will be interpreted as a virus and the utility will act to prevent the upgrade from occurring. If a warning message is displayed under normal circumstances, a full-feature anti-virus utility should be run on the system.

The *Features Setup* screen is used to configure different bootup options. These options include establishing the system's bootup sequence. The sequence can be set so that the system checks the floppy drive for a boot sector first, or so that it checks the hard drive without checking the floppy drive.

Other bootup options include: Floppy Drive Seek, Numlock Status, and System Speed settings. The **Swap Floppy Drive** option can be enabled to route commands for logical drive A to physical drive B. This option can be used to isolate FDD problems in dual-drive units. Likewise, the Drive A option should be enabled if the system cannot boot to the hard-disk drive.

```
              ROM PCI/ISA BIOS (2A5KFR3B)
                   STANDARD CMOS SETUP
                   AWARD SOFTWARE, INC.

Virus Warning          : Disabled   Video   BIOS Shadow : Enabled
CPU Internal Cache     : Enabled    C8000-CBFFF Shadow  : Disabled
External Cache         : Enabled    CC000-CFFF  Shadow  : Disabled
Quick Power On Self Test : Disabled D0000-D3FFF Shadow  : Disabled
Boot Sequence          : A,C, SCSI  D4000-D7FFF Shadow  : Disabled
Swap Floppy Drive      : Disabled   D8000-DBFFF Shadow  : Disabled
Boot Up Floppy Seek    : Enabled    DC000-DFFFF Shadow  : Disabled
Boot Up Numlock Status : On
Boot Up System Speed   : High
Gate A20 Option        : Fast
Memory Parity Check    : Disabled
Typematic Rate Setting : Disabled
Typematic Rate (Chars/Sec) : 6
Typematic Delay (Msec) : 250
Security Option        : Setup      ESC : Quit      ↑↓→← : Select Item
PCI/VGA Palette Snoop  : Disabled   F1  : Help      PU/PD/+/- : Modify
OS Select For DRAM > 64M : Non-OS2  F5  : Old Values  (Shift)F2  Color
                                    F6  : Load BIOS Defaults
                                    F7  : Load Setup Defaults
```

Figure 2-50: BIOS Features Setup Screen

The system board's cache memory organization is displayed in the screen's External Cache Memory field. The CMOS provides options for controlling the system's A20 line and **Parity Checking** functions. The operation of the A20 line is connected to the system's changeover from Real mode to Protected mode and back. When set to the Fast mode, the chipset controls the operation of the system's A20 line. If the Normal mode setting is selected, the keyboard controller circuitry controls the **Gate A20** function. The operating system uses this function to enable the Real mode changeover. The system's Parity Checking function is used to check for corruption in the contents of data read from DRAM memory.

The operation of the keyboard can be modified from this screen. **Typematic Action** refers to the keyboard's ability to reproduce characters when a key is held down for a period of time. This action is governed by two parameters set in the BIOS Features screen—Typematic Rate and Typematic Delay. **Typematic Rate** refers to the rate at which characters will be repeated when the key is held down, while **Typematic Delay** defines the amount of time between the initial pressing of the key and when the repeating action begins. Typematic action is normally enabled and values of six characters/second and 250 milliseconds are typical for these settings.

The system's **Shadow** feature is controlled through the *BIOS Features* screen. Shadowing can be used to copy various system firmware routines into high memory. This allows the system to read firmware from a 16-bit or 32-bit data bus instead of the normal 8-bit PC-compatible X-bus. This technique speeds up firmware read operations but reduces the high memory space available for loading device drivers. Shadowing should be enabled for individual sections of memory as needed.

| Swap Floppy Drive |

| Parity Checking |

| Gate A20 |

| Typematic Action |

| Typematic Rate |

| Typematic Delay |

| Shadow |

The Chipset Features Screen

The *Chipset Features* screen, depicted in Figure 2-51, contains advanced setting information that system designers and service personnel use to optimize the chipset.

```
            ROM PCI/ISA BIOS (2A5KFR3B)
              CHIPSET FEATURES SETUP
               AWARD SOFTWARE, INC.

Auto Configuration       : Enabled    Word Merge          : Enabled
AT Bus Clock             : CLK2/4     Byte Merge          : Disabled
Asysc. SRAM Write WS     : X-3-3-3    Fast Back-to-Back   : Disabled
Asysc. SRAM Read WS      : X-3-3-3    PCI Write Burst     : Enabled
EDO Read WS              : X-3-3-3    SDRAM Access Timing : Normal
Page Mode Read WS        : X-3-3-3    SDRAM CAS Latency   : 3
DRAM Write WS            : X-2-2-2    TAG [10-8] Config   : Default
CPU to DRAM Page Mode    : Disabled
DRAM Refresh Period      : 60 us
DRAM Data Integrity Mode : Parity
Pipelined Function       : Disabled
16 Bit ISA I/O Command WS  : 2 Wait
16 Bit ISA Mem Command WS: 2 Wait
Local Memory 15-16M      : Enabled
Passive Release          : Enabled
ISA Line Buffer          : Enabled   ESC : Quit        ↑↓→← : Select Item
Delay Transaction        : Enabled   F1  : Help        PU/PD/+/- : Modify
Primary Frame Buffer     : 2 MB      F5  : Old Values  (Shift)F2 : Color
VGA Frame Buffer         : Enabled   F6  : Load BIOS Defaults
Linear Merge             : Enabled   F7  : Load Setup Defaults
```

Figure 2-51: Chipset Features Screen

Auto Configuration

The **Auto Configuration** option selects predetermined optimal values for the chipset to start with. When this feature is enabled, many of the screen's fields are not available to the user. When this setting is disabled, the chipset's setup parameters are obtained from the system's CMOS RAM. Many of the system's memory configuration parameters are established in this screen.

These parameters include wait state timing for asynchronous SRAM read and writes, as well as EDO and page-mode RAM reads. Wait state settings for slower ISA I/O and memory devices can also be configured in this screen (16-bit ISA Memory and I/O Command WS options). The Local Memory 15-16M option sets up mapping in the chipset to shift slower ISA device memory into faster local bus memory to increase system performance.

Data Integrity

Error Checking and Correcting (ECC)

Special DRAM paging operations can be enabled in the *Chipset Features* screen. When this option is disabled, the chip set's memory controller closes the DRAM page after each access. When enabled, it holds the page open until the next access occurs. DRAM refresh period and **Data Integrity** functions are also established here. This particular chipset features both parity-error checking and **Error Checking and Correcting** (**ECC**) error handling modes.

Access to the system buses is controlled through the *Chipset Features* screen as well. The sample chipset uses internal buffers to control the flow of information between the system's different buses. The ISA Line Buffer, Primary Frame Buffer, and VGA Frame Buffer are manipulated by the chipset for speed matching purposes. When the **Passive Release** option is enabled, the system's microprocessor can access the DRAM during passive release periods. If not, only a PCI bus master can access the local memory.

Other options allow bytes on the data bus to be merged. Merge options include: *Linear Merge*, *Word Merge*, and *Byte Merge*. The chipset's memory controller checks the system's address bus enable lines to determine if items on the data bus can be used as a single unit.

┌─ **TEST TIP** ─────────────────┐
Be aware that parity checking only detects data errors whereas ECC can detect and correct data errors.
└────────────────────────────────┘

Finally, the *Chipset Features* screen supports three fast write modes. These are the Fast Back-to-Back, PCI Write Burst, and M1 Linear Burst modes. When enabled, these modes allow the system to conduct consecutive PCI Write cycles in fast or burst fashions.

The sample BIOS features Plug-and-Play (PnP) capability that makes adding options to the system more automatic. PCI devices feature PnP operation. They are questioned by the system during bootup, or when they are plugged into the system, to determine what their system resource requirements are. These requirements are compared to a listing of devices already in the system, and necessary system resources such as IRQ and DMA channels are allocated for them.

The PnP/PCI Configuration Screen

The BIOS holds information about the system's resource allocations and supplies it to the operating system as required. Figure 2-52 shows the *PCI Configuration* screen from the sample CMOS Setup utility. The operating system must be PnP-compatible in order to achieve the full benefits of the PnP BIOS. In most newer PCs, the standard operating system is Windows 95/98, which is PnP compliant.

```
                 ROM PCI/ISA BIOS (P155TVP4)
                      PNP AND PCI SETUP
                    AWARD SOFTWARE, INC.

Slot  1  (Right) IRQ   : Auto          DMA  1  Used By ISA       : No/ICU
Slot  2  IRQ           : Auto          DMA  3  Used By ISA       : No/ICU
Slot  3  IRQ           : Auto          DMA  5  Used By ISA       : No/ICU
Slot  4  IRQ           : Auto
PCI  Latency Timer     : 32 PCI Clock  ISA MEM Block BASE        : No/ICU

                                       NCR SCSI BIOS             : Auto
IRQ  3  Used By ISA  : No/ICU          USB Function              : Disabled
IRQ  4  Used By ISA  : No/ICU
IRQ  5  Used By ISA  : No/ICU
IRQ  6  Used By ISA  : No/ICU
IRQ  7  Used By ISA  : No/ICU
IRQ  8  Used By ISA  : No/ICU
IRQ  9  Used By ISA  : No/ICU
IRQ 10 Used By ISA   : No/ICU
IRQ 11 Used By ISA   : No/ICU
IRQ 12 Used By ISA   : No/ICU
IRQ 13 Used By ISA   : No/ICU         ESC  : Quit      ↑↓←→       : Select Item
IRQ 14 Used By ISA   : No/ICU         F1   : Help      PU/PD/+/-  : Modify
IRQ 15 Used By ISA   : No/ICU         F5   : Old Values  (Shift) F2 : Color
                                      F6   : Load BIOS Defaults
                                      F7   : Load Setup Defaults
```

Figure 2-52: PnP/PCI Configuration Options Screen

┌─ **TEST TIP** ──────┐

Know which portion of
the BIOS is responsible
for implementing the PnP
process.
└─────────────────────┘

PCI IRQ Map-to

This CMOS utility can automatically configure all PnP devices if the **Auto mode** is enabled. Under this condition, the system's IRQ and DMA assignment fields disappear as the BIOS assigns them to installed devices. When the configuration process is performed manually, each resource can be assigned as either a legacy device or a PnP/PCI device. The legacy device is one that is compatible with the original ISA slot and requires specific resource settings. The PnP/PCI device must be compliant with the Plug-and-Play specification.

With this chipset, the system board's IDE channels are coordinated with the operation of the PCI bus. The **PCI IRQ Map-to** function lets the user establish the PCI IRQ mapping for the system. Because the PCI interface in the sample chipset has two channels, it requires two interrupt services. The Primary and Secondary IDE interrupt fields default to values appropriate for two PCI IDE channels. The primary channel has a lower interrupt number than the secondary channel. Normally, ISA interrupts reserved for IDE channels are IRQ14 for the primary channel and IRQ15 for the secondary channel.

The secondary IDE channel can be deactivated through the PCI IDE Second Channel option. This setting is usually disabled so that an add-on IDE host adapter card can be added to the system. Only the secondary on-board IDE channel is disabled through this setting. The type of action required to trigger the interrupt can also be established in this screen. The PCI IRQ Activated by option is normally set to Level unless a device that requires an ISA-compatible, edge-triggered interrupt is added to the system.

The Integrated Peripherals Setup Functions

Integrated
Peripherals

In most Pentium-based systems, the standard I/O functions of the Multi-I/O card have been integrated into the system board. In these systems, the BIOS' **Integrated Peripherals** screen, depicted in Figure 2-53, provides configuration and enabling settings for the system board's IDE drive connections, floppy-disk drive controller, on-board UARTs, and on-board parallel port.

```
          ROM PCI/ISA BIOS (2A5KFR3B)
          INTEGRATED PERIPHERALS SETUP
              AWARD SOFTWARE, INC.

  On-Chip IDE Controller    : Enabled   Parallel Port Mode      : Normal
  The 2nd channel IDE       : Enabled
  IDE Primary Master PIO    : Auto
  IDE Primary Slave PIO     : Auto
  IDE Secondary Master PIO  : Auto
  IDE Secondary Slave PIO   : Auto
  IDE Primary Master FIFO   : Enabled
  IDE Primary Slave FIFO    : Disabled
  IDE Secondary Master FIFO : Disabled
  IDE Secondary Slave FIFO  : Disabled
  IDE HDD Block Mode        : Enabled

  Onboard FDC Controller    : Enabled
  Onboard UART 1            : Auto
  UART 1 Operation mode     : Standard
                                        ESC : Quit         ↑↓→← : Select Item
  Onboard UART 2            : Auto      F1  : Help      PU/PD/+/- : Modify
  UART 2 Operation mode     : Standard  F5  : Old Values   (Shift)F2 : Color
                                        F6  : Load BIOS Defaults
  Onboard Parallel Port     : 378/IRQ7  F7  : Load Setup Defaults
```

Figure 2-53: Integrated Peripherals Screen

The *Integrated Peripherals* screen is used to enable the on-board IDE controller. As mentioned earlier in this chapter, the second IDE channel can be enabled or disabled independently of the first channel, provided that the controller has been enabled. Any of the four possible devices attached to the interface can be configured for Master or Slave operation.

Each IDE device can also be enabled for **Programmed Input/Output (PIO)** modes and **First In/First Out (FIFO) buffering**. The PIO field permits the user to select any of four PIO modes (0-4) for each device. The PIO mode determines how fast data will be transferred between the drive and the system. The performance level of the device typically increases with each higher mode value.

Older BIOS versions provided for a manual PIO configuration setting. In Mode-0, the transfer rate is set at 3.3 MB/second with a 600 nanosecond (ns) cycle time. Mode-1 steps up to 5.2 MB/s with a 3.3 ns cycle time. Mode-2 improves to 8.3 MB/s using a 240 ns cycle time.

However, the newer ATA standards provide for different *Programmed I/O (PIO)* modes that offer higher performance capabilities. Most of the faster drives support PIO Modes-3 and -4 through the ATA-2 specification. These modes use 11.1 MB/s with a 180 ns cycle time and 16.6 MB/s using a 120 ns cycle time respectively. These modes require that the IDE port be located on a local bus, such as a PCI bus. Some system boards only place the IDE1 connection on this 64-bit bus, whereas the IDE2 connection is a function of the ISA bus. In these cases, devices installed on the IDE2 connector will only be capable of mode 2 operations. Newer BIOS versions do not offer manual PIO configuration capabilities.

If the *Auto mode* option is selected, the system will determine which mode is best suited for each device. If FIFO operation is selected, the system establishes special FIFO buffers for each device to speed up data flow between the device and the system.

The *IDE HDD Block mode* selection should be set to Enabled for most new hard drives. This setting, also referred to as Large Block Transfer, Multiple Command, and Multiple-Sector Read/Write mode, supports LBA disk drive operations so that partitions larger than 528 MB can be used on the drive.

The other on-board I/O functions supported through the CMOS utility include: enabling the FDD controller, selecting the logical COM port addressing and operating modes for the system's two built-in UARTs, and selecting logical addressing and operating modes for the parallel port.

The UARTs can be configured to support half-duplex or full-duplex transmission modes through an infrared port, provided the system board is equipped with one. This allows wireless communications with serial peripheral devices over short distances.

The parallel printer port can be configured for normal PC-AT compatible **Standard Parallel Port (SPP)** operation, for extended bi-directional operation (**Extended Parallel Port - EPP**), for fast, buffered bi-directional operation (**Extended Capabilities Port - ECP**), or for combined ECP+EPP operation. The normal setting should be selected unless both the port hardware and driver software support EPP and/or ECP operation.

Infrared Data Association (IrDA) ports provide short-distance wireless connections for different IrDA-compliant devices, such as printers and personal digital assistants. Because the IrDA port communicates by sending and receiving a serial stream of light pulses, it is normally configured to work with the UART of the system's second serial port. This arrangement is established through the Integrated Peripherals page of the CMOS Setup utility. In this manner, the infrared port is assigned the same system resources normally reserved for the COM2/COM4 serial ports.

Programmed Input/Output (PIO)

First In/First Out (FIFO) buffering

TEST TIP

Remember that ECP and EPP modes for the parallel port must be enabled through the CMOS Setup utility.

Standard Parallel Port (SPP)

Extended Parallel Port (EPP)

Extended Capabilities Port (ECP)

Infrared Data Association (IrDA)

To enable the IrDA port, the mode for the COM2 UART must be set to automatic and one of the infrared protocol settings (*HPSIR* or *ASKIR*) must be selected. In addition, the transmission duplex mode must be selected (normally half duplex). The operation of the infrared port and the second serial port are mutually exclusive. When the infrared option is enabled in CMOS, the second serial port will be disabled.

Power Management Functions

Power Management
Doze
Standby
Suspend

The **Power Management** fields allow the user to select from three power saving modes: **Doze**, **Standby**, and **Suspend**. These are green PC-compatible power saving modes that cause the system to incrementally step down from maximum power usage. The Doze setting causes the microprocessor clock to slow down after a defined period of inactivity. The Standby mode causes the hard drive and video to shut down after a period of inactivity. Finally, everything in the system except the microprocessor shuts down in Suspend mode. Certain system events, such as IRQ and DRQ activities, cause the system to wake up from these modes and resume normal operation.

Security Subsystem

security options
passwords
supervisory passwords

Newer BIOS offer a variety of **security options** that can be set through the CMOS Setup utility. Figure 2-54 displays a typical security configuration screen. Typically, these options include items such as setting **passwords** and **supervisory passwords** to control access. The password setting options permit the user to enter and modify password settings. Password protection can be established for the system, so that a password must be entered each time the system boots up or when the Setup utility is entered, or it can simply be set up so that it is only required to access the Setup utility.

```
                        PhoenixBIOS Setup Utility
                  Security
                                                    Item Specific Help
 Set User Password:        [Enter]
 Set Supervisor Password:  [Enter]
                                            Supervisor password
 Virus Check Reminder:     [Disabled]       controls access to Setup
 System Backup Reminder:   [Disabled]       utility.

 Password on boot:         [Disabled]
 Diskette access:          [Disabled]
 Fixed disk boot sector:   [normal]




 F1   Help        ↑↓ Select Item   -/+   Change Values   F9  Setup Defaults
 ESC  Exit        ←→ Select Menu    Enter Select > Sub-Menu  F10 Save and Exit
```

Figure 2-54: CMOS Security Configuration

The security configuration screen may also include options for setting virus check and backup reminders that will pop up periodically when the system is booted. In addition to enabling these settings, administrators can also specify the time interval between notices.

One of the main sets of security options in the CMOS Setup utility consists of those that can be used to control access to the system. For the most part, these options cover such things as access permitted through the floppy drive and access to the boot sector of the drive. This section may also provide for a password on bootup.

ADDING AND REMOVING FRU MODULES

The A+ Core objective 1.2 states that the test taker should be able to identify basic procedures for adding and removing field replaceable modules. As this A+ objective points out, every technician should be aware of typical personal computer components that can be exchanged in the field. They should be able to install, connect, and configure these components to upgrade or repair an existing system. The following sections of this chapter present standard procedures for installing and removing typical field replaceable units in a microcomputer system.

System Boards

System boards are generally removed for one of two possible reasons. Either the system board has failed, and needs to be replaced, or the user wants to install a new system board with better features. In either case, it will be necessary to remove the current system board and replace it. The removal procedure can be defined in five steps, as described in the following process:

1. Remove all external I/O systems.

2. Remove the system unit's outer cover.

3. Remove the adapter cards.

4. Remove the cables from the system board.

5. Remove the system board.

To replace a system board, it is necessary to disconnect several cables from the old system board and reconnect them to the new system board. The easiest method of handling this is to use tape (preferably masking tape) to mark the wires and their connection points (on the new system board) before removing them from the old system board.

Removing External I/O Systems

Unplug all power cords from the commercial outlet. Remove all peripherals from the system unit. Disconnect the mouse, keyboard, and monitor signal cable from the rear of the unit. Finally, disconnect the monitor power cable from the system (or the outlet). Figure 2-55 illustrates the system unit's back panel connections.

POWER INPUT

KEYBOARD AND MOUSE CONNECTORS

PRINTER ADAPTER CONNECTOR

SPEAKER OUT

GAME ADAPTER CONNECTOR

NETWORK CONNECTOR

MONITOR CONNECTOR

BACK OF SYSTEM UNIT

Figure 2-55: System Unit Back Panel Connections

Removing the System Unit's Outer Cover

Unplug the 120 Vac power cord from the system unit. Determine which type of case you are working on. If the case is a desktop model, does the cover slide off the chassis in a forward direction, bringing the front panel with it, or does it raise off the chassis from the rear? If the back lip of the outer cover folds over the edge of the back panel, then the lid raises up from the back after the retaining screws are removed. If the retaining screws go through the back panel without passing through the lip, then the outer cover will slide forward after the retaining screws have been removed.

Determine the number of screws that hold the outer cover to the chassis. Do not confuse the power supply retaining screws with those holding the back panel. The power supply unit requires four screws. Check for screws along the lower edges of the outer cover that hold it to the sides of the chassis. Remove the screws that hold the cover to the chassis. Store the screws properly.

Remove the system unit's outer cover, as illustrated in Figure 2-56, and set it aside. Slide the case forward. Tilt the case upward from the front and remove it from the unit. Or, lift the back edge of the outer cover to approximately 45 degrees, and then slide it toward the rear of the chassis.

Figure 2-56:
Removing the
Case

Removing the Adapter Cards

A wide variety of peripheral devices are used with PC-compatible systems. Many of these devices communicate with the main system through adapter cards that fit into expansion slot connectors on the system board.

Remove the retaining screws that secure the adapter cards to the system unit's back panel. Remove the adapter cards from the expansion slots. It is a good practice to place adapter cards back into the same slots they were removed from, if possible. Store the screws properly. Refer to Figure 2-57 to perform this procedure.

If the system employs an MI/O card, disconnect the floppy drive signal cable (smaller signal cable) and the hard drive signal cable (larger signal cable) from the card. Also disconnect any I/O port connections from the card before removing it from the expansion slot.

Figure 2-57: Removing
Adapter Cards

Removing the Cables from the System Board

The system board provides an operator interface through a set of front panel indicator lights and switches. These indicators and switches connect to the system board by BERG connectors, as depicted in Figure 2-58.

The front panel connectors must be removed in order to exchange the system board for a new one. Since it is quite easy to get these connections reversed, make sure that you mark them for identification purposes before removing them from their connection points. Record the color and function of each connection. Trace each wire back to its front panel connection to determine what its purpose is. This will ensure that all the wires are reinstalled correctly after the exchange is completed.

Disconnect the power supply connections from the system board as well.

Figure 2-58: Front Panel Connections

Removing the System Board

Verify the positions of all jumper and switch settings on the old system board. Record these settings and verify their meanings before removing the board from the system. This may require the use of the board's user's manual, if available. Remove the grounding screw (or screws) that secure the system board to the chassis. Store the screws properly.

In a desktop unit, slide the system board toward the left (as you face the front of the unit) to free its plastic feet from the slots in the floor of the system unit. Tilt the left edge of the board up, and then lift it straight up and out of the system unit, as illustrated in Figure 2-59.

Figure 2-59: Removing the System Board from a Desktop Case

In a tower unit, slide the system board toward the bottom of the system unit to free its plastic feet from the slots in the side panel. Tilt the bottom edge of the board away from the unit and pull it straight out of the chassis, as shown in Figure 2-60.

UNIT CASE

BRASS
STANDOFFS

SYSTEM
BOARD

SMALL
SCREWS

Figure 2-60: Removing the System Board from a Tower Case

System Board Devices

There are a few serviceable devices on the system board. These include:

- the microprocessor
- the system RAM modules
- specialized support ICs

As with the system board itself, there are really only two possible reasons for servicing any of these devices: to replace a failed unit or to upgrade the unit.

Microprocessors

PC manufacturers mount microprocessors in **sockets** so that they can be replaced easily. This enables a failed microprocessor to simply be exchanged with a working unit. More often though, the microprocessor is replaced with an improved version to upgrade the speed or performance of the system.

The notches and dots on the various ICs are important keys when replacing a microprocessor. They specify the location of the IC's number 1 pin. This pin must be lined up with the **pin-1 notch** of the socket for proper insertion. In older systems, the microprocessors had to be forcibly removed from the socket using an IC extractor tool. As the typical microprocessor's pin count increased, special Zero Insertion Force (ZIF) sockets were designed that allowed the microprocessor to be set in the socket without force and then be clamped in place. An arm-activated clamping mechanism in the socket shifts to the side, locking the pins in place. A microprocessor and ZIF socket arrangement is depicted in Figure 2-61.

Figure 2-61: A Microprocessor and ZIF Socket

To release the microprocessor from the socket, the lever arm beside the socket must be pressed down and away from the socket. When it comes free from the socket, the arm raises up to release the pressure on the microprocessor's pins.

A notch and dot in one corner of the CPU marks the position of the processor's #1 pin. The dot and notch should be located at the free end of the socket's locking lever for proper installation. Both the CPU and the socket have one corner that does not have a pin (or pin hole) in it. This feature prevents the CPU from being inserted into the socket incorrectly.

Pentium processors generate a considerable amount of heat during normal operation. To prevent this heat from reaching a destructive level, all Pentiums require that a CPU cooling fan and heat sink unit be installed on the microprocessor. These units are available in glue-on and snap-on models. A special heat-conducting grease is typically used with snap-on heat sinks to provide good thermal transfer between the microprocessor and the heat sink. Power for the fans is normally obtained from one of the system's options power connectors, or from a special jumper block on the system board. These items must be installed before operating the microprocessor.

Pentium microprocessors come in a number of speed ratings and many use a dual processor voltage arrangement. In addition, the processor unit may be a Pentium clone unit manufactured by a company other than Intel. The microprocessor's supply voltage is controlled by a **Voltage Regulator Module (VRM)** on the system board. On some system boards, jumpers are used to establish the proper +3V and **CPU Core voltage** settings for the particular type of microprocessor being installed in the system. On other systems, the PnP BIOS will communicate directly with the microprocessor to configure the system with the proper settings for that type of processor.

As stated earlier in this chapter, all Pentium processors up to Pentium II operated from one of three external clock frequencies—50 MHz, 60 MHz, or 66 MHz. Newer Pentium versions employ 100 MHz and 133 MHz clocks to produce processor speeds of up to 3.0 GHz. The *advertised speed rating* of a microprocessor is derived by multiplying its maximum allowable clock frequency by its maximum internal clock multiplier setting (e.g., 100 MHz clock signal applied to an internal bus multiplier of 20 will produce a processor speed of 2.0 GHz). If the processor is placed on a system board that is using a slower clock input, its actual operating speed will be decreased proportionally.

The front side bus frequency is determined by another multiplication process that is tied to the system clock. For example, the 100 MHz clock described in the previous example would be applied to a quadrature summation (4X) circuit in a Pentium 4 processor that produces a 400 MHz front side bus frequency. On older system boards, jumpers were used to establish the external/internal clock ratio for the microprocessor, as well as its external bus frequency. On newer boards, the BIOS establishes these parameters by default. However, they can be modified manually through the CMOS Setup utility.

Memory Modules

Modern system boards typically provide rows of **Single In-line Memory Module (SIMM)** sockets and a single **Dual In-line Memory Module (DIMM)** socket. These sockets accept small piggyback memory modules that can contain various combinations of DRAM devices. Both SIMMs and DIMMs use edge connectors that snap into a retainer on the system board. The SIMMs used on Pentium boards are typically 72-pin SIMMs whereas the DIMM socket accepts 168-pin DIMM units.

The SIMM modules can only be inserted in one direction because of a plastic safety tab at one end of the SIMM slot. The notched end of the SIMM module must be inserted into this end. To install a SIMM module, insert the module into the slot at a 45-degree angle, making sure that all of the contacts are aligned with the slot. Rock the module into a vertical position so that it snaps into place and the plastic guides go through the SIMM's mounting holes. The metal clip should lock into place. To release the SIMM module, gently push the metal clips outward and rotate the module out of the slot. The DIMM module simply slides vertically into the socket and is locked in place by a tab at each end. These processes are illustrated in Figure 2-62.

Figure 2-62: Installing SIMM and DIMM Modules

On most Pentium system boards, the SIMM sockets are organized so that slots 1 and 2 make up **bank-0**, while slots 2 and 3 form **bank-1**. Each bank can be filled with single-sided (32-bit) SIMMs, or double-sided (64-bit) SIMMs. The system can be operated with only bank-0 full. It will also operate with both banks full. However, it cannot be operated with a portion of any bank filled (a bank in use must be full).

SYSTEM UPGRADING AND OPTIMIZING

The A+ Core hardware objective 1.8 states that the test taker should be able to identify concepts and procedures relating to BIOS. It also states that the test taker should be able to identify hardware methods of system optimization and when to use them.

The modular design of the PC-compatible system enables portions of the system to be upgraded as new, or better, components become available, or as the system's application changes. As this A+ objective points out, computer technicians must be capable of upgrading the system's BIOS as part of a system upgrade. Technicians should also be able to optimize PC hardware to obtain the best performance possible for a given system configuration. The following sections cover upgradeable components found in common PC systems, including information about when and how to upgrade them.

System Board Upgrading

There are typically five serviceable components on the system board. These include:

- the microprocessor
- the RAM modules
- the CMOS backup battery
- the ROM BIOS
- the cache memory

> Of the five items listed, three—the microprocessor, the RAM modules, and the cache memory—can be exchanged to increase the performance of the system. These devices are normally mounted in sockets to make replacing or upgrading them an easy task.

Electrostatic Discharge (ESD)

Great care should be taken when exchanging these parts to avoid damage to the ICs from **Electrostatic Discharge (ESD)**. ESD prevention is covered in detail in Chapter 13—*Preventive Maintenance*. In addition, care should be taken during the extraction and replacement of the ICs to avoid misalignment and bent pins. Make sure to correctly align the IC's pin #1 with the socket's pin #1 position. In the case of microprocessors that plug into standard sockets, the force required to insert them may overstress the system board if it is not properly supported.

Microprocessor Upgrades

As stated earlier in this chapter, microprocessor manufacturers have devised upgrade versions for virtually every type of microprocessor in the market. It is also common for clone microprocessors to be pin-for-pin compatible with older Intel socket designs. This strategy enables the end-user to realize a speed increase by upgrading, along with an increase in processing power.

Actually upgrading the processor is a fairly easy operation after gaining access to the system board. In most cases, you simply remove the microprocessor from its socket and replace it with the upgrade. Two items must be observed when changing the microprocessor:

- Make sure the replacement microprocessor is hardware compatible with the original, or that the system board will support the new microprocessor type
- Make certain to properly orient the new processor in the socket so that its pin #1 matches the socket's pin #1

The physical upgrade should also be accompanied by a logical upgrade. For major upgrades, such as installing newer and faster processors, the BIOS may need to be upgraded as well. Later BIOS versions are often developed by the system board's manufacturer to permit installation of faster processors as they come on the market. Therefore, you should always check the manufacturer's Internet support site to determine whether the system board can support the processor type and speed you intend to upgrade to.

After the new processor has been installed, you should verify the operation of the upgrade. The initial test will be to boot up the system and see if you receive an error code, and to verify that the system recognizes the newly installed processor.

Installing Additional Processors

Some system boards provide multiple processor sockets or slots that permit additional processors to be added to distribute the processing load. You can use all, some, or just one of the available sockets by removing the terminator from the socket and installing the new processor. Adding additional processors represents the most effective means to upgrade the performance of the computer. However, there are several steps that should be taken before installing additional processors.

1. *Verify processor compatibility* — Ensure that that the processor you are adding is compatible with the socket type on the board (preferably the same brand that is already on the board). You should also check the production run number of the processor to ensure that it is within one production run of its companion processors. In the case of Intel processors, this is referred to as a "stepping level." For example, if you have a Pentium III 750 MHz processor from stepping level four, you should install additional processors that are defined as stepping 3, 4, or 5. For optimum stability you should install the same make, model, and clock speed for all processors. This would include using the same bus speed and multiplier settings and the same cache size to ensure there is no speed difference between cache feeds. Refer to the system board's manual or online documentation for detailed information about processor compatibility issues.

2. *Perform a BIOS upgrade* — Multiple processor system boards include a BIOS version with multiple processor support. This BIOS should be sufficient when installing directly compatible additional processors. However, for major upgrades, such as installing newer and faster processors, the BIOS may need to be upgraded. In many cases, newer BIOS versions are developed by the system board's manufacturer to permit the installation of faster processors as they enter the market. Therefore, check the manufacturer's Internet support site to determine whether your system board can support the processor type and speed you intend to use.

3. *Verify upgrade* — Verifying a processor upgrade is fairly simple. Boot up the system to see if an error code is generated and to verify that the system recognizes the newly installed processor.

> **NOTE**
>
> You should not interpret an automatic entry into the CMOS Setup utility as an error when the system is initially booted after adding an additional processor. This is the process that systems often use to recognize new processors. You can use the system's CMOS Setup utility (or an administrative tools package) to ensure that the system board is recognizing all the installed processors, and that they are working properly.

Firmware Upgrades

When the microprocessor is upgraded, the BIOS should also be *flashed* with the latest compatibility firmware. If the BIOS does not possess the flash option and does not support the new microprocessor, a new BIOS chip that does support it must be obtained. If not, the entire system board will typically need to be upgraded.

When you **flash** firmware, you direct the system board to send electrical charges into a ROM chip that will rewrite its programming. In order to flash the ROM device you must have a program from its vendor that can be downloaded into the IC. This program will write the updated information into the chip so that the physical device now holds the latest version of information.

The same technique is used for flashing the system's ROM BIOS, as well as the various ROM BIOS extensions associated with video cards, network cards, modem, and RAID controllers. Each peripheral device will have its own utility program for flashing their ROM devices.

While there are many different types of devices whose BIOS you can flash, the general process to do so remains the same:

- Document the CMOS settings

- Back up the original BIOS program. In case the process fails, you can use the original BIOS program to attempt to restore the settings back to its original form

- Flash the BIOS with the new program according to the directions of the device manufacturer

A graphical representation of this process is shown in Figure 2-63.

- **TEST TIP**

Know what precautions to take before upgrading the system's BIOS.

Figure 2-63:
Flashing BIOS

Cooling System Upgrades

In any modern PC, the cooling system will include a passive heat sink device and a processor cooling fan. These items work alongside the power supply fan to cool the system and the processor. A special thermal compound (thermal grease) is placed between the heat sink and the processor to increase the rate of heat transfer to the heat sink. In some situations, additional case fans are installed to increase or redirect the airflow through the chassis.

When microprocessors are upgraded (or overclocked) the processor cooling system may also need to be improved. In most cases, the new microprocessor comes with a properly sized heat sink and fan. These processors are referred to as boxed processors and provide longer warranties than stand-alone **OEM (original equipment manufacturer)** processors. However, OEM processors do not include a fan or heat sink and you must research and locate a proper cooling system for them.

OEM (original equipment manufacturer)

To accomplish this, you must find the microprocessor's operating temperature specification. For Pentium processors the recommended operating temperature was 30 degrees C. However, with the appearance of the Pentium III and Pentium 4 processors, Intel switched to 35 degrees C. The AMD processors typically run much hotter than Intel versions (i.e., 45 – 50 degrees C). You must find a fan that is rated to work with a particular processor's temperature/speed specification.

The Health configuration settings in the system's CMOS Setup utility can be set to automatically control the fan speed to provide optimum cooling. This setting can also be switched to permit manual configuration of the cooling system. These settings work in conjunction with fan speed control values obtained from the BIOS. If the cooling system fails to maintain the processor temperature, the system can be shut down and preventesd from starting back up. Optimizing the speed of the fan lowers the relative dust accumulation that can lead to thermal failure.

Some computer manufacturers include air baffles (guides) that channel air through the chassis in specific paths. Others include foam filters at chassis openings to filter the incoming air, removing dust particles that can accumulate on electronic devices and cause overheating.

At present, high-end servers are available with liquid cooled and refrigerated processor cooling systems. At present only serious hardware users employ these options with their PCs. However, future processor development plans (i.e., Pentium 5+) are considering liquid versus refrigerated cooling systems as standard equipment.

Memory Upgrades

Upgrading system board memory is also a fairly simple process. Having more RAM on board allows the system to access more data from extended or expanded memory, without having to access the disk drive. This speeds up system operation considerably. Normally, upgrading memory simply amounts to installing new memory modules in vacant SIMM or DIMM slots. If the slots are already populated it will be necessary to remove them to install faster or higher-capacity modules.

Consult the system board user's guide to determine what speed the memory devices must be rated for. You should be aware that RAM and other memory devices are rated in access time instead of clock speed. Therefore, a 70-nanosecond (ns) RAM device is faster than an 80-nanosecond device. The guide should also be checked for any memory configuration settings that must be made to accept the new memory capacity.

You must ensure that the memory type and size you want to install is supported by the system board and that the system board does not already have the maximum amount of memory installed. The system board's manual will include information on the type, configuration, and size of memory it will accept. In addition, verify that the memory you wish to install is compatible with the memory currently installed on the board. For example, if the memory currently installed in the machine is rated as PC133, you would not want to install an additional PC100-type memory module.

Normally you should use the same type, brand, and speed of memory devices for RAM upgrades. Since the information detailing the RAM module's type and speed is rarely annotated on the device, you may need to check the signal to clock rate (CAS) for comparison. For instance, if your current memory modules are described as CAS3 units, then you should get CAS3 type memory for a compatible replacement, or for adding additional memory. To verify the memory upgrade, attempt to observe the memory test display during the POST process to ensure that the system sees the additional memory. Afterwards, boot into the operating system and verify that it also recognizes the installed memory.

Cache Upgrades

If the system has socketed cache memory, some additional performance can be gained by optimizing the cache. Upgrading the cache on these system boards normally only requires that additional cache ICs be installed in vacant sockets. If the sockets are full but the system's cache size is less than maximum, it will be necessary to remove the existing cache chips and replace them with faster, higher-capacity devices. Make sure to observe the pin #1 alignment as well as check the system board's user's guide for any configuration jumper changes.

Before upgrading the system board's FRU units, compare the cost of the proposed component upgrade against the cost of upgrading the system board itself. In many cases, the RAM from the original board can be used on a newer, faster model that should include a more advanced microprocessor. Before finalizing the choice to install a new system board, however, make sure that the current adapters, software, and peripherals will function properly with the updated board. If not, the cost of upgrading may be unexpectedly higher than simply replacing an FRU component.

CHAPTER SUMMARY

The chapter picked up where the general system board discussion from Chapter 1 left off. The opening sections featured an expanded discussion of motherboards (components and architecture) roughly equivalent with CompTIA's Core Hardware objective 4.3. This section was used to start the chapter because it permitted the discussion of all the system board objectives to flow better. After completing this section, you should be able to describe the major architectural differences between system board types.

After completing the discussion of motherboard fundamentals, the chapter keyed in on its main component—the microprocessor. You should be able to describe the basic characteristics of popular microprocessors after examining this section.

Following the microprocessors section, the chapter moved into an extended discussion of system memory structures. This section should enable you to describe the different categories of RAM and identify their normal system-board locations and physical characteristics.

After leaving memory structures, the chapter next explored CMOS Setup utilities in detail. After completing this section, you should be able to describe the purpose of CMOS RAM, discuss what a typical CMOS utility contains, and explain how to change basic parameters.

The chapter concluded with a discussion of adding and removing various FRU modules.

At this point, review the objectives listed at the beginning of the chapter to be certain that you understand and can perform each item listed there.

KEY POINTS REVIEW

This chapter has examined the major components that make up typical PC-compatible system boards. These items include microprocessors, memory types, microprocessor support systems, and expansion buses. Review the following key points before moving into the Review and Exam Questions sections to make sure you are comfortable with each point. Afterward, answer the Review Questions that follow to verify your knowledge of the information.

- The system board contains the components that form the basis of the computer system.

- System boards fundamentally change for three reasons: new microprocessors, new expansion-slot types, and reduced chip counts. Reduced chip counts are typically the result of improved microprocessor support chipsets. Chipsets combine PC- and AT-compatible structures into larger integrated circuits.

- Since chipset-based system boards require much fewer IC devices to produce, printed-circuit-board manufacturers have been able to design much smaller boards.

- Chipset-based system boards and I/O cards tend to change often as IC manufacturers continue to integrate higher levels of circuitry into their devices.

- The system's expansion slots provide the connecting point for most of its I/O devices. Interface cards communicate with the system through the extended microprocessor buses in these slots.

- In order to speed up the operation of their systems, system board manufacturers began to add proprietary bus designs to their board to increase the speed and bandwidth for transfers between the microprocessor and a few selected peripherals. This was accomplished by creating special local buses between the devices that would enable the peripherals to operate at speeds close to that of the microprocessor.

- The main component in the PCI-based system is the PCI bus controller, called the host bridge. This device monitors the microprocessor's address bus to determine whether addresses are intended for devices on the system board, in a PCI slot, or in one of the system board's other expansion slots.

- The microprocessors used in the vast majority of all PC-compatible microcomputers include: the 8088/86, the 80286, the 80386, the 80486, and the Pentium (80586 and 80686) devices.

- The Pentium is a 32/64-bit microprocessor contained in a Ceramic Pin Grid Array package. The registers for the microprocessor and floating-point sections of the Pentium are identical to those of the 80486. It has a 64-bit data bus that allows it to handle Quad Word (or Qword) data transfers. The Pentium also contains two separate 8 kB caches, compared to only one in the 80486. One of the caches is used for instructions or code, and the other is used for data. The internal architecture of the Pentium resembles an 80486 in expanded form. The floating-point section operates up to five times faster than the FPU in the 80486.

- In the Pentium MMX processor, the multimedia and communications processing capabilities of the original Pentium device are extended by the addition of 57 multimedia-specific instructions to the instruction set.

- Intel departed from simply increasing the speed of its Pentium processor line by introducing the Pentium Pro processor. While compatible with all of the previous software written for the Intel processor line, the Pentium Pro is optimized to run 32-bit software.

- The Pentium II includes all of the multimedia enhancements from the MMX processor, as well as retaining the power of the Pentium Pro's dynamic execution and 512 kB L2 cache features. The L1 cache is increased to 32 kB, while the L2 cache operates with a half-speed bus.

- There are normally three types of semiconductor memory found on a typical system board. These include the system's ROM BIOS ICs, the system's RAM memory, and the second-level cache memory unit.

- The microprocessor, the RAM modules, and the cache memory can be exchanged to increase the performance of the system. These devices are normally mounted in sockets to make replacing or upgrading them an easy task.

- One method of increasing the memory access speed of a computer is called caching. This memory management method assumes that most memory accesses are made within a limited block of addresses. Therefore, if the contents of these addresses are relocated into a special section of high-speed SRAM, the microprocessor could access these locations without requiring any wait states.

- There are also other commonly used methods of organizing RAM memory so that it can be accessed more efficiently. Typically, memory accesses occur in two fashions: instruction fetches (which are generally sequential) and operand accesses (which tend to be random). Paging and interleaving memory schemes are designed to take advantage of the sequential nature of instruction fetches from memory.

REVIEW QUESTIONS

The following questions test your knowledge of the material presented in this chapter.

1. What part of the ATX Pentium system board is responsible for controlling the operating temperature of its microprocessor?

2. Identify two options that can be implemented to cool microprocessors that run outside their operating temperature range. Also, indicate what conditions might cause this to occur.

3. Where is the L1 cache located in the Pentium microprocessor?

4. How many pins does a MicroDIMM possess?

5. Compare the data transfer performance of the PCI local bus using a 32-bit bus versus a 64-bit bus.

6. Where would you expect WRAM to be used in a PC system?

7. What function does parity checking provide for the system?

8. What function does IRQ 2 serve in an AT-compatible system?

9. Which IRQ channel services the FDD in PC-compatible systems?

10. Can a Pentium MMX processor be used to upgrade a system board that has a Pentium 66 installed?

11. Which type of memory device comes in a 168-pin module?

12. To install an Intel Pentium 166 in the sample system board from this chapter, operating with an external clock frequency of 66 MHz, what conditions must be established at JP14 and JP15?

13. How are local buses different than other expansion buses?

14. Which memory device employs special clock signals and buffer storage to deliver data to the microprocessor in one clock cycle?

15. Name two advantages of using chipsets to design circuit boards.

EXAM QUESTIONS

1. What does the Suspend mode actually do?
   a. Suspend mode causes the microprocessor clock to slow down after a defined period of inactivity.
   b. Suspend mode causes everything in the system except the microprocessor to shut down.
   c. Suspend mode causes the microprocessor clock to slow down after a defined period of inactivity.
   d. Suspend mode causes system to stop its system clock until F5 is pressed.

2. What is the maximum data throughput of a video card that is AGP 8x compliant used in a motherboard with an AGP slot that is AGP 8x?
   a. 1.07 GBps
   b. 2.1 GBps
   c. 5.33 GBps
   d. 7.33 GBps

3. You install a Pentium processor rated to operate at 850 MHz in a system. When you start the system up, the speed is indicated as 600 MHz. Which part of the system should you most likely check?
   a. The microprocessor, because it has obviously been mislabeled
   b. The chip set is obviously not rated to manage this processor speed.
   c. The system's RAM must not be rated to run at this speed.
   d. The BIOS because it does not support this level of microprocessor operating speed

4. In a water-cooled system, what device is used to cool the water, and exhaust heat into the outside atmosphere?
   a. Water reservoir tank
   b. Water pump
   c. Condenser coil radiator
   d. CPU cooling block

5. A purchasing manager contacts you, and is confused by the different types of RAM that can be purchased. He is specifically looking for RAM that is only used for a laptop. What sort of RAM should he purchase?
   a. MicroDIMM
   b. DDR RAM
   c. RDRAM
   d. SODIMM

6. What function does IRQ0 play in a PC-compatible system?
   a. It drives the system's DRAM Refresh signal.
   b. It drives the system's time-of-day clock.
   c. It drives the system's FDD interrupt.
   d. It drives the system's keyboard interrupt.

7. How many DMA channels are included in a PC- or XT-compatible system?
   a. Eight
   b. Sixteen
   c. One
   d. Four

8. What grouping of the BIOS allows you to specify time intervals between notices to back up to pop up periodically when the system is booted?
   a. The Chipset Features Screen
   b. The PnP/PCI Configuration Screen
   c. Security Subsystem
   d. Power Management Functions

9. In a Pentium system that uses two IDE controllers (ID1 and ID2), what will the primary partition of the drive attached to ID2 be?
   a. C:\
   b. D:\
   c. E:\
   d. F:\

10. What type of device is used with microprocessors to supply special voltage levels for different types of microprocessors that might be installed?
    a. RAM
    b. Voltage Module Regulator
    c. Voltmeter
    d. Voltage Regulator Module

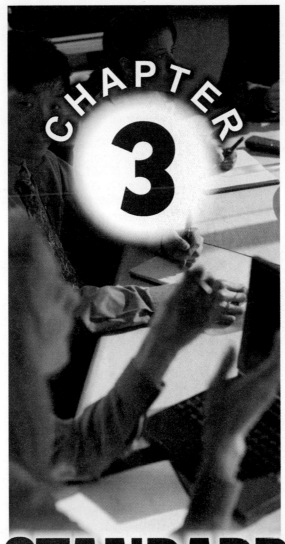

CHAPTER 3

STANDARD I/O SYSTEMS

OBJECTIVES

Upon completion of this chapter and its related lab procedures, you should be able to:

1. Define the overall function of the computer's input/output units.

2. Describe differences between parallel and serial ports.

3. Identify the various port connectors used in PC-compatible systems.

4. Describe the differences between synchronous and asynchronous transmissions, stating advantages and disadvantages for both.

5. Describe the need for parallel/serial conversions.

6. Explain the operation of an RS-232C serial communication port and define its signal lines.

7. Describe the operation of the Universal Serial Bus (USB).

8. List the events that occur when a key is depressed on the keyboard.

9. Describe the operation of the PC's keyboard.

10. Explain the operation of a mouse.

11. Describe the operation of a game port used with joysticks and game paddles.

12. Describe the operation of a flat-bed scanner.

13. Describe the physical aspects of a cathode-ray tube.

14. Explain how a single dot can be positioned anywhere on the face of the CRT, using raster scanning.

15. Describe how color displays are created on the screen.

16. Define the terms pixel and PEL.

17. Describe the function of a shadow mask in a CRT monitor.

18. State the characteristics of the VGA video standard, including the type of physical connector specified for this video standard.

19. Identify standard PC-compatible resource allocations.

20. Differentiate between the operating characteristics of IEEE-1394 and USB ports.

STANDARD I/O SYSTEMS

INTRODUCTION

Although the circuitry on the system board forms the nucleus of the personal computer system, it cannot stand alone. The computer must be able to acquire data from the outside world. In most applications, it must also be able to deliver results of operations it performs to the outside world in a useful format. Many different systems have been developed for both inputting and outputting data.

In a PC-compatible system more than 65,000 input and output addresses are available. Part of the previous chapter described how the system treats its on-board intelligent devices as I/O devices. This chapter examines peripheral I/O in detail. The first portion covers the standard I/O port assignments and configurations in PC systems. The second half of the chapter deals with typical I/O devices associated with PC systems.

SYSTEM RESOURCES

The A+ Core Hardware objective 1.4 states that the test taker should be able to identify typical IRQs, DMAs, and I/O addresses and procedures for altering these settings when installing and configuring devices. Choose the appropriate installation or configuration steps in a given scenario.

Contents may include the following:

- Legacy devices (e.g., ISA sound cards)
- Specialized devices (e.g., CAD/CAM)
- Internal modems
- Floppy drive controllers
- Hard drive controllers
- Multimedia devices
- NICs
- I/O ports
    - Serial
    - Parallel
    - USB ports
    - IEEE-1394/Firewire
    - Infrared

An IBM-compatible PC system is a very flexible tool because it can be configured to perform so many tasks. By selecting appropriate hardware and software options, the same basic system can be customized to be an inventory management business machine, a multimedia development system, or a simple game machine. As this A+ objective indicates, the computer technician must be able to determine what system resources are required for the component, what resources are available in the system, and how they may be allocated in order to successfully install hardware components in a PC. The following sections describe various standard I/O methods and peripheral connection schemes used to attach options to a PC system. However, installing and configuring floppy- and hard-disk drives is covered in the following chapter.

Input/Output

In addition to the millions of possible memory locations in a PC, there are typically thousands of addresses set aside for input and output devices in a system. In order for any device to operate with the system's microprocessor, it must have an address (or group of addresses) where the system can find it.

Referring to the computer system depicted in Figure 3-1, it can be seen that external input and output devices connect to the computer's bus systems through interfacing circuits. The job of the interfacing circuits is to make the peripherals compatible with the system. In the PC, standard interface circuits are provided by the system board's chipset or by an adapter card. The interface's physical connector is typically presented to the world on the system unit's back panel. In an ATX system, the system board provides all of the standard PC interfaces. The physical connectors for these ports (with the exception of the hard- and floppy-disk drives) are grouped into a block of I/O connectors at the back of the system board.

Figure 3-1: Basic Input/Output Organization

When discussing the standard PC I/O ports, also referred to as **legacy ports**, it is common to differentiate between traditional standard ports that include:

- Keyboard port
- Centronic parallel ports
- RS-232C serial ports
- Game ports

And newer standard ports that include:

- PS/2 mouse and keyboard ports
- USB ports
- Firewire ports
- Infrared ports
- Improved parallel ports

Interface circuits—interface **circuits** are necessary because the characteristics of most peripherals differ greatly from those of the basic computer. Most interface circuits in the PC-compatible world have been integrated into application-specific ICs.

The microcomputer is a completely solid-state, digital electronic device that uses parallel words of a given length and adheres to basic digital logic levels. However, computer peripherals generally tend to be more mechanical and analog in nature. Conversely, humans are analog in nature.

The computer's input and output units enable it to communicate with the outside world. The input units contain all of the circuitry necessary to accept data and programs from peripheral input devices such as keyboards, light pens, mice, joysticks, and so on, and convert the information into a form that is usable by the microprocessor. The input unit may be used to enter programs and data into the memory unit before execution, or it may be used to enter data directly into the microprocessor during execution.

The output units contain all of the circuitry necessary to transform data from the computer's language into a form that is more convenient for the outside world. Most often that is in the form of alphanumeric characters, which are convenient for humans to use. Common output devices include video display monitors, audio speakers, and character printers. Figure 3-2 depicts several common I/O devices associated with personal computers.

Some computer peripherals do double duty as both input and output units. These devices are collectively referred to as I/O devices and include secondary storage devices such as hard-disk drives, floppy-disk drives, and magnetic tape drives, as well as modems and sound cards. In these devices, the form that data takes is not for the convenience of human beings, but the form most suitable to carry out the function of the device.

Figure 3-2: Common I/O Devices Used with PCs

Moving Data

The most frequent operation performed in a computer is the movement of information from one location to another. This information is moved in the form of words. Basically, there are two modes in which the words can be transferred. These modes are **parallel mode**, where an entire word is transferred from location A to location B by a set of parallel conductors at one instant, and **serial mode**, where the bits of the word are transmitted along a single conductor, one bit at a time. Serial transfers require more time to accomplish than parallel transfers since a clock cycle must be used for each bit transferred.

parallel mode

serial mode

A parallel transfer requires only one clock pulse. Examples of both parallel and serial transfers are depicted in Figure 3-3. Since speed is normally of the utmost importance in computer operations, all data movements within the computer are conducted in parallel, as shown in (a). But when information is being transferred between the computer and its peripherals (or another computer), conditions may dictate that the transfer be carried out in serial mode, as shown in (b).

Peripherals may use parallel or serial transmission modes between themselves and the system board. Parallel buses are generally used for high-speed devices, such as disk drives and some printers. Conversely, serial transmission is used with remotely located devices or with devices whose operation is more compatible with serial data flow, such as monitors, modems, certain input devices, and some printers.

Figure 3-3: Parallel and Serial Data Transfers

Initiating I/O Transfers

During a program's execution, the microprocessor constantly Reads from or Writes to memory locations. The program may also call on the microprocessor to Read from or Write to one of the system's I/O devices. Regardless of how the peripheral is connected to the system (serial or parallel), one of four methods may be used to initiate data transfer between the system and the peripheral. These four methods are listed as follows:

Polling

Programmed I/O

Interrupt-driven I/O

DMA

- **Polling** is where the microprocessor examines the status of the peripheral under program control.

- **Programmed I/O** is where the microprocessor alerts the designated peripheral by applying its address to the system's address bus.

- **Interrupt-driven I/O** is where the peripheral alerts the microprocessor that it's ready to transfer data.

- **DMA** is where the intelligent peripheral assumes control of the system's buses to conduct direct transfers with primary memory.

Polling and Programmed I/O

Both polling and programmed I/O represent software approaches to data transfer whereas interrupt-driven and DMA transfers are basically hardware approaches.

In the polling method, the software periodically checks with the system's I/O devices to determine if any device is ready to conduct a data transfer. If so, it will begin reading or writing data to the corresponding I/O port. The polling method is advantageous in that it is easy to implement and reconfigure since the program controls the entire sequence of events during the transfer. However, polling is often inconvenient since the microprocessor must be totally involved in the polling routine and cannot perform other functions.

The programmed I/O method calls for the microprocessor to alert the desired peripheral of an I/O operation by issuing its address to the address bus. The peripheral can delay the transfer by asserting its Busy line. If the microprocessor receives a Busy signal from the peripheral, it continues to perform other tasks, but periodically checks the device until the Busy signal is replaced by a Ready signal.

In order to establish an orderly flow of data during the transfer, a number of **handshakes** may occur between the peripheral and the system. This prevents the microprocessor from sending or requesting data at a faster rate than the peripheral can handle. In both methods, the main system resource that is used is the microprocessor's time.

handshakes

Interrupts

In the course of normal operations, the various I/O devices attached to a PC, such as the keyboard and disk drives, require servicing from the system's microprocessor. Although I/O devices may be treated like memory locations, there is one big difference between the two; I/O devices generally have the capability to interrupt the microprocessor while it is executing a program. The I/O device does this by issuing an **Interrupt Request (IRQ)** input signal to the microprocessor. Each device in a PC-compatible system that is capable of interrupting the microprocessor must be assigned its own unique IRQ number. The system uses this number to identify which device is in need of service.

Interrupt Request (IRQ)

If the microprocessor is responding to INT signals and a peripheral device issues an interrupt request on an IRQ line, the microprocessor will finish executing its current instruction and issue an **Interrupt Acknowledge (INTA)** signal on the control bus. The microprocessor suspends its normal operation and stores the contents of its internal registers in a special storage area referred to as the stack.

Interrupt Acknowledge (INTA)

The interrupting device responds by sending the starting address of a special program called the **interrupt service routine** to the microprocessor. The microprocessor uses the interrupt service routine to service the interrupting device. After it finishes servicing the interrupting device, the contents of the stack are restored to their original locations, and the microprocessor returns to the original program at the point where the interrupt occurred. If two interrupt signals occur at the same instant, the interrupt that has the highest priority will be serviced first.

interrupt service routine

Two varieties of interrupts are used in microcomputers:

- **Maskable Interrupts (MI)**—which the computer can ignore under certain conditions.

- **Non-Maskable Interrupts (NMI)**—which it must always respond to.

Maskable Interrupts (MI)

Non-Maskable Interrupts (NMI)

A programmable interrupt controller, and its relationship to the system's microprocessor, is illustrated in Figure 3-4. The interrupt controller chip accepts prioritized IRQ signals from up to eight peripheral devices on IRQ lines 0 through 7. When one of the peripherals desires to communicate with the microprocessor, it sends an IRQ to the interrupt controller. The controller responds by sending an INT signal to the microprocessor. If two interrupt requests are received at the same time, the interrupt controller accepts the one that has the higher priority and acts on it first. As mentioned in Chapter 2, the priority order is highest for the device connected to the IRQ-0 line and descends in order, with the IRQ-7 input being given the lowest priority.

Figure 3-4: A Programmable Interrupt Controller Operation

INTC1

INTC2

In AT-compatible systems, the IRQ capabilities of the system are doubled by providing two 8-line interrupt controllers (**INTC1** and **INTC2**), each of which is equivalent to the original 8259 PIC used in the original PC. These interrupt controllers are internally cascaded together to provide the 15 interrupt channels necessary for AT-compatibility. IRQ channel 2 is used to cascade the second controller to the first. Because this channel is used for the cascade, the system sees IRQ channels 8 through 15 as channel 2.

Of the possible 15 interrupt channels available (IRQ0 through IRQ15), several are reserved for use inside the PC. Therefore, they do not have external IRQ pins. The internally connected channels are:

Channel 0 (IRQ0) Timer/Counter interrupt

Channel 1 (IRQ1) Keyboard buffer full

Channel 2 (IRQ2) Cascaded from INTC2

Channel 8 (IRQ8) Real-Time Clock interrupt

Channel 13 (IRQ13) Math Coprocessor interrupt

The other IRQ inputs are available to the system for user-definable interrupt functions. Each IRQ input is assigned a priority level. With this in mind, it is not difficult to see that the priority orders for IRQs in an AT-compatible machine begin with IRQ0 as the highest, followed by IRQ1, IRQ8 through IRQ15, and finally IRQ3 through IRQ7.

Table 3-1 shows the designations for the various interrupt levels in the system.

Table 3-1: System Interrupt Levels

INTERRUPT	DESCRIPTION	INTERRUPT	DESCRIPTION
NMI	I/O CHANNEL CHECK OR PARITY CHECK ERROR		
INTC1		INTC2	
IRQ0	TIMER/COUNTER ALARM	IRQ8	REAL-TIME CLOCK
IRQ1	KEYBOARD BUFFER FULL	IRQ9	CASCADE TO INTC1
IRQ2	CASCADE FROM INTC2	IR110	SPARE
IRQ3	SERIAL PORT 2	IRQ11	SPARE
IRQ4	SERIAL PORT 1	IRQ12	SPARE PS/2 MOUSE
IRQ5	PARALLEL PORT 2	IRQ13	COPROCESSOR
IRQ6	FDD CONTROLLER	IRQ14	PRIMARY IDE CTRL
IRQ7	PARALLEL PORT 1	IRQ15	SECONDARY IDE CTRL

TEST TIP

Memorize the system resources available in an ISA-compatible system and what their typical assignments are.

CHALLENGE #1

One of your co-workers is adding a wide carriage dot matrix printer to his workstation so that he can print multipart forms. He already has a color ink-jet printer attached to the computer using IRQ7. He has no idea of which resources to assign to the new printer. What will you tell him when he asks for help?

There are two system board-based conditions that will cause a **Non-Maskable Interrupt (NMI)** signal to be sent to the microprocessor. The first condition occurs when an active **IO Channel Check (IOCHCK)** input is received from an adapter card located in one of the board's expansion slots. The other event that will cause an NMI signal to be generated is the occurrence of a **Parity Check (PCK) Error** in the DRAM memory.

Non-Maskable Interrupt (NMI)

IO Channel Check (IOCHCK)

Parity Check (PCK) Error

As mentioned in Chapter 2, system boards that feature PCI bus technology bring four flexible PCI interrupt lines (INTa through INTd, or INT1 through INT4) to the system. Adapter cards in the PCI slots can use these lines to activate up to four different interrupts that are mapped to the system's IRQ channels (typically IRQ9 through IRQ12). You may see these interrupts described in the PnP and PCI Configuration screen of the CMOS Setup utility. In Windows-based systems, the operating system can manipulate the use of the PCI interrupts and steer them to different IRQ lines so that there is never a conflict between devices sharing them.

TEST TIP

Know what types of problems can cause an NMI to occur.

Direct Memory Access

**Direct Memory
Access (DMA)**

Another difference between memory and some intelligent, high-speed I/O devices is that the I/O devices may have the ability to perform Read and Write data transfers on their own. This type of operation is called **Direct Memory Access** (**DMA**). DMA generally involves a high-speed I/O device taking over the system's buses to perform Read and Write operations with the primary memory, without the intervention of the system microprocessor.

DMA Request (DREQ)

DMA controller

HOLD

Buses Available (BA)

**Hold Acknowledge
(HLDA)**

**DMA Acknowledge
(DACK)**

When the peripheral device has data ready to be transferred, it sends a **DMA Request** (**DREQ**) signal to a special IC device called a **DMA controller**, which in turn sends a **HOLD** input signal to the microprocessor. The microprocessor finishes executing the instruction it is currently working on and places its address and data pins in a floating state, effectively disconnecting the microprocessor from the buses. At this time, the microprocessor issues a **Buses Available** (**BA**) or **Hold Acknowledge** (**HLDA**) signal to the DMA controller. The DMA controller, in turn, issues a **DMA Acknowledge** (**DACK**) to the peripheral and the necessary R/W and enable signals for the data transfer to begin. The key to DMA operations is that the DMA controller has been designed specifically to transfer data bytes faster than the microprocessor can.

The PC-compatible DMA subsystem provides an AT-compatible PC with four channels for 8-bit DMA transfers (DMA1) and three channels (DMA2) for 16-bit DMA transfers. The DMA1 channels are used to carry out DMA transfers between 8-bit options adapters and 8- or 16-bit memory locations. These 8-bit transfers are conducted in 64 kB blocks and can be performed throughout the system's address space. The DMA2 channels (channels 5, 6, and 7) are used only with 16-bit devices and can only transfer words in 128 kB blocks. The first 16-bit DMA channel (DMA channel 4) is used internally to cascade the two DMA controllers together. Table 3-2 describes the system's DMA channel designations.

**Table 3-2:
System's DMA
Channel Designations**

CHANNEL	FUNCTION	CONTROLLER	PAGE REGISTER ADDRESS
CH0	SPARE	1	0087
CH1	SDLC (NETWORK)	1	0083
CH2	FDD CONTROLLER	1	0082
CH3	SPARE	1	0081
CH4	CASCADE TO CNTR 1	2	
CH5	SPARE	2	008B
CH6	SPARE	2	0089
CH7	SPARE	2	008A

PC Address Allocations

on-board I/O

In the PC system, there are two types of addresses to contend with—those that refer to locations in the system's memory map (i.e., RAM and ROM addresses) and those that apply to I/O device locations. In the case of I/O address allocations, most I/O devices and subsystems require at least a small block of addresses for their individual uses. The various I/O port addresses listed in Table 3-3 are used in the PC-compatible system. When dealing with PC-compatibles, there are two forms of I/O to contend with. These include the system board's **on-board I/O** systems (System), and peripheral devices that interact with the system through its expansion slots or port connectors (I/O).

Table 3-3:
I/O Port Addresses

HEX ADDRESS	DEVICE	USAGE
000–01F	DMA Controller (South Bridge)	System
020–03F	Interrupt Controller (South Bridge)	System
040–05F	Timer/Counter (South Bridge)	System
060–06F	Keyboard Controller	System
070–07F	Real-Time Clock, NMI Mask (South Bridge)	System
080–09F	DMA Page Register (South Bridge)	System
0A0–0BF	Interrupt Controller (South Bridge)	System
0F0	Clear Math Coprocessor Busy	System
0F1	Reset Math Coprocessor	System
0F8–0FF	Math Coprocessor	System
170–177	Second IDE Controller	I/O
1F0–1F7	First IDE Controller	I/O
200–207	Game Port	I/O
278–27F	Parallel Printer Port #2	I/O
2F8–2FF	Serial Port #2	I/O
378–37F	Parallel Printer Port #1	I/O
3B0–3BF	MGA/first Printer Port	I/O
3D0–3DF	CGA	I/O
3F0–3F7	FDD Controller	I/O
3F8–3FF	Serial Port #1	I/O
FF80-FF9F	USB Controller	I/O

┌─ **TEST TIP** ─┐

Memorize the I/O port addresses for the first and second IDE controllers.

redundant addressing

Table 3-4 provides an abbreviated listing of the standard PC memory map. Notice that these addresses are the same as those stated for the Interrupt Vectors in system memory. This method of dual addressing is referred to as **redundant addressing**.

Table 3-4:
System Memory Map

ADDRESS	FUNCTION
0–3FF	Interrupt Vectors
400–47F	ROM-BIOS RAM
480–5FF	BASIC and Special System Function RAM
600–9FFFF	Program Memory
A0000–BFFFF	VGA/EGA Display Memory
B0000–B7FFF	Monochrome Display Adapter Memory
B8000–BFFFF	Color Graphics Adapter Memory
C0000–C7FFF	VGA/SVGA BIOS
C8000-CBFFF	EIDE/SCSI ROM (also older HDD Types)
D0000–D7FFF	Spare ROM
D0000–DFFFF	LAN Adapter ROM
E0000–E7FFF	Spare ROM
E8000–EFFFF	Spare ROM
F0000–EFFFF	Spare ROM
F4000–EFFFF	Spare ROM
F8000–EFFFF	Spare ROM
FC000–FDFFF	ROM BIOS
FE000–FFFFF	ROM BIOS

Hexadecimal Addresses

Addresses in PC systems are always referred to by their hexadecimal value. The reason for this is that digital computers are built on components that only work with two logic levels: On/Off, High/Low, 1/0. This corresponds directly to the base-2 or binary numbering system. In the binary system, each piece of information represents a binary digit, or bit.

**Table 3-5:
Decimal, Binary, and
Hexadecimal Numbers**

The power of the digital computer lies in how it groups bits of information into words. The basic word length in PCs is the 8-bit word called a byte. Some computers can handle data as 16-, 32-, and 64-bit words. With the byte as the basic data unit it is easier for humans to speak of computer numbers in the base-16 or **hexadecimal** (**hex**) numbering system. In this system, groups of 4 bits can be represented directly by a single hex character (i.e., 1001 base2 = 09 base16). For human representation, the values in the hexadecimal numbering system run from 0 to 9 and then from A through F, as illustrated in Table 3-5.

DECIMAL (10)	BINARY (2)	HEXADECIMAL (16)
0	0000	0
1	0001	1
2	0010	2
3	0011	3
4	0100	4
5	0101	5
6	0110	6
7	0111	7
8	1000	8
9	1001	9
10	1010	A
11	1011	B
12	1100	C
13	1101	D
14	1110	E
15	1111	F
16	10000	10

While this may seem a little inconvenient for those of you not familiar with binary and hexadecimal systems, it is much easier to convey the number 3F8 to someone than it is 001111111000. The real difficulty of reconciling a hexadecimal value comes when you try to convert binary or hexadecimal values to the decimal (base 10) number system you are familiar with.

REFERENCE
SHELF

> For more in-depth information about computer-related numbering systems, refer to the Electronic Reference Shelf located on the CD that accompanies this book.

Typical I/O Resource Allocations

In a PC system every I/O device requires some type of physical interface to enable it to interact with the system. Each interface in turn requires certain system resources to support its operation and interaction with the system. For practical purposes, these resources can be summarized as:

- IRQ Interrupt channels
- DMA channels
- I/O Port address allocations
- Buffer memory address allocation (in system RAM)

Most intelligent devices in the PC system will require at least two of these resources.

On-Board I/O Resource Allocations

In a PC-compatible system, certain I/O addresses are associated with intelligent devices on the system board, such as the interrupt and DMA controllers, timer counter channels, and keyboard controller. The system treats its on-board intelligent devices as I/O addresses. The on-board address decoder, similar to the one displayed in Figure 3-5, converts addresses from the address bus into enabling bits for the system's intelligent devices. These addresses are included in the overall I/O addressing map of the system.

**Figure 3-5:
On-Board Address
Decoding**

Most of the I/O functions associated with PC-compatible systems have become so standardized that IC manufacturers produce them in single-chip ASIC formats. Figure 3-6 illustrates an ASIC for standard, AT-compatible system board functions.

**Figure 3-6:
On-Board I/O**

Peripheral I/O Resource Allocations

Some I/O ports and their interfaces may be located on optional plug-in cards. However, many have been incorporated directly into ATX system boards. In both cases, the I/O controllers integrated into the ASIC are responsible for matching signal levels and protocols between the system and the I/O device. Figure 3-7 illustrates how a system address is routed through the system to an I/O port location.

**Figure 3-7:
Address Routing to an
I/O Port**

Some I/O connections have become standards associated with PC-compatibles. These include the system's parallel printer ports, RS-232 serial ports, and the game port. Figure 3-8 depicts an Enhanced MI/O ASIC for standard peripheral control.

**Figure 3-8:
System I/O Resources**

The FDC portion of the system board's chipset provides a programmable, logical interface for up to two FDD units. It resides in the I/O address range between locations 3F0 and 3F7. The FDC receives and decodes instructions from the system to the floppy-disk drive at these addresses. In a PC system, the FDC operates in conjunction with the system's DMA controller and is assigned to the DRQ-2 and DACK-2 lines. In operation, the FDC presents an active DRQ-2 signal to the DMA controller for every byte of data to be transferred. After the last byte has been transferred, the FDC interrupt is generated. The floppy-disk drive controller is assigned the IRQ6 channel in PC-compatible systems.

Typical Pentium-based system boards include two enhanced IDE controllers to handle their hard-disk drive/CD-ROM hosting function. Each controller can handle up to two IDE drives. The first, or Primary IDE, controller is assigned IRQ14, whereas the Secondary controller uses IRQ15 to interrupt the system. Likewise, the first IDE drive controller responds to I/O addresses between 1F0 and 1F7, whereas the second answers to addresses between 170 and 177.

Whenever the system is booted up, the operating system searches the hardware for traditional parallel ports installed at hex addresses 3BC, 378, and 278 consecutively. The operating system links the addresses of any printer ports it find to the names — LPT1, LPT2, or LPT3. Normal IRQ settings for printer ports in a PC-compatible system are IRQ5 or IRQ7. IRQ7 is normally assigned to the LPT1 printer port, whereas IRQ5 typically serves the LPT2 port, if installed.

The RS-232 ports in a PC can be designated as COM1, COM2, COM3, or COM4, as long as both ports are not assigned the same COM port number. In most PCs, COM1 is assigned as port address hex 3F8 and uses IRQ channel 4. The COM2 port is typically assigned port address hex 2F8 and IRQ3. Likewise, COM3 uses IRQ4 and is assigned an I/O address of 3E8 while COM4 usually resides at 2E8 and uses IRQ3.

Most ATX system boards also include dual **Universal Serial Bus (USB)** connectors as a standard part of their I/O port offering. The onboard USB controller resides between the I/O addresses of FF80 and FF9F. The USB controller is also assigned an IRQ channel (such as IRQ10) by the PnP process.

| Universal Serial Bus (USB) |

A similar high-speed peripheral bus called the **IEEE-1394** or **Firewire bus** is not considered a standard part of the PC port package. However, these ports are often added to the system in the form of an adapter card. When these ports are installed in a system they require the same types of resources used by the USB bus. Because most Firewire ports are installed in the PC on a PCI adapter card, the resources allocated to the port are actually PCI resources. Therefore, the IRQ assignment for a Firewire host adapter is typically assigned by the operating system through the PnP process. From Windows 98 forward, the Microsoft line of operating systems have included drivers for Firewire ports. However, many times the drivers supplied with the adapter card work much better than those provided by Microsoft.

| IEEE-1394 |

| Firewire bus |

Infrared Data Association (IrDA) ports are very popular with notebook computers. These infrared light ports provide short-distance wireless connections for different IrDA-compliant devices, such as printers and personal digital assistants. Because the IrDA port communicates by sending and receiving a serial stream of light pulses, it is normally configured to work with the UART of the system's second serial port. In this manner, the infrared port is assigned the system resources normally reserved for the COM2/COM4 serial ports (that is, IRQ3, 2F8-2FF, or 2E8-2EF).

| Infrared Data Association (IrDA) |

Resources for Specialty Devices

The system resource allocations described in the preceding paragraphs represent those most commonly used in PC-compatible systems. However, it should be apparent that even if all of these ports had devices attached to them that were active, the PC system would still have additional resources available for attaching other, nonstandard devices to the system. Systems such as CAD/CAM machines can be attached to the system through one of the existing port types (i.e., serial/parallel/game ports), through one of the advanced bus interfaces (i.e., Firewire or USB), or through a proprietary adapter card that provides the interfacing required for the machine to work with the PC.

In most cases, specialty equipment comes with an adequate set of installation and configuration instructions for attaching the device to the PC and getting it to run properly. However, many of these products are not considered to be mainstream items for PCs so they may not have the latest technology available with them (i.e., PnP capabilities). In these cases, you must manually configure the device — probably using jumpers on the card — and then reserve the used resource settings through the *PnP and PCI Setup* screen in the CMOS Setup utility. This will notify the system at startup that these resources have been set aside and cannot be used in the PnP configuration process. Because the device is nonstandard, you should follow the installation manual closely and use any recommended settings. Chances are there is a lot more configuration flexibility in the PC than there is in a nonstandard peripheral device.

Resources for Legacy Devices

In a Pentium-based ATX system, the PnP BIOS will normally detect the ports and devices in the system and allocate the appropriate resources to each. The exception to this would be a non-PnP device, also referred to as a **legacy device**, installed in the system. Older ISA adapter cards typically had no PnP function and had to be configured manually. In these situations, the system has no way to reconfigure the card, so you must tell it which resources are required for it. This function is performed through the *PnP and PCI Setup* screens in the CMOS Setup routine and reserves certain resources so that they are available for the legacy device.

legacy device

When you manually configure such a device, you must be aware of which system resources it needs and what settings it can work with. This information can typically be found in the device's installation guide. If the guide is not available, you should check the Internet for the manufacturer's web site to determine whether any configuration information is available there. In addition, there may be third-party sites on the Internet that can supply the configuration information that you need for the device.

You will find that each of the I/O ports mentioned in the preceding paragraphs (and the devices that use them) is covered in more detail later in this chapter (i.e., parallel, serial, USB, Firewire and infrared ports, as well as modems, scanners and sound cards) or in subsequent chapters (i.e., floppy drives, hard drives, NICs, and modems). The main point of the information presented here is to show how the system divides up its available resources.

PORTS, CABLES, AND CONNECTORS

The A+ Core Hardware objective 1.5 states that the test taker should be able to identify the names, purposes, and performance characteristics of standardized/common peripheral ports, associated cables, and their connectors. Recognize ports, cabling and connectors by sight.

Content may include the following:

- Port Types
  - Serial
  - Parallel
  - USB ports
  - IEEE-1394/Firewire
  - Infrared
- Cable types
  - Serial (straight through vs. null modem)
  - Parallel
  - USB
- Connector types
  - Serial
    - DB-9
    - DB-25
    - RJ-11
    - RJ-45
  - Parallel
    - DB-25
    - Centronics (mini and 36-pin)
  - PS2/mini-DIN
  - USB
  - IEEE-1394

As mentioned earlier, a wide variety of peripheral devices can be added to a PC-compatible system. Most of these devices are designed to employ some type of PC-compatible I/O connection method. As this A+ objective indicates, the computer technician must be able to recognize what type of port the device requires, locate standard I/O port connections, and determine what type of cabling is required to successfully connect the port and the device in order to successfully add peripheral devices to a PC system. The following sections of the chapter describe standardized I/O ports and connections found in a PC-compatible system.

PC Port Connections

Although many different methods have been developed to connect devices to the PC-compatible system, there are three ports that have been standard since the original PCs were introduced. However, with the advent of several newer, faster, and more flexible ports, these ports are becoming legacy ports and will probably disappear from PCs in the near future. Table 3-6 summarizes the types of connectors typically found on the back panel of both AT and ATX system units, along with their connector and pin count information. These connector types are described in Figure 3-9.

Table 3-6: Typical I/O Ports

PORT	AT	ATX
Keyboard	5-pin DIN	PS/2 6-pin mini-DIN
Mouse	xxxxxxx	PS/2 6-pin mini-DIN
COM1	DB-9M	DB-9M
COM2	DB-25M	DB-9M
LPT	DB-25F	DB-25F
VGA	DB-15F (3 row)	DB-15F (3 row)
Game	DB-15F (2 row)	DB-15F (2 row)
Modem	RJ-11	RJ-11
LAN	BNC/RJ-45	BNC/RJ-45
Sound	RCA mini-jacks	RCA mini-jacks
SCSI	Centronics 50-pin	Centronics 50-pin
USB	xxxxxxx	4-pin USB Socket

**Figure 3-9:
Typical I/O Port
Connectors**

CHALLENGE #3

Your office is just getting networked, and you are in charge of making the physical connections to all the machines. In the CFO's office, you encounter a machine that has been running on a small accounting network for some time, but doesn't have an RJ-45 jack for the network cable. How can this be, and what should you do about it?

Parallel Ports

Parallel ports have been a staple of the PC system since the original PCs were introduced. They have traditionally been the most widely used port for connecting printers to the computer.

Parallel ports

In many instances, parallel ports are referred to as *parallel printer ports*. Due to the parallel port's ability to quickly transfer bytes of data in parallel mode, it has been adopted to interface a number of other peripheral devices to the computer. These devices include CNC mills and lathes; X-Y plotters; fast computer-to-computer transfer systems; high-speed, high-volume, removable disk backup systems; and optical scanners.

The Centronics Standard

Figure 3-10 shows a typical parallel printer connection, using the IBM version of the **Centronics standard**. This interface enables the computer to pass information to the printer, 8 bits at a time, across the 8 data lines. The other lines in the connection carry control signals (handshaking signals) back and forth between the computer and the printer.

**Figure 3-10:
Parallel-Port Connector
and Signals**

The original Centronics interface employed a 36-pin D-shell connector on the printer adapter and a 36-pin Centronics connector on the printer end. The Centronics connector on the printer features a female slotted connector with contacts embedded on the top and bottom of the slot. The IBM version of the interface, which became known as the **Standard Parallel Port (SPP)** specification for printers, reduced the pin count to 25 at the computer end of the connection. However, at the printer end of the cable, IBM continued with the standard 36-pin Centronics connector.

The PC-compatible parallel port interface offers 8-bit parallel data words and nine I/O control lines at a 25-pin, female D-shell connector at the rear of the system unit. The printer port connector may be provided through the I/O block of an ATX system board or mounted directly on the back plate of an I/O card, or its interface circuitry may be connected, via a ribbon cable, to the 25-pin D-shell connector on the unit's back panel. Newer printer connections often employ a 36-pin mini Centronic connector at the printer end of the cable.

When the port is used in SPP mode, all the printer port's signals are transmitted between the adapter card and the printer at standard **TTL (Transistor-Transistor Logic)** electronic levels. This means that the signals can deteriorate quickly with long lengths of cable. The cable length used for the parallel printer should be kept to less than 10 feet. If longer lengths are needed, the cable should have a low-capacitance value. The cable should also be shielded, to minimize **Electromagnetic Field Interference (EFI)** peripherals.

TEST TIP

Know the recommended length of a standard parallel printer cable.

LPT Handles

Microsoft operating systems keep track of the system's installed printer ports by assigning them the logical device names (handles) LPT1, LPT2, and LPT3. Whenever the system is booted up, DOS searches the hardware for parallel ports installed at hex addresses 3BC, 378, and 278 consecutively.

If a printer port is found at 3BC, then DOS assigns it the title of LPT1. If, however, no printer port is found at 3BC, but there is one at 378, then DOS will assign LPT1 to the latter address. Likewise, a system that has printer ports at physical addresses 378 and 278 would have LPT1 assigned at 378, and LPT2 at location 278.

The address of the printer port can normally be changed to respond as LPT1, LPT2, or LPT3, depending on the setting of address selection jumpers. The printer port can also be disabled completely through these jumper settings.

The interrupt level of the printer port may be set at a number of different levels by changing its configuration jumpers, or CMOS enabling setting. Normal interrupt settings for printer ports in a PC-compatible system are IRQ5 or IRQ7. IRQ7 is normally assigned to the LPT1 printer port, and IRQ5 typically serves the LPT2 port, if installed.

TEST TIP

Memorize the system resources that the PC typically assigns to parallel ports.

While the full implementation of the original SPP mode printer port could be used in a bi-directional manner, most PC manufacturers never implemented the two-way capabilities. Newer **Enhanced Parallel Port (EPP)** and **Extended Capabilities Port (ECP)** ports can be converted between unidirectional and bi-directional operation through the CMOS setup screen. If a bi-directional port is being used to support an I/O device, such as a local area network adapter or a high-capacity storage device, this feature would need to be checked at both the hardware and software levels.

Enhanced Parallel Port (EPP)

Extended Capabilities Port (ECP)

The parallel cable should also be checked to see that it complies with the *IEEE-1284* standard for use with bi-directional parallel ports. Using a traditional SPP cable could cause the device to operate erratically or fail completely.

TEST TIP

As you study the I/O ports in this chapter, be aware of which ports provide bi-directional, half-duplex, and full-duplex operation.

EPP and ECP Parallel Port Operations

When EPP mode is selected in the port's configuration register, the standard and bi-directional modes are enabled. The functions of the port's pins are redefined under the EPP specification. When the EPP mode is enabled, the port can operate either as a standard bi-directional parallel port, or as a bi-directional EPP port.

The software controlling the port will specify which type of operation is required. If no EPP read, write, or address cycle is being executed, the port and its control signals function as an SPP port. When the software calls for an EPP read, write, or address cycle, however, all the port's registers are enabled and the signal lines take on the functions defined by the selected EPP standard.

The ECP mode provides a number of advantages over the SPP and EPP modes. The ECP mode employs DMA operations to offer higher performance than either of the other two modes. As with the EPP mode, the pins of the interface are redefined when ECP mode is selected in the system's BIOS. Table 3-7 lists the standard, EPP, and ECP definitions for the parallel port's pins.

Table 3-7: SPP/EPP/EPC Pin Definitions

HOST CONNECTOR	PIN NO.	STANDARD	EPP	ECP
1	77	Strobe	Write	Strobe
2-9	71-68, 66-63	Data <0:7>	Data <0:7>	Data <0:7>
10	62	Ack	Intr	Ack
11	61	Busy	Wait	Busy, PeriphAck
12	60	PE	Not Used	PError nACKReverse
13	59	Select	Not Used	Select
14	76	Autofd	DSTRB	Autofd HostAck
15	75	Error	Not Used	Fault PeriphRequest
16	74	Init	Not Used	Init ReverseRqst
17	73	Selectin	Astrb	Selectin

In ECP mode, the parallel port operates in forward (host-to-peripheral) and reverse (peripheral-to-host) directions. It employs interlocked handshaking for reliable, half-duplex transfers through the port. The capabilities of the ECP port enable it to be used in peer-to-peer applications.

The ECP port is compatible with the standard LPT port and is used in the same manner when no ECP read or write operations are called for. However, it also supports high-throughput DMA operations for both forward- and reverse-direction transfers.

Prior to ECP operation, the system examines the peripheral device attached to the port to determine that it can perform ECP operations. This operation is carried out in SPP mode. Afterward, the system initializes the port's registers for operation. In particular, it sets a direction bit in the port controller to enable the ECP drivers and sets the port's mode to ECP.

The host computer may switch the direction of the port's operation by changing the mode value in the controller and then negotiating for the forward/reverse channel setting. Afterward, the mode is set back to ECP. During normal operation, commands and data may be passed through the port.

ECP transfers may be conducted in DMA or programmed I/O modes. DMA transfers use standard PC DMA services. To use this method, the host must set the port direction and program its DMA controller with the desired byte count and memory-address information.

TEST TIP

Remember that the ECP specification employs DMA operations to provide the highest data throughput for a parallel port.

Serial Ports

As the distance between the computer and a peripheral reaches a certain point (10 feet), it becomes less practical to send data as parallel words. An alternative method of sending data is to break the parallel words into their individual bits, and transmit them, one at a time, in a serial bit stream over a single conductor.

In this manner, the number of conductors connecting the computer and the peripheral is reduced from eight or more data lines, and any number of control lines, to one (or two) communications lines, a ground line, and maybe a few control lines. Therefore, when a peripheral device must be located at some distance from the computer, using serial communication techniques reduces the cost of connecting the equipment. In the PC, serial communications have traditionally been conducted using one of its standard RS-232 **communication (COM) ports**.

Serial Transmission Modes

The biggest problem encountered when sending data serially is keeping the transmitted data-bit timing synchronized between the two devices.

Two methods are used to provide the proper timing for serial transfers: the data bits may be sent **synchronously** (in conjunction with a synchronizing clock pulse), or **asynchronously** (without an accompanying clock pulse).

When data is transmitted synchronously, the bits of a word, or character, are synchronized by a common clock signal, which is applied to both the transmitting and receiving shift registers. The two registers are initialized before data transmission begins, when the transmitting circuitry sends a predefined bit pattern, which the receiver recognizes as the initialization command. After this, receiving circuitry processes the incoming bit stream by counting clock pulses, and dividing the bit stream into words of a predetermined length. If the receiver misses a bit for any reason, all the words that follow will be processed erroneously.

When data is transferred asynchronously, the receiving system is not synchronized with the sending system. The standard serial ports in a PC employ this transmission method. The transmitted material is sent character by character (usually ASCII), with the beginning and end of each character framed by character Start and Stop bits. Between these bits, the bits of the character are sent at a constant rate, but the time interval between characters may be irregular, as illustrated in Figure 3-11.

Figure 3-11: Asynchronous Transmission

Over a given period of time, synchronous communications are much faster than asynchronous methods. This is due to the extra number of bits required to send each character asynchronously. PC serial ports and analog modems use asynchronous communications methods, whereas digital modems and local area network adapters use synchronous methods.

Serial Interface ICs

Like the single-chip parallel ports, IC manufacturers have developed a number of single-chip devices that perform all of the functions necessary for serial transfers to occur. These serial port IC's are referred to as **Universal Asynchronous Receiver/Transmitters** or **UARTs**. Synchronous devices are usually called **USARTs** (**Universal Synchronous/Asynchronous Receiver/Transmitters**). Not only do these devices provide the parallel-to-serial and serial-to-parallel conversions required for serial data communications, but they also handle the parallel interface requirements for the computer's internal buses, and all the control functions associated with the transmission.

The original serial adapters featured 8250 UARTs with programmable baud rates from 50 to 9600 baud, a fully programmable interrupt system, and variable character lengths (5, 6, 7, or 8-bit characters). In addition, the adapter added and removed start, stop, and parity bits; had false start-bit detection, line-break detection, and generation; and possessed built-in diagnostics capabilities. As modems became faster and faster, upgraded UARTs were included, or integrated, to keep up.

Notable advanced UART versions include the 16450 and 16550. The 16450 was the 16-bit improvement of the 8250, and the 16550 was a high-performance UART, with an on-board 16-byte buffer. The buffer allows the UART to store, or transmit, a string of data without interrupting the system's microprocessor to handle them. This provides the 16550 with an impressive speed advantage over previous UARTs. These advanced UARTs allow serial ports to reach data transmission rates of up to 115 kbps. While some features have changed between these UARTs, and while they are sometimes integrated directly into an integrated I/O chip, they must still adhere to the basic 8250 structure to remain PC-compatible.

Serial Interfaces and Cables

Because of the popularity of asynchronous serial data transmissions and the number of devices that use them, such as printers and modems, standardized bit-serial signals and connection schemes have been developed to simplify the connecting of serial devices to computers. The most popular of these serial interface standards is the **Electronic Industry Association** (**EIA**) RS-232C interface standard.

Basically, the IBM version of the **RS-232C** standard calls for a 25-pin, male D-type connector, as depicted in Figure 3-12. It also designates certain pins for data transmission and receiving, along with a number of control lines. The standard was developed to cover a wide variety of peripheral devices, and therefore, not all the lines are used in any given application. Normally, only nine of the pins are active for a given application. The other lines are used for secondary, or backup, lines and grounds. Different device manufacturers may use various combinations of the RS-232C lines, even for peripherals of the same type.

Figure 3-12:
RS-232C Connector

In addition to defining the type of connector to be used, and the use of its individual pins, the RS-232 standard also establishes acceptable voltage levels for the signals on its pins. These levels are generally converted to and from standard digital logic levels. These levels can produce a maximum baud rate of 20,000 baud over distances less than 50 feet.

┌─ **TEST TIP** ─────────────────────┐
│ Know the maximum recommended │
│ length of an RS-232 cable. │
└─────────────────────────────────────┘

Since the advent of the PC AT, the system's first serial port has typically been implemented in a 9-pin D-shell male connector on the computer. Figure 3-13 depicts a typical 9-pin to 25-pin connection scheme. Notice the crossover wiring technique employed for the TXD/RXD lines displayed in this example. This type of connection became popular with the 9-pin PC AT serial port.

Figure 3-13: A 9-Pin to
25-Pin RS-232 Cable

In cases where the serial ports are located close enough to each other, a null modem connection can be implemented. A **null modem** connection allows the two serial ports to communicate directly without using modems. A typical null modem connection scheme is illustrated in Figure 3-14.

In any event, it should be apparent from the previous figures that all serial cables are not created equal. Incorrect serial cabling can be a major problem when attaching third-party communication equipment to the computer. Read the modem's user's manual carefully to make certain the correct pins are being connected together.

The RS-232C standard is becoming very old. Since its inception, the EIA has also adopted two more improved serial standards, the RS-422 and RS-423, which are enhancements of the RS-232C standard. The RS-422 uses twisted-pair transmission lines, and differential line signals to provide a high degree of noise immunity for transmitted data. The RS-423 standard uses coaxial cable to provide extended transmission distances and higher data transfer rates.

**Figure 3-14:
A Null Modem
Cable**

DOS Serial Port Names

As with parallel ports, DOS assigns COM port designations to the system's serial ports during bootup. COM port designations are normally **COM1** and **COM2** in most systems, but they can be extended to **COM3** and **COM4** in advanced systems.

Either RS-232 port may be designated as COM1, COM2, COM3, or COM4, as long as both ports are not assigned to the same COM port number. In most PCs, COM1 is assigned as port address hex 3F8 and use IRQ channel 4. The COM2 port is typically assigned port address hex 2F8 and IRQ3. Likewise, COM3 uses IRQ4 and is assigned an I/O address of 3E8, and COM4 usually resides at 2E8 and uses IRQ3.

TEST TIP

Know the system addresses and other resources that a PC-compatible system uses for serial ports. It may be helpful to remember that IBM set up these standards so that the odd-numbered COM ports use the even-numbered IRQ channel, and vice versa.

Game Ports

The **game control adapter** enables two joysticks to be used with the system. The adapter converts resistive input values into relative joystick positions, in much the same manner as described in the previous section. This adapter can also function as a general-purpose I/O converter, featuring four analog and four digital input points.

The input to the game port is generally a pair of resistive joysticks. Joysticks are defined as having two variable resistances, each of which should be variable between 0 and 100 kilohms. Joysticks may have one or two normally-open **fire buttons**. The order of fire buttons should correspond with that of the resistive elements (A and B, or A, B, C, and D). The wiring structure for the two-row, 15-pin D-shell female connector is shown in Figure 3-15.

Figure 3-15: Game-Port Connections

Universal Serial Bus

A new serial interface scheme, called the **Universal Serial Bus (USB)**, has been developed to provide a fast, flexible method of attaching up to 127 peripheral devices to the computer. The USB provides a connection format designed to replace the system's traditional serial- and parallel-port connections.

USB peripherals can be daisy-chained, or networked together using connection hubs that enable the bus to branch out through additional port connections. A practical USB PC connection scheme is presented in Figure 3-16.

Figure 3-16: USB PC Connection Scheme

In this example, some of the peripheral devices are simply devices, whereas others serve as both devices and connection hubs. The system provides a USB host connection that serves as the main USB connection.

USB devices can be added to or removed from the system while it is powered up and fully operational. This is referred to as hot-swapping or hot plugging the device. The Plug-and-Play capabilities of the system will detect the presence (or absence) of the device and configure it for operation.

USB Cabling and Connectors

USB transfers are conducted over a four-wire cable, as illustrated in Figure 3-17. The signal travels over a pair of twisted wires (D+ and D–) in a 90-ohm cable. The differential signal and twisted-pair wiring provide minimum signal deterioration over distances and high noise immunity.

Figure 3-17: The USB Cable

A Vbus and Ground (GND) wire are also present. The Vbus is the +5V (DC) power cord. The interface provides power to the peripheral attached to it. The root hub provides power directly from the host system to those devices directly connected to it. Hubs also supply power to the devices connected to them. Even though the interface supplies power to the USB devices, they are permitted to have their own power sources if necessary.

In these instances, the device must be designed specifically to avoid interference with the bus' power-distribution scheme. The USB host's power-management software can apply power to devices when needed and suspend power to them when not required.

The USB specification defines two types of plugs: series-A and series-B. Series-A connectors are used for devices where the USB cable connection is permanently attached to devices at one end. Examples of these devices include keyboards, mice, and hubs. Conversely, the series-B plugs and jacks are designed for devices that require detachable cabling (printers, scanners, and modems, for example). Both are four-contact plugs and sockets embedded in plastic connectors, as shown in Figure 3-18. The sockets can be implemented in vertical, right-angle, and panel-mount variations. The icon used to represent a USB connector is depicted by the centers of the A and B "plug connectors."

The connectors for both series are keyed so that they cannot be plugged in backward. All hubs and functions possess a single, permanently attached cable with a series-B connector at its end. The connectors are designed so that the A- and B-series connections cannot be interchanged.

Figure 3-18: USB Connectors

USB Architecture

When USB devices are daisy-chained together, the resulting connection architecture forms a tiered-star configuration, like the one depicted in Figure 3-19.

The USB system is composed of a USB host and USB devices. The devices category consists of hubs and nodes. In any system, there is one USB host. This unit contains the interface that provides the USB host controller. The controller is actually a combination of USB hardware, firmware, and software.

Hubs are devices that provide additional connection points for other USB devices. A special hub, called the **root hub**, is an integral part of the host system and provides one or more attachment points for USB devices.

Many newer AT and ATX system boards feature built-in USB host ports. In the AT-style boards, the port is furnished as part of a BERG pin connection, as illustrated in Figure 3-20. The ports are converted to standard connectors through an additional back panel cable set that mounts in an open back panel slot. On the other hand, ATX boards feature a pair of USB port connectors as part of the ATX port connection block as illustrated in the figure. There are also PCI card-mounted USB ports that can be added to the system to enable even more USB devices to be attached to the system. These host ports function as the system's root hub.

┌─ **TEST TIP** ─────────────────
Memorize the number of devices that can be attached to a USB port.

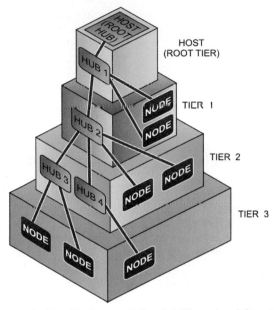

Figure 3-19: Universal Serial Bus Architecture

root hub

Figure 3-20: Implementing USB Ports in an AT Computer

In the case of built-in USB ports, the operation of the port connections is controlled by settings in the system board's CMOS Setup utility. In most cases, it will be necessary to access the CMOS Setup utility's PCI Configuration Screen and enable the USB function and assign the ports IRQ channels to use. If no USB device is being used with the system, the IRQ allocation should be set to "NA" to free up the IRQ line for use by other devices.

It is evident that some of the components of the system serve as both a function and as a hub (that is, the keyboard and monitor). In these devices, the package holds the components of the function, as well as providing an embedded hub that other functions can be connected to. These devices are referred to as compound devices.

Although the tiered architecture described in Figure 3-19 approaches the complexity and capabilities of the LAN architectures covered in Chapter 5 — *Data Communications*, the overhead for managing the port is much easier to implement. As mentioned earlier, USB devices can be added to or removed from the system while it is fully operational. In reality, this means that the USB organizational structure is modified any time a device is added to or removed from the system.

USB Data Transfers

Unlike traditional serial interfaces that transmit framed characters one at a time, data moves across the USB in the form of **data packets**. Packet sizes vary with the type of transmission being carried out. However, they are typically 8, 16, 32, or 64 bytes in length. All transmissions require that two or three packets of information be exchanged between the host, the source location, and the destination location.

All data transfers are conducted between the host and an **endpoint device**. The flow of data can occur in either direction. USB transactions begin when the **host controller** sends a token packet that contains information about the type of transaction to take place, the direction of the transmission, the address of the designated USB device, and an **endpoint number**. If the device is the source of the transaction, it either places a data packet on the bus, or informs the host that it has no data to send. If the host is the source, it just places the data packet on the bus.

In either case, the destination returns a handshake packet if the transfer was successful. If an error is detected in the transfer, a **not acknowledge (NACK)** packet is generated. Figure 3-21 demonstrates the USB's four packet formats: **token packet**, the **start-of-frame (SOF)** packet, the **data packet**, and the **handshake packet**.

data packets

endpoint device

host controller

endpoint number

not acknowledge (NACK)

token packet

start-of-frame (SOF)

data packet

handshake packet

packet ID (PID)

Cyclic Redundancy Check (CRC)

Each type of packet begins with an 8-bit **packet ID (PID)** section. The SOF packet adds an 11-bit frame-number section and a 5-bit **Cyclic Redundancy Check (CRC)** error-checking code section. In the data packet, a variable-length data section replaces the frame-number section, and the CRC frame is enlarged to 16 bits. The data section can range up to 1023 bytes in length. The handshake packet just consists of a PID byte.

Figure 3-21: USB Packet Formats

The USB management software dynamically tracks what devices are attached to the bus and where they are. This process of identifying and numbering bus devices is known as **bus enumerating**. The USB specification promotes **hot-swap** peripheral connections that do not require the system to be shut down. The system automatically detects peripherals and configures the proper driver. Instead of just detecting and charting devices at startup in a PnP style, the USB continuously monitors the bus and updates the list whenever a device is added to or removed from it.

The USB specification provides for the following four types of transfers to be conducted:

- **Control transfers** are used by the system to configure devices at startup or time of connection. Other software can use control transfers to perform other device-specific operations.

- **Bulk data transfers** are used to service devices that can handle large batches of data (scanners and printers, for example). Bulk transfers are typically made up of large bursts of sequential data. The system arranges for bulk transfers to be conducted when the bus has plenty of capacity to carry out the transfer.

- **Interrupt transfers** are small, spontaneous transfers from a device that are used to announce events, provide input coordinate information, or transfer characters.

- **Isochronous transfers** involve large streams of data. This format is used to move continuous, real-time data streams such as voice or video. Data delivery rates are predetermined and correspond to the sampling rate of the device.

USB devices are rated as full-speed and low-speed devices based on their communication specification. Under the USB 1.1 specification, **low-speed USB** devices run at 12 Mbps. The length limit for cables serving low-speed devices is 9 feet 10 inches (3 meters). On the other hand **full-speed USB** devices operate under the USB 2.0 specification (also referred to as high-speed USB) and support data rates up to 480 Mbps. The maximum cable length for full-speed USB communication is 16 feet 5 inches (5 meters).

The low-speed USB data rate is sufficient for many PC peripherals such as telephones, keyboards, mice, digital joysticks, floppy drives, digital speakers, and low-end printers. The higher bandwidth of high-speed USB enables peripherals such as higher resolution full motion video cameras, high-resolution scanners and printers, fast data storage devices, and broadband Internet connections to operate smoothly.

High-speed USB ports are available on PCI adapter cards for upgrading older PC systems. Likewise, USB drivers for Windows 2000 and Windows XP can be downloaded from the Microsoft Windows update web site.

IEEE-1394 Firewire Bus

While the USB specification was being refined for the computer industry, a similar serial interface bus was being developed for the consumer products market. Apple Computers and Texas Instruments worked together with the **IEEE (Institute of Electrical and Electronic Engineers)** to produce the **Firewire** (or **IEEE-1394**) specification. The new bus offers a very fast option for connecting consumer electronics devices, such as camcorders and DVDs, to the computer system.

---

bus enumerating

hot-swap

Control transfers

Bulk data transfers

Interrupt transfers

Isochronous transfers

TEST TIP
Be aware of the USB high-speed data streaming mode.

full-speed USB

low-speed USB

TEST TIP
Know the length limits for full- and low-speed USB devices. It should help you to remember that the low-speed distance is actually shorter than the high-speed length.

IEEE (Institute of Electrical and Electronic Engineers)

Firewire

IEEE-1394

TEST TIP
Be aware that the Firewire bus is faster than the USB bus.

The Firewire bus is similar to USB in that devices can be daisy-chained to the computer using a single connector and host adapter. It requires a single IRQ channel, an I/O address range, and a single DMA channel to operate. Firewire is also capable of using the high-speed Isochronous transfer mode described for USB to support data transfer rates up to 400 Mbps. This actually makes the Firewire bus superior to the USB 1.1 bus but slower than USB 2.0. Firewire's high-speed capabilities make it well suited for handling components, such as video and audio devices, which require real-time, high-speed data transfer rates.

A single IEEE-1394 connection can be used to connect up to 63 devices to a single port. However, up to 1023 Firewire buses can be interconnected. PCs most commonly use a PCI expansion card to provide the Firewire interface. While AV equipment typically employs 4-pin 1394 connectors, computers normally use a 6-pin connector, with a 4-pin to 6-pin converter. The maximum segment length for an IEEE-1394 connection is 4.5 m (14 ft). Figure 3-22 depicts the Firewire connector and plug most commonly used with PCs.

Figure 3-22: Firewire Plug and Connector

The IEEE-1394 cable is composed of two twisted-pair conductors similar to those used in the local area networks described later in the chapter. Like USB, it supports both PnP and hot-swapping of components. It also provides power to the peripheral devices through one pair of the twisted conductors in the interface cable.

Firewire operates in peer-to-peer mode and is supported in both the Windows 9x and Windows NT/2000 operating systems. Both operating systems support advanced Firewire operations by including support for three critical 1394-related specifications: OHCI, IEC61883, and SBP-2. The Open Host Controller Interface (OHCI) standard defines the way Firewire interfaces to a PC. The IEC 61883 standard defines the details for controlling specific audio-video devices over the IEEE-1394 bus. The Serial Bus Protocol - 2 (SBP-2) specification defines standard ways of encapsulating device commands over 1394 and is essential for DVD players, printers, scanners, and other devices. The Home AV interoperability (HAVi) standard is another layer of protocols for the Firewire specification. This standard is directed at making Firewire devices plug-and-play capable in networks where no PC host is present.

A proposed version of the IEEE-1394 standard (titled P1394b) provides an additional electrical signaling method that permits data transmission speeds of 800 Mbps and greater. The new version of the standard also supports new transport media including glass and plastic optical fiber, as well as Category 5 copper cable. With the new media come extended distances, for example, 100 meters over CAT 5 cabling.

CHALLENGE #4

Your company is moving strongly into multimedia systems that include professional electronic music and video devices. Your boss has asked you which type of interface the company should standardize on. What should you tell the boss about this?

Infrared Ports

The **Infrared Data Association (IrDA)** has produced a wireless peripheral connection standard based on infrared light technology, similar to that used in consumer remote control devices. Many system board designs include an IrDA-compliant port standard to provide wireless communications with devices such as character printers, Personal Digital Assistants, and notebook computers. Figure 3-23 illustrates an IrDA-connected device. The same technology has been employed to carry out transfers between computer communications devices such as modems and Local Area Network cards.

Figure 3-23: An IrDA Device Connection

The IrDA standard specifies four protocols that are used with different types of devices:

- *IrLPT* — used with character printers to provide a wireless interface between the computer and the printer.

- *IrDA-SIR* — the standard infrared protocol used to provide a standard serial port interface with transfer rates ranging up to 115 kbps.

- *IrDA-FIR* — The fast infrared protocol used to provide a high-speed serial port interface with transfer rates ranging up to 4 Mbps.

- *IrTran-P* — used to provide a digital image transfer standard for communications with digital image capture devices.

TEST TIP

Remember that the IrLPT port is a new, high-speed printer interface that can be used to print from a wide array of computing devices.

These protocols specify communication ranges up to 2 meters (6 feet), but most specifications usually state 1 meter as the maximum range. All IrDA transfers are carried out in half-duplex mode and must have a clear line of sight between the transmitter and receiver. The receiver must be situated within 15 degrees of center with the line of transmission.

The Windows operating system supports the use of infrared devices. The properties of installed IrDA devices can be viewed through its Device Manager. Likewise, connections to another IrDA computer can be established through the Windows Network Dialup Connections applet. By installing a **Point-to-Point Protocol** (PPP) or an **IrDA LAN protocol** through this applet, you can conduct wireless communications with other computers without a modem or network card.

Point-to-Point Protocol (PPP)

IrDA LAN protocol

CHALLENGE #5

Your assistant is setting up an IrDA printer in a remote location. He has called you because he cannot get the system to see the infrared printer connection. To check the printer, the assistant connected it to the host computer using a normal parallel interface and it ran successfully. Which items should you suggest that your assistant check to verify the operation of the infrared port?

INSTALLING AND CONFIGURING PERIPHERAL DEVICES

The A+ Core Hardware objective 1.8 states that the test taker should be able to identify proper procedures for installing and configuring common peripheral devices. Choose the appropriate installation or configuration sequence in given scenarios.

Content may include the following:

- Modems and transceivers (dial-up, cable, DSL, ISDN)
- External storage
- Digital cameras
- PDAs
- Wireless Access Points
- Infrared devices
- Printers
- UPS (Uninterruptible Power Supply) and suppressors
- Monitors

Likewise, the A+ Core Hardware objective 1.10 states that the test taker should be able to determine the issues that must be considered when upgrading a PC. In a given scenario determine when and how to upgrade system components.

While the A+ objective mentions three different types of peripherals that technicians must know how to install, there are many different devices that can be installed in a PC system. In this text, we have decided to cover the installation of these devices along with the other information about them. The procedures for installing external storage devices are presented in Chapter 4—*Mass Storage Systems*. Likewise, modems, transceivers and wireless access points are covered in Chapter 5—*Data Communications*. UPS and power line suppressors are considered to be system protection devices and are covered in Chapter 13—*Preventive Maintenance*. Finally, there is an entire domain concerning printers and all of this information is covered in Chapter 6—*Printers*. Therefore, the installation processes involved with these devices are covered in those chapters.

TYPICAL PERIPHERALS

Peripherals are devices and systems that are added to the basic system to extend its capabilities. These devices and systems can be divided into three general categories: **input systems**, **output systems**, and **memory systems**.

input systems

output systems

memory systems

Most peripheral devices interact with the basic system through adapter cards that plug into the system board's expansion slots. The peripheral devices connect to the adapter cards through expansion slot openings in the back of the system unit.

The standard peripherals associated with personal computers are the **keyboard** and the **CRT monitor**. With the rapid growth of GUI-oriented software, the **mouse** has become a common input peripheral as well. The next most common peripheral is the **character printer**. These peripherals are used to produce hard copy output on paper. Many other types of peripheral equipment are routinely added to the basic system. As long as there are open expansion slots, or other standard I/O connectors, it is possible to add compatible devices to the system. Figure 3-24 illustrates external connections for a basic system configuration.

keyboard

CRT monitor

mouse

character printer

Figure 3-24: External Connections

Input Devices

Input devices convert physical quantities into electronic signals that can be manipulated by interface units. The input devices typically used with microcomputers convert human physical activity into electronic impulses that can be processed by the computer. The chief devices of this type are keyboards, joysticks, mice, trackballs, and touch pads. Some of these devices are illustrated in Figure 3-25. Other types of input devices convert physical quantities (such as temperature, pressure, and motion) into signals that can be processed. These devices are normally found in industrial control applications.

Figure 3-25: Typical Input Devices

Keyboards

The alphanumeric keyboard is the most widely used input device for microcomputers. It provides a simple, finger-operated method of entering numbers, letters, symbols, and special control characters into the computer. Modern computer keyboards are adaptations of earlier typewriter-like keyboards used with teletypewriters. In addition to the alphabetic and numeric keys found on conventional typewriters, the computer keyboard may also contain any number of special function and command keys to extend its basic operation and provide special-purpose entry functions.

The pattern in which keyboards are arranged and constructed has traditionally sparked some debate among users. Everyone seems to have a favorite key pattern that they prefer in a keyboard. Obviously, an individual who is trained to touch-type on a standard QWERTY typewriter keyboard would prefer that the computer keyboard be laid out in the same manner. The contour of the key top, the amount of pressure, and the length of the stroke that must be applied to the key to actuate it are also important ergonomic considerations in keyboard design. Some keyboards offer a defined click at the bottom of the keystroke to identify a complete entry. Others offer shorter keystrokes with a soft bottom and no feedback click.

Inside, a keyboard is basically an X-Y matrix arrangement of switch elements, as shown in Figure 3-26. To produce meaningful data from a key depression, the keyboard must be capable of detecting and identifying the depressed key and then encoding the key closure into a form the computer can use.

Figure 3-26: 101-Key Keyboard

The 101 keys of the sample keyboard depicted in the figure are arranged in a matrix of 13 Strobe lines and 8 Sense lines. Computer keyboards employ a dedicated microprocessor, called a **keyboard encoder**, to scan the keyboard matrix and send an interrupt request signal to the system when a key closure occurs. The keyboard encoder scans the lines of the matrix sequentially at a scan rate much faster than it is humanly possible to close one of the key switches and release it. A typical encoder scans the entire keyboard within 3 to 5 milliseconds.

keyboard encoder

When a switch closure shorts a particular row to a particular column, an active signal appears at one of the keyboard encoder's sense inputs. When the active logic level is detected, the keyboard encoder pauses for a few milliseconds to enable the switch closure to settle out. Afterward, the keyboard encoder stores the closure in its buffer and continues scanning until all the rows have been scanned.

Each time the keyboard encoder receives a valid key closure from the matrix, it generates two serially coded characters: a scan code that corresponds to the key closure, and a break code that is generated when the key closure is broken. The encoder notifies the system unit that it is ready to transmit a scan code by sending it a start bit. The encoder then begins transmitting the codes to the system unit.

On most AT and ATX-compatible system boards, the keyboard-interfacing function is handled by an intelligent **keyboard controller** built into the system board chipset. When the keyboard controller receives serial data from the keyboard, it checks the parity of the data, converts it into a scan code, and generates a keyboard interrupt request (IRQ1) to the system. The keyboard encoder transmits the codes to the keyboard controller through the cable, as illustrated in Figure 3-27. The keyboard controller releases the code to the system's keyboard interrupt handler routine.

Figure 3-27: Moving Keyboard Data

Finally, the routine sends the ASCII character code to the program that called for it. The program delivers the code to the activated output device (monitor, modem, or printer). Sending a character to a display device through the CPU is called an echo and may be suppressed by programming so that the character is not displayed.

Installing Keyboards

Most ATX-style, detachable keyboards use a round, (quarter-inch) **6-pin mini-DIN** connector (also referred to as a **PS/2 connector**). Older AT-class systems employed a larger, half-inch, **5-pin DIN** connector to plug in to the PC's system board. Both of these connections are usually made through a round opening in the rear of the system unit's case. Figure 3-28 shows the various connection schemes used with detachable keyboards.

Figure 3-28: Connection Schemes for PC Keyboards

Although many newer peripheral devices can safely be unplugged and reattached to the system while power is applied, this is not so with the standard keyboard. Plugging the keyboard in to the system while power is applied can cause the system board to fail due to the power surge and **electrostatic discharge (ESD)** that might occur between the keyboard and the system board.

Pointing Devices

Mice, joysticks, trackballs, and touch pads belong to a category of input devices called **pointing devices**. They are all small, handheld input devices that allow the user to interact with the system by moving a cursor, or some other screen image, around the display screen to choose options from an on-screen menu, instead of typing commands from a keyboard. Pointing devices make it easier to interact with the computer than other types of input devices, and are, therefore, friendlier to the user.

electrostatic discharge (ESD)

pointing devices

The most widely used pointing device is the mouse. A mouse is a hand-held device that produces input data by being moved across a surface, such as a desktop. The mouse has become a standard input device for most systems due to the popularity of GUI-based software.

The most common mouse type is the trackball mouse, depicted in Figure 3-29. The trackball mouse detects positional changes through the movement of a rolling trackball that it rides on. As the mouse is moved across a surface, its circuitry detects the movement of the trackball, and creates pulses that the system converts into positional information.

The movement of the mouse causes the trackball to roll. Inside the mouse, the trackball drives two small wheels that are attached to the shafts of two potentiometers (one X and one Y). As the trackball rolls, the wheels turn and the resistance of the potentiometers varies proportionally. The varying resistance is converted to an analog signal that undergoes an analog-to-digital conversion process, by which it is changed into a digital input that represents the movement of the mouse.

The trackball mice use opto-coupling techniques to generate a string of digital pulses when the ball is moved. These devices are referred to as opto-mechanical mice. The trackball turns two perforated wheels by friction. Light from light emitting diodes shines through holes in the wheels (which are not attached to potentiometers) as the mouse moves. The light pulses are detected by a photoconductive device that converts them into digital voltage pulses. The pulses are applied to counters that tabulate the distance (both X and Y) that the mouse moves.

Figure 3-29: Typical Trackball Mouse

optical mouse

trackball

gimbal

Another popular type of mouse is the **optical mouse**. In these mice a light emitting diode and light sensor arrangement has replaced the **trackball**. The mouse detects motion by emitting an infrared light stream, which is reflected off the surface when the mouse moves. The sensor detects the movement and direction by subtle changes in the angle of the received light and converts it into X-Y position changes. Both trackball and optical mice have similar appearances, except for the trackball underneath the mouse.

There are two major types of joysticks that can be used with PC-compatible systems: analog and digital joysticks. The analog version employs two resistive potentiometer elements, one for the X-direction and one for the Y-direction. Both potentiometers are mechanically connected to the movable **gimbal** that causes the resistance elements to produce variable levels of output signal when the gimbal is moved along the X-axis, Y-axis, or at some angle between them (this varies both the X and Y voltages).

The computer's game port interface uses these analog signals to produce digital X-Y coordinate information for the system. When this type of joystick is used to position a screen image, the position of the image on the screen corresponds to the X-Y position of the gimbal.

A somewhat simpler design is used in the construction of digital joysticks. The gimbal is used to mechanically open and close different combinations of an internal, four-switch arrangement, as depicted in Figure 3-30. The joystick produces a single-byte output, which encodes the gimbal's movement in any of eight possible directions. Unlike analog joysticks, the position of the controlled image on the screen does not correspond to the X-Y position of the gimbal. Instead, the gimbal position only produces the direction of movement for the screen image. When the gimbal is returned to its neutral position, the screen image simply stops where it is.

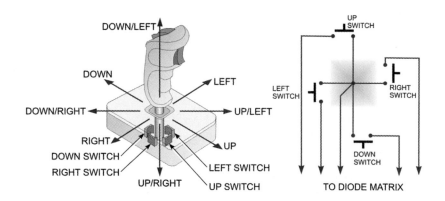

Figure 3-30: A Digital Joystick

Installing Mice

TEST TIP

Be aware that the mouse connector type is an important consideration in selecting a mouse for use.

In an ATX system, the mouse usually plugs into a 6-pin PS/2 mini-DIN connector on the back of the system unit. This connector is identical to the keyboard connector and can easily be confused with it. In AT-class systems, the mouse is plugged into a 9-pin serial port. This brings up a major point to consider when choosing a new mouse for an upgrade of an existing system or a replacement for a defective mouse—the type of connector that's required to attach it to the system.

In an ATX/Windows system, the steps for installing a mouse are simple — plug the mouse cable into the mouse connector at the back of the unit. Then, turn the system on and let the operating system detect and automatically configure the mouse. The only additional steps that might be required to get the mouse operational are to ensure that the port's hardware is properly selected and enabled, and that the mouse's driver software is installed.

When the ATX specification adopted the same connector for both the keyboard and mouse, it introduced an opportunity to plug these devices into the wrong connector. Later ATX models and peripherals have adopted an informal color coding system to differentiate between the mouse and keyboard connections — the keyboard connector and port are color coded purple, whereas the mouse connection is green.

— TEST TIP —

Be aware that it is quite possible to confuse the mouse and keyboard connections on an ATX system.

Touch-Sensitive Screens

Touch-sensitive screens, or simply **touch screens**, employ different sensing mechanisms to divide the display screen into rows and columns that correspond to X and Y coordinates and to detect the location of any contact made with the screen. When a user touches an area of the screen, the screen coordinates for the point are captured and passed to the system as input information. The supporting software application matches that coordinate with items displayed on the screen and determines what type of action is appropriate for the definition of the corresponding screen item.

These input devices are widely used in business settings for **Point of Sale (POS)** operations, such as computerized cashier stations. They are also popular as input devices for customer information and service **kiosks** (self-service computer stations). The lack of easily detachable items and mechanical mechanisms makes the touch screen very attractive for these applications.

Two techniques are commonly used to construct touch screens. The first technique employs see-through membranes arranged in rows and columns over the screen, as illustrated in Figure 3-31.

touch screens

Point of Sale (POS)

kiosks

Figure 3-31: Membrane Strip Touch Screen

When the user presses the touch-sensitive panel, the transparent strips are pressed together. When strips from a row and a column make contact with each other, their electrical qualities change. The signal generated between the two strips is decoded to an approximate X/Y position on the screen by the panel's decoding circuitry.

The second type of touch-sensitive screen technology employs infrared techniques to section the screen. Banks of LEDs and sensors arranged around the face of the monitor, as illustrated in Figure 3-32, divide the screen into a grid pattern. When an object interrupts the signal paths between a pair of horizontal and vertical LEDs and sensors, a decodable signal is produced that can be related to an X/Y coordinate on the screen.

**Figure 3-32:
LED Sensor Touch
Screen**

The main drawback associated with using touch screens involves the excessive arm movements required to operate the system. It is also true that the human fingertip is not a fine enough pointing device to select small points on the screen. Therefore, the location of a small item pointed to on the screen may not be exact due to the relative size of the fingertip. The software designer must create screen displays that take this possibility into account, and compensate for it where touch screens are used.

parallax errors

Touch-sensitive panels are available as built-in units on some monitors, whereas other units are designed as add-ons to existing monitors. These units clip, or strap, onto the body of the monitor, and hang down in front of the screen. In add-on units, the coordinate mismatch problem can be compounded by the addition of **parallax errors**. The distance between the screen and the sensors and the angle at which the user views the display are responsible for these types of errors. Parallax error causes the image to appear at a different location than it actually is. This concept is illustrated in Figure 3-33.

**Figure 3-33:
Parallax Error**

Scanners

Scanners convert pictures, line art, photographs, and text into electronic signals that can be processed by software packages such as desktop publishers and graphic design programs. These programs, in turn, can display the image on the video display or can print it out on a graphics printer.

Scanners are typically classified by the types of images they can reproduce. Some scanners can differentiate only between different levels of light and dark. These scanners are called **grayscale scanners**. **Color scanners**, on the other hand, include additional hardware that helps them distinguish among different colors. The software included with most scanners provides the user with at least a limited capability to manipulate the image after it has been scanned.

In a typical **flatbed scanner**, the scanner body remains stationary as a scan head moves past the paper. Figure 3-34 describes this process. The paper is placed face down on the scanner's glass window. The light source from the scanning mechanism is projected up through the glass and onto the paper. The lighter areas of the page reflect more light than the darker areas do.

Scanners

grayscale scanners

Color scanners

flatbed scanner

GLASS WINDOW

MIRROR

LIGHT BAR

SCAN HEAD MIRROR

LIGHT DETECTOR ARRAY

MIRROR

LENS

Figure 3-34: A Flatbed Scanner

A precision positioning motor moves the scan head below the paper. As the head moves, light reflected from the paper is captured and channeled through a series of mirrors. The mirrors pivot to continually focus the reflected light on a light-sensitive diode. The diode converts the reflected light intensity into a corresponding digital value.

A normal scanner resolution is 300 dots (or pixels) per inch. Newer flatbed scanners can achieve resolutions up to 4,800 dpi. At these resolutions, each dot corresponds to about 1/90,000 of an inch. The higher the selected scanning resolution, the slower the computer and printer operate, because of the increased amount of data that must be processed.

The digitized information is routed to the scanner adapter card in one of the PC's expansion slots. In main memory, the graphic information is stored in a format that can be manipulated by graphic design software.

Grayscale scanners can differentiate between varying levels of gray on the page. This capability is stated in shades. A good-quality grayscale scanner can differentiate between 256 levels of gray. Color scanners, on the other hand, use three passes to scan an image. Each scan passes the light through a different color filter to separate the colors from each other. The red, blue, and green filters create three different electronic images that can be integrated to form a complete picture. For intermediate colors, varying levels of the three colors are blended to create the desired shade. Figure 3-35 illustrates this concept.

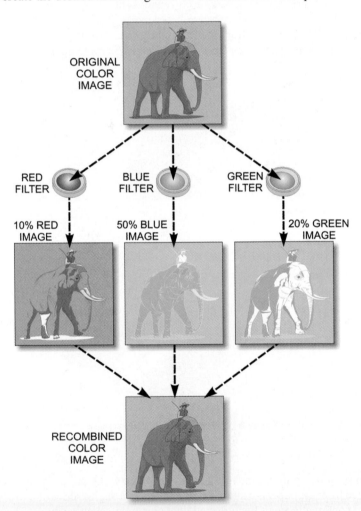

Figure 3-35:
Color Filters

Installing Scanners

Although some older scanners employed proprietary adapter cards, most of these devices typically connect to one of the system's standard I/O ports. For the most part, scanners are typically connected to their host computers in a permanent fashion and employ the system's EPP or ECP-enabled parallel port, as illustrated in Figure 3-36. In these cases, it is important to use an approved IEEE-1284 compliant cabling. Older parallel printer cables were designed for unidirectional low-speed communications and may prevent a bi-directional high-speed device like a scanner from working correctly.

Figure 3-36: Connecting an IEEE-1284 – Compliant Scanner

On the other hand, there are newer scanners available that connect to a SCSI bus extension, or to newer USB port connections. These scanners must be installed in accordance with the appropriate SCSI or USB installation procedures.

Output Devices

Common output devices are depicted in Figure 3-37. The most widely used output device for personal computers is the **Cathode-Ray Tube (CRT)** video display monitor. The most widely used display device for current PCs is the **Video Graphics Array (VGA)** color monitor. The monitor's signal cable connects to a 15-pin D-shell connector at the back of the system unit. After the monitor, the next most often added output device is the character printer. These peripherals are used to produce hard copy output on paper. They convert text and graphical data from the computer into print on a page.

Cathode-Ray Tube (CRT)

Video Graphics Array (VGA)

**Figure 3-37:
Typical Output
Devices**

SPEAKERS

MONITOR

LCD PROJECTOR

PRINTER

Video Displays

The video monitor has long been one of the most popular methods of displaying computer data. At the heart of the monitor is the cathode-ray tube (CRT), familiar to us from the television receivers we have in our homes. As a matter of fact, the early personal computers used televisions as video units. The basic difference between the television and a monitor is that no radio-frequency demodulation electronics are used in the video monitor.

As an output device, the monitor can be used to display alphanumeric characters and graphic images. Two possible methods are used to create these displays: the raster scan method and the X-Y, or vector scan, method. All television sets , and most video displays, are of the raster scan type, so this is the type on which this text focuses. An oscilloscope display is a prime example of vector scanning.

Desktop and tower computers normally employ a color CRT display monitor as standard video output equipment. The PC, PC/XT, and PC-AT often used monochrome (single-color) monitors. They could also use color monitors by simply adding a color video adapter card. The color CRT monitor is sometimes referred to as an RGB monitor, since the three primary colors that make a color CRT are red, green, and blue.

The popularity of portable computers has created a large market for lightweight display devices. The main devices used in this market are the Liquid Crystal Display (LCD) displays. These devices do not use a CRT tube or its supporting circuitry, so the weight associated with the CRT and its high-voltage components is not present. The flat-panel nature of these devices also works well in the portable computer due to its reduced size. LCDs are covered in detail in Chapter 7 — *Portable Systems*.

Basic CRT Display Operations

A CRT is an evacuated glass tube with an **electron gun** in its neck, and a fluorescent coated surface opposite the electron gun. A typical CRT is depicted in Figure 3-38. When activated, the electron gun emits a stream of electrons that strike the fluorescent coating on the inside of the screen, causing an illuminated dot to be produced.

Figure 3-38: A Cathode-Ray Tube

The sweeping electron beam begins at the upper left-hand corner of the screen, and moves across its face to the upper right-hand corner, leaving a line across the screen. This is called a **raster line**. Upon reaching the right side of the screen, the trace is blanked out, and the electron beam is repositioned to the left side of the screen, one line below the first trace in an operation called the **horizontal retrace**. At this point, the horizontal sweep begins producing the second display line on the screen. The scanning continues until the horizontal sweep reaches the bottom of the screen, as shown in Figure 3-39. At that point, the electron beam is blanked again and returned to the upper-left corner of the screen in a move referred to as the **vertical retrace**, completing one **field**.

As the beam moves across the screen, it leaves an illuminated trace, which requires a given amount of time to dissipate. The amount of time depends on the characteristics of the fluorescent coating and is referred to as **persistence**. Video information is introduced to the picture by varying the voltage applied to the electron gun as it scans the screen. The human eye perceives only the picture due to the blanking of the retrace lines, and the frequency at which the entire process is performed.

The video adapter's **Cathode-Ray Tube Controller (CRTC)** circuitry develops the video signals, and the horizontal (HSYNC) and vertical (VSYNC) synchronization signals for the CRT. Typically, a horizontal sweep requires about 63 microseconds to complete, while a complete field requires approximately 1/60 of a second, or 1/30 of a second per frame.

Figure 3-39: Raster Scan Video

The **National Television Standards Committee (NTSC)** specifies 525 lines per frame, composed of two fields of 262.5 lines, for television pictures. The two fields, one containing the even-numbered lines, and the other containing the odd-numbered lines, are interlaced to produce smooth, flickerless images. This method of creating display images is referred to as **interlaced scanning**, and is primarily used with television. Most computer monitors use **non-interlaced scanning** methods.

In text mode operations, the most common monitor arrangement calls for 25 lines of text, with 80 characters per line. This requires that the top row of 80 character blocks be serialized during the first horizontal trace of the CRT. Afterwards, the second line of 80 character blocks is serialized for the second horizontal trace. This serialization is repeated until all the horizontal traces have been made.

After a line, or a page, of text has been displayed on the screen, it must be rewritten periodically to prevent it from fading away. In order for the rewrite to be performed fast enough to avoid display **flicker**, the contents of the display are stored in a special memory, called the **screen memory**. This memory is typically located on the video adapter card. However, some newer systems use sections of the system's on-board memory for the video screen memory function. In our example of 25 lines of text at 80 characters per line, the memory must be able to hold at least 2000 bytes of screen data for a single display.

The 80 x 25 format listed above is for alphanumeric text mode. When the adapter is in text mode, it will typically require at least two bytes of screen memory for each character position on the screen. The first byte is for the ASCII code of the character itself, and the second byte is used to specify the screen attributes of the character and its cell. Under this scenario, the screen memory must be capable of holding at least 4000 bytes. The attribute byte specifies how the character is to be displayed. Common attributes include underlining, blinking, and the color of a text character for the color displays.

Color Monitors

The monitor we have been discussing so far is referred to as a monochrome monitor, because it is capable of displaying only shades of a single phosphor color. A color monitor, on the other hand, employs a combination of three color phosphors, red, blue, and green, arranged in adjacent trios of dots or bars, called **pixels** or **PELs**. By using a different electron gun for each element of the trio, the individual elements can be made to glow at different levels to produce almost any color desired. The electron guns scan the front of a screen in unison, in the same fashion as described earlier for a monochrome CRT. Color CRTs add a metal grid in front of the phosphor coating called a **shadow mask**. It ensures that an electron gun assigned to one color doesn't strike a dot of another color. The basic construction of a color CRT is shown in Figure 3-40.

ELECTRON GUNS
BLUE
GREEN
RED
ELECTRON
BEAMS
SHADOW
MASK
BLUE PHOSPHOR
RED PHOSPHOR
GREEN PHOSPHOR
GLASS
FACEPLATE

Figure 3-40: A Color CRT Construction

Screen Resolution

The quality of the image produced on the screen is a function of two factors: the speed at which the image is retraced on the screen, and the number of pixels on the screen. The more pixels on a given screen size, the higher the image quality. This quantity is called resolution, and is often expressed in an X-by-Y format. Using this format, the quality of the image is still determined by how big the viewing area is (e.g., an 800 x 600 resolution on a 14-inch monitor will produce much better quality than the same number of pixels spread across a 27-inch monitor).

Resolution can be expressed as a function of how close pixels can be grouped together on the screen. This form of resolution is expressed in terms of **dot pitch**. A monitor with a .28 dot pitch has pixels that are located .28 mm apart. In monochrome monitors, dot pitch is measured from center to center of each pixel. In a color monitor, the pitch is measured from the center of one dot trio to the center of the next trio.

For more in-depth information about how monitors work, refer to the Electronic Reference Shelf located on the CD that accompanies this book.

REFERENCE
SHELF

Installing Video/Monitor Systems

The video display system is one of the easiest systems to add to the computer. The components associated with the video display are depicted in Figure 3-41. The video adapter card typically plugs into one of the system's expansion slots. The monitor's signal cable plugs into the video adapter card. The monitor's power cable may be plugged into a commercial wall outlet, or it may be attached to the special power outlet provided by an AT-class power supply unit. Using this outlet enables the monitor to be turned on and off along with the system unit.

Most VGA cards employ the AGP form factor. However, some versions are still being produced on PCI boards. High-end video adapter cards typically include a heat sink and possibly a snap-on fan unit to cool the video controller IC. The operating speeds and complexity of these devices have increased to the point where active cooling methods are required. Cooling units that include fans require a power connection to drive the fan. This connection can be made on a special connector on the video card or to the system board.

Figure 3-41: Video System Components

Some very high-end video adapters have internal VGA-to-TV converters that enable them to deliver output directly to a typical television display. This output signal is provided through a standard RCA mini-jack mounted on the back of the card.

After the video card has been installed and the monitor has been connected to the video card and plugged into the power outlet, it will be necessary to install the correct drivers for the video card. The Windows 9x operating systems should detect the video card, start the system with basic VGA video drivers, and ask if you want to install the manufacturer's video drivers. The Windows 2000 operating system is even more proactive. It will detect the new video card, tell you that it has found the new card, and then automatically load its video drivers. The only time that you should need to be directly involved with the system's video drivers is when PnP fails or the video card is not recognized by the operating system.

Sound Cards

The sound-producing capabilities of early PCs were practically nonexistent. They included a single, small speaker that was used to produce beep-coded error messages. Even though programs could be written to produce a wide array of sounds from this speaker, the quality of the sound was never any better than the limitations imposed by its small size. This led various companies to design audio digitizer cards for the PC that could both convert sound into digital quantities that the computer could manipulate and play back digitized sound produced by the computer. These cards are referred to as **sound cards**.

A typical audio digitizer system is depicted in Figure 3-42. A microphone converts sound waves from the air into an encoded analog electrical signal. The analog signal is applied to the audio input of the sound card. On the card, the signal is applied to an A/D converter circuit, which changes the signal into corresponding digital values, as described in Figure 3-43.

**Figure 3-42:
A Typical Audio
Digitizer System**

**Figure 3-43:
Converting Analog
Signals to Digital Values**

The sound card takes samples of the analog waveform at predetermined intervals, and converts them into corresponding digital values. Therefore, the digital values approximate the instantaneous values of the sound wave.

The **fidelity** (the measure of how closely the original sound can be reproduced) of the digital samples is dependent on two factors: the accuracy of the samples taken, and the rate at which the samples are taken. The accuracy of the sample is determined by the **resolution** capabilities of the A/D converter. Resolution is the capability to differentiate between values (i.e., if the value of the analog waveform is 15.55 microvolts at a given point, how closely can that value be approximated with a digital value?).

The number of digital output bits an A/D converter can produce determines its resolution capabilities. For example, an 8-bit A/D converter can represent up to 256 (2^8) different values. On the other hand, a 16-bit A/D converter can represent up to 65,536 (2^{16}) different values. The more often the samples are taken, the more accurately the original waveform can be reproduced.

Playback of the digitized audio signal is accomplished by applying the digital signals to a D/A converter at the same rate the samples were taken. When the audio files are called for, the sound card's software driver sends commands to the audio output controller on the sound card. The digitized samples are applied to the audio output IC, and converted back into the analog signal.

The analog signal is applied to an audio preamplifier that boosts the power of the signal, and sends it to an RCA, or mini jack. This signal is still too weak to drive conventional speakers. However, it can be applied to an additional amplifier, or to a set of speakers that have an additional amplifier built into them.

A CD-quality audio signal requires a minimum of 16-bit samples, taken at approximately 44 kHz. If you calculate the disk space required to store all of the 16-bit samples collected in one minute of audio at this rate, the major consideration factor associated with using digitized audio becomes clear (16 x 44,000 x 60 x 8 = 5.28 MB). If you want stereo sound, this will double to a whopping 10.56 MB. Therefore, CD-quality audio is not commonly used in multimedia productions. The audio sampling rate used in multimedia titles is generally determined by the producer. An alternative to lowering the sampling rate is to limit the digitized audio used in a product to short clips.

Installing Sound Cards

Installing a sound card is similar to installing any other adapter card. Refer to the card's user guide to determine what hardware configuration settings might need to be made before inserting the card into the system. It might also be beneficial to run a diagnostic software package to check the system's available resources before configuring the card.

After the hardware configuration has been completed, simply install the card in one of the system's vacant expansion slots and secure it to the back panel of the system unit. Plug the microphone and speakers into the proper **RCA mini jacks** on the card's back plate. With the card installed, the system loads its software drivers according to the directions in the user guide. Figure 3-44 depicts the connectors located on the back of a typical sound card.

Figure 3-44: Sound Card Connections

Most sound cards support microphones through a stereo RCA jack. A very similar speaker jack is also normally present on the back of the card. Depending on the card, the jack might be designed for mono or stereo output. An on-board volume control wheel might also protrude through the card's back plate.

Personal Digital Assistants

Palmtop computers are a class of very small computers designed to fit in most users' hands. The palmtop market was diminished for some time because of the difficulty of running Windows on such small displays. **Human ergonomics** also come into play when dealing with smaller notebooks. The smaller display screens become difficult to see, and keyboards become more difficult to use as the size of the keys decreases.

However, the market was revived by the introduction of palm tops as **personal digital assistants (PDAs)**. Figure 3-45 depicts a typical PDA. These handheld devices use a special stylus, referred to as a pen, to input data and selections instead of a keyboard or mouse. Basically the PDA is an electronic time management system that can also include computer applications such as word processors, spreadsheets, and databases.

Figure 3-45: A Personal Digital Assistant

Two items have made PDAs popular—their size and their capability of communicating with the user's desktop computer system. The PDA's display is a touch-screen LCD display that works in conjunction with a graphical user interface running on top of a specialized operating system. Some PDAs employ a highly modified, embedded (on a chip) version of Microsoft Windows, called Windows CE, as their operating system. These devices are particularly well suited for exchanging and synchronizing information with larger Windows-based systems.

Early PDAs exchanged information with full-sized computers through standard serial port connections. Newer models communicate with the user's desktop computer through a USB port, an infrared communications link, or a docking cradle.

Installing Other Peripherals

The typical PC features built-in logic and physical connection support for the standard PC peripherals. The system board provides the controllers and connectors for the system's hard- and floppy-disk drives. It also furnishes the standard keyboard (and possibly the mouse) connection. As we have seen, newer systems provide industry standard parallel- and serial-port connections, and may supply a game port connector.

Adapter Card−Based Peripherals

In addition to installing hard drives and peripheral devices that connect to standard I/O ports, technicians must be able to successfully install and configure peripheral devices (or systems) that connect to the system in other ways—such as through the system's expansion slots. The steps for installing these types of peripherals and systems are generally very similar from device to device:

1. Remove the system unit's cover and take out an expansion slot cover.

2. Check the adapter card's user's manual for any manual configuration information and set up the card as required.

3. Insert the card into the empty expansion slot.

4. Connect any necessary cabling to the adapter card.

5. Connect any external power supply connections to the peripheral device.

6. Start the machine. The Windows operating system should detect the new device if it is PnP-compatible. If it does not, you will need to load drivers for the device from its installation media (disk or CD).

7. Shut down the system, turn it off, and reinstall the system unit's outer cover.

This process can be used to install diverse I/O devices such as modems and LAN adapters, as well as scanners and other devices that use adapter cards in expansion slots. However, for many devices, the advent of newer hot-swap I/O buses, such as USB and Firewire, has reduced this process to more or less just connecting the device to the bus.

Upgrading Adapters

Normally, updating adapters in a PC involves installing additional NIC cards, modems, or other proprietary adapter cards. You should always use the following guidelines for upgrading adapter card-based peripherals in a system:

1. *Verify compatibility* − When you are installing adapter cards, you should verify their compatibility with the system board, its adapter slot, and the other cards installed in the system. For example, if you are upgrading a PCI card, you should make sure that the voltage is compatible with the available PCI slot. If your PCI slots only support 3.3 V adapters, then the card you are upgrading to also needs to be 3.3 V.

   PCI cards that operate on 3.3 V and those that use 5 V are configured differently. Therefore, a 3.3 V card will only fit in a 3.3 V slot, whereas 5 V cards will only fit in a 5 V slot. The 3.3 V and 5 V PCI slot configurations were discussed in detail in Chapter 2 — *Advanced System Boards*. On the other hand, there are some PCI cards that support both 5 V and 3.3 V operation. There is less to worry about with such dual-voltage cards.

2. *Perform BIOS upgrade* — A system BIOS upgrade is not required when upgrading adapter cards, but some adapter cards contain their own specific BIOS. These BIOS may need to be upgraded to permit the adapter to work with the other components in the system. If in doubt, refer to the installation documentation and the manufacturer's web site for specific information pertaining to the adapters you are using.

3. *Obtain the latest drivers* — In most cases, the drivers that came with an adapter card include the necessary drivers for the operating system you are using. However, the latest driver on the CD-ROM or floppy disk supplied with the component is often not the latest driver available for the noted operating system. Check the manufacturer's web site for newer versions.

4. *Implement ESD best practices* — To prevent the adapter from being damaged, make sure that it is enclosed in an anti-shock bag when not in use. Make sure that you wear an anti-static device when handling the adapter. Most adapters include static sensitive components that can be damaged by very small electromagnetic shocks, so take extra care when handling or installing your adapter cards.

5. *Verify upgrade* — There are specific attributes that are common when verifying proper installation of a wide variety of adapter cards. For instance, all adapters use resources, such as IRQ, I/O memory, and/or base memory address. You must make sure that none of these settings conflict with those of other hardware devices in the system.

You can check this in Windows by checking the system properties in the Control Panel, and looking at the *Hardware* tab for hardware errors. Some adapter cards require jumper settings to be preset for these attributes, whereas others do not require jumpers, or include jumperless BIOS. The newer plug-and-play operating systems in use today usually automatically set up your adapter to preclude conflicts.

Specialized Video Cards

If you are designing a high-end computer, such as a computer to produce multimedia presentation (or view them), a high-end video display card is usually required. This type of video adapter card includes a heat sink and possibly a snap-on fan unit to cool its video controller IC. The operating speeds and complexity of these devices have increased to the point where active cooling methods are required. Cooling units that include fans require a power connection to drive the fan. This connection can be made on a special connector on the video card or to the system board.

Some very high-end video adapters provide internal VGA-to-TV converters that enable them to deliver output directly to a typical television display. In addition to standard VGA and SVGA compatible outputs, these cards generate NTSC-compatible (or European PAL compatible) raster scan video signals compatible with television sets. These signals can be delivered in the form of composite TV or analog S-Video formats.

Digital Visual Interface (DVI) cards are specialized video adapters that provide both analog and digital video signals to accommodate both analog and digital monitors The DVI standard specifies a single plug and connector arrangement that can accommodate traditional legacy VGA connections as well as newer digital interfaces. The DVI interface operates with signal bandwidths that support new **Ultra Extended VGA (UXGA)** video display specifications, as well as **High Definition TV (HDTV)** signals.

> Digital Visual Interface (DVI)
>
> Ultra Extended VGA (UXGA)
>
> High Definition TV (HDTV)

Installing Devices Using Advanced Buses and Ports

Most new I/O ports and buses (e.g., USB, IEEE-1394, PCMCIA, and IrDA) feature hot insertion and removal capabilities for their devices. These are in addition to the traditional PnP operation. The devices that connect to these ports and buses are designed to be plugged in and removed as needed. Installing these devices is practically a hands-off operation.

Installing a USB or Firewire device usually involves the following steps:

1. Enable the USB resources in the CMOS Setup screen, as illustrated in Figure 3-46. In some cases, this involves enabling the port and reserving an IRQ resource for the device.

2. Plug the device into an open USB connector.

3. Wait for the operating system to recognize the device and configure it through the PnP process.

Figure 3-46: Enabling the USB Resources

Microsoft's Windows 98, Windows 2000, or Windows XP will detect the presence of the USB or Firewire device and start their Found New Hardware Wizard program, shown in Figure 3-47, to guide the installation process. Simply follow the instructions provided by the wizard to set up the new device—there is no need to shut down or turn off the computer.

Installing an IrDA device in an infrared-enabled system is a fairly simple process. When an IrDA device is installed in the system, a *Wireless Link* icon appears in the Windows Control Panel as depicted in Figure 3-48. (Remember, infrared port operations must first be enabled through the CMOS Setup utility.) When another IrDA device comes within range of the host port, the *Infrared* icon will appear on the Windows desktop and in the taskbar. In the case of an IrDA printer, a printer icon will appear in the *Printer* folder.

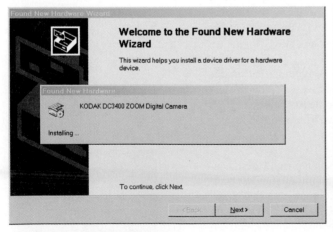

**Figure 3-47: The Windows
Found New Hardware Wizard**

Figure 3-48: The Windows Wireless Link Icon

Right-click the *Infrared* icon on the taskbar to turn on the infrared communication function. Make sure that the *Enable Infrared communication* check box is checked. To turn off infrared communications, make sure that this item is not checked. When infrared communication has been turned off, the *Search for Devices Within Range* and *Enable Plug and Play functions* are also turned off. To engage support for infrared Plug-and-Play devices, right-click the *Infrared* icon on the taskbar.

Make sure that the *Enable Plug and Play* option is checked. Conversely, to turn off support for Plug-and-Play device installation, make sure that this item is not checked. It will only be available if the infrared and searching functions are enabled. If the *Taskbar* icon is not visible, click on the *Related Topics* option.

Simply right-click the *Infrared* icon on the Taskbar to install software for an infrared device. Make sure that the *Enable Plug and Play* check box is checked and verify that the new device is within range. If you are not sure whether the device you are installing is Plug-and-Play capable, check its user's guide. If it is not a Plug-and-Play device, install its drivers by accessing the *Add New Hardware* icon in the Control Panel.

Infrared Monitor

Windows provides an **Infrared Monitor** utility that can be used to track the computer's activity. When this utility is running, it will alert you when infrared devices are within range of your computer by placing the Infrared icon on the taskbar. The Infrared Monitor not only notifies you when the computer is communicating with an infrared device, but it also indicates how well it is communicating. Other functions that can be performed through the Infrared Monitor include controlling how the system reports the status of the infrared activity it detects and what types of infrared activity it can conduct.

Infrared Monitor

Installing Digital Cameras

Digital cameras are mobile devices that are mostly plugged into the computer simply to download pictures. Therefore, most digital cameras feature the capability of being connected to parallel ports, serial ports, and USB ports. Some cameras can also communicate through IEEE-1394 Firewire ports. USB and Firewire ports feature hot-swap capabilities that permit the camera to be plugged into the system and removed while power is still applied. Figure 3-49 shows a typical digital camera connection scheme.

Digital cameras

Figure 3-49: Digital Camera Connection

Software applications for downloading the pictures from the camera must be loaded on the PC before any transfers can be conducted. Likewise, the software supplied with the camera can be used to display the images and typically offers a limited number of graphic manipulation features (e.g., rotate, color balance, crop, and resize). Most digital cameras deliver the images to the PC in a JPEG format. This format is compact, but it can be manipulated with virtually any commercial graphic design software.

Upgrading Peripheral Devices

Devices that come under this category include printers, external modems, external CD devices, and input devices, such as the keyboard and mouse. The steps involved in this process are similar to those listed for upgrading adapter cards presented earlier in this chapter. You should use the general procedure that follows when you are upgrading a system's peripheral devices.

1. *Verify compatibility* – Because peripheral devices can vary greatly in their configuration and use, you should always refer to the device's documentation to ensure that it will work properly with your system. Since external devices must connect to the computer through its interface ports (i.e., serial and parallel ports, USB, Firewire, and in some cases external SCSI connectors), you must ensure that the proper port is available for the device to be installed.

2. *Perform firmware upgrade* — Prior to installing a peripheral, consult the manufacturer's website for any updates that may exist for its firmware, or any updated device drivers that may be available. To apply firmware updates, you must first obtain the firmware update tool from the manufacturer.

3. *Obtain the latest drivers* — In most cases, the installation software that came with the peripheral will have the necessary drivers for the operating system you are using. The latest driver on the installation CD or floppy disk is usually only the latest driver available at the time the peripheral shipped.

4. *Implement ESD best practices* — Peripherals tend to be less sensitive to electrostatic damage than PC board devices and are often directly grounded through their power cords. However, since peripheral devices tend to be expensive, you may still want to properly ground yourself before working with them. It is always better to be safe than sorry.

5. *Verify the upgrade* — Because peripheral devices can vary greatly in their configuration and use, there are a variety of ways that you can test your upgrade. For instance, with a printer you can print a test page, print a page from a client, or print multiple print jobs to test the queue. For a zip disk, this may include moving data onto the disk and then trying to examine the data on another computer later.

6. *Check system resources* — Normally, peripherals use the resources associated with the port they are attached to. If the peripheral tests OK, you will normally not have to verify system resources.

CHAPTER SUMMARY

The first half of this chapter has examined standard I/O port assignments in a PC-compatible system. At this point, you should be able to identify the type of port being used from a description of its structure. In addition, you should be able to use the troubleshooting information provided for each port type to isolate and correct typical port problems in a PC-compatible system.

The second half of the chapter dealt with common I/O devices used with PCs. You should be able to describe the operation of each type of input and output device. You should also be able to list the types of devices that are normally associated with each I/O port type. As with the I/O ports in the first half of the chapter, you should be able to use the troubleshooting information provided for each input device to isolate and correct problems typically associated with that device.

At this point, review the objectives listed at the beginning of the chapter to be certain that you understand and can perform each item listed there.

KEY POINTS REVIEW

The first half of this chapter examined standard I/O port assignments in a PC-compatible system. The second half of the chapter dealt with common input/output devices used with purchase. Review the following key points before moving into the Review and Exam Questions sections to make sure you are comfortable with each point. Afterward, answer the Review Questions that follow to verify your knowledge of the information.

- In addition to the millions of possible memory locations in a PC, there are typically thousands of addresses set aside for input and output devices in a system. In order for any device to operate with the system's microprocessor, it must have an address (or group of addresses) where the system can find it.

- Interface circuits are necessary because the characteristics of most peripherals differ greatly from those of the basic computer. Most interface circuits in the PC-compatible world have been integrated into application-specific ICs.

- When dealing with a PC-compatible, there are two forms of I/O to contend with. These include the system board's on-board I/O, and peripheral devices that interact with the system through its expansion slots.

- Parallel ports have been a staple of the PC system since the original PCs were introduced. They are most widely used to connect printers to the computer.

- A typical parallel printer connection, using the IBM version of the Centronics standard, allows the computer to pass information to the printer, 8 bits at a time, across the 8 data lines. The other lines in the connection carry control signals (handshaking signals) back and forth between the computer and the printer.

- Microsoft operating systems keep track of the system's installed printer ports by assigning them the logical device names (handles) LPT1, LPT2, and LPT3. Whenever the system is booted up, the operating system searches the hardware for parallel ports installed at hex addresses 3BC, 378, and 278 consecutively.

- As the distance between the computer and a peripheral reaches a certain point (10 feet), it becomes less practical to send data as parallel words. An alternative method of sending data is to break the parallel words into their individual bits, and transmit them, one at a time, in a serial bit stream over a single conductor.

- Two methods are used to provide the proper timing for serial transfers: The data bits may be sent synchronously (in conjunction with a synchronizing clock pulse), or asynchronously (without an accompanying clock pulse).

- As with parallel ports, the operating system assigns COM port designations to the system's serial ports during bootup. COM port designations are normally COM1 and COM2 in most systems, but they can be extended to COM3 and COM4 in advanced systems.

- Peripherals are devices and systems that are added to the basic system to extend its capabilities. These devices and systems can be divided into three general categories: input systems, output systems, and memory systems.

- A new serial interface scheme, called the Universal Serial Bus (USB), has been developed to provide a fast, flexible method of attaching up to 127 peripheral devices to the computer. The USB provides a connection format designed to replace the system's traditional serial and parallel port connections.

REVIEW QUESTIONS

The following questions test your knowledge of the material presented in this chapter.

1. What is the maximum recommended length of a standard parallel printer cable?

2. Describe the standard system resources allocated to the LPT1 port in a PC.

3. Describe the standard system resources allocated to the COM1 serial port in a PC.

4. Which type of data transfer technique involves a high-speed device taking over the system busses from the microprocessor to conduct I/O read and write operations?

5. A technician is concerned about purchasing digital cameras for a company. Her main concern is the digital camera can connect to the workstation properly. List all the traditional connections that a digital camera can use to connect to a workstation.

6. What is the function of a shadow mask in a CRT display?

7. A user wishes to connect a Firewire-compatible video camera with his workstation. However, before he requests a purchase for all required devices, he wants to make sure that the cable segment is long enough so that he can place the video camera on a tripod in a specific place at his office, and still be connected to the workstation. What is the maximum segment length for an IEEE-1394 connection in terms of feet?

8. Which IRQ is normally used for a modem attached to the system's COM2 port?

9. How many USB devices can be attached to the USB port of a PC?

10. What is the maximum recommended distance for an IrDA link?

11. State the maximum segment lengths for low- and high-speed USB connections.

12. How many devices can be connected to a single IEEE-1394 port?

13. Which port types include high-speed data streaming modes that can transfer large streams of data such as audio or video information?

14. What type of device normally uses IRQ14 in an ATX system?

15. Where is the EPP mode enabled in an ATX system?

EXAM QUESTIONS

1. Which device or port uses IRQ8 in an ATX PC system?
   a. Keyboard Buffer
   b. Math Coprocessor
   c. RAM Refresh controller
   d. Real-Time Clock Module

2. At what I/O port addresses does the system communicate with the primary hard disk (IDE) controller?
   a. 0F8-0FF
   b. 1F0-1F7
   c. 200-207
   d. 278-27F

3. What type(s) of connector is usually found on PC-compatible keyboards? (Select all that apply.)
   a. A 6-pin mini-DIN connector
   b. A 5-pin DIN connector
   c. An RJ-11 connector
   d. An RJ-45 connector

4. Which type of I/O port employs a 2-row 15-pin, D-shell female connector?
   a. VGA port
   b. ATX mouse port
   c. LAN port
   d. Game port

5. Which printer port type employs DMA transfers for high-speed operation?
   a. SPP
   b. EPP
   c. ECP
   d. IrDA

6. What is the standard PC address given to a second parallel printer port?
   a. 378
   b. 3F8
   c. 278
   d. 0FF

7. Which type of I/O cable uses a 36-pin Centronics connector?
   a. USB cable
   b. Firewire cable
   c. RS-232C port cable
   d. SPP parallel cable

8. A user complains that he is unable to find a cord or plug to connect his brand-new PDA to the workstation. Reading through the PDA manual, you note no mention of additional cords to interface with the PDA. All other functions of the PDA appear to be working. What is most likely the problem?
   a. The PDA is defective.
   b. The PDA is missing cabling.
   c. The PDA uses wireless connections to transfer data.
   d. The PDA does not have batteries installed.

9. Which DMA channel has a dedicated function in a standard PC?
   a. Channel 6 for the FDD controller
   b. Channel 2 for the FDD controller
   c. Channel 3 for the EPP port controller
   d. Channel 1 for the keyboard controller

10. Choose the event that will cause an NMI error to occur.
   a. Adapter card error
   b. Hard drive failure
   c. Power failure port
   d. User error

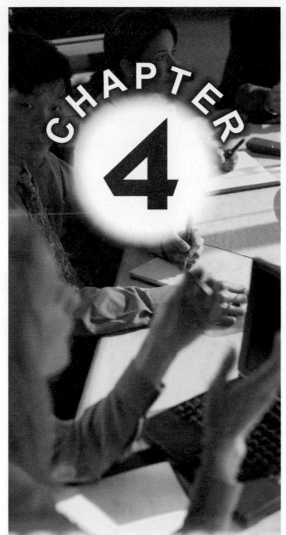

CHAPTER 4

MASS STORAGE SYSTEMS

OBJECTIVES

OBJECTIVES

Upon completion of this chapter and its related lab procedures, you should be able to:

1. Differentiate between different types of hard- and floppy-disk drives.

2. State reasons for the popularity of magnetic disks as computer data storage systems.

3. Describe the format or organization of a typical hard or floppy disk.

4. Identify the major physical blocks of the disk drive unit.

5. Explain why the DOS software is so important to the operation of a disk drive.

6. Differentiate between common connecting cables (e.g., SCSI, IDE, FDD).

7. Discuss the different RAID advisory levels and apply them to given applications.

8. Install IDE and EIDE devices, including setting Master/Slave/Single designations.

9. Install and configure single and complex SCSI device chains.

10. Establish proper addressing and termination for SCSI devices to avoid conflicts and problems.

11. Describe the operation of a Writable CD drive.

12. Differentiate between different types of CDs.

13. Install and configure a CD-ROM drive for operation.

MASS STORAGE SYSTEMS

INTRODUCTION

Nearly every microcomputer includes some type of mass information storage system that allows it to store data or programs for an extended period of time. Unlike primary memory devices, which are fast and have a relatively low storage capacity, mass storage systems are usually slower, and possess much larger storage potential. These systems are an acceptable alternative to the IC RAM and ROM devices used on system and video cards. Like the ROM devices, these systems must be able to hold information even when the computer is turned off. On the other hand, they are like RAM devices in that their information can be updated and changed often.

The most widely used mass storage systems have typically involved covering some medium with a magnetic coating. However, optical storage technologies such as compact discs and Digital Video Disks have made great inroads into the digital data storage market.

STORAGE DEVICES

The problem with electronic devices is that programs and data disappear from the system's memory when the device is turned off, or loses power. In addition, the costs associated with IC RAM devices tend to be too expensive for constructing large memories that can hold multiple programs and large amounts of data. Therefore, storage systems that can be used for long-term data storage are desirable as a second level of memory.

With this in mind, a number of secondary memory technologies have been developed to extend the computer's memory capabilities and store data on a more permanent basis. These systems tend to be too slow to be used directly with the computer's microprocessor. The secondary memory unit holds the information and transfers it in batches to the computer's faster internal memory when requested.

Magnetic Storage

From the early days of digital computers, most secondary memory systems have involved storing binary information in the form of magnetic charges on moving magnetic surfaces.

These systems include flexible Mylar disks (called floppy disks), rigid aluminum hard disks, and various widths of flexible Mylar tape, as illustrated in Figure 4-1. The information to be

stored on the medium is converted into electromagnetic pulses, which in turn are used to create tiny positive and negative magnetized spots on the magnetic surface. To retrieve, or read, the information back from the surface, the storage system needs only to detect the spots and decode them. The stored information can be changed at any time by remagnetizing the surface with the new information.

**Figure 4-1:
Typical Magnetic
Storage Systems**

Magnetic Disk Drives

Magnetic disks resemble grooveless phonograph records, and fall into two general categories: high-speed hard disks, and slower flexible disks. Data bits are recorded serially in concentric circles, called **tracks**, around the disk. Since the tracks toward the outer edge of the disk are longer than the inner tracks, all tracks are divided into an equal number of equal-size data blocks called **sectors**. Therefore, each block of data has an address, which is the combination of its track number and its sector number. Since each sector can be accessed for a read or write operation as fast as any other sector on the disk, disk memories are classified as Direct Access Memory.

The tracks of the disk are numbered, beginning with 00, from the outer edge of the disk inward. Each side of the disk may hold 80 or more tracks, depending on the type of disk and the drive being used. When disks are stacked, such as in a hard-disk drive, all of the tracks having the same number are referred to collectively as a **cylinder**. The number of sectors on each track runs between 8 and 50, also depending on the disk and drive type.

In floppy- and hard-disk systems, track and sector address information is contained in a track/sector identification code recorded on the disk. This method of address specification is known as **soft sectoring**, because the sector information is written in software. Figure 4-2 depicts a typical soft-sectored track and sector arrangement. PC-compatible systems use soft-sectored disks.

| tracks |
| sectors |

| cylinder |

| soft sectoring |

**Figure 4-2: Disk Tracks
and Sectors**

Each sector is separated from the previous and following sectors by a small gap of unrecorded space. A typical sector contains 256 (2^8) or 512 (2^9) bytes, but on some systems this value may range as low as 128 (2^7) or as high as 1024 (2^{10}) bytes per sector. The most common sector size in the IBM-compatible/Microsoft world is 512 bytes. Within these confines, the sector is segmented, beginning with an ID field header, which tells the controlling circuitry that an ID area containing the physical address information is approaching. A small data field header precedes the actual data field. The data field is followed by a postamble, containing error-checking and correcting codes for the data recorded in the sector.

In their original conditions, hard disks and soft-sectored disks, as well as magnetic tapes, are blank. The system must prepare them to hold data. The system's disk-drive control circuitry accomplishes this by writing track/sector identification and gap locations on the disk in a process known as **formatting**. This leads to some confusion when disk storage capacity is specified. Capacity may be stated for either formatted or unformatted conditions. Obviously, the capacity of an unformatted disk is greater, because no gap or ID information has been added to the disk.

formatting

Reading and Writing on Magnetic Surfaces

Data is read from, or written to, the disk one sector at a time. In order to perform a read or write operation, the address of the particular track and sector to be accessed is applied to a stepper motor, which moves a **Read/Write (R/W) head** over the desired track. As the desired sector passes beneath the R/W head, the data transfer occurs. Information read from, or written to, the disk is usually held in a dedicated part of the computer's RAM memory. The system then accesses the data from this memory location at microprocessor-compatible speeds.

Read/Write (R/W) head

The R/W head consists of a coil of wire wrapped around a soft iron core, as depicted in Figure 4-3. A small air gap in the core rides above the magnetic coating on the disk's surface. Data is written on the disk by applying pulses to the coil, which produces magnetic lines of flux in the soft iron core. At the air gap, the lines of flux dip down into the disk's magnetic coating, due to its low reluctance (compared to the air). This, in turn, causes the magnetic domains in the recording surface to align in a direction dictated by the direction of current flow through the coil. The magnetic domains of the surface can assume one of three possible states depending on the direction of current flow through the R/W head:

Figure 4-3: A Typical R/W Head

- Unmagnetized (randomly arranged domains)
- Magnetized in a positive direction
- Magnetized in a negative direction

Data is read from the disk in a reversal of this process. As the magnetized spots on the surface pass by the R/W head, changes in magnetic polarity of the spots induce lines of flux into the R/W head's core. This, in turn, induces a small voltage in the R/W head that is sensed and amplified to the proper digital logic levels by the drive's Read circuitry.

Contact vs. Non-Contact Recording

Depending on the nature of the magnetic medium being read from or written to, the R/W head may ride directly on the medium's surface (contact recording), or it may "fly" slightly above it on a thin cushion of air created by the moving surface (non-contact recording). Hard disks, whether fixed or removable, must use flying heads, whereas flexible media (tapes and disks) generally use contact recording.

Hard disks use non-contact heads that fly over the medium. The extremely high speed of the medium, and the thin and fragile nature of its magnetic oxide coating, makes almost any contact between the R/W head and the disk surface a cause of considerable damage to both the head and the disk. Such contact is known as **Head-to-Disk Interference (HDI)**, or simply as a **head crash**. Recent advances, such as smaller and lighter R/W heads, and ever-harder damage-resistant disk surfaces, have lowered the possibilities of damaging crashes somewhat. Because the medium is dimensionally stable, and spins at a high rate of speed, the data density associated with hard disks is relatively high.

Head-to-Disk Interference (HDI)

head crash

The flying R/W head glides over the disk at a height of approximately 50 microinches. This may seem like an unimportant measurement until you consider the size of a common dust particle or a human hair.

This relationship is illustrated in Figure 4-4. If the R/W head should strike one of these contaminants as the disk spins at high speed, the head would be lifted into the air and then crash into the disk surface, damaging the R/W head and/or the disk surface. To avoid this, hard disks are encased in sealed protective housings. It is important to realize that at no time should the disk housing be opened to the atmosphere. Repairs to hard disk drives are performed in special repair facilities having ultra-clean rooms. In these rooms, even particles the size of those described in the figure have been removed from the air.

Figure 4-4: Flying R/W Heads

Flexible media such as floppy disks and tape expand and shrink with temperature and humidity variations. This causes the data tracks on the media to migrate in terms of track-location accuracy of the R/W head. To compensate for such shifting, the R/W heads ride directly on the media's surface, the track density is kept low, and the heads are made more complex to create special zones in the track construction, which compensate for some of the misalignment due to shifting.

DISK DRIVE OPERATIONS

The basic organization of both hard- and floppy-disk drives is similar in many respects. Both have drive spindles, which are actuated by precision synchronous motors, and a set of movable R/W heads that are positioned by a digital stepper motor, or voice coil. In addition, both systems have intelligent control circuitry to position the R/W head and to facilitate the transfer of information between the disk and the computer's memory. Figure 4-5 depicts the major components of a typical disk drive system.

Figure 4-5: Disk Drive Components

The heart of the disk drive's circuitry is the **disk-drive controller**. The controller is responsible for providing the necessary interfacing between the disk drive and the computer's I/O channel. It does this by decoding the computer's instructions to the disk drive, and generating the control signals that the disk drive must have to carry out the instruction. The controller must also convert back and forth between the parallel data format of the computer's bus, and the serial format of the disk drive.

In addition, the controller must accurately position the R/W heads, direct the read and write operations, check and correct data received from the processor, generate error-correction codes for outbound data, and mark the location of defective sectors on the disk, closing them to use. After all of these responsibilities, the disk controller must also provide addressing for the tracks and sectors on the disk, and control the transfer of information to and from the internal memory.

disk-drive controller

INITIALIZATION

To transfer a file from the system to the disk (a Write operation), the operating system sends the disk-drive controller a Write command, along with parameters required to carry out the operation. It also specifies the track and sector number where writing will begin. It obtains this information by referring to the disk's file system table (FAT) and locating the address of the next available sector. Figure 4-6 illustrates the type of information used to initialize a disk drive for operation.

**Figure 4-6:
Disk Drive
Initialization**

Track-Seek Operations

track-seek

To position the drive's R/W heads over the desired track, the controller must conduct a **track-seek** operation. In this operation, the controller enables the drive and produces a burst of step pulses to position the R/W head over the proper track. The controller accomplishes this by keeping a record of the current track location of the drive's R/W heads.

direction

step

When the controller receives a Read or Write command from the system, it compares the current location information to the track number specified by the command. The controller decides which direction the head must be moved, issues a direction signal to the drive on its **direction** line, and begins producing step pulses on its **step** line. Each step pulse causes the drive unit to move the R/W heads over one track, in the direction specified by the direction signal. When the value of the present location matches the track number that was specified for the Read or Write operation, the step-pulses stop and the R/W heads settle over the desired track. The positioning of the R/W heads is illustrated in Figure 4-7.

**Figure 4-7:
A Track-Seek Operation**

Write Operations

When the system wants to send data to the disk drive for storage, it sends a **Write command** to the drive. But first, it performs a lookup operation on the drive's FAT to determine where to store the data. It then performs a track-seek operation to position the R/W heads over the designated track. When the head is over the track, the controller begins looking for the proper sector by reading the sector headers as they pass by. Once the sector is found, the controller changes from Read to Write operation and data serialization/transfer begins.

The drive controller requests a byte of data (DREQ) from the DMA controller, which places the byte on the data bus, and also sends a DACK signal to the disk controller. The disk controller obtains the byte from the data bus, encodes it into the proper form, and applies it to the R/W head, as illustrated in Figure 4-8.

If the data from the computer requires more than one sector to be written, as it usually does, these logically related sectors typically are not located sequentially on the disk. When data is transferred a block at a time, some time will be required to process each sector of data. In order to give the drive time to process the information, logically sequential sectors are **interleaved** (separated) by a fixed number of other sectors. This way, the motion of the disk is moving the second sector into position to be written (or read), while the drive is processing the previous sector of information. A common interleaving factor is 8 sectors between logically related sectors on a floppy drive, a factor of 3 on older hard disk systems, and a factor of 1 on newer systems.

Figure 4-8: Data Transfers

Read Operations

Read operation

When a **Read operation** is performed, the operating system examines the disk's directory to get the starting track/sector address of the data to be read. This address is loaded into the disk controller and a track-seek operation is performed. The R/W heads are stepped to the desired track and the designated head is enabled. After a few milliseconds delay to permit the R/W head to settle precisely over the track, the operating system gives the disk controller the command to Read the desired sector. The controller begins reading the sector ID headers, looking for the assigned sector.

When the sector is identified, the preamble is read and the controller synchronizes its operation with the incoming bit stream from the disk drive. At the beginning of the sector's data field, a data start marker coordinates the first bit of the first data byte with the controller's operation. At this point, the controller begins dividing the incoming bit stream into bytes for transmission to the system. The transfer may continue over multiple sectors or tracks until an end-of-file marker is encountered, indicating that the entire file has been transferred.

Figure 4-9 depicts the process of a typical disk drive Read operation.

**Figure 4-9:
The Read
Operation**

FLOPPY-DISK DRIVES

The discussion of general disk drive operations applies to both hard and floppy drives alike. However, the physical construction and operation of the drives are quite different. The FDD is an exposed unit, with an opening in the front to allow the floppy disk to be inserted and removed. In addition, the R/W heads are open to the atmosphere, and ride directly on the surface of the disk. Modern 3-1/2" floppy-disk drives have ejection buttons that kick the disk out of the drive when they are pushed. Table 4-1 provides a comparison of the two different formats used with 3-1/2" floppy drives.

**Table 4-1: FDD
Disk Parameters**

DIAMETER	DENSITY	CAPACITY	TRACK	SECTORS
3 ½"	DD	720 kB	80	9
3 ½"	HD	1.44 MB	80	18

Data moves back and forth between the system's RAM memory and the floppy disk surface. Along the way, it passes from the system RAM, to the **Floppy-Disk Controller (FDC)**, through the floppy drive signal cable, and into the floppy drive's analog control board. The analog control board converts the data into signals that can be applied to the drive's Read/Write heads, which in turn produce the magnetic spots on the disk surface.

In the original PCs and XTs, the FDC circuitry was located on an FDD controller card. In AT-compatible systems, it migrated onto a Multi I/O card along with parallel, serial, game, and HDD control ports. With ATX systems, all of this circuitry has been integrated into the system board. The circuitry on the floppy drive unit is usually distributed between two printed circuit boards: the analog control board and the drive's spindle motor control board.

Under direction of the operating system, the FDC divides the 3-1/2" floppy disk into 80 tracks per side, with nine or eighteen 512-byte sectors per track. This provides the system with 737,280 (720 kB) or 1,474,560 (1.44 MB) total bytes of storage on each disk. Table 4-2 lists the operating specifications for a typical 3-1/2" floppy-disk drive unit.

DRIVE UNIT PART	DSSD	DSHD
Track	80	80
Heads	2	2
Sectors per Track	9	18
Bytes per Sector	512	512
Formatted Capacity	720 kB	1.44 MB
Unformatted Capacity	1 MB	2 MB
Rotational Speed (RPM)	300	300
Recording Density (bits/inch)	8717	17,432
Tracks per Inch	135	135
Transfer Rate Unformatted (kbps)	250	500

Table 4-2: FDD Drive Specifications

The FDC also supplies interface signals that permit it to be connected to microprocessor systems with or without DMA capabilities. In most systems, however, the FDC operates in conjunction with the system's DMA controller, and is assigned to the DRQ2 and DACK2 lines. In operation, the FDC presents a DRQ2 request for every byte of data to be transferred. In addition, the disk-drive controller is assigned to the IRQ6 line. The FDC generates an interrupt signal each time it receives a Read, Write, or Format command from the system unit. An interrupt will also be generated when the controller receives a Ready signal from one of the disk drive units.

Floppy Drive Cables

A single ribbon cable is used to connect the floppy drive to the system board's FDD adapter connector. Generally, the cable has two 34-pin, two-row BERG headers along its length. The other end of the cable terminates in a 34-pin, two-row BERG header. A small colored stripe normally runs along one edge of the cable, as illustrated in Figure 4-10. This is the **Pin #1 indicator stripe** that marks the side of the cable, which should be aligned with the #1 pin of the FDD connector and the disk drive's signal connector. The location of this pin is normally marked on the drive's printed-circuit board.

The floppy-disk drive connected to the 34-pin header at the end of the cable will be assigned the drive A designation by the system. A floppy drive connected to the edge connector in the middle of the cable will be designated as the B drive. A small twist of wires between the A and B connectors reroutes key lines that determine which drive is which.

The 34-pin interface connection enables the FDC to manage two floppy-disk drive units. Figure 4-11 depicts the connections between the disk drive adapter and the disk drives. The directions of signal flow between the drives and the adapter are indicated by the arrow-tips.

Figure 4-10: The FDD Signal Cable

Figure 4-11: FDD Cable Signal Definitions

SIGNAL NAME	ADAPTER PIN NUMBER
GROUND (ODD NUMBERS)	1-33
DENSITY SELECT	2
UNUSED	4, 6
INDEX	8
MOTOR ENABLE A	10
DRIVE SELECT B	12
DRIVE SELECT A	14
MOTOR ENABLE B	16
DIRECTION	18
STEP	20
WRITE DATA	22
WRITE ENABLE	24
TRACK 0	26
WRITE PROTECT	28
READ DATA	30
SELECT HEAD 1	32
DISK CHANGE	34

DISK DRIVE

MULTI I/O

HARD-DISK DRIVES

Modern PC systems feature hard drives with storage capacities that typically range well into the gigabyte (GB) of storage as standard equipment. Physically, the hard drive is organized as a stack of rigid disks that turn in unison on a common spindle and are accessed by a bank of coordinated read/write heads. Each surface is divided into tracks, which are, in turn, divided into sectors. Each disk possesses a matching set of tracks on the top and bottom of the disk.

The disks are stacked on top of each other and the R/W heads move in and out between them. Since there are matching tracks on the top and bottom of each disk in the stack, the HDD controller organizes them into cylinders. For example, cylinder 1 of a four-platter HDD would consist of track 1 of each disk surface. The cylinder concept is described in Figure 4-12.

The physical make-up of a hard disk system is depicted in Figure 4-13. It involves a controller (either on an I/O card, or built into the system board), one or more signal cables, a power cable, and a disk drive unit. In some cases, floppy- and hard-disk drive signal cables may look similar. However, there are some slight differences in their construction that prevent them from being compatible. Therefore, great caution must be used when installing these cables. Many skilled technicians have encountered problems by not paying attention to which type of cable they were installing with a particular type of drive.

Figure 4-12: HDD Cylinders

Figure 4-13: Components of the HDD System

The system's CMOS Setup holds the HDD configuration settings. As with other configuration settings, these must be set correctly for the installed drive. Typical HDD information required for the CMOS setup includes its capacity, number of cylinders, number of R/W heads, number of sectors/track, amount of precompensation, and the track number to be used as the landing zone for the R/W heads when the drive is shut down. In Pentium-class systems, the PnP BIOS and operating system work with the newer system-level drives to **auto-detect** the drive and supply its configuration information to the CMOS Setup utility. Otherwise, this information must be obtained from the drive manufacturer, or a third-party maintenance. Table 4-3 shows typical HDD format information associated with a particular BIOS. Systems using other BIOS may have different values. Most BIOS tables also provide a user-definable HDD entry, where the values can be entered manually into the CMOS settings.

auto-detect

Table 4-3: Typical HDD Format Values

CYLINDERS	HEADS	WRITE-PRECOMPENSATE	CAPACITY
306	4	128	11
615	4	300	21
615	6	300	32
940	8	512	65
940	6	512	49
615	4	65535	21
462	8	256	32
733	5	65535	32
900	15	65535	118
820	3	65535	21
855	5	65535	37
855	7	65535	52
306	8	128	21
733	7	65535	45
*	*	*	*
612	4	*	21
977	5	300	43
977	7	65535	60
1024	7	512	62
733	5	300	32
733	7	300	45
733	5	300	32
306	4	*	11
925	7	*	56
925	9	65535	72
754	7	754	46
754	11	65535	72
699	7	256	43
823	10	65535	72
918	7	918	56
1024	11	65535	98
1024	15	65535	134
1024	5	1024	45
612	2	128	11
1024	9	65535	80
1024	8	512	71
615	8	128	43
987	3	987	26
987	7	987	60
820	6	820	43
977	5	977	43
981	5	981	43
830	7	512	51
830	10	65535	72
917	15	65535	120
1224	15	65535	160
16383	16	0	8456

The other important hard-disk drive specifications to consider are access time, seek time, data transfer rate, and storage capacity. These quantities designate how much data the drive can hold, how fast it can get to a specific part of the data, and how fast it can move it to the system.

Hard Drive Preparation

Unlike floppy drives, which basically come in four accepted formats, hard-disk drives are created in a wide variety of storage capacities. When the drive is created, its surface is electronically blank. To prepare the disk for use by the system, three levels of preparation must take place. These are, in order, the **low-level format,** the **partition**, and the **high-level format**.

A low-level format is very similar to a land developer sectioning off a field for a new housing development. The process begins with surveying the property, and placing markers for key structures such as roads, water lines, and electrical service. The low-level format routine is similar in that it marks off the disk into cylinders and sectors, and defines their placement on the disk. **System-level drive** types, such as IDE and SCSI drives, come with the low-level format already performed. Therefore, they do not require any low-level formatting from the user.

Attempts to perform low-level formats on IDE and SCSI drives may result in damage to the drive. This is not physical damage, but the loss of prerecorded bad track and sector information that would occur during a low-level format. The drive also contains alignment information used to control the R/W heads for proper alignment over the tracks. This alignment information would also be lost during a low-level format. If this occurs, it will normally be necessary that the drive be sent to the manufacturer to restore this information to the disk.

low-level format
partition
high-level format

System-level drive

Logical and Physical Drives

Before a disk drive can have a high-level format applied to it so that it can be used to perform useful functions for the system, the drive must be partitioned. **Partitioning** is the practice of dividing a physical drive into multiple logical storage areas and then treating each area as if it were a separate disk drive. This is normally done for purposes of organization and increased access speeds. However, drives may also be partitioned to enable multiple operating systems to exist on the same physical drive.

Partitioning

For example, the disk management capabilities of the oldest versions of MS-DOS (2.x, 3.x) imposed a limit on the size of a drive at 32 MB, which was huge at the time. However, as HDD technology steadily advanced, the capacities of the physical drives being produced eventually passed this limit. Fortunately, disk operating systems already had the ability to partition large physical drives into multiple logical drives. When this is done in the Microsoft operating system environment, each logical drive is assigned a different drive letter (such as C, D, E, and so on) to identify it to the system.

Figure 4-14 illustrates the concept of creating multiple **logical drives** on a single physical hard drive.

logical drives

Figure 4-14: Partitions on an HDD

Consumer-based Microsoft operating systems (i.e., MS-DOS and Windows 3.x up through Windows Me) have provided for two partitions on a physical hard-disk drive. The first partition is referred to as the **primary partition** and must be created on the disk first. After the primary partition has been established and properly configured, an additional partition referred to as an **extended partition** can be created on any unused disk space that remains. In addition, the extended partition may be subdivided into 23 logical drives (the letters of the alphabet minus a, b, and c). These drives are dependent on the extended partition, so it cannot be deleted if logical drives have been defined within it.

When the primary partition is created on a hard disk, a special table is created in its master boot sector called the **partition table**. This table is used to store information about the partitions and logical drives on the disk. It includes information about where each partition and logical drive begins and ends on the physical drive. This is expressed in terms of beginning and ending track numbers. Each time a logical drive is added to the system, a complete disk structure, including a boot sector and preliminary directory management structure, is created. Its beginning and ending locations are also recorded in the partition table when the new drive is created.

The table also includes a setting that identifies the partition or logical drive that is **active**. The active partition is the logical drive that the system will boot to. On a partitioned drive, only one logical drive can be active at a time. When the system checks the drive's master boot sector looking for an MBR during bootup, it encounters the partition table and checks it to determine which portion of the disk has been marked as active. With this information, the system jumps to the first track of the active partition and checks its boot sector for a **partition boot record** (an MBR for that partition). If an operating system has been installed in this partition, the boot sector will contain an MBR for it and the system will use it to boot up with. This arrangement enables a single physical disk to hold different operating systems that the system can boot to.

Most PCs can have multiple physical hard-disk drive units installed in them. In a system using a Microsoft operating system, the primary partition is on the first disk drive designated as drive C. The system files must be located in this partition, and the partition must be set to Active for the system to boot up from the drive.

In local and wide area networks, the concept of logical drives is carried a step further. A particular hard-disk drive may be a logical drive in a large system of drives along a peer-to-peer network. On the other hand, a very large centralized drive may be used to create several logical drives for a server/client type of network. Local area networks are covered in detail in Chapter 5 — *Data Communications*.

primary partition

extended partition

partition table

active

partition boot record

The partitioning program for MS-DOS, Windows 9x, and Windows Me is named **FDISK**. The FDISK utility in MS-DOS version 4.0 raised the maximum size of a logical drive to 128 MB, and version 5.0 raised it to 528 MB. The FDISK utility in Windows 9x provided upgraded support for very large hard drives. The original version of Windows 95 set a size limit for logical drives at 2 GB. The FDISK version in the upgraded OSR2 version of Windows 95 extended the maximum partition size to 8 GB.

FDISK

In Windows NT the partitioning process is performed through the **Disk Administrator** utility. In Windows 2000 and Windows XP, this function is performed using the **Disk Management** utility. These utilities perform all of the basic functions that the FDISK utility does. For instance, both utilities can be used to partition drives and both will show you the basic layout of the system's disks, including:

Disk Administrator

Disk Management

- The size of each disk

- The size and file system type used in each logical drive

- The size and location of any unformatted (free) space on the drive

However, these advanced disk utilities can also provide many advanced functions associated with enterprise (large-scale business-oriented) computing systems. The Disk Administrator and Disk Management utilities can be used to create both traditional primary and extended partitions for Windows NT/2000/XP systems. They can also be used to create **volumes** (partitions that involve space on multiple physical drives) like those shown in Figure 4-15. The subject of volumes is addressed in greater detail when we discuss RAID systems later in this chapter.

volumes

Figure 4-15: Volume Types

When newer operating system versions provided for partitions larger than 528 MB, another limiting factor for the size of disk partitions was encountered — the BIOS. The original AT-compatible BIOS featured a 504 MB capacity limit. To overcome this, newer BIOS include enhanced modes that employ special **Logical Block Addressing (LBA)** techniques to utilize the larger partition sizes available through newer operating systems. This technique — known as **Enhanced Cylinder, Heads, Sectors (ECHS)** — effectively increases the number of R/W heads the system can recognize from 16 to 256. The maximum allowable disk drive parameters of 1,024 cylinders, 63 sectors/track, and 512 bytes/sector remained unchanged.

Logical Block Addressing (LBA)

Enhanced Cylinder, Heads, Sectors (ECHS)

The high-level format procedure is performed by the operating system and fills in or recreates the preliminary logical structures on the logical drive during the partitioning process. These structures tell the system what files are in the logical disk and where they can be found. In MS-DOS and Windows 9x systems, the format process creates **File Allocation Table (FAT)** and **root directory** structures for the partition. In the case of Windows NT, Windows 2000, and Windows XP, the format operation may produce FATs and root directories, or it may produce more flexible **Master File Table (MFT)** structures. Chapter 8 provides more detailed information about the organization of disks, including FATs, MFTs, and directory structures.

CD-ROM Drives

Data is written on a CD digitally on a light-sensitive material by a powerful, highly focused laser beam.

The writing laser is pulsed with the modulated data to be stored on the disc. When the laser is pulsed, a microscopic blister is burned into the optical material, causing it to reflect light differently from the material around it. The blistered areas are referred to as **pits**, while the areas between them are called **lands**. Figure 4-16 illustrates the writing of data on the optical disc.

The recorded data is read from the disc by scanning it with a lower-power, continuous laser beam. The laser diode emits the highly focused, narrow beam that is reflected back from the disc. The reflected beam passes through a prism, and is bent 90 degrees, where it is picked up by the diode detector and converted into an electrical signal. Only the light reflected from a land on the disc is picked up by the detector. Light that strikes a pit is scattered and is not detected. The lower power level used for reading the disc ensures that the optical material is not affected during the read operation.

With an audio CD, the digital data retrieved from the disk is passed through a digital-to-analog converter (DAC) to reproduce the audio sound wave. However, this is not required for digital computer systems, since the information is already in a form acceptable to the computer. Therefore, CD players designed for use in computer systems are referred to as **CD-ROM drives**, to differentiate them from audio CD players. Otherwise, the mechanics of operation are very similar between the two devices.

Figure 4-16: Writing on a CD-ROM Drive

CD-ROM Discs

A typical CD-ROM disc is 4.7 inches in diameter, and consists of three major parts:

- acrylic substrate
- aluminized, mirror-finished data surface
- lacquer coating

The scanning laser beam comes up through the disc, strikes the aluminized data surface, and is reflected back. Since there is no physical contact between the reading mechanism and the disc, the disc never wears out. This is one of the main advantages of the CD system. The blisters on the data surface are typically just under 1 micrometer in length, and the tracks are 1.6 micrometers apart. The data is encoded by the length and spacing of the blisters, and the lands between them. This concept is illustrated in Figure 4-17.

Figure 4-17: Encoding Data on a CD-ROM

The information on a compact disc is stored in one continuous **spiral track**, unlike floppy disks, where the data is stored in multiple, concentric tracks. The compact disc storage format still divides the data into separate sectors. However, the sectors of a CD-ROM disc are physically the same size. The disc spins counterclockwise, and it slows down as the laser diode emitter/detector unit approaches the outside of the disc.

The disc begins spinning at approximately 500 RPM at its inner edge and slows down to about 200 RPM at its outer edge. The spindle motor controls the speed of the disc, so that the track is always passing the laser at between 3.95 and 4.6 feet per second. Therefore, CD-ROM drives must have a variable-speed spindle motor, which cannot just be turned on and off like a floppy drive's spindle motor. The variable speed of the drive allows the disc to contain more sectors, thereby giving it a much larger storage capacity. In fact, the average storage capacity of a CD-ROM disc is about 680 MB.

CD Writers

Another type of CD drive is a **Write Once, Read Many (WORM) drive**. As the acronym implies, these drives allow users to write information to the disc once, and then retrieve this information as you would with a CD-ROM drive. Once information is stored on a WORM drive, the data cannot be changed or deleted.

CD Writer technology has developed to the point where it is inexpensive enough to be added to CD-ROM drives used in typical PC systems. CD Writers record data on blank **CD-Recordable (CD-R)** discs. A CD-R is a *Write Once, Read Many* media that is generally available in 120 mm and 80 mm sizes. The drives are constructed using a typical 5.25" half-height drive form factor. This form factor is convenient in that it fits into a typical PC drive bay. The CD-R technology has continued to evolve into a recordable, ReWritable compact disc, called a **CD-RW disc**. These discs can be recorded, erased, and rewritten just like a floppy disk.

The physical construction of the CD-R disc is considerably different than that of the CD-ROM disc. The writable disc is constructed as described in Figure 4-18. The CD-R disc is created by coating a transparent polycarbonate substrate with an opaque polymer dye. The dye is covered with a thin layer of gold and topped with a protective lacquer layer and a label. The CD-R writing mechanism is not as strong as that of a commercial CD-ROM duplicator. Instead of burning pits into the substrate of the disc, the CD writer uses a lower-power laser to discolor the dye material.

Figure 4-18:
Writable CD-R Disc

The CD-R disc format is identical to that of a CD-ROM and information written on it can be read by a typical CD-ROM drive. The spiral track formation and sectoring are the same as those used with CD-ROM discs. In addition, the CD writer can produce recordings in the standard CD book formats (i.e., Red, Yellow, Orange, and Green).

During the write operation, the CD Writer uses a medium-intensity laser to write the data on the thermally sensitive media. The laser light is applied to the bottom side of the disc. It passes through the substrate to the reflective layer and is reflected back through the substrate. The light continues through the drive's optics system until it reaches the laser detector.

When the polymer is exposed to the light of the writing laser, it heats up and becomes transparent. This exposes the reflective gold layer beneath the polymer. During readback, the reflective layer reflects more light than the polymer material does. The transitions between lighter and darker areas of the disc are used to encode the data.

CD writers are typically able to write to the CD-R at either 4x or 8x CD speeds. These settings have nothing to do with playback speeds. CD-RW drives are specified in a Record x Write-once x Rewrite speed format (e.g., a 32 x 8 x 4 CD-RW can read at 32x, write at 8x, and rewrite at 4x speeds).

Digital Versatile Discs

DVD drives and discs are identical in form factor and appearance with CD-ROM drives and discs. As a matter of fact, DVD drives are backward compatible with old CD-ROM discs and newer DVD drives can be used to read CD-R and CD-RW discs. The discs are inserted into the front of the unit just like CD-ROM discs. The drive's circuitry senses the type of disc being used and automatically adjusts for it.

Within the DVD specification, there are several disc types that are associated with different DVD standards. These include:

- **DVD Recordable (DVD-R)** and **(DVD+R)** — Separate recordable DVD formats where the media can only be used to record data once and then the data becomes permanent on the disc. The disc cannot be recorded onto a second time.

- **DVD Rewritable (DVD-RW)** and **(DVD+RW)** — Separate re-recordable DVD formats where data on the disc can be erased and recorded over numerous times.

- **DVD-RAM** — A specialized DVD format where the media can be recorded and erased repeatedly. The DVD-RAM specification is nonstandard, so DVD-RAM discs can only be used with drives manufactured by the companies that support the format.

There are two variations of the DVD-R disc — DVD-RG and DVD-RA. The DVD-RG designation is associated with general-use media, and the DVD-RA standard is provided for authoring and mastering DVD video and data. DVD-RA media is generally not available for general use. The DVD-RAM format supports 2.6 GB of storage per disc, and the DVD-RW standards supports 3.0 GB per disc.

DVD Recordable (DVD-R) and (DVD+R)

DVD Rewritable (DVD-RW) and (DVD+RW)

DVD-RAM

HDD Interfaces

For the most part, all PCs employ one of two standard system-level interface types to communicate with their internal disk drive systems. These two system-level interface types are — **Integrated Drive Electronics (IDE)** and **Small Computer System Interface (SCSI)**. Both interfaces place most of the controller circuitry on the drive itself. Therefore, the system sees the entire HDD system as an attachment to its bus systems. These units come with the low-level format already in place.

Integrated Drive Electronics (IDE)

Small Computer System Interface (SCSI)

host adapter cards

In pre-Pentium systems, the SCSI and IDE drives employed **host adapter cards** that plugged into the system board's expansion slots. They are referred to as host adapters because most of the interface's control circuitry is actually on the drive — therefore, calling the card a controller would be incorrect.

In the Pentium environment, the IDE host adapter function has been integrated into the system board. Therefore, the IDE interface connectors are located on the system board. Typical PC system boards include two physical IDE connectors that represent two IDE channels. SCSI systems continue to use host adapter cards as their interface connectors. The host adapter provides a BERG pin connector for the system's internal SCSI ribbon cable. However, there are many versions of the SCSI standard and several types of SCSI connecting cables.

There are also two versions of the IDE interface: the original IDE specification and a newer Enhanced IDE, or EIDE standard. The EIDE interface has been redefined to allow faster transfer rates, as well as the handling of more storage capacity. It can also be used to control drive units such as a tape or CD-ROM. The EIDE interface is often described as an **ATAPI (AT Attachment Packet Interface)**, or a **Fast ATA (Fast AT Attachment)** interface. These standards are described in the "Installing and Configuring Disk Drives" section, presented later in this chapter.

ATAPI (AT Attachment Packet Interface)

Fast ATA (Fast AT Attachment)

External disk drive systems typically use SCSI interfaces, advanced buses (such as USB), or networks to communicate with the system.

CD-ROM/DVD Interfaces

With as many speed choices as there are, there are also several choices of architectures for CD-ROM drives. The choices include:

- SCSI interfaces
- IDE/EIDE interfaces
- USB interfaces
- IEEE-1394 interfaces
- proprietary interfaces

An internal SCSI CD-ROM drive must be capable of connecting to the type of SCSI cable being used. The SCSI interface that employs a Centronics-type connector is the most widely used method for connecting external CD-ROM drives to systems.

Controllers for proprietary interfaces are often included with the drive or with a sound card. To gain full advantage of a CD-ROM, it's essential to also have a sound card. Many sound cards include a CD-ROM drive interface as an integral part of their designs. However, these controllers may not be IDE or SCSI compatible. They often contain proprietary interfaces that work with only a few CD-ROM models.

Tape Drives

Tape drives

capstan

Tape drives are available in a variety of types and configurations. Tape drives intended for desktop computers are available in both 5-1/4" and 3-1/2" drive form factors. These units are designed for mounting inside the system unit as part of the system's permanent drive capabilities.

Removable tape cartridges like the one depicted in Figure 4-19 are inserted into the front of the drive and locked into place by an internal mechanism. The drive's R/W heads access the tape through an opening in the front of the cartridge. Likewise, a **capstan** in the drive is used to turn a drive wheel inside the cartridge, which in turn moves both tape spools simultaneously.

The drive also has a sensor, which detects the position of the tape's Write-Protect switch. This switch disables the drive's write circuitry so that important data on the tape cannot be written over by mistake.

Figure 4-19: Data Storage Cartridge

With the exception of their front panels, internally mounted tape drives share a great deal of their form with internal floppy and hard drive units. They feature a signal interface connection to connect them to their controller and standard options power supply connectors that deliver power to the drive.

Internal tape drives are available for most of the standard drive interface types (i.e., floppy drive connection as well as IDE and internal SCSI buses). In many cases, tape drives are supplied with proprietary controller cards that plug into one of the system's expansion slots. Other older models are even capable of using the system's B: drive floppy connection as their interface connection.

For portable systems, tape drives are designed as external units that connect to one of the portable's external port or bus connections. These units typically employ one of the PC's standard I/O port or extension bus connections to communicate with the system (i.e., external SCSI, USB, or IEEE-1394 buses). These units usually include an external housing for aesthetic purposes. They also normally derive power independently from the host computer through their own detachable power pack unit.

Because tape drives are not considered standard PC peripherals, they are not directly supported by the available operating systems. These operating systems support the bus or port operation, but not the drive. However, the Backup utility in newer versions of Windows will treat tape drives as another storage device after their drivers have been installed.

Tape drive manufacturers normally supply device drivers for their own tape drives. In most cases, the entire application software package for the tape drive is provided by the manufacturer. These packages are installed in the same manner as any other application package.

Tape Standards

As more users employed tape as a backup media, standards for tape systems were formed. The most widely-used tape standard is the **Quarter Inch Cartridge (QIC)** standard. This standard calls for a tape cartridge like the one depicted in Figure 4-20. Its physical dimensions are 6"x 4"x 5/8". The cartridge has a head access door in the front that swings open when it is inserted into the drive unit.

Quarter Inch Cartridge (QIC)

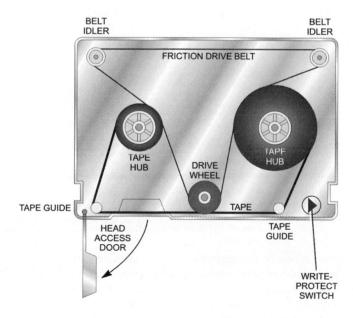

Figure 4-20: A 1/4" Tape Cartridge

Unlike audio cassette tapes, cartridge tapes are not driven by capstans that extend through their tape spools. Instead, they employ a belt drive system that loops through the cartridge and turns both spools synchronously. The belt is driven by a rubber drive wheel, which in turn is driven by the capstan. This design provides smoother, more precise operation than the audio cassette is capable of.

The R/W heads magnetize the tape as it passes by, in much the same manner as described for other magnetic storage media. The data is placed on the tape serially as it moves past the head. The tape is organized into sectors of data, separated by inter-gap blocks. The data can be applied in parallel tracks (using multiple R/W heads) in a continuous stream of data (streaming tape systems), or in a serpentine manner, where the data is applied to the tape in one direction for odd tracks, and in the other direction for even tracks.

Magnetic tape must be formatted before use, just like a magnetic disk. In the formatting process, the controller marks the tape off into sectors. In addition, it establishes a file allocation table in its header, similar to that of a floppy or hard disk. The header also contains a bad-sector table to prevent defective areas of the tape from being used. Some of the tape is devoted to the error-detection and correction information that must be used with tape systems.

Cartridge tapes formerly were referred to as DC-6000 style tapes. Their model numbers would normally include a reference to their tape capacity as the last digits (e.g., DC-6200 would be a 200 MB tape). As the cartridge tape industry matured, manufacturers came together to establish standards for tape formats and labeling. In the process, the DC-6000 number has been replaced in discussions about capacity and format.

For the most part, a series of QIC numbers have been used to describe different tape cartridges. Table 4-4 provides a sample list of QIC standard numbers.

Table 4-4: QIC Standard Numbers

SPECIFICATION	TRACKS	CAPACITY	CARTRIDGE
QIC-02	9	60 MB	DC-3000
QIC-24	9	60 MB	DC-6000
QIC-40	20	40 MB	DC-2000
QIC-80	32	80 MB	DC-2000
QIC-100	12 / 24	100 MB	DC-2000
QIC-150	18	250 MB	DC-6000
QIC-1000	30	1.0 GB	DC-6000
QIC-1350	30	1.35 GB	DC-6000
QIC-2100	30	2.1 GB	DC-6000

minicartridge

A **minicartridge** version of the quarter-inch tape cartridge, with dimensions of 3-1/4"x 2-1/2"x 5/8", has been developed to provide a more compact form factor to fit in 3-1/2" drive bays. The internal operation of the cartridge has remained the same, but the amount of tape inside has been reduced. The reduced amount of tape in the cartridge is offset by the use of more advanced data-encoding schemes that store more data on less tape. Minicartridges are referred to as DC-2000 style cartridges. Like the DC-6000 tapes, the DC-2000 model numbers will normally include a reference to their tape capacity as the last digits.

A number of QIC tape standards have developed over time. The original QIC standard was QIC-40. This standard called for a unit that could be connected to a floppy-disk drive interface so that it acted like a large drive B:. It specified a 20-track format, with each track consisting of 68 segments, having 29 sectors of 1024 bytes each. This format provided 40 MB of data storage. The specification treated the tape's sectors like the sectors of a floppy disk in that they were organized into files.

An updated QIC-80 specification was developed to replace the QIC-40 standard. Advanced R/W head designs enable the QIC-80 to place 32 tracks on the tape instead of 20. Coupled together with improved data-per-inch storage capabilities, the total capacity of the cartridge was boosted to 80 MB. The QIC-80 systems included data compression software that could effectively double the capacity of the drive from its stated value.

The QIC-80 standard has been superseded by the QIC-500M format, which allows for up to 500 MB of data to be stored on the cartridge. Newer standards for tape drives continue to emerge. Specifications that depart from the floppy-disk drive interface and use the IDE or SCSI interfaces are producing data storage potentials into the multiple gigabyte range.

Newer digital tape standards have appeared in the personal computer market as the need to back up larger blocks of data has increased. The most noteworthy of these is the *Digital Audio Tape (DAT)* and the *Digital Linear Tape (DLT)* formats.

DAT Drives

The **Digital Audio Tape (DAT)** format has found little success in the public market for the storage of audio, but has found great success in the computer storage industry. The unique design of the DAT drive allows it to back up large volumes of data onto small tape cartridges.

When performing a restore with DAT drives, the backup software first reads the entire directory of the tape. It then winds the tape to the appropriate spot and reads the contents into the controller's buffer. The controller uses CRC code to make sure the information is correct. If an error is detected, the ECC can be used to fix them. Once the data has been verified as correct, the contents are written to the hard disk.

The most popular format for DAT today in terms of data storage is the **Digital Data Storage (DDS)** standard. Table 4-5 shows the different DDS standards and technical information. All of these standards are backward compatible.

STANDARD	CAPACITY	MAX DTR
DDS	2 GB	55 kBps
DDS-1	2/4 GB	0.55/1.1 MBps
DDS-2	4/8 GB	0.55/1.1 MBps
DDS-3	12/24 GB	1.1/2.2 MBps
DDS-4	20/40 GB	2.4/4.8 MBps

Digital Audio Tape (DAT)

Digital Data Storage (DDS)

Table 4-5: DDS Standards

The increased data storage capacity provided by DAT drives comes at a price. A DAT drive can easily cost nearly twice as much as a QIC drive. Also, DAT drives only employ SCSI interfaces. However, the additional cost associated with DAT tape may be well worth it when comparing the usability of the tapes.

DLT Drives

Digital Linear Tape (DLT)

Digital Linear Tape (DLT) drives use half-inch wide metal particle tapes. The media is 60% wider than 8 mm tape. Data is recorded on these tapes in a serpentine pattern on parallel tracks that run the entire length of the tape. When data is recorded, the first set of tracks is recorded along the whole length of the tape. After reaching the end of the tape the heads are repositioned to record a new set of tracks in the opposite direction. The process continues until the tape is full. A DLT drive is shown in Figure 4-21.

Figure 4-21: A DLT Drive

On a DLT drive, data is recorded and read using multiple parallel channels simultaneously. DLT technology segments tape media into parallel, horizontal tracks and records data by running the tape past a stationary head. Current products record two channels simultaneously using two read/write elements in the head, effectively doubling the transfer rate possible at a given drive speed and recording density.

Another measure of tape performance is the time required to locate a file. This criterion is especially important in near-line applications, such as image manipulation, that frequently search for files and append or restore data. DLT technology minimizes search time through a file mark index located at the logical end of the tape. Using this index, the drive "steps" to the track containing the file and performs a high-speed streaming search to the file. This feature enables DLT products to find any file in a 20-gigabyte capacity tape in an average of 45 seconds.

Table 4-6 gives some examples of some of the more common formats.

Table 4-6: Some More Common DLT Formats

TYPE	DISK SPACE PER TAPE (NATIVE/COMPRESSED)	DATA TRANSFER BANDWIDTH
DLT 2000	15 GBs/30 GBs	2.5 MB/sec
DLT 4000	20 GBs/40 GBs	3 MB/sec
DLT 7000	35 GBs/70 GBs	10 MB/sec

Super Digital Linear Tape (SuperDLT)

The **Super Digital Linear Tape (SuperDLT)** specification is a natural progression of the DLT standard, increasing its capacity as well as its transfer rates. The general properties are comparable to DLT, and are backward compatible with the DLT standard. Drives based on SuperDLT technology will far exceed the 35 GB native capacity of the DLT 7000 format and be backward compatible.

As Table 4-7 illustrates, the ultimate goal is to cram up to 1.2 TB of uncompressed data onto a single cartridge with uncompressed transfer rates rising to an eventual 100 MBps. Initial products, however, offer a more modest 110 GB with sustained data transfer rates of 11 MBps in native mode.

Table 4-7:
SDLT Standards

	SDLT 220	SDLT 320	SDLT 640	SDLT 1280	SDLT 2400
Native Capacity	110 GB	160 GB	320 GB	640 GB	1.2 TB
Compressed Capacity (2:1 compression)	220 GB	320 GB	640 GB	1.28TB	2.4 TB
Native DTR	11 MBps	16 MBps	32 MBps	50+ MBps	100+ MBps
Compressed DTR	22 MBps	32 MBps	64 MBps	100+ MBps	200+ MBps
Interfaces	Ultra2 SCSI LVD HVD	Ultra2 SCSI Ultra160 SCSI	Ultra 320 SCSI Fiber channel	TBD	TBD

INSTALLING AND CONFIGURING DISK DRIVES

The A+ Core objective 1.6 states that the test taker should be able to identify proper procedures for installing and configuring common IDE/EIDE devices. Choose the appropriate installation or configuration sequences in given scenarios. Recognize the associated cables. Content may include the following:

- IDE Interface Types
  - EIDE
  - ATA/ATAPI
  - Serial ATA
  - PIO
- RAID (0, 1, and 5)
- Master/Slave/Cable Select
- Devices per channel
- Primary/Secondary
- Cable orientation requirements

Likewise, the A+ Core objective 1.6 states that the test taker should be able to identify proper procedures for installing and configuring common SCSI devices. Choose the appropriate installation or configuration sequences in given scenarios. Content may include the following:

- SCSI Interface Types
  - Narrow
  - Fast Wide
  - Wide Ultra
  - LVD
  - HVD
- Internal versus external
- SCSI IDs
  - Jumper block settings (binary equivalents)
  - Resolving ID conflicts
- RAID (0, 1, and 5)
- Cabling
  - Length
  - Type
  - Termination requirements (active, passive, auto)

Hard-disk drives are the mainstays of mass data storage in PC-compatible systems. In modern PC systems, IDE and SCSI drives are most commonly used. Therefore, the computer technician must be able to successfully install and configure both IDE and SCSI drives, as well as other devices that employ IDE and SCSI interfaces. The following sections of the chapter cover the characteristics of these two interfaces, including standard variations and common connector types associated with each.

Integrated Drive Electronics Interface

AT Attachment (ATA)

The Integrated Drive Electronics (IDE) interface, also referred to as an **AT Attachment (ATA)** interface, is a system-level interface designed to connect disk drive units to the system. The IDE interface places most of the controller electronics on the drive unit. Therefore, data travels in parallel between the computer and the drive unit. The controller circuitry on the drive handles all of the parallel-to-serial and serial-to-parallel conversions. This permits the interface to be independent of the host computer design.

An IDE drive stores low-level formatting information on itself. This information is placed on the drive by its manufacturer, and is used by the controller for alignment and sector sizing of the drive. The IDE controller extracts the raw data (format and actual data information) coming from the R/W heads and converts it into signal that can be applied to the computer's buses.

host adapter

The IDE interface uses a single 40-pin cable to connect the hard drive to the adapter card or system board. Its signal cable arrangement is depicted in Figure 4-22. In a system-level interface, the I/O card that plugs into the expansion slot is called a **host adapter** instead of a controller card. It should be apparent from the figure that the IDE host adapter is quite simple, since most of the interface signals originate directly from the system's extended bus lines.

34-PIN SIGNAL CABLE				CONNECTOR ENDS	20-PIN DATA CABLE			
Pin	Description	Pin	Description		Pin	Description	Pin	Description
1	Ground	2	Reduced Write Current		1	DRV SLCTD	2	Ground
3	Ground	4	Head Select 4		3	Reserved	4	Ground
5	Ground	6	Write Gate		5	Reserved	6	Ground
7	Ground	8	Seek Complete		7	Reserved	8	Ground
9	Ground	10	Track 00		9	Reserved	10	Reserved
11	Ground	12	Write Fault		11	Ground	12	Ground
13	Ground	14	Head Select 1		13	Mfm WR Data	14	Mfm Write Data
15	Ground	16	Reserved		15	Ground	16	Reserved
17	Ground	18	Head Select 2		17	Mfm RD Data	18	Mfm Read Data
19	Ground	20	Index		19	Ground	20	Ground
21	Ground	22	Ready					
23	Ground	24	Step					
25	Ground	26	Drive Select 1					
27	Ground	28	Drive Select 2					
29	Ground	30	Drive Select 3					
31	Ground	32	Drive Select 4					
33	Ground	34	Direction In					

Figure 4-22:
The IDE Signal Cable

Configuring IDE Drives

The IDE/EIDE interface has been the standard PC disk drive interface for some time. The IDE controller structure is an integrated portion of most PC system boards. This structure includes BIOS and chipset support for the IDE version the board will support, as well as the IDE host connector.

┌─ **TEST TIP** ─────────────────────┐

Remember that IDE bus driver support is built into the BIOS of system boards that have integrated IDE host adapters.
└────────────────────────────────────┘

The host adapter basically serves three functions. These include providing the select signals to differentiate between a **single-drive** system, or the **master** and **slave** drives. It also provides the 3 least significant address bits (A0-A2), and the interface Reset signal. The HDCS0 signal is used to enable the master drive, and the HDCS1 signal is used to enable the slave drive. The relationships between the host adapter, the system buses, and the IDE interfaces are described in Figure 4-23.

single-drive

master

slave

┌─ **TEST TIP** ─────────────────────┐

Remember the three configurations that can be set on an IDE drive.
└────────────────────────────────────┘

Figure 4-23: The Host Adapter, System Buses, and IDE Interface

MASTER (1 DRIVE)
DXX
DCF
CSEL
-C/D
1 2

SLAVE
DXX
DCF
CSEL
-C/D
1 2

CABLE (SELECT)
DXX
DCF
CSEL
-C/D
1 2

8-PIN USER CONFIGURATION JUMPER BLOCK

Figure 4-24: IDE Master/Slave Setting

Most IDE drives come from the manufacturer configured for operation as a single drive, or as the master drive in a multi-drive system. In order to install the drive as a second, or slave, drive, it is usually necessary to install, remove, or move a jumper block, as illustrated in Figure 4-24. Some hosts disable the interface's Cable Select pin for slave drives. With these types of hosts, it is necessary to install a jumper for the *Cable Select* option on the drive. Consult the system's user's manual to see if it supports this function.

In the MS-DOS system, the primary partitions of multiple IDE hard drives are assigned the first logical drive identifiers. If an IDE drive is partitioned into two logical drives, the system will identify them as drives C: and D:. If a second IDE drive is added as a slave drive with two additional logical drives, MS-DOS will reassign the partitions on the first drive to be logical drives C: and E:, and the partitions on the slave drive will be D: and F:.

CHALLENGE #1

You are installing IDE drives in a new system. The buyers want to include a large HDD, a standard CD-ROM drive and a rewritable CD-ROM drive. Their company needs to have Windows 2000 and MS-DOS operating systems on the machine, so they want you to divide the hard drive into two equal sized drives. You connect the hard drive to the system board's IDE1 connector and the two CD-ROM drives to the cable connected to its IDE2 connector. How will their drive-specific MS-DOS programs need to be configured if DOS is placed on the drive's extended partition?

Advanced EIDE Specifications

As mentioned earlier in this chapter, there are a variety of IDE-related specifications. The initial IDE standard was the IDE/ATA specification. (IDE and ATA are the same standard.) It supported a maximum throughout of 8.3 MBps through the 40-pin IDE signal cable.

Enhanced IDE (EIDE)

ATA-2

AT Attachment Packet Interface (ATAPI)

Updated IDE specifications have been developed to enable more than two drives to exist on the interface. This new IDE specification is called **Enhanced IDE (EIDE)**, or the **ATA-2** interface. The new standard actually includes the ATA-2/EIDE/ATAPI specifications (the ATAPI standard is a derivative of the ATA-2 standard). The **AT Attachment Packet Interface (ATAPI)** specification provides improved IDE drivers for use with CD-ROM drives and new data transfer methods. This specification provides maximum throughput of 16.7 MBps through the 40-pin IDE signal cable.

The ATA standards provide for different **Programmed I/O (PIO)** modes that offer higher performance capabilities, as illustrated in Table 4-8. Most IDE devices are now capable of operating in modes 3 or 4. However, the IDE port must be attached to the PCI bus to use these modes. Some system boards only place the IDE1 connection on this bus, while the IDE2 connection is a function of the ISA bus. In these cases, devices installed on the IDE2 connector will only be capable of mode-2 operation.

Programmed I/O (PIO)

PIO MODE	TRANSFER	ATA VERSION
0	3.3 MB/sec	ATA-1
1	5.2 MB/sec	ATA-1
2	8.3 MB/sec	ATA-1
3	11.1 MB/sec	ATA-2
4	16.6 MB/sec	ATA-2
4	33.3 MB/sec	ATA-3/Ultra DMA 33
4	66.6 MB/sec	ATA-4/Ultra DMA 66
4	100 MB/sec	ATA 100

**Table 4-8:
ATA PIO Modes**

An additional development of the ATA standard has provided the ATA-3/Ultra ATA 33 specification that boosts throughput between the IDE device and the system to 33.3 MBps. This standard still employs the 40-pin IDE signal cable. It relies on the system to support the 33.3 MBps burst mode transfer operation through the **Ultra DMA (UDMA)** protocol.

Ultra DMA (UDMA)

Newer IDE enhancements called ATA-4/Ultra ATA 66 and Ultra ATA 100 provide even higher data throughput by doubling the number of conductors in the IDE signal cable. The IDE connector has remained compatible with the 40-pin IDE connection, but each pin has been provided with its own ground conductor in the cable. The Ultra ATA 66 specification provides 66 MBps and the Ultra ATA 100 connection provides 100 MBps.

Both Ultra ATA versions support 33.3 MBps data rates when used with a standard 40-pin/40-conductor IDE signal cable. Therefore, Ultra ATA 66 and 100 devices can still be used with systems that don't support the new IDE standards.

TEST TIP

Remember how the Ultra ATA 66 interface cable can be identified.

These operating modes must be configured correctly through the system's CMOS Setup Utility. These settings are discussed under the "Integrated Peripherals Setup Functions" heading as described in Chapter 2.

Serial ATA

The newest ATA implementation from the IDE development community is the **Serial ATA** standard. This interface standard has been developed to compete with other interface types that employ serial data transmission types. In the computer industry, there is a race starting between interface camps to be the only interface in the computer. For now, the participants in this race include the USB bus, the IEEE-1394 bus, the Serial ATA interface, and the latest SCSI interface, which we will cover in the next section of this chapter. These interfaces and buses in turn compete with the different types of local area networks. All of these interfaces are based on serial data transmission methods.

Modern serial transmission modes are fast and provide high performance. The serial ATA specification currently conducts transfers at up to 150 MBps using 250 mV differential signaling techniques. Serial ATA needs only two data channels — one for sending and one for receiving. The seven-wire data cable used with the serial ATA connection is considerably different from the traditional ribbon cables used with parallel interfaces. They are thin and flexible and their connectors are just 8 mm wide. These cables can range up to a meter in length, meaning that there is no problem connecting a disk drive that is mounted in the top bay of a large tower case.

So far, only PCI card mounted interfaces are available for the serial ATA interface. This restricts their maximum data transfer rate of 150 MBps to the 133 MBps that can be provided by the PCI bus. Therefore, the performance of the Serial ATA interface is no better than that of the more established UltraATA/100 and UltraATA/133 interfaces.

Small Computer System Interface

Small Computer System Interface (SCSI)
scuzzy
SCSI host adapter

The **Small Computer System Interface (SCSI)**, often referred to as the "**scuzzy**" standard, like the IDE concept, provides a true system-level interface for the drive. Nearly all of the drive's controller electronics are located on the peripheral device. As with the IDE host adapter, the duties of the **SCSI host adapter** are reduced to mostly physical connection functions, along with some signal compatibility handling.

With this arrangement, data arrives at the system interface in a form that is already usable by the host computer. This can be seen through the SCSI interface description in Figure 4-25. Note that the original SCSI interface described in the figure only makes provisions for 8-bit parallel data transfers.

Figure 4-25:
The SCSI Interface Connection

The SCSI interface can be used to connect diverse types of peripherals to the system. As an example, a SCSI chain could connect a controller to a hard drive, a CD-ROM drive, a high-speed tape drive, a scanner, and a printer. Additional SCSI devices are added to the system by daisy-chaining them together: The input of the second device is attached to the SCSI output of the first device, and so forth.

SCSI Specifications

The original **SCSI-1** specification established a data bus width of 8 bits and permitted up to 8 devices to be connected to the bus (including the controller). The maximum speed of the SCSI-1 bus is 5 MBps (1 byte x 5 MHz = 5 MBps.) The maximum recommended length for a complete standard SCSI chain is 20 feet (6 m). However, unless the cables are heavily shielded, they become susceptible to data corruption caused by induced noise. Therefore, a maximum single SCSI segment of less than 3 feet (1 m) is recommended. Don't forget the length of the internal cabling when dealing with SCSI cable distances. You can realistically count on about three feet of internal cable, so reduce the maximum total length of the chain to about 15 feet (4.5 m). This specification became known as Narrow SCSI.

An updated SCSI specification was developed by the ANSI committee to double the number of data lines in the standard interface to 16 bits (2 bytes). It also adds balanced, dual-line drivers that allow much faster data transfer speeds to be used. This implementation is referred to as **Wide SCSI-2**. The specification expands the SCSI specification into a 16/32-bit bus standard and increases the cable and connector specification to 68 pins. This enhancement enabled the SCSI bus to transfer data twice as fast (2 bytes x 5 MHz = 10 MBps).

Wide SCSI-2

A different improvement to the original specification increased the synchronous data transfer option for the 8-bit interface from 5 Mbps to 10 Mbps. This implementation became known as **Fast SCSI-2**. Under this system, the system and the I/O device conduct non-data message, command, and status operations in 8-bit asynchronous mode. After agreeing on a larger, or faster file-transfer format, they conduct transfers using an agreed-upon word size and transmission mode. As the speed of the bus was increased, it caused **cross talk** to occur earlier, which cut the maximum usable cable length in half (from 6 meters to 3 meters, or about 10 feet). Fast SCSI-2 connections use 50-pin connectors.

Fast SCSI-2

cross talk

A third version brought together both improvements and became known as **Wide Fast SCSI-2**. This version of the standard doubles the bus size to 16 bits and employs the faster transfer methods to provide a maximum bus speed of 20 MBps (2 bytes x 10 MHz = 20 MBps) supporting a chain of up to 15 additional devices. The maximum cable length is still specified at 3 meters because the bus can run at 10 MHz.

Wide Fast SCSI-2

After increasing the bus width of the SCSI-2 specification to 16 bits, the next step in the evolution of the specification was to speed up the bus again. The newer version, referred to as **Ultra SCSI** (ultra meaning ultra-fast), pushed the bus speed from 10 MHz to 20 MHz, using the original SCSI-1 interface. Naturally, this move increased the maximum transfer rate from 5 MBps to 20 MBps (1 byte x 20 MHz), but it also reduced the maximum useful cable length of 1.5 meters. This distance tends to physically limit the number of devices that you can attach to the cable; however, it is still suitable for most installations. The Ultra SCSI specification also makes provisions for a special high-speed serial transfer mode and special communications media, such as fiber-optic cabling.

Ultra SCSI

This update has been combined with both wide and fast revisions to produce:

- Ultra SCSI

- Ultra2 SCSI

- Wide Ultra SCSI

- Wide Ultra2 SCSI

- Wide Ultra3 SCSI

Of course, the next logical SCSI standard advancement was to once again increase the data bus width. This revision is called Wide Ultra SCSI. The addition of the Wide specification doubles the number of devices that can be serviced by the interface. Likewise, the Ultra designation indicates a speed increase due to improved technology. Combining the two technologies yielded a 4X increase in data throughput (i.e., Wide Ultra SCSI = 40 MBps compared to Ultra SCSI = 20 MBps and Wide and Fast SCSI = 10 MBps), while still keeping the cable length at 1.5 meters.

At this point, the SCSI development community could not increase the speed of the bus using the existing hardware interface. Increasing the speed again would limit the maximum cable length to the point where it would be unusable in the real world. To increase the bus speed to 40 MHz, the specification switched to Low-Voltage Differential (LVD) signaling techniques described later in this section.

Ultra2 SCSI

By employing LVD technology, the **Ultra2 SCSI** specification doubled the data throughput of the 8-bit SCSI bus (1 byte x 40 MHz = 40 MBps). However, the presence of the LVD technology enabled the maximum cable length for this specification to be increased to 12 meters. Single LVD devices connected solely to a single controller may use up to 25 meters of cable.

Wide Ultra2 SCSI

Quickly, the SCSI community mixed the LVD technology with the increased bus width of the Wide SCSI specification to produce **Wide Ultra2 SCSI**. This specification increased the maximum data throughput to 80 MBps (2 bytes x 40 MHz = 80 MBps), while the cable length remained at 12 meters.

Double Transition (DT) clocking

ULTRA160 SCSI

The next improvement to the SCSI technology was the introduction of **Double Transition (DT) clocking** techniques. DT clocking enabled an **ULTRA160 SCSI** controller to send data on both the rising and falling edges of its clock cycles. Although the bus width remained at 16 bits and the bus clock frequency stayed at 40 MHz, the new technique increased the maximum throughput to 160 MBps (2 bytes x 40 MHz x 2 =160 MBps). The maximum cable length also remained at 12 meters with the new specification, although the specifications for the cable type had to be made more stringent.

Ultra 320 SCSI

Single Connector Attachment (SCA)

The latest SCSI specification, referred to as **Ultra 320 SCSI**, increased the clock speed from 40 MHz to 80 MHz, while still employing the DT clocking scheme. Together, these steps boosted the maximum bus speed to 320 MBps (2 bytes x 80 MHz x 2 = 320 Mbps), using a 16-bit bus and supporting up to 15 external devices. The Ultra 320 SCSI connection employs a special 80-pin **Single Connector Attachment (SCA)** connector.

ULTRA640 SCSI

There is currently a proposal in place for a new **ULTRA640 SCSI** specification. This specification proposes to increase the throughput of the interface to 640 MBps. While this proposal is currently in development, it may not be released for quite some time. In the development papers, it mentions that the cable length will need to be shortened to increase the standard's integrity, but does not mention by how much.

SCSI Cables and Connectors

The SCSI standard has been implemented using a number of different cable types. In PC-compatible systems, the SCSI interface uses a 50-pin signal cable arrangement. Internally, the cable is a 50-pin flat ribbon cable. However, 50-pin shielded cables, with Centronic connectors, are used for external SCSI connections. The 50-pin SCSI connections are referred to as **A-cables**.

Advanced SCSI specifications have created additional cabling specifications. A 50-conductor alternative cable using 50-pin D-shell connectors has been added to the A-cable specification for SCSI-2 devices. A second cable type, referred to as **B-cable**, was added to the SCSI-2 specification to provide 16- and 32-bit parallel data transfers. However, this arrangement employed multiple connectors at each end of the cable and never received widespread acceptance in the market. A revised 68-pin **P-cable** format, using D-shell connectors, was introduced to support 16-bit transfers in the SCSI-3 specification. A 68-pin **Q-cable** version was also adopted in SCSI for 32-bit transfers. The P and Q cables must be used in parallel to conduct 32-bit transfers.

For some PS/2 models, IBM used a special 60-pin Centronics-like connector for their SCSI connections. The version of the SCSI interface used in the Apple Macintosh employs a variation of the standard that features a proprietary miniature 25-pin D-shell connector.

These cabling variations create a hardware incompatibility between different SCSI devices. Likewise, there are SCSI devices that just will not work with each other due to software incompatibilities.

In addition, SCSI devices may be classified as internal or as external devices. An internal SCSI device has no power supply of its own and, therefore, must be connected to one of the system's options power connectors. On the other hand, external SCSI devices come with built-in or plug-in power supplies that need to be connected to a commercial ac outlet. Therefore, when choosing a SCSI device, always inquire about compatibility between it and any other SCSI devices installed in the system.

Figure 4-26 depicts a 25-pin D-shell, a 50-pin Centronics, and a 68-pin Centronics-type SCSI connector used for external connections. Inside the computer, the SCSI specification employs 50-pin and 68-pin ribbon cables with BERG pin connectors.

Figure 4-26: SCSI Connectors

SCSI Signaling

You should also be aware that two types of signaling are used with SCSI interfaces — **single-ended (SE)** and **differential**. Single-ended signaling transmits signals in a straightforward manner where the information is applied to a signal line and referenced to ground. Differential signaling applies reciprocal versions of the same signal to two wires in the cable and compares them at the other end of the cable. This differential signal technique provides exceptional noise rejection properties and enables the signal to be transmitted much further (from 3/6 meters using SE up to 25 meters using differential) before it significantly deteriorates. For this reason, single-ended interface uses half as many active conductors in the cable as differential cables do. The other conductors in the SE cable are used to provide grounds for the individual signal cables. In a differential cable the ground conductors are used to carry the differential portion of the signal.

SINGLE-ENDED (SE) LOW-VOLTAGE DIFFERENTIAL (LVD) LOW-VOLTAGE DIFFERENTIAL / MULTIMODE SINGLE-ENDED (LVD / MSE) HIGH-VOLTAGE DIFFERENTIAL (HVD)

**Figure 4-27:
SCSI Symbols**

Single-ended and differential SCSI cables are available for A, P, and Q applications. Since they are electrically different, confusing them with each other would be problematic (i.e., using a differential cable to connect single-ended devices together could damage the devices because of the missing ground capabilities). For this reason, the industry has adopted different symbols, as illustrated in Figure 4-27, to identify SE and differential cables and devices. These symbols are placed on the connectors of the cables and ports so that they are not confused with each other. Fortunately, most PC applications use single-ended connections and therefore you are unlikely to run into differential cables or devices.

There have been two different differential signal specifications used in the SCSI environment. These are:

- **High-Voltage Differential (HVD)**: The high differential refers to the +5 Vdc and 0 Vdc signal levels used to represent data bits. These voltage levels were implemented with the original SCSI-1 bus and have been included with all of the specifications up to the Wide Ultra SCSI version.

- **Low-Voltage Differential (LVD)**: This is similar to the move in microprocessors to reduce the core voltage to 3.3 V to make them run faster and consume less power. LVD interfaces operate on 3-volt logic levels instead of the older TTL-compatible 5-volt levels.

Unlike the earlier HVD interfaces that were incompatible with SE devices, LVD SCSI devices actually operate in what is known as **multimode** (i.e., they can shift back and forth between traditional SE mode and LVD mode). The LVD is backward compatible with single-ended SCSI. However, connecting one single-ended peripheral to a multimode LVD bus will cause the entire bus to switch to the single-ended mode for protection. With the switch, the single-ended limitations on data throughput and cable length come into play. **LVD mode was not defined in the original SCSI standards. If all devices on the bus support LVD, then operations at up to 12 meters are possible at full speed. However, if any device on the bus is singled-ended only, then the entire bus switches to single-ended mode and the distance is reduced to the 3/6** meters.

To add a single-ended peripheral to an LVD bus and preserve the data throughput and cable length of the LVD, you can add a SCSI expander called an LVD-to-SE or LVD/MSE-to-LVD/MSE converter. This converter divides the SCSI domain into two bus segments. One segment can operate at the LVD data throughput rate and cable length, while the other segment uses the single-ended data throughput and cable length ratings. Most LVD controllers employ a single-ended connector for connecting to slower tape drives so that they can preserve the speed and cable length of the LVD segment.

SCSI Addressing

The SCSI specification allows up to eight SCSI devices to be connected together. The standard SCSI1 port can be daisy-chained to permit up to six external peripherals to be connected to the system. To connect multiple SCSI devices to a SCSI host, all of the devices, except the last one, must have two SCSI connectors: one for **SCSI-In**, and one for **SCSI-Out**. Which connector is which does not matter. However, if the device has only one SCSI connector, it must be connected to the end of the chain.

It is possible to use multiple SCSI host adapters within a single system to increase the number of devices that can be used. The system's first SCSI controller can handle up to 7 devices, whereas the additional SCSI controller can boost the system to support up to 14 SCSI devices.

> **SCSI-In**
> **SCSI-Out**

> ## TEST TIP
> Remember how many devices can be daisy-chained on a standard SCSI interface, and which ID numbers are assumed automatically.

Each SCSI device in a chain must have a unique ID number assigned to it. Even though there are a total of eight possible **SCSI ID numbers** for each controller, only six are available for use with external devices. The SCSI specification refers to the SCSI controller as **SCSI-7** (by default), and then classifies the first internal hard drive as **SCSI-0**. If two devices are set to the same ID number, one or both of them will appear invisible to the system. This type of identification is also used for Wide SCSI. The difference is that the bus can now support up to sixteen devices with the bus being 16 bits wide. The addressing scheme changes to SCSI-0 to SCSI-15.

> **SCSI ID numbers**
> **SCSI-7**
> **SCSI-0**

> ## TEST TIP
> Be aware of how SCSI ID priorities are set.

With older SCSI devices, address settings were established through jumpers on the host adapter card. Each device had a SCSI number selection switch, or a set of configuration jumpers for establishing its ID number. Figure 4-28 illustrates a three-jumper configuration block that can be used to establish the SCSI ID number. In the figure, an open jumper pair is counted as a binary 0 and a shorted pair represents a binary 1. With a three-pair jumper block, it is possible to represent the numbers 0 through 7. In PnP systems, the BIOS will configure the device addresses using information obtained directly from the SCSI host adapter during the bootup process.

```
JUMPER
BINARY=  000   001   010   011   100   101   110   111
NUMBER=   0     1     2     3     4     5     6     7
```

**Figure 4-28:
Configuring a
SCSI ID Number**

CHALLENGE #2

You are installing a SCSI device on an AT-class machine and need to manually set the SCSI ID on the device. The device has a 3-position, 2-pin BERG jumper for configuration and you need to configure the device ID to 5. You have no documentation for the device, so you must guess at the setting. How would you arrange the three jumpers on the card? Explain your reasoning.

Before Plug-and-Play technology matured, SCSI hard drives were not configured as part of the system's CMOS setup function. However, newer BIOS versions are able to detect SCSI drives during the PnP process and can even be set to boot to a SCSI device. Older operating systems such as MS-DOS, Windows 3.x, and Windows 95 did not include support for SCSI devices. Therefore, SCSI drivers had to be loaded during the boot process before the system could communicate with the drive. However, Windows 9x and Windows 2000 do offer SCSI support. Because SCSI drives use a system-level interface, they require no low-level formatting. Therefore, the second step involved in installing a SCSI drive is to partition it.

SCSI Termination

terminated

The SCSI daisy chain must be **terminated** with a resistor network pack at both ends. Single-connector SCSI devices are normally terminated internally. If not, a SCSI terminator cable (containing a built-in resistor pack) must be installed at the end of the chain. SCSI termination is a major cause of SCSI-related problems. Poor terminations cause a variety of different system problems including:

- failed system startups

- hard drive crashes

- random system failures

Several different types of termination are commonly used with SCSI buses. They differ in the circuitry that is used to terminate the bus. The better the termination method, the better the quality of signal moving along the bus, making it more reliable. In general, the slower bus specifications are less particular in the termination method required, while the faster buses require better termination techniques. The different types of termination commonly used with SCSI systems include:

Passive Termination

- **Passive Termination:** This is the simplest and least reliable method of termination. It employs non-active resisters to terminate the bus. Passive termination is fine for short, low-speed SCSI-1 buses; however, it is not suitable for faster SCSI buses.

Active Termination

- **Active Termination:** Adding active elements such as voltage regulators to the resistors used in passive termination provides for more reliable and consistent termination of the bus. Active termination is the minimum requirement for any of the faster single-ended SCSI buses.

Forced Perfect Termination (FPT)

- **Forced Perfect Termination (FPT)**: FPT is a more advanced form of active termination, where the diode clamps are added to the circuitry to force the termination to the correct voltage. FTP virtually eliminates any signal reflections or other problems, and is the best form of termination for a single-ended SCSI bus.

multimode LVD

Newer SCSI buses that employ low-voltage differential signaling require special types of terminators. In addition, there are special LVD/SE terminators designed for use with **multimode LVD** devices that can function in either LVD or SE modes. When the bus is in single-ended mode, they behave like active terminators. LVDs are currently more popular than HVDs due to the fact that LVDs can support the Wide Ultra 2 SCSI, so the bandwidth is effectively doubled from 80 to 160 MB/sec.

Newer SCSI technologies often provide for automatic cable termination. Many of the latest internal SCSI cables provide the termination function on the cable itself. The terminator is permanently applied at the end of the cable. For this reason, you should always verify the type of SCSI cables and components you are using before installation. This will help to ensure that your SCSI installation process moves along as effortlessly as possible.

In these systems, after a SCSI component has been installed, the system queries the device to detect modifications to the SCSI configuration. It then provides termination as required to enable the system to operate properly. In addition, these intelligent systems can also assign SCSI IDs as required. Even in these systems you can still manually select ID numbers for the devices. In many cases, this is the best option because it enables you to document each SCSI component's ID for future reference.

CHALLENGE #3

You are installing SCSI devices in a new system. Inside the case, there is a SCSI host adapter card, a hard disk drive, and a CD-ROM drive. The SCSI cabling runs from the host adapter to the hard drive and ends at the CD-ROM drive. External to the case, you must make connections for a SCSI flat bed scanner and a SCSI printer. The external cabling runs from the host adapter to the scanner and ends at the printer. Where should the terminator packs be installed?

SCSI Adapter Cards

In the PC environment, SCSI devices are not standard. Even though newer system boards and operating systems do support SCSI operation, it has never been incorporated into the PC as a standard interface. Therefore, to use SCSI devices with a PC, you will typically need to install a SCSI host adapter card.

Older ISA SCSI adapters required considerable manual configuration effort and careful consideration for installing cabling and terminators (these activities are described in great detail in Chapter 6). With newer PCI SCSI host adapter cards, the installation and configuration process is much simpler. These cards possess PnP capabilities that enable the system to automatically configure them with the system resources they need to operate. PnP SCSI adapters are normally configured by default for ID=7. However, you can change this setting by using the card's OEM software to update the BIOS extension on the card. This will cause the PnP process to configure the card with resources for the new ID setting when it is started again.

After the SCSI host adapter card has been installed in the system and secured, the cables must be attached to the card and the devices it supports. These cables could be internal ribbon cables, external cables with D-shell connectors, or a combination of internal and external cables. As you will find in Chapter 6, one of the major tasks in getting SCSI systems installed and operating has been properly terminating the cables that run to the different SCSI devices in the system. Many newer SCSI adapters have auto termination capabilities built into them to reduce the effort required to achieve satisfactory termination. As with any type of device you are installing in a PC system, you should refer to the adapter's documentation to determine its termination and configuration needs.

Windows 9x and Windows NT did not directly support SCSI adapters and devices. All SCSI configuration and support had to be performed and installed manually. However, the Windows Me/2000/XP operating systems offer support for most SCSI adapters. If the PnP process does not recognize a given SCSI adapter, it will ask for the OEM driver disk so that it can upload the driver required to support the card. In some cases the driver may need to be loaded through the Windows Add/Remove Hardware applet in the Control Panel.

The increased speed capabilities of the SCSI interfaces make them attractive for intensive applications such as large file servers for networks, and multimedia video stations. However, the EIDE interface is generally more widely used due to its lower cost and nearly equal performance. Table 4-9 contrasts the specifications of the SCSI and IDE interfaces.

> **TEST TIP**
>
> Know the number of devices that can be attached to IDE, EIDE, and standard SCSI interfaces.

Table 4-9: SCSI/IDE Specifications

INTERFACE	BUS SIZE	# DEVICES	ASYNC. SPEED	SYNC. SPEED
IDE (ATA-1)	16 bits	2	4 MB/s	3.3/5.2/8.3 MB/s
EIDE (ATA-2)	16 bits	2	4 MB/s	11/16 MB/s
SCSI (SCSI-1)	8 bits	7	2 MB/s	5 MB/s
Wide SCSI (SCSI-2)	8/16 bits	15	2 MB/s	5 MB/s
Fast SCSI (SCSI-2)	8/16 bits	7	2 MB/s	5/10 MB/s
Wide Fast SCSI (SCSI-2)	8/16 bits	15	2 MB/s	10/20 MB/s
Ultra SCSI	8 bits	7	2 MB/s	10/20 MB/s
Wide Ultra SCSI (SCSI-3)	16 bits	15	2 MB/s	10/20/40 MB/s
Ultra2 SCSI	8 bits	7	2 MB/s	10/20/40 MB/s
Wide Ultra2 SCSI	16 bits	15	2 MB/s	10/20/40/80 MB/s
Wide Ultra3 SCSI	16 bits	15	2 MB/s	10/20/40/160 MB/s
Ultra320 SCSI	16 bits	15	2 MB/s	10/20/40/320 MB/s

INSTALLING STORAGE DEVICES

For installation purposes, storage devices fall into one of two categories: internal and external. Internal devices are typically mounted in the system unit's drive bays. External devices normally connect to adapter cards installed in the system board's expansion slots. Whereas internal devices typically derive their power from the system unit's power supply, external storage devices tend to employ separate, external power supply units.

Most internal storage devices conform to traditional disk drive form factors. Therefore, the hardware installation procedures for most storage devices are the same.

To install a storage device in a disk drive bay, disconnect the system's power cord from the back of the unit. Slide the device into one of the system unit's open drive bays, and install 2 screws on each side to secure the unit to the disk drive cage. If the unit is a 3-1/2" drive, and it is being installed into a 5-1/4" drive bay, you will need to fit the drive with a **universal mounting kit**. These kits attach to the drive and extend its form factor, so that it fits correctly in the 5-1/4" half-height space.

universal mounting kit

Connect the device's signal cable to the proper interface header on the system board (or on an I/O card). Then connect the signal cable to the storage device. Use caution when connecting the disk drives to the adapter. Make certain that the Pin #1 indicator stripe on the cable aligns with the Pin #1 position of the connectors on both the storage device and its controller. Proper connection of a signal cable is depicted in Figure 4-29. Finally, connect one of the power supply's optional power connectors to the storage device.

Figure 4-29: Connecting a Drive's Signal Cable

FDD Installation

The FDD installation procedure follows the sample procedure described earlier. Simply slide the FDD into one of the system unit's open drive bays, install 2 screws on each side to secure the drive to the system unit, and connect the signal and power cables to the drive. Figure 4-30 illustrates the steps required to install the floppy drive.

Figure 4-30: Installing a Floppy-Disk Drive

The PC-compatible FDD unit uses a 34-pin signal cable. The FDD signal cable is designed to accommodate two FDD units, as illustrated in Figure 4-31. If the drive is the only floppy in the system, or intended to operate as the A: drive, connect it to the connector at the end of the cable. If it is being installed as a B: drive, attach it to the connector toward the center of the cable. On older floppy drives, the cable connected to an edge connector on the drive's printed-circuit board. With newer units, the connection is made to a BERG connector.

```
┌─ TEST TIP ──────────────────────────────────────────────┐
│                                                          │
│  Know what makes a floppy drive an A: or B: drive in a PC system. │
│                                                          │
└──────────────────────────────────────────────────────────┘
```

Figure 4-31: Connecting Floppy Drives

On some Pentium system boards and on all-in-one system boards, check the system board's documentation for an FDD enabling jumper and make certain that it is set correctly for the FDD installed. In newer systems, the FDD enabling function should be set in the *Advanced CMOS Setup* screen.

Reinstall the system unit's power cord and boot up the computer. As the system boots, move into the CMOS Setup utility and configure the CMOS for the type of FDD being installed.

HDD Installation

The HDD hardware installation process is similar to that of other storage devices, as illustrated in Figure 4-32. Simply slide the hard drive unit into one of the system unit's open drive bays, install 2 screws on each side to secure the drive to the system unit, and connect the signal and power cables to it.

However, the configuration and preparation of a typical hard-disk drive is more involved than that of a floppy drive. It is a good idea to confirm the IDE drive's Master/Slave/Single, or the SCSI drive's ID configuration setting before installing the unit in the drive bay. These settings were described earlier in this chapter. If a replacement hard drive is being installed for repair or upgrading purposes, the data on the original drive should be backed up to some other media before replacing it (if possible).

When handling hard drives, make sure to practice proper **Electrostatic Discharge (ESD)** precautions to prevent damage to the drive's electronic control circuitry. For instance, the hard drive should be kept inside its anti-static bag until installation. Also, make sure that during installation, your technicians are wearing an anti-static device, such as a grounded wrist or ankle strap. These precautions and device are discussed in Chapter 13 — *Preventive Maintenance*.

Figure 4-32: Securing the Drive Unit

When you are installing the HDD signal cable in an IDE-based system, you should recall that there are two similar types cables used with IDE devices. The newer ATA-4/Ultra ATA 66, Ultra ATA 100, and Ultra ATA 133 IDE enhancements provide higher data throughput by doubling the number of conductors in the signal cable to 80. The IDE connector has remained compatible with the original 40-pin IDE connection, but each pin has been provided with its own ground conductor in the cable. All three Ultra ATA versions support 33.3 Mbps data rates when used with a standard 40-pin/40-conductor IDE signal cable. Therefore, Ultra ATA 66, 100, and 133 devices can still be used with systems that don't support the new IDE standards; but they will operate well below their potential.

Likewise, in a SCSI system, make sure that the drive is correctly configured and terminated for its position in the system. Verify that the SCSI host adapter and all the SCSI devices installed in the system are supported and will work together. For example, a standard SCSI-I host adapter will not support a Fast-Wide SCSI device. The physical cable and the communication speed differences between the two specifications will not match.

After completing the hardware installation process, the drive must be configured and formatted. Unlike floppy drives, which basically come in four accepted formats, hard-disk drives are created in a wide variety of storage capacities and geometries. When the disk is created its surface is electronically blank. With system-level drive types, the manufacturer performs the low-level formatting process. To prepare the disk for use by the system, three levels of preparation must take place. The order of these steps is as follows:

1. Verify the CMOS configuration for the drive.

2. Partition the drive.

3. High-level format the drive.

After the IDE hardware has been installed, its operating mode must be configured correctly through the system's CMOS Setup utility. The system's CMOS Setup holds the hard drive's configuration settings. As with other I/O devices, these settings must be established correctly for the type of drive being installed. Newer BIOS versions possess **auto-detection** capabilities that enable them to find and identify the drives in the system. The physical geometry of the drive might be different than the logical arrangement that the controller displays to the CMOS. The IDE controller handles the translation between the drive parameters the system believes to exist and the actual layout of the drive.

However, if the BIOS does not support auto-detection, you must move into the CMOS Setup utility and identify the drive type being installed. The Hard Disk C: Type entry is typically located in the CMOS Setup utility's main screen. Simply move to the entry and scroll through the HDD selections until an entry is found that matches the type of drive you are installing. In some cases, such as with SCSI drives, the CMOS configuration entry must be set to *None Installed* before the drive will operate correctly. Store this parameter in the CMOS configuration file by following the directions given on the menu screen. This utility can also be used to manually configure various IDE channel selections. Both IDE channels can be Enabled, Disabled, or placed in Auto-detect mode through the CMOS.

Programmed I/O (PIO)

low-level format

Older BIOS versions provide for a manual PIO configuration setting. The ATA standards provide for different **Programmed I/O (PIO)** modes that offer higher performance capabilities. Most EIDE devices are now capable of operating in modes 3 or 4. However, the IDE port must be attached to the PCI bus to use these modes. Some system boards only place the IDE1 connection on this 64-bit bus, whereas the IDE2 connection is a function of the ISA bus. In these cases, devices installed on the IDE2 connector will only be capable of mode 2 operations. Newer BIOS versions do not offer manual PIO configuration capabilities.

— NOTE —

A **low-level format** routine marks off the disk into cylinders and sectors and defines their placement on the disk. System-level interface devices, such as IDE and SCSI drives, come with automatic low-level formatting routines already performed. Therefore, no low-level formatting needs to be performed on these drives before they can be partitioned and high-level formatted. Low-level formatting will not produce physical damage, but it may cause the loss of prerecorded bad track and sector information, as well as loss of information used to control the R/W heads for proper alignment over the tracks. If this occurs, it will normally be necessary to send the drive to the manufacturer to restore this information to the disk.

Installing CD-ROM/DVD Drives

CD Input

Before installing an internal CD-ROM or DVD drive, confirm its Master/Slave/Single, or SCSI ID configuration setting. Afterwards, install the drive unit in one of the drive bays, connect the power and signal cables, and load the drive's driver software if needed. (Due to their widespread use with portable systems, the procedure for installing external CD-ROM drives is presented in Chapter 7 — *Portable Systems*.)

Figure 4-33 illustrates the installation of an internal CD-ROM drive. If the interface type is different than that of the HDD, it will be necessary to install a controller card in an expansion slot. Finally, refer to the drive's documentation regarding any necessary jumper or switch settings.

To connect the drive to the system, hook up the CD-ROM drive to the HDD signal cable, observing proper orientation. Connect the audio cable to the drive and to the sound card's **CD Input** connection (if a sound card is installed).

Figure 4-33: Installing an Internal CD-ROM Drive

Configuring CD-ROM Drives

As previously indicated, the CD-ROM drive must be properly configured for the system it is being installed in. In an IDE system, the Master/Slave setting must be confirmed. In a SCSI system, the ID setting must be correct. In a SCSI system, the only requirement is that a valid ID setting be configured. In an IDE system, however, some thought may be required as to how to configure the drive.

In a single-HDD system, the CD-ROM drive can be set up as the slave drive on the primary interface. However, the operation of the drives is much cleaner if the CD-ROM is set up as the Master drive on the secondary IDE interface. In this manner, each drive has access to a full IDE channel instead of sharing one. Likewise, in a two-HDD system, the CD-ROM drive would most likely be configured as the Master or Single drive on the secondary interface. If the system also contains a sound card that has a built-in IDE interface, it should be disabled to prevent it from interfering with the primary or secondary interfaces.

After the hardware has been installed, it will be necessary to install its software drivers.

Consult the drive's documentation for instructions on software installation. Typically, all that is required is to insert the OEM driver disk into the floppy drive, and follow the manufacturer's directions for installing the drivers. If the drive fails to operate at this point, reboot the system using single-step verification and check the information on the various boot screens for error messages associated with the CD-ROM drive.

In older PCs, you should check the system to determine whether it has AUTOEXEC.BAT and CONFIG.SYS files. If so, these files should be examined for updated information. In particular, check for the presence of the **Microsoft CD Extension (MSCDEX)** driver. This driver was used to provide access to the system's CD-ROM drives under older Microsoft operating system versions. It must be loaded from the CONFIG.SYS file using a DEVICE= or DEVICEHIGH command. This driver assigns the logical drive letters to all CD-ROM drives in the system along with a unique **driver signature** (name). The signature is used to differentiate one CD-ROM drive from another in the system.

> In Windows 95, an advanced CD-ROM driver called **CDFS (CD-ROM File System)** was implemented to provide protected-mode operation of the drive. Windows 9x retains the MSCDEX files for real-mode operation. If Windows 9x detects that the CDFS has taken over control of the CD-ROM on its initial bootup, it will REM any MSCDEX lines in the AUTOEXEC.BAT file.

> **Microsoft CD Extension (MSCDEX)**
>
> **driver signature**

> **TEST TIP**
> Remember what type of device the MSCDEX file is used with and where it should be located.

> **CDFS (CD-ROM File System)**

Installing CDRW and DVDRW Drives

The hardware installation process involved with rewriteable CD-ROM and DVD drives is identical to that used with standard CD-ROM and DVD drives. However, prior to the Windows XP operating system, rewriteable CDRW and DVDRW drives required third-party application packages to perform their write and rewrite functions. These applications had to be installed from the OEM CD that was packaged with the drive, or a CD obtained from an independent supplier.

In the Windows XP environment, rewriteable drives are supported directly from the operating system and don't require any third-party applications. When you insert a blank disc into one of these drives, the operating system detects it and pops up a dialog box that asks you what you want to do with the disc. Most users still prefer to install a third-party program to manage all of the functions of these drives.

Installing Peripheral Storage Devices

External storage devices normally connect to adapter cards installed in the system board's expansion slots. They also tend to employ separate, external power supply units. Several newer storage technologies, such as removable hard drive media, have been designed to take advantage of the enhanced parallel port specifications of modern systems. These devices can be connected directly to the system's parallel port, or can be connected to the system through another device that is connected to the port. The device's installation software is used to configure it for use in the system.

Installing External Storage Devices

The general procedure for installing external storage devices is:

1. Configure the device for operation.
   a. Refer to the device's user's manual regarding any IRQ and COM jumper or switch settings.
   b. Record the card's default IRQ and COM settings.
   c. Set the device's configuration jumpers to operate at the default setting.

2. Install the device's adapter card (if necessary).
   a. Turn the system off.
   b. Remove the cover from system unit.
   c. Locate a compatible empty expansion slot.
   d. Remove the expansion slot cover from the rear of the system unit.
   e. Install the adapter card in the expansion slot.
   f. Reinstall the screw to secure the card to the back panel of the system unit.

3. Make the device's external connections.
   a. Connect the device's signal cable to the appropriate connector at the rear of the system.
   b. Connect the opposite end of the cable to the device.
   c. Verify that the power switch or power supply is turned off.
   d. Connect the power supply to the external storage unit.

4. Configure the device's software.
   a. Turn the system on.
   b. Check the CMOS Setup to ensure that the port setting is correct.
   c. Run the device's installation routine.

Removable Storage

Removable storage includes all of the removable technologies we have already described (i.e., floppies, CD/CDRWs and DVD/DVDRWs, and tapes). However, there are still several other types of emerging and lesser-known removable storage systems. These systems include cartridge-mounted high-capacity floppy disks (Zip drives), solid-state USB drives (IC memory devices configured to operate like a mechanical disk drive), and PC Card drives. PC Card versions of removable storage can hold miniature (1.8 inch) mechanical or solid-state disk drives.

Most removable storage systems connect to and operate from standard I/O ports (i.e., ECP Parallel, SCSI, USB, Firewire). This permits the system's PnP operation to detect the new hardware attached to the system. However, most of the devices are nonstandard in nature and require that an OEM applications package be installed to control them. However, USB memory drives automatically load USB drivers and function as another drive in the system (e.g., drive e:). In the case of PC Card mounted removable storage systems, the entire peripheral is PnP and hot swappable.

RAID Systems

As applications pushed storage capacity requirements past available drive sizes, it became logical to combine several drives together to hold all of the data produced. In a desktop unit, this can be as simple as adding an additional physical drive to the system. Wide area and local area networks connect computers together so that their resources (including disk drives) can be shared. If you extend this idea of sharing disk drives to include several different drive units operating under a single controller, you have a **drive array**. A drive array is depicted in Figure 4-34.

Drive arrays have evolved in response to storage requirements for local area networks. They are particularly useful in client/server networks, in which the data for the network tends to be centrally located and shared by all of the users around the network.

Figure 4-34: A Drive Array

drive array

In the cases of multiple drives within a unit, and drives scattered around a network, each drive assumes a different letter designation. In a drive array, the stack of drives can be made to appear as a single large hard drive. The drives are operated in parallel so that they can deliver data to the controller in a parallel format. If the controller is simultaneously handling 8 bits of data from 8 drives, the system will see the speed of the transfer as being 8 times faster. This technique of using the drives in a parallel array is referred to as a striped drive array.

It is also possible to simply use a small drive array as a data backup system. This is referred to as a **mirrored drive array**, in which each drive is supplied with the same data. In the event that the data from one drive is corrupted, or one of the drives fails, the data is still safe. Both types of arrays are created through a blend of connection hardware and control software.

mirrored drive array

RAID

Redundant Arrays of
Inexpensive Disks
(RAID)

RAID Advisory Board

RAID 0

RAID 1

The RAID Advisory Board designated the classic striped array described above as RAID level-0 (**RAID 0** - *Striped Disk Array without Fault Tolerance*). Likewise, the mirrored drive array described above is labeled RAID 1. The operation of a striped disk array is shown in Figure 4-35.

> The most common drive arrays are **RAID** systems. RAID is an acronym for **Redundant Arrays of Inexpensive Disks**. Later usage of the term RAID exchanges the word Independent for Inexpensive. Five levels of RAID technology specifications are given by the **RAID Advisory Board**.

RAID 1 (*Mirroring and Duplexing*) is a redundancy scheme that uses two equal-sized drives, where both drives hold the same information. Each drive serves as a backup for the other. Figure 4-36 illustrates the operation of a mirrored array used in a RAID 1 application.

Figure 4-35: A Striped Disk Array

Figure 4-36: A Mirrored Array

RAID 2

Figure 4-37: Interleaved Data on Parallel Drives

error-detection and correction functions

Duplicate information is stored on both drives. When a file is retrieved from the array, the controller reads alternate sectors from each drive. This effectively reduces the data read time by half.

The **RAID 2** (*Data Striping with Error Recovery*) strategy interleaves data on parallel drives, as shown in Figure 4-37. Bits or blocks of data are interleaved across the disks in the array. The speed afforded by collecting data from the disks in a parallel format is the biggest feature of the system. In large arrays, complete bytes, words, or double words can be written to, and read from, the array simultaneously.

The RAID 2 specification uses multiple disks for **error-detection and correction functions**. Depending on the error-detection and correction algorithms used, large portions of the array are used for non-data storage overhead. Of course, the reliability of the data being delivered to the system is excellent, and there is no need for time-consuming corrective read operations when an error is detected. Arrays dealing with large systems may use between 3 and 7 drives for error-correction purposes. Because of the high hardware overhead, RAID 2 systems are not normally used with microcomputer systems.

When the array is used in this manner, a complex **error-detection and correction algorithm** is normally employed. The controller contains circuitry based on the algorithm that detects, locates, and corrects the error without re-transmitting any data. This is a very quick and efficient method of error-detection and correction.

In Figure 4-37, the data block being sent to the array is broken apart and distributed to the drives in the array. The data word already has a parity bit added to it. The controller generates parity for the block, and stores it on the error-detection drive. When the controller reads the data back from the array, it regenerates the error-check character, and compares it to the one written on the error-check drive. By comparing the error-check character to the rewritten one, the controller can detect the error in the data field, and determine which bit within the field is incorrect. With this information in hand, the controller can simply correct that bit as it is being processed.

In a **RAID 3** (*Parallel Transfer with Parity Striping*) arrangement, the drives of the array operate in parallel like a RAID 2 system. However, only parity checking is used for error-detection and correction, requiring only one additional drive. If an error occurs, the controller reads the array again to verify the error. This is a time-consuming, low-efficiency method of error correction.

A **RAID 4** (*Independent Data Disks with Shared Parity Disk*) controller interleaves sectors across the drives in the array. This creates the appearance of one very large drive. The RAID 4 format is generally used for smaller drive arrays, but can be used for larger arrays as well. Only one parity-checking drive is allotted for error control. The information on the parity drive is updated after reading the data drives. This creates an extra write activity for each data read operation performed.

The **RAID 5** scheme (*Independent Data Disks with Distributed Parity Blocks*) alters the RAID 4 specification by allowing the parity function to rotate through the different drives. Under this system, error checking and correction is the function of all the drives. If a single drive fails, the system is capable of regenerating its data from the parity information on the other drives. RAID 5 is usually the most popular RAID system, since it can be used on small arrays, and it has a high level of error recovery built in. The operation of a RAID 5 array is shown in Figure 4-38.

A variation of RAID 5 that implements two independent error-correcting schemes (Independent Data Disks with two Independent Distributed Parity Schemes) has been devised and labeled **RAID 6**. This format is relatively expensive, but it provides an extremely high fault tolerance level for critical applications. This RAID level requires at least two additional drives to operate.

The **RAID 10** (*Very High Reliability/High Performance RAID*) specification combines mirroring and striping to produce a high-performance, high-reliability backup system. This arrangement combines RAID 1 striped array segments with mirroring to provide increased performance to a RAID 1 installation.

A variation of RAID 3 referred to as **RAID 53** (*High I/O Rates and Data Transfer Performance RAID*) combines RAID 0 striped arrays with RAID 3 parallel segments. The result is a high-performance RAID 3 system.

Figure 4-38: A RAID 5 Array

DISK DRIVE UPGRADING AND OPTIMIZING

The A+ Core Hardware objective 1.8 states that the test taker should be able to identify hardware methods of upgrading system performance, procedures for replacing basic subsystem components, unique components, and when to use them. One of the components listed under this objective is the hard drive unit. CD-ROM drives are also good candidates for periodic upgrading.

As with other modules in the PC, the hard disk and CD-ROM drives can be upgraded as new, or better, components become available, or as the system's application changes. As this A+ objective points out, computer technicians must be capable of upgrading the various components of the system — including its disk drives. The technician should also be able to optimize the operation of the drive to obtain the best performance possible for a given system configuration.

HDD Upgrading

One of the key components in keeping the system up to date is the hard disk drive. Software manufacturers continue to produce larger and larger programs. In addition, the types of programs found on the typical PC are expanding. Many newer programs place high demands on the hard drive to feed information, such as large graphics files or digitized voice and video, to the system for processing.

CHKDSK

SCANDISK

DEFRAG

Invariably, the system will begin to produce error messages that say that the hard drive is full. The first line of action is to use software disk utilities to optimize the organization of the drive. These utilities, such as **CHKDSK**, **SCANDISK**, and **DEFRAG**, are covered in detail in Chapter 12 — *Operating System Troubleshooting*. The second step is to remove unnecessary programs and files from the hard drive. Programs and information that are rarely, or never, used should be moved to an archival media, such as removable disks or tape.

In any event, there may come a time when it is necessary to determine whether the hard drive needs to be replaced in order to optimize the performance of the system. One guideline suggests that the drive should be replaced if the percentage of unused disk space drops below 20%.

Another reason to consider upgrading the HDD involves its ability to deliver information to the system. If the system is constantly waiting for information from the hard drive, replacing it should be considered as an option. Not all system slowdowns are connected to the HDD, but many are. Remember that the HDD is the mechanical part of the memory system, whereas everything else is electronic.

As with the storage space issue, HDD speed can be optimized through software configurations, such as a disk cache. However, once it has been optimized in this manner, any further speed increases must be accomplished by upgrading the hardware.

When considering an HDD upgrade, determine what the real needs are for the hard drive. Multimedia-intensive applications can place heavy performance demands on the hard-disk drive. Moving large image, audio, and video files into RAM on demand requires high performance from the drive. Critical HDD specifications associated with disk drive performance include:

- **Access Time** — The average time, expressed in milliseconds, required to position the drive's R/W heads over a specified track/cylinder and to reach a specified sector on the track.

- **Track-Seek Time** — The amount of time required for the drive's R/W heads to move between cylinders and settle over a particular track following the seek command being issued by the system.

- **Data Transfer Rate** — The speed, expressed in megabytes per second (MBps), at which data is transferred between the system and the drive.

Access Time

Track-Seek Time

Data Transfer Rate

These factors should be checked thoroughly when upgrading an HDD unit for speed-critical applications. In contemporary systems, the choice of hard drives for high-performance applications is between IDE/EIDE drives and SCSI drives. The EIDE drives are competitive and relatively easy to install, whereas the high-end SCSI specifications offer additional performance, but require additional setup effort and an additional host adapter card. Refer to Table 4-9 for comparisons of SCSI and IDE specifications.

When upgrading an IDE hard drive, make sure that that the system board supports the type of IDE drive you are installing. If your system board only supports ATA-66 drives, there is little reason to purchase an ATA-100 drive, unless you plan to upgrade the system board in the near future. Also verify that the correct cabling is being used to connect the new drive to the system. You should know that installing a new ATA-66 or ATA-100 drive in a system using the old IDE cable will cause the drive's operation to be diminished to the level of the old drive. Without new cables, communications with the drives will be limited to the lesser standard determined by the 40-conductor signal cable. Check the Master/Slave jumper settings to see that they are correct for the new system before the drive is actually mounted in the system.

When upgrading SCSI systems, prepare a scheme for SCSI identification and termination ahead of time, and ensure that you have the necessary cabling and terminators. Take care to ensure that the new drive is correctly configured and terminated for its position in the system. Verify that the SCSI host adapter will support the new drive type. For example, a standard SCSI-I host adapter will not support a Fast-Wide SCSI drive. The physical cable and the communication speed differences between the two specifications will not match.

Likewise, when you upgrade a SCSI component, you should be aware that the SCSI host controller and the SCSI devices have the ability to adapt to lower functionality. If you upgrade one or more SCSI devices in a system, but do not upgrade the SCSI host adapter, then the devices will probably operate, but they will only operate at the maximum performance level of the adapter.

On the other hand, if you update the SCSI adapter and one or more SCSI devices, but you still have some older SCSI devices installed, devices that can operate at higher performance levels will attempt to do so. However, slower devices will work at their designated speed. The fact that the controller must slow down to work with the slower devices will effectively slow the operation of the entire SCSI system.

TEST TIP

Be aware of the effects of using newer EIDE devices with older IDE signal cables.

Before upgrading the HDD unit, make certain that the existing drive is providing all of the performance that it can. Check for SMARTDRV or VCACHE arrangements at the software configuration level and optimize them if possible. Also, determine how much performance increase can be gained through other upgrading efforts before changing out the hard drive.

If the drive is being upgraded substantially, such as from a 500 MB IDE drive to a 10 GB EIDE drive, check the capabilities of the system's ROM BIOS. If the system's BIOS does not support large LBA or ECHS enhancements, the drive capacity of even the largest hard drive will be limited to 528 MB. All newer BIOS support large LBA and ECHS enhanced drives.

If the current BIOS does not support the drive type or size you intend to install, you must upgrade it to support the new hard drive installation. The best place to find out the type and size of hard drives your current BIOS supports is the system board's documentation. The best place to find out whether a new BIOS version is available to support the new hard drive is the system board manufacturer's Internet support site. This website typically makes provisions for downloading the new BIOS material and loader utility.

After the drive upgrade has been performed, you should verify its operation. When you boot up the system, its POST will examine the drive's configuration and notify you if it has been detected. This is the most basic verification. An additional level of verification occurs at bootup. After the operating system starts up, you can open a file manager to see if the drive exists and how much space it presents to the system. You can also see the file system structure on the drive. In Figure 4-39, you can see the Windows 2000/XP Disk Management utility displaying information about a connected hard drive.

Finally, determine how much longer the unit in question is likely to be used before being replaced. If the decision to upgrade the HDD stands, ultimately, the best advice is to get the biggest, fastest hard drive possible. Don't forget that a different I/O bus architecture might add to the performance increase.

Figure 4-39:
Windows 2000 Disk
Management Utility

CHALLENGE #4

Your EIDE hard drive is continually producing "Out of Hard Drive Space" error messages. These messages continue to be a problem even after you have optimized the drive through the Defrag utility and removed as much old information as possible. You are thinking of upgrading to a new high-speed, high-capacity 20 GB ATA-100 drive. What system considerations do you need to resolve before buying this drive?

Disk Drive Subsystem Enhancements

If you are installing IDE hard drives, ensure that the jumper(s) are correctly configured, and that the system board supports the type of IDE drives you are installing. If the IDE controller on the system board will only support up to ATA-66 drives, there is little reason to purchase ATA-100 drives, unless you plan to upgrade the system board in the near future.

Likewise, when you upgrade a SCSI component you must be aware that the SCSI controller and the devices have the ability to adapt to lower functionality. If you upgrade one or more SCSI devices in a system, but do not upgrade the SCSI host adapter, then the devices will very likely operate, but they will only operate at the maximum performance level of the adapter.

On the other hand, if you update the adapter and one or more devices, but still have some older SCSI devices installed, those devices that can operate at higher performance levels will attempt to do so, while the slower devices will work at their level. However, the fact that the controller must slow down to work with the slower devices will effectively slow down the operation of the entire SCSI system.

You may need to upgrade the BIOS to support the new hard drive installation if the current BIOS does not support the type or size of drive you intend to install. The best place to determine the type and size hard drives your current BIOS will support is the system board's documentation. The best place to see whether an updated BIOS is available to support the new hard drive (and to download the BIOS loader routine) is the system board manufacturer's support Internet site.

> **TEST TIP**
>
> Be aware of how conducting partial upgrades on IDE and SCSI systems affects the performance of the devices involved and the drive system.

RAID Adapter Enhancements

RAID systems are available in two basic varieties — IDE and SCSI RAID systems. In each case the components of the system include a RAID controller (usually an adapter card) and the RAID drives. At the center of each system is the RAID controller card. Therefore, the speed and efficiency of the RAID system cannot be upgraded by upgrading the adapter card.

If you are working with an ATA66 IDE RAID adapter and you install new EIDE drives, the system will be limited to the operating speed and characteristics of the controller card. Likewise, if the RAID system is built on Wide SCSI 2 devices and you upgrade the drives to Wide Fast SCSI 2 devices, the system would still function as a Wide SCSI 2 system.

CHAPTER SUMMARY

The first section of the chapter explained the fundamentals of recording and reading data with magnetic media. This introductory information was followed by an extensive explanation of general disk drive operations. The third section dealt with installation and operation of disk drive systems.

The final sections of the chapter covered other magnetic storage devices and strategies commonly used with personal computer systems. Modern PCs typically employ IDE disk drives for their mass storage needs. A second type of system-level devices has also been adapted to PC-compatible systems—these are devices that employ versions of the SCSI interface. This chapter covered the installation and configuration of these two types of devices in some detail. It began with discussions of the IDE and EIDE interface standards commonly associated with PC-compatible systems. The remainder of the chapter turned to installing and configuring the more complex (and less widely used) array of SCSI interface standards.

At this point, review the objectives listed at the beginning of the chapter to be certain that you understand and can perform each item listed there.

KEY POINTS REVIEW

This chapter has explored the use of magnetic media to provide long-term, high-volume data storage for personal computer systems. Review the following key points before moving into the Review and Exam Questions sections to make sure you are comfortable with each point. Afterward, answer the Review Questions that follow to verify your knowledge of the information.

- From the beginning, most secondary memory systems have involved storing binary information in the form of magnetic charges on moving magnetic surfaces.

- The most common drive arrays are RAID systems. RAID is an acronym for Redundant Arrays of Independent (Inexpensive) Disks. Five levels of RAID technology specifications are given by the RAID Advisory Board.

- Soon after the Compact Disc (CD) became popular for storing audio signals on optical material, the benefits of storing computer information in this manner became apparent. With a CD, data is written digitally on a light-sensitive material by a powerful, highly focused laser beam.

- The information on a compact disc is stored in one continuous spiral track, unlike floppy disks, where the data is stored in multiple, concentric tracks. The compact disc storage format still divides the data into separate sectors. However, the sectors of a CD-ROM disc are physically the same size. The disc spins counterclockwise, and it slows down as the laser diode emitter/detector unit approaches the outside of the disc.

- Another type of CD drive is a Write Once, Read Many (WORM) drive. As the acronym implies, these drives allow users to write information to the disc once, and then retrieve this information as they would with a CD-ROM drive. With WORM drives, once data is stored on a disc, it cannot be changed or deleted.

- Tape drive units are another popular type of information storage system. These systems can store large amounts of data on small tape cartridges.

- Tape drives are generally used to store large amounts of information that will not need to be accessed often, or quickly. Such information includes backup copies of programs and data. This type of data security is a necessity with records such as business transactions, payroll, artwork, and so on.

- Before a high-level format can be performed, the drive must be partitioned. The disk management capabilities of the oldest versions of MS-DOS (2.x, 3.x) imposed a limit on the size of a drive at 32 MB. However, as HDD technology steadily increased, the capacities of the physical drives eventually passed this limit. Fortunately, operating systems can partition, or divide, large physical drives into multiple logical drives. Each logical drive is identified by a different drive letter (such as C, D, E, etc.).

- The high-level format procedure is performed by the operating system. This format routine creates a blank File Allocation Table (FAT) and root directory on the disk.

- In Windows 95, an advanced CD-ROM driver called CDFS (CD-ROM File System) was implemented to provide protected-mode operation of the drive. Windows 95 retains the MSCDEX files for real-mode operation. If Windows 95 detects that the CDFS has taken over control of the CD-ROM on its initial bootup, it will REM the MSCDEX lines in the AUTOEXEC.BAT file.

REVIEW QUESTIONS

The following questions test your knowledge of the material presented in this chapter.

1. What is the logical structure that replaces the function of the FAT on an NTFS drive?

2. Which interrupt request channel is normally used with floppy-disk drives in a PC-compatible system?

3. Name the tool that is used to perform partitioning in an NTFS system such as Windows 2000.

4. How can the A: and B: floppy drives be differentiated by looking into the system unit?

5. Name two types of HDD interfaces most commonly used with PC systems.

6. If you are installing an EIDE drive in a new computer, how should it be configured so that it is the only drive in the system to be drives C:, D:, and E:?

7. What MS-DOS utility is used to partition drives in Windows 9x systems?

8. What protected-mode driver did the Windows operating system use to replace the real-mode MSCDEX driver?

9. Describe how data is stored on a magnetic disk.

10. List the steps that you would use for the installation of a hard-disk drive in a desktop system.

11. Describe the differences between the two types of drive array applications.

12. How and why is a cartridge tape different from a standard audio cassette tape?

13. What is formatting as it applies to a magnetic disk?

14. What is the major procedural difference between installing a floppy drive and a hard drive?

15. What is the main function of the high-level format?

1. RAID 0 is also known as ___.
   a. Striped Disk Array
   b. mirroring
   c. duplexing
   d. parity

2. What action should always be taken before upgrading a hard-disk drive?
   a. Use the MS-DOS VER command to determine what version of MS-DOS is currently in use.
   b. Use the FDISK command to locate any lost cluster chains on the original drive.
   c. The contents of the installed drive should be backed up to some other media.
   d. Save the values of the installed drive's CMOS setup values for use with the new drive.

3. Head-to-Disk Interference (HDI) is also referred to as _____.
   a. a head crash
   b. R/W head bounce
   c. interleaving
   d. data compression

4. Identify the function that you would not employ on a SCSI drive when installing it.
   a. Low-level formatting
   b. Partitioning
   c. Formatting
   d. Installing the operating system on it

5. What protocol enables the EIDE interface to support a CD-ROM drive?
   a. MSCDEX
   b. ATAPI
   c. Host Adapter
   d. SCA

6. The _____ partition is the partition that the system will boot to.
   a. active
   b. primary
   c. system
   d. extended

7. Which of the following is not a disk optimization utility?
   a. CHKDSK
   b. DEFRAG
   c. FDISK
   d. SCANDISK

8. What is the main purpose of a RAID 1 drive array?
   a. To act as an error-checking and correction method
   b. To create the appearance of one very large drive
   c. To act as a redundant data-backup method
   d. To act as a high-speed retrieval system

9. Which type of SCSI signal specification uses a core voltage of 3.3 V?
   a. LVD
   b. HVD
   c. Wide Ultra
   d. Single-Edged

10. Which IDE interface version employs an 80-wire, 40-pin cable?
    a. IDE
    b. ATA-2
    c. ATA-66
    d. EIDE

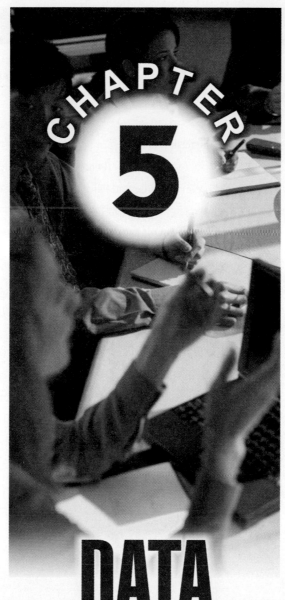

CHAPTER
5

DATA
COMMUNICATIONS

OBJECTIVES

OBJECTIVES

Upon completion of this chapter and its related lab procedures, you should be able to perform these tasks:

1. Define the term modem.

2. Define the term baud.

3. Compare hardware- and software-oriented (code control) protocols.

4. Describe the operation and hardware of an Ethernet LAN system.

5. Differentiate among typical LAN topologies.

6. Differentiate among different types of network media (10Base-2, 10Base-5, and so on).

7. Define the term wide area network (WAN).

8. Describe the function of routers, hubs, and bridges in network systems.

9. Discuss basic concepts relating to Internet access (i.e., dial-up, ISP connections, browsers).

10. Discuss ISDN, DSL and cable modem connections.

11. Describe FTP operations.

12. Discuss common Internet concepts and terminology (such as e-mail).

13. Discuss the purpose and use of an Internet browser.

DATA COMMUNICATIONS

INTRODUCTION

The most explosive area of personal computer use is in the realm of data communications. Increasingly, personal computers are being connected to one another. Data communications can be as simple as connecting two units together so they can talk to each other. This can be accomplished by wiring their serial, or parallel, ports together when they are in close physical proximity to each other (up to a few feet). Communicating over longer distances requires additional hardware in the form of a modem, or a network card, and software, in the form of drivers and protocols.

When more than two computers are linked together so that they can share information, a network is formed. Networks in a relatively confined geographical area are called Local Area Networks (LANs), and networks distributed over wider geographical areas are referred to as Wide Area Networks (WANs).

BASIC NETWORKING CONCEPTS

The A+ Core Hardware objective 6.2 states that the test taker should be able to identify basic networking concepts including how a network works.

Concepts include:

- Installing and configuring network cards
- Addressing
- Bandwidth
- Status indicators
- Protocols
- TCP/IP
- IPX/SPX (NWLINK)
- Cabling — Twisted pair, coaxial, fiber optic, RS-232

- AppleTalk
- NETBEUI/NETBIOS
- Full-duplex, half-duplex
- Networking models
- Peer-to-peer
- Client/server
- Infrared
- Wireless

Within a very short time span, the use of local area networks has grown immensely. They have become such an integral part of commercial computer systems, that, as the A+ objective points out, the PC technician must understand how they function. The following sections will present basic local area networking concepts and practices.

LOCAL AREA NETWORKS

Local area networks (LANs) are systems designed to connect computers together in relatively close proximity. These connections enable users attached to the network to share resources such as printers and modems. LAN connections also enable users to communicate with each other and share data among their computers.

When discussing LANs, there are two basic topics to consider: the LAN's **topology** (hardware connection method) and its **protocol** (communication control method). In concept, a minimum of three stations must be connected to have a true LAN. If only two units are connected, point-to-point communications software and a simple null modem could be employed.

LAN Topologies

Network topologies are physical connection/configuration strategies. LAN topologies fall into four types of configurations:

- **Bus**
- **Ring**
- **Star**
- **Mesh**

Figure 5-1 illustrates all four topologies. In the **bus topology**, the **nodes**, or **stations**, of the network connect to a central communication link. Each node has a unique address along the bus that differentiates it from the other users on the network. Information can be placed on the bus by any node. The information must contain the network address of the node, or nodes, that the information is intended for. Other nodes along the bus will ignore the information.

**Figure 5-1:
Star, Bus, Ring, and
Mesh Configurations**

Sidebar labels (left margin):

Local area networks (LANs)

topology

protocol

Bus

Ring

Star

Mesh

bus topology

nodes

stations

TEST TIP

Be able to recognize network topologies from this type of drawing.

In a ring network configuration, the communication bus is formed into a closed loop. Each node inspects the information on the LAN as it passes by. A repeater, built into each ring LAN card, regenerates every message not directed to it and sends it to the next appointed node. The originating node eventually receives the message back and removes it from the ring.

Ring topologies tend to offer very high data transfer rates but require additional management overhead. The additional management is required for dependability. If a node in a ring network fails, the entire network fails. To overcome this, ring designers have developed rings with primary and secondary data paths as depicted in Figure 5-2. If a break occurs in a primary link, the network controller can reroute the data onto the secondary link to avoid the break.

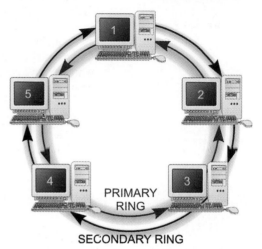

In a **star topology**, the logical layout of the network resembles the branches of a tree. All the nodes are connected in branches that eventually lead back to a central unit. Nodes communicate with each other through the central unit. The central station coordinates the network's activity by polling the nodes, one by one, to determine whether they have any information to transfer. If so, the central station gives that node a predetermined slice of time to transmit. If the message is longer than the time allotted, the transmissions are chopped into small packets of information that are transmitted over several polling cycles.

Figure 5-2: Primary/Secondary Ring Topologies

The **mesh design** offers the most basic network connection scheme. In this design, each node has a direct physical connection to all the other nodes in the network. While the overhead for connecting a mesh network topology together in a LAN environment is prohibitive, this topology is employed in two very large network environments—the public telephone system and the Internet.

Logical Topologies

It would be easy to visualize the connections of the **physical topologies** just described if the nodes simply connected to each other. However, this is typically not the case in newer LAN arrangements. This is due to the fact that most LAN installations employ connection devices,

such as **hubs** and **routers**, which alter the appearance of the actual connection scheme. Therefore, the **logical topology** will not match the appearance of the physical topology. The particulars of the connection scheme are hidden inside the connecting device. As an illustration, Figure 5-3 shows a typical network connection scheme using a router. The physical topology appears as a star. However, the internal wiring of the connecting router provides a logical bus topology.

It is not uncommon for a logical ring or mesh topology to be implemented in a physical star topology.

Figure 5-3: Logical Topologies

Network Control Strategies

When you begin to connect computers to other computers and devices so that they can share resources and data, the issue of how and who will control the network comes up very quickly. In some applications, such as developing a book like this one, it is good for the author, artists, and pagination people to be able to share access to text and graphics files, as well as access to devices such as printers. However, in a business network, companies must have control over who can have access to sensitive information and company resources, as well as when and how much.

Control of a network can be implemented in two ways:

peer-to-peer network

client/server network

file server

1. As a **peer-to-peer network** where each computer is attached to the network in a ring or bus fashion and is equal to the other units on the network.

2. As a **client/server network** where dependent workstations, referred to as clients, operate in conjunction with a dedicated master computer (**file server**).

Figure 5-4 illustrates a typical peer-to-peer network arrangement. In this arrangement, the users connected to the network can share access to different network resources, such as hard drives and printers. However, control of the local unit is fairly autonomous. The nodes in this type of network configuration usually contain local hard drives and printers that the local computer has control of. These resources can be shared at the discretion of the individual user. A common definition of a peer-to-peer network is one in which all of the nodes can act as both clients and servers of the other nodes under different conditions.

Figure 5-5 depicts a typical client/server LAN configuration. In this type of LAN, control tends to be very centralized. The server typically holds the programs and data for its client computers. It also provides security and network policy enforcement.

Figure 5-4: A Peer-to-Peer Network

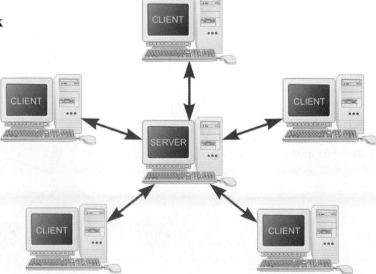

**Figure 5-5:
A Client/Server
Network**

In some cases, the client units do not even include a local hard drive or floppy drive unit. The bootup process is performed through an on-board BIOS, and no data is stored at the client machine. This type of client is referred to as a diskless **workstation**.

The major advantages of the client/server networkingarrangement include:

- Centralized administration
- Data and resource security

CHALLENGE #1

You are setting up a new production room for creating textbooks and multimedia presentations. You will employ writers, artists, document layout and paste up professionals, multimedia animators, and multimedia presentation designers. Your board of directors has asked you for input about how to set up the system. They anticipate tying everyone into the company's existing client/server network, but someone has suggested looking into peer-to-peer networks. What will you recommend to them and why?

CHALLENGE #2

Your board of directors has asked you to give them a report on implementing a peer-to-peer network for the entire company. This would include the development room from challenge 1 and would also include the accounting office, the technical services department, and the warehouse/shipping department. They have been told that peer-to-peer networks are relatively inexpensive and very flexible. What would you tell them about implementing this idea?

Network Transmission Media

Basically four media are used to transmit data between computers. These media include:

- Copper cabling
- Fiber-optic cabling
- Infrared light
- Wireless radio frequency (RF) signals

Each media type offers advantages that make them useful for networking in certain conditions. The main media-related considerations include their cost to implement, maximum data transmission rates, and noise immunity characteristics.

In the implementation phase of a network, the cost to install the medium is a primary concern. This cost exists in two facets—the actual relative cost of the media and its adapter/connections, and the cost associated with installing and configuring the network.

Likewise, each media type has some limitations on its ability to transfer information. This factor is also wrapped up in two considerations — its bandwidth and its attenuation. Bandwidth is the media's total ability to carry data at a given instance. Attenuation is a measure of how much signal loss occurs as the information moves across the medium. As you will see in the following sections, some media types can literally carry a signal for miles and still deliver it as recognizable information.

Unshielded Twisted Pair (UTP)

Shielded Twisted Pair (STP)

The final media-related consideration is noise immunity capabilities. Stray electrical energy (referred to as noise) moves through the atmosphere as a natural course. Electrical machines and devices also generate electronic noise. These stray signals can interfere with organized data signals and make them unrecognizable. Therefore, cabling used to transmit data is expected to have some resistance to these stray signals.

Under the heading of copper cabling, there are basically two categories to consider twisted-pair cabling and coaxial cabling. Twisted-pair cabling consists of two or more pairs of wires twisted together to provide noise reduction. The twist in the wires causes induced noise signals to cancel each other out. In this type of cabling, the number of twists in each foot of wire indicates its relative noise immunity level.

When discussing twisted-pair cabling with data networks, there are two basic types to consider: **Unshielded Twisted Pair (UTP)** and **Shielded Twisted Pair (STP)**. UTP networking cable contains four pairs of individually insulated wires as illustrated in Figure 5-6. STP cable is similar with the exception that it contains an additional foil shield that surrounds the four-pair wire bundle. The shield provides extended protection from induced electrical noise and cross talk by supplying a grounded path to carry the induced electrical signals away from the conductors in the cable.

Figure 5-6: UTP and STP Cabling

Coaxial Cable

Coaxial cable

Coaxial cable (often referred to simply as "coax") is familiar to most people as the conductor that carries cable TV into their homes. Coaxial cable is constructed with an insulated solid or stranded wire core surrounded by a dielectric insulating layer and a solid or braided metallic shield. Both the wire and shield are wrapped in an outer protective insulating jacket, as illustrated in Figure 5-7.

Figure 5-7: Coaxial Cable

In the past coaxial cable was widely used for Ethernet LAN media. However, because the thickness and rigidity of coaxial cable make it difficult and time consuming to install, the networking industry and network standards development groups have abandoned coaxial cable in favor of unshielded twisted pair cabling.

However, coax cable continues to be used for some applications, such as Internet service delivered to residential settings through the commercial cable television (CATV) system. In addition, several varieties of coaxial cable are available for transporting video and high-data-rate digital information. This comes into play as computers, audio/video equipment, and intelligent home products with residential networks.

Fiber-Optic Cable

Fiber-optic cable is plastic or glass cable designed to carry voice or digital data in the form of light pulses. The signals are introduced into the cable by a laser diode and bounce along its interior until they reach the end of the cable, as illustrated in Figure 5-8. At the end, a light detecting circuit receives the light signals and converts them back into usable information. This type of cabling offers potential signaling rates in excess of 200,000 Mbps. However, current access protocols still limit fiber-optic LAN speeds to 100 Mbps.

Because light moving through a fiber-optic cable does not attenuate (lose energy) as quickly as electrical signals moving along a copper conductor, segment lengths between transmitters and receivers can be much longer with fiber-optic cabling. In some fiber-optic applications, the maximum cable length can range up to 2 kilometers.

Figure 5-8: Transmitting Over Fiber-Optic Cable

Fiber-optic cable also provides a much more secure data transmission medium than copper cable because it cannot be tapped without physically breaking the conductor. Basically, light introduced into the cable at one end does not leave the cable except through the other end. In addition, fiber-optic cable electrically isolates the transmitter and receiver so that no signal level matching normally needs to be performed between the two ends.

Getting the light out of the cable without significant attenuation is the key to making fiber-optic connections. The end of the cable must be perfectly aligned with the receiver and be free from scratches, film, or dust that would distort or filter the light.

Wireless Infrared Links

The **IrDA** infrared transmission specification makes provisions for multiple IrDA devices to be attached to a computer so that it can have multiple, simultaneous links to multiple IrDA devices. Figure 5-9 shows how IrDA links can be used to share computers and devices through a normal Ethernet hub. In these scenarios, the IrDA link provides the high-speed transmission media between the Ethernet devices.

**Figure 5-9:
IrDA Networking**

One drawback of infrared transmissions in general is that they only provide line-of-sight communications over short distances and can be interfered with easily. In addition, they have very narrow lines of site (15 degrees of center with the line of transmission). IrDA devices cannot offer dependable communication paths if an object, such as a person, interrupts the path of the light from the transmitter to the receiver. And they also cannot penetrate walls or other solid objects and cannot communicate around corners.

Wireless RF Links

Recently, a variety of **Wireless Local Area Networking** (**WLAN** or **LAWN**) specifications have been introduced into the market. These networks connect computer nodes together using high-frequency radio waves. The IEEE organization has presented a specification titled IEEE-802.11 to describe its wireless networking standard. The IEEE-802.11b wireless standard has gained wide acceptance as the preferred wireless networking technology for both business and home network applications. Most current wireless LANs are based on this specification and operate at transfer rates in the range of 1 Mbps.

The wireless networking community is working with two **spread spectrum** technologies as the basis of their transmission method. In spread spectrum transmissions, the frequency of the radio signal hops in a random, defined sequence that is known to the receiving device. These technologies are referred to as **Frequency Hopping Spread Spectrum (FHSS)** and **Direct Sequence Spread Spectrum (DSSS)**. The FHSS method spreads the signal across the time spectrum using **Time Division Multiplexing (TDM)** techniques. The DSSS method combines the data with a faster carrier signal according to a predetermined frequency spreading ratio for transmission.

Time Division Multiple Access (TDMA) technology employs TDM to divide a radio carrier signal into time-slices, called **cells**, and then funnel data from different sources into the cells. This technique enables a single frequency signal to serve a number of different customers simultaneously. A similar technology known as **CDMA (Code Division Multiple Access)** does not assign users a specific frequency. Instead, it spreads the user's data across a range of frequencies in a random digital sequence.

Another interesting wireless networking specification is known as **Bluetooth**. This specification was originally put forth by a consortium made up of Ericsson, IBM, Intel, Nokia, and Toshiba as a short-range wireless radio technology designed to coordinate communications between network devices and the Internet. The meshing together of personal computers, cell phones, web devices, LAN devices, and other intelligent devices in a common forum is referred to as **convergence**. The Bluetooth specification is intended to promote convergence of these systems.

A typical wireless LAN, depicted in Figure 5-10, consists of a device known as an **access point** and any number of wireless network-capable devices. The wireless access point acts as a bridging device that connects the wireless network computers with the wired network. Wireless network computers use a network interface card that has a radio transmitter, receiver, and antenna integrated into the card.

| spread spectrum |
| Frequency Hopping Spread Spectrum (FHSS) |
| Direct Sequence Spread Spectrum (DSSS) |
| Time Division Multiplexing (TDM) |
| Time Division Multiple Access (TDMA) |
| CDMA (Code Division Multiple Access) |
| Bluetooth |
| convergence |
| access point |

**Figure 5-10:
A Wireless LAN**

Each computer that has a wireless card installed can communicate with other wireless equipped computers or with the access point. The access point has antennas and a radio receiver/transmitter that it uses to communicate with the other devices through radio frequency signals in the unlicensed 2.4 GHz radio band. Conversely, it communicates with the host computer through a physical interface known as an Ethernet hub. The hub provides connectivity between the access point and the wired Ethernet LAN.

Wireless LAN (WLAN) adapters

On the other hand, **Wireless LAN (WLAN) adapters** for PCs are typically available in the form of plug-in PCI and PCMCIA cards, or as attachable USB devices. Wireless network computers are also able to communicate with wired network computers on an Ethernet LAN using the access point as the connection between the two networks.

The IEEE-802.11b wireless standard has gained wide acceptance as the preferred wireless networking technology for both business and home network applications.

The access point is the key component of wireless networks. It has antennas, a radio receiver/transmitter that it uses to communicate with the other devices through radio frequency signals in the unlicensed 2.4 GHz radio band. Conversely, it communicates with the host computer through a physical interface known as an Ethernet hub. The hub provides connectivity between the access point and the wired Ethernet LAN.

While wireless networks are gaining popularity for their ease of installation, some security issues remain concerning using them to communicate personal or otherwise sensitive information. The following list describes the fundamental pros and cons associated with wireless networking:

- Installation flexibility — Wireless LANs provide the maximum amount of flexibility for connecting home and office networking components. Because no wires are required to connect devices to the wireless network, the users have considerable mobility. Laptop computers may be used throughout the home as long as they are within range of other wireless terminals or the access point. Installing the needed adapter cards and network software is all that is necessary to start sharing data and resources.

- Services for mobile users — Typical distances covered by wireless LANs are limited to specific indoor office locations or retail business locations called "hot spots." These are WiFi-enabled locations where customers with wireless-equipped portable computers can connect to the Internet while enjoying a coffee break or snack such as an airport, hotel lobby, fast food restaurant, or coffee shop. WiFi is a trademark used by wireless LANs that operate on unlicensed radio spectrum and are therefore restricted to limited transmitter power covering an area of 200–300 feet from the antenna.

Wired Equivalent Privacy (WEP)

- Security issues – Transmissions from wireless network devices cannot simply be confined to the local environment of a home or business. Although the range is limited to a few hundred feet, radio signals can easily be intercepted even outside the vicinity of the stated security perimeter. Any other unauthorized mobile terminal can accomplish this using an 802.11 receiver. In order to minimize the risk of security compromise on a wireless LAN, the IEEE-802.11b standard provides a security feature called **Wired Equivalent Privacy (WEP)**. WEP provides a method for encrypting data transmissions and authenticating each computer on the network. The 802.11b standard is discussed in detail later in this chapter.

- Multipath problems and signal strength — Signal strength at the received nodes on a wireless LAN can be impacted by signals bouncing off walls and objects in an indoor environment. The radio waves may arrive from multiple directions and in some cases can cancel or severely reduce the signal strength between portable users.

This effect is called multipath and is eliminated by analyzing the signals with test instruments or moving the nodes to a different location. Microwave radio emissions from other devices using the unlicensed 2.4 GHz radio spectrum are also a source of electromagnetic interference. The WLAN adapter cards and the access point should be installed in such a way that they provide the maximum exposure for the antenna to maximize signal strength.

Although there are still problems to overcome, the wireless network is becoming a popular option for connecting devices in the home and small office environments. It is also becoming an economical choice for locations where installing cable is not practical or is prohibited by historic building codes or other restrictions. Home networks where maximum flexibility and mobility for the network devices is desired also make wireless LAN technology an attractive technology.

INSTALLING AND CONFIGURING LANS

A portion of the A+ Core Hardware objective 6.2 states that the test taker should be able to identify procedures for swapping and configuring network interface cards. Because PC technicians are typically responsible for maintaining the portion of the network that attaches to the computer, they must be able to install, configure, and service the network adapter card and cable. The following sections deal with installing and configuring LAN cards.

LAN Adapter Cards

In a LAN, each computer on the network requires a **network adapter card** (also referred to as a **Network Interface Card** or **NIC**) and every unit has to be connected to the network by some type of cabling. These cables are typically either twisted-pair wires, thick or thin coaxial cable, or fiber-optic cable.

LAN adapter cards must have connectors that are compatible with the type of LAN cabling being used. Many Ethernet LAN cards come with both an RJ-45 and a BNC connector, so the cards can be used in any type of Ethernet configuration.

Figure 5-11 depicts a typical LAN card. In addition to its LAN connectors, the LAN card may have a number of configuration jumpers that must be set up.

> **network adapter card**
>
> **Network Interface Card (NIC)**

Figure 5-11: A
Typical LAN Card

bootup ROM

Another item that can be found on many LAN cards is a vacant ROM socket. This socket is included so that it can be used to install a **bootup ROM** that will enable the unit to be used as a diskless workstation. One or more activity lights may also be included on the card's back plate. These lights can play a very important part in diagnosing problems with the LAN connection. Check the card's user manual for definitions of its activity lights.

Each adapter must have an adapter driver program loaded in its host computer to handle communications between the system and the adapter. These are the Ethernet and Token Ring drivers loaded to control specific types of LAN adapter cards.

In addition to the adapter drivers, the network computer must have a network protocol driver loaded. This program may be referred to as the **transport protocol**, or just as the protocol. It operates between the adapter and the initial layer of network software to package and unpackage data for the LAN. In many cases, the computer may have several different protocol drivers loaded so that the unit can communicate with computers that use other types of protocols.

transport protocol

Internetworking Packet Exchange/ Sequential Packet Exchange (IPX/SPX)

Transmission Control Protocol/Internet Protocol (TCP/IP)

ARPA

Typical protocol drivers include the **Internetworking Packet Exchange/Sequential Packet Exchange (IPX/SPX)** model produced by Novell, and the standard **Transmission Control Protocol/Internet Protocol (TCP/IP)** developed by the U.S. military for its **ARPA** network. Figure 5-12 illustrates the various LAN drivers necessary to transmit, or receive, data on a network.

Figure 5-12: Various LAN Drivers

Installing LAN Cards

Installing a LAN card in a PC follows the basic steps of installing most peripheral cards. Check the system for currently installed drivers and system settings. Consult the LAN card's installation guide for the default settings, and compare them to those of the devices already installed in the system. If there are no apparent conflicts between the default settings and those already used by the system, place the adapter card in a vacant expansion slot and secure it to the system unit's back plate.

Connect the LAN card to the network as directed by the manufacturer's installation guide, and load the proper software drivers for the installed adapter (see Table 5-1). Figure 5-13 illustrates connecting the computer to the LAN, using UTP or coaxial cable. If UTP cable is being used, the line drop to the computer would come from a concentrator like the one depicted.

Figure 5-13: Connecting the Computer to the LAN

The following three important pieces of information are required to configure the LAN adapter card for use:

- The Interrupt Request (IRQ) setting the adapter will use to communicate with the system.

- The **I/O port address** the adapter will use to exchange information with the system.

- The **base memory address** that the adapter will use as a starting point in memory for DMA transfers.

Some adapters may require that a DMA channel be defined.

Typical configuration settings for the network card's IRQ, I/O port address, and base memory are as follows:

```
IRQ=5
Port Address=300
Base Memory=D8000
```

Table 5-1: LAN Card Configuration Settings

I/O ADDRESS OPTIONS	INTERRUPT REQUEST CHANNELS	EXTENDED MEMORY ADDRESSING
240	IRQ3	C400
280	IRQ4	C800
2C0	IRQ10	CC00
320	IRQ11	D000
340	IRQ12	D400
360	IRQ15	DC00

If a configuration conflict appears, reset the conflicting settings so that they do not share the same value. Which component's configuration gets changed is determined by examining the options for changing the cards involved in the conflict. A sound card may have many more IRQ options available than a given network card. In that case, it would be easier to change sound card settings than network card settings.

After the card has been installed and physically connected to the network transmission media, the driver and protocols described in the previous section must be installed. These items are operating system specific, so we will deal with them in the networking sections of the various operating system chapters later in the book.

Optimizing Network Adapters

In a networked system, by design all the nodes in the network run at the same speed. That means that the performance of the network is limited by its slowest component. If the system is using mostly adapter cards and devices rated for 100 MHz operation, but one or more of the cards are only rated for 10 MHz operation, then the system will be limited to 10 MHz operation. Therefore, all of the adapters in the system should be updated to use the 100 MHz speed.

Installing Wireless LANs

Wireless LANs provide the maximum amount of flexibility for connecting home and office networking components. Because no wires are required to connect devices to the wireless network, the users have considerable mobility. The wireless network is becoming a popular option for connecting devices in residential and small office environments. It is also becoming an economical choice for locations where installing cable is not practical or is prohibited by historic building codes or other restrictions.

As Figure 5-14 illustrates, the access point is the mainstay of the wireless network. These devices serve as the central connection point for all the network devices within its range. The access point also provides the physical connection with wired networks. The access point can be connected to a host computer that is a node on an existing hard-wired network, or it can be connected directly into a connectivity device such as a network hub or router. Installing the access point is normally a matter of connecting it to the network host, installing its power adapter, and loading its network drivers and protocols on the host computer.

**Figure 5-14:
A Typical
Ethernet Frame**

The antennas in the access point establish a range of transmission around the access point called a hot spot. Other wireless computing devices (clients) may access the network throughout the hot spot as long as they are within range of other wireless terminals or the access point. Wireless clients can be any type of computer or peripheral designed to use the same wireless protocol that the access point is using. These devices include desktop computers with wireless PCI cards, laptop computers using PCMCIA cards, and wireless peripheral equipment using built-in wireless interfaces.

For most computers, all that is necessary to start sharing data and resources wirelessly is to install the proper wireless adapter cards and network software. Intel has recently unveiled its new Centrino mobile technology that will be included in a wide variety of network computers and network devices.

However, while wireless networks are gaining popularity for their ease of installation, there are a number of security issues concerning using them to communicate personal or otherwise sensitive information. Transmissions from wireless network devices cannot simply be confined to the local environment of a residence or business. Although their range is typically limited to a few hundred feet, RF signals can easily be intercepted even outside the vicinity of the stated security perimeter. Any other unauthorized mobile terminal can accomplish this using an 802.11 receiver.

In order to minimize the risk of security compromise on a wireless LAN, the IEEE-802.11b standard provides a security feature called Wired Equivalent Privacy (WEP). This standard provides a method for encrypting data transmissions and authenticating each computer on the network.

While the physical installation and configuration of wireless networks is typically easy when computers are close to each other and there are no physical barriers to their line-of-sight transmissions, installations can become more difficult when you have clients located at distances from the access point or when there are physical barriers of any type (e.g., walls).

The RF signal strength at wireless LAN clients can be negatively impacted by signals bouncing off walls and objects in an indoor environment. The radio waves may arrive from multiple directions and in some cases can cancel or severely reduce the signal strength between portable users. This effect is called **multipath** and is eliminated by analyzing the signals with test instruments or moving the nodes to a different location. Most access points include software-based signal strength analysis tools as part of their support package. These tools can be used to test for signal strength when the computer has been installed and brought on line.

multipath

Microwave radio emissions from other devices using the unlicensed 2.4 GHz radio spectrum are also a source of electromagnetic interference. The WLAN adapter cards and the access point should be installed in such a way that they provide the maximum exposure for the antenna to maximize signal strength.

Network Architectures

Networks are complex, multifaceted structures that require a tremendous amount of interaction between computer designers, network equipment designers, operating system manufacturers, and networking application providers. Several initiatives have been put forward to provide models to serve as blueprints for these groups to follow in designing their products. While you should be aware that different hierarchical networking models exist, the most widely discussed initiative is the Open Systems Interconnection (OSI) model put forward by the International Standards Organization.

The layers of this model are shown in Figure 5-15. In the figure, each layer on the left is matched with a group of protocols that operate within it on the right. As you can see, there are many protocols at work in network architectures. Local area networking environments are primarily concerned with the first four layers of the model, while layers four through seven are more widely dealt with in wide area network environments. Basically, there are two de facto network architectures in use with local area networks: Ethernet and Token Ring.

Figure 5-15: The OSI Networking Model

NOTE

Don't worry about memorizing the layers of the OSI model and their related protocols. The OSI model is not tested for on the A+ exam, but it puts the following discussions of different protocols in perspective. You should be aware as we describe different protocols in subsequent discussion that they work together to get data where it is supposed to go. However, you may want to start getting familiar with the OSI model if you intend to pursue the Network+ and i-Net+ exams after you complete the A+ exams.

Ethernet

Xerox developed **Ethernet** in 1976. The standard specification for Ethernet has been published by the **International Electrical and Electronic Association (IEEE)** as the **IEEE-802.3 Ethernet protocol** (refer to the *Data Link* layer of the OSI model). Local area networks are designed so that the entire network runs synchronously at one frequency. Therefore, only one set of electronic signals may be placed on the network at one time. However, data can move in both directions between network locations. By definition, this makes local area network operations half-duplex in nature (i.e., information can travel in both direction, but not at the same time).

In a network, some method must be used to determine which node has use of the network's communications paths, and for how long it can have it. The network's access protocol handles these functions, and it is necessary to prevent more than one user from accessing the bus at any given time. If two sets of data are placed on the network at the same time, a data collision occurs and data is lost.

Ethernet

International Electrical and Electronic Association (IEEE)

IEEE-802.3 Ethernet protocol

The Ethernet methodology for access control is referred to as **carrier sense multiple-access with collision detection (CSMA/CD)**. Using this protocol, a node that wants to transfer data over the network first listens to the LAN to determine whether it is in use. If the LAN is not in use, the node begins transmitting its data. If the network is busy, the node waits for the LAN to clear for a predetermined time, and then takes control of the LAN.

If two nodes are waiting to use the LAN, they will periodically attempt to access the LAN at the same time. When this happens, a data collision occurs, and the data from both nodes is rendered useless. The receiver portion of the Ethernet controller monitors the transmission to detect collisions. When it senses the data bits overlapping, it halts the transmission, as does the other node. The transmitting controller generates an abort pattern code that is transmitted to all the nodes on the LAN, telling them that a collision has occurred. This alerts any nodes that might be waiting to access the LAN that there is a problem.

The receiving node (or nodes) dump any data that it might have received before the collision occurred. Other nodes waiting to send data generate a random timing number and go into a holding pattern. The timing number is a waiting time that the node sits out before it tries to transmit. Because the number is randomly generated, the odds against two of the nodes trying to transmit again at the same time are very low.

The first node to time out listens to the LAN to determine whether any activity is still occurring. Because it almost always finds a clear LAN, it begins transmitting. If two of the nodes do time out at the same time, another collision happens and the abort pattern/number generation/time-out sequence begins again. Eventually, one of the nodes will gain clear access to the network and successfully transmit its data.

Limitations of Ethernet — The Ethernet strategy provides for up to 1,024 users to share the LAN. From the description of its collision-recovery technique, however, it should be apparent that with more users on an Ethernet LAN, more collisions are likely to occur, and the average time to complete an actual data transfer will be longer.

The Ethernet Frame

Under the Ethernet standard, information is collected into a package called a **frame**. Figure 5-16 depicts a typical Ethernet frame. The frame carries the following six sections of information:

- A preamble
- A destination address
- An originating address
- A type field
- The data field
- The frame check error-detection and correction information

Figure 5-16: A Typical Ethernet

This organizational structure is very similar to that of a sector on a hard disk. The preamble synchronizes the receiver's operation to that of the transmitter. This action also tells the other nodes that a transmission is under way. The Ethernet preamble is a 64-bit string made up of alternating 1s and 0s, and ending in two consecutive 1s.

The destination address field is 6 bytes long, and is used to define one of three address locations. This number can represent the individual node address of the intended receiver or the address of a grouping of nodes around the LAN, or it can be a broadcast code that allows the node to send a message to everyone on the LAN.

The originating address field contains the identification address for the transmitting node. The type field is a 2-byte field that identifies the user protocol of the frame.

The data field is a variable-length field that contains the actual information. Because it is sent in a synchronous mode, the data field can be as long as necessary. The Ethernet standard does not allow for data fields less than 46 bytes, however, or longer than 1,500 bytes.

The frame-check block contains an error-detection and correction word. Like parity and other error-detection schemes, the receiver regenerates the error code from the received data (actually the data, the address bytes, and the type field), and compares it to the received code. If a mismatch occurs, an error signal is generated from the LAN card to the system.

Token Ring

Token Ring

In 1985, IBM developed a token-passing LAN protocol called **Token Ring**. As its name implies, Token Ring is a token-passing protocol operating on a ring topology. The token is a small frame that all nodes can recognize instantly. This access protocol standard specification is referred to as the IEEE-802.5 Token Ring Protocol (refer to the Data Link layer of the OSI model in Figure 5-15).

In a token-passing system, contention for use of the LAN between different nodes is handled by passing an electronic enabling code, called a token, from node to node. Only the node possessing the token can have control of the LAN. Figure 5-17 illustrates this concept.

The token is passed from node to node along the LAN. Each node is allowed to hold the token a prescribed amount of time. After sending its message, or after its time runs out, the node must transfer the token to the next node. If the next node has no message, it just passes the token along to the next designated node. Nodes do not have to be in numeric sequence; their sequences are programmed in the network management software. All nodes listen to the LAN during the token-passing time.

Figure 5-17: A Token-Passing Scheme

In a token-passing network, new or removed nodes must be added to, or deleted from, the rotational list in the network-management software. If not, the LAN will never grant access to the new nodes. Token Ring management software and cards are built so that each device attached to the LAN is interrogated when the LAN is started up. In this way, the rotational file is verified each time the network is started.

New nodes that start up after the LAN has been initialized transmit a reconfiguration burst that can be heard by all the nodes. This burst grabs the attention of all the installed nodes, and erases their token destination addresses. Each node goes into a wait state determined by its station number. The node with the highest station number times out first and tries to access the LAN.

The highest numbered node is responsible for starting the token-passing action after a new unit is added to the LAN. This is accomplished by broadcasting a signal to all nodes telling them what it believes is the lowest numbered node in the LAN, and asking whether it will accept the token. If no response is given, the node moves to the next known address in the LAN management software's roster and repeats the request. This action continues until an enabled node responds. At this point, the token is passed to the new node and the forwarding address is stored in the LAN manager's list. Each successive node goes through the same process until all the nodes have been accessed.

The node passing the token must always monitor the LAN. This is done to prevent the loss of the token during its passage. If the node remains inactive for a predetermined amount of time, the transmitting node must reclaim the token and search for the next active node to pass it to. In this case, the transmitting node just increments its next-node address by one, and then attempts to make contact with a node at that address. If not, it will increment the count by one again, and retry, until it reaches an enabled node. This new node number is stored in the transmitting node and will be the pass-to number for that node, until the system is shut down or reconfigured.

When the ring is idle, the token just passes counterclockwise from station to station. A station can transmit information on the ring any time that it receives the token. This is accomplished by turning the token packet into the start of a data packet and adding the node's data to it.

At the intended receiver, the packet is copied into a buffer memory, serially, where it is stored. The receiver also places the packet back on the ring so that the transmitter can get it back. Upon doing so, the transmitter reconstructs the token and places it back on the ring. Figure 5-18 depicts this concept.

The Token Ring cabling is a two-pair, shielded twisted-pair cable. The main cable is called the **trunk cable**, and the individual drops are referred to as the interface cables. The cables are grouped together by hardware units called **concentrators**. Internally, the concentrator's ports are connected into a ring configuration. In this manner, the concentrator can be placed in a convenient area, and have nodes positioned where they are needed. Some Token Ring adapters provide 9-pin connectors for **Shielded Twisted Pair (STP)** cables as well.

Figure 5-18: Token Ring Concept

| trunk cable |
| concentrators |
| Shielded Twisted Pair (STP) |

The data-transfer rate stated for Token Ring systems is 4 to 16 Mbps. Token-passing is less efficient than other protocols when the load on the network is light. It evenly divides the network's usage among nodes, however, when traffic is heavy. It can also be extremely vulnerable to node crashes when a node has the token. LAN adapter cards are typically designed to monitor the LAN for such occurrences so that they can be corrected without shutting down the entire network.

The IEEE specifications for both Ethernet (802.3) and **Token Ring (802.5)** make provisions for a high-speed, full-duplex mode (two-way simultaneous communication). This mode is normally encountered in large networks that have multiple servers. Its primary use is to perform backup functions between the large system servers where lots of data must be moved through the network. In full-duplex mode, the standard Ethernet transfer rate of 10 Mbps is boosted to 20 Mbps and the Token Ring rate is raised to 32 Mbps. This mode is rarely encountered on desktop client units. These units tend to operate in half-duplex mode (providing two-way communication, but in only one direction at a time).

Networking Protocols

When more than two computers are involved in the communications pathway, a network is formed and additional controls must be put into place to make certain that information is sent to the correct member of the network. This is in addition to controlling the flow of information on the network connection. A **network protocol** is a set of rules that governs how communications are conducted across a network. These protocols operate at the Network and Transport layers of the OSI model (as shown in Figure 5-15). In order for devices to communicate with each other on the network, they must all use the same network protocol.

While there are many different types of network protocols in use throughout the world, there are four that are widely accepted and must typically be dealt with in normal network environments:

- *NetBEUI* – **NetBIOS Enhanced User Interface (NetBEUI)** is a fast, efficient protocol, suitable for use on smaller Microsoft networks. It doesn't require any configuration to implement and is very simple to administer. NetBEUI is the fastest networking protocol because it has very low non-data overhead. However, NetBEUI is not a routable protocol and therefore it cannot be used in complex, multisegment networks that use routers. Therefore, the NetBEUI protocol is not used much anymore because the TCP/IP protocol has become the protocol of choice for most networks.

- *NWLink* – NWLink is Microsoft's version of the **Internetwork Packet Exchange/Sequenced Packet Exchange (IPX/SPX)** network protocol used in Novell NetWare environments. While NetWare has used IPX/SPX for the majority of its networking functions, with the release of Netware 5.0 Novell changed Netware's primary protocol from IPX/SPX to TCP/IP. Even so, the majority of the installed NetWare networks continue to run IPX/SPX for at least some networking functions. IPX/SPX is a routable protocol, and therefore is suitable for use in larger multisegment network environments.

NWLink is relatively easy to install and manage and is also a routable protocol. While IPX/SPX nearly became the most widely used network protocol, it has taken second place behind TCP/IP because of the Internet. The IPX/SPX protocol is slower than NetBEUI, but it is faster than TCP/IP.

- *Appletalk* – **Appletalk** is used to communicate with Apple Macintosh computers. Historically, Apple has used Appletalk for the majority of the functions in their networking environment. However, Apple now supports TCP/IP as well. Appletalk is a routable protocol. In a PC environment, the Appletalk protocol is normally only implemented to communicate with Macintosh computers on your network.

- *TCP/IP* – **Transmission Control Protocol/Internet Protocol (TCP/IP)** Transport Control Protocol/Internet Protocol (**TCP/IP**) is the most popular network protocol currently in use due largely to the fact that the Internet is based on it. However, TCP/IP has rapidly become the protocol of choice for corporate networks because most operating systems support this protocol. This fact becomes very useful when you are trying to network different types of systems (e.g., Windows, Apple Macs, Linux machines) to one another. Also, TCP/IP is a routable protocol, so its packets can be transferred across many different types of networks before they reach their final destination.

While TCP/IP is much slower than either IPX/SPX or NetBEUI, because it is aa very reliable protocol it has the ability to ensure that data will be delivered to the receiver correctly. These network protocols will be visited again later in this chapter as we apply them to the Internet, and then again in Chapters 9 and 10 when we set up LAN and WAN connections for different operating systems.

NETWORKING MEDIA

The A+ Core Hardware objective 6.1 states that the test taker should be able to identify the common types of network cables, their characteristics, and connectors.

Cable types include:

- Coaxial
- RG-6
- RG-8

- RG-58
- RG-59
- Plenum/PVC

- UTP
- CAT 3
- CAT 5/e

- CAT 6
- STP
- Fiber

- Single-mode
- Multimode

Connector types include:

- BNC
- RJ-45
- AUI
- ST/SC
- DC/UDC

In the previous sections of this chapter we have only touched on the different network media in general terms. However, as this objective points out, there are many variations of network media that an A+ technician may be required to deal with.

Coaxial Cable Specifications

Typically coax cable is specified by an **RG rating** that is appropriate for a given application (such as RG-58 cable for use in Ethernet data network applications or RG-59 for CATV). The "RG" designation stands for radio grade, a term used in military specifications. Some grades of coaxial cable have similar outer appearances (i.e., RG-58 and RG-59). However, it is not advisable to mix different cable and terminator specifications as we once did when we switched from an older ArcNet LAN to an Ethernet LAN. Make sure that you have the correct grade of cable and the corresponding correct terminator for the intended coaxial application.

Coaxial cables are typically categorized according to their size (diameter), shielding and core construction, type of dielectric, impedance, velocity factor, fire rating, and attenuation rating.

- *RG-6* – RG-6 coaxial cable is the preferred type of coaxial cable for residential structured wiring. It is widely used for video distribution and also for connecting satellite receiving antenna systems to standard, digital, and high-definition television (HDTV) receivers. RG-6 cable has an impedance of 75 ohms and uses 18-gauge wire. This type of coaxial cable connects to equipment through a threaded "F" connector.

Thicknet

Medium Attachment Unit (MAU)

Attachment Unit Interface (AUI)

- *RG-8* – Referred to as **Thicknet** coax cabling, RG-8 was widely used in 10Base-5 Ethernet networking. RG-8 cable has an impedance of 50 ohms and uses 19/10-gauge wire centers. The Thicknet cable does not actually connect to the network adapter in the computer. Instead, a device called a **Medium Attachment Unit (MAU)** is inserted in line with the cable as illustrated in Figure 5-19. An interface cable referred to as an **Attachment Unit Interface (AUI)** connects the MAU to the network adapter card through a 15-pin AUI cable.

Figure 5-19: Thicknet Connections

Thinnet

- *RG-58* – **Thinnet** Ethernet cabling used for 10Base-2 networks. RG-58 cable has an impedance of 50 ohms and uses 24-gauge wire centers. These cables attach to equipment through BNCs (British Naval Connectors). In 10Base-2 LANs, the node's LAN adapter card is usually connected directly to the LAN cabling, using a T-connector for peer-to-peer networks, or a BNC connector in a client/server LANs.

- *RG-59* – RG-59 cable is widely used for CATV and video services. It is very similar in appearance to RG-58 cabling.

Twisted-Pair Cabling

EIA/TIA-568

Unshielded Twisted Pair (UTP)

category (CAT) ratings

One of the specifications associated with the Physical layer of the OSI model is the **EIA/TIA-568** specification for network wiring. Two groups have established this specification jointly — the Electronic Industry Association and the Telecommunications Industry Association (TIA) — to standardize the use of **Unshielded Twisted Pair (UTP)** cable for different networking applications. These organizations have categorized different grades of cable along with connector, distance, and installation specifications to produce the EIA/TIA UTP wiring **category (CAT) ratings** for the industry (i.e., CAT 3 and CAT 5 cabling).

Table 5-2 lists the industry's various CAT cable ratings that apply to UTP data communications cabling. CAT 5 cabling is currently the most widely used specification for data communication wiring.

The connector and color-coded connection schemes specified for 4-pair, EIA/TIA 568-A and 568-B CAT 5 UTP network cabling configurations is illustrated in Figure 5-20. In both cases, the UTP cabling is terminated in an 8-pin RJ-45 plug. The color code for attaching the connector to the cable is also provided in the figure.

UTP LAN connections are made through modular RJ-45 registered jacks and plugs. RJ-45 connectors are very similar in appearance to the RJ-11 connectors used with telephones and modems. However, the RJ-45 connectors are considerably larger than the RJ-11 connectors. Some Ethernet adapters include 15-pin sockets that enable special systems, such as fiber-optic cabling, to be interfaced to them. Other cards provide specialized ST connectors for fiber-optic connections.

Table 5-2: UTP Cable Category Ratings

CATEGORY	MAXIMUM BANDWIDTH	WIRING TYPES	APPLICATIONS
3	16 MHz	100 Ω UTP Rated Category 3	10 Mbps Ethernet 4 Mbps Token Ring
4	20 MHz	100 Ω UTP Rated Category 4	10 Mbps Ethernet 16 Mbps Token Ring
5	100 MHz	100 Ω UTP Rated Category 5	100 Mbps TPDDI 155 Mbps ATM
5E	160 MHz	100 Ω UTP Rated Category 5E	1.2 Gbps 1000Base-T High-Speed ATM
6 Proposed	200-250 MHz	100 Ω UTP Rated Category 6	1.2 Gbps 1000Base-T High-Speed ATM and beyond
7 Proposed	600-862 MHz	100 Ω UTP Rated Category 7	1.2 Gbps 1000Base-T High-Speed ATM and beyond

T568A STANDARD

T568B STANDARD (MORE COMMON)

─ **TEST TIP** ─

Know what type of cabling is involved in the CAT 5 cable rating.

Figure 5-20: UTP Cable Connection Specifications

IDC Connections

While UTP cabling is typically terminated in an RJ-45 connector at the computer end of the network, other types of connectors are used when the cables become part of the structured wiring of a facility. These connections are normally made in areas of the facility designated as the entrance facility or the telecommunications closet.

A standard method for terminating telecommunications wiring at these locations is to route all the data/telecommunications wiring to a connection block that employs an **Insulation Displacement Connector (IDC)**. This connection method offers faster installation and more reliable connections.

Insulation Displacement Connector (IDC)

IDCs do not require the conductors to be stripped of their insulation. Instead, the conductor is forced into a terminal strip, which not only holds it firmly in place, but also pierces the insulation to make an electrical connection.

The two most common styles of IDC are the **type-66** and **type-110 termination blocks**, depicted in Figure 5-21. Older type-66 blocks are insulation displacement system designed to wire up telephones and similar communications systems. They usually contain 200 metal slots (for interfacing 50 pairs from two sources), and come in various formats for those pins.

TYPE-66 IDC BLOCK

TYPE-110 IDC BLOCK

Figure 5-21:
IDC Connection

They are designed to work with solid wire (22- to 26-gauge), which is forced or "punched" into each slot, displacing the insulation and making the connection. While they were not originally intended for use in data connections, some newer versions are used for this purpose.

Type-110 blocks are newer types of IDC blocks that occupy less space than type-66 blocks for an equal number of connections. These blocks are more likely to be rated for CAT 5 wire than type-66 blocks, and often have RJ-11 or RJ-45 connectors already attached to them.

Computer and network technicians are not typically involved with these connections, but should be aware that they exist as part of the communications infrastructure that enables them to communicate outside their local facility.

UDC Connections

Universal Data Connectors (UDCs)

Some Token Ring networks employ special connectors called **Universal Data Connectors (UDCs)** to interconnect their four-wire STP (Type-1A) cables in very noisy electronic environments. The UDC device was developed as a part of IBM's Token Ring networking standard to provide highly dependable connections even under adverse conditions.

Most Token Ring networks have resorted to using UTP cable and RJ-45 connectors, but in some environments UDCs are still preferred. Figure 5-22 depicts a UDC connector being attached to a UTP adapter.

Figure 5-22: A UDC Connection

Fiber-Optic Cables

As indicated earlier in this chapter, fiber-optic cabling offers the prospect of very high performance links for LAN implementation. It can handle much higher data-transfer rates than copper conductors, and can use longer distances between stations before signal deterioration becomes a problem. In addition, fiber-optic cable offers a high degree of security for data communications: Because it does not radiate EMI signal information that can be detected outside the conductor, it does not tap easily, and it shows a decided signal loss when it is tapped into.

There are two basic types of fiber-optic cabling used in networking applications. These are:

- *Multimode Fiber-Optic Cable* — **Multimode fiber-optic cable** is designed so that light travels in many paths from the transmitter to the receiver. Light rays that enter the cable reflect off the cladding at different angles as they move along the length of the cable. These rays disperse in the cladding and are useless as signals. Only those light rays introduced to the core of the cable within a range of critical angles will travel down the cable. Even with the excessive signal attenuation created by this method, it is still the most commonly used cable type because it is cheaper and will transmit light over sufficient distances for use in local area networks.

- *Single-Mode Fiber-Optic Cable* — In a **single-mode fiber-optic cable**, the diameter of the core is reduced so that just one wavelength of the light source travels down the wire. The light source for this type of cable is a laser. Laser diodes (LDs) produce the in-phase, single-frequency, unidirectional light rays required to travel down such a cable. These cables are normally reserved for use in high-speed, long-distance cable runs.

Multimode fiber-optic cable

single-mode fiber-optic cable

TEST TIP
Know that single-mode and multimode are the two types of fiber-optic cable.

SC connector

Straight Tip (ST) connector

Figure 5-23: Fiber-Optic Cable Connectors

SC CONNECTOR

ST CONNECTOR

Figure 5-23 depicts two types of fiber-optic connectors. The connector on the top is a **SC connector** and the one on the bottom is a **Straight Tip (ST) connector**. The SC connector is the dominant connector for fiber-optic Ethernet networks. In both cases, the connectors are designed so that they correctly align the end of the cable with the receiver.

Plenum Cable

Another important rating for all cable types comes into play when you must install a cable in a space that is primarily involved in moving air throughout a facility. According to the National Electrical Code 1999 (NEC), a **plenum** is "a compartment or chamber to which one or more air ducts are connected and that forms part of the air distribution system." Likewise, the BICSI (Building Industry Consulting Services International) standards organization defines plenum as "a designated closed or open area that is used for transport of environmental air."

plenum

According to the *National Electrical Code*, when you install cables in plenums you must use special plenum rated cables that are listed as "Type CMP" (Communications Plenum) cable. In certain cases, "Type MPP" (Multipurpose Plenum) Cables offer an acceptable substitute for Type CMP cables. **Plenum rated cables** are suitable for use in ducts, plenums, and other spaces used for environmental air because they have adequate fire-resistant and low smoke-producing characteristics. The reason for this requirement is that when the protective insulation placed around cabling burns, it gives off toxic gases. If these cables are located in a plenum area, the dangerous gases will spread throughout the facility as part of the air circulation system.

Plenum rated cables

Ethernet Specifications

In earlier discussions, the Ethernet and Token Ring architectures were described in terms of where they operated on the OSI model, but no mention was made of how those protocols were implemented at the *Physical* layer.

Ethernet is classified as a bus topology that has been implemented across several different network media, including:

- Coaxial cable
- Twisted-pair copper cable
- Fiber-optic cable
- Wireless RF

Figure 5-24 depicts typical coaxial and UTP connections.

**Figure 5-24:
Typical Coax and
UTP Connections**

Coaxial Ethernet Specifications

The original Ethernet scheme was classified as a 10 Mbps transmission protocol. The maximum length specified for Ethernet is 1.55 miles (2.5 km), with a maximum segment length between nodes of 500 meters. This type of LAN is referred to as a 10Base-5 LAN by the IEEE organization.

The XXBaseYY IEEE nomenclature designates that the maximum data rate across the LAN is 10 Mbps, that it is a baseband LAN (versus broadband), and that its maximum segment length is 500 meters. One exception to this method is the 10Base-2 implementation. The maximum segment length for this specification is 185 meters (almost 200).

Coaxial Ethernet connections can be made through 50-ohm RG-8 thicknet coaxial cable (10Base-5) or thinnet coaxial cable (10Base-2). The original 10Base-5 connection scheme required that special transceiver units be clamped to the cable. A pin in the transceiver pierced the cable to establish electrical contact with its conductor. An additional length of cable, called the drop cable, was then connected between the LAN adapter card and the transceiver. The 10Base-2 Ethernet LAN uses thinner, industry-standard RG-58 coaxial cable, and has a maximum segment length of 185 meters.

Both coaxial connection methods require that a terminating resistor be installed at each end of the transmission line. Ethernet systems use 52-ohm terminators.

> **TEST TIP**
>
> Be aware that the 10Base-xx system roughly uses the xx value to represent the distance (in meters) that a network segment can be (the notable exception is the 185 meter Base-2 value—it's almost 200 meters).

Twisted-Pair Ethernet Specifications

Unshielded Twisted Pair (UTP)

The **Unshielded Twisted Pair (UTP)** specifications are based on telephone cable and are normally used to connect a small number of PCs together. The twisted pairing of the cables uses magnetic-field principles to minimize induced noise in the lines. The original UTP LAN specification (10Base-T) had a transmission rate that was stated as 1 Mbps. Using UTP cable, a LAN containing up to 64 nodes can be constructed with the maximum distance between nodes set at 250 meters. Newer Ethernet implementations are producing LAN speeds of up to 100 Mbps using UTP copper cabling.

For these networks, the IEEE adopted 10Base-T, 100Base-T, and 100Base-TX designations, indicating that they operate on twisted-pair cabling and depend on its specifications for the maximum segment length. The 100Base designation is referred to as Fast Ethernet. The TX version of the Fast Ethernet specification employs two pairs of twisted cable to conduct high-speed, full-duplex transmissions. The cables used with the TX version can be CAT 5 UTP or STP. There is also a 100Base-FX Fast Ethernet designation that indicates the network in using fiber-optic cabling. This specification is described later in this chapter.

TEST TIP

Know what type of cable 10Base-T and 100Base-T use.

Network cards capable of supporting both transmission rates are classified as 10/100 Ethernet cards. The recommended maximum length of a 10/100Base-T segment is 100 meters (actually, the maximum segment length of any Ethernet connection designated with a T is 100 meters).

concentrators

UTP systems normally employ **concentrators** or hubs, like the one in Figure 5-25, for connection purposes.

Figure 5-25: UTP Between a Computer and a Concentrator

100VG (Voice Grade) AnyLAN

demand priority

Hewlett-Packard and AT&T have jointly developed a completely different 100 Mbps standard referred to as the **100VG (Voice Grade) AnyLAN**. The 100VG AnyLAN runs on UTP cabling. It simultaneously employs four pairs of cable strands for transfers. Instead of using CSMA/CD for collision avoidance, the 100VG AnyLAN employs an access protocol called **demand priority**. This scenario requires that the network nodes request and be granted permission before they can send data across the LAN. The overwhelming popularity of the Fast Ethernet specification has caused 100VG AnyLAN to nearly disappear from the market.

Fiber Ethernet Standards

The IEEE organization has created several fiber-optic variations of the Ethernet protocol. They classify these variations under the **IEEE-803** standard. These standards are referenced as the **10/100Base-F** specification. Variations of this standard include:

- **10Base-FP**. This specification is used for passive star networks running at 10 Mbps. It employs a special hub that uses mirrors to channel the light signals to the desired node.

- **10Base-FL**. This specification is used between devices on the network. It operates in full-duplex mode and runs at 10 Mbps. Cable lengths under this specification can range up to 2 kilometers.

- **100Base-FX**. This protocol is identical to the 10Base-FL specification with the exception that it runs at 100 Mbps. This particular version of the specification is referred to as *Fast Ethernet* since it can easily run at the 100 Mbps rate.

Table 5-3 summarizes the different Ethernet specifications. Other CSMA/CD-based protocols exist in the market. Some are actually Ethernet compatible. However, these systems may, or may not, achieve the performance levels of a true Ethernet system. Some may actually perform better.

IEEE-803
10/100Base-F
10Base-FP
10Base-FL
100Base-FX

TEST TIP

Know the types of connectors and physical cable used with each network type.

CLASSIFICATION	CONDUCTOR	MAX. SEGMENT LENGTH	NODES	MAX. LENGTH	TRANS. RATE
10Base-2	RG-58	185 m	30/1024	250 m	10 Mbps
10Base-5	RG-8	500 m	100/1024	2.5 km	10 Mbps
10Base-T	UTP/STP	100 m/200 m	2/1024	2.5 km	10 Mbps
100Base-T	UTP	100 m	2/1024	2.5 km	100 Mbps
100Base-FX	FO	412 m	1024	5 km	100 Mbps

Table 5-3: Ethernet Specifications

The FDDI Ring Standard

There is a Token Ring-like network standard that has been developed around fiber-optic cabling. This standard is the **Fiber Distributed Data Interface (FDDI)** specification. The FDDI network was designed to work almost exactly like a Token Ring network, with the exception that it works on two counter-rotating rings of fiber-optic cable, as illustrated in Figure 5-26. All other differences in the two specifications are associated with their speed differences.

FDDI employs token-passing access control and provides data-transfer rates of 100 Mbps. Using the second ring, FDDI can easily handle multiple frames of data moving across the network at any given time. This provides the FDDI system a type of **full-duplex communication** capability (i.e., data can travel in both directions at the same time—in this case on two different conductors). Of course, the dual ring implementation provides additional network dependability since it can shift over to a single ring operation if the network controller senses that a break has occurred in one of the rings.

Fiber Distributed Data Interface (FDDI)
Full-duplex communication

Figure 5-26: An FDDI Network

FDDI employs token-passing access control and provides data-transfer rates of 100 Mbps. Using the second ring, FDDI can easily handle multiple frames of data moving across the network at any given time. Of course, the dual ring implementation provides additional network dependability since it can shift over to a single ring operation if the network controller senses that a break has occurred in one of the rings.

WIDE AREA NETWORKS

Wide Area Network (WAN)

Bulletin Board Service (BBS)

A **Wide Area Network (WAN)** is very similar in concept to a widely distributed client/server LAN. In a wide area network, some distances typically separate computers. A typical WAN is a local city- or countywide network, like the one in Figure 5-27. This network links network members together through a **Bulletin Board Service (BBS)**. Users can access the bulletin board's server with a simple telephone call.

Figure 5-27: County-Wide Network

links

Metropolitan Area Networks (MANs)

Several different types of communication systems connect WANs together. These communication paths are referred to as **links**. In some areas, high-speed intermediate-sized networks, referred to as **Metropolitan Area Networks (MANs)**, are popping up. These networks typically cover areas up to 30 miles (50 kilometers) in diameter and are operated to provide access to regional resources. They are like LANs in speed and operation, but use special high-speed connections and protocols to increase the geographic span of the network, like a WAN.

Internet Concepts

The most famous WAN is the **Internet**. The Internet is actually a network of networks, working together. The main communication path for the Internet is a series of networks, established by the U.S. government, to link supercomputers together at key research sites.

This pathway is referred to as the **backbone**, and is affiliated with the **National Science Foundation (NSF)**. Since the original backbone was established, the Internet has expanded around the world, and offers access to computer users in every part of the globe.

The TCP/IP protocol divides the transmission into packets of information, suitable for retransmission across the Internet. Along the way, the information passes through different networks that are organized at different levels. Depending on the routing scheme, the packets may move through the Internet using different routes to get to the intended address. At the destination, however, the packets are reassembled into the original transmission.

This concept is illustrated in Figure 5-28.

As a message moves from the originating address to its destination, it may pass through LANs, mid-level networks, routers, repeaters, hubs, bridges, and gateways. A mid-level network is simply another network that does not require an Internet connection to carry out communications.

Figure 5-28: Packets Moving Through the Internet

A router receives messages, amplifies them, and retransmits them to keep the messages from deteriorating as they travel. Hubs are used to link networks together, so that nodes within them can communicate with each other. **Bridges** connect networks together, so that data can pass through them as it moves from one network to the next. A special type of bridge, called a **gateway**, translates messages as they pass through, so that they can be used on different types of networks (e.g., Apple networks and PC networks).

Internet Service Providers

Some service providers, such as **America On-Line (AOL)** and **Earthlink**, have become very well known. However, there are thousands of lesser-known, dedicated Internet access provider companies offering services around the world. Figure 5-28 illustrates the service provider's position in the Internet scheme, and shows the various connection methods used to access the Internet.

INTERNET SERVICE
PROVIDER SERVER

Figure 5-28: Service Provider's Position

When you connect to a service provider, you are connecting to its computer system, which, in turn, is connected to the Internet through devices called routers. A router is a device that intercepts network transmissions and determines for which part of the Internet they are intended. It then determines the best routing scheme for delivering the message to its intended address. The routing schedule is devised based on the known available links through the Internet and the amount of traffic detected on various segments. The router then transfers the message to a **Network Access Point** (**NAP**).

Services that most ISPs deliver to their customers include:

- Internet identity through IP addresses
- E-mail services through POP3 and SMTP servers
- Internet News Service through USENET archive servers
- Internet routing through DNS servers

Internet Service Providers (ISPs)

America On-Line (AOL)

Earthlink

Network Access Point (NAP)

TEST TIP

Be aware of common services that ISPs provide to their Internet customers.

All of these services will be discussed in detail later in this chapter.

No matter which connection technology is employed for Internet access, most users are actually connecting to Internet Service Provider (ISP) organizations at the other end of their connection. Only very large businesses and organizations can afford to act as their own ISPs and provide a technical gateway to the Internet. These companies own blocks of access addresses that they assign to their customers to give them an identity on the network.

In addition to e-mail and Usenet services, the ISP's main responsibility is to provide its customers with access to the Internet. At the root, this involves providing users with an IP address that gives them an Internet identity. IP addresses and the TCP/IP protocol that drives the Internet are described later in this chapter.

The customer's Internet identity can be permanent if the ISP provides the user with a static IP address from its stockpile of IP addresses, or it can be assigned dynamically to customers as they initiate contact with the ISP. The Dynamic Host Configuration Protocol (DHCP) is typically used to provide this function. The DHCP protocol issues and tracks IP addresses from the ISP's store of IP addresses. The DHCP protocol is covered in some detail later in this chapter.

The other key function that ISPs perform is to act as the first stop in the Internet routing process. The structure of the Internet is built on a hierarchical system of servers that route transmissions according to a standard called the Domain Naming System. DNS servers keep track of who is where and act as traffic cops on the Internet. The DNS system is also described later in this chapter.

INTERNET ACCESS METHODS

The A+ Core Hardware objective 6.3 states that the test taker should be able to identify common technologies available for establishing Internet connectivity and their characteristics.

Technologies include:

- LAN
- DSL
- Cable
- ISDN
- Dial-up
- Satellite
- Wireless

Characteristics include:

- Definition
- Speed
- Connections

Most users connect to the Internet and other wide area networks via standard telephone lines, using dial-up modems. **Dial-up connections** are generally the slowest way to connect to a network, but they are inexpensive to establish and use. Other users, who require quicker data transfers, contract with the telephone company to use special high-speed **Digital Subscriber Line (DSL)** or **Integrated Service Digital Network (ISDN)** lines. These types of links require a **digital modem** to conduct data transfers. Because the modem is digital, no analog conversion is required. These technologies are covered in detail later in this chapter.

| Dial-up connections |
| Digital Subscriber Line (DSL) |
| Integrated Service Digital Network (ISDN) |
| digital modem |

Users who require very high volumes lease dedicated **T1 and T3 lines** from the telephone company. These applications generally serve businesses that put several of their computers or networks on-line. Once the information is transmitted, it may be carried over many types of communications links on its way to its destination. These interconnecting links can include fiber-optic cables, satellite up and down links, UHF, and microwave transmission systems. Figure 5-30 illustrates different ways to access WANs.

Figure 5-30: Methods of Accessing Wide Area Networks

LAN Access to the Internet

As the figure illustrates, there are several methods of contacting an ISP to gain access to the Internet. You can dial them up directly using an analog modem and the **plain old telephone system (POTS)**. Or you can make special arrangements with service providers for special always-on services such as DSL, ISDN, **cable**, or **satellite services**. These services can be obtained through direct links to the phone company or an ISP that represents such services. Most residential users access the Internet in this manner.

However, in commerce and industrial settings it is more common for users to work in a LAN environment. In these environments, Internet access is generally provided through the existing local area network structure. One or more of the LAN's network devices are used to provide some type of **gateway** to the Internet as illustrated in Figure 5-31. This arrangement may involve a third-party ISP, or in large organizations, the company may act as its own ISP.

gateway

Figure 5-31: Internet Gateways

The network device that offers the gateway service may be a stand-alone router, or it could be one of the LAN's servers acting as a router for the LAN. The example of using a router as a gateway to the outside world has led to the terms router and gateway being used interchangeably. When the router is used as the gateway, the outside world only sees the router—not the individual computers attached to the LAN.

When a computer is used to serve as the gateway it may actually be configured to perform several connection functions. Of course the server's first function is to perform all of the routing services for the LAN. This includes properly routing incoming messages to the proper node on the LAN and forwarding outgoing messages to the Internet. To accomplish this, the server must possess an **Internet connection sharing** utility that will enable it to represent the other computers on the LAN.

Internet connection sharing

The server may also act as a **proxy server** for the LAN. A proxy server is a computer used to perform services locally and then forward requests for services that it cannot fulfill to an appropriate server. In this case, the proxy server function of the gateway computer could be used to cache (store) web pages that have recently been accessed from the Internet, so that if they are needed again, they can be accessed locally instead of trying to reach them over the Internet. This improves network performance by reducing the load placed on the bandwidth capabilities of the link between the company and the Internet. If the requested page is not in the proxy cache, the server forwards the request to the Internet for resolution.

proxy server

The gateway computers may also act as a **firewall**. A firewall is a combination of hardware and software components that provide a protective barrier between networks with different security levels (e.g., the LAN and the Internet). Rules for transmitting and receiving information to and from the other network can be established for the firewall so that specific types of items or addresses will not be allowed to pass between the networks.

firewall

In some versions of this LAN connection scheme, a router is placed between the gateway computer and the Internet. In this case, the router is the only device seen by the outside world, but its function is single-ended in that the LAN server still represents the other computers on the LAN. However, the router can still be used to provide the firewall services referred to earlier.

always-on

The physical connection between the LAN and the Internet can be a dial-up connection using the telephone network, or it may involve one of the newer faster **always-on** access methods — ISDN, DSL, cable, or satellite. Corporate customers and large organizations may lease special multichannel T1 or T3 telephone lines for direct access to the Internet or ISP. The following sections of this chapter deal with these various Internet connectivity technologies.

Dial-Up Networking

Dial-Up Networking (DUP)

The world's largest communications network is the public telephone system. When computers use this network to communicate with each other it is referred to as **Dial-Up Networking (DUP)**. Computers connect to the phone system through devices, called modems, and communicate with each other using audio tone signals. In order to use the telephone system, the modem must duplicate the dialing characteristics of a telephone and be able to communicate within the frequencies that occur within the audible hearing range of human beings (after all, this is the range that telephone lines are set up to accommodate).

Modems

modem

If the peripheral is located at some distance from the computer (greater than 100 ft), the connection cannot be made by simply getting a longer cable. As the connecting cable gets longer, its natural resistance and distributive capacitance tend to distort digital signals until they are no longer digital.

In order to overcome this signal deterioration, a device called a **modem** (short for modulator/demodulator) is used to convert the parallel, digital signals of the computer into serial, analog signals that are better suited for transmission over wire. A modem allows a computer to communicate with other computers through the telephone lines, as depicted in Figure 5-32.

Figure 5-32: Modem Communications

In its simplest form, a modem consists of two major blocks, a modulator and a demodulator. The modulator is a transmitter that converts the parallel/digital computer data into a serial/analog format for transmission. The demodulator is the receiver that accepts the serial/analog transmission format and converts it into a parallel/digital format usable by the computer, or peripheral.

When a modem is used to send signals in only one direction, it is operating in **simplex mode**. Modems capable of both transmitting and receiving data are divided into two groups, based on their mode of operation. In **half-duplex mode**, modems exchange data, but only in one direction at a time, as illustrated in Figure 5-33. Multiplexing the send and receive signal frequencies will allow both modems to send and receive data simultaneously. This mode of operation is known as **full-duplex mode**.

simplex mode

half-duplex mode

full-duplex mode

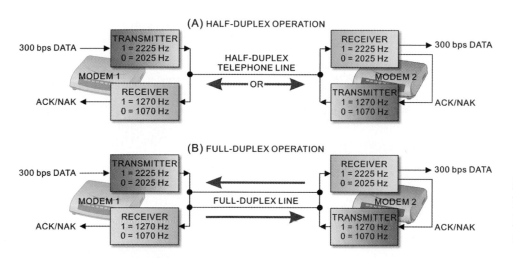

Figure 5-33:
Half-Duplex and
Full-Duplex
Communications

As the distance between terminals increases, it soon becomes impractical to use dedicated cabling to carry data. Fortunately, there is already a very extensive communications network in existence — the public telephone network. Unfortunately, the phone lines were designed to carry analog voice signals instead of digital data. The design of the public phone system limits the frequency at which data may be transmitted over these lines.

TEST TIP

Be able to state the difference between simplex, half-duplex, and full-duplex transmissions and as you move through the text, be able to identify which communications systems use each type.

A modem can be either an internal or an external device, as illustrated in Figure 5-34. An **internal modem** is installed in one of the computer's expansion slots, and has its own interfacing circuitry. The **external modem** is usually a box that resides outside the system unit and is connected to one of the computer's serial ports by an RS-232 serial cable. These units depend on the interfacing circuitry of the computer's serial ports. Most PC-compatible computers contain two serial-port connections. External modems also require a separate power source.

internal modem

external modem

Figure 5-34:
Internal and
External Modems

Registered Jack

In both cases, the modem typically connects to the telephone line through a standard 4-pin RJ-11 telephone jack. The RJ designation stands for **Registered Jack**. A second RJ-11 jack in the modem allows an additional telephone to be connected to the line for voice usage. A still smaller 4-pin RJ-12 connector is used to connect the telephone handset to the telephone base. Be aware that an RJ-14 jack looks exactly like the RJ-11, but that it defines two lines to accommodate advanced telephone features such as Caller ID and Call Waiting.

How Modems Work

bandwidth

The standard telephone system accommodates a range of frequencies between 300 and 3300 Hz, or a **bandwidth** of 3000 Hz. This is quite adequate to transmit voice, but severely distorts digital data. In order to use the audio characteristics of the phone lines to their best advantage, the modem encodes the digital 1s and 0s into analog signals within this bandwidth.

baud rate

Modems are generally classified by their **baud rate**. Baud rate is used to describe the number of signal changes that occur per second during the transfer of data. Since signal changes are the quantity that is actually being limited by the telephone lines, the baud rate is the determining factor. Most modems encode data into different transmission formats, so that a number of data bits can be represented by a single signal change. In this way, the bit rate can be high, while the baud rate is still low. Common bit rates for telecommunications include 2400, 9600, 14400, 28800, and 33600 bits per second. To complete a successful connection at maximum speed, the other party involved must have a compatible modem capable of using the same baud rate.

local command state

on-line state

To understand the operation of the modem, it is important to understand that it must function in two different modes — the **local command state** and the **on-line state**. Between these two states, there are basically three functions that the modem carries out:

- Dialing
- Data exchange (the call)
- Answering

Figure 5-35 describes the Dial/Answer/Disconnect cycles of a typical modem.

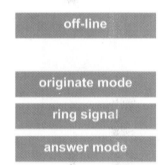

Figure 5-35:
AutoDial/AutoAnswer
Modem Cycle

In the local command state, the modem is **off-line** and communicates with the host system to receive and process commands. In the on-line state, the modem facilitates the transfer of data between the host computer and a remote computer or device.

There are two events that can cause the modem to shift from the off-line state to the on-line condition. The system can prompt the modem to go on-line and dial out to another unit. To accomplish this, the host computer places the modem in **originate mode**. The second event involves the modem receiving a **ring signal** from a remote device. In this situation, the host system shifts the modem into **answer mode**.

The modem will automatically shift from the on-line state to the local command state whenever the carrier signal from the incoming line is not detected within a given amount of time, or if it is lost after the connection has been made. An embedded code in the transmitted data can also be used to shift the modem into the local command state.

Dialing

In order to place a call using the modem, the same series of events must occur as for placing a voice telephone call. When the handset is removed from its cradle, a switch inside the telephone closes, connecting the phone to the line. At this point, the phone is off-hook, but it is not yet on-line. When the modem's relay closes, and the dial tone is detected, the modem notifies the host computer that it is connected to the line.

To place a call, the communication software places the modem in originate mode. In this mode, most modems can automatically place calls by issuing the digital tones equivalent to the desired phone number. The number may come from the keyboard, or it may be one that has previously been entered into memory. Some auto-dial modems are capable of producing both pulse and touch-tone dialing equivalents.

Answering

When a call comes in, the ring voltage is detected by the modem if it is turned on. If so, the modem notifies the host computer that a call is coming in, and, depending on its configuration, will answer the call after some preset number of rings. If the receiving computer informs the modem that it is ready to communicate, the modem goes off-hook, and begins the handshaking routine.

The Conversation

After the line connection has been established, a **handshaking sequence** occurs between the modems and their computers. The originating modem signals its computer that the receiving modem is on-line. This is followed by a signal from the remote modem indicating that its computer is ready to transmit and receive data. The originating modem responds by issuing its own carrier tone frequency, which the answering modem must detect in order to notify its computer that the originating modem is on-line and ready for data. If both tones have been received successfully, the greetings and handshakes are completed, and the transfer of information begins.

While the modem is in the on-line state, no commands can be given to it from the keyboard. However, the local command state can be re-entered while still maintaining the connection by using an escape-code sequence.

For more in-depth information about how modems actually work, refer to the Electronic Reference Shelf on the CD that accompanies this book.

REFERENCE
SHELF

INSTALLING MODEMS

Portions of the A+ Core Hardware objectives 1.2 and 1.8 states that the test taker should be able to identify proper procedures for installing and configuring common field replaceable units and peripheral devices. The data communications-related devices include modems — internal (i.e., adapter cards) and external (i.e., peripheral devices).

The following sections of the chapter deal with installing the system's video output components, internal and external modems, and alternative data storage systems. The steps for installing a modem vary somewhat depending on whether it is an internal or external device. The steps of both procedures are covered in the following sections.

Installing an Internal Modem

Use the following steps to install an internal modem.

1. Prepare the system for installation.
    a. Turn the system OFF.
    b. Remove the cover from system unit.
    c. Locate a compatible empty expansion slot.
    d. Remove the expansion slot cover from the rear of the system unit.

2. For ISA modems, configure the modem's IRQ and COM settings.
    a. Refer to the modem user's manual regarding any IRQ and COM jumper or switch settings.
    b. Record the card's default IRQ and COM settings.
    c. Set the modem's configuration jumpers to operate the modem as COM 2.

3. Install the modem card in the system.
    a. Install the modem card in the expansion slot.
    b. Reinstall the screw to secure the modem card to the back panel of the system unit.
    c. Connect the phone line to the appropriate connector on the modem, as shown in Figure 5-36.
    d. Connect the other end of the phone line to the commercial phone jack.

**Figure 5-36:
Installing an
Internal Modem**

4. Disable any competing COM ports.
    a. For ISA modems, disable COM2 on the system board.

    NOTE: PCI modems should automatically be configured through the Plug-and-Play procedure.

5. Finish the hardware installation.
    a. Replace the system unit cover.

It is necessary to disable the COM2 port on older systems because the system looks to see how many COM ports are available when it boots up. Even if there is no device connected to a COM port, the computer knows the port is there. By disabling this setting, possible interrupt conflict problems are avoided. In addition, some communication software will assign a COM port to an empty serial port. By disabling the port, software that assigns empty COM ports will not see the port at all and, therefore, no conflict will occur.

Installing an External Modem

Use the following steps to install an internal modem.

Hands-on Activity

Installing an External Modem

1. Make the modem connections.
   a. Connect the serial cable to the 9- or 25-pin serial or COM port (depending on the modem) at the rear of the system.
   b. Connect the opposite end of the cable to the RS-232 connector of the external modem unit.
   c. Connect the phone line to the appropriate connector on the modem.
   d. Connect the other end of the phone line to the phone system jack.
   e. Optionally, connect the phone to the appropriate connector on the modem.
   f. Verify that the power switch or power supply is turned off.
   g. Connect the power supply to the external modem unit.
   h. Verify this connection arrangement in Figure 5-37.

**Figure 5-37:
Installing an External
Modem**

2. Enable the system's internal support circuitry.
   a. Remove the cover from system unit.
   b. Enable COM2 on the MI/O adapter.
   c. Replace the system unit cover.

Modem Configuration

Most ISA modems had to be configured manually. However, with newer PCI-based internal modems, the installation and configuration process is much simpler. These cards possess PnP capabilities that enable the system to automatically configure them with the system resources they need to operate.

While all Windows operating systems since Windows 95 have provided PnP support for modems, if the PnP process does not recognize a given modem, the operating system will request that the OEM driver disk be inserted into the floppy or CD-ROM drive so that it can obtain the driver required to support the modem. In some cases, the driver may need to be loaded through the Windows Add/Remove Hardware applet in the Control Panel.

Establishing Modem Protocols

As with other facets of networking and data communications, a **protocol**, or set of rules governing the transfer of information, must be in place in order to maintain an orderly flow of information between the computer and the modem and between the modem and another modem. All of the participants in the "conversation" must use the same protocols to communicate.

protocol

At the *Physical* layer, there are two distinct classes of protocols in widespread use with modems today. These include:

- **Hardware-oriented protocols**
- **Control-code-oriented protocols**

Hardware-oriented
protocols

Control-code-oriented
protocols

Hardware-Oriented Protocols

Hardware-oriented protocols are tied to the use of particular interface pins to control data flow. As far as stand-alone modems are concerned, the most basic hardware standard is the RS-232C serial interface standard. But within the realm of the RS-232 standard a proliferation of communication methods exists.

The RS-232C standard begins by identifying communication equipment using two categories:

Data Terminal Equipment (DTE)

Data Communication Equipment (DCE)

- **Data Terminal Equipment (DTE)**, usually a computer
- **Data Communication Equipment (DCE)**, usually a modem

The term DTE is applied to any equipment whose main purpose is to process data. On the other hand, any communication equipment that changes data during transmission is referred to as DCE. Figure 5-38 illustrates a typical DTE/DCE relationship.

Figure 5-38: The DTE/DCE Relationship

Transmit Data (TXD)

Receive Data (RXD)

Data Terminal Ready

Request To Send

Clear to Send (CTS)

Data Set Ready (DSR)

Data Carrier Detect (CD)

Speed Indicator (SI)

Ring Indicator (RI)

In its most basic form, the RS-232C interface makes provision for a full-duplex operating mode through its **Transmit Data (TXD)** and **Receive Data (RXD)** pins. Normally, data passes from the DTE to the DCE on the TXD line, and from the DCE to the DTE on the RXD line, although these two pins may sometimes be reversed.

The two most common forms of hardware protocols are DTR and RTS, named after the interface's **Data Terminal Ready** and **Request To Send** pins. These lines are toggled On and Off to control when to send, and not send, data. The DTE uses the RTS pin to inform the DCE that it is ready to send data.

The DCE uses a trio of reciprocal lines, **Clear to Send (CTS)**, **Data Set Ready (DSR)**, and **Data Carrier Detect (CD)** to signal the Data Terminal Equipment. It uses the CTS line to inform the DTE that it is ready to accept data. The modem uses the DSR line to notify the DTE that it is connected to the phone line.

The RS-232C standard also designates a number of other lines that can be used for specialized functions. The **Speed Indicator (SI)** line is used by the DCE to indicate whether the modem is in low- or high-speed mode. The DCE may also use the **Ring Indicator (RI)** line to indicate that ring-in voltage is being received. The complete RS-232C interface specification, and its variations, is described in the "Serial Ports" section of Chapter 3 — *Standard I/O Systems*.

Control-Code-Oriented Protocols

Most data-flow control is performed using the control-code class of protocols. In this class of protocols, three types are in widespread use:

- X-ON/X-OFF
- ACK/NAK
- ETX/ACK

In these protocols, control codes are sent across the data lines to control data flow, as opposed to using separate control lines. The **X-ON/X-OFF** protocol, where X represents two special control characters, is a relatively simple concept used to regulate data flow. This control is necessary to prevent buffer memories from overflowing. When data overflows the buffer, the result is usually an error code. The X-ON/X-OFF protocol uses special control characters to start, and stop, data flow.

The **ACK/NAK** and **ETX/ACK** protocols are considered to be high-level protocols because they require special interface programs called device drivers to be installed. In both cases, these protocols use special control characters, and escape code sequences, to provide functions such as data transmission integrity, flow control, requests for retransmission, and so forth.

The ACK/NAK protocol derives its title from the ASCII control characters for ACKnowledge, and Not ACKnowledge. It uses these characters to provide error correction for transmitted data. Basically, the ACK/NAK protocol expects a block of data to be preceded by a Start-Of-Text (STX) character, and to be followed by both an End-Of-Text (ETX) character and an error-checking code, as depicted in Figure 5-39. At the receiving end, the **Block Check Character (BCC)** is checked for errors. Depending on the outcome of the check, either an ACK signal, indicating a successful transmission, or a NAK signal, indicating an error has occurred, will be returned. If a NAK signal is returned, the transmitting device responds by retransmitting the entire block.

X-ON/X-OFF

ACK/NAK

ETX/ACK

Block Check
Character (BCC)

Figure 5-39: ACK/NAK Transmission

The ETX/ACK protocol is somewhat simpler than ACK/NAK, in that no character check is performed. If the receiving device does not return an ACK signal within a predetermined length of time, the sending device assumes that an error, or malfunction, has occurred, and retransmits the character block.

Error-Correcting Protocols

Several error-correcting file transfer protocols have been developed for modem communications packages. Some of the more common protocols include:

- Xmodem
- Ymodem
- Zmodem
- Kermit

checksum

Cyclic Redundancy Checks (CRCs)

These protocols use extensive error detection schemes to maintain the validity of the data as it's being transmitted. Error-detecting and correcting protocols generate more exotic error detection algorithms, such as **checksum** and **Cyclic Redundancy Checks** (**CRCs**), to identify, locate, and possibly correct data errors.

Compression Protocols

compression

Advanced communication protocols use data **compression** techniques to reduce the volume of data that must be transmitted. Each protocol involves a mathematical algorithm that reads the data, and converts it into encoded words. The modem at the receiving end must use the same algorithm to decode the words and restore them to their original form.

Comite Consultatif International Telegraphique et Telephonique (CCITT)

Microcom Networking Protocol

Some modem compression standards reach ratios as high as 4 to 1. The major standards for modem data compression have come from a company named Microcom, and the **Comite Consultatif International Telegraphique et Telephonique** (**CCITT**) worldwide standards organization. The **Microcom Networking Protocol** level7 (MNP7) standard can produce 3:1 compression ratios, and the CCITT V.42bis standard reaches 4:1.

The CCITT standards are identified by a v.xx nomenclature. The original CCITT standard was the v.22 protocol that established transfers at 1200 bps using 600 baud. The v.22bis standard followed providing 2400 bps transfers at 600 baud. The v.32 protocol increased the bps rate to 4800 and 9600.

The CCITT standards also include an error correction protocol and a data compression protocol. The v.42 standard is the error correction protocol and the v.42bis protocol is the CCITT equivalent of the MNP5 and MNP7 protocols. Both protocols run as modules along with the v.32 and v.32bis protocols to provide additional transmission speed.

The MNP Microcom standards began with protocols MNP2 through MNP4. These standards dealt with error correction protocols. The MNP5 and MNP 7 standards followed as the first data compression protocols. The MNP10 standard introduced the first Adverse Channel Enhancement protocol. This type of protocol is designed to provide maximum performance for modems used in typically poor connection applications, such as cellular phones. It features multiple connection attempts and automatically adjusted transmission rates. Like the advanced CCITT protocols, the MNP 10 protocol module runs along with a V.42 protocol to maximize the data transmission rate. Newer CCITT and MNP protocols provide modems with 56 kbps transmission capabilities.

During a special training period conducted at lower speeds, the modem tests the integrity of the transmission medium. The modem then negotiates with the remote modem to determine the maximum transfer rate for the existing line conditions.

Character Framing

Within a particular protocol there are a number of parameters that must be agreed upon before an efficient exchange of information can occur. The most significant of these parameters are **character-type** and **character framing**. Basically, character-type refers to the character set, or alphabet, understood by the devices. Depending on the systems, the character set may be an 8-bit, ASCII line code; a 7-bit, ASCII code (with an error-checking bit); or an EBCDIC code.

Character framing refers to the total number of the bits used to transmit a character. This includes the length of the coded character, and the number and type of overhead bits required to send the character. A common character-framing scheme calls for a start bit, seven data bits, an odd-parity bit, and a stop bit, as depicted in Figure 5-40. An additional bit is often added to the frame for error-checking purposes.

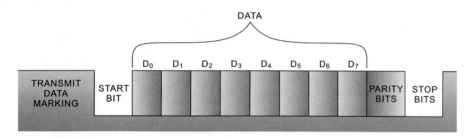

Figure 5-40: Asynchronous Character Format

Although this is a typical character-framing technique, it is not universal throughout the industry. The problem here is one of device comprehension. The local unit may be using a 10-bit character frame consisting of a start bit, seven data bits, an odd-parity bit, and a stop bit. However, if the remote system is using something besides 7-bit, odd-parity ASCII with one stop bit, the response from it would be unintelligible as anything written in English. The composition of the character frame must be the same at both the sending and receiving ends of the transmission.

ISDN Connections

As discussed earlier in the chapter, ISDN service offers high-speed access to the public telephone system. However, ISDN service requires digital modems (also referred to as **Terminal Adapters**, or **TAs**). Not only does the end-user require a digital modem, the telephone company's switch gear equipment must be updated to handle digital switching. This fact has slowed implementation of ISDN services until recently.

Three levels of ISDN service are available: **Basic Rate Interface (BRI)** services, **Primary Rate Interface (PRI)** services, and **Broadband ISDN (BISDN)** services.

BRI services are designed to provide residential users with basic digital service through the existing telephone system. The cost of this service is relatively low, although it is more expensive than regular analog service. BRI service is not available in all areas of the country, but it is expanding rapidly.

Typical residential telephone wiring consists of a four-wire cable. Up to seven devices can be connected to these wires. Under the BRI specification, the telephone company delivers three information channels to the residence over a two-wire cable. The two-wire system is expanded into the four-wire system at the residence through a **network terminator**. The ISDN organizational structure is depicted in Figure 5-41.

Figure 5-41:
ISDN Organizational
Structure

The BRI information channels exist as a pair of 64 kbps channels and a 16 kbps control channel. The two 64 kbps channels, called **bearer** or **B channels**, can be used to transmit and receive voice and data information. The 16 kbps **D channel** is used to implement advanced control features such as call waiting, call forwarding, caller ID, and others. The D channel also can be used to conduct packet-transfer operations.

PRI services are more elaborate ISDN services that support the very high data rates needed for live video transmissions. This is accomplished using the telephone company's existing wiring and advanced ISDN devices. The operating cost of PRI service is considerably more expensive than BRI services. The higher costs of PRI tend to limit its usage to larger businesses.

The fastest, most expensive ISDN service is broadband ISDN. This level of service provides extremely high transfer rates (up to 622 Mbps) over coaxial or fiber-optic cabling. Advanced transmission protocols are also used to implement broadband ISDN.

ISDN modems are available in both internal and external formats. In the case of external devices, the analog link between the computer and the modem requires D-to-A and A-to-D conversion processes at the computer's serial port and then again at the modem. Of course, with an internal digital modem these conversion processes are not required.

Digital Subscriber Lines

The telephone companies have begun to offer a new high-bandwidth connection service to home and business customers in the form of **Digital Subscriber Lines (DSL)**. This technology provides high-speed communication links by using the existing telephone lines to generate bandwidths ranging up to 9 Mb/s or more. However, distance limitations and line quality conditions can reduce the actual throughput that can be achieved with these connections.

DSL Modems and Splitters

As with ISDN connections, DSL communications requires a special **DSL modem** (also known as an **ADSL Terminal Unit (ATU)**) to provide the interface between the computer (or the computer network) and the DSL phone line. DSL modem connections are illustrated in Figure 5-42. DSL modems are available in both internal and external configurations. Internal DSL modems are installed in one of the host computer's expansion slots, similar to an analog dial-up modem. External DSL modems connect to the computer through a USB port, or network adapter card. In many cases, an Ethernet router is installed between the DSL modem and the LAN to provide equal access to the Internet connection. Normally, a CAT 5 UTP cable is used to connect the DSL modem to a port on the router.

**Figure 5-42:
DSL Modem
Connections**

Installing a device called a **POTS splitter** in the DSL connection separates the telephone voice band (0−4 kHz) and the DSL band used to transmit digital information. This enables the DSL phone line connection to be used for both telephone/voice and data communications. Depending on the DSL service provider, the splitter may be manually installed at the subscriber location (**splitter-based DSL**), or the signal splitting may be provided remotely from the telephone exchange carrier local office (**splitter-less DSL**). A splitter variation referred to as *Distributed Splitter DSL service* lowers the complexity at the subscriber location but is more complex to implement at the local office.

TEST TIP

Be aware of the consequences of placing a line filter inline with the computer and network equipment in a DSL installation.

With most new DSL installations line splitters are not required. Instead, telephone line filters are used to separate voice information from communications data. This is achieved by placing line filters on all the lines used by telephones. These filters are placed inline with the phones, as illustrated in Figure 5-43, so that users do not hear the sound of the digital communications going on. It is important to note that no line filter should be placed inline with the network and computer equipment since it will prevent the digital data from reaching it.

**Figure 5-43:
DSL Line Filters**

There are several advantages to using a DSL connection over standard dial-up connections. Some of these advantages include:

- The speed of DSL connections (1.5 Mbps) is much higher than that of dial-up connections using regular modems (56 kbps).

- The Internet connection can remain open while the phone line is used for voice calls.

- DSL service employs existing telephone wires between the home and the telephone-switching center (referred to as the local office).

- The local exchange carrier that offers DSL usually provides the DSL modem as part of the installation.

However, there are disadvantages associated with using DSL technology:

- A DSL connection works better when you are closer to the provider's central office.

- The connection is faster for receiving data than it is for sending data over the Internet.

- DSL service is not available in all locations.

DSL Versions

The term **xDSL** is used to refer to all types of DSL collectively. There are two main categories of DSL — **Asymmetric DSL (ADSL)** and **Symmetric DSL (SDSL)**. Two other types of xDSL technologies that have some promise are **High-data-rate DSL (HDSL)** and **Symmetric DSL (SDSL)**.

SDSL is referred to as symmetric because it supports the same data rates for upstream and downstream traffic. Conversely, ADSL (also known as rate-adaptive DSL) supports different data transfer rates when receiving data (referred to as the downstream rate) and transmitting data (known as the upstream rate). SDSL supports data transfer rates up to 3 Mbps in both directions and ADSL supports data transfer rates of from 1.5 to 9 Mbps downstream and from 16 to 640 kbps upstream. Both forms of DSL require special modems that employ sophisticated modulation schemes to pack data onto telephone wires. However, you should be aware that access speeds may also vary from provider to provider, even if they are using the same central office to provide service.

xDSL is similar to the ISDN arrangements just discussed in that they both operate over existing copper **POTS (Plain Old Telephone System)** telephone lines. Also, they both require short geographical cable runs (less than 20,000 feet) to the nearest central telephone office. However, as we've just stated, xDSL services offer much higher transfer speeds. In doing so, the xDSL technologies use a much greater range of frequencies on the telephone lines than the traditional voice services do. In addition, DSL technologies use the telephone lines as a constant connection so that users can have access to the Internet and e-mail on a 24/7 basis. There is no need to connect with an ISP each time you want to go on-line.

| xDSL |
| Asymmetric DSL (ADSL) |
| Symmetric DSL (SDSL) |
| High-data-rate DSL (HDSL) |
| Symmetric DSL (SDSL) |

TEST TIP
Be aware that ADSL provides different upload and download speeds.

| POTS (Plain Old Telephone System) |

TEST TIP
Know that the maximum distance that is specified between the subscriber location and the local office for ADSL is 18,000 feet.

Asymmetric DSL Versions

Asymmetric DSL (ADSL) works by splitting the phone line into two frequency ranges. The frequencies below 4 kHz are reserved for voice, and the range above that is used for data. This makes it possible to use the line for phone calls and data network access at the same time. This type of DSL is called "asymmetric" because more bandwidth is reserved for receiving data than for sending data. Asymmetrical variations include ADSL, G.lite ADSL, RADSL, and VDSL. The collection of ADSL standards facilitates interoperability between all standard forms of ADSL.

- *Asymmetric DSL (ADSL)* — Full Rate ADSL offers differing upload and download speeds and can be configured to deliver up to six megabits of data per second (6000K) from the network to the customer, that is, up to 120 times faster than dial-up service and 100 times faster than ISDN. ADSL enables voice and high-speed data to be sent simultaneously over the existing telephone line.

- *G.lite ADSL* — The G.lite standard was specifically developed to meet the plug-and-play requirements of the consumer market. It is a medium bandwidth version of ADSL that provides Internet access at up to 1.5 megabits downstream and up to 500 kilobits upstream.

TEST TIP

Be aware that ADSL has the slowest upstream rate and VDSL has the fastest upstream rate.

- *Rate Adaptive DSL (RADSL)* – RADSL is a non-standard version of ADSL, although standard ADSL also permits the ADSL modem to adapt speeds of data transfer.

- *Very High Bit Rate DSL (VDSL)* – VDSL offers transfer rates of up to 26 Mbps, over distances up to 50 meters on short loops such as from fiber to the curb. VDSL lines are normally served from neighborhood cabinets that link to a Central Office through fiber-optic cabling. This type of DSL is particularly useful for campus type environments.

Table 5-4: ADSL Performance vs. Local Loop Length

CABLE LENGTH (FEET)	BANDWIDTH AVAILABILITY (kbps)
18,000	1,544
16,000	2,048
12,000	6,312
9,000	8,448

Table 5-4 illustrates the downstream performance of ADSL as a function of the distance from the subscriber to the local office.

One disadvantage of ADSL service is that when the ADSL local loop length increases, the available bandwidth decreases for both upstream (not shown) and downstream traffic. These numbers assume 24-gauge wire; performance decreases significantly if 26-gauge wire exists on the local loop.

Symmetric DSL Versions

Symmetric DSL

As with ASDSL, there are several varieties of **Symmetric DSL**. These versions include SHDSL, HDSL, HDSL-2, and IDSL. The equal upstream and downstream speeds make Symmetric DSL versions useful for LAN access, video-conferencing, and for locations that host their own web sites.

TEST TIP

Know that SDSL has the slowest downstream rate and VDSL has the fastest downstream rate.

- *Symmetric DSL (SDSL)* – SDSL is a vendor-proprietary version of symmetric DSL that may include bit-rates to and from the customer ranging of 128 kbps to 2.32 Mbps. SDSL is an umbrella term for a number of supplier-specific implementations over a single copper pair providing variable rates of symmetric service.

- *Symmetric HDSL (SHDSL)* – (also known as G.shdsl) SHDL is the newest, industry standard symmetric DSL version. This service can operate at bit-rates ranging from 192 kbps up to 2.3 Mbps, depending on the type of customer and installation parameters. Overall, it achieves 20% better useful distance than previous versions of symmetric DSL (i.e., 1.2 Mbps transmissions at distances over 20,000 feet using 26 AWG wire).

voice-over-DSL

SHDSL is designed for data-only applications that require high upstream bit-rates. Though SHDSL does not carry voice like ADSL, new **voice-over-DSL** techniques permit these services to be used for transmitting digitized voice and data.

- *High Data Rate DSL (HDSL)* – This DSL variety delivers symmetric service at speeds up to 2.3 Mbps in both directions. Available at 1.5 or 2.3 Mbps, this symmetric fixed rate application does not provide standard telephone service over the same line.

TEST TIP

Be aware that HDSL does not use phones and data on the same lines.

- *High Data Rate DSL* – 2nd generation (HDSL2) – This HDSL delivers 1.5 Mbps service each way, supporting voice, data, and video using either ATM (asynchronous transfer mode), private-line service, or frame relay over a single copper pair. This standard for this symmetric service gives a fixed 1.5 Mbps rate both upstream and downstream. HDSL2 does not provide standard voice telephone service on the same wire pair. The HDSL2 standard employs one pair of wires to transmit data at 1.5 Mbps whereas HDSL requires two pairs.

- *Integrated Services Digital Network DSL (IDSL)* — This DSL type supports symmetric data rates of up to 144 kbps using existing phone lines. It is unique in that it has the ability to deliver services through a remote device, called a Digital Loop Carrier (DLC), that is positioned in planned neighborhoods to simplify the distribution of cable and wiring from the phone company.

Cable Modems

Another competitor in the high-speed Internet connection market involves the local cable television service companies. These companies act as ISPs and provide Internet access through their existing **broadband** cable television networks. To accomplish this, the cable companies offer special **cable modems** that attach the computer to an existing **cable TV** (**CATV**) network connection in the home.

The cable modem typically features two main connections — one to the host computer's USB port or 10/100 Ethernet network adapter and the other to the CATV coaxial cable outlet on the wall. A CAT 5 UTP cable normally provides the communication path between the cable modem and the NIC card. The cable modem has a BNC connector that is used to attach the coaxial cable from the cable system to the cable modem. Figure 5-44 illustrates this connection scheme.

broadband
cable modems
cable TV (CATV)

Figure 5-44: A Cable Modem

When a cable modem subscriber configures multiple computers in a LAN environment, the connection between the cable modem and the network may be made through a gateway/router. This places the router between the modem and the other computers on the network. As with the LAN/Internet connection scheme described earlier, the router provides each computer on the LAN with equal access to the Internet through the modem.

The cable modem is similar to an ASDL modem because it establishes two different transmission rates. They provide for the uploading of data (information leaving the subscriber PC to the server) to have a slightly slower speed than downloading information (the server sending information to the subscriber). The typical cable modem transfers data at speeds up to 38 Mbps downstream and 10 Mbps upstream. For comparison, this is about 1,000 times faster than the fastest analog modem connections using dial-up service. However, these rates vary depending upon the number of users on the cable (because cable Internet access is a shared service).

DOCSIS (Data Over Cable Service Interface Specification)

There is a standard for cable modems in North America called **DOCSIS (Data Over Cable Service Interface Specification)**. To deliver DOCSIS data services over a cable television network, one 6 MHz radio frequency (RF) channel is typically allocated for downstream traffic to residential subscribers. Another frequency channel is used to carry upstream signals.

Satellite Internet Access

Two major companies (DirecTV and Dish Network) have successfully entered the market for television distribution using signals delivered to the customer via satellite. In these distribution systems, television signals are transmitted up to a satellite in orbit around the earth (**up linked**) and then retransmitted to satellite receiver dishes installed in residences and offices (**down linked**). These companies have not been content to simply compete for television distribution markets. They have also taken on the cable distribution companies by providing Internet access via satellite link.

up linked

down linked

These services have been provided using two methods—two-way satellite link and separate up- and down-link channels using satellite and dialup telephone lines. In most systems, the satellite dish has no uplink capabilities, so users cannot send data to retrieve information from the web. This function must be supplied through the telephone connection. Download speeds are very good (up to 1.5 Mbps), but upload speeds are limited to the 56 kbps speed of the dial-up modem. In other systems, the dish is equipped with multiple transceivers that provide both up and down links through the satellite link.

Figure 5-45 depicts a typical satellite/Internet communications configuration.

Figure 5-45: Satellite Internet Access

As the figure illustrates, the satellite dish is the transmitter and the receiver for both the television and Internet signals. The dish holds a device known as a **Low Noise Block** (**LNB**) converter that receives the satellite signal, removes the noise from it, and converts it into a digital signal that is compatible with the **satellite receiver**. RG-6 coaxial cable is used to connect the LNBs and the satellite receiver. The receiver unit separates the received demodulated signal into the individual television and Internet channels. It typically furnishes multiple methods for connecting to the television sets in the facility, including through RG-59 coaxial cabling and S-video/Optical audio cabling options.

Most receiver models employ a dial-up connection for the uplink portion of the Internet operation but employ the satellite channel to provide very high-speed downloads and streaming media service. However, some more expensive models provide an "always-on" uplink through the satellite system as well. On the downlink side, the Internet access signal is considered to be just another channel coming from the satellite that gets filtered out and sent to the computer system, normally through a standard USB port. However, when satellite uplink method is included, two USB satellite units are required. These units include the receiver (also called the Indoor Receive Unit or IRU) and an additional Indoor Transmit Unit (ITU). The ITU unit is connected to a digital-to-RF converter mounted on the dish that performs the uplink function. The IRU unit shares the USB connection to the computer with the ITU unit.

Low Noise Block (LNB)

satellite receiver

Wireless Internet Access

In a wireless network environment, the access point is the key component of wireless networks. As described earlier in this chapter, the access point can be connected to a hub or a computer in the LAN that will act as its host for the wired network.

hot spot

WiFi enabled

WiFi (Wireless Fidelity)

Several industries are beginning to employ this concept to provide Internet services to their customers that carry Internet-ready wireless computing devices. In these settings, service providers such as restaurants, hotels, and airports install access points that provide their customers with Internet access within the **hot spot** they establish. Customers with wireless-equipped portable computers can connect to the Internet while in a **WiFi enabled** hot spot such as an airport, hotel lobby, fast food restaurant, or coffee shop. **WiFi (Wireless Fidelity)** is a trademark used by wireless LANs that operate on unlicensed radio spectrum and are therefore restricted to limited transmitter power covering an area of 200–300 feet from the antenna. In most cases, this Internet connectivity is a for-pay service that the customer signs up for.

Tablet PCs

There are a number of computing devices that have moved into the wireless Internet access market. In particular, cellular telephones, personal digital devices, and **Tablet PCs** have become major technologies involved in the wireless Internet market. Cell phones are widely used to send and receive text messages, e-mail, graphics transmissions, and Internet downloads. In the same vein, many PDA manufacturers have included wireless Internet access capabilities with their devices. Tablet PCs are small computer systems that offer a tradeoff between PDAs and notebooks. They feature touch-screen operation like a PDA, but tend to include items such as multiple-gigabyte hard drives and USB ports. They typically work with docking stations just like a laptop to provide removable drives and usually have built-in wireless networking. National ISPs or telephone providers typically supply the actual Internet access service.

Transmissions from wireless network devices cannot simply be confined to the local environment of a home or business. Although the range is limited to a few hundred feet, radio signals can easily be intercepted even outside the vicinity of the stated security perimeter.

Wired Equivalent Privacy (WEP)

Any unauthorized mobile terminal can accomplish this using an 802.11 receiver. In order to minimize the risk of security compromise on a wireless LAN, The IEEE-802.11b standard provides a security feature called **Wired Equivalent Privacy (WEP)**. WEP provides a mathematical method for encrypting data transmissions and authenticating each computer on the network. Enabling the WEP function adds security for data being transmitted by the workstations.

┌─ **TEST TIP** ─────────────────────────────────┐
│ Be aware of the security-related problems associated with wireless │
│ networking and know how to compensate for them. │
└──┘

INTERNET CONCEPTS

The A+ Operating System Technologies objective 4.2 states that the test taker should be able to identify the basic Internet Protocols and terminologies. Identify procedures for establishing Internet Connectivity. In a given scenario configure the operating system to connect to and use Internet resources.

The tremendous popularity of the Internet, and its heavy concentration on PC platforms, requires that the PC technician understand how the Internet is organized and how the PC relates to it. The successful technician must be able to establish and maintain Internet connections for customers using the major operating systems and dial-up networking software. The remainder of this chapter focuses on wide area networking/Internet concepts.

TCP/IP

The key to the Internet is the **Transmission Control Protocol/Internet Protocol (TCP/IP)**. The U.S. Department of Defense originally developed the TCP/IP protocol as a hacker-resistant, secure protocol for transmitting data across a network. It is considered to be one of the most secure of the network protocols. Because the U.S. government developed TCP/IP, no one actually owns the TCP/IP protocol, and so it was adopted as the transmission standard for the Internet. Due to its ability to connect to many different types of computers and servers TCP/IP is used in the majority of all computer networks and is the preferred network protocol for Windows 2000.

However, the main reason that TCP/IP is the most widely used network protocol today is the Internet. No matter what type of computer platform or software is being used, information must move across the Internet in the form of TCP/IP packets. This protocol calls for data to be grouped together in bundles called **network packets**. The TCP/IP packet is designed primarily to allow for message fragmentation and reassembly. It exists through two **header fields**, the **IP header** and the **TCP header**, followed by the data field, as illustrated in Figure 5-46.

The TCP/IP protocol was so widely accepted by the Internet community that virtually every network operating system supports it, including Apple, MS-DOS/Windows, UNIX, LINUX, OS/2, and even networked printers. It can also be used on any topology (e.g., Ethernet, Token Ring, etc.). Therefore, all of these computer types can exchange data across a network using the TCP/IP protocol.

| Transmission Control Protocol/Internet Protocol (TCP/IP) |
| network packets |
| header fields |
| IP header |
| TCP header |

TEST TIP
Know what TCP/IP is and what it does.

TEST TIP
Know the advantages of using the TCP/IP protocol.

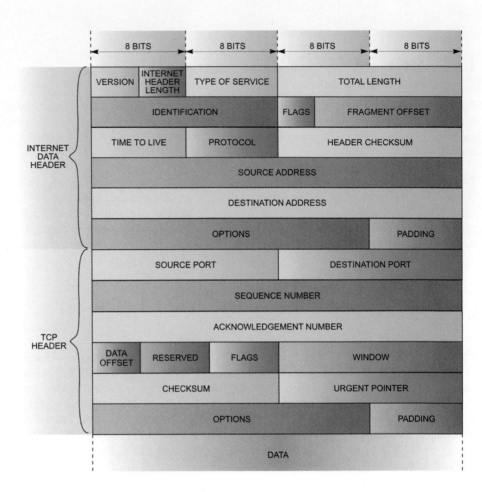

**Figure 5-46:
TCP/IP Packet**

The TCP/IP Suite

Over time, the TCP/IP protocol has expanded to include many options that network technicians and administrators must understand to ensure proper configuration and operation of TCP/IP systems. First of all, the TCP/IP protocol is not a single protocol — it is actually a suite of protocols that were originally developed by the Department of Defense in 1969. TCP/IP consists of two main parts—Transmission Control Protocol (TCP) and Internet Protocol (IP). These protocols work together with a number of other protocols in a structure referred to as a protocol stack.

As was mentioned earlier, the most important function of the network protocol is to make sure that information gets to the network location it is intended for. Ultimately this is the real function of the TCP/IP protocol. It accomplishes this by routing packets of information to locations specified by Internet Protocol (IP) addresses. In Figure 5-46 you should have noticed that the TCP/IP header contained two addresses — the source address that the message comes from and the destination address that it is being sent to.

Because humans don't relate to strings of numbers very well, computers are typically identified by name. For information to get to the address humans want it to go, there has to be some resolution between the numerical IP addresses understood by computers and the alphanumeric names we give them. To accomplish this, TCP/IP relies on a group of protocols and services that represent special advanced name and address resolution functions. These protocols and services include:

- DNS (Domain Name System) service – a service that works with the hierarchical DNS naming system employed by the Internet

- WINS (Windows Internet Name Service) – a service that works with the Microsoft naming system used with earlier Microsoft networks

- DHCP (Dynamic Host Configuration Protocol) – a protocol that is used by ISPs and other networks to automatically assign users IP addresses from a rotating pool of available addresses

- ARP (Address Resolution Protocol) – this protocol/utility is used to modify tables that translate IP-to-Ethernet addresses

In addition to these supporting protocols associated with IP/computer name resolution, the TCP/IP protocol suite includes support for:

- electronic mail transportation

- file and print services

- web browsing

- network troubleshooting

The information in the remainder of this chapter deals primarily with IP address issues. However, the other TCP/IP components will be examined in the different operating system chapters, Chapters 9 and 10, while the troubleshooting tools are described in Chapter 12 — *Operating System Troubleshooting*.

IP Addresses

The blocks of Internet access addresses that ISPs provide to their customers are called Internet Protocol addresses, or IP addresses. The IP address makes each site a valid member of the Internet. This is how individual users are identified to receive file transfers, e-mail, and file requests.

IP addresses exist in the numeric format of XXX.YYY.ZZZ.AAA. Each address consists of four 8-bit fields separated by dots (.). This format of specifying addresses is referred to as **dotted decimal notation**. The decimal numbers are derived from the binary address that the hardware understands. For example, a binary network address of:

> dotted decimal notation

    10000111.10001011.01001001.00110110 (binary)

corresponds to:

    135.139.073.054 (decimal)

Each IP address consists of two parts: the network address and the host address. The network address identifies the entire network; the host address identifies an intelligent member within the network (a router, a server, or a workstation).

Three classes of standard IP addresses are supported for LANs: Class A, Class B, and Class C. These addresses occur in four-octet fields like the example shown earlier.

- **Class A addresses** are reserved for large networks and use the last 24 bits (the last three octets or fields) of the address for the host address. The first octet always begins with a 0, followed by a 7-bit number. Therefore, valid Class A addresses range between 001.x.x.x and 126.x.x.x. This allows a Class A network to support 126 different networks with nearly 17 million hosts (nodes) per network.

- **Class B addresses** are assigned to medium-sized networks. The first two octets can range between 128.x.x.x and 191.254.0.0. The last two octets contain the host addresses. This enables Class B networks to include up to 16,384 different networks with approximately 65,534 hosts per network.

- **Class C addresses** are normally used with smaller LANs. In a Class C address, only the last octet is used for host addresses. The first three octets can range between 192.x.x.x and 223.254.254.0. Therefore, the Class C address can support approximately 2 million networks with 254 hosts each.

> **┌─ NOTE ─┐**
>
> The 127.x.x.x address range is a special block of addresses reserved for testing network systems. The U.S. government owns some of these addresses for testing the Internet backbone. The 127.0.0.1 address is reserved for testing the bus on the local system.

Subnets are created by masking off (hiding) the network address portion of the IP address on the units within the subnet. This, in effect, limits the mobility of the data to those nodes within the subnet because they can reconcile only addresses from within their masked range. There are three common reasons to create a subnet:

- To isolate one segment of the network from all the others − Suppose, for example, that a large organization has 1,000 computers, all of which are connected to the network. Without segmentation, data from all 1,000 units would run through every other network node. The effect of this would be that everyone in the network would have access to all the data on the network, and the operation of the network would be slowed considerably by the uncontrolled traffic.

- To efficiently use IP addresses − Because the IP addressing scheme is defined as a 32-bit code, there are only a certain number of possible addresses. Although 126 networks with 17 million customers might seem like a lot, in the scheme of a worldwide network system, that's not a lot of addresses to go around.

- To utilize a single IP address across physically divided locations − For example, subnetting a Class C address between remotely located areas of a campus would permit half of the 253 possible addresses to be allocated to one campus location, and the other half to be allocated to hosts at the second location. In this manner, both locations can operate using a single Class C address.

Internet Domains

The IP addresses of all the computers attached to the Internet are tracked using a listing system called the **Domain Name System** (**DNS**). This system evolved as a way to organize the members of the Internet into a hierarchical management structure.

The DNS structure consists of various levels of computer groups called **domains**. Each computer on the Internet is assigned a **domain name**, such as mic-inc.com. The "mic-inc" is the user-friendly domain name assigned to the Marcraft site.

domains

domain name

In the example, the .com notation at the end of the address is a top-level domain that defines the type of organization, or country of origin associated with the address. In this case, the .com designation identifies the user as a commercial site. The following list identifies the Internet's top-level domain codes:

* .com = Commercial Businesses	* .au = Australia
* .edu = Educational Institutions	* .ca = Canada
* .gov = Government Agencies	* .fr = France
* .int = International Organizations	* .it = Italy
* .mil = Military Establishments	* .es = Spain
* .net = Networking Organizations	* .tw = Taiwan
* .org = Nonprofit organizations	* .uk = United Kingdom

On the Internet, domain names are specified in terms of their **Fully Qualified Domain Names (FQDN)**. An FQDN is a human-readable address that describes the location of the site on the Internet. It contains the host name, the domain name, and the top-level domain name. For example, the name "www.oneworld.owt.com" is an FQDN.

Fully Qualified Domain Names (FQDN)

The letters "www" represent the **host name**. The host name specifies the name of the computer that provides services and handles requests for specific Internet addresses. In this case, the host is the World Wide Web. Other types of hosts include ftp and http sites.

host name

The .owt extension indicates that the organization is a domain listed under the top-level domain heading. Likewise, the .oneworld entry is a subdomain of the .owt domain. It is very likely one of multiple networks supported by the .owt domain.

At each domain level, the members of the domain are responsible for tracking the addresses of the domains on the next-lower level. The lower domain is then responsible for tracking the addresses of domains, or end-users, on the next level below it.

In addition to its domain name tracking function, the DNS system resolves (links) individual domain names of computers to their current IP address listings. Some IP addresses are permanently assigned to a particular domain name so that whenever the domain name is issued on the Internet it always accesses the same IP address. This is referred to as **static IP addressing**. However, most ISPs use a **dynamic IP addressing** scheme for allocating IP addresses.

static IP addressing

dynamic IP addressing

If an ISP wanted to service 10,000 customers within its service area using static IP addressing, it would need to purchase and maintain 10,000 IP addresses. However, because most Internet customers are not on line all of the time, their IPs are not always in use. This allows the ISP to purchase a reasonable number of IP addresses that it can hold in a bank and dynamically assign to its users as they log on to their service. When the user logs out, the IP address returns to the bank for other users.

Point-to-Point
Protocol (PPP)

UNIX

Serial Line Internet
Protocol (SLIP)

The Internet software communicates with the service provider by embedding the TCP/IP information in a **Point-to-Point Protocol (PPP)** shell for transmission through the modem in analog format. The communications equipment, at the service provider's site, converts the signal back to the digital TCP/IP format. Older units running the **UNIX** operating system used a connection protocol called **Serial Line Internet Protocol (SLIP)** for dial-up services.

Dynamic Host Configuration Protocol

Dynamic Host
Configuration
Protocol (DHCP)

The **Dynamic Host Configuration Protocol (DHCP)** is an Internet protocol that can be used to automatically assign IP addresses to devices on a network using TCP/IP. Using DHCP simplifies network administration because software, rather than an administrator, assigns and keeps track of IP addresses. For this reason, many ISPs use the dynamic IP addressing function of DHCP to provide access to their dial-up users. The protocol automatically delivers IP addresses, subnet mask and default router configuration parameters, and other configuration information to the devices on the network.

The dynamic addressing portion of the protocol also means that computers can be added to a network without manually assigning them unique IP addresses. As a matter of fact, the devices can be issued a different IP address each time they connect to the network. In some networks, the device's IP address can even change while it is still connected. DHCP also supports a mix of static and dynamic IP addresses.

Internet Engineering
Task Force (IETF)

DHCP is an open standard, developed by the **Internet Engineering Task Force (IETF)**. It is a client-server arrangement in which a DHCP client contacts a DHCP server to obtain its configuration parameters. The DHCP server dynamically configures the clients with parameters appropriate to the current network structure.

The most important configuration parameter carried by DHCP is the IP address. A computer must be initially assigned a specific IP address that is appropriate to the network to which the computer is attached, and that is not assigned to any other computer on that network. If a computer moves to a new network, it must be assigned a new IP address for that new network. DHCP can be used to manage these assignments automatically. The DHCP client support is built into Windows 9x, Windows NT 4.0 Workstation, and Windows 2000 Professional. Windows NT 4 and Windows 2000 Server versions include both client and server support for DHCP. These operating systems and DHCP are covered in greater detail in Chapters 9 and 10.

CHALLENGE #3

You work as a service representative for an Internet service provider. One day, you receive a call from a customer wondering why her IP address changes periodically. She doesn't have a problem with the operation of her computer, so what do you tell her?

Internet Resources

World Wide Web

The Internet is constructed of resources, or services, offered to users. The range of services available includes file transfers, database access, e-mail, or access to linked documents on the World Wide Web.

A **uniform resource locator (URL)** is used to access services on the Internet. A URL is composed of two parts. The first part specifies an Internet resource that's to be accessed. HTTP or FTP are examples of an Internet resource. Frequently, the resource is the name of a particular protocol. For example, both FTP and HTTP are well-established protocols used on the Internet. The second part of a URL lists the name of the server. The server name is followed by the directory path and file name of a particular document.

For example, consider the URL HTTP:\\help.com/documents/security.txt. The URL consists of the following parts:

- **HTTP:** The protocol, or service, that will be accessed.
- **help.com:** The server name (also called the host name or domain name) that is accessed for files.
- **/documents/:** The directory path from which one, or many specific files may be accessed.
- **security.txt:** The name of the file to be accessed.

Other common ways of referring to an Internet name are to call it a web address, Internet address, or web site. This is a reference to the static IP addresses assigned to the server name.

The World Wide Web

The **World Wide Web (WWW)** is a menu system that ties together Internet resources from around the world. These resources are scattered across computer systems everywhere. **Web servers** inventory the web's resources and store address pointers, referred to as links, to them.

To access a web site, the user must place the desired URL on the network. Each URL begins with http:// or https://. These letters stand for Hypertext Transfer Protocol and identify the address as a web site. The rest of the address is the name of the site being accessed (e.g., http://www.mic-inc.com is the home page of Marcraft, located on a server at One World Telecommunications). Each web site begins with a home page. The home page is the menu to the available contents of the site.

There are numerous types of resources available on the Internet. Typical Internet resources include:

- The **HyperText Transfer Protocol (HTTP)** is used to access linked documents on the World Wide Web. The documents are prepared with the HyperText Markup Language (HTML).
- The **HyperText Transfer Protocol Secure (HTTPS)** is used to access linked documents on the World Wide Web that are located on a secure server. A secure server typically requires that a password be entered before access is granted. In some applications, https:// means that documents are encrypted (using the Secure Socket Layer protocol as described in detail later in this chapter) before sending them to a user that connects to the secure site.
- The **File Transfer Protocol (FTP)** is used to copy files to and from a remote server. When a URL has the ftp:// prefix, it means that the user is accessing a site from which files can be downloaded, or uploaded.

    The mailto: prefix is used to access an e-mail server. Once the e-mail server is accessed (usually after entering a username and password), the e-mail application is started and the user can read or write e-mail.

news:

gopher://

telnet://

Simple Mail Transfer Protocol (SMTP)

file://

- The **news:** prefix starts the newsgroup application on the Internet. A newsgroup is a bulletin board arranged by specific discussion group titles such as the Internet, Networking, or Computers. There are thousands of newsgroups on the Internet.

- The **gopher://** prefix is used to access the database area of the Internet. Largely replaced by the World Wide Web, Gopher consists of a series of linked menu items.

- The **telnet://** prefix is used to connect a user to a remote server. Once the connection is established, the user has access to software or tools located on the server. When telnet is specified, a separate telnet application begins on the user's workstation. Like Gopher, telnet is being used less and less. Network operating systems like Windows NT and Novell NetWare contain remote access services that have largely replaced telnet.

- The **Simple Mail Transfer Protocol (SMTP)** is used to send e-mail across the Internet. E-mail uses conventions that are somewhat different than those used with other services.

- The **file://** prefix is used to access a file on a local server that supports Internet applications. For example, assume the URL http://inet.com/document/help.txt is accessed. Once the help.txt file is open, it may include references to other documents on the inet.com server. The file:// prefix can be used to directly connect to one of the other documents.

**Figure 5-47:
E-Mail Account
Configurations**

E-mail utilities must be accessed through the *Tools* option of the *Outlook Express* applet. From the *Tools* option on the Outlook Express menu bar, select the *Accounts* entry, highlight an account name, and click on the *Properties* tab. Finally, click the *Servers* tab to access the e-mail account configuration, as depicted in Figure 5-47.

Table 5-5 summarizes common Internet protocols and includes the well-known port number for each resource. Port numbers are discussed in greater detail later in this chapter.

Table 5-5 Common Internet Protocols and Well-Known Port Numbers

URL PREFIX	DESCRIPTION	PORT NUMBER
http://	Specifies an address on the World Wide Web	80
https://	Specifies a secure address on the World Wide Web	443
ftp://	Specifies file transfers	20/21
mailto:	Initiates e-mail	24
news:	Initiates access to newsgroups	144
gopher://	Initiates access to database information	70
telnet://	Initiates direct access to a remote computer	23
SMTP:	Initiates e-mail over the Internet	25
file://	Initiates access to a file on a local server	59

File Transfer Protocol

A special application, called the **File Transfer Protocol (FTP)**, is used to upload and download information to, and from, the Net. FTP is a client/server type of software application. The server version runs on the host computer, and the client version runs on the user's station.

To access an FTP site, the user must move into an FTP application and enter the address of the site to be accessed. After the physical connection has been made, the user must log on to the FTP site by supplying an account number and password. When the host receives a valid password, a communication path opens between the host and the user site, and an FTP session begins.

Around the world, thousands of FTP host sites contain millions of pages of information that can be downloaded free of charge. However, most FTP sites are used for file transfers of things like driver updates and large file transfers that are too large for e-mail operations.

FTP Authentication

FTP sites exist on the Internet in two basic formats—private and public. To access most **private FTP sites**, you must connect to the site and input a username and password designated by the FTP host. Most **public FTP sites** employ **anonymous authentication** for access to the site. Anonymous authentication is an interaction that occurs between the local browser and the FTP host without involving the remote user. (That is, no username or passwords are required to gain access.)

E-Mail

One of the most widely used functions of WANs is the **electronic mail (e-mail)** feature. This feature enables Internet users to send and receive electronic messages to each other over the Internet. As with the regular postal service, e-mail is sent to an address, from an address. With e-mail, however, you can send the same message to several addresses at the same time, using a mailing list.

On the Internet, the message is distributed in packets, as with any other TCP/IP file. At the receiving end, the e-mail message is reassembled and stored in the recipient's mailbox. When the recipient opens his e-mail program, the e-mail service delivers the message and notifies the user that it has arrived. The default e-mail reader supported by the Windows 9x Outlook Express applet is the **POP3** standard. Likewise, it includes a standard **Simple Mail Transfer Protocol (SMTP)** e-mail utility for outgoing e-mail.

When setting up an e-mail account, you must supply the following configuration information:

- Account name
- Password
- POP3 Server address
- SMTP Server address

| File Transfer Protocol (FTP) |

TEST TIP
Memorize the different file types associated with Internet operations and know what their functions are.

| private FTP sites |
| public FTP sites |
| Anonymous authentication |

TEST TIP
Be aware that FTP sites employ anonymous authentication for access.

| electronic mail (e-mail) |

| POP3 |
| Simple Mail Transfer Protocol (SMTP) |

Secure Socket Layer Protocol

The **Secure Socket Layer** (SSL) protocol is used to authenticate users or e-commerce servers on the Internet, and to encrypt/decrypt messages (particularly credit card purchases) by using a security process called **public-key encryption**. SSL encrypts data that moves between the browser and the server.

The SSL protocol consists of a digital certificate that the e-commerce site must possess before a web browser can authenticate web servers at the e-commerce site. The digital certificate is issued by a Certificate Authority (CA). The role of the CA in the SSL session is to authenticate the holder of a certificate (such as an e-commerce server), and to provide a digital signature that will reveal whether the certificate has been compromised. CA certificates are pre-installed in all modern web browsers.

The reason sites need to be authenticated is that it's relatively easy to copy a complete web site and then repost it using a domain name that's very similar to the "real" site. For example, it is easy to mistake the site *micrsoft.com*, for *microsoft.com*. A purchaser may be lured to the first site, make a purchase, and never receive the purchased item.

A connection to a certificate server that uses SSL will use a URL that begins with https://. For example, a site called *https://buy.now.com* is a secure site in which messages between the browser and server are encrypted. The browser indicates that the connection is secure by displaying a locked padlock, or key, near the bottom corner of the browser.

Telnet

Telnet is a service that enables you to "telephone-net" into another computer so that you can utilize the resources of the computer in a command-line interface environment. While most web browsers do not include a client for telnet access, most operating systems include a utility that will enable you to launch telnet. In Windows, you can enter telnet from the command line. In other operating systems, a terminal emulator utility may be required in addition to a telnet client. A terminal emulator is a software package that allows a computer to mimic a dumb terminal.

Telnet enables users at remote computers to connect to a remote server. The client computer doesn't have to be running the same operating system as the remote server. This is an ideal situation for a PC-to-mainframe connection where the PC environment is radically different than that of the mainframe.

Web Browsers

As the Internet network has grown, service providers have continued to provide more user-friendly software for exploring the World Wide Web. These software packages are called browsers, and are based on **hypertext links**. Browsers use hypertext links to interconnect the various computing sites in a way that resembles a spider's web.

Browsers are to the Internet what Windows is to operating environments. Graphical browsers such as Netscape Navigator and Microsoft Internet Explorer enable users to move around the Internet and make selections from graphically designed pages and menus, instead of operating from a command line. The original Internet operating environment was a command-line program called UNIX. Fortunately, the UNIX structure and many of its commands were the basis used to create MS-DOS. Therefore, users who are DOS literate do not require extensive training to begin using UNIX. With the advent of a variety of browsers, however, it is unlikely that most users will become involved with UNIX.

The **National Center for Supercomputing Applications** introduced the first graphical browser in 1993. This program was known as Mosaic. As its name implies, Mosaic allowed graphical pages to be created using a mixture of text, graphics, audio, and video files. It translated the **Hypertext Markup Language (HTML)** files that were used to create the web, and that ultimately link the various types of files together.

Mosaic was quickly followed by the **Netscape Navigator** and the **Microsoft Internet Explorer** browsers. Figure 5-48 depicts the home page (presentation screen) for the Netscape Navigator from Netscape Communications Corporation.

Figure 5-49 illustrates the Microsoft Internet Explorer. Its features are similar to those of the Netscape Navigator. Both provide a graphical interface for viewing web pages. Links to **search engines** are useful for finding information on the Internet. Both have links to built-in e-mail facilities, and to their respective creator's home pages.

National Center for Supercomputing Applications

Hypertext Markup Language (HTML)

Netscape Navigator

Microsoft Internet Explorer

┌─ **TEST TIP** ────
Be aware of the different file types used with the Internet.
────────────────────

Figure 5-48:Netscape Navigator Home Page

search engines

┌─ **TEST TIP** ────
Memorize the Internet-related abbreviations and acronyms.
────────────────────

**Figure 5-49:
Internet Explorer
Home Page**

Figure 5-50: IE Security Tab

In the Netscape navigator, searches look at Netscape-recommended sites, while the Explorer first checks out Microsoft sites. Operating either browser in Windows versions before Windows 95 requires an external **Windows socket** program to be loaded before running the browser. With Windows 95, the socket was integrated directly into the operating environment.

Several software packages allow users to generate their own web pages. Programs such as word processors and desktop publishers have included provisions for creating and saving HTML files called **applets** that can be used as home pages. Internet browsers, such as Netscape and Internet Explorer, include facilities for generating home page documents. **Scripting languages**, such as **Java**, also are used to create HTML applets.

Configuring Internet Options

The original version of Windows 95 came without a built-in web browser. Customers routinely chose between installing the Netscape Navigator or the Microsoft Internet Explorer (IE) browsers. However, with Windows 98, Microsoft began to include IE as an integral part of the operating system. For the most part, there is no need to configure the IE browser to use it.

However, there are a variety of user-selectable options that can be established for web browsers. Some of these options are personal preferences — such as colors, fonts and toolbars. In older browser versions, you could typically find these settings under the Preferences option in a drop-down menu. In newer versions of Microsoft IE, these settings are grouped under the browser's *Tools/Internet Options* path.

There are some browser functions that you may need to configure for users in a workplace environment. Technicians need to be able to configure scripting, proxies, and security levels through the user's browser.

Configuring Security Settings

There are a variety of security-related activities that involve the browser and searching the Internet. In Microsoft IE these functions are located on the *Security* tab under the *Tools/Internet Options* path, shown in Figure 5-50.

Highlighting the *Intranet*, *Trusted Sites*, or *Restricted Sites* icons will enable the *Sites* button. This button can be used to add or remove sites to each of these different zone classifications. The security settings attached to these different zone types can be modified by clicking on the *Custom Level* button. The *Internet* icon enables security settings to be established for all web sites that have not been classified as one of the other zone types.

In each zone type, clicking on the *Custom Level* button will produce a list of individual controls that can be enabled, disabled, or configured to present a user prompt when the browser encounters a related objects. These objects represent web page components that may be encountered by accessing or viewing a given web site (such as animated scripts, file downloads, and user identification logins).

The *Reset Custom Settings* dialog box features a drop-down window for establishing general levels of security settings for all of the items in the selected zone type's list.

Configuring Script Support

Scripts are executable applications that provide interactive content on web sites. They are also capable of retrieving information in response to user selections. However, the user may not have to do anything to run a script program — they are simply embedded in the website that they access. There are a couple of reasons why you would consider controlling scripts encountered on web sites. Scripts are one of the main sources of virus infections. Hackers configure scripts to contain viruses that clients may download unwittingly. Scripts also facilitate automatic pop-up windows that appear without warning on the client's browser. These windows typically contain unrequested advertisements that tend to annoy users.

The ability to load and run scripts in a browser can be controlled through the browser's *Tools/Internet Options/Security* tab. The list of individual web page components that you can control includes different script types, such as ActiveX and Javascript. As with the other Security objects, you can configure the browser to enable, disable, or present a user prompt whenever it encounters one of these scripted items.

Configuring Proxy Settings

A **proxy server** is a barrier that prevents outsiders from entering a local area network. All addressing information sent to the Internet will use the IP address of the proxy server. Because the IP address of the workstation that's connecting to the Internet isn't used, an outside intruder has no way of accessing the workstation.

Client access is configured from the web browser of the workstation. To configure a workstation using the Microsoft Internet Explorer browser for a proxy server, follow these steps:

1. Start Microsoft Internet Explorer. From the toolbar menu, choose *Tools*, then *Internet Options*.

2. Select the *Connection* tab and click on the *LAN Setting* button. The *Local Area Network (LAN) Settings* dialog box will appear similar to Figure 5-51.

3. Check the *Use a proxy server for your LAN* option and enter the name of the proxy server in the *Address* field. An IP address may be entered in the *Address* field instead of the server name.

4. Enter the port number of the server in the *Port* field. The port number is usually a well-known port number.

5. Click on the *Apply* button, followed by the *OK* button.

When fully configured, the proxy server will supply the client with the addresses and port numbers for Internet services (HTTP, FTP, etc.) that are available to it.

Figure 5-51: Internet Explorer Proxy Configuration

Most commercial web browsers provide for proxy configuration in a manner that's similar to the steps described above. For example, follow these steps to configure the workstation proxy settings for Netscape Navigator:

1. From the Netscape Navigator toolbar menu, choose *Options* and then select the *Network Preferences* entry from the menu. Click on the *Proxies* tab in the *Preferences* dialog box.

2. Click on the *Manual Proxy Configuration* radio button, then click on the *View* button.

3. Enter the name or IP address of the proxy server for each service, along with the port number of the service.

4. Click on the *Apply* button, followed by the *OK* button.

Navigator also permits you to use an automatic proxy configuration for workstations by entering the address where the proxy configuration file is located. Enter the address in the *Automatic Proxy Configuration* field of the *Preferences* dialog box.

CHAPTER SUMMARY

This chapter has investigated the two major areas of data communications associated with personal computer systems — Local Area Networks and Wide Area Networks. The chapter opens with a short section on basic networking concepts.

The first major section of the chapter dealt with LANs. In this portion of the chapter, the major local area network topologies were described. These included Ethernet, Token Ring, and fiber-optic LANs. Major topics covered in this section included basic LAN installation and operation, as well as LAN troubleshooting procedures.

The second major section of the chapter covered dial-up networking. In particular, it dealt with basic modem installation and operation. Modems are the most widely used data communication devices today. This material works very well with the I/O port information delivered in Chapter 3. As a matter of fact, both sections should be covered when troubleshooting serial communications problems. The steps for troubleshooting modem problems were presented in this section of the chapter.

Dial-up networking is the basis of wide area networking, which invariably leads to the Internet. The final sections of the chapter moved quickly into subjects surrounding the Internet. These subjects included File Transfer Protocol (ftp), e-mail, the World Wide Web, and browsers. As with all the other major sections of this text, a troubleshooting section occurred at the end of the section to cap it off.

At this point, review the objectives listed at the beginning of the chapter to be certain that you understand each point and that you can perform each task listed there. Afterward, answer the Review Questions that follow to verify your knowledge of the information.

KEY POINTS REVIEW

This chapter has investigated the two major areas of data communications associated with personal computer systems: LANs and WANs. Review the following key points before moving into the Review and Exam Questions sections to make sure you are comfortable with each point. Afterward, answer the Review Questions that follow to verify your knowledge of the information.

- Local Area Networks (LANs) are systems designed to connect computers together in a relatively close proximity. These connections allow users attached to the network to share resources such as printers and modems. LAN connections also allow users to communicate with each other, and share data between their computers.

- Control of the network can be implemented in two ways: as peer-to-peer networks, in which each computer is equal to the other units on the network, or as client/server networks, in which dependent workstations (referred to as clients) operate in conjunction with a dedicated master computer (server).

- In a network, some method must be used to determine which node has use of the network's communications paths, and for how long it can have it. The network's protocol handles these functions, and it is necessary to prevent more than one user from accessing the bus at any given time.

- The Ethernet strategy allows up to 1024 users to share the LAN. However, from the description of its collision-recovery technique, it should be clear that with more users on an Ethernet LAN, more collisions are likely to occur, and the average time to complete an actual data transfer will be longer.

- Ethernet is classified as a bus topology. The original Ethernet scheme was classified as a 10 Mbps transmission protocol. The maximum length specified for Ethernet is 1.55 miles (2.5 km), with a maximum segment length between nodes of 500 meters. This type of LAN is referred to as a 10Base-5 LAN by the IEEE organization.

- In 1985, IBM developed a token-passing LAN protocol called the Token Ring. As its name implies, Token Ring is a token-passing protocol operating on a ring topology. The token is a small frame that all nodes can recognize instantly.

- In a LAN, each computer on the net requires a network adapter card (also referred to as a NIC), and every unit is connected to the network by some type of cabling. These cables are typically either twisted-pair wires, thick or thin coaxial cable, or fiber-optic cable.

- In its simplest form, a modem consists of two major blocks, a modulator and a demodulator. The modulator is a transmitter that converts the parallel/digital computer data into a serial/analog format for transmission. The demodulator is the receiver that accepts the serial/analog transmission format and converts it into a parallel/digital format usable by the computer, or peripheral.

- The standard telephone system accommodates a range of frequencies between 300 and 3300 Hz, or a bandwidth of 3000 Hz. This is quite adequate to transmit voice, but severely distorts digital data. In order to use the audio characteristics of the phone lines to their best advantage, the modem encodes the digital 1s and 0s into analog signals within this bandwidth.

- In order to maintain an orderly flow of information between the computer and the modem, and between the modem and another modem, a protocol, or set of rules governing the transfer of information, must be in place. All of the participants in the "conversation" must use the same protocols to communicate.

- A wide area network is very similar in concept to a widely distributed client/server LAN. In a wide area network, computers are typically separated by distances that must be serviced via modems instead of network cards.

- The most famous wide area network is the Internet. The Internet is actually a network of networks working together. The main communication path for the Internet is a series of networks, established by the U.S. government, to link supercomputers together at key research sites.

- Connecting all of the users and individual networks together are Internet Service Providers (ISPs). ISPs are companies that provide the technical gateway to the Internet. These companies own blocks of access addresses that they assign to their customers to give them an identity on the network.

- The IP addresses of all the computers attached to the Internet are tracked using a listing system called the Domain Name Service (DNS). This system evolved as a method of organizing the members of the Internet into a hierarchical management structure.

- The TCP/IP protocol divides the transmission into packets of information, suitable for retransmission across the Internet. Along the way, the information passes through different networks that are organized at different levels. Depending on the routing scheme, the packets may move through the Internet using different routes to get to the intended address. At the destination, however, the packets are reassembled into the original transmission.

- ISDN service offers high-speed access to the public telephone system. However, ISDN service requires digital modems (also referred to as Terminal Adapters (TAs)). Not only does the end-user require a digital modem, the telephone company's switch gear equipment must be updated to handle digital switching. This fact has slowed implementation of ISDN services until recently.

- A special application, called the File Transfer Protocol (FTP), is used to upload and download information to, and from, the Internet.

- One of the most widely-used functions of wide area networks is the electronic mail (e-mail) feature. This feature allows Internet users to send, and receive, electronic messages to and from each other over the Internet.

- The World Wide Web (WWW) is a menu system that ties together Internet resources from around the world. These resources are scattered across computer systems everywhere. Web servers inventory the web's resources and store address pointers, referred to as links, to them.

- As the Internet has grown, service providers have continued to provide more user-friendly software for exploring the World Wide Web. These software packages are called browsers and are based on hypertext links.

REVIEW QUESTIONS

The following questions test your knowledge of the material presented in this chapter.

1. What is the primary difference between a client/server type of network and a peer-to-peer network?

2. Describe the three important configuration settings associated with a network adapter card.

3. What element determines the active unit in a Token Ring network?

4. What is TCP/IP, and what does it mean?

5. The CIO of the company asks you for technical assistance about choosing an Internet Service Provider for your company. Due to cost cutting, she is interested in choosing a satellite Internet access solution, but is unfamiliar with how up linked versus down linked satellites operate. Explain how up linked versus down linked satellites function.

6. You join a new division as part of the technical staff of a large company. This new division integrates Windows XP workstations with an older network that uses Netware 4.0 and older software. Due to software incompatibility, TCP/IP is not a viable option. What sort of networking protocol should the network be using?

7. A fellow technician receives an order to purchase coaxial cable from a supplier. The supplier offers RG-6, RG-58, and RG-59 coaxial cable. The technician is unable to tell the difference between the three and enlists your help. Explain the difference between all three cable types.

8. Describe the function of the World Wide Web.

9. What is the purpose of a router in a network?

10. Your network consists of PCs and a number of older Macintosh computers that are used for digital editing purposes. The users would like to have the PCs and Macintosh computers networked together; however, the Macintosh computers are unable to use the TCP/IP protocol. What protocol should you attempt to try next?

11. Describe the function of the DNS.

12. Define the acronym URL and describe what it is used for.

13. Describe the functions of an Internet Service Provider.

14. What protocol is used to send large files on the Internet?

15. Describe plenum cabling, and explain why it's required for specific situations.

EXAM QUESTIONS

1. You install a new wireless network for a client. However, your client has been reading about network security, and asks you to increase the security of the network while maintaining the wireless nature of the network. What do you suggest to accomplish this?
    a. Connect all workstations to the wireless access point using CAT5.
    b. Turn on Wired Equivalent Privacy.
    c. Install more Wireless Access Points throughout the network.
    d. Change encryption from 40-bit keys to 16-bit keys.

2. What type of topology is typically used by Ethernet?
   a. A token-passing topology
   b. A star topology
   c. A ring topology
   d. A bus topology

3. State the maximum segment length of a 10Base-2 Ethernet network.
   a. 100 feet
   b. 185 meters
   c. 185 feet
   d. 100 meters

4. What does the designation 100Base-T tell you about a network?
   a. Its maximum cable segment length is 100 meters and it uses BNC T connectors.
   b. Its maximum data rate is 100 Mbps and it uses UTP cabling.
   c. Its maximum data rate is 100 MHz and it uses BNC-type T connectors.
   d. Its maximum cable segment length is 100 feet and it uses UTP cabling.

5. In a client/server network, _____.
   a. at least one unit is reserved just to serve the other units
   b. at least one unit depends on the other units for its information
   c. each unit has its own information and can serve as either client or server
   d. each unit handles some information for the network

6. What sort of special connection is used in conjunction with Token Ring networking?
   a. IDC connections
   b. UDC connections
   c. USB connection
   d. TCP/IP connection

7. What popular networking protocol is also the protocol that the Internet uses?
   a. TCP/IP
   b. Appletalk
   c. IPX/SPX
   d. NetBEUI

8. The maximum segment length of a 10Base-5 network connection is _____.
   a. 15 meters
   b. 185 meters
   c. 500 meters
   d. 1000 meters

9. Which file type is associated with the Internet?
   a. HTML
   b. COM
   c. EPS
   d. DLL

10. In order to connect to the Internet, a computer must be able to use the protocol _____.
    a. MAU
    b. NIC
    c. PPP
    d. TCP/IP

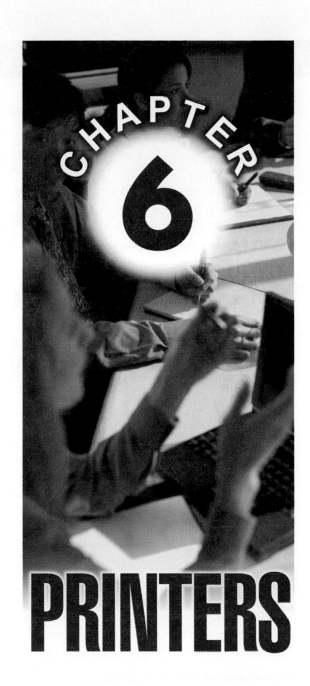

CHAPTER 6

PRINTERS

OBJECTIVES

OBJECTIVES

Upon completion of this chapter and its related lab procedures, you should be able to perform the following tasks:

1. Describe the various methods currently used to place computer print on paper.

2. Discuss characteristics of dot-matrix characters.

3. Discuss the types of paper handling common to different printer technologies.

4. Install and configure a printer.

5. List special considerations that must be observed when installing or repairing serial printers.

6. Identify a given type of cable connection between the printer and the computer.

7. Discuss data flow-control methods as they apply to serial printers.

8. Identify the major components of a dot-matrix printer.

9. Describe troubleshooting techniques associated with dot-matrix printers.

10. Relate symptoms to associated components in a dot-matrix printer.

11. Describe general alignment procedures for printhead mechanisms.

12. Describe the operation of a typical ink-jet printer.

13. Identify the major components of an ink-jet printer.

14. Describe troubleshooting techniques associated with ink-jet printers.

15. Relate symptoms to associated components in an ink-jet printer.

16. Describe the process for applying print to a page in a laser printer.

17. Identify the major components of a laser printer.

18. Describe troubleshooting techniques associated with laser printers.

19. Relate symptoms to associated components in a laser printer.

PRINTERS

INTRODUCTION

There are many instances when a permanent copy of a computer's output may be desired. The leading hard-copy output device is the **character printer** (that is, letters, numbers, and graphic images). This definition distinguishes the character printer from the other hard copy output device referred to as an **X-Y plotter**. Plotters are typically used to create complex graphics and drawings.

character printer

X-Y plotter

Character printers are the second most common output peripheral used with PCs (behind the video display). As this A+ objective indicates, computer technicians must understand how the different types of printers operate, what their typical components are, and what printer components can be serviced in the field.

As computer systems and their applications have diversified, a wide variety of printer systems have developed to fill the particular printing needs created by the marketplace. These developments have yielded faster and higher quality printing capabilities than ever before. In addition, these printers are now much less expensive than they have ever been before.

PRINTER FUNDAMENTALS

The A+ Core Hardware objective 5.1 states that the test taker should be able to identify printer technologies, interfaces, and options/upgrades. The opening sections of this chapter introduce basic printer-related terminology as well as the operation and organization of the most common printer types.

Technologies include:

- Laser
- Ink dispersion (ink jet)
- Dot matrix
- Solid ink
- Thermal
- Dye sublimation

Currently, laser and ink dispersal printers are the most widely used printing technologies in the personal computer environment. In times past, dot matrix printers were the printer technology of choice because they were relatively inexpensive and fast. However, advanced functionality—such as color and graphical printing—has combined with decreasing costs of laser and inkjet technology to relegate dot matrix printers to multipart continuous-form printing operations.

impact

non-impact

low speed

high speed

letter quality

near-letter quality

draft quality

fully formed

dot-matrix

The other categories of printer technologies also represent different niche areas of the PC printing market. Thermal printing techniques are very old and at one point had nearly vanished. However, they continue to remain in use with specialized peripherals such as credit card receipt printers. Thermal wax printing is used to produce near photographic reproductions of images. Similarly, professional graphics companies have used dye sublimation printing to produce high quality reproductions of photographic images. However, smaller versions designed for the consumer market have been introduced to provide personal printing capabilities for digital camera users.

Along with the diversity of printer systems have come various methods of classifying printers. Printers may be classified in a number of ways:

- Their method of placing characters on a page (**impact** or **non-impact**)

- Their speed of printing (**low speed** and **high speed**)

- The quality of the characters they produce (**letter quality**, **near-letter quality**, or **draft quality**)

- Or, how they form the character on the page (**fully formed** or **dot-matrix**)

Printing Methods

The first method of differentiating printers is by how they deliver ink to the page. Impact printers produce the character by causing the print mechanism, or its ink ribbon, to impact the page. Conversely, non-impact printers deliver ink to the page without the print mechanism making contact with the page.

Impact Printers

Impact printers

Impact printers place characters on the page by causing a hammer device to strike an inked ribbon. The ribbon, in turn, strikes the printing surface (paper).

The print mechanism may have the image of the character carved on its face, or it may be made up of a group of small print wires, arranged in a matrix pattern. In this case, the print mechanism is used to create the character on the page by printing a pattern of dots resembling it.

Generally, the quality, and therefore the readability of a fully formed character is better than that of a dot-matrix character. However, dot-matrix printers tend to be less expensive than their fully formed character counterparts. In either case, most printers in use today are of the impact variety. Figure 6-1 depicts both fully formed and dot-matrix type characters.

FULLY FORMED   DOT-MATRIX

Figure 6-1: Fully Formed and Dot-Matrix Characters

Non-Impact Printers

Several non-impact methods of printing are used in computer printers. Older, non-impact printers relied on special **heat-sensitive** or **chemically reactive paper** to form characters on the page. Newer non-impact methods use ink droplets, squirted from a jet-nozzle device (**ink-jet printers**), or a combination of laser/xerographic print technologies (laser printers) to place characters on a page. Currently, the most popular non-impact printers use ink-jet or laser technologies to deliver ink to the page.

In general, non-impact printers are less mechanical than impact counterparts. Therefore, they tend to be more dependable. Also, to their advantage, non-impact printers tend to be very quiet, and faster than comparable impact printers. The major disadvantage of non-impact printers is their inability to produce **carbon copies**.

Character Types

Basically, there are two methods of creating characters on a page. One method places a character on the page that is fully shaped, and fully filled-in. This type of character is called a fully formed character. The other method involves placing dots on the page in strategic patterns to fool the eye into seeing a character. This type of character is referred to as a dot-matrix character.

A fully formed impact print mechanism is depicted in Figure 6-2. The quality of **fully formed characters** is excellent. However, creative choices in print fonts and sizes tend to be somewhat limited. To change the size or shape of a character, the print mechanism would need to be replaced. Conversely, the flexibility of using dots to create characters allows them to be altered as the document is being created. The quality of dot matrix characters runs from extremely poor to extremely good, depending on the print mechanism.

**Figure 6-2:
A Fully Formed
Character
Mechanism**

Dot-matrix characters are not fully formed characters. Instead, they are produced by printing a pattern of dots to represent the character, as illustrated in Figure 6-3. The reader's eye fills in the gaps between the dots. Today's dot-matrix printers offer good speed and high-quality characters that approach those created by good typewriters, and nearly limitless printing flexibility.

**Figure 6-3:
Dot-Matrix
Characters**

┌─ **TEST TIP** ─┐
Remember the number of print wires in typical dot-matrix printheads.
└──────────────┘

Basically, the printhead in a dot-matrix printer is a vertical column of print wires that are controlled by electromagnets, as depicted in Figure 6-4. Dots are created on the paper by energizing selected electromagnets, which extend the desired print wires from the printhead. The print wires impact an ink ribbon, which impacts the paper. It's important to note that the entire character is not printed in a single instant of time. A typical printhead may contain 9, 18, or 24 print wires. The number of print wires used in the printhead is a major determining factor when discussing a printer's character quality.

**Figure 6-4:
Dot-Matrix Printer
Pinheads**

character cells

pitch

The matrix portion of this printer's name is derived from the manner in which the page is subdivided for printing. The page is divided into a number of horizontal rows, or text lines. Each row is divided into groups of columns, called **character cells**. A character cell defines the area in which a single character is printed. The size of the character cell is expressed in terms of **pitch**, or the number of characters printed per inch. Within the print cell, the matrix dimensions of the character are defined.

The density of the dots within the character cell determines the quality of the character printed. Common matrix sizes are 5 x 7, 24 x 9, and 36 x 18, to mention only a few of those available. The more dots that the printhead produces within the character cell, the better the character looks. This is because the dots are closer together, making the character more fully formed and easier to read.

Fonts

The term **font** refers to variations in the size and style of characters. With true fully formed characters, there is typically only one font available without changing the physical printing element. With all other printing methods, however, it is possible to include a wide variety of font types and sizes.

There are three common methods of generating character fonts. These are as bit-mapped, or raster-scanned fonts, as vector-based fonts, and as TrueType outline fonts. **Bit-mapped fonts** store dot patterns for all of the possible size and style variations of the characters in the set. Since a complete set of dots must be stored for each character and size that may be needed, this type of font tends to take up large amounts of memory. For this reason, the number of character sizes offered by bit-mapped fonts is typically limited. Font styles refer to the characteristics of the font, such as **normal**, **bold**, and **italic** styles. Font size refers to the physical measurement of the character. Type is measured in increments of 1/72 of an inch. Each increment is referred to as a **point**. Common text sizes are 10-point and 12-point type.

> **TEST TIP**
>
> Be aware of the benefits and drawbacks of bit-mapped characters.

Vector-based fonts store the outlines of character styles and sizes as sets of starting points and mathematical formulas. Each character is composed of a set of reference points and connecting lines between them. When a particular character is needed, the character generator sets the starting point for the character in the print cell and generates its outline from the formula. These types of fonts can be scaled up and down to achieve various sizes.

The vector-based approach requires much less storage space to store a character set and all of its variations than would be necessary for an equivalent bit-mapped character set. In addition, vector-based fonts can be scaled and rotated while bit-mapped fonts typically cannot. Conversely, bit-mapped characters can be printed out directly and quickly, while vector-based characters must be generated when called for.

> **TEST TIP**
>
> Know which font types are generated by establishing starting points and then calculating mathematical formulas.

TrueType fonts are a newer type of outline fonts that are commonly used with Microsoft Windows. These fonts are stored as a set of points and outlines that are used to generate a set of bit maps. Special algorithms adjust the bit maps so that they look best at the specified resolution. Once the bitmaps have been created, Windows stores them in a RAM cache that it creates. In this manner, the font is only generated once when it is first selected. Afterwards, the fonts are simply called out of memory, thus speeding up the process of delivering them to the printer. Each TrueType character set requires an **.FOT** and a **.TTF** file to create all of its sizes and resolutions.

Print Quality

The last criterion for comparing printers is the quality of the characters they produce. This is largely a function of how the characters are produced on the page. Printers that produce fully formed characters are described as **Letter Quality (LQ)** printers. All elements of the character appear to be fully connected when printed. On the other hand, printers that produce characters by forming a dot pattern are simply referred to as matrix printers. Upon close inspection of a character, one can see the dot patterns. The characters produced on some matrix printers are difficult to distinguish from fully formed characters. These printers have been labeled **Correspondence Quality (CQ)**, or **Near-Letter Quality (NLQ)** printers. Often, dot-matrix printers have two printing modes, one being standard dot matrix (sometimes called **utility** or **draft mode**), and the other a Near-Letter Quality mode.

Printer Mechanics

> By the very nature of their operation, printers tend to be extremely mechanical peripherals. During the printing operation, the print mechanism must be properly positioned over each character cell in sequence.

Loss of synchronization in impact printers can lead to paper jams, tearing, smudged characters, and/or printhead damage. Non-impact printers may produce totally illegible characters if synchronization is lost. The positioning action may be produced by moving the paper under a stationary printhead assembly, or by holding the paper stationary and stepping the printhead carriage across the page. In the latter operation, the **printhead carriage** rides on rods extending across the front of the page, as shown in Figure 6-5.

**Figure 6-5:
The Printhead
Carriage**

Depending upon the type of print mechanism used, the carriage may be stepped across the page at a rate of one character cell at a time (fully formed characters), or in sub-character-cell steps (dot-matrix characters). Printing may occur in only one direction (unidirectional), or in both directions (bi-directional). In bi-directional printers, the second line of characters is stored in the printer's buffer memory and printed in the opposite direction, saving the time that would normally be used to return the carriage to the start of the second line.

The printhead carriage assembly is stepped across the page by a **carriage motor/timing belt** arrangement. With many printer models, the number of character columns across the page is selectable, producing variable character spacing (expressed in **characters per inch**, or **cpi**), which must be controlled by the carriage position motor. Dot-matrix printers may also incorporate variable dot-densities (expressed as **dot-pitches**). Dot-pitch is also a function of the carriage motor control circuitry. Obviously, this discussion excludes continuous-stream, ink-jet printers, in which printing is done by electromagnetic deflection of the ink drops, and laser printers, in which the beam is reflected from a revolving mirror.

| carriage motor/timing belt |
| characters per inch (cpi) |
| dot-pitches |

Paper Handling

In addition to positioning the print mechanism for printing, all printer types must feed paper through the print area. The type of **paper handling mechanism** in a printer is somewhat dependent on the type of form intended for use with the printer, and its speed.

| paper handling mechanism |
| continuous forms |
| single-sheet forms |
| Friction-feed |
| platen |
| Pin-feed |
| tractor |

Paper forms fall into two general categories, **continuous forms**, which come in folded stacks and have holes along their edges, and **single-sheet forms**, such as common typing paper. There are two common methods of moving paper through the printer:

- **Friction-feed** – uses friction to hold the paper against the printer's **platen**. The paper advances through the printer as the platen turns.

- **Pin-feed** – pulls the paper through the printer by a set of pins that fit into the holes along the edge of the form, as shown in Figure 6-6. The pins may be an integral part of the platen, or mounted on a separate, motor-driven **tractor**.

Figure 6-6: A Pin-Feed Tractor Mechanism

Friction-feed is normally associated with single sheet printers. The sheet feeding system can be manual or automatic. Platen pin-feed and pin tractors are usually employed with continuous and multi-layer forms. These mechanisms can control paper slippage and misalignment created by the extra weight imposed by continuous forms. Platen pin-feed units can handle only one width of paper whereas tractors can be adjusted to handle various paper widths. **Tractor feeds** are used with very heavy forms, such as multiple-part continuous forms, and are most commonly found on dot-matrix printers. Most ink-jet and laser printers use single-sheet feeder systems.

Tractor feeds

┌─ **TEST TIP** ─┐

Know the major purpose of a tractor-feed mechanism and where it is most commonly used.

The gear trains involved in the paper handling function can be treated as an FRU item in some printers. While it is possible to replace the gears, or gear packs, in dot-matrix and ink-jet printers (if they can be obtained from the manufacturer as separate items), it is usually not economical to do so. Laser printers, on the other hand, are normally expensive enough to warrant replacing the gear trains and clutch assemblies that handle the paper movement through the printer.

Printer Controls

Although printers vary considerably from type to type, and model to model, there are some elements that are common to all printers. These elements are depicted in Figure 6-7.

**Figure 6-7:
Common Printer
Components**

interface/controller

Like most other peripherals, the heart of a character printer is its **interface/controller** circuitry. The interface circuitry accepts data and instructions from the computer's bus systems, and provides the necessary interfacing (serial or parallel) between the computer and the printer's control circuitry. This includes decoding the computer's instructions to the printer, converting signal logic levels, and passing data to the printer's controller.

Parallel-port connections are most efficient when the printer is located in close proximity to the computer. If the printer must be located remotely, the serial interface becomes more appropriate. Many manufacturers offer both connections as standard equipment. Others offer the serial connection as an option. More is said about these two interfaces later in this section. A third less common method of connecting printers to computers uses the SCSI interface as the connection port. As with other SCSI devices, the printer must be set up as a unique SCSI device, and proper connection and termination procedures should be observed.

The controller section receives the data and control signals from the interface section, and produces all of the signals necessary to select, or generate, the proper character to be printed. It also advances the print mechanism to the next print position, and feeds the paper at the proper times. In addition, the controller generates status and control signals that tell the computer what is happening in the printer.

Due to the complexity of most character printers, a dedicated **microcontroller** is typically employed to oversee the complete operation of the printer. The presence of the dedicated microprocessor provides greater flexibility, and additional options, for the printer.

microcontroller

Along with the dedicated processor, the printer normally contains IC memory in the form of RAM, ROM, or both. A speed mismatch exists between the computer and the printer, since the computer is usually capable of generating characters at a much higher rate than the printer can print them. In order to minimize this speed differential, printers typically carry **on-board RAM** memory buffers to hold characters coming from the computer. In this way, the transfer of data between the computer and the printer occurs at a rate that is compatible with the computer's operating speed. The printer obtains its character information from the on-board buffer.

on-board RAM

In addition to character print information, the host computer can also store printer instructions in the buffer for use by the dedicated processor. The printer may also contain **on-board ROM** in the form of **character generators**, or **printer initialization programs** for start-up. Some printers contain EPROM, instead of ROM, to provide a greater variety of options for the printer, such as **downloadable type fonts** and **variable print modes.**

on-board ROM
character generators
printer initialization programs
downloadable type fonts
variable print modes

Basically, the controller must produce signals to drive the print mechanism, the paper feed motor, the carriage motor, and possibly optional devices, such as single-sheet feeders and add-on tractors. Most of these functions are actually performed by precision stepper motors. There are usually hardware driver circuits between the motors and the controller to provide current levels high enough to activate the motors.

The controller also gathers information from the printer through a variety of sensing devices. These include position sensing switches and user-operated, front-panel-mounted, mode-control switches. Some of the more common sensing switches include the **home-position sensor**, the **end-of-paper sensor**, and the **carriage position sensor**. The controller also responds to manual input command switches, such as **On/Off Line**, **Form Feed (FF)**, and **Line Feed (LF)**.

home-position sensor
end-of-paper sensor
carriage position sensor
On/Off Line
Form Feed (FF)
Line Feed (LF)

The sensors and switches can be treated as FRUs in many printers. This is particularly true with more expensive laser printers. In most printers, the entire **operator control panel** can be exchanged for another unit. This effectively changes all of the user-operated input switches at one time.

operator control panel

Dot-Matrix Printers

At one time, dot-matrix impact printers were the stalwarts of the microcomputer printing market. The components of a typical dot-matrix printer are depicted in Figure 6-8. They consist of a **power supply board,** a **main control board**, a **printhead assembly**, a **ribbon cartridge**, a **paper feed motor** (along with its mechanical drive gears), and a **printhead positioning motor** and mechanisms.

POWER SUPPLY BOARD   POWER TRANSFORMER   MAIN CONTROL BOARD   PAPER FEED MOTOR

HOME POSITION SENSOR   TIMING BELT   PRINTHEAD ASSEMBLY   PRINTHEAD POSITIONING MOTOR   CONTROL PANEL

Figure 6-8:
Parts of a Dot-Matrix
Printer

power supply board

main control board

printhead assembly

ribbon cartridge

paper feed motor

printhead positioning motor

The Power Supply

The power supply board is called on to provide various voltages to power the electronics on the control board. It also drives both the printhead positioning and paper feed motors, and energizes the wires of the printhead so that they will strike the ribbon as directed by the control board.

The Main Control Board

The control board is typically divided into four functional sections, as described in Figure 6-9. These functional blocks include:

- interface circuitry
- character generation circuitry
- printer controller circuitry
- motor control circuitry

**Figure 6-9:
Logical Parts of
the Control Board**

The control board contains the logic circuitry required to convert the signals received from the computer's adapter card into character patterns, as well as to generate the proper control signals to position the printhead properly on the page, fire the correct combination of printhead wires to create the character, and to advance the paper properly. The on-board microcontroller, character generators, RAM, and ROM are found on the control board.

The status of the printer's operation is monitored by the control board through a number of sensors. These sensors typically include:

- Paper Out

- Printhead Position

- Home Position (for the printhead carriage)

Input from the printer's operator panel is also routed to the control board. Operator panel information includes:

- On-line

- Form Feed

- Line Feed

- Power/Paper Out

The control panel may contain a number of other buttons and indicator lights, whose functions are specific to that particular printer. Always consult the printer's user's manual for information about control panel buttons and indicators.

The printer's interface may contain circuitry to handle serial data, parallel data, or a combination of the two. At the printer end of a **Centronics parallel port**, a 36-pin connector, like the one depicted in Figure 6-10, is used. Of course, the computer end of the cable should have a DB-25M connector to plug into the system's DB-25F LPT port.

Figure 6-10: A Parallel Connection at the Printer

┌─ **TEST TIP** ───┐
Remember the types of connectors used at both the computer and the printer ends of a parallel printer cable.
└──┘

Dot-matrix printers process bit patterns in much the same way that CRT controllers do. The dot patterns are accessed from a character generator ROM. In addition to the standard ASCII character set, many printers feature preprogrammed sets of block-graphics characters that can be used to create non-text images on a page. Most manufacturers use EPROM (erasable-programmable ROM) character generators instead of the older ROM type. This allows their units to accept downloadable fonts from software.

Where used with a high-quality printhead, a variety of typefaces, such as **Roman Gothic**, Italic, and foreign language characters, can be loaded into the programmable character generator from software. In addition, it is possible for users to create their own character sets, typefaces, and graphic symbols. Some manufacturers even offer standard bar-code graphics software sets for their machines.

Printhead Mechanisms

The **printhead** is a collection of print wires set in an electromagnetic head unit. The printhead assembly is made up of a permanent magnet, a group of electromagnets, and a housing. In the printhead, the permanent magnet keeps the wires pulled in until electromagnets are energized, causing them to move forward.

The printhead is mounted in the **printhead carriage assembly**. The carriage assembly rides on a bar that passes along the front of the platen. The printhead carriage assembly is attached to the printhead positioning motor by a **timing belt**.

The **printhead positioning motor** is responsible for moving the printhead mechanism across the page, and stopping it in just the right places to print. The printhead rides back and forth across the printer on a pair of carriage rods. A timing belt runs between the printhead assembly and the printhead positioning motor, and converts the rotation of the motor into the linear movement of the printhead assembly. The printhead must stop each time the print wires strike the paper. If this timing is off, the characters will be smeared on the page, and the paper may be damaged. The motor steps a predetermined number of steps to create a character within a character cell. Figure 6-11 illustrates a dot-matrix printhead delivering print to a page.

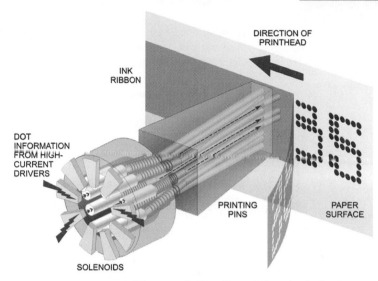

Figure 6-11: Dot-Matrix Printhead

Paper Handling

The **paper feed motor** and **gear train** move the paper through the printer. This can be accomplished by driving the **platen assembly**. The platen can be used in two different ways to move the paper through the printer. After the paper has been wrapped halfway around the platen, a set of rollers are used to pin the paper to the platen as it turns. This is **friction-feed paper handling**. As described earlier, the platen may have small pins that can drag the paper through the printer as the platen turns. In either case, the paper feed motor drives the platen to move the paper.

The feed motor's gear train can also be used to drive the extended gear train of a **tractor assembly** when it is installed. The gears of the feed motor mesh with those of the tractor, causing it to pull, or push, the paper through the printer. To use a tractor, the friction-feed feature of the platen must be released. Otherwise, the tractor and the platen may not turn at the same rate, and the paper will rip or jam. The installation of a tractor assembly is illustrated in Figure 6-12.

Figure 6-12: Installing a Tractor Assembly

Thermal Printers

As mentioned earlier in this section, thermal printing techniques were at one time widely used with PC printing. These printers use heated elements to burn or melt dot pattern characters on special paper. There are two types of thermal printers:

Direct thermal printers

Thermal wax transfer printers

- **Direct thermal printers**

- **Thermal wax transfer printers**

Direct thermal printers work in much the same manner as the ink cartridge dot-matrix printers described in the preceding section. The major difference between the two technologies is that the print wires are heated in the thermal printer so that they can burn dot patterns into special thermal paper. Early facsimile (fax) machine technology was based on this type of thermal printing. Even now, thermal printers are widely used for bar code printing, battery-powered hand-held printing devices, and credit card receipt printers.

The other difference between direct thermal and dot-matrix printers is that in the thermal printer, the printhead does not move across the page. Instead, different pins in a row of heating elements are extended as the paper passes over the print bar. This makes thermal printing quiet and efficient. There is also no ink ribbon to change or run out of.

The drawback to direct thermal printing is the special thermal paper required for operation (using regular paper would present a fire hazard). In addition, the paper does not age well. Over time the entire page will darken and become difficult to read.

thermal wax transfer printer

The other variation of thermal printers is the **thermal wax transfer printer**. In these units, a thermal printhead melts dots of wax-based ink from the transfer ribbon onto the paper. When the wax cools, it is permanently attached to the page. Unlike the direct thermal printer, thermal wax transfer printers do not require special paper to print on.

These printers are available in monochrome (one color) and multicolor versions. The multicolor versions can be three-color printers (Cyan, Magenta, and Yellow — CMY color) or four-color printers (CMY + black = CMYK color). These thermal printers use a high volume of wax to print each page. Each page requires a complete covering of wax to print regardless of how many characters are placed on the page.

In Figure 6-13, the thermal printer feeds a sheet of paper into the thermal printing mechanism. In the print mechanism the paper is brought together with a roll of color film that is coated with successive sheets of inked wax. Each sheet on the roll contains one of the basic colors (CYM and K) and is equal to the length and width of the sheet of paper. As the paper moves through the print engine the first time, it is matched with one of the color sheets as it passes through a compression roller and a strip of thermal print heating elements (pins). The heating elements are turned on and off to melt selected dots of colored wax onto the paper. After completing the first pass, the paper and the film are separated from each other, the paper is repositioned for another run using the second color sheet, and the process is repeated to place the second set of color dots on the page. This cycle is repeated until all the colors have been applied to the page. This type of printer is used in professional color printing because it provides vivid reproductions of picture and artwork. However, they can't actually produce images that approach real photographic quality because they use color dots to create the image of the picture and photographs are made up of continuous tones.

Figure 6-13:
Color Thermal
Printing

Ink-Jet Printers

Ink-jet printers produce characters by squirting a precisely controlled stream of ink drops onto the paper, as shown in Figure 6-14. The drops must be controlled very precisely in terms of their aerodynamics, size, and shape, or the drop placement on the page becomes inexact and the print quality falters.

Figure 6-14:
Ink-Jet Printers

The drops are formed by one of two methods:

- **thermal shock** − heats the ink in a capillary tube, just behind the nozzle. This increases the pressure of the ink in the tube and causes it to explode through the opening.

thermal shock

- **mechanical vibration** − uses vibrations from a piezoelectric crystal to force ink through a nozzle.

The ink jet nozzle is designed to provide the proper shape and trajectory for the ink drops so that they can be directed precisely toward the page. The nozzle is also designed so that the surface tension of the ink keeps it from running out of the nozzle uncontrollably.

1. NO VOLTAGE IS APPLIED

2. VOLTAGE IS APPLIED

3. AFTER EJECTION OF AN INK DROPLET

4. INK LEFT IN THE NOZZLE TIP IS PULLED BACK BY THE SURFACE TENSION

Figure 6-15: Drop-on-Demand Printing

Two methods are used by ink-jet printers to deliver the drops to the page: the **interrupted-stream** (**drop-on-demand**) method and the **continuous-stream** method. The drop-on-demand system forms characters on the page in much the same manner as a dot-matrix printer does. As the printhead mechanism moves across the character cells of the page, the controller causes a drop to be sprayed, only where necessary, to form the dot pattern of a character. Drop-on-demand printing is illustrated in Figure 6-15.

Continuous-stream systems, like the one shown in Figure 6-16, produce characters that more closely resemble fully formed characters. In these systems, the printhead does not travel across the page. Instead, the drops are given a negative charge in an ion chamber and are passed through a set of deflection plates, similar to the electron beam in a CRT tube. The plates deflect the drops to their proper placement on the page, and unused drops are deflected off the page into an ink recirculation system.

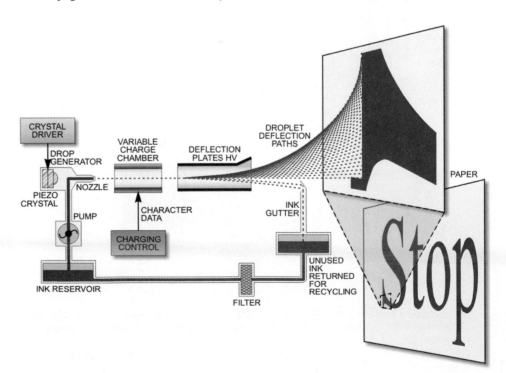

Figure 6-16: Continuous-Stream Printing

While capable of delivering very high-quality characters at high speeds, continuous-stream systems tend to be expensive, and therefore are not normally found in printers for the consumer market. Instead, they are reserved for high-volume commercial printing applications. The ink-jet printers in the general consumer market use drop-on-demand techniques to deliver ink to the page.

Some ink-jet printers incorporate multiple jets to permit color printing. Four basic colors may be mixed to create a palette of colors by firing the ink jets in different combinations.

A special variety of ink-jet printers referred to as **solid ink-jet printers** (also called *wax-jet printers*) combines thermal printer technology with ink-jet type operations to produce brilliantly colored pictures and images. Instead of working with inks, these printers melt dyed waxes and then spray them on the page using ink-jet—like dispersal methods. The wax base used for the printing process produces exceptionally bright colors on all types of paper; however, because these printers are slow and relatively expensive, they are typically only found in professional reproduction and advertising settings.

Ink-Jet Printer Components

Aside from the printing mechanism, the components of a typical ink-jet printer are very similar to those of a dot-matrix printer. Its primary components are:

- the printhead assembly
- the power board
- the control board
- the printhead positioning motor and timing belt
- the paper feed motor and gear train
- the printer's sensors

These components are shown in Figure 6-17.

Figure 6-17: Ink-Jet Printer Components

The Printhead Assembly

The ink cartridge snaps into the printhead assembly that rides in front of the platen on a rail or rod. The printhead assembly is positioned by a timing belt that runs between it and the positioning motor. A flexible cable carries ink-jet firing information between the control board and the printhead. This cable folds out of the way as the printhead assembly moves across the printer.

Paper Handling

The paper feed motor turns a gear train that ultimately drives the platen, as depicted in Figure 6-18. The paper is friction-fed through the printer, between the platen and the pressure rollers. Almost all ink-jet printers used with microcomputer systems are single-sheet, friction-feed systems. The control board, power supply board, and sensors perform the same functions in an ink-jet printer that they did in the dot-matrix printer.

Figure 6-18: Ink-Jet Paper Handling

Laser Printers

The **laser printer** modulates a highly focused laser beam to produce CRT-like raster-scan images on a rotating drum, as depicted in Figure 6-19.

Figure 6-19: A Typical Laser Printer

The **drum** is coated with a photosensitive plastic, which is given a **negative electrical charge** over its surface. The modulated laser beam creates spots on the rotating drum. The spots written by the laser take on a **positive electrical charge**. A negatively charged **toner material** is attracted to the positively charged, written areas of the drum. The paper is fed past the rotating drum and the toner is transferred to the paper. A pair of compression rollers is combined with a high-temperature lamp to fuse the toner to the paper. Thus, the image, written on the drum by the laser, is transferred to the paper.

The laser beam scans the drum so rapidly that it is not practical to do the scanning mechanically. Instead, the beam is bounced off a rotating, **polygonal** (many-sided) **mirror**. The faces of the mirror cause the reflected beam to scan across the face of the drum as the mirror revolves. Using the highest dot densities available, these printers produce characters that rival typeset text in quality. Larger laser printers produce characters at a rate of 20,000 lines per minute. Laser printers intended for the personal computer market generate 6 to 45 pages per minute.

| drum |
| negative electrical charge |
| positive electrical charge |
| toner material |
| polygonal mirror |

Laser Printer Components

From manufacturer to manufacturer, and model to model, the exact arrangement and combinations of components may vary in laser printers. However, the order of operations is always the same. The six stages of operation in a laser printer include:

- Cleaning
- Conditioning
- Writing
- Developing
- Transferring
- Fusing

TEST TIP

Memorize the stages of a typical laser printer.

To accomplish these objectives, all laser printers possess the following logical blocks:

- Power supply
- Control board
- Laser writing unit
- Drum unit

- Fusing assembly
- Paper feed motor and gear train
- System's sensors
- Control panel board

The blocks of the typical laser printer are illustrated in Figure 6-20.

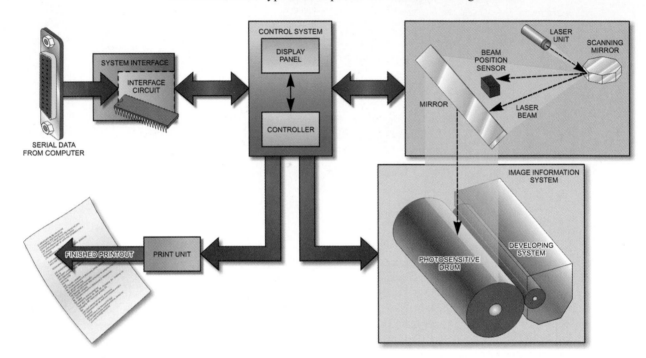

Figure 6-20: Block Diagram of a Laser Printer

ac power

high-voltage dc supply

static charges

dc operating voltages

registration

The laser printer power supply unit is the most complex found in any type of printer. It must deliver **ac power** to the fuser unit. This unit requires power for its fusing heaters and image erase lamps. The power supply also delivers a **high-voltage dc supply** (+1000 Vdc) to the toner transfer mechanisms in the drum area. The high voltages are used to create the **static charges** required to move toner from one component to another (i.e., from the drum to the paper). Finally, the power supply unit must deliver **dc operating voltages** to the scanning and paper handling motors, as well as the digital electronic circuitry on the control board.

The control board contains all of the circuitry required to operate the printer and control its many parts. It receives control signals from the computer, and formats the data to be printed. The control board also monitors the conditions within the printer, and responds to input from the its various sensors.

When data is received from the host computer, the control board generates all of the enabling signals needed to place the information on the page as directed. The character information is converted into a serial bit stream, which can be applied to the scanning laser. The photosensitive drum rotates as the laser beam is scanned across it. The laser creates a copy of the image on the photosensitive drum in the form of a relatively positive-charged drawing. This operation is referred to as **registration**.

Laser Printing Operations

Before the laser writes on the drum, a set of erase lamps shine on the drum to remove any residual traces of the previous image. This leaves the drum with a neutral electrical charge. A high voltage, applied to the **primary corona wire**, creates a highly charged negative field that **conditions** the drum to be written on by applying a uniform negative charge (−1000 V) to it.

primary corona wire

conditions

As the drum is written on by the laser it turns through the **toner powder**, which is attracted to the more positively charged image on the drum.

toner powder

Toner is a very fine powder, bonded to iron particles that are attracted to the charges written on the drum. The **developer roller** in the toner cartridge turns as the drum turns, and expels a measured amount of toner past a **restricting blade**, as illustrated in Figure 6-21. A regulating ac voltage assists the toner in leaving the cartridge, but also pulls back some excess toner from the drum. Excess toner is recycled within the toner cartridge so that it can be used again.

developer roller

restricting blade

Figure 6-21: The Developer Roller

Great care should be taken when installing a new drum unit. Exposing the drum to light for more than a few minutes may damage it. The drum should never be touched, as this too can ruin its surface. Keep the unit away from dust and dirt, as well as away from humidity and high-temperature areas.

TEST TIP

Know that you should never expose the drum of a laser printer to sunlight, or any other strong light source.

The **transfer corona wire (transfer roller)** is responsible for transferring the toner from the drum to the paper. The toner is transferred to the paper because of the highly positive charge that the transfer corona wire applies to the paper. The positive charge attracts the more negative toner particles away from the drum, and onto the page. A special, static-eliminator comb acts to prevent the positively-charged paper from sticking to the negatively-charged drum.

transfer corona wire

transfer roller

TEST TIP

Know the functions of the two corona wires in a laser printer.

compression rollers

fusing unit

fusing roller

After the image has been transferred to the paper, a pair of **compression rollers** in the **fusing unit** act to press the toner particles into the paper, while they melt them to it. The top compression roller, known as the **fusing roller**, is heated by a quartz lamp. This roller melts the toner to the paper as it exits the fusing unit, while the lower roller applies pressure to the paper. A cleaning pad removes excess particles, and applies a silicon lubricant to prevent toner from sticking to the Teflon-coated fusing roller. The complete transfer process is shown in Figure 6-22.

Figure 6-22: The Transfer Process

Component Variations

electrophotographic cartridge

toner supply

corona wire

drum assembly

developing roller

In Hewlett-Packard printers, the main portion of the printing system is contained in the **electrophotographic cartridge**. This cartridge contains the **toner supply**, the **corona wire**, the **drum assembly**, and the **developing roller**. The HP cartridge configuration is depicted in Figure 6-23.

TEST TIP

Memorize the parts of a typical laser printer cartridge.

Figure 6-23: The HP Cartridge Configuration

In other laser printers, like the one depicted in Figure 6-24, the basic components are combined so that the printer consists of a **developer unit**, a **toner cartridge**, a **drum unit**, a **fuser unit**, and a **cleaning pad**. In this case, the developer unit and toner cartridge are separate units. With this configuration, changing the toner does not involve changing some of the other wear-prone components. While it is less expensive to change toner, attention must be paid to how much the other units are wearing. Notice that the photosensitive drum is also a separate component.

Color laser printers operate on the same principles as the monochrome version we have described as an example. However, color lasers use four different color toners. From earlier discussions of other color printers, you may be able to guess that the four toners are combined in different ratios on the page to form the different colors in the spectrum. Likewise, from the description of how images are written on the drum of a laser printer and transferred to the paper, you can probably imagine that the voltages used to control the attraction properties of the toner to the drum and paper are much more complex than they are for a single-color laser printer. However, for the technician color laser printers still work like their single-color relatives.

developer unit

toner cartridge

drum unit

fuser unit

cleaning pad

Color laser printers

**Figure 6-24:
Basic Components
of a Laser Printer**

Paper Handling

Laser printers are very mechanical in nature. The paper handling motor and the gear train assembly perform a tremendous number of operations to process a single sheet of paper. The **paper transport mechanics** must pick up a page from the paper tray, and move it into the printer's registration area. After the drum has been written with the image, the paper handling mechanism moves the paper into registration. A roller system moves the page past the drum, and into the fusing unit. When the page exits through the fusing rollers, the printer senses that the page has exited, and resets itself to wait for another page to print.

paper transport mechanics

In addition to the motor and gear train, the printer uses a number of sensors and solenoid-actuated clutches to control the paper movement. It uses solenoids to engage and disengage different gear sets, and clutches, at appropriate times during the printing process.

Laser printer sensors—A typical laser printer has sensors to determine what paper trays are installed, what size paper is in them, and whether the tray is empty. It also uses sensors to track the movement of the paper through each stage of the printer. This allows the controller to know where the page is at all times, and to sequence the activities of the solenoids and clutches properly.

Laser printer sensors

Figure 6-25 gives a summary of the sensors found in a typical laser printer.

Figure 6-25:
Sensor Summary

If the page does not show up at the next sensor at the appropriate time, the printer will know that a paper jam has occurred, and will create an error message that indicates the area of the printer it is in. When a paper jam occurs, it will be necessary to remove the paper from the inside of the printer, and reset the print operation. Gaining access to the area where the jam is usually requires direction from the printer's user's manual. The printer should always be allowed to cool, and should always be turned off before reaching inside the unit.

Another set of sensor switches monitor the printer's access doors to protect personnel from potentially dangerous conditions inside the printer. The **interlock switch** blocks the laser beam as a vision-protection measure. Likewise, the high-voltage supplies to various printer components are also shut down. To observe the operation of the printer, it will be necessary to locate, and bypass, these interlocks. However, you should always be aware that these interlocks are present for protection, and great care should be taken when working with them defeated.

Still other sensors are used to monitor the temperatures within different sections of the printer. A **thermal sensor** in the fusing unit monitors the temperature of the unit. This information is applied to the control circuitry so that it can keep the fuser temperature between 140°C and 230°C. If the temperature of the fuser is not controlled correctly, it may cause severe damage to the printer, as well as present a potential fire hazard.

A **thermal fuse** protects the fuser assembly from overheating and damaging the printer. The thermal fuse should normally snap back after the temperature condition is cleared. If the switch is open under cool conditions, it will need to be replaced. This is normally an indication that the thermal sensor has failed, or that the fuser assembly has been installed improperly.

When the laser beam is turned on, a **beam detector sensor** in the writing unit alerts the control circuitry that the writing process has begun. This signal synchronizes the beginning of the laser-modulating data with the beginning of the scan line.

interlock switch

thermal sensor

thermal fuse

TEST TIP

Remember the purpose of the thermal fuse in laser printers.

beam detector sensor

Paper Specifications

One reason for faint printing is that the paper thickness lever is set to the wrong position for the weight of paper being used.

> **Paper weight**—Paper is specified in terms of its **weight** per 500 sheets at 22" x 17" (e.g., 500 sheets of 22" x 17", 21-pound bond paper weighs 21 pounds).

Paper weight

weight

The thickness setting will also cause smudged characters when the paper is too thick for the actual setting. In this case, adjust the thickness lever one or two notches away from the paper.

```
┌─ TEST TIP ──────────────────────┐
│ Know how paper weight is specified and │
│ how many sheets are involved.    │
└──────────────────────────────────┘
```

Dye Sublimation Printers

Earlier in this chapter we discussed thermal wax printers that could produce vivid high-quality graphics. However, the images they produce can never approach photographic quality because of their dot composition. A variation of that printer type, referred to as a **dye sublimation printer**, has been produced to provide photographic quality, continuous tone images.

dye sublimation printer

Figure 6-26 illustrates the dye sublimation process. While the printing mechanism appears similar to the thermal wax printer described earlier, there are some distinct differences. In a dye sublimation printer, sheets of special paper or transparencies are fastened securely to a print drum. Clamping the page to the drum ensures good **registration** between the different colors that will be printed on the paper in successive color passes.

registration

The drum with the paper is rotated in conjunction with a continuous roll of plastic film containing successive CYMK color sheets that have the same dimensions as the page. At the point where the paper and film come together, a heating element strip is used to heat the color substance on the film so that it vaporizes (sublimates) and is absorbed into the paper. The heating element contains thousands of small heat points that can create extremely fine patterns of color dots. In addition, each element can be used to supply hundreds of different temperatures, which leads to hundreds of different amounts of ink transferred to the page and results in hundreds of different shades that can be produced.

Figure 6-26: Dye Sublimation Printing

After the length of the page has been printed with one color, the drum cycles again and the process is repeated until all the colors have been transferred to the page.

These printers tend to be very slow and expensive. However, due to their ability to produce continuous tone quality images, these printers are widely used by professional graphics businesses to produce posters and large-scale reproductions.

With the popularity of digital cameras continuing to increase, users have many more options for how they handle, view, and display their photographs. Because digital photographs can be viewed without sending them to a print house, many users simply store their images on an electronic storage medium such as a disk drive or CD. However, there are always some photographs that people want to create hard copies of. For these occasions, some small consumer versions of the dye sublimation printer have been introduced to the market to enable users to reproduce electronic photographs without using a print service.

PRINTER CONNECTIONS AND CONFIGURATIONS

A portion of A+ Core Hardware objective 5.1 states that the test taker should be able to identify printer technologies, interfaces, and options/upgrades.

Interfaces include:

- Parallel
- Network
- SCSI
- USB
- Infrared
- Serial
- IEEE-1394/Firewire
- Wireless

Printers used with personal computers are available in many types and use various connection schemes. As this A+ objective points out, the computer technician must be able to connect any make of printer to any make of computer and configure it for operation.

The connection method between the printer and the computer will affect many of the troubleshooting steps necessary to isolate printing problems. Likewise, connecting a printer to a network will affect how the technician approaches its configuration and troubleshooting. The following sections of this chapter concentrate on the various printer connection methods commonly used in personal computer environments.

Printer Installation

Generally speaking, one of the least difficult I/O devices to add to a microcomputer system is a parallel printer. This is largely due to the fact that, from the beginning of the PC era, a printer has been one of the most standard pieces of equipment to add to the system. Historically, the printer has been primarily attached to the computer through a standard parallel printer port. However, special printer installation requirements, such as remotely located printers, often led to using standard RS-232 serial interfaces to connect the computer and printer together. However, both of these interface standards are beginning to age and be surpassed by newer interface types.

This standardization has led to fairly direct installation procedures for most printers: Obtain an IBM Centronics printer cable, plug it into the appropriate LPT port on the back of the computer, connect the Centronic-compatible end to the printer, plug the power cord into the printer, load a device driver to configure the software for the correct printer, and print.

One note of caution concerning parallel printer cables — the IEEE has established specifications for bi-directional parallel printer cables (**IEEE-1284**). These cables affect the operation of EPP and ECP parallel devices. Refer to the "Enhanced Parallel Port Operations" section of Chapter 3 — *Standard I/O Systems*, for additional information about these ports. Using an older, non-compliant unidirectional cable with a bi-directional parallel device will prevent the device from communicating properly with the system and may prevent it from operating.

IEEE-1284

Some failures will produce error messages, such as "**Printer Not Ready**," while others will simply leave the data in the computer's **print spooler**. The symptom normally associated with this condition is that the parallel device simply refuses to operate. If an ECP or EPP device successfully runs a self test, but will not communicate with the host system, check the Advanced BIOS Setup screens to make certain that bi-directional printing has been enabled for the parallel port. If so, check the printer cable by substituting a known 1284-compliant cable for it.

Printer Not Ready

print spooler

CHALLENGE #1

You are called out to a customer's site to check his laser printer. The printer sits on the desk next to the host computer and is attached to the 25-pin D-shell connector on the back of the system. When you start the printer, it shows no startup errors and prints a page from a self-test. So, you check the system's CMOS settings to verify that the printer port is enabled and that it is set for ECP operation. Still, you cannot get the system to print a page from the printer. What should you check next?

Setting up serial printers—Serial printers are slightly more difficult to set up, since the communication definition must be configured between the computer and the printer. The serial port will need to be configured for speed, parity type, character frame, and protocol.

Regardless of the type of printer being installed, the steps for adding a printer to a system are basically the same: Connect the printer to the correct I/O port at the computer system. Make sure the port is enabled. Set up the appropriate printer drivers. Configure the port's communication parameters, if a serial printer is being installed. Install the paper. Run the printer's self-test, and then print a document. These steps are summarized in Figure 6-27.

Figure 6-27: Printer Installation Steps

Printer Drivers

All peripheral devices require device driver programs to coordinate their operation with the system. These programs are installed on the host computer and create a software interface between the operating system's printing subsystem, the port, and the printer's intelligent devices. For the most part, modern operating systems supply a wide variety of device drivers (including **printer drivers**) as an integral part of their packages.

printer drivers

When a new printer is installed, it should be detected by the system's PnP process then next time the system is started. In many cases, the operating system will be able to determine which type of printer is attached and automatically load a standard driver for it. In other cases, the PnP process will request that the user insert an OEM driver disk so that it can load a driver for the new printer.

When the new printer is not detected, the user must manually install the printer (and its driver program) through a configuration program (wizard) in the operating system. Figure 6-28 illustrates the functional position of a printer driver in the system.

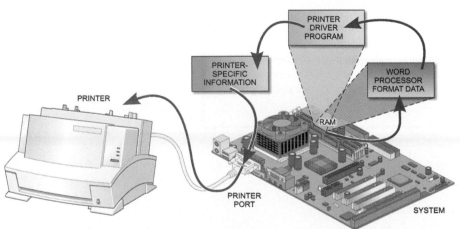

Printer drivers can be a source of many printing problems and are generally one of the first things checked when a new printer installation does not function. These programs can also become corrupted in some operating systems when new devices are installed that write over .dll portions of their code. Therefore, it may be necessary to reload printer drivers in these situations.

Figure 6-28: Printer Driver Position

Faulty or incorrect printer drivers typically produce garbled print (because the driver is not giving the printer information that it can recognize) or no print at all. If you suspect that a printer driver problem is occurring, you must reinstall or replace the driver. In a PnP system, you can remove the existing driver through the installation wizard and restart the system so that it can detect the printer and install a new copy of the driver. In a non-PnP system you must manually reinstall the driver.

If you are going to reinstall the driver, you should check the printer manufacturer's web site for new updated drivers for the printer you are working with. Printer manufacturers typically supply proprietary driver programs that may be newer than the drivers in your operating system. Theoretically, these newer drivers should work better or offer improved features over the older version.

Serial Printer Considerations

In some applications, it is simply impossible to locate the printer close enough to the host computer to use the parallel connection. In these cases, serially interfaced printers come into play. Printers using a serial interface connection add an extra level of complexity to the system. Unlike the parallel printer interface that basically plugs and plays on most systems, serial interface connections require additional hardware and software configuration steps. Serial printer problems basically fall into three categories:

- Cabling problems
- Configuration problems
- Printer problems

Cabling Problems

Not all serial cables are created equal. In the PC world, RS-232 serial cables can take on several configurations. First of all, they may use either 9-pin or 25-pin D-shell connectors. The cable for a particular serial connection will need to have the correct type of connector at each end. Likewise, the connection scheme inside the cable can vary from printer to printer. Normally, the Transmit Data line (TXD - pin 2) from the computer is connected to the Receive Data line (RXD - pin 3) of the printer. Also, the Data Set Ready (DSR - pin 6) is typically connected to the printer's **Data Terminal Ready** (DTR - pin 20) pin. These connections are used as one method to control the flow of information between the system and the printer. If the printer's character buffer becomes full, it will signal the computer to hold up sending characters by deactivating this line.

Different or additional pin interconnections can be required for other printer models. The actual implementation of the RS-232 connection is solely up to the printer manufacturer. Figure 6-29 depicts typical connection schemes for both 9-pin and 25-pin connections to a typical printer. The connection scheme for a given serial printer model is usually provided in its user's manual.

Figure 6-29: Serial Printer Connection Schemes

The other limiting factor for printer cables, both serial and parallel, is length. While cables purchased from reputable suppliers are typically correct in length and contain all of the shielding and connections required, cheaper cables and home-made cables are often lacking in some of these areas. The recommended signal cable lengths associated with parallel and serial printers are:

- *Standard Parallel Printers*: 0–10 ft (3 meters), although some equipment manufacturers specify 6 ft (1.8 meters) maximum for their cables. You should believe these recommendations when you see them.

- *RS-232 Serial Printers*: 10 – 50 ft (15.25 meters). However, some references use 100 ft as the acceptable length of an RS-232C serial cable. Serial connections are tricky enough without problems generated by the cable being too long. Make the cable as short as possible.

CHALLENGE #2

Your warehouse manager has come to you asking for a 20-foot printer cable so that he can move his wide carriage dot-matrix printer out of his office and into the warehouse where the noise level caused by the dot-matrix printer will not be a problem. He must use the dot-matrix printer because he has to print multipart invoice forms. What can you suggest to the warehouse manager that would solve his problem?

Configuration Problems

After the correct connector and cabling scheme has been implemented, the printer configuration must be established at both the computer and the printer. The information in both locations must match in order for communications to go on. On the system side of the serial-port connection, the software printer driver must be set up to match the settings of the printer's receiving section.

First, the driver must be directed toward the correct serial port. In a Windows-based system, this is typically COM2. Second, the selected serial port must be configured for the proper character framing. The number of start, stop, data, and parity bits must be set to match what the printer expects to receive. These values are often established through hardware configuration switches located on the printer.

The printer driver must also be set up to correctly handle the flow of data between the system and the printer. Incorrect flow control settings can result in slow response, lost characters, or continuous errors and retries. **Flow control** can be established through **software** or **hardware handshaking**. In a hardware handshaking mode, the printer tells the port that it is not prepared to receive data by deactivating a control line, such as the DTR line. Conversely, in a software handshaking environment, control codes are sent back and forth between the printer and the computer to enable and disable data flow.

Flow control

software handshaking

hardware handshaking

Software data flow control—Two popular methods of implementing software flow control are Xon/Xoff and ETX/ACK. In the Xon/Xoff method, special ASCII control characters are exchanged between the printer and the computer to turn the data flow on and off. In an ETX/ACK protocol, ASCII characters for End-of-Text (ETX) and ACKnowledge (ACK) are used to control the movement of data from the port to the printer.

Basically, the computer attaches the ETX character to the end of a data transmission. When the printer receives the ETX character, it checks the incoming data, and when ready, returns an ACK character to the port. This notifies the system that the printer is capable of receiving additional characters. This concept is illustrated in Figure 6-30. In any event, the devices at both ends of the interface connection must be set to use the same flow control method.

Serial communications standards and procedures were covered in the "Character Framing" section of Chapter 5 — *Data Communications*. Consult that section for more information about character framing, error detection and correction methods, and serial transmission protocols.

**Figure 6-30:
Software Flow
Control**

Serial Printer Problems

Problems associated with serial printers differ from those of parallel printers only in the area of the serial interface configuration. As mentioned in the preceding section, "Configuration Problems," the protocol, character framing, and baud rate of the printer must match those of the system's interface. After ensuring that the interface settings match, and that the interface is working, the steps of troubleshooting a serial printer are identical to those given for parallel interfaced printers. Therefore, the only steps that need to be added to the Troubleshooting sections later in this chapter are those needed to validate the operation of the serial interface.

Infrared Printer Ports

The LrLPT IrDA standard provides specifications for implementing an infrared printer connection as illustrated in Figure 6-31. In this example, the printer connection is an IrDA printer connector and a receiver that is placed in line with the standard parallel printer port connection. The receiver has power supplied to it through its own power adapter.

Figure 6-31: IrDA Printer Connections

The computer and printer communicate with each other over the infrared link that is established between their IrDA ports. The printer receives data and control signals from the computer and responds with status and error information. As with all IrDA connections, the distance and angle of transfer are limited. The recommended clear distance between the two devices is 1 meter, and the maximum angle between the transmitters and receivers is 15 degrees. The driver for the IrDA port of the printer must be loaded in the host machine for communications to occur.

Networked Printers

local computer

remote computers

print sharing

network-ready printers

network printers

If a printer is installed in a computer system that is part of a network, it is possible for any other computer on the network to send work to the printer. Historically, the **local computer** has been attached to the printer through one of the normal printing interfaces (i.e., parallel, serial, or USB) and also connected to the other **remote computers** through its network connection. In addition to the signal cable, the local computer's operating system must be configured to permit the remote stations on the network to print through it to its printer. This relationship is known as **print sharing**.

Newer printers, referred to as **network-ready printers**, or simply as **network printers**, come with built-in network interfacing that enables them to be connected directly into the local area network. Most network printers contain an integrated network controller and Ethernet LAN adapter that enables it to work on the LAN without a supporting host computer.

Other printers may be connected directly to the local area network through a device called a **print server port**. This device resembles a network hub in appearance and can be used to connect up to three printers directly into the network.

print server port

While some older network printers used coaxial cable connections, newer network printers feature RJ-45 jacks for connection to twisted-pair Ethernet networks.

It is relatively easy to determine whether a printer is networked by the presence of a coaxial or a twisted-pair network signal cable connected directly to the printer. The presence of the RJ-45 jacks on the back of the printer also indicate that the printer is network capable, even if it is not being used in that manner. These cables are covered in the section titled "Network Cabling" in Chapter 5 *Data Communications*. In Windows, you can determine that a printer is networked by the appearance of its icon in the *Printers* folder. The icon will graphically illustrate the network connection. You can also check the *Details* tab of the printer in its *Windows Properties* page.

TEST TIP
Know how to determine whether a printer is networked or not.

While parallel printers are easy to set up and check, and serial printers require a little more effort to set up, networked printers add another set of variables to the configuration and troubleshooting processes. To avoid dealing directly with the complexity of the network, it is normal to handle printer configuration and troubleshooting at the local level first. Once the operation of the local computer/printer interface has been established, or verified, the network portion of the system can be examined. The "Network Troubleshooting Basics" section of Chapter 11 deals with typical network troubleshooting procedures, while Windows-related network printing problems are covered extensively in the "Troubleshooting Local Area Networks" section of Chapter 12.

TEST TIP
Know how to identify the presence of a network-ready printer.

Other Printer Interfaces

As was mentioned earlier in this chapter, traditional parallel and serial ports are slowly fading from prominence as newer, faster, more powerful interfaces are gaining acceptance. As a matter of fact, there is somewhat of an interface/bus war going on for supremacy of the personal computer world. (These buses and interfaces were discussed in Chapter 3 and include SCSI buses, USB ports, Firewire ports, and Infrared ports along with direct-connect and wireless network adapter technologies.) Therefore, it is not uncommon for printers to feature a variety of different connection options.

Many organizations that design and support given technologies are working to develop a single dominant connection method that will permit any type of device to be plugged directly into the connection channel (buses and ports), be recognized by the system, and begin functioning without any further human intervention. For example, the USB port (and bus) can support up to 127 hot swappable devices on a single port hub. One can hardly imagine what 127 devices you would connect to your PC today. However, these groups are planning for a future where everything can be connected to the PC, including residential systems and automotive devices.

Printer Options and Upgrades

A portion of A+ Core Hardware objective 5.1 states that the test taker should be able to identify printer technologies, interfaces, and options/upgrades.

Options/upgrades include:

- Memory

- Hard drives

- NICs

- Trays and feeders

- Finishers (e.g., stapling, etc.)

- Scanners/fax machines/copiers

Printer FRU modules

Printer FRU modules — In some printers, the microcontroller, RAM modules, and ROM/EPROM devices may be treated as FRU components. Many laser printers come with something less than their maximum amount of RAM installed. However, they also provide optional hardware to permit the memory to be upgraded if desired. Many high-speed laser printers require additional RAM to be installed to handle printing of complex documents, such as desktop-published documents containing large Encapsulated Post Script (EPS) graphics files.

Similarly, ROM and EPROM devices that contain BIOS or character sets have often been placed in sockets so that they can be replaced or upgraded easily. However, newer printers have followed the ROM technologies used in computers and installed ROM devices that can be flashed. As with the gears and gear trains discussed earlier in the chapter, how replaceable these units are depends on the ability to source them from a supplier. In most cases, the question is not whether the device can be exchanged, but whether it makes economical sense to do so. For a given printer type and model, the manufacturer's service center can provide information about the availability of replacement parts.

In many cases, printers in business environments are becoming their own node of the company network. Increasingly, these printers are being equipped with their own built-in network adapters and computer-like peripherals so that they can function in a stand-alone manner. Figure 6-32 depicts a high-end laser printer intended for multiple-user or network printer applications.

Initially, these units were only equipped with an Ethernet network adapter and enough electronics to let them function as a network node and provide printing services for other network nodes. However, it has become common to integrate other computer peripherals such as hard drives into the printer unit to make them more efficient. For example, the hard-disk drive unit is used in a high-volume printer to store information coming to it from across the network. The HDD unit makes it possible for the printer to spool large amounts of data that it receives so that the network does not get congested waiting for the printer to print users' documents.

Figure 6-32: Stand-Alone Multiple-User Printer

In all but the most basic printer installation, several time- and labor-saving peripherals and devices may be attached to printers. The technician must be aware of these devices and their functions because they can fail in printer installations. It is not unusual for commercial office printers to offer several types of add-on components for their machines such as the following:

- *an automatic sheet feeder* — a device that mounts on the printer to enable special paper types to be fed directly into the printer. This unit can be combined with a scanner unit so that hard copy documents can be scanned directly into the printer for printing.

- *multiple paper trays* — storage bins that can be used to supply different sizes and types of papers to the printer without having to manually load them, or change paper in a single tray. They can also be used to store large volumes of standard paper so that the printer does not need human attention as often.

- *a duplexer* — a device that reroutes paper through the printer so that copies can be made on both sides.

- *a collator* — a device that sorts multi-page documents as they are printed so that they are in a prescribed order (page 1, page 2, etc.)

- *a stapler/stacker* — an add-on that is used to staple multi-page documents after they have been sorted and collated and stack them for distribution.

As mentioned earlier in this chapter, laser printers share their basic technologies with other office machines such as copiers, scanners, and plain paper faxes. Because of this, combination products have been developed to bring all of these functions together in a single unit, like the one depicted in Figure 6-33. These units offer considerable savings over buying separate machines for each function.

Figure 6-33: Office Automation Unit

In combination units, the ELP drum provides the central function for each operation. In a scanner operation, the image is scanned from an inserted document and digitized. The digitized image can then be stored as an electronic file. Since the document is in a digital form, it can also be converted to a proper format for faxing to another fax machine. And yes, the unit can act as a laser printer that accepts information from a host computer, scans it on the drum, and prints it out.

SERVICING PRINTERS

The A+ Core Hardware objective 5.2 states that the test taker should be able to recognize common printer problems and techniques used to resolve them. Content may include the following:

- Printer drivers
- Firmware updates
- Paper feed and output
- Calibrations
- Printing test pages
- Errors (printed or displayed)
- Memory
- Configuration

- Network connections
- Connections
- Paper jams
- Print quality
- Safety precautions
- Preventive maintenance
- Consumables
- Environment

Printers are connected to personal computers and they break down. Therefore, the computer technician should be familiar with common printer problems and be able to demonstrate current service techniques. The following sections of this chapter deal with typical problems encountered with dot-matrix, ink-jet, and laser printers. They also include troubleshooting methods associated with each type of printer.

Troubleshooting Dot-Matrix Printers

The classical first step in determining the cause of any printer problem is to determine which part of the printer-related system is at fault — the **host computer**, the **signal cable**, or the **printer**.

host computer

signal cable

printer

built-in self-test

Nearly every printer is equipped with a **built-in self-test**. The easiest way to determine whether the printer is at fault is to run its self-test. Consult the printer's user's manual for instructions on running its self-test. Some printers are capable of producing audible tones to indicate the nature of an internal problem. Refer to the printer's user's manual for the definitions of the coded beep tones, if they are available.

If a printer runs the self-test, and prints clean pages, then most of the printer has been eliminated as a possible cause of problems. The problem could be in the computer, the cabling, or the interface portion of the printer. However, if the printer fails the self-test, it will be necessary to diagnose the printer's problem. The following section presents typical problems encountered in dot-matrix printers.

The following are symptoms for dot-matrix printer problems:

- No lights or noise from printer

- Light or uneven print being produced

- Printhead moving, but not printing

- Dots missing from characters

- Printhead is printing, but does not move

- Paper will not advance

┌─ **TEST TIP** ─────────┐
Know what it means if the printer produces a satisfactory self-test printout, but does not print from the computer.
└────────────────────────┘

Dot-Matrix Printer Configuration Checks

The presence of on-board microcontrollers allows modern printers to be very flexible. Like other peripheral devices, printers can be configured to operate in different modes. Operating configuration information can be stored in CMOS RAM on the control board. Some configuration settings may be made through DIP switches mounted inside the printer. These switches are read by the printer's microcontroller at startup.

In the case of dot-matrix printers, the configuration settings are normally entered into the printer through the buttons of its control panel. Typical dot-matrix configuration settings include:

- Printer mode

- Perforation skip (for continuous forms)

- Automatic line feed at the bottom of the page

- Paper handling type

- ASCII character codes (7-bit or 8-bit)

- Basic character sets

Other quantities that can be set up include:

- Print font

- Character pitch

- Form length

Most dot-matrix printers contain two or three on-board fonts (character styles) that can be selected through the printer's configuration routines. In many dot-matrix printer models, it is also possible to download other fonts from the computer. Typical fonts included in dot-matrix printers are:

- Draft

- Courier

- Prestige

- Bold Prestige

character pitch

The **character pitch** refers to the number of characters printed per inch. Common pitch settings include 10, 11, 12, and 14 characters per inch. Consult the printer's user's guide to find the definitions of such settings.

Dot-Matrix Printer Hardware Checks

To perform work inside the printer, it will be necessary to disassemble its case. Begin by removing any add-on pieces, such as dust covers and paper feeders. Next, remove the paper advancement knob located on the right side of most dot-matrix printers. Turn the printer over, and remove the screws that hold the two halves of the case together. These screws are sometimes hidden beneath rubber feet and compliance stickers. Finally, it may be necessary to disconnect the printer's front panel connections from the main board to complete the separation of the two case halves. This procedure is shown in Figure 6-34.

**Figure 6-34:
Disassembling the
Printer**

Dot-Matrix Printer Power Supply Problems

If the printer does not function, and displays no lights, no sounds, and no actions, the power supply is generally involved. Troubleshoot printer power supply problems in the same manner as you would a computer power supply problem. As a matter of fact, the power supply troubleshooting routine is the same.

Check the on-line light. If the printer is off-line, no print action will occur. A missing, or improperly installed, ribbon cartridge will also prevent the unit from printing. Install the ribbon correctly. Check the power outlet to make certain that it is live. Plug a lamp, or other device, into the outlet to verify that it is operative. Check to see that the power cord is plugged securely into the printer and the socket. Make sure the power switch is on.

If everything is plugged in and in the on position, but still not working, turn OFF the power, and unplug the printer from the outlet. Remove the top of the printer's case, and find the power supply board. Check the power supply's fuse to make sure that it is good. If the fuse is blown, replace it with a fuse of the same type and rating. Do not replace a blown fuse with a conductor, or a slow-blow fuse. Doing so could lead to more extensive damage to the printer, and possibly unsafe conditions.

Also, check the power supply and control boards, as well as the paper feed and printhead positioning motors for burnt components, or signs of defect. Fuses usually do not blow, unless another component fails. Another possible cause of excessive current occurs when a motor (or its gear train) binds, and cannot move. Check the drive mechanisms and motors for signs of binding. If the gear train or positioning mechanisms will not move, they may need to be adjusted before replacing the fuse.

If none of the printer sections work when everything is connected and power is applied, it will be necessary to exchange the power supply board for a new unit. Unlike the computer's power supply, the typical printer power supply is not enclosed in a protective housing and, therefore, presents a shock hazard anytime it is exposed.

To exchange the power supply board, disconnect the power cable from the printer. Disconnect and mark the cabling from the control board, and any other components directly connected to the power supply. Remove any screws or clips that secure the power supply board to the case. Lift the board out of the cabinet. Install the new board, and reconnect the various wire bundles to it.

Ribbon Cartridges

The single item in a dot-matrix printer that requires the most attention is the **ribbon cartridge**. It is considered a consumable part of the printer and must be changed often. The ink ribbon is stored in a controlled wad inside the cartridge, and moves across the face of the platen, as depicted in Figure 6-35. A take-up wheel draws new ribbon out of the wad as it is used. As the ribbon wears out, the printing will become faint and uneven. When the print becomes noticeably faint, the cartridge should be replaced. Most dot-matrix printers use a snap-in ribbon cartridge.

Figure 6-35:
The Printer
Cartridge

To replace a typical ribbon cartridge, move the printhead carriage assembly to the center of the printer. Remove the old cartridge by freeing it from its clips or holders, and then lifting it out of the printer.

Tighten the ribbon tension by advancing the tension knob on the cartridge, in a counterclockwise direction, until the ribbon is taut. Snap the cartridge into place, making certain that the ribbon slides between the printhead and the ribbon mask. Slide the printhead assembly back and forth on the rod to check for proper ribbon movement.

Printhead Not Printing

If the printhead is moving, but not printing, begin by checking the printer's **head gap lever** to make sure that the printhead is not too far back from the paper. If the printhead does not operate, components involved include:

head gap lever

- the printhead

- the flexible signal cable between the control board and the printhead

- the control board

- possibly the power supply board

Run the printer's self-test to see if the printhead will print from the on-board test. Check the flexible signal cable to make sure that it is firmly plugged into the control board, and that it is not damaged or worn through. If none of the print wires are energized, then the first step should be to exchange the control board for a known good one of the same type. If the new control board does not correct the problem, replace the printhead. A power supply problem could also cause the printhead to not print.

A related problem occurs when one, or more, of the print wires does not fire. If this is the case, check the printhead for physical damage. Also check the flexible signal cable for a broken conductor. If the control board is delivering any of the other print wire signals, the problem is most likely associated with the printhead mechanism. Replace the printhead as a first step. If the problem continues after replacing the printhead, however, exchange the control board for a new one.

If the tops of characters are missing, the printhead is misaligned with the platen. It may need to be reseated in the printhead carriage, or the carriage assembly may need to be adjusted to the proper height and angle.

> **TEST TIP**
>
> Know what causes tops of characters to be missing from dot-matrix characters and how to correct the problem.

To exchange the printhead assembly, make sure that the printhead assembly is cool enough to be handled. These units can get hot enough to cause a serious burn. Unplug the printhead assembly from the control board. Slide the printhead assembly to the center of the printer, and rotate the **head-locking lever** to release the printhead from the assembly. Remove the printhead by lifting it straight up. Install the new printhead by following the disassembly procedure in reverse. Adjust the new printhead for proper printing. In some printers, the printheads are held in the printhead assembly with screws. To remove the printhead from these units it will be necessary to remove the screws so that the printhead can be exchanged. Refer to the printer's documentation for directions concerning exchanging the printhead mechanism.

head-locking lever

> **TEST TIP**
>
> Remember that the printhead of a dot-matrix printer generates a great deal of heat and can be a burn hazard when working on these units.

If the output of the printer gets lighter as it moves from left to right across the page, it may become necessary to adjust the spacing of the printhead mechanism to obtain proper printing. This procedure is illustrated in Figure 6-36. To print correctly, the printhead should be approximately 0.6 mm from the platen when the head position lever is in the center position. Move the printhead to the center of the printer. Adjusting this setting requires that the nut at the left end of the rear carriage shaft be loosened. Using a feeler-gauge, set the distance between the platen and printhead (not the **ribbon mask**). Tighten the nut, and check the spacing between the printhead and platen at both ends of the printhead travel.

ribbon mask

Figure 6-36:
Adjusting the Printhead
Spacing

Finally, check the distance between the platen and the ribbon mask. This space should be 0.3 mm. If not, loosen the screws that hold the ribbon mask to the printhead assembly, and adjust the gap with feeler gauges. There should also be a 0.1 mm space between the printhead and the ribbon mask. After setting the various gaps, run the printer's self-test to check for print quality.

Printhead Not Moving

If the printhead is printing but not moving across the page, a single block of print will be generated on the page. When this type of problem occurs, the related components include the printhead positioning motor, the timing belt, the **home position** and **timing sensors**, the control board, and possibly the power supply board.

home position

timing sensors

With the power off, manually move the printhead to the center of the printer. Turn the printer on to see if the printhead seeks the home position at the far left side of the printer. If it moves to the left side of the printer, and does not shut off, or does not return to the center of the printer, then the home position sensor is malfunctioning and should be replaced. If the printhead moves on startup, and will not move during normal printing, the control board should be replaced. In the event that the printhead assembly will not move at any time, the printhead positioning motor should be replaced. If the print is skewed from left to right as it moves down the page, the printer's bi-directional mode settings may be faulty, or the home-position/end-of-line sensors may be defective.

Testing the timing sensor would require test equipment, in the form of a logic probe or an oscilloscope, to look for pulses produced as the printhead is manually moved across the printer. Figure 6-37 depicts the components associated with the printhead's timing belt. Replacing the timing belt requires that it be removed from the printhead assembly. In many cases, the belt is secured to the printhead assembly with adhesive cement. This will require that the adhesive seal be cut with a single-edged razor blade, or a hobby knife.

Figure 6-37: Printhead Timing Belt

After the seal has been broken, it should be possible to shove the belt out of the clips that secure it to the printhead assembly. Next, remove the belt from the drive pulley assembly at the positioning motor. It may be necessary to remove the positioning motor from the case to gain access to the pulley.

To reinstall the timing belt, apply a small drop of adhesive to the belt, and reattach it to the printhead assembly. Wrap the belt around the positioning motor's drive pulley, and reinstall the motor. Following this, it will be necessary to adjust the tension on the belt. To set the tension on the belt, loosen the adjustment screw on the belt-tension adjustment plate. Tighten the timing belt until it will not move more than 1/4" when the printhead is at either end of the carriage shaft and the belt is pressed inward. Tighten the retaining screw to lock the tension plate in place. Run the printer's self-test, and check the distance between the characters. If the character spacing is not uniform, replace the belt and perform the check again.

Paper Not Advancing

When the paper does not advance, the output will normally be one line of dark blocks across the page. Examine the printer's **paper feed selector lever** to make sure that it is set properly for the type of paper feed selected (i.e., friction feed, pin feed, or tractor feed). If the paper feed is set correctly, the printer is on-line, and the paper still does not move, it will be necessary to troubleshoot the paper handling motor and gear train. Check the motor and gear train by setting the printer to the off-line mode and holding down the Form Feed (FF) button.

If the feed motor and gear train work from this point, the problem must exist in the **control board**, the **interface cable**, the **printer's configuration**, or the **computer system**. If the motor and/or gear train does not respond, unplug the paper feed motor cable, and check the resistance of the motor windings. If the windings are open, replace the paper feed motor.

paper feed selector lever

control board

interface cable

printer's configuration

computer system

To replace the paper feed motor and/or gear train, remove the screws that hold the paper feed motor to the frame of the printer. Create a wiring diagram that describes the routing of the feed motor's wiring harness. Disconnect the wiring harness from the control board.

Prepare a drawing that outlines the arrangement of the gear train (if multiple gears are used). Remove the gears from the shafts, taking care not to lose any washers, or springs, that may be located behind the gears. After reinstalling the gears and replacing the motor, adjust the motor and gear relationships to minimize the **gear lash** so that they do not bind or lock up. Use the printer's self-test to check the operation of the motor and gears.

gear lash

CHALLENGE #4

You get a call from your warehouse manager complaining about the serial printer you installed in his warehouse in the previous chapter. It seems that soon after you installed the new dot-matrix printer, the text on the multipart forms became uneven from side to side and printed with an uphill slant. When you check out the printer, you determine that the paper is slipping from the weight of the multipart continuous forms. What can you do to fix this printing problem on the new printer?

Troubleshooting Ink-Jet Printers

host computer

signal cable

printer

As with the dot-matrix printer, the first step in determining the cause of an ink-jet printer problem is to determine which part of the printer system is at fault — the **host computer**, the **signal cable**, or the **printer**.

computer

cabling

interface

Ink-jet printers are equipped with built-in self-tests. The easiest way to determine if the printer is at fault is to run its self-tests. Consult the printer's user's manual for instructions in running its self-tests. If the printer runs the self-tests, and prints clean pages, then most of the printer has been eliminated as a possible cause of problems. The problem could be in the **computer**, the **cabling**, or the **interface** portion of the printer.

However, if the printer fails the self-tests, it will be necessary to diagnose the printer problem. The following section presents typical problems encountered in ink-jet printers.

The following are symptoms of ink-jet printer problems:

- No lights or noise from the printer

- Light or uneven print being produced

- Printhead is moving, but is not printing, or is printing erratically

- Lines on the page

- Printhead is printing, but does not move

- Paper will not advance

Ink-Jet Printer Configuration Checks

The presence of an on-board microcontroller allows modern printers to be very flexible. Like other peripheral devices, printers can be configured to operate in different modes. Operating configuration information can be stored in RAM, on the control board.

In the case of ink-jet printers, the configuration settings are normally entered into the printer through software. Typical configuration information includes:

- **Paper Size**
- **Page Orientation (landscape or portrait)**
- **Print Quality**
- **Collation**

Landscape printing is specified when the width of the page is greater than the length of the page. **Portrait printing** is specified when the length of the page is greater than the width. In an ink-jet printer, the quality of the printout is specified in the number of dots per inch (dpi) produced. Typical ink-jet resolutions run from 180 x 180 dpi to 720 x 720 dpi. Ink-jet printers have the capability to download additional fonts from the host computer.

```
┌─ TEST TIP ─────────────────┐
│ Be aware that print density can │
│ be adjusted through software in │
│ an ink-jet printer.            │
└────────────────────────────┘
```

You can also configure the basic appearance of color and **grayscale** images produced by the ink-jet printer. A color ink-jet printer uses four ink colors to produce color images. These are **Cyan**, **Magenta**, **Yellow**, and **Black** (referred to as **CMYK color**). To create other colors, the printer prints a predetermined percentage of the basic colors in close proximity to each other.

The different percentages determine what the new color will be. The eye does not differentiate the space between them, and perceives only the combined color. This is referred to as **halftone color**. Typical color configurations include setting up the **brightness**, the **contrast**, and the **saturation** settings of images.

Paper Size

Page Orientation

Print Quality

Collation

Landscape printing

Portrait printing

grayscale

Cyan

Magenta

Yellow

Black

CMYK color

halftone color

brightness

contrast

saturation

Ink-Jet Printer Hardware Checks

To perform work on the printer's hardware, it will be necessary to disassemble the printer's case. Begin by removing all of the add-on pieces, such as dust covers and paper feeders. Remove the screws that hold the outer panels of the case to the printer frame. Removing the access panels of a typical ink-jet printer is shown in Figure 6-38. The retaining screws are sometimes hidden beneath rubber feet and compliance stickers. Finally, it may be necessary to disconnect the printer's front panel connections from the control board to complete the disassembly of the case.

Figure 6-38: Printer Case

Power Supply Problems

If the printer does not function, and displays no lights, no sounds, and no actions, the power supply is generally involved. Check the on-line light. If the printer is off-line, no print action will occur. A missing, or improperly installed, ink cartridge will prevent the unit from printing. Install the ink cartridge correctly. Check the power outlet to make certain that it is live. Plug a lamp or some other device into the outlet to verify that it is operative. Check to see that the power cord is plugged securely into the printer and the socket. Make sure the power switch is ON.

If the unit is plugged in and turned ON, but still not working, turn it off and unplug it. Remove the top of the printer's case, and locate the power supply board. Check the power supply's fuse to make sure that it is good. If the fuse is blown, replace it with a fuse of the same type and rating. Do not replace a blown fuse with a conductor, or a slow-blow fuse. Doing so could lead to more extensive damage to the printer, and possible unsafe conditions.

Also, check the power supply and control boards, as well as the paper feed and printhead positioning motors, for burnt components or signs of defect. Fuses usually do not blow unless another component fails. Another possible cause of overcurrent occurs when a motor (or its gear train) binds and cannot move. Check the drive mechanisms and motors for signs of binding. If the gear train, or positioning mechanisms, do not move, they may need to be adjusted, or replaced, before replacing the fuse.

If none of the printer sections work, everything is connected, and power is applied, it will be necessary to exchange the power supply board for a new unit. Unlike the computer's power supply, the typical power supply in a printer is not enclosed in a protective housing and therefore presents a shock hazard any time it is exposed.

To exchange the power supply board, disconnect the power cable from the printer. Disconnect and mark the cabling from the control board, and any other components directly connected to the power supply. Remove any screws or clips that secure the power supply board to the case. Lift the board out of the cabinet. Install the new board, and reconnect the various wire bundles to it.

Ink Cartridges

ink cartridge

> The single item in an ink-jet printer that requires the most attention is the **ink cartridge** (or cartridges). As the ink cartridge empties, the printing will eventually become faint and uneven, and the resolution of the print on the page will diminish.

The density of the printout from an ink-jet printer can be adjusted through its printing software. However, when the print becomes noticeably faint, or the resolution becomes unacceptable, the cartridge will need to be replaced. Most ink-jet printers use a self-contained, snap-in ink cartridge, like the one shown in Figure 6-39. Some models have combined ink cartridges that replace all three colors and the black ink at the same time. Other models use individual cartridges for each color. In this way, only the colors that are running low are replaced.

The ink cartridge can be popped out of the printhead assembly to inspect the ink jets. If any of the jets is clogged, it is normally possible to clear them by gently wiping the face of the cartridge with a swab. A gentle squeeze of the ink reservoir can also help to unblock a clogged jet. Using solvents to clear blockages in the jets can dilute the ink and allow it to flow uncontrollably through the jet.

To replace a typical ink cartridge, move the printhead carriage assembly to the center of the printer. Remove the old cartridge by freeing it from its clips or holders and lifting it out of the printer.

After replacing the ink cartridge, you should cycle the printer on so that it will go through its normal warmup procedures. During these procedures, the printer does a thorough cleaning of the ink jet nozzles and gets the ink flowing correctly from the nozzles. Afterward, print a test page to verify the output of the new ink cartridge.

Figure 6-39:
Self-Contained, Snap-in
Ink Cartridge

Printhead Not Printing

If the printhead is moving, but not printing, begin by checking the ink supply in the print cartridge. The reservoir does not have to be completely empty to fail. Replace the cartridge(s) that appear(s) to be low. Some or all of the jets may be clogged. This is particularly common if the printer has not been used for a while. If there are cleaning instructions in the user's manual, clean the jets and attempt to print from the self-test.

If the printer will not print from the self-test, the components involved include:

- the printhead
- the flexible signal cable (between the control board and the printhead)
- the control board
- possibly the power supply board

Check the flexible signal cable to make sure it is firmly plugged into the control board, and that it is not damaged or worn through. If none of the ink jets are firing, the first step should be to exchange the ink cartridges for new ones. If a single ink jet is not firing, replace the cartridge that is not working.

Next, use the ohmmeter function of a multimeter to check the continuity of the conductors in the flexible wiring harness that supplies the printhead assembly. If one of the conductors is broken, a single jet will normally be disabled. However, if the broken conductor is a ground, or common connection, all of the jets should be disabled. Exchange the control board for a known-good one of the same type. If the new control board does not correct the problem, replace the printhead. A power supply problem could also cause the printhead to not print.

If a single jet is not functioning, the output will appear as a white line on the page. If one of the jets is activated all of the time, then black or colored lines will be produced on the page. Use the following steps to isolate the cause of these problems — replace the print cartridge; check the flexible cabling for continuity and for short circuits between adjacent conductors; exchange the control board for a known good one; and finally, check the power supply.

Printhead Not Moving

If the printhead is printing, but not moving across the page, a single block of print will normally be generated on the page. When this problem occurs, the related components include the printhead positioning motor, the timing belt, the **home position sensor**, the control board, and possibly the power supply. These components are depicted in Figure 6-40.

Figure 6-40: Printhead Positioning Components

With the power off, manually move the printhead to the center of the printer. Turn the printer on to see if the printhead seeks the home position at the far end of the printer. If the printhead moves to the end of the printer, and does not shut off, or does not return to the center of the printer, then the home position sensor is malfunctioning and should be replaced. If the printhead moves on startup, and will not move during normal printing, the control board should be replaced. In the event that the printhead assembly will not move at any time, check to see if the printer is in **Maintenance mode**. In this mode, the printer typically keeps the printhead assembly in the home position. If no mode problems are present, the printhead positioning motor should be replaced.

If characters are unevenly spaced across the page, the timing sensor may be failing. To test the timing sensor would require test equipment, such as a logic probe or an oscilloscope, to look for pulses produced as the printhead is manually moved across the printer.

Replacing the timing belt requires that the belt be removed from the printhead assembly. In many cases, the belt will be secured to the printhead assembly with adhesive cement. This will require that the adhesive seal be cut with a single-edged razor blade, or a hobby knife. After the seal has been broken, it should be possible to shove the belt out of the clips that secure it to the printhead assembly. Next, remove the belt from the drive pulley assembly at the positioning motor. It may be necessary to remove the positioning motor from the case to gain access to the pulley.

Paper Not Advancing

When the paper does not advance, the output will normally be a thick, dark line across the page. Check the control panel to see that the printer is on-line. If the printer is on-line, and the paper will not move, it will be necessary to troubleshoot the paper handling motor and gear train. Check the motor and gear train by setting the printer to the off-line mode and holding down the Form Feed button.

If the feed motor and gear train work from this point on, the problem must exist in the control board, the **interface cable**, the printer configuration, or the computer system. If the motor and/or gear train does not respond, unplug the paper feed motor cable and check the resistance of the motor windings. If the windings are open, replace the paper feed motor.

To replace the paper feed motor and/or gear train, remove the screws that hold the paper feed motor to the frame of the printer. Create a wiring diagram that describes the routing of the feed motor's wiring harness. Disconnect the wiring harness from the control board.

Draw an outline of the gear train arrangement (if multiple gears are used). Remove the gears from their shafts, taking care not to lose any washers or springs that may be located behind the gears. After reinstalling the gears and replacing the motor, adjust the motor and gear relationships to minimize the gear lash so that they do not bind or lock up. Use the printer's self-test to check the operation of the motor and gears.

If the printer's paper thickness selector is set improperly, or the rollers in its paper feed system become worn, the paper can slip as it moves through the printer and cause wavy graphics to be produced. Check the printer's paper thickness settings. If they are correct and the print output is disfigured, you will need to replace the paper feed rollers.

> **TEST TIP**
> Know what types of problems can cause disfigured print in an ink-jet printer.

Troubleshooting Laser Printers

Many of the problems encountered in laser printers are similar to those found in other printer types. For example, notice that most of the symptoms listed in the following section relate to the printer **not printing**, or **not printing correctly**, and **not moving paper**.

Due to the extreme complexity of the laser printer's paper handling system, **paper jams** are a common problem. This problem tends to increase in frequency as the printer's components wear from use. Basically, paper jams occur in all three main sections of the printer. These sections are:

- the **pickup area**
- the **registration area**
- the **fusing area**

If the rubber separation pad in the pickup area is excessively worn, more than one sheet of paper may be drawn into the printer, causing it to jam.

> **TEST TIP**
> Memorize places where paper jams are likely to occur in a laser printer.

If additional paper handling features, such as **duplexers** (for double-sided copying) and **collators** (for sorting) are added to the printer, they will contribute to the possibility of jams as they wear. Paper problems can also cause jams to occur. Using paper that is too heavy or too thick can result in jams, as can overloading paper trays. Similarly, using the wrong type of paper can defeat the separation pad and allow multiple pages to be drawn into the printer. In this case, the multiple sheets may move through the printer together, or they may result in a jam. Using coated paper stock can be hazardous since the coating may melt or catch fire.

WARNING

Laser printer dangers — Unlike other printer types, the laser printer tends to have several high-voltage and high-temperature hazards inside it. To get the laser printer into a position where you can observe its operation, it will be necessary to defeat some interlock sensors. This action will place you in potential contact with the high-voltage, high-temperature areas mentioned above. Take great care when working inside the laser printer.

The following are symptoms of laser printer problems:

- Printer dead: power on, but no printing

- The print on the page is light, or washed out

- A blank page is produced

- Stains, or black dust, on paper

- Vertical lines on paper

- The printer will not load paper

- Paper jams in printer

- A paper jam has been cleared, and the unit still indicates a jam is present

---

Laser Printer Configuration Checks

Like other complex peripheral equipment, laser printers must be configured for the desired operational characteristics. The printer is an extension of the computer system and, therefore, must be part of the overall configuration. In order to make the system function as a unit, **configure the computer**, **configure the printer**, and **configure the software**. Review and record the computer's configuration information for use in setting up the printer and software. Configure the printer with the parameters that you want it to use, record these settings, and then set up the software to match. Consult the printer's user's manual for configuration information specific to setting up that particular printer.

Laser Printer Hardware Checks

Variations in the hardware organization of different laser printers makes it impossible to write a general troubleshooting routine that can be applied to all of them without being specific to one model. The following troubleshooting discussions are general, and will require that the user do some interpretation to apply them to a specific laser printer.

Fortunately, laser printer hardware has become highly modularized. This allows entire sections of hardware to be checked by changing a single module. Unfortunately, the mechanical gear train and sensor systems are not usually parts included in the modules. Therefore, their operation will need to be checked individually.

Printer Is Dead or Partially Disabled

As usual, when the printer appears to be dead, the power supply is suspected. Again, as usual, the power supply can affect the operation of basically every section of the printer. In the laser printer, this is particularly complicated, since there are three types of power being delivered to the various printer components.

If the printer does not start up, check all of the usual power supply—related check points (e.g., **power cord, power outlet, internal fuses**, etc.). If the printer's fans and lights are working, other components that are associated with a defective power supply include:

| **power cord** |
| **power outlet** |
| **internal fuses** |

- Main motor and gear train

- High-voltage corona wires

- Drum assembly

- Fusing rollers

There are four basic reasons why the main motor does not run when the printer is supposed to print. These include:

- the portion of the power supply that supplies the motor is defective

- the control circuitry is not sending the enabling signals to turn the motor on

- the motor is dead

- the gear train is bound, and will not let the motor turn

In these instances, there should be sounds from the fan running, and lights on the control panel. Isolate the failure, and troubleshoot the components involved in that section.

If the high-voltage portion of the power supply that serves the corona wires and drum sections is defective, the image delivered to the page will be affected. If the high-voltage section of the power supply fails, then transfers of toner to the drum, and then to the paper, cannot occur. The contrast control will not be operational either.

In cases of partial failure, the image produced will have a washed-out appearance. Replace the high-voltage section of the power supply and/or the drum unit. If a separate corona wire is used, let the printer cool off sufficiently, and replace the wire. Never reach into the high-voltage, high-temperature corona area while power is applied to the printer. Also, avoid placing conductive instruments in this area.

If the dc portion of the power supply fails, the laser beam will not be produced, creating a **Missing Beam** error message. The components involved in this error are the **laser/scanning module**, the control board, and the dc portion of the power supply. Replace the laser/scanning module, the dc portion of the power supply, and the main control board.

Missing Beam

laser/scanning
module

When the heating element or lamp in the fusing area does not receive adequate ac power from the power supply, the toner will not affix to the page as it should. This condition will result in smudged output.

If the printer remains in a constant state of starting up, this is equivalent to the computer not passing the POST portion of the bootup process. If the printer starts up to an off-line condition, there is likely a problem between the printer and the host computer's interface. Disconnect the interface cable, and check to see if the printer starts up to a ready state. If so, then the problem is in the host computer, its interface, its configuration, or its signal cable. Troubleshoot the system accordingly.

If the printer still does not start up, note the error message produced, and check the sections of the printer related to that message. Check to see if the printer is connected to the system through a print-sharing device. If so, connect the printer directly to the system and try it. It is not a good practice to use laser printers with this type of device.

A better arrangement is to install, or simply use an LPT2 port to attach an additional printer to the system. If you need more than two printers, it would be better to network the printers to the system.

Print on Page Is Missing or Bad

Many of the problems encountered in laser printers are associated with missing or defective print on the page. Normal print delivery problems fall into eight categories. These include:

- Black pages

- White (blank) pages

- Faint print

- Random specks on the page

- Faulty print at regular intervals on the page

- White lines along the page

- Print missing from some portion of the page

- Smudged print

A **black page** indicates that toner has been attracted to the entire page. This condition could be caused by a failure of the **primary corona**, the laser scanning module, or the main control board. If the laser is in a continuous on condition, the entire drum will attract toner. Likewise, if the primary corona is defective, then the uniform negative charge will not be developed on the drum to repel toner. Replace the primary corona and/or drum assembly. If the problem continues, replace the laser scanning module and the main control board.

On the other end of the spectrum, a **white page** indicates that no information is being written on the drum. This condition basically involves the laser scanning module, the control board, and the power supply. Another white page fault occurs when the corona wire becomes broken, contaminated, or corroded, so that the attracting charge between the drum and paper is severely reduced.

Specks and **stains** on the page may be caused by a worn-out cleaning pad, or a defective corona wire. If the cleaning pad is worn, it will not remove excess toner from the page during the fusing process. If the corona wire's grid does not regulate the charge level on the drum, dark spots will appear in the print. To correct these situations, replace the corona assembly by exchanging the toner cartridge or drum unit. Also, replace the cleaning pad in the fusing unit. If the page still contains specks after changing the cartridge, run several pages through the printer to clear excess toner that may have collected in the printer.

White lines along the length of the page are generally caused by poorly distributed toner. Try removing the toner cartridge and gently shaking it to redistribute the toner in the cartridge. Other causes of white lines include damaged or weakened corona wires. Check and clean the corona wires, if accessible, or replace the module containing the corona wires.

Faint print in a laser printer can be caused by a number of different things. If the contrast control is set too low, or the toner level in the cartridge is low, empty, or poorly distributed, print quality can appear washed-out. Correcting these symptoms is fairly easy; adjust the contrast control, remove the toner cartridge, inspect it, shake it gently (if it is a sealed unit), and retry it. If the print does not improve, try replacing the toner cartridge. Other causes of faint print include a weakened corona wire, or a weakened high-voltage power supply that drives it. Replace the unit that contains the corona wire. Replace the high-voltage power supply. Make sure that latent voltages have been drained off the high-voltage power supply before working with it.

Faults in the print that occur at regular intervals along the page are normally caused by mechanical problems. When roller and transport mechanisms begin to wear in the printer, bad registration and print appear in cyclic form. This can be attributed to the dimensions of cyclic components such as the drum, the developing roller in the toner cartridge, or the fusing rollers. Examine the various mechanical components for wear or defects.

Missing print is usually caused by a bad or misaligned laser scanning module. If this module is not correctly installed, then it will not be able to deliver lines of print to the correct areas of the page. Likewise, if the scanning mirror has a defect, or is dirty, portions of the print will not be scanned on the drum. Another cause of missing print involves the toner cartridge, and low or poorly distributed toner. If the toner does not come out of the cartridge uniformly, areas of missing print can be created. A damaged or worn drum can also be a cause of repeated missing print. If areas of the drum do not hold the charge properly, toner will not transfer to it, or the page, correctly.

Smudged print is usually a sign of a failure in the fusing section. If the fusing roller's temperature or pressure is not sufficient to bond the toner to the page, the print will smudge when touched. Examine the fuser unit, the power supply, and the fusing roller's heating unit.

TEST TIP

Know what types if problems produce blank pages from a laser printer.

Specks

stains

White lines

Faint print

Missing print

Smudged print

Paper Will Not Feed or Is Jammed

paper trays

If the paper will not feed at all, then the place to begin checking is the paper tray area. The **paper trays** have a complex set of sensors and pickup mechanisms that must all be functioning properly to begin the paper handling. Due to the complexity of the paper pickup operation, jams are most likely to occur in this area. Check each paper tray to make sure that there is paper in it, and that it has the correct size of paper in it. Each tray in a laser printer has a set of tabs that contact sensor switches to tell the control circuitry that the tray is installed, and what size paper is in it. A mechanical arm and photodetector are used to sense the presence of paper in the tray. If these switches are set incorrectly, the printer could print a page that is sized incorrectly for the actual paper size. The various paper tray sensors are illustrated in Figure 6-41.

┌─ **TEST TIP** ─────────────

Be aware of the consequences of incorrectly setting the paper tray switches in a laser printer.

Figure 6-41: Paper Tray Sensors

Paper-Out error

pickup roller

If the printer's display panel indicates a **Paper-Out error** message, locate and actuate the paper detector by hand (lift it up). While holding the paper sensor, check the sensor switches by pressing each one individually. If the Paper Out message does not go out when any of the individual switches is pressed, replace that switch. If none of the switches show good, replace the paper sensor and arm. Also, check the spring-loaded plate in the bottom of the tray to make sure that it is forcing paper up to the **pickup roller** when the tray is installed in the printer.

The paper pickup roller must pull the top sheet of paper off the paper stack in the tray. The controller actuates a solenoid that engages the pickup roller's gear train. The pickup roller moves the paper into position against the registration rollers. If the printer's display panel shows a jam in the pickup area, check to make sure that the paper tray is functional, and then begin troubleshooting the pickup roller and main gear train. If the gear train is not moving, then the main motor and controller board need to be checked. The power supply board may also be a cause of the problem.

If the paper feeds into the printer, but jams after the process has begun, troubleshoot the particular section of the printer where the jam is occurring — **pickup**, registration, fusing area, and **output devices** (collators and duplexers). This information is generally presented by the laser printer's display panel. Figure 6-42 shows the paper path through a typical laser printer.

**Figure 6-42:
The Paper Path**

In each stage, you will need to check the action of the gear train in the area. Also, inspect the various rollers in that stage for wear or damage. If the motor and gear train operate, but no action occurs in the pickup roller or registration rollers, check the solenoid and clutches for these units.

Another cause of jams is the presence of some obstruction in the paper path. Check for pieces of paper that have torn loose and lodged in the printer's paper path. In most laser printers, mechanical components are part of a replaceable module (i.e., the drum unit, the developing unit, or the fusing unit). If the motor and all the exposed gears are working, replace these units one at a time.

Many times, a paper-jam error will remain even after the paper has been removed from the laser printer. This is typically caused by an interlock error. Simply opening the printer's main access door should clear the error.

CHAPTER SUMMARY

The focus of this chapter has been printers. The opening section of the chapter presented an introduction to the different types of printers and provided a fundamental course in general printer structure and organization.

Following the general discussions of dot matrix, ink-jet, and laser printer operations, the chapter focused on common types of printer connections and configurations. The largest portion of the chapter presented troubleshooting procedures for each type of printer. Each procedure was divided into logical areas associated with typical printer symptoms.

The final section of the chapter featured preventive maintenance procedures that apply to the different printer types.

KEY POINTS REVIEW

The focus of this chapter has been printers. Review the following key points before moving into the Review and Exam Questions sections to make sure you are comfortable with each point. Afterward, answer the Review Questions that follow to verify your knowledge of the information.

- Impact printers place characters on the page by causing a hammer device to strike an inked ribbon. The ribbon, in turn, strikes the printing surface (paper).

- Several non-impact methods of printing are used in computer printers. Older non-impact printers relied on special heat-sensitive, or chemically reactive paper to form characters on the page. Newer methods of non-impact printing use ink droplets squirted from a jet-nozzle device (ink-jet printers), or a combination of laser/xerographic print technologies (laser printers), to place characters on a page. Currently, the most popular non-impact printers use ink-jet or laser technologies to deliver ink to the page.

- Basically, there are two methods of creating characters on a page. One method places a character that is fully shaped and fully filled-in. This type of character is called a fully formed character. The other method involves placing dots on the page in strategic patterns to fool the eye into seeing a character. This type of character is referred to as a dot-matrix character.

- The term font refers to variations in the size and style of characters. With true fully formed characters, there is typically only one font available without changing the physical printing element. However, with all other printing methods, it is possible to include a wide variety of font types and sizes.

- By the very nature of their operation, printers tend to be extremely mechanical peripherals. During the printing operation, the print mechanism must be properly positioned over each character cell in sequence.

- In addition to positioning the print mechanism for printing, all printer types must feed paper through the print area. The type of paper handling mechanism in a printer is somewhat dependent on the type of form intended for use with the printer and the printer's speed.

- Like most other peripherals, the heart of a character printer is its interface/controller circuitry. The interface circuitry accepts data and instructions from the computer's bus systems, and provides the necessary interfacing (serial or parallel) between the computer and the printer's control circuitry.

- In some printers, the microcontroller, RAM chips or modules, and ROM/EPROM devices may be treated as FRU components.

- The components of a typical dot-matrix printer are depicted in Figure 6-8. They consist of a power supply board, a main control board, a printhead assembly, a ribbon cartridge, a paper feed motor (along with its mechanical drive gears), and a printhead positioning motor and mechanisms.

- The printhead is a collection of print wires set in an electromagnetic head unit. The printhead assembly is made up of a permanent magnet, a group of electromagnets, and a housing. In the printhead, the permanent magnet keeps the wires pulled in until electromagnets are energized, causing them to move forward.

- Ink-jet printers produce characters by squirting a stream of ink drops onto the paper. The drops must be controlled very precisely in terms of their aerodynamics, size, and shape, or their placement on the page becomes inexact, and the print quality falters.

- The laser printer modulates a highly focused laser beam to produce CRT-like raster-scan images on a rotating drum.

- As the drum is written on by the laser, it turns through the toner powder, which is attracted to the charged image on the drum.

- A typical laser printer has sensors to determine what paper trays are installed, what size paper is in them, and whether a tray is empty. It will also use sensors to track the movement of the paper through each stage of the printer. This allows the controller to know where a page is at all times, and sequence the activities of the solenoids and clutches properly.

- Paper is specified in terms of its weight per 500 sheets at 22" x 17" (e.g., 500 sheets of 22" x 17", 21-pound bond paper weighs 21 pounds).

- Generally speaking, one of the least difficult I/O devices to add to a microcomputer system is a parallel printer. This is largely due to the fact that, from the beginning of the PC era, a parallel printer has been a standard piece of equipment to add to the system.

- Serial printers are slightly more difficult to set up, since the communication definition must be configured between the computer and the printer. The serial port will need to be configured for speed, parity type, character frame, and protocol.

- Like mice, printers require device driver programs to oversee their operation.

- Not all serial cables are created equal. In the PC world, RS-232 serial cables can take on several configurations. First of all, they may use either 9-pin or 25-pin D-shell connectors. The cable for a particular serial connection will need to have the correct type of connector at each end. Likewise, the connection scheme inside the cable can vary from printer to printer. Normally, the Transmit Data line (TXD - pin 2) from the computer is connected to the Receive Data line (RXD - pin 3) of the printer. Also, the Data Set Ready (DSR - pin 6) is typically connected to the printer's Data Terminal Ready (DTR - pin 20) pin. These connections are used as one method to control the flow of information between the system and the printer. If the printer's character buffer becomes full, it will signal the computer to hold up sending characters by deactivating this line.

- Two popular methods of implementing software flow control are Xon/Xoff and ETX/ACK. In the Xon/Xoff method, special ASCII control characters are exchanged between the printer and the computer to turn the data flow on and off. In an ETX/ACK protocol, ASCII characters for End-of-Text (ETX) and ACKnowledge (ACK) are used to control the movement of data from the port to the printer.

- The classical first step in determining the cause of any printer problem is to determine which part of the printer-related system is at fault — the host computer, the signal cable, or the printer.

- As with the dot-matrix printer, the first step in determining the cause of an ink-jet printer problem is to determine which part of the printer system is at fault—the host computer, the signal cable, or the printer.

- You can configure the basic appearance of color and grayscale images produced by the ink-jet printer. A color ink-jet printer uses four ink colors to produce color images. These are Cyan, Magenta, Yellow, and Black (referred to as CMYK color). To create other colors, the printer prints a predetermined percentage of the basic colors in close proximity to each other.

- The single item in an ink-jet printer that requires the most attention is the ink cartridge (or cartridges). As the ink cartridge empties, the printing will eventually become faint and uneven, and the resolution of the print on the page will diminish.

- Many of the problems encountered in laser printers are similar to those found in other printer types. For example, notice that most of the symptoms listed relate to the printer not printing, or not printing correctly, and not moving paper.

- Unlike other printer types, the laser printer has several high-voltage and high-temperature hazards inside it. To get the laser printer into a position where you can observe its operation, it will be necessary to defeat some interlock sensors. This action will place you in potential contact with the high-voltage, high-temperature areas mentioned above. Take great care when working inside the laser printer.

REVIEW QUESTIONS

The following questions test your knowledge of the material presented in this chapter.

1. Describe the function of the transfer corona wire in a laser printer.

2. What common transmission parameters must be established for a serial printer interface?

3. Describe the purpose for using platen pin-feed mechanisms to move paper through the printer.

4. Describe the reason for using tractor-feed paper handling.

5. If the resolution of an ink-jet printer becomes unacceptable, what action should be taken?

6. Describe the function of the fuser unit in a laser printer.

7. Compare how a direct thermal printer operates versus a thermal wax transfer printer.

8. If a laser printer continues to show a paper jam after the paper has been cleared, what type of problem is indicated, and what action should be taken?

9. List the three primary areas where paper jams occur in a laser printer, as well as any other areas where jams are likely to occur.

10. Describe two methods used by ink-jet printers to put ink on the page.

11. Does a successful self-test indicate that the printer is not the cause of the problem? List the parts of the system that can still be problem causes if the self-test runs successfully.

12. Describe how a dye sublimation printer operates.

13. What functions does the printer's controller typically perform?

14. List four things that can be damaging to the photosensitive surface of the laser printer's drum.

15. List the basic components of an ink-jet printer.

EXAM QUESTIONS

1. List three common pin configurations for dot-matrix printers.
   a. 10, 20, and 30 pins
   b. 5, 10, and 15 pins
   c. 9, 18, and 24 pins
   d. 3, 6, and 9 pins

2. Name the four basic components of a Hewlett-Packard electrophotographic cartridge.
   a. Laser, toner supply, drum, and fuser
   b. Toner supply, corona wire, drum assembly, and developing roller
   c. Laser, toner supply, corona wire, and drum
   d. Toner supply, corona wire, drum assembly, and fuser

3. What is the purpose of the primary corona wire in a laser printer?
   a. It cleans the paper as it enters the printer.
   b. It conditions the drum for printing.
   c. It transfers toner from the drum to the paper.
   d. It fuses the toner to the paper.

4. What is the first action that should be taken if the print generated by a dot-matrix printer becomes faded or uneven?
   a. Change the ribbon cartridge.
   b. Add ink.
   c. Adjust the print carriage.
   d. Add toner.

5. What is the purpose of a printer driver?
   a. Energizes the pins to strike the ribbon
   b. Translates between the application and the printer hardware
   c. Moves paper through the printer
   d. Moves the print mechanism across the page

6. What type of electrical charge must be placed on the corona wire to transfer toner from the drum to the paper?
   a. Negative
   b. None
   c. Neutral
   d. Positive

7. List the six stages of a typical laser printer.
   a. Pick up, registration, transfer, printing, fusing, and finishing
   b. Pick up, conditioning, transfer, developing, fusing, and finishing
   c. Cleaning, conditioning, writing, developing, transferring, and fusing
   d. Cleaning, registration, writing, transferring, fusing, and finishing

8. List the fundamental parts of a dot-matrix printer.
   a. Power supply, microprocessor, tractor feed motor, printhead mechanism, and printhead positioning motor
   b. Power supply, interface board, paper feed motor, printhead mechanism, and printhead positioning motor
   c. Interface board, ink cartridge, printhead mechanism, printhead positioning motor, and sensors
   d. Controller, paper feed motor, ribbon cartridge, and printhead positioning motor

9. What type of ink delivery system is typically found in ink-jet printers built for personal computers?
   a. Drop-on-demand ink delivery
   b. Continuous stream ink delivery
   c. Impact ink delivery
   d. Compact spray ink delivery

10. The specification for 60-pound bond paper means that _____.
    a. 100 22"x 17" sheets weigh 60 pounds
    b. 500 8.5"x 11" sheets weigh 60 pounds
    c. 100 11"x 17" sheets weigh 60 pounds
    d. 500 22"x 17" sheets weigh 60 pounds

CHAPTER
7

PORTABLE
SYSTEMS

OBJECTIVES

OBJECTIVES

Upon completion of this chapter and its related lab procedures you will be able to perform the following tasks:

1. Identify the unique components of portable systems and their unique problems.

2. Describe basic procedures for adding and removing FRU modules associated with portable systems.

3. Identify proper procedures for installing peripheral devices commonly used with portable systems.

4. Describe the applications that the three types of PCMCIA cards can be used to perform.

5. Discuss and recognize the different PCMCIA devices currently available.

6. Describe the purpose of a docking station.

PORTABLE SYSTEMS

INTRODUCTION

Portable computers represent a large and growing portion of the personal computer market. Therefore, the computer technician must be aware of how they vary from traditional desktop units and how their service requirements are different from the norm.

The A+ Core Hardware objective 1.3 states that the test taker should be able to identify basic procedures for adding and removing field-replaceable modules for portable systems. Given a replacement scenario, choose the appropriate sequences.

Portable components:

- Storage device
  - FDD
  - HDD
  - CD/CDRW
  - DVD/DVDRW
  - Removable storage
- Power sources
  - AC adapters
  - DC adapter
  - Batteries
- Memory
- Display device
- Input devices
  - Keyboard
  - Mouse/pointer devices
  - Touch screen

- PCMCIA adapters
  - Network Interface Card (NIC)
  - Modem
  - SCSI
  - IEEE-1394/Firewire
  - USB
  - Storage (memory and hard drive)
- Docking station/port replicators
- LCD panel
- Wireless
  - Adapter/controller
  - Antenna

PORTABLE COMPUTER TYPES

luggables

The original portables were called **luggables**. Although they were smaller than desktop computers they were not truly convenient to transport. The first portables included small built-in CRT displays and detachable keyboards. Their batteries and CRT equipment made them extremely bulky and heavy to carry. Therefore, they never really had a major impact on the PC market. However, they set the stage for the development of future portable computer systems. Examples of different portable computer designs are shown in Figure 7-1.

Figure 7-1: Portable Computers

laptops

With advancements in battery design and the advent of usable, large-screen, flat-panel displays, the first truly portable PCs, referred to as **laptops**, were introduced. These units featured all-in-one, AT-compatible PC boards. The system board included the I/O and video controller functions. Laptops featured built-in keyboards and hinged LCD display panels that flipped up from the case for use. They also used an external power supply and a removable, rechargeable battery.

The battery life of typical laptops was minimal and their size was still large enough to be inconvenient at times. However, the inclusion of LCD viewing screens and external power supply/battery arrangements made them useful enough to spawn a healthy portable computer market. Even though these units could weigh in excess of seven pounds, the user could easily take work from the office to the home, or to a hotel room while traveling. Users could also get work done at traditionally nonproductive times, such as on long automobile or airplane rides. An occasional game of computerized cards or golf was always at hand as well.

notebook computers

Continued advancements in integrated circuitry and peripheral technology allowed the PC's circuitry to be reduced. This allowed portable sizes to be reduced further so that they could achieve sizes of 8.75"d x 11"w x 2.25"h and smaller. Portables in this size range are referred to as **notebook computers**. The weight of a typical notebook dropped down to 5 or 6 pounds.

Even smaller **sub-notebook PCs** have been created by moving the disk drives outside the case and reducing the size of the display screen. These units tend to be slightly thinner than traditional notebooks and weigh in the neighborhood of 3 to 4 pounds. Very small sub-notebooks, referred to as **palmtop PCs**, were produced for a short time in the pre-Windows days. These units limited everything as far as possible to reach sizes of 7"w x 4"d x 1"h and weights of 1 to 2 pounds. Sub-notebooks have decreased in popularity as notebooks have continued to decrease in weight and cost.

Personal Digital Assistants

The palmtop market was diminished for some time because of the difficulty of running Windows on such small displays. Human **ergonomics** also come into play when dealing with smaller notebooks. The smaller display screens are difficult to see and keyboards become more difficult to use as the size of the keys decreases.

However, the market was revived by the introduction of palmtops known as **Personal Digital Assistants (PDAs)**. Figure 7-2 depicts a typical PDA. These handheld devices use a special stylus, referred to as a pen, to input data and selections instead of a keyboard or mouse. Basically the PDA is an electronic time management system that may also include computer applications such as word processors, spreadsheets, and databases.

The PDA's display is a touch-screen **Liquid Crystal Display (LCD)** that works in conjunction with a graphical user interface running on top of a specialized operating system. Some PDAs employ a highly-modified, embedded (on a chip) version of Microsoft Windows, called **Windows CE**, as their operating system. These systems are particularly well suited for exchanging and synchronizing information with larger Windows-based systems.

Two items have made PDAs popular: their size and their ability to communicate with the user's desktop computer system. Early PDAs exchanged information with full-sized computers through serial port connections. Newer models communicate with the user's desktop computer through high-speed USB ports, infrared communications links, or docking stations.

Figure 7-2: A Personal Digital Assistant

Inside Portables

Portable computers have two ideal characteristics: They are compact and light-weight. Portable computer designers work constantly to decrease the size and power consumption of all the computer's components. Special low-power ICs and disk drives have been developed to extend battery life.

Likewise, cases have been designed to be as small as possible while providing as many standard features as possible. Figure 7-3 shows the inside of a typical portable computer. Notice how the components are interconnected by the design. The system board is designed so that it wraps around other components whose form factors cannot be altered — such as the disk drive units. The components also tend to be layered in portable designs. Disk drives cover portions of the system board, whereas the keyboard unit covers nearly everything. The internal battery may slide into a cutout area of the system board, or more likely, it may be located beneath the system board.

Figure 7-3: Inside a Portable Computer

Portable System Boards

A typical notebook system board is depicted in Figure 7-4. The first thing you should notice about it is its unusual shape. As noted earlier, system boards for portable computers are not designed to fit a standardized form factor. Instead they are designed to fit around all of the components that must be installed in the system. Therefore, system boards used in portable computers tend to be proprietary to the model they are designed for. Mounting hole positions are determined by where they will best suit the placement of the other system components.

Figure 7-4: Typical
Notebook System
Board

The second item to notice is that none of the "standard" expansion slots or adapter cards are present on the portable's system board. These system board designs typically include the standard MI/O and video circuitry as an integral part of the board. They also provide the physical connections for the unit's parallel and serial I/O ports, as well as on-board connectors for the disk drives, display unit, and keyboard units.

The computer's external I/O connections, such as serial- and parallel-port connectors, are arranged on the system board so that they align with the corresponding openings in the portable case. It is highly unlikely that a system board from another portable would match these openings. On the maintenance side, a blown parallel-port circuit would require that the entire system board be replaced in order to correct the problem. In a desktop unit, a simple I/O card could be installed in an expansion slot to overcome such a situation.

> The I/O ports included in most notebook computers consist of a single parallel port, a single serial port, an external VGA monitor connector, an external keyboard connector, and a docking port expansion bus. Some models can be found with a second serial-port connector, but they are not common.

Figure 7-5 shows the port connections associated with most portable systems. This example places the connectors on the back of the unit, just as in a typical desktop. Other units may place some of these connectors on each side of the unit instead. High-end portables may include an array of other connectors, such as external microphone and speaker jacks. Some connectors may be hidden behind hinged doors for protection. These doors usually snap closed.

Figure 7-5:
Notebook Backpanel
Connections

Microprocessors in Portables

The portable computer market is so large that it even influences the microprocessor and IC manufacturers. They produce special low-power-consumption microprocessors and chipsets just for portable computer systems. These power-saving IC devices are typically identified by an "SL" designation (i.e., 80486SLC).

In Chapter 2 — *Advanced System Boards*, it was pointed out that Pentium microprocessors produce large amounts of heat, even by desktop standards. Most of the portables currently in the market are based on Pentium devices. To minimize the heat buildup condition, Intel has produced a complete line of **mobile Pentium processors** for use in portable systems. Mobile devices differ from standard microprocessor devices in terms of both their internal construction and their external packaging. In mobile microprocessors, both design aspects have been optimized to provide minimum size and power consumption, as well as maximum heat reduction.

Figure 7-6 depicts a mobile Pentium MMX processor. It is constructed using Intel's **Voltage Reduction Technology**, which enables the processor to run at lower core voltages (1.8 − 2.0 Vdc) and, thereby, consume less energy and generate less heat. The package style created for the mobile Pentium is referred to as a **Tape Carrier Package** (TCP). The microprocessor chip is embedded in a polyimide film (tape) that is laminated with a copper foil. The leads of the IC are etched into the foil and attached to the processor.

mobile Pentium processors

Voltage Reduction Technology

Tape Carrier Package (TCP)

Figure 7-6:
The Mobile Pentium

The tape package arrangement makes the mobile package much smaller and lighter than the PGA and SPGA packages used with the standard Pentium devices. It also mounts directly to the PC board instead of plugging into a bulky heavy socket. A special insertion machine cuts the strip of microprocessors into individual 24 mm units as it is soldered to the system board. The system board furnishes a heat sink area beneath the processor that helps to dissipate heat. A layer of thermal conductive paste is applied to this connection prior to the soldering process to increase the heat transfer away from the processor. This design enables the full-featured Pentium processor to run at competitive speeds without additional heat sinks and fan modules. The cross section of the complete mobile Pentium attachment is depicted in Figure 7-7.

Figure 7-7: The Mobile Pentium Installation

The attachment of the mobile microprocessor to a system board makes the arrangement permanent for all practical purposes. To allow for microprocessor upgrading, portable system boards often employ mobile processors mounted on plug-in daughter boards, or modules. Intel has produced two Pentium plug-in variations. One of these is a mobile Pentium on a 4" x 2.5" x 0.3" **mobile module**, referred to as an **MMO**. This module is attached to the system board via screws and plugs through a 280-pin connector. The other Intel module is a mini-cartridge for the Pentium II.

> mobile module
> (MMO)

Memory for Portables

It is not a common practice for notebook and other portable computer manufacturers to use traditional SIMM and DIMM modules in their designs. Instead, these types of computers routinely use the smaller SODIMMs and MicroDIMMs form factor memory modules described in Chapter 2. The key to upgrading or replacing internal RAM in a portable computer can be found in its documentation. Only memory modules recommended by the portable manufacturer should be installed, and only in the configurations suggested.

The voltage level support for the memory devices in portable computers is very critical. Using RAM devices that electrically overload this supply will cause memory errors to occur.

If the type of RAM device being installed is not one of the recommended types, the notebook might not be able to recognize the new memory. If the new RAM is being added to expand the existing banks of memory, the system might not recognize this additional RAM. The problem will show up in the form of a short memory count during the POST routines. However, if only the new RAM type is installed, the system could present a number of different symptoms, including:

- Not working at all
- Giving beep coded error messages
- Producing soft-memory errors
- Producing short memory counts in the POST
- Locking up while booting the operating system

As with disk drives, changing memory in a portable PC involves disassembling the computer case. Figure 7-8 shows the replacement of a SODIMM module in a particular notebook computer. The location of, and process of accessing the memory in the unit varies from manufacturer to manufacturer and model to model.

Figure 7-8: Replacing a SODIMM Module

In notebook computers, it is also possible to increase memory by installing PC-Card based memory cards—described later in this chapter. These memory units can increase the portable computer's memory capabilities without the need to take it apart. In addition, they can be removed when additional memory space is not in high demand. A newer memory add-on technology that has found some favor in the notebook computer arena is the USB plug-in memory module.

Portable Drives

Smaller 2.5" form factor hard drives, low-profile 3.5" floppy drives, and combination FDD/CD-ROM drives have been developed to address the portable computer market's need for compact devices. Older portables included one FDD and one HDD as standard equipment. Newer models tend to include a CD-ROM drive and an HDD as standard internal units.

More expensive notebook computers may substitute a DVD or CDRW drive for the standard CD-ROM drive. While it is possible to install internal DVDRW drives in portable computers, these tend to only be installed in very high-end versions. On the other hand, external CDRW and DVDRW units are also widely used with portable computers. These drive units are described in greater detail later in this chapter. Figure 7-9 shows the placement of drives in a high-end notebook unit that includes one of each drive type.

HARD-DISK DRIVE

CD-ROM DRIVE

FLOPPY-DISK DRIVE

Figure 7-9:
Portable Disk Drives

Newer portable models include swappable drive bays that permit the combination of internal drives in the unit to be changed as dictated by the work being performed. In some units, a disk drive that is not needed for a particular task may be removed and replaced by an extra battery.

There are basically three considerations that should be observed when replacing disk drives in portable computers. These are its physical size and layout, its power consumption, and whether the existing BIOS will support it.

BASIC I/O

Personal computer users are creatures of habit as much as anyone else. Therefore, as they moved toward portable computers, they wanted the types of features they had come to expect from their larger desktops and towers. These features typically include an alphanumeric keyboard, a video display, and a pointing device.

Portable Display Types

Notebook and laptop computers use non-CRT displays, such as **Liquid Crystal Display (LCD)** and **gas-plasma panels**. These display systems are well suited to the portability needs of portable computers. They are much lighter and more compact than CRT monitors and require much less electrical energy to operate. Both types of display units can be operated from batteries.

TEST TIP
Know that notebook display panels are powered by low-voltage DC power sources such as a battery or converter.

Portable computers continue to gain popularity due to their ability to travel with the user. This has been made possible by the development of different flat-panel display technologies. Early attempts at developing portable microcomputers used small CRTs that minimized the size of the unit. However, these units quickly gained the label of luggables, due to their weight. The high-voltage circuitry required to operate a CRT device is heavy by nature, and could be reduced only slightly.

Liquid Crystal Displays

Liquid Crystal Displays — The most common flat-panel displays used with portable PC's are Liquid Crystal Displays. They are relatively thin, flat, and lightweight, and require very little power to operate. In addition to reduced weight and improved portability, these displays offer better reliability and longer life than CRT units.

The LCD, illustrated in Figure 7-10, is constructed by placing **thermotropic** liquid crystal material between two sheets of glass. A set of electrodes is attached to each sheet of glass. Horizontal (row) electrodes are attached to one glass plate, and vertical (column) electrodes are fitted to the other plate. These electrodes are transparent and let light pass through. A **picture element**, or **pixel**, is created in the liquid crystal material at each spot where a row electrode and a column electrode intersect. A special plate called a **polarizer** is added to the outside of each glass plate. There is one polarizer on the front, and another on the back of the display.

Figure 7-10: LCD Construction

GLASS
POLARIZER
COLUMN ELECTRODE
LIQUID CRYSTAL MATERIAL
ROW ELECTRODE
GLASS
POLARIZER

The display is designed so that when the pixel is off, the molecules of the liquid crystal twist from one edge of the material to the other, as depicted in Figure 7-11. The spiral effect created by the twist polarizes light, and prevents it from passing through the display. When an electric field is created between a row and column electrode, the molecules move, lining up perpendicular to the front of the display. This allows light to pass through the display, producing a single dot on the screen.

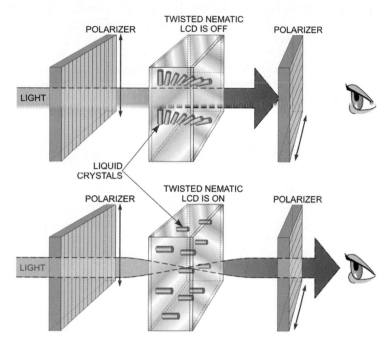

**Figure 7-11:
LCD Operation**

Depending on the orientation of the polarizers, the energized pixels can be made to look like a dark spot on a light screen, or a light dot on a dark screen. In most notebook computers, the display is lit from behind the panel. This is referred to as **back lighting**. Some units are constructed so that the display can be removed from the body of the computer, and used with an overhead projector to display computer output on a wall or large screen.

back lighting

Because no current passes through the display to light the pixels, the power consumption of LCD displays is very low. The screen is scanned using IC multiplexers and drivers to activate the panel's row and column electrodes. The scanning circuitry addresses each row sequentially, column by column. Although the column electrode is activated for a short portion of each horizontal scan, the pixels appear to be continuously lit because the scanning rate is very high. The electrodes can be controlled (turned on and off) using standard TTL voltage levels. This translates into less control circuitry required to operate the panel. LCDs using this type of construction are referred to as **dual scan**, or **passive matrix** displays. Advanced passive matrix technologies are referred to as **Color Super-Twist Nematic (CSTN)** and **Double-layer Super-Twist Nematic (DSTN)** displays.

dual scan

passive matrix

Color Super-Twist
Nematic (CSTN)

Double-layer
Super-Twist Nematic
(DSTN)

An improved LCD approach is similar in design to the passive matrix designs, except that it adds a transistor at each of the matrix's row-column junctions to improve switching times. This technology produces an LCD display type referred to as an **active matrix display**. In these displays, a small current is sent to the transistor through the row-column lines. The energized transistor conducts a larger current, which, in turn, is used to activate the pixel seen on the screen. The active matrix is produced by using **Thin Film Transistor (TFT)** arrays to create between one and four transistors for each pixel on a flexible, transparent film. TFT displays tend to be brighter and sharper than dual scan displays. However, they also tend to require more power to operate and to be more expensive.

active matrix display

Thin Film Transistor
(TFT)

Color LCD displays are created by adding a three-color filter to the panel. Each pixel in the display corresponds to a red, blue, or green dot on the filter. Activating a pixel behind a blue dot on the filter will produce a blue dot on the screen. Like color CRT displays, the dot color on the screen of the color LCD panel is established by controlling the **relative intensities** of a three-dot (RGB) pixel cluster.

The construction of LCD displays prevents them from providing multiple resolution options like an adapter-driven CRT display can. The resolution of the LCD display is dictated by the construction of the LCD panel.

The life and usefulness of the portable's LCD panel can be extended through proper care and handling. The screen should be cleaned periodically with a glass cleaner and a soft, lint-free cloth. Spray the cleaner on the cloth and then wipe the screen. Never spray the cleaner directly on the screen. Also, avoid scratching the surface of the screen. It is relatively easy to damage the front polarizer of the display. Take care to remove any liquid droplets from the screen since they can cause permanent staining. After cleaning, allow 30 minutes for complete drying.

The screen should be shielded from bright sun light and heat sources. Moving the computer from a warm location to a cold location can cause damaging moisture to condense inside the housing (including the display). It should also be kept away from ultraviolet light sources and extremely cold temperatures. The liquid crystals can freeze in extremely cold weather. A freeze/thaw cycle may damage the display and cause it to be unusable.

Keyboards

The most widely used notebook keyboard is the 84-key version. The keys are slightly smaller and shorter than those found in full-size keyboards. A number of keys or key functions may be combined or deleted from a notebook keyboard.

A typical notebook keyboard is illustrated in Figure 7-12.

Figure 7-12: 84-Key Notebook Keyboard

Since a portable keyboard tends to be more compact than the detachable models used with desktop units, many of its keys are typically given dual or triple functions. The portable keyboard normally contains an **Fn** function key. This key activates special functions in the portable, such as display brightness and contrast. Other common Fn functions include Suspend mode activation and LCD/external-CRT device selection.

Newer keyboard models may also include left and right Windows keys (**WIN keys**), and an **application key**, as identified in Figure 7-13. The WIN keys are located next to the ALT keys and provide specialized Windows functions, as described in Table 7-1. Similarly, the application key is located near the right WIN key, or the CTRL key, and provides context-sensitive help for most applications.

WIN KEY   APPLICATION KEY

**Figure 7-13:
WIN and Application
Keys**

KEY STROKE	ACTION
WIN/E	Start Windows Explorer
WIN/F	Start Find files or folders
Ctrl/WIN/F	Find the computer
WIN/M	Minimize All
Shift/WIN/M	Undo Minimize All
WIN/R	Display Run dialog box
WIN/F1	Start Help
WIN/Tab	Move through Taskbar objects
WIN/Break	Show System Properties dialog box

**Table 7-1:
WIN Key Definitions**

Most portables offer standard connectors to enable full-size keyboards and VGA monitors to be plugged in, as shown in Figure 7-14. The VGA connector is usually the standard 15-pin D-shell type, while the external keyboard connector is generally the 6-pin mini-DIN (PS/2) type. When an external keyboard is plugged in, the built-in keyboard is disabled. The portable's software may allow both displays to remain active while the external monitor is connected.

MONITOR

KEYBOARD

Figure 7-14: Attaching Standard I/O Devices

Trackballs

In some systems, such as notebook computers, it is desirable to have a pointing device that does not require a surface to be moved across. The **trackball** can be thought of as an inverted mouse that allows the user to directly manipulate it. Trackballs, like the one depicted in Figure 7-15, may be separate units that sit on a desk, or clip to the side of the computer, and connect to one of the system's serial ports. In many laptop and notebook computers, trackballs are frequently built directly into the system housing and connected directly to its I/O circuitry. Like mice, trackballs may come with one to three buttons.

**Figure 7-15:
A Trackball Unit**

Touch Pads

Hewlett-Packard introduced the **first touch screen monitor** in 1983. These screens divide the display into rows and columns that correspond to X and Y coordinates on the screen. This technology has been adapted to notebook computers in the form of **touch pad** pointing devices, like the one illustrated in Figure 7-16.

**Figure 7-16: A
Touch Pad**

This pointing device normally takes the place of the mouse as the pointing device in the system. The user controls the screen cursor by moving a finger across the pad surface. Small buttons are included near the pad to duplicate the action of the mouse buttons. With some touch pads, single- and double-clicking can be simulated by tapping a finger on the pad.

The touch pad contains a gridwork of electric conductors that organize it in a row and column format, as described in Figure 7-17. When the user presses the touch pad, the protective layer over the grid flexes and causes the capacitance between the two grids within the pad to change. This produces a signal change that is detected by the touch pad controller at one X-grid line and one Y-grid line. The controller converts the signal generated between the two strips into an approximate X/Y position on the video display.

Figure 7-17: Inside a Touch Pad

The human fingertip is broad and does not normally provide a fine enough pointing device to select precise points on the screen. Therefore, accurately locating a small item on the screen may be difficult. Touch pad software designers have created drivers that take this possibility into account and compensate for it.

Touch pads are available as built-in units in some portables, while others are designed as add-ons to existing units. These units clip onto the body of the computer, or sit on a desktop, and plug into one of the system's serial ports, just as a mouse or trackball does.

When troubleshooting touch pad problems, there are really only three components to consider. These are the touch-sensitive pad, the I/O port the pad is attached to, and its driver software. Review the user's manual for the pad to check its software setup for possible configuration problems. Examine the I/O port connection and configuration to make sure it is properly set up to support the pad. If the pad is an add-on unit, check the port specification to make sure that it is compatible with the touch pad unit. Reinstall the touch pad driver software, carefully reviewing each step. Check for the presence of diagnostic routines in the touch pad's software. Check the I/O port settings.

As with the portable's LCD panel, the life and usefulness of a touch pad can be extended through proper care and handling. The panel should be cleaned periodically with mild soap and water and a soft, lint-free cloth. Rinse the residue from the pad by wiping it with a cloth dampened in clear water. Never pour or spray liquids directly on the computer or the touch pad. After cleaning, allow 30 minutes for complete drying.

Like the other portable components, the touch pad should be shielded from bright sunlight and heat sources, as well as extremely cold temperatures. Never use sharp or pointed objects to tap the pad as these items may damage the surface of the pad.

EXTENDED I/O

As more and more desktop users began to use laptop and notebook computers, they demanded that additional peripheral systems be included. With the limited space inside these units, it became clear that a new method for installing options would need to be developed.

At first, laptop and notebook manufacturers included proprietary expansion connections for adding such devices as fax/modems, additional memory, and additional storage devices. Of course, these devices tended to be expensive since they were proprietary to a single vendor. In addition, they were not useful as the user upgraded to newer or more powerful units.

PC Cards (PCMCIA)

In 1989, the **PCMCIA** bus standard was introduced primarily to accommodate the notebook and sub-notebook computer markets. A small form-factor expansion-card format, referred to as the **PC Card** standard, was also adopted for use. This format was derived from earlier proprietary laptop/notebook memory card designs. It is based on the 68-pin JEIDA connector, depicted in Figure 7-18.

**Figure 7-18:
PCMCIA Connector
Standard**

The definitions of the PCMCIA connector's 68 pins are listed in Table 7-2.

The interface is designed so that cards can be inserted into the unit while it is turned on (**hot insertion**). Although the PC Card connection scheme was never intended for use with a full-size unit, its design is compatible with all the other expansion bus types. As a matter of fact, PCMCIA adapters have been mounted on PCI cards so that they can be used in desktop and tower units. The PCI card is placed in one of the system board's expansion slots and the removable PC Cards can be inserted and removed through an opening in the PCI card's slot cover.

The PC Card standard defines a methodology for software programmers to write standard drivers for PC Card devices. The standard is referred to as **socket services** and provides for a software head to identify the type of card being used, its capabilities, and its requirements. Although the card's software driver can be executed directly on the card (instead of moving it into RAM for execution), the system's PC Card enablers must be loaded before the card can be activated. This is referred to as **execute-in-place mode**. In addition, PC Cards can use the same file allocation system used by floppy- and hard-disk drives. This also makes it easier for programmers to write code for PCMCIA devices.

PIN	NAME	DESCRIPTION	PIN	NAME	DESCRIPTION
1	GND	Ground	35	GND	Ground
2	D3	Data bit 3	36	CD1	Card detect 1
3	D4	Data bit 4	37	D11	Data bit 11
4	D5	Data bit 5	38	D12	Data bit 12
5	D6	Data bit 6	39	D13	Data bit 13
6	D7	Data bit 7	40	D14	Data bit 14
7	CE1	Card enable 1	41	D15	Data bit 15
8	A10	Address bit 10	42	CE2	Card enable 2
9	OE	Output enable	43	RFSH	Refresh input
10	A11	Address bit 11	44	IORD	I/O read strobe
11	A9	Address bit 9	45	IOWR	I/O write strobe
12	A8	Address bit 8	46	A17	Address bit 17
13	A13	Address bit 13	47	A18	Address bit 18
14	A14	Address bit 14	48	A19	Address bit 19
15	WE/-PGM	Write enable	49	A20	Address bit 20
16	IREQ	Interrupt request	50	A21	Address bit 21
17	VCC	Card power	51	VCC	Card power
18	VPP1	Programming supply voltage 1	52	VPP2	Programming supply voltage 2
19	A16	Address bit 16	53	A22	Address bit 22
20	A15	Address bit 15	54	A23	Address bit 23
21	A12	Address bit 12	55	A24	Address bit 24
22	A7	Address bit 7	56	A25	Address bit 25
23	A6	Address bit 6	57	RFU	Reserved
24	A5	Address bit 5	58	RESET	Card reset
25	A4	Address bit 5	59	WAIT	Extend bus cycle
26	A3	Address bit 3	60	INPACK	Input port acknowledge
27	A2	Address bit 2	61	REG	Register and I/O select enable
28	A1	Address bit 1	62	SPKR	Digital audio waveform
29	A0	Address bit 0	63	STSGNG	Card status changed
30	D0	Data bit 0	64	D8	Data bit 8
31	D1	Data bit 1	65	D9	Data bit 9
32	D2	Data bit 2	66	D10	Data bit 10
33	IOIS16	IO port is 16 bits	67	CD2	Card detect 2
34	GND	Ground	68	GND	Ground

**Table 7-2:
68-Pin Connector
Definitions**

PC Card Types

Three types of PCMCIA adapters currently exist. The **PCMCIA Type I** cards, introduced in 1990, are 3.3 mm thick and work as memory expansion units. In 1991, the **PCMCIA Type II** cards were introduced. They are 5 mm thick and support virtually any traditional expansion function, except removable hard drive units. Type II slots are backward compatible so that Type I cards will work in them. Currently, **PCMCIA Type III** cards are being produced. These cards are 10.5 mm thick and are intended primarily for use with removable hard drives. Both Type I and Type II cards can be used in a Type III slot.

PCMCIA Type I

PCMCIA Type II

PCMCIA Type III

All three card-types adhere to a form factor of 2.12"w x 3.37"l and use a 68-pin, slide-in socket arrangement. They can be used with 8-bit or 16-bit data bus machines and operate on +5 V or +3.3 V supplies. The card's design allows it to be installed in the computer while it is turned on and running. Figure 7-19 shows the three types of PCMCIA cards.

─ TEST TIP ─

Memorize the physical sizes of the three card standards. Also, know what applications each type of card is capable of.

**Figure 7-19:
PCMCIA Cards**

PC Card versions of most adapter types are available in the market place. Even PC Card hard drives (with disks the size of a quarter) can be found. Other common PC Card adapters include fax/modems, SCSI adapters, network adapters, and IDE host adapters. The PCMCIA standard allows up to 255 adapters, each capable of working with up to 16 cards. If a system implemented the standard to its extreme, it could, theoretically, work with over 4,000 PC cards installed. Most portable designs only include two PC Card slots.

Cardbus

The latest variation of the PCMCIA standard is Cardbus. Cardbus is a redefined and enhanced 32-bit version of the PC Card standard. The main purpose of this new specification is to extend the PCMCIA bus to higher speeds with more powerful devices, and to provide support of 32-bit I/O and memory data paths.

The cardbus slot has intelligent software that interrogates a card when it is inserted into the slot. If the slot finds that the card is a PC Card, then it configures itself to function like a conventional PCMCIA slot. However, if an advanced CardBus card has been inserted, the slot reconfigures itself to use the 32-bit bus width, increased speeds and low voltage capabilities of the Cardbus specification.

While the Cardbus slot is designed to work with older PCMCIA and PC Card devices, the same is not true concerning using Cardbus cards in older slot types. The Cardbus card is keyed with a physical sheath around its pins so that it will not plug into the traditional PC Card socket. On the software side, for a Cardbus device to work in a given system, the operating system must support 32-bit data paths.

You can use the following procedure to determine whether a particular system is a Cardbus-enabled system:

1. Insert the Cardbus card into your system's PC Card slot, if it doesn't insert completely, then the slot is not a Cardbus slot.

2. Check the system BIOS setup and verify that the *PC Card* option is set to the *CardBus* option. If there is no option for Cardbus, then the system does not support Cardbus devices.

3. Check the version of Windows installed on your system under the *Settings/Control Panel/System/General* path. If you do not have version 4.00.950B or later, you do not have the necessary software to use CardbBus PC Cards.

Installing PC Cards

Although portable computers do not include standard desktop expansion slots for adding peripheral devices to the system, they do typically include a couple of PC Card slots. Most notebooks provide two PCMCIA slots that can accept a wide variety of I/O device types. PC Cards are relatively easy to install in a PnP system that has the PCMCIA card services function running. Simply slide the card into an open PC Card slot and turn the machine on. The PnP function should detect the card in the slot and configure it with the proper drivers.

The operating system must support the PCMCIA slots at two levels — at the socket level (universal support for all PCMCIA devices) and at the card level (specific drivers to handle the function of the particular card installed). Because PCMCIA cards are hot swappable, the operating system's socket service must update the system when a new card is installed or an existing card is removed. If not, the system would lose track of its actual resources. The card service portion delivers the correct device driver for the installed PC Card (that is, when a PC Card modem is removed and replaced with a LAN card, the operating system must automatically update its capability of controlling and using the new card).

In many cases, the PC Card must furnish a standard I/O connector for connection to the full sized world. Often, these connections are made through nonstandard connectors at the PC Card end but terminate in standard connectors at the I/O device end. For example, a PC Card LAN card, such as the one depicted in Figure 7-20, is not physically thick enough to accommodate a standard RJ-45 plug used with Ethernet networks. To overcome this, a thin connector is attached to the card and a standard connector is used at the other end of the cable. Depending on their specific function, some PC Cards require an external power supply to acquire enough power to operate efficiently.

Figure 7-20: PC Card Connections

Installing PC Card Support

There are three ways in which the card services utility delivers the proper drivers to the card:

- The operating system, such as Windows 9x or Windows 2000, immediately recognizes the card and installs the driver without restarting.

- The operating system recognizes the card and has its driver, but needs to reboot in order to load the driver.

- The operating system does not recognize the card and requires that an external driver be loaded. Under Windows 9x, a PC Card Wizard is started to guide the user through the driver installation process. Windows 2000 does not supply a PC Card Installation wizard.

To install the PC Card (PCMCIA) Wizard on your Windows 9x system, you must navigate the *Start/Settings/Control Panel* path and access the *Add/Remove Programs* applet. Click on the *Windows Setup* tab, select a category, and then click on the *Details* tab. If you don't see the component listed in the *Add/Remove Programs* dialog box, it might be one that is only present on the Windows 9x distribution CD. In this case, you can download the component from an online service, such as the Microsoft Network, or from the Microsoft Download Service at the main Microsoft web site.

At different times, you might want to stop a PC Card driver from being loaded. To turn off support for a PC Card, access the *Device Manager* tab and expand the PC Card slot node. Then, double-click the PC Card controller and in the Device usage area, check the *Disable in This Hardware Profile* check box option.

The proper procedure for removing a PC Card from the computer begins with clicking on the PC Card status indicator on the taskbar. Then, select the command to stop the operation of the PC Card you want to remove. When the operating system prompts you, physically remove the PC Card from the system.

CHALLENGE #1

You are traveling away from your office, and you want to get as much work done on the airplane as possible. You notice that the notebook takes several minutes during the PnP configuration portion of the boot process. Your notebook has a PCMCIA modem and network card, and you want to disable these devices while you are traveling so that their drivers are not loaded. How can you do this without permanently removing them? (You want to use them when you get back to the office.)

Networking Portables

When the portable computer returns to the office, there is usually a gap between what is on the portable and what is on the desktop machine. One alternative is to use a docking station to allow the notebook to function as both a portable and as a desktop system. This concept is explored later in this chapter. The other alternative is to make the portable computer network-ready so that it can plug into the network in the office.

There are PC Card network adapters that can be used with a network socket device to enable the portable to be connected into the office network. The socket device has internal circuitry that prevents the open net connection from adversely affecting the network when the portable is removed. Some network adapters use the system's parallel port and a pocket LAN adapter to connect portables to the network. The LAN adapter actually works between the network, the computer, and its printer, as shown in Figure 7-21.

Figure 7-21: A LAN Adapter

Notebook computers are natural selections for use as wireless networking clients. Because they are portable, they can be used anywhere within any wireless access point's hot spot. As mentioned in Chapter 5, many enterprises are creating hot spots to enable traveling computer users to access their access point—for a fee.

For the most part, the installation process involves inserting the wireless card in the PCMCIA slot and supplying the OEM drivers from the manufacturer's CD. Notebook computers typically use PC Card—based wireless network adapters like the one depicted in Figure 7-22. The wireless PC Card adapter slides into one of the notebook's PCMCIA slots and should be auto-detected by the system. The card communicates with a remote access point through the embedded antenna that sticks out of the computer's PC Card slot.

Figure 7-22: A Wireless Network Adapter PC Card

Part of configuring the drivers involves identifying the name of the access point that the card should use. Afterward, you simply need to configure networking support in the operating system. The device should be capable of functioning on the wireless LAN provided the card's driver and the operating system's networking components have been set up properly for communications.

Because wireless units can and do move, there are certain wireless connectivity issues that you must be aware of. Type 802.11b cards have a limited range of operation (i.e., about 500 ft). This estimation relies on a clear line-of-sight pathway existing between the card and the access point. The signals used under this wireless specification do not travel well through objects. In addition, if the card is used in a multiple access point environment, it will always try to communicate with the access point it has been configured to use. To switch to another access point, this setting must be reconfigured.

Many wireless configuration applications include a built-in power meter program that shows the relative signal strength being received from the access point. When you're positioning a computer that has a wireless network card, you should use this tool to maximize the location of the computer. Likewise, if you are operating in a multiple access point environment you can use this tool to identify the best access point to use in a given location.

Notebook computers can also be used in dial-up networking environments by installing a PC Card modem as shown in Figure 7-23. These modems slide into Type II PCMCIA slots and connect to the telephone jack through a special phone cable. The cable plugs into a small slot on the card and into the phone jack using a standard RJ-11 connector.

Figure 7-23: A PC Card Modem

EXTERNAL DEVICES

The basic portable should contain all of the devices that the user needs to do work while away from the office. However, there are always additional items that users have become accustomed to using with their computers. For this reason, portable computers typically offer a full range of I/O port types.

Power Supplies

Notebooks and other portables use a detachable, rechargeable battery and an external power supply, as illustrated in Figure 7-24 (battery sizes will vary from manufacturer to manufacturer). They also employ power-saving circuits and ICs designed to lengthen the battery's useful time. The battery unit contains a recharging regulator circuit that allows the battery to recharge while it is being used with the external power supply. As with other hardware aspects of notebook computers, there are no standards for their power supply units. They use different connector types and possess different voltage and current delivery capabilities. Therefore, a power supply from one notebook will not necessarily work with another portable model.

**Figure 7-24:
Laptop/Notebook
Power Supplies**

Since the premise of portable computers is mobility, it can be assumed that they should be able to run without being plugged into an ac outlet. The question for most portables is how long it will run without being plugged in. This is the aspect in which portable designs lead the industry. They continuously push forward in three design areas:

- better battery design

- better power-consumption devices

- better power management

TEST TIP

Be aware that the external power supply used with portable systems basically converts ac voltage into a dc voltage that the system can use to power its internal components and recharge its batteries.

Batteries

To be honest, the desktop world doesn't really pay much attention to power conservation issues. Conversely, portable computer designers must deal with the fact that portable computers are tied to a battery. Older portable designs included the battery as an external, detachable device, as depicted in the previous figure. These units normally contained rows of **Nickel Cadmium (Ni-Cad)** batteries wired together to provide the specified voltage and current capabilities for the portable. The housing was constructed both to hold the Ni-Cads and to attach to the portable case.

Typical Ni-Cad batteries offer operating times approaching two hours in some models. As with other devices that rely on Ni-Cads, computer battery packs constructed with this type of battery suffer from the charge/discharge cycle "memory effect" problem associated with Ni-Cads. A full recharge for some Ni-Cad packs could take up to 24 hours to complete. For these reasons, Ni-Cad battery packs have all but disappeared from the portable computer market.

Newer portable designs have switched to **Nickel Metal-Hydride (NiMH)**, **Lithium-Ion (Li-ion)**, or **Lithium-Ion Polymer** batteries. These batteries are housed in a plastic case that can be installed inside the portable's case, as illustrated in Figure 7-25. These types of batteries typically provide up to 2 or 3 hours of operation. It is best to run the battery until the system produces a low battery warning message, indicator, or chime.

It should take about 2 to 3 hours to fully recharge the typical Ni-MH battery pack and about 4 to 5 hours for a Li-ion pack. The battery packs should always be fully recharged before using. When the ac adapter is used, a trickle charge is applied to the battery pack to keep it in a fully charged condition. The ac adapter should be used whenever possible to conserve the battery.

Nickel Cadmium
(Ni-Cad)

Nickel Metal-Hydride
(NiMH)

Lithium-Ion (Li-ion)

Lithium-Ion Polymer

BATTERY

BATTERY
RELEASE
LATCH

Figure 7-25: Removing Battery Packs

Fuel Cells

A relatively new power source for portable computers and hand-held devices is the **fuel cell**. Fuel cells are power-generating technologies that use electrochemical reactions between hydrogen and oxygen to produce electrical power. One fuel cell technology does this using hydrogen extracted from methanol whereas the other major fuel cell technology employs pure hydrogen. In both cases, the reaction between hydrogen and oxygen produces water vapor, heat, and electrical power.

fuel cell

Fuel cells small enough to be used with mobile computing systems are still primarily in the development stage, although some companies have produced prototypes already. Mobile computer manufacturers plan to routinely include fuel cells in their mobile products, including notebook PCs, digital still cameras, PDAs, and cell phones, by 2004. These units will act as small wireless rechargers for the high-density lithium batteries already being used in notebook computers and PDAs. Current fuel cell designs in this category have about ten times the energy capacity of a similar-size typical portable computer battery.

Power Consumption

standby mode

suspend mode

As mentioned earlier, power consumption consideration has been built into most devices intended for use with portable computers. Many of the Pentium chipsets provide a **standby mode** that turns off selected components, such as the hard drive and display, until a system event, such as a keyboard entry or a mouse movement, occurs. An additional power-saving condition called **suspend mode** places the system in a shutdown condition except for its memory units.

hibernate mode

An additional power-saving mode, known as **hibernate mode**, writes the contents of RAM memory to a hard drive file and completely shuts the system down. When the system is restarted, the feature reads the hibernate file back into memory and normal operation is restarted at the place it left off.

Power Management

Each sector of the portable computer market has worked to reduce power consumption levels, including software suppliers. Advanced operating systems include power management features that monitor the system's operation and turn off some higher-power-consumption items when they are not in use (Standby mode), and will switch the system into a low-power-consumption **sleep mode** (Suspend mode) if inactivity continues.

sleep mode

Advanced Power Management (APM)

green mode

These modes are defined by a Microsoft/IBM standard called the **Advanced Power Management (APM)** standard. The hardware producers refer to this condition as a **green mode**. The standard is actually implemented through the cooperation of the system's chipset devices and the operating system. Control of the APM system is provided through the BIOS' CMOS Setup utility, as described in Chapter 2—*Advanced System Boards*.

Most newer portable computers possess a number of automatic power-saving features to maximize battery life. Some can be controlled through the Power menu of the Advanced CMOS Setup utility. If the Hard Disk Timeout value is set to 3 minutes, the Standby Timeout to 5 minutes, and the Auto Suspend value to 10 minutes, the following activities will occur:

1. The hard disk will spin down after 3 minutes of inactivity.

2. After 2 additional minutes of inactivity, the system will enter the standby mode.

3. After 10 additional inactive minutes, the system will store the hibernation file on the hard drive and enter suspend mode.

The suspend mode can also be entered by pressing a key combination for those times when the user must step away from the computer for a few minutes, but does not want to shut down. The POWER.EXE command must be loaded in a Device= line of the CONFIG.SYS file for APM to work properly under DOS 6.x or Windows 3.x. This command is not needed to run APM in Windows 9x.

When the system suspends operation, the following events take place:

- The video screen is turned off.
- The CPU, DMA, clocks, and math coprocessor are powered down.
- All controllable peripheral devices are shut down.

The amount of time the unit can remain in suspend mode is determined by the remaining amount of battery power. For this reason, data should be saved to the hard drive before voluntarily going to suspend mode. Pressing the computer's power button will return the system to its previous operational point.

External Drive Units

The first laptops and notebooks incorporated the traditional single floppy drive and single hard drive concept that was typical in most desktop units. However, as CD-ROM drives and discs became the norm for new operating systems and software packages, a problem arose. There is simply not enough room in most notebook computers for three normal-size drive units. Even with reduced size drives, the size limitations of most portables require that one of the three major drives be external.

External FDDs

Typically, the first item to be left out of a new notebook design is the internal floppy drive. So much of the latest software is distributed on CD-ROM that CD-ROM drives now have preference in newer designs. Even so, there are still so many applications that use floppies that an external FDD is almost always an add-on option for a new notebook. There continue to be software components, such as OEM device drivers and utilities that are distributed on floppy disks. Likewise, many users have volumes of cherished data stored on floppies. In these cases, having an external floppy drive for a portable computer makes sense.

The external floppy comes as a complete unit with an external housing and a signal cable. As with other external devices, it requires an independent power source, such as an ac adapter pack. The external floppy drive's signal cable generally connects to a special FDD connector, such as the one shown in Figure 7-26.

Figure 7-26: An External Floppy Drive

External CD-ROM and DVD Drives

Prior to the CD-ROM drive becoming an accepted part of the notebook PC, some manufacturers produced external CD-ROM drives for use with these machines. Now, external DVD drives have become popular add-ons for notebook computers. External CD-ROM drives typically connect to a SCSI host adapter, or to an enhanced parallel port on the host computer. The latter connection requires a fully functional bi-directional parallel port and a special software device driver to operate properly.

Figure 7-27 illustrates the installation of an external SCSI CD-ROM drive. Since the drive is external, connecting the CD-ROM unit to the system usually involves simply connecting a couple of cables together. First, connect the CD-ROM's power supply to the external drive unit. Before making this connection, verify that the power switch, or power supply, is turned off. Connect the signal cable to the computer. Finally, connect the opposite end of the cable to the external CD-ROM unit. Complete the installation by installing the CD-ROM driver software on the system's hard-disk drive.

Figure 7-27: Installing an External CD-ROM Drive

Docking Stations

docking station

docking port

A **docking station**, or **docking port**, is a specialized structure that allows the notebook unit to be inserted into it. Once the notebook is inside, the docking port extends its expansion bus so that it can be used with a collection of desktop devices, such as an ac power source, a full-sized keyboard and CRT monitor, as well as modems, mice, and standard PC port connectors. A typical docking station is depicted in Figure 7-28.

Figure 7-28:
A Docking Station

The notebook and the docking station communicate with each other through a special docking port connector in the rear of the notebook. When the notebook is inserted into the docking station, the extension bus in the docking station plugs into the expansion connector in the notebook. Most docking stations provide standard PC expansion slots so that non-notebook peripheral devices, such as network adapters and sound cards, can be used with the system.

When the notebook is in the docking station, its normal I/O devices (keyboard, display, and pointing device) are disabled and the docking station's peripherals take over.

For the most part, docking stations are proprietary to the portable they were designed to work with. The docking port connection in the docking station must correctly align with the connector in the notebook. The notebook unit must also fit correctly within the docking station opening. Since there are no standards for these systems, the chances of two different manufacturers locating the connectors in the same places and/or designing the same case outline are very remote.

Port Replicators

Many notebook computer manufacturers offer devices similar to docking stations that are called **port replicators**. These devices plug into the notebook computer and contain common PC ports, such as serial and parallel ports. The purpose of these devices is to enable users to attach portable computers to standard, non-portable devices such as printers and monitors.

port replicators

Notebook manufacturers typically offer port replicators as additional proprietary options for their computers. Although these systems are similar to docking stations, they do not provide the additional expansion slots for adding adapter cards and disk drives found in docking stations.

TROUBLESHOOTING PORTABLE SYSTEMS

From a service point of view, the greatest drawback of portable computers is that conventions and compatibility disappear. The continued minimization of the system comes at a cost. Most notably, the number of I/O ports, memory, and disk drive expansion capabilities are limited. In addition, there is no chance to use common, full-sized adapter cards that are inexpensive and easy to find.

One of the biggest problems for portable computers is heat buildup inside the case. Since conventional power supplies (and their fans) are not included in portable units, separate fans must be designed into portables to carry the heat out of the unit. The closeness of the portable's components and the small amount of free air space inside their cases also adds to heat-related design problems.

The internal PC boards of the portable computer are designed to fit around the nuances of the portable case and its components, rather than to match a standard design with standard spacing and connections. Therefore, interchangeability of parts with other machines or makers goes by the wayside. The only source of most portable computer parts, with the exception of PC cards and disk drive units, is the original manufacturer. Even the battery case may be proprietary. If the battery dies, you must hope that the original maker has a supply of that particular model.

PULL UP
FROM THESE
CORNERS

REMOVE
THE SCREWS

Figure 7-29: Disassembling a Notebook Computer

Access to the notebook's internal components is normally challenging. Each case design has different methods for assembly and disassembly of the unit. Even the simplest upgrade task can be difficult with a notebook computer. Although adding RAM and options to desktop and tower units is a relatively easy and straightforward process, the same tasks in notebook computers can be difficult.

In some notebooks, it is necessary to disassemble the two halves of the case and remove the keyboard in order to add RAM modules to the system. In other portables, the hinged display unit must be removed to disassemble the unit. Once inside the notebook you may find that several of the components are hidden behind other units. Figure 7-29 demonstrates a relatively simple disassembly process for a notebook unit.

In this example, a panel in front of the keyboard can be removed to gain access to the notebook's internal user-serviceable components. Four screws along the front edge of the unit's lower body must be removed. Afterward, the LCD panel is opened and the front panel of the notebook's chassis is pulled up and away to expose a portion of the unit's interior.

Troubleshooting PCMCIA

To overcome the shortfalls of miniaturization, a wide variety of specialty items aimed at the portable computer market have emerged. One of the mainstays of portable computer products is the credit card–like PCMCIA cards described in Chapter 3. The process for troubleshooting PC Cards is nearly identical to troubleshooting other I/O adapter cards.

PCMCIA cards can be plugged into the system at any time and the system should recognize them. In most cases, Windows 9x/Me and Windows 2000/XP have a copy of the necessary driver software for the PCMCIA adapter being installed and will install it automatically when it detects the adapter. Most Windows operating system versions will display messages telling you that they are installing the drivers required. However, Windows 2000 and Windows XP just install the drivers without a notice.

In cases where the operating system does not have the necessary driver software, it will display a prompt asking the user for a path to the location where the driver can be loaded, when it detects the adapter. PCMCIA manufacturers typically supply drivers for various operating systems on a floppy disk or a CD that comes with the adapter.

To verify that the PC Card device is working, access the Device Manager under the Windows Control Panel's System applet. If there is a problem with the PC Card device it will appear in the Device Manager. If the adapter's icon shows an exclamation mark on a yellow background, the card is not functioning properly. Turn the system off and reinsert the device into a different PCMCIA slot. If the same problem appears, there are three possible causes — the card may be faulty, the PC card controller in the PC may be faulty, or the operating system may not support the device in question.

If the Windows Device Manager displays the PCMCIA socket but no name for the card, then the card insertion has been recognized, but the socket could not read the device's configuration information from the card. This indicates that there is a problem with the PCMCIA socket installation. To correct this problem, remove the PCMCIA socket listing from the device manager, reboot the computer, and allow the Windows PnP process to detect the socket and install the appropriate driver for it. If the names of the PCMCIA cards do not appear after the restart, then the reinstallation process was not successful. Therefore, the PCMCIA socket you are using is not supported by the operating system version.

If the names of other PCMCIA cards do appear in the Device Manager, but the card in questions does not, it is likely that the card has been damaged. To test the PC Card device, insert a different PC Card device of any type into the slot. If the other card works, it is very likely that the card in question has been damaged.

Troubleshooting Portable Unique Storage

As with other PCMCIA devices, PC Card hard drives are self contained. Plug them into the PCMCIA slot and the system should detect them (they are hot swappable). If the system does not detect the PC Card hard drive, use the troubleshooting steps described for other PCMCIA devices.

Troubleshooting Batteries

If you turn your portable computer on and nothing happens, the first things to check out include the power supply and the battery. If the power supply is plugged in, the computer should start up when the On/Off switch is engaged. However, if the computer is running on battery power and the system will not start up, the battery could be bad or need to be charged up.

Verify that the battery doesn't need a recharge by trying to start the system with the ac power adapter plugged in. Check the power indicator in the system display panel. If it is on, then power is being supplied to the portable. If the indicator is not on, make sure that the power cord is securely connected to a live power source. Check all the power connections to make sure that the AC adapter jack is securely connected to the AC adapter port. If the portable still won't start up, you must troubleshoot the system board. If the system runs from the ac adapter, then the battery needs to be recharged or replaced.

While a dead system is a classic battery/power supply problem, there are several other battery-related problems that you may encounter with portable computers. These include problems that present the following types of symptoms:

- Receiving warning messages about the battery not charging

- Intermittent system shutdowns when operating with only on the battery

- The computer does not recognize its network connection when operating with only the battery

- The computer and input devices are slow when operating with only the battery

- The computer loses the time and date information when operating on battery power

A loose or improperly installed battery can cause these problems. They can also appear when the battery is toward the end of its charge/recharge cycle. Check the installation and attempt to recharge the battery using the portable computer's ac adapter.

The actual life of a laptop computer battery varies from just under one hour to over two hours in each sitting. If you are experiencing battery life cycles that are significantly shorter than this (i.e., 10 to 15 minutes), you may have a problem referred to as battery memory. Battery memory is a condition that occurs with some types of batteries where the battery becomes internally conditioned to run for less time than its designed capacity (i.e., if you routinely operate the computer using the battery for an hour and then plug it back into an ac source, the battery can become conditioned to only run for that amount of time).

To correct battery memory problems, you must fully discharge the battery and then recharge it. To accomplish this, turn the portable's Power Management feature off by accessing the Power Management icon in the Windows Control Panel. Then restart the computer and access the CMOS Setup utility during bootup. Disenable the power management functions in the CMOS settings. Finally, start the portable computer using only the battery and allow it to run until it completely discharges the battery and quits. Then recharge the battery for at least 12 hours. Repeat this process several times, watching for consistently increasing operating times.

Troubleshooting Docking Stations/Port Replicators

Most docking stations offer an internal power supply that can operate the portable and its peripheral attachments. They typically include an external parallel port for printers, a serial port for serial devices (mice and modems), USB ports, external VGA/DVI video and full-size keyboard connections, and audio connections for external speakers. In addition, the docking station can host several types of external storage devices including full-sized FDD/HDD/CD-ROM/DVD drives. Docking stations may also include 1 or 2 PCI slots that allow full-sized desktop adapter cards (SCSI or specialized video or LAN card) to be added to the system when it is docked. A docking station may also provide multiple PCMCIA slots that add to the existing PC Card capabilities of the portable it is supporting.

For the most part, these connections are simply physical extensions of the ports provided by the portable. Therefore, if the port works on the portable and doesn't when connection is made through the docking station, then there is generally something wrong with the docking station/port replicator. However, many portable computers employ special keystroke combinations (Fn + some other key) to activate external devices such as video display monitors or full-size keyboards.

For example, some portables will detect that the external video display has been attached. Others will use an Fn key combination to switch the display to the external monitor only, and then use another Fn key combination to send the display to both the LCD panel and the external display. If a peripheral device is not working, one of the first steps to take is to refer to the portable's documentation to ensure that the external device has been activated.

For audio problems, make sure the speakers are connected to the correct RCA mini-jacks (not the Line-in or microphone jacks). Check the documentation to make sure the sound output has not been muted by using an Fn key combination.

Under Windows operating systems, the hardware profile information for the portable computer can be configured differently for docked and undocked situations. When the computer is docked and turned on, its configuration is reset and the *Eject PC* option will appear on the Start menu. However, when the computer is not docked, the *Eject PC* option is automatically removed from the Start menu.

The Windows XP Professional operating system uses hardware profiles to determine which drivers to load when the system hardware changes (docked or undocked). It uses the Docked Profile to load drivers when the portable computer is docked and the Undocked Profile when the computer starts up without the docking station. These hardware profiles are created by the Windows XP operating system when the computer is docked and undocked if the system is PnP compliant. If a portable is not PnP-compliant, you must manually configure the profile by enabling and disabling various devices present when docked and undocked.

The first check to make when you encounter docking station/port replicator problems is the same as with any other electronic device—check the power cord and docking power supply. Next, verify that the portable has been properly inserted into the docking station or port replicator.

If a single connection does not work, bypass the docking station/replicater and try to operate the peripheral directly with the portable unit. Check the power supply for both the docking station and the peripheral device and make sure that both are turned on. Reboot the portable while it is attached to the docking station. Then check any signal cables between the docking station and the peripheral.

If the PS/2 mouse connection does not work, verify that it has not been installed in the PS/2 keyboard connector by mistake. Make sure the mouse port is enabled in the CMOS Setup utility. Likewise, if you are using a serial mouse, make sure the port is enabled in CMOS and that it is connected to the correct port. Check the serial port's configuration settings to verify that a proper device driver has been installed for the serial mouse. If the portable's touch pad works but the external mouse does not, check the documentation for an Fn key combination requirement for the mouse.

CHAPTER SUMMARY

This chapter has dealt expressly with aspects of portable computer systems. It has documented how portable units differ from conventional personal computer units. After completing the chapter, you should be able to identify the components of portable systems and describe how they differ from typical desktop components. You should also be able to identify their unique problems.

At this point, review the objectives listed at the beginning of the chapter to be certain that you understand and can perform each item listed there.

KEY POINTS REVIEW

The focus of this chapter has been portable computer systems. Review the following key points before moving into the Review and Exam Questions sections to make sure you are comfortable with each point. Afterward, answer the Review Questions that follow to verify your knowledge of the information.

- Continued advancements in IC and peripheral technology allowed the PC's circuitry to be reduced. This allowed portable sizes to be reduced further so that they could achieve sizes of 8.75"d x 11"w x 2.25"h and smaller. Portables in this size range are referred to as notebook computers. The weight of a typical notebook dropped down to 5 or 6 pounds.

- However, the market was revived by the introduction of palmtops known as Personal Digital Assistants (PDAs). These handheld devices use a special stylus, referred to as a pen, to input data and selections instead of a keyboard or mouse. Basically the PDA is an electronic time management system that may also include computer applications such as word processors, spreadsheets, and databases.

- The drawback of portable computers from a service point of view is that conventions and compatibility disappear. Therefore, interchangeability of parts with other machines or makers goes by the wayside.

- One of the biggest problems for portable computers is heat buildup inside the case. Since conventional power supplies (and their fans) are not included in portable units, separate fans must be designed into portables to carry the heat out of the unit. The closeness of the portable's components and the small amount of free air space inside its case also adds to heat-related design problems.

- Portable computers have two ideal characteristics: They are compact and light weight. Portable computer designers work constantly to decrease the size and power consumption of all the computer's components. Special low-power consumption ICs and disk drives have been developed to extend battery life.

- The I/O ports included in most notebook computers consist of a single parallel port, a single serial port, an external VGA monitor connector, an external keyboard connector, and a docking port expansion bus. Some models with a second serial port connector can be found, but they are not common.

- It is not a common practice for notebook and other portable computer manufacturers to use traditional SIMM and DIMM modules in their designs. Instead, these types of computers routinely use the smaller SODIMMs and MicroDIMMs form factor memory modules. The key to upgrading or replacing internal RAM in a portable computer can be found in its documentation. Only memory modules recommended by the portable manufacturer should be installed, and only in the configurations suggested.

- The most common flat-panel displays used with portable PC's are Liquid Crystal Displays (LCDs). They are relatively thin, flat, and lightweight, and require very little power to operate. In addition to reduced weight and improved portability, these displays offer better reliability and longer life than CRT units.

- The most widely used notebook keyboard is the 84-key version. Its keys are slightly smaller and shorter than those found in full-size keyboards. A number of keys or key functions may be combined or deleted from a notebook keyboard.

- Three types of PCMCIA adapters currently exist. The PCMCIA Type I cards, introduced in 1990, are 3.3 mm thick and work as memory expansion units. In 1991, the PCMCIA Type II cards were introduced. They are 5 mm thick and support virtually any traditional expansion function, except removable hard drive units. Type II slots are backward compatible so that Type I cards will work in them. Currently, PCMCIA Type III cards are being produced. These cards are 10.5 mm thick and are intended primarily for use with removable hard drives. Both Type I and Type II cards can be used in a Type III slot.

- The PCMCIA bus was developed to accommodate the space conscious notebook and sub-notebook computer market.

- Notebook computer designers work constantly to decrease the size and power consumption of the computer's components.

- The drawback of portable computers from a service point of view is that conventions and compatibility disappear. Therefore, interchangeability of parts with other machines or makers goes by the wayside.

REVIEW QUESTIONS

The following questions test your knowledge of the material presented in this chapter.

1. How are mobile processors optimized for use in portable units?

2. List three considerations that must be taken into account when replacing disk drives in a portable.

3. What is the purpose of a docking station?

4. List three power management modes and describe how they are different.

5. What is the purpose of the Fn key on a portable computer keyboard?

6. How are notebook and laptop computers different?

7. Where is the network adapter normally located in a portable computer?

8. Describe some of the major maintenance problems that are associated with notebook computers.

9. How are active and passive matrix LCD displays different?

10. What type of device is a touch pad?

11. Describe two typical connection methods for adding an external CD-ROM drive to a portable system.

12. Which type of LCD panel uses less power than the others?

13. Describe two methods of connecting a portable computer to a network.

14. Describe what a port replicator does.

15. What functions do socket services provide for PC Cards in a notebook computer?

EXAM QUESTIONS

1. What form factor does a notebook computer's system board conform to?
   a. AT
   b. Baby AT
   c. ATX
   d. None

2. A Type I PCMCIA card is _____ thick.
   a. 3.3 mm
   b. 5.0 mm
   c. 7.5 mm
   d. 10.5 mm

3. A Type II PCMCIA card is _____ thick.
   a. 3.3 mm
   b. 5.0 mm
   c. 7.5 mm
   d. 10.5 mm

4. A Type III PCMCIA card is _____ thick.
   a. 3.3 mm
   b. 5.0 mm
   c. 7.5 mm
   d. 10.5 mm

5. Where would you usually expect to find a PCMCIA card?
   a. In an ISA expansion slot
   b. In a serial port
   c. In a notebook computer
   d. In an MCA expansion slot

6. Which of the following functions can be served by a Type I PCMCIA card?
   a. Memory expansion functions
   b. Serial port functions
   c. Parallel port functions
   d. Game port functions

7. Which of the following functions cannot be performed with a Type II PCMCIA card?
   a. Memory expansion functions
   b. Removable hard drive functions
   c. Serial port functions
   d. Parallel port functions

8. Select the battery technology that would not likely be used to provide power to a notebook computer.
   a. Nickel Metal-Hydride
   b. Lithium-Ion
   c. Nickel Cadmium
   d. Lithium-Ion Polymer

9. What sort of power source uses electrochemical reactions between hydrogen and oxygen to produce electrical power?
   a. Lithium batteries
   b. NiCad batteries
   c. Solar Power batteries
   d. Fuel cells

10. Which of the following items cannot be used with portable computer systems?
    a. Full-size keyboards
    b. VGA monitors
    c. 3-button mice
    d. PCI modem

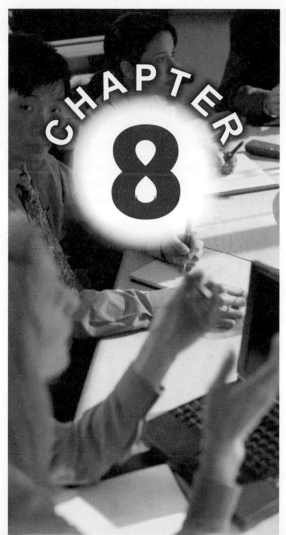

CHAPTER
8

OPERATING SYSTEM FUNDAMENTALS

OBJECTIVES

OBJECTIVES

Upon completion of this chapter and its related lab procedures you will be able to perform the following tasks:

1. Describe the basic functions of an operating system.

2. Differentiate between single-process and multiple-process systems.

3. Differentiate between multiuser, multitasking, and multiprocessor operations.

4. Identify FAT-based operating system functions, structures, and major system files.

5. Describe procedures for locating, accessing, and retrieving information in a command-line environment.

6. Identify basic concepts and procedures for creating and managing files and directories in an FAT-based system.

7. List the events that occur during the bootup process.

8. Explain the basic organization of a FAT-based disk.

9. Describe the operation of the Microsoft command line.

10. Identify and use disk-level commands.

11. Create, delete, and navigate through various directories.

12. Discuss naming conventions as they apply to various types of files.

13. Find, copy, rename, delete, and move files.

14. Manipulate file attributes from the Microsoft command line.

15. Describe the methods used to bypass and correct inoperable MS-DOS startup sequences.

16. Describe the sequence of events associated with the MS-DOS configuration during bootup.

17. Describe the different types of DOS memory.

18. Use the AUTOEXEC.BAT and CONFIG.SYS files to optimize system performance.

19. Load driver software for any devices added to the system.

OPERATING SYSTEM FUNDAMENTALS

INTRODUCTION

The general responsibilities of an operating system were presented in Chapter 1. This chapter will build on that description by presenting concepts that are fundamental to all operating systems.

Every portion of the computer system must be controlled and coordinated so that the millions of operations that occur every second are carried out correctly and on time. In addition, it is the job of the operating system to make the complexity of the personal computer as invisible as possible to the user.

Operating systems are programs designed to control the operation of a computer system. As a group, they are easily some of the most complex programs devised. Likewise, the operating system acts as an intermediary between software applications nearly as complex, and the hardware they run on. Finally, the operating system accepts commands from the computer user, and carries them out to perform some desired operation.

OPERATING SYSTEM BASICS

> Literally thousands of different operating systems are in use with microcomputers. The complexity of each operating system typically depends on the complexity of the application the microcomputer is designed to fill.

There are two basic types of operating systems used with personal computers:

- **single-process systems** — Systems that can work on only one task at one time

- **multiple-process systems** — Systems that can work on several tasks at one time

In a single-process system, the operating system works with a single task only. These operating systems can operate in **batch mode** or **interactive mode**. In batch mode, the operating system runs one program until it is finished. In interactive mode, the operation of the program can be modified by input from external sources, such as sensors, or a user interface device.

single-process
systems

multiple-process
systems

batch mode

interactive mode

Multiple-process operations can be organized in three different ways:

multiuser

multitasking

multiprocessor

threads

tasks

- **multiuser** – Systems that accommodate more than one user at once

- **multitasking** – Systems that work on more than one task at a time

- **multiprocessor** – Systems that divide the processing load into **threads** and distribute them between different processors

In multiuser and multitasking operations, the appearance of simultaneous operation is accomplished by switching between different **tasks** in a predetermined order.

The multiuser system switches between different users at multiple locations, whereas multitasking systems switch between different applications at a single location. In the large, multiple-user system, the operating system is likely to be stored on disk and have sections loaded into RAM when needed. This type of operating system must control several pieces of hardware, manage files created and used by various users, provide security for each user's information, and manage communications between different stations. The operating system is also responsible for presenting each station with a user interface that can accept commands and data from the user. This interface can be a command-line interpreter or a Graphical User Interface (GUI).

parallel processing

In a multiprocessor operating system, tasks are divided among multiple microprocessors. This type of operation is referred to as **parallel processing**. All three types of multiple-process operating systems are described in Figure 8-1.

Figure 8-1:
Multiple-Process
Operating Systems

While simple microcomputers store the entire operating system in ROM, most microcomputers use a **bootstrapping** process to load the operating system into RAM. Bootstrapping describes an arrangement where the operating system is loaded into memory by a smaller program called the **bootstrap loader**. The operating system can be loaded from a ROM chip, a floppy disk, a hard-disk drive, or another computer. The term bootstrap refers to the system pulling itself up by its own bootstraps, because in loading the more-powerful operating system files from the disk it increases its on-board intelligence considerably. In personal computers, the bootstrap operation is one of the functions of the ROM BIOS.

BOOTING THE OPERATING SYSTEM

The bootstrap process is primarily used in disk drive−based systems to load an operating system to assume control of the system. **MS-DOS** was the original disk operating system for IBM PC-compatible computers. In its day, it was easily the most popular operating system in the world. As with any other operating system, its function is to oversee operation of the system by providing support for executing programs, controlling I/O devices, handling errors, and providing the user interface.

MS-DOS was a disk-based, single-user, single-task operating system that featured Microsoft's original FAT-based disk management system. This system continues as the basis from which the Windows 9x/Me operating systems derive their underlying bootup, command-line operations, and file management systems. Therefore the remainder of the chapter will use these features of the Microsoft FAT-based system to describe basic operating system architecture and operation.

The Hardware Startup Process

The system startup sequence was described briefly in Chapter 1. This is basically a hardware-related operation until the bootstrap process begins. At this point, the hardware begins looking for an operating system to take over control of the hardware to increase its functionality. This process represents the starting point of everything related to operating systems. With the exception of some hardware configuration information that is collected during the initialization phase of the startup process and is eventually passed to the operating system, modern operating systems do not care what goes on prior to the bootup process. As a matter of fact, until the bootstrap process occurs the system runs exactly the same no matter which operating system may eventually be started to take over control of the system.

At this point, we will review the basic hardware startup sequence. The key components and events of the PC-compatible hardware system are:

- *System Startup or Reset* − When the system is started up or reset, the microprocessor is reset so that it begins taking instructions from a specified location in the ROM BIOS address range to test and initialize the system for operation.

- *POST* — The POST is actually a series of tests that are performed each time the system is turned on. The different tests check the operation of the microprocessor, the keyboard, the video display, the floppy- and hard-disk drive units, as well as both the RAM and ROM memory units.

  - *Initial POST Checks* — The first instruction that the microprocessor executes causes it to jump to the POST test, where it performs standard tests such as the ROM BIOS **checksum** test (that verifies that the BIOS program is accurate), the system's various **DRAM tests** (that verify the bits of the memory), as well as a test of the system's CMOS RAM (to make certain that its contents have not changed due to a battery failure). During the memory tests, the POST displays a running memory count to show that it is testing and verifying the individual memory locations.

During these tests, the BIOS determines whether the system is being started from an off condition, or being reset from some other state. When the system is started from an off condition, a cold boot is performed. However, simultaneously pressing the CTRL, ALT, and DEL keys while the system is in operation will generate a reset signal in the system and cause it to perform a shortened bootup routine. This operation is referred to as a **warm boot**, and allows the system to be shut down and restarted without turning it off. This function also allows the computer's operation to be switched to another operating system.

- *System Initialization* — During this part of the program, startup values stored in the ROM BIOS IC are moved into the system's programmable devices to make them functional. These include the IRQ and DMA channel configurations along with the standard I/O addresses that make the system PC-compatible.

  - *Plug-and-Play Configuration* — During the initialization process, the **Plug and Play (PnP)** BIOS checks the devices installed in the expansion slots to see what types they are, how they are configured, and which slots they are in. It then assigns each adapter a **software handle** (**name**) and stores its name and configuration information in a RAM table. Next, the BIOS performs an enumeration process to verify the adapter information against the system's basic configuration for **resource conflicts**. If no conflicts are detected, all the devices required for bootup will be activated.

  - *CMOS Setup Checks* — During the initialization process, the BIOS checks the battery-powered CMOS RAM configuration storage area to determine what types of options are installed in the system. In PnP systems these settings are established by the PnP process's autodetect functions. However, the CMOS settings can be entered for manual configuration during this period.

- *Additional POST Checks* — After the final memory test and basic system configuration steps have been performed, the remaining I/O devices and adapters are tested.

  - *BIOS Extensions* — After the POST and initialization processes have been completed, the BIOS checks the area of memory between C0000 and DFFFF for **BIOS extension** programs. IBM system designers created this memory area so that new or nonstandard BIOS routines could be added to the basic BIOS structure. BIOS extensions are created in 512-byte blocks that must begin at a 2 kB marker (e.g., **C8000**, C8200, C8400, **C8800**, etc.), as illustrated in Figure 8-2. These extended firmware routines match software commands from the system to the hardware they support. Therefore, the software running on the system does not have to be directly compatible with the hardware.

checksum

DRAM tests

warm boot

Plug and Play (PnP)

software handle (name)

resource conflicts

BIOS extension

C8000h

C8800h

**Figure 8-2:
BIOS Extension
Blocks**

Advanced video cards contain **Video BIOS** code, either in a ROM IC or built directly into the video controller ASIC. The IBM EGA and VGA standards allow for on-board ROM that uses addresses between C0000 and C7FFF. Likewise, different types of HDD controller cards contain a BIOS extension IC that uses the address space between C8000 and C9FFF. Some current HDD controllers, such as SCSI adapters, reserve memory blocks between C8000 and CBFFF.

Video BIOS

Another type of device that commonly uses the C000-D000 blocks are network adapter cards. These cards enable the computer to be connected to other computers in the local area. The BIOS extension code on a network card may contain an **Initial Program Load** (IPL) routine that will cause the local computer to load up and operate with an operating system from a remote computer. This is the principle behind diskless workstations that boot up to remote computers and have no local disk drives.

Initial Program Load (IPL)

At the successful completion of these tests, most systems produce a single beep tone through the system speaker to announce the end of the hardware portion (POST/Initialization) phase of the startup process and the beginning of the software portion (bootup) of the startup sequence.

FAT System Bootup

A portion of the Operating System technologies objective 1.2 states that the test taker should be able to identify the names, locations, purposes, and contents of major system files.

Content may include the following:

- Windows 9x–specific files
- IO.SYS
- MSDOS.SYS
- AUTOEXEC.BAT
- COMMAND.COM
- CONFIG.SYS
- HIMEM.SYS

- EMM386.exe
- WIN.COM
- SYSTEM.INI
- WIN.INI
- Registry data files
    - SYSTEM.DAT
    - USER.DAT

After the POST and initialization phases have been completed, the BIOS will begin the process of booting up to the operating system. As has already been mentioned, this operation can occur on a local computer through its disk drives, or it can be performed from a remote computer across a network. A simple, single-operating system, single-disk bootup process is described in Figure 8-3. As you can see, it is a multiple-access operation that uses two different bootstrap routines to locate and load two different boot records.

Figure 8-3: The Bootstrap Operation

bootup

Master Boot Record (MBR)

boot sector

Starting the Bootup Process — The **bootup** process starts when the BIOS begins looking through the system for a **Master Boot Record** (**MBR**). This record can reside on drive A: or C:, or at any other location.

The very first section on any logical disk is called the **boot sector**. This section contains information about how the disk is organized. It may also contain the small optional master boot record that can access a larger, more powerful bootstrap loader program located on the drive.

bootable disk

system disk

data disk

Supplemental disk

In most systems, the master boot record is found at sector-1, head-0, and track-0 of the first logical hard drive. Some texts may refer to the first sector as Sector zero, in keeping with the idea that the first of anything in a digital system is 0. If the disk possesses a master boot record, it can boot up the hardware system to the operating system. The disk is then referred to as a **bootable disk**, or a **system disk**. If not, the disk is simply a **data disk** that can be used for storing information.

The usage of the term "system disk" has changed somewhat over time. In the old days, when MS-DOS came on two disks labeled "System disk" and "**Supplemental disk**," the System disk was the one that contained the files necessary to boot the system. Now, the term is used generally to specify any floppy disk that has a master boot record so that it can boot the system — regardless of the type of operating system it carries.

primary bootstrap loader

Traditionally, BIOS programs would search for the master boot record in floppy-disk drive A: first. If a bootable disk was found in the floppy-disk drive, the BIOS would execute the **primary bootstrap loader** routine to move the master boot record into RAM and then begin the process of loading the operating system. In the original IBM PC, if the boot record was not located on the floppy, the BIOS routine turned over control to a BASIC program located in the PC's ROM BIOS IC.

In the PC-XT, the BIOS looked first in the floppy drive, or drives, and then in the hard-disk drive. If neither location contained the boot record, the system loaded up the ROM BASIC program. In clone systems, there was no ROM BIOS present to default to when no boot record was found. If the BIOS did not locate the boot record in the floppy or hard drive, it simply displayed a **Non-System Disk or Disk Error**, or **ROM BASIC Interpreter Not Found** message on the screen.

In newer systems, the order in which the BIOS searches through the system drives for the boot record is governed by information stored in the system's CMOS configuration RAM. The order can be set to check the floppy drive first and then the hard drive, or to check the hard drive first, or to check the hard drive only. It can also be set to check the CD-ROM drive for a bootable disc.

In a networked system, a bootstrap loader routine can also be located in the ROM extension of a network card as described earlier. When the system checks the BIOS extensions, the bootstrap routine redirects the bootup process to look for a boot record on the disk drive of another computer. Any boot record on the local drive will be bypassed.

The next BIOS instruction executes a *Disk Drive Interrupt Service Routine* to activate the Primary Bootstrap Loader program. This routine searches for the master boot record in the first sector of the floppy and hard disks. When it locates the master boot record, it loads it into system RAM to be executed. This step marks the end of the BIOS routine.

The master boot record contains the **secondary bootstrap loader**, also called the **operating system loader**. This routine looks for an **operating system boot record**, typically located on the disk. When it finds it, it loads the bigger boot record into RAM and begins executing it.

This boot record brings special operating system files into memory so that they can control the operation of the system (i.e., the operating system). In the case of Microsoft FAT-based operating systems, the special files in the OS boot record are the **IO.SYS** and **MSDOS.SYS** files.

The operating system loader looks for a command processor file. The command processor can belong to any operating system, such as Microsoft MS-DOS, UNIX, IBM PC-DOS, Novell NetWare, and so forth. The default command processor for DOS is a system file called **COMMAND.COM**. This file interprets the input entered at the DOS prompt. When the bootstrap program finds the command processor, it moves it into system RAM along with the operating system support files. In DOS systems, the command processor provides the basic user interface, called the **command line**.

In the original PC-DOS from IBM, the system files were titled IBMBIO.COM, IBMDOS.COM, and COMMAND.COM. The three system files must be found in the root directory (the starting point for any disk-based operations) in order to successfully boot the FAT-based operating system. The total bootup process is shown in Figure 8-4.

Non-System Disk or Disk Error

ROM BASIC Interpreter Not Found

secondary bootstrap loader

operating system loader

operating system boot record

IO.SYS

MSDOS.SYS

COMMAND.COM

command line

**Figure 8-4: The
Bootup Process**

If the system has performed a standard FAT bootup without any modifications, it should print Date and Time prompts on the monitor screen, followed by the DOS **command-line prompt** (A:\ or C:\). The prompt indicates that the operating system is functional and the currently active drive is the A: floppy drive or the C: hard drive.

Now the operating system will control the movement of data and overall operation of the system. In a command line–based system, the operating system waits for the user to do something, such as enter commands and instructions that will run application programs from the other two software categories. Up to this point, the user hasn't had anything to do with the operation of the system. This is why operating system software is referred to as system software.

FAT Disk Files

As indicated in the previous section, the main portions of Microsoft's FAT-based operating systems are the IO.SYS, MSDOS.SYS, and COMMAND.COM files. IO.SYS and MSDOS.SYS are special **hidden system files** that do not show up in a normal directory listing.

The IO.SYS file moves the system's basic I/O functions into memory and then implements the operating system's default control programs, referred to as **device drivers**, for various hardware components. These include:

- the boot disk drive

- the console display and keyboard

- the system's time-of-day clock

- the parallel and serial communications port

Conversely, the MSDOS.SYS file provides default support features for software applications. These features include:

- memory management

- character input and output

- real-time clock access

- file and record management

- execution of other programs

There is a little known MS-DOS system requirement that the MSDOS.SYS file must maintain a size in excess of 1 kB.

The COMMAND.COM command interpreter contains the operating system's most frequently used commands. When a DOS command is entered at the DOS prompt, the COMMAND.COM program examines it to see if it is an **internal DOS command**, or an **external DOS command**. Internal commands are understood directly by COMMAND.COM, while external commands are stored in a directory called DOS. If it is one of the internal commands, the COMMAND.COM file can execute it immediately. If not, COMMAND.COM looks in the \DOS directory for the command program.

When MS-DOS runs an application, COMMAND.COM finds the program, loads it into memory, and then gives it control of the system. When the program is shut down, it passes control back to the command interpreter. The remainder of the operating system consists of utility programs to carry out DOS operations such as formatting disks (Format), printing files (Print), and copying files (XCOPY).

MS-DOS Configuration Files

In the MS-DOS operating systems, two special configuration files, called CONFIG.SYS and AUTOEXEC.BAT, were included in the startup process. These programs were used to optimize the system for operations in particular functions, or with different options.

As the FAT-based system moves through the bootup procedure, the BIOS checks in the root directory of the boot disk for the presence of the CONFIG.SYS file. Afterward, it searches for the COMMAND.COM interpreter, and finally looks in the root directory for the AUTOEXEC.BAT file. Both the CONFIG.SYS and AUTOEXEC.BAT files play key roles in optimizing the system's memory and disk-drive usage. Their involvement in the FAT-based bootup process can be summarized as follows:

1. The BIOS performs a software interrupt routine to search drives for the master boot record.

2. The primary Bootstrap Loader moves the master boot record into memory.

3. The system executes the Secondary Bootstrap Loader from the master boot record.

4. The secondary Bootstrap Loader moves IO.SYS and MSDOS.SYS into memory.

5. IO.SYS runs the MSDOS.SYS file to load memory and file management functions.

6. IO.SYS checks for CONFIG.SYS file in root directory.

7. If CONFIG.SYS is found, IO.SYS uses it to reconfigure the system in three read sequences (device, install, and shell).

8. IO.SYS loads COMMAND.COM.

9. COMMAND.COM checks for the AUTOEXEC.BAT file in the root directory.

10. If the AUTOEXEC.BAT file is found, COMMAND.COM carries out the commands found in the file.

11. If no AUTOEXEC.BAT file is found, COMMAND.COM displays the MS-DOS Time and Date prompt on the display.

**Figure 8-5:
DOS/BIOS
Relationships**

While the system is operating, the BIOS continues to perform several important functions. It contains BIOS service routines that the operating system calls on to carry out basic services. These services include providing BIOS interrupt service routines for operations such as printer, video, and disk-drive accesses.

In older machines the BIOS and operating systems were constantly handing control of the system back and forth as normal system functions were carried out. This relationship is illustrated in Figure 8-5. These BIOS interrupt calls were also responsible for most of the drawbacks of the PC system; that's why so much effort is exerted in newer operating system versions to avoid handing control over to the BIOS interrupts.

Disk Preparation

A portion of the A+ Operating System Technologies Objective 1.4 indicates that the test taker should be able to identify basic concepts and procedures for creating, viewing, and managing disks, directories and files. This includes procedures for changing file attributes and the ramifications of those changes (for example, security issues).

Content may include the following:

- Disks
- Partitions
    - Active Partition
    - Primary Partition
    - Extended Partition
    - Logical partition

Now that we have described the major components of a disk operating system, it is important to understand how operating systems see disks. When a disk is manufactured, its surface is electronically blank. Several levels of preparation must take place to prepare the disk for use by the system. Installing the operating system on a new hard drive has evolved into the four basic steps outlined in this A+ objective:

1. Partition the drive for use with the operating system.

2. Format the drive with the basic operating system files.

3. Run the appropriate setup utility to install the complete operating system.

4. Load all the drivers necessary to enable the operating system to work with the system's installed hardware devices.

Drive Partitioning

Physical hard-disk drives can be divided into multiple logical drives. This operation is referred to as partitioning the drive. From the beginning, the consumer-oriented operating systems from Microsoft have been based on a disk/file management system known as FAT (File Allocation Table). With earlier versions of MS-DOS, partitioning became necessary because the capacity of hard drives exceeded the ability of the existing FAT structure to track all of the possible sectors.

Dividing the physical disk space into multiple logical drives where each new drive contains another complete file tracking structure solved this dilemma. The operating system sees each logical drive on the hard drive as a completely new disk that it assigns a new, unique drive letter to.

Figure 8-6 illustrates the concept of creating multiple logical drives on a single hard drive. This is usually done for purposes of organization and increased access speeds. The partitioning program for MS-DOS, Windows 9x, Windows Me, UNIX, and LINUX is named **FDISK**. This program creates the disk's boot sector and establishes partition parameters (partition table) for the system's use.

Figure 8-6: HDD Partitions

primary partition

extended partition

Basically, DOS provides for two partitions on an HDD unit. The first, or the **primary partition**, must exist as drive C. After the primary partition has been established and properly configured, an additional partition, referred to as an **extended partition**, is also permitted. However, the extended partition may be subdivided into 23 logical drives. The extended partition cannot be deleted if logical drives have been defined within it.

```
┌─ TEST TIP ──────────────────────────────┐
│                                          │
│  Be aware of how the primary partition,  │
│  the extended partition, and the active  │
│  partition are related.                  │
│                                          │
└──────────────────────────────────────────┘
```

The active partition is the logical drive that the system will boot to. The system files must be located in this partition, and the partition must be set to "Active" for the system to boot up from the drive.

In local and wide area networks (LANs and WANs), the concept of logical drives is carried a step further. A particular hard-disk drive may be a logical drive in a large system of drives along a peer-to-peer network. On the other hand, a very large, centralized drive may be used to create several logical drives for a client/server type of network. This is accomplished by creating a logical **mapping** between the operating system and the desired drive, so that the local system handles the mapped drive as one of its own drives.

mapping

In some applications, partitioning is used to permit multiple operating systems to exist on the same physical drive. Since each partition on the drive contains its own boot sector, FAT, and root directory, each partition can be set up to hold and boot up to a different operating system.

partition table

On a partitioned drive, a special table, called the **partition table**, is created in the boot sector at the very beginning of the disk. This table holds information about the location and starting point of each logical drive on the disk, along with information about which partition has been marked as active and a master boot record.

The partition table is located at the beginning of the disk because this is the point where the system looks for bootup information. When the system checks the MBR of the physical disk during the boot process, it also checks to see which partition on the disk has been marked as active. It then jumps to that location, reads the information in that partition boot record, and boots to the operating system in that logical drive.

High-Level Formatting

The high-level format procedure is used to load the operating system into the partition. On a FAT (MS-DOS, Windows 9x) disk, the high-level format can be performed using the Format command from the command prompt or as part of the operating system installation process. In a FAT-based system, this operation re-creates the two **file allocation tables (FATs)** along with a **Root Directory** on the disk. These elements tell the system what files are on the disk and where they can be found. Modifying the Format command with a /S after the drive letter designation moves the operating system files to the drive.

Figure 8-7 describes the organization of a FAT disk and illustrates the position of the boot sector, the file allocation tables, and the root directory. The remainder of the disk is dedicated to data storage. As mentioned previously, the first area on each logical disk or partition is the boot sector. While all formatted partitions have this sector, they do not all have the optional master boot record located in the sector. Only disks created to be bootable disks have this record.

| File Allocation Tables (FATs) |
| Root Directory |

Figure 8-7: FAT Disk Organization

File Allocation Tables

The second logical section of a FAT disk is occupied by the file allocation tables. This area consists of information about how the disk is organized. Basically, the system logs the use of the space on the disk in these tables.

In older versions of MS-DOS, the amount of space dedicated to tracking the sectors on the disk was 16 bits. Therefore, only 65,536 sectors could be accounted for. This parameter limited the size of an MS-DOS partition to 32 MB (33,554,432 bytes). To more effectively manage the space on larger disks, later versions of MS-DOS divided the disk into groups of logically related sectors, called **allocation units**, or **clusters**. In a FAT-based system, the cluster is the smallest piece of manageable information.

The sectors on a FAT disk hold 512 bytes each. Files, on the other hand, can be any length. Therefore, a single file may occupy several sectors on the disk. The operating system's disk handling routine breaks a file into sector-sized chunks and stores it in a cluster of sectors. In this manner, DOS uses the cluster to track files instead of sectors. Since the file allocation table only has to handle information for a cluster, instead of for each sector, the number of files that can be tracked in a given length table is greatly increased.

The organization of a typical FAT is described in Table 8-1. The first two entries are reserved for DOS information. Each cluster after that holds a value. Each value may represent one of three conditions. A value of 0 indicates that the cluster is available and can be used for storage. Any number besides 0 or FFF indicates that the cluster contains data, and the number provides the location of the next cluster in a chain of clusters. Finally, a value of FFF (or FFFF in a 16-bit entry) indicates the end of a cluster chain.

Table 8-1: File Allocation Table Structure

CLUSTER NUMBER	CONTENTS
Cluster 0	Reserved for DOS
Cluster 1	Reserved for DOS
Cluster 2	3 (contains data; go to cluster 3)
Cluster 3	4 (contains data; go to cluster 4)
Cluster 4	7 (contains data; go to cluster 7)
Cluster 5	0 (free space)
Cluster 6	0 (free space)
Cluster 7	8 (contains data; go to cluster 8)
Cluster 8	FFF (end cluster chain)
Cluster 9	0 (free space)
✴	✴
Cluster X	0 (free space)
Cluster Y	0 (free space)
Cluster Z	0 (free space)

On floppy disks, common cluster sizes are one or two sectors long. With hard disks, the cluster size may vary from 1 to 16 sectors in length. The FAT keeps track of which clusters are used and which ones are free. It contains a 12- or 16-bit entry for each cluster on the disk. The 12-bit entries are used with floppy disks and hard disks that are smaller than 17 MB. The 16-bit entries are employed with hard disk drives larger than 17 MB. Obviously, the larger entries allow the FAT to manage more clusters.

In free clusters, a value of zero is recorded. In used clusters, the cluster number is stored. In cases where a file requires multiple clusters, the FAT entry for the first cluster holds the cluster number for the next cluster used to store the file. Each subsequent cluster entry has the number of the next cluster used by the file. The final cluster entry contains an end-of-file marker code that tells the system that the end of the file has been reached.

These **cluster links** enable the operating system to store and retrieve virtually any size file that will fit on the disk. However, the loss of any link will make it impossible to retrieve the file and use it. If the FAT becomes corrupted, chained files can become **cross-linked** with each other, making them useless. For this reason, two complete copies of the FAT are stored consecutively on the disk under the FAT-based disk structure. The first copy is the normal working copy while the second FAT is used as a backup measure in case the contents of the first FAT become corrupted.

cluster links

cross-linked

The Root Directory

The next section following the FAT tables is the disk's root directory. This is a special directory that is present on every FAT-based disk. It is the main directory of every logical disk, and serves as the starting point for organizing information on the disk.

The location of every directory, subdirectory, and file on the disk is recorded in this table.

Each directory and subdirectory (including the root directory) can hold up to 512 32-byte entries that describe each of the files in them. The first eight bytes contain the file's name, followed by three bytes for its filename extension.

The next 11 bytes define the file's **attributes**. Attributes for DOS files include:

- Read Only
- System File
- Volume Label
- Subdirectory Entry
- Archive (backup) status

— TEST TIP —
Remember the number of entries that directories in a FAT-based system can hold.

attributes

Two bytes are used to record the time the file was created or last modified. This is followed by two additional bytes that record the date the file was created or last modified. The final four bytes are divided equally between the value for the **starting cluster number** and a **byte count number** for the file. Unlike the previous information in the directory, the information associated with the last four bytes is not displayed when a directory listing is displayed on the screen.

starting cluster number

byte count number

Since each root directory entry is 32 bytes long, each disk sector can hold 16 entries. Consequently, the number of files or directories that can be listed in the root directory is dependent on how many disk sectors are allocated to it. On a hard-disk drive, there are usually 32 sectors set aside for the root directory. Therefore, the root directory for such a disk can accommodate up to 512 entries. A typical 3-1/2" 1.44 MB floppy has 16 sectors reserved for the root directory and can hold up to 224 entries.

On a floppy disk the logical structure usually has a group of files located under the root directory. Directory structures can be created on floppies, but due to their relatively small capacity, this is not normally done. A hard drive, however, is another matter. With hard drives, it is normal to organize the disk into directories and subdirectories as described earlier in the previous chapter.

Technically, every directory on a disk is a subdirectory of the root directory. All additional directories branch out from the root directory in a tree-like fashion. Therefore, a graphical representation of the disk drive's directory organization is called a **directory tree**. Figure 8-8 depicts the directory organization of a typical hard drive.

directory tree

Figure 8-8: The Microsoft Directory Tree Structure

NAVIGATING FROM THE COMMAND LINE

While MS-DOS is a thing of the past, you should not take this to mean that command-line operations have gone away — quite the contrary. Computer technicians are regularly required to perform tests at the command-line level because the system is broken and cannot support convenient graphical displays. Therefore, you must understand how Microsoft organizes disks so that you can navigate through their systems to find need information and tools during the troubleshooting process. The organizational structure of a computer's logical disks or partitions is typically described as being like a common office file cabinet, similar to the one depicted in Figure 8-9. Think of the drives in a computer as the filing cabinet structure. Our example has three drawers that can be opened. Think of these drawers as **disk drives** labeled A, B, and C/D. Inside each drawer are hanging folders that can hold different types of items. Think of these as **directories** (although Microsoft refers to them as folders in their Windows products).

disk drives

directories

Figure 8-9: Microsoft Disk Organizational Structure

The hanging folders may contain different types of items or other individual folders. Think of these individual folders as **subdirectories**. For organizational purposes, each hanging folder and each individual folder must have a unique label on it.

Inside each hanging folder, or individual folder, are the items being stored. In a real filing cabinet, these items in the folders are usually documents of different types. However, pictures and tapes and other items related to the folders can also be stored in them.

Think of the items inside the folders as **files**. Disk-based systems manage data blocks by giving them file names. Recall that a file is simply a block of logically related data, given a single name, and treated as a single unit. Like the contents of the folders, files can be programs, documents, drawings or other illustrations, sound files, and so on.

In order to find an item in the cabinet, you simply need to know which drawer, hanging folder, and folder it is located in. This concept can be translated directly to the computer system. To locate a particular file, you simply need to know which drive, directory, and subdirectory it is located in. In MS-DOS, the **path** to any file in the system can be written as a direction to the computer so that it will know where the file is that it is being directed toward. This format for specifying a path is as follows:

C:\directory name\subdirectory_name\filename

where the C: specifies the C disk drive. The directory name, subdirectory name, and filename would naturally be replaced by real names. The **back slashes** (\) after each item indicate the presence of a directory or subdirectory. The first slash indicates a special directory, called the root directory, which is present on all logical disks.

If the direction is to a file, the **filename** is always placed at the end of the path. MS-DOS allows for basic filenames of up to eight characters. It also provides for an **extension** of up to three characters. The extension is separated from the main portion of the filename by a period and is used to identify what type of file it is (e.g., the file name file1.ltr could be used to identify a letter created by a word processor).

NOTE

Filename extensions are not actually required for most files. However, they become helpful in sorting between files in a congested system. You should be aware that the operating system reserves some three-letter combinations, such as **.COM** and **.SYS**, for its own use. More information about filenames and extensions is presented in the subsequent section concerning file-level commands.

The operating system is responsible for providing the system's user interface. The main user interface for DOS is the command line. The command line is the space immediately following the DOS prompt on the screen. All DOS commands are typed in this space. They are executed by pressing the ENTER key on the keyboard.

The operating system is responsible for providing the system's user interface. The main user interface for DOS is the command line. The command line is the space immediately following the command prompt on the screen. All commands are entered in this space. They are executed by pressing the ENTER key on the keyboard.

Command-Line Functions

The A+ Operating System Technologies objective 1.3 states that the test taker should be able to demonstrate the ability to use command-line functions and utilities to manage the operating system, including the proper syntax and switches.

Command-line functions and utilities include:

- Command/CMD
- DIR
- ATTRIB
- VER
- MEM
- SCANDISK
- DEFRAG
- EDIT
- XCOPY
- COPY
- FORMAT

- FDISK
- SETVER
- SCANREG
- MD/CD/RD
- Delete/Rename
- DELTREE
- TYPE
- ECHO
- SET
- PING

user interface

Graphical User Interfaces (GUIs)

The operating system is responsible for providing the system's **user interface**. All operating systems for PCs provide some type of command-line user interface. The command line was the user interface for MS-DOS systems and remains the interface of choice for many LINUX and UNIX users. In the PC environment, different **Graphical User Interfaces (GUIs)** are the interfaces of choice for consumers. However, technicians routinely use the command-line environment for troubleshooting and repair purposes.

The command line is the space immediately following the command line's drive letter prompt on the screen. All command-line functions and actions are typed in the space immediately to the right of the prompt. These commands are executed by pressing the ENTER key on the keyboard. The command prompt for using the C: hard-disk drive as the active directory is displayed in Figure 8-10.

```
Mouse Version 8.00
1988 - 1993

Driver Installed : Mouse Systems Mode
Dynamic Resolution OFF
Mouse setup on COM1:

C:\MOUSE>
```

Figure 8-10: The Command Prompt

From the command prompt, all command-line functions can be entered and executed. Application programs can also be started from this prompt. These files can be discerned by their filename extensions. Files with .COM, **.EXE**, or **.BAT** extensions can be started directly from the prompt. The .COM and .EXE file extensions are reserved by Microsoft operating systems and can only be generated by programs that can correctly configure them. BAT files are simply ASCII text files that have been generated using command-line functions. Since .BAT files contain operating system commands mixed with .COM and .EXE files, Microsoft operating systems can execute them from the command line.

Programs with other types of extensions must be **associated** with one of these three file types to be operated. The user can operate application software packages such as graphical user interfaces, word processors, business packages, data communications packages, and user programming languages (e.g., QBASIC and DEBUG) As an example, the core component of a word processor could be a file called WORDPRO.EXE. Document files produced by word processors are normally given filename extensions of .DOC (for document) or .TXT (for text file).

In order to view a document electronically, you would first need to run the executable file and then use its features to load up, format, and display the document. Likewise, a BASIC file normally has an extension of .BAS assigned to it. In order to execute a file with this extension, it is necessary to run a BASIC interpreter, such as QBASIC.EXE, and then use it to load the .BAS file and then run it.

The user can also enter operating system user commands on the command line to perform different functions. These commands can be grouped into drive-level commands, directory-level commands, and file-level commands. The format for using command-line statements in a Microsoft command-line environment is:

COMMAND (space) SOURCE location (space) DESTINATION location

COMMAND (space) location

COMMAND

The first example illustrates how DOS operations that involve a source and a final destination, such as moving a file from one place to another, are entered.

The second example illustrates how single-location operations, such as formatting a disk in a particular disk drive, are specified. The final example applies to commands that occur in a **default location**, such as obtaining a list of the files on the current disk drive.

The performance of various commands can be modified by placing one or more software **switches** at the end of the basic command. A switch is added to the command by adding a space, a **fore-slash** (/), and a single letter after it:

COMMAND (space) option /switch

.EXE

.BAT

─ **TEST TIP** ─────────
Know which file types can be executed directly from the command-line prompt.

associated

default location

switches

fore-slash (/)

─ **NOTE** ─────────────
Common MS-DOS command switches include /P for page, /W for wide format, and /S for system. Different switches are used to modify different command functions. You can obtain definitions for switches that can be added to a given command by typing "/?" after the command.

Drives and Disks

In a Microsoft FAT-based system, each disk drive in the system is identified by a single-letter name (such as A:). This name must be specified when giving the system commands, so that they are carried out using the proper drive. The format for specifying which drive will perform a command-line function uses the drive's identifier letter in the command, followed by a colon (e.g., A: or C:).

Figure 8-11 illustrates how the various disk drives are seen by a typical stand-alone system. Microsoft operating systems reserve the letters A: and B: for the first and second floppy drives. Multiple hard-disk drive units can be installed in the system unit, along with the floppy drives. The Microsoft operating systems recognizes a single hard-disk unit in the system as **drive C:**. Disk management utilities can be used to partition a single physical hard disk drive into two or more **volumes** that the system recognizes as logical drives C:, D:, and so on.

drive C:

volumes

Figure 8-11: The System's Disk Drives

> ## NOTE
>
> The figure shows a CD-ROM drive as drive D: since this is the most common PC configuration. In the case of networked systems, logical drive letters may be extended to define up to Z drives. These drives are actually hard drives located in remote computers. The operating system in the local machine treats them as additional logical drives (e.g., F:, G:, etc.).

Conversely, a second hard-disk drive can be added to the system and set up as logical drive D:. It may also be partitioned into smaller logical drives that the system recognizes as drives E:, F:, and so on.

Some command-line operations are simplified by allowing the system to choose the location for the command to be carried out through the use of **default settings** (special predetermined settings that are automatically used by the system when no specific directions are given to change the settings). These settings are remembered in the operating system and used by the system when the operator does not specify a particular location for events to happen. The default drive in most systems is the A: drive. In systems with two or more drives, it is imperative that the user specify exactly where the specified action is to occur.

Drive-Level DOS Operations

A portion of the A+ Operating System Technologies objective 1.4 indicates that the test taker should be able to identify basic concepts and procedures for creating, viewing, and managing disks, directories and files. This includes procedures for changing file attributes and the ramifications of those changes (for example, security issues).

Content may include the following:

- Directory structures (root directory, subdirectories, etc)
- Create folders
- Navigate the directory structure
- Maximum depth

The following command-line functions pertain to **drive-level operations**. They must be typed at the command prompt, and they carry out the instruction along with any drive modifiers given.

- **FORMAT**: This command is used to prepare a new disk for use with an operating system. Actual data locations are marked off on the disk for the tracks and sectors, and bad sectors are marked. In addition, the directory is established on the disk. New disks must be formatted before they can be used.

> C:\>FORMAT A creates the tracks, sectors, and file system structure on the specified disk (in this case the A: floppy drive).
>
> C:\>FORMAT A:/S causes three system files (boot files—IO.SYS, MSDOS.SYS, and COMMAND.COM) to be copied into the root directory of the disk after it has been formatted. The new disk will now boot up without a DOS disk.
>
> C:\>FORMAT A:/Q causes the system to perform a quick format operation on the disk. This amounts to removing the FAT and root directory from the disk.

- **SETVER**: This command sets the operating system version number that the system reports to an application. Programs designed for previous DOS versions may not operate correctly under newer versions unless the version has been set correctly:

> C:\>SETVER C:

This entry will cause all of the files on the C: drive to be listed in the operating system version table. Note, however, that the SETVER command must be enabled by loading it in the CONFIG.SYS file before it can be used from the command line.

- **VER:** If the current operating system version is not known, typing **VER** at the command prompt will display it on the screen. These commands are particularly useful in networking operations in which multiple computers are connected together to share information. In these applications, several versions of operating systems may exist on different machines attached to the network.

Directories

As mentioned earlier, in hard drive–based systems it is common to organize related programs and data into areas called directories. This makes them easier to find and work with, since modern hard drives are capable of holding large amounts of information. As described earlier, most directories can hold up to 512 directory or filename entries.

The following list of commands is used for **directory-based operations** in Microsoft systems. The format for using them is identical to that for the disk-related commands discussed earlier.

- **DIR:** The Directory command gives a listing of the files on the disk that is in the drive indicated by the drive specifier.

> C:\>DIR or DIR B: (If DIR is used without any drive specifier, the content of the drive indicated by the prompt will be displayed.) The command may also be used with modifiers to alter the way in which the directory is displayed.
>
> C:\>DIR/W displays the entire directory at one time across the width of the display.
>
> C:\>DIR/P displays the content of the directory one page at a time. You must press a key to advance to the next display page.

- **MKDIR (MD):** Will create a new directory in an indicated spot in the directory tree structure.

> C:\>MD C:\DOS\XXX will create a new subdirectory named XXX in the path that includes the ROOT directory (C:\) and the DOS directory.

- **CHDIR (CD):** Will change the location of the active directory to a position specified by the command.

> C:\>CD C:\DOS will change the working directory from the C: root directory to the C:\>DOS directory.

TEST TIP

Be aware that Microsoft directories can hold up to 512 directory or filename entries.

directory-based operations

DIR

MKDIR (MD)

CHDIR (CD)

- **RMDIR (RD)**: Remove Directory will erase the directory specified in the command. You cannot remove a directory until it is empty or if it is currently active.

> C:\>RD C:\DOS\forms would remove the DOS subdirectory "forms", provided it were empty.

- **PROMPT**: Changes the appearance of the DOS prompt.

> C:\>PROMPT PG will change the form of the prompt from simply C: to C:\ and will cause the complete path from the main directory to the current directory to be displayed at the DOS prompt (i.e., C:\>DOS).

- **TREE**: Lists all of the directory and subdirectory names on a specified disk.

> C:\>TREE C: will display a graphical representation of the organization of the C hard drive.

- **DELTREE**: Removes a selected directory and all the files and subdirectories below it.

> C:\>DELTREE C:\DOS\DRIVER\MOUSE will delete the subdirectory "Mouse" and any subdirectories it may have.

CREATING AND MANAGING FILES

The A+ Operating System Technologies objective 1.4 states that the test taker should be able to identify basic concepts and procedures for creating, viewing, and managing disks, directories and files, including procedures for changing file attributes and the ramifications of those changes (for example, security issues).

It also states that the content under this objective may include the following items:

- Files
    - Creating files
    - File naming conventions (most common extensions, 8.3, maximum length)
    - File attributes — Read Only, Hidden, System, and Archive attributes
    - File compression
    - File encryption

- File permissions
- File types (text vs. binary file)

The operating systems of disk-based computers handle information in the form of files. Therefore, the computer technician must be aware of the methods that different operating systems use to create and manipulate files. The following sections of the chapter will begin the discussion of files in a disk-based system. It will describe files and file handling from the MS-DOS perspective. Subsequent chapters will expand these ideas to illustrate how they apply to the Windows 9x and Windows 2000 operating systems.

Files and Filenames

filenames

Disk-based systems store and handle related pieces of information in groups called files. The system recognizes and keeps track of the different files in the system by their **filenames**. Therefore, each file in the system is required to have a filename that is different from that of any other file in its directory.

If two files having the same name were present within the same directory of the system, the computer would become confused and fail to operate properly. This is because it could not tell which version of the file it should work on. Each time a new file of information is created, it is necessary to give it a unique filename by which the operating system can identify and store it.

name

Files are created through programming packages, or by applications. When they are created, they must be assigned a filename. In the MS-DOS environment, there are a few rules that you must remember when creating new filenames. As described earlier in this chapter, the filename consists of two parts: a **name** and an extension. The filename is a combination of alphanumeric characters and is between one and eight characters in length. The extension is an optional addition to the name that begins with a period, and is followed by one to three characters.

Extensions are not required on filenames, but they often prove useful in describing the content of a file, or in identifying different versions of the same file. If a filename that already exists is used to store another file, the computer will write the information in the new file over that of the old file, since it will assume that they are both the same file. Therefore, only the new file will still exist. The information in the old file will be lost.

Many software packages automatically generate filename extensions for files they create. The software does this so that other parts of the program, which may work with the same file, will be able to identify where the file came from, or what form it is in.

In any event, you should remember the following seven items when assigning and using filenames:

1. All files must have a filename.

2. All filenames must be different than any other filename in the system, or on the disk presently in use.

3. DOS filenames are up to 8 characters long with an optional 3-character extension (separated from the basic filename by a period).

4. When using a filename in a command, you must also use its extension, if one exists.

5. Some special characters are not allowed in filenames. These are: [,], :, ;, +, =, \, /, <, >, ?, and ,.

6. When telling DOS where to carry out a command, you must tell it on which disk drive the operation is to be performed. The drive must be specified by its letter name followed by a colon (A:, B:, C:, etc.).

7. The complete and proper way to specify a file calls for the drive specifier, the filename, and the filename extension, in that order (i.e., B:filename.ext).

The following commands are used to carry out file-level operations. The format for using them is identical to that for the disk and directory-related commands discussed earlier. However, the command must include the filename and its extension at the end of the directory path. Depending on the operation, the complete path may be required, or a default to the currently active drive will be assumed.

- **COPY**: The file copy command copies a specified file from one place (disk or directory) to another.

  C:\>COPY A:filename.ext B:filename.ext

  C:\>COPY A:filename.ext B: is used if the file is to have the same name in its new location; the second filename specifier can be omitted.

- **XCOPY**: This command copies all the files in a directory, along with any subdirectories and their files. This command is particularly useful in copying files and directories between disks with different formats (e.g., from a 1.2 MB disk to a 1.44 MB disk):

  C:\>XCOPY A: B: /s

  This command would copy all of the files and directories from the disk in drive A: (except hidden and system files) to the disk in drive B:. The /s switch instructs the XCOPY command to copy directories and subdirectories.

DEL

ERASE

- **DEL** or **ERASE**: This command allows the user to remove unwanted files from the disk when typed in at the DOS prompt:

  C:\>DEL filename.ext

  C:\>ERASE B:filename.ext

  A great deal of care should be taken when using this command. If a file is erased accidentally, it may not be retrievable.

REN

- **REN**: Enables the user to change the name or extension of a filename:

  C:\>REN A:filename.ext newname.ext

  C:\>COPY A:filename.ext B:newname.ext

  Using this command does not change the contents of the file, only its name. The original filename (but not the file) is deleted. If you wish to retain the original file and filename, a copy command, using different filenames, can be used.

TYPE

- **TYPE**: Shows the contents of a designated file on the monitor screen.

  C:\>TYPE AUTOEXEC.BAT will display the contents of the AUTOEXEC.BAT file

FC

- **FC**: This file-compare command compares two files to see if they are the same. This operation is normally performed after a file copy has been performed to ensure that the file was duplicated and located correctly:

  C:\>FC A:filename.ext B:

  If the filename was changed during the copy operation, the command would have to be typed as:

  C:\>FC A:filename.ext B:newname.ext

ATTRIB

Read-only

Archive

System

Hidden

- **ATTRIB**: Changes file attributes such as **Read-only** (+R or –R), **Archive** (+A or –A), **System** (+S or –S), and **Hidden** (+H or –H). The + and – signs are to add or subtract the attribute from the file.

  C:\>ATTRIB +R C:\DOS\memos.doc

  This command sets the file MEMOS.DOC as a read-only file. Read-only attributes protect the file from accidentally being overwritten. Similarly, one of the main reasons for giving a file a Hidden attribute is to prevent it from accidentally being erased. The System attribute is reserved for use by the operating system and marks the file as a system file.

A common error message encountered when working with command-line operations is the "bad command or file name" error message. This type of error message generally occurs when the path specified to the location of a file is incorrect, or when the filename is missing or misspelled.

Command-Line Shortcuts

Microsoft operating systems provide some **command-line shortcuts** through the keyboard's function keys. Some of the most notable are the F1 and F3 function keys. The F1 key will bring the previous command back from the command-line buffer, one character at a time. Likewise, the F3 key will bring back the entire previous command through a single keystroke.

When using filenames in command-line operations, the filename appears at the end of the directory path in the source and destination locations.

The * notation is called a **wild card** and allows operations to be performed with only partial source or destination information. Using the notation as *.* tells the software to perform the designated command on any file found on the disk using any filename and extension.

A question mark (?) can be used as a wild card to represent a single character in a filename or extension. Multiple question marks can be used to represent multiple characters in a filename or extension.

Data from a command can be modified to fit a prescribed output format through the use of **filter commands**. The main filter commands are **More**, **Find**, and **Sort**. The filter command is preceded by a **pipe symbol** (|) on the command line, when output from another command is to be modified. For example, to view the contents of a batch file that is longer than the screen display can present at one time, type **Type C:\xxx.bat|more**. If the information to be modified is derived from another file, the less than (<) symbol is used.

SYSTEM MEMORY MANAGEMENT

The A+ Operating System Technologies objective 2.5 says that the test taker should be able to identify procedures necessary to optimize the operating system and major operating system subsystems.

Content may include the following:

- Virtual memory management
- Disk defragmentation
- Files and buffers
- Caches
- Temporary file management

Traditional PC Memory Allocations

When the original PC was designed, certain decisions were made in dividing up the 8088's one megabyte of memory address space. These decisions were implemented by the original PC-DOS and MS-DOS operating systems. Due to compatibility issues, these decisions have carried over into the address allocations of all PC-compatibles, as described in Figure 8-12.

Figure 8-12:
PC Memory
Allocations

MS-DOS memory

MS-DOS memory—Basically, MS-DOS could recognize the following classifications of memory: conventional memory, upper memory blocks, high memory area, expanded memory, extended memory, and virtual memory.

Conventional Memory

Conventional memory (locations 00000 through 9FFFF) is the standard memory area for all PC-compatible systems. It traditionally holds the operating system, the interrupt vector tables, and relocated ROM BIOS tables. The remaining space in the conventional memory area is referred to as DOS Program Memory. (Programs written to operate under PC-DOS or MS-DOS use this area for program storage and execution.)

Conventional memory

The Upper Memory Area

The **upper memory area (UMA)** occupies the 384 kB portion of the PC's address space from A0000 to FFFFF. This space is not normally considered as part of the computer's total address space because programs cannot store information in this area. Instead, the area is reserved to run segments of the system's hardware. Address spaces from A0000 through BFFFF are dedicated addresses set aside for the system's video display memory. The system's ROM BIOS occupies the address space between locations FE000 and FFFFF.

upper memory area (UMA)

Between the video memory and system BIOS areas, addresses are reserved to hold BIOS extension programs for add-on hardware adapters. Typical BIOS extensions include those for hard drive adapters, advanced video adapters, and network adapters. After the BIOS extensions are in place, the typical UMA still has many unused memory areas that can have information mapped (copied) into them. This space is segmented into 64 kB sections called **upper memory blocks (UMBs)**. The primary use for these blocks is to hold installable device drivers and other memory resident programs moved out of the conventional memory area. By moving these programs out of the conventional memory area, more space is made available there for use by application programs.

upper memory blocks (UMBs)

PCs also use this area to incorporate a memory-usage scheme called **Shadow RAM** to improve their overall performance. With this feature, the contents of the system BIOS and/or adapter BIOS are rewritten (shadowed) into faster extended memory RAM locations. The operating system then re-maps the ROM addresses to the corresponding RAM locations through unused portions of the UMA. Shadowing enables the system to operate faster when application software uses any of the BIOS' CALL routines.

Shadow RAM

Extended Memory

With the advent of newer microprocessors that employ protected operating mode, it became possible to access physical memory locations beyond the 1-megabyte limit of the 8088. Memory above this address is generally referred to as **extended memory**. Modern operating systems can take full advantage of extended memory through the Protected Addressing modes of the more advanced microprocessors. This capability to manage higher memory enables the system to free up more of the base memory area for use by application programs.

extended memory

Flat Memory Models

Unlike MS-DOS, Windows 3.x, or Windows 9x, other operating systems, such as Windows NT, Windows 2000, Windows XP, UNIX, and LINUX, do not employ the address segmentation features of the Intel microprocessors to divide up the computer's memory allocations. Because segments can overlap, memory usage errors can occur when an application attempts to write data into a space being used by the operating system, or by another application.

Using the Flat Memory Model, the memory manager sections map each application's memory space into contiguous pages of physical memory. Using this method, each application is mapped into a truly unique address space that cannot overlap any other address space. The lack of segment overlap reduces the chances of applications interfering with each other and helps to ensure data integrity by providing the operating system and other processes with their own memory spaces.

Figure 8-13 illustrates the Flat Memory Model concept. In this example, the 32-bit address produced by the microprocessor contains three parts dictated by the operating system. The highest 10 bits of the address point to the Page Table Directory. This table sets the address boundaries for each page of memory in the memory. This guarantees that there is only one method of entering the page space — through this table. Therefore, there is no chance for poorly written software to stray into a page it has not been assigned. The lower 22 bits of the address are used to access a particular page within the block of addresses specified in the Page Table Directory (bits 12-21), and then to select a particular physical address within the page (bits 0-11).

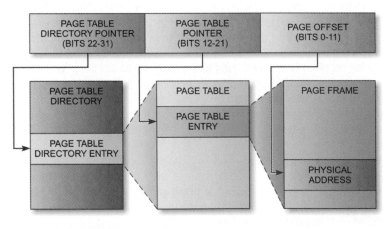

Figure 8-13: Flat Memory Model

Virtual Memory

virtual memory

swapping files

The term **virtual memory** is used to describe memory that isn't what it appears to be. Virtual memory is actually disk drive space that is manipulated to seem like RAM. Software creates virtual memory by **swapping files** between RAM and the disk drive, as illustrated in Figure 8-14. This memory management technique effectively creates more total memory for the system's applications to use. However, since there is a major transfer of information that involves the hard-disk drive, an overall reduction in speed is encountered with virtual memory operations.

Figure 8-14: Virtual Memory Operations

Most operating systems since Windows 3.x (Windows 9x, Windows NT, Windows 2000, UNIX, and LINUX) feature virtual memory operations. Within these systems, three types of swap files are used—temporary, permanent, and variable. Some operating systems will permit either a permanent or a **temporary swap file** to be established on the system's hard drive. A **permanent swap file** is always present and is a constant size. It is composed of contiguous clusters on the drive and cannot be established in fragmented drive space. It also cannot be established on a compressed partition. The following list shows the types of swap files supported by the various Microsoft operating systems:

- Temporary swap files — Windows 3.x

- Permanent swap files — Windows 3.x, NT, 2000

- Variable swap files — Windows 9x

Windows 9x swap drives do not require contiguous drive space and can be established on compressed drives that use virtual device drivers. The size of the Windows 95 swap file is variable and is dynamically assigned. The Windows 9x swap file is **WIN386.SWP**.

Control of Windows 9x Virtual Memory operations is established through the Control Panel's System\Performance tab. Clicking on the *Virtual Memory* button produces the *Virtual Memory* options screen shown in Figure 8-15. The default and recommended setting is *Let Windows manage my virtual memory settings*.

> temporary swap file

> permanent swap file

> WIN386.SWP

Figure 8-15: The Windows 95 Virtual Memory Dialog Box

In Windows NT, 2000, and XP, the virtual memory functions are located under the Control Panel's *System* icon. Simply click on its *Advanced* tab followed by the *Performance Options* button to view the dialog window depicted in Figure 8-16.

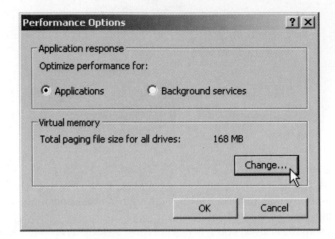

Figure 8-16: The System Performance Options Window

Clicking on the *Change* button in the dialog window will produce the *Virtual Memory* dialog window shown in Figure 8-17. Through this dialog window, you can establish and configure an individual swap file for each drive in the system. By highlighting a drive, you can check its virtual memory capabilities and settings. Entering new values in the dialog windows and clicking on the *Set* button will change the values for the highlighted drive.

pagefile.sys

The Windows NT/2000/XP pagefile (named **pagefile.sys**) is created when the operating system is installed. Its default size is typically set at 1.5 times the amount of RAM installed in the system. It is possible to optimize the system's performance by distributing the swap file space between multiple drives. It can also be helpful to relocate the swap file away from slower or heavily used drives. The swap file should not be placed on mirrored or striped volumes. Also, don't create multiple swap files on logical disks that exist on the same physical drive.

Figure 8-17: The Virtual Memory Dialog Window

┌─ **TEST TIP** ─────────┐
│ Memorize the filenames of the │
│ virtual memory swap files used │
│ in each operating system. │
└────────────────────────┘

CONFIG.SYS

Another convention that remains from older MS-DOS systems is a special configuration file called **CONFIG.SYS**. MS-DOS versions from 5.0 forward created this file when they were installed. This particular filename is reserved by Microsoft's operating systems for use with the special file that contains setup (configuration) instructions for the system. When the consumer Microsoft operating systems (MS-DOS, Windows 3.x, Windows 9x, and Windows Me) are loaded into the system during the bootup process, they will automatically search in the default drive for a file named CONFIG.SYS.

Originally, the commands in this file were used to configure the MS-DOS operating system for use with options devices and application programs in the system. Why are we discussing an old MS-DOS file when those operating systems have been out of sight for some time? Well, for compatibility reasons, the Windows consumer operating systems also check for this file during the bootup process. If this file is found, its contents will be used to configure the system instead of those generated by the operating system's configuration files. This often creates problems with systems that have been upgraded to newer operating systems and still have the old CONFIG.SYS file. Some of the filenames and functions that are used in the CONFIG.SYS file have also been carried over into these more advanced operating systems.

The CONFIG.SYS program is responsible for:

1. Setting up any memory managers being used.

2. Configuring the DOS program for use with options devices and application programs.

3. Loading device-driver software, and installing memory-resident programs into memory.

These activities are illustrated by the sample CONFIG.SYS file:

1. Device=C:\DOS\HIMEM.SYS
   Device=C:\DOS\EMM386.EXE 1024 RAM

2. FILES=30
   BUFFERS=15
   STACKS=9,256

3. DEVICE=C:\DOS\SMARTDRV.SYS 1024
   DOS=HIGH,UMB
   DEVICEHIGH=C:\MOUSE\MOUSE.SYS
   DEVICEHIGH=C:\DOS\RAMDRIVE.SYS 4096/a

Memory Managers

HIMEM.SYS

In the first section, the system's memory-manager programs are loaded. In this case, the **HIMEM.SYS** command loads the DOS extended memory (XMS) driver. This driver manages the use of extended memory installed in the system so that no two applications use the same memory locations at the same time. This **memory manager** should be listed in the CONFIG.SYS file before any other memory managers or device drivers. HIMEM.SYS also creates a 64 kB area of memory just above the 1 MB address space called the **High Memory Area (HMA)**. With this, the DOS=HIGH statement is used to shift portions of DOS from conventional memory into the HMA.

memory manager

High Memory Area (HMA)

Upper Memory Area (UMA)

The EMM386.EXE program provides the system's microprocessor with access to the **Upper Memory Area (UMA)** of RAM. Operating together with the HIMEM.SYS program, this program enables the system to conserve conventional memory by moving device drivers and memory-resident programs into the UMA. This concept is described in Figure 8-18.

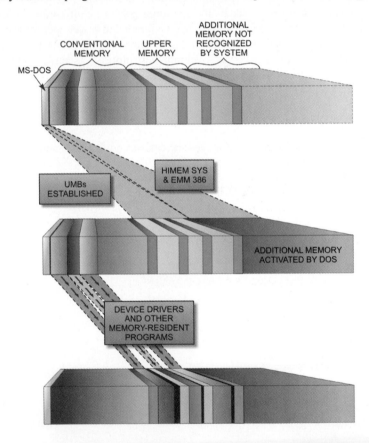

Figure 8-18: Loading Memory Managers

The EMM386.EXE command can also be used to simulate expanded memory mode operations in RAM above the 1 MB mark. In this case, the 1024 RAM switch in the command directs the EMM386 driver to provide upper memory access and establish a 1024-byte area above the 1 MB mark to simulate expanded memory operations. If the CONFIG.SYS file contains commands to load another expanded memory manager, the presence of a **NOEMS** switch in the EMM386.EXE line will prevent it from implementing expanded mode operation when the line is encountered. When this switch is used, the command provides access to the upper memory area, but prevents access to expanded memory.

NOEMS

Files, Buffers, and Stacks

The second section of the CONFIG.SYS file consists of the commands that define the operating system for operation with optional devices and applications. The **FILES command** causes the operating system to establish the number of files that operating systems can handle at any one time at 30. This just happens to be the minimum number required to load Windows for operation. The **BUFFERS command** sets aside 15 blocks of RAM memory space for storing data being transferred to and from disks. Similarly, the **STACKS command** establishes the number and length of some special RAM memory storage operations at 9 memory stacks, with each being 256 bytes long.

FILES command

BUFFERS command

STACKS command

Device Drivers

Device drivers are loaded in the third part of the file. Device drivers are programs that tell the operating system how to control specific devices. DEVICEHIGH=C:\MOUSE\MOUSE.SYS is a command that loads a third-party device driver supporting the particular mouse being used with the system. The order in which device drivers appear in the CONFIG.SYS file is important. The recommended order for listing device drivers is: (1) HIMEM.SYS, (2) the expanded memory manager, if installed, (3) the EMM386.EXE command, and (4) any other device drivers being used.

Device drivers

The **SMARTDRV.SYS** driver establishes a disk cache in an area of extended memory as a storage space for information read from the hard-disk drive. A **cache** is a special area of memory reserved to hold data and instructions recently accessed from another location. A **disk cache** holds information recently accessed from the hard-disk drive. Information stored in RAM is much quicker to access than if it were on the hard drive.

SMARTDRV.SYS

cache

disk cache

When a program or command-line operation requests more data, the SMARTDRV program redirects the request to check in the cache memory area to see if the requested data is there. If SMARTDRV finds the information in the cache, it will operate on it from there. If the requested information is not in the cache, the system will access the hard drive for it. Using this technique, the overall operating speed of the system is improved. When the system is shut down, SMARTDRV copies the most current information onto the hard drive. Therefore, no data is lost due to being stored in RAM. Figure 8-19 describes the idea behind SMARTDRV operations.

- ① THE PROGRAM REQUESTS INFORMATION FROM MEMORY.
- ② THE SYSTEM CHECKS THE DISK CACHE AREA OF RAM FOR THE INFORMATION.
- ③ IF THE INFORMATION IS NOT IN THE CACHE, THE SYSTEM CHECKS THE HARD DRIVE FOR IT.
- ④ THE SYSTEM MOVES THE INFORMATION INTO THE DISK CACHE AREA WHERE THE SYSTEM CAN WORK WITH IT.

Figure 8-19: How SMARTDRV Works

RAMDRIVE.SYS

virtual disk

DEVICEHIGH=

DEVICE=

DOS=HIGH,UMB

┌─ **TEST TIP** ─────
Know which statements and commands are normally located in the CONFIG.SYS file.
└─────────────

KEYBOARD.SYS

DISPLAY.SYS

code page

ANSI.SYS

DRIVER.SYS

PRINTER.SYS

The 1024 modifier establishes a memory cache size of 1 MB (1024 kB of memory) in extended memory. This is a typical cache size for SMARTDRV; however, 2 MB (2048 kB) is probably the most efficient size for the cache. This is because the larger the cache size, the greater the chance that the requested information will be in the cache.

The **RAMDRIVE.SYS** driver simulates the organization of a hard-disk drive in RAM memory. This type of drive is called a **virtual disk**. In this case, the **DEVICEHIGH=** command loads the RAMDRV into the upper memory area instead of the base memory area, where a simple **DEVICE=** command would run it. Likewise, the **DOS=HIGH,UMB** command shifts the operation of DOS into the high memory area, and gives the application access to the upper memory area.

MS-DOS had several other standard device driver programs that it employed to communicate with standard peripheral devices used in early PC systems. These included:

- KEYBOARD.SYS
- DISPLAY.SYS
- ANSI.SYS
- DRIVER.SYS
- PRINTER.SYS

KEYBOARD.SYS is the MS-DOS default keyboard definition file. The **DISPLAY.SYS** driver supports code-page switching for the monitor type used by the system. A **code page** is the set of 256 characters that the operating system can handle at one time when displaying, printing, and manipulating text.

ANSI.SYS supports ANSI escape-code sequences used to modify the function of the system's display and keyboard. This file is also required to display colors on the monitor in MS-DOS. The **DRIVER.SYS** file creates the logical drive assignments for the system's floppy drives (that is, A: and B:). Finally, the **PRINTER.SYS** driver supports code-page switching for parallel ports.

AUTOEXEC.BAT

After completing the CONFIG.SYS operation, the operating system searches for the presence of the AUTOEXEC.BAT file. This file contains a **batch** of commands that are automatically carried out when the operating system is loaded into the system.

batch

This file can also be re-executed from the command prompt by simply typing the command "AUTOEXEC". This is not true of the CONFIG.SYS file however: The system must be re-started in order to perform the commands in this file.

Refer to the following sample AUTOEXEC.BAT file:

```
DATE
TIME
PROMPT=$P$G
SET TEMP=C:\TEMP
PATH=C:\;C:\DOS;C:\MOUSE
SMARTDRV.EXE 2048 1024
CD\
DIR
```

The first two commands cause the operating system to prompt you for the date and time (since MS-DOS did not automatically do this when an AUTOEXEC.BAT file was present). The **PROMPT=PG** command causes the active drive and directory path to be displayed on the command line. The SET TEMP= line sets up an area for holding data temporarily in a directory named **TEMP**.

PROMPT=PG

TEMP

The **PATH command** creates a specific set of paths that the operating system will use to search for executable (.EXE, .COM, and .BAT) files. In this example, the operating system will search for these files first in the root directory (C:\), followed by the DOS directory (C:\DOS), and finally through the Mouse directory (C:\MOUSE).

PATH command

This statement effectively lets a Mouse.com or Mouse.exe driver program — normally located in the Mouse directory — be executed from anywhere in the system. Upon receiving the mouse command, the operating system looks through all of the directories in the path until it finds the specified filename.

The **syntax** (punctuation and organization) of the PATH command is very important. Each entry must be complete from the root directory and must be separated from the previous entry by a semicolon. There should be no spaces in the PATH command. Pressing the **Pause** key on the keyboard interrupts the execution of the steps in the AUTOEXEC.BAT file. Pressing any key restarts it.

syntax

Pause

You can use MS-DOS batch file commands to construct elaborate startup procedures. Other programs designed to test ports and peripherals can be constructed using these commands. These test files can be named using the MS-DOS filename conventions. They must be stored with a .BAT extension to be executable from the command prompt, but the extension does not need to be entered in order to run the program.

Neither the CONFIG.SYS nor the AUTOEXEC.BAT file is required for normal operation of the computer. However, they can prove to be very useful in tailoring the operation of the system to your personal use, or to the requirements of different software applications packages. To determine whether either of these files already exists on a given disk, simply type the DIR command at the command prompt for the designated drive.

Altering Configuration and Startup Sequences

The loading of the CONFIG.SYS file can be altered or bypassed by pressing selected keyboard keys during the bootup process. Holding the **Shift** key, or pressing the **F5** key while the MS-DOS message "**Starting DOS...**" was on the screen would cause the bootup process to skip all the commands in the CONFIG.SYS file. This action could also be used to bypass all of the steps of the AUTOEXEC.BAT file.

When this option was used, the system would boot up with a complete set of default settings. No installable device drivers were installed, the current directory was set to C:\>DOS, and a "**Bad or missing command interpreter**" message sometimes appeared. If this message was received, the system would also ask you to manually enter the path to the COMMAND.COM file.

Similarly, pressing the **F8** function key while the *Starting DOS* message was on the screen would cause the system to stop between each CONFIG.SYS command and ask for verification before proceeding. This is referred to as a **single-step** startup option and was very helpful in troubleshooting configuration and bootup problems. Beginning with MS-DOS version 6.2, the F8 interactive bypass procedure used with the CONFIG.SYS file was extended to include the AUTOEXEC.BAT file. This action would also cause the system to ask the user whether the AUTOEXEC.BAT file should be run, or skipped. Placing a question mark after a CONFIG.SYS command (before the = sign) would cause the system to automatically seek verification whenever the system was booted up.

These features were very valuable tools for isolating and correcting bad configuration settings and corrupt driver files. Now, all of Microsoft's operating systems (except for Windows Me) feature shortcut key functions that can be used to start up the system without any nonstandard drivers and to go through each configuration step one at a time. Interestingly, these functions are also based on variations of using the F5/F8 keys. You will be introduced to these tools in Chapter 12 — *Operating System Troubleshooting*.

The special function keys available during the MS-DOS startup are summarized as follows:

- F5 (also Left Shift key) — Skips the CONFIG.SYS and AUTOEXEC.BAT files.

- F8 — Proceeds through the CONFIG.SYS and AUTOEXEC.BAT files one step at a time waiting for confirmation from the user.

Windows Initialization Files

Another type of file that has been held over from previous consumer versions of Microsoft operating system is the **Initialization (INI) file**. When Microsoft added the Windows 3.x **operating environment** to an underlying MS-DOS structure, it did so by creating several INI files that established and controlled the parameters of the various Windows components. These files were installed in the \Windows directory with a file extension of .INI. The INI files carried the default, or current, startup settings for various Windows components. The major Windows 3.x initialization files were as follows:

Initialization (INI) file

operating
environment

- WIN.INI
- CONTROL.INI
- WINFILE.INI
- PROGMAN.INI
- SYSTEM.INI

Current versions of Windows 9x and Windows 2000 continue to include these files for compatibility reasons. The \Windows directory may also contain several other INI files. In fact, when a new Windows application is installed, it may very well install its own INI file at that time. These files can be modified to customize, or optimize, the program's execution.

Parameters in INI files are typically modified through normal Windows menus, or through pop-up dialog boxes. Other parameters can only be changed by directly modifying the INI files. The files are broken into sections that contain the individual parameters that can be altered. Changes to the files are automatically updated whenever Windows is exited.

Normal system functions that alter INI settings include changing Control Panel, Desktop, or Windows Explorer entries. However, INI files are basically text files that users can alter with a standard text editor utility such as SysEdit. This utility can also be used to modify the SYSTEM.INI, WIN.INI, CONFIG.SYS, and AUTOEXEC.BAT files. The SysEdit utility can be accessed by simply typing Sysedit in the Windows Start/Run dialog box.

The format of all the INI files is consistent. Each INI file is divided into logical sections. Each section consists of a list of entries in the format of keyname=value. Each section has a name enclosed in brackets. The keyname is simply a name that describes the function of the entry and is normally followed by an equals sign. It can be any combination of characters and numbers. The value entry can be any integer or string. Typical enabling entries include On, True, Yes, and 1. Conversely, disabling entries are Off, False, No, and 0.

Optimizing Memory

The real objective in memory management in MS-DOS and Windows 9x is to free up as much conventional memory as possible for use by DOS-based programs. The first step in this process is to use the DOS **MEM command** to determine how much memory is actually in the system and how it is organized. Figure 8-20 shows a typical **memory map** displayed by the MEM command.

MEM command

memory map

```
C:\>

C:\>mem
Memory Type          Total  =  Used  +  Free

Conventional          640K      47K      593K
Upper                   0K       0K       0K
Reserved              384K     384K       0K
Extended (XMS)      7,168K   2,112K    5,056K

Total memory        8,192K   2,559K    5,633K

Total under 1 MB      640K      47K      593K

Largest executable program size        593K   (607,312 bytes)
Largest free upper memory block          0K       (0 bytes)
MS-DOS is resident in the high memory area.
```

Figure 8-20:
The MEM Display

When the MEM command is executed without any modifying switches, the system's free and used memory are displayed. Adding a Page (/p) switch to the line causes the output to stop at the end of each screen of information. In versions of MS-DOS before release 6.0, the /p switch produced a program function that displayed the status of programs currently loaded into memory. Likewise, using a Debug (/d) switch with the MEM command will show the status of currently loaded programs and internal drivers. Another switch, called the Classify (/c) switch, displays the status of programs in conventional memory and the UMA. In addition, it provides each program's size in decimal and hex notation, along with a summary of memory usage and the largest memory blocks available. The MEM command can only be used with one switch at a time.

Even using the setup steps just listed, the system's performance will deteriorate over time. Most of this deterioration is due to unnecessary file clutter and segmentation on the system's hard disk drive. The following steps can be used to periodically tune up the performance of the system.

1. Periodically remove unnecessary .TMP and .BAK files from the system.

2. Check for and remove lost file chains and clusters using the CHKDSK and CHKDSK /f commands.

3. Use the DEFRAG utility to realign files on the drive that may have become fragmented after being moved back and forth between the drive and the system.

Temporary (TMP)

backup (BAK) files

Temporary (TMP) files and **backup (BAK) files** are special versions of files that the operating system creates when it is performing functions in which it needs to store an original copy of the file along with an updated copy. Over time, these types of files can accumulate and take up space on the hard drive. Removing these files and performing a defragmentation operation can improve the disk drive's access and delivery times dramatically. The Check Disk and Defrag utilities are covered in detail in Chapter 12 — *Operating System Troubleshooting*.

CHAPTER SUMMARY

After completing this chapter, you should be able to demonstrate your knowledge of fundamental operating system terminology, components, and principles. In particular, you should be able to describe the basic functions of a typical disk-based operating system.

You should also be able to differentiate between different types of operating systems and state their characteristics. This includes differentiating between single-process and multiple-process systems, between batch-mode and interactive mode processes, and between multiuser, multitasking, and multiprocessor operations.

The chapter has used the structure of the MS-DOS operating system as an example of a typical disk-based operating system. It has also described methods of managing files and running applications in a DOS-based system, as well as navigating through the operating system from a command line, and has presented procedures for accessing and retrieving information. Finally, the chapter has presented procedures for creating and managing files and directories in a FAT-based system.

At this point, review the objectives listed at the beginning of the chapter to be certain that you understand and can perform each item listed there.

KEY POINTS REVIEW

This chapter has discussed basic attributes associated with operating systems. In particular, it used the FAT-based MS-DOS operating system as an example of basic operating system functions, structure, operation, and file management. Review the following key points before moving into the Review and Exam Questions sections to make sure you are comfortable with each point. Afterward, answer the Review Questions that follow to verify your knowledge of the information.

- There are literally thousands of different operating systems in use with microcomputers. The complexity of each operating system typically depends on the complexity of the application the microcomputer is designed to fill.

- In multiuser and multitasking operations, the appearance of simultaneous operation is accomplished by switching between different tasks in a predetermined order. The multiuser system switches between different users at multiple locations, whereas multitasking systems switch between different applications at a single location.

- The POST is actually a series of tests that are performed each time the system is turned on. The different tests check the operation of the microprocessor, the keyboard, the video display, the floppy- and hard-disk drive units, as well as both the RAM and ROM memory units.

- After the intial set of POST checks, the BIOS routine initializes the system's intelligent devices. During this part of the program, startup values stored in the ROM chip are moved into the system's programmable devices to make them functional.

- After the initialization and POST are completed, the BIOS checks the area of memory between C0000 and DFFFF for BIOS extension programs.

- If an error or setup mismatch is encountered, the BIOS will issue an error code, either in message form on the display screen, or in beep-coded form through the system's speaker.

- The bootup process starts when the BIOS begins looking through the system for a Master Boot Record (MBR). This record can reside on drive A: or C:, or at any other location.

- While the system is operating, the BIOS continues to perform several important functions. It contains routines on which the operating system calls to carry out basic services. These services include providing BIOS interrupt calls (software interrupt routines) for such operations as printer, video, and disk drive accesses.

- The disk's file allocation tables occupy the second section of a FAT disk. This area contains information about how the disk is organized. Basically, the system logs the use of the space on the disk in these tables.

- The next section following the FAT tables is the disk's root directory. This is a special directory that is present on every FAT disk. It is the main directory of every logical disk, and serves as the starting point for organizing information on the disk.

- The operating system is responsible for providing the system's user interface. The main user interface for MS-DOS was the command line. The command line is the space immediately following the drive letter prompt on the screen. All commands are typed in this space. They are executed by pressing the ENTER key on the keyboard.

- Disk-based systems store and handle related pieces of information in groups called files. The system recognizes and keeps track of the different files in the system by their filenames. Therefore, each file in the system is required to have a filename that is different from that of any other file in its directory.

- In any event, you should remember the following seven items when assigning and using filenames:

  1. All files must have a filename.

  2. All filenames must be different from any other filename in the system, or on the disk presently in use.

  3. MS-DOS filenames are up to 8 characters long with an optional 3-character extension (separated from the basic filename by a period).

  4. When using a filename in a command, you must also use its extension, if one exists.

  5. Some special characters are not allowed in filenames. These are: [,], :, ;, +, =, \, /, <, >, ?, and ,.

  6. When telling MS-DOS where to carry out a command, you must tell it on which disk drive the operation is to be performed. The drive must be specified by its letter name followed by a colon (A:, B:, C:, etc.).

  7. The complete and proper way to specify a file calls for the drive specifier, the filename, and the filename extension, in that order (i.e., B:filename.ext).

- Basically, MS-DOS could recognize the following classifications of memory: conventional memory, upper memory blocks, high memory area, expanded memory, extended memory, and virtual memory.

- Conventional memory (locations 00000 through 9FFFF) is the standard memory area for all PC-compatible systems. It traditionally holds DOS program memory, interrupt vector tables, and relocated ROM BIOS tables.

- The remaining space in the conventional memory area is referred to as DOS Program Memory. (Programs written to operate under PC-DOS or MS-DOS use this area for program storage and execution).

- The upper memory area occupies the 384 kB portion of the PC's address space from A0000 to FFFFF. This space is not normally considered as part of the computer's total address space because programs cannot store information in this area. Instead, the area is reserved to run segments of the system's hardware. Address spaces from A0000 through BFFFF are dedicated addresses set aside for the system's video display memory. The system's ROM BIOS occupies the address space between locations FE000 and FFFFF.

- With the advent of the microprocessor with protected operating modes, it became possible to access physical memory locations beyond the 1-megabyte limit of the 8088. Memory above this address is generally referred to as extended memory.

- The term virtual memory is used to describe memory that isn't what it appears to be. Virtual memory is actually disk drive space that is manipulated to seem like RAM. Software creates virtual memory by swapping files between RAM and the disk drive. This memory management technique effectively creates more total memory for the system's applications to use. However, since there is a major transfer of information that involves the hard disk drive, an overall reduction in speed is encountered with virtual memory operations.

- After completing the CONFIG.SYS operation, the operating system searches for the presence of a file called the COMMAND.COM file.

- The COMMAND.COM file searches the default drive for a file called AUTOEXEC.BAT that contains a batch of DOS commands that will automatically be carried out when it is loaded into the system.

REVIEW QUESTIONS

The following questions test your knowledge of the material presented in this chapter.

1. Where is the Path statement located?

2. What type of operating system breaks the tasks associated with a process into various threads for execution?

3. In a CONFIG.SYS file, which memory manager should always be listed before any other memory managers or device drivers?

4. What does the "*" character stand for when used in a Microsoft filename?

5. Write a command-line statement that can be inserted into the AUTOEXEC.BAT file to cause the active path and directory to be shown on the command line.

6. What does the BUFFERS= command in the CONFIG.SYS file do?

7. In a PC system, where is the High Memory Area located?

8. From the system startup point of view, how do a cold and a warm boot differ?

9. Which key can be pressed to skip the CONFIG.SYS and AUTOEXEC.BAT files during MS-DOS startup?

10. What is the primary function of the IO.SYS file?

11. What are the three main files in the MS-DOS operating system structure?

12. What does the System attribute indicate about the file?

13. A _____ is the standard method of organizing files into directories and subdirectories on magnetic disks.

14. How many files or entries can be included in the root directory?

15. What system components are involved in virtual memory operations?

EXAM QUESTIONS

1. Which DOS command prepares a disk to function as a self-booting disk?
   a. Boot /s
   b. FDISK /s
   c. Format /s
   d. MEM /s

2. In terms of managing processes, what type of operating system is MS-DOS?
   a. A single-process, batch-mode operating system
   b. A multiple-process, interactive-mode operating system
   c. A multiple-process, batch-mode operating system
   d. A single-process, interactive-mode operating system

3. Where would you find the system's memory managers listed?
   a. In the CONFIG.SYS file
   b. In the boot record
   c. In the AUTOEXEC.BAT file
   d. In the COMMAND.COM file

4. Which of the following items is located in the root directory of a hard-disk drive?
   a. The drive letter
   b. The file attributes
   c. The primary OS boot loader
   d. The IO.SYS file

5. What does HIMEM.SYS do?
   a. It governs the use of shadow RAM.
   b. It governs the use of conventional memory.
   c. It governs the use of extended memory.
   d. It governs the use of base memory.

6. In which type of memory do MS-DOS applications run?
   a. Upper memory
   b. Expanded memory
   c. Conventional memory
   d. Extended memory

7. Which file is the primary operating system loader looking for during the bootup process?
   a. An OS loader
   b. A primary bootstrap loader
   c. A master boot record
   d. The root directory

8. List the three files that must be located in the root directory in order to successfully boot MS-DOS.
   a. MSDOS.SYS, IO.SYS, and COMMAND.COM
   b. CONFIG.SYS, COMMAND.COM, and AUTOEXEC.BAT
   c. FILES, STACKS, and BUFFERS
   d. HIMEM.SYS, EMM386.EXE, and COMMAND.COM

9. What is the smallest piece of manageable information in a Microsoft disk system?
   a. The cluster
   b. The sector
   c. The word
   d. The track

10. The value of having virtual memory is that _____.
    a. it creates more total memory for applications.
    b. it moves applications into the upper memory area.
    c. it shadows applications so that they can be recovered if the operating system crashes.
    d. it creates additional extended memory for applications to operate in.

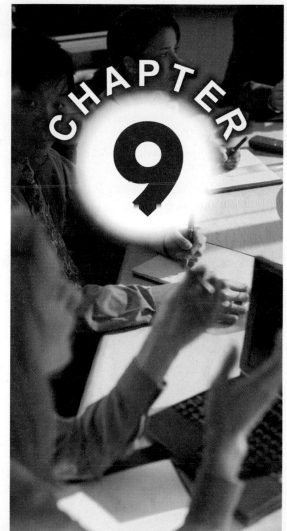

CHAPTER 9

WINDOWS 9X

OBJECTIVES

Upon completion of this chapter and its related lab procedures you will be able to perform the following tasks:

1. Identify the procedures for installing Windows 9x and bringing the software to a basic operational level.

2. Identify the basic Windows 9x boot/startup sequence and alternative ways to boot the system software.

3. Identify the steps to create a Windows 9x Startup Disk with helpful utilities installed.

4. Identify the procedures for loading/adding device drivers and the necessary software for certain devices in a Windows 9x system.

5. Identify procedures for changing options, configuring, and using the Windows 9x printing subsystem.

6. Identify the procedures for installing and launching typical Windows and non-Windows applications in a Windows 9x system.

7. Identify Windows 9x operating system functions, structure, and major system files.

8. Describe the major system files of a Windows 9x system, indicating where they are located and how they are used.

9. Identify ways of navigating through the Windows 9x operating system and how to get to needed technical information.

10. Describe procedures for locating, accessing, and retrieving information in a Windows 9x system.

11. Identify basic concepts and procedures for creating and managing files and folders in a Windows 9x system.

12. Identify the local area networking capabilities of Windows 9x.

13. Describe procedures for connecting to the network from a Windows 9x system.

14. Describe procedures for sharing disk drives, and print and file services in a Windows 9x system.

15. Identify concepts and capabilities relating to the Internet.

16. Describe basic procedures for setting up a Windows 9x system for Internet access.

WINDOWS 9X

INTRODUCTION

This chapter will help you to prepare for the Windows 9x portions of the A+ certification examination's Operating Systems Technology module. The previous chapter explored basic operating systems in some detail. Most of the information covered BIOS operations and the command-line structure. Domain 1.0 of the A+ Operating System Technologies exam states that the test taker should be able to identify major desktop components and interfaces. It also includes being able to navigate through the operating system from command-line prompts, and use Windows procedures to access and retrieve information, as well as to manage the operating system. Therefore, this chapter continues the exploration of operating system software by examining Microsoft's Windows 9x programs.

It may be natural to think that the Microsoft Windows programs evolved out of the existing MS-DOS program, but this is not the case. Microsoft first introduced Windows in 1984, 10 years before it introduced its final version of MS-DOS. The pressure for a GUI operating system to work with PCs was actually generated by the popularity of the Apple operating system.

WINDOWS EVOLUTION

A portion of A+ Operating System Technology objective 1.1 indicates that the test taker should be able to identify the major desktop components and interfaces, and their functions. Differentiate the characteristics of Windows 9x/Me, Windows NT 4.0 Workstation, Windows 2000 Professional, and Windows XP. It also says the content may include contrasts between Windows 9x/Me, Windows NT 4.0 Workstation, Windows 2000 Professional, and Windows XP.

Over time, the consumer market 9x version of Windows has developed into five distinct products:

- Windows 95
- Windows 95 OSR2
- Windows 98
- Windows 98SE
- Windows Millennium Edition

The following material describes each of these products and explains some of their key differences.

Windows 95

In 1995, Microsoft released a radically different looking Windows environment called **Windows 95**. It offered improved multimedia support for video and sound file applications, Plug-and-Play hardware support, 32-bit advanced multitasking functions, improved **e-mail** and **fax** capabilities through Microsoft Exchange, and the Microsoft Network for easy wide area network usage.

Windows 95 offered full built-in Plug-and-Play capability. When it was combined with a hardware system that implemented PnP BIOS, expansion slots, and adapter support, and that was supported with PnP adapter drivers, fully automated configuration and reconfiguration could take place.

Even though Windows 95 was optimized for running 32-bit applications, it was still fully compatible with 16-bit Windows 3.x and MS-DOS applications. It could be installed over either of these operating system versions as a direct upgrade. The only real concern when installing Windows 95 over either of these operating systems was that the existing system had the hardware resources needed to run Windows 95.

Windows 95 OSR2

Windows 95 OSR2, also known as **Windows 95 (b)**, is an upgrade of the original Windows 95 package and includes patches and fixes for version 1, along with Microsoft Internet Explorer 3.0 and Personal Web Server. It also includes an enhanced file allocation table system, referred to as **FAT32**.

In addition to the FAT32 system, **OSR2** offered improved **power management (APM)** functions, **bus mastering** support, **MMX** multimedia support, and enhanced PCMCIA functions over version 1 (which was referred to as **OSR1**, or **Service Pack 1**). Also new in OSR2 was HDD/CD-ROM DMA access support. This feature was located in the Control Panel/System/Device Manager/Disk Drives window.

Windows 98

Microsoft's **Windows 98** replaced the Windows 95 operating system. While many of its features remained basically the same as those of Windows 95, Windows 98 did bring certain new items to the system. Most notably, it extended the desktop to the Internet, creating a web-based desktop environment. This feature was designed to make Internet (or intranet) access as seamless as possible for the user. It also enabled Windows 98 to perform unattended self-upgrades directly from the Microsoft web site when new items or repairs were released.

In 1999, Microsoft produced an improved version of Windows 98 that became known as **Windows 98SE** (Second Edition). This edition was basically the original Windows 98 platform with all of the patches incorporated. However, it did transform a relatively unstable operating system into a very stable platform. Along with the patches, Windows 98SE offered additional device drivers and Internet Explorer repair tools. Its only notable new feature was built-in *Internet connection sharing*. This feature enabled a Windows 98 machine to act as a **proxy server** for other nodes in a network. The proxy acted as the connection point to the Internet for all of the computers on the LAN.

Windows Millennium

Windows **Millennium Edition** (**Me**) is the latest variation of the Windows 9x line of consumer operating systems. Although it operates in a manner similar to Windows 98, it incorporates more of the look and feel of the Windows 2000 commercial operating system discussed in the next chapter.

Windows Me minimizes the user's access to the command prompt functions. It also includes a number of new self-repair capabilities that perform some of the technician's repair functions automatically.

Several of the items we will discuss in this chapter and in the Operating System Troubleshooting chapter have been moved to new (Windows 2000-like) locations in Windows Me. The integration of Microsoft Internet Explorer is even tighter in Windows Me than it was in the Windows 98 package. All of these additional features and functionality ultimately have produced an operating system whose memory footprint (requirements) is much larger than the Windows 98 operating system that it is replacing. This can be a major consideration when considering whether to upgrade a system with marginal capacity to the new operating system.

INSTALLING WINDOWS 9X

A+ Operating System Technologies objective 2.1 states that the test taker should be able to identify the procedures for installing Windows 9x/Me, Windows NT 4.0 Workstation, Windows 2000 Professional, and Windows XP, and bringing the operating system to a basic operational level. In this chapter we will cover the installation of Windows 9x operating systems. Windows NT, 2000 and XP installation processes will be discussed in the next chapter.

Installing Windows 95

Windows 95 must be installed in an existing FAT16 partition (i.e., one formatted by an operating system, such as MS-DOS or Windows 3.x). This prevents it from being mistakenly installed over some other type of operating system, such as Windows NT or Novell NetWare.

TEST TIP

Remember that Windows 9x requires that a FAT 16 partition exist on the drive on which it is being installed.

TEST TIP

Memorize the minimum, recommended, and preferred CPU specifications for running Windows 9x.

The Windows 95 system must be at least an 80386DX or higher machine, operating with at least 4 MB of RAM (8 MB is recommended). The 80386DX is the listed minimum microprocessor for running Windows 95, and the recommended processor is the 80486DX, but the Pentium processors are actually the preferred microprocessor for running Windows 95. Likewise, 4 MB may be the minimum RAM option, with 8 MB being the recommended option, but 16 MB, 32 MB, or 64 MB are preferred for running Windows 95.

The system should also possess a mouse and a VGA monitor or better. The system's hard drive should have at least 20 MB of free space available to successfully install Windows 95. The actual requirements for successfully installing Windows 95 depend on the type of installation being conducted and what level it is being conducted from. As already mentioned, Windows 95 must be installed on a hard drive that already has a FAT16 structure in place (i.e., MS-DOS, Windows 3.1, and Windows for Workgroups systems).

In addition, the Windows 95 Setup installation routine provides for different types of installations, including Typical, Portable, Compact, and Custom, all of which install different combinations of the possible Windows 95 system. Therefore, they all have different system requirements for proper installation.

TEST TIP

Memorize the minimum and recommended amounts of memory specified to start Windows 95.

To perform a Typical installation in a DOS system requires a minimum of 40 MB of free drive space. Conversely, conducting a Compact installation on the same system would only require 30 MB. When the installation is being conducted from a Windows 3.1 or Windows for Workgroup environment, the free space requirements drop to 30 MB Typical/20 MB Compact for Windows 3.1 and 20 MB Typical/10 MB Compact for Windows for Workgroups. The total required free space can range up to 85 MB when a Custom installation is conducted using all of the Windows 95 options.

To run the Windows 95 Setup program from the command line,

1. Boot the computer.

2. Insert the Windows 95 Start Disk (Disk 1) in the A: drive, or place the Windows 95 CD in the CD-ROM drive.

3. Move to the drive that contains the Windows 95 Installation files.

4. At the command prompt, type *Setup* and press the *ENTER* key.

5. Follow the directions from the screen and enter the information requested by the program for the type of installation being performed.

Installing Windows 98

Unlike Windows 95, Windows 98 does not need to be installed over an existing operating system. Only the Upgrade version of Windows 98 requires an existing operating system such as MS-DOS, Windows 3.1x, or Windows 95. The distribution CD for the full version of Windows 98 can be used to boot the system and provide options to partition and format the drive.

To install Windows 98, the system hardware must be at least an 80486DX/66 or higher machine, operating with at least 16 MB of RAM. The system should also possess a modem, a mouse, and a 16-color VGA monitor or better. The system's hard drive should have between 120 and 355 MB of free space available to successfully install Windows 98. The actual amount of disk space used depends on the type of installation being performed (Typical, Custom, Portable, Compact, New, Upgrade, etc.). Typical installations use between 170 and 225 MB of disk space.

Several possible circumstances determine how Windows 98 should be installed. If Windows 98 is being installed in a new unit, or to a disk drive that has been reformatted, it will be necessary to boot the system from the Windows distribution CD or run the SETUP.EXE program from the command prompt. This method is also employed when Windows 98 is used to upgrade a system from Windows 95 using new settings.

Using this approach, the Windows 98 Setup program runs a real-mode version of the ScanDisk utility on the drive. This requires that the CD-ROM or network drive's real-mode driver be present and loaded. This ScanDisk version performs FAT, directory, and file checks on the drive and creates a ScanDisk log file. If an error is detected, the program displays an error message indicating that the log file should be checked. The file can be accessed through the ScanDisk View Log selection.

After the ScanDisk inspection has been completed, the Setup program initializes the system and begins copying installation files to the drive. The installation is carried out in the five-step procedure as follows:

1. *Preparing to Run Windows 98 Setup* — During this portion of the procedure, Setup performs the following steps to prepare the Windows 98 Setup Wizard to guide the user through the installation process.

2. *Collecting Information About the Computer* — After the Setup files have been extracted to the hard drive, the Setup Wizard begins operation by presenting the Microsoft Licensing Agreement and asking the user to enter the Product Key number, as illustrated in Figure 9-1. The product key can be found on the software's Certificate of Authenticity, or on the CD's jewel case. On stand-alone machines, this number must be entered correctly to continue the installation. Conversely, there will not be any Product Key request when Windows 98 is installed across a network.

Figure 9-1: Windows 98 Product Key Entry Screen

After the registration information has been gathered, Setup begins to collect information about the system.

After gathering this information, the Setup routine stops to prompt the installer to create an *Emergency Startup Disk* and then begins installing Windows 98 files to the selected drive.

3. *Copying Windows 98 Files to the Computer* — This portion of the operation begins when the Start Copying Files dialog box appears on the screen. The complete operation of this phase is automated so that no external input is required. However, any interruption of the Setup operation during this period might prevent the system from starting up again. In this event, it will be necessary to run the Setup routine again from the beginning.

4. *Restarting the Computer* — After Setup has copied the Windows 98 files into their proper locations, it will present a prompt to restart the system. Doing so enables the newly installed Windows 98 functions to become active. The restart will be conducted automatically if no entry is detected within 15 seconds.

5. *Setting Up Hardware and Finalizing Settings* — After the system has been restarted, Setup finalizes the installation of the operating system.

Upon completion of these steps, Setup again restarts the system and presents a log-on prompt. After the log-on process, Setup establishes a database of system driver information, updates the system's settings, establishes personalized system options, and presents a "Welcome to Windows 98" page on the screen.

Installing Window Me

The Windows Me operating system can be installed on any computer that has a Pentium 150 MHz or equivalent microprocessor, with at least 32 MB of RAM installed. The system should also possess a mouse, a CD-ROM or DVD drive, and a 16-color VGA monitor or better. The system's hard drive should have between 200 MB of free space available to successfully install Windows Me. The actual amount of disk space used depends on the type of installation being performed (Typical, Custom, Portable, Compact, New, Upgrade, etc.). Typical installations use about 350 MB of disk space. A Custom installation that includes all the available Windows components will require up to 400 MB of space.

1. Like Windows 98, the distribution CD for the full version of Windows Me can be used to boot the system and provide options to partition and format the drive. Since an underlying FAT structure is not needed to install Windows Me, the system will be ready to load when the hard drive has been partitioned. The first step in this installation process is to ensure that the system will check the CD-ROM drive for a bootable disc. This is accomplished through the Boot Sequence setting in the CMOS Setup utility.

2. After verifying the boot sequence, the next step is typically to partition the drive for the operating system. At the command prompt type *FDISK* to open the FDISK and press the *ENTER* key to enable large disk support. From the FDISK menu screen, select the options to create a partition, set the active partition, exit the FDISK utility, and restart the computer.

3. Open the CD-ROM tray, insert the Windows Me CD-ROM in the tray and then close it. When the Windows Me CD-ROM Startup Menu is displayed, select the *Boot from CD-ROM* option and press the *ENTER* key.

4. If the system does not autostart the Windows Me CD, restart the computer. At this point, you should insert the Windows Me CD-ROM into the appropriate drive and boot the computer to the CD-ROM. At the Startup menu, select the *Start computer with CD-ROM support* option and press the *ENTER* key.

5. Run the Windows Millennium Setup program. Reboot the computer to the CD-ROM, select the *Start Setup From CD-ROM* option, and press the *ENTER* key. At the *Welcome to Windows Me Setup* screen, shown in Figure 9-2, press *ENTER*. The Setup program will prompt you to format the hard-disk drive. Press *ENTER* again to begin the formatting process.

Figure 9-2: Microsoft Window Me Setup Screen

6. Next, the Setup process will perform some routine system checks. Press *ENTER* to continue the installation.

7. Click on the *Next* button on the *Welcome to Windows Me Setup* screen to start the Windows Me installation process.

8. When prompted, select the directory where the Windows Me operating system should be installed. It is strongly recommended that you use the Windows default selection (click on the *Next* button to accept the default C:\Windows directory for the install).

9. The *Setup Option* screen lists four types of installations to choose from. Select the appropriate installation type and click on the *Next* button.

10. In the *Windows Components Setup* window, select the Install the most common components option and click on the *Next* button.

11. When prompted at the *Network Identification* screen, enter the Computer Name and accept the default Workgroup Name (or enter the appropriate name). Click on the *Next* button to proceed.

12. Establish the Country/Region where the computer is located and click on the *Next* button.

13. Establish the Time zone setting for the computer system and click on *Next*. You should now be prompted that Windows Me is ready to begin copying files. Click on the *Finish* button to begin Copying Files. After the system reboots and installs drivers you will be prompted to enter User information. When ready, click on the *Next* button to move forward.

14. When the License Agreement screen appears click on the *I accept the Agreemen*t radio button and click on the *Next* button.

15. On the *Product Key* page, enter the product key number and click on the *Next* button.

16. Click on *Finish* to complete the Windows Millennium Edition setup. The computer will reboot at this point. When Windows restarts, it resumes the setup and begins checking and setting up the hardware, then automatically restarts the system.

17. Windows continues its setup process and configures the system software. When the Restart timer appears, click on the *Restart Now* button, or let Windows restart the system to complete the installation.

18. When the system restarts, an *Enter Windows Password* window may appear. Enter Marcraft as the username and, if desired, enter a password. Otherwise, click on *OK*.

NOTE

The Product Key can generally be found either on the sleeve that the CD-ROM came in, or on the CD itself.

NOTE

When the Windows Me operating system installation has been completed, it installs any hardware it found and personalizes the system. The operating system is now installed and ready for you to investigate some of its basic features.

Operating System Upgrading

The A+ Operating System Technologies objective 2.2 states that the test taker should be able to identify steps to perform an operating system upgrade from Windows 9.x/Me, Windows NT 4.0 Workstation, Windows 2000 Professional, and Windows XP. Given an upgrade scenario, choose the appropriate next steps. The reason for this objective is that it is not uncommon for a computer to have its operating system upgraded, possibly several times, during its life span. The following sections of this chapter cover upgrading from MS-DOS, Windows 3.x, or Windows 95 environments to the Windows 98/Me operating systems. Upgrading to Windows 2000 and Windows XP is covered in the next chapter.

Upgrading to Windows 98/Me

In order to upgrade to Windows 98 or Windows Me from an existing Windows version, and retain the current system settings, the Setup program should be executed from the Windows 95 user interfaces. Windows 98 and Windows Me Setup routines will execute the same basic five-step procedure described earlier from either interface. However, the events that occur within each step are dependent on the operating system information that is already available.

When Windows 98 or Windows Me is installed on a current Windows 95 machine, using the
existing settings, the Setup program acquires information about the system's hardware, applications, and utilities from the existing Registry entries. The existing information is simply
migrated into the new Windows 98/Me structure. In this manner, a lot of time is saved since
the system does not have to run a full hardware detection routine, or configure the system's
hardware. The Setup routine also skips to the option of selecting a Setup type (i.e., Custom,
Typical, etc.).

During Phase 1 of the Windows 98/Me upgrade, the system checks for the presence of
anti-virus software in the system. The Setup routine may fail if CMOS Anti-virus is enabled.
If this occurs, the SETUPLOG.TXT file should be checked for information about the
anti-virus test. In some cases, the Setup program may ask that the anti-virus software be disabled so that it can have access to the Master Boot Record. Setup will also modify the
AUTOEXEC.BAT file, causing it to run a file called SUWARN.BAT. This file reboots the
system in case of a failure, and presents an explanation of why the Setup failed.

In Phase 2 of the upgrade, the real-mode ScanDisk operation is carried out, and Setup runs
the **SCANREGW.EXE** file to check the existing Registry for corruption during this phase.
The Setup routine also provides a prompt that permits the current MS-DOS or Windows System Files to be saved in case an uninstall operation is required for Windows 98 or Windows
Me at some future time.

The Setup routine copies the Windows 98/Me files to the computer during Phase 3. This segment of the process begins with the appearance of the Start Copying Files dialog box on the
screen. This phase is completely automated and requires no external intervention. However,
any interruption of the Setup operation during this period may prevent the system from starting up again. In this event, it will be necessary to repeat the entire Setup routine from the
beginning.

In Phase 4, the Restart operation includes a step where the Setup routine modifies the
WIN.INI, SYSTEM.INI, and Registry files to include the appropriate Windows 98/Me entries. Likewise, an existing AUTOEXEC.BAT or CONFIG.SYS file will be examined for
device drivers and Terminate and Stay Resident programs that may be incompatible with the
upgraded installation. TSR programs can be quite problematic and should be deactivated before conducting any operating system upgrade. The results of this check are logged in a hidden file at *C:\Windows\Inf_folder\Setupc.inf.* The Setup routine disables the questionable
entries in these files by using REM statements.

You should be aware that active anti-virus software may prevent Windows 98 or Windows
Me from installing to a system. These utilities see the changes to the new operating system's
core files as a virus activity and will work to prevent them from occurring. Any anti-virus
program should be disabled prior to running Windows 98/Me Setup. The program can be
re-enabled after the setup process has been completed.

In cases where it is desirable to install Windows 98 or Windows Me into some directory other than the C:\Windows directory, click on the *Other Directory* button in the *Select Directory* dialog box, depicted in Figure 9-3, and click on *Next*. This will produce the *Change Directory* dialog box. Type the new directory name in the dialog box, and click on *Next*. The new directory will be created automatically, if it does not already exist.

Figure 9-3: The Select Directory Dialog Box

If Windows 98 or Windows Me is installed in a new directory, it will be necessary to reinstall any Windows-based applications in the system. This will be required in order for the applications to function properly. The applications' support DLLs will not be able to automatically access the Windows 98/Me structure in the new directory. Likewise, existing .GRP and .INI files will not work unless Windows 98 or Windows Me has been installed in the Windows directory.

If Setup detects the presence of a Windows 3.x operating system, it will ask if it should install its files in the same directory. If the prompt is answered with "Yes", then Windows 9x will act as an upgrade over the existing Windows structure. It will obtain existing configuration information from the SYSTEM.INI, WIN.INI, and PROTOCOL.INI files and move it into the Windows 9x **Registry**. This will enable these settings to work automatically when Windows 9x is first started.

Registry

If the answer to the installation directory question is "No", then you will be asked where the Windows 9x files should be installed. By installing Windows 9x in a new directory, it will be possible to preserve and use the old MS-DOS or Windows environment. In order to boot to either operating system it will be necessary to configure the system with dual boot options.

Dual Booting with Windows 9x/Me

dual-boot system

In a **dual-boot system**, a startup menu is established that can be used to boot the system into different operating systems on the disk. Depending on which OS option the user selects from the menu, the system will retrieve the correct set of files and then use them to boot the system.

Establishing a dual-boot configuration makes it possible to install Windows 9x or Windows Me and some other operating system on an existing system and then be able to select which operating system to boot the system with. To accomplish this, Windows 9x swaps versions of the boot files back and forth between their standard names and a designated set of backup names.

The first step in establishing a Windows 9x/Me dual-boot system is to install the Windows 9x/Me operating system into a new directory. The Windows 9x/Me Setup routine locates and stores existing MS-DOS files under .DOS extensions when it is installed as an upgrade over a previous operating system. In particular, the AUTOEXEC.BAT, COMMAND.COM, CONFIG.SYS, IO.SYS, and MSDOS.SYS files are stored with this extension.

The original IO.SYS, MSDOS.SYS, COMMAND.COM, CONFIG.SYS, and AUTOEXEC.BAT files are stored in the root directory using a **.DOS extension**. If the system is started with the other operating system, the Windows 9x versions of AUTOEXEC.BAT, COMMAND.COM, CONFIG.SYS, IO.SYS, and MSDOS.SYS are stored under .W40 extensions, and the renamed DOS versions of the files are returned to their normal extensions.

.DOS extension

They will also need to be handled as any other hidden, read-only, system files. Use the **ATTRIB command** to read and copy them (e.g., attrib -h -s -r IO.SYS). It will be necessary to perform the same copy/rename/copy operations to create CONFIG.DOS and AUTOEXEC.DOS files that are appropriate for the version of MS-DOS you are using in the system. Simply restart the system and perform the necessary steps to start and run the MS-DOS or Windows 9x operating system.

ATTRIB command

Windows 9x Startup

A portion of A+ Operating System Technology objective 2.3 indicates that the test taker should be able to identify the basic system boot sequences and boot methods, including the steps to create an emergency boot disk with utilities installed for Windows 9x/Me, Windows NT 4.0 Workstation, Windows 2000 Professional, and Windows XP. It also states that the content may include the boot sequence, the files required to boot, and the boot steps for Windows 9.x and NT-based systems.

Windows 9x takes over the complete bootup function as a normal part of its operation. This seamless bootup might be convenient for users, but it can offer some interesting problems when the system will not boot—there's no stable command-line level to fall back to for troubleshooting purposes. Special actions must be taken to overcome this problem. Basically, the Windows 98 bootup sequence occurs in the same five phases as the Windows 9x bootup did:

- Phase 1 — bootstrap with the BIOS

- Phase 2 — loading DOS drivers and TSR files

- Phase 3 — Real-mode initialization of static **Virtual Device Drivers (VxDs)**

Virtual Device Drivers (VxDs)

- Phase 4 — Protected-mode switchover

- Phase 5 — loading of any remaining VxDs

Phase 1: The Bootstrap Process

During the bootstrap process, the Plug-and-Play BIOS checks the system's CMOS RAM to determine which PnP devices should be activated, and where their PnP information should be stored. Each card's DMA, IRQ, and I/O addressing assignments are also collected. After all of the configuration information has been gathered, the BIOS configures the PnP cards and the intelligent system board devices. It then performs the traditional POST and initialization functions for the rest of the system. These functions are illustrated in Figures 9-4, 9-5, and 9-6.

Figure 9-4: Reading PnP Information from CMOS

Figure 9-5: Initializing PnP Cards

Figure 9-6: Programming the On-Board Devices

The BIOS then moves into the bootup process. The bootstrap loader routine searches for the Master Boot Record as it does with every other operating system. When the MBR is found, the system loads the IO.SYS and MSDOS.SYS files from the disk into memory, and turns over control to the IO.SYS file.

IO.SYS has the capability to display the Windows 9x Startup Menu, shown in Figure 9-7. The menu can be set up to be displayed each time the system boots by setting the BootMenu=1 option in the MSDOS.SYS file. Pressing the **left CTRL key** during bootup will retrieve the same menu. The "Starting Windows 9x" message will not appear on the screen using this key. The F8 function key will perform this function as well.

left CTRL key

```
Microsoft Windows 98 Startup Menu

    1. Normal
    2. Logged (\BOOTLOG.TXT)
    3. Safe Mode
    4. Step -by -Step Confirmation
    5. Command prompt only
    6. Safe Mode Command prompt only


Enter a choice:  3




F8 = Safe Mode  Shift + F5 = Command prompt  Shift + F8 = Step -by -Step Confirmation [N]
```

Figure 9-7: Windows 98 Startup Menu

Phase 2: Loading DOS Drivers and TSR Files

After the disk boot operation, IO.SYS checks the system's hardware profile to determine its actual configuration. This profile is a function of the BIOS' detection process during the initialization phase.

IO.SYS begins loading default drivers that were previously taken care of by the CONFIG.SYS file. These files include HIMEM.SYS, IFSHLP.SYS, SETVER.EXE, and DBLSPACE.BIN, as well as files, buffers, stacks, and dos=high settings.

If the F8 option for Step-by-Step startup has been selected, the system begins to generate a BOOTLOG.TXT file. This file, described in greater detail later in this chapter, tracks the Windows 9x components and drivers that are successfully loaded and initialized during the startup process.

At this point, IO.SYS begins looking for a CONFIG.SYS file. If found, the lines of the file are executed, and any values that are different than those loaded by the IO.SYS file are used instead. The CONFIG.SYS values for buffers, files, and stacks must be set to at least equal the default values in the IO.SYS file. The EMM386.EXE function must be initiated from the CONFIG.SYS file for any programs that require this memory manager.

Next, IO.SYS checks the MSDOS.SYS file for paths to find other Windows directories and files. These include such items as the selected location of the Windows 9x directory and startup files, including the Registry. The [Options] section of the file allows selected bootup events to be altered. This section can contain items to automatically display the Boot Menu, and to enable or disable key bootup features.

This is followed by executing the COMMAND.COM file. As with previous Microsoft operating systems, the Windows 9x COMMAND.COM extends the I/O functions of the system, supplies the command interface for the system, and looks for the AUTOEXEC.BAT file. If found, the AUTOEXEC.BAT commands are executed, loading device drivers and TSR programs in Real mode.

In the Windows 9x environment, the CONFIG.SYS and AUTOEXEC.BAT files primarily exist to maintain compatibility with applications written for earlier operating systems and environments. If neither of these files is present, the system will still start and run fine.

Phase 3: Initializing Static VxDs

The system next checks the SYSTEM.DAT file for the first part of the Registry file and processes it. SYSTEM.DAT is a hidden file that contains all of the system's hardware configuration information, including the PnP and application settings. It is always located under the C:\Windows directory. If the Windows 95 system does not find the SYSTEM.DAT file, it will refer to the SYSTEM.DA0 file, created during the previous bootup, as a backup. Likewise, Windows 98 refers to the rb000 Registry backup file located in C:\Windows\Sysbckup.

Afterward, IO.SYS loads the **WIN.COM** file to control the loading and testing of the Windows 9x core components. Next, the **VMM32.VXD virtual machine manager** is loaded and, finally, the SYSTEM.INI file. SYSTEM.INI is loaded so that its information can be used to maintain compatibility with non-dynamic VxDs.

The VMM32.VXD file creates the virtual environment and loads the system's VxD files. It contains a list of all the VxD files the system requires. These files are stored in the **Hkey_Local_Machine\System\CurrentControlSet\Services\VxD** branch of the Windows 98 Registry. The virtual machine manager searches this branch of the Registry looking for static drivers. If the value in the listing is represented by a StaticVxD= statement, the VMM32.VXD file loads and initializes it in Real mode. It also statically loads any VxDs that have a device=xxxVxD entry. Conversely, the dynamic VxD files in the Registry are not loaded by the VMM32.VXD file.

VMM32 also checks the [386enh] section of the SYSTEM.INI file for static VxDs (device=xxxVxD). If it finds a VxD in the SYSTEM.INI file, that version will be used instead of any version found in the Registry.

Phase 4: Protected Mode Changeover

After loading all of the static VxDs, the VMM32.VXD file shifts the microprocessor into Protected mode operation and begins loading the Protected-mode components of the system. The Configuration Manager is loaded and initialized with configuration information from the PnP BIOS' earlier detection efforts. If no PnP information is available, the Configuration Manager develops a PnP tree by loading dynamically loadable drivers. Once the tree is in place, the Configuration Manager reconciles the configuration information for each device, resolves any conflicts, and then reconfigures any necessary devices.

Phase 5: Loading Remaining Components

Following the initialization process, the final Windows 98 components are loaded into the system. During this period:

- The KERNEL32.DLL and KERNEL386.EXE files are executed
- The GDI.EXE and GDI32.EXE files are executed
- The USER.EXE and USER32.EXE files are executed
- All fonts and other associated resources are loaded
- The WIN.INI file values are checked
- The Win 98 shell and machine policies are loaded
- The desktop components are loaded

The **KERNEL32.DLL** contains the Windows 9x core components, and the **KERNEL386.EXE** file loads the Windows 9x device drivers. The **GDI files** provide the base of the graphical device interface, and the **USER** files provide the user interface. The GDI files graphically represent and manage the system hardware devices.

| WIN.COM |

| VMM32.VXD virtual machine manager |

| Hkey_Local_ Machine\System\ CurrentControl Set\Services\VxD |

| KERNEL32.DLL |

| KERNEL386.EXE |

| GDI files |

| USER |

The WIN.INI and SYSTEM.INI files are included in the Windows directory to maintain compatibility functions with older software. These files are retained for use with older 16-bit applications and are not necessary for the operation of Windows 9x applications. However, these files will need to be checked if the Windows 9x system has conflicts with any 16-bit applications.

When the shell and desktop components are loaded, the system may display a prompt on the screen for the user to log on. This logon process allows the operating system to configure itself for specific users. Normal logon involves entering a **user name** and **password**. If no logon information is entered, then default values will be loaded into the system. The logon screen only appears if the system is in use with a network, or when there are settings that the user can customize.

If the system is connected to a network, the network logon screen appears, as depicted in Figure 9-8. Logging onto a network is becoming more common every day. Therefore, one of the most common startup actions for Windows 9x users is entering their information into the logon window. After the user logs on, the system's user-specific setup instructions are carried out.

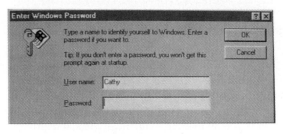

**Figure 9-8: Windows 9x
Network Logon Screen**

Windows 9x searches the Hkey_Local_Machine key and the user's home directory for user profile information. Windows 9x creates a folder for each user who logs on to the system. This profile is held in the \Windows\Profiles subdirectory. Each profile contains a USER.DAT file (the second half of the Registry) that holds the Registry information for that user. It also contains a number of other files that customize the desktop just for that user. As with the SYSTEM.DAT file, the USER.DAT file is backed up as USER.DA0 each time the Windows 95 system is rebooted. Under Windows 98, the USER.DAT backup is part of the rb000x.cab files.

┌─ **TEST TIP** ─────────────────┐
│ Be aware of the two files that make up the │
│ different Windows 9x Registries and │
│ where they are located. │
└────────────────────────────────┘

Earlier in this chapter we mentioned that the USER.DAT and SYSTEM.DAT files were located in the \Windows folder. The difference between that statement and the preceding one is that for single-user systems, these files are located in the \Windows folder. However, in multiple-user systems, Windows keeps profile information about all of its users in the \Windows\Profiles folder.

The Windows 9x startup sequence can be summarized as follows:

1. POST tests.

2. PnP configuration.

3. OS bootstrap looks for MBR.

4. System loads IO.SYS.

5. IO.SYS loads and executes CONFIG.SYS (if present).

6. IO.SYS loads MSDOS.SYS.

7. IO.SYS loads and executes COMMAND.COM.

8. COMMAND.COM looks for and executes AUTOEXEC.BAT (if present).

9. Windows 9x core files are loaded (Starting Windows notice displayed).

10. Windows 9x checks the Startup folder.

NAVIGATING WINDOWS 9X

A portion of the A+ Operating System Technologies objective 1.1 says that the test taker should be able to identify the major desktop components and interfaces, and their functions. Differentiate the characteristics of Windows 9x/Me, Windows NT 4.0 Workstation, Windows 2000 Professional, and Windows XP. It also indicates that content may include the major operating system interfaces.

When Windows 95, Windows 98, or Windows Me is started, it produces the basic **desktop** screen depicted in Figure 9-9. The desktop is the primary graphical user interface for all Windows 9x versions. As with previous Windows products, the desktop uses **icons** to quickly locate and run applications. In Windows 9x, however, the **Start button** provides the starting point for most functions.

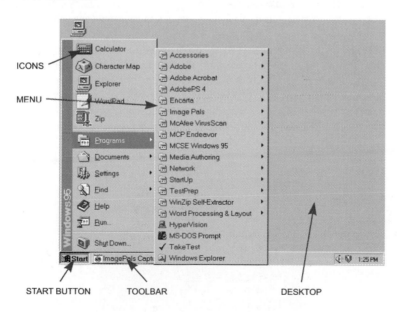

Figure 9-9:
The Windows 9x
Desktop Screen

Windows is a **task-switching** environment. Under this type of environment, several applications can run at the same time. In some cases, a particular application might be running on the desktop while others are running out of view. When you have multiple applications open in Windows, the window currently being accessed is called the active window and appears in the foreground (on top of the other windows). The activity of the other open windows is suspended, as denoted by their gray color, and their applications run in the background.

Select key combinations can be used to navigate through the Windows environment using the keyboard. The most common keys include the ALT, ESC, TAB, and ENTER keys. These keys are used to move between the different Windows structures and make selections (that is, the TAB key is used to move forward through different options, whereas the SHIFT+TAB combination is used to move backward through available options).

TEST TIP

Memorize the desktop's shortcut key combinations.

Special key combinations enable the user to move between tasks easily. By pressing the ALT and TAB keys together, you can quickly select one of the open applications. Similarly, the ALT+ESC key combination enables the user to cycle through open application windows. Pressing the CTRL+ESC keys will pop up the Start menu.

The Windows 95 Desktop

The desktop interface provides an easy method for starting tasks and making resource connections. Desktop icons are referred to as shortcuts (since the primary method of accessing applications is through the *Start* menu). Double-clicking the icon starts the application, or brings up its window.

In addition to the normal Windows left-click and double-click functions, Windows 95, Windows 98, and Windows Me all employ the right mouse button for some activities. This is referred to as **right-clicking**, or as **alternate-clicking** for right-handed users, and is used to pop up a menu of functions on the screen. The right-click menus in Windows 95 are context-sensitive, so the information they contain applies to the item that is being clicked on.

Alternate-clicking on an item produces a pop-up menu, similar to the left-hand menu in Figure 9-10. These menus enable the user to open, cut, or copy a **folder** (an icon that represents a directory), create a **shortcut**, delete or rename a folder, or examine **properties** of the folder. In the case of clicking on one of the system's hardware devices, the menu will permit you to perform such functions as sharing the device or checking its properties. These menus may have additional items inserted in their lists by applications that they serve.

Figure 9-10:
Right-Click Menus

Right-clicking in an open area of the desktop produces a pop-up menu, similar to the one displayed in the right-hand side of the figure. This menu enables the user to arrange icons on the desktop, create new folders and shortcuts, and see the properties of the system's video display.

The Windows 98/Me Desktop

In its basic form, the Windows 98/Me desktop is very similar to the Windows 95 desktop. The basic icons are located along the left border of the screen, the Taskbar runs across the bottom of the screen, and the Start menu pops up from the *Start* button on the Taskbar. However, some additional features of the new desktop, depicted in Figure 9-11, enable the user to quickly access a wide variety of resources.

**Figure 9-11:
Windows 98 Desktop**

Because the new desktop integrates the old Windows 95 desktop functions with the **Internet Explorer (IE) browser**, it can display the icons and windows typically found on the desktop, as well as HTML-based documents. This feature effectively places the desktop on-line, and creates an Active Desktop. As a matter of fact, web pages can be loaded into the desktop and automatically updated from the web. This type of operation is referred to as an **Active Channel**. On the desktop, the system displays icons representing the web links to these channels on the Channel Bar. The web sites listed on the Channel Bar can be located on an intranet or on the Internet (external organization), and are updated automatically from the server. This enables the user to always have access to the most recent information directly from the desktop.

> **Internet Explorer (IE) browser**

> **Active Channel**

The other items of interest on the Windows 98 desktop include an extended icon system, a **QuickLaunch toolbar**, user-defined toolbars, and Active Desktop elements. Windows 98 enables the user to establish toolbars for easy access to user-specific files. This can be done in any of three ways, as illustrated in Figure 9-12. The user can customize the QuickLaunch toolbar, customize the Windows 98 Taskbar, or create a new toolbar. The new toolbar can be a traditional toolbar that displays on the Taskbar, or it can be a floating toolbar that displays on the Active Desktop.

Figure 9-12: Windows 98 Toolbars

Active Desktop elements can be HTML files, JPEG files, GIF files, or an Internet Explorer window. Some of the items that appear on the desktop are a function of what the system finds as it looks for user profiles at the end of the bootup process. As mentioned earlier, the \Windows folder holds the system's default USER.DAT file. However, in a multiple-user system, the \Windows\Profiles directory contains a folder for each user that logs onto the system. These folders contain the individual user's USER.DAT files, along with a number of their desktop-related folders. These include each user's:

- Internet Explorer Cookies folder

- Desktop folder

- Favorites folder

- History folder

- My Documents folder

- NetHood folder

- Recent folder

- Start Menu folder

- Temporary Internet Files folder

NOTE

Cookies are collections of information samples from different users' visits to a web site.

Windows Me brought subtle changes to the Windows 9x system to make it more similar to the interfaces Microsoft was implementing in their Windows 2000 enterprise products, which are described in the next chapter. In particular, Windows Me changed the name of the Network Neighborhood applet to My Network Places to match the name and functions incorporated in Windows 2000. Figure 9-13 shows the standard Windows Me desktop.

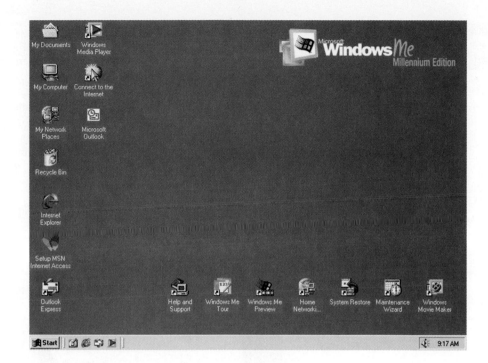

**Figure 9-13:
The Windows Me
Desktop**

Locating, Accessing, and Retrieving Information in Windows 9x

As the previous sections have shown, the Windows 9x/Me desktops feature three standard icons: My Computer, Network Neighborhood (My Network Places), and Recycle Bin. The major user interfaces in Windows 9x include:

- My Computer

- Pop-up dialog boxes

- The Start menu

- Windows Explorer

- Internet Explorer

- Network Neighborhood (My Network Places)

My Computer

The **My Computer** icon is the major user interface for Windows 9x. It enables the user to see the local system's contents and manage its files.

My Computer

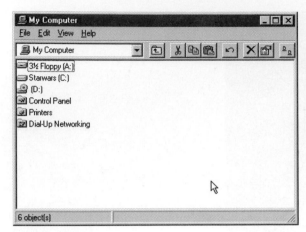

Figure 9-14:
My Computer Window

Double-clicking the *My Computer* icon will produce the *My Computer* window, shown in Figure 9-14. This window displays all the system's disk drives as icons, and represents the Control Panel and system printers as folders.

Double-clicking one of the drive icons produces a display of its contents onscreen. This information can also be displayed in several different formats using the *View* option. Selecting the *Options* entry in the View menu produces the *Folder Options* window displayed in Figure 9-15. This window consists of three tabs (screens): General, View, and File Types.

Figure 9-15: The Folder Options Window

General

Show Hidden Files

TEST TIP

Know how to show hidden files in the Windows 9x system.

Control Panel

Printers

The **General** tab supplies information about how the desktop will display windows as the user browses through multiple windows. The *View* window is used to define how the folders and files in the selected window will be displayed onscreen. This screen also determines which types of files will be displayed. To see hidden and system files, select the *View* tab and click on the **Show Hidden Files** button. Files with selected extensions will be hidden. The *File Types* screen lists the types of files that the system can recognize. New file types can be registered in this window.

The **Control Panel** and **Printers** folders under My Computer contain information about the system and its printers. The Windows 95 Control Panel is the user interface employed to manage hardware devices attached to the system. The Windows 98/Me Control Panel is explored in greater detail in a later section of this chapter.

The *Printers* folder displays the computer's installed printer types. As with other icons in the *My Computer* window, the printers can be displayed as small icons, large icons, in a simple list, or in a list with details. Details include such items as printer type, number of documents to print, current status, and any comments generated by the print controller.

Windows 9x Pop-up Menus

Most Windows 9x windows have **menu bars** that provide pop-up menus on the screen when they are accessed by clicking on their titles, or by pressing the ALT key and their underlined character (e.g., the ALT/F combination will pop up the File menu). Typical menu bar options include File, Edit, View, and Help. Options that apply to the current window are displayed as dark text. Options that are not applicable to the window are grayed out.

The *File* option on the My Computer menu bar can be used to perform many disk maintenance procedures. When a disk drive icon is selected, clicking on the *File* option will produce a menu that includes provisions for formatting the disk, sharing a drive with the network community, backing up the contents of the drive, or displaying its properties.

The File menu's **Properties** option displays general information about the drive, such as FAT type, capacity, free space, and used space. This option also provides a notice of how much time has elapsed since the last error-checking, backup, and defragmentation operations were performed on the selected drive.

The Windows 95 **View** menu option, shown in Figure 9-16, is one of the most used features of the menu bar. It can be used to alter the manner in which the contents of the window are displayed. The drives and folders in Figure 9-14 are displayed as **Small Icons**. However, they can be reduced to **Large Icons**, displayed as a **List**, or displayed with Name, Type, Size, and Free Space **Details**. Other options in the menu can be used to organize the icons within the window.

Figure 9-16:
The View Menu

A check mark located next to the menu option indicates that the item is currently in use. A large dot next to the item indicates that it is the currently selected option.

Double-clicking one of the drive icons produces a display of its contents on the screen. This information can also be displayed in several different formats using the *View* option. Selecting the **Options** entry in the View menu produces the *Options* window displayed in Figure 9-17. This window consists of three tabs (screens) — Folder, View, and File Types.

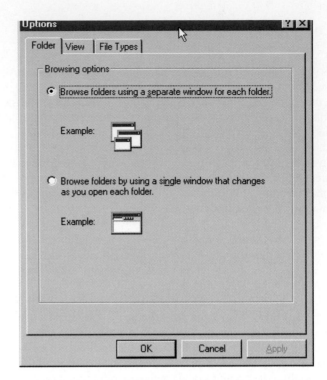

Figure 9-17: The View\Options Window

Formatting

Share

Backup

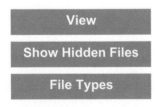

View

Show Hidden Files

File Types

The *File* option on the My Computer Menu Bar can be used to perform many disk maintenance procedures. When a disk drive icon is selected, clicking on the *File* option will produce a menu that includes provisions for **Formatting** the disk, **Share** a drive with the network community, **Backup** the contents of the drive, or displaying its properties.

The *Properties* option displays general information about the drive, such as FAT type, Capacity, Free Space, and Used Space. This option also provides a notice of how much time has elapsed since the last Error Checking, Backup, and Defragmentation operations were performed on the selected drive.

The *Folder* window supplies information about how the desktop will display windows as the user browses through multiple windows.

The **View** window is used to define how the folders and files in the selected window will be displayed on the screen. This screen also determines which types of files will be displayed. To see hidden and system files, select the *View* tab and click on the **Show Hidden Files** radio button. Files with selected extensions will be hidden. The **File Types** screen lists the types of files that the system can recognize. New file types can be registered in this window.

Right-clicking the *My Computer* icon produces a menu listing, similar to the one shown in the left-hand side of Figure 9-10. This menu provides options for opening the *My Computer* window, exploring the system drives and files through the Windows Explorer, working with network drives, creating shortcuts, renaming the selected folders and files, and accessing the properties of the system's installed devices.

```
┌─ TEST TIP ──────────────────────────────
│  Know how to navigate to various parts of Windows 9x
│  through the My Computer icon.
└──────────────────────────────────────────
```

In Windows 98 and Windows Me, the My Computer options have been rearranged slightly from those of the Windows 95 My Computer window. In particular, the Options entry under the *View* menu has been replaced by *Folder Options*. The tabs in this window are titled General, View, and File Types. As with the Windows 95 version, the View/Folder Options/View window is used to define how folders and files will be displayed and to determine which types of files will be displayed.

The Network Neighborhood

The **Network Neighborhood** icon in Windows 95 and Windows 98 provides quick information about the world around the system when it's used in a networked environment.

Double-clicking either of these icons will produce the *Network Neighborhood* window illustrated in Figure 9-18. Small computer icons represent the various computers attached to the network. They enable the user to browse through the network. Double-clicking on any of the icons will produce a listing of the resources the selected computer offers, such as disk drives and printers. Under Windows Me, the *Network Neighborhood* icon has been renamed "My Network Places".

**Figure 9-18:
Network
Neighborhood**

The Recycle Bin

The **Recycle Bin** is a storage area for deleted files that enables you to retrieve files if they are deleted by mistake. When you delete a folder or file from the Windows system, it removes the first three letters of its name from the drive's FAT so that it is invisible to the system. However, the system records its presence in the Recycle Bin. The system is free to reuse the space on the drive since it does not know that anything is there. As long as it hasn't been overwritten with new data, or it hasn't been removed from the Recycle Bin, it can be restored from the information in the Recycle Bin. If it has been thrown out of the bin but has not been overwritten, it can be recovered using a third-party software utility for recovering deleted files.

TEST TIP

Know what happens to files moved into the Recycle Bin.

The Recycle Bin icon should always be present on the desktop. It can only be removed through the Registry. If its icon is missing, there are two alternatives for restoring it: establish a shortcut to the Recycle Bin using a new icon, or just reinstall Windows 9x. This action will always place the Recycle Bin on the desktop.

TEST TIP

Know how to replace the Recycle Bin's icon in a Windows 9x system.

In the case of removable media, such as floppy disks and removable hard drives, the Recycle Bin does not retain the files deleted from these media. When a file or folder is removed from one of these devices, the information is deleted directly from the system.

TEST TIP

Be aware that information deleted from a removable media is not moved into the Recycle Bin. Therefore, no recovery is possible for this information.

The Taskbar

The *Start* button, located at the bottom of the screen, is used to accomplish several different tasks depending on the context of the operation. For example, the *Start* button is used to start programs, alter system settings, and open documents. Clicking on the *Start* button produces a Start menu onscreen.

Taskbar

Just to the right of the *Start* button is an area called the **Taskbar**. This area is used to display all the applications currently open. Each time a program is started, or a window is opened, a corresponding button appears on the Taskbar. To switch between applications, just click on the desired program button to make it the active window. The button will disappear from the Taskbar if the program is closed.

notification area

systray

A small window at the extreme right side of the Taskbar shows programs and events that occur in the background (mouse drivers, anti-virus programs, volume control, etc.). This area is referred to as the **notification area** or more commonly as the **systray**. On most systems at least the time of day clock will be displayed here. The icons in this area provide quick links to programs and services, such as the volume control icon, that are running in the background.

Right-clicking on the Taskbar at the bottom of the screen produces a menu that can be used to control the appearance of the Taskbar and open windows onscreen.

The Taskbar can be moved around the display by clicking and dragging it to the left, right, or top of the screen. It can be hidden just off screen by clicking on its edge and then dragging it toward the edge of the display. If the Taskbar is hidden, pressing the CTRL+ESC key combination will retrieve it. This will pop up the Start menu along with the Taskbar. Enter the Start/Settings/Taskbar & Start Menu option to change the Taskbar settings so that it will not be hidden. You can also locate an absent Taskbar by moving the mouse around the edges of the screen until the shape of the cursor changes. Likewise, pressing the TAB key will cycle control between the Start menu, the Quick launch icons, the Taskbar, and the desktop icons. The TAB key can be helpful in navigating the system if the mouse fails.

TEST TIP

Know how to move around the desktop, Start menu, and Taskbar using the keyboard.

The Start Menu

All operations begin from the *Start* button. When you click on the button, a pop-up menu of options appears, as illustrated in Figure 9-19. This menu normally contains the options Programs, Documents, Settings, Find, Help, Run, and Shut Down.

Placing the cursor over designated menu items will cause any submenus associated with that option to pop up onscreen. An arrow to the right of the option indicates a submenu is available. To open the selected item, just left-click on it and its window will appear on the desktop.

The Programs submenu, depicted in Figure 9-20, has several options that include Accessories, StartUp, MS-DOS Prompt, and Windows Explorer.

Figure 9-19: The Start Button Menu

Figure 9-20: The Programs Submenu

The Programs/Accessories entry is of particular interest to technicians because it provides access to some of the most frequently used Windows operating system tool groups and utilities. These groups include the Communications utilities, the Internet Tools, the Entertainment controls, and the System Tools. The System Tools group contains many utilities that are used to maintain and optimize the system, as illustrated in Figure 9-21. All of the tools in this area are covered in detail in Chapter 12 — *Operating System Troubleshooting*.

Figure 9-21: The Programs/Accessories/ System Tools Menu

The System Tools menu in Windows Me includes an option called *System Restore*. This utility is included as one of the system tools because in Windows Me, Microsoft removed the F5/F8 access to configuration and single-step startup tools. Instead, this tool enables users to create known good **Restore points** that the computer can be restored to if its configuration becomes corrupt. This tool is described in some detail in Chapter 12.

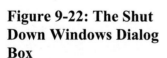

The Start menu's *Documents* entry displays a list of documents previously opened.

The *Settings* option displays values for the system's configurable components. It combines previous Windows functions, such as copies of the Control Panel and Print Manager folders, as well as access to the Windows 9x Taskbar.

The Find utility is used to locate folders, files, mail messages, and shared computers. The Find function can be accessed directly from the *Start* menu, or it can be reached by right-clicking on the *My Computer* icon. The selection from the *Start* menu allows searches for files, folders, and computers. The My Computer version searches only for files and folders. To locate a file, just type its name in the *Named* window, tell the system which drive or drive to look in, and click on the *Find* option. Standard MS-DOS wildcards can be included in the search name.

The Help file system provides extensive information about many Windows 9x functions and operations. It also supplies an exhaustive list of guided troubleshooting routines for typical system components and peripherals.

The *Run* option is used to start programs or open folders from a command-line dialog box. To start an Executable file, simply type its filename in the dialog box and click on the *OK* button. The *Browse* button can be used to locate the desired file by looking through the system's file structure.

The **Start button** is also used to correctly shut down Windows 9x. The *Shut Down* option from the *Start* menu shuts down the system, restarts the computer, or logs the user off. It must be used to avoid damaging files and to ensure that your work is properly saved. When it is clicked, the *Shut Down Windows* dialog box shown in Figure 9-22 appears. After you select an option from the dialog box, the operating system will tell you to wait, and then it will give you a screen message telling you that it is okay to turn off the system.

Figure 9-22: The Shut Down Windows Dialog Box

The Windows 98 Start Menu

The Windows 98 *Start* button remains on the Taskbar at the bottom of the screen. Clicking on the button produces the *Start* menu, similar to the one depicted in Figure 9-23. While most of the entries are carryovers from Windows 95, the *Log Off User* and *Favorites* entries are new.

Windows 98 enables individuals in multiuser systems to log onto, and operate in, Windows 98 environments that have been specifically configured to their work needs. The *Log Off User* option is used to return the system to its natural setup. The *Log Off* entry may not appear in some installations, such as stand-alone machines that are not connected to a network environment.

The Favorites entry is included to allow the user to store locations of often-used files. These files can be local to the machine, located on a local area network, or remotely located on the Internet. The Internet Explorer checks web sites specified in the Favorites folder regularly for updated information.

The *Shut Down* option from the menu has been changed so that there are only three possible methods listed for shutting down the session. They are *Shut Down*, *Restart* (warm boot), and *Restart in MS-DOS mode*. Windows 98 also includes a *Standby* option in the *Shut Down* menu. This option enables the user to put the system in a power conservation mode when it will not be active for some time. Standby keeps Windows ready to go when an event happens, but does not keep the system's I/O devices awake.

Figure 9-23: Windows 98 Start Menu

Additional items can be added to the *Start* menu so that they can be used directly from this menu. By doing so, the normal method of clicking on *Start*, pointing to the *Program* option, and moving through submenus can be avoided. To move a frequently used item to the top of the *Start* menu, simply drag its icon to the *Start* button on the Taskbar.

In Windows 98 and Windows Me it is also possible to move all of your frequently used programs to the *Programs* submenu. Frequently used items can be moved to the Windows 98 Taskbar, the QuickLaunch toolbar, or user-created toolbars for easy access.

```
┌─ TEST TIP ─────────────────────┐
│ Know how to navigate to various parts of │
│ Windows 9x through the Start menu.        │
└────────────────────────────────┘
```

Windows 9x Control Panels

The Windows **Control Panel** is the primary user interface for managing the Windows system. It contains a collection of Windows-specific applications and utilities (referred to as *applets*) that control different components of the operating system.

Control Panel

The Control Panel in Windows 95 can be accessed from multiple locations within the system. One *Control Panel* folder is located under the *My Computer* icon and another copy can be found under the *Start/Settings* path. Both folders access the *Control Panel* window, shown in Figure 9-24. This window contains icons for every device attached to the system. The *Control Panel* icon provides access to the configuration information for each of the system's installed devices specific to its type.

Figure 9-24: The Windows 95 Control Panel

Properties dialog box

Double-clicking on any of the device icons will produce a **Properties dialog box** for that device. Each box is different in that it contains information specific to the selected device. These dialog boxes may have a number of different folder tabs along their tops. Each tab is labeled with the type of information it holds. Clicking on a tab will display additional information for that dialog page. The most important uses of the Control Panel are:

- Adding or removing new hardware or software components to the system

- Modifying system device settings

- Modifying desktop items

Control Panel

The Windows 98/Me **Control Panel** remains the user's primary interface for configuring system components. It has been enlarged to control a number of new functions, as illustrated in Figure 9-25. In addition to the Windows 95 configuration icons, Windows 98 and Me add infrared device control options, an Internet configuration tool, a Power Management utility, support for scanners/digital cameras, and additional modem and communication control functions in the form of a Telephony utility. The final addition to their Control Panels is the *Users* icon that provides tools to establish and manage profiles for multiple users on the system.

The Windows 98/Me Control Panel can be accessed through the *My Computer* icon on the desktop, or through the *Settings* entry in the *Start* menu.

Figure 9-25: Windows 98 Control Panel Icons

Installation Wizards

The *Add New Hardware* icon brings the Add New Hardware Wizard into action. It will immediately ask the user if Windows should search for the new hardware through a PnP-style detection process. Clicking the *Next* option will cause Windows to conduct the hardware detection operation. If the device is not PnP, or if it must be installed manually because Windows 9x could not detect it, selecting the *No* option and clicking on *Next* will produce a hardware component list similar to the one shown in Figure 9-26. The Add New Hardware Wizard will guide the manual installation process from this point, and prompt the user for any necessary configuration information. If Windows 9x does not support the device, click on the **Have Disk button** to load drivers supplied by the device's manufacturer.

Have Disk button

TEST TIP

Know what action is required to install hardware devices not directly supported by Windows 9x.

Figure 9-26: The Hardware Wizard's Device Selection Page

The *Add/Remove Programs* icon leads to the *Install/Uninstall* screen illustrated in Figure 9-27. This page can be used to install new programs from floppies or CDs by simply clicking on the *Install* button. Conversely, programs listed in the programs window can be removed from the system by highlighting their title and clicking on the *Add/Remove* button.

The **Windows Setup** tab is used to add or remove selected Windows 9x components, such as communications packages or additional system tools. The Windows **Startup Disk** tab is used to create a clean startup disk for emergency start purposes after a crash. This disk can be used to boot the system to the command prompt (not the Windows desktop) so that you can begin troubleshooting failed startups. The Windows 98 Start disk provides CD-ROM support that is not available with the Windows 95 Start disk.

Windows Setup

Startup Disk

TEST TIP

Remember the location of the Control Panel screen that is used to create a Windows Startup Disk.

Figure 9-27: The Install/Uninstall Wizard Window

The System Icon

System icon

System Properties

One of the main Control Panel icons is the **System icon**. Clicking this icon produces the **System Properties** window displayed in Figure 9-28. This window features tabs for General information, the Device Manager, Hardware Profiles, and system Performance.

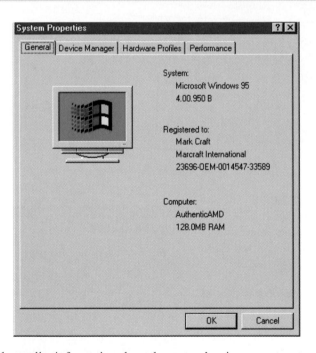

**Figure 9-28:
The System Properties
Window**

General

The **General** tab supplies information about the system's microprocessor type and RAM capacity, as well as its ownership and registration.

┌─ **TEST TIP** ─────────────────────────────┐
│ Memorize the types of information provided by the │
│ *General* tab of the System Properties page. │
└──┘

Device Manager

The **Device Manager** utility, shown in Figure 9-29, provides a graphical representation of the devices configured in the system. This interface can be used to identify installed ports, update device drivers, and change I/O settings. It can also be used to manually isolate hardware and configuration conflicts. The problem device can be examined to see where the conflict is occurring. In Windows 9x, the Device Manager can be accessed through the *Start/Settings/Control Panel/System* path.

Device Manager

TEST TIP
Memorize the pathway to the Device Manager's Properties screens.

User Selection Conflict

Conflicting devices

The Device Manager will display an exclamation point (!) inside a yellow circle whenever a device is experiencing a direct hardware conflict with another device. Similarly, when a red "X" appears at the device's icon, the device has been disabled due to a User Selection Conflict.

If a conflict is suspected, click on the offending device in the listing, make sure that the selected device is the current device, and then click on the **User Selection Conflict** tab to examine its **Conflicting devices** list. Make sure that the device has not been installed twice.

**Figure 9-29:
The Windows 9x
Device Manager**

The Device Manager contains a set of buttons that permit its various functions to be accessed. These buttons include: *Properties*, *Refresh*, *Remove*, and *Print*.

Typical *Device Manager Properties* pages provide tabs that can be used to access general information, device settings, device drivers information, and device resources requirements and usage. Each device may have some or all of these tabs available depending on what type of device it is and what its requirements are.

The information under the tabs can be used to change the properties associated with the selected device. This often becomes necessary when resource conflicts occur in a system that has legacy devices installed. The Device Manager can be used to identify possible causes of these IRQ, DMA, I/O, and memory settings conflicts.

Hardware Profiles

The *System* icon's **Hardware Profiles** tab provides a window that can be used to establish different hardware configuration profiles to be implemented at startup. Most systems do not require any additional profiles. The *System* icon's **Performance** tab displays information about the system's installed RAM, system resource usage, virtual memory settings, and disk FAT type.

The final major Control Panel function is to enable users to customize the Windows 9x desktop. This customization includes such things as setting screen colors, changing the Windows **wallpaper**, and selecting **screen savers**. Wallpaper is the pattern that shows behind the various application windows. Screen savers are screen displays that remain in motion while the system is setting idle. This utility prevents a single display from remaining on the screen for a prolonged time. This keeps the image from being "burned into" the screen. When this happens, the image becomes a permanent ghost on the screen and the monitor is ruined.

Windows 9x Files

A portion of the A+ Operating System Technologies objective 1.4 indicates that the test taker should be able to identify basic concepts and procedures for creating, viewing, and managing disks, directories, and files. This includes procedures for changing file attributes and the ramifications of those changes (for example, security issues).

The Windows 9x file system does away with the 8+3 character filename system implemented under MS-DOS. In Windows 9x, **long filenames** of up to 255 characters can be used, so that they can be more descriptive in nature. When these filenames are displayed in non-Windows 9x systems, they are **truncated** (shortened) to fit the 8.3 DOS character format and identified by a tilde character (~) followed by a single-digit number.

The tilde character is placed in the seventh character position of the filename to show that the filename is being displayed in a shortened manner as an alias for the full-length filename. The number following the mark will have a value of 1 assigned to it, unless another file has already been assigned the alias with a 1 value. Customers with older operating systems may overlook files because they are saved in this manner. Consider the following examples:

- oldlongfile.txt = oldlon~1.txt
- oldlongtable.txt = oldlon~2.txt
- oldlonggraphic.txt = oldlo~63.txt

The tilde character is inserted into the seventh character space for up to 9 iterations of similar filenames. After that, Windows will replace the sixth character for iterations up to 99. Windows 9x applies this same convention to the naming of directories as well. To change a log directory name from the command line requires that quote marks be placed around the name. Additional characters can be used in the Windows 9x long filenames. These characters include: + , : = [and]. Blank spaces can also be used in long filenames.

Windows Explorer

File Management

Windows Explorer

The **File Management** function in Windows 9x/Me and NT/2000/XP is performed through the **Windows Explorer** interface. This manager is located under the *Start/Programs* path from the Windows 9x/Me and NT 4.0 desktops. In Windows 2000 and XP, the Windows Explorer interface is located under *Start/Programs/Accessories*.

By clicking on the *Windows Explorer* entry, the system's directory structure will appear, as shown in Figure 9-30. You can access the Windows Explorer by right-clicking on the *Start* button, or by clicking on the *My Computer* icon and selecting the *Explore* option.

Figure 9-30: The Windows 9x Explorer Screen

The Windows Explorer enables the user to copy, move, and erase files on any of the system's drives. Its screen is divided into two parts. The left side displays the system's directory tree, showing all of the directories and subdirectories of its available drives.

In Windows 9x, directories and subdirectories are referred to, and depicted as, folders (and **subfolders**). Any drive or directory can be selected by clicking on its icon or folder. You can expand the content of a folder by clicking on the (+) sign beside it. Conversely, you can contract the same folder by clicking on the minus (-) sign in the same box.

subfolders

The Windows Explorer is not limited to simply showing the directories, subdirectories, and files on local drives. It will also display drives and folders from throughout the network environment. The contents of the local drives are displayed at the top of the directory tree. If the system is connected to a network, the additional resources available through the network are displayed below those of the local system as a continuation of its tree structure. One noticeable difference exists between the Windows 9x, Me, and Windows 2000/XP main tree structures in Windows Explorer—the *Printers* folder has been removed from the main tree and placed as a sub-branch of the *Control Panel* folder.

The right side of the Windows Explorer screen displays the files of the selected directory. Applications can be started from this window by double-clicking their executable file. Double-clicking on a file produced by an associated application will cause Windows to open the application and load the selected file. The **Status bar** at the bottom of the screen provides information about the number and size of the files in the selected directory. The *View* menu on the Windows Explorer menu bar can be used to set the display for large or small icons, as well as simple or detailed lists. The Explorer's View functions are the same as those described for the My Computer menu bar.

The Windows Explorer is also used to perform DOS-like functions, such as formatting and copying disks. Right-clicking on a folder icon will produce a menu that includes a **Send To** option, as shown in Figure 9-31. Moving the mouse to this entry will produce a submenu that can be used to send a selected folder or file to a floppy drive, or to the desktop. Several files or folders can be selected for copying using the SHIFT key.

Figure 9-31: The Send To Option

The contents of the right-click menu change in the Windows Explorer, depending on the item that is selected. Since the right-click function is context-sensitive, the menu produced for a folder will be different than the one displayed for a document file. Each menu will have options that apply to the selected item.

Right-clicking on a document file will produce options that enable the user to Copy, Cut, Rename, Open, or Print the document from the Windows Explorer. This menu also provides options to Create a Shortcut for the document, or to Change its Attributes.

By default, Windows Explorer does not show SYS, INI, or DAT files. To change file attributes from the Explorer, right-click on the desired file, select the *Properties* option from the pop-up list, move to the *General* page, and click on the desired attribute boxes. To see hidden and system files in Windows Explorer, click on the *View* menu option, select the *Folder Options* entry, click on the *View* tab, and check the **Show All Files** box. If you experience difficulty with this operation from the Windows environment, you can always access the file from the command prompt and change its attributes with the ATTRIB command.

Status bar

Send To

Show All Files

TEST TIP
Be familiar with efficient methods of changing file attributes from the Windows Explorer.

TEST TIP
Know which file types are normally not shown in Windows Explorer.

If Windows cannot identify the application associated with the selected file, the operator will need to start the application and then manually open the file. However, the user can also register the file's extension type under the *View/Folders* option from the menu bar. This will produce the Registered file types dialog box shown in Figure 9-32.

┌─ **TEST TIP** ────────────┐
Know how to navigate to various parts
of Windows 9x through the Windows
Explorer.
└─────────────────────────┘

**Figure 9-32:
The Registered
File Types Window**

The Windows File Menu

The Windows 9x/Me drop-down **File menu** performs basic file management-related functions for files and folders. These functions include the typical *Open*, *Close*, and *Save* operations that users constantly perform on files. In addition, the menu provides options that enable the user to rename the file or folder, create a shortcut for it, or establish properties for it. The *File* menu also includes an entry at the top of the menu titled *New*. Clicking on this option produces the *New* options submenu shown in Figure 9-33. This menu is used to create new folders, shortcuts, and files.

File menu

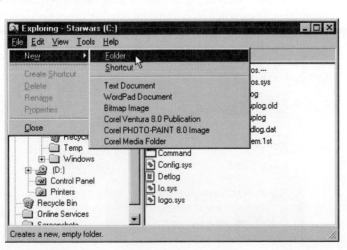

**Figure 9-33: The
New Options**

shortcut

To create a new folder in Windows Explorer, select a parent directory by highlighting it in the left window. Then click on the *File* menu button, move the cursor to the *New* entry, slide across to the *Folder* option, and click on it. A new unnamed folder icon will appear in the right *Explorer* window.

The same process is used to create new files. A file icon can be produced for any of the file types registered. Alternate-clicking on the new icon will produce the menu with options for renaming the icon, creating a shortcut for it, and establishing its properties (including its attributes).

A small arrow in the lower-left corner of an icon identifies it as a **shortcut**. When a shortcut is created, Windows does not place a copy of the file or application in every location that references it. Instead, it creates an icon in each location and defines it with a link to the actual location of the program in the system. This reduces the amount of disk space required to reference the file from multiple locations.

WINDOWS 9X/ME STRUCTURE

A portion of the A+ Operating System Technologies objective 1.1 says that the test taker should be able to identify the major desktop components and interfaces, and their functions. Differentiate the characteristics of Windows 9x/Me, Windows NT 4.0 Workstation, Windows 2000 Professional, and Windows XP. It also indicates that content may include the major operating system components.

When Windows 9x/Me starts, several major files are loaded into the system. These include:

GDI.EXE

GDI32.EXE

USER.EXE

USER32.EXE

WIN.COM

- the KERNEL32.DLL and KERNEL386.EXE files
- the **GDI.EXE** and **GDI32.EXE** files
- the **USER.EXE** and **USER32.EXE** files
- all fonts and other associated resources
- the WIN.INI file
- the Windows 9x shell and desktop files

The Windows 9x/Me program is loaded when the startup routine locates and executes the file named **WIN.COM**. This file resides in the *\Windows* folder and is responsible for loading the Windows operating system. When fully installed, the Windows 9x/Me structure is depicted in Figure 9-34.

Figure 9-34: The Windows 9x/Me Organizational Structure

The Windows 9x/Me core consists of three components: the **Kernel**, the **GDI**, and the **USER** files. Their functions are basically the same for both Windows 95 and Windows 98 architectures. The Kernel is the foundation of the system. It includes basic memory and I/O management, task scheduling, error (exception) handling, and program execution functions. The USER files manage input from hardware devices and output to the user interface components (that is, to the icons and screen structures). The GDI components control what appears on the video display and from the printer.

The Kernel files (KERNEL32.DLL and KERNEL386.EXE) contain the Windows 9x/Me core and load its device drivers. The GDI files provide the base of the graphical device interface; the USER files provide the user interface. The GDI files graphically represent and manage the system's hardware devices.

Any **WIN.INI**, **SYSTEM.INI**, and **WINFILE.INI** files that previously existed are included in the Windows directory to maintain compatibility functions with older software. These files are retained for use with older 16-bit applications and are not necessary for the operation of Windows 9x applications. These files must be checked if the Windows 9x system has conflicts with any 16-bit applications. The Windows 9x/Me shell program is normally the Windows 9x desktop.

Windows 9x/Me possesses system bootup files that replace the MS-DOS files described earlier in this chapter. The Windows 9x version of IO.SYS is a real-mode operating system that replaces the DOS version. It also takes over many of the functions associated with the CONFIG.SYS file. An MSDOS.SYS file is created to retain compatibility with older applications. However, the Windows 9x/Me VMM32 and VxD files take over control of the system from the IO.SYS file during the startup process. Windows 9x supplies its own version of COMMAND.COM as well.

No CONFIG.SYS or AUTOEXEC.BAT files are created when Windows 9x/Me is installed in a new system. These files are also not required by Windows 9x to start up or to run. Even so, both files will be retained from the previous operating system in upgraded systems to maintain compatibility with older applications. However, entries in the CONFIG.SYS file override the values in the Windows 9x/Me IO.SYS file.

The Windows 9x IO.SYS file also handles some of the AUTOEXEC.BAT commands. In both cases, the system uses *REM* statements to deactivate those CONFIG.SYS and AUTOEXEC.BAT functions implemented in the IO.SYS file. Similarly, the functions of the SYSTEM.INI and WIN.INI files have been moved to the *Windows 9x/Me Registry*.

Windows 9x/Me provides a mechanism for automatically starting programs whenever the operating system starts by adding them to the system's **Startup** folder. You can accomplish this by accessing the Start Menu's *Programs* tab and then selecting the *Add* option. From here you can simply browse until the desired program is found and then double-click on it. Finish the addition by clicking on the *Next* button and then double-clicking on the *Startup* folder. These programs can be bypassed for troubleshooting purposes by pressing the *left-SHIFT* key during startup.

Kernel

GDI

USER

TEST TIP

Be aware of the file that is used to load the Windows environment into memory.

WIN.INI

SYSTEM.INI

WINFILE.INI

Startup

TEST TIP

Remember how to prevent the items in the Windows 9x Startup folder from running at startup.

Windows 98/Me Components

The Windows 98/Me structure is organized as depicted in Figure 9-35. The Windows Registry, Configuration Manager, Virtual Machine Manager, and **Installable File System (IFS)** Manager operate between the Windows 9x core and the device drivers that service the system's hardware. On the other side of the Windows 9x core, applications running on the system are accessed through the new **32-bit Shell** and **User Interface tools**.

Figure 9-35: The Windows 98/Me Organizational Structure

The 32-bit Windows 98 and Windows Me structures basically build on the Windows 95 structure. However, Windows 98 and Me add enhanced video display support, power management functions, and additional hardware support. They also feature built-in Internet Explorer functions.

Windows 9x/Me Registries

Registry

In Windows 9x and Windows Me, the system's configuration information is held in a large hierarchical database called the **Registry**. The Registry structure is primarily used to hold information about system hardware that has been identified by the enumeration or detection processes of the Plug-and-Play system. When a device is installed in the system, Windows 9x detects it, either directly or through the system's bus managers, and searches the Registry and installed media sources for an appropriate driver. When the driver is found, it is recorded in the Registry along with its selected settings.

TEST TIP

Know what type of database Windows uses for its Registry.

The Registry also holds information that enables the system to serve and track multiple users. It does this by retaining user- and configuration-specific information that can be used to customize the system to different users, or to different configuration situations. This includes the local hardware configuration, the network environment, file associations, and user configurations.

USER.DAT

SYSTEM.DAT

The contents of the Registry are located in two files located in the \Windows directory. These are the **USER.DAT** and **SYSTEM.DAT** files. The USER.DAT file contains user-specific information, while the SYSTEM.DAT file holds hardware- and computer-specific profiles and setting information.

When applications were removed from the system in earlier Windows versions, the configuration information distributed between the various .INI files remained, unless the user, or a special Windows Uninstall program, looked them up and removed them individually. With Windows 9x versions, applications' headings and their associated configuration information are all removed from the Registry, unlike the old .INI method of tracking this information.

Each time Windows 95 boots up successfully, Registry files are backed up with a **.DA0 extension**. The content of the Registry can be viewed and altered through the **Registry Editor (Regedit.exe)** utility, as depicted in Figure 9-36. If the system experiences a Registry corruption problem, the USER.DA0 and SYSTEM.DA0 files can be renamed to .dat files and used to restore the Registry to its previous working configuration.

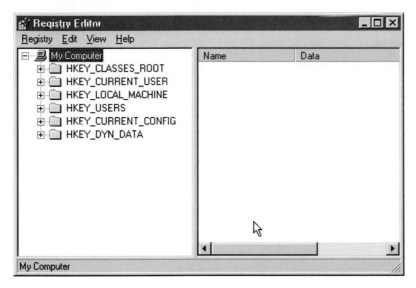

**Figure 9-36:
The Windows 9x
Registry Edit Window**

The content of the Registry is not backed up in the same way under Windows 98 and Windows Me that it was in Windows 95. The Windows 98/Me system makes up to five backup copies of the Registry structure each time it successfully starts Windows. The backed-up content of the Registry is stored in the *\Windows\Sysbckup* directory in the form of **cabinet (.CAB) files** (not as .da0 files). These files contain the following Registry-related files:

- System.dat

- System.ini

- User.dat

- Win.ini

The *Sysbckup* folder is a hidden folder. To examine its content, you must remove the hidden attribute from it. Inside the folder, the backup files are stored under an **RB0XX.CAB** format, where XX is a sequential backup number given to the file when it is created. Running the Scanreg /restore command will also produce a listing of the available backup files to select from for troubleshooting purposes.

Headkeys

Keys

Subkeys

Values

RegEdit

DWORDS

strings

The Registry uses English-language descriptions and a hierarchical organization strategy. The hierarchy is divided into **Headkeys**, **Keys**, **Subkeys**, and **Values**. Keys are descriptive section headers that appear at the left side of the **RegEdit** window. Values, on the other hand, are definitions of topics organized under the keys. This organization can be thought of in the same terms as the organization of any book; the head keys are similar to chapter titles, the keys and subkeys are equivalent to the major and minor headings of the chapters, and values are equal to the sentences that convey information.

Values can contain a wide variety of information types. They can contain interrupt and port address information for a peripheral system, or simply information about an installed application program. The information can be encoded into binary, **DWORDS**, or **strings**. Values are always located at the right side of the *RegEdit* window.

If you examine the My Computer heading using the *RegEdit* option, you will find six categories listed. The head keys all start with an HKEY_ notation.

Under My Computer the categories are:

- HKEY_CLASSES_ROOT
- HKEY_CURRENT_USER
- HKEY_USERS
- HKEY_LOCAL_MACHINE
- HKEY_DYN_DATA
- HKEY_CURRENT_CONFIG

Classes_Root

Current_User

Most of the HKEY titles should appear very descriptive of their contents. The **Classes_Root** key divides the system's files into two groups by file extension type and by association. This key also holds data about icons associated with the file.

The **Current_User** key holds data about the user-specific configuration settings of the system, including color, keyboard, desktop, and start settings. The values in the Current_User key reflect those established by the user that is currently logged into the system. If a different user logs in, then the content of the Users key is moved into the Current_User key.

Users

The **Users** key contains the information about the various users that have been defined to log into the system. The information from the Current_User key is copied into this section whenever a user logs off the system, or when the system is shut down.

Local_Machine

The **Local_Machine** key contains information about the system's hardware. All of the hardware drivers and configuration information is contained in this key. The system will not be able to use peripheral devices that are not properly documented in the Local_Machine key.

Dyn_Data

Current_Config

The **Dyn_Data** key and **Current_Config** keys work with the Local_Machine key. The Dyn_Data key works with the branch of the Local_Machine key that holds PnP dynamic status information for various system devices including current status and problems. The Current_Config key works with the Local_Machine branch containing current information about hardware devices.

The Windows Registry structure is primarily used to hold information about system hardware that has been identified by the enumeration or detection processes of the Plug-and-Play system. When a device is installed in the system, the operating system detects it, either directly or through the system's bus managers, and searches the Registry and installed media sources for an appropriate driver. When the driver is found, it is recorded in the Registry along with its selected settings.

Some devices, such as PCMCIA devices, can be inserted and removed under hot conditions (while power is on). The system will detect the removal or insertion of the device, and adjust its Registry configuration on the fly. Legacy, or PnP ISA, devices must be installed in the system before startup, and go through the PnP process.

The Registry also holds information that enables the system to serve and track multiple users. It does this by retaining user- and configuration-specific information that can be used to customize the system to different users, or to different configuration situations.

TEST TIP

Memorize the basic function of each Registry key.

CHALLENGE #3

One of your friends calls you to get some advice about his computer. He was reading an article about changing his Windows 98 system so that it would run games faster. The article mentioned making changes in the Registry, so he did — through the Registry Editor. Now his system will not run, and he does not know how to get it going again. What can you do to help him?

Windows 9x System Policies

Because Windows 9x provides multiuser operations, operational system policies are necessary to govern the rights and privileges of different users. Windows 9x **System Policies** establish guidelines to restrict user access to the options in the Control Panel and desktop. They also allow an administrator to customize the desktop and configure network settings.

System Policies

When a user logs on to the system, Windows 9x checks that user's configuration information. When found, the policy information associated with that user is moved into the Registry and replaces the existing settings. This information is held in the CONFIG.POL file. Policies can be established for individual users, for defined groups of users, for a specific computer, for a network environment, or for default settings.

The system policies that govern these functions are established and modified using an editor similar to the Registry Editor, called the **System Policy Editor (PolEdit)**. The Policy Editor is another tool that can be used to access the information in the Registry. Unlike the RegEdit utility, the Policy Editor can access only subsets of keys. The Registry Editor can access the entire Registry.

System Policy Editor (PolEdit)

Normally, the use of the PolEdit tool is restricted to the network administrator. Therefore, it is not normally installed on users' computers. This utility is located on the Windows 9x CD under the **Admin** folder so that only the keeper of the CD can adjust the system's policies. The path to access the Policy Editor on the CD is *Admin\Apptools\Poledit*. Once located, it can be executed by entering **PolEdit** in the Run box. This causes the Policy Editor screen to display, as depicted in Figure 9-37.

Figure 9-37: The Windows 9x Policy Editor

With any multiuser system, it may be necessary to establish various working environments for different users. Some users are entrusted with access to more of the system than other users. As described earlier, this is the purpose of logon procedures. The Windows 9x policy file tracks policies for different users in a file named CONFIG.POL. The contents of this file are moved into the USER.DAT and SYSTEM.DAT files when a user logs on.

The Policy editor enables system administrators to configure the Windows desktop differently for different users. Some users may not need to have access to certain system options, such as printers or Registry editing tools. Through the Policy Editor, access to these options can be removed from the desktop for a given user.

The window in Figure 9-37 contains an icon for a default user and a default computer. When the user logs onto the system, Windows searches for a user profile that matches the user logging in. If none is found, the default policies are copied into the new user's profile and used until modified by a system administrator. The editing screen used to modify the Default User's policies is shown in Figure 9-38.

Like the Registry Editor, the branches of the Policy Editor can be expanded or contracted by clicking on the plus (+) and minus (−) signs in the nodes of the tree. Three options can be selected for each setting: checked, cleared, or dimmed (grayed out). When a policy is checked, it is being implemented. If it is cleared (open), the policy is not implemented. When the policy is grayed out, the policy has not been changed since the last time the user logged on, Windows will not make any related changes to the system configuration, and users can make changes to the settings.

Figure 9-38: Inside the Policy Editor

As an example of the effects of these settings, consider the system's *Wallpaper* setting in the Control Panel. If the setting is checked, the designated wallpaper will be displayed. If the setting is cleared, no wallpaper will be displayed. Finally, if the setting is grayed out, Windows will not enforce the policy and the user can select his or her own wallpaper pattern through the Control Panel.

The FAT32 File System

Earlier versions of MS-DOS and Windows supported what is now called **FAT16** (or **FAT12**). The OSR2 version of Windows 9x introduced the FAT32 file management system. As described earlier, the size of the operating system's FAT determines the size of the clusters for a given size disk partition. Of course, smaller cluster sizes are better because even a single byte stored in a cluster will remove the entire cluster from the available storage space on the drive. This can add up to a lot of wasted storage space on larger drives. Table 9-1 describes the relationships between clusters and maximum partition sizes for various FAT entry sizes.

FAT16

FAT12

FAT TYPE	PARTITION SIZE	CLUSTER SIZE (IN BYTES)
FAT12	16 MB	4096
FAT16	32 MB	2048
FAT16	128 MB	2048
FAT16	256 MB	4096
FAT16	512 MB	8192
FAT16	1 GB	16384
FAT16	2 GB	32768
FAT32	<260 MB	512
FAT32	8 GB	4096
FAT32	16 GB	8192
FAT32	32 GB	16384
FAT32	>32 GB	32768

**Table 9-1:
FAT Relationships**

In order to use the FAT32 system, the hard drive must be formatted using the FDISK/FORMAT functions in OSR2. This makes FAT32 incompatible with older versions of Windows (even Windows 95(a) and Windows NT) and with disk utilities and troubleshooting packages designed for FAT12/16 systems.

To use the **FAT32 FDISK** function in OSR2, it is necessary to enable the **Large Disk Support** option. After completing the FDISK function and exiting, it is necessary to manually reboot the system. After this, it is usually a simple matter of performing a FORMAT operation using the OSR2 CD, or Start Disk, to install the FAT32 drive. Failure to reboot between the FDISK and FORMAT operations will produce an error.

FAT32 FDISK

Large Disk Support

To verify that the hard drive is formatted with FAT32, select the *My Computer* option from the desktop and right-click on the *C: drive* icon. This will produce the *[C:] Properties* window displayed in Figure 9-39. The *Type* entry should read *Local Disk [FAT 32]*. The hard drive usage pie chart will not work correctly with drives larger than 2 GB. It will show the drive as empty until at least 2 GB of space is used.

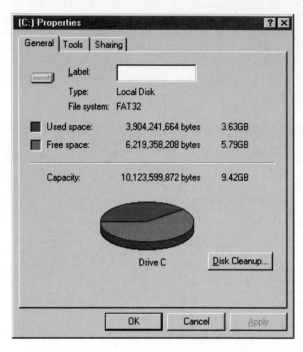

Figure 9-39: Showing FAT32 in the HDD Properties Window

OSR2 does not require that FAT32 be used. It will operate just as well, if not better using the FAT16 format. Depending on the application of the system, it may run slower with FAT32. Remember that FAT32 is designed to optimize storage space, not performance. The simple fact that FAT32 offers the potential for more clusters makes it slower than a drive with fewer clusters. With this in mind, the decision to use FAT32 or FAT16, or to use different cluster sizes in FAT32, usually depends on the balance the user establishes between performance and storage. The default cluster size set by Microsoft for FAT32 is 4 kB.

┌─ **TEST TIP** ─────────────┐
│ Know how to convert FAT16 partitions │
│ to FAT32 partitions. │
└──────────────────────────────┘

In Windows 9x, it is possible to convert partitions created on a FAT16 drive into a FAT32 file system using the CVT.EXE utility. The main drawback to doing this is that there is some possibility of data corruption and loss. Not surprisingly, there is no utility for converting FAT32 partitions to FAT16.

Virtual File Allocation Table

Windows 9x versions streamline the 32-bit file and disk access operations by removing the BIOS from the access equation, as illustrated in Figure 9-40. This enables Windows 9x to always run in Protected Memory mode, so that no mode switching need occur.

Figure 9-40: 32-Bit Access in Windows 9x

Because the system does not normally have to exit and reenter Protected mode, performance is increased considerably. The logical blocks of the VFAT are described in Figure 9-41.

Figure 9-41: The Windows 9x VFAT Interface

Microsoft refers to this portion of the system as the **Protected Mode FAT File System**. It is also called the **Virtual File Allocation Table** or **VFAT**. As its full name implies, the VFAT provides a Protected mode method of interacting with the file system on the disk drive. VFAT operates in 32-bit mode; however, the actual FAT structure of the disk remains as 12-bit or 16-bit allocations.

Protected Mode FAT
File System

Virtual File Allocation
Table (VFAT)

VCACHE

The VFAT system replaces the SMARTDRV disk caching utility with a protected-mode driver named **VCACHE**. Under VCACHE, the size of the cache data pool is based on the amount of free memory in the system instead of a fixed amount. The program automatically allocates blocks of free memory to caching operations as needed. Under Windows 9x, the VCACHE driver controls the cache for the system's CD-ROM drive, as well as for hard disk and file operations.

When a file or disk access request is received by Windows 9x, a subsection of the interface known as the **Installable File System (IFS)** processes the request by passing it to the proper **File System Driver (FSD)**.

Installable File System (IFS)

File System Driver (FSD)

I/O Supervisor Layer (IOS)

The FSDs communicate with the IFS manager and the drivers that work directly with the hardware device controllers. These device-specific drivers work within the **I/O Supervisor Layer (IOS)**. The IOS layer handles I/O systems that transmit and receive data in multiple-byte transfers. Devices in this category include hard-disk drives, CD-ROM drives, tape drives, and network controllers.

LOADING AND ADDING DEVICE DRIVERS

The A+ Operating System Technologies objective 2.4 states that the test taker should be able to identify procedures for installing/adding a device, including loading, adding, and configuring device drivers, and required software.

One of the reasons for the success of the PC-compatible system is its open architecture and its versatility. This versatility is the result of an architecture that enables all types of devices to be added to it. In the PC world, this is accomplished through the use of software device drivers that interface diverse equipment to the basic system. Although the process for installing equipment and their drivers in a PC has become increasingly easy, the technician must still be able to install whatever drivers are necessary. Therefore, the following sections of this chapter are dedicated to device-driver installations.

> The PnP-compliant design of Windows 9x/Me makes installing most new hardware nearly automatic (as long as the new device is also PnP compliant). The PnP function will automatically detect the presence of any new PnP-compliant hardware when the system is started. If the device is PnP compliant, the operating system will attempt to load a driver for it from its own list of drivers. If the system cannot find a suitable driver for the device, it will stop and ask for a location where the driver files can be found. If Windows does not detect a new Plug and Play device, either the device is not working properly or it is not installed correctly.

Add New Hardware Wizard

If the device is not PnP compliant, or the system just can't detect it for some reason, it will be necessary to use the Windows 9x **Add New Hardware Wizard**. The Add New Hardware Wizard is a series of screens that will guide the installation process for the new device. The new card or device should already be physically installed in the system before running this procedure. The *Add New Hardware* icon can be found under the *Control Panel* option of the *Settings* menu. It can also be accessed through the *Hardware* tab of the *System Properties* window.

Setting Up New Hardware—Windows 9x is designed to assist the user in setting up any new hardware components that may be added to the system. The *Add New Hardware* icon is found under the *Control Panel* option of the Settings menu.

Double-clicking on this icon will activate the Windows 9x Add New Hardware Wizard, shown in Figure 9-42. The wizard is designed to guide you through hardware setup steps. The new card or device should already be installed in the system before running this procedure.

Figure 9-42: The Windows 9x Add New Hardware Wizard

The Add New Hardware Wizard is a series of screens that will guide the installation process for the new device. The first user-selectable option is to use the *AutoDetect* function, shown in Figure 9-43. The progress indicator bar at the bottom of the page displays the progress of the detection operation in bar-chart format. When it has filled the opening, Windows will indicate what hardware it has found that can be installed. Clicking on the *Details* button will show which hardware it found.

┌─ **TEST TIP** ──────────────┐
Know where the Add New Hardware applet is located in the Windows 9x and Windows 2000 environments.
└────────────────────────────┘

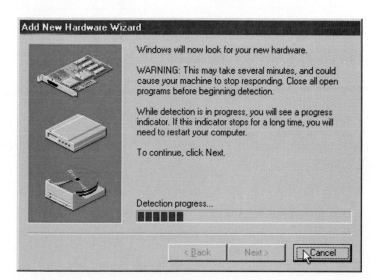

Figure 9-43: Windows 9x Detecting New Hardware

If the wizard does not detect the hardware, the user can attempt to locate the device in the wizard's list of supported devices, as shown in Figure 9-44. The only other option for installing hardware devices is to obtain an OEM disk or CD for the device that has Windows 9x drivers. If the driver disk does not have an AutoStart function, it will be necessary to click on the *Have Disk* button and supply the file's location to complete the installation process.

**Figure 9-44:
Windows 9x Supported
Hardware Listing**

Finish

Clicking on the **Finish** button will conclude the installation process. This will cause Windows to install the drivers for the new hardware in the system. It may also request configuration information from the user before finishing. Afterward, the system will need to be rebooted for the configuration changes to take effect.

TEST TIP

Be aware of your options for installing drivers that are not directly supported by the Windows 9x operating system.

WINDOWS 9X APPLICATIONS

Another factor that makes PC-compatible systems so widely accepted is the fact that so many software applications are available for them. Therefore, the technician must be able to successfully install application software and configure it according to the customer's specifications. The following sections deal with application installations under Windows 9x.

Like the Hardware Wizard, Windows 9x offers the user assistance in installing new programs. The *Add/Remove Programs* icon under the Control Panel is used to install new programs automatically. The **Add/Remove Programs** screen is depicted in Figure 9-45.

Add/Remove
Programs

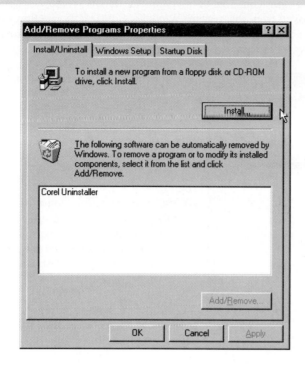

Figure 9-45: The Windows 9x Add/Remove Programs Window

The main page of the *Add/Remove Programs* window is the Install/Uninstall page used to add and remove the desired software package. The upper half of the page contains the **Install** button that is clicked to start the software installation process. The lower half of the page lists the Windows 9x software packages that are already installed in the system. However, non-Windows 9x—compliant software packages will not appear in the list. Only those programs that the Windows 9x Install/Uninstall utility can uninstall appear here.

Install

In old MS-DOS systems, adding a program to the system was normally a simple process of copying it to the hard drive. Removing the program was also simple—just delete its directory and files. However, in Windows 3.x removing a program would typically leave several .INI and .DLL files scattered around the hard drive. Not only did these files take up disk space, they could also become a source of conflict with new software added to the system.

Some Windows 9x applications may share support files with other applications. In these instances, the Uninstall utility will produce a dialog box asking about deleting the shared files. The best response is to keep the shared files to avoid disabling the other application. If the files are to be deleted, then a backup should be made before running the Uninstall utility so that the files can be replaced if needed.

┌─ **TEST TIP** ─────────────────────────┐
│ Be aware of the best response to the possibility of │
│ deleting shared files in a Windows system. │
└──────────────────────────────────────┘

Windows Setup

The Windows 9x *Setup* tab, depicted in Figure 9-46, is also located under the Control Panel's *Add/Remove Programs* icon. This utility permits different Windows 9x components to be added to or removed from the system. Windows Configuration settings can be changed through its dialog boxes. The window in the center of the Setup page provides a list of the standard Windows 9x groups, along with their total sizes.

**Figure 9-46:
The Windows 9x
Setup Page**

An empty box beside the option indicates that it has not been installed. Conversely, a checkmark inside the box indicates that the complete group has been installed in the system. Finally, a gray checkmark indicates that some of the files in the group have been installed.

Highlighting a group title with the cursor, and then clicking on the *Details* button will cause a listing of the group's files to appear. Items in this list may be added to the system by checking on the box next to them. Once the options to be added have been checked, the system will need to be restarted in order for the new options to become active.

Most software manufacturers include a proprietary setup program for their Windows 9x applications. These programs normally run directly from the CD-ROM when they are inserted into the drive for the first time (unless the AutoPlay function is disabled).

For applications that don't feature the automatic installation function, or if the AutoPlay function is disabled, the software must be installed manually. This is accomplished through the *Have Disk* button. Clicking on this button will produce a dialog box asking for the name and location of the application's installation file. Most software suppliers will provide a SETUP.EXE or INSTALL.EXE file to handle the actual installation and configuration process for their software.

One of the optional groups that you might typically leave out is the *Accessibility options*. This group contains programs that modify the operations of the Windows keyboard—audio and video output for use by those who have physical conditions that inhibit their use of the computer. If you require visual warning messages for hearing disabilities or special color controls for visual difficulties, install this component and select the options that you need access to. When the *Accessibility* options are installed, the icon appears in the Control Panel, and when they're removed, it disappears. These options use 4.6 MB of disk space when they are installed.

Launching Windows Applications

In the command-line environment, starting or launching an application was a simple matter of typing the name of its executable file at the command prompt of the directory that it was installed in. Special startup batch files could also be used. However, in the Windows 3.x environment starting an application became as simple as double-clicking on its icon. In Windows 9x versions there are several acceptable methods of launching an application. These include:

- From the *Start* menu, select the *Applications* entry, click on the folder where the desired application is, and double-click its filename.

- From the *Start* menu, select the *Run* entry, and then enter the full path and filename for the desired executable file.

- Double-click the application's filename in *Windows Explorer* or in *My Computer*.

- Click on the *File* menu option from the Menu Bar in *My Computer* or *Windows Explorer*, and select the *Open* option. (You can also alternate-click on the application and choose *Open*.)

- Create a shortcut icon on the desktop for the application so that it can be started directly from the desktop by simply double-clicking its icon.

In Windows, an application can be set up to run by association. Using this method, the application will be called into action any time that an associated file (such as a document and its related word processor) is double-clicked. This is accomplished by defining the file's type in the Registry. Because the Registry is a delicate place to operate, you can also associate an application program with a given file using the following steps:

> **TEST TIP**
>
> Be aware of the various methods of launching an application in the Windows environment.

Hands-on Activity

1. Click on the *Folder Options* entry in the *My Computer* (or Windows Explorer) *View* menu.

2. Click on the *File Types* tab.

3. Select the file type you want to change from the list.

4. Click on the *Edit* button.

5. In the *Actions* dialog window, click on the *Open* option.

6. Click on the *Edit* button.

7. In the *Application used to perform action* dialog box, enter the name of the program you want to use to open files that have the designated extension.

8. Click on the *OK* button to complete the association process. The settings for selected file types are shown in File type details.

MS-DOS and Windows 9x

APPS.INF

MS-DOS-based applications can be installed in Windows 9x by simply running their executable file from the *Run* dialog box, or from the Windows 9x Explorer. If the file has never been run under Windows 9x, the operating system creates a default entry in its **APPS.INF** file for that program. A copy of the new entry is also used to create a Program Information File (PIF) for the application. A PIF file is created to serve as a bridge between an MS-DOS−based application and the Windows environment in older versions of Windows. PIF files contain information about how much memory the application requires and which system resources it needs.

Nearly every DOS-based program should run successfully in Windows 9x. Even MS-DOS programs that require access to all of the system's resources can run successfully in the Windows 9x **MS-DOS mode**. In this mode, basically all but a small portion of Windows exits from memory. When the application is terminated, Windows restarts and returns to the desktop screen.

MS-DOS mode

Advanced

**Figure 9-47:
Establishing MS-DOS
Mode in Windows 95**

MS-DOS mode is established for the application by configuring its properties in the **Advanced** dialog box under the *My Computer/application name/Properties/Program* tab, as illustrated in Figure 9-47. This tab only exists for MS-DOS specific files. To enter MS-DOS mode, select the *Shut Down* option in the *Start* menu, and then click on the *Restart in MS-DOS* mode option.

It is also possible to adjust the memory allocated to the program through the *My Computer/Properties/Memory* tab. This function is accessed by right-clicking its executable file name, moving to the *Memory* window, and increasing or decreasing the memory available, as illustrated in Figure 9-48.

When Windows is restarted in MS-DOS mode, a batch file named **DOSSTART.BAT** runs automatically. It is used to load real-mode DOS drivers for devices such as mice, sound cards, and joysticks. You will find it located in the \Windows directory, provided that you have installed software that requires real-mode DOS drivers. If not, the file might be absent from the directory. As time passes, fewer applications remain that require a real-mode DOS environment. Therefore, most computers will never have their DOSSTART.BAT programs activated.

If an MS-DOS application takes up the entire screen in Windows 9x, it will be necessary to press the ALT+ENTER key combination to switch the application into a window. The ALT+TAB key combination switches the screen to another application. Some applications might grab the entire screen and cover the **Toolbar** and *Start* menu button when maximized. When this occurs, it will be necessary to resize the application's window through the Screen tab to access the Toolbar. You can press the CTRL+ESC keys at any time to access the Windows 9x *Start* menu.

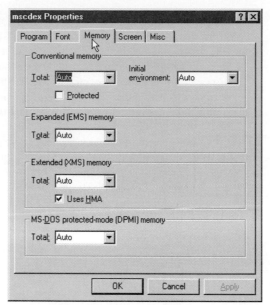

DOSSTART.BAT

TEST TIP
Be aware of the DOSSTART.BAT file's function.

Figure 9-48: Establishing MS-DOS Mode in Windows 95

TEST TIP
Know the consequences of running MS-DOS utilities from a Windows environment and how to solve problems associated with running DOS applications in the Windows environment.

Toolbar

CHALLENGE #5

Your boss has started up an old MS-DOS game program, and it has taken over his entire screen. He does not know how to regain control of his system to get out of the game and get back to the Windows 9x GUI that he is familiar with. He has called you for advice about getting back to his desktop. What should you tell him to do?

mkcompat.exe

In some cases, old MS-DOS and Windows 3.x applications will not run well under Windows 9x platforms. This is usually due to the application being written specifically to run under these older operating systems. In Windows 98, Microsoft included a *Make Compatible utility* that can be used to establish compatibility between the application and the operating system. This utility can be executed from the *Start/Run* path by typing **mkcompat.exe** in the *Run* dialog box.

TEST TIP
Know how to bring applications written specifically for older Microsoft operating systems into compatibility with Windows 9x.

Printing in Windows 9x

In Windows 9x, the Print Manager function and its support components have been integrated into a single print-processing architecture, referred to as the **print spooler**. This integration provides smooth printing in a background mode and quick return-to-application time. The key to this operation is in how the print spooler sends data to the printer. Data is only moved to the printer when it is ready. Therefore, the system is never waiting for the printer to digest data that has been sent to it.

print spooler

To print an open file in Windows 9x, simply move to the application's *File* menu and click on the *Print* option. If the file is not open, it is still possible to print files in Windows 9x. Under the *My Computer* icon, right-clicking on a selected file will produce a *Print* option in a pop-up menu. Files can be printed using the same right-click menu method from the *Windows Explorer* screen. Documents can also be dragged and dropped onto a printer icon in the *Printers* folder, in the *Network Neighborhood* listing, or on the desktop. Obviously, this option can be performed with both local and remote networked printers.

┌─ **TEST TIP** ─────────

Be aware of the various methods of printing documents in Windows 9x.

The settings for any printer can be changed through the *My Computer* icon on the desktop or through the *Printers* option under the *Start* menu's *Settings* entry. The process is the same for both routes, just double-click on the *Printer* folder, right-click on the desired printer, and select its *Properties* entry from the pop-up menu as illustrated in Figure 9-49.

Figure 9-49: Printer Right-Click Pop-Up Menu

┌─ **TEST TIP** ─────────

Know where and how to change the settings for a printer under the Windows 9x operating system.

To view documents waiting to be printed from the print spooler, double-click on the desired printer's icon in the *Printer* folder. This will display the existing print queue, as illustrated in Figure 9-50. Unlike earlier Windows Print Managers, closing the *Print* window does not interrupt the print queue in Windows 9x. The fact that the print spooler runs in its own 32-bit virtual environment means that printer hang-ups will not lock up the system. The print jobs in the queue will be completed unless they are deleted from the list.

┌─ **TEST TIP** ─────────

Know the value that the Print Spooler provides for printing operations in Windows 9x.

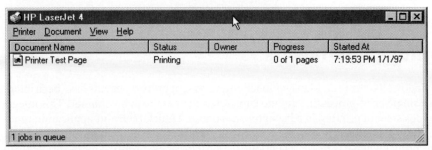

Figure 9-50: Windows 9x Print Queue Display

You have sent a document to your local printer for printing when you notice that you have not included some key information in the document. Nothing has come out of the printer, so you check the Windows 9x printer queue in an attempt to delete the document before it prints. However, nothing is there. What can you do to get the document back?

The *Print Spooler* window's menu bar items permit printing to be paused and resumed. They can also be used to delete print jobs from the queue. Right-clicking on a printer icon will produce a pop-up menu that can also be used to control printing operations being performed by that printer. Both options offer a *Properties* option that can be used to access the printer's configuration and connection information. One of the most important *Printer Properties* tabs is the *Details* page depicted in Figure 9-51.

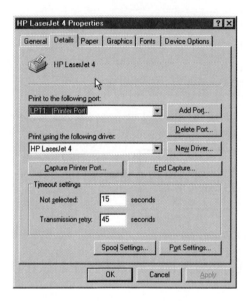

**Figure 9-51:
Typical Printer
Properties/Details Page
in Windows 9x**

Installing Printers in Windows 9x

Windows 9x/Me automatically adopts any printers that have been established prior to its installation. If no printers are already installed, the Setup program will run the new **Add Printer Wizard** to allow a printer to be installed. Each printer in the system has its own print window and icon to work from. The wizard can be accessed at any time through the Windows 9x *My Computer* icon or *Start* menu. In the *Start* menu, move to the Settings entry and click on Printers. Likewise, through the *My Computer* icon, or the *Control Panel* window, double-click on the *Printers* folder or icon.

> **Add Printer Wizard**

To install a printer, open the *Printers* folder and double-click the *Add Printers* icon. From this point, the Add Printer Wizard guides the installation process. Because Windows 9x has built-in networking support, the printer can be a local unit (connected to the computer) or a remote unit located somewhere on the network. If the physical printer is connected to a remote computer, referred to as a print server, the remote unit must supply the printer drivers and settings to control the printer. Likewise, the print server must be set up to share the printer with the other users on the network.

> ┌─ **TEST TIP** ─┐
> Know the identifying feature of a print server.

To install the network printer, access the *Network Neighborhood* icon on the desktop, select the remote computer's network name and the remote unit's printer name, and right-click on the *Install* option, as illustrated in Figure 9-52. After the remote printer has been installed, the local computer can access it through the *Network Neighborhood* icon.

Figure 9-52: Installing a Network Printer in Windows 9x

OEMSETUP.INF

If the printer is not recognized as a model supported by the Windows 9x driver list, OEM drivers can be installed from a device manufacturer's installation disk, which contains the **OEMSETUP.INF** file. After locating the appropriate INF file, simply right-click on the file and select the *Install* option from the context-sensitive menu.

OPTIMIZING WINDOWS 9X PERFORMANCE

A portion of the A+ Operating System Technology objective 2.5 states that the test taker should be able to identify procedures necessary to optimize the operating system and major operating system subsystems. In a purely 32-bit Windows 9x environment, very little memory management is needed. In these systems, new 32-bit virtual device drivers (VxDs) are automatically loaded into extended memory during the bootup process. This eliminates the need for DEVICE= and LOADHIGH commands for devices that have VxDs and Windows 9x application programs. When 16-bit device drivers or MS-DOS applications are being used, however, Windows 9x must create a Real-mode DOS environment for them. For this reason, Windows 9x will execute a CONFIG.SYS and/or AUTOEXEC.BAT file it encounters during bootup.

If no MS-DOS-based drivers or applications are in the system, the CONFIG.SYS and AUTOEXEC.BAT files are not necessary. However, the Windows 9x version of the IO.SYS file will automatically load the Windows 9x version of the HIMEM.SYS file during bootup. This file must be present for Windows 9x to boot up. Even though Windows loads its own version of HIMEM.SYS, a DEVICE=HIMEM.SYS line must be present in a CONFIG.SYS file if a DEVICE=EMM386 line or a 16-bit device driver is required. There are usually multiple versions of the HIMEM.SYS file in a Windows 9x system (there could be three or more versions).

If a Windows 9x system has a CONFIG.SYS, AUTOEXEC.BAT, or .INI file that has been held over from a previous operating system, you should be aware that any unneeded commands in these files have the potential to reduce system performance. In particular, the SMARTDRV function from older operating systems will inhibit dynamic **VCACHE** operation and slow the system down. The VCACHE driver establishes and controls a disk cache in an area of RAM as a storage space for information read from the hard-disk drive, CD-ROM, other drives, and file operations.

The SYSTEM.INI, WIN.INI, PROTOCOL.INI, CONFIG.SYS and AUTOEXEC.BAT files can be modified through the System Editor (Sysedit) in Windows 9x. You can access this utility by typing the **Sysedit** command in the Start/Run dialog box.

If the system runs slowly, check the CONFIG.SYS and AUTOEXEC.BAT files for SMARTDRV and any other disk cache software settings. Remove these commands from both files to improve performance. Also, remove any SHARE commands from the AUTOEXEC.BAT file.

The most obvious cure for most Windows 9x memory errors is to install extra RAM for extended memory. RAM has become very inexpensive to add to most systems and the Windows 9x memory-management system is very stable. If the system has troublesome DLL and/or TSR programs installed, remove them and reinstall them one by one until the offending files have been identified. Check with the application manufacturer for updated versions of these files.

VCACHE

TEST TIP
Know what function the VCACHE utility performs in a Windows 9x system.

Sysedit

TEST TIP
Be aware of the affect that active commands in a CONFIG.SYS, AUTOEXEC.BAT, or INI file can have on the operation of an advanced Windows operating system.

TEST TIP
Know how to optimize the operation of a CD-ROM drive in Windows 9x.

NETWORKING WITH WINDOWS 9X

The A+ Operating System Technologies objective 4.1 states that the test taker should be able to identify the networking capabilities of Windows. Given configuration parameters, configure the operating system to connect to a network.

The prevalence of local area networks (LANs) in businesses requires that PC technicians know how to install and maintain LAN equipment and software. This is evident by the increased weight of the "Networking" domain in the new A+ exams. The following sections of this chapter deal with the software side of local area networking. LAN hardware installation and troubleshooting were discussed in Chapter 5 — *Data Communications*. Taken together, these two chapters provide a comprehensive study of desktop networking.

Network Hardware

Networking PCs begins with the network type and card. Although the hardware side of networking was covered in Chapter 5 — *Data Communications*, some information about the network type and the network card must be obtained before the software side of the network can be addressed. The type of network determines which transfer protocol you need to load, and the network card determines which adapter driver you can install. You can find the network card's information in its user manual or installation guide. You also can find information on the network type that the network adapter can support in these guides.

Network interface cards (NICs) must be configured to communicate with the system software before installing them in the system. On older network cards, you accomplish this by setting hardware jumpers to a specified pattern on the card. With software-configured ISA and PCI cards, you accomplish this through configuration software that downloads information to a configuration EEPROM on the card. The typical parameters that must be established for the NIC include the following:

IRQ5

300

D0000

- IRQ level (**IRQ5**/10/11/15)

- Base I/O port address (**300**/210/220)

- Base memory address (**D0000**/C800)

Typical values used for these parameters in a PC are presented in parentheses, with the typical default values in bold. The address values presented in literature may drop the last zero. You also might have to find alternative settings for one or more of the parameters if those default values are already being used in the system. Record the hardware setting so that there is less chance for mix-ups when setting the corresponding software parameters.

Resource Sharing

network operating system (NOS)

The concept of sharing directories, files, and hardware resources is central to the design of any **network operating system** (**NOS**). The overriding features that distinguish a NOS system from a DOS system are the sharing and security features of the NOS. These features are typically manifested in passwords, permission levels, and access rights for the system's users.

Initially, MS-DOS made no provision for sharing resources across LANs. The only computer-to-computer communications practiced in the early days of the PC were point-to-point communications between two units. This could be performed through a direct, null-modem connection between the serial ports of the two systems, or through a pair of modems.

SHARE.EXE

Windows for Workgroups (WfW)

In later versions of MS-DOS, however, Microsoft added the **SHARE.EXE** command to provide file-sharing and file-locking capabilities for files on a local hard-disk drive. These capabilities enabled multiple users to access the same file at the same time in a networked or multitasking environment. With version 3.11, the Windows operating system added built-in, peer-to-peer networking capabilities to the operating environment and titled it **Windows for Workgroups** (**WfW**).

TEST TIP

Know what the MS-DOS SHARE command does.

In a network environment, only shared directories and resources can be accessed across the network. The sharing function is instituted at the remote computer. In Windows, the presence of a hand under the folder or device icon notifies other potential users that this resource or directory has been shared and can be accessed.

To access a shared remote resource, the local operating system must first connect to it. When the connection is established with a remote drive or folder, the local operating system creates a new logical drive on the local machine to handle the shared directory. Normally, the local file management system assigns the directory the next available drive letter in the local system.

The path to the shared resource contains a little more information than the path to a local directory. The remote path must include the remote computer's name and shared resource name (directory or printer). It also must be expressed using the **Universal Naming Convention (UNC)** Format. This format begins with a pair of back slashes followed by the computer name and the resource name. Each name in the path is separated by a single backslash. Therefore, the format of a shared path is *computer_name\directory_name*.

Universal Naming Convention (UNC)

Valid computer names in Windows 9x can be up to 15 characters in length and cannot contain any blank spaces. In Windows 2000 using the TCP/IP protocol, computer names can range up to 63 characters in length and should be made up of the letters A through Z, numbers 0 through 9, and hyphens.

┌─ **TEST TIP** ────────────────┐
│ Know the specifications for setting up computer │
│ names in a given operating system. │
└──────────────────────────────┘

Network Neighborhood

In Windows 9x, the peer-to-peer local area networking function is an integral part of the system. The heart of the Windows 95 and 98 networking systems is contained in the desktop's **Network Neighborhood** icon and the Control Panel's *Network* icon. Under Windows Me the *My Network Places* icon provides this function.

Network Neighborhood

The *Network Neighborhood* display, shown in Figure 9-53, is the primary network user interface for Windows 9x. This screen is used to browse the organization of the LAN and access its shared resources in a method similar to that used with the Windows Explorer for a local hard drive. As a matter of fact, most directory and file-level activities, such as opening and saving files, can be performed through the *Network Neighborhood* screen.

Figure 9-53: The Network Neighborhood Window

workgroups

Microsoft networks group logically related computers together in **workgroups** for convenient browsing of resources. The local computer is a part of a workgroup. Double-clicking the *Network Neighborhood* icon displays the printers and folders available in the workgroup in either a list or an icon format. As with the Windows Explorer, you can change the format through the *View* menu options.

Entire Network

If the desired computer does not display, double-click the **Entire Network** icon. This action produces any other workgroups in the system and displays additional printers and folders that are available.

If the *Network Neighborhood* (or *My Network Places*) window is empty, or if its icon is missing, networking connections have not been established. If this is the case, you must correctly configure networking on the local unit to connect to any other computers on the network. This is done through the Control Panel's *Network* icon. After you have located the desired computer, double-click its icon (or entry) to view its resources.

The Network Neighborhood applet also provides an easy way to connect to and use other network resources. If the local computer is connected to the network, double-click any remote computer in the list to connect to it. This action displays its content in the neighborhood. In this condition, it is possible to copy files between the local and remote computers.

Mapping a Drive

mapping the drive

It is possible for the local system to assign a logical drive letter to the remote unit or folder. This is referred to as **mapping the drive** letter to the resource. This mapping enables non-Windows 9x applications running on the local computer to use the resource across the network.

A drive map is a very important tool in a network environment. It allows a single computer to act as though it possesses all the hard drives that reside in the network. The operating system coordinates the access to various systems so that drives located on other physical machines show up as logical drives on the local machine. This shows up in the Windows Explorer and My Computer screens, as illustrated in Figure 9-54.

Figure 9-54: A Mapped Drive Display

The primary reason to map a drive in a network environment is because some applications cannot recognize volume names. They can see only drive letters. In Windows 9x, the number of recognizable drive letters is 26 (A-Z). Some network operating systems can recognize an extended number of drive letters (for example, A-Z and AA-ZZ). By using unique volume names to identify drives, however, the Windows 2000 system is capable of recognizing a vast number of network drives.

For a local system to access a remote resource, the resource must be shared, and the local user must have a valid network user ID and password. The user's assigned rights and permissions are tied to his or her password throughout the network—either through individual settings or through group settings.

To **map** (assign) a drive letter to a remote network computer or folder, open the Windows Explorer. From the *Tools* menu, select the **Map Network Drive** option. The *Map Network Drive* dialog box is displayed in Figure 9-55.

Figure 9-55: Map Network Drive Dialog Box

Windows 9x attempts to assign the next available drive letter to the computer or folder indicated in the *Path* dialog box. Establishing the map to the resource is a simple matter of entering the required path and share name in the dialog box using the **Universal Naming Convention** (**UNC**) format (i.e., *\\Path\Remote_name\folder_name*). The format always begins with double slashes \\.

Windows produces a prompt for a password if the remote unit requires one. You can map a computer or a folder that has been used recently by clicking on the down arrow beside the *Path* window and then choosing the desired resource from the pop-up list.

The *Reconnect at logon* option must be selected in the *Map Network Drive* page for the drive mapping to become a permanent part of the system. If the option is not selected when the user logs off, the mapped drive information disappears and needs to be remapped for any further use. If a red X appears on the icon of a properly mapped drive, this indicates that the drive is no longer available. The drive's host computer may be turned off, the drive may have been removed, or it may no longer be on the same path. If the drive was mapped to a particular folder and the folder name has been changed, the red X will also appear.

The Network Icon in Control Panel

The Control Panel's *Network* page, shown in Figure 9-56, provides configuration and properties information about the system's networks. The system's installed **network components** are listed under the *Configuration* tab.

> **map**
>
> **Map Network Drive**

> **Universal Naming Convention (UNC)**

> ┌ **TEST TIP** ───
> Know what will cause a mapped drive to disappear from a system when it is shut down and restarted.
> └────────────────

> **network components**

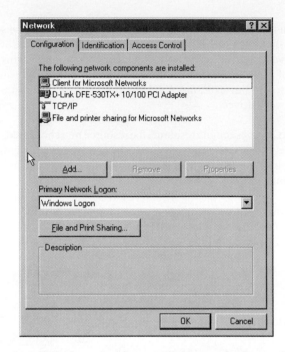

Figure 9-56: The Network Control Panel Screen

Double-clicking an installed adapter's driver, or clicking on the *Properties* button when the driver is highlighted, produces its *Configuration information* page. The *Add* and *Remove* buttons on this page are used to install and remove network drivers from the system.

Primary Network Logon

The **Primary Network Logon** window is used to establish which type of network Windows 9x will enter when it starts up. This proves particularly helpful on systems that may be working in multiple network environments (e.g., a computer that may need to access Microsoft network resources in some situations, and Novell network resources at other times).

The **File and Print Sharing** button is used to select the first level of resource sharing for the local unit. Sharing can be individually enabled/disabled for file and printer accesses from remote computers.

File and Print Sharing

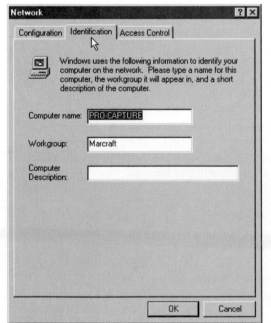

Identification

The page's **Identification** tab is used to establish a network identity for the local computer, as illustrated in Figure 9-57. This page establishes the local computer's share name and workgroup association.

Access Control

Similarly, the **Access Control** tab enables the local user to set the level of access control that is applied to remote accesses. The possible options include: assign a password requirement for each access, or grant access to selected groups or users.

Figure 9-57: Network Identification Page

As mentioned earlier, double-clicking a driver in the *Configuration* tab opens a series of pages describing its properties. The **Resources** section of an NE-2000−compatible network adapter's configuration (common in Ethernet installations) is shown in Figure 9-58.

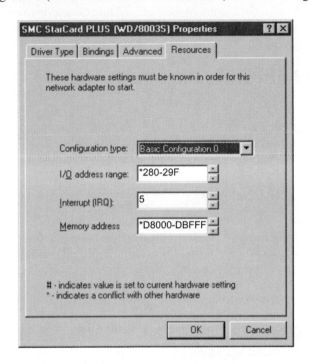

Figure 9-58:
NE-2000 Compatible
Resources Screen

This page shows the adapter's current system resource allocations (using IRQ5, I/O addresses 280–29F, and memory addresses D8000–DBFFF).

Windows 9x/Me Resource Sharing

In Windows 9x/Me peer-to-peer systems, resource sharing is performed at the user level. The user can use the *File and Print Sharing* button of the *Network* applet's *Configuration* tab (shown in Figure 9-56) to enable resource sharing on the local computer. This option makes it possible for you to grant other network users access to your files, printers, or both. After sharing has been enabled, you can set sharing on several levels—the entire computer, complete disk drives, folders, and files.

To share a folder or file in Windows 9x/Me, access the Windows Explorer or My Computer interface and click on the resource you want to share. From the drop-down File menu, select the *Properties* option and click on the *Sharing* tab. On this tab, click on the *Shared As* option and select the *Access Type* you want to implement. In a peer-to-peer environment, you are given the options to share, share in a read-only mode, or share with password protection. There is no additional mechanism for limiting access by individual users.

However, when Windows 9x/Me systems are used in a domain based-network environment, sharing is governed by the capabilities of the domain controller. In these network environments, users can be individually given access to local resources, and what they are permitted do with those resources can also be restricted in different ways.

To share a local printer resource in the Windows 9x/Me environment, navigate the *Start/Settings* path and then click on the *Printers* entry. From the *Printers* window, select the printer you want to share, drop down the File menu, and click on the *Properties* entry. From the printer's *Properties* page, click on the *Sharing* tab, and then click on the *Shared As* button.

Installing Network Components

After the network adapter card has been configured and installed, the next step in setting up the computer on the network is to load its drivers, protocols, and services. In most Windows 9x installations, simply rebooting the computer and permitting Windows to detect the network adapter will accomplish the majority of these steps.

The Windows networking utilities should produce an adapter driver, a **Microsoft Client protocol**, and a **Novell NetWare Client protocol** in the *Network Configuration* window in a typical installation. A default set of file and print services also are loaded. The only items that must be installed manually are the protocols for the particular type of network in which the computer is being used. Clicking on the *Add* button in the *Network Configuration* page brings up the **Select Network Component Type** screen shown in Figure 9-59.

Figure 9-59: The Select Network Component Type Screen

The types of networking components include four categories:

- **Client**. Software that enables the system to use files and printers shared on other computers

- **Adapter**. Drivers that control the physical hardware connected to the network

- **Protocol**. Rules that the computers use to govern the exchange of information across the network

- **Service**. Utilities that enable resources and provide support services, such as automated backup, remote registry, and network monitoring facilities

Each entry contains a list of primary and alternative drivers, protocols, and configuration settings that can be viewed by clicking on the title in the window. These alternatives are included because there are many non-Microsoft networks in use, and Windows 9x attempts to support the most common ones.

If a particular network type is not supported in the standard listings, the Components page features a *Have Disk* button that permits the system to upload Windows-compatible drivers and protocols.

Configuring Clients in Windows 9x/Me

Any network computer that uses the resources of another computer in the network is acting as its client. To use these resources, the local computer must have client software installed that will enable it to work with the other computer. In some networks, this may mean working with computers that have other types of operating systems running on them. In Windows 9x/Me systems, you are offered Microsoft and Novell clients that will enable the computer to use resources that belong to these types of systems.

To add a new client to the computer, highlight the *Client* option in the *Select Network Component Type* screen, select the desired client from the list, and click on the *Add* button. The new Client will appear in the *Installed Network Components* window of the *Network* page.

Configuring Adapters in Windows 9x/Me

The Adapters portion of the TCP/IP configuration refers to loading drivers for the LAN and dial-up hardware devices used to connect to the communication media. As with the clients components, adapters are added to the system and configured through the *Select Network Component Type* screen. From this screen, select the *Adapters* option and click on the *Add* button to produce the *Select Network Adapters* dialog window.

In this window you should first select the manufacturer of the device and then select the specified adapter type. If the device does not appear in the listing, you can click on the *Have Disk* button to load OEM drivers for the device from a manufacturer's disk.

Configuring Protocols in Windows 9x/Me

Because the bootup detection process loads the adapter driver, two types of clients to choose from, and a set of sharing parameters, most installation procedures require only that the appropriate protocols be loaded for the network type. In Windows-based client/server LANs, TCP/IP has become the leading choice of networking protocols. Therefore, the TCP/IP protocol must be activated and configured properly for the computer to function on the LAN.

However, you may need to add the NetBEUI, Appletalk, and IPX/SPX (also known as NWLink) protocols if the LAN contains computers with older Windows operating systems, Apple/Mac computers, or computers running Novell operating systems. You should also be aware that Microsoft offers separate TCP/IP protocols for local area and wide area networking. The additional TCP/IP protocol is used for dial-up Internet support.

The procedure for adding protocols is the same as that described for adding clients.

Configuring TCP/IP in Windows 9x/Me LANs

When the TCP/IP protocol is installed, it can require several pieces of configuration information to fully implement. In a simple local area network, such as a peer-to-peer network, only an IP address and a subnet mask setting are required. However, in larger networks, such as multisegment client/server LANs, you may also be required to provide a Default Gateway (router) address, as well as an IP address for a DNS or WINS server.

TEST TIP

Know where TCP/IP properties are established in Windows.

To configure these TCP/IP values, select the TCP/IP protocol for the LAN from the listing in the Network Control Panel and click on the *Properties* button. This will produce the *TCP/IP Properties* page as illustrated in Figure 9-60. There are several tabs on this page that may need to be filled out.

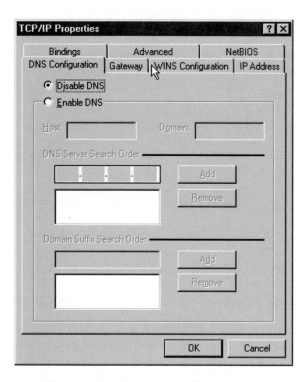

Figure 9-60: The TCP/IP Properties Page

- *IP Address tab* – Through this tab you can configure the computer to obtain an IP address through an automatic service, such as DHCP, or you can manually configure a static address for the computer. Every computer on a network must have a unique IP address that identifies who it is.

Each computer on the network must also have a subnet mask entry to limit the mobility of the transmission to those nodes within the subnet (without subnets, every TCP/IP communication could range across every connected network link in the world—the traffic would be unbelievable).

If the *Obtain an IP address automatically* option is selected, the computer will attempt to locate a DHCP server when it boots onto the network. The DHCP server has the ability to provide it with all the TCP/IP configuration information it needs. If no DHCP server is found, Windows computers will default to a random IP address in the range of 169.254.XX.XX and a subnet mask of 255.255.0.0. This is referred to as Automatic IP Addressing (AIPA). This feature is very useful in smaller single-segment networks because it effectively auto-configures such a network.

To use the manual configuration option, you must know the IP address and subnet mask settings you want to use.

- *DNS Configuration tab* – this tab enables you to specify the IP addresses of Domain Name System servers that are responsible for reconciling DNS computer names to actual IP addresses. In a LAN this is typically the domain server for your network. In a wide area network environment, such as the Internet, this is typically the IP address of the ISP.

Various DNS suffixes can be attached to enable the DNS system to attempt to resolve incomplete domain names. This listing will attach specified domain suffixes (e.g., mic-inc.net, mic-inc.com, etc.) to names it receives. These suffixes will be attached to the received name and tried in the order they are entered in the list.

- *WINS Configuration tab* – this tab is used to specify the IP address of a Windows Name System server that is used to resolve the NetBIOS/NetBEUI names associated with older Windows operating systems to IP addresses.

- *Gateway tab* – this tab is used to specify the IP address of the router (or other gateway device) that separates your network segment from other segments. The computer uses this address to communicate with IP addresses outside the local segment.

In a Windows network, the set of rules that govern the exchange of data between computers is the **NetBIOS Extended User Interface (NetBEUI)** protocol. This protocol works in most purely Windows networks, so another protocol is rarely called for. If an additional protocol is required, choose the *Add Protocol* option in the *Network Components* dialog box to add another protocol. Network adapters can typically handle up to four different protocols. The key to protocol selection is that the devices on the network must use the same protocol to be able to talk with each other.

NetBIOS Extended
User Interface
(NetBEUI)

Although NetBEUI is easy to implement, it is a non-routable protocol. Because NetBEUI uses broadcast techniques to find other nodes on the network, it has no inherent capabilities to access nodes outside the immediate physical network segment. Therefore, it is not used in wide area networking applications. However, NetBEUI is required to support dial-up **Remote Access Services (RAS)** through a modem. The RAS service uses the NetBEUI protocol to navigate through a network after you have dialed into it. Both the calling client and the receiving server in the LAN must be running NetBEUI. If either computer does not have this protocol active, the client will be able to connect with the LAN, but will not be able to navigate through it.

┌─ **TEST TIP** ─────────┐
│ Remember the meaning of the term NetBEUI and │
│ know what type of network operating system it │
│ belongs to. │
└──────────────────┘

Remote Access
Services (RAS)

IPX/SPX is a Novell network protocol for LANs, and TCP/IP is the Internet protocol supported by Windows 9x/Me and Windows NT/2000/XP.

┌─ **TEST TIP** ─┐
│ Be aware that NetBEUI │
│ is required to navigate a │
│ dial-up connection to a │
│ local area network. │
└──────────┘

Network Printing with Windows 9x/Me

Printers folder

Network printing in Windows 9x/Me is a matter of creating and linking an icon on the local computer with a shared physical device attached to a remote computer. The standard method of installing a printer in Windows 9x is to activate the Add Printer Wizard through the **Printers folder**. This folder provides a central location for adding and managing printer operations. The *Printers* folder can be accessed from:

- Start/Settings/Printers
- My Computer/Printers
- Control Panel/Printers

To install a network printer on the local computer, access the local *Printers* folder and double-click the *Add Printer* option. This action starts the Windows 9x Add Printer Wizard shown in Figure 9-61. This wizard asks a number of questions about how the printer will be used. Since you are installing a remote network printer, you will need to supply the complete path to the printer, or browse for the network to find its location.

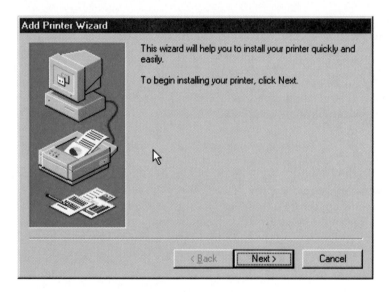

Figure 9-61: The Add Printer Wizard

You can also use the *Network Neighborhood* icon to browse the network until you locate the desired computer. Then double-click on it so that its designated printer displays. The presence of a hand under the icon indicates a shared printer. You can also install the desired remote printer by clicking and dragging its icon to the local *Printers* window and then dropping it anywhere inside the window.

The Add Printer Wizard performs three basic tasks in setting up the local unit to use the remote printer. First it establishes the printing path for DOS-based applications. Because these programs do not handle UNC-based paths, a logical **port name**, such as LPT2, must be established for them.

port name

If the Yes option is selected, Windows captures a local port for those applications to use. Clicking on the *Capture Printer Port* button produces the **Capture Printer Port** dialog box shown in Figure 9-62. This is a logical port designation and does not need to actually be installed in the system. As a matter of fact, any actual port in the local unit that has been assigned that handle will be disabled.

Figure 9-62:
The Capture Printer
Port Dialog Box

The next step in setting up the remote printer is to assign it a unique printer name. In a network environment, this name should have some relevance to what type of printer it is, or what relationship it has to the local unit.

The final step in setting up the printer is to configure its icon properties as if it were a local printer. Right-click the printer icon and select *Properties*. Enter all the information required to bring the printer to operation.

WIDE AREA NETWORKING WITH WINDOWS 9X/ME

A portion of A+ Operating System Technologies objective 4.2 indicates that the test taker should be able to identify the basic Internet protocols and terminologies. Identify procedures for establishing Internet connectivity. In a given scenario, configure the operating system to connect to and use Internet resources.

The Internet is the most famous example of wide area networking. The primary way to connect to the Internet with Windows 9x and Windows Me is through a **dial-up networking** connection (using a modem). The dial-up communications system in Windows 9x/Me offers many improvements over previous operating system versions. Under Windows 9x and Windows Me, applications can cooperatively share the dial-up connections through its **Telephony Application Programming Interface (TAPI)**. This interface provides a universal set of drivers for modems and COM ports to control and arbitrate telephony operations for data, fax, and voice.

TEST TIP
Know what the Telephony Application Programming Interface (TAPI) is and what it does.

The Windows 9x/Me Internet Connection

To establish dial-up Internet connection using the Windows 9x/Me operating systems, follow the steps in the following Hands-on Activity:

Hands-on Activity

1. Configure the Windows Dial-up Networking feature.

2. Establish the Windows modem configuration.

3. Set up the ISP dial-up connection information.

4. Establish the server address for the connection (if required by the ISP).

5. Set up the Internet Explorer (or other browser).

6. Connect to the Internet.

The following sections discuss each of these steps in more detail.

Welcome to Dial-Up Networking

Make New Connection

Internet Service Provider (ISP)

Configuring the Dial-up Networking Feature

To set up dial-up networking to connect to the Internet, turn on the computer, double-click the *My Computer* icon on the desktop, and click on the *Dial-Up Networking* icon. You can also reach this icon through the *Start* button. Choose the *Programs* option from the *Start* menu, point at the *Accessories* entry, and click on the *Dial-Up Networking* entry.

If this option has never been set up before, a **Welcome to Dial-Up Networking** message comes up. Click on the *Next* button to advance into the **Make New Connection** screen, illustrated in Figure 9-63. At this point, enter the name of the **Internet Service Provider (ISP)** in the *Type* window.

Figure 9-63: The Make New Connection Window

Establishing the Windows 9x/Me Modem Configuration

Click on the **Configure** button and set the maximum speed value to its fastest available setting to allow compression and smoother connection. Next, click on the *Connection* tab to see the modem **Connection preferences** information, as illustrated in Figure 9-64.

Click on the **Port Settings** button and set the **Receive Buffer** speed setting to 75%. Also, set the **Transmit Buffer** speed setting to 100%. You must set the Receive buffer speed below the Transmit buffer speed, otherwise the modem will try to receive as fast as it sends and will end up filling the buffer, slowing the operation of the connection.

Click on the *OK* button to return to the *Connection* tab. Select the *Advanced* button and add any extra settings desired for the installed modem. For example, an M0 setting should turn the volume on your modem off so that it is quiet when connecting to the Internet. Click on the *OK* button to return to the *Modem Properties/Connection* tab.

**Figure 9-64:
The Modem
Properties Window**

Setting Up the ISP Dial-up Connection Information

From the *Modem Properties* window, click on the *OK* button to move into the *Make New Connection* entry. Click on the *Next* button to advance to the phone number entry page shown in Figure 9-65.

**Figure 9-65:
ISP Connection
Window**

**Figure 9-66:
The Dial-Up
Networking
Window**

Type in the dial-in phone number of your ISP—area code and local number. If a dialing prefix is required, such as 9, set this up as well. If the number is a long-distance number, Windows detects this during dialing and automatically enters the appropriate long-distance prefix (i.e., a 1 in the United States). Click on the *Next* button to record the information and click on *Finish*. Then an icon displays in the *Dial-Up Networking* window, similar to the one shown in Figure 9-66.

NOTE

When using dial-up networking functions outside the U.S. several configuration settings must be changed. Most international telephone systems do not feature the same dial tone/ ring characteristics used in the U.S. If your modem fails to detect a dial tone in a foreign country, you will need to disable the modem's dial tone detection feature. Accessing the *Connections* tab under the *Control Panel/Modems* path and then clearing the check box beside the *Wait for dial tone before dialing* option will accomplish this. You may also need to increase the cancel call waiting period if connections take a relatively long time from where you are calling. This is accomplished by increasing the number of seconds in the *Cancel the Call If Not Connected* setting under the *Connection* tab.

Establishing the IP and Server Addresses

**Dynamic Host
Configuration
Protocol (DHCP)**

As described in Chapter 5—*Data Communications*, most ISPs use dynamic IP address assignments for their customers. The **Dynamic Host Configuration Protocol (DHCP)** service makes this possible by dynamically assigning IP addresses to the server's clients. This service is available in both Windows 9x and Windows NT/2000 and must be located on both the server and the client computers. In Windows 9x, the path to the TCP/IP Properties window is *Start/Settings/Control_Panel/Network/TCP/IP_Properties*. In Windows 2000, the path is *Start/Settings/Network_and_Dial-Up_Connections/desired_connection/Properties/TCP/IP_Properties*.

name server

The ISP will also have one or more **name server** computers to route traffic onto and off of the Internet, and to reconcile IP addresses to domain names. These are the computers that users dial into to establish and conduct their Internet communications. Each name server has a DNS number/name, just as every other Internet computer does. Like IP addresses, the domain **server address** can be static, or dynamic. If the ISP has several servers, the ISP may allow traffic to be routed to the servers with the lightest workload instead of waiting for a particular server to become free.

server address

With some ISPs, it may be necessary to manually enter server addresses and IP information that they supply. Some users require that their IP address not be changed. Therefore, they purchase an IP address from the ISP that is always assigned to them. Of course, this removes an assignable address from the ISP's bank of addresses, but the customer normally pays a great deal more for the constant address. In these situations, it may be necessary to enter the IP address information into the Internet connection's TCP/IP configuration.

Likewise, some ISPs may assign static server addresses that must be entered manually, while others assign their server addresses dynamically and, therefore, do not require that this information be entered into the TCP/IP configuration.

In both cases, Windows 9x/Me provides for the local unit to assign values to IP and server addresses, or for the server to assign those values after the connection has been made. In dial-up situations, the ISP typically determines which option is used.

In those situations in which the ISP requires a server and/or IP address to be supplied, just move into the *Dial-Up Networking* window and right-click the *Internet Connection* icon. Select the *Properties* option from the list and move into the **Server Types** page, shown in Figure 9-67. From this page, verify the **Dial-Up Server type** — usually PPP for Windows 9x/Me, Windows NT, and Windows 2000/XP — and click on the **TCP/IP Settings** button. Set the TCP/IP settings as directed by the ISP's instructions. If a specific set of values is entered into this page, the ISP connects the system to the Internet through a specific server address.

Server Types

Dial-Up Server type

TCP/IP Settings

Figure 9-67: The Server Types Page

Click on the **Specify name server addresses** radio button and enter the **Primary DNS** and **Secondary DNS** addresses provided to you by the ISP. The screen should be similar to the one depicted in Figure 9-68. Return to the *Dial-Up Networking* window.

Specify name server addresses

Primary DNS

Secondary DNS

Figure 9-68: TCP/IP Settings Numbers

Although DNS is the naming service used by the Internet, it is not the only name-resolution service used with PCs. In the case of Windows LANs, the Microsoft preferred naming system is the **Windows Internet Naming Service (WINS)**. This service can be used to translate IP addresses to NetBIOS names within a Windows LAN environment. The LAN must include a Windows name server running the WINS server software that maintains the IP address/NetBIOS name database for the LAN.

Each client in the WINS LAN must contain the WINS client software and be WINS enabled. In Windows 9x/Me, you can establish the WINS client service through the Control Panel's *Network* icon. On the *Network* page, select the *TCP/IP LAN adapter* from the list and click on the *Properties* button. Select the **WINS Configuration** tab to obtain the page shown in Figure 9-69, and enable the WINS resolution function. Then, enter the IP address of the WINS server.

Windows Internet Naming Service (WINS)

WINS Configuration

TEST TIP

Know what DNS and WINS are, what they do, and how they are different.

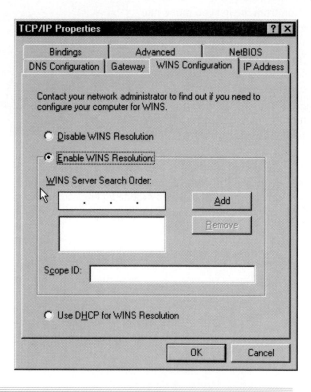

**Figure 9-69:
WINS Enabling**

Setting Up the Internet Explorer Browser

As mentioned previously in this chapter, Internet browsers make the Internet much easier to navigate. Nearly every Internet connection is made through a browser of some type. Windows 98 and Windows Me include a default browser called **Internet Explorer (IE)**. Unless a different browser is installed, all the Windows 9x versions after Windows 95 place the *IE* icon on the desktop and automatically use this browser for Internet access. In order to browse the Internet using the IE, it will be necessary to configure it for use. This process varies somewhat between Windows versions and Internet Explorer versions. In general, you can access the Internet Explorer in three different ways to configure it:

Internet Explorer (IE)

- From the *IE Tools* menu (the *View* menu in Windows 95) select the *Internet Options* entry

- Right-click the desktop *Internet Explorer* icon (*Internet* icon in Windows 95) and click on the *Properties* tab

- Click on the *Internet Explorer* icon under the *Start/Settings/Control Panel* path

Selecting one of these options leads to an **Internet Options** page or on **Internet Properties** page. From either page, choose the *Connection* tab and click on the *Setup* button to bring up the Windows **Internet Connection Wizard** and feature the *Welcome to the Internet Connection Wizard* page. This page lists three possible options for setting up the Internet connection and the browser:

Internet Options

Internet Properties

Internet Connection Wizard

- I want to sign up for a new Internet account. (My telephone line is connected to my modem.)

- I want to transfer my existing Internet account to this computer. (My telephone line is connected to my modem.)

- I want to set up my Internet connection manually, or I want to connect through a local area network (LAN).

If you choose either of the first two options, the Internet Connection Wizard asks for the first three digits of the local phone number and tries to dial the **Microsoft Internet Referral Service** for known Internet service providers in your local area. In most cases this will be a Microsoft Network (MSN) connection. Simply select one of the options provided in the list and provide the user information requested by the wizard to set up a new Internet account.

Microsoft Internet Referral Service

If you do not want to use any of the service providers recommended by Microsoft, click on the *My Internet service provider is not listed* option and click on the *Next* button. This will shift the Internet Connection Wizard into manual Internet account setup mode. The wizard will produce a guided setup sequence for configuring the new connection.

If you select the *I want to set up my Internet connection manually, or I want to connect through a local area network (LAN)* option, the I*nternet Connection Wizard* page, similar to the one in Figure 9-70, should appear.

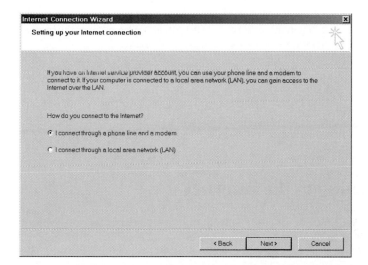

**Figure 9-70:
The Internet
Connection Wizard**

Under this option, the wizard asks whether the connection will be made through a phone line and modem, or a through local area network. Most home-use and small-business connections still use dial-up modems for their connection type. Small, medium, and large businesses typically use LAN-based connections.

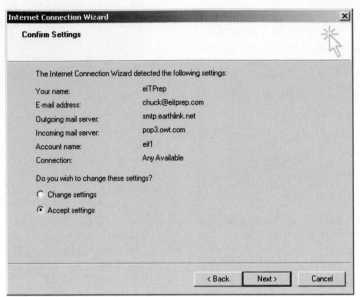

In dial-up situations, click on the *I connect through a phone line and a modem* option and advance to the next page. In three successive steps, the wizard will ask you to enter the telephone number of the dial-up connection (normally an ISP), the user name and password to access the remote account, and the name of the account, as you want it to appear in the *Dial-Up Networking* folder.

Next, the wizard will ask you if you want to establish an e-mail account. To do so, you must already have a mail account established with an ISP and have the relevant account information to enter into the wizard.

At the end of the process, the *Confirm Settings* page, shown in Figure 9-71 will appear and you will be asked to confirm the connection information listed. If the information is correct, simply click on the *Next* button, which will lead to the Internet Connection Wizard *Completion* page. However, you also have the option to click on the *Change settings* radio button to update the information.

Figure 9-71: The Windows 9x/Me Internet Connection Wizard Confirm Settings Page

Installing Other Browsers

Although Windows 9x and Windows Me include the Microsoft Internet Explorer, there are other browsers that the public may prefer to use. To use another browser in the system, it will be necessary to install it in the system. This is typically a function of the browser's Windows Install Wizard.

If the install process detects an existing Dial-Up Networking configuration in Windows, it normally imports those values into its structure. If not, the Windows Dial-Up Connection Wizard runs as a part of the third-party installation process. The user manual for the browser normally provides exact instructions for installing its software in a Windows 9x/Me system.

Connecting to the Internet

Double-click the icon of the new connection. Enter the username and password supplied by your ISP. Click on the **Connect** option. You should hear the modem dialing at this point (unless the M0 parameter was specified in the *Modem Properties - Extra Settings* dialog windows to silence the modem's volume). A *Connecting To* window should appear on the screen, displaying the status of the modem. When it comes up, the *Connected To* window should minimize to the Taskbar. The system is now connected to the Internet.

Setting Up Internet E-Mail

Windows systems that run Microsoft Internet Explorer 4.0 or newer have a built-in e-mail manager called **Outlook Express** that resides on the desktop Taskbar. To set up an e-mail account, open Outlook Express and click on the drop-down *Tools* menu. From the menu, choose the *Account* option, click on the *Add* button, and select the *Mail* entry. On successive screens you will need to enter:

Outlook Express

- your display name (the name that will be displayed to those receiving e-mails from you)

- e-mail address

- **Internet Mail Server** information (POP3 and SMTP server names) for incoming and outgoing mail

Internet Mail Server

- the ISP-supplied mail account name and password

At the end of the setup process you simply click on the *Finish* button to complete the e-mail setup.

All e-mail managers require these pieces of information. If you are using a different e-mail manager (Eudora, Netscape Mail, etc.) you will need to enter this information in the appropriate spaces provided by the particular manager.

Accessing the Internet Explorer

After the hardware has been installed and the Internet connection has been arranged, click on the desktop *Internet* icon to access the Internet. In the **Connect To** window, click on the *Connect* button. You should hear the modem communications sounds again. The *Internet Explorer* main screen displays, as depicted in Figure 9-72.

Connect To

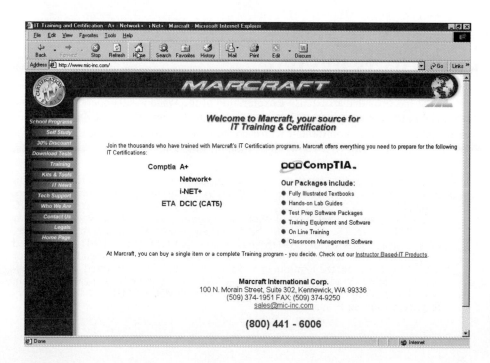

Figure 9-72:
Internet Explorer
Main Screen

CHAPTER SUMMARY

This chapter has presented an extensive discussion covering the Microsoft Windows 95, 98, and Me operating systems. The chapter opened by discussing the installation and configuration of the different Windows 9x operating systems and the steps required for bringing them to a basic operational level. After completing this material, you should be able to identify the basic Windows 9x boot/startup sequence and alternative ways to boot the system software.

As with other operating systems, there are normally three elements involved in bringing the system to a fully functional status. These include employing procedures for loading/adding device drivers and the necessary software for devices, changing options, configuring and using the Windows 9x printing subsystem, and installing and launching typical Windows and non-Windows applications in a Windows 9x system.

The second portion of the chapter covered the Windows 9x operating systems in terms of their function and structure, as well as methods of managing files and running applications. This section included procedures for navigating through the operating system from the Windows 9x desktop, as well as methods of accessing and retrieving information.

The next section of the chapter dealt with networking Windows 9x systems. This discussion began by describing topics associated with Local Area Networking with Windows 9x operating systems.

The final sections of the chapter covered the Internet, including its capabilities, as well as basic concepts related to Internet access. You should be able to identify concepts and capabilities relating to the Internet and describe basic procedures for setting up a system for Internet access with Windows 9x.

At this point, review the objectives listed at the beginning of the chapter to be certain that you understand and can perform each item listed there.

KEY POINTS REVIEW

This chapter has provided an extensive exploration of the Windows 9x operating systems. Review the following key points before moving into the Review and Exam Questions sections to make sure you are comfortable with each point. Afterward, answer the Review Questions that follow to verify your knowledge of the information.

- Windows 9x must be installed over an existing operating system, such as MS-DOS or Windows 3.x. In particular, the Windows 9x installation program must find a recognizable MS-DOS FAT16 partition on the drive. This prevents it from being installed over some other type of operating system, such as Windows NT/2000 or Novell NetWare. The system must be at least an 80386DX or higher machine, operating with at least 4 MB of RAM (8 MB is recommended). The 80386DX is the listed minimum microprocessor for running Windows 9x, and the recommended processor is the 80486DX, but the Pentium processors are actually the preferred microprocessor for running Windows 9x. Likewise, 4 MB may be the minimum RAM option, with 8 MB being the recommended option, but 16 MB, 32 MB, or 64 MB are preferred for running Windows 9x.

- By establishing a dual-boot configuration, it is possible to install Windows 9x, or some other operating system, on an existing system and still retain the original operating system.

- The My Computer icon is the major user interface for Windows 9x. It enables the user to see the local system's content and manage its files.

- The Network Neighborhood icon provides quick information about the world around the system when it's used in a networked environment.

- One of the main Control Panel icons is the System icon. Clicking on this icon produces the System Properties window. This window features tabs for General information, the Device Manager, Hardware Profiles, and system Performance.

- The Device Manager utility provides a graphical representation of the devices configured in the system. This interface can be used to identify installed ports, update device drivers, and change I/O settings. It can also be used to manually isolate hardware and configuration conflicts. The problem device can be examined to see where the conflict is occurring.

- The Windows 9x file system does away with the 8+3 character filename system implemented under DOS. In Windows 9x, long filenames of up to 255 characters can be used, so that they can be more descriptive in nature. When these filenames are displayed in non-Windows 9x systems, they are truncated (shortened) to fit the 8.3 DOS character format and identified by a tilde character (~) followed by a single-digit number.

- The File management functions in Windows 9x and NT/2000 are performed through the Windows Explorer interface. This manager is located under the *Start/Programs* path from the desktop.

- In Windows 9x, the system's configuration information is held in an area known as the Registry. This includes the local hardware configuration, the network environment, file associations, and user configurations. Many of Windows 3.1's SYSTEM.INI, CONTROL.INI, PROGRAM.INI, and WIN.INI management functions have been relocated to the Registry.

- The content of the Registry is located in two files located in the Windows directory. These are the USER.DAT and SYSTEM.DAT files. The USER.DAT file contains user-specific information, and the SYSTEM.DAT file holds hardware- and computer-specific profiles and setting information.

- The Configuration Manager oversees the complete Plug-and-Play configuration process for Windows 9x. Its primary purpose is to ensure that each device in the system can access an interrupt request channel without conflict and that it has a unique I/O port address.

- As its full name implies, the Virtual File Allocation Table or VFAT provides a Protected-mode method of interacting with the file system on the disk drive. VFAT operates in 32-bit mode; however, the actual FAT structure of the disk remains as 12-bit or 16-bit allocations.

- The Plug-and-Play−compliant design of Windows 9x makes installing most new hardware nearly automatic (as long as the new device is also PnP compatible). The PnP function will automatically detect new PnP-compliant hardware when it is started. If the device is not PnP compliant, or the system just can't detect it for some reason, it will be necessary to use the Windows 9x Add New Hardware Wizard.

- Windows 9x is designed to assist the user in setting up any new hardware components that may be added to the system. The Add New Hardware icon can be found under the Control Panel option of the Settings menu.

- In addition to the Hardware Wizard, Windows 9x offers the user assistance in installing new programs. The Add/Remove New Programs icon under the Control Panel is used to install new programs automatically.

- DOS-based applications are installed in Windows 9x by simply running their executable file from the Run dialog box, or from the Windows 95 Explorer. If the file has never been run under Windows 9x, the operating system creates a default entry in its APPS.INF file for that program. A copy of the new entry is also used to create a .PIF file for the application.

- In later versions of DOS, Microsoft added the SHARE.EXE command to provide file-sharing and file-locking capabilities for files on a local hard disk drive. These capabilities enabled multiple users to access the same file at the same time in a networked or multitasking environment. The Share command should be loaded in the CONFIG.SYS file using an Install= statement (e.g., Install=Share /f:4096 /l:25).

- In Windows 9x, the peer-to-peer local area networking function is an integral part of the system. The heart of the Windows 9x networking system is contained in the desktop's Network Neighborhood icon and the Control Panel's Network icon.

- It is possible for the local system to assign a logical drive letter to the remote unit or folder. This is referred to as mapping the drive letter to the resource. This will enable non-Windows 9x applications running on the local computer to use the resource across the network.

- After the network adapter card has been configured and installed, the next step in setting up the computer on the network is to load its drivers, protocols, and services. In most Windows 95 installations, the majority of these steps are accomplished simply by rebooting the computer and allowing Windows to detect the network adapter.

REVIEW QUESTIONS

The following questions test your knowledge of the material presented in this chapter.

1. Describe the steps required to change a file's attributes in Windows 9x Explorer.

2. What action must be taken to see hidden files in Windows 9x?

3. Why are drives mapped in Windows 9x?

4. What type of File Allocation Table must be located on the partition that Windows 9x will be installed in?

5. If a DOS application is running in Windows 9x but it is taking up the entire screen, and you wish to switch to another application, what action should be taken?

6. What action should be taken if an older application covers the Taskbar and the Start menu button in a Windows 9x system?

7. In Windows 9x, a filename can be up to _____ characters long.

8. Which Windows 9x utility permits simultaneous editing of the SYSTEM.INI, WIN.INI, AUTOEXEC.BAT, CONFIG.SYS, and PROTOCOL.INI?

9. Which Control Panel is used to check protocols installed in a Windows 9x system?

10. If a properly mapped drive disappears when the system is rebooted, what could be wrong?

11. What condition would cause a user to be unable to connect to a remote system over the network in Windows 9x?

12. When Windows 95 boots up successfully, the Registry files are backed up with the _____ extension.

13. Describe the procedure used to view information about the network's connections through the Network Neighborhood icon.

14. What is the minimum microprocessor type that can be used to run Windows 98?

15. Which disk utility does Windows 98 run on the system during the installation process? What items does it check?

EXAM QUESTIONS

1. Where are you likely to encounter the NetBEUI protocol?
   a. In a Novell LAN
   b. In a Windows Internet environment
   c. In a Novell Internet environment
   d. In a Windows LAN

2. What is IPX/SPX and what is its function?
   a. Novell LAN protocol
   b. Windows Internet protocol
   c. Novell Internet protocol
   d. Windows LAN protocol

3. Which of the following structures recognize, configure, and allocate system resources under Windows 9x?
   a. The Registry
   b. Plug-and-Play
   c. The Windows Explorer
   d. The Control Panel

4. Which of the following best describes the boot sequence for Windows 9x systems?
   a. IO.SYS, MSDOS.SYS, COMMAND.COM, SYSTEM.DAT, USER.DAT, WIN.COM
   b. IO.SYS, SYSTEM.DAT, USER.DAT, MSDOS.SYS, COMMAND.COM, CONFIG.SYS, AUTOEXEC.BAT
   c. IO.SYS, MSDOS.SYS, COMMAND.COM, SYSTEM.DAT, USER.DAT, CONFIG.SYS, WIN.COM
   d. IO.SYS, MSDOS.SYS, COMMAND.COM, WIN.COM

5. Windows 98 stores Registry backup files in which format?
   a. XXXX.DAT
   b. XXXX.ZIP
   c. XXXX.TAR
   d. XXXX.CAB

6. During the startup process, which key should you press to access the Windows 9x Startup Menu?
   a. the F5 key
   b. the F8 key
   c. the F3 key
   d. the F4 key

7. If you save the file MYDOCUMENT.TXT in Windows 9x, how will it look in a DOS directory?
   a. MYDOCUME.NTT
   b. MYDOCU~T.TXT
   c. MYDOCU~1.TXT
   d. MYDOCUME.~XT

8. A customer complains that Windows 9x does not detect new hardware that has been installed in the system. Possible causes for this condition include:
   a. The hardware detection mechanism is disabled in CMOS.
   b. The BIOS is not PnP-compatible.
   c. The detection drivers have not been loaded for the hardware.
   d. Windows 9x does not support automatic hardware detection.

9. In Windows 9x, the _____ networking components provide the rules that the computer will use to govern the exchange of information across the network.
   a. client
   b. adapter
   c. protocol
   d. service

10. Which of the following is a format for providing a common telephony control system for Windows 9x communications products?
    a. ATAPI
    b. SCSI
    c. TAPI
    d. WINS

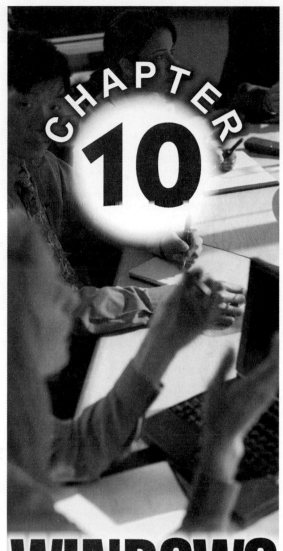

CHAPTER 10

WINDOWS NT/2000/XP

OBJECTIVES

OBJECTIVES

This chapter focuses on the Windows NT, Windows 2000, and Windows XP operating systems. After completing this chapter and its associated lab procedures, you will be able to:

1. Install Windows NT 4.0, Windows 2000, and Windows XP on new systems.

2. Upgrade systems from Windows 9x or Windows NT 4.0 to Windows 2000 or Windows XP.

3. Describe the bootup sequence employed by Windows NT/2000/XP.

4. Navigate through the Windows NT/2000/XP system, including the Internet Explorer.

5. Explain the structure of Windows NT/2000/XP.

6. List the core files in the Windows NT and Windows 2000 structures.

7. Identify the components of the Windows NT/2000/XP Registry structure.

8. Install and access printers in Windows NT 4.0, 2000, and XP.

9. Install and access software applications in Windows NT, 2000, and XP.

10. Install and configure hardware devices and drivers in Windows NT, 2000, and XP.

11. Install and configure local area networking functions in Windows NT, 2000, and XP.

12. Install and configure wide area networking and Internet functions in Windows NT 4.0, 2000, and XP.

WINDOWS NT/2000/XP

INTRODUCTION

While Microsoft developed and improved the Windows 3.x and Windows 9x products for desktop use by the general population, it also developed a more robust and complicated operating system for corporate client/server networking installations. This new operating system was introduced as **Windows New Technology**, or **Windows NT**.

Although the consumer-oriented Windows 3.x and 9x operating systems attempted to retain compatibility with the original MS-DOS platform, Windows NT made no such attempt. Instead, the new operating system was built around a completely new kernel that focused on enhanced reliability, scalability, and security elements required for corporate applications, while retaining the ease-of-use strengths associated with the Windows operating system.

In like manner, the Windows NT line of operating systems made no attempt to be compatible with a wide array of hardware and software components. Instead, the Windows NT line of operating systems offers fairly specific sets of software and hardware requirements that must be met for proper operation. Fortunately, more Windows NT compatible hardware and software systems have become available over time. With Windows 2000, Microsoft introduced an even wider range of compatible hardware and software options for the Windows NT platform. Even so, Windows 2000 and Windows XP still do not support nearly as many hardware and software options as Windows 95/98/Me.

Instead of being designed to operate on a single type of computer, the Windows NT operating system was designed to be portable between systems using different microprocessor architectures. By exchanging a single component, the Windows NT kernel can be used to exploit advances in PC hardware including 32-bit microprocessors, **Reduced Instruction Set Computer (RISC) architectures**, and multiprocessor (parallel processing) systems, as well as high-capacity RAM and disk storage for the purposes of creating advanced line-of-business platforms. The Windows NT operating system actually exists as three distinct products:

- A Workstation operating system

- A Server operating system

- An Extended Server operating system to manage large enterprise networks

Although all three Windows NT product types are referenced in this chapter, the scope of the A+ examination deals with the Workstation versions of the software. Therefore, the discussions in this chapter will primarily be aimed at these portions of the Windows NT platform. When aspects of the Server side of the package must be mentioned, this will be pointed out.

Even though there have been several versions of each Windows NT operating system version, the A+ examination has limited its involvement to the three most recent versions. These are **Windows NT 4.0**, **Windows 2000**, and the newest Windows NT version, called **Windows XP**. Throughout most of this chapter, these three versions will be referenced as a single topic.

WINDOWS NT NETWORKING

Microsoft designed the Windows NT operating system for corporate business networking environments. Unlike its mainstream Windows 3.x and 9x packages that included peer-to-peer networking functions, the Windows NT line of operating systems has been designed specifically to perform in a client/server network environment.

You should recall from Chapter 5 that a client/server network is one in which stand-alone computers, called **clients**, are connected to, and administered by, a master computer called a **server**. Collectively, the members of the group make up a network structure called a **domain**. Figure 10-1 depicts a typical domain-based network arrangement. The members of the domain share a common directory database and are organized in levels. Every domain is identified by a unique name and is administered as a single unit having common rules and procedures.

Figure 10-1:
A Client/Server or
Domain-Based
Network

Enterprise Networks

Windows NT 4.0 is sold in two different versions, a Standard NT Server version and an extended Enterprise Server package.

Enterprise networks

Enterprise networks are designed to facilitate business-to-business, or business-to-customer operations. Because monetary transactions and customers' personal information travel across the network in these environments, enterprise networks feature facilities for additional, highly protective security functions. These networks consist of multiple domains (called trusted domains) that are linked together, but managed independently.

Most enterprise networks are actually **intranets**.

intranets

An intranet is a network built on the TCP/IP protocol that belongs to a single organization. It is in essence a private Internet. Like the Internet, intranets are designed to share information and services, but they are accessible only to the organization's members, with authorization.

Figure 10-2 depicts an intranet structure where a local web server provides Internet applications, such as e-mail, FTP, and web browsing, for the network without using the public telephone system.

**Figure 10-2:
An Intranet**

A relatively new term, **extranet**, is being used to describe intranets that grant limited access to authorized outside users such as corporate business partners, as illustrated in Figure 10-3. This makes the extranet a partially private, partially public network arrangement. In this example, a customer web server is placed between the company's intranet and the Internet. Part of this server's job is to authenticate users from the outside by asking them for a valid password before they can access the contents of the server. A hardware or software **firewall** is typically employed to block unauthorized outside users from accessing the intranet site.

extranet

firewall

Figure 10-3: An Extranet

Primary Domain Controllers (PDC)

Backup Domain Controllers (BDC)

User Accounts

Group Accounts

Computer Accounts

Security Accounts Manager (SAM)

Authentication

Windows NT Network Structures

In the Windows NT Client/Server environment, two types of domain controllers exist—**Primary Domain Controllers (PDC)** and **Backup Domain Controllers (BDC)**. The PDC contains the directory database for the network. This database contains information about **User Accounts**, **Group Accounts**, and **Computer Accounts**. You may also find this database referred to as the **Security Accounts Manager (SAM)**. BDCs are servers within the network that are used to hold read-only backup copies of the directory database. As illustrated in Figure 10-4, a network may contain one or more BDCs. These servers are used to authenticate user logons. **Authentication** is the process of identifying individuals as being who they claim to be. This process is normally based on user names and passwords.

Figure 10-4: A PDC/BDC Arrangement in a Network

Windows 2000 Active Directory

The central feature of the Windows 2000 network architecture is the **Active Directory (AD)** structure. Active Directory is a distributed database of user and resource information that describes the makeup of the network (i.e., users and application settings). It is also a method of implementing a distributed **authentication process**. The Active Directory replaces the domain structure used in Windows NT 4.0-based networks, described earlier in this chapter. This feature helps to centralize system and user configurations, as well as data backups on the server in the Windows 2000 network.

Windows 2000 remains a domain-dependent operating system. It uses domains as boundaries for administration, security, and replication purposes. Each domain must be represented by at least one domain controller. Recall that a domain controller is a server set up to track the names of all of the objects and requests for resources within a domain.

In Windows 2000, the peer-server networking model has replaced the Primary and Backup Domain Controller structure from Windows NT. Under this model, individual servers can be promoted to Active Directory domain controllers without shutting down the system to reinstall their operating systems.

The Active Directory structure employs two common Internet standards — the **Lightweight Directory Access Protocol (LDAP)** and **Domain Name Service (DNS)**. The LDAP protocol is used to define how directory information is accessed and exchanged. DNS is the Internet standard for resolving domain names to actual IP addresses. It is also the standard for exchanging directory information with clients and other directories.

> The Active Directory arranges domains in a hierarchy and establishes trust relationships among all of the domains in a tree-like structure, as illustrated in Figure 10-5.

Active Directory (AD)

authentication process

Lightweight Directory Access Protocol (LDAP)

Domain Name Service (DNS)

Figure 10-5: Basic Active Directory Structure

| **tree** | A **tree** is a collection of objects that share the same DNS name. Active Directory can subdivide domains into organizational units (sales, admin, etc.) that contain other units, or leaf objects, such as printers, users, and so on. |

| **forest** | Conversely, Windows 2000 can create an organizational structure containing more than one tree. This structure is referred to as a **forest**. Figure 10-6 expands the AD structure to demonstrate these relationships. |

Figure 10-6: Active Directory Relationships

The Windows 2000 operating system automatically joins all of the domains within a tree through two-way trusts.

| **Trusts** | **Trusts** are relationships that enable users to move between domains and perform pre-scribed types of operations. |

If a trust relationship is established between the sales and marketing domains in the example and a similar trust exists between the sales and admin domains, then a trust relationship also exists between the marketing and admin domains. Trusts enable administrators to provide users and groups with different rights to objects.

| **Rights** **Administrative rights** | **Rights** are permission settings that control a user's (or groups of users') authority to access objects and perform operations (such as reading or writing a file). **Administrative rights** provide authority to users down to the Organizational Unit level. |

| **user rights** | Administrative rights do not cross boundaries established at the domain level but can be inherited by other OUs having subordinate positions within the same tree. On the other hand, **user rights** must be established for individual users or for members of groups. Using groups allows common rights to be assigned to multiple users with a single administrative action (as opposed to setting up and maintaining rights for each individual in, say, a 150-person accounting staff). |

Managing user and group rights in Windows NT/2000/XP is discussed in greater detail later in this chapter.

THE WINDOWS NT PRODUCT LINE

A portion of A+ Operating System Technologies objective 1.1 states that the test taker should be able to identify the major desktop components and interfaces, and their functions. Differentiate the characteristics of Windows 9x/Me, Windows NT 4.0 Workstation, Windows 2000 Professional, and Windows XP. As mentioned earlier, the Windows NT package was originally developed in two parts — the **NT Workstation** and the **NT Server** operating systems. The server software has become known simply as NT Server. However, with the advent of Windows 2000 and then Windows XP, Microsoft changed the name of the workstation software to **Windows 2000 Professional** and **Windows XP Professional**.

> **NT Workstation**
>
> **NT Server**
>
> **Windows 2000 Professional**
>
> **Windows XP Professional**

Windows NT Workstation

The Windows NT Workstation operating system can be employed as a client workstation in a client/server network, or it can be used as an operating system for a stand-alone computer that's not connected to anything. However, Windows NT was designed to work in a strong network environment. As such, many of the features that make Windows 9x packages easier to use are not located in Windows NT Workstation.

Windows NT 4.0 Workstation supports advanced multitasking and multiprocessor operations. It can maintain different hardware profiles for multiple configurations within the same system. The Windows NT memory management system does a much better job of protecting applications from violating each other's space than the Windows 9x products do. Finally, Windows NT Workstation provides a much higher level of file, folder, and resource security than the 9x versions do. Windows NT can control access to these resources through passwords and logins on the desktop, or through a central network controller called a server in a client/server relationship.

Windows NT Server

The Windows NT 4.0 Server package provides the same features and functions found in the Windows NT Workstation. However, the Server package also provides the tools necessary to administer and control a network from its central location.

Recall that in a peer-to-peer workgroup setting, all of the nodes may act as servers for some processes and clients for others. In a domain-based network, the network is controlled from a centralized server (**domain controller**). In a Windows NT network, this concept is embodied by the location where the Administration and Security databases are kept. In the workgroup, each machine maintains its own security and administration databases. In a domain environment, the server is responsible for keeping the centralized user account and security databases.

> **domain controller**

With some network operating systems, servers cannot function as active workstations in the network. With the Windows NT operating system, however, both the Workstation and Server versions can be used as nodes in peer-to-peer (workgroup) networks, and as workstations in domain-based, client/server networks. While you can use Windows NT Server as a workstation, doing so would be a very expensive waste of its capabilities.

Windows 2000

Windows 2000 is the successor of the Windows NT 4.0 operating system. As a matter of fact, it was originally titled Windows NT 5. This operating system brings together the stability and security of Windows NT 4.0 and the Plug-and-Play capabilities of Windows 9x.

Windows 2000 also includes built-in support for many new technologies including DVD drives, USB devices, Accelerated Graphics Ports, multifunction adapter cards, and a full line of PC Cards. Finally, Windows 2000 provides a new distributed directory service for managing resources across an enterprise, FAT 32 support, and the Internet Explorer 5 web browser.

As with previous NT versions, Windows 2000 comes in two basic variations: the corporate workstation version, titled Windows 2000 Professional, and the network server version, called Windows 2000 Server. The server product is also available in two extended enterprise versions — **Windows 2000 Advanced Server** and **Windows 2000 Datacenter Server**.

**Windows 2000
Advanced Server**

**Windows 2000
Datacenter Server**

Windows 2000 Professional

**Windows 2000
Professional**

The workstation side of Windows 2000 is named **Windows 2000 Professional**. This operating system is designed to be the reliable, powerful desktop for the corporate computing world. It has been designed to be easier to set up and configure than previous Windows NT platforms. Windows 2000 Professional employs several wizards, such as the New Hardware Wizard and the Network Connection Wizard, to make installation and configuration processes easier for users.

Windows 2000 Professional extended and improved the Windows 95/98 user interface. It also brought Plug-and-Play to the NT workstation. The hardware supported by Windows 2000 Professional has been upgraded to include those items commonly found in newer systems.

While it offers many improvements over previous Windows NT versions, Windows 2000 Professional is still be too complex for most general consumer usage. For this reason, Microsoft has continued to upgrade its Windows 9x product for the general consumer market with its release of Windows Me. They have followed this up with a later release of Windows XP Professional that represents their most consumer-oriented version of the NT operating system line.

Windows 2000 Server

On the server side, Windows 2000 offers a more scalable and flexible server platform than its Windows NT predecessors. **Windows 2000 Server** actually comes in three versions that correspond to the size and complexity of the network environment they are used in. These versions include the standard Server edition, the Advanced Server edition, and the Windows 2000 Datacenter Server edition.

Windows 2000 Server

The Standard Server edition offers a more scalable and flexible file server platform. It also functions as an application server that handles large data sets. It can be used to implement a standards-based, secured Internet/intranet server.

> **─ NOTE ─**
>
> Recall that an intranet is simply a private, web-based network, typically established by an organization for the purpose of running an exclusive web site not open to the public (i.e., company web sites for internal company use only). Intranets can be based on local or wide area networks, or constructed as combinations of the two.

The standard Windows 2000 Server package can manage up to 4 GB of RAM and is capable of distributing work between two microprocessors at a time. This type of operation is referred to as **Symmetrical Multiprocessing (SMP)**. If Windows 2000 Server has been installed as an upgrade to an existing Windows NT 4.0 Server, it can support up to four different microprocessors simultaneously.

Symmetrical Multiprocessing (SMP)

The Advanced Server edition can support up to 8 symmetrical processors and up to 8 GB of memory. These features enable it to function well in medium-size networks running between 100 and 500 concurrent users.

In other respects, the Advanced Server product is the same as the standard Server version. However, some enterprise versions of applications will run only on the Enterprise version of the operating system.

The Windows 2000 Datacenter Server edition can handle up to 64 GB of RAM and 32 processors. This will enable it to support up to 1000 simultaneous users with heavy processing demands.

Both the Advanced and Datacenter Server editions employ a pair of high-availability features that allow them to effectively handle the traffic levels found on medium and large web sites. These features are **Network Load Balancing (NLB)** and **Microsoft Cluster Server (MSCS)**. The load-balancing feature enables the operating system to distribute IP requests to the most available web server in a cluster of up to 32 web servers.

Network Load Balancing (NLB)

Microsoft Cluster Server (MSCS)

Windows XP Professional

Windows XP

Windows XP is the current version of Microsoft's desktop operating system. Windows XP represents another level of meshing the stable kernel of the Windows NT operating system line with the consumer-oriented ease of use associated with the Windows 9x products. The Windows XP operating system is available in three versions:

XP Home Edition

- *Windows XP Home Edition* — The Windows **XP Home Edition** is designed to replace the Windows 95/98 and Windows Me operating systems. It is primarily intended for consumer and entertainment markets and provides many enhancements, such as more powerful and streamlined Internet access than any of its predecessors.

XP Professional

- *Windows XP Professional* — Windows **XP Professional** is designed and positioned to compete with Windows NT Workstation and Windows 2000 Professional operating systems. It contains features that make it more suitable as a client in enterprise network. These features include such items as simpler remote access and domain membership, enhanced security and reliability features, multiple processor support, and multiple language availability. The A+ certification focuses primarily on this Windows XP version.

Windows XP 64-bit edition

- *Windows XP 64-bit Edition* — The **Windows XP 64-bit edition** is a high-end version of the operating system designed to run on Intel Itanium processors. These processors are employed in high-data-volume environments. This Windows XP version supports up to 16 GB of physical memory and 16 TB of virtual memory. Unlike its NT predecessors, Windows XP does not feature matching workstation and server operating system versions.

Windows 2003 Server

Windows Server 2003

While Microsoft decided to call their next workstation operating system Windows XP, the next version of the Windows NT Server product is called **Windows Server 2003**. As with the Windows 2000 series of server operating systems, the 2003 series will include Standard, Enterprise (advanced), and Datacenter editions. The capabilities and qualities of these editions are similar to those stated for their Windows 2000 predecessors.

Windows Server 2003 - Web edition

In addition to those editions already mentioned, Microsoft is producing a **Windows Server 2003 - Web edition** that is designed for web services and hosting support. It only contains features required specifically to support development and deployment of web services and applications.

> ### — NOTE —
> Remember that information about specific server operating systems is not part of the A+ certification objective map. These systems are mentioned here for your information and knowledge base.

NAVIGATING WINDOWS NT/2000/XP

A portion of A+ Operating System Technologies objective 1.1 states that the test taker should be able to identify the major desktop components and interfaces, and their functions. Differentiate the characteristics of Windows 9x/Me, Windows NT 4.0 Workstation, Windows 2000 Professional, and Windows XP. It also states that the content may include major operating system interfaces.

Many of the Windows NT/2000/XP structures and navigation methods should appear very familiar after reading the Windows 9x material in Chapter 9— *Windows 9x*. With Windows NT Version 4.0, Microsoft introduced a Windows 9x—like user interface to the Windows NT operating system. This includes the desktop with its icons, the pop-up Start menu, and the Taskbar.

Windows NT/2000/XP Desktops

The Windows NT/2000 desktops include most of the same features found in their Windows 9x counterpart. The standard desktop icons are the same as those mentioned for Windows 9x (i.e., *My Computer*, *My Network Places*, *Inbox*, and the *Recycle Bin*). If the operating system is installed on a stand-alone unit that does not have a network card installed, the *Network Neighborhood* icon will not be presented on the desktop. The functions of these icons are identical to those described for the Windows 9x versions. In its originally installed state, the Windows XP desktop only shows the Recycle Bin and the Start menu/Taskbar. Figure 10-7 depicts the Windows 2000 desktop with the Start menu expanded. Notice that the standard desktop icons for Windows 2000 include *My Computer*, *My Network Places*, and the *Recycle Bin.*.

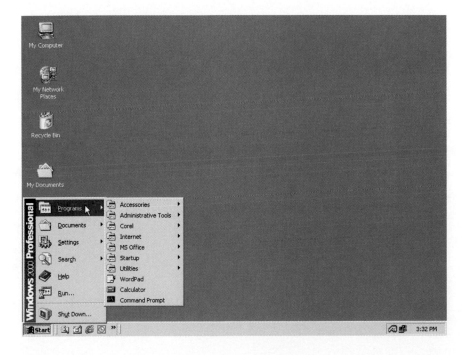

Figure 10-7: Windows 2000 Desktop

Locating, Accessing, and Retrieving Information in Windows 2000 and XP

Locating, accessing, and retrieving information in the different Windows NT operating system versions is virtually the same as with the Windows 9x operating systems.

The major Windows 2000/XP user interfaces are:

- My Computer
- Start menu/Taskbar
- Windows Explorer
- Internet Explorer
- My Network Places
- Windows 2000/XP dialog boxes (windows)

These interfaces provide user access to all of the major areas of the system. For the most part, these interfaces are graphical enhancements of the Windows 9x interfaces with the same name. In the following discussions we will treat them as the same except where we specifically point out differences between operating system versions. Most of the time, these occurrences will involve the Windows XP version.

Right-clicking techniques are also employed in the Windows NT platforms to access context-sensitive options on the screen. Right-clicking on an item produces a pop-up menu, similar to the one depicted in Figure 10-8. As with Windows 9x operating systems, these Windows 2000 and XP menus enable the user to copy a file, create a shortcut, close a folder, or examine properties of the system's installed devices. Right-click menus may also contain additional items that have been inserted by applications that they serve.

**Figure 10-8:
Windows NT
Right-Click Menu**

Right-clicking over an open area of the desktop produces a pop-up menu that enables the user to arrange icons on the desktop, create new folders and shortcuts, and see the properties of the system's video display.

As with the Windows 9x/Me version, the *Windows NT/2000/XP My Computer* window enables users to access every hardware device in the system.

In Windows NT, 2000 and XP, the Taskbar is located at the bottom of the display by default. The Taskbar displays icons that represent programs running in the system. Even though the Taskbar is normally located at the bottom of the screen, it can be moved to either side of the screen, or to the top of the display. When moved to the top of the screen, the *Start* menu will drop down from above instead of pop up from the bottom.

Windows NT, Windows 2000, and Windows XP operations typically begin from the *Start* menu that pops up when the *Start* button is clicked. The *Start* menu provides the user with access to the system regardless of what else is occurring in the system. In doing so, it provides access to the system's installed applications, a search engine for finding data in the system, and the operating system's Help file structure.

The Windows NT and 2000 Start menus contain entries for *Programs, Documents, Settings, Find, Help, Run*, and *Shut Down* options. Selecting one of these options from the menu will cause a pop-up submenu or dialog box to be displayed. As with the desktop icons, the functions of the Windows NT/2000 Start menu options are identical to those of their Windows 9x counterparts.

The Windows NT 4.0 Programs menu pops out from the *Start* menu in a fully extended manner. However, Windows 2000 and Windows XP feature intelligent, personalized *Programs* menus. These operating systems monitor the user's program usage, and after the first six accesses arrange the menu options according to those most frequently used. The menu options displayed change based on their usage. Less frequently used programs are not displayed in the list, but can be accessed by clicking on the double arrow at the bottom of the list. The hidden portion of the list will appear after a short delay. When this occurs, the six most frequently used applications are highlighted. This reduces screen clutter and makes it easier for users to access their most used items.

Start menu items can easily be renamed in Windows 2000. You can accomplish this by right-clicking on the menu item and choosing the *Rename* option from the context-sensitive pop-up menu. Then, the user types the new name in the text entry box. This is all accomplished without opening the *Start* menu.

The contents of the Windows 2000 and Windows XP Control Panels can be cascaded as a submenu of the *Start* button for quick access. The *My Documents* menu can also be cascaded off the *Start* menu for fast access to documents.

The My Documents concept has been expanded to include a *My Pictures* folder that acts as the default location to hold graphic files. The *Windows 2000* and *Windows XP* dialog boxes include an image preview function that allows the user to locate graphic files efficiently. The dialog box *View menu* option enables the user to toggle between Large and Small Icons, Details, and Thumbnail views. The dialog boxes can be resized to accommodate as many Thumbnail images as desired.

The Windows 2000/XP Windows Explorer graphically displays the entire computer system in a hierarchical tree structure. This enables the user to manipulate all of the system's software and hardware. Similarly, the *Network Neighborhood* window extends the Windows Explorer structure to include network and domain structures. The Internet Explorer supplies the system with a tightly linked web connection.

In Windows 2000 and XP, the *My Network Places* icon replaces the *Network Neighborhood* folder employed in previous Windows NT and 9x versions. This applet enables the user to create shortcut icons to network shares on the desktop. A network share is an existing shared resource (i.e., printer, drive, modem, or folder) located on a remote system. The new icon acts as an alias to link the system to the share point on the remote unit.

> Windows 2000 and XP versions offer extended common dialog boxes for *File/Open*, *File/Print*, and *File/Save* options. These dialog boxes provide easy organization and navigation of the system's hard drives, as well as providing navigation columns that grant quick access to frequently used folders, such as the *My Documents* and *My Pictures* folders.

Figure 10-9 depicts the *File/Open*, *File/Save As*, and *File/Print* common dialog boxes. The navigation column also provides easy access to the *My Network Places* folder.

Figure 10-9: Windows 2000/XP Common Dialog Boxes

Full Screen

Windows 2000/XP folders include a customizable toolbar with Windows 98−like navigation buttons. The Windows Explorer toolbar, depicted in Figure 10-10, comes with a collection of about 20 add-on buttons that can be used to customize its available options. You can modify the toolbar by alternate-clicking on the toolbar, and then selecting the *Customize* option from the pop-up menu. Additional buttons include *Move To*, *Copy To*, *Search*, *Map Drive*, *Favorites*, and *Full Screen*. The **Full Screen** option is new and can be used to toggle between maximized and normal window sizes.

Windows 2000 and XP versions also include powerful search capabilities for searching the local hard drive and the web. The HTML-like **Search function** in Windows 2000 and XP replaces the *Start* menu's *Find* option from previous Windows desktops. The Search feature provides three distinct search options:

1. For Files and Folders

2. On the Internet

3. For People

The **For Files and Folders** option opens a dual-page version of the Windows 98/NT 4 *Find Files and Folders* dialog window. This window provides all of the old Windows search functions and adds powerful new ones, such as case-sensitive searches. These options are available through the *Advanced* button.

Selecting the **On the Internet** option brings up a search bar that establishes a link to a predetermined Internet search engine such as Yahoo or AOL. The **Search for People** option opens a **Lightweight Directory Access Protocol (LDAP)** dialog window that resembles the one in Windows 98 or Internet Explorer.

Enabling the **Microsoft Index Server** function produces particularly fast searches. The **Indexing Service** runs in the background to provide content indexing on the local hard drive. Windows 2000 and XP Professional versions include a local version of the indexing service that operates with the local hard drive. In a network environment that uses Windows 2000 Servers, the server can perform the content indexing service. The **Index Service Management** tools are located in the *Start/Programs/Administrative Tools* path.

Searching with the context index feature enabled allows the user to write Boolean logic expressions (such as AND, OR, and NOT) for finding specific content quickly.

Figure 10-10: Windows 2000 Explorer Toolbar

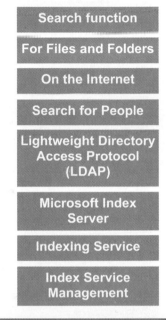

Windows XP Variations

While the Windows XP desktop and Start menu can be configured to look like the old 9x/2000 Start menus (referred to as the *Classic* theme), they have really been redesigned to offer a more compartmentalized arrangement as illustrated in Figure 10-11. To be more appealing to consumers, the "My..." collection has been expanded to include Documents (and Recent Documents), Pictures, Music, Favorites, Computer, and Network Places. These represent the personalized settings for the logged-in user. They also make up one of the biggest sections of the revised *Start* menu.

Figure 10-11: The Windows XP Start Menu

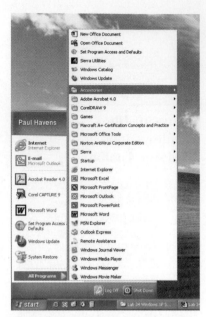

Figure 10-12: The Windows XP Programs Menu

Remote Assistance

Remote Desktop Connection Wizard

System Tools

Most of the other *Start* menu items are similar to those that users are familiar with from previous 9x or NT versions of Windows. This includes quick-access applications along the left side of the menu, the *Control Panel/Printers and Faxes* options, and the *Help and Support/Search and Run* options at the bottom right side of the menu. The *Log off* and *Shut Down* buttons have been set off to themselves at the bottom of the menu. The one item that looks significantly different is the *All Programs* entry. This button is the new version of the *Programs* option from previous menu versions.

Simply resting the cursor over the green arrow icon will pop up the *Programs* menu, as illustrated in Figure 10-12. As the figure shows, the Windows XP *All Programs* menu contains the usual entries from previous Programs menus. Technicians should be most familiar with the contents of the *Accessories* and *Administrative Tools* options. These two locations provide the most direct access to most of the diagnostic and maintenance tools provided by the Windows XP operating system.

One additional technician-related entry to note in the *All Programs* menu is the **Remote Assistance** icon. This utility can be used to let remote computer users, such as remote technicians or administrators, take over the local computer and operate it from their desktop. This feature must be activated locally and usually involves turning control over to a trusted individual for assistance purposes.

Figure 10-13 shows the *Accessories* menu listings. The most interesting entries in the *Accessories* menu include *Communications*, *Entertainment*, and *System Tools*. The *Communications* entry provides tools and wizards that assist in setting up local area and dialup networking functions. A new entry in this location is the **Remote Desktop Connection Wizard** that enables you to access desktops on remote computers and use them as if you were setting in front of those machines. The *Entertainment* option primarily involves audio and video functions associated with the PC. The **System Tools** submenu is a very important area for technicians. This entry can be used to access the disk and system management tools used to perform preventive maintenance on the system and to optimize its performance.

Figure 10-13: Key XP Programs Menu Extensions

One other entry that you may need to be aware of in the *Accessories* menu is the *Accessibility* option. This entry provides system customization features that can be implemented to accommodate users who have physical barriers to using the computer system.

The **Administrative Tools** menu, whose contents are displayed in Figure 10-14, is another key location for technicians. This applet provides access to the system's major administration and management tools. Important entries in this submenu include the **Computer Management applet** that has tools for managing the system's disk systems as well as both local and remote computers, the *Local Security Policy* option that is used to configure local security policies, and the *Event Viewer* and *Performance* tools that are used to monitor system events and performance so that problems can be spotted and corrected before major failures occur. These tools and their usage are described in greater detail in Chapter 12—*Operating System Troubleshooting*.

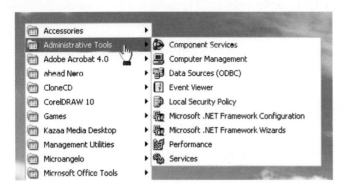

Figure 10-14: Windows XP Administrative Tools

Windows XP Control Panel

The Windows XP Control Panel, depicted in Figure 10-15, also offers some additional features and functionality not found in previous Windows 9x and NT/2000 versions. In Windows XP, the *Control Panel* option is included directly on the Start menu instead of in a submenu. Under the native Windows XP version of the Control Panel, the applets are organized into nine related categories.

When you access some of these options, two corresponding dialog windows pop up in the left window — *See Also* and *Troubleshooters*. The *See Also* window lists other related topics that might be important to the activity you are attempting to perform. The *Troubleshooters* window provides direct access to related Windows Help Troubleshooters to solve context-specific problems. The *Add or Remove Programs* and *User Accounts* options do not have either of these two options when they are accessed. Similarly, the *Date, Time...* and *Accessibility Options* only provide a *See Also* window.

If you select the *Switch to Classic View* option in the upper-left dialog box, you should see all of the normal 9x/NT options for adding and removing hardware and software components, as well as a collection of individual control panels for different devices and Windows services. The Windows XP Control Panel also features a Windows 2000 Administrative Tools applet that performs the same function as the entry from the *Start/Programs* menu of the same name.

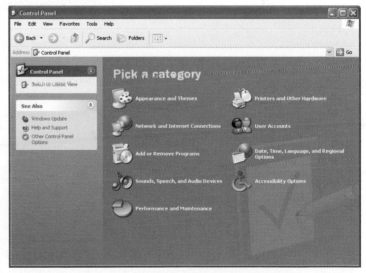

Figure 10-15: Windows XP Control Panel

In addition, the Windows 2000 Control Panel includes advanced applets for Wireless networking and Speech functions not found in other versions, as well as *Taskbar* and *Start Menu* options that can be used to customize these structures and control what items are displayed through them. A new feature provided in this applet is the ability to lock the Taskbar so that it cannot be moved or changed.

For the technician, one of the most important options in the Windows XP Control Panel is the Performance and Maintenance group depicted in Figure 10-16. This group contains the *Administrative Tools* and *System* icons. As mentioned previously in this chapter, the Administrative Tools are discussed in detail in Chapter 12 — *Operating System Troubleshooting*. However, the *System* icon is the link to information about the computer system and to the device manager that is used to change the properties of the system's hardware devices. This tool is also described later in this chapter and in the *Operating System Troubleshooting* chapter.

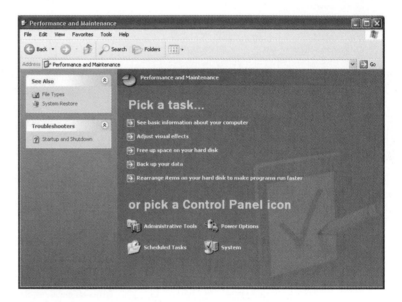

Figure 10-16: Windows XP Control Panel/ Performance and Maintenance Group

---

WINDOWS NT/2000/XP FILES

A portion of the A+ Operating System technology objective 1.4 says that the test taker should be able to identify basic concepts and procedures for creating, viewing, and managing disks, directories, and files. This includes procedures for changing file attributes and the ramifications of those changes (for example, security issues). It also indicates that the content may include working with files in a given operating system.

From Windows NT 4.0 forward, the Windows NT operating systems have been able to handle long filenames. Filenames in Windows 2000 and XP can be up to 215 characters long (NT 4.0 names could be a maximum of 256 characters long) including spaces. Windows 2000 and XP employ a proprietary method for reducing long filenames to MS-DOS−compatible 8.3 filenames. Instead of simply truncating the filename, inserting a tilde, and then assigning a number to the end of the filename, the Windows 2000 and XP systems perform a mathematical operation on the long name to generate a truly unique MS-DOS−compatible filename. Windows 2000/XP filenames cannot contain the following characters: /\:*?"|.

Basically, the Windows 2000 and Windows XP algorithms employed to produce MS-DOS−compatible filenames remove any characters that are illegal under MS-DOS, remove any extra periods from the filename, truncate the filename to six characters, insert a tilde, and add an ID number to the end of the name.

However, when five or more names are generated that would result in duplicate short names, Windows NT changes its truncation method. Beginning with the sixth filename, the first two characters of the name are retained, the next four characters are generated through the mathematical algorithm, and, finally, a tilde with an ID number is attached to the end of the name. This method is used to create MS-DOS−compliant short filenames for MS-DOS, Windows 3.x, and Windows 9x-compliant FAT systems, as well as the proprietary **Windows NT file system** (**NTFS**).

Windows NT file system (NTFS)

Windows 2000 and XP create properties sheets for each file and folder in the system. These sheets contain information about the file (or folder) such as its size, location, and creation date. When you view the file's properties, you can also see its attributes, file type, the program that is designed to open it, and when the file was last opened or modified.

CHALLENGE #1

A customer has an important business file on his Windows 2000 machine that has boot problems. He can gain access to the drive using a Start disk. However, when he views the disk from the command line, he cannot find the FutureBusinessPlansandMarketing.doc file. He has asked you to help him locate the file because he must give a presentation based on it in one hour. When you view the drive, there are literally several hundreds of files on the drive. What can you do for him?

File Encryption and Compression

The NTFS file system employed in Windows 2000 and Windows XP provides two new file types that technicians must deal with. These are **encrypted files** and **compressed files**. The Windows 2000 NTFS system provides an **Encrypted File System** (**EFS**) utility that is the basis of storing encrypted files on NTFS volumes. Once a file or folder has been encrypted, only the user who encrypted it can access it. The original user can work with the file or folder just as they would a regular file. However, other users cannot open or share the file (although they can delete it).

encrypted files

compressed files

Encrypted File System (EFS)

decrypted

For other users to be able to access the file or folder, it must first be **decrypted**. The encryption protection disappears when the file or folder is moved to a non-NTFS partition. Only files on NTFS volumes can be encrypted. Conversely, system files and compressed files cannot be encrypted.

Files and folders can be encrypted from the command line using the **cipher** command. Information about the cipher command and its many switches can be obtained by typing *cipher /?* at the command prompt. Files can also be encrypted through the Windows Explorer. Encryption is treated as a file attribute in Windows 2000 and Windows XP. Therefore, to encrypt a file you simply need to access its properties page by right-clicking on it and selecting its *Properties* option from the pop-up menu. Move to the *Advanced* screen under the *General* tab and click on the *Encrypt contents to secure data* check box, as illustrated in Figure 10-17. Decrypting a file is a simple matter of clearing the check box.

**Figure 10-17:
Encrypting a File**

NTFS compression

┌─ **TEST TIP** ─────────┐
│ Know how to encrypt a file │
│ from the Windows 2000 │
│ command line. │
└────────────────────────┘

The Windows Explorer can also be used to compress files and folders on NTFS volumes. Like encryption, Windows 2000 and Windows XP treat **NTFS compression** as a file attribute. To compress a particular file or folder, right-click on it in the Windows Explorer, and then select the *Properties* option, followed by the *Advanced* button to access its advanced properties screen, as illustrated in Figure 10-18. Click in the *Compress contents to save disk space* check box to compress the file or folder. Likewise, an entire drive can be compressed through the *My Computer* icon. From the *File* menu, select the *Properties* option, and click in the *Compress drive to save disk space* check box.

**Figure 10-18:
Compressing
a File**

As with the encryption function, Windows 2000 and XP files and folders can only be compressed on NTFS volumes. If you move a file into a compressed folder, the file will be compressed automatically. These files cannot be encrypted while they are compressed. Compressed files can be marked so that they are displayed in a second color for easy identification. This is accomplished through the *Folder Options* setting in the *Control Panel*. From this page, select the *View* tab and click in the *Display compressed files and folder with alternate color* check box. The only other indication that you will have concerning a compressed or encrypted file or folder is an attribute listing when the view setting is configured to display in web style.

┌─ **TEST TIP** ─────────────────────┐
│ Know how to identify a compressed file in │
│ Windows 2000. │
└────────────────────────────────────┘

Windows NT/2000/XP Structures

A portion of the A+ Operating System Technologies objective 1.1 says that the test taker should be able to identify the major desktop components and interfaces, and their functions. Differentiate the characteristics of Windows 9x/Me, Windows NT 4.0 Workstation, Windows 2000 Professional, and Windows XP. It also indicates that content may include the major operating system components.

When fully installed, the Windows NT logical structure exists as depicted in Figure 10-19. It is a modular operating system that allows for advances in computing technology to be integrated into the system. The operating system exists in two basic layers referred to as Modes. These two levels are the **Kernel Mode** and the **User Mode**.

Kernel Mode

User Mode

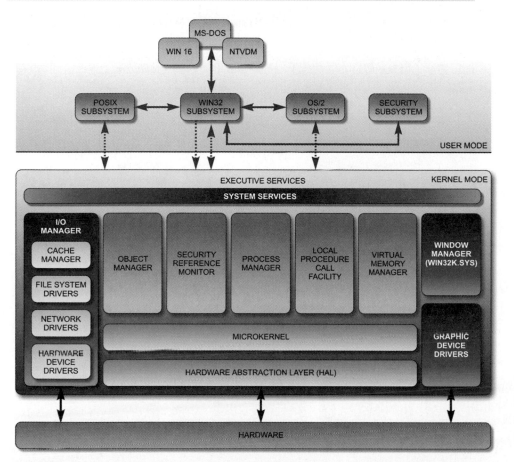

**Figure 10-19:
The Windows NT
Organizational
Structure**

Basically, the operating system runs in the *Kernel Mode*, whereas applications run in the *User Mode*. The Kernel Mode is the operating mode in which the program has unlimited access to all memory, including those of system hardware, the User Mode applications, and other processes (such as I/O operations). The User Mode is a more restrictive operating mode in which no direct access of hardware is permitted.

**Application
Programming
Interfaces (APIs)**

**Hardware Abstraction
Layer (HAL)**

Application Programming Interfaces (APIs) are routines, protocols, and tools built into the operating system that provide application designers with consistent building blocks to design their applications with. For the user, these building blocks lead to consistent interfaces being designed for all applications.

Likewise, the Windows NT **Hardware Abstraction Layer (HAL)** is a library of hardware drivers that operate between the actual hardware and the rest of the system. These software routines act to make the architecture of every device look the same to the operating system. The Microkernel works closely with the HAL to keep the system's microprocessor as busy as possible. It does this by scheduling threads for introduction to the microprocessor on a priority basis.

The Win32k Executive Services block provides all the basic operating system functions for the NT environment. It is made up of a number of managers that support activities such as basic operating system services, application environments, and APIs for the various types of applications that the Windows NT system can handle.

It should be apparent that the organizational structure of Windows 2000 and Windows XP, depicted in Figure 10-20, is very similar to the Windows NT structure depicted in Figure 10-19. However, Windows 2000 and XP add two additional managers to the Executive section. These are the *Plug-and-Play Manager* and the *Power Manager*.

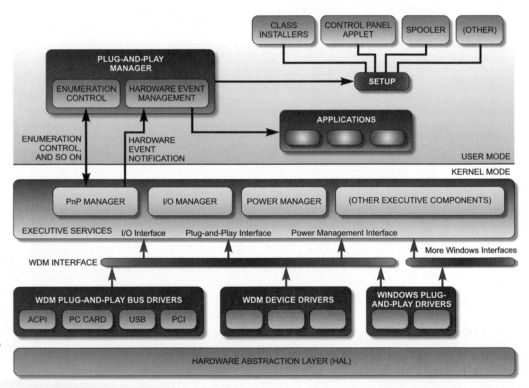

**Figure 10-20:
Windows 2000/XP
Organizational
Structure**

The PnP manager employs the enumeration process to discover PnP devices installed in the system. Afterwards, it loads appropriate drivers and creates Registry entries for those devices. These drivers and entries are based on Information (INF) scripts developed by Microsoft and the hardware vendors for the device being configured. The PnP manager then allocates the system's resources (IRQ settings, DMA channels, and I/O addresses) to the devices that require them.

The Power Manager interacts with key system components to conserve energy (especially useful for portable computers) and reduce wear on system devices. Both managers depend on PnP-compliant system components as well as the APM and ACPI power management standards described in Chapter 7 — *Portable Systems*.

Windows NT/2000/XP Memory Management

A portion of the A+ Operating system Technologies objective 2.5 indicates that the test taker should be able to identify procedures necessary to optimize the operating system and major operating system subsystems. It indicates that content may include Virtual Memory Management.

The Windows NT memory management scheme employs a full 32-bit architecture with a flat memory model. In the Windows NT model, the **Virtual Memory Manager (VMM)** assigns unique memory spaces to every active 32-bit and 16-bit application. Unlike MS-DOS, Windows 3.x, or Windows 9x, Windows NT operating system versions do not employ the address segmentation features of the Intel microprocessors. Because segments can overlap, memory usage errors can occur when an application attempts to write data into a space allocated to the operating system or another application.

The VMM maps each application's memory space into contiguous 4 kB pages of physical memory. Using this method, each application is mapped into a truly unique address space that cannot overlap any other address space. The lack of segment overlap reduces the chances of applications interfering with each other and helps to ensure data integrity by providing the operating system and other processes with their own memory spaces.

Virtual Memory Manager (VMM)

Windows NT Virtual Memory

When the VMM has exhausted the physical RAM locations available, it maps memory pages into virtual memory addresses, as described in Figure 10-21. Windows NT establishes virtual memory by creating a **PAGEFILE.SYS** file on the disk. The VMM shifts data between RAM memory and the disk in 4 kB pages. This theoretically provides the operating system with a total memory space that equals the sum of the system's physical RAM and the capacity of the hard-disk drive.

PAGEFILE.SYS

To take advantage of high RAM capacity, Windows NT automatically tunes itself to take advantage of any available RAM. The VMM dynamically balances RAM between paged memory and the virtual memory disk cache.

Figure 10-21: Virtual Memory in Windows NT

Windows NT/2000/XP Registries

A portion of A+ Operating System Technologies objective 1.1 states that the test taker should be able to identify the major desktop components and interfaces, and their functions. Differentiate the characteristics of Windows 9x/Me, Windows NT 4.0 Workstation, Windows 2000 Professional, and Windows XP. It also states that the content may include major operating system components such as the Registry.

Like Windows 9x, Windows NT, Windows 2000, and Windows XP use a multipart database, called the *Registry*, to hold system and user configuration information. However, the Windows NT Registry versions are not compatible with the Windows 9x Registries. The Windows NT Registry is depicted in Figure 10-22. As with the Windows 9x Registry discussed in the previous chapter, the Windows NT Registry is organized into Headkeys, Subkeys, and Values. Comparing Figure 10-22 to Figure 9-36, you should notice that both Registries contain the same HKEYs, except that no HKEY_DYN_DATA key is present in the Windows NT Registry.

Figure 10-22: The Windows NT/2000 Registry

| subtrees |
| tree |
| values |
| hives |
| SAM hive |
| Security hive |
| Software hive |
| System hive |
| Default hive |

In the Windows NT world, the HKEYs are also referred to as **subtrees**, while the Registry itself is referred to as the **tree**. Under each subtree are one or more subkeys, which, in turn, will have one or more **values** assigned to them.

The contents of the Windows NT Registries are physically stored in five files referred to as **hives**. Hives represent the major divisions of all the Registry's keys, subkeys, subtrees, and values.

The hives of the Windows NT Registry are:

- The **SAM hive**
- The **Software hive**
- The **Default hive**
- The **Security hive**
- The **System hive**

These files are stored in the *\Winnt\System32\Config* directory along with a backup copy and log file for each hive.

Configuration information about every user who has logged into the system is maintained in a named subfolder of the *\Winnt\Profiles* directory. The actual user configuration file is named **Ntuser.dat** (i.e., *\Winnt\Profiles\Charles\Ntuser.dat*). In Windows 2000 and XP, the *Ntuser.dat* file is stored in *\Documents and Settings\username*. The major Windows NT hives and their files are described in Table 10-1.

Ntuser.dat

SUBTREE/KEY	FILE	LOG FILE
HKEY_LOCAL_MACHINE\SOFTWARE	SOFTWARE	SOFTWARE.LOG
HKEY_LOCAL_MACHINE\SECURITY	SECURITY	SECURITY.LOG
HKEY_LOCAL_MACHINE\SYSTEM	SYSTEM	SYSTEM.LOG
HKEY_LOCAL_MACHINE\SAM	SAM	SAM.LOG
HKEY_CURRENT_USER	NTUSER.DAT	NTUSER.DAT.LOG
HKEY_USERS\DEFAULT	DEFAULT	DEFAULT.LOG

Table 10-1: Major Windows NT Hives and Their Files

The HKEY_LOCAL_MACHINE subtree is the Registry's major branch. It contains five major keys. The SAM and SECURITY keys hold information such as user rights, user and group information for domain or workgroup organization, and password information. The HARDWARE key is a database built by device drivers and applications during bootup. The database is updated each time the system is rebooted. The SYSTEM key contains basic information about startup including the device drivers loaded and which services are in use. The **Last Known Good configuration** settings are stored here. Finally, the SOFTWARE key holds information about locally loaded software, including file associations, OLE information, and configuration data.

Last Known Good configuration

The second most important subtree is HKEY_USERS. It contains a subkey for each local user that accesses the system. These subkeys hold desktop settings and user profiles. When a server logs in across a domain, the subkey is stored on the domain controller.

The Windows NT/2000/XP Control Panel wizards are designed to correctly make changes to the Registry in a manner that the operating system can understand. Editing the Registry directly opens the possibility of changing an entry in a manner that Windows NT cannot accept, and thereby, of crashing the system. In either event, it is a good practice to back up the contents of the Registry before installing new hardware or software, or modifying the Registry directly. The **Rdisk.exe** utility, located in the *\Winnt\System32* folder, can be used to create a backup copy of the Registry in the *\Winnt\Repair* folder.

Rdisk.exe

Windows 2000 and XP rely on the same Registry structure used in previous Windows NT versions. For this reason, it is not compatible with Windows 9x Registries. As with Windows NT 4.0, the user settings portion of the Registry is stored in the NTUSER.DAT file located in the *\Documents_and_Settings\userxxx* folder. The System portions of the Registry are stored in the SOFTWARE, SYSTEM, SECURITY, and SAM hives. These files are stored in the *\Winnt\System32\Config* folder.

┌─ **TEST TIP** ─────────
Know how to make a backup copy
of the Registry in Windows NT 4.0.
└──────────────────────

TEST TIP

Be aware of the utility used to directly edit Registry entries of the various operating systems.

The contents of the Registry can be edited directly using the Windows NT/2000/XP RegEdit utility — **Regedt32.exe**. Although there is a RegEdit tool in Windows 2000, this tool was designed to work with Windows 9x clients. The editor used to manage the Windows 2000/XP Registry is Regedt32. However, in some instances, such as Registry searches, the RegEdit utility offers superior operation, even in Windows 2000 and XP. This file is located in the *\Winnt\System32* folder. As with the Windows 9x packages, most changes to the Registry should be performed through the Wizards in the Windows NT/2000/XP Control Panels.

CHALLENGE #2

You have been sent to a customer site to upgrade one of his old Windows NT 4.0 workstations to Windows 2000 Professional. Because the equipment is getting a little old, you want to protect the system in case you need to reinstall it. You are not too familiar with Windows NT, but you know that there is a utility for creating a backup of the system's Registry. What is this utility named and where can you access it?

Windows 2000/XP Device Manager

Windows NT Diagnostic

Both the Windows 2000 and Windows XP operating systems employ the Windows 9x−like Device Manager illustrated in Figure 10-23. The Device Manager replaces the **Windows NT Diagnostic** utility found in Windows NT 4.0. As with Windows 9x, the Windows 2000/XP Device Manager plays a major role in modifying hardware configurations and troubleshooting hardware problems encountered in Windows 2000 and Windows XP systems.

**Figure 10-23:
The Windows 2000
Device Manager**

You can access the Windows 2000 or Windows XP Device Manager utilities by clicking on their buttons located under the *Hardware* tab of the Control Panel's System *Properties* page. However, in Windows 2000 and Windows XP, the Device Manager is usually accessed through the *Computer Management Console*.

The operation of the Device Manager is very similar to that of its Windows 9x counterparts. It can be used to identify installed ports, update device drivers, and change I/O settings for hardware installed in the system. Even though entries in the Registry can be altered through the RegEdt32 and RegEdit utilities, the safest method of changing hardware settings is to change their values through the Device Manager. Steps for using the Device Manager are covered in some detail in Chapter 12—*Operating System Troubleshooting*.

Symmetric Multiprocessing

The Windows NT/2000/XP task scheduling capabilities enable it to control multiple microprocessors on a single system board. In the case of hardware with multiple microprocessors, the Windows NT Microkernel provides synchronization between the different processors. The **Symmetrical Multiprocessing (SMP)** function enables threads of any process to be applied to any available processor in the system. The SMP function also enables microprocessors within a system to share memory space with and assign threads to the next available microprocessor.

Using SMP, the processing load is distributed evenly among all the installed processors, regardless of what type of task is being performed. However, in an **Asymmetrical Multiprocessing (AMP)** scheme, each processor is capable of processing only a particular type of task. Therefore, the processing load is distributed based on the tasks that each processor can perform. This technique permits conditions to occur where one processor is very busy while others are idle.

Windows 2000 Professional and XP Professional both offer SMP support for dual (2x) processor operations. Similarly, Windows 2000 Server can support up to 4 (4x) simultaneous processors, while the Advanced and Datacenter versions of the Server package support 8x and 16x SMP respectively (or 32 processors using a special OEM version of Windows 2000 Datacenter). With versions of the Server running more than 4 processors, the hardware manufacturer must supply a special, proprietary version of the Windows 2000 HAL.DLL file for their machines.

If you upgrade a system to use additional processors, or you upgrade the existing processors on a multiprocessor board, you will need to update the HAL file. This operation is performed through the Device Manager utility as follows.

1. Access the Device Manager and expand the Computer node. The currently installed HAL will be displayed, as illustrated in Figure 10-24.

2. To update the installed HAL, right-click on the existing HAL and select the *Update Driver* option from the menu.

Figure 10-24: Updating the HAL in a Multiple-Processor System

WINDOWS NT FILE SYSTEM

All Windows NT operating system versions can employ two very different disk management structures. Like MS-DOS, Windows 3.x, and Windows 9x, it can employ the MS-DOS FAT system.

Windows NT File System (NTFS)

In addition, Windows NT versions offer their own proprietary **Windows NT File System (NTFS)**. The NTFS structure is designed to provide better data security and to operate more efficiently with larger hard drives than FAT systems do.

NTFS Advantages

Compact Disk File System (CDFS)

The Windows 2000 operating system supports several file management system formats including FAT, FAT16, FAT32, **CDFS** (the **Compact Disk File System** is used on CD-ROM disks), and NTFS4, along with the new improved NTFS format referred to as *NTFS5*. This version enables administrators to establish user hard disk quotas limiting the amount of hard drive space users can have access to. The new NTFS system also offers enhanced system security. NTFS5 provides an encrypted file system and secure network protocol and authentication standards.

Although Windows 2000 and XP both support several different file systems (i.e., FAT, FAT16, FAT32, CDFS, NTFS4, and NTFS5), in most situations, the NTFS system offers better performance and features than a FAT16 or FAT32 system. The exceptions to this occur when smaller drives are being used, other file systems are being used on the same drive, or the operating system crashes.

In most other situations, the NTFS system offers:

- More efficient drive management due to its smaller cluster size capabilities

- Support for very large drives made possible by its 64-bit clustering arrangement

- Increased folder and file security capabilities

- Disk quotas governing how much disk space individual users can take up

- Disk compression that enables the system to create more available disk space by compressing folders and files

- File encryption that encodes data that is stored on the hard drive, making it much more difficult for data to be stolen

- Recoverable file system capabilities

- Built-in RAID support

TEST TIP

Be aware of the different file system types supported by Windows 2000 and Windows XP.

TEST TIP

Memorize the advantages associated with using the NTFS file system.

The NTFS structure breaks away from the disk-size and cluster-size limitations inherent with the FAT file management structure by relying on a more flexible **Master File Table (MFT)** format for tracking clusters and files on the disk. This system replaces the fixed length FAT tables with a flexible table that can be linked to areas of the disk outside the table to store file and directory information.

Master File Table (MFT)

Windows NT 4 employs an NTFS version known as NTFS4, which provides access and use controls for the disk at the directory level. Users' rights to an individual files cannot be manipulated in Windows NT 4. However, in Windows 2000 and Windows XP, the administrator has been given new tools that can be used to limit what the user can do to any given file or directory. This is accomplished through two types of security permissions — **share permissions** and **NTFS permissions**. Both of these permission types are discussed in the Administrating Windows section of this chapter.

share permissions

NTFS permissions

Windows 2000 and Windows XP both feature an improved NTFS referred to as NTFSv5. This NTFS version enables administrators to establish user hard disk quotas limiting the amount of hard drive space users can have access to. The new NTFS system also offers enhanced system security. Windows 2000/XP NTFS version provides an encrypted file system and secure network protocol and authentication standards.

The NTFS structure provides recoverable file system capabilities including a hot-fix function and a full recovery system to quickly restore file integrity. The NTFS system maintains a copy of the critical file system information. If the file system fails, the NTFS system will automatically recover the system from the backup information as soon as the disk is accessed again. In addition, NTFS maintains a transaction log to ensure the integrity of the disk structure even if the system fails unexpectedly.

Security is a very big issue in large business networks. The Windows NT file system provides security for each file in the system, as well as complete file access auditing information to the system administrator. NTFS files and folders can have permissions assigned to them whether they are shared or not. Data security is also improved by Windows NT's ability to support mirrored drives.

You should recall from the RAID discussions in Chapter 4 — *Mass Storage Systems*, that mirroring is a technique of storing separate copies of data on two different drives. This protects the data from loss due to hard drive failures. This is a very important consideration when dealing with server applications. Additional fault tolerance capabilities such as disk mirroring, drive duplexing, striping, RAID, and support for UPS are provided with the Windows NT LAN Manager.

CHALLENGE #3

You have a physical disk in your computer that has two partitions — both of which are formatted with FAT 16. In one partition you are running Windows 95, and in the other you are running Windows NT 4.0. Because Windows 95 is becoming very old and you do not want to keep it up, you upgrade the Windows 95 partition to Windows 2000 and use the NTFS5 file system. When you start up the system using the Windows 2000 partition, there is no problem. However, when you boot into the Windows NT 4.0 partition, the new partition is not available. What should you do to correct this problem?

NTFS Organization

Master File Table
(MFT)

The NTFS structure uses 64-bit entries to keep track of storage on the disk (as opposed to the 16- and 32-bit entries used in FAT and FAT32 systems). The core component of the NTFS system is the **Master File Table (MFT)**. This table replaces the FAT in an MS-DOS—compatible system and contains information about each file stored on the disk. In order of occurrence, this information includes:

- Header information
- Standard information
- Filename
- Security information
- Data

When a volume is formatted in an NTFS system, several system files and the MFT are created on the disk. These files contain the information required to implement the file system structure on the disk. The system files produced during the NTFS formatting process include:

1. A pair of MFT files (the real one and a shorter backup version).
2. A Log file to maintain transaction steps for recovery purposes.
3. A Volume file that includes the volume name, NTFS version, and other key volume information.
4. An Attribute definition table file.
5. A Root Filename file that serves as the drive's root folder.
6. A Cluster Bitmap that represents the volume and shows which clusters are in use.
7. The partition boot sector file.
8. A Bad Cluster file containing the locations of all bad sectors identified on the disk.
9. A Quota Table for tracking allowable storage space on the disk for each user.
10. An Upper Case Table for converting lowercase characters to Unicode uppercase characters.

Unicode

Unicode is a 16-bit character code standard, similar to 8-bit ASCII, used to represent characters as integer numbers. The 16-bit format allows it to represent over 65,000 different characters. This is particularly useful for languages that have very large character sets.

Partition Boot Sector

BIOS Parameter Block

Code section

NTLDR

Figure 10-25 illustrates the organization of an NTFS disk volume. The first information in the NTFS volume is the 16-sector **Partition Boot Sector**. The sector starts at physical sector-0 and is made up of two segments—the **BIOS Parameter Block** and the **Code section**. The BIOS Parameter Block holds information about the structures of the volume and disk file system. The Code section describes the method to be used to locate and load the startup files for the specified operating system. This code loads the Windows NT bootstrap loader file **NTLDR** in Intel-based computers running Windows NT.

**Figure 10-25:
The Organization of an
NTFS Disk Volume**

Standard Information

Security Descriptor

The MFT contains information about each folder and file on the volume. The NTFS system relates to folders and files as a collection of attributes. All the folder's, or file's, elements (i.e., filename, security information, and data) are considered to be attributes. The system allocates space in the MFT for each file or folder based on the cluster size being used on the disk.

Figure 10-26 shows a typical MFT record. The first section of the record contains **Standard Information** about the file or folder, such as its date and time stamp and number of links. The second section contains the file's or folder's name. The next section contains the file or folder's **Security Descriptor** (which holds information about who can access the file, who owns it, and what they may do with it).

**Figure 10-26: Basic
NTFS Master File Table
Record**

resident attributes

data runs

Virtual Cluster
Numbers (VCNs)

non-resident
attributes

Attribute List

The next section of the MFT record is the Data (or Index) area. The information for smaller files and folders is stored in the MFT itself. The data area is 2 kB long on smaller drives, but can be bigger on larger drives. When the data fits within the MFT record, the various portions of the file are referred to as **resident attributes**.

For larger files and folders that cannot be stored in a single MFT, the NTFS may resort to two other methods of using the MFT. For medium-size folders and files, the system stores standard information about the folder or file, such as its name and time information, in the MFT and then establishes Index links to external cluster locations to store the rest of the data. The external clusters are referred to as **data runs** and are identified by 64-bit **Virtual Cluster Numbers (VCNs)** assigned to them. The attributes stored outside the MFT are referred to as **non-resident attributes**. An **Attribute List** attribute that contains the locations of all the file or folder's non-resident attributes is created in the data area of the MFT record. This arrangement is depicted in Figure 10-27.

Figure 10-27:
Extended MFT
Record Organization

For extremely large files that cannot be identified by a single MFT record, multiple MFT records are employed. The first record contains a pointer to the additional MFT records. The original MFT record contains the file's or folder's standard information, followed by index links to other MFT records that, in turn, have index links to the actual data runs. In these cases, the data is stored outside the table and can theoretically range up to 16 **EB (exabytes** − 2^{60}).

All entries in the MFT are stored in alphabetical order by filename. Like FAT systems, NTFS systems use the cluster as the basic unit of disk storage. In Windows 4.0, NTFS clusters can range between 512 bytes and 64 kB, depending on the size of the drive and how the disk was prepared. Clusters can range up to 64 kB when established using the FORMAT command from the command prompt. However, cluster sizes are limited to a maximum of 4 kB when using the **Windows NT Disk Manager** to handle the disk organization. Clusters are numbered sequentially on the disk from start to end. These numbers are referred to as **Logical Cluster Numbers (LCNs)**. The default cluster size is determined by the volume size and can be specified in the Disk Administrator utility. Table 10-2 lists the default cluster sizes for NTFS systems in Windows 4.0 environments.

EB (exabytes)

Windows NT Disk Manager

Logical Cluster Numbers (LCNs)

Table 10-2:
NTFS Cluster Sizes

The smaller cluster size of the NTFS format makes it more efficient than FAT formats for storing smaller files. It also supports larger drives (over 1 GB) much more efficiently than FAT16 or FAT32 structures. The NTFS system is more complex than the FAT systems and, therefore, is not as efficient for smaller drives.

PARTITION SIZE	SECTORS/CLUSTER	CLUSTER SIZE
<512 MB	1	512 bytes
512 MB-1 GB	2	1 kB
GB-2 GB	4	2 kB
2 GB-4 GB	8	4 kB
4 GB-8 GB	16	8 kB
8 GB-16 GB	32	16 kB
16 GB-32 GB	64	32 kB
>32 GB	128	64 kB

Traditional Windows NT Disk Partitions

Windows NT can be used to partition a hard drive so that different operating systems can be used in each partition (and in extended partitions). However, the NTFS format lacks compatibility with other operating systems. Therefore, it will not permit other operating systems to access files on the NTFS drive. This can be a problem on partitioned drives that support multiple operating systems.

Windows NT employs very difficult terminology when referring to types of disk partitions. The disk partition where the BIOS looks for the master boot record is called the **system partition or system volume,** whereas the partition containing the Windows NT operating system is called the **boot partition** or **boot volume.**

Either, or both, types of partitions/volumes can be formatted as FAT or NTFS file systems. In actual practice, both partition types can be assigned to a single partition, or they can exist as separate partitions. Figure 10-28 depicts the Windows NT partitioning scheme applied to a two-partition disk.

system partition
system volume
boot partition
boot volume

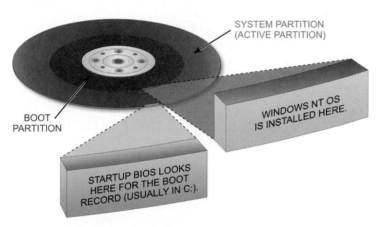

SYSTEM PARTITION
(ACTIVE PARTITION)

BOOT PARTITION

WINDOWS NT OS IS INSTALLED HERE.

STARTUP BIOS LOOKS HERE FOR THE BOOT RECORD (USUALLY IN C:).

Figure 10-28: Windows NT Partitions

Before you can install Windows NT, 2000, or XP, the hard disk must contain as least one partition to hold the system and boot files. Several disk partition options are available when performing Setup from the Windows XP distribution CD. Partitioning can also be performed with a partitioning utility prior to the installation of Windows 2000 or XP Professional. Some partitioning utilities, such as the FDISK utility, are limited in the size and number of partitions that they can create. Third-party disk partitioning utilities tend to be much more flexible.

When you are partitioning the disk during the Setup process, you will be given the following options:

- *Create a new partition* if the hard disk does not have any partitions, or if it has existing partitions but also has free (unpartitioned) space.

- *Delete partitions* if the hard disk has existing partitions that you do not want to preserve. Then you can create a new partition to install the operating system in. However, when you delete a partition, all the existing information in it is lost.

- *Bypass the partitioning process* if the hard disk has existing partitions that you want to install Windows XP into. Any other existing partitions will remain intact.

> **NOTE**
>
> During the Setup procedure, you should only create the partition that will hold the operating system. In Windows 2000 or XP it is more efficient to create any additional partitions using the Disk Management utility after the installation has been completed.

Managing Windows 2000/XP NTFS

As mentioned earlier, Windows 2000 and Windows XP are based on NTFS Version 5.0. This version of NTFS enables the user to establish disk space quotas for users and locate files by owner. The new NTFS system provides administrator with tools to manage user access and usage rights to individual files and directories. As mentioned earlier, file-level control was not possible in earlier NT versions. A special administrative list called the **Access Control List (ACL)** is used to view which files a user can have access to. This feature was new to the NT environment, but had been available in the Novell NetWare products for some time.

Access Control List (ACL)

Disk Management

Dynamic Volume Management

basic disks

dynamic disks

dynamic volumes

The Windows 2000/XP **Disk Management** utility contains a **Dynamic Volume Management** feature that permits the capacity of an existing volume to be extended without rebooting or reformatting. The Disk Management utility also features a new user interface that enables administrators to configure drives and volumes located in remote computers. Disk Management is a graphical tool that handles two distinctive types of disks — **basic disks** and **dynamic disks**. This tool enables the administrator to handle **dynamic volumes**, created on dynamic disks.

A basic disk is a physical disk that contains partitions, drives, or volumes created with Windows NT 4.0 or earlier operating systems.

Dynamic disks are physical disks created through the Windows 2000 Disk Management utility. These disks can only hold dynamic volumes (not partitions, volumes, or logical drives). However, with dynamic disks the four-volume limit inherent with other Microsoft operating system versions has been removed. There are five different types of dynamic volumes:

- Simple
- Spanned
- Mirrored
- Striped
- RAID 5

Only systems running Windows 2000 or Windows XP can access dynamic volumes. Therefore, basic volumes should be established on drives that Windows 9x or Windows NT 4.0 systems need to access. If a dynamic volume is present on a drive, the file management systems associated with the other operating systems will not be able to see or access the dynamic drives or volumes.

To install Windows 2000 or Windows XP on a dynamic volume, it must be either a simple or a mirrored volume and it must be a volume that has been upgraded from a basic volume. Installing Windows 2000 on the volume requires that it have a partition table, which dynamic volumes do not have unless they have been upgraded from a basic volume. Basic volumes are upgraded by upgrading a basic disk to a dynamic disk. Under Windows 2000, basic volumes are converted to dynamic volumes using the Disk Management tool (follow the path *Start/Run*, enter *DISKMGMT.MSC* into the text box, and then click on the *OK* button). Windows 2000 and XP will not support dynamic volumes on portable computers. Likewise, mirrored and RAID-5 volumes are only supported on Windows 2000 Servers.

┌─ **TEST TIP** ─────────────────┐
│ Know what the requirements are for creating │
│ a dynamic volume in Windows 2000. │
└─────────────────────────────┘

Dynamic volumes are managed through the Windows 2000/XP **Disk Management snap-in** tool, depicted in Figure 10-29, located under the Computer Management console. To access the Disk Manager, follow the *Start/Settings/Control Panel/Administrative Tools* path. Double-click the *Computer Management* icon and click on the *Disk Management* entry. Because working with dynamic volumes is a major administrative task, you must be logged in as an administrator or as a member of Windows 2000's **Administrators group** in order to carry out the procedure. Also, system and boot volumes cannot be formatted as dynamic volumes.

Figure 10-29: Windows 2000 Disk Management Snap-in

Formatting Volumes in Windows 2000/XP

Formatting a partition or volume prepares the logical structure to accept data by creating the file system in it. If a partition or volume has not been formatted, it does not contain a file system and cannot be accessed through the operating system or any applications. In the Windows 2000/XP environment, many actions can be performed to initiate formatting. These include:

- Use the Volume Creation wizard in the Disk Management utility when the volume is created

- In the Disk Management utility, right-click on a volume that has already been created and select the *Format* option from the action menu

- In Windows Explorer, right-click on the desired drive letter and select the *Format* option from the action menu

- At a command prompt, type the command *Format* along with the appropriate switches

┌───┐
│ **WARNING** │
│ │
│ If you format an existing partition or volume, any data residing │
│ in the structure will be lost. The Windows XP Professional oper- │
│ ating system protects its system files by preventing the system │
│ and boot partitions from being formatted. │
└───┘

Typical options that will be presented during the formatting process include:

- *Volume label* – an 11-character name for the volume that will be displayed in Disk Management, Windows Explorer, and other utilities to identify it. You should make the label descriptive of the type of information that is stored on the volume.

- *File system* – This option permits you to choose FAT (for FAT16), FAT32, or NTFS for the file system type that will be installed in the partition or volume.

- *Allocation unit size* – This setting enables you to manipulate the default cluster size for any of the file systems. This setting should be left at the default value unless you are highly skilled at manipulating disk parameters.

- *Perform a quick format* – This option is used when you want to remove the files and folders on the volume without checking for bad sectors. This should only be selected if you have previously performed a full format and verified that the disk does not have damaged areas.

- *Enable file and folder compression* – The compression option is only available for partitions or volumes that are formatted with NTFS. It specifies that all files placed on the disk will be compressed by default. The compression option is always available on NTFS volumes and can be enabled at any time.

High Performance File System

IBM followed their successful PC-AT system with a line of personal computers called PS/2 (Personal System 2). The line was advertised around a proprietary 32-bit bus, called Micro Channel Architecture (MCA), and a new GUI-based operating system called OS/2 (Operating System 2). The PS/2 line has long since faded into the background of PC hardware, but OS/2 software continues to be used in some circles.

High Performance File System (HPFS)

At the heart of the OS/2 operating system is the **High Performance File System** (**HPFS**). It provided a very robust file system for its time. The HPFS structure retained the FAT directory structure, but featured long filenames (up to 254 characters) and volume sizes up to 8 GB. Under HPFS, the unit of management was changed to physical sectors rather than clusters.

HPFS's other attributes include good performance when directories contain several files, built-in fault tolerance, fragmentation resistance, and good effectiveness when working with large partitions.

HPFS employs banding to organize the disk efficiently. Using this arrangement, HPFS segments the drive into 8 MB bands with 2 kB allocation bitmaps between each band. The bitmaps are used to record which sectors have been used within a band. Whenever possible, the operating system tries to retain files within a single band. In doing so, the drive's R/W head does not have to return to track-0 for reference. The HPFS file system is only accessible under the OS/2 and Windows NT 3.51 operating systems.

> **— NOTE —**
>
> **High Performance File System** — Although HPFS is listed in the objectives for this section, it does not seem to actually appear as a question topic in the exam. However, it has been used as an incorrect answer in many of the questions.

INSTALLING WINDOWS NT/2000/XP

A portion of A+ Operating System Technologies objective 2.1 states that the test taker should be able to identify the procedures for installing Windows 9x/Me, Windows NT 4.0 Workstation, Windows 2000 Professional, and Windows XP, and bringing the operating system to a basic operational level.

Likewise, a portion of Objective 2.1 states that the test taker should be able to identify steps to perform an operating system upgrade from Windows 9.x/ME, Windows NT 4.0 Workstation, Windows 2000 Professional, and Windows XP. Given an upgrade scenario, choose the appropriate next steps.

The installation process for Windows NT versions, including Windows NT/2000/XP, can be a little more difficult than that of the Windows 9x versions. In particular, the lack of extensive hardware and software compatibilities requires some advanced planning before installing, or upgrading to Windows NT/2000/XP.

The first issue to deal with is hardware compatibility. Windows NT/2000/XP makes no claim to maintaining compatibility with a wide variety of hardware devices. Check to ensure that the hardware being used is supported by the intended version of Windows 2000 or Windows XP. If the current hardware does not appear in the Microsoft **Hardware Compatibility List (HCL)** of the new version, you are on your own for technical support.

> **Hardware Compatibility List (HCL)**

The second factor to sort out is which file management system should be used. Windows NT/2000/XP can be configured to use either a typical FAT-based file system, or its own proprietary NTFS file system. Review the "NTFS Advantages" section from earlier in this chapter to determine which file system is better suited to the particular situation.

Installation Methods

Windows NT/2000/XP operating systems can be installed using two different methods. These are:

- from the Windows distribution CD

- across a network connection using a copy of the installation files obtained from a network server.

In both cases, the installer must have access to the operating system's installation files. This primarily means the equivalent of the \I386 folder on the distribution CD. If the local unit has a bootable CD-ROM drive, you can simply insert the CD in the drive and boot directly to it. When the system starts, the CD will load and the installation can take place locally straight from the CD. If the system does not support a bootable CD, then you will need to start the system using a boot floppy, load the CD-ROM drivers, and run the setup utility from the CD. This will require running the *Winnt.exe* or *Winnt32.exe* files from the \I386 folder on the Windows CD.

In a network environment, it is possible to perform installs from a network server across the network connection. This is particularly efficient when you need to perform multiple installations of the operating system around the network (such as when a new operating system version is rolled out across a business or office environment). In these settings, the operating system files are placed on a **distribution server** and executed from the **destination** (receiving) **computer**.

distribution server

destination

computer

To do this you simply boot the destination computer to a start disk that has the *MS-DOS Client for Microsoft Networks* utility on it, connect to the shared folder on the server that holds the setup files, and execute the Winnt.exe or Winnt32.exe file, as illustrated in Figure 10-30. Of course, the disk drive of the destination drive must be partitioned and formatted before engaging the installation routine.

**Figure 10-30:
Network-Based
Windows Installation**

In a large corporate network it could take weeks to perform a network operating system upgrade for all the systems on the network. For these environments, all of the network operating system manufacturers have provided options for automating the installation process using the network and one or more *distribution servers*. Two automation methods are offered for Windows 2000 and XP networks:

- Unattended automated installations using answer files

- Disk cloning using disk images

answer files

Uniqueness Database File (UDF)

In an unattended installation using **answer files**, administrators run scripted answer files that have been created to provide automatic answers to all the questions normally asked by the Setup/Install routine. In this manner, an administrator can run multiple installations across the network at one time. If circumstances require different answers for different computers in the network, a **Uniqueness Database File (UDF)** must also be created to supply the unique settings required for those computers.

Disk cloning

reference computer

Sysprep

disk image

The second high-volume automated installation method employs clone copies of a given installation and simply re-creates that exact installation on multiple computers across the network. **Disk cloning** requires that a disk image be created of a **reference computer**. This computer must be an exact copy of the hardware and software that you want to clone. The **Sysprep** tool is used to prepare the reference computer for cloning. Third-party cloning software is required to actually create and distribute the **disk image** file that is used to clone the installation process on the remote computers.

The Windows 2000/XP **Setup Manager Wizards** can be used to create answer files for un-attended Windows installations and for Sysprep disk image cloning. In addition, this wizard can be used to create answer files for use with Windows **Remote Installation Services (RIS)** server. This service is available to conduct RIS image-based installations across the network. It can only be used to deploy Windows 2000 Professional and Windows XP Professional operating systems. This system involves establishing an RIS server in the network and then booting up systems as RIS clients that can download the image from the server. These images can be **CD-based** images or **Remote Installation Preparation (RIPrep)** images created with the Windows RIPrep wizard.

Setup Manager Wizards

Remote Installation Services (RIS)

CD-based

Remote Installation Preparation (RIPrep)

These automated installation techniques are usually the responsibility of the network administrator and are well beyond the scope of the A+ certification. Therefore, the following sections deal primarily with attended, local installations of the Windows 2000 and XP operating systems.

> **— NOTE —**
>
> Be aware that RIS can only be used to deploy Windows XP Professional and Windows 2000 Professional. It cannot be used to deploy Windows 2000 Server or any down-level operating systems.

Patches and Service Packs

In the Windows environment, there are actually three parts of the operating system that you must address when installing a new version or upgrade. These are:

- the operating system release version
- operating system patches and service packs
- third-party device drivers

The **operating system release** is the version of the installation media produced and distributed as a complete unit. However, due to the nature of product development and the pressures on software producers to bring new products to the market, new releases never seem to be complete or perfect. Therefore, manufacturers continue to develop and upgrade their operating systems after they have been released.

operating system release

Rather than provide customers with a new version of the operating system when new features are added or major problems are corrected, software manufacturers provide **OEM patches** for their products. Microsoft typically releases patches in the form of updates, or in collections that include additional functionality or new device drivers, that they refer to as **service packs**. Patches and service packs are not typically required to run an operating system release. The fact that an operating system exists as a release means that it is a complete operating system.

OEM patches

service packs

When you install a fresh copy of an operating system that has been on the market for some time, or when you upgrade an existing operating system to a new version, there is a definite order for installing the new components:

1. Install the Operating System release.

2. Install the OEM patches or the latest service pack.

3. Install the best device driver choices.

When the new version or the upgrade is installed, it should automatically install its own drivers for the devices it detects. In most cases, these drivers are the best choice for the installed devices because they have been tested to work with the operating system and should provide the least amount of problems. OEM drivers may not be written as well and tested as thoroughly as those supplied with the operating system.

If the device is not listed in the operating system's HCL, the device manufacturer's driver offers the only choice for operating the device. The other condition that calls for using the equipment manufacturer's driver occurs when the device does not operate correctly with the Windows-supplied drivers. New drivers delivered in service packs may offer a better choice than using the original operating system drivers. However, if they do not produce the operation desired, then the OEM drivers must be reinstalled.

Installing Windows 2000 Professional

The minimum hardware requirements for installing Windows 2000 Professional on a PC-compatible system are:

- Microprocessor — 133 MHz Pentium (P5 equivalent or better)
- RAM — 64 MB (4 GB maximum)
- HDD Space — 650 MB or more free on a 2 GB drive
- VGA monitor

TEST TIP

Memorize the minimum system requirements for installing Windows 2000 Professional.

For installation from a CD-ROM, a 12x drive is required. If the CD-ROM drive is not bootable, a high-density 3.5-inch floppy drive is also required.

checkupgradeonly

upgrade.txt

Before installing Windows 2000 Professional from the CD, it is recommended that the Windows 2000 version of the **checkupgradeonly** be run. This file is located on the installation CD under \i386\winnt32 and checks the system for possible hardware compatibility problems. The program generates a text file report named **upgrade.txt** that can be found under the \Windows folder. It contains Windows 2000 compatibility information about the system along with a list of potential complications.

If your system has hardware devices that are not on the Windows 2000 Hardware Compatibility List, you should contact the manufacturer of the device to determine whether they have new, updated Windows 2000 drivers for their device. Many peripheral makers have become very proactive in supplying updated drivers for their devices. Often, they post their latest drivers and product compatibility information on their Internet web sites, where customers can download them. This is a good place to begin looking for needed drivers. The second alternative is to try the device with Windows NT or Windows 9x drivers to see if it will work. The final option is to get a device that is listed on the Windows 2000 HCL.

TEST TIP

Know what to do if you encounter hardware devices not listed on the Windows 2000 HCL.

If Windows Professional is to be installed across a network, a Windows 2000 Professional—compatible NIC is required.

HCL.TXT

A list of Microsoft-verified network cards can be obtained from the **HCL.TXT** file on the Windows 2000 Professional distribution CD. The system must also have access to the network share that contains the Setup files.

If several machines in an organization are being upgraded to the same status, the Windows 2000 Scripting capabilities can be put to good use. This feature can be used to create installation routines that require no user interaction. Microsoft has also increased support for third-party disk copying and imaging utilities that perform multiple installs within a networked system.

To conduct a New Windows 2000 Professional installation, you will need the Windows 2000 Professional distribution CD. If the installation is being performed on a system that cannot boot to the CD-ROM drive, you will also need the Windows 2000 Professional Setup disks.

Hands-on Activity

1. To initiate the installation from a floppy disk, turn the system off, place the Windows 2000 Professional Startup Disk #1 in the floppy drive, and turn the system on. When the Setup program starts, it brings the Windows 2000 Setup Wizard, shown in Figure 10-31, to the screen. The Setup Wizard collects information, including Names, Passwords, and Regional Settings, and writes the information to files on the hard drive. Afterwards, the Wizard checks the system's hardware and properly configures the installation.

2. The first step in the Setup process is to choose whether the installation is a *Clean Install* or an *Upgrade*. If a new installation is being performed, the Setup program will install the Windows 2000/XP files in the *\WINNT* folder.

3. Follow the instructions the Wizard places on the screen, entering any information required. The choice made concerning the type of setup being performed and user-provided input determines the exact path the installation process will take.

Figure 10-31: Windows 2000 Setup Wizard

Hands-on Activity

1. For a CD-ROM install, boot the system to the existing operating system and then insert the Windows 2000 Professional distribution CD into the CD-ROM drive.

2. If the system detects the CD in the drive, simply click the *Install Windows 2000 (XP)* option. If not, start Setup through the *Run* command. In Windows 9x and NT 4.0, click on *Start* and then *Run*. In Windows 3.x and NT 3.51 click on *File* and then *Run*.

3. At the prompt, enter the location on the Windows 2000/XP start file (*Winnt.exe* or *Winnt32.exe*) on the distribution CD (i.e., *d:\i386\Winnt32.exe*). In the case of Windows 3.x, the *Winnt.exe* option should be used.

4. Choose whether the installation is a *New Install* or an *Upgrade*.

5. Follow the instructions the Wizard places on the screen, entering any information required.

To install Windows 2000 or Windows XP Professional across a network, it will be necessary to establish a shared connection between the local unit and the system containing the Windows 2000/XP Professional Setup files.

Hands-on Activity

1. Boot the local unit to the existing operating system and establish a connection with the remote unit.

2. At the command prompt, enter the path to the remote *Winnt32.exe* file (use the *Winnt.exe* file if an older 16-bit operating system is being used on the local unit).

3. Choose whether the installation is a *Clean Install* or an *Upgrade*.

4. Follow the instructions the Setup Wizard places on the screen, entering any information required.

The Windows 2000 Setup Wizard collects information about the system and the user during the installation process. The most important information that must be provided includes the type of file management system that will be used (FAT or NTFS), Computer Name and Administrator Password, Network Settings, and Workgroup or Domain operations.

Upgrading to Windows 2000

Systems can be upgraded to Windows 2000 Professional from Windows 9x versions, as well as Windows NT 3.5 and 4.0 workstations versions. This includes older NTFS, FAT16, and FAT32 installations. When you install Windows 2000, it can recognize all three of these file system types.

If the computer is running a different Microsoft operating system, that OS version must be upgraded to one of these versions before it can be upgraded to Windows 2000. Otherwise, a clean install must be performed from a full version of the operating system. Table 10-3 lists the acceptable Windows 2000 upgrade routes.

CURRENT OPERATING SYSTEM	UPGRADE PATH
Windows 95 and Windows 98	Windows 2000 Professional only
Windows NT 3.51 and 4.0 Workstation	Windows 2000 Professional only
Windows NT 3.51 and 4.0 Server	Any Windows 2000 product
Windows NT 3.1 and 3.5	Must be upgraded to NT 3.51 or 4.0 first, and then to Windows 2000
Windows 3.x	Must be upgraded to Windows 95 or 98 first, then to Windows 2000 Professional

Table 10-3: Windows 2000 Upgrade Routes

The easiest upgrade path to Windows 2000 is from the Windows NT 4.0 operating system. Upgrading from Windows 9x is potentially more difficult.

┌─ **TEST TIP** ─────────────
Memorize the acceptable paths for upgrading from older Windows operating systems to Windows 2000.
└───────────────────────────

The process of upgrading to Windows 2000 can be performed in incremental steps. This enables network administrators to bring network machines up to Windows 2000 status over time. During the system upgrade process the Windows NT 4.0 units can interact with the Windows 2000 units because they see them as NT 4.0 systems. Upgrading Windows 2000 from a Windows NT 4.0 or Windows 9x base is quicker than performing a new installation. When a system is upgraded to Windows 2000 Professional, the Setup utility replaces any existing Windows files with Windows 2000 Professional versions. However, existing settings and applications will be preserved in the new environment.

> As with previous Windows NT products, Windows 2000 does not attempt to remain compatible with older hardware and software. Therefore, some applications may not be compatible with Windows 2000 and may run poorly, or may fail completely after an upgrade.

CHALLENGE #5

One of your customers has an office network made up of a Windows 4.0 Server with three Windows NT 3.5 workstations, two Windows 98 workstations, one Windows NT 4.0 workstation, and one Windows 3.51 workstation. He wants to test out Windows 2000 Professional on one of his computers to see how it works and to begin getting his users accustomed to Windows 2000. He wants to do this with as little hassle as possible. What would you suggest he do to accomplish these goals?

Upgrading to Windows 2000 is suggested for those using an existing Windows operating system that is compatible with Windows 2000 and who wish to maintain their existing data and preference settings.

Hands-on Activity

1. To upgrade a system to Windows 2000 from a previous operating system using a CD-ROM install, boot the system to the existing operating system and then insert the Windows 2000 Professional distribution CD into the CD-ROM drive.

2. If the system detects the CD in the drive, simply click on the *Install Windows 2000* option. If not, start Setup through the *Run* command. In Windows 9x and NT 4.0, click on *Start* and then *Run*. In Windows 3.x and NT 3.51, click on *File* and then *Run*.

3. At the prompt, enter the location on the Windows 2000 start file (*Winnt.exe* or *Winnt32.exe*) on the distribution CD (i.e., *d:\i386\Winnt32.exe*). In the case of Windows 3.x, the *Winnt.exe* option should be used.

4. Choose whether the installation is a *Clean Install* or an *Upgrade*.

5. Follow the instructions the Wizard places on the screen, entering any information required.

┌─ **TEST TIP** ─┐

Be aware that in a current Windows 2000 system, you should be able to reinstall Windows 2000 by simply starting the system with the Windows 2000 distribution CD in the drive so that it can be auto-detected.

To upgrade Windows 2000 Professional from a previous operating system across a network, it will be necessary to establish a shared connection between the local unit and the system containing the Windows 2000 Professional Setup files.

Hands-on Activity

1. Boot the local unit to the existing operating system and establish a connection with the remote unit.

2. At the command prompt, enter the path to the remote *Winnt32.exe* file (use the *Winnt.exe* file if an older 16-bit operating system is being used on the local unit). The Winnt command is used with 16-bit operating systems such as DOS or Windows 3.x. The Winnt32 version is used with 32-bit operating systems including Windows 95, 98, NT 3.5, and NT 4.0.

3. Choose the *Upgrade your computer to Windows 2000* option.

4. Follow the instructions the Setup Wizard places on the screen, entering any information required.

During the installation process, the Windows 2000 Setup Wizard collects information about users and the system. Most of this information is collected automatically. However, some information must be provided by the user or technician. The most important information required during the setup process is the file management system to be used, the computer name and administrator password, network settings, and Workgroup/Domain selection.

CHALLENGE #6

You place the Windows 2000 Professional distribution CD into the drive of a Windows 98 machine, and nothing happens. You want to upgrade the system to Windows 2000, but there is no auto-detection or self-starting feature for the CD-ROM. What do you need to do to install the Windows 2000 OS?

Installing Windows XP Professional

The installation process for Windows XP is considerably different from previous Windows installation processes in that Windows XP requires you to activate your copy of the operating system within 30 days after installing it. This process is electronic and is meant to ensure that the copy of XP being used is legitimate and that it is being used on only one computer. If you attempt to install it on a second computer and activate it, an error message will be generated notifying you that the registration is already active.

For technicians this does not become a problem until an extensive system upgrade is performed or a hard drive must be replaced. When these events occur it will be necessary to deal with Microsoft's licensing department to reactivate the license. The licensing agreement that comes with Windows XP enables a single copy to be legally installed on one desktop and one portable computer.

The minimum hardware requirements for installing Windows XP Professional on a PC-compatible system are:

- *Microprocessor* – Pentium II 233 MHz or higher or compatible processor required/ Pentium II 300 MHz or compatible processor recommended. Dual-processor configurations are also supported with Windows XP.

- *RAM* – 64 MB required/128 MB recommended. The more memory installed, the better. Maximum supported RAM is 4 GB.

- *HDD Space* – 2 GB with 650 MB of free space required/2 GB of free hard disk space recommended. A 1.5 GB partition size is required, with 2 GB recommended. Additional disk space is required for installing over a network. The maximum hard disk space supported for a partition is 2 TB.

- *Display device* – A VGA-compatible or higher display adapter with a monitor capable of 800 x 600 resolution required/SVGA-compatible display adapter recommended.

- *Input devices* – Keyboard and mouse (or other pointing device) required.

- *CD-ROM* – 12x or faster CD-ROM drive recommended (this item is required to perform Setup from CD-ROM). If the CD-ROM drive is not bootable, a high-density 3.5-inch floppy drive is also required.

Other installation hardware requirements associated with network installations include a high-density 3.5" drive for performing Setup across the network using a network client or boot disk along with an appropriate network adapter card.

As with the Windows NT and Windows 2000 systems, all hardware devices included in a Windows XP Professional system must be listed on Microsoft's **Windows XP HCL**. These devices have been tested and are supported by Microsoft. As with Windows NT and 2000, copies of the Windows XP HCL can be obtained at two locations:

- The Windows XP Professional distribution CD contains a file is named Hcl.txt in the *\Support* folder.

- On the Microsoft web site at *http://www.microsoft.com/hcl*. The HCL version on the Microsoft web site typically represents the most up-to-date listing.

Before installing Windows XP Professional from the CD, you should run the Windows XP version of the *checkupgradeonly* utility. This file is located on the installation CD under *\i386\winnt32* and checks the system for possible hardware compatibility conflicts. It generates a text file report named upgrade.txt that contains Windows XP compatibility information, along with potential complications for the system. This report can be accessed in the *\Windows* folder.

If the system has a hardware device that is not on the Windows XP HCL, then Microsoft has not tested or approved it and, therefore, will not support it. You should contact the device manufacturer to determine whether they have new or updated Windows XP drivers for their device. Most peripheral makers are aware of the importance of supplying updated drivers for their devices. So, they typically post the latest drivers and product compatibility information on their corporate Internet sites.

Upgrading to Windows XP

As time passes, many corporate workstations that are already running different versions of Windows will be upgraded to Windows XP Professional. These workstations can be migrated to the new operating system by either upgrading them, or by performing a clean install of Windows XP Professional. Upgrading is preferable in many situations, because it provides for the preservation of existing users and groups, user settings, data, and installed applications.

If a computer is currently running Windows 98, Windows Me, Windows NT Workstation 4.0 (with Service Pack 6 installed), or Windows 2000 Professional, it can be upgraded directly to Windows XP. This includes older FAT16, FAT32, and NTFS systems. As was the case with Windows 2000, the Windows XP operating system can recognize all three file-system types when it is installed. However, systems running Windows 95 or Windows NT Workstation 3.51 operating systems cannot upgrade directly to XP. Instead, they must have intermediate upgrades to bring them up to a Windows version that does support direct upgrading to Windows XP.

> **NOTE**
>
> Although older Windows operating systems can be upgraded using interim upgrades, the computer hardware that they are running on probably does not satisfy the minimum hardware requirements for Windows XP Professional.

As with new Windows operating system installations, it is a good idea to generate a system compatibility report prior to running the upgrade process. This will permit potential problems to be detected and analyzed and allow solutions to be implemented. The report can be generated through the WINNT32 *checkupgradeonly* command, or by selecting the *Check system compatibility* option on the Setup menu. Either action will launch Setup for the purpose of generating the compatibility report only—the computer will not be modified in any way.

Some portions of upgrading from Windows 98 to Windows XP Professional can be difficult. While most operating system and user configuration settings upgrade easily, other items such as applications and device drivers may create problems. Most of these issues will show up when the Compatibility Report is generated. If any hardware or software incompatibilities are detected, the proper updates should be obtained and applied before proceeding with the upgrade. Any incompatible software detected should be uninstalled from the system until new compatible replacements can be loaded. Because Windows XP is relatively new, you should take the time to check the system BIOS version to verify that it is the latest revision available.

> **NOTE**
>
> As with Windows 2000 upgrades, remember to verify that BIOS-based virus protection is disabled before performing the Windows XP upgrade. This BIOS feature causes the Setup process to fail because it will interpret Setup's attempts to modify the boot sector as a virus activity.

You should always back up any important files and data before performing an upgrade to avoid losing them. You should also scan for viruses and remove them from the system before conducting an upgrade. Finally, make sure to uncompress any drive compressed with anything other than NTFS compression before performing the upgrade. The only compression type supported by Windows XP Professional is NTFS compression. Third-party compression formats are not supported.

Performing Local Upgrades

To initiate a local upgrade from a bootable CD-ROM drive, simply insert the Windows XP Professional distribution CD into the drive and select the *Install Windows XP* option from the Setup menu, as illustrated in Figure 10-32. If the menu is not displayed automatically, run the Setup utility from Windows XP CD. If you are upgrading from a distribution server, run the WINNT32 utility command.

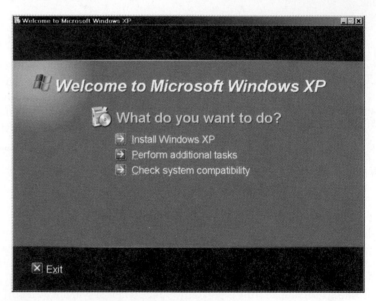

Figure 10-32: Windows XP Setup Menu

Figure 10-33: Windows Setup

The opening Windows Setup page, depicted in Figure 10-33, asks for verification of whether an upgrade of the existing operating system is being conducted, or a new version of Windows XP is being installed. If the *New Installation* option is specified, the existing operating system settings will be overwritten along with any existing applications. These applications must be reinstalled to retain their use.

There are two types of upgrades — express and custom. An express upgrade will automatically upgrade the existing Windows installation and maintain all current settings. A custom upgrade enables you to change the following:

- Installation partition
- Installation folder
- Language options
- File system type (NTFS conversions allowed)

Upgrading to Windows XP requires a minimum of administrative intervention, and can be fully automated using answer files as previously discussed in this chapter. The information required to perform a standard upgrade is very similar to that involved with the standard Setup process.

Windows XP has special tools called the **User State Migration Tools (USMT)** that administrators can use to transfer user configuration settings and files from systems running Windows 9x and NT systems to a clean Windows XP installation. This enables user information to be preserved without going through the upgrade process. In a USMT operation, user state information is backed up from the old operating system to a network server and then restored to the new Windows XP system. The following list describes the default settings transferred from the older system to the new Windows XP system by the USMT utility:

> **User State Migration Tools (USMT)**

- The contents of all the *My Documents*, *My Pictures*, *Desktop*, and *Favorites* folders

- Most user interface settings, including display properties, fonts, mapped network drives, network printers, browser settings, folder options, Taskbar options, and files and settings associated with the Microsoft Office applications

- Files with industry standard extensions such as — .doc, .ppt, .txt, and .xls

Dual Booting with NT Operating Systems

Windows NT can be set up to dual boot with MS-DOS or Windows 9x operating systems. This provides the option for the system to boot up into a Windows NT environment, or into an MS-DOS/Windows 9x environment. In such cases, a startup menu appears on the display that asks which operating system should be used. Establishing either of these dual-boot conditions with Windows NT requires that the MS-DOS or Windows 9x operating systems be installed first.

While it is possible for Windows 2000 or Windows XP to share a partition with Windows 9x or Windows NT 4.0, this produces some potentially undesirable situations. You should install Windows 2000 or XP and the other operating system in separate partitions.

The major drawback of dual booting with Windows NT is that neither operating system is capable of using applications installed in the other operating system's partition. Therefore, software to be used by both operating systems must be installed in the system twice — once for each operating system's partition. Even when you permit Windows 2000 or Windows XP to share the same partition with a Windows 9x or Windows NT OS, you will need to reinstall the system's applications so that their installation programs can modify the Windows 2000/XP Registry.

Care must also be taken when formatting a logical drive in a Windows NT dual-boot system. The native file management formats of Windows NT and the other operating systems are not compatible. If the disk is formatted with NTFS, the MS-DOS or Windows 9x operating systems will not be able to read the files in the NTFS partition. These operating systems are not "*NTFS Aware*." However, Windows NT can operate with the FAT file systems used by MS-DOS and Windows 3.x/9x. As a matter of fact, Windows 2000 and Windows XP can be installed on FAT16, FAT32, or NTFS partitions. Windows 2000 and Windows XP also supports the CDFS file system used with CD-ROM drives in PCs. Therefore, it is recommended that logical drives in a dual-boot system be formatted with the FAT system.

One reason to configure a dual-boot arrangement occurs when some of your key applications are not Windows XP compatible. In these situations, you can simply boot the computer into an older operating system to use those applications and then run all the other applications under Windows XP. However, there are a few items to consider when dual booting. You should be aware that the system's *active partition* must be formatted with a file system that all the operating systems in the system can use. For example, Windows NT 4.0 does not support the FAT32 file system and cannot boot from a FAT32 partition. Likewise, Windows 98 does not support NTFS and cannot boot from an NTFS partition.

NOTE

If you want to set up a dual-boot configuration with your current operating system, you will need to select the new installation option to preserve the existing operating system.

If drive C: is formatted as NTFS, you will be unable to dual boot with any other operating system without employing a third-party boot manager utility. Therefore, Windows XP Professional should be the last operating system installed. The Windows XP boot manager is backward compatible with previous Microsoft operating systems; however, their boot managers are not compatible with Windows XP. For example, if you were to install Windows NT 4.0 as a second operating system in a dual-boot scenario after Windows XP Professional had been installed, the Windows NT 4.0 boot manager would overwrite the Windows XP boot manager, making it unbootable.

You should make sure that each operating system is installed into a different folder. If possible, they should even be placed in different volumes (drive letters). For example, if you install Windows XP in a folder where another operating system exists, the XP files will overwrite the previous operating system so that it will not boot. However, if you install Windows XP in a different folder on the same volume as an existing operating system, then all the operating systems will function.

WINDOWS NT STARTUP MODES

A portion of A+ Operating System Technology objective 2.3 indicates that the test taker should be able to identify the basic system boot sequences and boot methods, including the steps to create an emergency boot disk with utilities installed for Windows 9x/Me, Windows NT 4.0 Workstation, Windows 2000 Professional, and Windows XP. It also states that the content may include the boot sequence, the files required to boot, and the boot steps for Windows 9x and NT-based systems.

Unlike the Windows 9x products, Windows NT 4.0 provides very few options when it starts up. The user is normally offered two options. The NTLDR file causes the system to display a selection menu of which operating system to boot from, along with an option to start the system in VGA mode. The menu listing is based on what NTLDR finds in the Boot.ini file. If the *VGA* option is selected, the system will start up as normal, with the exception that it will only load the standard VGA driver to drive the display.

The second option presented is the **Last Known Good Hardware Configuration mode** option. Selecting this option will cause the system to start up using the configuration information that it recorded the last time a user successfully logged onto the system. The option appears on the screen for a few seconds after the operating system selection has been made. You must press the SPACEBAR while the option is displayed on the screen to select this startup mode. If no selection is made, the system continues with a normal startup as previously outlined, using the existing hardware configuration information.

Last Known Good
Hardware
Configuration mode

Windows NT Startup

The sequence of steps in the Windows NT bootup and startup processes is similar to that presented in the previous chapters for FAT-based systems. The main differences lay in terminology and the names of the files that Windows NT employs.

Like any other PC system, the Windows NT-based PC starts up by running its POST, performing an initialization of its intelligent system devices, and performing a system boot process. It is in the boot process that the descriptions of the two operating systems diverge.

When the BIOS accesses the Master Boot Record on the hard drive, the MBR examines the disk's partition table to locate the active partition. The boot process then moves to the boot sector of that partition (referred to as the **partition boot sector**) located in the first sector of the active partition. Here the MBR finds the code to begin loading the secondary bootstrap loader from the root directory of the boot drive.

partition boot sector

In the case of a Windows NT partition, the bootstrap loader is the **NT Loader** file named **NTLDR**. This file is the Windows NT equivalent of the MS-DOS IO.SYS file and is responsible for loading the NT operating system into memory. Afterwards, NTLDR passes control of the system over to the Windows NT operating system.

NT Loader

NTLDR

When Windows NT gains control of the system, its first action is to initialize the video hardware and switch the microprocessor into protected mode. In the Windows NT system, the microprocessor is switched into the 32-bit flat memory mode described earlier in this chapter.

Next, a temporary miniature file system that can read both FAT and NTFS file structures is loaded to aid NTLDR in reading the rest of the system. Recall that Windows NT has the capability to work in either FAT or proprietary NTFS partitions. However, at this stage of the boot process, the operating system is still uncertain as to which system it will be using.

With the minifile system in place, the NTLDR can locate and read a special hidden boot loader menu file named **BOOT.INI**. NTLDR uses this text file to generate the **Boot Loader Menu** that is displayed on the screen. If no selection has been made after a given time delay, the default value is selected.

BOOT.INI

Boot Loader Menu

If Windows NT is designated as the operating system to be used, the NTLDR program executes a hardware detection file called **NTDETECT.COM**. This file is responsible for collecting information about the system's installed hardware devices and passing it to the NTLDR program. This information is later used to upgrade the Windows NT Registry files.

NTDETECT.COM

BOOTSECT.DOS

NTOSKRNL.EXE
HAL.DLL

If a different operating system is to be loaded, as directed by the Boot Loader Menu entry, the NTLDR program loads a file called **BOOTSECT.DOS** from the root directory of the system partition and passes control to it. From this point, the BOOTSECT file is responsible for loading the desired operating system.

Finally, the NTLDR program examines the partition for a pair of files named **NTOSKRNL.EXE** and **HAL.DLL**. NTOSKRNL.EXE is the Windows NT kernel file that contains the Windows NT core and loads its device drivers. HAL.DLL is the Hardware Abstraction Layer driver that holds the information specific to the CPU that the system is being used with.

Even though NTLDR reads the NTOSKRNL and HAL files at this time, it does not load or execute them. Instead, it uses a file named NTDETECT.COM to gather information about the hardware devices present and passes it to the NTLDR. This should not be confused with the PnP enumeration process that occurs later in the Windows 2000/XP bootup process. The information gathered by NTDETECT is stored to be used later for updating the Hardware Registry hive. In particular, the NTDETECT program checks for information concerning:

- Machine ID
- Bus types
- Keyboard
- Mouse

- Video type
- Floppy drives
- Parallel ports
- COMM ports

┌─ **TEST TIP** ─────────┐
Know what the swap file in
Windows NT/2000 is called.
└────────────────────┘

BOOTVID.DLL
Session Manager
SMSS.EXE
AUTOCHK
PAGEFILE.SYS
WINLOGON.EXE
Local Security Authority Subsystem (LSASS.EXE)
SPOOLS.EXE
Service Controller (SCREG.EXE)

Once the information has been passed back to NTLDR, it opens the System Hive portion of the Registry to find the Current Control Set. At this point, the system displays the Starting Windows NT logo on the display along with a sliding progress bar that shows the degree of progress being made in loading the drivers. After the drivers have been loaded, the NTLDR program passes control to the NTOSKRNL file to complete the bootup sequence.

When NTOSKRNL gains control of the system, it initializes the HAL.DLL file along with the **BOOTVID.DLL** file and shifts the video display to graphics mode. It then initializes the drivers prepared by NTLDR and uses the NTDETECT information to create a temporary Hardware Hive in memory. Finally, NTOSKRNL executes a **Session Manager** file titled **SMSS.EXE** to carry out pre-start functions such as running a boot-time version of CHKDSK called **AUTOCHK**. It also establishes parameters concerning the Windows NT paging file (**PAGEFILE.SYS**) to hold RAM memory swap pages.

After these tasks have been performed, the Session Manager loads the console logon service file (**WINLOGON.EXE**) to begin the authentication verification process. WINLOGON starts the **Local Security Authority Subsystem (LSASS.EXE)** and the print spooler (**SPOOLS.EXE**) along with their supporting files. Finally, WINLOGON loads the **Service Controller (SCREG.EXE)** that completes the loading process by bringing in the remaining devices and services.

┌─ **TEST TIP** ──────────────────────────────┐
Memorize the names and functions of the files involved in the
Windows NT/2000 boot process and know which order they are
executed in.
└──┘

Windows 2000/XP Startup

The Windows 2000/XP boot process is almost identical to the Windows NT bootup. The major events in the Windows 2000 startup include:

1. NTLDR looks into memory and the OS loader V5.0 message appears on the screen.

2. NTLDR switches the processor to 32-bit flat memory mode.

3. NTLDR starts a mini-file system (FAT or NTFS) to read disk files.

4. NTLDR reads the Boot.ini file and displays the Advanced Boot Options menu on the screen.

5. NTLDR runs Ntdetect.com to gather system hardware information. Ntdetect checks for the following hardware items:

   - Machine ID
   - Video type
   - Keyboard
   - Parallel ports
   - SCSI adapters
   - Bus types
   - Floppy drives
   - Pointing devices
   - COMM ports
   - Math coprocessor

6. NTLDR loads Ntoskrnl and HAL files into memory and passes the hardware information to it.

7. NTLDR reads the SYSTEM Registry key, places it in memory, and implements the hardware profile (configuration and control set) from the proper Registry.

8. NTLDR loads startup device drivers into memory.

9. NTLDR passes control to the Ntoskrnl file.

10. Ntoskrnl creates the Registry's HARDWARE key from the information gathered earlier by Ntdetect.

11. Ntoskrnl executes additional device drivers.

12. Ntoskrnl starts the SMSS.EXE session file.

13. The Win32 subsection runs the WINLOGON.EXE and LSASS.EXE programs, the CTRL+ALT+DEL window is presented on the display, and the logon screen is displayed.

14. The SCREG.EXE service controller program starts and loads all remaining services specified in the Registry, including the Windows 2000 shell and desktop.

As with Windows 9x, the Windows 2000 and Windows XP shell program is the **Windows desktop**. When the shell and desktop components are loaded, the system displays a prompt on the screen for the user to log in, as shown in Figure 10-34.

**Figure 10-34:
The Windows
NT Logon
Dialog Box**

The Windows NT/2000/XP logon process enables the operating system to configure itself for specific users. Normal logon involves entering a user name and password. If no logon information is entered, then default values will be loaded into the system.

In Windows 2000, the login screen always appears even if the system is not being used with a network.

WINDOWS NT/2000/XP DEVICE DRIVERS

The A+ Operating System Technologies objective 2.4 says that the test taker should be able to identify procedures for installing/adding a device, including loading, adding, and configuring device drivers, and required software. It also indicates that content may include obtaining, installing, manipulating, and uninstalling device drivers.

─ **NOTE** ─

*This information can be obtained from the Microsoft web site (*www.microsoft.com/st/hcl*), shown in Figure 10-35.

As mentioned earlier in the chapter, the Windows NT/2000/XP operating systems do not support as many hardware devices as the Windows 9x platforms do. However, the Windows NT versions still offer support for a fairly wide range of disk drive types, VGA video cards, network interface cards, tape drives, and printers. To determine what components Windows NT versions support, it is necessary to consult the Hardware Compatibility List for the version of Windows NT/2000/XP being used.*

**Figure 10-35:
Windows NT/2000/XP
Drivers Page**

If drivers for the device being installed are not listed at this location, there is a good chance the device will not operate well, if at all, in the Windows NT environment. If this is the case, the only recourse is to contact the device's manufacturer for *Windows NT drivers*. It is a good idea to check the manufacturer's web site for updated drivers that can simply be downloaded.

CHALLENGE #7

You are working in a music production facility that uses high-end MIDI devices (high-end professional sound cards and devices) to generate and manipulate musical instruments and sounds. You want to upgrade your production computers, but you worry that these specialized sound cards will not be compatible with the Windows 2000 Professional operating system. The cards and devices work under Windows 98 and they tend to be somewhat expensive compared to other computer devices. How can you determine whether this is a good thing to do?

Adding new devices to Windows 2000 or Windows XP is typically performed automatically through the system's Plug-and-Play process. However, devices can be manually added to a Windows 2000 system through the *Add /Remove Hardware* icon located in the Control Panel. In Windows XP the icon is simply labeled *Add Hardware*. Double-clicking this icon will produce the Add/Remove Hardware (Add Hardware) Installation Wizard that will guide the installation process or aid in troubleshooting problems with the new hardware component. In cases where the device came with an Installation CD, Microsoft recommends that you use the CD instead of the Add Hardware Wizard.

Windows NT 4.0 does not possess Plug-and-Play capabilities, although it does feature some auto-detection capabilities. It also has no Add/Remove Hardware Wizard. Devices must be installed manually under Windows NT 4.0—either through the icons in the Control Panel or through installation routines provided by the equipment manufacturer.

Double-clicking on a device icon in the Control Panel will produce a *Properties* dialog box for that device. The dialog box holds configuration information specific to that device. The tabs located along the tops of the dialog boxes can be used to review and change settings and drivers for the device.

Finding Drivers

Device manufacturers often continue to develop improved device drivers for their products after they have been released into the market. In addition, there is relatively little cooperation between hardware manufacturers and operating system companies. Therefore, you may need to locate new drivers for existing equipment that is not included in an early release of an operating system such as Windows 2000 or Windows XP.

To find new or updated drivers for a specific device, you should contact the product vendor's web site and search for your specific network operating system. Typically, you will need to know the specific make and model of your device. In most cases, the appropriate device drivers can be downloaded directly from the vendor's web site or obtained through mail. However, some vendors will only supply their drivers by shipping them to the user on CD.

There are also several third-party web sites on the Internet where device drivers can be obtained for various pieces of hardware. These sites tend to be especially useful for finding device drivers for older pieces of hardware, where original copies of drivers have been lost.

Driver Signing

Windows 2000 and Windows XP support a relatively wide array of newer hardware devices. These devices include DVD, USB, and IEEE-1394 devices. Microsoft works with hardware vendors to certify their drivers. These drivers are digitally signed so that they can be loaded automatically by the system.

Because poorly written device drivers had traditionally been a third-party problem, Microsoft created a Windows Hardware Quality Labs (WHQL) approval system for hardware manufacturers. Manufacturers who want to ensure their customers that their products will work with Windows 2000 and XP operating systems can submit their equipment and drivers to Microsoft for certification. Microsoft grants tested drivers a digital signature that is embedded in the driver to show that it has been approved. When Windows 2000 or Windows XP load the driver, they check it for the signature.

Driver signing is controlled through the Windows 2000/XP Control Panel's *System* icon. In the System applet, select the Hardware tab and click on the *Driver Signing* button. The *Driver Signing Options* page will appear. On this page you can establish how the system should react when it detects an unsigned driver. The options are:

- *Warn* – this setting will cause Windows to notify the user when an unsigned driver has been detected. It will also produce an option to load or not load the driver.

- *Block* – as its title implies, this option will not permit any unsigned drivers to be loaded into the system.

- *Disable* – this option disables the digital signature check and automatically loads any driver without providing a warning to the user.

If you check the Apply setting as system default checkbox, the signature verification setting will be applied to anyone who logs onto the system. Otherwise, only the currently logged-on user will be affected.

Because Windows 2000 and Windows XP are designed with centralized network security in mind, there are some administrative control issues that may be encountered when loading device drivers into one of these systems. If the system detects a valid digital signature, or the Designed for Windows Logo, when it checks the driver, it will usually accept the driver without any problems. However, if there is no digital signature or logo, then administrative privileges are required to load the driver into the system.

You must also be a member of the Administrators group to install drivers using the Add Hardware Wizard or when a network policy setting has been established to restrict who can install devices.

ADMINISTERING WINDOWS 2000/XP NETWORKS

Windows NT, 2000, and XP are all designed for use in an administrated LAN environment. As such, they must provide network administrators with the tools necessary to control users and data within the network. To empower the network administrator, Windows 2000 and XP furnish five powerful administrative tools:

- System Policies
- User Profiles
- Groups and Group Policies
- Network Share Permissions
- NTFS Rights

Each of these tools is designed to enable administrators to limit, or grant, users' access to files, folders, services, and administrator-level services.

Windows NT/2000/XP Policies

As with other Windows versions, the overall operation of the Windows 2000 and Windows XP environments is governed by **System Policies**. Basically, policies give administrators control over users. Using System Policies, the network administrator can give or limit users' access to local resources, such as drives and network connections. Administrators can establish policies that force certain users to log in during specified times and lock them out of the system at all other times. System Policies also enable the administrator to send updates and configure desktops for network clients. Fundamentally, any item found in the Control Panel can be regulated through System Policies.

> **System Policies**

User Profiles

Each Windows NT user is assigned a profile directory under their username the first time they log into a given Windows NT/2000/XP system. This **profile** contains system information and settings that become particular to the user and is stored under the Documents and Settings directory. Inside the directory, the system creates the Ntuser.dat file, along with various other data files. As discussed previously, this file contains the User portion of the Windows NT Registry. This file contains the user-specific settings that have been established for this user. When the user logs onto the system, the User and System hive portions of the Registry are used to construct the user-specific environment in the system.

> **profile**

The first time a user logs onto a system, the default **User Profile** directory is copied into the directory established under the user's name. When the user makes changes to the desktop, Start menu, My Documents, and so on, the data is stored in the appropriate files under the username. Windows NT, Windows 2000, and Windows XP provide methods of storing user profiles on the server in a networked environment. This prevents the user's profile directories from being re-created at each machine the user logs into. Instead, these operating systems provide roaming profiles that are downloaded from the server to the client when the user logs in. Changes made during sessions are uploaded to the server when the user logs out.

> **User Profile**

As with previous versions of Windows NT, Windows 2000 and Windows XP employ profiles to provide customized operating environments for users. These profiles are stored in different locations, hold more information, and are more customizable than previous Windows NT versions, but they perform the same functions. However, you should be aware that Windows 2000/XP policies work very differently under the Active Directory structure than they do in the Windows NT Domain structure.

Active Directory Users and Computers

Organizational Units (OUs)

The primary tool for working with the Active Directory is the **Active Directory Users and Computers**, depicted in Figure 10-36. The organizational units of a domain contain users, groups, and resources. The Active Directory Manager tool is used to add users, groups, and **Organizational Units (OUs)** to the directory.

**Figure 10-36:
Active Directory Users
and Computers**

Although the Active Directory structure is designed primarily to help manage a network, it can also be a valuable desktop tool. The Active Directory Service running on a Windows 2000 Server enables Windows 2000 and XP Professional installations to locate printers, disk drives, and other network devices across the network.

Group Policies

Group Policy Objects (GPOs)

While Windows NT relied on system policies, the Windows 2000 and XP environments function on **Group Policy Objects (GPOs)**. Group Policies are the Windows 2000/XP tools for implementing changes for computers and users throughout an enterprise. The Windows 2000 and XP Group Policies can be applied to individual users, domains, organizational units, and sites. In addition, the Windows 2000/XP policies are highly secure.

In Windows 2000 and Windows XP systems, policies are established through the Group Policy Editor (GPE) shown in Figure 10-37. Administrators use this editor to establish which applications different users have access to, as well as to control applications on the user's desktop.

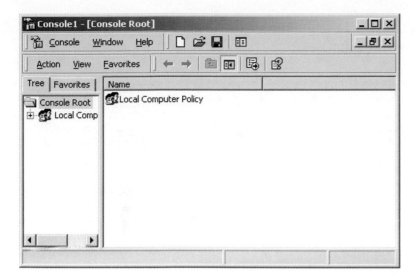

Figure 10-37: The Windows 2000 Group Policy Editor

With Group Policies, administrators can institute a large number of detailed settings for users throughout an enterprise, without establishing each setting manually. GPOs can be used to apply a large number of changes to machines and users through the Active Directory. These changes appear in the GPE under three headings:

- **Software Installation Settings**

- **Windows Settings**

- **Administrative Templates**

Each heading appears in two places — the first version is listed under Computer Configuration and the second copy is found under User Configuration. Values will usually differ between the versions of the headings since the user and computer settings will be different.

- The *Software Installation Settings* heading can be used to install, update, repair, and remove applications.

- The *Windows Settings* portion of the GPO contains startup and shutdown scripts as well as security settings. The Security Setting portion of this heading covers such topics as Account policies, Password policies, and User Right Assignments, to name a few.

- The *Administrative Templates* portion of the GPO stores changes to the Registry settings that pertain to the HKEY_LOCAL_MACHINE. Figure 10-38 shows the hierarchy of items in the *Computer Configuration Administrative Templates* window of the Group Policy Editor.

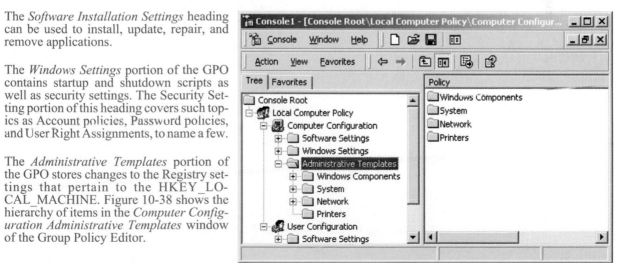

Figure 10-38: Computer Configuration Administrative Templates

Network Shares

In a network environment, only network shares (shared directories and resources) can be accessed across the network. The sharing function is implemented at the computer that hosts the folder or resource (resources are devices capable of holding or manipulating data). In Windows operating systems you can establish sharing for a folder by right-clicking on it and selecting the *Sharing* option from the menu. This will produce the *Sharing* tab of the file or folder's *Properties* page, as illustrated in Figure 10-39.

Similarly, for resources such as disk drives and printers, you can institute sharing by right-clicking on the device's icon and select the *Sharing* option from the menu. This will produce the *Sharing* tab from the device's *Properties*. In both cases, the presence of a hand symbol under the folder or device's icon indicates that it has been shared. To configure a shared folder's Properties, click on the *Share this folder* radio button and fill in the *Share name:* dialog box. Then click on the *Permissions* button to open the folder's *Permissions* dialog box to produce the *Share Permissions* dialog window shown in Figure 10-40.

**Figure 10-39:
File and Folder
Sharing Tab**

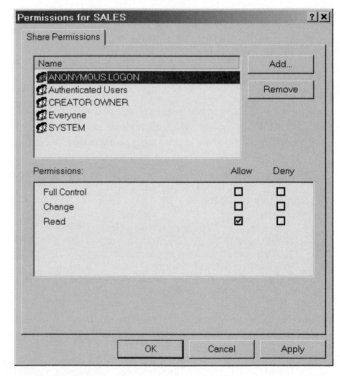

**Figure 10-40: Share
Permissions Dialog
Window**

Standard share permission options in Windows 2000 and XP are:

- *Read* — This setting enables the user to view file and folder names, run applications, read files, view file and folder attributes, and to navigate through the directory tree at levels beneath this folder.

- *Change* — This setting provides complete Read permissions, as well as the ability to create and delete files and folders, to edit files, and to change file and folder attributes.

- *Full Control* — This option enables the user to perform all of the functions available through the Change permission and provides the ability to modify permissions and to take ownership of the folder.

It is possible for users to receive these permissions from different sources (i.e., as members of different groups that have been assigned different permissions to the folder or resource). When this occurs, the different settings combine and the user receives the highest *Allow* option setting. However, *Deny* option settings override any Allow setting. For example, if a user has Full Control permissions for a certain folder from one group and only Read permissions from another group, then the result will be Full Control. However, if a *Deny* permission is assigned for Full Control from another group, then the user will receive only Read permissions for the folder.

To access the shared remote resource, the local operating system must first connect to it. After the connection has been established, the local operating system creates a new logical drive on the system to accommodate the new folder in the system.

Share permissions can only be assigned to the folder level. Windows NT, 2000, and XP NTFS permissions are much more robust than share permissions. NTFS permissions can be set at the file level in NTFS systems. However, share permissions are the only network access control option available for non-NTFS partitions.

NTFS Permissions

The NTFS5 system includes security features that enable **permission levels** to be assigned to files and folders on the disk. These permissions set parameters for operations that users can perform on the designated file or folder.

permission levels

Standard NTFS permissions include:

- **Read (R)**. This permission enables the user to display a file or folder along with its attributes and permissions.

Read (R)

- **Write (W)**. This permission enables the user to add files or folders, change file and folder attributes, add data to an existing file, and change display attributes.

Write (W)

- **Execute (X)**. The Execute permission enables users to make changes to subfolders, display attributes and permissions, as well as to run executable file types.

Execute (X)

- **Delete (D)**. The Delete permission makes it possible for users to remove files and folders.

Delete (D)

- **Change Permission (P)**. This permission enables users to change permission assignments of files and folders.

Change Permission (P)

- **Take Ownership (O)**. Ownership permission enables the user to take ownership of the file or folder.

Take Ownership (O)

No Access (none)

Read (RX)

Change (RWXD)

Add (WX)

Add & Read (RWX)

List (RX)

Full Control
(RWXDPO)

Some of these permission settings apply only to file-level objects, whereas others apply to both files and folders. Some combinations of the permissions are woven together in Standard NTFS file and folder permissions. These include:

- **No Access (none)**. File and Folder levels
- **Read (RX)**. File and Folder levels
- **Change (RWXD)**. File and Folder levels
- **Add (WX)**. Folder level only
- **Add & Read (RWX)**. Folder level (RX) File level
- **List (RX)**. Folder level only
- **Full Control (RWXDPO)**. File and Folder levels

While the NTFS system provides permission-level security for files and folders, other operating systems under Windows NT do not. For example, when a file is moved from an NTFS partition to a FAT partition, the NTFS-specific attributes are discarded. However, NTFS permissions do apply over a network connection.

Permissions can be assigned directly by the administrator, or they can be inherited through group settings. If a user only has Read permissions to a particular file, but is assigned to a group that has wider permissions, then that individual would gain those additional rights through the group. In a server environment, the default permission setting for files is *No Access*.

Administrative Tools

Administrative Tools

Computer
Management Console

Microsoft
Management
Consoles (MMCs)

The Windows 2000 and Windows XP operating system versions have taken a different approach to system administration and preventive maintenance by concentrating many of the system's administration tools in a single location, under the Control Panel's **Administrative Tools** icon. The tools are combined in the Windows 2000/XP **Computer Management Console**, shown in Figure 10-41. You can access the Management Console by right-clicking the My Computer icon and selecting the Manage option from the pop-up menu. As the figure illustrates, the console includes three primary **Microsoft Management Consoles** (MMCs):

- System Tools
- Storage
- Services and Applications

The contents of the different consoles vary depending on which snap-in tools administrators decide to add to them.

**Figure 10-41:
The Windows
2000 Computer
Management
Console**

The **System Tools** console, shown in Figure 10-42, provides a collection of tools that can be used to view and manage system objects. They can also be used to track and configure all of the system's hardware and software. They can also be used to configure network options and view system events.

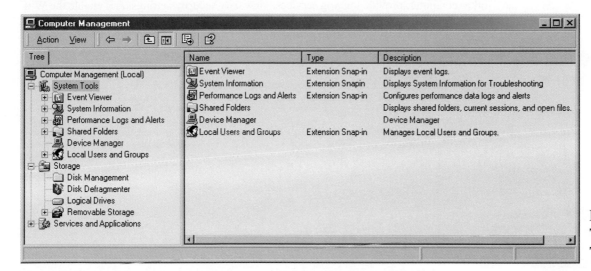

Figure 10-42: The System Tools Options

Likewise, the *Storage* console provides a standard set of tools for maintaining the system's disk drives. These tools include the **Disk Management** tool, the Disk Defragmenter utility, and a **Logical Drives** utility. The *Disk Management* tool enables the user to create and manage disk partitions and volumes. The organization of the Storage console is illustrated in Figure 10-43. The *Disk Defragmenter* is used to optimize file operations on disks by rearranging their data into the most effective storage pattern for reading and writing. Finally, the *Logical Drives* tool shows a listing of all the logical drives in the system, including remote drives that have been mapped to the local system.

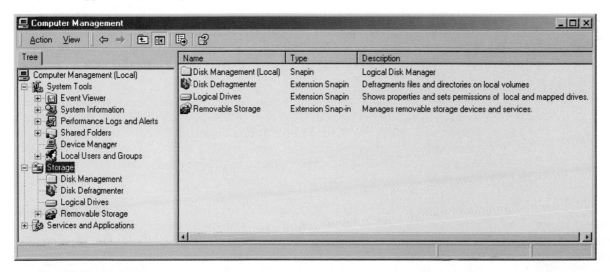

Figure 10-43: The Storage Console Options

TEST TIP

Be aware of where the Disk Management tools are located in Windows 2000.

The *Services and Applications* entry includes an advanced set of system management tools. These tools include the **Windows Management Instrumentation (WMI)** tools, a listing of all the system's available services, and access to the Windows 2000 Indexing functions, as shown in Figure 10-44. The WMI tools are used to establish administrative controls with another computer, provide logging services, view user security settings, and enable the Windows 2000/XP advanced scripting services.

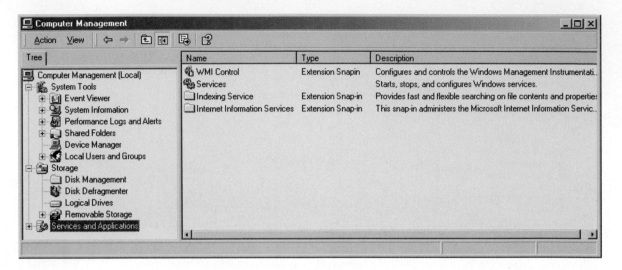

**Figure 10-44:
The Services and
Applications Options**

Some of the Windows 2000/XP management consoles are not loaded when the operating system is installed. However, they are available for installation from the Windows 2000/XP CDs. These consoles are referred to as snap-ins. In addition to the Control Panel path, all of the installed MMCs can be accessed under the *Start/Programs/Administrative Tools* path. Extended discussions of these tools are presented throughout the remainder of the text as they apply to managing and troubleshooting the operating system.

Windows NT Command-Prompt Procedures

Although "DOS is dead" for most consumers, technicians must often resort to using the command-line interface to isolate and correct problems within an operating system. Windows NT, Windows 2000, and Windows XP provide a *Command Prompt* window. However, unlike Windows 9x, when this feature is engaged in Windows NT, no separate DOS version is being accessed. Windows NT simply provides a DOS-like interface that enables users to perform some command-line functions.

There is also no convenient *MS-DOS* icon that can be clicked in the Windows NT system. To access the MS-DOS emulator in Windows 9x or Windows NT 4.0, select the *Run* option from the *Start* menu and type the word *COMMAND* in the *Run* dialog box. To access this function in Windows 2000 or XP, you must select the *Run* option from the *Start* menu and then type the command **CMD** (or **COMMAND**) into the dialog box.

```
┌─ TEST TIP ─────────────────────────────────┐
│                                             │
│  Know how to access the Command Prompt interface in │
│  Windows NT and Windows 2000/XP.            │
│                                             │
└─────────────────────────────────────────────┘
```

PRINTING IN WINDOWS 2000/XP

Windows 2000 and Windows XP employ a print spooler processing architecture similar to that found in Windows 9x. This structure provides smooth printing in a background mode and quick return-to-application time. The key to this operation is in how the print spooler sends data to the printer. Data is moved to the printer only when it is ready to receive more. Therefore, the system never waits for the printer to digest data that has been sent to it.

The Windows 2000 print spooler, depicted in Figure 10-45, is actually a series of 32-bit virtual device drivers and DLLs. In the figure, the spooler consists of the logical blocks between the client computer and the print device. These blocks process threads in the background and pass them to the printer when it is ready. In essence, the application prints to the Windows printer driver, the driver controls the operation of the spooler, and the driver prints to the printer from the spooler.

In a network printing operation, the print spooler must run on both the local server and the remote client systems. The user can start and stop the local print spooler process in Windows 2000 and XP through the Control Panel's *Administrative Tools/Services* icon. Clicking on this icon produces the Services listing, which contains the *Print Spooler* entry. Simply select the *Print Spooler* entry from the list to access the *Print Spooler Properties*, as illustrated in Figure 10-46. After the user stops the spooler service, it will be necessary to restart it before printing can occur again, unless the printer driver has been configured to bypass the spooler. Also, the local user is not capable of controlling the print operation to a server. The server print function is managed independently.

Figure 10-45: The Windows 2000 Print Spooler

Figure 10-46: Windows XP Print Spooler Properties

To print an open file in Windows 2000 or Windows XP, simply move to the application's *File* menu as usual and click on the *Print* option. If the file is not open, it is still possible to print files in Windows 2000 and Windows XP. Under the *My Computer* icon, access the desired file, right-click on it, and select the *Print* option from the pop-up menu as shown in Figure 10-47. Files can be printed from the *Windows Explorer* screen by employing the same right-click menu method. The document can also be dragged-and-dropped onto a printer icon in the *Printers* folder, in the *My Network Places* listing, or on the desktop. Obviously, this option can be performed with both local and remote networked printers.

Figure 10-47: Printing from My Computer Pop-up Menu

In Windows 2000, the settings for any printer can be changed through the *My Computer* icon on the desktop or through the *Printers* option under the *Start* menu's *Settings* entry. The process is the same for both routes: simply double-click on the *Printer* folder, right-click on the desired printer, and select its *Properties* entry from the menu. In Windows XP, you can access these settings through the *Printers and Faxes* option in the *Start* menu. The rest of the process is the same as that used in Windows 2000.

To view documents waiting to be printed from the print spooler, double-click on the desired printer's icon in the *Printer* folder. This will display the existing print queue, as illustrated in Figure 10-48. Closing the print window does not interrupt the print queue in Windows 2000 or XP.

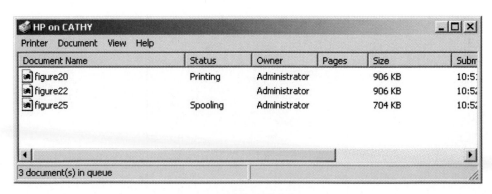

Figure 10-48: Windows 2000 Print Queue

The fact that the print spooler runs in its own 32-bit virtual environment means that printer stalls will not lock up the system. The print jobs in the queue will be completed unless they are deleted from the list.

The print spooler window's menu bar contains the same basic tool set as the one described for the Windows 9x Print Spooler. The menu items permit printing to be paused and resumed. They can also be used to delete print jobs from the queue. Right-clicking a printer icon will produce a pop-up menu that can also be used to control printing operations that are performed by that printer. Both options offer a *Properties* option that can be used to access the printer's configuration and connection information.

The Windows 2000 and Windows XP Printers dialog boxes enable users to sort between different printers based on their attributes. Windows 2000 Professional possesses the capability of printing across the Internet using the new standards-based **Internet Printing Protocol** (**IPP**). Using this protocol Windows 2000 Professional and Windows XP can print to a URL, view the print queue status using an Internet browser, and install print drivers across the Internet.

Internet Printing Protocol (IPP)

> Windows 2000 Professional and Windows XP also support a new universal font format called **OpenType**. This font type combines the best features of TrueType and Type 1 fonts. OpenType is supported by subsetting and compression technology that makes it efficient for transmission over the Internet.

OpenType

Establishing Printers in Windows 2000/XP

Like Windows 9x, Windows 2000 and Windows XP will automatically adopt any printers that have been established prior to their installation in the system. If no printers have been installed, the Setup routine will run the **Add Printer Wizard**, shown in Figure 10-49, to enable a printer to be installed. Each printer in the system possesses its own print window and icon to work from. The wizard can be accessed at any time through the *Start* menu.

Add Printer Wizard

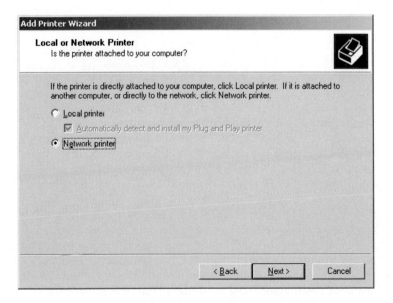

Figure 10-49: The Windows 2000/XP Add Printer Wizard

To use the *Start* menu in Windows 2000 for this purpose, move to the *Settings* entry and click on *Printers*. To install a printer, open the *Printers* folder and double-click the **Add Printer icon**. In Windows XP click on the *Start* button and then click on the *Printers and Faxes* icon. To access the Printer wizard in Windows XP, select the *Add a Printer* option from the *Printer Tasks* window. From this point, the Printer Wizard guides the installation process. Because Windows 2000 and Windows XP have built-in networking support, the printer can be a local unit (connected to the computer), or a remote unit located somewhere on the network.

To install local printers, choose the *Local Printer* (*Local printer attached to this computer in XP*) option and click on the *Next* button. In the Windows XP dialog window you should also have the *Automatically detect and install my Plug and Play printer* option checked. Normally, the LPT1 options should be selected from the list of **Printer Port** options. Next, the Add Printer Wizard will produce a list of manufacturers and models to choose from. This list will be similar to the one shown in Figure 10-50. Simply select the correct manufacturer and then the desired model from the list and inform the wizard about the location of the *\I386* directory to fetch the driver from. If the *\I386* directory has been copied to the hard drive, it will be faster to access the driver there. If not, the Windows 2000 or Windows XP distribution CD will be required.

**Figure 10-50:
A List of Printer Manufacturers and Models**

If the printer is not recognized as a model supported by the Windows 2000 or Windows XP driver lists, OEM drivers can be installed from a disk containing the OEMSETUP.INF file. Select the *Have Disk* option from the *Add Printer Wizard* screen. In Windows XP, you can also select the *Windows Update* option to search for updated drivers. After loading the driver, the wizard will request a name for the printer to identify it to the network system. Enter a unique name or use the default name supplied by Windows and continue.

> ┌─ **TEST TIP** ─────────┐
> Know how to install device drivers in Windows 2000 if the particular device is not listed in the standard Windows driver listings.
> └────────────────────────┘

Finally, the Add Printer Wizard will ask whether the printer is to be shared with other units on the network. If so, the printer must have a unique name to identify it to others on the network and must be set as *Shared*. The shared printer must also be set up for the different types of operating systems that may want to use it. The wizard will display a list of operating system types on the network. Any or all of the operating system types may be selected. The installation process is completed when the *Finish* button is clicked.

In Windows 2000, the Add Printer Wizard can also be accessed through the *My Computer* icon, the Control Panel, or by double-clicking on the *Printers* folder or icon. However, in Windows XP the My Computer path does not exist.

Printer Properties

Printer properties are all of the defining features about a selected printer and include information that ranges from which port it uses, to what security features have been implemented with it.

To examine or change the properties of a printer in Windows 2000, select the *Printers* option from the *Start/Settings* menu. In Windows XP the path is *Start/Printers and Faxes*. Inside the printer window, click on the desired printer to select it. From the *File* menu option, select the *Properties* entry to display the printer's properties sheet, as depicted in Figure 10-51. Right-clicking on the printer icon and then selecting the *Properties* option from the menu will also access the printer *Properties*.

The *General* tab provides general information about the printer. This includes such information as its description, physical location, and installed driver name. The *Ports* tab lists the system's physical ports, and the *Scheduling* tab displays the printer's availability, priority level, and spooling options. In Windows XP the *Scheduling* tab has been replaced with a tab named *Advanced*. The *Sharing* tab shows the printer's share status and share name.

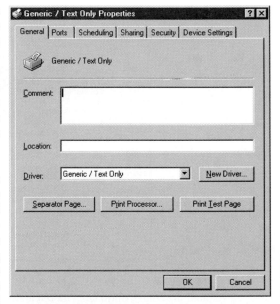

Figure 10-51: Printer Properties Sheet

The *Security* tab provides access to three major components. These are the *Permissions* button, the *Auditing* button, and the *Ownership* button. The *Permissions* button enables the system administrator to establish the level of access for different users in the system. The *Auditing* button provides user and event tracking capabilities for the administrator. Finally, the *Ownership* button displays the name of the printer's owner.

The *Device Settings* tab provides a wide array of information about the printer, including such items as paper tray sizes and font substitution tables. This feature is used to import downloadable font sets, install font cartridges, and increase the printer's virtual memory settings. The *Device Settings* tab, shown in Figure 10-52, is one of the most important tabs in the Printer *Properties* page.

Figure 10-52: Windows 2000 Printer Properties/Device Settings Tab

WINDOWS NT/2000/XP APPLICATIONS

The Windows 2000 and Windows XP environments employ an Add/Remove Programs wizard (actually *Add or Remove Programs* in Windows XP) to assist users in installing new applications. The Windows 2000/XP *Add/Remove Programs* icon is located in the Control Panel.

Double-clicking on the *Add/Remove Programs* icon produces the *Add/Remove Programs* dialog window, as illustrated in Figure 10-53. Any application that employs a *Setup.exe* or *Install.exe* installation routine can be installed through this window. Clicking on the *Install* button will cause the system to request the location of the installation program.

**Figure 10-53: Windows
XP Add or Remove
Programs Window**

In addition to third-party applications, the Windows Components Wizard can be used to install or remove optional components of the Windows 2000/XP operating system. Clicking on the Windows 2000 or Windows XP *Setup* tab under the *Properties* box produces a list of components, like the one shown in Figure 10-54. The individual components can be selected for inclusion in, or removal from Windows 2000 or Windows XP systems.

**Figure 10-54: Windows XP Optional
Components Window**

In Windows 2000 networks, application software can be installed remotely across the network. This enables the network administrator to control user application software across the network and keep it uniform throughout an enterprise. Likewise, the network administrator can assign applications to users so that they appear on their Start menus. When the application is selected for the first time, it will be installed on the local machine. The administrator can also place optional applications on the *Add/Remove Programs* dialog box in the Control Panel. The user can install these applications from this location at any time.

Windows 2000/XP Application Installer

Windows 2000 and Windows XP both feature a versatile MSI applications installer called the **Windows Application Installer**. This program is designed to better handle DLL files in the Windows 2000/XP environments. In previous versions of Windows, applications would copy similar versions of shared DLL files, and other support files, into the *\Windows* folder. When a new application overwrites a particular DLL file that another application requires for proper operation, a problem is likely to occur with the original software package.

The Windows 2000 Application Installer enables applications to check the system before introducing new DLLs to the system. Software designers who want their products to carry the Windows 2000/XP logo must write code that does not place proprietary support files in the \Windows directory—including DLL files. Instead, the DLL files are located in the application's folder.

Windows Installer—compatible applications can repair themselves if they become corrupted. When the application is started, the operating system checks the properties of its key files. If a key file is missing, or appears to be damaged, it will invoke the Installer and prompt the user to insert the application distribution CD. When the CD has been inserted, the Installer automatically reinstalls the file in question.

Launching Applications in Windows 2000/XP

In Windows 2000 and Windows XP there are several acceptable methods of launching an application. These include:

- Select the application from the extended *Start* menu, click on the folder containing the application, and double-click its filename.

- Select the *Run* entry from the *Start* menu, and then enter the full path and filename for the desired executable file.

- Double-click the application's filename in the Windows Explorer or in *My Computer*.

- Click on the *File* menu option from the My Computer menu bar or through the Windows Explorer, and select the *Open* option. (You can also alternate-click on the application and choose *Open*).

- Create a shortcut icon on the desktop for the application, so that simply double-clicking on its icon will start it.

In the Windows NT/2000/XP operating systems, an application can also be set up to run by association. Using this method, the application will be started whenever an associated file is double-clicked. This is accomplished by defining the file's type in the **Open With** dialog box. The first time you attempt to open a non-associated application, the *Open With* dialog box, shown in Figure 10-55, will appear. The *Open With* option can also be accessed by holding the left SHIFT key and alternate-clicking the file's icon.

Open With

Figure 10-55: The Windows 2000 Open With Dialog Box

Windows 9x and Windows NT

Microsoft did not intend for the Windows NT and Windows 9x systems to be compatible with each other. There is no direct pathway between the two and no direct upgrade path from Windows 9x to Windows NT. Because both rely on Registry structures and because those structures are incompatible with each other, there is no way to bring them together.

Hardware support is another difference that prevents the two Windows operating systems from working with each other. While some Windows 9x device drivers require direct access to system hardware, the Windows NT HAL cannot tolerate such operations. Therefore, Windows 9x drivers simply will not work in Windows NT and neither will the devices they support. Windows NT also lacks support for the **Virtual Device Drivers (VxDs)** employed by Windows 9x.

For these reasons, Microsoft does not recommend or support dual-booting operation of the two operating systems. However, both the Windows 2000 and Windows XP designs do provide for upgrading from Windows 9x platforms.

MS-DOS and Windows NT

Under Windows NT, 16-bit MS-DOS applications run in special NTVDM environments. Likewise, Win16 applications run in special Win16-on-Win32 NTVDMs. These environments prevent the 16-bit applications from interacting with any other applications while providing full access to all of the system's resources through the APIs in the Win32 Subsystem.

After placing a 16-bit application on the system's hard drive, the next step in establishing a NTVDM environment for it is to create a shortcut for the program on the desktop. This is accomplished through the Windows NT Explorer utility. Start the Explorer and then click-and-drag the application's executable filename to the desktop to create the shortcut icon. Click on the shortcut text box to edit its name.

The Properties of the shortcut must be edited through the shortcut icon. Alternate-click on the icon, select the *Properties* option from the floating menu, click on the *Program* tab, and click on the *Windows NT* button. This should produce the **Windows NT PIF Settings** dialog box shown in Figure 10-56.

Figure 10-56: Windows NT PIF Settings Dialog Box

Custom MS-DOS initialization files

Autoexec filename: %SystemRoot%\SYSTEM32\AUTOEXEC.NT

Config filename: %SystemRoot%\SYSTEM32\CONFIG.NT

OK   Cancel

☐ Compatible timer hardware emulation

Notice that **AUTOEXEC.NT** and **CONFIG.NT** initialization files exist to support DOS applications. These files mimic the functions of the AUTOEXEC.BAT and CONFIG.SYS files found in MS-DOS and Windows 3.x environments. While it's possible to establish separate initialization files for each DOS application, normally all such applications use the default files. The MS-DOS commands inside the files are executed by the NTVDM when it is first loaded.

The next step in setting up an MS-DOS application to run in Windows NT is to configure memory for it. This is accomplished by clicking on the *Memory* tab in the *MS-DOS Properties* page. This should produce the *Memory* screen shown in Figure 10-57. The Auto mode settings are normally selected so that Windows NT retains control over memory usage.

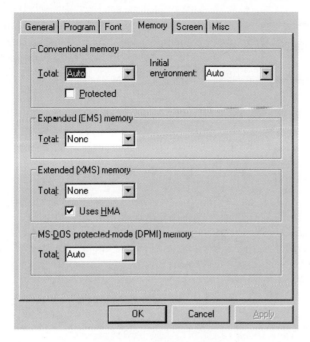

**Figure 10-57:
Windows NT Memory
Usage Screen**

In the case of 16-bit Windows applications, select the *Shortcut* tab from the *Shortcut Properties* window. To run the application in a private NTVDM, click on the *Run* option and select Run in the *Separate Memory Space* box.

NETWORKING WITH WINDOWS 2000/XP

The A+ Operating System Technologies objective 4.1 states that the test taker should be able to identify the networking capabilities of Windows. Given configuration parameters, configure the operating system to connect to a network.

During the Windows 2000 or Windows XP setup processes, the system must be configured to function as a workgroup node, or as part of a domain. A workgroup is a collection of networked computers assigned the same workgroup name. Any user can become a member of a workgroup by specifying the particular workgroup's name during the setup process. Conversely, a domain is a collection of networked computers established and controlled by a network administrator. As mentioned earlier in this chapter, domains are established for security and administration purposes.

The Setup routine requires that a computer account be established before a computer can be included in the domain. This account is not the same as the user accounts that the system uses to identify individual users.

If the system has been upgraded from an existing Windows NT version, Windows 2000 or XP will adopt the current computer account information. If the installation is new, the Setup utility will request that a new computer account be established. The network administrator normally assigns this account prior to running Setup. Joining the domain during setup requires a username and password.

<table>
<tr><td>
━ TEST TIP ━━━━━━━━━━
Know the specifications for setting up computer names in a given operating system.
</td><td>
In Windows 2000 or Windows XP systems using the TCP/IP protocol, computer names can range up to 63 characters in length and should be made up of the letters A through Z, numbers 0 through 9, and hyphens.
</td></tr>
</table>

My Network Places

My Network Places

Add Network Place

In the Windows 2000 and Windows XP operating systems, the *Network Neighborhood* folder has been replaced with a more powerful **My Network Places** folder, shown in Figure 10-58. The new folder includes a convenient new *Computers Near Me* view. The **Add Network Place** options enable you to more easily establish connections to other servers on the network. The user can establish shortcuts to virtually every server on the network.

Figure 10-58:
My Network Places

In the Windows XP operating system, the *My Network Places* icon opens to a display of the local network as shown in Figure 10-59. As the figure illustrates, the Network Tasks pane offers options to *Add a network place* and *View network connections*. In larger network environments, you may also have a *Search Active Directory* option.

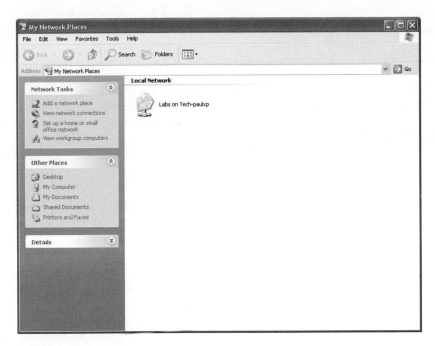

Figure 10-59: The Windows XP Local Network Window

The *Add a network place* option can be used to create shortcuts to network locations and web sites. It can also be used to sign up for personal web storage space. The *View network connections* option enables you to see all of the network connections that exist for the local computer. As its name indicates, the *Search Active Directory* option enables the user to search the Active Directory structure for network shares, computers, and users.

Mapping a Drive

As illustrated in the previous chapter, a drive map is a very important tool in a network environment. It allows a single computer to act as though it possesses all the hard drives that reside in the network. The **Network File Service (NFS)** portion of the operating system coordinates the systems so that drives located on other physical machines show up as logical drives on the local machine. This shows up in the *Windows Explorer* and *My Computer* screens, as illustrated in Figure 10-60. It also makes the additional drives available through the command-line prompt.

Network File Service (NFS)

> The primary reason to map a drive in a network environment is because some applications cannot recognize volume names. They can see only drive letters. In Windows, the number of recognizable drive letters is 26 (A–Z).

Figure 10-60: A Mapped Drive Display

Some network operating systems can recognize an extended number of drive letters (i.e., A-Z and AA-ZZ). However, by using unique volume names to identify drives, the system is capable of recognizing a large number of network drives.

For a local system to access a remote resource, the resource must be shared, and the local user must have a valid network user ID and password. The user's assigned rights and permissions are tied to his or her password throughout the network, either through individual settings or through group settings.

The Network Icon in Windows 2000/XP Control Panels

In Windows 2000, the *Network* icon under the Control Panel has been changed to the *Network and Dial-up Connections* folder. It provides access to the *Network and Dial-up Connections* window shown in Figure 10-61. This window provides several key functions associated with local and wide area networking. It is used to install new network adapter cards and change their settings, change network component settings, and to install TCP/IP.

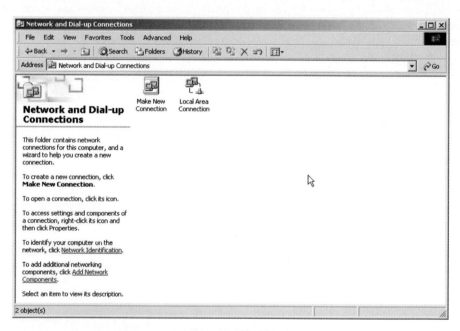

**Figure 10-61:
The Network and
Dial-up Connections
Window**

In Windows XP, the *Network* icon has been changed to the *Network Connections* icon. It does not offer the dial-up networking function included in the Windows 2000 applet, but it is used to configure and manage LAN and high-speed Internet access connection (i.e., DSL and cable modem connections). Clicking on the icon produces the *LAN or High-Speed Internet* window shown in Figure 10-62.

Figure 10-62: Windows XP LAN or High-Speed Internet Window

The *Network Tasks* pane of the *Network Connections* window provides options for creating, viewing, repairing, renaming, and reconfiguring the displayed connection as well as for disabling a network device.

Right-clicking on the connection will produce a pop-up menu that contains the *Properties* option for the connection. Selecting this option in either operating system version will produce the connection's *Properties* window. The organization of the Windows 2000 *Network and Dial-up Connections* and Windows XP *LAN or High-Speed Internet Properties* windows differs somewhat from that of the Windows 9x Network Control Panel. The Windows 2000 and XP versions consolidate the Services, Protocols, and Adapters function under a single tab, as illustrated in Figure 10-63.

Figure 10-63: Windows 2000/XP Local Area Connection Properties

The functions associated with the Windows 2000 Local Area Connection Properties include the following:

Services

- **Services**. Used to add, remove, or configure network services such as DNS, WINS, and DHCP functions.

Protocols

- **Protocols**. Used to add, remove, or configure network protocols for specific types of network environments.

Adapters

- **Adapters**. Used to add, remove, or configure NIC cards for operation with the system. This includes loading drivers and assigning system resources to the adapter.

To configure any of these functions for a given component, access the Local Area Connection Properties page, highlight the desired component, and click on the *Install* button. Other functions affecting the networking and dial-up connections in Windows 2000 and Windows XP include the following:

Network Identification

- **Network Identification**. Specifies the computer name and the workgroup or domain name to which the computer belongs. Under TCP/IP, computer names can be up to 63 characters but should be limited to 15 characters or less. They can use the numbers 0-9, letters A-Z (and a-z), as well as hyphens. Using other characters may prevent other nodes from finding your computer or the network. This option is located under the System icon in the Control Panel.

Bindings

- **Bindings**. Establishes a potential pathway between a given network service, a network protocol, and a given network adapter. The order of the bindings can affect the efficiency of the system's networking operations. To establish bindings, access the *Network and Dial-Up Connections* (*Network Connections* in XP) page and click on the *Advanced* entry on its drop-down menu bar. Then select the *Advanced Settings* option from the menu.

TEST TIP

Memorize which network items can be set through the Windows 2000 Network and Dial-up Connections applet's Local Area Connection Properties.

The Windows XP *Local Area Connections Properties* window offers two tabs not available in the Windows 2000 version. These are the *Advanced* tab and the *Authentication* tab. The *Advanced* tab is used to enable the Windows XP **Internet Connection Firewall**. This feature is embedded in Windows XP so that it can act as an Internet firewall for itself or for a local area network attached to it. This feature is described in more detail at the end of this chapter.

Internet Connection Firewall

Authentication protocols

**Figure 10-64:
Windows XP
Authentication Tab**

The *Authentication* tab is used to configure **authentication protocols** for conducting local area and wide area communications across a network. Recall that authentication is the process of identifying an individual as who they claim to be. This page, shown in Figure 10-64, is used to select standard protocols associated with particular network types, including Ethernet and 802.1x Wireless protocols.

Although the organization of the Network or Network Connections Control Panels are different in Windows 2000 and XP, the sequence of events involved in installing network components is identical to that used in the Windows 9x environment.

Networking with Novell NetWare

In a Novell NetWare system, the root directory of the workstation should contain the files **NETBIOS** and **IPX.COM**. The NETBIOS file is an emulation of IBM's Network Basic Input/Output System (NetBIOS), and represents the basic interface between the operating system and the LAN hardware. This function is implemented through ROM ICs, located on the network card. The Internetworking Packet Exchange (IPX) file passes commands across the network to the file server.

The NETBIOS and IPX protocols must be bound together in order to navigate the Novell network from a computer using a Windows operating system. This is accomplished by enabling the NETBIOS bindings in the IPX protocol properties in the *Network Properties* window.

The **Open Datalink Interface (ODI)** file is the Novell network shell that communicates between the adapter and the system's applications. Older versions of NetWare used a shell program called NETx. These files should be referenced in the AUTOEXEC.BAT or NET.BAT files.

| NETBIOS |
| IPX.COM |

| Open Datalink Interface (ODI) |

TEST TIP

Be aware of the elements that are required to navigate through a Novell network from a computer running a Microsoft operating system.

CHALLENGE #8

You are working on a Windows 2000 Professional client computer that has IPX loaded. You are working in a Novell LAN, however, and you find that you cannot browse the network. What should you check to gain access to the LAN?

Installing Netware Clients and Protocols

For Windows computers to be able to communicate with Novell servers in a network, they must have the client service for NetWare installed and configured. As indicated earlier in this chapter, clients are installed through the *Select Network Component Type* dialog window. This window is located under the connection's properties.

In Windows 9x/Me systems you should install the Novell Client for Windows 95/98 that is supplied by Novell. This client can be loaded through the Network Control Panel. In the *Network* page, click on the *Add* button, select the *Client* option from the list, click on the *Add* button, and select the *Have Disk* option. At this point you must enter a path to the location on the disk where the Novell client installation files are located.

Similarly, in Windows 2000 and Windows XP systems, you must install the *Client Service for Netware (CSNW)* option to provide the Windows client with the ability to communicate with NetWare servers. CSNW requires that the IPX/SPX protocol be installed on the client. It can be installed manually beforehand, or it will be installed automatically when the CSNW client is installed.

There are actually two pieces to the IPX/SPX implementation in Windows — the *NWLink NetBIOS* and *NWLink IPX/SPX/NetBIOS Compatible Transport Protocol* options. Both are required for interaction with Novell systems. To configure the IPX/SPX protocol, select the *NWLink IPX/SPX/NetBIOS Compatible Transport Protocol* option from the list in the dialog window and click on the *Properties* button.

In certain instances, you may need to enter an internal network number and a frame type setting on the *General* tab of the *IPX/SPX Properties* page. The network number is used when certain NetWare-specific applications are installed. This number is generally obtained form the NetWare administrator. The *Frame Type* setting is used in Ethernet networks to identify the type of Ethernet packets that are being used. The *Auto frame type detection* option permits the IPX function to determine what type of frame is actually being used on the network.

Installing Other Network Protocols

There are two other protocols of interest that you can install in a Windows system — Appletalk and NetBEUI. As mentioned earlier, Appletalk is required for the Windows computers to communicate with Apple Macs running Apple operating systems in the network, and NetBEUI is required when the network contains computers running older Windows operating systems. Both of these protocols are available through the *Select Network Component Type* dialog window. As with the other protocols, they are installed by simply clicking on the Install button, selecting the *Protocol* option, clicking on the *Add* button, selecting the desired protocol from the list, and clicking on the *OK* button.

Network Printing with Windows 2000/XP

As with the Windows 9x operating systems, Windows NT 4, Windows 2000, and Windows XP provide installation wizards to guide the network printer installation. If the physical printer is connected to a remote computer, referred to as a print server, the remote unit must supply the printer drivers and settings to control the printer. Likewise, the print server must be set up to share the printer with the other users on the network.

To install the network printer, access the *My Network Places* icon on the desktop, navigate the network to locate and open the remote computer's network name, right-click on the remote unit's printer name, select the *Connect* option from the pop-up menu, and follow the directions provided by the Windows *Add Printer Wizard*. When the wizard produces a dialog box asking whether to install the selected printer, click on the *OK* button. This should produce the *Add Printer Wizard* driver selection dialog box, shown in Figure 10-65. After the remote printer has been installed, the local computer can access it through the *My Network Places* icon.

Figure 10-65: Installing a Network Printer in Windows 2000/XP

Windows 2000 includes a printing feature called **Autopublish** (or point and print). This feature enables the user to install a printer driver on a client PC from any application. The Active Directory also enables the user to browse the network for a specific printer type or location.

Autopublish

Windows 2000 and Windows XP both feature Internet printing capabilities. This function enables the user to print to a remotely located printer using the Internet as the network. Microsoft designed this feature to compete with document faxing. Instead of faxing a document to a remote fax machine, just print it out on a printer at that location. Any standard printer can be used for this operation, as long as a Windows 2000 Server is hosting it.

The *File/Print* window, shown in Figure 10-66, includes a *Find Printer* button that you can use to search for printers locally, connected to the LAN, or connected across the Internet. After a printer has been located, Windows 2000 or XP will automatically install the driver for that printer on the client PC.

Both Windows 2000 and Windows XP include a library of more than 2500 printer drivers. If the local unit is not set up for the type of printer selected, it is possible to add these files and initiate the print job without leaving the *Print* dialog box.

Figure 10-66: The Windows 2000 File/Print Window

Sharing Printers in Windows 2000/XP

Shared printers

networked printers

Shared printers, also referred to as **networked printers**, receive data from computers throughout the network and direct it to a local printer. As in other networks, these printers must be configured as shared printers in the Windows 2000/XP environment to allow remote computers to access them.

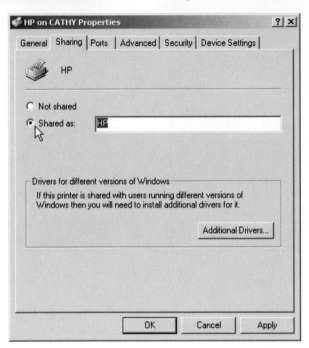

**Figure 10-67:
Sharing a Printer
in Windows 2000**

To share a printer under Windows 2000, select the *Printers* option from the *Start/Settings* path. In Windows XP, select the *Faxes and Printers* option from the *Start* menu. Alternate-click the printer to be shared and select the *Sharing* option. This action produces the *Sharing* tab shown in Figure 10-67. From this page, click the *Shared As* option, enter a share name for the printer, and click on the *OK* button to complete the sharing process. Unlike the Windows 9x systems, you must have administrative rights to make these changes in Windows 2000.

To connect to a printer on the network in Windows 2000, select the *Printers* option from the *Start/Settings* path and double-click the *Add Printer* icon. In Windows XP you must select the *Printers and Faxes* option from the *Start* menu and click on the *Add a printer* option. The *Welcome to the Add Printer Wizard* page will be displayed. Click on the *Next* button to move forward in the connection process. In the *Local or Network Printer* page, select the *Network Printer* (or *A Network Printer or Printer attached to another computer*) option, and click on the *Next* button to access the *Specify a Printer* dialog window, shown in Figure 10-68.

In Windows 2000, you can enter the network printer name in this window. You should also use the UNC format to specify the path to the printer being connected to (that is, *\\computer_name\share_name*). If the printer's name is not known, click on the *Type the Printer Name* option or click on the *Next* button to use the *Browse for a Printer* option.

**Figure 10-68: The Windows XP
Specify a Printer Dialog Window**

In Windows XP, you have additional options to enter the UNC path and printer name or connect to a printer on the Internet (or a SOHO network). There is also a radio button that will enable you to find a printer using the Active Directory.

To link up with a printer over the Internet (or the company intranet), select the *Connect to Printer on the Internet* or *Your Intranet* option and enter the URL address of the printer. The URL must be expressed in standard HTTP addressing format (i.e., *http://servername/printer/*). The connection wizard guides the connection from this point.

> ┌─ **TEST TIP** ─
> Know how to correctly write a UNC
> path to a shared directory located on a
> remote computer.

WIDE AREA NETWORKING WITH WINDOWS NT/2000/XP

A portion of A+ Operating System Technologies objective 4.2 indicates that the test taker should be able to identify the basic Internet protocols and terminologies. Identify procedures for establishing Internet connectivity. In a given scenario, configure the operating system to connect to and use Internet resources.

Older versions of Windows NT refer to all aspects of the dial-up networking function as **Remote Access Services (RAS)**. With Windows NT 4.0, however, Microsoft changed the nomenclature to *Dial-up Networking* on its client-side elements. Microsoft did so to maintain compatibility with Windows 9x descriptions. The server-side elements are still referred to as RAS. This same convention continues in the Windows 2000 and Windows XP products.

Windows NT Workstation provides all the software tools required to establish an Internet connection. These include a TCP/IP network protocol and the Windows NT Workstation *Dial-up Networking* component. The *Dial-up Networking* component is used to establish a link with the ISP over the public telephone system. This link also can be established over an ISDN line. Windows NT versions from 4.0 forward feature the built-in Microsoft Internet Explorer web browser and a personal Web Server.

The Windows 2000/XP Internet Infrastructure

The Windows 2000 operating system replaces the *Network Settings* item from the Windows NT 4.0 Control Panel with a *New Network Connections* folder, located in the My Computer window.

To create a dial-up connection in Windows 2000, click on the *Make New Connection* icon in the *My Computer/Network Connections* folder.

To create a new connection in Windows XP, you must navigate the *Start/My Network Places/View network connections* path and click on the *Create a new connection* option in the Network Tasks pane as illustrated in Figure 10-69.

These actions will open the Windows 2000/XP *Network Connection Wizard* (*New Connection Wizard* in XP) that guides the connection process. The wizard requires information about the type of connection, modem type, and the phone number to be dialed. The connection types offered by the wizard include private networks, virtual private networks, and other computers. The *Network Connection Wizard* enables users to employ the same device to access multiple networks that may be configured differently. This is accomplished by enabling users to create connection types based on who they are connecting to rather than on how they are making the connection.

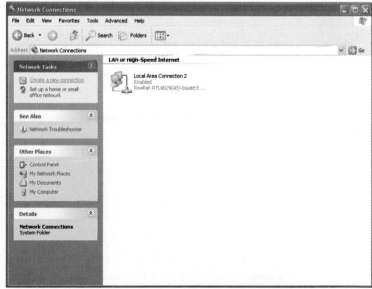

Figure 10-69: Creating a New Network Connection

Establishing the Windows 2000/XP Dial-up Configuration

Under Windows 2000 and Windows XP, the operating system should detect (or offer to detect) the modem through its Plug-and-Play facilities. It may also enable you to select the modem drivers manually from a list in the Control Panel's *Phone and Modem Options* applet. After the modem has been detected, or selected, it appears in the *Windows 2000* or *Windows XP Modems* tab. The settings for the modem can be examined or reconfigured by selecting it from the list and clicking on its *Properties* tab. In most cases, the device's default configuration settings should be used.

Configuring the modem to operate properly with an ISP is much easier in Windows 2000 and XP than it was in Windows NT 4.0. The *Connection Settings* tab from the *Windows NT 4.0 Modem Properties* dialog window has been replaced by the *Advanced* tab with space to enter the initialization string received from the ISP.

Establishing Dialing Rules

dialing rules

For Windows 2000 or XP to connect to a network or dial-up connection, it must know what rules to follow to establish the communication link. These rules are known as the **dialing rules**. In Windows 2000 and XP, the dialing rules are configured through the *Phone and Modem Options* icon in the Control Panel. If the connection is new, a *Location Information* dialog window displays, enabling you to supply the area code and telephone system information.

To create a new location, click on the *New* button on the *Dialing Rules* tab and move through the *General*, *Area Code Rules*, and *Calling Card* tabs, shown in Figure 10-70, to add information as required. The default rules for dialing local, long-distance, and international calls are established under the *General* tab. These rules are based on the country or region identified on this page. Ways to reach an outside line (such as dialing 8 or 9 to get an outside line in a hotel or office building) are established here. Similarly, the *Area Code Rules* information modifies the default information located under the *General* tab. As its name implies, the information under the *Calling Cards* tab pertains to numbers dialed using a specific calling card or long-distance company.

Figure 10-70: The Windows 2000 Phone and Modem Options/New Location Dialog Window

Establishing Dial-up Internet Connections

The Windows 2000 **Internet Connection Wizard**, shown in Figure 10-71, provides an efficient way to establish Internet connectivity. In Windows XP, the Internet connection is established through the New Connection Wizard. You can use the Internet or New Connection Wizard to set up the web browser, the Internet e-mail account, and the newsgroup reader. To create the Internet connection for an existing account with an ISP, you need to know the following:

- The ISP's name
- The user name and password
- The ISP's dial-in access number

Figure 10-71: The Windows 2000 Internet Connection Wizard

If the system is equipped with a **cable modem** or an **Asymmetrical Digital Subscriber Line** (**ADSL**), the ISP will need to furnish any additional connection instructions. The cable modem is a device that transmits and receives data through cable television connections. Conversely, ADSL is a special, high-speed modem technology that transmits data over existing telephone lines. The Internet Connection Wizard collects this information and then creates the Internet connection.

To connect to the Internet in Windows 2000, select *the Internet Connection Wizard* option from the *Start/Programs/Accessories/Communications* path. Likewise, to connect to the Internet in Windows XP, you must select the *New Connection* option from the *Accessories/Communications* menu. If the connection is new, the *Location Information* dialog boxes, shown in Figure 10-72, along with the dialing rules defined in the preceding section of this chapter will appear. You also need to click on the *I want to sign up for a new Internet account* option, click on the *Next* button, and follow the wizard's instructions.

Figure 10-72: The Location Information Dialog Box

In a Windows XP system, the New Connection Wizard produces the *Network Connection Type* screen shown in Figure 10-73. In this screen you can choose to *Connect to the Internet*, *Connect to a network at my workplace*, or *Set up an advanced connection*.

Figure 10-73: Windows XP Network Connection Type Page

Establishing Internet Connection Sharing

Sharing an Internet connection enables several computers to be connected to the Internet through a single dial-up connection. These connections can be made individually, or simultaneously, with each user maintaining the ability to use the same services it did when it was connected directly to the Internet.

To establish **Internet Connection Sharing (ICS)**, you must log on to the computer using an account that has Administrator rights. In a Windows 2000 system, click on *Start/Settings* and select the *Network and Dial-up Connections* option. Right-click the connection to be shared and then select the *Properties* option from the pop-up menu. The Internet connection's *Sharing* screen displays, as shown in Figure 10-74.

Under the *Internet Connection-Sharing* tab, select the *Enable Internet Connection Sharing for this connection* check box. If the connecting computer is supposed to dial in to the Internet automatically, click on the *Enable on-demand dialing* check box. Clicking on the *OK* button causes protocols, services, interfaces, and routes to be configured automatically.

In Windows XP, access the Network Connections, select the connection you want to share, and then select the *Change settings of this connection* option from the Network Tasks pane. On the *Advanced* tab, enable the *Allow other network users to connect through this computer's Internet connection* setting. On this tab you can also enable settings that will automatically dial out when another computer on the network tries to access the Internet and permit other network users to control the shared Internet connection.

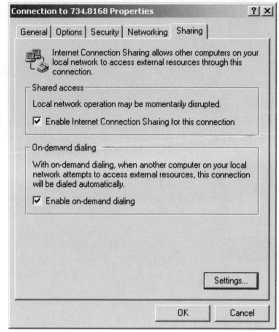

Figure 10-74: The Internet Connection Sharing Screen

WINDOWS NT SECURITY

One of the main features of all the Windows NT operating system versions has been their array of security options. As an operating system designed to work in business networks, **data security** is one of the most important functions of Windows NT.

The Windows 2000 and XP operating systems provide security in four forms:

- User security in the form of **User Logon** and **Passwords** is required to access the system

- User security between users of the same computer to control access to local data

- Identification of attempted security breaches through audit trails

- Memory usage protection between applications running on the same hardware

User Account

In a Windows NT system, a user must have a **User Account** on a particular computer to gain access to its operation. In a workgroup setting, this account must be set up on each computer. However, in a domain environment, the account can be established on the domain server.

Administrator Account

When Windows 2000 or XP is first installed, a master **Administrator Account** is established.

> The administrator has rights and permissions to all of the system's hardware and software resources. The administrator in turn grants rights and permissions to other users as necessary.

groups

The administrator can deal with users on an individual basis, or may gather users into **groups** that can be administered uniformly. In doing so, the administrator can assign permissions or restrictions on an individual or an entire group. The value of using groups lies in the time saved by being able to apply common rights to several users instead of applying them one by one.

profile

Each user and group in the NT environment has a **profile** that describes the resources and desktop configurations created for them. Settings in the profile can be used to limit the actions users can perform, such as installing, removing, configuring, adjusting, or copying resources. When users log into the system, it checks their profile and adjusts the system according to their information. In Windows NT 4.0, this information is stored in the *\WINNT\login_name\NTUSER.DAT* file. In Windows 2000 this file has been moved to *\Documents and Settings\login_name\NTuser.dat*.

The Windows 2000 Server operating system can be used to establish profiles for the entire network from a central location. Its administration package can also be used to establish roaming profiles that enable users to log into any workstation on the network and work under their own profile settings. The administrator can also cause the content of each user's local *My Documents* folder to reside on the server instead of the local desktop. This option provides safe, centralized storage for user files by enlisting the server's security and backup functions to safeguard the data.

User Manager

The Windows NT 4.0 **User Manager** utility can be accessed through the *Start* button's *Start/Programs/Administrative Tools* path. Clicking on the *User Manager* entry should produce the User Manager window. To create a new user, select the *New User* option from the User pull-down menu to produce the *New User* window displayed in Figure 10-75. Enter the necessary user information in the *New User* dialog box. The user's Username and Password will need to be supplied to them at least the first time they log in. If the *User Must Change Password...* option is selected, the user will be able to change the password to something more personal as soon as they log in.

Figure 10-75: The New User Window

Selecting the *Groups* icon at the bottom of the screen brings up the *Group Memberships* dialog box shown in Figure 10-76. Groups that the designated user is a part of are listed in the left-hand window. Groups that the user is not a part of are listed in the right-hand window. To add the user to a group, simply highlight the desired group in the right-hand window and click on the *Add* button.

Figure 10-76: The Group Memberships Dialog Box

Windows 2000/XP Security

Windows 2000 and Windows XP offer much improved security structure over previous Windows versions. The new security features apply to both LAN and wide area communications. The main security improvement is the adoption of the **Kerberos** authentication protocol.

> **Authentication** is a process that determines that users on the network are who they say they are.

The Kerberos protocol enables users to authenticate without sending a password over the network. Instead, the user acquires a unique key from the network's central security authority at login. The domain controller referred to as the **Key Distribution Center (KDC)** provides the security authority.

When a client makes a request to access a network resource or program, it authenticates itself with the KDC as described in Figure 10-77. The KDC responds by returning a session ticket to the client that is used to establish a connection to the requested resource. The ticket can only be used to authenticate the client's access to services and resources for a limited amount of time. During that time, the client presents the ticket to the application server that verifies the user and provides access to the requested program.

Kerberos

Authentication

Key Distribution Center (KDC)

Figure 10-77: Kerberos Protocol Operations

The key is cached on the local machine so that the user can reuse the key at a later time to access the resource. Keys are typically good for about eight hours, so there is no need for repeated interaction between the user and the KDC. This reduces the number of interactions that must be made across the network and, thereby, reduces the traffic load on the network in general. In addition, no passwords are circulated during the process, so there is no chance of compromising them.

Digital certificates are another major security feature in the Windows 2000 and Windows XP operating systems.

> Digital certificates are password-protected, encrypted data files that include data that identifies the transmitting system and can be used to authenticate external users to the network through **Virtual Private Networks** (**VPNs**).

VPNs use message encryption and other security techniques to ensure that only authorized users can access the message as it passes through public transmission media. In particular, VPNs provide secure Internet communications by establishing encrypted data tunnels across the WAN that cannot be penetrated by others.

When the certificates are combined with security standards such as the **IP Security Protocol** (**IPSec**) secure, encrypted TCP/IP data can be passed across public networks, such as the Internet. IPSec is a secure, encrypted version of the IP protocol. IPSec client software connects remote users to a VPN server by creating an encrypted tunnel across the Internet to the remote user as illustrated in Figure 10-78.

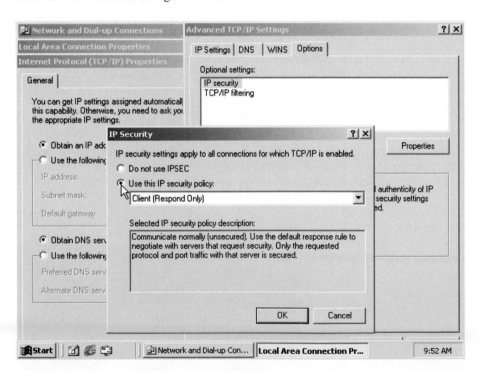

**Figure 10-78:
IP Security Protocol
Operations**

In addition to IPSec, Windows 2000 and Windows XP continue to offer **Point-to-Point Tunneling Protocol** (**PPTP**) and **Layer 2 Tunneling Protocol (L2TP)** as alternative security technologies for VPNs. L2TP can be used in conjunction with IPSec to pass the IPSec packets through routers that perform **Network Address Translation**.

In addition to the outstanding network security features, Windows 2000 and Windows XP both provide effective local hard drive security through its **Encrypted File System (EFS)** feature. The EFS feature enables the user to encrypt files stored on the drive using keys only the designated user (or an authorized recovery agent) can decode. This prevents theft of data by those who do not have the password or a decoding tool. EFS is simple to use because it is actually an attribute that can be established for files or folders.

Encrypted File System (EFS)

The Windows XP Firewall

Windows XP Professional provides a new **Internet Connection Firewall (ICF)** feature that is designed to provide protection from outside attacks by preventing unwanted connections from Internet devices. Computers connected directly to the Internet are vulnerable to attacks from the outside. Recall that a firewall is a device (or program) that is placed between an internal network, such as a corporate intranet, and an outside network (i.e., the Internet). The firewall is used to inspect all traffic going to and coming from the outside network, and can be programmed to control traffic flow between the networks based on desirable properties.

Internet Connection Firewall (ICF)

The Windows XP ICF service is designed to protect individual computers that are directly connected to the Internet through dial-up, LAN, or high-speed Internet connections. Proper installation and configuration of the ICF service can provide a strong protective barrier between Windows XP Professional and the outside network. When combined with the Windows ICS service, the XP firewall can be configured to provide Internet access to multiple computers through a single connection. ICF should be enabled on the shared external connection to secure communication for all internal clients.

Firewalls work by examining the front end (header) of network packets as they are received. Depending on how the firewall is configured, it may look at the header information and permit it to pass through the firewall or block it from going through. By default, the Windows XP ICF service will block all connection requests initiating from outside its network. It will only permit incoming traffic to come through that it recognizes as a response to a request from inside the network. The ICF knows which responses are acceptable because it maintains a table of outgoing connection information for itself and any computers on the local network that are sharing the ICF connection.

However, the ICF function can be configured with filters to enable specific traffic to enter the network. For example, if there are services such as web or FTP services running on the internal network that must be made available to external customers, then you can configure a filter to open the firewall to let just that service pass through.

Normally, these filters are configured around services recognized by the TCP and UDP networking protocols. These protocols use port numbers to identify specific processes such as HTTP or FTP. These ports are 16-bit numbers that refer incoming messages to an application that will process them. Many of the port numbers are standardized, and are referred to as **well-known ports**. Similarly, their associated applications are called *well-known services*.

well-known ports

Table 10-4 lists several well-known port numbers, and their provided services. The **Internet Assigned Numbers Authority (IANA)** has assigned standard port numbers ranging from 0 to 1023 to specific services. Port numbers from 1024 through 65535 are called ephemeral ports and are not assigned by the organization. Instead, they are frequently employed in user-developed programs.

Table 10-4:
Well-Known Ports

SERVICE	WELL-KNOWN PORT NUMBER
FTP	21, 20
Telnet	23
SMTP Mail	25
HTTP (WWW)	80
POP3 (Mail)	110
News	144
HTTP	443
PPTP	1723
IRC	6667

When the firewall examines the incoming packet, it can read the source and destination IP addresses of the packet and any TCP/UDP port numbers. It will use the IP address and port information in the packet headers to determine if an incoming packet should be routed into the internal network. If you have configured the firewall with the IP address of an internal computer that provides FTP services and opened ports 20 and 21, the firewall will recognize the IP address and port numbers in the incoming header as valid and route the packet to that computer. However, all other incoming requests will still be blocked.

To enable the Internet Connection Firewall function in Windows XP, open the *Network Connections* applet and right-click the connection (dial-up, LAN, or high-speed Internet) that you want to protect, and select the *Properties* option from the menu. Then, in the *Internet Connection Firewall* section of the *Advanced* tab, check the *Protect my computer and network by limiting or preventing access to this computer from the Internet* checkbox and click on the *OK* button.

In a network that is using Internet Connection Sharing, only the outgoing Internet connection should use the ICF feature. The other computers in the internal network should not have their ICF enabled.

Portable Design

The Windows 2000 and XP operating systems bring many new features for portable computers to the Windows NT line. In addition to furnishing the power management and Plug-and-Play features discussed earlier, Windows 2000 and Windows XP both provide increased data security functions and greater administrator control over mobile PCs.

Portable computer users in the business world typically spend some time connected to a company network and other times traveling away from the network connection. The Windows 2000 Synchronization Manager enables the user to select network files and folders and to travel without an active connection to a server.

When the client wishes to take files, the files are moved from the server to the portable and the Synchronization Manager synchronizes the time and date version information concerning the files. While the portable client is off-line, the user can continue to use the files under their network names. When the user returns to the network environment, the client resynchronizes the files with the server versions and the newer copy overwrites the older version. The synchronization process is described in Figure 10-79.

The Windows 2000/XP EFS feature further enhances the security of files on portable computers by enabling users to designate files and folders so that they can only be accessed using the proper **encryption key**. Public key encryption techniques employ two keys to ensure the security of the encrypted data — a **public key** and a **private key**. The public key (known to everyone) is used to encrypt the data, and the private or secret key (known only to the specified recipient) is used to decrypt it. The public and private keys are related in such a way that the private key cannot be decoded simply by possessing the public key.

Windows 2000/XP portability features are not limited to mobile computers. Many organizations have mobile employees that work at different computers within a given location. To accommodate this type of mobility, Windows 2000 and Windows XP provide for **roaming profiles** that can be employed to store each user's desktop, *Start* menu setup, and *My Document* folder on the server and redirect them to the local client where the user logs in. Windows 2000 and XP can also automatically install applications the user requires on the local client when they log on.

**Figure 10-79:
Windows 2000
Synchronization Manager**

CHAPTER SUMMARY

This chapter has presented an extensive technical exploration of the Windows NT, Windows 2000, and Windows XP operating systems. It has explored both operating systems in terms of their functions and structures. In many instances, the material in this chapter has built on, or contrasted with, the Windows 9x material from the previous chapter.

Having completed the chapter, you should able to describe the processes for installing or upgrading systems with Windows NT 4.0 and Windows 2000. You should also be able to describe the bootup sequence employed by Windows NT/2000.

Secondly, you should be able to describe the structure of Windows NT/2000/XP operating systems, including their core files and Registry components. In addition, you should be able to describe accepted methods for navigating through either system, including the Internet Explorer.

Finally, you should be able to successfully install, configure, and access software applications, peripheral systems such as printers, local area networking functions, as well as wide area networking and Internet functions in Windows NT 4.0, 2000, and XP.

At this point, review the objectives listed at the beginning of the chapter to be certain that you understand and can perform each item listed there.

KEY POINTS REVIEW

This chapter has investigated the structure and operation of the Windows NT, Windows 2000, and Windows XP operating systems. Review the following key points before moving into the Review and Exam Questions sections to make sure you are comfortable with each point. Afterward, answer the Review Questions that follow to verify your knowledge of the information.

- While Microsoft improved the Windows 3.x and Windows 9x products for use by the general population, it also developed a more robust and complicated Windows New Technology, or Windows NT, operating system for corporate client/server networking installations.

- It was built around a new operating system kernel that focused on enhanced reliability, scalability, and security elements required for corporate applications, while retaining the strengths of the Windows operating system.

- The Windows NT Server package provides the same features and functions found in the Workstation, except the Server package also provides the tools necessary to administer and control a network from a central location.

- Enterprise networks are designed to facilitate business-to-business, or business-to-customer operations. Because monetary transactions and personal information travels across the network in these environments, enterprise networks feature facilities for additional, highly protective security functions.

- An intranet is a network built on the TCP/IP protocol that belongs to a single organization — in essence a private Internet. Like the Internet, intranets are designed to share information and are only accessible to the organization's members, with authorization.

- Windows 2000 is the successor of the Windows NT 4.0 operating system. It brings together the stability and security of Windows NT 4.0 and the Plug-and-Play capabilities of Windows 9x.

- The Windows 2000 Server product is also available in two extended enterprise versions — Windows 2000 Advanced Server and Windows 2000 Datacenter Server.

- The standard Server package supports four-way symmetrical microprocessor operations (i.e., it can distribute work between four different microprocessors at a time) and can manage up to 4 GB of RAM.

- The Advanced Server edition can support up to 8 symmetrical processors and up to 8 GB of memory. These features enable it to function well in medium-size networks running between 100 and 500 concurrent users.

- The Windows 2000 Datacenter Server edition can handle up to 64 GB of RAM and 32 processors. This enables it to support up to 1000 simultaneous users with heavy processing demands.

- The Windows NT desktop includes most of the same features found in its Windows 9x counterpart (i.e., My Computer, Network Neighborhood, Inbox, and the Recycle Bin).

- The Windows NT Start Menu contains Programs, Documents, Settings, Find, Help, Run, and Shut Down options.

- Locating, accessing, and retrieving information in Windows NT is virtually the same as with the Windows 9x operating systems.

- Instead of simply truncating the filename, inserting a tilde, and then attaching a number to the end of the filename, Windows NT performs a mathematical operation on the long name to generate a truly unique MS-DOS—compatible filename.

- When five or more names are generated that would result in duplicate short names, Windows NT changes its truncation method. Beginning with the sixth filename, the first two characters of the name are retained, the next four characters are generated through the mathematical algorithm, and, finally, a tilde with an ID number is attached to the end of the name.

- Windows 2000 and Windows XP feature an intelligent, personalized Programs menu. It monitors the user's program usage, and after the first six accesses, arranges the menu options according to those most frequently used.

- A network share is an existing shared resource (i.e., printer, drive, modem, or folder) located on a remote system.

- Windows 2000 and Windows XP offer extended common dialog boxes for the File/Open, File/Print, and File/Save options. These dialog boxes provide easy organization and navigation of the system's hard drives, as well as navigation columns that grant quick access to frequently used folders.

- The Windows NT logical structure is a modular system that allows for advances in computing technology to be integrated into the system. It exists in two basic layers referred to as Modes — the Kernel Mode and the User Mode.

- Basically, the operating system runs in the Kernel Mode while applications run in User Mode. User Mode is a more restrictive operating mode where no direct access of hardware is permitted.

- The Windows NT HAL is a library of hardware drivers that operate between the actual hardware and the rest of the system. These software routines act to make every architecture look the same to the operating system.

- The Windows NT Registry is not compatible with the Windows 9x Registries.

- The content of the Registry is physically stored in five files referred to as Hives. Hives represent the major divisions of all the Registry's keys, subkeys, subtrees, and values.

- The NT Registry hive files are stored in the \Winnt\System32\Config directory along with a backup copy and log file for each hive.

- The content of the Registry can be edited directly using Regedt32.exe. This file is located in the \Winnt\System32 folder. As with the Windows 9x packages, most changes to the Registry should be accomplished through the wizards in the Windows NT Control Panel.

- The Rdisk.exe utility, located in the \Winnt\System32 folder, can be used to create a backup copy of the Registry in the \Winnt\Repair folder.

- The overall operation of Windows NT 4.0 is governed by System Policies that give administrators control over users. Using System Policies, the network administrator can give or limit users' access to local resources, such as drives and network connections.

- The central feature of the Windows 2000 architecture is the Active Directory structure. Active Directory is a distributed database of user and resource information that describes the makeup of the network (i.e., users and application settings).

- In Windows 2000 and XP, policies are established through the Group Policy Editor. Administrators use this editor to establish which applications different users have access to, as well as to control applications on the user's desktop.

- With Group Policies, administrators can institute a large number of detailed settings for users throughout an enterprise, without establishing each setting manually.

- Windows NT offers its own proprietary NTFS file system that is designed to provide better data security and to operate more efficiently with larger hard drives than FAT systems do.

- The Windows NT file system provides security for each file in the system, as well as complete file access auditing information to the system administrator. NTFS files and folders can have permissions assigned to them whether they are shared or not.

- The NTFS system includes security features that allow permission levels to be assigned to files and folders on the disk. These permissions set parameters for activities that users can conduct with the designated file or folder.

- A member server is most often referred to as a stand-alone server. As such, the member server maintains a local domain database that only it uses. These servers are most commonly used as application and file servers.

- The Primary Domain Controller server is the first domain controller installed in a Windows NT domain and maintains the working security and account databases for the domain.

- The Backup Domain Controller server maintains backup copies of the PDC's security and account databases. These copies are used to assist in authenticating user account logins.

- The minimum hardware requirements for installing Windows 2000 Professional on a PC-compatible system are:

  - *Microprocessor* — 133 MHz Pentium (P5 equivalent or better)

  - *RAM* — 64 MB (4 GB maximum)

  - *HDD Space* — 650 MB or more free on a 2 GB drive

  - *VGA Monitor*

- For installation from a CD-ROM, a 12x drive is required. If the CD-ROM drive is not bootable, a high-density 3.5-inch floppy drive is also required. If Windows Professional is to be installed across a network, a Windows 2000 Professional–compatible NIC is required.

- Systems can be upgraded to Windows 2000 Professional from Windows 3.x and 9x, as well as Windows NT 3.5 and 4.0 workstations. This includes older NTFS, FAT16, and FAT32 installations. When you install Windows 2000, it can recognize all three of these file system types.

- As with previous Windows NT products, Windows 2000 does not attempt to remain compatible with older hardware and software. Therefore, some applications may not be compatible with Windows 2000 and may run poorly, or fail completely after an upgrade.

- Windows NT can be set up to dual boot with DOS or Windows 9x operating systems.

- The Windows NT logon allows the operating system to configure itself for specific users. Normal logon involves entering a user name and password. If no logon information is entered, then default values will be loaded into the system.

- Windows 2000 and XP support a wide array of newer hardware devices. These devices include DVD, USB, and IEEE-1394 devices. Microsoft works with hardware vendors to certify their drivers. These drivers are digitally signed so that they can be loaded automatically by the system.

- Windows NT and Windows XP employ a print spooler processing architecture similar to that found in Windows 9x. This structure provides smooth printing in a background mode and quick return-to-application time.

- Windows 2000 Professional and Windows XP also support a new universal font format called OpenType. This font type combines the best features of TrueType and Type 1 fonts and is supported by subsetting and compression technology that makes it efficient for transmission over the Internet.

- Printer properties are all of the defining features about a selected printer and include information that ranges from which port it should use, to what security features have been implemented with it.

- Active Directory arranges domains in a hierarchy and establishes trust relationships among all of the domains in a tree-like structure.

- In AD, a tree is a collection of objects that share the same DNS name. Active Directory can subdivide domains into organizational units that contain other units, or leaf objects, such as printers, users, and so on.

- Windows 2000 can create an organizational structure containing more than one tree. This structure is referred to as a forest.

- Trusts are relationships that enable users to move between domains and perform prescribed types of operations.

- Rights are the permission settings that control a user's (or group of users') authority to access objects and perform operations (such as reading or writing a file). Administrative rights provide authority to users down to the Organizational Unit level.

- In the Windows 2000 and Windows XP systems, the Network Neighborhood folder has been replaced with a more powerful My Network Places folder. The new folder includes new Recently Visited Places and Computers Near Me views.

- The primary reason for mapping a drive in a network environment is that some applications cannot recognize volume names. They can only see drive letters. In Windows NT/2000/XP, the number of recognizable drive letters is 26 (A-Z).

- Windows 2000 includes a printing feature called Autopublish (or point and print). This feature enables the user to install a printer driver on a client PC from any application. The Active Directory also enables the user to browse the network for a specific printer type, or location.

- Windows 2000 replaces the Network Settings item from the Windows NT 4.0 Control Panel with a New Network Connections folder, located in the My Computer window.

- Windows 2000 and XP make it possible to share resources such as printers, folders, and Internet connections across a network. Sharing the connection permits several computers to access the Internet through a single dial-up connection. These connections can be made individually, or simultaneously, with each user maintaining the ability to use the same services it did when it was connected directly to the Internet.

- Since its creation, one of the main features of the Windows NT operating system has been its security capabilities. As an operating system designed to work in business networks, data security is one of the most important functions of Windows NT.

- The administrator has rights and permissions to all of the system's hardware and software resources. The administrator in turn grants rights and permissions to other users as necessary.

- Authentication is a process that determines that users on the network are who they say they are.

- Digital certificates are password-protected, encrypted data files that include data that identifies the transmitting system and can be used to authenticate external users to the network through Virtual Private Networks.

REVIEW QUESTIONS

The following questions test your knowledge of the material presented in this chapter.

1. A user wants to use his new hard drive to store sensitive company data. His computer is running Windows XP Professional. He plans on encrypting all data in his folder so that only a few select users may access the data. From the properties window of the folder, what tab do you suggest that the user utilize to protect his data?

2. List the two types of domain controllers employed in Windows NT networks.

3. Describe four types of security found in the Windows 2000 environment.

4. A new Windows XP Professional workstation is built for the company accountant. The accountant is very concerned about security of his data, and wishes to have his data protected via the Windows XP Firewall. How do you enable the Windows XP Firewall?

5. Describe the sequence of events required to upgrade a Windows 9x Registry HKEY to a Windows NT 4.0 HKEY.

6. How much memory is required to install Windows 2000 Professional?

7. You are installing a new network for a company. The company recently acquired workstations with the Windows XP Professional operating system, and has a hub and a DSL modem. Due to costs, the company does not wish to pay for a new server or a router, but would still like to have the Internet available to all workstations, and would therefore be willing to pay for extra cabling and Network Interface card costs. What is the best solution for this scenario?

8. Which file contains user-related configuration information for Windows NT?

9. Where should changes to Registry items be made from?

10. To ensure that existing hardware will work after a Windows 2000 upgrade, what reference should be examined before beginning the upgrade process?

11. What is the function of the BOOT.INI file in a Windows XP system?

12. Name two factors that must be taken into account when considering upgrading a system to a Windows NT or Windows 2000 operating system.

13. _____ is the Windows 2000 tool for implementing changes for computers and users throughout an enterprise.

14. Name three advantages of the Windows NT file system over FAT16 and FAT32 file management structures.

15. Which Windows 2000 utility can be used to create a backup copy of the Registry? Where is the utility located and where will the backup copy be stored?

EXAM QUESTIONS

1. Which Windows NT file is responsible for guiding the Windows NT bootup process?
   a. NTLDR
   b. NTDETECT.COM
   c. NTOSKRNL.EXE
   d. BOOT.INI

2. What is the name of the virtual memory file used by Windows XP Professional?
   a. Winswp.386
   b. Pagefile.sys
   c. Swap file
   d. Winswp.XP

3. What is the basic unit of storage in an NTFS system?
    a. The file
    b. The cluster
    c. The MFT
    d. The organizational unit

4. For Windows XP, the Local Connection properties window offers two tabs not available in the Windows 2000 version. What are the two tabs called?
    a. General and Advanced
    b. Authentication and Encryption
    c. Advanced and Encryption
    d. Advanced and Authentication

5. _____ are relationships that enable users to move between domains and perform certain types of operations.
    a. Trusts
    b. Permissions
    c. Rights
    d. Privileges

6. The portion of the Windows NT structure that communicates directly with the system hardware is _____.
    a. the Win32 Executive
    b. the User Mode
    c. the HAL
    d. the Hardware Subsystem

7. How many drives can be mapped in a Windows 2000 system?
    a. 10
    b. 26
    c. 4
    d. 16

8. What is the maximum length of a Windows 2000 filename?
    a. 8 characters
    b. 215 characters
    c. 255 characters
    d. 256 characters

9. Where will the Windows NT Setup utility install the Windows NT files in a typical installation?
    a. The \Winnt directory
    b. The \I386 folder
    c. The \Windows\system folder
    d. The \Windows directory

10. The members of a _____ share a common directory database and are organized in levels.
    a. workgroup
    b. tree
    c. group
    d. domain

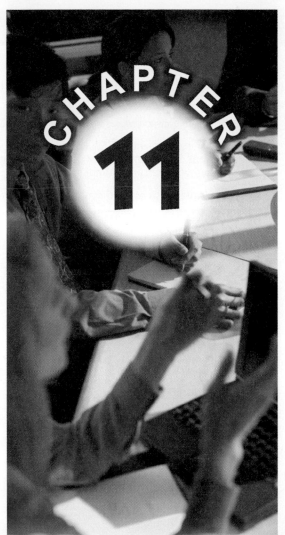

CHAPTER 11

BASIC SYSTEM TROUBLESHOOTING

OBJECTIVES

OBJECTIVES

Upon completion of this chapter and its related lab procedures, you should be able to perform these tasks:

1. Describe the characteristics of a good workspace.

2. Outline steps for using a digital multimeter to perform voltage, resistance, and current checks on a system, as well as identify common DMM tests associated with personal computers.

3. List preliminary steps for diagnosing computer problems.

4. Perform visual inspections of a system.

5. Describe the three general categories of problems into which symptoms can be grouped, and differentiate between them.

6. Differentiate between software- and hardware-based troubleshooting techniques.

7. Use disk-based diagnostic tools to isolate system problems.

8. Describe the function of a POST card.

9. Describe quick checks that can be used to determine the nature of system hardware problems.

10. Describe FRU-level troubleshooting.

11. Describe the steps for isolating power supply problems.

12. Outline checks to isolate problems that produce a dead system.

13. Discuss methods of dealing with symptoms that are not defined well enough to point to a particular component.

BASIC SYSTEM TROUBLESHOOTING

INTRODUCTION

Effective troubleshooting of electronic equipment is a matter of combining good knowledge of the equipment and its operation with good testing techniques and deductive reasoning skills. In general, the process of troubleshooting microprocessor-based equipment begins outside the system and moves inward. The first step always involves trying the system to see what symptoms are produced. Second, you must isolate the problem as either a software- or hardware-related issue. After this, the problem can be isolated to a particular section of the hardware or software. Finally, the problem must be isolated to the offending component.

The information in this chapter instructs you in the theory behind tools and methods you will need to effectively troubleshoot microprocessor-based equipment.

BASIC TROUBLESHOOTING TECHNIQUES

The A+ Core Hardware objective 2.2 states that the test taker should be able to identify basic troubleshooting procedures and tools, and how to elicit problem symptoms from customers. Justify asking particular questions in a given scenario.

Content may include the following:

- Troubleshooting/isolation/problem determination procedures
- Determining whether the problem is a hardware or software problem
- Gathering information from user
- Customer environment
- Symptoms/error codes
- Situation when the problem occurred

One of the most important aspects of troubleshooting anything is the gathering of information about the problem at hand and the symptoms it is showing. One of the best sources for this type of information is the computer user. As this A+ objective states, the computer technician should be able to effectively acquire information from the customer (user) concerning the nature of a problem and then be able to practice basic troubleshooting methods to isolate and repair the problem. To this end, the following sections of the chapter address these topics. A place to start this discussion is with your tools and workspace.

Work Space

The first order of business when working on any type of electronic equipment is to prepare a proper work area. You need a clear, **flat work space** on which to rest the device. Make sure that your work space is large enough to accommodate the work piece. Confirm that you have an adequate number of power receptacles to handle all of the equipment you may need. Try to locate your work space in a low-traffic area.

Good lighting is a prerequisite for the work area since the technician must be able to see small details, such as part numbers, cracked circuit foils, and solder splashes. An adjustable lamp with a shade is preferable. Fluorescent lighting is particularly desirable. In addition, a magnifying glass helps to read small part numbers.

Diagnostic and Repair Tools

Anyone who wants to work on any type of equipment must have the proper tools for the task. The following sections discuss the tools and equipment associated with the testing and repair of digital systems. A well-prepared technician's tool kit should contain a wide range of both **flat-blade** and **Phillips-head screwdriver** sizes. At a minimum it should have a small jeweler's and a medium-sized flat-blade screwdriver, along with a medium-size Phillips screwdriver. In addition, you may want to include a set of miniature nut drivers and a set of **Torx drivers**.

You also should have a couple of pairs of **needle-nose pliers**. These pliers are available in a number of sizes. You need at least one pair with a sturdy, blunt nose and one pair with a longer, more tapered nose. You also might wish to get a pair that has a cutting edge built into its jaws. You may perform this same function with a different type of pliers called **diagonals**, or crosscuts. Many technicians carry a pair of surgical forceps in addition to their other pliers. Figure 11-1 depicts **hand tools** commonly associated with microcomputer repair.

**Figure 11-1:
Hand Tools**

In addition to these hardware tools, the technician should have a collection of software tools at his disposal. Typical software tools used by computer technicians include:

- Emergency boot/start disks to get broken systems started
- Anti-virus utilities
- Hardware diagnostic utility packages

Using a Multimeter

In addition to a good selection of hand tools, there are a number of test instruments that can help you to isolate problems. One of the most basic pieces of electronic troubleshooting equipment is the **multimeter**. These test instruments are available in both analog and digital readout form and can be used to directly measure values of **voltage (V)**, **current** in milliamperes (mA) or amperes (A), and **resistance** in ohms (Ω). Therefore, these devices are referred to as **VOMs (Volt-Ohm-Milliammeters)** for analog types, or **DMMs (Digital MultiMeters)** for digital types. Figure 11-2 depicts a digital multimeter.

With a little practice, you can use this device to check diodes, transistors, capacitors, motor windings, relays, and coils. This particular DMM contains facilities built into the meter to test transistors and diodes. These facilities are in addition to its standard functions of current, voltage, and resistance measurement.

The first step in using the multimeter to perform tests is to select the proper function. For the most part, you should never need to use the current functions of the multimeter when working with computer systems. However, the voltage and resistance functions can be very valuable tools.

multimeter
voltage (V)
current
resistance
VOMs (Volt-Ohm-Milliammeters)
DMMs (Digital MultiMeters)

**Figure 11-2:
Digital Multimeter**

In computer and peripheral troubleshooting, fully 99% of the tests made are dc voltage readings. These measurements most often involve checking the dc side of the power supply unit. You can make these readings between ground and one of the expansion slot pins, or at the P8/P9 power supply connectors. It is also common to check the voltage level across a system-board capacitor to verify that the system is receiving power. The voltage across most of the capacitors on the system board is 5 Vdc. The dc voltages that can normally be expected in a PC-compatible system are +12 V, +5 V, −5 V, and −12 V. The actual values for these readings may vary by 5% in either direction.

WARNING

Setting the meter—It is normal practice to *first set the meter to its highest voltage range* to make certain that the voltage level being measured does not damage the meter.

The **dc voltage function** is used to take measurements in live dc circuits. It should be connected in parallel with the device being checked. This could mean connecting the reference lead (black lead) to a ground point and the measuring lead (red lead) to a test point to take a measurement, as illustrated in Figure 11-3.

Figure 11-3: dc Voltage Check

As an approximate value is detected, you can decrease the range setting to achieve a more accurate reading. Most meters allow for over-voltage protection. However, it is still a good safety practice to decrease the range of the meter after you have achieved an initial value.

The second most popular test is the resistance, or **continuity test**.

WARNING

Power off—Unlike the voltage check, resistance checks are always made with power removed from the system.

Failure to turn off the power when making resistance checks can cause serious damage to the meter and can pose a potential risk to the user. Resistance checks also require that you electrically isolate the component being tested from the system. For most circuit components, this means desoldering at least one end from the board.

The resistance check is very useful in isolating some types of problems in the system. One of the main uses of the resistance function is to test fuses. You must disconnect at least one end of the fuse from the system. You should set the meter on the 1-kilohm resistance setting. If the fuse is good, the meter should read near 0 ohms. If it is bad, the meter reads infinite. The resistance function also is useful in checking cables and connectors. By removing the cable from the system and connecting a meter lead to each end, you can check the cable's continuity conductor by conductor to verify its integrity. You can also use the resistance function to test the system's speaker. To check the speaker, just disconnect the speaker from the system and connect a meter lead to each end. If the speaker is good, the meter should read near 8 ohms. If the speaker is defective, the resistance reading should be 0 for an electrical short or infinite for an open circuit.

Only a couple of situations involve using the **ac voltage function** for checking microcomputer systems. The primary use of this function is to check the commercial power being applied to the power supply unit. As with any measurement, it is important to select the correct measurement range. However, the lethal voltage levels associated with the power supply call for additional caution when making such measurements. The second application for the ac voltage function is to measure ripple voltage from the **dc** output side of the power supply unit. This particular operation is very rarely performed in field service situations.

TEST TIP

Know what readings to expect from a multimeter when testing fuses, speakers, and typical power-supply voltages in a PC.

CHALLENGE #1

One of your network administrator friends has called you about a problem she is having with her computer at home. She is not getting sound from her speaker and has checked all her software. She has asked you to explain to her how to check her speaker hardware. What should you tell her?

Information Gathering

Careful observation — The most important thing to do when checking a malfunctioning device is to be observant. Begin by talking to the person who reported the problem. You can obtain many clues from this person. Careful listening also is a good way to eliminate the user as a possible cause of the problems. Part of the technician's job is to determine whether the user could be the source of the problem—either trying to do things with the system that it cannot do, or not understanding how some part of it is supposed to work.

TEST TIP

Be well aware that the user is one of the most common sources of PC problems. In most situations, your first troubleshooting step should be to talk to the user.

Situations

Gather information from the user regarding the environment the system is being used in, any symptoms or error codes produced by the system, and the situations that existed when the failure occurred. Ask the user to demonstrate the procedures that led to the malfunction in a step-by-step manner. This communication can help you narrow down a problem to a particular section of the computer. It does no good to check the video display when the user is having trouble using the disk drive. Gain an understanding of the process they are trying to complete.

Finally, remove the operator from the situation and observe the symptoms of a malfunction to verify the problem for yourself. Attempt to limit the problem to the hardware involved, the software package being used, and then to the operator.

Environment

Take note of the environment that the equipment is being used in and how heavy its usage is. If the system is located in a particularly dirty area, or an area given to other environmental extremes, it may need to be cleaned and serviced more frequently than if it were in a clean office environment. The same is true for systems subjected to heavy or continuous use. In an industrial environment, check with the management to see whether any office or industry maintenance standards for servicing apply.

Finally, use simple observation of the wear and tear on the equipment to gauge the need for additional or spot maintenance steps. Look for signs of extended use (such as frayed cords, missing slot covers, keyboards with letters worn off, etc.) to spot potential problems resulting from age or usage.

CHALLENGE #2

You have been called to a business to repair a printing problem. When you arrive, you are told that the user is having trouble printing spreadsheets from his Microsoft Excel program. You are not an Excel or spreadsheet guru, so how do you go about servicing this problem?

Symptoms/Error Codes

Most PCs have reasonably good built-in self-tests that are run each time the computer is powered up. These tests can prove very beneficial in detecting hardware-oriented problems within the system.

beep code

> **Error message formats**—Whenever a self-test failure or setup mismatch is encountered, the BIOS may indicate the error through a blank screen, or a visual error message on the video display, or an audio response (**beep code**) produced by the system's speaker.

Some PCs issue numerically coded error messages on the display when errors occur. Conversely, other PCs display a written description of the error. Figure 11-4 defines the error messages and beep codes produced by a BIOS version from American Megatrends. The error messages and codes will vary among different BIOS manufacturers and from version to version.

BEEP CODE MESSAGES

1 beep - DRAM refresh failure

2 beeps - RAM failure (base 640 kB)

3 beeps - System Timer failure

5 beeps - Microprocessor failure

6 beeps - Keyboard Controller failure

7 beeps - Virtual Mode Exception failure

9 beeps - ROM BIOS checksum failure

1 long, 2 short beeps - Video controller failure

1 long, 3 short beeps - Conventional and extended test failure

1 long, 8 short beeps - Display test failure

VISUAL DISPLAY ERROR MESSAGES

SYSTEM HALTED ERRORS

CMOS INOPERATIONAL - Failure of CMOS shutdown register test

8042 GATE A20 ERROR - Error getting into protected mode

INVALID SWITCH MEMORY FAILURE - Real/Protected mode change over error.

DMA ERROR - DMA controller failed page register test

DMA #1 ERROR - DMA device # 1 failure

DMA #2 ERROR - DMA device # 2 failure

NON-FATAL ERRORS - WITH SETUP OPTION

CMOS BATTERY LOW - Failure of CMOS battery or CMOS checksum test

CMOS SYSTEM OPTION NOT SET - Failure of CMOS battery or CMOS checksum test

CMOS CHECKSUM FAILURE - CMS battery low or CMOS checksum test failure

CMOS DISPLAY MISMATCH - Failure of display type verification

CMOS MEMORY SIZE MISMATCH - System Configuration and Setup failure

CMOS TIMER AND DATE NOT SET - System Configuration and Setup failure in timer circuitry

NON-FATAL ERRORS - WITHOUT SETUP OPTION

CH-X TIMER ERROR - Channel X (2, 1, or 0) TIMER failure

KEYBOARD ERROR - Keyboard test failure

KB/INTERFACE ERROR - Keyboard test failure

DISPLAY SWITCH SETTING NOT PROPER - Failure to verify display type

KEYBOARD IS LOCKED - Unlock it

FDD CONTROLLER ERROR - Failure to verify floppy disk setup by System Configuration file

HDD CONTROLLER FAILURE - Failure to verify hard disk setup by System Configuration file

C:DRIVE ERROR - Hard disk setup failure

D:DRIVE ERROR - Hard disk setup failure

Figure 11-4: Error Messages and Beep Codes

Initial Troubleshooting Steps

Successful troubleshooting results from careful observation, deductive reasoning, and an organized approach to solving problems. These techniques apply to the repair of any type of defective equipment.

To be an effective computer troubleshooter, you must combine good equipment knowledge with good testing techniques and deductive reasoning skills. Always try the system to see what symptoms you produce. Second, you must isolate the problem to either software- or hardware-related problems. Finally, you should isolate the problem to a section of the hardware or software.

Observe the Bootup Procedure

Unless the system is on fire, the first real diagnostic step is normally to turn the system on and carefully observe the steps of the bootup process. This procedure can reveal a great deal about the nature of any problems in a system. Faulty areas can be included or excluded as possible causes of errors during the bootup process.

The observable actions of a working system's cold-boot procedure are listed as follows, in their order of occurrence:

1. When power is applied, the power supply fan activates.

2. The keyboard lights flash as the rest of the system components are being reset.

3. A BIOS message displays on the monitor.

4. A memory test flickers on the monitor.

5. The floppy-disk drive access light comes on briefly (if enabled in the CMOS boot sequence).

6. The hard-disk drive access light comes on briefly.

7. The system produces a single beep, indicating that it has completed its Power On Self Tests and initialization process. After this point, the operation of the machine has shifted to looking for and loading an operating system.

8. The floppy-disk drive access light comes on briefly before switching to the hard drive. At this point in the process, the BIOS is looking for additional instructions (boot information) — first from the floppy drive and then from the hard drive (assuming that the CMOS setup is configured for this sequence).

9. When the system finds the boot files, the drive light will come on, indicating that the system is loading the operating system and configuration files.

10. For Windows machines, the "Starting Windows message" appears on the screen.

11. Windows loads its GUI components and takes over control of the system.

┌─ **TEST TIP** ─┐
Memorize the order of the series of observable events that occur during the normal (DOS) bootup.
└─────────────┘

If a section of the computer is defective, you will observe just some (or possibly none) of these events. By knowing the sections of the computer involved in each step, you can suspect a particular section of causing the problem if the system does not advance past that step. For instance, it is illogical to replace the floppy-disk drive (step 5) when a memory test (step 4) has not been displayed on the monitor.

Determining Hardware/Software/Configuration Problems

One of the earliest steps in troubleshooting a computer problem (or any other programmable system problem) is to determine whether the problem is due to a hardware failure or to faulty software.

In most PCs, you can use a significant event that that occurs during the bootup process as a key to separating **hardware problems** from **software problems**: the single beep that most PCs produce between the end of the POST and the beginning of the bootup process (step 7 in the preceding list).

> **hardware problems**
>
> **software problems**

Errors that occur, or are displayed, before this beep indicate that a hardware problem of some type exists. Up to this point in the operation of the system, only the BIOS and the basic system hardware have been active. The operating system does not come into play until after the beep occurs.

> **NOTE**
>
> If the system produces an error message (such as The System Has Detected Unstable RAM at Location x) or a beep code before the beep, for example, the system has found a problem with the RAM hardware. In this case, a bad memory device is indicated.

Normally, symptoms can be divided into three sections: **configuration problems, bootup problems**, and **operational problems**. Typically, if the bootup process reaches the point where the system's CMOS configuration information displays onscreen, you can safely assume that no hardware failures or configuration conflicts exist in the system's basic components. After this point in the bootup process, the system begins loading drivers for optional devices and additional memory. If the error occurs between these two events, then a configuration problem probably exists with one of the optional components. If the error occurs after the CMOS screen displays and before the bootup tone, you must clean boot the system and single-step through the remainder of the bootup sequence.

> **configuration problems**
>
> **bootup problems**
>
> **operational problems**

You can group errors that occur before the beep into two distinct categories:

> **Configuration errors**
>
> **Hardware failures**

- **Configuration errors**

- **Hardware failures**

Configuration or setup problems tend to occur whenever a new hardware option is added to the system, or when the system is used for the very first time. These problems result from mismatches between the system's programmed configuration, held in CMOS memory, and the actual equipment installed in the system. You can trace most problems that occur in computer systems back to configuration settings.

It is usually necessary to access and configure the system's CMOS Setup utility in the following situations:

1. The first situation occurs when the system is first constructed.

2. The second occurrence happens if it becomes necessary to replace the CMOS backup battery on the system board.

3. Whenever a new or different option is added to the system (such as a hard drive, floppy drive, or video display), it may be necessary to run the Setup utility.

In most systems, the BIOS and operating system use **Plug-and-Play** (**PnP**) techniques to detect new hardware that has been installed in the system. These components work together with the device to allocate system resources for the device. In some situations, the PnP logic will not be able to resolve all the system's resource needs and a configuration error will occur. In these cases, the user must manually resolve the configuration problem.

When you are installing new hardware or software options, be aware of the possibility of this type of error. If you encounter configuration (or setup) errors, refer to the installation instructions found in the new component's user's manual. Table 11-1 lists typical configuration error codes and messages produced when various types of configuration mismatches occur.

Table 11-1: Common Configuration Error Messages

CONFIGURATION ERROR MESSAGE	MEANING
CMOS System Option Not Set	Failure of CMOS battery or CMOS Checksum test
CMOS Display Mismatch	Failure of display type verification
CMOS Memory Size Mismatch	System configuration and setup failure
Press F1 to Continue	Invalid configuration information

┌─ **TEST TIP** ─┐
Know the situations that cause a Press F1 to Continue error message to display.
└───────────────┘

The system's configuration settings are normally checked first. It is important to observe the system's symptoms to determine in which part of the system's operation the fault occurs. The configuration error messages described in Table 11-1 occur and are reported before the single beep tone is produced at the end of the POST routines. These errors occur and are reported before the single beep tone is produced at the end of the POST routines.

If you cannot confirm a configuration problem, the problem most likely is a defective component. The most widely used repair method involves substituting known-good components for suspected bad components. Other alternatives for isolating and correcting a hardware failure that appears before the bootup depend on how much of the system is operable.

After the beep tone has been produced in the startup sequence, the system shifts over to the process of booting up and begins looking for and loading the operating system. Errors that occur between the beep and the presentation of the operating system's user interface (command prompt or GUI) generally have three possible sources. These sources are summarized in the following list that includes the typical error messages associated with each source.

- Hardware failure (physical problem with the boot drive)
  - General Failure Error Reading Drive x

- Corrupted or missing boot files
  - Bad or Missing Command Interpreter
  - Non-System Disk or Disk Error
  - Bad File Allocation Table
- Corrupted or missing operating system files

CHALLENGE #3

A friend is having trouble starting up her computer and she has asked you for help. When you turn the system on, the video display comes on and you can hear the disk drive spinning. Several different screens display and then you hear a single beep from the computer. From your knowledge of system bootups, what can you tell your friend about her system?

Procedures for diagnosing and troubleshooting problems associated with typical PC hardware components are presented throughout the Symptoms and Troubleshooting section in this chapter. Conversely, bootup problems are typically associated with the operating system. Steps for isolating and correcting operating system problems are presented in Chapter 12 — *Operating System Troubleshooting*. In these cases, checking the drive hardware is generally the last step of the troubleshooting process. Unless some specific symptom indicates otherwise, you should check for missing or corrupted boot files and operating system files first.

CHALLENGE #4

A remote customer calls and complains that she is receiving a Bad or Missing Command Interpreter error message and the system stops operating. She thinks she should replace her hard drive and wants you to order it for her. What should you tell her?

Software Diagnostic Packages

Many companies produce disk-based diagnostic routines that check the system by running predetermined tests on different areas of its hardware. The diagnostic package evaluates the response from each test and attempts to produce a status report for all of the system's major components. Like the computer's self-tests, these packages produce visual and beep-coded error messages. Figure 11-5 depicts the Main menu of a typical self-booting software diagnostic package.

Figure 11-5: The Main Menu

This menu is the gateway to information about the system's makeup and configuration, as well as the entryway to the program's Advanced Diagnostic Test functions. You can find utilities for performing low-level formats on older hard drive types and for managing SCSI interface devices through this menu. Additionally, options to print or show test results are available here, as is the exit point from the program.

The most common software-troubleshooting packages test the system's memory, microprocessor, keyboard, display monitor, and the disk drive's speed. If at least the system's CPU, disk drive, and clock circuits are working, you may be able to use one of these special software-troubleshooting packages to help localize system failures. They can prove especially helpful when trying to track down non-heat-related intermittent problems.

If a diagnostic program indicates that multiple items should be replaced, replace the units one at a time until the unit starts up. Then, replace any units removed prior to the one that caused the system to start. This process ensures that there were not multiple bad parts. If you have replaced all the parts, and the unit still does not function properly, the diagnostic software is suspect.

For enterprises that repair computers, or build computers from parts, diagnostic programs that perform continuous burn-in tests are valuable tools. After the system has been built or repaired, these programs are used to run continuous tests on the system for an extended **burn-in period**, without any intervention from a technician or operator.

The tests performed in a burn-in situation are similar to standard software utility tests. However, they are normally used for reliability testing instead of general troubleshooting. Different parts of the system can be selected for the burn-in tests. Since the burn-in tests are designed for use in an unattended manner, you must be careful to select only tests that apply to hardware that actually exists in the system. The diagnostic keeps track of how many times each test has been run, and how often it failed during the designated burn-in period, as depicted in Figure 11-6.

**Figure 11-6:
The Burn-in
Test Report**

POST Cards

Most BIOS program chips do not have an extensive set of on-board diagnostics built into them. Therefore, several companies produce **POST cards** and diagnostic software to aid in hardware troubleshooting. A POST card is a diagnostic device that plugs into the system's expansion slot and tests the operation of the system as it boots up. These cards can be as simple as interrupt and DMA channel monitors, or as complex as full-fledged ROM BIOS diagnostic packages that carry out extensive tests on the system.

POST cards are normally used when the system appears to be dead, or when the system cannot read from a floppy or hard drive. The firmware tests on the card replace the normal BIOS functions and send the system into a set of tests. The value of the card lies in the fact that the tests can be carried out without the system resorting to software diagnostics located on the hard disk or in a floppy drive.

The POST routines located in most BIOS chips will report two types of errors: fatal and nonfatal. If the POST encounters a fatal error, it stops the system. The error code posted on the indicator corresponds to the defective operation. If the POST card encounters a nonfatal error, however, it notes the error and continues through the initialization routine to activate as many additional system resources as possible. When these types of errors are encountered, the POST card must be observed carefully, because the error code on its indicator must be coordinated with the timing of the error message or beep code produced by the BIOS routines.

Simple POST cards come with a set of light-emitting diodes (LEDs) on them that produce coded error signals when a problem is encountered. Other cards produce beep codes and seven-segment LED readouts of the error code. Figure 11-7 depicts a typical XT/AT-compatible POST card.

Figure 11-7: A Typical POST Card

Field-Replaceable Unit Troubleshooting

Field-Replaceable Units (FRUs) are the portions of the system that you can conveniently replace in the field. Typical microcomputer FRUs are depicted in Figure 11-8. FRU troubleshooting involves isolating a problem within one section of the system. A section consists of one device such as a keyboard, video display, video adapter card, I/O adapter card, system board, disk drive, printer, and so on. These are typically components that can simply be exchanged for a replacement on site and require no actual repair work.

```
┌─ TEST TIP ────────────────
│  Know which devices in a typical PC system
│  are FRU devices.
└────────────────────────────
```

ATX POWER SUPPLY

MONITOR

FLOPPY DISK DRIVE

CD-ROM DRIVE

FDD SIGNAL CABLE

MONITOR VIDEO CABLE

VIDEO CARD

CD-ROM SIGNAL CABLE

HDD SIGNAL CABLE

HARD DISK DRIVE

KEYBOARD

PRINTER

SYSTEM BOARD

PS/2 MOUSE

PRINTER CABLE

**Figure 11-8:
The Typical FRUs
of a Microcomputer
System**

known-good ones

Exchanging FRUs is the level of troubleshooting most often performed on PCs. Due to the relative low cost of computer components, it is normally not practical to troubleshoot failed components to the IC level. The cost of using a technician to diagnose the problem further, and repair it, can quickly exceed the cost of the new replacement unit.

> **Exchanging FRU components** — After a hardware error has been indicated, start troubleshooting the problem by exchanging components (cards, drives, etc.) with **known-good ones**. Turn off the power and exchange suspected or indicated devices from the system one at a time. Make sure to restore the power and retry the system after each exchange.

If a diagnostic tool indicates that multiple components have failed, use the one-at-time exchange method, starting with the first component indicated, to isolate the original source of the problem. Test the system between each component exchange and work backward through the exchanged components after the system has started to function again.

Always check cabling connections after plugging them in. Look for missed connections, bent pins, and so on. Also, check the routing of cables. Try to establish connections that do not place unnecessary strain on the cable. You should attempt to route cables away from major IC devices as much as possible. Some ICs, such as microprocessors, can become so hot that they may eventually damage cables. Avoid routing cables near cooling fans as well since they produce high levels of EMI that can be introduced into the signal cables as electrical noise.

Work backwards — After you have isolated the problem and the computer boots up and runs correctly, work backwards through the troubleshooting steps and reinstall any original adapters and other components removed during the troubleshooting process. Working backwards, one component at a time, through components that have been removed from the system enables you to make certain that only one failure occurred in the machine. If the system fails after installing a new card, check the card's default configuration settings against those of the devices already installed in the system.

SYMPTOMS AND TROUBLESHOOTING

The A+ Core Hardware objective 2.1 states that the test taker should be able to recognize common problems associated with each module and their symptoms, and identify steps to isolate and troubleshoot the problems. Given a problem situation, interpret the symptoms and infer the most likely cause.

Content may include the following:

- I/O ports and cables
- Serial
- Parallel
- USB ports
- IEEE-1394/Firewire
- Infrared
- SCSI
- Motherboards
- CMOS/ BIOS settings
- POST audible/visual error codes
- Peripherals
- Computer case
- Power supply
- Slot covers
- Front cover alignment
- Storage devices and cables
- FDD
- HDD
- CD/CDRW
- DVD/DVDRW
- Tape drive
- Removable storage
- Cooling systems

- Fans
- Heat sinks
- Liquid cooling
- Temperature sensors
- Processor/CPU
- Memory
- Display device
- Input devices
- Keyboard
- Mouse/pointer devices
- Touch screen
- Adapters
- Network Interface Card (NIC)
- Sound card
- Video card
- Modem
- USB
- Portable systems
- PCMCIA
- Batteries
- Docking stations/port replicators
- Portable unique storage

One of the primary responsibilities of every PC technician is to diagnose and troubleshoot computer problems. As this A+ objective points out, the technician should be able to identify common symptoms associated with computer components, and to use those symptoms to effectively troubleshoot and repair the problem. Numerous sources of problems and symptoms are discussed below, beginning with those that relate to the power supply.

Isolating Power Supply Problems

Typical symptoms associated with power-supply failures include:

- No indicator lights visible, with no disk drive action, and no display on the screen. Nothing works, and the system is dead.

- The ON/OFF indicator lights are visible, but there is no disk drive action and no display on the monitor screen. The system fan may or may not run.

- The system produces a continuous beep tone.

The power supply unit is one of the few components in the system that is connected to virtually every other component in the system. Therefore, it has the ability to affect all of the other components if it fails. Figure 11-9 illustrates the interconnections of the power supply unit with the other components in the system.

Figure 11-9: Power Supply Interconnections

Checking a Dead System

Special consideration must be taken when a system is inoperable. In a totally inoperable system, there are no symptoms to give clues where to begin the isolation process. In addition, it is impossible to use troubleshooting software or other system aids to help isolate the problem.

The following discussion is a standard method of troubleshooting dead microprocessor-based equipment. The first step in troubleshooting any dead system is to visually inspect the system. Check for unseated cards, loose cables, or foreign objects within the system unit.

When the system exhibits no signs of life — including the absence of lights — *the best place to start looking for the problem is at the power supply*. The operation of this unit affects virtually every part of the system. Also, the absence of any lights working usually indicates that no power is being supplied to the system by the power supply.

external connections

1. Begin by checking the **external connections** of the power supply. This is the first step in checking any electrical equipment that shows no signs of life.

2. Confirm that the power supply cord is plugged into a functioning outlet.

3. Check the position of the ON/OFF switch.

4. Examine the power cord for good connection at the rear of the unit.

5. Check the setting of the 110/220 switch setting on the outside of the power supply. The normal setting for equipment used in the United States is 110.

6. Check the power at the commercial receptacle using a voltmeter, or by plugging in a lamp (or other 110-volt device) into the outlet.

> **TEST TIP**
> Remember the first step of checking out electrical equipment that appears dead.

If power is reaching the power supply and nothing is happening, the most likely cause of a totally dead system is the power supply itself. However, be aware that in an ATX system, if the cable that connects the system board to the power switch has become loose, the power supply will appear dead. Use a voltmeter to check for the proper voltages at one of the system's option's power connectors. (All system voltages should be present at these connectors.) If any voltage is missing, check the power supply by substitution.

WARNING

Turn It Off First! — Before changing any board or connection, always turn the system off first. In an ATX-style system, you should also disconnect the power cable from the power supply. This is necessary because even with the power switch off, there are still some levels of voltages applied to the system board in these units.

Other Power Supply Problems

If the front panel lights are on and the power-supply fan is running, but no other system action is occurring, you should consider the power supply as one of the most likely sources of such a problem. The presence of the lights and the fan operation indicate that power is reaching the system and that at least some portion of the power supply is functional. This type of symptom results from the following two likely possibilities:

1. A portion of the power supply has failed, or is being overloaded. One or more of the basic voltages supplied by the power supply is missing while the others are still present.

2. A key component on the system board has failed, preventing it from processing, even though the system has power. A defective capacitor across the power input of the system board can completely prevent it from operating.

Adding and Removing Power Supplies

Figure 11-10 illustrates the steps involved in removing the power supply from a PC. To exchange the power supply, all of its connections to the system must be removed.

Figure 11-10: Removing a Power Supply

Hands-on Activity

Typical steps for removing a power supply:

1. Disconnect the exterior power connections from the system unit.
   a. Unplug the power cable from the commercial receptacle.
   b. Disconnect the monitor's power cable from the power supply.

2. Disconnect the interior power connections.
   a. Disconnect the power supply connections from the system board.
   b. Disconnect the power supply connector from the floppy-disk drive.

c. Disconnect the power supply connector from the hard-disk drive.

d. Disconnect the power supply connector from the CD-ROM/DVD drive (if present).

e. Disconnect the power supply connector to the front panel switches

3. Remove the power supply unit from the system.

a. Remove the four retaining screws that secure the power supply unit to the rear of the system unit. (Note: In some AT style cases, an additional pair of screws are used along the front edge of the power supply to secure it to the metal bracket it is mounted on.)

b. Store the screws properly.

c. Remove the power supply from the system unit by lifting it out.

These steps would be reversed for the installation of a power supply.

Power Supply Upgrade Considerations

One consideration that may not be apparent when system components are being upgraded is the power supply. The power supply unit in a computer comes with a given power rating (in watts). The voltage level for a given location in the world is fixed (i.e., 120 or 220 Vac) and the power required can be calculated by multiplying the voltage level by the maximum current rating (in amperes) of all the devices in the system.

In the field, it is difficult to accumulate the current values for all the devices in a system. Therefore, each time a new drive or device is added to the system, more current is required. For example, upgrading the processor can easily increase the power consumption in the system by more than 20 watts. A typical Pentium processor may require 65 watts of power to operate. Advanced Pentium processors have increased their power consumption to over 80 watts.

Likewise, replacing RAM with faster or bigger RAM devices tends to increase power consumption as well. Simply increasing the installed memory from 128 MB to 256 MB by adding an additional DIMM will almost double the power consumption of the system's memory (i.e., from 6 watts to 12).

Adding adapter cards to the system also significantly increases the amount of power the power supply must deliver to the system board. A typical adapter card may require 12 to 15 watts with good connections to the slot. A high-end video adapter used for games may consume up to 100 watts.

However, disk drive devices tend to consume more power than most other system devices, simply because they use motors to spin the disk or disc and to position the read/write mechanism. A typical hard-disk drive can require up to 20 or 30 watts.

As you can see from the previous paragraphs, it is relatively easy to consume hundreds of watts of power with a normal system. The typical power supply used with basic Pentium desktop systems is 300 watts. One-third of this value must be reserved simply for startup of the computer. During this time, the system will require more power than it does when it is running. For systems using the high-end video card mentioned earlier, the power supply might need to be capable of delivering 500 watts of power.

In any event, there are two ways to determine whether a system needs a power supply upgrade. The first is to approximate how much power each device will require and double that value to provide for operating safety and the startup surge. The second method involves purchasing all of the upgrade items and turning on the system to discover that it will not start.

TROUBLESHOOTING THE SYSTEM BOARD

Troubleshooting problems related to the system board can be difficult to solve because of the system board's relative complexity. So many system functions at least partially rely on the system board that certain symptoms can be masked by other symptoms. Observe the steps that lead to the failure and determine under what conditions the system failed. Were any unusual operations in progress? Note any error messages or beep codes. Refer to the documentation for the system board and peripheral units to check for configuration problems. Examine the CMOS setup entries for configuration problems. In Pentium systems, also check the advanced CMOS setup parameters to make certain that all the appropriate system board–enabling settings have been made.

Remember that the microprocessor, RAM modules, ROM BIOS, and CMOS battery are typically replaceable units on the system board. If enough of the system is running to perform tests on these units, you can replace them. If symptoms suggest that one or more of these devices may be defective, you can exchange them with a known-good unit of the same type.

System Board Symptoms

So much of the system's operation is based on the system board that a system board problem can have several different types of symptoms. Typical symptoms associated with system board hardware failures include:

- The On/Off indicator lights are visible, the display is visible on the monitor screen, but there is no disk drive action and no bootup.

- The On/Off indicator lights are visible and the hard drive spins up, but the system appears dead and there is no bootup.

- The system locks up during normal operation.

- The system produces a beep code with 1, 2, 3, 5, 7, or 9 beeps.

- The system produces a beep code of 1 long and 3 short beeps.

- The system will not hold date and time.

- An "8042 Gate A20 Error" message displays — Error getting into Protected mode.

- An "Invalid Switch Memory Failure" message displays.

- A "DMA Error" message displays — DMA Controller failed page register test.

- A "CMOS Battery Low" message displays, indicating failure of CMOS battery or CMOS checksum test.

- A "CMOS System Option Not Set" message displays, indicating failure of CMOS battery or CMOS checksum test.

- A "CMOS Checksum Failure" message displays, indicating CMOS battery low or CMOS checksum test failure.

- A 201 error code displays, indicating a RAM failure.

- A parity check error message displays, indicating a RAM error.

Typical symptoms associated with system board setup failures include:

- A "CMOS Inoperational" message displays, indicating failure of CMOS shutdown register.

- A "Display Switch Setting Not Proper" message displays — Failure to verify display type.

- A "CMOS Display Mismatch" message displays — Failure of display type verification.

- A "CMOS Memory Size Mismatch" message displays — System Configuration and Setup failure.

- A "CMOS Time & Date Not Set" message displays — System Configuration and Setup failure.

- An IBM-compatible error code displays, indicating that a configuration problem has occurred.

Typical symptoms associated with system board I/O failures include the following:

- Speaker doesn't work during operation. The rest of the system works, but no sounds are produced through the speaker.

- Keyboard does not function after being replaced with a known-good unit.

Most of the hardware problems that occur with PCs involve the system board. Because the system board is the center of virtually all the computer's operations, it is only natural that you must check it at some point in most troubleshooting efforts. The system board normally marks the end of any of the various troubleshooting schemes given for different system components. It occupies this position for two reasons. First, the system board supports most of the other system components, either directly or indirectly. Second, it is the system component that requires the most effort to replace and test.

Configuration Checks

Normally, the only time a configuration problem occurs is when the system is being set up for the first time, or when a new option is installed. The other condition that causes a configuration problem involves the system board's CMOS backup battery. If the battery fails, or has been changed, the contents of the CMOS setup will be lost. After replacing the battery, it is always necessary to run the CMOS Setup utility to reconfigure the system. The values stored in CMOS must accurately reflect the configuration of the system; otherwise, an error occurs. You can access these values for change by pressing a predetermined key combination during the bootup procedure.

> In Pentium-based systems, check the advanced CMOS configuration and enabling settings in the BIOS and Chipset Features screens. These settings, illustrated in Figure 11-11, usually include the disk drives, keyboard, and video options, as well as on-board ports and buses.

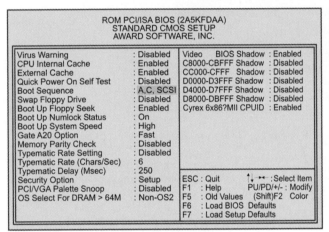

Figure 11-11: BIOS Enabling Settings

In addition, the user can turn on or off certain sections of the system's RAM for shadowing purposes and establish parity or non-parity memory operations. Incorrectly set BIOS-enabling parameters cause the corresponding hardware to fail. Therefore, check the enabling functions of the advanced CMOS settings as a part of every hardware configuration troubleshooting procedure.

The many configuration options available in a modern BIOS require the user to have a good deal of knowledge about the particular function being configured. Refer to the discussions of these advanced CMOS setup options in Chapter 2 — *Advanced System Boards*. In cases where there are serious configuration circumstances, don't forget that you normally have the option to select default configuration options through the CMOS Setup utility.

clean boot

single-step

> Typically, if the bootup process reaches the point where the system's CMOS configuration information is displayed onscreen, you can safely assume that no hardware configuration conflicts exist between the system's basic components. After this point in the bootup process, the system begins loading drivers for optional devices and additional memory. If errors occur after the CMOS screen has been displayed and before the bootup tone, you must **clean boot** the system and **single-step** through the remainder of the bootup sequence to locate the cause of the failure. These techniques are described in detail in Chapter 12 — *Operating System Troubleshooting*.

Hardware Checks

If the system's CMOS configuration setup appears to be correct and a system board hard-ware problem is suspected, you probably need to exchange the system board for a working unit. Because most of the system must be dismantled to exchange it, however, a few items are worth checking before doing so.

Check the system board for signs of physical problems, such as loose cables and devices. If nothing is apparently wrong, check the power-supply voltage levels on the system board. Check for +5 V and +12 V (DC) on the system board, as illustrated in Figure 11-12. If these voltages are missing, turn off the system, disconnect power to all disk drives, and swap the power-supply unit with a known-good one.

Figure 11-12: The System Board Voltage Check Location

RAM

The system board's memory is a very serviceable part of the system. RAM failures basically fall into two major categories and create two different types of failures:

- **Soft-memory errors** – Errors caused by infrequent and random glitches in the oper-ation of applications and the system. You can clear these events just by restarting the system.

- **Hard-memory errors** – These errors are caused by permanent physical failures that generate NMI errors in the system and require that the memory units be checked by substitution.

soft-memory errors

hard-memory errors

Observe the bootup RAM count to see that it is correct for the amount of physical RAM actu-ally installed in the system. If not, swap RAM devices around to see if the count changes. Use logical rotation of the RAM devices to locate the defective part. The burn-in tests in most di-agnostic packages can prove helpful in locating borderline RAM modules.

TEST TIP

Know what type of failures hard- and soft-memory errors are and how they affect the system.

You can swap the RAM modules out one-at-a-time to isolate defective modules. These modules are also swapped out when a system upgrade is being performed. Take care when swapping RAM into a system for troubleshooting purposes to make sure that the new RAM is the correct type of RAM for the system and that it meets the system's bus speed rating. Also, make sure that the replacement RAM is consistent with the installed RAM. Mixing RAM types and speeds can cause the system to lock up and produce hard memory errors.

Microprocessor

In the case of the microprocessor, the system may issue a slow, single beep, with no display or other I/O operation as a symptom. This indicates that an internal error has disabled a portion of the processor's internal circuitry (usually the internal cache). Internal problems also may allow the microprocessor to begin processing, but then cause it to fail as it attempts operations. Such a problem results in the system continuously counting RAM during the bootup process. It also may lock up while counting RAM. In either case, the only way to remedy the problem is to replace the microprocessor.

TEST TIP

Know the effects on the system of heat buildup and microprocessor fan failures.

If the system consistently locks up after being on for a few minutes, this is a good indication that the microprocessor's fan is not running or that some other heat buildup problem is occurring. You also should check the microprocessor if its fan has not been running, but the power is on. This situation may indicate that the microprocessor has been without adequate ventilation and has overheated. When this happens, you must replace the fan unit and the microprocessor. Check to make certain that the new fan works correctly; otherwise, a second microprocessor will be damaged.

corrosion

The fact that most microprocessors are mounted in sockets or slots brings up another point. These items should be pulled and reseated in their sockets or slots if they appear to be a possible cause of problems. Sockets and slots are convenient for repair and upgrade purposes, but they can also attract **corrosion** between the pins of the device, and those of the socket. Over time, the corrosion may become so bad that the electrical connection becomes too poor for the device to operate properly.

ROM

As with the microprocessor, a bad or damaged ROM BIOS will typically stop the system completely. When you encounter a dead system board, examine the BIOS chip(s) for physical damage. When these devices overheat, they usually crack or blow a large piece out of the top of the IC package. Another symptom of a damaged BIOS is indicated by the bootup sequence automatically moving into the CMOS configuration, but never returning to the bootup sequence. In any case, you must replace the defective BIOS with a version that matches the chipset used by the system.

In situations where new devices (microprocessors, RAM devices, hard drives, etc.) have been added to the system, there is always a chance that the original BIOS will not be able to support them. In these situations, the system may or may not function depending on which device has been installed and how its presence affects the system. To compensate for these possible problems, always check the web sites of the device and the system board manufacturers to obtain the latest BIOS upgrade and support information.

Problems with key system board components produce symptoms similar to those described for a bad power supply. Both the microprocessor and the ROM BIOS can be sources of such problems. You should check both by substitution when dead system symptoms are encountered but the power supply is good.

Cooling Systems

Microprocessors-based equipment is designed to provide certain performance levels under specified environmental conditions. One of the key design elements for microprocessor performance is operating temperature. With Pentium class microprocessors, PC systems are designed to maintain the operating temperature for the device in the range of 30^0 to 40^0 C.

To accomplish this, Pentium class computers employ a microprocessor temperature control system that operates as part of the system chipset. A temperature-sensing **thermocouple** device is embedded in the system board under the microprocessor socket (or in the microprocessor cartridge). The thermocouple senses the current temperature of the microprocessor and produces an analog voltage signal that is proportional to the temperature. A special **health controller** IC monitors this signal and supplies the microprocessor with a digital representation of the temperature measurement.

> **thermocouple**

> **health controller**

The microprocessor compares this reading to an ideal setting established in the CMOS configuration and sends a digital code to the health controller, which in turn generates an analog speed control signal that is applied to the microprocessor fan. This signal slows the fan down if the measured temperature is too low, and speeds it up if it's too hot.

The ideal operating temperature setting varies between microprocessor types and manufacturers. In addition, the location of the CMOS configuration setting varies between BIOS versions. Some CMOS setup utilities provide a separate Health screen while others integrate it into their Power Management screen. Many systems include an additional fan control circuit for use with an optional chassis (case) fan. In these cases, the system board features additional berg connectors for the chassis temperature sensor and fan control cable.

If temperature-related problems like those described in the previous section occur, you should access the CMOS Hardware Health configuration screen, like the one depicted in Figure 11-13, and check the fan speed and processor temperature readings. If they are outside the designated range, you may enter a different value for the temperature set point. If no fan speed measurement is shown, check to see if the fan is actually turning. If not, you should turn the system off as soon as possible, check the operation of the fan, and replace it before the microprocessor is damaged.

Other alternatives when dealing with thermal problems in a PC include installing an additional chassis fan to help move cooler air through the system unit, changing the microprocessor fan for one that runs faster over a given range of temperatures, and flashing the BIOS to provide different fan control parameters.

Figure 11-13: The CMOS Setup Health Screen

Also, check for missing slot covers that can disrupt air flow in the case, and route internal signal cables so that they do not block the flow of air through the case.

CMOS Batteries

┌─ **TEST TIP** ─────┐
│ Be aware that a defective
│ battery can cause the system
│ to continually lose track of
│ time.
└────────────────────┘

The second condition that causes a configuration problem involves the system board's CMOS backup battery. If a system refuses to maintain time and date information, the CMOS backup battery, or its recharging circuitry, is normally faulty. After the backup battery has been replaced, check the contacts of the battery holder for corrosion.

CHALLENGE #5

You receive a call from a customer who complains that his Windows system constantly loses the time and date information. What advice can you give this customer about his system?

If the battery fails or if it has been changed, the content of the CMOS configuration will be lost. After replacing the battery, it is always necessary to run the CMOS Setup utility to reconfigure the system.

Exchanging the System Board

If symptoms indicate that the system board is the source of problems and you have done the following:

- Used the CMOS Setup utility to check the system's configuration for accuracy (and possibly used default CMOS configuration options to start the system)

- Checked the BIOS version to verify that it supports the system's installed hardware components

- Examined the system board's FRU components for possible problem causes

Then, you must exchange the system board with a known good one. If possible, back up the contents of the system's hard drive to some other media before removing the system board. Also, record the CMOS configuration settings, along with the settings of any jumpers and switches, before exchanging the system board.

Exchange the system board with a known-good one. Reconnect all of the power-supply, disk drive, and front-panel connections to the system board. Reinstall the video card and any other adapter cards and try to reboot the system. Reconfigure the system board to operate with the installed peripherals. When the system boots up, reinstall any options removed from the system and replace the system unit's outer cover.

Troubleshooting Keyboard Problems

Most of the circuitry associated with the computer's keyboard is contained in the keyboard itself. However, some keyboard interface circuitry is located on the system board. Therefore, the steps required to isolate keyboard problems are usually confined to the keyboard, its connecting cable, and the system board.

This arrangement makes isolating keyboard problems relatively easy. Just check the keyboard and the system board. Figure 11-14 depicts the components associated with the keyboard.

KEYBOARD

SYSTEM
BOARD

**Figure 11-14:
Keyboard-Related
Components**

Keyboard Symptoms

Typical symptoms associated with keyboard failures include the following:

- No characters appear onscreen when entered from the keyboard.

- Some keys work, whereas others do not work.

- A "Keyboard Is Locked — Unlock It" error displays.

- A "Keyboard Error — Keyboard Test Failure" error displays.

- A "KB/Interface Error — Keyboard Test Failure" error displays.

- An error code of 6 short beeps is produced during bootup.

- Wrong characters display.

- An IBM-compatible 301 error code displays.

┌─ **TEST TIP** ─┐
Memorize the IBM-
compatible error codes.
└────────────────┘

Keyboard Configuration Checks

While keyboard configuration settings do not generally cause keyboard failures, you should be aware that several keyboard configuration settings are stored in CMOS that can affect the operation of the keyboard. In most systems, the CMOS setup information includes keyboard enabling, NumLock key condition at startup, typematic rate, and typematic delay. The typematic information applies to the keyboard's capability to repeat characters when the key is held down. The typematic rate determines how quickly characters are repeated, and the delay time defines the amount of time the key can be held before typematic action occurs. A typical typematic rate setting is 6 characters per second; the delay is normally set at 250 milliseconds.

Basic Keyboard Checks

One quick test to determine basic keyboard problems is to watch the keyboard's NumLock and ScrollLock lights during the bootup process. These lights should flash when the system attempts to initialize the keyboard. The system's POST routines may also return keyboard-related error messages and codes.

The keys of the keyboard can wear out over time. This may result in keys that don't make good contact (no character is produced when the key is pushed) or that remain in contact (stick) even when pressure is removed. A stuck key will produce an error message when the system detects it. However, the system has no way of detecting an open key. If you detect a stuck key, or keys, you can desolder and replace the individual key switches with a good key from a manufacturer or a similar keyboard. However, the amount of time spent repairing a keyboard quickly drives the cost of the repair beyond the cost of a new unit.

If the keyboard produces odd characters on the display in a Windows operating system environment, check the Windows keyboard settings in the Control Panel's Device Manager. If the keyboard is not installed, or is incorrect, install the correct keyboard type. Also, make certain that you have the correct language setting specified under the Control Panel's keyboard icon.

Keyboard Hardware Checks

If you suspect a hardware problem, you must first isolate the keyboard as the definite source of the problem (a fairly easy task). Because the keyboard is external to the system unit, detachable, and inexpensive, begin by exchanging the keyboard with a known-good keyboard.

If the new keyboard works correctly, return the system to full service and service the defective keyboard appropriately. Remove the back cover from the keyboard and check for the presence of a fuse in the +5 V (DC) supply and check it for continuity. Disconnecting or plugging in a keyboard with this type of fuse while power is on can cause it to fail. If the fuse is present, simply replace it with a fuse of the same type and rating.

If replacing the keyboard does not correct the problem, and no configuration or software reason is apparent, the next step is to troubleshoot the keyboard receiver section of the system board. On most modern system boards, this ultimately involves replacing the system board with another one. Refer to the system board removal and installation instructions in Chapter 2 — *Advanced System Boards* to carry out this task.

Troubleshooting Mouse Problems

Most of the problems with mice are related to a few items:

- Its port connection

- The mouse driver

- The trackball in a trackball mouse or a trackball unit

- The operation of the mouse buttons

In newer systems, the mouse is typically connected to the dedicated PS/2 mouse port on the back of the unit. Unfortunately, the PC industry forgot an old design problem that they eradicated long ago — they used the same type of connector for two different connections. The original IBM PCs used the same connector for monochrome and color video monitors – with sometimes disastrous consequences. In ATX systems, the keyboard and mouse have been given the same 6-pin mini-DIN connector and unfortunately they do not work interchangeably. While plugging the mouse into the keyboard connector should not cause any physical damage, it will cause problems with the operation of the system. These connections tend to be color-coded, so check to make sure the mouse is connected to the *green* connector.

Older mice used one of the PC's serial ports. These ports had to be properly configured for the serial mouse to work properly. Refer to the *Mouse Configuration Checks* section that follows for information about manually configuring a serial mouse.

The second reason for mouse failures was using the wrong driver for the mouse or its port. For ATX-compatible mice, installation and configuration has become a fairly routine process. Connect the mouse to the PS/2 mouse port and let the system auto-detect it and install the basic Windows mouse drivers. However, specialty mice — including USB connected mice, wireless mice, and infrared mice — along with other pointing devices require special drivers that must be supplied by the manufacturer and loaded from the disk or disc that accompanies the device.

When a trackball mouse is moved across the table, the trackball picks up dirt or lint, which can hinder the movement of the trackball, typically evident by the cursor periodically freezing and jumping onscreen. On most mice, you can remove the trackball from the mouse by a latching mechanism on its bottom. Twisting the latch counterclockwise enables you to remove the trackball. Then you can clean dirt out of the mouse.

```
┌─ TEST TIP ──────────────────────┐
│ Be aware of the condition that causes the cursor │
│ to jump and freeze on the display. │
└──────────────────────────────────┘
```

The other mechanical part of the mouse is its buttons. These can wear out under normal use. When they do, the mouse should simply be replaced. However, before doing so, make sure to check the properties of the mouse in the operating system to make sure that the button functions have not been altered. It would be a shame to throw away a perfectly good mouse because it had been set up for left-hand use in the operating system. Refer to the *Mouse Configuration Checks* section that follows for instructions on checking the mouse configuration settings in a Windows-based system.

Mouse Hardware Checks

For most systems, the hardware check for the mouse involves isolating it from its connection port. Simply replace the mouse to test its electronics. If the replacement mouse works, the original mouse is probably defective. If its electronics are not working properly, few options are available for actually servicing the mouse. It may need a cleaning, or a new trackball. However, the low cost of a typical mouse generally makes it a throwaway item if simple cleaning does not fix it.

If the new mouse does not work either, chances are very high that the mouse's electronics are working properly. In this case, the mouse driver or the port hardware must be the cause of the problem. If the driver is correct for the mouse, the port hardware and CMOS configuration must be checked.

The system board typically contains all of the port hardware electronics and support, so it must be replaced to restore the port/mouse operation at that port. However, if the system board mouse port is defective, another option is to install a mouse that uses a different type of port (e.g., use a USB mouse to replace a PS/2 mouse).

Mouse Configuration Checks

When a mouse does not work in a Windows system, restart it and move into Safe Mode by pressing the F5 function key while the "Starting Windows" message is displayed. This will start the operating system with the most basic mouse driver available. If the mouse does not operate in this mode, you must check the mouse hardware and the port that the mouse is connected to.

If the mouse works in Safe Mode, then the problem exists with the driver you are trying to use with it. It may be corrupt or it could be having a conflict with some other driver. To check the driver, consult the Device Manager entry under the Control Panel's System icon. If the Device Manager shows a conflict with the mouse, remove the driver and allow the system's PnP process to reinstall it. If the correct driver for the installed mouse is not available, you will need to install one from the manufacturer. This typically involves placing the manufacturer's driver disk or disc in the appropriate drive and load the driver using the Update Driver (requires disk from OEM) option on the Device Manager Mouse Properties page. If the OEM driver fails to operate the mouse in Windows, you should contact the mouse manufacturer for an updated Windows driver.

For serial mice, select the *Ports* option, click on the *COM x properties* option in the menu, and click on *Resources*. Make certain that the selected IRQ and address range match those of the port. Click on the *Mouse* entry in the Device Manager and double-click its driver to obtain the *Mouse Properties* page shown in Figure 11-15. Move to the *Resources* tab as illustrated and check the IRQ and base address settings for the mouse in Windows. Compare these settings to the actual configuration settings of the hardware. If they differ, change the IRQ or base address setting in Windows to match those of the installed hardware. Windows normally supports serial mice only on COM1 and COM2. If several serial devices are being used in the system, you might have to establish alternative IRQ settings for COM3 and COM4.

**Figure 11-15:
Mouse Properties**

In older systems, check the directory structure of the system for a Mouse directory. Also, check for AUTOEXEC.BAT and CONFIG.SYS files that may contain conflicting device drivers. Two common driver files may be present: the MOUSE.COM file called for in the AUTOEXEC.BAT file; and the MOUSE.SYS file referenced in the CONFIG.SYS file. If these files are present and have mouse lines that do not begin with a REM statement, they could be overriding the settings in the operating system. In particular, look for a DEVICE= command associated with the mouse.

CHALLENGE #6

When you upgrade your mouse to one of those new two-button wheel mice, you cannot get it to work. You return it to the distributor and exchange it for another one. It also does not work. When you try one from your co-worker's machine, it works fine. What should you conclude about the wheel mouse?

Troubleshooting Video

Figure 11-16 depicts the components associated with the video display. It may be most practical to think of the video information as starting out on the system board. In reality, the keyboard, one of the disk drives, or some other I/O device may be the actual originating point for the information. In any case, information intended for the video display monitor moves from the system board to the video adapter (usually through a video card installed in one of the system board's expansion slots). Finally, the information is applied to the monitor through the video signal cable.

Figure 11-16: Video-Related Components

Basically, there are two levels of troubleshooting that apply to video problems: configuration and hardware problems. As the figure indicates, in the case of hardware problems, the components involved include the video adapter card, the monitor, and, to a lesser degree, the system board. Common symptoms associated with display problems include the following:

- No display

- Wrong characters displayed onscreen

- Diagonal lines onscreen (no horizontal control)

- Display scrolls (no vertical control)

- An error code of 1 long and 6 short beeps is produced by the system

- A "Display Switch Setting Not Proper — Failure to verify display type" error displays

- A "CMOS Display Mismatch — Failure to verify display type" error displays

- An error code of 1 long and 2 short beeps is produced by the system (indicates a display adapter problem)

The following sections cover the digital portion of the video system. Troubleshooting the actual monitor is discussed immediately following the video adapter troubleshooting sections. Only experienced technicians should participate in troubleshooting internal monitor problems because of the very high voltages present there.

Video Hardware Checks

The video monitor should come on fairly quickly after power has been applied to it. With newer monitors, the monitor is normally only asleep and is awakened through the video adapter card when power is applied to the system. When the system is shut down, the monitor's circuitry senses that no signal is present from the video adapter card and slips into a monitoring mode as long as its power switch is left in the On position.

If the monitor does not wake up early in the system's startup process and present a display, you should assume that there is some type of hardware problem—the bootup action and operating system have not been introduced to the system before the single beep tone is produced. However, video problems that occur after the single beep are more likely to be related to operating system configuration settings.

If you suspect a video display hardware problem, the first task is to check the monitor's On/Off switch to see that it is in the On position. Also, check the monitor's power cord to see it is plugged either into the power supply's monitor outlet, or into an active 120 V (AC) commercial outlet. Also check the monitor's intensity and contrast controls to make certain that they are not turned down.

The next step is to determine which of the video-related components is involved. On some monitors, you can do this by just removing the video signal cable from the adapter card. If a raster appears onscreen with the signal cable removed, the problem is probably a system problem, and the monitor is good. If the monitor is an EPA-certified Energy Star–compliant monitor, this test may not work. Monitors that possess this power-saving feature revert to a low-power mode when they do not receive a signal change for a given period of time.

Check the components associated with the video display monitor. Start by disconnecting the monitor's signal cable from the video controller card at the rear of the system unit, and its power cord from the power supply connector or the 120 V (AC) outlet. Then, exchange the monitor for a known-good one of the same type (i.e., VGA for VGA).

If there is still a video problem, exchange the video controller card with a known-good one of the same type. Remove the system unit's outer cover. Disconnect the monitor's signal cable from the video controller card. Swap the video controller card with a known-good one of the same type. Reconnect the monitor's signal cable to the new video adapter and reboot the system.

Other symptoms that point to the video adapter card include a shaky video display and a high-pitched squeal from the monitor or system unit. If the system still does not perform properly after swapping the video adapter card, the source of the problem may be in the system board.

Windows Video Checks

If you can read the contents of the display through the startup process, but then cannot see it after the system boots up, you have an operating system-related video problem. Because Windows operating systems are graphically based programs, navigation can be nearly impossible if video problems are severe enough to prevent you from seeing the display.

If the Windows video problem prevents you from being able to work with the display, restart the system, press the F8 function key when the "Starting Windows" message appears, and select the *Safe Mode* option. This should load Windows with the standard 640 x 480 x 16–color VGA driver (the most fundamental driver available for VGA monitors), and should furnish a starting point for installing the correct driver for the monitor being used.

After you have gained access to a display that you can use, the next step in isolating Windows video problems involves checking the installed video drivers. You can access the Windows video information through the Control Panel's *System* icon. Inside the *System Properties* page, access the Device Manager and select the *Display Adapters* entry from the list. Double-click the monitor icon that appears as a branch.

The adapter's *Properties* page should pop up onscreen. From this page, the *Driver* tab reveals the driver file in use. If the video driver listed is not correct, reload the correct driver. Selecting the *Resources* tab displays the video adapter's register address ranges and the video memory address range, as described in Figure 11-17. You can manipulate these settings manually by clicking on the *Set Configuration Manually* button. You also can obtain information about the monitor through the *System* icon.

Figure 11-17: Video Adapter's Resources

You can also gain access to the Windows video information by double-clicking the Control Panel's *Display* icon. At the top of the *Display* page, there are a series of file folder tabs. Of particular interest is the *Settings* tab. Under this tab, the *Change Display Type* button provides access to both the adapter type and monitor type settings.

In the Adapter type window, information about the adapter's manufacturer, version number, and current driver files is given. Clicking on the *Change* button beside this window brings a listing of available drivers to select from. You also can use the *Have Disk* button with an OEM disk to install video drivers not included in the list. You also can alter the manner in which the list displays by choosing the *Show Compatible Devices* or the *Show All Devices* options.

In the *Monitor type* window, there is an option list for both manufacturers and models. You also can use this function with the *Have Disk* button to load OEM settings for the monitor.

If the video problem disappears when lower settings are selected, but reappears when a higher resolution setting is used, refer to the *Color Palette* box under the Control Panel's *Display option/Settings* tab, and try the minimum color settings. If the problem goes away, contact the Microsoft Download Service (MSDL) or the adapter card maker for a compatible video driver. If the video problem persists, reinstall Windows. If the video is distorted or rolling, try an alternative video driver from the list.

CHALLENGE #7

One of your customers has called you to his facility to repair a desktop computer that doesn't show anything on the display. When you start it up, you hear the system fans come on and the hard drive spin up. You also hear the system beeps when they are supposed to occur. The monitor power light is on. What piece of equipment should you retrieve from your repair kit for these symptoms?

Working with Monitors

All the circuitry discussed so far is part of the computer or its video adapter unit. The circuitry inside the monitor is responsible for accepting, amplifying, and routing the video and synchronizing information to the CRT's electron guns and the deflection coils.

Figure 11-18 shows the components located inside a typical CRT color monitor. Of particular interest is the high-voltage anode that connects the tube to the high-voltage sections of the signal-processing board. This is a very dangerous connection that is not to be touched.

WARNING

Lethal voltage levels — You must exercise great caution when opening or working inside the monitor. The voltage levels present during operation are lethal. Electrical potentials as high as 25,000 V are present inside the unit when it is operating.

CRT NECK

POWER SUPPLY

SIGNAL PROCESSING BOARD HIGH-VOLTAGE SECTION

DEFLECTION YOKE ASSEMBLY

HIGH-VOLTAGE ANODE

POWER SUPPLY BOARD

CRT TUBE

**Figure 11-18:
The Circuitry Inside a
Typical CRT**

Operation of a monitor with the cover removed poses a shock hazard from the power supply. Therefore, anyone unfamiliar with the safety precautions associated with high-voltage equipment should not attempt servicing.

The high voltage levels do not necessarily disappear because the power to the monitor is turned off. Like television sets, monitors have circuitry capable of storing high-voltage potentials long after power has been removed. Always discharge the anode of the picture tube to the receiver chassis before handling the CRT tube. Due to the high voltage levels, you should never wear antistatic grounding straps when working inside the monitor.

An additional hazard associated with handling CRTs is that the tube is fragile. Take extra care to prevent the neck of the tube from striking any surface. Never lift the tube by the neck —especially when removing or replacing a CRT tube in the chassis. If the picture tube's envelope is cracked or ruptured, the inrush of air will cause a high-velocity **implosion**, and the glass will fly in all directions. Therefore, you should always wear protective goggles when handling picture tubes.

implosion

X-rays

Color monitors produce a relatively high level of **X-rays**. The CRT tube is designed to limit X-rays at its specified operating voltage. If a replacement CRT tube is being installed, make certain to replace it with one of the same type, and with suffix numbers that are the same. You can obtain this information from the chassis schematic diagram inside the monitor's housing.

Diagnosing Monitor Problems

Examine the power cord to see that it is plugged in and check to see that the monitor's power switch is in the On position. Verify the external settings to see that the brightness and contrast settings are not turned off. If the problem produces a blank display, disconnect the monitor's signal cable from its video adapter card. If a raster appears, a video card problem is indicated. The final step in isolating the video monitor as the cause of the problem is to exchange it for a known-good one. If the replacement works, the problem must be located in the monitor.

Some display problems can actually be caused by incorrectly set front panel display settings. The monitor's front panel controls (either analog or digital) establish parameters for brightness, contrast, screen size and position, and focus. Typical problems associated with these controls include fuzzy characters, poor or missing colors, and incomplete displays.

Actually, there can be several causes of fuzzy characters on the display. The first step in troubleshooting this problem is to reset the display resolution to standard VGA values. If the fuzzy characters remain, check the intensity and contrast controls to see if they are out of adjustment. Finally, you might need to remove built-up electromagnetic fields from the screen through a process called **degaussing**. This can be done using a commercial degaussing coil. However, newer monitors have built-in degaussing circuits that can be engaged through their front panel controls. These monitors normally perform a degauss operation each time they are turned on. However, sometimes the user might need to perform this operation.

degaussing

The front panel controls can also be used to adjust the Red/Green/Blue color mixture for the display. If the monitor is showing poor colors, or only one color, examine the color settings using the front panel controls. If these settings are responsive to change, the problem exists in either the video adapter or the signal cable (broken or bad pin or conductor), or the monitor's color circuitry is deteriorating.

Troubleshooting FDDs

Typical symptoms associated with floppy-disk drive (FDD) failures during bootup include the following:

- FDD errors are encountered during bootup.

- The front-panel indicator lights are visible, and the display is present on the monitor screen, but there is no disk drive action and no bootup.

- An IBM-compatible 6xx (i.e., 601) error code displays.

- An FDD Controller Error message displays, indicating a failure to verify the FDD setup by the System Configuration file.

- The FDD activity light stays on constantly, indicating that the FDD signal cable is reversed.

Additional FDD error messages commonly encountered during normal system operation include:

- Disk Drive Read Error messages

- Disk Drive Write Error messages

- Disk Drive Seek Error messages

- No Boot Record Found message, indicating that the system files in the disk's boot sector are missing or have become corrupt

- The system stops working while reading a disk, indicating that the contents of the disk have become contaminated

- The drive displays the same directory listing for every disk inserted in the drive, indicating that the FDD's disk-change detector or signal line is not functional

A number of things can cause improper floppy-disk drive operation or failure. These items include the use of unformatted disks, incorrectly inserted disks, damaged disks, erased disks, loose cables, drive failure, adapter failure, system board failure, or a bad or loose power connector. Basically three levels of troubleshooting apply to FDD problems: the configuration, the software, and the hardware. No Windows-level troubleshooting applies to floppy-disk drives. Figure 11-19 depicts the components associated with the operation of the floppy-disk drive.

TEST TIP

Memorize the IBM error codes for different types of hardware devices.

**Figure 11-19:
FDD-Related
Components**

Basic FDD Checks

If there is a problem booting the system, insert the bootable disk into the new A: drive and turn on the system. If the system does not boot up to the floppy, examine the advanced CMOS Setup to check the system's boot order. It may be set so that the FDD is never examined during the bootup sequence.

If the system still will not boot up with the CMOS setting established to check the FDD first in the boot seek order, check the disk drive cables for proper connection at both ends. In many systems, the pin-1 designation is difficult to see. Reversing the signal cable causes the FDD activity light to stay on continuously. The reversed signal cable will also erase the master boot record from the disk, making it non-bootable. Because this is a real possibility, you should always use an expendable backup copy of the boot disk for troubleshooting FDD problems.

If there is a problem reading or writing to a particular disk, try the floppy disk in a different computer to see whether it works in that machine. If not, there is most likely a problem with the format of the disk or the files on the disk. In the case of writing to the disk, you could be dealing with a write-protected disk, but the system will normally inform you of this when you attempt to write to it. However, if the other computer can read and write to the disk, you must troubleshoot the floppy drive hardware.

> **NOTE**
>
> If the system has a second floppy-disk drive, turn off the computer and exchange its connection to the floppy-disk drive's signal cable so that it becomes the A: drive. Try to reboot the system using this other floppy-disk drive as the A: drive.

Hardware troubleshooting for floppy-disk drives primarily involves exchanging the FDD unit for another one that is working. If necessary, exchange the signal cable with a known-good one. Finally, the only other option with most PC-compatible systems is to exchange the system board with a known-good one.

Troubleshooting HDDs

Typical symptoms associated with hard-disk drive failures include:

- The computer does not boot up when turned on.

- The computer boots up to a system disk in the A: drive, but not to the hard drive, indicating that the system files on the HDD are missing or have become corrupt.

- No motor sounds are produced by the HDD while the computer is running. (In desktop units, the HDD should always run when power is applied to the system—this also applies to portables because of their advanced power-saving features.)

- An IBM-compatible 17xx error code is produced on the monitor screen.

- An HDD Controller Failure message displays, indicating a failure to verify hard disk setup by system configuration file error.

- A C: or D: Fixed Disk Drive Error message displays, indicating a hard disk CMOS setup failure.

- An Invalid Media Type message displays, indicating that the controller cannot find a recognizable track/sector pattern on the drive.

- A No Boot Record Found, a Non-System Disk or Disk Error, or an Invalid System Disk message displays, indicating that the system boot files are not located in the root directory of the drive.

- The video display is active, but the HDD's activity light remains on and no bootup occurs, indicating that the HDD's CMOS configuration information is incorrect.

- An Out of Disk Space message displays, indicating that the amount of space on the disk is insufficient to carry out the desired operation.

- A Missing Operating System, a Hard Drive Boot Failure, or an Invalid Drive or Drive Specification message displays, indicating that the disk's master boot record is missing or has become corrupt.

- A No ROM BASICS — System Halted, or ROM BASIC Interpreter Not Found message displays, followed by the system stopping, indicating that no master boot record was found in the system. This message is produced only by PCs, XTs, and some clones.

- A Current Drive No Longer Valid message displays, indicating that the HDD's CMOS configuration information is incorrect or has become corrupt.

TEST TIP

Be able to describe the conditions indicated by the Invalid Drive or Drive Specification, Missing Operating System, and Hard Drive Boot Failure error messages.

Figure 11-20 depicts the relationship between the hard-disk drive and the rest of the system. It also illustrates the control and signal paths through the system.

Figure 11-20: Hard-Disk Drive-Related Components

Hard Drive Systems—Hard drive systems are very much like floppy drive systems in structure—they have a **controller**, one or more signal cables, a **power cable**, and a drive unit. The troubleshooting procedure typically moves from setup and configuration, to formatting, and, finally, to the hardware component isolation process.

The system board is a logical extension of the components that make up the HDD system. However, unless the HDD controller is integrated into it, the system board is typically the least likely cause of HDD problems.

Notice that as with a floppy drive, there is no Windows component to check with a hard-disk drive. Windows relies on the system's BIOS and PnP routines to handle HDD operations.

HDD Configuration Checks

While booting up the system, *observe the BIOS's IIDD type information* displayed on the monitor. Note the type of HDD(s) that the BIOS believes is installed in the system. The values stored in this CMOS configuration must accurately reflect the actual HDD(s) format installed in the system; otherwise, an error occurs. Possible error messages associated with HDD configuration problems include the **Drive Mismatch Error** message and the **Invalid Media Type** message.

Check the drive to make sure that it is properly **terminated**. Every drive type (both IDE and SCSI) requires a termination block somewhere in the interface. On IDE drives, check the Master/Slave jumper setting to make sure that it is set properly for the drive's logical position in the system.

TEST TIP
Know that there can be only one master drive selection on each IDE channel.

If you have more than one device attached to a single interface cable, make sure that they are of the same type (i.e., all are EIDE devices or all are ATA100 devices). Mixing device types creates a situation where the system cannot provide the different types of control information each device needs. The drives are incompatible and you may not be able to access either device.

TEST TIP
Be aware that mixing drive types on a single signal cable can disable both devices.

If the drive is a SCSI drive, check to see that its ID has been set correctly and that the SCSI chain has been terminated correctly. Either of these errors will result in the system not being able to see the drive. Also, check the CMOS Setup utility to make sure that SCSI support has been enabled, along with large SCSI drive support.

TEST TIP
Know that in newer systems, SCSI drive support and large drive support are both enabled in the BIOS.

CHALLENGE #8

You are updating a working computer for your boss. The upgrade consists of adding a new microprocessor to the system, along with additional RAM and a second EIDE hard drive. When you restart the system, the system will not boot to the original hard drive. As a matter of fact, neither drive works. What should you check first?

Basic HDD Checks

startup disk

boot the system

If you suspect that a hard-disk drive problem exists, the first task is to determine how extensive the problem is. Place an appropriate **startup disk** in the A: drive and try to clean **boot the system**. Depending on the operating system installed, this may be a simple boot disk, an Emergency Start disk, or a setup/Distribution CD. These items are discussed in detail in Chapter 12 — *Operating System Troubleshooting*.

After you get the system started and can look around inside, the next objective is to determine whether the hard-disk drive problem is a simple boot problem, or something more serious. The quickest way to determine this is to attempt to access the primary partition of the drive. This can be accomplished by executing a directory (DIR) command to access the C: drive. If the system can see the content of the drive, the boot files have simply been lost or corrupted, but the architecture of the disk is intact.

DOS DIR command

Modify the **DOS DIR command** with an /AH or /AS switch (i.e., DIR C: /AH or DIR C: /AS) to look in the root directory for the system files. You will need to be familiar with the different files used by the different operating systems. These are covered in detail in the operating system chapters. If any of these files are missing, you will typically receive some type of **Disk Boot Failure** message onscreen. The *No (or Missing) ROM BASIC Interpreter* message presented in the symptoms list may also be produced by this condition.

Disk Boot Failure

In Windows 9x/Me systems, if the clean boot disk has a copy of the FDISK program on it, you can attempt to restore the drive's master boot record (including its partition information) by typing the following at the A: prompt:

FDISK /MBR

       FDISK /MBR

Emergency Startup disk

Provided that the hard disk can be accessed with the DIR command, type and enter the following command at the command prompt (with the **Emergency Startup disk** still in the A: drive):

SYS C:

       SYS C:

┌─ **TEST TIP** ─────────┐
│ Know how and when to use the │
│ **FDISK /MBR** and **SYS C:** │
│ commands. │
└──────────────────────┘

This command copies the IO.SYS, MSDOS.SYS, and COMMAND.COM system files from the boot disk to the hard-disk drive. Turn off the system, remove the boot disk from the floppy drive, and try to re-boot the system from the hard drive.

Three conditions will produce a Bad or Missing Command Interpreter (i.e., COMMAND.COM) error message. These conditions include the following:

1. The command interpreter file cannot be found on the hard drive (because it has become corrupted), and no bootable disk is present in drive A:.

2. The command interpreter file is not located in the hard drive's root directory. This message is likely when installing a new hard drive, or a new operating system on a new drive.

3. If the user inadvertently erases the command interpreter file from the root directory of the hard drive.

If the system cannot see the drive after booting to the floppy-disk drive, an "Invalid Drive" message or an "Invalid Drive Specification" message should be returned in response to any attempt to access the drive. Under these conditions, you must examine the complete HDD system. In Windows 9x systems, use the FDISK utility to partition the drive. Next, use the FORMAT /S command to make the disk bootable. Any data that was on the drive will be lost in the formatting process, but it was already gone because the system could not see the drive.

The process for checking the hard drive on a Windows NT, Windows 2000, or Windows XP computer is similar to the one for checking a Windows 9x–based system. The file management systems in these versions can be slightly different than the one used in Windows 9x. Therefore, different tools, or tools that use different names, must be employed to perform the different checks listed. These tools and techniques for using them are described in Chapter 12 – *Operating System Troubleshooting*

HDD Hardware Checks

If you cannot access the hard-disk drive and its configuration settings are correct, you must troubleshoot the hardware components associated with the hard-disk drive. These components include the drive, its signal cable, and the HDC (on the system board).

Check the HDD signal cable for proper connection at both ends. Exchange the signal cable for a known-good one.

Verify the *Master/Slave* jumper settings to make sure that they are set correctly, as illustrated in Figure 11-21. Check to see whether the system might be using the **Cable Select** option, also depicted in the figure. This setting requires a special **CSEL** signal cable designed to determine the master/slave arrangements for multiple IDE drives. Likewise, check the ID configuration settings and terminator installations for SCSI drives. Exchange the HDD power connector with another one from the power supply to make certain that it is not a source of problems.

> **Cable Select**
>
> **CSEL**

Figure 11-21: IDE Master/Slave Settings

The next logical step may seem to be to replace the hard drive unit. However, it is quite possible that the hard drive may not have any real damage. It may just have lost track of where it was, and cannot find its starting point. In this case, the most attractive option is to reformat the hard disk. This action gives the hard drive a new starting point to work from. Unfortunately, it also destroys anything that you had stored on the disk.

If the reformatting procedure is not successful, or the system still doesn't boot from the hard drive, you must replace the hard-disk drive unit with a working one. Disconnect the signal, control, and power cords from the HDD unit, and exchange the HDD with a known-good one of the same type. Reconnect the signal, control, and power cords to the replacement HDD unit.

Troubleshooting CD-ROM and DVD Drives

configuration level

The troubleshooting steps for CD-ROM and DVD drives are nearly identical to those of an HDD system. The connections and data paths are very similar. Basically, three levels of troubleshooting apply to CD-ROM problems. These are the **configuration level**, the operating system level, and the hardware level. Figure 11-22 shows the parts, and drivers, associated with CD-ROMs.

Figure 11-22: Components and Drivers Associated with CD-ROMs

Basic Checks

In most systems, the CD-ROM and DVD drives share a controller or host adapter with the hard-disk drive. Therefore, you should verify their *Master/Slave* jumper settings to make sure that they are set correctly. Normally, the CD-ROM or DVD drive should be set up as the Master on the Secondary IDE channel. In this manner, each drive has its own communications channel and does not need to share. If three or four IDE devices are installed in the system, you must determine which devices can share the channels most effectively.

Windows Checks

In the Windows operating systems, you can access the contents of the CD-ROM or DVD through the CD icon in the desktop's *My Computer* applet. The CD-ROM drive's information is contained in the Control Panel's *System* icon. The properties of the installed CD-ROM drive are located under the **Settings** tab. Figure 11-23 shows a typical set of CD-ROM specifications in Windows 9x.

Settings

**Figure 11-23:
CD-ROM Drive
Properties**

If the correct drivers are not installed, load the correct driver, or contact the CD-ROM manufacturer for the correct Windows driver. Check the system for old AUTOEXEC.BAT and CONFIG.SYS files that could contain commands concerning older CD-ROM drives. These commands will overrule the Windows CD-ROM configurations and can create problems. Make a copy of the AUTOEXEC.BAT or CONFIG.SYS file for backup purposes and remove the MSCDEX lines from the original file.

CD-ROM/DVD Hardware Checks

If the configuration and software checks do not remedy the CD-ROM or DVD problem, you must troubleshoot the drive's related hardware. Basically, the hardware consists of the drive unit, the signal cable, the power cord, the media, and the controller or host adapter. The controller may be mounted on a host adapter card or in a Pentium system on the system board. For external drives, you must also check the plug-in power adapter.

In most systems, the CD-ROM and DVD drives share a controller or host adapter with the hard-disk drive. Therefore, if the hard drive is working and the CD-ROM drive is not, the likelihood that the problem is in the CD-ROM or DVD drive unit is very high.

Before entering the system unit, check for simple user problems:

- Is there a CD or DVD in the drive?
- Is the label side of the disk facing upward?
- Is the disk a CD-ROM or some other type of CD?

If the drive is inoperable and there is a CD or DVD locked inside, you should insert a straightened paper clip into the tray-release access hole that's usually located beside the ejection button. This will release the spring-loaded tray and pop out the disc.

If no simple reasons for the problem are apparent, exchange the CD-ROM drive with a known-good one of the same type. For external units, simply disconnect the drive from the power and signal cables, and then substitute the new drive for it. With internal units, you must remove the system unit's outer cover and disconnect the signal and power cables from the drive. Remove the screws that secure the drive unit in the drive bay. Install the replacement unit, start the system, and attempt to access the CD-ROM drive.

If the new drive does not work, check the drive's signal cable for proper connection at both ends. Exchange the signal cable for a known-good one.

If the controller is built into the system board and becomes defective, it is still possible to install an IDE host adapter card in an expansion slot and use it without replacing the system board. This action can also be taken to upgrade older IDE systems to EIDE systems so that they can use additional IDE devices. The onboard IDE controller may need to be disabled before the system will address the new host adapter version.

Writable Drive Problems

An additional set of problems come into play when a write or rewrite function is added to the CD-ROM or DVD drive. These problems are concentrated in three basic areas:

- The quality of the drive's controller circuitry
- The makeup and version of the drive's Read/Write application interface software
- Compatibility with the operating system's multimedia support systems

The quality of the drive is actually based on the controller IC that oversees the operation of the drive. In less expensive drives, the BIOS extension on the drive may not support all of the R/W functions needed to coordinate with the application package or the operating system's drivers. While all newer CD-ROM and DVD drives are ATAPI compatible, they may not have an effective method of controlling **buffer underrun** errors. These errors occur when the system transfers data to the drive faster than the drive can buffer and write it to the disc. The ATAPI compatibility of the chipset ensures that the CD-ROM and DVD read functions work fine, but the non-standard writing part of the drive may not produce satisfactory results.

buffer underrun

There are a few techniques that can be used to minimize buffer underruns. These include placing the CD-ROM or DVD writer on an IDE channel of its own. This keeps the drive from competing with other drives for the channel's available bandwidth. Also, conducting the write operation on the same drive as the read operation and using reduced write speed options in the R/W application software can minimize data flow problems.

In addition, the R/W application software for the drive may not be compatible with the operating system version in use, or with the controller chip on the drive. Likewise, the operating system's multimedia enhancement drivers (**DirectX** in Windows operating systems) may not be compatible with the controller, or the R/W application. It is best to consult the operating system's hardware and software compatibility lists before buying and installing a CDRW or DVDRW drive in a system. This typically means using a more expensive drive, but for now you do seem to get what you pay for when it comes to rewritable drives.

DirectX

If the drive has already been purchased and installed, check the drive's documentation for suggestions and check the drive manufacturer's web site for newer R/W applications and driver versions. You may also be able to locate a flash program for the drive's BIOS to upgrade it so that it provides better support for the write function.

In the end, there are some CD-ROM and DVD R/W applications that are incompatible with different drive BIOS versions or DirectX versions. Check all of the parties involved to find a collection of components that are all compatible with each other.

Troubleshooting Port Problems

The PC compatible computer features a wide array of peripheral connection ports. Figure 11-24 illustrates the components involved in the operation of the legacy serial, parallel, and game ports. Failures in these ports tend to end with poor or no operation of the peripheral. Generally, there are only four possible causes for a problem with a device connected to an I/O port:

- The port is defective.

- The software is not configured properly for the port.

- The connecting signal cable is bad.

- The attached device is not functional.

Figure 11-24: Components Associated with I/O Ports

Port Problem Symptoms

Typical symptoms associated with serial, parallel, or game port failures include:

- A 199, 432, or 90x IBM-compatible error code displays on the monitor (printer port).

- The on-line light is on, but no characters are printed by the printer.

- An 110x IBM-compatible error code displays on the monitor (serial port).

- "Device not found" error message displays, or you have an unreliable connection.

- Input device does not work on the game port.

As you can see from the symptoms list, I/O ports do not tend to generate many error messages onscreen.

Basic Port Checks

With newer Pentium systems, you must check the advanced CMOS setup to determine whether the port in question has been enabled, and, if so, whether it has been configured correctly.

Check the PC board that contains the I/O port circuitry (and its user guide) for configuration information. This normally involves LPT, COM, and IRQ settings. Occasionally, you must set up hexadecimal addressing for the port addresses; however, this is becoming rare as PnP systems improve.

For example, a modern parallel port must be enabled and set to the proper protocol type to operate advanced peripherals. For typical printer operations, the setting can normally be set to SPP mode. However, devices that use the port in a bi-directional manner need to be set to EPP or ECP mode for proper operation. In both cases, the protocol must be set properly for both the port and the device to carry out communications.

If serial or parallel port problems are occurring, the CMOS configuration window is the first place to look. Read the port assignments in the boot-up window. If the system has not detected the presence of the port hardware at this stage, none of the more advanced levels will find it either. If values for any of the physical ports installed in the system do not appear in this window, check for improper port configuration.

Because the system has not loaded an operating system at the time the configuration window appears, the operating system cannot be a source of port problems at this time. If all configuration settings for the ports appear to be correct, assume that a hardware problem exists.

Basic Parallel Ports Check

Run a **software diagnostic** package to narrow the possible problem causes. This is not normally a problem because port failures do not generally affect the main components of the system. Software diagnostic packages normally require you to place a loopback test plug in the parallel port connector to run tests on the port. The loopback plugs simulate a printer device by redirecting output signals from the port into port input pins. Figure 11-25 describes the signal-rerouting scheme used in a parallel port loopback plug.

**Figure 11-25:
Parallel Port Loopback
Connections**

You can use a live printer with the port for testing purposes. However, this action elevates the possibility that the printer might inject a problem into the troubleshooting process. If there is a *printer switch box* between the computer and the printer, remove the print-sharing equipment, connect the computer directly to the printer, and try to print directly to the device.

┌─ **TEST TIP** ─────────────────
Be aware that print-sharing equipment (such as switch boxes) can be responsible for parallel port/printer problems and should be removed as part of port testing.
└───────────────────────────

Figure 11-26: Serial Port Loopback Connections

Basic Serial Ports

As with parallel ports, diagnostic packages typically ask you to place a loopback test plug in the serial port connector to run tests on the port. Use the diagnostic program to determine whether any IRQ or addressing conflicts exist between the serial port and other installed options. The serial loopback plug is physically connected differently from a parallel loopback plug so that it can simulate the operation of a serial device. Figure 11-26 describes the signal-rerouting scheme used in a serial port loopback plug.

You can use a live serial device with the port for testing purposes but, as with the printer, this elevates the possibility that non-port problems can be injected into the troubleshooting process.

Windows Printer Checks

You can reach the I/O port functions in Windows (9x, 2000, XP) through two avenues. You can access port information through the desktop's Start/Settings buttons. You also can reach this information through the My Computer icon on the desktop. Printer port information can be viewed through the *Printers* icon; serial port information is accessed through the System/Device Manager entries under the *Control Panel* icon.

Windows Parallel Ports

Check to determine whether the Print option from the application's File menu is unavailable (gray). If so, check the My Computer/Printers window for correct parallel port settings. Make certain that the correct printer driver is selected for the printer being used. If no printer (or the wrong printer type) is selected, use the Add Printer Wizard to install and set up the desired printer.

The system's printer configuration information is also available through the *Device Manager* tab under the *System* icon in the Control Panel. Check this location for printer port setting information. Also, check the definition of the printer under the Control Panel's *Printer* icon.

Troubleshooters

Print Troubleshooter

The Windows operating systems come with embedded tools called **Troubleshooters,** one of which is designed to help solve printing problems. To use the Printing Troubleshooter, access the Windows *Help* system through the Start menu, as illustrated in Figure 11-27, and navigate to the **Print Troubleshooter** (or Printing Troubleshooter in Windows XP). The Troubleshooter asks a series of questions about the printing setup. After you have answered all of its questions, the Troubleshooter returns a list of recommendations for fixing the problem.

Figure 11-27: Print Troubleshooter

If the conclusions of the Troubleshooter do not clear up the problem, try printing a document to a file. This enables you to separate the printing software from the port hardware.

Continue troubleshooting the port by checking the printer driver to ensure that it is the correct driver and version number. Click on the *Printer* icon and select the *Properties* entry from the menu. Click on the *Details* tab to view the driver's name. Click on the **About** entry under the **Device Options** tab to verify the driver's version number.

Click on the printer port in question (under the *Printer* icon) to open the *Print Manager* screen. Check the Print Manager for errors that have occurred and that might be holding up the printing of jobs that follow it. If an error is hanging up the print function, highlight the offending job and remove it from the print spool by clicking on the *Delete Document* entry of the Document menu.

Windows 9x Serial Ports

Information on the system's serial ports is contained in their properties pages under the **Device Manager**. The *COM port Properties* page contains three tabs. The **Resources** tab displays port address ranges and IRQ assignments. The **Driver** tab displays the names of the installed device drivers and their locations. The **Port Settings** tab, shown in Figure 11-28, contains speed and character frame information for the serial ports. The *Advanced* button under Port Settings enables you to adjust the transmit and receive buffer speeds for better operation.

Check under the Device Manager for correct serial port settings.

Figure 11-28: Port Settings Entry

Hands-on Activity

1. Click on the *Port Settings* option to see the setup for the ports. Most serial printers use settings of 9600 Baud, No Parity, 8 Bits, 1 Stop Bit, and Hardware Handshaking (Xon-Xoff).

2. Click on the *Resources* button to determine the IRQ setup for the port.

3. Check the user's manual to document the correct settings for the device using the port in question.

USB Port Checks

Because nearly any type of peripheral device can be added to the PC through the USB port, the range of symptoms associated with USB devices can include all the symptoms listed for peripheral devices in this chapter. Therefore, problems associated with USB ports can be addressed in three general areas:

- The USB hardware device
- The USB controller
- The USB drivers

Figure 11-29: The USB Controller Properties Page

The first step in troubleshooting USB problems is to check the CMOS setup screens to make sure that the USB function is enabled there. If the USB function is enabled in BIOS, check in the Windows Control Panel/System/Device Manager to make certain that the USB controller appears there. In Windows 2000, the USB controller should be listed under the *Universal Serial Bus Controllers* entry, or in the *Human Interface Devices* entry (using the default *Devices by Type* setting).

If the controller does not appear in Device Manager, or a yellow warning icon appears next to the controller, the system's BIOS may be outdated. Contact the BIOS manufacturer for an updated copy of the BIOS.

If the controller is present in the Device Manager, right-click the *USB controller* entry and click on the *Properties* tab. If there are any problems, a message appears in the *Device status* window, shown in Figure 11-29, describing any problems and suggesting what action to take.

If the BIOS and controller settings appear to be correct, the next items to check are the USB port drivers. These ports have a separate entry in the Device Manager that you can access by clicking on the *Universal Serial Bus Controllers* option, right-clicking the *USB Root Hub* entry, and then clicking on the *Properties* tab.

If a USB device does not install itself automatically, you may have conflicting drivers loaded for that device and you may need to remove them.

> **Authority Needed** — To use the Windows 2000 Device Manager utility to trouble-shoot USB problems, you must be logged on as an administrator, or as a member of the Administrators group.

Hands-on Activity

Removing Potentially Conflicting USB Drivers

1. Disconnect any USB devices connected to the system and start the system in Safe Mode.

2. Under Windows 2000, you are asked about which operating system to use. Use the up- and down-arrow keys to highlight Windows 2000 Professional or Windows 2000 Server, and then press *ENTER*.

   If alert messages appear, read each alert and then click on the *OK* button to close it.

3. Open the Device Manager, click on the USB device, and then click on the *Remove* option.

   Your particular USB device may be listed under the Universal Serial Bus Controller, Other Devices, Unknown Devices, or a particular device category (such as the Modem entry if the device is a USB modem).

4. Click on the *Start* menu, select the *Shut Down* option followed by the *Restart* entry, and then click on the *OK* button.

5. Connect the USB device directly to the USB port on your computer. If the system does not auto-detect the device, you must install the drivers manually. You may need to obtain drivers from the device manufacturer to perform this installation.

Troubleshooting Tape Drives

Because the fundamentals of recording on tape are so similar to those used with magnetic disks, the troubleshooting process is also very similar. The basic components associated with the tape drive include the tape drive, the signal cable, the power connection, the controller, and the tape drive's operating software. The tape itself can be a source of several problems. Common points to check with the tape include:

- Is the tape formatted correctly for use with the drive in question?

- Is the tape inserted securely in the drive?

- Is the tape write-protected?

- Is the tape broken or off the reel in the cartridge?

As cartridge tapes are pulled back and forth, their mylar base can become stretched over time. This action can cause the tape's format to fail before the tape actually wears out. To remedy this, you should retention the tape periodically using the software's retention utility. Cartridge tapes are typically good for about 150 hours of operation. If the number of tape errors begins to increase dramatically before this time, try reformatting the tape to restore its integrity. After the 150-hour point, just replace the tape.

If the tape is physically okay and properly formatted, the next item to check is the tape drive software. Check the software setup and configuration settings to make sure they are correct for any hardware settings. Refer to the tape drive's documentation for a list of system requirements, and check the system to make sure they are being met.

If any configuration jumpers or switches are present on the controller, verify that they are set correctly for the installation. Also, run a diagnostic program to check for resource conflicts that may be preventing the drive from operating (such as IRQ and base memory addressing).

The software provided with most tape drives includes some error-messaging capabilities. Observe the system and note any tape-related error messages it produces. Consult the drive's documentation for error-message definitions and corrective suggestions. Check for error logs that the software may keep. You can view these logs to determine what errors have been occurring in the system.

Because many tape drives are used in networked and multiuser environments, another problem occurs when you are not properly logged in, or enabled to work with files being backed up or restored. In these situations, the operating system may not allow the tape drive to access secured files, or any files, because the correct clearances have not been met. Consult the network administrator for proper password and security clearances.

If you have Read/Write problems with the drive, begin by cleaning its R/W heads. Consult the user's guide for cleaning instructions, or use the process described in the *Preventive Maintenance* chapter for manual cleaning of floppy and tape drive R/W heads. The R/W heads should be cleaned after about 20 backups or restores. Also, try to use a different tape to see whether it works. Make certain that the tape is properly formatted for operation. It should also be a clean tape, if possible, to avoid exposing any critical information to potential corruption. If cleaning does not restore the drive to proper operation, continue by checking the drive's power and signal cables for good connection and proper orientation.

CHALLENGE #9

You have installed a new sound card in your desktop computer. When you attempt to perform your weekly backup to tape, the sound card fails. When you reboot the system, the sound card begins working again. What type of troubleshooting steps should you employ?

Troubleshooting Modems

A section on troubleshooting modems has to be subdivided into two segments:

- internal modems
- external modems

An internal modem is checked out in the same basic sequence as any other I/O card. First, check the modem's hardware and software configuration, check the system for conflicts, and check for correct drivers. Improper software setup is the most common cause of modems not working when they are first installed. Inspect any cabling connections to see that they are correct and functioning properly, and test the modem's hardware by substitution. If an external modem is being checked, it must be treated as an external peripheral, with the serial port being treated as a separate I/O port. Figure 11-30 shows the components associated with internal and external modems.

Figure 11-30: Internal and External Modem Components

Modem Problem Symptoms

Typical symptoms associated with modem failures include:

- No response from the modem
- Modem does not dial out
- Modem does not connect after number has been dialed
- Modem does not transmit after making connection with a remote unit
- Cannot get modem installed properly for operation
- Garbled messages are transmitted
- Cannot terminate a communication session
- Cannot transfer files

COM Port Conflicts

As stated earlier, every COM port on a PC requires an IRQ line in order to signal the processor for attention. In most PC systems, two COM ports share the same IRQ line. The IRQ4 line works for COM1 and COM3, and the IRQ3 line works for COM2 and COM4. This is common in PC compatibles. The technician must make sure that two devices are not set up to use the same IRQ channel. If more than one device is connected to the same IRQ line, a conflict occurs, because it is not likely that the interrupt handler software can service both devices.

Therefore, the first step to take when installing a modem is to check the system to see how its interrupts and COM ports are allocated. You can alleviate this particular interrupt conflict by using a bus mouse rather than a serial mouse, thus freeing up a COM port.

To install a non-PnP device on a specific COM port (e.g., COM2), you must first disable that port in the system's CMOS settings in order to avoid a device conflict. If not, the system may try to allocate that resource to some other device, since it has no way of knowing that the non-PNP device requires it.

Windows Modem Checks

In Windows, you can find the modem configuration information in the Control Panel under the *Modems* icon. There are two tabs that appear on the *Modem Properties* page — *General* and *Diagnostics*. The *Properties* button on the *General* tab provides port and maximum-speed settings. The *Diagnostics* tab's dialog box, shown in Figure 11-31, provides access to the modem's driver and additional information. The PnP feature reads the modem card and returns its information to the screen, as demonstrated in the figure.

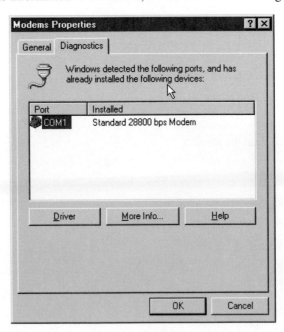

Figure 11-31: The Diagnostics Tab of the Modem Properties Dialog Box

Clicking on the *Properties* button in the *Modem Properties* page will produce the *Standard Modem Properties* page. This page contains two or more tabs that apply to the port associated with the selected modem. The *Connection* tab provides character-framing information and Call Preferences information, as illustrated in Figure 11-32. Recall that character-framing information includes items such as the number of data bits to be included in a character frame as well as the number and type of Start and Parity bits to be used. Clicking on the *Advanced* button will provide error and flow-control settings, as well as modulation type.

Figure 11-32: The Connection Tab of the Standard Modem Properties Dialog Box

The Windows program contains an application called **HyperTerminal** that can be used to control the operation of the system's modem with **TelNet services**. HyperTerminal is capable of operating with several different modem configurations. This flexibility enables it to conduct transfers with a wide variety of other computer systems on the Internet, such as UNIX and LINUX, without worrying about operating system differences.

Using HyperTerminal with TelNet to access other locations is much quicker than browsing web sites with a graphical browser. The *HyperTerminal New Connection* window, shown in Figure 11-33, provides the options for configuring the communications settings. This program can be accessed through the *Start/Programs/Accessories/Communications* path in Windows 98.

Figure 11-33: HyperTerminal

Windows also provides fundamental troubleshooting information for wide area networking through its system of *Help* screens. Just select *Help* from the Control Panel's toolbar, and click on the topic that you are troubleshooting.

Communication Software

All modems require software to control the communication session. This software is typically included with the purchase of the modem and must be configured to operate in the system the modem will be used in. To communicate with other computers, some information about how the communication will proceed must be agreed on. In particular, it is necessary to match the protocol of the remote unit, as well as its parity, character framing, and baud rate settings. In the case of online services, the information comes with the introductory package the user receives when joining the service.

Hayes-compatible command set

At the fundamental instruction level, most modem software employs a set of commands known as the **Hayes-compatible command set**. This set of commands is named for the Hayes Microcomputer Products company that first defined them.

In the Hayes command structure, the operation of the modem shifts back and forth between a Command mode and a Communications mode. In the Command mode, the modem exchanges commands and status information with the host system's microprocessor. In Communications mode, the modem facilitates sending and receiving data between the local system and a remote system. A short guard period between Communications mode and Command mode allows the system to switch smoothly without interrupting a data transmission.

The AT Command Set

The Hayes command set is based on a group of instructions that begin with a pair of attention characters followed by command words. Because the attention characters are an integral part of every Hayes command, the command set is often referred to as the **AT command set**.

AT command set

AT commands are entered at the command line using an AT*Xn* format. The *Xn* nomenclature identifies the type of command being given (*X*) and the particular function to be used (*n*). Except for ATA, ATDn, and ATZn commands, the AT sequence can be followed by any number of commands. The ATA command forces the modem to immediately pick up the phone line (even if it does not ring). The Dn commands are dialing instructions, and the Zn commands reset the modem by loading new default initialization information into it. Table 11-2 provides a summary of the Hayes-compatible AT command set.

Table 11-2: AT Command Set Summary

COMMAND		FUNCTION
A/		Re-execute command.
A		Go off-hook and attempt to answer a call.
B0		Select V.22 connection at 1200 bps.
B1	*	Select Bell 212A connection at 1200 bps.
C1	*	Return OK message.
Dn		Dial modifier (see Dial Modifier).
E0		Turn off command echo.
E1		Turn on command echo.
F0		Select auto-detect mode (equivalent to N1).
F1	*	Select V.21 of Bell 103.
F2		Reserved.
F3		Select V.23 line modulation.
F4		Select V.22 or Bell 212A 1200 bps line speed.
F5		Select V.22bis 7200 line modulation.
F6		Select V.32bis or V.32 4800 line modulation.
F7		Select V.32bis 7200 line modulation.
F8		Select V.32bis or V.32 9600 modulation.
F9		Select V.32bis 12000 line modulation.
F10		Select V.32bis 14400 line modulation.
H0		Initiate a hang-up sequence.
H1		If on-hook, go off-hook and enter command mode.
I0		Report product code.
I1		Report computed checksum.
I2		Report OK.
I3		Report firmware revision, model, and interface type.
I4		Report response.
I5		Report the country code parameter.
I6		Report modem data pump model and code revision.
L0		Set low speaker volume.
L1		Set low speaker volume.
L2	*	Set medium speaker volume.
L3		Set high speaker volume.
M0		Turn off speaker.
M1	*	Turn speaker on during handshaking, and turn speaker off while receiving carrier.
M2		Turn speaker on during handshaking and while receiving carrie.r
M3		Turn speaker off during dialing and receiving carrier, and turn speaker on during answering.
N0		Turn off Automode detection.
N1	*	Turn on Automode detection.
O0		Go online.
O1		Go online and initiate a retrain sequence.
P		Force pulse dialing.
Q0	*	Allow result codes to PC.
Q1		Inhibit result codes to PC.
Sn		Select S-Register as default.
Sn?		Return the value of S-Register n.
=v		Set default S-Register to value v.
?		Return the value of default S-Register.
T		Force DTMF dialing.
V0		Report short form (terse) result codes.
V1	*	Report long form (verbose) result codes.
W0	*	Report PC speed in EC mode.
W1		Report line speed, EC protocol, and PC speed.
W2		Report modem speed in EC mode.
X0		Report basic progress result codes, OK, CONNECT, RING, NO CARRIER (also for busy, If enabled, and dial tone not detected), NO ANSWER, and ERROR.
X1		Report basic call progress result codes and connection speeds such as OK, CONNECT, RING, NO CARRIER (also for busy, if enabled, and dial tone not detected), NO ANSWER, CONNECT XXXX, and ERROR.
X2		Report basic call progress result codes and connection speeds such as OK, CONNECT, RING, NO CARRIER (also for busy, if enabled, and dial tone not detected), NO ANSWER, CONNECT XXXX, and ERROR.
X3		Report basic call progress result codes and connection rate such as OK, CONNECT, RING, NO CARRIER, NO ANSWER, CONNECT XXXX, BUSY, and ERROR.

* Default

Table 11-3: AT Command Result Codes

After a command has been entered at the command line, the modem attempts to execute the command and then returns a result code to the screen. Table 11-3 describes the command result codes.

RESULT	CODE	DESCRIPTION
0	OK	The OK code is returned by the modem to acknowledge execution of a command line.
1	CONNECT	The modem sends this result code when line speed is 300 bps.
2	RING	The modem sends this result code when incoming ringing is detected on the line.
3	NO CARRIER	The carrier is not detected within the time limit, or the carrier is lost.
4	ERROR	The modem could not process the command line (entry error).
5	CONNECT 1200	The modem detected a carrier at 1200 bps.
6	NO DIAL TONE	The modem could not detect a dial tone when dialing.
7	BUSY	The modem detected a busy signal.
8	NO ANSWER	The modem never detected silence (@ command only).
9	CONNECT 0600	The modem sends this result code when line speed is 7200 bps.
10	CONNECT 2400	The modem detected a carrier at 2400 bps.
11	CONNECT 4800	Connection is established at 4800 bps.
12	CONNECT 9600	Connection is established at 9600 bps.
13	CONNECT 7200	The modem sends this result code when the line speed is 7200 bps.
14	CONNECT 12000	Connection is established at 12000 bps.
15	CONNECT 14400	Connection is established at 14400 bps.
17	CONNECT 38400	Connection is established at 38400 bps.
18	CONNECT 57600	Connection is established at 57600 bps.
22	CONNECT 75TX/1200RX	The modem sends this result code when establishing a V.23 Originate.
23	CONNECT 1200TX/75RX	The modem sends this result code when establishing a V.23 answer.
24	DELAYED	The modem returns this result code when a call fails to connect and is considered delayed.
32	BLACKLISTED	The modem returns this result code when a call fails to connect and is considered blacklisted.
40	CARRIER 300	The carrier is detected at 300 bps.
44	CARRIER 1200/75	The modem sends this result code when V.23 backward channel carrier is detected.
45	CARRIER 75/1200	The modem sends this result code when V.23 forward channel carrier is detected.
46	CARRIER 1200	The carrier is detected at 1200 bps.
47	CARRIER 2400	The carrier is detected at 2400 bps.
48	CARRIER 4800	The modem sends this result code when either the high or low channel carrier in V.22bis modem has been detected.
49	CARRIER 7200	The carrier is detected at 7200 bps.
50	CARRIER 9600	The carrier is detected at 9600 bps.
51	CARRIER 12000	The carrier is detected at 12000 bps.
52	CARRIER 14400	The carrier is detected at 14400 bps.
66	COMPRESSION: CLASS 5	MNP Class 5 is active CLASS 5.
67	COMPRESSION: V.42bis	COMPRESSION: V.42bis is active V.42bis.
69	COMPRESSION: NONE	No data compression signals NONE.
70	PROTOCOL: NONE	No error correction is enabled.
77	PROTOCOL: LAPM	V.42 LAP-M error correction is enabled.
80	PROTOCOL: ALT	MNP Class 4 error correction is enabled.

Using the AT Command Set

Run All Tests

ATZ

OK code

Many of the software diagnostic packages available include a utility for testing modems. If such a program is available, run the equivalent of its **Run All Tests** entry to test the modem. If all of the configuration settings are correct, attempt to run the modem's command line–based communications package to test the modem's operation. At the command line, type **ATZ** to reset the modem and enter the Command mode using the Hayes-compatible command set. You should receive a 0, or OK response, if the command was processed.

If no result code is returned to the screen, check the modem's configuration and setup again for conflicts. Also, check the speed setting of the communication software to make sure it is compatible with that of the modem. On the other hand, a returned **OK code** indicates that the modem and the computer are communicating properly.

Other AT-compatible commands can be used to check the modem at the DOS level. The **ATL2** command sets the modem's output volume to medium, to make sure that it is not set too low to be heard. If the modem dials, but cannot connect to a remote station, check the modem's speed and DTR settings. Change the DTR setting by entering **AT&Dn**. When:

> n = 0 the modem ignores the DTR line
>
> n = 1 the modem goes to async command state when DTR goes off
>
> n = 2 DTR off; switches modem to off-hook and back to Command mode
>
> n = 3 DTR switching off initializes modem

ATL2

AT&Dn

If the modem connects, but cannot communicate, check the character framing parameter of the receiving modem, and set the local modem to match. Also, match the terminal emulation of the local unit to that of the remote unit. ANSI terminal emulation is the most common. Finally, match the file transfer protocol to the other modem.

During the data transfer, both modems monitor the signal level of the carrier to prevent the transfer of false data due to signal deterioration. If the carrier signal strength drops below some predetermined **threshold level**, or is lost for a given length of time, one or both modems will initiate automatic disconnect procedures.

threshold level

Use the **ATDT*70** command to disable call waiting if the transmission is frequently garbled. The +++ command should interrupt any activity the modem is engaged in, and bring it to the Command mode.

ATDT*70

Modem Hardware Checks

Most serial ports and modems can perform self-tests on their circuitry. Modems have the capability to perform three different kinds of self-diagnostic tests:

- The local digital loopback test

- The local analog loopback test

- The remote digital loopback test

In a **local digital loopback test**, data is looped through the registers of the port's UART. When testing the RS-232 port itself, a device called a **loopback plug** (or **wrap-plug**) channels the output data directly back into the received data input, and only the port is tested.

local digital
loopback test

loopback plug

wrap-plug

Many modems can extend this test by looping the data through the local modem, and back to the computer (the **local analog loopback test**). Some modems even possess the ability to loopback data to a remote computer through its modem (**remote digital loopback test**). In this manner, the entire transmit and receive path can be validated, including the communication line (i.e., the telephone line). One of the most overlooked causes of transmission problems is the telephone line itself. A noisy line can easily cause garbled data to be output from the modem. Figure 11-34 illustrates port, analog, and digital loopback tests.

local analog
loopback test

remote digital
loopback test

LOCAL DIGITAL LOOPBACK TEST

LOCAL ANALOG LOOPBACK TEST

SERIAL PORT LOOPBACK TEST PLUG

DATA

TxD

RxD

SERIAL PORT

TxD

RxD

SERIAL PORT

LOCAL MODEM

REMOTE MODEM

PHONE LINE

LOCAL MODEM

TxD

RxD

SERIAL PORT

REMOTE DIGITAL LOOPBACK TEST

**Figure 11-34:
Loopback Tests**

**Local Digital
Loopback Test with
Self Tests**

**communications
software**

If transmission errors occur frequently, you should use the various loopback tests to locate the source of the problem. Begin by running the remote digital loopback test. If the test runs successfully, the problem is likely to be located in the remote computer.

If the test fails, run the **Local Digital Loopback Test with Self Tests**. If the test results are positive, the problem may be located in the local computer. On the other hand, you should run the local analog loopback test if the local digital test fails.

If the local analog test fails, the problem is located in the local modem. If the local analog test is successful, and problems are occurring, you should run the local analog test on the remote computer. The outcome of this test should pinpoint the problem to the remote computer or the remote modem.

If the modem is an internal unit, you can test its hardware by exchanging it with a known-good unit. If the telephone line operates correctly with a normal handset, only the modem, its configuration, or the **communications software** can be causes of problems. If the modem's software and configuration settings appear correct and problems are occurring, the modem hardware is experiencing a problem and it will be necessary to exchange the modem card for a known-good one.

> With an external modem, you can use the front panel lights as diagnostic tools to monitor its operation. You can monitor the progress of a call, and its handling, along with any errors that may occur.

Figure 11-35 depicts the front panel lights of a typical external modem.

**Figure 11-35:
Modem Front Panel
Indicators**

FRONT PANEL LIGHTS:

MR - MODEM READY
HS - HIGH SPEED
AA - AUTO ANSWERING
CD - DATA CARRIER DETECT

OH - OFF-HOOK
SD - SEND DATA
RD - RECEIVE DATA
TR - TERMINAL READY

The **Modem Ready (MR)**, **Terminal Ready (TR)**, and **Auto Answer (AA)** lights are preparatory lights that indicate that the modem is plugged in, powered on, ready to run, and prepared to answer an incoming call. The MR light becomes active when power is applied to the modem and the modem is ready to operate. The TR light becomes active when the host computer's communication software and the modem contact each other. The AA light just indicates that the Auto Answer function has been turned on.

The **Off-Hook (OH)**, **Ring Indicator (RI)**, and **Carrier Detect (CD)** lights indicate the modem's on-line condition. The OH light indicates that the modem has connected to the phone line. This action can occur when the modem is receiving a call, or when it is commanded to place a call. The RI light becomes active when the modem detects an incoming **ring signal**. The CD light activates when the modem detects a carrier signal from a remote modem. As long as this light is on, the modem can send and receive data from the remote unit. If the CD light does not activate with a known-good modem, a problem with the data communication equipment exists.

The final three lights indicate the status of a call in progress. The **Send Data (SD)** light flickers when the modem transmits data to the remote unit, and the **Received Data** light flickers when the modem receives data from the remote unit. The **High Speed (HS)** light becomes active when the modem is conducting transfers at its highest possible rate. If an external modem does not operate at its highest rated potential, check the specification for the UART on the adapter card to make certain that it is capable of operating at that speed.

Modem Ready (MR)
Terminal Ready (TR)
Auto Answer (AA)

Off-Hook (OH)
Ring Indicator (RI)
Carrier Detect (CD)
ring signal

Send Data (SD)
Received Data
High Speed (HS)

Troubleshooting Sound Cards

Some very basic components are involved in the audio output of most computer systems: a **sound card**, some **speakers**, the **audio-related software**, and the **host computer system**. Several software diagnostic packages enable you to test sound card operation. Most sound cards perform two separate functions. The first is to **play** sound files; the second is to **record** them. You might need to troubleshoot problems for either function.

sound card
speakers
audio-related software
host computer system
play
record

Sound Card Configuration Checks

If sound problems are occurring in the multimedia system, two of the first things to check are the hardware and audio software configuration settings. Refer to the sound card manufacturer's documentation for proper hardware settings. These items usually include checking the card's jumper settings for IRQ and I/O address settings. However, with more plug-and-play cards in the market, software configuration of IRQ and I/O addressing is becoming more common.

In the past, sound cards have been notorious for interrupt conflict problems with other devices. Because these conflicts typically exist between peripheral devices, they may not appear during bootup. If the sound card operates correctly except when a printing operation is in progress, for example, an IRQ conflict probably exists between the sound card and the printer port. Similar symptoms would be produced for tape backup operations if the tape drive and the sound card were configured to use the same IRQ channel. Use a software diagnostic program to check the system for interrupt conflicts.

Checking the system for resource conflicts in Windows is relatively easy. Access the Control Panel and select the *System* icon. From this point, click on the *Device Manager* and select the *Sound, video, and game controller* option. If the system detects any conflicts, it places an exclamation point within a circle on the selected option.

From the Device Manager, choose the proper sound card driver from the list and move into its *Resource* window. The page's main window displays all the resources the driver is using for the card. The Conflicting devices list window provides information about any conflicting resource that the system has detected in conjunction with the sound card.

If the Windows PnP function is operating properly, you should be able to remove the driver from the system, reboot the computer, and allow the operating system to re-detect the sound card and assign new resources to it.

Check to verify that the multimedia icon is installed in the Control Panel, and available through the *Start/Programs/Accessories* path. Also check the Control Panel's Device Manager to see that the correct audio driver is installed, and that its settings match those called for by the sound card manufacturer. If the drivers are missing, or wrong, add them to the system through the Control Panel's Add/Remove Hardware wizard.

If the driver is not installed, or is incorrect, add the correct driver from the available drivers list. If the correct driver is not available, reinstall it from the card's OEM disk, or obtain it from the card's manufacturer.

Sound Card Hardware Checks

Figure 11-36 depicts the system's sound card–related components. Provided that the sound card's configuration is properly set, and the software configuration matches it, the sound card and speakers will need to be checked out if problems exist. Most of these checks are very simple. They include checking to see that the speakers are plugged into the speaker port. It is not uncommon for the speakers to be mistakenly plugged into the card's MIC (microphone) port. Likewise, if the sound card does not record sound, make certain that the microphone is installed in the proper jack (not the speaker jack), and that it is turned on. Check the amount of disk space on the drive to ensure that there is enough to hold the file being produced.

MICROPHONE

MICROPHONE
JACK

SOUND
CARD

HARD-DISK
DRIVE

SPEAKER
JACK

HDD
SIGNAL
CABLE

EXTERNAL
SPEAKERS

SYSTEM BOARD

**Figure 11-36: Sound
Card—Related
Components**

In the case of stereo speaker systems, it is possible to place the speakers on the wrong sides. This will produce a problem when you try to adjust the balance between them. Increasing the volume on the right speaker will instead increase the output of the left speaker. The obvious cure for this problem is to physically switch the positions of the speakers.

If the system does not produce sound, troubleshoot the audio output portion of the system. Do the speakers require an external power supply? If so, is it connected, and are the speakers turned on? If the speakers use batteries for their power source, check them to see that they are installed and good. Check the speakers' volume setting to make certain it is not turned down.

┌─ **TEST TIP** ─────────┐
│ Know how to correct a balance │
│ problem that occurs with │
│ add-on stereo speakers. │
└────────────────────┘

NETWORK REPAIR

Begin troubleshooting a general network problem by determining what has changed since it was running last. If the installation is new, it will need to be inspected as a setup problem. Check to determine whether any new hardware or software has been added to the system. Has any of the cabling been changed? Have any new protocols been added? Has a network adapter been replaced or moved? If any of these events has occurred, begin by checking them specifically.

Network Troubleshooting Basics

If the problem does not appear in, or is not related to, the stand-alone operation of the unit, it will be necessary to check the portions of the system that are specific to the network. These elements include the network adapter card, the network-specific portions of the operating system, and the **network drop cabling**. Figure 11-37 depicts the network-specific portions of a computer system.

network drop cabling

**Figure 11-37:
Network-Related
Components**

Be aware that in a network environment, no unit really functions alone. Unlike working on a stand-alone unit, the steps performed on a network computer may affect the operation of other units on the network.

For example, disconnecting a unit from a network that uses coaxial cable creates an unterminated condition in the network. This condition can cause several different types of problems:

- Data moving through the network can be lost.
- A general slowdown of data movement across the network can occur due to reduced bandwidth.
- Nodes may not be able to "see," or connect to, each other.

─ **TEST TIP** ─

Be aware of the effects that a missing terminator or bad cable/connector can have on an Ethernet network.

If a unit must be removed from the network, it is a good practice to place a terminator in the empty connector where the unit was attached. This should allow the other units to function without the problems associated with an open connection. Care must be taken to ensure that the proper value of terminating resistor is used. Substituting a terminator from an obsolete ArcNet network into an Ethernet system may create as many problems as the open connection would have, and the problems may be harder to track down. Systems that use concentrators have fewer connection problems when a unit needs to be removed for servicing.

Even if the unit does not need to be removed from the network, diagnostic efforts and tests run across the network can use a lot of the network's bandwidth. This reduced bandwidth causes the operation of all the units on the network to slow down. This is due simply to the added usage of the network.

Because performing diagnostic work on the network can affect so many users, it is good practice to involve the network administrator in any such work being performed. This person can run interference for any work to be performed that could disable the network or cause users to lose data.

LAN Configuration Checks

As with any peripheral device, the LAN card's configuration must be correct for the software that is driving the peripheral, and for the adapter card it is communicating through. An improperly configured network adapter card can prevent the system from gaining access to the network. Many newer network cards possess plug-and-play capabilities. With other non-PnP network cards, such as most ISA NIC cards, it is necessary to configure the card through hardware jumpers, or through logical configuration switches in BIOS Extension EPROM.

Security Access Problems

One of the major concerns in most network environments is data security. Since all of the data around the network is potentially available to anyone attached to the net, all LAN administration software employs different levels of security. Passwords are typically used at all software levels to lock people out of hardware systems, as well as out of programs and data files.

Log-on passwords and **scripts** are designed to keep unauthorized personnel from accessing the system, or its contents. Additional passwords may be used to provide access to some parts of the system, and not others (e.g., lower-level accounting personnel may be allowed access to accounts receivable and payable sections of the business management software package, but not allowed into the payroll section). A series of passwords may be used to deny access to this area.

> **Log-on passwords**
>
> **scripts**

In other LAN management packages, the **network administrator** is normally responsible for establishing user **access and privileges** to programs and data through the operating system's security subsystem. These settings can be established to completely provide access to everything, deny access to certain information, or to allow limited **access rights** to specific resources. An example of limited rights would be the ability to read data from a file, but not to manipulate it (write, delete, print, or move it) in any way.

> **network administrator**
>
> **access and privileges**
>
> **access rights**

The reason for discussing security at this point is because established security settings can prevent the technician from using any, or all, of the system's resources. In addition, having limited access to programs can give applications the appearance of being defective. Because of this, you, the service technician, must work with the network administrator when checking a networked machine. The administrator can provide the access, and the security relief, needed to repair the system. The administrator can also keep you away from data that may not be any of your business.

Refer to Chapter 12—*Operating System Troubleshooting*, which covers the Operating System Technologies module for in-depth network software troubleshooting information.

LAN Hardware Checks

Check the activity light on the back plate of the LAN card (if available) to see if the network recognizes the adapter. If the lights are active, the connection is alive. If not, check the adapter in another node. Check the cabling to make sure that it is the correct type, and that the connector is properly attached. A LAN cable tester is an excellent device to have in this situation.

Check the system for concentrators, routers, and bridges that may not be functioning properly. Check the protocol's frame settings to make sure that they are compatible from device to device, or that they are represented on the file server. The operation of these devices will have to be verified as separate units.

No Network Node is an Island — In a network, no node is an island, and every unit has an impact on the operation of the network when it is on line. Changes made in one part of a network can cause problems, and data loss, in other parts of the network. You should be aware that changing hardware and software configuration settings on an adapter might have adverse effects when the system is returned to the network. In addition, changing hard drives in a network node can have a negative impact on the network when the unit is brought back on line.

CHALLENGE #10

You have been called to a customer site to repair a networking problem. The user cannot see any other computers on her network. You check the drivers for the NIC, and you check the protocols that are installed in the operating system, and they appear to be okay. You also check the NIC and see that the light on its back panel is not glowing. What items should you check next?

Testing Cable

As we mentioned earlier in this chapter, the most frequent hardware-related cause of network problems involves bad cabling and connectors. There are several specialized, handheld devices designed for testing the various types of data communication cabling. These devices range from inexpensive continuity testers, to moderately priced data cabling testers, to somewhat expensive **Time Domain Reflectometry (TDR)** devices.

Time Domain Reflectometry (TDR)

The inexpensive continuity testers can be used to check for broken cables. This function can also be performed by the simple DMM described in Chapter 2. Data cabling testers are designed to perform a number of different types of tests on twisted pair and coaxial cables. These wiring testers normally consist of two units — a master test unit and a separate load unit, as illustrated in Figure 11-38.

The master unit is attached to one end of the cable and the load unit is attached at the other. The master unit sends patterns of test signal through the cable and reads them back from the load unit. Many of these testers feature both RJ-45 and BNC connectors for testing different types of cabling. When testing twisted pair cabling, these devices can normally detect such problems as broken wires, crossed wiring, shorted connections, and improperly paired connections.

Figure 11-38: Cable Tester

TDRs are sophisticated testers that can be used to pinpoint the distance to a break in a cable. These devices send signals along the cable and wait for them to be reflected. The time between sending the signal and receiving it back is converted into a distance measurement. The TDR function is normally packaged along with the other cable testing functions just described. TDRs used to test fiber-optic cables are known as **Optical Time Domain Reflectometers (OTDRs)**.

Optical Time Domain Reflectometers (OTDRs)

CHAPTER SUMMARY

This chapter has covered fundamental troubleshooting tools and techniques. The first half of the chapter presented the basic tools and investigative techniques used to troubleshoot computer systems. It dealt with the early steps of computer problem solving, including differentiating hardware versus software problems and identifying configuration problems. The final portion of this section focused on software diagnostic packages and their use. Upon completion of this material, you should be able to identify basic troubleshooting procedures and good practices for eliciting problem symptoms from customers.

The second half of the chapter presented typical symptoms and standard troubleshooting procedures for various system components. It included FRU troubleshooting procedures that included software, configuration, and hardware segments for each device. The procedures for most of the devices included related troubleshooting information associated with command prompt and Windows problems. After completing the chapter, you should be able to identify common symptoms and problems associated with each module and know how to troubleshoot and isolate the problems.

A portion of A+ Core Hardware objective 2.1 states that the test taker should be able to recognize common problems associated with each module and their symptoms. A portion of the contents listed in the objective includes "Portable Systems." The devices referenced in this section were described in Chapter 7 — *Portable Systems*.

At this point, review the objectives listed at the beginning of the chapter to be certain that you understand and can perform each item listed there.

KEY POINTS REVIEW

This chapter has discussed basic troubleshooting and diagnostic methods associated with the system hardware. Review the following key points before moving into the Review and Exam Questions sections to make sure you are comfortable with each point. Afterward, answer the Review Questions that follow to verify your knowledge of the information.

- It is normal practice to first set the meter to its highest voltage range to make certain that the voltage level being measured does not damage the meter.

- Unlike the voltage check, resistance checks are always made with power removed from the system.

- The most important thing to do when checking a malfunctioning device is to be observant. Begin by talking to the person who reported the problem. Many clues can be obtained from this person. Careful listening is also a good way to eliminate the user as a possible cause of the problems occurring. Part of the technician's job is to determine whether the user could be the source of the problem—either trying to do things with the system that it cannot do, or not understanding how some part of it is supposed to work.

- Whenever a self-test failure or setup mismatch is encountered, the BIOS may indicate the error through a blank screen, or a visual error message on the video display, or through an audio response (beep code) produced by the system's speaker.

- Carefully observing the steps of a bootup procedure can reveal a great deal about the nature of problems in a system. Faulty areas can be included or excluded as possible causes of errors during the bootup process.

- Most problems that occur in computer systems are in the area of configuration settings.

- In most newer systems, the BIOS and operating system use Plug-and-Play techniques to detect new hardware that has been installed in the system. These components work together with the device to allocate system resources for the device. In some occasions, the PnP logic will not be able to resolve all of the system's resource needs and a configuration error will occur. In these cases, the user will be required to manually resolve the configuration problem.

- Field Replaceable Units (FRUs) are the portions of the system that can be conveniently replaced in the field.

- Once you have isolated the problem, and the computer boots up and runs correctly, work backwards through the troubleshooting routines, reinstalling any original boards and other components removed during the troubleshooting process.

- Special consideration must be taken when a system is inoperable. In a totally inoperable system, there are no symptoms to give clues where to begin the isolation process. In addition, it is impossible to use troubleshooting software or other system aids to help isolate the problem.

- In Pentium-based systems, check the Advanced CMOS configuration and enabling settings in the BIOS and Chipset Features screens. These settings usually include the disk drives, keyboard, and video options, as well as on-board serial and parallel ports.

- Typically, if the bootup process reaches the point where the system's CMOS configuration information is displayed on the screen, it can be assumed that no hardware configuration conflicts exist in the system's basic components. After this point in the bootup process, the system begins loading drivers for optional devices and additional memory. If the error occurs after the CMOS screen is displayed and before the bootup tone, it will be necessary to clean boot the system and single-step through the remainder of the bootup sequence.

- A number of things can cause improper floppy-disk drive operation or failure. These items include the use of unformatted disks, incorrectly inserted disks, damaged disks, erased disks, loose cables, drive failure, adapter failure, system board failure, or a bad or loose power connector.

- There are basically three levels of troubleshooting that apply to FDD problems: configuration, the software level, and the hardware level. There is no Windows-level troubleshooting that applies to floppy drives.

- Hard drive systems are very much like floppy drive systems in structure—they have a controller, one or more signal cables a power cable, and a drive unit. The troubleshooting procedure typically moves from setup and configuration, to formatting, and, finally, to the hardware component isolation process.

- The troubleshooting steps for a CD-ROM drive are almost identical to those of an HDD system. The connections and data paths are very similar. There are basically three levels of troubleshooting that apply to CD-ROM problems. These are the configuration level, the operating system level, and the hardware level.

- There are basically three levels of testing that apply to troubleshooting port problems. These are the DOS level, the Windows level, and the hardware level.

- With newer Pentium systems, it will be necessary to check the Advanced CMOS Setup to determine whether the port in question has been enabled, and, if so, whether it has been enabled correctly.

- The basic components associated with the tape drive include the tape drive, the signal cable, the power connection, the controller, and the tape drive's operating software.

- Every COM port on a PC requires an IRQ line in order to signal the processor for attention. In most PC systems, two COM ports share the same IRQ line. The IRQ4 line works for COM1 and COM3, and the IRQ3 line works for COM2 and COM4. This is common in PC-compatibles. The technician must make sure that two devices are not set up to use the same IRQ channel.

- During the data transfer, both modems monitor the signal level of the carrier to prevent the transfer of false data due to signal deterioration. If the carrier signal strength drops below some predetermined threshold level, or is lost for a given length of time, one or both modems will initiate automatic disconnect procedures.

- Modems have the capability to perform three different kinds of self-diagnostic tests.

- With an external modem, the front panel lights can be used as diagnostic tools to monitor its operation. The progress of a call, and its handling, can be monitored along with any errors that may occur.

- The components involved in the audio output of most computer systems are very simple. There is a sound card, some speakers, the audio-related software, and the host computer system. Several software diagnostic packages are available that have the capability of testing sound card operation.

- Be aware that in a network environment, no unit really functions alone. Unlike working on a stand-alone unit, the steps performed on a network computer may affect the operation of other units on the network.

- One of the major concerns in most network environments is data security. Since all of the data around the network is potentially available to anyone connected to the network, all LAN administration software employs different levels of security. Passwords are typically used at all software levels to lock people out of hardware systems, as well as out of programs and data files.

- In a network, no node is an island, and every unit has an impact on the operation of the network when it is online. Changes made in one part of a network can cause problems, and data loss, in other parts of the network. You should be aware that changing hardware and software configuration settings for the adapter can have adverse effects when the system is returned to the network. In addition, changing hard drives in a network node can have a negative impact on the network when the unit is brought back online.

- All modems require software to control the communication session. This software is typically included with the purchase of the modem and must be configured to operate in the system the modem will be used in. At the fundamental instruction level, most modem software employs a set of commands known as the Hayes-compatible command set.

REVIEW QUESTIONS

The following questions test your knowledge of the material presented in this chapter.

1. If the system issues a single beep and the C:\> prompt appears on the screen, what condition is indicated?

2. List the FDD-related hardware components that should be checked when floppy disk problems are suspected.

3. List three situations that would normally require that the CMOS Setup routines be run.

4. What type of problem is indicated by a "Press F1 to continue" message during bootup?

5. What is the recommended method of using a digital multimeter to check voltage in a computer system?

6. If you are replacing components one at a time and the system suddenly begins working properly, what can be assumed?

7. List three items commonly tested using the resistance function of a multimeter.

8. What resistance reading would normally be expected from a fuse if it is functional?

9. If you are measuring across a capacitor on the system board with a DMM, what voltage reading would you normally expect to see?

10. Which non-computer possibility should be eliminated early in the troubleshooting process?

11. What range should the voltage function of a DMM be set to for an initial measurement?

12. Logon passwords and scripts are designed to _____.

13. In a LAN environment, access and privileges to programs and data can be established by the _____.

14. What is the first step in checking a networked computer?

15. To what type of communications products do Hayes-compatible commands pertain?

EXAM QUESTIONS

1. If an error occurs before the single beep tone in the bootup sequence, what type of failure is probable?
    a. The problem is probably associated with the operating system.
    b. The BIOS code has become corrupted.
    c. A setup or configuration problem.
    d. The problem is hardware related.

2. If an error occurs after the single beep in the bootup process, what type of problem is likely?
    a. The problem is probably associated with the operating system.
    b. The BIOS code has become corrupted.
    c. A setup or configuration problem.
    d. The problem is hardware related

3. If the system refuses to boot up after a new component is installed, what type of problem is normally assumed?
    a. The problem is probably associated with the operating system.
    b. The BIOS code has become corrupted.
    c. A setup or configuration problem has occurred.
    d. A hardware-related problem has occurred.

4. What component has the ability to affect the operation of all the other sections of the computer system?
    a. The power supply
    b. The ROM BIOS
    c. The microprocessor
    d. The system board

5. What multimeter reading would be appropriate for checking a system's speaker?
    a. Infinity
    b. Near zero ohms
    c. 4 ohms
    d. 8 ohms

6. What type of problem is indicated by a continuous beep tone from the system?
   a. A power supply failure
   b. An undefined problem
   c. A configuration problem
   d. A bootup problem

7. If a system appears to be completely dead, what item should be checked first?
   a. The system board
   b. The microprocessor
   c. The hard-disk drive
   d. The power supply

8. The error message "Bad File Allocation Table" indicates _____ problem.
   a. an operating system
   b. a Run Time
   c. a configuration
   d. a bootup

9. If a "CMOS Display Type Mismatch" message appears on the screen, what type of error is indicated?
   a. An operating system problem
   b. A Run Time error
   c. A setup or configuration problem
   d. A bootup failure

10. Which of the following is not normally considered an FRU that would be changed in the field?
    a. A system board
    b. A floppy-disk drive
    c. A power supply
    d. A video controller IC

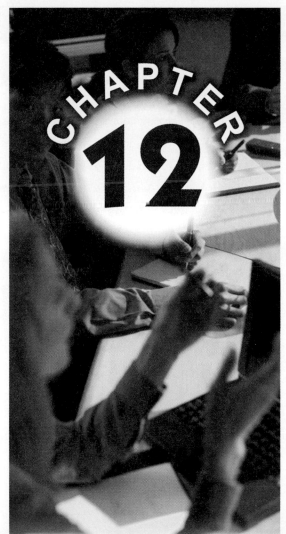

CHAPTER
12

OPERATING SYSTEM TROUBLESHOOTING

OBJECTIVES

OBJECTIVES

Upon completion of this chapter and its related lab procedures, you should be able to perform the following tasks:

1. Identify and solve Windows 9x Setup problems.

2. Locate and solve Windows 9x startup problems.

3. Locate and solve Windows 9x operational problems.

4. Identify and solve Windows 2000/XP Setup problems.

5. Locate and solve Windows 2000/XP startup problems.

6. Locate and solve Windows 2000/XP operational problems.

7. Describe Windows 9x/NT/2000/XP system tools, disk management tools, and TCP/IP tools.

8. Use the Policy Editor to change Windows NT/2000/XP policy settings.

9. Use various Windows 9x/2000/XP Safe Mode startup scenarios.

10. Use the Windows XP Automated System Recovery and System Restore functions.

11. Use log files to determine the location of Windows 9x/2000/XP operating system problems.

12. Employ Microsoft On-line Help utilities in Windows 9x and 2000/XP.

OPERATING SYSTEM TROUBLESHOOTING

INTRODUCTION

As you have seen in previous chapters, operating systems are tremendous collections of complex programming code brought together to control and link every operation of the computer hardware to the software applications that users want to employ. As with anything so complex, operating systems fail from time to time — some more than others — and although potentially millions of things can go wrong with complex software systems, you should be happy to know that you can group operating system problems into three basic areas:

- Setup problems (those that occur during installation or upgrading)

- Startup problems (those that occur when the system is booting up)

- Operational problems (those that occur during the normal course of operations)

By isolating a particular software problem to one of these areas, the troubleshooting process becomes less complex.

Setup problems typically involve failure to complete an OS install or upgrade operation. In some cases, this can leave the system stranded between an older OS version and a newer OS version, making the system unusable.

Startup problems usually produce conditions that prevent the system hardware and software from coming up and running correctly. These problems fall into two major groups:

- Hardware configuration problems

- OS bootup problems

Operational problems occur after the system has booted up and started running. These problems fall into three main categories:

- When performing normal application and file operations

- When printing

- When performing network functions

TROUBLESHOOTING SETUP PROBLEMS

Setup problems are errors that occur during the process of installing the operating system on the hard-disk drive. With early DOS versions, installation was a simple matter of making a \DOS directory on the hard drive and copying the contents of the DOS disks into it. For operating system versions from MS-DOS 5.0 forward, however, the installation procedure became an automated process requiring an Install or Setup program to be run.

One of the most common OS setup problems involves situations in which the system's hard drive does not have enough free space to carry out the installation process. When this occurs, you must remove files from the disk until you have cleared enough room to perform the installation. Unless you can remove enough obsolete files from the drive to make room for the new operating system, it is recommended that the files be backed up to some other media before erasing them from the drive.

Setup problems also occur when the system's hardware does not support the operating system that is being installed. These errors can include the following:

- Microprocessor requirements

- Memory speed mismatches

- Insufficient memory problems

- Incompatible device drivers

Windows Protection Error

The memory speed mismatch or mixed RAM-type problem produces a **Windows Protection Error** message during the installation process. This error indicates that the operating system is having timing problems that originate from the RAM memory used in the system. Correcting this problem involves swapping the system's RAM for devices that meet the system's timing requirements.

It is not uncommon for mouse or video drivers to fail during the installation of an operating system. If the video driver fails, you must normally turn off the system and attempt to reinstall the operating system from scratch. Conversely, if the mouse driver fails during the install, it is possible to continue the process using the keyboard. This problem is usually self-correcting after the system reboots.

A similar problem occurs when the operating system is looking for a PS/2 mouse and the system is using a serial mouse. It will not detect the serial mouse, and you will need to complete the installation process using the keyboard. Afterward, you can check the CMOS Port Settings for the serial port the mouse is connected to and install the correct driver for the serial mouse if necessary.

The best way to avoid hardware-compatibility problems is to consult Microsoft's web site to ensure that the hardware you are using is compatible with the operating system version you are installing.

Most error messages produced during an operating system installation stop the system. However, some errors offer to continue the process. It is our experience that continuing the installation rarely works out. Instead, just shut down the system, attempt to solve the problem, and then reinstall the operating system.

Windows 9x Setup Problems

Windows 9x draws from the existing FAT structure when it is being installed. Therefore, an interruption, or a crash during the installation process may leave the system with no workable operating system in place. If this occurs, you must boot the system from a bootable floppy disk and reinstall Windows 9x from that point.

If the system crashes during the hardware detection phase of a Windows 9x install, Microsoft recommends that you simply reboot the system until the installation process is successful. The Windows Setup wizard will mark startup steps that have failed and will bypass that step the next time you attempt to install the operating system. The failed steps are recorded in the Setuplog text file.

The Windows 9x installation files are stored on the installation disk in a compressed **Cabinet (CAB) file** format. Therefore, they cannot just be copied over to the hard drive to repair files damaged in an aborted installation. The best recovery method for this situation is to boot the system to a floppy disk, run **FDISK** to repartition the drive, format the drive, and run the Windows 9x Setup utility (provided your data was backed up beforehand).

If some programs or hardware options fail to run properly after a system has been upgraded to a Windows 9x operating system, you must determine whether they require specific real-mode drivers to be retained in the CONFIG.SYS and AUTOEXEC.BAT files. Recall that during the Restart phase of the installation process, Windows 9x deactivates files that it perceives as incompatible or unnecessary by placing a **Remark (REM) statement** at the beginning of the line. This may cause different applications or hardware to fail if they require these specific entries for operation. Be aware that restoring the driver can cause other problems within Windows 9x. The best choice is always to contact the software or hardware manufacturer for a Windows 9x driver.

> Cabinet (CAB) file

> FDISK

> Remark (REM) statement

> Blue Screen of Death (BSOD)

Windows NT/2000 Setup Problems

When an attempt to install Windows NT, Windows 2000, or Windows XP fails, a *Stop screen* error usually results. Stop errors occur when Windows NT or Windows 2000 detects a condition from which it cannot recover. The system stops responding, and a screen of information with a blue or black background displays, as illustrated in Figure 12-1. Stop errors are also known as Blue Screen errors, or the **Blue Screen of Death (BSOD)**. Troubleshooting these types of errors is discussed in more detail later in the chapter.

Figure 12-1: Stop Error or Blue Screen Error

Some other problems can typically occur during the Windows 2000 installation process. These problems include items such as the following:

- Noncompliant hardware failures
- Insufficient resources
- File system type choices
- The installation process starts over after rebooting
- WINNT32.EXE will not run from the command-line errors

Ways to correct these particular installation-related problems include the following:

- *Verify Hardware Compatibility* — The hardware-compatibility requirements of Windows NT, Windows 2000, and Windows XP are more stringent than those of the Windows 9x platform. When either of these operating systems encounters hardware that is not compatible during the setup phase, they fail. In some cases, the system incorrectly detects the hardware, whereas in other cases the system produces a **blue screen error**.

  Make certain to check the **Hardware Compatibility List** to ensure that your hardware is compatible with Windows 2000. If the hardware is not listed, contact the hardware vendor to determine whether they support Windows 2000/XP before starting the installation.

- *Verify Minimum System Resource Requirements* — Also, make certain that your hardware meets the minimum hardware requirements, including the memory, free disk space, and video requirements. When the Windows NT, Windows 2000, or Windows XP Setup routine detects insufficient resources (that is, processor, memory, or disk space), it either informs you that an error has occurred and halts, or it just hangs up and refuses to continue the install.

- *Establish the File System Type* — During the installation process, you must decide which file system you are going to use. If you are going to dual boot to Windows 98, and have a drive that is larger than 2 GB, you must choose FAT32. Choosing NTFS for a dual-boot system renders the NTFS partition unavailable when you boot to Windows 98. FAT16 does not support drives larger than 2 GB. You can upgrade from FAT16 to FAT32 or from FAT32 to NTFS; however, you can never revert to the older file system after you have upgraded. You should also be aware that Windows NT 4.0 does not support FAT32 partitions. Therefore, Windows NT 4.0 or earlier cannot be used on a Windows 9x drive. Consider using the lowest common file system during installation and upgrading later.

- *Installation process reboots* If you discover after the initial installation of Windows 2000, and the subsequent rebooting of the system to finish the installation, that the installation program seems to start over again, check the CD-ROM drive for the installation disc. Leaving the bootable CD-ROM in the CD player normally causes this condition because the BIOS settings instruct the computer to check for a bootable CD-ROM before looking on the hard drive for an operating system. To correct this problem, remove the Windows 2000 CD from the player, or change the System Setup configuration to not check the CD player during bootup.

- *WINNT32 will not run from the command prompt* — The **WINNT32.EXE** program is designed to run under a 32-bit operating system and will not run from the command line. It is used to initiate upgrades from Windows 9x or Windows NT to Windows 2000 or Windows XP. From a 16-bit operating system, such as MS-DOS or Windows 95, you must run the **WINNT.EXE** program from the command line to initiate the installation of Windows 2000.

In most cases, a failure during the Windows 2000 setup process produces an unusable system. When this occurs, you usually must reformat the disk and reinstall the system files from the Windows 2000 Setup (boot) disks.

Windows XP Setup Problems

As with the other operating system versions, there are many things that can cause Windows XP installations to fail. If a setup attempt fails during the installation process, you will be left with a system that has no workable operating system in place. If this occurs, you must first of all investigate to determine whether there are any hardware/software application conflicts that could keep the system from starting. If not, you should start up the system from some type of bootable media and attempt to determine what might be keeping Windows XP from installing. Finally, if nothing appears as a likely cause of the problem, attempt to reinstall the Windows XP operating system from scratch.

If the Windows Setup wizard does not detect sufficient hard disk space on the drive, a stop error will be created. If this occurs, try to remove files and programs to free up the needed disk space. You can also create an additional partition to hold Windows XP, or delete the existing partition and create a larger partition.

You should also verify that the system's hard drive and CD-ROM drives are on the **Windows XP HCL**. If the drives are not acceptable to the system, it will be difficult to conduct the install and you will receive errors during the text-based portion of the Windows XP Setup routine. If the drives are not on the HCL, you can attempt to load **OEM drivers** for the devices from an OEM CD-ROM or floppy by pressing the F6 key when prompted and accessing the drivers on the disk.

BIOS-based anti-virus utilities can prevent operating systems from being installed or upgraded. When the Setup utility attempts to make the hard disk Windows XP bootable, a **BIOS-based virus scanner** will interpret this action as an attempt by a virus to infect the system. In these cases, the system will produce an error message indicating that a virus is attempting to infect the boot sector. To prevent this from happening, disable the virus protection through the CMOS Setup utility and then enable it again after the operating system has been installed.

Generally, most other failures during the installation process involve hardware detection problems or component installation errors. If the Windows XP installation process fails during the hardware detection phase of the process, check the system for devices that are not listed on the Windows XP HCL. Because of Windows NT/2000/XP's relative intolerance for unapproved devices, you should verify that all the system's hardware components are listed on the HCL. If any component is not on the list, remove it, restart the installation process, and see whether the process advances past the error.

| Windows XP HCL |

| OEM drivers |

| BIOS-based virus scanner |

Upgrade Problems

You will encounter many of the same problems performing an operating system upgrade that you do when performing a clean install. To review, these problems are normally related to the following:

- Insufficient hard drive or partition sizes
- Memory speed mismatches
- Insufficient memory problems
- Incompatible device drivers

While performing upgrade operations, you can also encounter problems created by version incompatibilities. New versions of operating systems are typically produced in two styles: full versions and upgrade versions. In some cases, you cannot use a full version of the operating system to upgrade an existing operating system. Doing so will produce an **Incompatible Version error** message telling you that you cannot use this version to upgrade. You must either obtain an upgrade version of the operating system, or partition the drive and perform a new installation (thus losing your existing data).

You also must have the appropriate version of the upgrade for the existing operating system. (That is, Windows 98SE comes in two versions—one upgrades both Windows 95 and Windows 98, whereas the other version upgrades only Windows 98.)

TEST TIP

Know how to display the current version of Windows information for a system.

In order to determine the current version of a Windows operating system running on a computer, alternate-click on the *My Computer* icon, select the *Properties* option from the pop-up menu, and select the *General* tab of the *System Properties* window. Another way to get the version of Windows is to open Windows Explorer, click on the *Help* menu, and select *About Windows*.

TROUBLESHOOTING STARTUP PROBLEMS

A portion of A+ Operating System Technologies objective 3.2 states that the test taker should be able to recognize when to use common diagnostic utilities and tools. Given a diagnostic scenario involving one of these utilities or tools, select the appropriate steps needed to resolve the problem. It also says that utilities and tools may include the following:

- Startup disks
- Required files for a boot disk
- Boot disk with CD-ROM support
- Startup modes
- Safe Mode
- Safe Mode with command prompt
- Safe Mode with networking
- Step-by-Step/Single-step mode

Fortunately, only a few problems can occur during the startup process of a disk-based computer. These problems include the following:

- Hardware problems
- Configuration problems
- Bootup (or operating system startup) problems
- Operating system desktop GUI won't load.

NOTE

Bootup Process Single Beep—A key troubleshooting point occurs at the single beep in the bootup process of most computers. If the system produces an error message or a beep-coded error signal before the beep, the problem is hardware related. On the other hand, if the error message or beep code is produced after the single beep occurs, the problem is likely to be associated with starting up the operating system. At this point, the problem becomes an operating system startup problem.

All four of the previously listed problem types can result in startup failures. Some prevent any activity from appearing in the system, others produce symptoms that can be tracked to a cause, and yet others produce error messages that can be tracked to a source. When dealing with starting up a disk operating system, the following four things can prove very useful to help you isolate the cause of startup problems:

- Error messages and beep codes
- Clean boot disks (Emergency Start disks)
- Single-step startup procedures
- System log files

The following Hands-On Activity identifies the preliminary ways to troubleshoot startup problems.

Hands-on Activity

Troubleshooting Startup Problems

1. Try to reboot the system.

2. Check system log files if available to determine where the process was interrupted.

3. Perform a clean boot with minimal configuration settings to remove nonessential elements from the process.

4. Perform a single-step bootup to isolate any driver problems that are preventing bootup from taking place.

If the system does not boot up correctly, you must boot the system to a minimum configuration and establish a point to begin troubleshooting the problem. This startup method enables you to bypass any unnecessary configuration and normally involves using a clean boot disk or the **Emergency Start disk** to start the system.

If the system boots up from the minimal condition, the problem exists in the bypassed files. Restart the system and select a startup mode that single-steps through the configuration and startup file sequence.

The **single-step startup procedure** enables you to isolate the problem command. If the system crashes while trying to execute a particular command, restart the bootup process and skip the offending command. Repeat the process until the system reaches bootup. Track all offending commands so that you can correct them individually. Check the **syntax** (spelling, punctuation, and usage) of any offending lines.

When the system boots to the clean boot disk, but does not boot up to the hard drive, and has no configuration or startup file errors, a problem exists in the operating system's boot files. These errors typically return some type of **Bad or Missing Command Interpreter** message, or a Disk Boot Failure message. Basically, three conditions produce these types of error messages:

Emergency Start disk

single-step startup procedure

syntax

Bad or Missing Command Interpreter

- The Master Boot Record or command interpreter file cannot be found on the hard drive, and no bootable disk is present in the A: drive.

- The Master Boot Record or operating system's command interpreter file is not located in the partition's root directory. This message usually occurs when installing a new hard drive or a new operating system version.

- The user has inadvertently erased the Master Boot Record or operating system command interpreter file from the hard drive, possibly during the process of establishing a dual-boot disk or when setting up a multiple operating system environment.

Often, you can repair the Missing Command Interpreter error by restoring the boot record and operating system files to the hard disk. To do so, simply copy or extract the files from the clean boot disk to the hard drive. In a FAT environment, if the boot disk contains a copy of the FDISK command, you can use the *FDISK /MBR* command to restore the hard drive's Master Boot Record, along with its partition information. The command SYS:*X* (where *X* is the drive designation) is used to restore the command interpreter.

Windows 9x Startup Problems

Safe Mode

troubleshooting Help file

Windows 9x includes several built-in troubleshooting tools. These tools include several **Safe Mode** startup options, a trio of system log files, and an extensive interactive **troubleshooting Help file** system. Windows 9x also includes three important tools that can be used when a Windows 9x system is having startup problems: the Emergency Start disk, Safe Modes, and the step-by-step startup sequence. With Windows 9x, the clean boot disk is referred to as an Emergency Start disk. To access the Safe Modes and the single-step with confirmation startup process, press the SHIFT and F8 function keys simultaneously when the "Starting Windows 9x" message appears onscreen.

The special function keys available during the Windows 9x startup are:

- F5 – Safe Mode
- F6 – Safe Mode with Network Support
- F8 – Step-by-Step Confirmation mode
- SHIFT+F5 – Safe Mode Command Prompt Only

Typical Windows 9x startup error messages include the following:

- HIMEM.SYS not loaded.
- Unable to initialize display adapter.
- Device referenced in WIN.INI could not be found.
- Bad or missing COMMAND.COM.
- Swap file corrupt.
- Damaged or missing core files.
- Device referenced in SYSTEM.INI could not be found.

These and other Windows 9x–related startup messages indicate the presence of problems that must be corrected before the system can boot up and run correctly. The generic process for isolating the cause of a Windows 9x startup problem is as follows:

1. Use the Emergency Start disk to gain access to the system and the hard drive.

2. If necessary, repair the system files and command interpreter files as described earlier in this chapter.

3. Attempt to boot up into Safe Mode to see if the problem is driver-related.

4. Reboot the system into the step-by-step confirmation startup mode to isolate configuration and driver problems. Continue single stepping through the startup process until all offending steps have been identified and corrected.

5. Review the Windows 9x log files for problem steps.

Be aware that the MSDOS.SYS file in Windows 9x is used to provide startup options, load some drivers, and establish paths for certain system files. You should check these entries if Windows 9x does not start properly.

HIMEM.SYS Problems

HIMEM.SYS error

In the case of the **HIMEM.SYS error**, use the System Editor to check the syntax and correctness of the entry in the CONFIG.SYS file, if present. With Windows 9x, the HIMEM.SYS statement must be present and correct for the operating system to run. Also check the HIMEM.SYS file to make sure it is the correct version and in the correct location. In a system that has been upgraded to Windows 9x, there may be as many as three different versions of HIMEM.SYS present.

TEST TIP

Know where to go and how to correct HIMEM.SYS errors in MS-DOS and Windows 9x environments.

Initializing the Display Adapter

The **"Unable to Initialize Display Adapter" error** message is indicative of errors that occur during the hardware-detection phase of the Windows 9x PnP boot-up routine. These errors usually occur either because the Windows 9x PnP function cannot detect the hardware component, or because it cannot reconcile the adapter's needs to the available system resources. However, do not assume that PnP is in effect and running just because Windows 9x is running. The system's BIOS and the peripheral device also must be PnP compliant for the auto-detection function to work.

Unable to Initialize Display Adapter error

You should be able to sort out problems that occur during the detection phase by starting the system in **step-by-step confirmation mode** (pressing F8 during the bootup) and then single stepping through the driver loading process to sort out the display driver/hardware problem. You must use the Control Panel's Add New Hardware Wizard to install device drivers when the PnP detection function does not work.

step-by-step confirmation mode

Windows 9x Boot Problems

Key Windows 9x files can prevent the system from starting up if they become corrupted. These files include those associated with the Master Boot Record, the boot sector, the FATs, and the Windows core files. Errors that occur between the single beep that marks the end of the POST and the appearance of the "Starting Windows 9x" message on the screen are associated with the boot sector. Problems that show up between the Starting Windows message and the appearance of the desktop involve the Windows core files. In any event, if disk corruption is detected, you must rebuild the corrupted file structures.

When IO.SYS is corrupted in Windows 9x, the system hangs up before the Starting Windows message appears and produces a **System Disk Invalid error** message onscreen.

If the MSDOS.SYS file is missing or corrupted, Windows displays a blue screen with an **Invalid VxD Dynamic Link message** and fails to start up. Other MSDOS.SYS-related problems relate to the Registry, the **Extended Memory Manager (XMS)**, and the Installable File System Manager (IFSMGR). These problems produce errors that appear during startup and are caused by syntax errors in the [Paths] section of the file.

Likewise, the COMMAND.COM problem produces an error message onscreen and fails to start up Windows. You can repair the missing COMMAND.COM error by using the MS-DOS COPY and SYS commands, as described in Chapter 11. These commands copy the COMMAND.COM and system files from the clean boot disk to the hard drive. Similarly, if the boot disk contains a copy of the FDISK command, you can use the FDISK/MBR command to restore the hard drive's Master Boot Record, along with its partition information.

As mentioned earlier, the following conditions produce a Bad or Missing COMMAND.COM error message:

- The COMMAND.COM file cannot be found on the hard drive, and no bootable disk is present in the A: drive.

- The COMMAND.COM file is not located in the hard drive's root directory. This message is likely when installing a new hard drive or a new DOS version.

- The user inadvertently erases the COMMAND.COM file from the hard drive.

To correct these problems, start the system using the Emergency Start disk. At the command prompt, type SYS C: to copy the IO.SYS, MSDOS.SYS, and COMMAND.COM files onto the hard disk. You can use the MS-DOS **Attribute command** to verify that the hidden system files have been successfully copied to the disk (i.e., Attrib -r -s -h c:\IO.SYS and Attrib –r –s –h C:\MSDOS.SYS to make them visible and to remove their read-only and system status).

The COMMAND.COM file can also be restored from the command line or through the Windows Explorer. To restore the COMMAND.COM file from the command line, start the system from the startup disk and use the **Copy command** to transfer the file manually. The COMMAND.COM file can also be dragged from the startup disk to the root directory of the hard drive using the Windows 9x My Computer or Windows Explorer functions. As with the manual copy procedure, the COMMAND.COM file's read-only, system, and hidden attributes must be removed so that it can be manipulated within the system.

System Disk Invalid error

Invalid VxD Dynamic Link message

Extended Memory Manager (XMS)

Attribute command

Copy command

┌─ **TEST TIP** ─────────┐
│ Know what causes bad or missing │
│ COMMAND.COM errors and how │
│ to correct them. │
└────────────────────────┘

Missing Windows Core File Problems

To locate and correct the "**Missing Core File**" **problem** cited earlier, check for corrupted files on the disk drive. To accomplish this, start the system in Safe Mode using the **Command Prompt Only option**. When the command prompt appears, move to the Windows Command directory and run the **ScanDisk** utility. If ScanDisk detects corrupted files, you must replace them. The ScanDisk utility can locate and fix several types of problems on the hard drive. These problems include corrupted FATs, long filenames, lost clusters, cross-linked files, tree structure problems, and bad sectors on the drive.

> **Check the Versions** — The ScanDisk version used with a Windows 9x system must be the one specifically designed for that operating system (i.e., a Windows 95 ScanDisk version should not be used on a Windows 98 system). Other versions may not work correctly and could result in data loss. When using ScanDisk to isolate startup problems, the Windows 9x version used should be the version that is located on the particular computer's Emergency Start disk and that runs from the command prompt.

You can use the Windows 9x Setup function to verify or repair damaged Windows operating system files. To accomplish this, run the Setup utility and select the *Verify* option when presented by the Setup procedure. You then can repair damaged system files without running a complete reinstall operation.

If corrupted Windows 9x files are found in the system, you cannot simply copy new ones onto the drive from the CD. Instead, you must run Setup using the distribution CD and the **Validate/Restore option**.

You also can run the **EXTRACT.EXE** command from the Windows Command directory to extract selected compressed cabinet files from the Windows CD. The preferable method is the *Setup* option. In most cases, however, it is simpler to reinstall Windows than to search for individual files and structures.

CHALLENGE #1

One of your assistants has deleted a print manager file from his Windows 98 workstation. How can you restore this file to the system from the Windows CD so that he can print out his normal documentation?

Swap File Problems

The Windows 9x swap file is controlled through the *System* icon in the Control Panel. From this point, enter the *Performance* page and click on its *Virtual Memory* button. Typically, the *Let Windows Manage Virtual Memory* option should be selected. If the system locks up and does not start, the swap file may have become corrupted, or the Virtual Memory setting may have been changed to *Disabled*. In either case, you must reinstall Windows 9x to correct the problem.

> **Missing Core File problem**

> **Command Prompt Only option**

> **ScanDisk**

> **Validate/Restore option**

> **EXTRACT.EXE**

TEST TIP

Know the effects of checking the Disable Virtual Memory setting in Windows 9x.

Initialization File Problems

missing INI files error

The device or driver files referenced in the **missing INI files error** messages should be checked to make certain that they have been properly identified and that their locations and paths are correct. If they are not, use the System Editor to make the necessary changes by installing the specified device driver in the designated INI file. If the path and syntax are correct for the indicated files, you should reload them from the Emergency Start disk.

Error in CONFIG.SYS Line XX

Error in AUTOEXEC.BAT Line XX

SYSEDIT

Errors in the CONFIG.SYS and AUTOEXEC.BAT files will produce the **Error in CONFIG.SYS Line XX** or **Error in AUTOEXEC.BAT Line XX** messages described in the A+ objectives. The line specified by the XX in the error message contains a syntax (spelling, punctuation, or usage) error that prevents it from running. Syntax errors can also produce an "Unrecognized command in CONFIG.SYS" message. Missing or corrupted files referenced in the CONFIG.SYS or AUTOEXEC.BAT files can also cause these errors. To correct these errors, use one of the system's text editors, such as **SYSEDIT**, to correct the designated line in the file, reload the indicated file with a known-good copy, and restart the computer.

TEST TIP

Know how to correct problems that cause an error message about a particular line in a CONFIG.SYS or AUTOEXEC.BAT file.

Figure 12-2 provides a graphic illustration of the Windows 9x startup sequence. It lists the order of event occurrences in each major startup stage and provides typical types of problems that might be encountered in each stage.

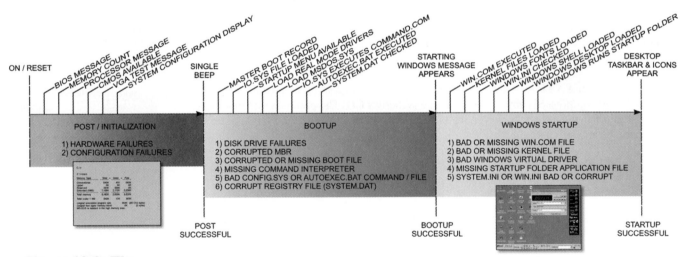

Figure 12-2: The Windows 9x Startup Sequence

password

One of the final problems that could affect startup in Windows 9x is the **password**. Normally, when a user forgets his local Windows logon password, he can click on the *Cancel* option and gain access to most of the local resources. However, the user will not be able to see any network resources, or access resources restricted through the System Policy setting. The system declares network resources "Unavailable" to the user.

The most direct way to get around a local logon password is to access the local machine and delete the *username.PWL* file in the *C:\Windows* directory. You could also create a new user account in Windows 9x to establish another password. To get around a forgotten network password, remove the *Client for Microsoft Networks* protocol from the *Network Components* window and then reinstall it. When you restart the system, it asks you to establish a new user who will have a new password.

Creating a Windows 95 Emergency Start Disk

A portion of the A+ Operating System Technologies objective 2.3 indicates that the test taker should be able to identify the steps to create an emergency boot disk with utilities installed for Windows 9x/Me, Windows NT 4.0 Workstation, Windows 2000 Professional, and Windows XP.

In the event that Windows becomes nonfunctional, it will be necessary to use the start disk to gain access to the system so that you can restore it to proper operation. The Windows 95 Startup disk will only boot the system up to the command prompt. From this point you must be familiar with command-line operations so that you can employ tools and utilities that will get the system up and running again.

During the Windows setup operation, the software provides an option for creating an emergency startup disk. This option should be used for every Windows 95 installation. Setup copies the operating system files to the disk along with utilities for troubleshooting startup problems. The disk can then be used to boot up the system in Safe Mode and display a command-line prompt. The Emergency Start disk can also be used to replace lost or damaged system files on the hard disk.

An Emergency Start disk can also be created through the Control Panel's *Add/Remove Programs* icon. This option is normally used to create a new startup disk after new hardware has been installed, or when configuration information has been changed. In addition to creating a startup floppy disk, Windows 95 transfers a number of diagnostic files to the disk, including the following:

> **TEST TIP**
> Be aware of the two methods of creating Emergency Start disks in Windows 9x and know when these disks should be employed.

- IO.SYS
- MSDOS.SYS
- COMMAND.COM
- SYS.COM
- FDISK.EXE

- FORMAT.COM
- EDIT.COM
- REGEDIT.EXE
- ATTRIB.EXE
- SCANDISK.EXE and .INI

> **TEST TIP**
> Know which files should be present on a Windows 9x Emergency Start disk.

These utilities are particularly helpful in getting a Windows 95 machine operational again. This disk provides one of the few tools for the technician to service a down machine with this operating system. The steps involved in creating the Emergency Start disk are as follows:

Hands-on Activity

Creating the Emergency Start Disk

1. Click on the *Start* button.

2. Move to the *Settings* option in the *Start* menu.

3. Select the *Control Panel* from the list.

4. Double-click on the *Add/Remove Programs* icon.

5. Select the *Startup Disk* tab.

6. Click on the *Create Disk* button.

7. Place the Windows 95 CD in the CD-ROM drive when prompted.

8. Follow the menu items as directed.

9. Place a blank disk in drive A: when prompted.

10. Remove the Windows 95 CD from the drive when the operation is complete.

SYSTEM.DAT

USER.DAT

RegEdit

Because the Windows 95 system settings are basically contained in the two Registry files **SYSTEM.DAT** and **USER.DAT**, it is not uncommon to back them up on the Emergency Start disk. This operation is performed with the **RegEdit** utility's Export function. The Export function can be used to save a selected branch or the entire Registry as a REG text file.

The steps for exporting the Registry are as follows:

Hands-on Activity

Exporting the Registry

1. Start the RegEdit function.

2. Select the *Run* option from the *Start* menu.

3. Type *REGEDIT* in the Filename dialog box and click on *OK*.

4. From the RegEdit toolbar, select the *Registry* menu.

5. Choose the *Export Registry file* option from the drop-down menu.

6. In the *Export* window, click on the *All* button.

7. Type the filename *REGBACK* in the *Filename* window.

8. Select the 3.5 Floppy (A:) entry from the *Save In* window.

9. Click on the *Save* button.

10. Check the contents of the A: drive to make certain that the REGBACK.REG file is there.

In addition to the .DAT Registry files, you might want to include copies of any CONFIG.SYS, AUTOEXEC.BAT, WIN.INI, SYSTEM.INI, and CD-ROM driver files on the Emergency Start disk. These files can be quite useful for maintaining compatibility with installed hardware and software applications. The real mode CD-ROM driver (that is, MSCDEX.EXE) should be included to provide CD-ROM support for access to the utilities on the Windows distribution CD.

The Registry backup file can be used to restore the Registry to the system after a crash. Once again, this involves using the RegEdit Import function to restore the Registry for use. The RegEdit Import function can be performed using the Windows-based version, or it can be conducted from the command line using the real-mode version located on the Emergency Start disk. For the purposes of this text, this discussion focuses on the version needed in a troubleshooting-and-repair scenario.

To restore the Registry, follow these steps:

Hands-on Activity

Restoring the Registry

1. Restart the system.

2. Place the emergency start disk into the A: drive.

3. Turn the computer on.

4. Import the original Registry into Windows 95 to return it to its original condition.

5. Place the disk containing the REGBACK.REG file in the floppy drive.

6. From the RegEdit toolbar, select the *Registry* menu.

7. At the A:\> prompt, type *REGEDIT /C REGBACK*.

8. Wait for the file to be imported.

9. Remove the floppy disk from the A: drive.

10. Turn the system off and then back on again.

The system should be restored to the same operating parameters that it had when the Registry backup file was created.

Registry Restoration Caveat — The **REGEDIT /C** command should not be used except for cases where the Registry is heavily corrupted. It must have a complete image of the Registry to be used in this manner. Also realize that Windows 9x backs up the Registry files each time it is started. There should be several iterations of the Registry files that could be renamed and copied over the existing Registry files to repair them.

REGEDIT /C

The Windows 95 Emergency Start disk should be stored in a convenient place and clearly labeled so that it is easy to find when you need it.

The Windows 98 Emergency Start Disk

TEST TIP

Know where to make Emergency Start disks in Windows 9x.

Like the Windows 95 Emergency Start disk, the Windows 98 version is basically a boot disk with key utilities included, which can be used to assist in restarting the system when Windows 98 doesn't boot. This disk can be created during the installation process, or by accessing the *Startup disk* tab in the Control Panel's *Add/Remove Programs* window. From this point, creating the emergency disk is simply a matter of inserting a blank disk into the floppy drive and clicking on the *Create Disk* button. As always, store the Start disk in an obvious, but safe location.

TEST TIP

Know that real-mode drivers must be available to support CD-ROM drive operation in Safe Mode.

In addition to the necessary system files required to start the system in a minimal, real-mode condition, the Windows 98 Emergency Start disk provides a number of diagnostic programs and a trio of real-mode CD-ROM drivers (MSCDEX.EXE for IDE drives and BTDCDROM.SYS and ASPICD.SYS for SCSI drives) to enable the CD-ROM drive to operate in Safe Mode.

CHALLENGE #2

You have started a customer's computer in Safe Mode because it has repeatedly failed to start Windows 95. After reaching Safe Mode, you put the Windows CD into the drive but cannot access it. What do you need to do to access the CD-ROM drive so that you can run repair utilities from it?

Extract command
(EXT.EXE)

EXTRACT.EXE

The Windows 98 Emergency Start disk includes real-mode SCSI CD-ROM support, provides a RAMDrive, and features a new **Extract command (EXT.EXE)** to work with **EXTRACT.EXE**. The Extract command is used to pull necessary files from the *cabinet* (*.CAB*) files on the Windows 98 distribution CD.

TEST TIP

Be aware of the function of the Extract command and of the file type used to store files on the Windows 9x distribution CD.

CHALLENGE #3

A customer has accidentally erased the SCANDISK.EXE file from her Windows 98 notebook computer. What is the least intrusive method that you can use to recover her file and get the ScanDisk function back in operation?

You should be aware that Windows 98 will not run if the system is started with an Emergency Start disk from another Windows version. The machine can be started on the older versions of the Start disk, and some repair operations can be carried out; but the new version will not be able to be started, and some items could become corrupted with the older operating system.

Alternative Windows 9x Startup Modes

The Windows 9x **Startup menu** (not to be confused with the desktop's *Start* menu), depicted in Figure 12-3, can be obtained on a non starting system by holding down the F8 function key when the "Starting Windows 9x" message is displaying onscreen. The menu offers several startup options including Normal, Logged, Safe, Step-by-Step Confirmation, and Command Prompt Modes. These startup modes play an important role in getting the Windows 9x operating system up and running when it fails to start.

```
┌─ TEST TIP ──────────────────────────────────────────────────┐
│                                                              │
│   Be aware that the BOOTLOG.TXT file is not normally created during startup. │
│   It has to be initiated with the Logged mode.               │
│                                                              │
└──────────────────────────────────────────────────────────────┘
```

```
Microsoft Windows 95 Startup Menu

    1. Normal
    2. Logged C\BOOTLOG.TXT
    3. Safe Mode
    4. Safe Mode with network support
    5. Step -by -Step Confirmation
    6. Command prompt only
    7. Safe Mode Command prompt only

Enter a choice: 3




F8 = Safe Mode  Shift + F5 = Command prompt  Shift + F8 = Step -by -Step Confirmation [N]
```

Figure 12-3: The Windows 9x Startup Menu

If the Normal mode option is selected, the system simply tries to restart as it normally would, loading all of its normal startup and Registry files. The **Logged mode** option also attempts to start the system in Normal mode, but keeps an error log file that contains the steps performed and outcome. You can read this text file (**BOOTLOG.TXT**) with any text editor, or you can print it out on a working system.

Safe Mode

Safe Mode

If Windows determines that a problem prevents the system from starting has occurred, or if it senses that the Registry is corrupt, it automatically attempts to restart the system in **Safe Mode**. This mode bypasses several startup files to provide access to the system's configuration settings. In particular, any existing CONFIG.SYS and AUTOEXEC.BAT files are bypassed, along with the Windows 9x Registry and the [Boot] and [386enh] sections of the SYSTEM.INI file. The contents of these files are employed to retain compatibility with older hardware and applications.

TEST TIP

Know what files are loaded into the system when it is started in Safe Mode.

> **What's active in Safe Mode?** — In Safe Mode, the minimal device drivers (keyboard, mouse, and standard-mode VGA drivers) are active to start the system. However, the CD-ROM drive will not be active in Safe Mode.

You also can access Safe Mode by pressing the F5 function key while the "Starting Windows 9x" message is displaying onscreen. Windows 9x also reverts to this mode if an application requests it.

Unless modified, the *Safe Mode* screen appears as shown in Figure 12-4. Active functions appear onscreen along with the "Safe mode" notice in each corner. However, there is no Taskbar in Safe Mode.

Safe Mode with Network Support

Safe Mode Command Prompt Only

Safe Mode Without Compression

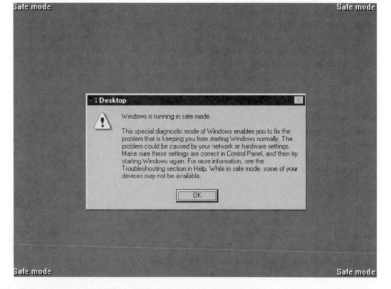

Figure 12-4: The Safe Mode Startup Screen

Windows 9x has four Safe Mode startup options: Safe Mode, **Safe Mode with Network Support**, **Safe Mode Command Prompt Only**, and **Safe Mode Without Compression**. Each option is customized for specific situations and disables selected portions of the system to prevent them from interfering with the startup process.

NOTE

Windows 98 does not officially support Safe Mode with Network Support. However, you can press the F6 function key during the startup process to access this option.

The standard Safe Mode startup is used when the system:

- Will not start after the "Starting Windows 9x" message appears onscreen

- Stalls repeatedly or for long periods of time

- Cannot print to a local printer after a complete troubleshooting sequence

- Has video display problems

- Slows down noticeably, or does not work correctly

In standard Safe Mode startup, Windows bypasses certain startup and configuration files and loads a standard set of device drivers to start the system. The bypassed files include the following:

- The Registry

- The CONFIG.SYS and AUTOEXEC.BAT files

- The [boot] and [386enh] sections of the SYSTEM.INI file

The only device drivers loaded in Safe Mode are the mouse driver, the standard keyboard driver, and the standard VGA driver. This should enable enough of the Windows structure to operate so that the offending portions can be isolated and repaired using step-by-step checking procedures.

The **Step-by-Step Confirmation** option enables you to check each line of the startup procedure individually. In doing so, the *Step-by-Step* option enables you to verify which drivers are being loaded, temporarily disable any offending drivers, and check other startup errors that may be indicated through error messages. This option is obtained by pressing the F8 function key at the Startup Menu and should be employed when the system:

Step-by-Step
Confirmation

- Fails while loading the startup files

- Needs to load real-mode drivers

- Displays a Registry Failure error message

As the startup process moves forward, the system asks whether each line is correct. Press the ENTER key to confirm the line, or press the ESC key to skip a line. Keep track of any skipped lines so that you can check them individually. If the system crashes after a line has been confirmed, mark it as a problem and restart the system using the *Step-by-Step* option. Bypass the offending line on the next attempt to reach bootup. Record all lines that prevent the bootup process and troubleshoot them one by one.

The *Step-by-Step* option provides an opportunity to create a startup log file called BOOTLOG.TXT. This file will help you isolate startup problems — such as real-mode, 16-bit adapter drivers that refuse to load and prevent the system from booting. You can check the content of the log file for offending entries that stop the system. More information is provided concerning the BOOTLOG.TXT file later in this chapter.

Responses for the CONFIG.SYS and AUTOEXEC.BAT prompts are Y and N for individual lines. You can use the TAB key to accept the entire file. An N answer to the *Load All Windows Drivers* prompt results in Windows operating in Safe Mode. Otherwise, answering Y to all the prompts starts Windows 9x as normal, with the exception that the Windows logo does not appear at startup.

The *Safe Mode with Network Support* option typically bypasses the CONFIG.SYS and AUTOEXEC.BAT files and loads the COMMAND.COM processor. It then loads HIMEM.SYS and IFSHLP.SYS, followed by any drive-compression drivers, the Windows 9x core and Registry files, and the basic network driver files. This mode is used in networked environments when the system:

- Stops responding when a remote network is accessed
- Cannot print to a remote printer
- Stalls during startup and cannot be started using a normal Safe Mode startup

Because this mode loads the Windows Registry, it cannot be used if the Registry has been corrupted. If the system loads Windows in standard Safe Mode, but not with the *Network Support* option, check the network configuration settings. Also be aware that Windows 9x uses the MSDOS.SYS file to establish paths for some options. In the case of real-mode networking, the [Paths] entry, WINDIR=, must be defined for the NETSTART.BAT file used to start the network. If this file does not run, Windows will fail to load.

CHALLENGE #4

You attempt to change the video driver on a customer's Windows 98 computer because you believe that he should be able to get more performance out of his video card. However, when you reboot the machine, you only have horizontal streaks across the screen. You know that you should restart the system in a mode that will permit you to access the display setup, but you are not sure which mode you should select. Which Windows 9x startup mode is the best choice to accomplish this without wasting a lot of extra time?

Command Prompt Modes

Other startup options may also be available from the menu depending on the configuration of the system. Some options start the system and bring it to a command prompt. Selecting the *Command Prompt Only* mode causes the system to boot up to the command line, using the startup files and the Registry.

If this option will not start the system, reboot the computer and select the *Safe Mode Command Prompt Only* option from the Startup menu. This option performs the same function as pressing the SHIFT and F5 keys simultaneously (SHIFT+F5) during the bootup process. The system will start in Safe Mode with minimal drivers (while not executing any of the startup files) and will produce the DOS command-line prompt.

The *Safe Mode Command Prompt Only* option loads just two items — the command interpreter (COMMAND.COM in Windows 9x and **CMD.EXE** in Windows NT/2000) and, if present, the disk-compression utility files (DriveSpace or DoubleSpace). It does not load any of the Windows 9x files, HIMEM.SYS, or IFSHLP.SYS. This option should be chosen when the system fails to start in Safe Mode. You can enter this mode directly during the startup process by pressing the SHIFT and F5 keys simultaneously (SHIFT+F5) when the "Starting Windows 9x" message is onscreen. You also can use it to:

CMD.EXE

- Employ command-line switches, such as WIN d/x
- Employ command-line tools, such as DOS editors
- Avoid loading HIMEM.SYS or IFSHLP.SYS

The *Safe Mode without Compression* option only appears in systems that are using compressed drives. In operation, it is similar to the *Command Prompt Only* option with the exception that no compression drivers are loaded. The following list provides reasons for selecting this option.

- The system stops responding when a compressed drive is accessed.
- A Corrupt CVF (**Compressed Volume File**) error displays during startup.
- When Safe Mode and Safe Mode Command Prompt Only options fail to start the system.

Compressed Volume File

If the *BootMulti=* option was set to 1 during the Windows 9x setup, the menu will contain an option to *Start Using the Previous Version of MS-DOS*. As its name indicates, this option starts the system with the version of MS-DOS that was on the hard drive before Windows 9x was installed. Dual booting must be enabled in the MSDOS.SYS file for this option to function.

CHALLENGE #5

When you attempt to start a client's Windows 9x computer, the system reaches the "Starting Windows..." prompt and then locks up. You try to start the system in standard Safe Mode, but it still locks up when the desktop GUI come to the screen. What could be causing this problem, and how should you repair it?

WIN Switches

When Windows 9x refuses to start up, a number of options are available for starting it from the command line. Starting Windows using the **WIN command** with a /D switch is often helpful in isolating possible areas of the operating system as problem sources (that is, WIN /D). You can modify the /D switch to start Windows in a number of different configurations:

WIN command

- Using a /D:F switch disables 32-bit disk access.
- The /D:M and /D:N switches start Windows in Safe Mode, or Safe Mode with Networking.
- A /D:S switch inhibits Windows from using address space between F0000 and FFFFF.

- The /D:V switch prevents Windows from controlling disk transfers. Instead, HDD interrupt requests are handled by the BIOS.

- The /D:X switch prevents Windows from using the area of memory between A000 and FFFF.

Other switches can be used with the WIN command. The WIN /B switch causes Windows to start in Logged mode and to produce a BOOTLOG.TXT file during startup. This option enables you to determine whether specific device drivers are stalling the system. Logged mode can also be selected by pressing the F8 key while the "Starting Windows 9x" message is onscreen. After selecting the *Logged* option, restart the system using the *Safe Mode Command Prompt Only* option. Then, use a text editor to examine the contents of the BOOTLOG.TXT file and determine which driver has failed to load.

Using a question mark as a switch with the WIN command (i.e., WIN /?) shows a listing of all the switches associated with the command. You can use these switches to start Windows with various portions of the operating system disabled. If the system runs with a particular section disabled, at least some portion of the problem can be linked to that area.

CHALLENGE #6

A client has called you up from her hotel room. She is traveling to a convention and her Windows 9x notebook computer hangs up after displaying the "Starting Windows" notice. She does not know how to begin troubleshooting the problem, and there is no technical support around the hotel. She needs the notebook to be running tomorrow so that she can give a Power Point slide show presentation at the convention. What two things can you suggest for getting past the "Starting Windows" message so that she can try to repair her computer?

Windows 9x Log Files

log files

Windows 9x maintains four **log files**: BOOTLOG.TXT, SETUPLOG.TXT, DETLOG.TXT, and DETCRASH.LOG. These files maintain a log of different system operations and enable you to see what events occurred leading up to a failure. The TXT files can be read with Notepad, DOS Editor, or any other text editor. Their filenames are indicative of the types of information they log. As described earlier, the BOOTUPLOG.TXT file tracks the events of the startup procedure. Likewise, SETUPLOG.TXT tracks the events of the setup process. The DETLOG.TXT file monitors the presence of detected hardware devices and identifies the parameters for them. This file just happens to be a very good description of the system's PnP operations.

BOOTLOG.TXT

- *BOOTLOG.TXT* – The **BOOTLOG.TXT** file contains the sequence of events conducted during the startup of the system. The original BOOTLOG.TXT file is created during the Windows 9x setup process. You can update the file by pressing the F8 key during Startup, or by starting Windows 9x with a WIN /b switch. It is not updated automatically each time the system is started.

- *SETUPLOG.TXT* − The **SETUPLOG.TXT** file holds setup information that was established during the installation process. The log file exists in seven basic sections, as described in the following sample sections. Entries are added to the file as they occur in the setup process. Therefore, the file can be read to determine what action was being taken when a setup failure occurred. The file is stored on the system's root directory and is used in Safe Recovery situations.

- *DETCRASH.LOG* − This **Detect Crash log** file is created when the system crashes during the hardware detection portion of the startup procedure. It contains information about the detection module that was running when the crash occurred. This file is a binary file and cannot be read directly. However, a text version of the file, named *DETLOG.TXT*, is available under the root directory of the drive.

SETUPLOG.TXT

Detect Crash log

DETLOG.TXT

DETCRASH.LOG

Detlog and the PnP Process

The **DETLOG.TXT** file holds the text equivalent of the information in the **DETCRASH.LOG** file. This file can be read with a text editor to determine which hardware components have been detected by the system and what its parameters are. This printout is really a detailed explanation of the hardware-detection phase of the system's PnP operation.

The following section of a sample DETLOG.TXT file demonstrates the type of information logged in this file. This listing is actually a reflection of how the PnP process works and how it allocates resources (compare the resource values to those listed in the Standard I/O chapter.

```
[System Detection: 11/07/97 - 12:05:11]
Parameters "", InfParams "", Flags=01004233
SDVer=0400.950, WinVer=0700030a, Build=00.00.0, WinFlags=00000419
LogCrash: crash log not found or invalid
SetVar: CDROM_Any=
Checking for: Programmable Interrupt Controller
QueryIOMem: Caller=DETECTPIC, rcQuery=0
    IO=20-21,a0-a1
Detected: *PNP0000\0000 = [1] Programmable interrupt controller
    IO=20-21,a0-a1
    IRQ=2
Checking for: Direct Memory Access Controller
QueryIOMem: Caller=DETECTDMA, rcQuery=0
    IO=0-f,81-83,87-87,89-8b,8f-8f,c0-df
Detected: *PNP0200\0000 − [2] Direct memory access controller
    IO=0-f,81-83,87-87,89-8b,8f-8f,c0-df
    DMA=4
*
Checking for: Standard Floppy Controller
QueryIOMem: Caller=DETECTFLOPPY, rcQuery=0
    IO=3f2-3f5
QueryIOMem: Caller=DETECTFLOPPY, rcQuery=0
    IO=372-375
Detected: *PNP0700\0000 = [11] Standard Floppy Disk Controller
    IO=3f2-3f5
    IRQ=6
    DMA=2
Checking for: Serial Communication Port
QueryIOMem: Caller=DETECTCOM, rcQuery=0
    IO=3f8-3ff
```

```
GetCOMIRQ: IIR=1
Detected: *PNP0500\0000 = [12] Communications Port
   IO=3f8-3ff
   IRQ=4
SetVar: COMIRQ3f8=4,0
SetVar: COMIRQ2f8=3,0
Checking for: Serial Mouse
QueryIOMem: Caller=DETECTSERIALMOUSE, rcQuery=2
   IO=3f8-3ff
Serial mouse ID: M (004d)
Detected: *PNP0F0C\0000 = [14] Standard Serial Mouse
SetVar: COMIRQ3f8=4,0
*
```

PnP hardware detection

Referring to the information in the sample file, it should be easy to see the type of information that is logged about the system. The **PnP hardware detection** routine cycles through a three-part process; first it identifies the activity it is about to perform (i.e., Checking for: Serial Mouse), and then it queries the system at addresses normally allocated to that type of device (IO=3f8-3ff), and finally verifies that it was detected (or not). Some entries also include a listing of the IRQ and DMA resources allocated to the device.

The sample list includes information about many of the system and I/O devices found in a typical PC system. In each case, the PnP system inquires about particular system devices and logs the parameters of the device it detects. The sample also shows that, at least in this case, no crash log has been created. To use the file for crash-detection purposes, simply check the last entry created in the log. To determine exactly where a problem has occurred, it may be necessary to compare this information to the listing in a file named DETLOG.OLD. This file is the old version of the DETLOG file that was renamed before the latest detection phase began.

Using the Windows 98 Startup Disk

If the system does not make it to the Startup menu, you must boot the system with the Startup disk and begin checking the operating system on the boot drive. When the system is booted from a Windows 98 Startup disk, a menu such as the following displays:

1. Start the computer with CD-ROM support.

2. Start the computer without CD-ROM support.

3. View the Help file.

If the *CD-ROM support* option is selected, the system will execute the portion of the CONFIG.SYS file that loads the CD-ROM driver, and will set up a 2 MB RAMdrive. Use the Startup disk to boot the system and gain access to the operating system's files. After gaining access to the system, you can use the built-in troubleshooting aids on the Windows 9x Startup disk to isolate the cause of the problem.

Using Windows 98 System Tools on Startup Problems

A portion of the A+ Operating System Technologies objective 3.2 states that the test taker should be able to recognize when to use common diagnostic utilities and tools. Given a diagnostic scenario involving one of these utilities or tools, select the appropriate steps needed to resolve the problem. It also indicates that the content will include the following utilities and tools:

- Automatic skip driver (ASD.exe)
- Diagnostic tools, utilities, and resources
- User/Installation manuals
- Internet/web resources
- Training materials

- Task Manager
- Dr. Watson
- Boot disk
- Event Viewer

In addition to the clean-boot, Safe Mode, and log file functions previously described, Windows 98 contains a wealth of other troubleshooting tools that you can use to isolate and correct problems.

If a startup problem disappears when the system is started using any of the Safe Modes, use the **System Configuration** utility (**MSCONFIG.EXE**) to isolate the conflicting items. Of course, you may need to enter this command from the command line.

Select the *Diagnostic Startup* option to interactively load device drivers and software options from the *General tab* screen. When the Startup menu appears, select the *Step-by-Step* option. Begin by starting the system with only the CONFIG.SYS and AUTOEXEC.BAT files disabled. If the system starts, move into those tabs and step through those files, one line at a time, using the selective startup option. The step-by-step process is used to systematically enable or disable items until all the problem items are identified. If an entry is marked with a Microsoft Windows logo, it is used when the *Selective Startup* option is disabled.

> **System Configuration**
>
> **MSCONFIG.EXE**

If the problem does not go away, you can use the *Advanced* button from the *General* tab to inspect lower level configuration settings, such as real-mode disk accesses, and VGA standard video settings. You also can start the Device Manager from the *MSCONFIG View* option. This will allow the protected mode device drivers to be inspected. The MSINFO-Problem Devices section also should be examined to check for possible problem-causing devices. Other items to check include missing or corrupted system files (using the *System File Checker* utility), corrupted Registry entries (using the *Registry Checker*), viruses (using a virus checker program), and hardware conflicts using the CMOS Configuration screens.

> ┌─ **TEST TIP** ─────────────────┐
> │ Know what types of problems the │
> │ MSCONFIG.EXE utility is used for. │
> └──────────────────────────────────┘

When a potential problem setting has been identified in CONFIG.SYS, AUTOEXEC.BAT, or the Registry, use the **Automatic Skip Driver** (**ASD**) utility to automatically isolate and disable the suspect line. Just select the *ASD* option from the *System Information's Tools* menu. Select the operation that has failed by marking it in the *Hardware Troubleshooting Agent* dialog box, and then select the *Details* option. This action should cause the *Enumerating a Device* dialog box to provide recommendations for correcting any problems. This normally involves replacing the driver disabled by the ASD utility. This series of automated tests basically replaces the manual isolation method performed with the *Step-by-Step Startup* option.

> **Automatic Skip Driver (ASD)**

The Windows 98 system may contain up to five backup copies of the Registry structure. If the system fails to start up after installing some new software or hardware component, run the **Registry Checker** utility using the *Restore* option (**ScanReg /Restore**) to return the Registry to its previous condition. Just type *ScanReg /Restore* at the MS-DOS prompt to view a list of available backup copies. Generally, the most recent version should be selected for use. These tools are discussed in greater detail later in this chapter.

TEST TIP

Know which Windows 9x utility can be used to restore backup copies of the Registry to the system.

WINDOWS 2000/XP STARTUP PROBLEMS

For Windows 2000 and Windows XP, you can build on the operating system troubleshooting methodology previously discussed. If Windows 2000/XP fails to boot, the first troubleshooting step is to determine whether the computer is failing before or after the operating system takes control. If the startup process makes it to the beep that indicates the end of the POST, but you do not see the operating system's Advanced Options Menu, the problem is probably one of the following:

- System partition
- Master Boot Record
- Partition boot sector

These types of problems are usually the result of hard disk media failure or a virus, and must be repaired before the operating system can function. Typical symptoms associated with these failures include the following:

- The blue screen or Stop message appears.
- Bootup stops after the POST.
- The Boot Selection menu is never reached.
- An error message is produced.

Windows 2000 displays a number of error messages related to these problems, including the following:

- Missing Operating System
- Disk Read Error
- Invalid Partition Table
- Hard Disk Error (or Absent/Failed)
- Insert System Disk
- Error Loading Operating System

The "Error Loading Operating System" message indicates that the system partition was located but could not start the operating system. The system partition on that drive could be missing or misidentified. Use the FDISK utility to search for and set the system partition properly.

The **BOOT.INI** file enables Windows 2000/XP to boot to separate operating systems. If this file is missing or corrupt you will not be able to boot to the Previous version of Windows. The computer will only boot to Windows 2000/XP. To correct this condition copy the BOOT.INI file from a backup, or from another machine running the same setup and using the same installation directories.

The **NTDETECT.COM** or **NTLDR files** could also be missing or have become corrupt. If you receive the message "**NTLDR is missing**" or "**NTDETECT failed**", the partition boot sector is okay, but the NTLDR or NTDETECT.COM file is missing or corrupt. To correct these errors, you must reinstall Windows 2000 or Windows XP, or boot to the **Recovery Console** and copy the missing or corrupt file from a backup.

> **TEST TIP**
> Know which files must be present to boot Windows NT/2000/XP and how to correct problems associated with the Windows NT boot sequence.

The **Missing Operating System** and **Invalid Partition Table** errors indicate a problem with the Master Boot Record. Use the **FIXMBR** command in the Recovery Console to replace the Master Boot Record. Although this command works well on a stand-alone drive, it does not work with disks that contain partitions or logical drives that are part of striped or volume sets. You also should not perform this procedure on drives that use third-party translation, partitioning, or dual-boot programs.

Figure 12-5 illustrates the Windows 2000/XP startup process. In addition to listing the order of events that occur in each distinct startup stage, it also describes various types of problems typically encountered during each stage.

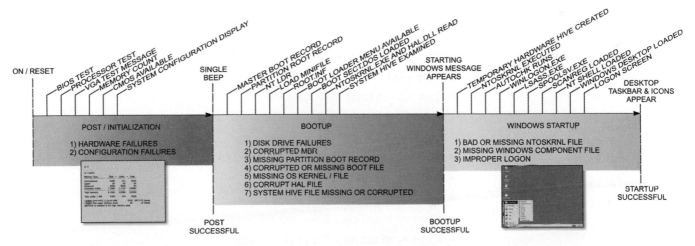

If the startup problem occurs at some point after the screen clears and the operating system selection menu appears, or after selecting Windows 2000 or Windows XP from the boot menu, the issue is probably with the operating system. Most likely, some necessary files are missing or have been corrupted.

Figure 12-5: The Windows 2000/XP Startup Sequence

Windows NT/2000/XP Startup Tools

Windows 2000 and Windows XP provide a wealth of tools for recovering from a startup problem, including the following:

- Windows NT 4.0 startup options
- Windows 2000/XP Safe Mode options
- Windows 2000/XP Recovery Console
- Windows 2000 Emergency Repair Disk
- Windows XP System Restore Function
- Windows XP Automated System Recovery
- Windows XP Driver Rollback option

The following sections describe these tools and their use in detail.

Windows NT Startup Modes

A portion of the A+ Operating System Technologies objective 2.3 indicates that the test taker should be able to identify the basic system boot sequences and boot methods, including the steps to create an emergency boot disk with utilities installed for Windows 9x/Me, Windows NT 4.0 Workstation, Windows 2000 Professional, and Windows XP. It also indicates that content should include:

- Alternative boot methods
- Using a Startup disk
- Safe/VGA-only mode
- Last Known Good Configuration
- Command Prompt mode
- Booting to a system restore point
- Recovery Console
- Boot.ini switches
- Dual booting
- Creating Emergency disks with OS utilities
- Creating Emergency Repair Disk (ERD)

Unlike the Windows 9x products, Windows NT 4.0 provides very few options when it starts up. The user is normally offered two options. The NTLDR file causes the system to display a selection menu of which operating system to boot from, along with an option to start the system in **VGA mode** or the **Last Known Good Hardware Configuration mode**. The menu listing is based on what NTLDR finds in the BOOT.INI file.

If the *VGA* option is selected, the system will start up as normal, with the exception that it will only load the standard VGA driver to drive the display. This option was introduced with the Windows NT 4.0 version for the express purpose of managing video driver problems.

VGA mode

Last Known Good Hardware Configuration mode

The second option presented is the *Last Known Good Hardware Configuration mode* option. Selecting this option will cause the system to start up using the configuration information that it recorded the last time a user successfully logged onto the system. The option appears on the screen for a few seconds after the operating system selection has been made.

These options are extremely valuable for sorting out Windows NT/2000 configuration problems. You must press the SPACEBAR while they are displayed on the screen to select one of the optional startup modes. If no selection is made, the system will continue with a normal startup sequence as previously outlined, using the existing hardware configuration information.

Altering BOOT.INI

The BOOT.INI file in Windows NT/2000/XP systems is a special, hidden read-only boot text file that is used to generate the Advanced Boot Options menu during the NT/2000/XP startup process. The system reads this file during the bootup process and places the Advanced Boot Options menu on the screen to permit the user to select different bootup options. If no selection is made within a specified time frame, the bootup process continues on in default mode.

The settings in the BOOT.INI file are used to select an operating system to boot to. It supports the starting of different Windows NT versions as well as providing for starting one non-NT operating system. The BOOT.INI file contains two sections of text that can be read and modified. This enables technicians and administrators to configure the system so that the Boot Options menu will display the different operating system options available.

The default values of the BOOT.INI file are generated automatically by the system when the Windows NT/2000/XP operating system is installed. You can access this file by using a text editor. Before doing this you must change its attributes so that it becomes visible and so you can open it. This can be done through My Computer, Windows Explorer, or by using the Attrib command.

There are many switches available for use with the Windows NT entries in the menu to change the bootup process. Some of the switches that are particularly interesting for trouble-shooting purposes are the:

- /BASEVIDEO switch that forces the computer to start up using the Standard VGA driver.

- /DEBUG switch that starts the system in Debug mode as described in the later Windows 2000/XP Startup Modes section in this chapter.

- MAXMEM:n switch that can be used to specify the maximum amount of RAM that the system will start up with.

- /SOS switch that displays the different drive names as they are loaded (similar to the step-by-step startup option in Safe Mode).

One of the major Windows Me/XP Recovery Console commands is the Bootcfg command. This command can be used to change the configuration of the BOOT.INI file or to recover from bootup problems. The Bootcfg file is only available for use in the Recovery Console.

DUAL BOOTING

In a dual-boot system a startup menu is established that can be used to boot the system into different operating systems located on the disk. Depending on which operating system option the user selects from the menu, the system will retrieve the correct set of files and then use them to boot the system.

To accomplish this, Windows 9x swaps versions of the boot files back and forth between their standard names and a designated set of backup names. In Windows NT/2000/XP systems you should place the operating systems in different partitions and access them through the Advanced Options Menu at startup.

If the system has been configured for dual booting, the option to do so will appear in the Boot Options menu (or the Advanced Options Menu in Windows 2000/XP systems), which appears whenever you boot up. This is the same startup menu that can be accessed by pressing the F8 function key during the boot process.

Windows 2000/XP Startup Modes

The Windows 2000 and Windows XP operating systems incorporate a number of Windows 9x – like startup options that can be engaged to get the system up and running in a given state to provide a starting point for troubleshooting operations. The **Advanced Options Menu**, shown in Figure 12-6, contains several options that can be of assistance when troubleshooting startup failures. To display this menu, press F8 at the beginning of the Windows 2000/XP startup process.

Advanced Options Menu

```
Windows 2000 Advanced Options Menu
Please select an option:

Safe Mode
Safe Mode with Networking
Safe Mode with Command Prompt

Enable Boot Logging
Enable VGA Mode
Last Known Good Configuration
Directory Services Restore Mode (Windows 2000 domain controllers only)
Debugging Mode

Boot Normally
Return to OS Choices Menu


Use ↑ and ↓ to move the highlight to your choice.
Press Enter to choose.
```

**Figure 12-6:
The Advanced Options
Menu**

The Windows 2000/XP Startup Menu basically provides the same Safe Mode options as the Windows 9x operating systems — Boot Normally, **Safe Mode**, **Safe Mode with Networking**, and **Safe Mode with Command Prompt**. However, the Windows 2000 and Windows XP menus also provide a number of Windows NT—like options:

Safe Mode
Safe Mode with Networking
Safe Mode with Command Prompt
Enable Boot Logging
NTBTLOG.TXT
Enable VGA Mode
Last Known Good Configuration
Debugging Mode

- **Enable Boot Logging** — which creates a log file called **NTBTLOG.TXT** in the root folder. This log is very similar to the BOOTLOG.TXT file described earlier in that it contains a listing of all the drivers and services that the system attempts to load during startup and can be useful when trying to determine what service or driver is causing the system to fail.

- **Enable VGA Mode** — when selected, this option boots the system normally, but uses only the standard VGA driver. If you have configured the display incorrectly and are unable to see the desktop, booting into VGA Mode will enable you to reconfigure those settings.

- **Last Known Good Configuration** — this option will start Windows 2000 using the settings that existed the last time a successful user logon occurred. All system setting changes made since the last successful startup are lost. This is a particularly useful option if you have added or reconfigured a device driver that is causing the system to fail.

- **Debugging Mode** — will start Windows 2000 in a kernel debug mode that will enable special debugger utilities to access the kernel for troubleshooting and analysis.

CHALLENGE #7

While you are working on a customer's Windows 2000 system, you notice that the display resolution is running well below what you expect from his video card. When you attempt to change the video driver to get better display performance out of it, you only see horizontal streaks across the screen after you reboot the machine. Which Windows 2000 startup mode provides the best choice for quickly accessing the display setup so you can correct it?

Windows 2000/XP Recovery Console

The **Recovery Console** available in Windows 2000 and Windows XP is a command-line interface that provides you with access to the hard disks and many command-line utilities when the operating system will not boot (i.e., after the *Last Known Good Configuration* and *Safe Mode* options have been tried). The Recovery Console can access all volumes on the drive, regardless of their file system type. However, if you have not added the *Recovery Console* option prior to a failure, you will not be able to employ it and will need to use the Windows 2000 Setup disks or the Windows 2000/XP distribution CD instead. You can use the Recovery Console to perform tasks such as the following:

Recovery Console

- Copy files from a floppy disk, CD, or another hard disk to the hard disk used for booting, enabling you to replace or remove files that may be affecting the boot process. Because of the security features in Windows 2000 and Windows XP, you are only granted limited access to certain files on the hard drive. You cannot copy files from the hard drive to a floppy or other storage device under these conditions.

- Control the startup state of services, enabling you to disable a service that could potentially be causing the operating system to crash

- Add, remove, and format volumes on the hard disk

- Repair the MBR or boot sector of a hard disk or volume

- Restore the Registry

The Recovery Console can be permanently installed on a system and be made accessible from the *Advanced Options* menu. The Recovery Console can be started at any time by booting from the Windows 2000 Setup disks or the Windows 2000/XP distribution CDs, choosing to repair an installation, and selecting *Recovery Console* from the repair options.

To install the Recovery Console on a computer, follow these steps:

1. Put the Windows 2000 or Windows XP distribution CD into the CD-ROM drive, or connect to an installation share on the network.

winnt32 /cmdcons

2. Run the **winnt32 /cmdcons** command. Windows 2000/XP Setup will start up, as illustrated in Figure 12-7, and install the Recovery Console.

3. The Recovery Console will automatically be added to the Advanced Options Menu.

Figure 12-7: Installing the Recovery Console Using winnt32 /cmdcons

You can run the Recovery Console from the distribution CD for both Windows 2000 and Windows XP. To do so, start the system with the distribution CD in the drive and choose the option to *Repair* (by pressing the R key) the installation. Enter the administrator's password to access the Recovery Console. The password protection for the Recovery Console only permits two incorrect attempts by default. On the third incorrect attempt, the system will stop accepting further entries for a predetermined amount of time (referred to as **lockout time**).

lockout time

Calling for Help — When you start the Recovery Console, you are prompted to choose the folder that contains the Windows 2000 or Windows XP installation that you are trying to repair, and then to log on as Administrator. The commands that can be used with the Recovery Console include most of the MS-DOS—based commands covered in Chapter 8 — *Operating System Fundamentals*. After you have logged on to the system, you can type HELP at the command line to obtain a list of available commands.

One of the primary uses of the Recovery Console is to restore the Registry. Every time you back up the System State data with the Windows 2000 or Windows XP Backup utilities, a copy of the Registry is placed in the *\Repair\RegBack* folder. If you copy the entire content of this folder or only particular files to *\System32\Config* (which is the folder where the working copy of the Registry is stored), you can restore the Registry to the same condition as the last time you performed a **System State data backup**. It is recommended that you create a copy of the files in *\System32\Config* prior to restoring the other files from backup so that you can restore the Registry to its original condition if necessary.

System State data backup

Windows XP System Restore

The Windows XP **System Restore** utility enables administrators to **roll back** Windows XP Professional operating system to a previous operational state and configuration — without affecting any user's personal data. This feature extends the *Last Known Good Configuration* mode by allowing the system to be rolled back to predetermined **restore points**.

System Restore

roll back

restore points

Restore points are records of information that are created at specific intervals and when certain events occur. Some restore points are created automatically on a 24-hour/daily basis. Others are created when significant events occur, such as when you upgrade the system hardware or software, perform a recovery operation, or when a new driver is loaded. However, restore points can also be created manually as a method of preserving the current state of the operating system prior to performing management activities. Such activities include:

- When you are updating a driver and it appears to cause problems with the system that rolling back the driver does not resolve

- When you are installing a new software program and it creates problems with the system that uninstalling the software does not resolve

- Anytime you need to get back to a point where you know the system was functioning correctly

You should actually create a restore point anytime you are making changes to the system that might make it unstable or that might disable it.

Using System Restore

To activate the Windows XP **System Restore feature**, navigate the *Start/All Programs/Accessories/System Tools* path, and then select the *System Restore* option from the menu. The *Welcome* screen will be displayed as shown in Figure 12-8.

System Restore feature

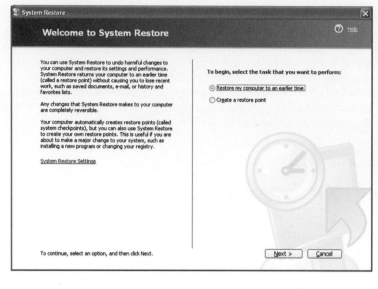

Figure 12-8: System Restore Welcome Screen

Help and Support Center

To manually create Restore points simply select the *Create a restore point* option from the *Welcome to System Restore* screen (the *Create a restore point* option can also be accessed through the *Start* menu's **Help and Support Center** option). Click on the *Next* button and enter the name for the restore point in the *Restore point description* text box, as illustrated in Figure 12-9. The System Restore utility will automatically add this name, along with the time and date, to the restore point list. Click on *Create* to finish the process.

Figure 12-9: Creating a Restore Point

Selecting the *Restore my computer to an earlier time* option from the *Welcome* screen will enable you to select a restore point from a calendar and a listing, as illustrated in Figure 12-10. Unless you simply need a restore point from earlier in the day, select the date on the calendar that you wish to roll the system back to and if there are multiple restore points for that day, choose the restore point you want to use.

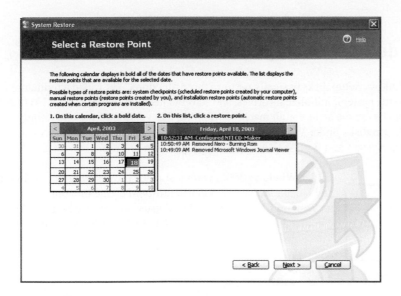

Figure 12-10: The Select a Restore Point Screen

After you have confirmed the restore point, the system will conduct the rollback and the system will automatically restart. There is an *Undo* option (undo my last restoration) available that can be used if the restore operation did not solve the problem, or the problem is worse.

To access the System Restore utility through the Start menu's *Help and Support* option, select the *Performance and Maintenance* option from its menu, click on the *Using System Restore to Undo changes* entry, and click on the *Run the System Restore Wizard* option.

Windows NT/2000 Emergency Repair Disks

In the Windows NT/2000 arena, there are two different types of troubleshooting-related disks that the technician should have on hand. These are:

- The Setup disks

- The Emergency Repair Disk

Setup disks are the equivalent of the Windows 9x Startup Disk. Windows 2000 creates a four-disk set. Unlike the Windows 9x Start Disk, the Setup disks do not bring the system to a command prompt. Instead, they initiate the Windows Setup process.

Both Windows NT 4.0 and Windows 2000 provide for an **Emergency Repair Disk (ERD)** to be produced. The ERD is different than the Setup disks in that it is intended for use with an operational system when it crashes. It is not a bootable disk and must be used with the Setup disks, or the distribution CD. While the Setup disks are uniform for a given version of Windows NT, the ERD is specific to the machine it is created from. It contains a copy of the Registry in Windows 2000. When dealing with the Windows 2000 ERD, it is necessary to manually copy the Registry files to the disk.

Emergency Repair Disk (ERD)

Windows NT Setup Disks

The Windows Setup disks basically perform three functions. They load a miniature file system into the system, initialize its drives, and start the installation process. All **Windows NT Setup disks** are the same for all machines running that version of the operating system. To create Setup disks under Windows NT 4.0, you must install the Windows NT distribution CD in the system and type **WINNT /ox** at the command prompt.

> ┌─ **TEST TIP** ─────────
> Be aware of the different ways that Setup disks are created in Windows NT 4.0 and Windows 2000.

Under Windows 2000, you must place the distribution CD in the drive and launch the MakeBootDisk utility to create the four disk images for its Windows 2000 Setup disks. You can also create Setup disks from the command prompt using the **MAKEBT32.EXE** file for Windows 2000. These disks can also be made from the *Start/Run/Browse/CD-ROM* path. From the CD, select the *BOOTDISK* option followed by the *MAKEBT32.EXE* command.

Windows NT 4.0 ERD

Repair Disk

RDISK.EXE

During the installation process, Windows NT Setup asks whether you want to create an Emergency Repair Disk. You can also create an ERD later using the **Repair Disk** program (**RDISK.EXE**). To do so, select the *Run* option from the *Start* menu, enter the *CMD* command in the *Run* dialog box, and then type *rdisk* at the command prompt.

> ┌─ **TEST TIP** ─────────
> Know what the RDISK command is used for in a Windows NT 4.0 system.

When Windows NT is installed, the Setup routine stores Registry information in the *%systemroot%\system32\config* folder and creates a *%systemroot%\repair* folder to hold key files.

Windows 2000 ERD

> ┌─ **TEST TIP** ─────────
> Know where ERDs are created in Windows NT 4.0 and in Windows 2000.

The Windows 2000 Setup routine prompts you to create an ERD during the installation process. The ERD can also be created using the Windows 2000 Backup utility located under the *Programs/Accessories/System Tools* path. Choosing this option will activate the Windows 2000 ERD creation box, shown in Figure 12-11. The Windows 2000 ERD disk contains configuration information that is specific to the computer that will be required during the emergency repair process.

Figure 12-11: The ERD Creation Box

Performing an Emergency Repair

The Emergency Repair Disk provides another troubleshooting tool that can be used when Safe Mode and the Recovery Console do not enable you to repair the system. If you have already created an ERD, you can start the system with the Windows 2000 Setup CD or the Setup floppy disks, and then use the ERD to restore core system files. The emergency repair process enables you to do the following:

- Repair the boot sector
- Replace the system files
- Repair the startup files

> **Limited to the operating system**—The emergency repair process is designed to repair the operating system only, and cannot assist in repairing application or data problems.

To perform an emergency repair, follow these steps:

Hands-on Activity

Performing an Emergency Repair

1. Boot the system from the Window 2000 CD. If the system will not boot from the CD, you must boot with the Setup Boot Disk, which is the first of four Setup floppy disks that are required. You create the Setup floppy disks with MAKEBOOT.EXE, which is in the *\BOOTDISK* folder in the Windows 2000 CD root directory.

2. When the text-mode portion of setup begins, follow the initial prompts. You will reach the *Welcome To Setup* screen, as shown in Figure 12-12.

3. When prompted, choose the *Emergency Repair Process* by pressing *R*.

4. When prompted, press *F* for fast repair.

5. Follow the instructions, and insert the Emergency Repair Disk into the floppy disk drive when prompted.

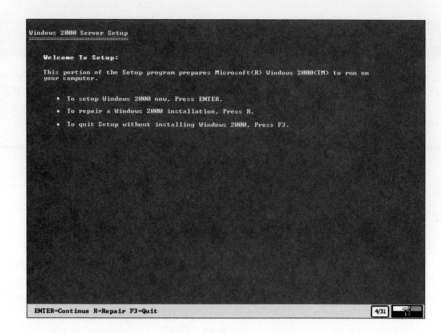

**Figure 12-12:
The Welcome To Setup
Screen**

Windows XP Automated System Recovery

In the Windows XP operating system, the Emergency Repair Disk has been replaced with an emergency startup tool called **Automated System Recovery (ASR)**. The ASR tool can be used to back up and restore the system state information, along with all the files stored on the system volume. As with the Windows NT/2000 Emergency Repair Disk, the ASR feature is considered to be the last resort that is used when you have been unable to recover the system using other methods, including Safe Mode, Last Known Good Configuration mode, and the Recovery Console.

The ASR utility is a function of the backup utility (NTBackup.exe). As with other backup options, ASR is a two-part system— backup and restore operations. **ASR backups** should be performed periodically to keep them up-to-date. On the other hand, an **ASR restore** operation is usually performed only in the case of a system failure. The contents of an ASR backup operation include:

- the System State data
- the system services
- the system components for all disks

In addition, an ASR floppy disk is created during the backup operation that contains additional information required for the ASR restore process. This disk contains two files:

- *Asr.sif* — which contains hard disk, partition, and volume configuration information along with general system information.

- *Asrpnp.sif* — which contains PnP device configuration data.

Conducting ASR Backups

ASR backup operations are performed through the Windows XP Backup Utility as follows:

1. Access the Windows XP Backup Utility and click on the *Next* button on the *Backup and Restore Wizard Welcome* window.

2. From the *Welcome* window, switch to *Advanced mode*.

3. Click on the *Automated System Recovery Wizard* button, as shown in Figure 12-13, and click on the *Next* button.

4. Select a backup media type, specify the backup name, and click on the *Finish* button to complete the ASR backup operation.

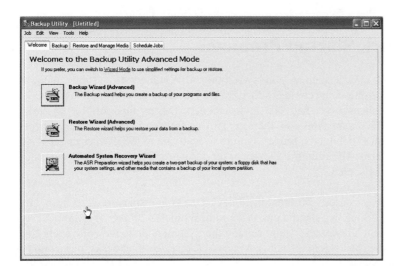

**Figure 12-13:
Launching the ASR
Wizard**

You should not place the ASR backup on the system or boot volume when specifying a location for the backup. The system volume is reformatted during an ASR restore, and depending on the condition of the system, the boot volume may be reformatted as well. You should also be aware that performing a restore operation from network shares is not an option with ASR. You must use local devices such as another hard disk, a CD-ROM, or a tape drive to hold the ASR backup.

> **— NOTE —**
>
> If the ASR backups are being used as a method of system restore, make sure that they are performed on a regular schedule.

ASR Restore Operations

The ASR restore process is launched from Windows XP Professional Setup as a part of the operating system install process (i.e., the operating system is reinstalled and then the ASR backup information is used to complete the restoration of the system).

Three items are required to conduct the ASR restore operation. These items are:

- The Windows XP distribution CD

- The ASR floppy disk

- The ASR backup

You should make sure that you have access to these items prior to launching an ASR restore operation.

To perform an ASR restore, boot the system using the Windows XP Professional CD and press the F2 function key when the *Welcome To Setup* screen is displayed. The ASR process should automatically start at this point. Then, when prompted, insert the ASR floppy disk and simply follow the on-screen prompts.

In the event that the ASR floppy disk is lost or damaged, the *Asr.sif* and *Asrpnp.sif* files can be recovered from the ASR backup. The *Asf.inf* and *Asrpnp.inf* files must reside at the root of the ASR floppy disk in order for them to be found during the ASR restore process.

Network Startup Problems

For network clients, such as Windows 2000 and Windows XP systems, there is one additional startup phase that could produce errors. This is the network logon phase (which is automatic in client/server network environments). During this period, the desktop should appear on the screen. However, there are still several communication services being loaded into the system behind the scenes. Failure to load one of these services (or the device that supports them) will result in a "Device or service has failed to start" error message being displayed on the screen.

In most of these cases, you should still have a desktop display to work from. However, the system is working in a stand-alone fashion. In Windows 2000 or Windows XP systems, access the Event Viewer utility and expand the System node to view the event log of system events — such as loading the networking services. Even if no desktop is available, you can restart the system in Safe Mode and access the Event Viewer to use this log to isolate the cause of the error.

Logon Problems

logon problem

One last problem that can occur during startup (even though it is not actually a startup problem) is a **logon problem**, in which users cannot log on to systems when they have the proper authorization to do so. These problems tend to be very common in secure environments such as those that use Windows 2000 or Windows XP.

The most common logon problem is a forgotten or invalid username and password. Invalid usernames and passwords typically result from poor typing, or from having the Caps Lock function turned on. Users also can be prevented from logging on due to station or time restrictions. Check with the network administrator to see whether the user's rights to the system have been restricted.

COMMON OS OPERATIONAL PROBLEMS

The A+ Operating System Technologies objective 3.3 states that the test taker should be able to recognize common operational and usability problems and determine how to resolve them. It also says that content may include the following:

- Troubleshooting Windows-specific printing problems
- Print spool is stalled
- Incorrect/incompatible driver for print
- Incorrect parameter
- Other common problems
- General Protection Faults
- Blue screen error (BSOD)
- Illegal operation
- Invalid working directory
- System lock up
- Option device (i.e., sound card, modem, input device) will not function
- Application will not start or load
- Cannot log on to network (option – NIC not functioning)
- Applications don't install
- Network connection

The technician should be able to recognize common problems and determine how to resolve them. Once the operating system has been started up and is functional, there are particular types of problems that come into play. Many of these problems are documented in this A+ objective. It indicates that the technician must be able to identify and correct operational problems associated with the operating system. To this end, the following sections deal specifically with OS operational symptoms and problems, including the following:

- Memory usage
- Application
- Printing
- Networking

Memory Usage Problems

Memory usage problems occur when the operating system, or one of its applications, attempts to access an unallocated memory location. When these memory conflicts occur, the data in the violated memory locations is corrupted and may crash the system. In Windows 3.x, these types of problems were labeled **General Protection Faults** (**GPF**) and were generally the product of data protection errors induced by poorly written programs. These programs typically use stray pointers or illegal instructions that access areas of memory that have been protected.

General Protection
Faults (GPF)

Although the Windows 9x structure provides a much better multitasking environment than its predecessor did, applications can still attempt to access unallocated memory locations, or attempt to use another application's space. When these memory conflicts occur, the system can either return an error message or just stop processing. Due to the severity of the GPF problems in Windows 3.x, Microsoft chose to provide memory usage error messages in Windows 9x that say "**This Application Has Performed an Illegal Operation and Is About to Be Shut Down**".

Some memory usage errors are nonfatal and provide an option to ignore the fault and continue working, or to just close the application. These errors are generally caused by poorly written Windows applications and can sometimes be tracked to **dynamic link library** (**DLL**) files associated with a particular application. Although the application may continue to operate, it is generally not stable enough to continue working on an extended basis. It is recommended that the application be used only long enough to save any existing work and properly shut down the system.

Windows NT and Windows 2000 employ a flat memory management scheme that does not use the segmented memory mapping features associated with the Intel microprocessors. Therefore, these operating systems have very few memory usage problems.

> **This Application Has Performed an Illegal Operation and Is About to Be Shut Down**
>
> **dynamic link library (DLL)**

Optional Devices Will Not Operate

The system's basic devices are configured as part of the system's PnP startup process in both Windows 9x and Windows NT/2000 systems. However, this doesn't mean that all the system's devices are in working order or that they will remain in working order while the system is on. Optional devices such as modems, sound cards, and advanced I/O devices might configure properly as part of the PnP process and then fail to operate after the system starts.

As an example, many video cards are capable of displaying very high-resolution screens at high refresh rates. However, some monitors do not have the same capabilities. When you configure the video card with settings that the monitor cannot display, symptoms can range from a simple blank screen to several ghost images being displayed onscreen. After the initial installation, the video drivers are always changed while Windows is operating.

To correct this problem under Windows 9x, start the system in Safe Mode. This action causes Windows to load a basic VGA video driver, enabling you to then change the display properties of the video card. In a Windows 2000 or Windows XP system, you should select the *VGA Mode* option to gain access to the video configuration by loading a standard VGA driver.

Similarly, adding input devices, such as a new mouse or joystick, can create problems where the new device does not work under the Windows environment. In the Windows operating system, there are several tools to help identify and isolate hardware-related problems. These tools include the Device Manager (located under the Control Panel's *System* icon), the Hardware Troubleshooter procedures (located under the *Help* entry of the *Start* menu), and the various hardware-related icons in the Control Panel.

You believe your video display can produce a much higher resolution display than it is currently providing, so you change the video driver in your Windows 2000 Professional system. When you apply the new setting, you cannot see anything on the display. What should you do to regain control of your display?

As mentioned earlier, Windows XP offers *Device Driver Rollback, System Restore,* and *Disable the Device* options that can be used to replace an updated driver (other than a printer driver) that may be causing problems. This option reinstalls the driver that was being used previous to the current driver and restores any driver settings that were updated when the driver was installed.

The *System Restore* feature can be used to restore the system and its applications to a previous operating configuration that was known to be working correctly at that point. You would resort to this method of changing the device driver in Windows XP if the *Device Driver Rollback* option does not repair the system.

The *Disable the Device* option should be used when you believe that a specific device is causing a system problem. This option simply disables the device and its drivers so that you can verify that it is the cause of whatever problem the system is experiencing.

Applications Will Not Install

In Windows 9x, Windows 2000, and Windows XP systems, most applications will autorun when their distribution CD is placed in the drive. The **Autorun feature** presents a user interface on the display that will guide the user through the installation process. If the Autorun feature in Windows 2000 or Windows XP systems can be disabled in the drive's *Properties* page, the automatic interface will not start and the installation will not be performed. In Windows 9x, the Autorun feature is a function of the Registry and is not generally available to the user.

Autorun feature

You should check the distribution CD for the presence of the *Autorun.inf* file. If it is present and no Autorun action occurs, you should examine the CD-ROM drive's *Properties* page to ensure that the Autorun function is enabled.

Some applications do not include the Autorun function as part of their installation scheme and are typically installed through the Control Panel's *Add/Remove Programs* applet. If the application is not on the *Windows 2000 Application Compatibility Toolkit (ACT)*, the software equivalent of the HCL listing, the application might not install on the system or operate properly. This tool can be downloaded from the Microsoft Upgrade web page.

Windows 9x Operating Problems

Aside from the application, printing, and networking problem categories listed earlier, if the Windows 9x operating system starts up properly, only a limited number of things can go wrong afterward. The disk drive can run out of space, files can become corrupt, or the system can lock up due to software exception errors. When these problems occur, the system can either return an error message or just stop processing.

Drive Space and Memory Problems

System Information

The **System Information** utility in the */Programs/Accessories/System Tools* path can be used to view the disk drive's space parameters. You also can check the drive's used/available space information by performing a CheckDisk operation on it.

Out of Memory error

If the system produces an **Out of Memory error** in Windows 9x, it is very unlikely that the system is running out of RAM, unless you are running DOS-based applications. In Windows 9x, this error indicates that the system is running out of memory space altogether — RAM and virtual.

MEMMAKER utility

Run the Windows System Monitor utility described later in this chapter to observe system memory usage and determine the nature of the error. If you are running MS-DOS—based applications, you can optimize the system's use of conventional memory by running the old DOS **MEMMAKER utility** from the *\Tools\Oldmsdos* directory on the Windows distribution CD.

lost clusters

You can view the drive's swap file settings through the Control Panel's *System/Performance/Virtual Memory* option or through the System Tool's System Information utility. As always, any **lost clusters** taking up space on the drive can be identified and eliminated using the ScanDisk utility. A heavily used, heavily fragmented hard drive can affect the system's virtual memory and produce memory shortages as well. Run the Defrag utility to optimize the storage patterns on the drive.

CVT1.EXE

If the system is running a FAT16 drive, you can free up additional space by converting it to a FAT32 drive. The command-line utility for this is **CVT1.EXE**. The smaller sector clustering available through FAT32 frees up wasted space on the drive. The drawbacks of performing this upgrade are that you run some risk of losing data if a failure occurs in the conversion process, and that larger files will have slightly slower read/write times than they did under FAT16.

> **TEST TIP**
>
> Be aware of the part that the disk drive plays in Windows 9x memory management and how to optimize its use.

If these corrective actions do not clear the memory error, you will need to remove unnecessary files from the drive, or install a larger drive.

> **TEST TIP**
>
> Memorize which command-line utility can be used to convert the disk drive file system from FAT16 to FAT32.

If the system begins to run out of hard disk space, remember that there may be up to five backup copies of the Registry on the drive. This is a function of using the **SCANREGW** utility to check out the Registry structure for corruption. Each backup can be up to 2 MB in size and can be removed to free up additional disk drive space.

SCANREGW

Stalled Applications

If the system locks up, or an application stalls, it is often possible to regain access to the **Close Program** dialog box by pressing the CTRL+ALT+DEL key combination. Once the *Close Program* dialog box is onscreen, you can close the offending application and continue operating the system without rebooting.

Close Program

┌─ **TEST TIP** ─────────┐
Know how to clear a stalled application in the Windows environment.
└────────────────────────┘

As an example, in Windows 9x the Windows Explorer shell (EXPLORER.EXE) may crash and leave the system without a *Start* button or Taskbar to work with. To recover from this condition, use the CTRL+ALT+DEL combination to access the *Close Programs* dialog box and shut the system down in a proper manner. The ALT+F4 key combination can also be used to close active windows. Pressing this key combination in an application stops the application and moves to the next active application in the task list. If the ALT+F4 combination is pressed when no applications are active, the Windows **Shut Down menu** will appear on the display. This will enable you to conduct an orderly shutdown or restart of the system.

Shut Down menu

Dr. Watson

┌─ **TEST TIP** ─────────┐
Memorize the functions associated with the ALT+F4 key combination.
└────────────────────────┘

If the application repeatedly locks the system up, you must reinstall it and check its configuration settings. The **Dr. Watson** utility also proves very useful in detecting application faults. When activated, Dr. Watson intercepts the software actions, detects the failure, identifies the application, and provides a detailed description of the failure. The information is automatically transferred to the disk drive and stored in the *\Windows\Drwatson*.WLG* file. You can view and print the information stored in the file from a word processor.

┌─ **TEST TIP** ─────────┐
Know the function of the Dr. Watson utility and where its information is stored in the system.
└────────────────────────┘

CHALLENGE #10

You are using a number of different applications on a Windows 9x system, but when you open a spreadsheet program, it hangs up and the system will not do anything. What is the best method to safely restart the system and retain the information you have in the other open applications?

If an MS-DOS—based program is running and the system locks up, you must restore Windows 9x. To accomplish this, attempt to restart the system from a cold boot. If the system starts in Windows 9x, check the properties of the DOS application. This information can be obtained by locating the program through My Computer or through the Windows Explorer interfaces, right-clicking on its filename, and selecting the *Properties* option from the pop-up menu. From the *Properties* window, select the *Programs* tab and then click on the *Advanced* button to view the file's settings, as shown in Figure 12-14. If the application is not already set for MS-DOS mode operation, click on the box to select it. Also select the *Prevent MS-DOS—based programs from detecting Windows* option. Return to the failing application to see whether it will run correctly in this environment.

Figure 12-14: MS-DOS Program Properties

Windows 98 occasionally produces an error message that says you are running out of resources. This message indicates that the operating system believes that it has exhausted all the system's real and virtual memory. Although the message tells you to correct the problem by shutting down applications, and it provides an endless series of application shutdown dialog windows, this process almost never works. Even shutting the applications down through the *Close Program* dialog box will not restore the system. Therefore, you should shut down the system and restart it. This action normally clears the problem.

Windows 2000 Operating Problems

You should be aware of some typical symptoms that can pop up during the normal operation of the Windows 2000 operating system, including the following:

- User cannot log on.
- You cannot recover an item that was deleted by another user.
- You cannot recover any items deleted.
- The video adapter supports higher resolution than the monitor does.
- Personalized menus are not working.

Administrator account

Guest account

When Windows NT, 2000, or XP is first installed, the only usable account is the **Administrator account**; the **Guest account** is disabled by default. If a user cannot log on, check the user's password. The password is case sensitive, so verify that the Caps Lock key is not an issue. If you have forgotten the Administrator password and you have not created any other accounts with Administrator privileges, you must reinstall Windows NT, 2000, or XP. Some third-party utilities may be able to help you recover the Administrator password, but you will usually find it easier to just reinstall the operating system at this point.

TEST TIP

Be aware that files deleted from remote and removable storage devices do not appear in the Recycle Bin.

You cannot recover an item that was deleted by another user because the Recycle Bin is maintained on a user-by-user basis. If one user deletes something, only that user can recover it. You must log on as the user who deleted the items. Files and folders deleted from a floppy disk or network drive are permanently deleted and cannot be recovered. When the Recycle Bin fills to capacity, any newly deleted file or folder added causes older deleted items to be automatically deleted from the Recycle Bin.

Troubleshooting Application Problems

A portion of the A+ Operating System Technologies objective 3.3 states that the test taker should be able to recognize common operational and usability problems and determine how to resolve them. It also says that the content may include:

- Application will not start or load
- Applications don't install

One of the other major operational problems that affect operating systems involves the application programs running in the system. In the Microsoft world, if the application is a BAT, EXE, or COM file, it should start when its name is properly entered on the command line. If such an application will not start in a command-line environment, you have a few basic possibilities to consider: It has been improperly identified; it is not located where it is supposed to be; or the application program is corrupted.

Check the spelling of the filename and reenter it at the command prompt. Also, verify that the path to the program has been presented correctly and thoroughly. If the path and filename are correct, the application may be corrupted. Reinstall the program and try to start it again.

Other possible reasons for application programs not starting in a command-line environment include low conventional memory or disk space, and file attributes that will not let the program start. In client/server networks, permission settings may not permit a user to access a particular file or folder.

Windows 9x Application Problems

If an application will not start in Windows 9x, you have four basic possibilities to consider: The application is missing; part or all of the application is corrupted; the application's executable file is incorrectly identified; or its attributes are locked.

As with other GUI-based environments, Windows 9x applications hide behind icons. The properties of each icon must correctly identify the filename and path of the application's executable file; otherwise, Windows will not be able to start it. Likewise, when a folder or file, accessed by the icon or by the shortcut from the Windows 9x Start menu, is moved, renamed, or removed, Windows will once again not be able to find it when asked to start the application. Check the application's properties to verify that the filename, path, and syntax are correct. **Application properties** can be accessed by right-clicking on the application's desktop icon, as well as by right-clicking its entry in the *Start* menu, *My Computer* page, or *Windows Explorer* screen.

| Application properties |

Most applications require Registry entries in order to run. If these entries are missing or corrupt, the application will not start. In addition, Windows 9x retains the DLL structure of its Windows 3.x predecessor under the *\Windows\System* directory. Corrupted or conflicting DLL files prevent applications from starting. To recover from these types of errors, you must reinstall the application.

TEST TIP
Be aware of the different methods of accessing an application's properties.

Windows 2000/XP Application Problems

Windows 2000 and Windows XP may suffer the same types of application problems as those described for the Windows 9x versions:

- Incorrect application properties (filename, path, and syntax)

- Missing or corrupt Registry entries

- Conflicting DLL files

TEST TIP
Know what items to look for when applications will not start.

Because Windows NT, 2000, and XP are typically used in client/server networks, some typical administrative problems are associated with files, folders, and printers and can pop up during their normal operations. These problems include such symptoms as:

- Users cannot gain access to folders.

- Users send a print job to the printer, but cannot locate the documents.

- Users have Read permissions to a folder, but they can still make changes to files inside the folder.

- Users complain that they can see files in a folder, but cannot access any of the files.

- Users complain that they cannot set any NTFS permissions.

A user's inability to gain access to folders can occur for many reasons. In the Windows NT/2000/XP environment, the user might not have permissions that will enable them to access different files and folders. This is an administrative decision and can only be overcome by an administrator establishing **permission levels** that will permit access.

permission levels

print server

Print Pooling

If the print job is not still in the local spooler or the **print server**, but **Print Pooling** is enabled, check all the printers in the pool. You cannot dictate which printer receives the print job. If the print job is visible in the spooler but does not print, this can be caused by the printer availability hours being set for times other than when you submitted the print job.

If users have Read permission for a folder, but can still make changes to files inside the folder, their file permissions must be set to Full Control, Write, or Modify. These permissions are set directly to the file and override the folder permissions of Read. You can correct this by changing the permissions on the individual files or at the folder level and allow the permissions to propagate to files within the folder.

┌─ **TEST TIP** ─────────────┐
│ Know what items to look for when │
│ applications will not start. │
└──────────────────────────┘

When users complain that they can see files in a folder but cannot access any of the files, they have most likely been assigned the List permission at the folder level. The List permission enables users to view the contents of the folder only, and denies them all other permissions, including Read and Execute.

NTFS permissions

With users who complain that they cannot set any **NTFS permissions**, the first item to check is that the file or folder is on an NTFS partition. FAT16 and FAT32 have no security options that can be assigned. If the partition is NTFS the user must have *Full Control permission* to set any security permissions to a file or folder.

CHALLENGE #11

You have just installed a new Windows 2000 Professional operating system upgrade on a co-worker's machine. In the process of testing it, you discover that her word processor application will not start from the desktop icon. How should you go about troubleshooting this problem?

Locating Hidden Files

By default, Windows 2000 hides known filename extensions. If you cannot see filename extensions, open the Windows Explorer, click on *Tools*, click on *Folder Options*, click on the *View* tab, and then locate and deselect the *Hide File Extensions for Known Files* option.

Likewise, Windows 2000 and Windows XP, by default, do not display hidden or system files in Explorer. To see hidden or system files in Windows 2000, open the Windows Explorer, click on *Tools*, click on *Folder Options*, click on the *View* tab, and then locate and select the *Show Hidden Files and Folders* option.

Windows 2000 Task Manager

In Windows NT, Windows 2000, and Windows XP, the *Close Program* dialog window is referred to as the **Task Manager**. This utility can be used to determine which applications in the system are running or stopped, as well as which resources are being used. You can also determine general microprocessor and memory usage levels.

Task Manager

When an application hangs up in these operating systems, you can access the *Task Manager* window shown in Figure 12-15 and remove it from the list of tasks. The Windows 2000 and Windows XP Task Managers can be accessed by pressing CTRL+ALT+DEL or by pressing CTRL+SHIFT+ESC.

You can also access the Task Manager by right-clicking the system tray and selecting *Task Manager* from the pop-up contextual menu. The CTRL+SHIFT+ESC key sequence moves directly into Task Manager while the CTRL+ALT+DEL selection opens the Windows Security menu screen, which offers *Task Manager* as an option.

To use the Task Manager, select the application from the list on the *Applications* tab and click on the *End Task* button. If prompted, click on the *End Task* button again to confirm the selection. The *Performance* tab provides a graphical summary of the system's CPU and memory usage. The *Process* tab provides information that can be helpful in tracking down problems associated with slow system operation.

Figure 12-15: Task Manager

Applying Task Manager to Application Problems

In Windows 2000 and XP, the Task Manager can be used to monitor the condition and operation of application programs and key Windows operating system services and components. In these operating systems, the Task Manager is available at any time and can be accessed by pressing the CTRL+ALT+DEL key combination.

When the Task Manager appears, the *Applications* tab will show by default. This tab displays the applications that are currently running in the system along with a description of their status (i.e., Running or Not Running). When an application is present in this window and shows a Not Running status, it has stalled and you should remove it. You can use this tab to remove these applications from the active system by highlighting the task and clicking on the *End Task* button.

You should consult the Task Manager's *Processes* tab if the system is running slow to determine whether an application is using more of the system's resources than it should. If the memory usage number for a given application consistently grows, the application may have a programming problem known as a memory leak. Over time, memory leaks can absorb all of the system's free memory and crash the system.

CHALLENGE #12

You are using a commercial customer tracking database application on a Windows 2000 Professional system when the system hangs up and will not do anything. What is the best method to safely gain control of the system and remove the offending application?

Applying Event Viewer to Application Problems

Although blue screen stop errors are primarily associated with setup and configuration problems involving new hardware or software products, they can happen at any time. When a stop error occurs during the normal operation of a Windows NT/2000/XP system, you should restart the system and see if it reoccurs. When the system restarts, use the Event Viewer utility to look for the source of the problem.

The Windows 2000 and Windows XP Application logs can be used to examine the operation of the higher end applications and some operating system services. The contents of this log can be examined through the Event Viewer utility to determine what conditions the system logged leading up to a failure, such as an application failing to start or stalling. The Event Viewer will show whether the application or service ran correctly or not. It may also indicate that there are conditions present which you should take note of before they become failures.

Another indicator of application-related problems is the appearance of an "Event Log is full" error message. The Event Logs have a specified maximum file size that they can become before they are considered full. By default, the Event Logs are set to overwrite any log data that is more than seven days old if they become full. Therefore, if events are occurring so quickly that the logs fill up before the default time, this indicates that an excessive number of system errors (events) are occurring. You should examine the full Event Log to determine what activity is accounting for so many loggable events.

In the case of failure events, the system will usually generate a user alert through a pop-up dialog box on the screen. The information in the box will indicate the nature of the problem and refer you to the Event Viewer for details. The Event Viewer is available through the *Start/Programs/Administrative Tools/Event Viewer* path.

Troubleshooting Stop Errors

Stop errors occur most frequently when new hardware, or their device drivers have been installed, or when the system is running low on disk space. Also, stop errors can occur on a system that has been running without a problem for months, but for whatever reason experiences a hardware error of some sort that causes the system to crash. You need to be aware that stop errors can happen for a variety of other reasons and can be very difficult to troubleshoot.

Stop errors

There is no set procedure for resolving stop errors, but you can do many things to potentially eliminate the error, or to gain additional information about what caused the error.

Use the following steps to troubleshoot stop errors:

1. Restart the system to see whether the error will repeat itself. In many cases, an odd series of circumstances within the system can cause the error, and simply restarting the system will correct the condition. If the stop error appears again, however, you will need to take additional action.

2. If you have recently installed new hardware in the system, verify that it has been installed correctly and that you are using the most current version of its device drivers.

3. Check the HCL to verify that any newly installed hardware and device drivers are compatible with Windows 2000 or Windows XP.

4. Remove any newly installed hardware to see whether that relieves the stop error. If Windows 2000 starts, immediately use the Event Viewer to view any additional error messages that were generated before the stop error occurred. These messages will provide further information as to why the hardware caused the system to crash.

5. Try to start the operating system in Safe Mode. If you can start the system in Safe Mode, then you can remove any newly installed software that could be causing the stop error. You can also remove or update device drivers that could be causing the stop error.

6. Attempt to start the system using the Last Known Good Configuration. This resets the system configuration to whatever the hardware configuration was the last time you were able to successfully boot the system, and gives you the opportunity to try to install or configure a new hardware device again.

7. Verify that the latest operating system **Service Pack** has been installed.

Service Pack

8. Use TechNet or visit the Microsoft Support Center web site and search for the particular stop error number to see whether you can get any additional information. The stop error number is noted in the upper-left corner of the *Stop* screen.

9. Disable memory caching or shadowing options in the system CMOS Setup.

10. If possible, run diagnostic software on the system to check for memory errors.

11. Use a virus utility to check for viruses and eliminate any viruses if found.

12. Verify that the system's BIOS is the latest revision. If not, contact the manufacturer of your system to determine how to update the BIOS.

One of these steps should enable you to resolve the error, or pinpoint it to a particular component that you can eliminate from the system to clear up the symptom.

Troubleshooting Printing Problems

A portion of the A+ Operating System Technologies objective 3.3 states that the test taker should be able to recognize common operational and usability problems and determine how to resolve them. It also says that the content may include:

- Troubleshooting Windows-specific printing problems
- Print spool is stalled
- Incorrect/incompatible driver for print
- Incorrect parameters

Determine whether the *Print* option from the application's File menu is unavailable (gray). If so, check the Windows *Control Panel/Printers* window (or *Printers and Faxes* in Windows XP) for correct parallel port settings.

In a Windows-based system, the Windows environment controls the printing function through its drivers. Make certain that the correct printer driver is selected for the printer being used. If no printer type, or the wrong printer type is selected, simply set the desired printer as the default printer and try to print a document.

Check to determine whether there is a printer switch box between the computer and the printer. If so, remove the print sharing equipment and connect the computer directly to the printer.

Troubleshooting Windows Printing Problems

If a printer is not producing anything in a Windows 9x/NT/2000/XP environment, even though print jobs have been sent to it, check the **Print Spooler** to see whether any particular type of error has occurred. To view documents waiting to be printed, double-click the desired *printer's* icon. Return to the *Printer* folder, right-click the *printer's* icon, click on *Properties*, and then select *Details*. From this point, select *Spool Settings* and select the *Print Directly to the Printer* option. If the print job goes through, there is a spooler problem. If not, the hardware and printer driver are suspect.

To check spooler problems, examine the system for adequate hard disk space and memory. If the **Enhanced Metafile (EMF) Spooling** option is selected, disable it, clear the spooler, and try to print. To check the printer driver, right-click the *printer's* icon, select the *Properties* option, and click on the *Details* option. Reload or upgrade the driver if necessary.

If a Windows printer operation stalls, or crashes, during the printing process, some critical condition must have been reached to stop the printing process. The system was running but stopped. Restart the system in Safe Mode and try to print again. If the system still does not print, check the print driver, the video driver, and the amount of space on the hard-disk drive. Delete backed up spool and temp files (SPL and TMP) in the *System/Spool/Printers* directory.

Print Spooler

Enhanced Metafile (EMF) Spooling

┌─ **TEST TIP** ─┐
Remember how to test the operation of the Windows Print Spooler when the printer will not print.
└───────────────┘

When you arrive at the customer's machine, he tells you that he has been sending files to the local printer but nothing comes out. When you check the local print queue, you see the files sitting there and determine that they are not moving. What steps should you take to get the printer back into operation?

Troubleshooting Local Area Networks

Figure 12-16 depicts the system components associated with LAN troubleshooting. Generally, the order of isolating LAN problems is as follows:

1. Check the local networking software.

2. Check the cabling and connectors.

3. Check the NIC adapter.

The order of checking is based on convenience and speed of isolating problems. The configuration checks performed on the operating system do not require that any hardware be disassembled. Likewise, cables and connectors are easier and faster to check than internal hardware.

Most network adapter cards come from the manufacturer with a disk or CD-ROM of drivers and diagnostic utilities for that particular card. You can run these diagnostic utilities to verify that the LAN hardware is functioning properly. However, it may be easier to run the Windows **PING utility** from the command prompt and attempt to connect to the network. In a LAN environment, you will need to know the IP address, or the name of a computer in the network that you can direct the PING to. Both PING and TRACERT can be used to identify the IP address of a known network address. These utilities are discussed in detail later in this chapter.

**Figure 12-16:
LAN Components**

PING utility

Cabling is one of the biggest problems encountered in a network installation. Is it connected? Are all the connections good? Is the cable type correct? Has there been any termination, and if so, has it been done correctly? The most efficient way to test network cable is to use a line tester to check its functionality.

With UTP cabling, simply unplug the cable from the adapter card and plug it into the tester. If coaxial cable is used, you must unplug both ends of the cable from the network, install a terminating resistor at one end of the cable, and plug the other end into the tester. The tester performs the tests required to analyze the cable and connection.

— TEST TIP —
Know which network utility can be used to identify the address of a known remote location.

— TEST TIP —
Be aware that cabling faults represent the number one reason for LAN failures.

— TEST TIP —
Know what type of device is commonly used to make checks on LAN cables.

Windows 9x Networking Problems

There are several possible reasons why users cannot log on to a network in Windows 9x. Some of these reasons are hardware related. Running the Add New Hardware Wizard and allowing it to detect the network hardware should point out these types of problems. However, also click the *Network* icon in the Control Panel to review the NIC settings. Use the *Advanced* tab under the *Properties* window to confirm that the Transceiver Type value is correct for the type of physical network being used. Also, check under the *Resources* tab to confirm the adapter card's settings. Use the **Detected Config** option, illustrated in Figure 12-17, if the NIC settings are not known.

If the network adapter card is installed in the system and the cabling is connected correctly, the operating system's network support must be checked. The most obvious items to check are those found in the *Properties* pages of the *Network Neighborhood* window. Possible reasons for not being able to log on to the network include the following:

- Incorrect Services Settings (Configuration page)
- Incorrect Protocol Settings (Configuration page)
- Incorrect Adapter Settings (Configuration page)
- Incorrect Primary Network Logon Settings (Configuration page)
- Missing Computer Name (Identification page)
- Missing Workgroup Name (Identification page)

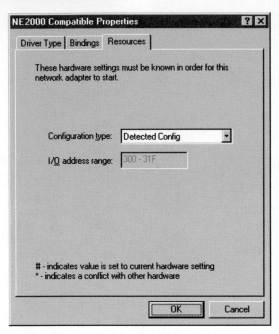

Figure 12-17: The Detected Config Option

Begin the troubleshooting by checking the system for resource conflicts that might involve the network adapter card. You can obtain this information by accessing the Control Panel's Device Manager. If a conflict exists, an exclamation point (!) should appear beside the network adapter card in the listing. If Windows thinks the card is working properly, the Device Manager displays a normal listing.

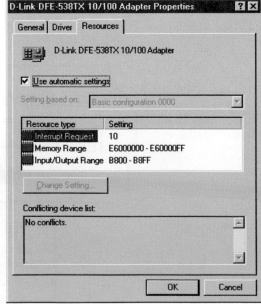

Figure 12-18: Network Adapter Properties Page

If a conflict is detected, move into the network adapter's *Properties* page, shown in Figure 12-18, and check the adapter's resources against those indicated by the card's diagnostic utility. The conflict must be resolved between the network adapter and whatever device is using its resources.

If the adapter resources are okay, the next step depends on the type of symptom being encountered:

- Can any units be seen on the network?

- Can other units be seen but not used?

If the network cannot be seen in the Network Neighborhood, or the network cannot be browsed from this utility, the network protocols and drivers should be checked. Network adapters and protocols are checked through the Control Panel's *Network* icon. Check the protocols listed in the *Configuration* tab's *Installed Components* window. Compare these to those listed on working units in the workgroup. Each machine must have all the clients and protocols other machines are using; otherwise it will not be possible to browse the network. The local computer and the *Entire Network* icon should be present, but the other units will not be visible.

If you can browse the network but cannot use certain resources in other locations, sharing is not turned on in the remote unit, or the local unit does not have proper access rights to that resource. To use the remote resource across the network, the system's File and Print functions must be turned on, and its Share function must be enabled. Turning on the file and print functions places the local resources in the network's Browse listing.

CHALLENGE #14

You are working in a Windows 2000 Client/Server network, and you discover that you cannot use a shared drive on another computer. What should you do to troubleshoot access to the drive?

However, this does not enable the Share function. The Share function is established by supplying the system with a valid Share Name. In addition, the computer must be running Client for Microsoft Networks for the File and Print functions to be available on a Microsoft network. If this client service is not installed, the File and Print functions will be unavailable for use (grayed out). The Client for Microsoft Networks services component must be installed in the *Select Network Component Type* screen.

Windows NT/2000/XP Networking Problems

Because Windows NT/2000/XP systems are typically involved in client/server networks, the types of problems encountered are somewhat different from those found in Windows 9*x* network environments. Some typical networking problems can occur during normal Windows 2000 or Windows XP operations, including such things as the following:

- The user cannot see any other computers on the local network.

- The user cannot see other computers on different networks.

- The clients cannot see the DHCP server, but do have an IP address.

- The clients cannot obtain an IP address from a DHCP server that is on the other side of a router.

TEST TIP

Know what the presence of a light on the NIC card indicates.

As mentioned earlier, a major cause of connectivity problems is the physical layer. Check to see that the computer is physically connected to the network and that the status light is glowing (normally green). The presence of the light indicates that the NIC sees network traffic.

If a client cannot see any other computers on the network, improper IP addressing may be occurring. This is one of the most common problems associated with TCP/IP. Users must have a valid IP address and subnet to communicate with other computers. If the IP address is incorrect, invalid, or conflicting with another computer in the network, you will be able to see your local computer, but will not be able to see others on the network.

TCP/IP network

DHCP server

One reason for an incorrect IP address problem would be that the local system in a **TCP/IP network** is looking for a **DHCP server** that is present. In some LANs, a special server called a DHCP server is used to dynamically assign IP addresses to its clients in the network. In large networks, each segment of the network requires its own DHCP server to assign IP addresses for that segment. If the DHCP server were missing, or not functioning, none of the clients in that segment would be able to see the network.

Likewise, if a DHCP client computer were installed in a network segment that did not use DHCP, it would need to be reconfigured manually with a static IP address. The DHCP settings are administered through the *TCP/IP Properties* window. This window is located under the *Start/Settings/Networking and Dial-up Connections* option. From this point, open the desired Local Area or Dial-up Connection and click on the *Properties* button. DHCP operations are covered in more detail later in this chapter.

IPCONFIG/ALL

WINIPCFG

TEST TIP

Know the primary TCP/IP tools used to troubleshoot network problems.

Begin the troubleshooting process for this type of problem by checking the *TCP/IP Properties* under the *Network* icon. Next, check the current TCP/IP settings using the command-line **IPCONFIG/ALL** (or **WINIPCFG**) utility. They will display the current IP settings and offer a starting point for troubleshooting. Afterwards, use the PING utility to send test packets to other local computers that you find. The results of this action indicate whether the network is working.

CHALLENGE #15

You have installed a new Windows 2000 Professional client in your network and manually assigned it a valid IP address. However, when you try to browse the network, nothing shows up. What network utilities should you use to get the new system into operation?

If users can see other local computers in a TCP/IP network, but cannot see remote systems on other networks, the problem may be routing. Check to make certain that the address for the default gateway listed in the TCP/IP properties is valid. Use the NET VIEW command to see whether the remote computer is available. If the user is relying on the My Network Places feature to see other computers, a delay in updating the Browse list may cause remote systems to not be listed. The **NET VIEW** command directly communicates with the remote systems and displays available shares.

NET VIEW

If the clients have an IP address of 169.254.xxx.xxx, it is because they cannot communicate with the DHCP server. Windows 2000 automatically assigns the computer an IP address in the 169.254 range if it cannot be assigned one from a DHCP server. Check the previously discussed procedures to determine what the problem may be.

Many routers do not pass the broadcast traffic generated by DHCP clients. If clients cannot obtain an IP address from a DHCP server that is on the other side of a router, the network administrator must enable the forwarding of DHCP packets, or place a DHCP server on each side of a router.

CHALLENGE #16

You work in a large corporation that has just converted all of its Windows NT Workstation client computers in your network over to Windows 2000 Professional. The network uses a DHCP server to provide IP addresses for the clients. In the process of upgrading the system, you have also moved one of the workstations to a new location in the network. However, when you bring the network back up, all the clients come up perfectly except the unit that was relocated — it cannot connect to the network. What should you look for as you try to get the unit back in operation?

Troubleshooting Network Printing Problems

The complexity of conducting printer operations over a network is much greater because of the addition of the network drivers and protocols. Many of the problems encountered when printing over the network involve components of the operating system. Therefore, its networking and printing functions must both be checked.

When printing cannot be carried out across the network, verify that the local computer and the network printer are set up for remote printing. In the Windows operating systems, this involves sharing the printer with the network users. The local computer that the printer is connected to, referred to as the print server, should appear in the Windows 9x *Network Neighborhood* window of the remote computer. If the local computer cannot see files and printers at the print server station, file and print sharing may not be enabled there.

In Windows 9x, file and printer sharing can be accomplished at the print server in a number of ways. First, double-click the printer's icon in the *My Computer* window, or the *Windows Explorer* screen. Select the *Printer/Properties/Sharing* option and then choose the desired configuration. The second method uses a right-click on the printer's icon, followed by selecting *Share* in the *Context* menu, and choosing the desired configuration. The final method is similar except that you right-click the printer's icon and click on *Properties*, *Sharing*, and then choose the configuration.

TEST TIP

Be aware that not having file and print sharing enabled will cause computers to not "see" the other computers across the network.

Run a printer's self-test to verify that its hardware is working correctly. If it will not print a test page, there is obviously a problem with the printer hardware. Next, troubleshoot the printer hardware. When the operation of the hardware is working, attempt to print across the network again.

Next, determine whether the print server can print directly to the printer. Open a document on the print server and attempt to print it. If the file will not print directly to the local printer, there is a problem in the local hardware. Troubleshoot the problem as a local, stand-alone printer problem.

If the local print server operation is working, verify the operation of the network by attempting to perform other network functions, such as transferring a file from the remote unit to the print server. In Windows 9x, open the Control Panel's *Printer* folder and select the *Properties* entry in the drop-down *File* menu. Check the information under the *Details* and *Sharing* tabs.

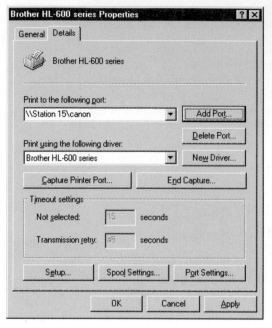

If other network functions are operational, verify the printer operation of the local computer. If possible, connect a printer directly to the local unit and set its print driver up to print to the local printer port. If the file prints to the local printer, a network/printer driver problem still exists. Reload the printer driver and check the network print path, as shown in Figure 12-19. The correct format for the UNC network path name is *computer_name\\shared device_name*.

If the printer operation stalls or crashes during the printing process, a different type of problem is indicated. In this case, the remote printer was functioning, the print server was operational, and the network was transferring data. Some critical condition must have been reached to stop the printing process. Check the print spooler in the print server to see whether an error has occurred. Also, check the hard disk space and memory usage in the print server.

**Figure 12-19:
Checking the
Printer Path**

TEST TIP

Know how to create a UNC path from a local computer to a remote printer, or a directory located on a remote computer.

Troubleshooting WAN Problems

**Fully Qualified
Domain Names**

The quickest items to check in a WAN application are the dial-up network software settings. Check the spelling of **Fully Qualified Domain Names** to make sure they are spelled exactly as they should be. If the spelling is wrong, no communications will take place. The major difference in checking WAN problems occurs in checking the Internet-specific software, such as the browser.

Most of the WAN troubleshooting steps from the local computer level involve the modem. The modem hardware should be examined as described in Chapter 11. If the hardware is functional, the operating system's driver and resource configuration settings must be checked.

In Windows 9x, you can find the modem configuration information in the Control Panel under the *Modems* icon. This icon has two tabs: the *General* tab and the *Diagnostics* tab. The Properties button in the *General* window provides Port and Maximum Speed settings. The *Connection* tab provides character-framing information, as illustrated in Figure 12-20. The *Connection* tab's *Advanced* button provides Error and Flow Control settings, as well as Modulation Type.

Figure 12-20: The Connection Dialog Box

The *Diagnostics* tab's dialog box, shown in Figure 12-21, provides access to the modem's driver and additional information. The PnP feature reads the modem card and returns its information to the screen, as demonstrated in the depiction.

Each user should have received a packet of information from his or her ISP when the service was purchased. These documents normally contain all the ISP-specific configuration information needed to set up the user's site. This information should be consulted when installing and configuring any Internet-related software.

The ISP establishes an Internet access account for each user. These accounts are based on the user's account name and password that are asked for each time the user logs onto the account. Forgetting or misspelling either item will result in the ISP rejecting access to the Internet. Most accounts are paid for on a

Figure 12-21: The Diagnostics Dialog Box

monthly schedule. If the account isn't paid up, the ISP may cancel the account and deny access to the user. In either of these situations, if the user attempts to log onto the account they will repeatedly be asked to enter their account name and password until a predetermined number of failed attempts has been reached.

TEST TIP

Be aware of reasons that ISP accounts become invalid and what the consequences of this situation are.

The most common communication error is the Disconnected message. This message occurs for a number of reasons, including a noisy phone line or random transmission errors. You can normally overcome this type of error by just retrying the connection. Other typical error messages include the following:

- *No Dial Tone.* This error indicates a bad or improper phone-line connection, such as the phone line plugged into the modem's line jack rather than the phone jack.

- *Port In Use.* This error indicates a busy signal or an improper configuration parameter.

- *Can't Find Modem.* This error indicates that the PnP process did not detect the modem, or that the modem has not been correctly configured to communicate with the system.

If the system cannot find the modem, you should reboot the system and allow Windows to redetect the modem. If rebooting does not detect the modem, run any diagnostics available for the modem. In particular, use the utility disk or CD-ROM that comes with the modem to run tests on the hardware. Check any hardware configuration settings for the modem and compare them to the settings in the Control Panel's Device Manager. These values can be checked through the Control Panel's *Modems/Properties* page, but the Device Manager must be used to make changes.

If the modem is present, move into the Device Manager and check the modem for resource conflicts. If there is a conflict with the modem, an exclamation point (!) should appear beside the modem listing.

If you detect a conflict, move into the modem's *Properties* page and check the modem's resources. Also, record the Connection Preferences from the *Connection* page and make certain the character-framing configuration is correct. The conflict must be resolved between the modem and whatever device is using its resources.

If no conflict is indicated, move into the *Diagnostics* page and highlight the installed device. Click on the *More Info* button. This action causes Windows to communicate with the modem hardware. If no problems are detected by this test, Windows 9x displays the modem's port information, along with a listing of the AT commands that it used to test the hardware, as illustrated in Figure 12-22. If an error is detected during the Windows testing, an error message displays onscreen. These messages are similar to those previously listed.

Figure 12-22: Modem Properties More Info Response

If the modem tests are okay, check the User Name and Password settings. This can be accomplished through the *My Computer/Dial-up Networking* path, or through the *Start/Programs/Accessories/Communications/Dial-up Networking* path in Windows 98.

In the *Dial-up Networking* window, right-click the desired connection icon and select the *Properties* option from the list. Check the phone number and modem type on the *General* page. Next move into the *Server Types* page and check the type of dial-up server installed. For Windows Internet dial-up service, this is typically a "PPP, Internet, Windows NT, Windows 98" connection. Also, disable the NetBEUI and IPX/SPX settings from the page and make certain that the TCP/IP setting is enabled.

Most ISPs use DHCP to assign IP, DNS, and Gateway addresses to clients for dial-up accounts. Therefore, in a dial-up situation, the *Server Assigns IP Address* option and the *Server Assigns Name Server Address* option are normally enabled. Check the ISP-supplied package to make sure that these settings do not need to be set manually. If they do, set up the page to match the ISP-specified settings. In the case of intranets with "in-house" clients, the network administrator determines how the values are assigned — statically or via DHCP.

NETWORK TROUBLESHOOTING TOOLS

A portion of A+ Operating System Technologies objective 4.1 states that the test taker should be able to identify the networking capabilities of Windows. Given configuration parameters, configure the operating system to connect to a network.

Understand the use of the following tools:

- IPCONFIG.EXE
- WINIPCFG.EXE
- PING
- TRACERT.EXE
- NSLOOKUP.EXE

When TCP/IP is installed in a Windows 9x, Windows 2000, or Windows XP system, a number of TCP/IP troubleshooting tools are automatically installed with it. All TCP/IP utilities are controlled by commands entered and run from the command prompt. These TCP/IP tools include the following:

- **Address Resolution Protocol (ARP) command** – This utility enables you to modify IP-to-Ethernet address-translation tables.

- **FTP** – This utility enables you to transfer files to and from FTP servers.

- **PING** – This utility enables you to verify connections to remote hosts.

- **NETSTAT** – This utility enables you to display the current TCP/IP network connections and protocol statistics. A similar command, called NBTSTAT, performs the same function using NetBIOS over the TCP/IP connection.

TEST TIP
Know where TCP/IP utilities are run from.

Address Resolution Protocol (ARP) command

FTP

PING

NETSTAT

┌─ **TEST TIP** ──────────┐

Know which TCP/IP utility can
be used to display the path of a
transmission across a network.
└────────────────────────┘

• **Trace Route (TRACERT)** − This utility enables you to display the route and a hop count, taken to a given destination. The route taken to a particular address can be set manually using the ROUTE command.

• **IPCONFIG** − This command-line utility enables you to determine the current TCP/IP configuration (MAC address, IP address, and subnet mask) of the local computer. It also may be used to request a new TCP/IP address from a DHCP server. IPCONFIG is available in both Windows 98 and Windows 2000. Windows 95 did not support IPCONFIG. The IPCONFIG utility can be started with two important option switches—/renew and /release. These switches are used to release and update IP settings received from a DHCP server. The /all switch is used to view the TCP/IP settings for all the adapter cards that the local station is connected to.

┌─ **TEST TIP** ──┐

Know which TCP/IP utilities can be used to release and renew IP address information from a DHCP server.
└───┘

• **WINIPCFG** − This is a GUI version of the IPCONFIG command available only in Windows 95. The various command-line switches available with the IPCONFIG command are implemented in graphical buttons. Like IPCONFIG, WINIPCFG can be used to release and renew IP addresses leased from a DHCP server.

┌─ **TEST TIP** ──────────────────────────┐

Know which TCP/IP utilities show the host IP address.
└───┘

• **NSLOOKUP.EXE** − This is a Windows 2000/XP TCP/IP utility that can be entered at the command prompt to query Internet (DNS) name servers interactively. It has two modes—interactive and non-interactive. In interactive mode, the user can query name servers for information about various hosts and domains. Non-interactive mode is used to print just the name and requested information for a host or domain. *NSLOOKUP* is only available when the TCP/IP protocol has been installed.

┌─ **TEST TIP** ──────────────────────────┐

Know where TCP/IP utilities are run from.
└───┘

Although all of these utilities are useful in isolating different TCP/IP problems, the most widely used commands are PING and TRACERT.

CHALLENGE #18

You are setting up a network of old Windows 95 and 98 computers that have been donated to a school by a local company. Which utilities must you use to view the TCP/IP settings for all the adapter cards in the network?

┌─ **TEST TIP** ──────────┐

Know which Windows tools
to employ to check out network-related problems.
└────────────────────────┘

The **PING** utility sends **Internet Control Message Packets (ICMP)** to a remote location and then waits for echoed response packets to be returned. The command waits for up to one second for each packet sent and then displays the number of transmitted and received packets. You can use the command to test both the name and IP address of the remote unit. A number of switches can be used to set parameters for the PING operation. Figure 12-23 shows the information displayed by a typical PING operation.

Figure 12-23:
A PING Operation

Most Internet servers do not respond to ICMP requests created by pinging. However, you can use the PING utility to access *www.somewebsitename.com*. By doing so, you can get a reply that will verify that TCP/IP, DNS, and gateway are working. The **TRACERT** utility traces the route taken by ICMP packets sent across the network, as illustrated in Figure 12-24. Routers along the path return information to the inquiring system and the utility displays the host name, IP address, and round trip time for each hop in the path.

TRACERT

Figure 12-24:
TRACERT Operation

Because the TRACERT report shows how much time is spent at each router along the path, it can be used to help determine where network slowdowns are occurring.

Verifying TCP/IP Configurations

There are two TCP/IP utilities that are very important for troubleshooting a new TCP/IP configuration. These are the IPCONFIG and PING utilities. To test the configuration of a new TCP/IP installation, run the IPCONFIG utility from the command prompt to verify that the connection has been properly initialized.

Then, use the PING utility to test the TCP/IP operations. This is accomplished by pinging different IP addresses in order:

1. PING address 127.0.0.1 to perform a loopback test that will verify that TCP/IP has successfully been loaded in the local computer.

2. PING the local adapter's IP address to ensure that it has been initialized.

3. PING the default gateway (router) address to verify that TCP/IP is working on both devices.

4. PING the address of another computer on the same network segment to make sure that the default gateway is functional.

```
┌─ TEST TIP ─────────────────┐
│ Know which Windows tools to use to │
│ check out network-related problems. │
└────────────────────────────┘
```

If only one of the PINGed devices does not return a reply, then it has a problem. If neither device replies, then the local computer may have a problem. Recheck your TCP/IP configuration settings to make sure no values have been transposed during entry.

CHALLENGE #19

You are supposed to demonstrate the operation of the company's network to some executives and you want to display the path that your TCP/IP packets are traveling to get to a remote network location. Which utilities can you use to accomplish this?

OPERATING SYSTEM UTILITIES

A portion of A+ Operating System Technologies objective 1.5 indicates that the test taker should be able to identify the major operating system utilities, their purpose, location, and available switches. Successful troubleshooting of operating systems requires tools. In addition to the startup tools already described (clean boot disks and single-step bootup utilities), a number of other utilities are available through the Windows operating systems to isolate and correct operating system problems.

Many of these utilities can be added directly to the startup disk so that they will be readily available in emergency situations. Some of the utilities that should be added to the startup disk include the following:

```
SCANDISK.EXE
```

```
cross-linked files
```

- **SCANDISK.EXE** – Checks the disk for lost clusters and **cross-linked files** and can examine disks and their contents for errors.

- **DEFRAG.EXE** – Realigns the file structure on the disk to optimize its operation.

- **MEM.EXE** – Used to view system memory organization.

- **SYSEDIT.EXE/REGEDIT.EXE** – These utilities can be used to edit Windows 9x system structures such as CONFIG.SYS, AUTOEXEC.BAT, and INI files, as well as the Windows 9x Registry structure.

- **FDISK.EXE** – Used to create, view, and manage partitions on a hard disk.

- **ATTRIB.EXE** – Can be employed to change the attribute of files (such as hidden, read-only, and system files) so that they can be seen and manipulated for troubleshooting purposes.

- **FORMAT.COM** – Used to establish the high level format on disk drives.

- **SYS.COM** – Used to copy key system files to a disk so that it will be self-booting.

| DEFRAG.EXE |
| MEM.EXE |
| SYSEDIT.EXE/ REGEDIT.EXE |
| FDISK.EXE |
| ATTRIB.EXE |
| FORMAT.COM |
| SYS.COM |
| Microsoft Diagnostic |

In the case of Windows 9x, the *Create Startup Disk* option under the *Add/Remove Programs* tab installs most of these utilities on the Emergency Start disk when it is created. Other utilities that can be very helpful for troubleshooting operating system problems include the **Microsoft Diagnostic** program and the Windows Device Manager.

Windows 98 Troubleshooting Tools

Microsoft includes an extensive set of troubleshooting system tools in Windows 98. It has also expanded the built-in Troubleshooting menu located in the Windows 98 Help functions. Both of these items are included to assist in the location and correction of many problems.

The System Tools

A portion of A+ Operating System Technologies objective 1.5 indicates that the test taker should be able to identify the major operating system utilities, their purpose, location, and available switches. It also indicates that content will include the System Management Tools. The following list identifies the major Windows 98 troubleshooting tools:

- Microsoft System Information
- Windows Report Tool
- MS-DOS Report Tool
- Dr. Watson
- System File Checker
- Registry Checker
- System Configuration Utility
- Automatic Skip Driver Agent

- Version Conflict Manager
- Scheduling Tasks
- Maintenance Wizard
- Microsoft Backup
- Microsoft System Recovery
- Digital Signal Check
- Signature Verification Tool
- Windows Update

The Microsoft **System Information** tool (**MSINFO32.EXE**) is the replacement for the Microsoft Diagnostic (MSD) and Windows MSD command-line utilities used with the MS-DOS and Windows 3.x operating systems. You can use this utility to view system hardware resources, installed devices, and drivers. It can also be used to view reports generated by web-based Windows and MS-DOS Report Tools. This tool enables remote service providers to inspect MSINFO information from local units across a LAN or WAN. The Windows 9x/Me MS-DOS Report Tool is located at *Program Files\Common Files\Microsoft Shared\MSINFO*.

MSINFO is typically started by clicking on the *System Information* option in the *Programs/Accessories/System Tools* path from the *Start* menu. If Windows 98 does not run, the program can be executed by typing *MSINFO32* at the DOS command prompt. When the utility starts, the Windows 9x System Information screen shown in Figure 12-25 appears.

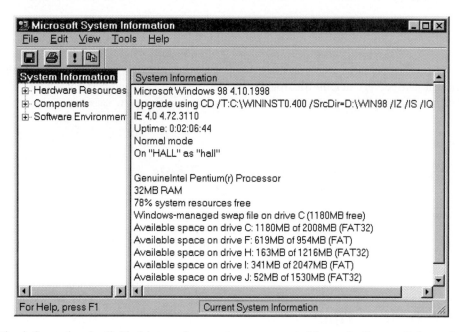

**Figure 12-25:
Windows 9x System
Information Screen**

The information is divided into a four-part arrangement. The main *System Information* screen displays general system information. The *Hardware Resources* entry provides information about system hardware settings, including IRQ, DMA, I/O, and memory addresses. The *Components* entry shows information about multimedia-related software, networking software, and device drivers. The final entry, *Software Environment*, lists the software loaded into the system's memory.

The **Windows Report Tool (WINREP.EXE)** is located in the *Windows* directory and provides a copy of the MSINFO information in HTML format. The **MS-DOS Report Tool** (**DOSREP.EXE**), also located in the Windows directory, provides a snapshot of the system files and can upload it to an FTP site when Windows is not working.

The **Dr. Watson** function, which has been around since the days of Windows 3.1x, is alive and well in the Windows 98 and Windows XP versions. As before, it is used to trace problems that appear under certain conditions, such as starting, or using a certain application. When Dr. Watson is started, it runs in the background with only an icon appearing on the Taskbar to signify that it is present. When a system error occurs, Dr. Watson logs the events that were going on up to the time of the failure. In many cases, the program will describe the nature of the error, and possibly suggest a fix. However, Dr. Watson is less than perfect. In some cases, the utility will completely miss the failing event.

The Dr. Watson utility is not located in any of the Windows 98 menus. To use the utility, it is necessary to execute the program from the *Start* menu's *Run* option. Just type the name drwatson in the dialog box, and click on *OK* to start the log file. The *Dr. Watson* icon should appear on the Taskbar. Dr. Watson also can be started through the *Tools* menu in the *System Information* screen. This option is located in the *Programs\Accessories\System Tools* path.

To see the resulting log file, alternate-click the icon. This action produces the Dr. Watson main screen, shown in Figure 12-26. From this screen, select the *System* tab. This information also can be viewed from the System Information section of the *System Tools* menu.

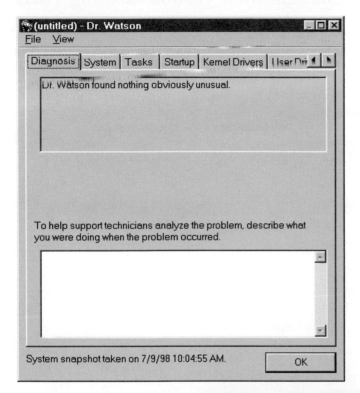

**Figure 12-26:
Dr. Watson's
Main Screen**

System File Checker
utility (SFC.EXE)

The **System File Checker utility (SFC.EXE)** checks the system files for changed, deleted, or possibly corrupt files. If it finds such files, it attempts to extract the original version of the file from Windows files. This file can be found at *Windows\System*.

Clicking on the *System File Checker* entry in the *System Information Tools* menu will activate the System File Checker utility, illustrated in Figure 12-27. This utility provides two options: scanning for altered system files, or extracting a file from the Windows 98 distribution CD.

Figure 12-27: System File Checker's Main Menu

Windows 98 also includes a pair of Registry checker utilities (**SCANREG.EXE** and **SCANREGW.EXE**) to scan, fix, back up, and restore Registry files. The SCANREG file is a DOS-based program, whereas SCANREGW is a Windows-based version. The DOS version is located in the *Windows\Command* directory, whereas the Windows version is just in the *Windows* directory.

System Configuration Troubleshooting Tools

Windows 98 has a collection of configuration-related troubleshooting tools. These utilities include the **System Configuration Utility (MSCONFIG.EXE)**, the **Automatic Skip Driver Agent (ASD.EXE)**, and the **Version Conflict Manager (VCMUI.EXE)**.

The **System Configuration Utility** enables you to examine the system's configuration through a check-box system. By turning different configuration settings on and off, problem settings can be isolated and corrected by a process of elimination. You can access this utility through the *System Information* screen. From the *Tools* menu, select the *System Configuration Utility*. This action brings up the System Configuration Utility's main screen, shown in Figure 12-28.

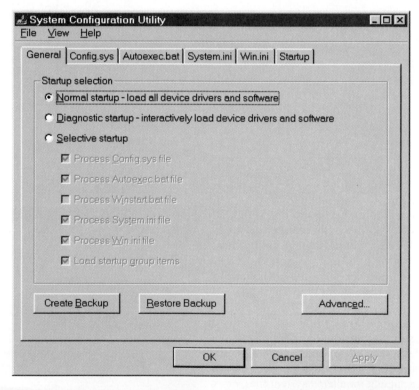

Figure 12-28: System Configuration Utility's Main Screen

The screen is divided into six tabs that correspond to the files that run during the startup process. The information under the *General* tab enables you to select the type of startup. For most troubleshooting efforts, the *Diagnostic Startup* is selected first to provide a clean environment. When the *Selective Startup* option is chosen, complete sections of the bootup sequence can be disabled. Once an offending section has been isolated, you can use the individual tabs to enter that section and selectively disable individual lines within the file.

Device Driver Tools

In cases in which the configuration problem is more severe, you can use the Automatic Skip Driver Agent. This utility senses, and skips, configuration steps that prevent Windows 98 from starting. The Version Conflict Manager automatically installs Windows 98 drivers over other drivers that it finds, even if these drivers are newer. The System Configuration Manager is located in the *Windows\System* directory, whereas the other two utilities are found under the *Windows* directory.

To minimize the adverse affects of poorly written device drivers on the system, Microsoft works with hardware suppliers and signs (certifies) their drivers for Windows 98 compatibility by adding special digital codes to them. This **Driver Signing** tool is valuable to administrators who do not want users to introduce questionable devices and drivers into the system.

The **Signature Verification Tool (SIGVERIF.EXE)** is used to check files to determine whether Microsoft has signed them. It also determines whether the files have been modified since they were signed.

Finally, the **Windows Update** utility **(WUPDMGR.EXE)** is a Windows 98 extension located on the Microsoft web site (*www.microsoft.com/windowsupdate*). It enables you to update the system's files and drivers with new or improved versions over the web.

TEST TIP

Be aware of driver signing and know why it is implemented.

Driver Signing

Signature Verification Tool (SIGVERIF.EXE)

Windows Update (WUPDMGR.EXE)

System Monitor

System Resource Meter

System Monitor

Two other valuable utilities in Windows 9x are the **System Monitor** and the **System Resource Meter** programs. The System Monitor can be used to track the performance of key system resources for both evaluation and troubleshooting purposes. If system performance is suspect but there is no clear indication of what might be slowing it down, the System Monitor can be used to determine which resource is operating at capacity, thereby limiting the performance of the system.

Typical resources that the System Monitor is capable of tracking include those associated with processor usage and memory management. Results can be displayed in real-time using Statistical mode, Line Chart mode, or Bar Chart mode. Figure 12-29 illustrates the System Monitor operating in Line Chart mode. The System Monitor can be set up to run on top of other applications so that the user can see what effect they are having on the system.

Figure 12-30: Using the Resource Meter

The Resource Meter, shown in Figure 12-30, is a simple bar chart display that shows the percent usage of the system resources, user resources, and GDI resources. When activated, the meter normally resides as an icon on the extreme right side of the Taskbar, at the bottom of the desktop. Double-clicking the icon brings the bar chart display to the desktop. As with the System Monitor, the Resource Meter can be used to evaluate hardware and software performance.

Figure 12-29: Using the System Monitor

TEST TIP

Be aware of which Windows 9x utility can be used to monitor certain resource activities.

Both the System Monitor and the Resource Meter are installed through the *Setup* tab under the Control Panel's *Add/Remove Programs* applet. From the *Setup* tab, highlight the *System Tools* entry and click on the *Details* button. Select the utilities and click on the *Apply* button.

Windows 2000 System Tools

A portion of A+ Operating System Technologies objective 1.5 indicates that the test taker should be able to identify the major operating system utilities, their purpose, location, and available switches. It also indicates that content will include the System Management Tools. As mentioned earlier, Windows 2000 and XP cluster a number of administrative, diagnostic, and troubleshooting tools under the Control Panel's Microsoft Management Console.

Event Viewer

Event Viewer

In Windows 2000 and Windows XP, significant events (such as system events, application events, and security events) are routinely monitored and stored. These events can be viewed through the **Event Viewer** utility shown in Figure 12-31. As described earlier, this tool is located under the *Control Panel/Administrative Tools/Computer Management* path.

Figure 12-31: Windows 2000 Event Viewer

System events include items such as successful and failed Windows component startups, as well as successful loading of device drivers. Likewise, application events include information about how the system's applications are performing. Not all Windows applications generate events that the Event Viewer will log. Finally, security events are produced by user actions such as logons and logoffs, file and folder accesses, and creation of new Active Directory accounts.

Three default event logs track and record the events just mentioned. The system log records events generated by the operating system and its components. The application log tracks events generated by high-end applications. Likewise, the security log contains information generated by audit policies that have been enacted in the operating system. If no audit policies are configured, the security log will remain empty.

In addition to the default logs, some special systems such as domain controllers and DNS systems will have specialized logs to track events specifically related to the function of the system.

The Event Viewer produces three categories of system and application events:

- **Information events** – Events that indicate that an application, service, or driver has loaded successfully. These events require no intervention.

- **Warning events** – Events that have no immediate impact, but that could have future significance. These events should be investigated.

- **Error events** – Events that indicate that an application, service, or driver has failed to load successfully. These events require immediate intervention.

Notice in the figure that the Information events are denoted by a small "i" in a balloon, whereas exclamation marks (!) and Xs are used to identify Warning and Error events respectively.

> Information events

> Warning events

> Error events

Windows 2000/XP System Information

The **Windows 2000/XP System Information** utility, shown in Figure 12-32, provides five subfolders of information about the system. These folders include a System Summary, a list of Hardware Resources being used, a list of I/O Components in the system, a description of the system's current Software Environment, and a description of the Windows Internet Explorer.

> Windows 2000/XP
> System Information

Figure 12-32: The Windows 2000 System Information Utility

As with the Windows 98 System Information tool, the Windows 2000 and Windows XP versions can be used to enable remote service providers to inspect the system's information across a LAN environment. To save system information to a file, right-click the *System Information* entry and select the *Save As* option from the resulting menu. Saving this information enables you to document events and conditions when errors occur. You can use the results of different system information files to compare situations and perhaps determine what changes may have occurred to cause the problem.

In Windows XP systems, the System Information tool can be accessed through the *Start/Run* menu by typing *msinfo32.exe* in the *Run* dialog box. You can also access the Windows XP System Information tool by navigating the *Start/All Programs/ Accessories/ System Tools* path and selecting the *System Information* option. Both methods will produce the Windows XP System Information console shown in Figure 12-33.

The content of the System Information utility can be saved or exported to a file so that it can be saved for troubleshooting or optimization purposes. Both of these functions can be performed through the utility's *File* menu. Using the *Save* option stores the data in a (.NFO) format that can read again by the System Information utility. The export function saves the information to a text file that can be read with any standard text editor (e.g., Notepad).

Figure 12-33: Windows XP System Information

One of the biggest reasons to save the System Information is for troubleshooting use when system errors occur. By saving System Information when the system is functioning properly, you can compare it to information obtained when a failure occurs. Another reason to save System Information is to establish performance baselines that can be used to measure the effectiveness of changes that are made to the system. If an upgrade is performed and the System Information report shows diminished performance characteristics, then you can reverse the upgrade effort.

The Windows XP System Information *Tools* menu, shown in Figure 12-34, provides additional access to many of the system's troubleshooting and administrative tools.

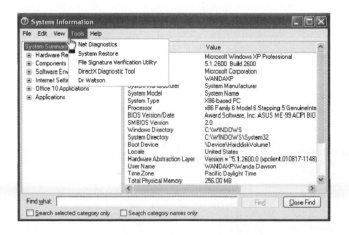

Figure 12-34: Windows XP System Information/ Tools Menu

Using Device Manager

Hardware and configuration conflicts also can be isolated manually using the Windows 9x/2000/XP **Device Manager** from the Control Panel's *System* icon. This utility is basically an easy-to-use interface for the Windows 9x and Windows 2000/XP Registries. You can use the Device Manager, shown in Figure 12-35, to identify installed ports, update device drivers, and change I/O settings. From this window, the problem device can be examined to see where the conflict is occurring.

Figure 12-35: The Device Manager's Display

Two radio buttons on the *Device Manager* page can be used to alter the way it displays the devices installed in the system. Clicking on the left button (the page's default setting), displays the system's devices alphabetically by device type. The rightmost radio button shows the devices by their connection to the system. As with the Registry and Policy Editors, the presence of plus (+) and (−) signs in the nodes of the devices indicates expandable and collapsible information branches at those nodes.

The Device Manager will display an exclamation point (!) inside a yellow circle whenever a device is experiencing a direct hardware conflict with another device. The nature of the problem is described in the device's *Properties* dialog box. Similarly, when a red X appears at the device's icon, the device has been disabled due to a user-selection conflict.

This situation can occur when a user wishes to disable a selected device without removing it. For example, a user that travels and uses a notebook computer may want to temporarily disable device drivers for options that aren't used in travel. This can be accomplished through the Device Manager's *Disable in this hardware profile* option. This will keep the driver from loading up until it is re-activated. Clicking on the *Properties* button at the bottom of the *Device Manager* screen produces the selected device's *Properties* sheet. The three tabs at the top of the page provide access to the device's general information, driver specifications, and system resource assignments.

TEST TIP

Memorize symbols used by the Windows Device Manager.

TEST TIP

Be aware of how to temporarily disable device drivers that are not needed in certain situations, yet retain them in the system for future use.

When a device conflict is suspected, just click on the offending device in the listing, make sure that the selected device is the current device, and then click on the *Resources* tab to examine the conflicting device's list, as shown in Figure 12-36.

Figure 12-36: The Device Manager Resources Page

To change the resources allocated to a device, click on the resource to be changed, remove the check mark from the *Use automatic settings* box, click on the *Change Setting* button, and scroll through the resource options. Take care when changing resource settings. The *Resource Settings* window displays all the available resources in the system, even those that are already spoken for by another device. You must know which resources are acceptable for a given type of device and which ones are already in use.

┌─ **TEST TIP** ─────────────────┐
│ Know how to find conflicts using │
│ the Windows Device Manager.   │
└──────────────────────────────────┘

Figure 12-37: The Device Manager Computer Properties Page

To determine what resources the system already has in use, click on the *Computer* icon at the top of the Device Manager display. The *Computer Properties* page, shown in Figure 12-37, provides ways to view and reserve system resources.

Through this page, you can click on radio buttons to display the system's usage of four key resources: IRQ channels, DMA channels, I/O addresses, and memory addresses. The Reserve Resources page is used to set aside key resources to avoid conflicts with the PnP configuration operations. If a resource is reserved and Windows detects that it as already in use, a warning dialog box displays onscreen and asks for a confirmation.

Normal causes for conflict include devices sharing IRQ settings, I/O address settings, DMA channels, or base memory settings. The most common conflicts are those dealing with the IRQ channels. Nonessential peripherals, such as sound and network adapters, are most likely to produce this type of conflict.

When a device conflict is reported through the *Resources* tab's conflicting device list, record the current settings for each device, refer to the documentation for each device to determine what other settings might be used, and change the settings for the most flexible device. If either device continues to exhibit problems, reset the configurations to their original positions and change the settings for the other device.

Make sure that the same device has not been installed twice. When this occurs, it is normally impossible to determine which driver is correct. Therefore, it will be necessary to remove both drivers and allow the PnP process to redetect the device. If multiple drivers are present for a given device, remove the drivers that are not specific to the particular device installed in the system.

Windows XP Driver Rollback Feature

The Windows XP operating system includes a new option that can be used to revert to an older device driver when a driver upgrade causes problems with a device. This feature is called **Driver Rollback** and can be implemented through the Windows XP Device Manager.

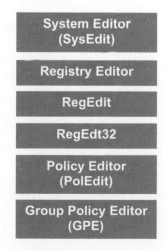

To roll back the driver, simply right-click on the device in the Device Manager listing and select the *Properties* option. Click on the *Driver* tab followed by the *Roll Back Driver* button, shown in Figure 12-38.

Figure 12-38: Device Manager/ Roll Back Driver Option

System Editors

The Windows operating systems contain three important editors: the **System Editor (SysEdit)**, the **Registry Editor (RegEdit** and **RegEdt32)**, and the **Policy Editor (PolEdit)**. Windows 2000 and XP also include a very powerful **Group Policy Editor (GPE)**.

Later versions of MS-DOS contained a small text editor program (EDIT.COM) that enabled users to easily modify text files. You can start this utility by typing the EDIT command and the filename at the command prompt. In Windows, this editor is named the System Editor (SYSEDIT.EXE), shown in Figure 12-39.

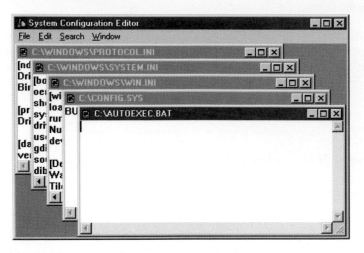

Figure 12-39: The Windows System Editor Screen

To start the SysEdit function, select the *Run* option from the *Start* menu. Type *SYSEDIT* in the *Run* dialog box and click on the *OK* button. The SysEdit commands are similar to those of other Windows-based text editing programs, such as Notepad or Write.

Windows 9x contains three important editors: the System Editor (SysEdit), the Registry Editor (RegEdit), and the Policy Editor (PolEdit). The Windows 9x SysEdit function is used to modify text files, such as any INI files in the system, as well as the CONFIG.SYS and AUTOEXEC.BAT files.

Windows 2000 and Windows XP include two Registry editors: RegEdit and RegEdt32. Both utilities enable you to add, edit, and remove Registry entries and to perform other basic functions. However, specific functions can be performed only in one editor or the other.

TEST TIP

Be aware of which Windows utilities can be used to make changes to the Registry in Windows 2000 and Windows XP.

RegEdt32 is the Registry editor that has historically been used with Windows NT. It presents each subtree as an individual entity in a separate window. RegEdit is the Registry editor that was introduced with Windows 95, and also was included with Windows NT 4.0. The subtrees are presented as being part of the same entity in a single window, as illustrated in Figure 12-40.

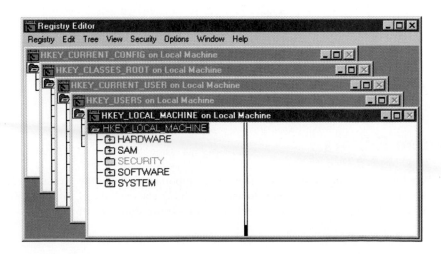

Figure 12-40: RegEdt32 Registry Editor

The Registry has a permissions system that is similar to NTFS permissions, which enables you to control access to the keys and assigned values. RegEdt32 enables you to view and set permissions through the *Security* menu. RegEdit does not allow you to access the permissions system.

The Find capabilities of RegEdt32 are accessed from the *View* menu, and are very limited. You can search only for keys, not assigned values or their corresponding data. This is the equivalent of being able to search for folders in the file system, but not for files. Also, you can initiate a search in only one subtree at a time. The Find capabilities of RegEdit are accessed through the *Edit* menu, and are very strong. You have the option to search for keys and assigned values, and you can search all subtrees at once. RegEdit also enables you to save frequently accessed Registry locations as favorites to enable quicker access.

WARNING

Editing the Registry with RegEdit or RegEdt32 should be done only when you have no alternative. These editors bypass all the safeguards provided by the standard utilities, and allow you to enter values that are invalid or that conflict with other settings. Incorrect editing of the Registry can cause Windows 2000 to stop functioning correctly, prompting a significant amount of troubleshooting or a reinstall of the operating system.

Using Dr. Watson

The main tool for isolating and correcting *General Protection Faults* (*GPFs*) is the *Dr. Watson* utility provided in all Windows versions. It is used to trace problems that appear under certain conditions, such as starting or using a certain application. When Dr. Watson is started, it runs in the background with only an icon appearing on the Taskbar to signify that it is present. For problems such as a GPF that cannot be directly attributed to the Windows operating system, an application program might be the source of the problem and the Dr. Watson utility should be set up to run in the background as the system operates.

As the system operates, the Dr. Watson utility monitors the code moving through the system and logs its key events in the **DRWATSON.LOG** file. When a system error occurs, the Dr. Watson log contains a listing of the events that were going on up to the time of the failure. This log provides programmers with a detailed listing of the events that led up to the failure. The information is automatically stored in the log file that can be provided to software developers, or to Microsoft, so that they can debug their software and produce patches for it. In many cases, the program will describe the nature of the error and possibly suggest a fix.

DRWATSON.LOG

TEST TIP

Know which Windows utility can be used to monitor the operation of application packages and to log errors so that they can be reported to software developers for repairing their programs.

The Dr. Watson utility is not located in any of the Windows 98 menus. To use it, you must execute the program from the *Start* menu's *Run* option by typing the name *drwatson* in the dialog box, and clicking on *OK* to start the log file. This will cause the *Dr. Watson* icon to appear on the Taskbar. Dr. Watson also can be started through the *Tools* menu in the *System Information* screen. This option is located in the *Programs/Accessories/System Tools* path.

Using Windows HDD Utilities

The operation of hard drives can slow down with general use. Files stored on the drive can be erased and moved, causing parts of them to be scattered around the drive. This causes the drive to reposition the R/W heads more often during read and write operations, thereby requiring more time to complete the process.

Four important Windows utilities can be used to optimize and maintain the operation of the hard-disk drive. These are the CHKDSK, ScanDisk, Defrag, and Backup utilities. With the exception of ScanDisk, which is a Windows utility, all of these utilities have been available since early MS-DOS versions.

In Windows 9x, these functions are located in several areas of the system. The icons for Backup, ScanDisk, and Defrag are located in the *Programs/Accessories/System Tools* path. The executable file for ScanDisk can be found in *C:\Windows\Command*; the Defrag program is under *C:\Windows*. The Backup utility is located in the *C:\Program Files\Accessories* applet in Windows 9x and is located in *C:\WINNT\SYSTEM32* in Windows NT/2000/XP.

The simplest way to access the HDD tools in Windows 9x is to open My Computer and right-click on the icon for the hard-disk drive you want to use. Next, select the *Properties* option from the context-sensitive pop-up menu. Then, simply click on the *Tools* tab to gain access to the three most useful Windows HDD utilities: ScanDisk, Backup, and Defrag.

You should use these HDD utilities periodically to tune up the performance of the system. To do so, perform these steps:

1. Periodically remove unnecessary TMP and BAK files from the system.

2. Check for and remove lost file chains and clusters using the CheckDisk or ScanDisk utilities.

3. Use the Defrag utility to realign files on the drive that may have become fragmented after being moved back and forth between the drive and the system.

DISK MANAGEMENT TOOLS

The operation of hard drives can slow down with general use. Files stored on the drive may be erased, and moved, causing parts of them to be scattered around the drive. This causes the drive to reposition the R/W heads more often during read and write operations, thereby requiring more time to complete the process.

Five important utilities can be used to optimize and maintain the operation of the hard-disk drive. These are the CHKDSK, ScanDisk, Defrag, Backup, and anti-virus utilities. With the exception of ScanDisk, which is a Windows utility, all these utilities have been available since early MS-DOS versions.

In different versions of Windows, these functions are located in several areas of the system. The icons for Backup, ScanDisk, and Defrag are located in the *Programs/Accessories/System Tools* path. The executable file for ScanDisk can be found in *C:\Windows\Command*; the Defrag program is under *C:\Windows*. The Backup utility is located in *C:\Program Files\Accessories* in Windows 9x, and is located in *C:\WINNT\SYSTEM32* in Windows NT/2000/XP. Microsoft does not supply a built-in anti-virus utility with its operating systems, so a third-party add-on should be used.

The simplest way to access the HDD tools in Windows 9x/Me/2000/XP is to open *My Computer* and right click on the icon for the hard-disk drive you want to use. Next, select the *Properties* option from the context-sensitive pop-up menu. Then, simply click on the *Tools* tab to gain access to the three most useful Windows HDD utilities: ScanDisk, Backup, and Defrag.

In Windows 2000 and Windows XP, these disk drive tools are located in the Computer Management console under the Control Panel's Administrative Tools icon. The Storage node in the Computer Management console offers direct access to the Disk Management and Defragmentation utilities. The other tools are available through the *Start/Programs/Accessories/System Tools* menu path.

CHKDSK

The **CHKDSK (Check Disk)** command is a command-line utility that has remained in use with Windows 3.x, 9x, NT, 2000, and XP and is used to recover **lost allocation units** from the hard drive. Lost allocation units occur when an application terminates unexpectedly and causes the file management system to lose track of where some parts of the program files are stored. The files become segmented into undefined pieces that can still be read by the utility, but cannot be associated with a particular filename in the FAT or MFT.

Files can also become cross-linked when the file management system loses track of some portion of the files. In these cases, part of a second file might be written into a sector that actually belonged to another file, and the files become linked to each other at that spot. Figure 12-41 depicts a typical CHKDSK display. CHKDSK locates lost clusters and, when used with an /F switch, converts them to files that can be viewed with a text editor.

> **TEST TIP**
>
> Remember where the main HDD utility programs are located in the Windows 9x environments.

> CHKDSK (Check Disk)
>
> lost allocation units

```
Corrections will not be written to disk

    1,202 lost allocation units found in 2 chains.
    9,846,784 bytes disk space would be freed

527,654,912 bytes total disk space
 24,510,464 bytes in 21 hidden files
    442,368 bytes in 54 directories
198,885,376 bytes in 1,552 user files
293,969,920 bytes available on disk

      8,192 bytes in each allocation unit
     64,411 total allocation units on disk
     35,885 available allocation units on disk

    655,360 total bytes memory
    494,784 bytes free

Instead of using CHKDSK, try using SCANDISK.  SCANDISK can reliably detect
and fix a much wider range of disk problems.  For more information,
type HELP SCANDISK from the command prompt.

C:\DOS>
```

Figure 12-41: A CheckDisk Display

Over a period of time, lost units can pile up and occupy large amounts of disk space. To remove these lost units from the drive, an /F switch is added to the command so that the lost units will be converted to files that can be investigated, and removed if necessary. In some cases, the converted file is a usable data file that can be rebuilt for use with an application. The Windows 9x CHKDSK /F command is often used before running a drive defragmentation program.

In Windows 9x, the CHKDSK command can be run from the command prompt at any time. However, in Windows 2000 and Windows XP, the CHKDSK command is only available when working from the command line in the Recovery Console. The Windows 2000/XP version only provides the /P switch for performing an exhaustive check of the drive, and /R for finding bad sectors and recovering readable information from them, if possible. The Windows 2000/XP version also requires that the file Autochk.exe be present in the root directory of the drive to operate.

ScanDisk

A similar program, called **ScanDisk,** is available in DOS 6.x and Windows 9x. ScanDisk searches the disk drive for disconnected file clusters and converts them to a form that can be checked and manipulated. This enables the user to determine whether there is any information in the lost clusters that can be restored. ScanDisk also detects, and deletes if necessary, cross-linked files. Cross-linked files occur when information from two or more files is mistakenly stored in the same sector of a disk.

In addition to locating and converting lost clusters on the disk drive, the ScanDisk utility can detect and delete cross-linked files from the drive. It also can make corrections to file and disk errors that it detects. ScanDisk can be run from the MS-DOS command line or as a Windows utility program. As with other disk utilities, only a Windows version of ScanDisk should be used on a Windows system. Using a command line−based version of ScanDisk may cause data loss rather than optimization, because the command-line version does not lock out the system when the file structure is being modified. By default, the command-line version of ScanDisk runs automatically during startup whenever the operating system detects that the system has not been shut down correctly.

Windows 9x actually provides two ScanDisk utilities: a command-line version that remains on the Windows 9x Startup disk, and a Windows-compatible graphics-based version (ScanDskw) that can be run from the Windows 9x environment. The command-line version (ScanDisk) is designed to be run from the Startup disk's command line in emergency recovery operations.

The Windows version of ScanDisk is located in the *Start/Programs/Accessories/System Tools* path. It can be run from the System Tools location, or it can be started through the *Start/Run* dialog box by typing *ScanDisk*. The Windows version repairs long filenames and is the recommended version for repairing disks. Figure 12-42 shows a typical Windows ScanDisk main page.

TEST TIP

Be aware of what events will cause ScanDisk to run automatically.

Figure 12-42: A ScanDisk Display

In the ScanDisk main window, select the drive to be examined, choose the type of test to be performed (Standard or Thorough), and set ScanDisk so that it will automatically attempt to fix errors it finds. The Standard test checks the folders and files on the drive for errors; the Thorough test also examines the disk's physical surface for problems.

Selecting the *Thorough* option will pop up the *Surface Scan Options* page shown in Figure 12-43. This page is used to control the scope of the surface scan, and therefore the time involved in checking it. The entire disk may be checked, or the test can be limited to only the data or system areas of the disk.

Clicking on the *Advanced* button on the ScanDisk main page produces another options page, shown in Figure 12-44. The *Advanced Options* page is used to determine how ScanDisk will deal with errors it finds. Its options include what to do with lost and cross-linked clusters, how to handle the log file, and how to display its results.

Figure 12-43: Surface ScanDisk Options

Figure 12-44: ScanDisk Advanced Options Page

HDD Defragmentation

In the normal use of the hard-disk drive, files become fragmented on the drive, as illustrated in Figure 12-45. This file fragmentation creates conditions that cause the drive to operate more slowly. Fragmentation occurs when files are stored in non-contiguous locations on the drive. This happens when files are stored, retrieved, modified, and rewritten, resulting in differences in the sizes of the before and after files.

**Figure 12-45:
Data Sectors**

■ – USED   FRAGMENTED HARD-DISK DRIVE
■ – UNUSED
X – UNMOVABLE
1 BLOCK = 53 CLUSTERS

Because fragmented files do not permit efficient reading by the drive, it takes longer to complete multisector read operations. The **defragmentation** process optimizes the operation of the disk drive by reorganizing its data into logically contiguous blocks. When data is arranged in this manner, the system does not need to reposition the drive's read/write heads as many times to read a given piece of data.

defragmentation

Some portions of files may become lost on the drive when a program is unexpectedly interrupted (such as when software crashes, for example, or during a power failure). These lost allocation units (chains) will also cause the drive to operate slowly. Therefore, it is customary to use the command-line CHKDSK command to find these chains and remove them before performing a defrag operation.

It may also be necessary to remove some data from the drive in order to defragment it. If the system is producing "Out of Disk Space" error messages, the defragmentation utility will not have enough room on the drive to realign clusters. When this happens, some of the contents of the drive need to be transferred to a backup media (or discarded) to free up some disk space for the realignment process to occur.

**Disk Defragmenter
utility**

The Defrag utility has been available since the later versions of MS-DOS (with the exception of Windows NT). In Windows 9x and Windows 2000 the **Disk Defragmenter utility** is located under the *Start/Programs/Accessories/System Tools* path. In Windows XP the correct path is *Start/All Programs/ Accessories/System Tools*. In Windows 2000 and Windows XP, the Disk Defragmenter can also be accessed through the *Control Panel/Administrative Tools/Computer Management* path. To use the Disk Defragmenter tool from this point:

1. Click on the *Disk Defragmenter* option.

2. Click on the desired drive to highlight it.

3. Click on the *Defragment* button to begin the operation.

The Disk Defragmenter main screen should appear, similar to that shown in Figure 12-46.

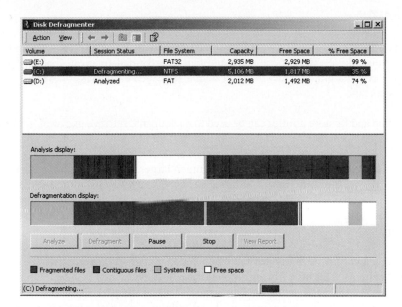

Figure 12-46: The Disk Defragmenter Main Screen

The Disk Defragmenter contains a disk analysis tool that reports the current status of the volume's key parameters. Figure 12-47 shows a sample analysis report.

Figure 12-47: The Disk Defragmenter Analysis Report Advanced Options Page

Viewing the defragmentation operation is possible through the *My Computer* window. Just right-click the drive icon and select the *Properties* option. From this point, click on the *Tools* option and select *Defrag*. However, viewing the operation of the defragmentation process makes the operation longer. It is better to run this utility in a minimized condition.

Backups

Backup utilities enable the user to quickly create extended copies of files, groups of files, or an entire disk drive. This operation is normally performed to create backup copies of important information, for use if the system's hard drive crashes, or when its content becomes corrupt.

The Backup and Restore utilities can be used to back up and retrieve one or more files to another disk.

Because a backup of related files is typically much larger than a single floppy disk, serious backup programs allow information to be backed up to a series of disks; they also provide file compression techniques to reduce the size of the files stored on the disk. Of course, it is impossible to read or use the compressed backup files in this format. To be usable, the files must be decompressed (expanded) and restored to the MS-DOS file format.

The Backup and Restore utility has been included in Windows 9x systems and in Windows 2000/XP systems. This utility is not automatically installed when Windows 95 is set up. If the user decides to install this feature, the actual Backup file (BACKUP.EXE) is placed in the *C:\Program Files\Accessories* directory. Windows also creates a shortcut icon for the Backup utility in the *C:\Windows\Start Menu\Programs\Accessories\System Tools* directory.

Backup Types

Most backup utilities provide a number of different options for conducting backups. Typically, backups fall into four categories:

- Full or total
- Incremental
- Selective
- Differential (or modified only)

total backup

In a full, or **total backup** process, depicted in Figure 12-48, the entire content of the designated disk is backed up. This includes directory and subdirectory listings and their contents. This backup method requires the most time each day to back up, but also requires the least time to restore the system after a failure. Only the most recent backup copy is required to restore the system.

Figure 12-48: Full Backup

Partial backups are often used instead of full backups to conserve space on the backup media and consume less time for the administrator. Three partial backup techniques are used to store data, but yet conserve space on the storage media: incremental backups, selective backups, and differential backups.

- *Incremental Backup* — In an **incremental backup** operation, shown in Figure 12-49, the system backs up files that have been created or changed since the last backup. Restoring the system from an incremental backup requires the use of the last full backup and each incremental backup taken since then. This method requires the least amount of time to back up the system, but the most amount of time to restore it.

Figure 12-49: Incremental Backup

- *Selective or Copy Backup* — To conduct a **selective backup** the operator moves through the tree structure of the disk and marks or tags directories and files to be backed up. After all the desired directories/files have been marked, they are backed up in a single operation. This form of backup is very labor-intensive and may inadvertently miss important data. A selective backup is illustrated in Figure 12-50.

Figure 12-50: Selective Backup

- *Differential or Modified Only Backup* — Specifying a **differential backup** causes the backup utility to examine each file to determine whether it has changed since the last full backup was performed. If not, it is bypassed. If the file has been altered, however, it will be backed up. This option is a valuable time-saving feature in a periodic backup strategy. To restore the system, you need a copy of the last full backup and the last differential backup. A differential or modified only backup operation is depicted in Figure 12-51.

TEST TIP

Know which backup type requires the least amount of time to perform and the least amount of effort to restore the system.

Figure 12-51:
Differential Backup

Data Backup

Use the CHKDSK/F command to clean up lost file clusters. Instruct the program to convert any lost chains into files that can be checked later. The operation of the Microsoft Windows 98/2000/XP Backup utility is described in the following paragraphs.

— NOTE —

If you do not see the Backup entry in a Windows 95 system, it has not been installed. You can add the Backup utility to the *System Tools* menu through the *Windows Setup* tab. Click on the *Start* button, point to *Settings*, click on *Control Panel*, and double-click the *Add/Remove Programs* icon. This will open the *Add/Remove Programs Properties* screen. Click on the *Windows Setup* tab to access the list of available utilities. If you used a compact disc to install Windows, you will be prompted to insert it into your computer.

To start the Backup program from the *Start* menu, navigate to the *System Tools* menu and select the *Backup* option from the menu. This will start the Backup wizard and display the *Backup Welcome* screen, shown in Figure 12-52. If you select the *Create a new backup job* option, the Windows Backup wizard will appear to guide you through the Backup setup process. The wizard will ask you questions about which items to back up (entire computer or selected folder and files), what to backup (selected files or only new/changed files), and where to backup to. It will also ask you to supply a name for the backup job.

Figure 12-52:
Welcome to Backup

If you select the *Open an existing backup job* option you will be asked to select the name of the existing backup job from a pop-up dialog box. Select a job and the *Backup* screen, similar to that shown in Figure 12-53, should appear. Under this option, you can accept the parameters of the existing job, or change them to new values.

Figure 12-53: The Backup Screen

To set new backup parameters:

Hands-on Activity

1. Click on the desired radio button in the *What to back up* area (i.e., All selected files or New and changed files)

2. Select the desired drive in the left pane by clicking on its icon. Expand or contract the branches of the directory tree to gain access to any particular folders or files that you wish to back up. Checking an object will mark all of its subfolders and files. To unmark any selected files of folders you must click on the check box next to it.

3. Identify where to back up by specifying that the backup will be a file and the path to the location where it should be stored. Select the backup options by clicking on the *Options* button. This will provide access to the *Backup Job Options* screen shown in Figure 12-54. Select the desired backup options from the window by clicking on the radio button next to each option. Under the *Type* tab, verify the *All selected files* or *New and changed files only* option. Click on the *OK* button to accept the new options.

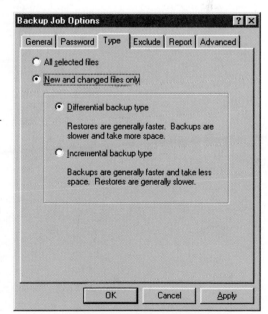

Figure 12-54: The Backup Job Options Screen

4. Click on the *Job* option on the menu bar and select the *Save As* or *Save* option. If you select the *Save As* option, you will be required to supply a new name for the job. If you select *Save*, the job, along with any new parameters, will be saved under its existing name.

5. Click on the *Start* button to begin the backup operation.

Restoring Data

To restore data, start the Backup/Restore utility from the System Tools submenu.

Hands-on Activity

1. From the *Backup Welcome* screen, select the *Restore* option by checking its radio button and then clicking on the *OK* button.

2. The Restore Wizard will appear, as shown in Figure 12-55. Supply the file and path of where the restore should come from in the dialog boxes. Click on the *Next* button to continue with the restore operation.

Figure 12-55: The Restore Wizard

3. Check the parameters of the backup job. Make any changes to the job by manually checking on any items that you do not want to restore.

4. In the *Where to Restore* dialog box, you can select to use the *Original location for the restore*, or you can select an *Alternate location* option for the restored folders and files. If you select this option, you will need to specify the new location in the drop-down dialog window.

5. Under the *How to Restore* option, click on the *Options* button to access the *Restore Options* screen shown in Figure 12-56. Select the restore options from the window by checking the box next to each option. Click on the *OK* button to return to the *Restore* screen.

6. Click on the *Start* button to restore the specified directories and files from the backup location.

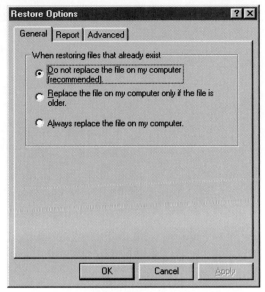

Figure 12-56: The Restore Options Screen

System State Data Backups

In addition to backing up data files and applications, it is often convenient to back up the key system configuration and information as well. This type of data is called **System State data** and is stored so that the system can be rebuilt quickly in case of a failure. Windows 2000 and Windows XP Backup utilities provide an option specifically to perform System State data backup, as illustrated in Figure 12-57. The System State data can be backed up by itself, or as part of the regularly scheduled system backup operation.

System State data

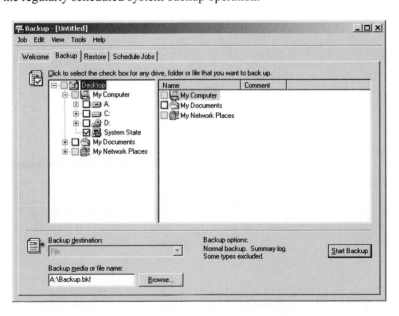

Figure 12-57: System State Data Backup Option

Under Windows 2000 and XP operating systems, backing up the System State data includes:

- The contents of the Registry

- The System startup files

- Files under Windows File Protection in Windows XP

- The COM+ Class registration database (a database of information about Component Services applications)

When the System State data checkbox is checked, its individual components are listed in the details pane of the display. The components are dependent on one another and can only be backed up and restored as a set (i.e., there is no way to back the components up individually).

When the System State data is restored to a machine, any existing system state information will be overwritten and destroyed. This can be a problem if an older version of the System State data is copied back into the system (any newer configuration information would be lost).

Backup Scheduling

In business environments, backup operations are a very important part of most company preventive maintenance programs. In these environments, the backup process is scripted into a schedule and a method for performing the backup function. To develop an acceptable backup schedule, you must consider a variety of issues, including when and what type of backup is required to ensure acceptable recovery in case of system failure. As a minimum, you must ask yourself the following questions when considering what type of backup method to use:

- How critical is your data?

- Can the business tolerate losing records for the past 24 hours?

- What systems must be reinstated first?

- How far back should you retain system settings?

- How far back might you be asked to go to recover a file?

Time is also a critical element in deciding your backup schedule. While a full system backup would give you the best assurance of a quick system recovery, it also takes a fair amount of server down time to perform. Can you afford to have productivity stop just to perform backups? This may not be an issue when backing up a small server system that is measured in megabytes, but when your overall system's data is large, measured in multiple gigabytes or terabytes, your server down time for full backups could adversely affect overall company productivity.

When determining your backup method, you must consider when to do your backups, and the form of media rotation you will use. The following provides you with a brief discussion on these issues.

- *Daily Backup* – Daily full-system backup provides the best assurance of at least being able to quickly recover all but the last 24 hours of your data. This is only feasible for small systems or portions of a system. For larger systems, a daily regimen of incremental or differential backups would at least assure recovery of your system, again excluding up to the last 24 hours. If your organization determines that specific data is too critical to potentially lose 24 hours worth of information, you may need to back up that specific data on a more rigorous schedule.

- *Weekly Backup* – Normally you can schedule weekly full-system backups during weekends, as long as your company requirements for uptime allow. The overall time required for your weekly backups will depend upon size of your system, and the frequency you apply. Very large companies may require maximum uptime, even during weekend timeframes. In these cases, more aggressive data distribution, backup methods, and more controlled backup scheduling need to be applied

- *Unscheduled Backups* – Unscheduled backups occur whenever there is a need that is either unanticipated or does not fit into your regular schedule of backups. A good example is when your server is exhibiting symptoms of potential failure, or you are upgrading portions of the system. At these times, or any time you are concerned that the normal backup schedule may not cover a potential loss of data, you should perform an unscheduled backup.

Backup Media Rotation

backup media rotation

Once you ensure that your backup plan has the necessary attributes to ensure initial system recovery, you must determine the need of your company to retrieve historical copies of their data. The **backup media rotation** method you employ will determine the historical timeframe in which you will be able to retrieve data. There are numerous media rotation methods that can be employed, each having its own timeframe of recovery. The *Grandfather-Father-Son* method, shown in Figure 12-58, is the most common method employed today.

The Grandfather-Father-Son method uses three different groupings of backup tapes: The *Grandfather* for monthly backups, the *Father* for weekly backups, and the *Son* for daily backups.

Figure 12-58: The Grandfather-Father-Son Method

The Son uses four tapes, one for every weekday, usually Monday through Thursday, typically applying the incremental backup method. The Father's weekly backup, normally performed on Friday, uses one tape applying the differential method of backup. After this, you reuse the corresponding Son tapes for the following daily backups. At month's end, you will use one tape to run the Grandfather backup. This backup would be a full backup of the system. Depending upon your company's needs, you may store these tapes to support an ongoing historical backup library, or reuse the tape for future backups.

OPTIMIZING WINDOWS PERFORMANCE

Windows operating systems have evolved to the point where they adapt well to most system settings and changes. Most of these adaptations are automatic in nature. However, as this Operating System Technologies objective 2.5 points out, there are still some areas of the Windows system that can be optimized by users and administrators. These areas involve the following activities:

- Optimizing virtual memory management

- Performing disk defragmentation when appropriate

- Maintaining Files and Buffers

- Establishing and optimizing various memory caches

- Effective temporary file management

- Optimizing Windows 9x/Me performance

Establishing a supplemental cache for the CD-ROM drive can enhance the efficiency of a Windows 9x system. This cache enables data to be paged between the CD and the system (or hard disk). The supplemental cache is established through the Control Panel's System icon:

1. Under the *System* icon, click on the *Performance* tab and select the *File System* button.

2. Set the *Supplemental Cache Size* slider to the desired cache size.

3. Set the *Optimize Access Pattern* setting to the Quad-speed or higher option (unless you have an old single- or double-speed drive). This will establish a 1238 kB supplemental cache (provided the system's RAM size is larger than 12 MB).

4. Click on the *OK* button and restart the system to create the cache.

Optimizing Windows 9x/Me Memory

The real objective in memory management in Windows 9x/Me systems is to free up as much conventional memory as possible for use by legacy applications. The first step in this process is to use the command-line MEM utility, to determine how much memory is actually in the system and how it is organized. Figure 12-59 shows a typical memory map displayed by the MEM command.

When the MEM command is executed without any modifying switches, the system's free and used memory are displayed. Adding a Page (/p) switch to the line causes the output to stop at the end of each screen of information. In versions of MS-DOS before release 6.0, the /p switch produced a program function that displayed the status of programs currently loaded into memory. Likewise, using a Debug (/d) switch with the MEM command shows the status of currently loaded programs and internal drivers. Another switch, called the Classify (/c) switch, displays the status of programs in conventional memory and the UMA. In addition, it provides each program's size in decimal and hex notation, along with a summary of memory usage and the largest memory blocks available. The MEM command can only be used with one switch at a time.

```
C:\>

C:\>mem
Memory Type          Total  =  Used  +  Free
-------------------- ------    ------    ------
Conventional          640K      47K      593K
Upper                   0K       0K        0K
Reserved              384K     384K        0K
Extended (XMS)      7,168K   2,112K    5,056K
-------------------- ------    ------    ------
Total memory        8,192K   2,559K    5,633K

Total under 1 MB      640K      47K      593K

Largest executable program size      593K   (607,312 bytes)
Largest free upper memory block        0K         (0 bytes)
MS-DOS is resident in the high memory area.
```

Figure 12-59: The MEM Display

Even using the setup steps just listed, the system's performance will deteriorate over time. Most of this deterioration is due to unnecessary file clutter and segmentation on the system's hard-disk drive. The following steps can be used to periodically tune up the performance of the system.

1. Periodically remove unnecessary .TMP and .BAK files from the system.

2. Check for and remove lost file chains and clusters using the CHKDSK and CHKDSK /f commands.

3. Use the DEFRAG utility to realign files on the drive that may have become fragmented after being moved back and forth between the drive and the system.

Temporary (TMP) files and backup (BAK) files are special versions of files that the operating system creates when it is performing functions in which it needs to store an original copy of the file along with an updated copy. Over time, these types of files can accumulate and take up space on the hard drive.

Removing these files and performing a defragmentation operation can improve the disk drive's access and delivery times dramatically.

Optimizing Windows 9x/Me Systems that Have Legacy Files

In a pure 32-bit Windows 9x/Me environment, very little memory management is needed. In these systems, new 32-bit virtual device drivers (VxDs) are automatically loaded into extended memory during the boot-up process. This eliminates the need for DEVICE= and LOADHIGH commands for devices that have VxDs and Windows 9x/Me application programs. However, when 16-bit device drivers or MS-DOS applications are being used, Windows must create a Real-mode MS-DOS environment for them. For this reason, Windows 9x will execute a CONFIG.SYS and/or AUTOEXEC.BAT file if it encounters them during the bootup process.

If no MS-DOS−based drivers or applications are in the system, the CONFIG.SYS and AUTOEXEC.BAT files are not necessary; however, the Windows 9x/Me version of the IO.SYS file will automatically load the Windows 9x version of the HIMEM.SYS file during bootup. This file must be present for Windows 9x/Me to boot up. There are usually multiple versions of the HIMEM.SYS file in a Windows 9x/Me system (there could be three or more versions).

If a Windows 9x or Windows Me system has a CONFIG.SYS, AUTOEXEC.BAT, or .INI file that has been held over from a previous operating system, you should be aware that any unneeded commands in these files have the potential to reduce system performance. In particular, the SMARTDRV function from older operating systems will inhibit dynamic VCACHE operation and slow the system down. The VCACHE driver establishes and controls a disk cache in an area of RAM as a storage space for information read from the hard-disk drive, CD-ROM, and other drives and file operations.

If the system runs slowly, check any CONFIG.SYS and AUTOEXEC.BAT files for SMARTDRV and any other disk cache software settings. Remove these commands from both files to improve performance. Also, remove any Share commands from the AUTOEXEC.BAT file. Likewise, the SYSTEM.INI, WIN.INI, PROTOCOL.INI, CONFIG.SYS, and AUTOEXEC.BAT files can be modified through the System Editor (SysEdit) in Windows 9x. You can access this utility by typing Sysedit in the *Start/Run* dialog box.

Optimizing Windows 2000/XP Systems

As with Windows 9x/Me systems, you can optimize the performance of Windows 2000 and Windows XP machines by defragmenting the system drives, removing unwanted or unused files, and maintaining the operating system's various caches.

Cross-linked files can accumulate and cause the system to slow down. Use the Chkdsk or ScanDisk utilities to find and remove or repair cross-linked files that may be using up disk space.

The Windows 2000/XP Defragmenter utility is available through the Administrative Tools/Computer Management console and is used to reposition related files/sectors on a disk drive so that they are located in the most advantageous pattern for being found and read by the system.

The Windows 2000/XP Windows Cleanup utility can be used to identify optional applications and certain types of temporary files that are not required for operation of the system. The temporary files that you can normally afford to remove from the system to gain needed disk space include Windows, Internet, and multimedia temp files.

Removable Storage Utility

Removable Storage utility

Windows 2000 and XP provide a **Removable Storage utility**, shown in Figure 12-60, that provides a variety of services to system administrators. It enables them to set up, share, and manage the removable media devices attached to the computer. Both the Windows 2000 and third-party backup applications use the Removable Storage utility to keep track of the identity of all backup media they use. The utility facilitates the actual mounting of the media when requested by the application, while the application itself keeps track of the actual data written or retrieved from the media.

Figure 12-60: Microsoft Removable Storage Utility

Windows Troubleshooting Help Files

Windows Troubleshooters

Windows 9x, NT 4.0, 2000, and XP come with built-in troubleshooting Help file systems. The **Windows Troubleshooters** are a special type of context-specific help that is available in Windows 9x, 2000, and XP. These interactive files enable you to pinpoint problems and identify solutions to problems by asking a series of questions and then providing you with detailed troubleshooting information based on your responses to those questions. This feature includes troubleshooting assistance for a number of different Windows problems.

The *Windows 9x* and *Windows 2000/XP Troubleshooters* are much more expansive than the Windows NT Troubleshooters. In all three systems, the Troubleshooter utilities can be accessed from the Start menu, from the Help menu entry on the toolbar, or through the Device Manager. Selecting the **Help** (or *Help and Support* option in Windows XP) entry from the Start or toolbar menus produces the *Help Topics* window, shown in Figure 12-61.

Figure 12-61: The Windows 9x Help Topics Window

The local Help screens are manipulated by making selections from the various tabs (i.e., Contents, Index, and Search). Double-clicking the *Troubleshooting* entry on the *Contents* tab will access the *Windows XX Troubleshooters* listing. Selecting this option will produce the window shown in Figure 12-62. This window contains a list of several entries with information about common Windows problems and situations. Clicking on one of the listed topics will produce an interactive troubleshooting process in the right-hand pane of the window that is associated with that particular problem (for instance, modem problems). The interactive text contains a step-by-step procedure for isolating the problem listed. Simply follow the questions and suggestion schemes provided.

Figure 12-62: Windows 98 Help Window

The *Index* tab provides an index of topics that can be searched using key words (i.e., Hardware/Conflict Troubleshooting) as illustrated in Figure 12-63. Several troubleshooting procedures can be accessed through this tab. Simply type the word "troubleshooting" in the keyword dialog box and select the appropriated topic from the list.

Figure 12-63: Using the Help/Index Tab

The *Search* tab can be used to conduct a search of all the Windows help and support materials for key topics such as troubleshooting. Enter the word and click on the *List Topics* button to conduct the search.

Other Information and Troubleshooting Resources

You can turn to many resources outside the operating system for information and troubleshooting assistance, such as Windows Resource Kits, the Internet, and Microsoft TechNet. The following sections discuss these additional resources.

Windows 2000 Resource Kits

The Windows 95, 98, NT 4.0, 2000, and XP **Resource Kits** provide thousands of pages of in-depth technical information on these Windows operating systems, as well as hundreds of additional utilities that you can use to enhance deployment, maintenance, and troubleshooting of your Windows network. The Resource Kits are excellent printed references for Windows, and also come with searchable electronic versions.

Resource Kits

There are two different versions of the Resource Kit for each NT operating system: one for Windows NT Workstation, and one for Windows NT Server (as well as one for Windows 2000 or Windows XP Professional, and one for Windows 2000 Server. The Resource Kits are published by Microsoft Press and are available from major book retailers.

Internet Help

online Help

You can activate the Windows 98 and Windows 2000/XP **online Help** functions by selecting a topic from the menu and then clicking on the *Web Help* button. Afterward, you must click on the *Support Online* option at the lower right of the *Help* window. This action brings up the *Internet Sign-in* dialog box, if the system is not already logged on to the Internet. After signing in, the Microsoft Technical Support page appears, as shown in Figure 12-64.

Figure 12-64: Microsoft Online Help Window

Microsoft's online **Product Support Services** provide a wealth of information about Microsoft products, including their operating systems. The URL for Product Support Services is *www.Microsoft.com/support*. Features of Microsoft Product Support include the following:

- **Microsoft Knowledge Base**, which is a searchable database of information and self-help tools. The Knowledge Base is used by Microsoft Technical Support to support their customers and is made available to you free of charge.

- **Download Center**, which enables you to search all available downloads for any Microsoft product, including service packs, patches, and updates.

- *Facts by Product*, which enables you to browse for information by product, and includes a list of most frequently asked questions about each product.

- Listing of support phone numbers that can be used to access live assistance. A charge applies for phone support.

- *Online Support Requests*, which permits you to submit questions to Microsoft support personnel. A charge applies for online support.

Microsoft TechNet

Microsoft's **TechNet** web site is designed to support IT professionals. The URL for this site is *www.Microsoft.com/technet*. This is an excellent site for getting the latest information about Windows 2000 (and all other Microsoft products and technologies).

TechNet

TechNet features include the following:

- Search capabilities for the Technical Information database and the Knowledge Base

- A What's New section that highlights new issues every month

- Access to the Product Support Services web site

- Information categorized by product to help you troubleshoot, maintain, and deploy software

- Chats, user groups, and Feedback Central for communicating with your peers and with Microsoft

Microsoft also provides a TechNet subscription service. For an annual fee, the Technical Information database, Knowledge Base, service packs, patches, fixes, software utilities, product enhancements, Resource Kits, beta versions of future Microsoft products, training information, and many other useful items will be shipped to you each month in CD-ROM format. A TechNet subscription can be purchased at the TechNet web site.

CHAPTER SUMMARY

This chapter has focused on diagnosing and troubleshooting operating system problems. The first section of the chapter examined installation and startup problems associated with Windows 9x, Windows NT, Windows 2000, and Windows XP systems. Typical startup error messages were related to probable causes for each type of system. Full discussions of Safe Mode startups and Windows log files were also presented in this section.

The second section of the chapter contained materials that pertain to operational problems associated with Microsoft operating systems. This topic explored memory usage problems, application problems, printing problems, and networking problems. Once again, Windows 9x and Windows 2000/XP systems were discussed, and typical error messages and symptoms were related to probable causes for each type of problem, along with procedures for correcting them.

The final section of the chapter provided an extended discussion of Windows file and disk management utilities, including methods and occasions of using them.

At this point, review the objectives listed at the start of the chapter to be certain that you understand each point and can perform each task listed there.

KEY POINTS REVIEW

This chapter has discussed troubleshooting and diagnostic methods associated with the Windows operating systems. Review the following key points before moving into the Review and Exam Questions sections to make sure you are comfortable with each point. Afterward, answer the Review Questions that follow to verify your knowledge of the information.

- During the bootup process, an interesting troubleshooting point occurs at the single beep in the bootup process of most computers. If the system produces an error message, such as "The system has detected unstable RAM at location XXXX", or a beep-coded error signal before the beep, the problem is hardware related.

- On the other hand, if the error message or beep code is produced after the single beep occurs, the problem is likely to be associated with starting up the operating system. At this point, the problem becomes an operating system startup problem.

- Windows 9x offers many improved features over previous operating systems. However, it can suffer many of the same problems as any other operating system. To overcome some of the typical system problems, Windows 9x includes several built-in troubleshooting tools. These tools include several Safe Mode startup options, a trio of system log files, and an extensive interactive troubleshooting help file system.

- Since Windows 9x does not start up through DOS, it will be very difficult to gain access to the system if Windows becomes disabled. Therefore, it is helpful to have an Emergency Start disk to troubleshoot Windows 9x–related problems. In the event that the Windows program becomes nonfunctional, it will be necessary to use the Start disk to restore the system to proper operation.

- When Windows 9x fails to start up properly, there is no separate underlying DOS platform that can be accessed to separate bootup/configuration problems from operating environment problems. However, Windows 9x provides the Safe Mode startup utility that can be employed to isolate and repair startup problems.

- When Windows 9x refuses to start up, a number of options are available for starting it from the command line. Starting Windows using a /D switch is often helpful in isolating possible areas of the operating system as problem sources (i.e., WIN /D). You can modify the /D switch to start Windows in a number of different configurations:

- Windows 9x maintains four log files named BOOTLOG.TXT, SETUPLOG.TXT, DETLOG.TXT, and DETCRASH.LOG. These files maintain a log of different system operations and can be used to see what events occurred leading up to a failure.

- The BOOTLOG.TXT file contains the sequence of events conducted during the startup of the system. The original BOOTLOG.TXT file is created during the Windows 9x Setup process. The file can be updated by pressing the F8 key during startup, or by starting Windows 9x with a WIN /B switch. It is not updated automatically each time the system is started. The log information is recorded in five basic sections.

- The SETUPLOG.TXT file holds setup information that was established during the installation process. The file is stored on the system's root directory and is used in Safe Recovery situations.

- The DETLOG.TXT file holds the text equivalent of the information in the DETCRASH.LOG file. This file can be read with a text editor to determine which hardware components have been detected by the system and what their parameters are.

- The Windows 9x structure provides a much improved multitasking environment over Windows 3.x. However, applications can still attempt to access unallocated memory locations, or attempt to use another application's space. When these memory conflicts occur, the system can either return an error message, or simply stop processing.

- Windows 9x produces a "This program has performed an illegal operation and is about to shut down" message when a memory conflict occurs. When this happens, Windows may take care of the error and allow you to continue operating by simply pressing a key.

- If nothing is being produced by the printer, even though print jobs have been sent to it, check the Print Spooler to see if any particular type of error has occurred. To view documents waiting to be printed, double-click on the desired printer's icon. Return to the Printer folder, right-click on the printer's icon, click on Properties, and then select Details. From this point, select Spool Settings and select the Print Directly to the Printer option. If the print job goes through, there is a spooler problem. If not, the hardware and printer driver are suspect.

- The complexity of conducting printer operations over a network becomes much greater due to the addition of network drivers and protocols. Many of the problems encountered when printing over the network involve components of the operating system. Therefore, the system's networking and printing functions must both be checked.

- In a client/server system such as a Novell NetWare or Windows NT system, the computer professional's main responsibility is to get the local station to boot up to the network's Login Prompt. At this point, the network administrator, or network engineer, becomes responsible for directing the troubleshooting process.

- Windows 9x comes with a built-in Troubleshooting Help file system. This feature includes troubleshooting assistance for a number of different Windows 9x problems.

- Hardware and configuration conflicts can also be isolated manually using the Windows 9x Device Manager from the Control Panel's System icon. This utility is basically an easy-to-use interface for the Windows 9x Registry.

REVIEW QUESTIONS

The following questions test your knowledge of the material presented in this chapter.

1. Using a Windows XP Professional Workstation, what sort of functions does the Recovery Console perform?

2. List the four preliminary steps used to troubleshoot operating system startup problems.

3. If an application will not start in a Windows 9x environment, list four possible causes.

4. What type of error is indicated by a "This Program Has Performed an Illegal Operation..." message?

5. Why are defragmentation programs run on computers?

6. What is the purpose of running a CHKDSK operation before performing a backup or defrag operation on the hard drive?

7. Which Windows utility can be used to examine and change ASCII text files such as CONFIG.SYS and Windows INI files?

8. If an application will not start in Windows 9x when its icon is clicked, what action should be taken?

9. What utility is used in a Windows XP environment to list a System Summary, a list of I/O Components in the system, and a description of the Windows Internet Explorer?

10. Name two important tools for solving startup problems in Windows 9x.

11. Which devices are loaded in Safe Mode startup?

12. If a printer is not producing anything in a Windows 9x/NT/2000 environment, even though print jobs have been sent to it, what should you check first?

13. Why would a Step-by-Step Confirmation mode startup be performed?

14. Which Windows 9x tool can be used to determine the configuration settings of a network card?

15. Which TCP/IP utility can be used to display the current TCP/IP network connections and protocol statistics?

EXAM QUESTIONS

1. What action occurs if the HIMEM.SYS file is missing in Windows 9x?
   a. Windows will not start.
   b. Windows will start in DOS mode.
   c. Windows will start in Standard mode.
   d. Windows will start in Safe Mode.

2. A Windows XP Professional workstation has had problems during operation lately. Which application will allow you to review any sort of conflicts and problems that have occurred over time?
   a. AUTOEXEC.BAT
   b. CONFIG.SYS
   c. Event Viewer
   d. Services and Applications

3. What Windows 9x utility can be used to change Registry entry values?
   a. SysEdit
   b. Polyedit
   c. Device Manager
   d. Edit

4. What is the Close Program dialog window now referred to as in Windows XP?
   a. The Task Manager
   b. Close Programs
   c. Task List
   d. Program Administration

5. An "X" is displayed by an entry in the Windows 9x Device Manager. What is indicated?
   a. The device has been disabled by a user selection conflict.
   b. The device is experiencing a direct hardware conflict with another device.
   c. The device's real-mode driver is not being loaded.
   d. The device's virtual-mode driver is not being loaded.

6. What function does the BOOTUPLOG.TXT file serve?
   a. It tracks the events of the Startup procedure.
   b. It carries out the steps of the Startup procedure.
   c. It tracks the events of the Shut Down procedure.
   d. It tracks the events of the POST sequence.

7. If one computer cannot see another computer on the network, what might the problem be?
   a. The Device Manager does not recognize the adapter.
   b. The IP address is incorrect, invalid, or conflicting with another computer.
   c. The Network Control Panel has not been enabled.
   d. The Networking Services have not been installed.

8. Plug-and-Play is not working in a Windows 9x system. Where can a device driver be installed from?
   a. The Start menu
   b. The Device Manager
   c. The Add/Remove Programs Wizard
   d. The Add New Hardware Wizard

9. A modem listed in the Device Manager indicates a resource conflict. What action should be taken to clear up the situation?
   a. Run MSD.EXE.
   b. Run MEM.EXE.
   c. Click on the Resources tab and check for conflicts.
   d. Change the IRQ setting for the device.

10. What is the proper path to activate the Windows XP System Restore wizard?
    a. Start/All Programs/Accessories/System Tools
    b. Start/Programs/Accessories/System Tools
    c. Start/All Programs/Administrative Tools/Backup
    d. Start/All Programs/Backup/System Restore

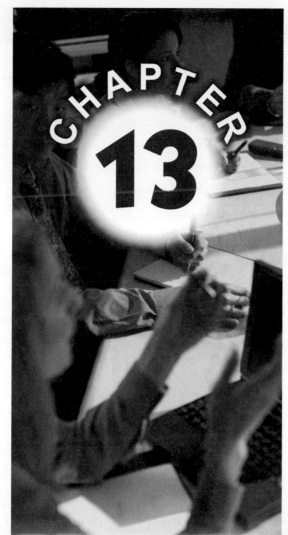

CHAPTER 13

PREVENTIVE MAINTENANCE

OBJECTIVES

Upon completion of this chapter and its related lab procedures, you should be able to perform the following tasks:

1. Demonstrate proper cleaning procedures for various system components.

2. Describe electrostatic discharge hazards and methods of preventing ESD.

3. List the steps for proper IC handling.

4. Define the term ground.

5. Describe the two types of uninterruptible power supplies (UPS) and state their qualities.

6. State typical precautions that should be observed when working on computer equipment.

7. Perform generic preventive maintenance routines as required (for example, remove excess toner, defragment hard drives, and create backup copies).

8. Detail routine preventive maintenance procedures as they apply to hard and floppy disks.

9. Perform basic disk management functions on a hard drive, including using ScanDisk, CHKDSK, and Defrag utilities.

10. Use backup software to create backups of important data.

11. Use software utilities to identify and remove viruses from computer systems.

12. List precautionary steps that should be taken when handling floppy disks.

13. List steps to clean a dot-matrix, ink-jet, or laser printer.

14. Establish and maintain preventive maintenance schedules for users.

15. Differentiate between various UPS specifications and state how they apply to a given situation.

16. State potential hazards that are present when working with laser printers, monitors, and other equipment.

PREVENTIVE MAINTENANCE

INTRODUCTION

This domain requires the test taker to show knowledge of safety and preventive mainte-nance. With regard to safety, it includes the potential hazards to personnel and equipment when working with lasers, high-voltage equipment, ESD, and items that require special dis-posal procedures that comply with environmental guidelines. With regard to preventive maintenance, this includes knowledge of preventive maintenance products, procedures, en-vironmental hazards, and precautions when working on microcomputer systems.

PREVENTIVE MAINTENANCE

The A+ Core objective 3.1 states that the test taker should be able to identify the various types of preventive maintenance measures, products, and procedures and when and how to use them.

Content may include the following:

- Liquid cleaning compounds

- Types of materials to clean contacts and connections

- Non-static vacuums (chassis, power supplies, fans)

- Cleaning monitors

- Cleaning removable media devices

- Ventilation, dust, and moisture control on the PC hardware interior.

- Hard disk maintenance (defragging, ScanDisk, CHKDSK)

- Verifying UPS (Uninterruptible Power Supply) and suppressors

It has long been known that one of the best ways to fix problems with complex systems is to prevent them before they happen. This is the concept behind preventive maintenance proce-dures. Breakdowns never occur at convenient times. By planning for a few minutes of nonproductive activities, hours of repair and recovery work can be avoided.

Cleaning

Cleaning

chamois

Cleaning is a major part of keeping a computer system healthy. Therefore, the technician's tool kit should also contain a collection of cleaning supplies. Along with hand tools, it will need a lint-free, soft cloth (**chamois**) for cleaning the plastic outer surfaces of the system.

TEST TIP
Know the common methods of cleaning various computer components.

Outer surface cleaning can be accomplished with a simple soap and water solution, followed by a clear water rinse. Care should be taken to make sure that none of the liquid splashes or drips into the inner parts of the system. A damp cloth is easily the best general-purpose cleaning tool for use with computer equipment.

antistatic spray

antistatic solution

oxidation

The cleaning should be followed by the application of an **antistatic spray** or **antistatic solution** to prevent the buildup of static charges on the components of the system. A solution composed of 10 parts water and one part common household fabric softener makes an effective and economical antistatic solution. To remove dust from the inside of cabinets, a small paint brush is handy.

TEST TIP
Know what types of materials/techniques can be used to clean different areas of the computer system.

Another common problem is the buildup of **oxidation**, or corrosion, at electrical contact points. These buildups occur on electrical connectors and contacts, and can reduce the flow of electricity through the connection. Some simple steps can be used to keep corrosion from becoming a problem. The easiest step in preventing corrosion is observing the correct handling procedures for printed circuit boards and cables, as shown in Figure 13-1. Never touch the electrical contact points with your skin, since the moisture on your body can start corrosive action.

**Figure 13-1:
How to Handle a
PC Board**

**electrical contact
cleaner**

Even with proper handling, some corrosion may occur over time. This oxidation can be removed in a number of ways. The oxide buildup can be sanded off with emery cloth, rubbed off with a common pencil eraser or special solvent-wipe, or dissolved with an **electrical contact cleaner** spray. Socketed devices should be reseated (removed and reinstalled to establish a new electrical connection) as part of an anti-corrosion cleaning. However, they should be handled according to the MOS handling guidelines in this chapter to make certain that no static discharge damage occurs.

If you use emery cloth or a rubber eraser to clean the contacts, always rub towards the outer edge of the board, or connector, to prevent damage to the contacts. Rubbing the edge may lift the foil from the PC board. Printed-circuit board connectors are typically very thin. Therefore, rub hard enough to remove only the oxide layer. Also, take time to clean up any dust or rubber contamination generated by the cleaning effort.

Cleaning other internal components, such as disk drive Read/Write heads, can be performed using lint-free foam swabs and isopropyl alcohol or methanol. It's most important that the cleaning solution be one that dries without leaving a residue.

PM (Preventive Maintenance) Procedures

The environment around a computer system and the manner in which the computer is used determine greatly how many problems it will have. Occasionally dedicating a few moments of care to the computer can extend its **Mean Time Between Failures (MTBF)** period considerably. This activity, involving maintenance not normally associated with a breakdown, is called **Preventive Maintenance (PM)**.

Mean Time Between Failures (MTBF)

Preventive Maintenance (PM)

The following sections of this chapter describe PM measures for the various areas of the system.

As with any electronic device, computers are susceptible to failures caused by dust buildup, rough handling, and extremes in temperature.

TEST TIP
Know what environmental conditions or activities are most likely to lead to equipment failures.

Dust

Over time, dust builds up on everything it can gain access to. Many computer components generate static electrical charges that attract dust particles. In the case of electronic equipment, dust forms an insulating blanket that traps heat next to active devices and can cause them to overheat. Excessive heat can cause premature aging and failure. The best dust protection is a dust-tight enclosure. However, computer components tend to have less than dust-tight seals. Power supply and microprocessor fans pull air from outside through the system unit.

Another access point for dust is uncovered expansion slot openings. Missing expansion slot covers adversely affect the system in two ways. First, a missing cover permits dust to accumulate in the system, forming the insulating blanket described above, which causes component overheating. Second, the heat problem is complicated further by the fact that the missing slot cover interrupts the designed airflow patterns inside the case, causing components to overheat due to missing or inadequate airflow.

TEST TIP
Be aware of the effect that missing expansion slot covers have on the operation of the system unit.

Smoke is a more dangerous cousin of dust. Like dust particles, smoke collects on all exposed surfaces. The residue of smoke particles is sticky and clings to the surface. In addition to contributing to the heat buildup problem, smoke residue is particularly destructive to moving parts such as floppy disks, fan motors, and so forth.

Smoke

Dust buildup inside system components can be taken care of with a soft brush. A **static-free vacuum** can also be used to remove dust from inside cases and keyboards. Be sure to use a static-free vacuum, since normal vacuums are by their nature static generators. The static-free vacuum has special grounding to remove the static buildup it generates. Dust covers are also helpful in preventing dust problems. These covers are simply placed over the equipment when not in use and removed when the device is needed.

> **TEST TIP**
>
> Know that computer vacuums have special grounding to dissipate static buildup that can damage computer devices.

Heat Buildup Problems

Identifying and controlling heat buildup problems can require some effort and planning. Microcomputers are designed to run at normal room temperatures. If the ambient temperature rises above about 85 degrees F, heat buildup can become a problem. High humidity can also lead to heat-related problems.

To combat heat problems, make sure that the area around the system is uncluttered so that free airflow around the system can be maintained. Make sure the power supply's fan is operational. If it is not, replace the power supply unit. Likewise, be sure that the microprocessor fan is plugged in and operational. It is very easy for a high-speed microprocessor to fry if its fan fails. A good rule of thumb is to install a fan on any microprocessor running above 33 MHz.

If heat buildup still exists, check to make sure that the outer cover is secured firmly to the machine and that all of the expansion clot covers are in place. These items can disrupt the designed airflow characteristics of the case. Finally, add an additional case fan to draw more air through the system unit.

CHALLENGE #1

When you arrive at a customer's office to repair one of their key computers, you trace the problem down to a defective microprocessor. The system has apparently been upgraded several times over its lifetime — there are several open expansion slots and loose cables inside the system unit. There is also a layer of dust on all the internal components. What should you tell the manager when she asks you about what you have found?

Handling Techniques

Rough handling is either a matter of neglect, or a lack of knowledge about how equipment should be handled. Therefore, overcoming rough handling problems requires that technicians be aware of proper handling techniques for sensitive devices, such as hard-disk drives and monitors, and that they adjust their component handling practices to compensate.

Protecting Monitors

The PM associated with video display **monitors** basically consists of **periodic cleaning**, **dusting**, and good **common-sense practices** around the monitor. The monitor's screen and cabinet should be dusted frequently, and cleaned periodically. Dust and smoke particles can build up very quickly around the monitor's screen, due to the presence of static charges on its face. When cleaning the screen, some caution should be used to avoid scratching its surface, and in the case of antiglare screens, to preserve its glare-reduction features.

Aerosol sprays, solvents, and commercial cleaners should be avoided, because they can damage the screen and cabinet. The simple cleaning solution, described earlier, is also fine for cleaning the monitor. Make sure that the monitor's power cord is disconnected from any power source before washing. The monitor's screen should be dried with a soft cloth after rinsing.

The monitor should not be left on for extended periods with the same image displayed on the screen. Over a period of time, the image will become permanently "burnt" into the screen. If it is necessary to display the same information on the screen for a long period of time, turn the intensity level of the monitor down, or install a **screen saver** program to alter the screen image periodically.

Inside the monitor's housing are very dangerous voltage levels (in excess of 25,000 volts, more than enough to kill or badly injure someone). Therefore, you should only remove the monitor's outer cabinet if you are fully qualified to work on CRT-based units. Even if the monitor has been turned off and unplugged for a year, it may still hold enough electrical potential to be deadly. Figure 13-2 shows the areas of the monitor that should be avoided, if you must work inside its housing.

| monitors |
| periodic cleaning |
| dusting |
| common-sense practices |

| screen saver |

Figure 13-2:
Caution Areas Inside
the Monitor

Video display monitors often include a tilt/swivel base that allows the users to position it at whatever angle is most comfortable. This offers additional relief from eyestrain by preventing the users from viewing the display at an angle. Viewing the screen at an angle causes the eyes to focus separately, which places strain on the eye muscles.

Protecting Hard-Disk Drives

Hard-disk drives don't require much preventive maintenance, since the Read/Write (R/W) heads and disks are enclosed in sealed, dust-tight compartments. However, there are some things that can be done to optimize the performance and life span of hard disk systems. Rough handling is responsible for more hard-disk drive damage than any other factor.

The drive should never be moved while you can still hear its disks spinning. The disk is most vulnerable during startup and shutdown, when the heads are not fully flying. Even a small jolt during these times can cause a great deal of damage to both the platters and the R/W heads. If the drive must be moved, a waiting period of one full minute should be allotted after turning the system off.

box-within-a-box

clean room

software backup

If the drive is to be transported or shipped, make sure to pack it properly. The forces exerted on the drive during shipment may be great enough to cause the R/W heads to slap against the disk surfaces, causing damage to both. Pack the drive unit in an oversized box, with antistatic foam all around the drive. You may also pack the drive in a **box-within-a-box** configuration, once again using foam as a cushion. This concept is illustrated in Figure 13-3.

At no time should the hard drive's housing, which protects the platters, be removed in open air. The drive's disks and R/W heads are sealed in the airtight housing under a vacuum. The contaminants floating in normal air will virtually ruin the drive. If the drive malfunctions, the electronic circuitry and connections may be tested, but when it comes to repairs within the disk chamber, factory service or a professional service facility with a proper **clean room** is a must!

To recover quickly from hardware failures, operator mistakes, and acts of nature, some form of **software backup** is essential with a hard disk system. The most common backup for larger systems is high-speed, streaming-tape cartridges, which can automatically back up the contents of the entire disk drive on magnetic tape. In the event of data loss on the disk, a full reinstall from the tape is possible in a matter of a few minutes.

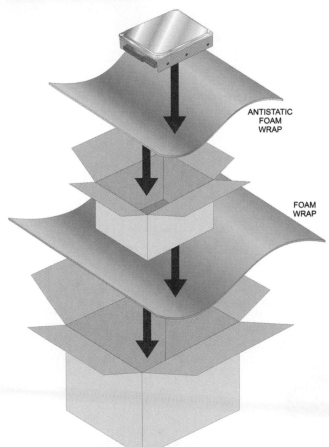

ANTISTATIC
FOAM
WRAP

FOAM
WRAP

Figure 13-3: Proper Packing of a Hard Drive for Shipment

High-volume disk-based devices, such as **optical drives** and **removable hard drives**, have become attractive methods for backing up the contents of large hard drives. CD-R and CD-RW drives provide an attractive option for storing limited amounts (680 MB) of critical data. Their high capacities allow large amounts of information to be written on a single disc. The major drawback of using a CD-R disc is that after the disc has been written to, it cannot be erased or reused. Various backup methods are depicted in Figure 13-4. In any case, failure to maintain backups will eventually result in a great deal of grief when the system goes down due to a hardware or software failure.

ZIP DISK

HARD-DISK DRIVE

OPTICAL DISC

3.5" FLOPPY DISKS

RAID SYSTEM

TAPE CARTRIDGE

Figure 13-4: Data Backup Systems

Copies of the system backup should be stored in a convenient, but secure place. In the case of secure system backups, such as client/server networks, the backup copies should be stored where the network administrators can have access to them, but not the general public (e.g., a locked file cabinet). Left unsecured, these copies could be used by someone without authority to gain access to the system or to its data. Even Emergency Repair Disks associated with Windows NT and Windows 2000 should be stored in a secure location. These disks can also be used by people other than administrators to gain access to information in client/server networks. Many companies maintain a copy of their backup away from the main site. This is done for protection in case of disasters such as fire.

TEST TIP

Be aware of the precautions that should be employed with storing system backups.

There are a number of hard-disk drive software utilities designed to optimize and maintain the operation of the hard-disk drive. They should be used as part of a regular preventive maintenance program. The primary HDD utilities are the CHKDSK, **ScanDisk**, **Defrag**, **Backup**, and **Antivirus** utilities that have been available with different versions of DOS and Windows since early MS-DOS versions.

Protecting Removable Media Drives

Unlike hard-disk drives, tape drives, floppy drives, and CD-ROM/DVD drives are at least partially open to the atmosphere, and their media may be handled on a regular basis. This opens these drive units up to a number of maintenance concerns not found in hard disk drives. Also, the removable cartridges, disks, or discs can be adversely affected by extremes in temperature, exposure to magnetic and electromagnetic fields, bending, and airborne particles that can lead to information loss.

Protecting Removable Media

Since magnetic tapes and floppy disks store information in the form of magnetized spots on their surfaces, it is only natural that external magnetic fields will have an adverse effect on their stored data. Never bring tape cartridges or floppies near magnetic-field-producing devices, such as CRT monitors, television sets, or power supplies. They should also never be placed on or near appliances such as refrigerators, freezers, vacuum cleaners, and other equipment containing motors. All of these items produce electromagnetic fields that can alter the information stored on their media.

Radio Frequency
Interference (RFI)

Proper positioning of the drive and proper connection of peripheral interface cables help to minimize noise and **Radio Frequency Interference (RFI)**. RFI can cause the drive to operate improperly. Magnetic fields generated by power supplies and monitors can interfere with the magnetic recording on disks and tapes. The drive and signal cables should be positioned away from these magnetic-field sources as well. Magnets should never be brought near any type of computer-related drive unit.

Additional measures to protect tape cassettes, disks, and discs include storing them in a cool, dry, clean environment, out of direct sunlight. Excessive temperature will cause the disk and its jacket, or the tape and cartridge to warp. Also, you should never physically touch the surface of the magnetic tape, floppy disk, or CD\DVD disc. In all cases, the natural oils from your skin can cause physical damage to the disk's coating and partially block the laser beam in a CD-ROM or DVD drive, causing the disk to be unreadable. Take care when inserting the disk into the drive so as not to damage the disk, its jacket, or the drive's internal mechanisms.

Maintaining Removable Media Drives

So far, each preventive action has involved disks. However, periodic manual cleaning of the R/W heads of tapes and floppies, or the laser reading mechanism in CD-ROMs and DVDs can prevent failures and bigger maintenance problems. Cleaning the R/W heads in tape and floppy drives removes residue and oxide buildup from the face of the head to ensure accurate transfer of data from the head to the media. Likewise, cleaning CD-ROM and DVD drives removes contaminants and buildup from the laser lens in the drive.

There are cleaning kits available for both floppy drives and CD/DVD drives, as well as for different types of tape drives. In the case of floppies and tape drives, cleaning should be done by manually cleaning the heads, as depicted in Figure 13-5. Automatic cleaning kits often include abrasive disks that scrub the faces of the R/W heads to remove buildup. These kits can eventually wear away the R/W head and damage it. On the other hand, CD-ROM/DVD drive cleaning kits offer cleaning discs that brush the laser lens to remove dust and other contaminants. It is also common practice to keep discs free from smudges and dust by wiping them gently with a soft cloth.

Manual cleaning operations involve removing the cover of the drive, gaining access to the R/W heads, and cleaning them manually with a swab that has been dipped in alcohol. Together, these steps provide an excellent preventive maintenance program that should ensure effective, long-term operation of the drive.

Figure 13-5: Cleaning the R/W Heads

alcohol

The cleaning solution for manual cleaning can be isopropyl alcohol, methanol, or some other solvent that does not leave a residue when it dries. Common cotton swabs are not recommended for use in manual cleaning, because they tend to shed fibers. These fibers can contaminate the drive and, in certain circumstances, damage the R/W mechanisms. Instead, **cellular foam swabs** or **lint-free cloths** are recommended for manual head cleaning. The interval of time between cleanings is dependent on several factors, such as the relative cleanliness of your computer area, and how often you use your disk drive.

cellular foam swabs
lint-free cloths

Protecting Input Devices

Input peripherals generally require very little in the way of preventive maintenance. An occasional **dusting** and cleaning should be all that's really required. There are, however, a few common-sense items to keep in mind when using an input device that should prevent damage to the device, and ensure its longevity.

dusting
soft brush
lint-free swab

The keyboard's electronic circuitry is open to the atmosphere and should be vacuumed, as shown in Figure 13-6, when you are cleaning around your computer area. Dust buildup on the keyboard circuitry can cause its ICs to fail due to overheating. To remove dirt and dust particles from inside the keyboard, disassemble the keyboard, and carefully brush particles away from the board with a **soft brush**. A **lint-free swab** can be used to clean between the keys. Take care not to snag any exposed parts with the brush or swab. To minimize dust collection in the keyboard, cover your keyboard when it is not in use.

┌─ **TEST TIP** ─────────────
│ Remember that dust can settle into the keyboard through the cracks between the keys.
└────────────────────────

SMALL HAND-HELD VACUUM

Figure 13-6: Cleaning the Keyboard

Never set keyboards, or pointing devices, on top of the monitor, or near the edge of the desk, where they may fall off. To prevent excessive wear on special keys, avoid applications and game programs that use keys in a repetitive manner. For these applications, use an appropriate pointing device, such as a mouse or joystick, for input.

When using a mouse, keep its workspace clear, dry, and free from dust. With a trackball mouse, the trackball should be removed and cleaned periodically. Use a lint-free swab to clean the X and Y trackball rollers inside the mouse, as shown in Figure 13-7.

**Figure 13-7:
Cleaning the Rollers
in a Mouse**

As with detachable keyboards, keep the connecting cables of all pointing devices out of harm's way.

PRINTER PM AND SAFETY ISSUES

Because printers tend to be much more mechanical than other types of computer peripherals, they require more effort to maintain. Printers generate pollutants, such as paper dust and ink droplets, in everyday operation. These pollutants can build up on mechanical parts and cause them to wear. As the parts wear, the performance of the printer diminishes. Therefore, printers require periodic cleaning and adjustments to maintain good performance.

The conditions and environment around the printer will also affect its usefulness and life cycle. The environmental requirements for printers are identical to those for a computer or any other electronic device. Therefore, the PM procedures described in Chapter 11 should also be applied to printers.

Dot-Matrix Printers

Adjust the printhead spacing, as described in Chapter 6. If the printhead is too far away from the platen, the print will appear washed-out. The tension on the printhead positioning belt should be checked periodically. If the belt is loose, the printer's dot positioning will become erratic. The belt should be reset for proper tension.

Clean the printer's roller surfaces. Use a damp, soft cloth to clean the surface of the platen. Rotate the platen through several revolutions. Do not use detergents, or solvents, on the rollers.

WARNING

Cleaning the printer and its mechanisms periodically adds to its productivity by removing contaminants that cause wear. Vacuum the inside of the unit, after applying antistatic solution to the vacuum's hose tip. Wipe the outside with a damp cloth, also using antistatic solution. Brush any contaminant buildup from the printer's mechanical components, using a soft-bristled brush. ***Never lubricate the platen assembly of the printer.***

Use a nonfibrous swab, dipped in alcohol, to clean the face of the dot-matrix printhead. This should loosen up paper fibers and ink that may cause the print wires to stick. Apply a small amount of oil to the face of the printhead.

Clean the paper-handling motor's gear train. Use a swab to remove buildup from the teeth of the gear train. If the gear train has been lubricated before, apply a light oil to the gears, using a swab. Turn the platen to make sure the oil gets distributed throughout the gear train. Apply a light coating of oil to the rails that the head-positioning carriage rides on. Move the carriage assembly across the rails several times to spread the lubricant evenly.

The cleaning of a dot-matrix printer is described in the following steps:

Hands-on Activity

Cleaning a Dot-Matrix Printer

1. Adjust the printhead spacing.

2. Check the tension on the printhead positioning belt.

3. Clean the printer and its mechanisms.

4. Clean the printer's roller surfaces.

5. Clean the surface of the platen.

6. Clean the surface of the dot-matrix printhead.

7. Clean the paper-handling motor's gear train.

8. Apply light oil to the gears using a swab.

9. Turn the platen to distribute the oil.

10. Apply a light coating of oil to the rails.

11. Move the carriage assembly to distribute the oil.

Ink-Jet Printers

The printheads in some ink-jet printers require cleaning and adjustment similar to those described for dot-matrix printers. Clean the paper-handling motor's gear train. Use a swab to remove buildup from the teeth of the gear train. If the gear train has been lubricated before, apply a light oil to the gears using a swab. Turn the platen to make sure the oil gets distributed throughout the gear train. Apply a light coating of oil to the rails that the printhead-positioning carriage rides on. Move the carriage assembly across the rails several times to spread the lubricant evenly.

The steps to cleaning an ink-jet printer are provided by the following:

Hands-on Activity

Cleaning an Ink-Jet Printer

1. Adjust the printhead spacing.

2. Check the tension on the printhead positioning belt.

3. Clean the printer and its mechanisms.

4. Clean the printer's roller surfaces.

5. Clean the surface of the platen.

6. Clean the surface of the ink-jet printhead.

7. Clean the paper-handling motor's gear train.

8. Apply light oil to the gears using a swab.

9. Turn the platen to distribute the oil.

10. Apply a light coating of oil to the rails.

11. Move the carriage assembly to distribute the oil.

Laser Printers

Use a vacuum cleaner to remove dust buildup and excess toner from the interior of the laser printer. Care should be taken to remove all excess toner from the unit. Vacuum the printer's ozone filter. Since water can mix with the toner particles in the printer, using wet sponges or towels to clean up toner inside the laser printer can create a bigger mess than the original one you were cleaning up. Remove the toner cartridge before vacuuming.

Clean the laser printer's rollers using a damp cloth or **denatured alcohol**. Also, clean the paper-handling motor's gear train. Use a swab to remove buildup from the teeth of the gear train. If the gear train has been lubricated before, apply a light coating of oil to the gears using a swab. Make sure the oil gets distributed throughout the gear train.

Clean the writing mechanism thoroughly. Use **compressed air** to blow out dust and paper particles that may collect on the lenses and shutters. If possible, wipe the laser lens with lint-free wipes to remove stains and fingerprints.

If accessible, use a swab, dipped in alcohol, to clean the corona wires. Rub the swab across the entire length of the wires. Take extra care to not break the strands that wrap around the corona. If these wires are broken, the printer will be rendered useless until new **monofilament wires** can be reinstalled.

Steps to cleaning a laser printer are described in the following hands-on activity:

denatured alcohol

compressed air

monofilament wires

TEST TIP

Remember acceptable methods for cleaning laser printers.

Hands-on Activity

Cleaning an Laser Printer

1. Remove dust buildup, and excess toner, from the interior.

2. Clean the laser printer's rollers.

3. Clean the paper-handling motor's gear train.

4. Apply light oil to the gears, using a swab.

5. Distribute the oil throughout the gear train.

6. Clean the corona wires.

In some laser printer models, the toner cartridges are designed so that they can be refilled. At this time, **third-party refill cartridges** are not typically as good as those from the manufacturer. However, they tend to be much cheaper than original equipment cartridges. If the output from the printer does not have to be very high quality, then refilled toner cartridges might be an interesting possibility to consider. To date, there are no regulations governing the disposal of laser printer cartridges.

third-party refill cartridges

Preventive Maintenance Scheduling

There is no perfect preventive maintenance (PM) schedule; however, the following is a reasonable schedule that can be used to effectively maintain most computer equipment. The schedule is written from the point of view of a personal computer. From an outside maintenance perspective, some of the steps will need to be shared with the daily users. As a matter of fact, for the most part, users carry out the daily and weekly PM activities.

Daily Activities

Back up important data from the unit. This can be done to floppy disks, backup tape, another network drive, or some other backup media. Check computer ventilation to make sure that papers and other desk clutter are not cutting off airflow to the unit. Check for other sources of heat buildup around the computer and its peripherals. These sources include:

- Direct sunlight from an outside window

- Locations of portable heaters in the winter

- Papers/books piled up around the equipment

Weekly Activities

Clean the outside of the computer and its peripheral equipment. Wipe the outside of the equipment with a damp cloth. The cloth can be slightly soapy. Wipe dry with an antistatic cloth. Clean the display screen using a damp cloth with the antistatic solution described earlier in this chapter. An antistatic spray can also be used for static buildup prevention.

CHKDSK/f

Run **CHKDSK/f** on all hard drives to locate and remove any lost clusters from the drives. This utility is available in all of the Microsoft operating systems including Windows 9x, Windows NT, and Windows 2000. The CHKDSK command must be run from the command prompt in all versions. Run a current virus-check program to check for hard drive infection. Back up any revised data files on the hard drive. Inspect the peripherals (mice, keyboard, etc.), and clean them if needed.

Monthly Activities

Clean the inside of the system. Use a long-nozzle vacuum cleaner attachment to remove dust from the inside of the unit. Wipe the nozzle with antistatic solution before vacuuming. A soft brush can also be used to remove dust from the system unit.

Clean the inside of the printer using the same equipment and techniques as those used with the system unit. Check system connections for corrosion, pitting, or discoloration. Wipe the surface of any peripheral card's edge connectors with a lubricating oil to protect it from atmospheric contamination.

Vacuum the keyboard out. Clean the X and Y rollers in the trackball mouse using a lint-free swab and a non-coating cleaning solution, as illustrated in Figure 13-7.

.TMP

Defragment the system's hard drive using the Defrag utility. Remove unnecessary temporary (**.TMP**) files from the hard drive. Check software and hardware manufacturers for product updates that can remove problems and improve system operation. Back up the entire hard-disk drive.

Semiannual Activities

Every six months, perform an extensive PM check. Apply an antistatic wash to the entire computer/peripheral work area. Wipe down books, the desktop, and other work area surfaces with antistatic solution. Disconnect power and signal cables from the system's devices, and reseat them. Clean the inside of the printer. Run the printer's self-tests.

Use a software diagnostic package to check each section of the system. Run all system tests available, looking for any hint of pending problems.

Annual Activities

Reformat the hard drive by backing up its contents and performing a high-level format. If the drive is an MFM, RLL, or ESDI drive, a low-level format should also be performed annually. Reinstall all the application software from original media, and reinstall all user files from the backup system. Check all floppy disks in the work area with a current anti-virus program.

Clean the R/W heads in the floppy drive, using a lint-free swab. Cotton swabs have fibers that can hang up in the ceramic insert of the head and damage it. Perform the steps outlined in the monthly and semiannual sections.

While this is a good model PM schedule, it is not the definitive schedule. Before establishing a firm schedule there are several other points to take into consideration. These points include any manufacturer's guidelines for maintaining the equipment. Read the user's guides of the various system components and work their suggested maintenance steps into the model.

Over time, adjust the steps and frequency of the plan to effectively cope with any environmental or usage variations. After all, the objective isn't to complete the schedule on time; it's to keep the equipment running and profitable.

SYSTEM PROTECTION

A portion of the A+ Core objective 3.1 states that the test taker should be able to identify the various types of preventive maintenance measures, products, and procedures and when and how to use them.

Content may include the following:

- Verifying UPS (uninterruptible power supply) and suppressors

As this A+ objective indicates, computer technicians should be aware of potential environmental hazards and know how to prevent them from becoming a problem. A good place to start checking for environmental hazards is with the incoming power source. The following sections of the chapter deal with power line issues and solutions.

Power Line Protection

Avoid power variations — Digital systems tend to be sensitive to power variations and losses. Even a very short loss of electrical power can shut a digital computer down, resulting in a loss of any current information that has not been saved to a mass storage device.

Typical power supply variations fall into two categories:

- **Transients** – an overvoltage condition, while sags are an undervoltage condition. Overvoltage conditions can be classified as **spikes** (measured in nanoseconds), or as **surges** (measured in milliseconds).

- **Sags** – can include **voltage sags** and **brownouts**. A voltage sag typically lasts only a few milliseconds, whereas a brownout can last for a protracted period of time.

┌─ **TEST TIP** ─┐
Be aware of how undervoltage and overvoltage situations are categorized (i.e., time lengths).
└─────────────┘

The effects of these power supply variations are often hard to identify as power issues. Brownouts and power failures are easy to spot because of their duration. However, faster-acting disturbances can cause symptoms that are not easily traced to the power source. Spikes can be quite harmful to electronic equipment, damaging devices such as hard drives and modems. Other occurrences will simply cause data loss. Sags may cause a system to suddenly reboot because it thinks the power has been turned off. These disturbances are relatively easy to detect since they typically cause any lights in the room to flicker.

In general, if several components go bad in a short period of time, or if components go bad more often than usual at a given location, these are good indicators of power-related issues. Likewise, machines that crash randomly and often could be experiencing power issues. If "dirty" power problems are suspected, a voltage-monitoring device should be placed in the power circuit and left for an extended period of time. These devices observe the incoming power over time and will produce a problem indicator if significant variations occur.

Surge Suppressors

Inexpensive **power line filters**, called **surge suppressors**, are good for cleaning up dirty commercial power. These units passively filter the incoming power signal to smooth out variations. There are two factors to consider when choosing a surge suppressor:

┌─ **TEST TIP** ─┐
Know what type of devices will protect systems from minor power sags and power surges.
└─────────────┘

- Clamping speed
- Clamping voltage

These units will protect the system from damage, up to a specified point. However, large variations, such as surges created when power is restored after an outage, can still cause considerable data loss and damage. In the case of startup surges, making sure that the system is turned off, or even disconnected from the power source, until after the power is restored is one option. In the case of a complete shutdown, or a significant sag, the best protection against losing programs and data is an **Uninterruptible Power Supply (UPS)**.

┌─ **TEST TIP** ─┐
Know what type of device prevents power interruptions that can corrupt data.
└─────────────┘

Uninterruptible Power Supplies

Uninterruptible power supplies are battery-based systems that monitor the incoming power and kick in when unacceptable variations occur in the power source. The term **UPS** is frequently used to describe two different types of power backup systems.

The first is a **standby power system**, and the second is a truly **uninterruptible power system**. A typical UPS system is depicted in Figure 13-8.

Figure 13-8: UPS System

The standby system monitors the power input line, and waits for a significant variation to occur. The batteries in this unit are held out of the power loop, and only draw enough current from the AC source to stay recharged. When an interruption occurs, the UPS senses it and switches the output of the batteries into an inverter circuit that converts the DC output of the batteries to an AC current and voltage that resemble the commercial power supply. This power signal is typically applied to the computer within 10 milliseconds.

The uninterruptible systems do not keep the batteries offline. Instead, the batteries and converters are always actively attached to the output of UPS. When an interruption in the supply occurs, no switching of the output is required. The battery/inverter section simply continues under its own power. Figure 13-9 shows how a UPS connects into a system.

**Figure 13-9:
Connecting the
UPS in the System**

Standby systems don't generally provide a high level of protection from sags and spikes. However, they do include additional circuitry to minimize such variations. Conversely, an uninterruptible system is an extremely good power-conditioning system. Since it always sits between the commercial power and the computer, it can supply a constant power supply to the system.

When dealing with either type of UPS system, the most important rating to be aware of is its **Volt-Ampere (VA)** rating. The VA rating indicates the ability of the UPS system to deliver both voltage (V) and current (A) to the computer, simultaneously. This rating is different than the device's **wattage rating**, and the two should not be used interchangeably.

The wattage power rating is a factor of multiplying the voltage and current use, at any particular time, to arrive at a power consumption value. The VA rating is used in AC systems because peak voltage and current elements do not occur at the same instant. This condition is referred to as being **out-of-phase**, and makes it slightly more difficult to calculate power requirements. In general, always make sure that the UPS system has a higher wattage capability than the computer requires, and likewise that the VA rating of the UPS is higher than that required by the computer.

**Volt-Ampere (VA)
rating**

wattage rating

out-of-phase

The other significant specification for UPS systems is the length of time they can supply power. Since the UPS is a battery-powered device, it uses an **ampere-hour rating**. This is the same time notation system used for automobile batteries and other battery-powered systems. The rating is obtained by multiplying a given current drain from the battery by a given amount of time (i.e., a battery capable of sustaining 1.5 amps of output current for 1 hour would be rated at 1.5 ampere-hours).

ampere-hour rating

The primary mission of the UPS is to keep the system running when a power failure occurs (usually, long enough to conduct an orderly shutdown of the system). Because it's battery-based, it cannot keep the system running infinitely. For this reason, you should not connect nonessential, power-hungry peripheral devices such as a laser printer to the UPS supply. If the power goes out, it is highly unlikely that you will really have to print something before shutting the system down. If the UPS is being used to keep a critical system in operation during the power outage, the high current drain of the laser printer would severely reduce the length of time that the UPS could keep the system running.

┌─ **TEST TIP** ─────────────────┐

Remember that nonessential peripheral devices should not be connected to UPS supplies.

└────────────────────────────────┘

If the UPS were simply connected in line with the computer's power source, the UPS would simply kick in when a power line disruption occurred and keep the computer running until the batteries were drained or the power was restored. However, UPS systems have the ability to communicate with a host computer so that an orderly shutdown of the system can be performed. The host computer can be a stand-alone desktop/tower unit that the UPS is guarding, or in a network environment, it can be a server that has network management capabilities for all of the computers on the network. The host computer is typically connected to the UPS through a serial interface cable.

When a disruption occurs, the UPS notifies the power management system in the host computer's operating system of the failure. The power management utility for most operating systems can be configured to begin a prescribed shutdown schedule. This option is designed to give the system enough time to safely store any key information and prepare to be shut down. In the case of a server-managed network situation, the server can shut down different programs, computers, and support equipment at different times to conserve the battery life of the UPS, yet stay online as long as possible.

The server can also be configured to notify system users that a shutdown will be occurring so that they can complete their tasks and shut down properly. At the same time the host computer can issue a page or e-mail alert to an administrator or service person to notify them that a problem has occurred and needs to be investigated.

The host computer sees the UPS device as another peripheral device. As a matter of fact, when the UPS is first installed, the system's PnP process should detect the UPS as it would any other peripheral attached to one of its serial ports. Afterward, the system will simply see the UPS as another one of its installed devices.

Checking UPS Operation

A UPS system is a major component of any server system that must have a high level of availability. The UPS provides continued operation when power problems arise and provides safety for data in process. However, a UPS is still an electronic device and is subject to failure. If the safety component of a system fails, then the entire system becomes vulnerable.

Therefore, the UPS should be tested at regular intervals to ensure that it is functioning properly. The simplest UPS test is to unplug the UPS from the wall while the computer is running to make it supply power to the system through its batteries alone. You should measure the performance of the system against its configured shutdown schedule.

> **NOTE**
>
> Of course, you should be aware that any UPS testing should be performed while the computer is not in active use and when there is no chance of data loss due to unexpected test results.

If the UPS does not supply the expected amount of backup time when it's tested, it may be overloaded, or its batteries may be wearing out. The first option is to unplug less important equipment, such as laser printers, from the UPS. Afterward, attempt to recharge the batteries and retest the system. If this does not restore backup time to acceptable levels, consider replacing the batteries in the UPS.

Other common problems that can occur with UPS systems include the UPS not turning on, the UPS not turning off, the host computer running only on the UPS batteries, and the UPS not controlling the shutdown of the host computer. If the UPS system does not come on, there are several items that should be checked. These items include:

- The On/Off switch
- The commercial AC power supply
- The UPS input circuit breaker
- The UPS battery connector

All of these items can cause the UPS to fail. Verify the function of the UPS On/Off switch. If it functions properly, check the AC supply to the UPS by substituting a lamp or other handheld AC device in its outlet to verify that power is reaching the outlet. If power is available at the outlet, check the AC power cord at the outlet and the UPS. Next, check the input circuit breaker UPS, if present, to determine whether it is set or tripped. Finally, check the battery connector to make certain that it is fully engaged.

If the UPS operates on battery power even though AC power is available, the input circuit breaker may be tripped or the unit's input voltage sensitivity may be set to high. You should reduce the load on the UPS by unplugging any unnecessary items. After the auxiliary devices have been removed, reset the breaker. Some inexpensive power generators can distort the input voltage to the UPS. To combat this, you may need to move the UPS to a different outlet on a different power circuit, or adjust the UPS unit's voltage sensitivity setting.

Likewise, if the UPS does not turn off, an internal UPS fault has occurred and the unit should not be used. Instead, the UPS unit should be replaced and serviced immediately.

UPS systems do not always use standard serial cables for communication. If the cable is incorrect, loose, or missing, the computer's power management functions will not be able to communicate with the UPS to control it.

Protection during Storage

The best storage option for most computer equipment is the original manufacturer's box. These boxes are designed specifically to store and transport devices safely. They include form-fitting protective foam to protect the device from shock hazards. The device is normally wrapped in a protective antistatic bag or wrapper to defeat the effects of ESD.

Printed circuit boards are normally shipped on a thin piece of antistatic foam. The board is typically placed solder-side down on the foam. Both the foam and the board are placed in an antistatic bag and then into a storage box.

Hard-disk drives are usually placed directly into a static bag and then placed in a thick foam box. The foam box is then inserted into a storage carton. FDDs typically receive less padding than HDD units do.

Monitors, printers, scanners, and other peripheral equipment should be stored in their original boxes, using their original packing foam and protective storage bag. The contours in the packing foam of these devices are not generally compatible from model to model, or device to device. If the original boxes and packing materials are not available, make sure to use sturdy cartons and cushion the equipment well on all sides before shipping.

All electronic devices should be stored in dry, cool areas away from heat sources and direct sunlight. Low-traffic areas are also preferable for storage since there is less chance of incidental damage from people and/or equipment passing by.

HAZARDS AND SAFETY PROCEDURES

A portion of the A+ Core objective 3.2 states that the test taker should be able to identify various safety measures and procedures, and when/how to use them.

Content may include the following:

- Situations that could present a danger or hazard
- Potential hazards and proper safety procedures relating to:
    - High-voltage equipment
    - Power supply
    - CRTs

Avoiding High-Voltage Hazards

In most IBM compatibles, there are only two potentially dangerous areas. One of these is inside the **CRT display**, and the other is inside the power supply unit. Both of these areas contain electrical voltage levels that are lethal. However, both of these areas reside in self-contained units, and you will usually not be required to open either unit.

As a matter of fact, you should never enter the interior of a CRT cabinet unless you have been trained specifically to work with this type of equipment. The tube itself is dangerous if accidentally cracked. In addition, extremely **high voltage levels** (in excess of 25,000 volts) may be present inside the CRT housing, even up to a year after electrical power has been removed from the unit.

Never open the power supply unit either. Some portions of the circuitry inside the power supply carry extremely high voltage levels and have very high current.

Generally, there are no open shock hazards present inside the system unit. However, you should not reach inside the computer while power is applied to the unit. Jewelry and other metallic objects do pose an electrical threat, even with the relatively low voltage present in the system unit.

Never have liquids around energized electrical equipment. It's a good idea to keep food and drinks away from all computer equipment at all times. When cleaning around the computer with liquids, make certain to unplug all power connections to the system and its peripherals beforehand. When cleaning external computer cabinets with liquid cleaners, take care to prevent any of the solution from dripping or spilling into the equipment.

Do not defeat the safety feature of three-prong power plugs by using two-prong adapters. The equipment ground of a power cable should never be defeated or removed. This plug connects the computer chassis to earth ground through the power system. This provides a reference point for all of the system's devices to operate from, as well as supplying protection for personnel from electrical shock. In defeating the ground plug, a very important level of protection is removed from the equipment.

Periodically examine the power cords of the computer and peripherals for cracked or damaged insulation. Replace worn or damaged power cords promptly. Never allow anything to rest on a power cord. Run power cords and connecting cables safely out of the way, so that they don't become **trip** or **catch hazards**. Remove all power cords associated with the computer and its peripherals from the power outlet during thunderstorms.

Don't apply liquid or aerosol cleaners directly to computer equipment. Spray cleaners on a cloth, and then apply the cloth to the equipment. Freon-propelled sprays should not be used on computer equipment, since they can produce destructive electrostatic charges.

Check equipment vents to see that they are clear and have ample free-air space to allow heat to escape from the cabinet. Never block these vents, and never insert or drop objects into them.

Avoiding Laser and Burn Hazards

Laser printers contain many hazardous areas. The laser light can be very damaging to the human eye. In addition, there are multiple high-voltage areas in the typical laser printer, and a high-temperature area to contend with as well.

The technician is normally protected from these areas by interlock switches built into the unit. However, it is often necessary to bypass these interlocks to isolate problems. When doing so, proper precautions must be observed, such as avoiding the laser light, being aware of the high temperatures in the fuser area, and taking proper precautions with the high-voltage areas of the unit. The laser light is a hazard to eyesight, the fuser area is a burn hazard, and the power supplies are shock hazards.

Another potential burn hazard is the printhead mechanism of dot-matrix, thermal wax, and dye sublimation printers. During normal operations these elements become hot enough to be a burn hazard if touched.

> **TEST TIP**
> Know the areas of the computer system that are dangerous for personnel and how to prevent injury from these areas.

Since computers do have the potential to produce these kinds of injuries, it is good practice to have a well-stocked **first-aid kit** in the work area. In addition, a **Class-C fire extinguisher** should be on hand. Class-C extinguishers are the type specified for use around electrical equipment. You can probably imagine the consequences of applying a water-based fire extinguisher to a fire with live electrical equipment around. The class, or classes, that the fire extinguisher is rated for are typically marked on its side.

first-aid kit

Class-C fire extinguisher

You may think that there's not much chance for a fire to occur with computer equipment, but this is not so. Just let a capacitor from a system board blow up and have a small piece land in a pile of packing materials in the work area. It becomes a fire.

> **TEST TIP**
> Remember the type of fire extinguisher that must be used with electrical systems, such as a PC.

This covers the major safety precautions and considerations that you need to be aware of while working on computer equipment. Most of all, use common sense and sound safety practices around all electronic equipment.

DISPOSAL PROCEDURES

The A+ Core objective 3.3 states that the test taker should be able to identify environmental protection measures and procedures, and when/how to use them.

Content may include the following:

- Special disposal procedures that comply with environmental guidelines
- Batteries
- CRTs
- Chemical solvents and cans
- MSDS (Material Safety Data Sheet)

As with any mechanical device, a computer eventually becomes obsolete in the application that it was originally intended for. Newer machines, with improved features, arise to replace earlier models. And, slowly, but surely, components fail and get replaced. Then comes the question: What do we do with the old stuff? Can it simply be placed in the garbage bin so that it is hauled to the landfill and buried?

In today's world of environmental consciousness, you might not think so. Computers and peripherals contain some environmentally unfriendly materials.

local regulations

While all of these materials can be classified as hazardous materials, so far there are no widespread regulations when it comes to placing them in the landfill. Conversely, **local regulations** concerning acceptable disposal methods for computer-related components should always be checked before disposing of any electronic equipment.

hazardous substances

Most computer components contain some level of **hazardous substances**. Printed circuit boards consist of plastics, precious metals, fiberglass, arsenic, silicon, gallium, and lead. CRTs contain glass, metal, plastics, lead, barium, and rare earth metals. Batteries from portable systems can contain lead, cadmium, lithium, alkaline manganese, and mercury.

TEST TIP

Remember that toner cartridges from a laser printer should be recycled.

Laser printer toner cartridges can be refilled and recycled. However, this should only be done in draft mode operations where very good resolution is not required. Ink cartridges from ink-jet printers can also be refilled and reused. Like laser cartridges, they can be very messy to refill and often do not function as well as new cartridges do. In many cases, the manufacturer of the product will have a policy of accepting spent cartridges.

recycling

drop site

nonhazardous, sub-title D dump sites

Chamber of Commerce

For both batteries and cartridges, the desired method of disposal is **recycling**. It should not be too difficult to find a **drop site** that will handle recycling these products. On the other hand, even **nonhazardous, sub-title D dumpsites** can handle the hardware components if need be. Sub-title D dumpsites are nonhazardous, solid waste dumpsites that have been designed to meet EPA standards set for this classification. Sub-title C dumpsites are those designed to hold hazardous materials safely.

Fortunately, there seem to be several charitable organizations around the country that take in old computer systems and refurbish them for various applications. Contact your local **Chamber of Commerce** for information about such organizations. The Internet also has several computer disposal organizations that will take old units and redistribute them. In addition, there are a few companies that will dispose of your old computer components in an "environmentally friendly" manner — for a fee.

TEST TIP

Remember that the proper disposal method for batteries is to recycle them.

---

cleaning substances

In addition to the computer parts that provide hazardous materials, many of the **cleaning substances** used on computer equipment can be classified as hazardous materials. When it comes to the chemical solvents used to clean computers, as well as the containers they come in, it will normally be necessary to clear these items with the local waste management agencies before disposing of them. Many dumpsites will not handle **free liquids**. Free liquids are those substances that can pass through a standard paint filter. If the liquid passes through the filter, it is a free liquid and cannot be disposed of in the landfill. Therefore, solvents and other liquid cleaning materials must be properly categorized and disposed of at an appropriate type of disposal center.

free liquids

All hazardous materials are required to have **Material Safety Data Sheets (MSDS)** that accompany them when they change hands. They are also required to be on-hand in areas where hazardous materials are stored and commonly used. The MSDS contains information about:

- What the material is
- Its hazardous ingredients
- Its physical properties
- Fire and explosion data
- Reactivity data
- Spill or leak procedures
- Health hazard information
- Any special protection information
- Any special precaution information

The supplier of the hazardous material must provide this information sheet. If you supply this material to a third party, you must also supply the MSDS for the material. The real reason for the sheet is to inform workers and management about hazards associated with the material and how to handle it safely. The MSDS also provides instructions about what to do if an accident occurs involving the material. For this reason, employees should know where the MSDSs are stored in their work area.

Material Safety Data
Sheets (MSDS)

ELECTROSTATIC DISCHARGE

A portion of the A+ Core objective 3.2 states that the test taker should be able to identify various safety measures and procedures, and when/how to use them.

Content may include the following:

- ESD (Electrostatic Discharge) precautions and procedures
- What ESD can do, how it may be apparent or hidden
- Common ESD protection devices

The first step in avoiding ESD (Electrostatic Discharge) is being able to identify when and why it occurs.

Identifying and Avoiding Electrostatic Discharge

What is ESD — **Electrostatic Discharges (ESD)** are the most severe form of **Electromagnet Interference (EMI)**. The human body can build up static charges that range up to **25,000 volts**. These buildups can discharge very rapidly into a electrically grounded body, or device. Placing a 25,000-volt surge through any electronic device is potentially damaging to it.

Electrostatic
Discharges (ESD)

Electromagnet
Interference (EMI)

25,000 volts

TEST TIP

Remember what the acronym ESD stands for.

Static can easily discharge through digital computer equipment. The electronic devices that are used to construct digital equipment are particularly susceptible to damage from ESD. As a matter of fact, ESD is the most damaging form of electrical interference associated with digital equipment.

The most common causes of ESD are:

- Moving people
- Improper grounding
- Unshielded cables
- Poor connections
- Moving machines
- Low humidity (hot and dry conditions)

┌─ **TEST TIP** ─────────
Memorize the conditions that make ESD more likely to occur.

┌─ **TEST TIP** ─────────
Be aware that compressed air can be used to blow dust out of components and that it does not create ESD.

Elementary school teachers demonstrate the principles of static electricity to their students by rubbing different materials together. When people move, the clothes they are wearing rub together, and can produce large amounts of electrostatic charge on their bodies. Walking across carpeting can create charges in excess of 1,000 volts. Motors in electrical devices, such as vacuum cleaners and refrigerators, generate high levels of ESD.

┌─ **TEST TIP** ─────────
Memorize conditions and actions that produce electrostatic discharge.

ESD is most likely to occur during periods of **low humidity**. If the relative humidity is below 50%, static charges can accumulate easily. ESD generally does not occur when the humidity is above 50%. Anytime the charge reaches around 10,000 volts, it is likely to discharge to grounded metal parts.

low humidity

Metal Oxide Semiconductor (MOS)

While ESD won't hurt humans, it will destroy certain electronic devices. A high-voltage pulse can burn out the inputs of many IC devices. This damage may not appear instantly. It can build up over time and cause the device to fail. Electronic logic devices, constructed from **Metal Oxide Semiconductor (MOS)** materials, are particularly susceptible to ESD. The following section describes the special handling techniques that should be observed when working with equipment containing MOS devices.

You may be a little confused by the fact that we warn you about the lethal 25,000 volts present inside the monitor and then say that the 10,000 to 25,000 volts of ESD is not harmful to humans. The reason for this is the difference in current-delivering capabilities created by the voltage. For example, the circuitry in the monitor and the power supply is capable of delivering amps of current, while the current-producing capability of the electrostatic charge is less than a thousandth of that. Therefore, the 120 Vac, 1-amp current produced by the power supply unit is lethal, while the 25,000 Vdc, microamps of current produced by ESD is not.

┌─ **TEST TIP** ─────────
Remember that the current capabilities of electrical devices establish the potential danger levels associated with working around them.

MOS Handling Techniques

In general, MOS devices are sensitive to voltage spikes and static electricity discharges. This can cause many problems when you have to replace MOS devices, especially **Complementary-Symmetry Metal Oxide Semiconductor (CMOS)** devices. The level of static electricity present on your body is high enough to destroy the inputs of a CMOS device if you touch its pins with your fingers.

In order to minimize the chances of damaging MOS devices during handling, special procedures have been developed to protect them from static shock. ICs are generally shipped and stored in special **conductive-plastic tubes** or trays. You may want to store MOS devices in these tubes, or you may simply ensure their safety by inserting the IC's leads into aluminum foil or **antistatic** (conductive) **foam** — not styrofoam. PC boards containing static-sensitive devices are normally shipped in special **antistatic bags**. These bags are good for storing ICs and other computer components that may be damaged by ESD. They are also the best method of transporting PC boards with static-sensitive components.

Professional service technicians employ a number of precautionary steps when they are working on systems that may contain MOS devices. These technicians normally use **grounding straps**, like the one depicted in Figure 13-10. These antistatic devices may be placed around the wrists or ankle to ground the technician to the system being worked on. These straps release any static present on the technician's body, and pass it harmlessly to ground potential.

Complementary-Symmetry Metal Oxide Semiconductor (CMOS)

conductive-plastic tubes

antistatic foam

antistatic bags

grounding straps

**Figure 13-10:
Typical Antistatic
Devices**

Antistatic straps should never be worn while working on higher-voltage components, such as monitors and power supply units. Some technicians wrap a copper wire around their wrist or ankle, and connect it to the ground side of an outlet. This is not a safe practice, since the resistive feature of a true wrist strap is missing. As an alternative, most technicians work areas include **antistatic mats** made out of rubber or other antistatic materials that they stand on while working on the equipment. This is particularly helpful in carpeted work areas, since carpeting can be a major source of ESD buildup. Some antistatic mats have ground connections that should be connected to the safety ground of an AC power outlet.

To avoid damaging static-sensitive devices, the following procedures will help to minimize the chances of destructive static discharges:

- Before touching any components inside the system, touch an exposed part of the chassis or the power supply housing with your finger, as illustrated in Figure 13-11. Grounding yourself in this manner will ensure that any static charge present on your body is removed. This technique should be used before handling a circuit board or component. Of course, you should be aware that this technique will only work safely if the power cord is attached to a grounded power outlet. The ground plug on a standard power cable is the best tool for overcoming ESD problems.

**Figure 13-11:
Discharging Through the
Power Supply Unit**

- Do not remove ICs from their protective tubes (or foam packages) until you are ready to use them. If you remove a circuit board or component that contains static-sensitive devices from the system, place it on a conductive surface, such as a sheet of aluminum foil.

- In the event that you have to replace a hard-soldered IC, you may want to install an IC socket along with the chip. Be aware that normal operating vibrations and **temperature cycling** can degrade the electrical connections between ICs and sockets over time. This gradual deterioration of electrical contact between chips and sockets is referred to as **chip creep**. It is a good practice to reseat any socket-mounted devices when handling a printed circuit board. Before removing the IC from its protective container, touch the container to the power supply of the unit in which it is to be inserted.

temperature cycling

chip creep

TEST TIP

Be aware of the effects that temperature cycling can have on socket-mounted devices.

- Use antistatic sprays or solutions on floors, carpets, desks, and computer equipment. An antistatic spray or solution, applied with a soft cloth, is an effective deterrent to static.

- Install **static-free carpeting** in the work area. You can also install an antistatic floor mat as well. Install a conductive tabletop to carry away static from the work area. Use antistatic tablemats.

- Use a room humidifier to keep the humidity level above 50% in the work area.

static-free carpeting

Understanding Grounds

The term **ground** is often a source of confusion for the novice, because it actually encompasses a collection of terms. Generically, ground is simply any point from which electrical measurements are referenced. However, the original definition of ground actually referred to the ground. This ground is called **earth ground**.

ground

earth ground

The movement of the electrical current along a conductor requires a path to return to its source. In early telegraph systems and even modern power transmission systems, the earth provides a return path and, hypothetically, produces an electrical reference point of absolute zero. This type of ground is shown in Figure 13-12.

Figure 13-12: Power Transmission System

Many electronic circuits use an actual conductor as a return path. This type of ground is referred to as a **signal ground**. Electronic devices may also contain a third form of ground called **chassis ground**, or **protective ground**. In any event, ground still remains the reference point from which most electrical signals are measured. In the case of troubleshooting computer components, measurements referenced to ground may be made from the system unit's chassis.

signal ground

chassis ground

protective ground

The other measurement reference is the signal ground point on the printed circuit board, where the test is being performed. This point isn't too difficult to find in a circuit board full of ICs, because most DIP-style chips use the highest-numbered pin for the positive supply voltage, and the last pin on the pin-1 side of the chip as the ground pin. This type of ground is illustrated in Figure 13-13. Some caution should be used with this assumption, since not all ICs use this pin for ground. However, if you examine a number of ICs and connectors on the board, you should be able to trace the ground foil and use it as a reference.

**Figure 13-13:
Grounds on IC Chips**

Grounding is an important aspect of limiting EMI in computer systems. Left unchecked, EMI can distort images on the video display, interfere with commercial communication equipment (such as radios and televisions), and corrupt data on floppy disks. In addition, EMI can cause signal deterioration and loss from improper cable routing. If a signal cable is bundled with a power cable, radiation from the power cable may induce current into the signal cable, affecting the signals that pass through it. Good grounding routes the induced EMI signals away from logic circuitry and toward ground potential, preventing them from disrupting normal operations. Unlike ESD, which is destructive, the effects of EMI can be corrected without damage.

TEST TIP

Remember that ESD is destructive and EMI is not.

Because the computer system is connected to an actual earth ground, it should always be turned off and disconnected from the wall outlet during electrical storms. This includes the computer and all of its peripherals. The electrical pathway through the computer equipment can be very inviting to lightning on its way to earth ground. The extremely high electrical potential of a lightning strike is more than any computer can withstand.

TEST TIP

Know the best protection for a computer system during an electrical storm.

VIRUSES

Computer viruses are destructive programs designed to replicate and spread on their own. Viruses are created to sneak into personal computers. Sometimes these programs take control of a machine to leave a humorous message, and sometimes they destroy data. After they infiltrate one machine, they can spread into other computers through infected disks that friends and coworkers pass around or through local and wide area network connections.

Common Viruses

There are basically three types of viruses, based on how they infect a computer system:

- A **boot-sector virus** — This type of virus copies itself onto the boot sector of floppy and hard disks. The virus replaces the disk's original boot-sector code with its own code. This allows it to be loaded into memory before anything else is loaded. Once in memory, the virus can spread to other disks.

- A **file infector** — File infectors are viruses that add their virus code to executable files. After the file with the virus is executed, the virus spreads to other executable files. A similar type of virus, called a macro virus, hides in the macro programs of word processing document files. These files can be designed to load when the document is opened or when a certain key combination is entered. In addition, these types of viruses can be designed to stay resident in memory after the host program has been exited (similar to a TSR program), or they might just stop working when the infected file is terminated.

- A **Trojan horse** — This type of virus appears to be a legitimate program that might be found on any system. Trojan horse viruses are more likely to do damage by destroying files, and they can cause physical damage to disks.

A number of different viruses have been created from these three virus types. They have several different names, but they all inflict basically the same damage. After the virus file has become active in the computer, it basically resides in memory when the system is running. From this point, it might perform a number of different types of operations that can be as complex and damaging as the author designs them to be.

As an example, a strain of boot-sector virus, known as **CMOS virus**, infects the hard drive's Master Boot Record and becomes memory resident. When activated, the virus writes over the system's configuration information in the CMOS area. Part of what gets overwritten is the HDD and FDD information. Therefore, the system cannot boot up properly. The initial infection comes from booting from an infected floppy disk. The virus overwrites the CMOS once in every 60 bootups.

A similar boot-sector virus, referred to as the **FAT virus**, becomes memory resident in the area of system memory where the IO.SYS and MSDOS.SYS files are located. This allows it to spread to any non—write-protected disks inserted into the computer. In addition, the virus moves the system pointers for the disk's executable files to an unused cluster and rewrites the pointers in the FAT to point to the sector where the virus is located. The result is improper disk copies, inability to back up files, large numbers of lost clusters, and all executable files being cross-linked with each other.

┌─ **TEST TIP** ─────┐
Know how the different types
of viruses attack the system.
└────────────────────┘

In another example, a file infector virus strain, called the **FAT table virus**, infects EXE files but does not become memory resident. When the infected file is executed, the virus rewrites another EXE file.

Likewise, **Terminate and Stay Resident (TSR)** viruses create copies of themselves in system memory. Then, they intercept system events such as a disk access and use this operation to infect files and sectors on the disk. In this manner TSR viruses are active both when an infected program runs and after it terminates. Since the resident copy of these viruses remain viable in memory, even if all the infected files are deleted from disk, it is very difficult to fully remove these viruses from the system. Removing TSR viruses by restoring all the files from distribution disks or backup copies does not work well because the resident copy of virus remains active in RAM and infects the newly created files.

Virus Symptoms

Because viruses tend to operate in the background, it is sometimes difficult to realize that the computer has been infected. Typical virus symptoms include the following:

- Hard disk controller failures.
- Disks continue to be full even when files have been deleted.
- System cannot read write-protected disks.
- The hard disk stops booting, and files are corrupted.
- The system will boot to floppy disk, but will not access the HDD.
- An Invalid Drive Specification message usually displays when attempting to access the C: drive.
- CMOS settings continually revert to default even though the system board battery is good.
- Files change size for no apparent reason.
- System operation slows down noticeably.
- Blank screen when booting (flashing cursor).
- Windows crashes.
- The hard drive is set to DOS compatibility, and 32-bit file access suddenly stops working.
- Network data transfers and print jobs slow down dramatically.

Common practices that increase the odds of a machine being infected by a virus include use of shareware software, software of unknown origin, or bulletin board software. One of the most effective ways to reduce these avenues of infection is to buy shrink-wrapped products from a reputable source.

Anti-Virus Software

Another means of virus protection involves installing a **virus-scanning (anti-virus) program** that checks disks and files before using them in the computer. Several other companies offer third-party virus-protection software that can be configured to operate in various ways. If the computer is a stand-alone unit, it might be nonproductive to have the anti-virus software run each time the system is booted up. It would be much more practical to have the program check floppy disks or writable CD-ROM disks only because this is the only possible non-network entryway into the computer.

A networked or online computer has more opportunity to contract a virus than a stand-alone unit because viruses can enter the unit over the network or through the modem. In these cases, setting the software to run at each bootup is more desirable. Most modern anti-virus software includes utilities to check e-mail and files downloaded to the computer through dial-up connections, such as from the Internet.

With Windows 95, Microsoft abandoned their integrated anti-virus protection utilities. Therefore, you must use third-party anti-virus programs with Windows 9x, Windows NT, Windows 2000, and Windows XP. Special versions of these programs are also available for use with Apple Macintoch machines and LINUX-based computers.

Most of these suppliers provide their products in multiple formats. They usually sell boxed commercial versions as well as Internet download versions. In addition, they typically provide automatic update services that periodically notify you of new threats and provide new virus definition databases (these programs work by comparing the characteristics of received files to profiles associated with known virus types). A subscription service is normally provided to continue the update service after the intial usage period has expired.

As indicated earlier, when an anti-virus application is installed on the system, it can be configured to provide different levels of virus protection. You will need to configure when and under what circumstances you want the anti-virus software to run.

CHALLENGE #3

A customer calls you to his site complaining that the wide-carriage, dot-matrix printer in his accounting department is running very slowly and that they cannot get all their invoices printed for today's shipping purposes. When you check their print queue, you see that the print jobs for the invoices are stacked up in the queue but are being processed. The accounting manager tells you that they typically don't have any problems getting their invoices printed and that nothing out of the ordinary has been done to the computer to make it slow down. What items should you check to determine the cause of the slowdown?

CHAPTER SUMMARY

The focus of this chapter has been to present important points for inclusion in preventive maintenance programs associated with personal computer systems. The first section of the chapter dealt with typical cleaning chores. It also featured preventive maintenance procedures for the system's different components. A suggested PM schedule was also presented. This is time-proven information and should always be shared freely with customers.

The second major section of the chapter focused on environmental hazards that affect the operation of computer equipment. The majority of this section dealt with problems that revolve around fluctuations in the computer's incoming power line. Different types of Uninterruptible Power Supplies were discussed, along with other power line conditioning devices. The remainder of the section discussed proper storage methods for computer components.

Potentially hazardous areas of the computer and its peripherals were presented in the third major section of the chapter. Although a computer system is not an intrinsically unsafe environment, there are some areas that can be harmful if approached unawares.

Disposal of old and defective equipment, as well as cleaning materials, was discussed in the fourth section of the chapter. MSDS records for hazardous materials were also introduced.

The final section of the chapter described the danger and causes of electrostatic discharges, as well as providing information about how to eliminate them.

At this point, review the objectives listed at the beginning of the chapter to be certain that you understand and can perform each item listed there.

KEY POINTS REVIEW

The focus of this chapter has been to present important points for inclusion in the preventive maintenance programs associated with personal computer systems. Review the following key points before moving into the Review and Exam Questions sections to make sure you are comfortable with each point. Afterward, answer the Review Questions that follow to verify your knowledge of the information.

- Cleaning is a major part of keeping a computer system healthy. Therefore, the technician's tool kit should also contain a collection of cleaning supplies. Along with hand tools, it will need a lint-free, soft cloth (chamois) for cleaning the plastic outer surfaces of the system.

- The environment around a computer system and the manner in which the computer is used determine greatly how many problems it will have. Occasionally dedicating a few moments of care to the computer can extend its Mean Time Between Failures (MTBF) period considerably. This activity, involving maintenance not normally associated with a breakdown, is called Preventive Maintenance (PM).

- Unlike hard-disk drives, floppy drives are at least partially open to the atmosphere, and they may be handled on a regular basis. This opens floppy-disk drives to a number of maintenance concerns not found in hard-disk drives. Also, the removable disks are subject to extremes in temperature, exposure to magnetic and electromagnetic fields, bending, and airborne particles that can lead to information loss.

- Input peripherals generally require very little in the way of preventive maintenance. An occasional dusting and cleaning should be all that's really required.

- Because printers tend to be much more mechanical than other types of computer peripherals, they require more effort to maintain. Printers generate pollutants, such as paper dust and ink droplets, in everyday operation. These pollutants can build up on mechanical parts and cause them to wear. As the parts wear, the performance of the printer diminishes. Therefore, printers require periodic cleaning and adjustments to maintain good performance.

- Digital systems tend to be sensitive to power variations and losses. Even a very short loss of electrical power can shut a digital computer down, resulting in a loss of any current information that has not been saved to a mass storage device.

- Uninterruptible power supplies are battery-based systems that monitor the incoming power and kick in when unacceptable variations occur in the power source. The term UPS is frequently used to describe two different types of power backup systems.

- In most IBM compatibles, there are only two potentially dangerous areas. One of these is inside the CRT display, and the other is inside the power supply unit. Both of these areas contain electrical voltage levels that are lethal. However, both of these areas reside in self-contained units, and you will usually not be required to open either unit.

- Laser printers contain many hazardous areas. The laser light can be very damaging to the human eye. In addition, there are multiple high-voltage areas in the typical laser printer, and a high-temperature area to contend with as well.

- Most computer components contain some level of hazardous substances. Printed circuit boards consist of plastics, precious metals, fiberglass, arsenic, silicon, gallium, and lead. CRTs contain glass, metal, plastics, lead, barium, and rare earth metals. Batteries from portable systems can contain lead, cadmium, lithium, alkaline manganese, and mercury.

- Electrostatic Discharges (ESD) are the most severe form of Electromagnet Interference (EMI). The human body can build up static charges that range up to 25,000 volts. These buildups can discharge very rapidly into a electrically grounded body or device. Placing a 25,000-volt surge through any electronic device is potentially damaging to it.

- In general, MOS devices are sensitive to voltage spikes and static electricity discharges. This can cause many problems when you have to replace MOS devices, especially Complementary-Symmetry Metal Oxide Semiconductor (CMOS) devices. The level of static electricity present on your body is high enough to destroy the inputs of a CMOS device if you touch its pins with your fingers.

- The term ground is often a source of confusion for the novice, because it actually encompasses a collection of terms. Generically, ground is simply any point from which electrical measurements are referenced. However, the original definition of ground actually referred to the ground. This ground is called earth ground.

REVIEW QUESTIONS

The following questions test your knowledge of the material presented in this chapter.

1. List the two most dangerous areas of a typical microcomputer system, and explain why they are dangerous.

2. Name three devices used to minimize ESD in the repair area.

3. The best general-purpose cleaning tool for computer equipment is _____.

4. List at least three environmental conditions that can adversely affect microcomputer equipment.

5. A short undervoltage condition, lasting milliseconds, is called _____.

6. Are there any restrictions on disposing of a spent toner cartridge?

7. Which type of IC device is most likely to be damaged by ESD?

8. Can an effective ESD strap be constructed by simply wrapping a grounded bare wire around your wrist?

9. What is the most effective method of dealing with EMI problems?

10. The best method of protecting computer equipment from a thunderstorm is to _____.

11. The best method for transporting electronic devices is _____.

12. List computer-related PM items that should be performed annually.

13. Name two characteristics that should be checked carefully before purchasing a UPS for a given computer system.

14. Describe the normal duration of a voltage spike.

15. Once a virus has infected a computer, where does it normally reside?

EXAM QUESTIONS

1. Do viruses normally attack the system's CMOS settings?
   a. Yes, this is how a virus attacks most computers.
   b. No, viruses do not normally attack CMOS settings.
   c. Yes, this is how viruses attack all computers.
   d. No, viruses never attack CMOS settings.

2. How are most computer viruses spread from computer to computer?
   a. By downloading programs from networks
   b. By sharing infected files between individuals
   c. By not formatting disks before use
   d. By transferring files over modems

3. What is the most common cause of ESD in microcomputer systems?
   a. Moving people
   b. High humidity
   c. Rubber mats
   d. Grounded power supply cables

4. Where would it be inappropriate to use an ESD wrist strap?
   a. While working on hard-disk drives
   b. While working on system boards
   c. While working on CRT video monitors
   d. While working on printers

5. What is one of the best methods for protecting computer systems from ESD?
   a. A water and fabric softener solution
   b. A water and ammonia solution
   c. A water and bleach solution
   d. A hydrogen tetrachloride solution

6. A short overvoltage occurrence (nanoseconds) is called _____.
   a. a spike
   b. a surge
   c. a brownout
   d. a sag

7. ESD is most likely to occur during periods of _____.
   a. low humidity
   b. high humidity
   c. medium humidity
   d. rain

8. The best protection against power-failure data loss is _____.
   a. a tape backup
   b. a surge suppressor
   c. a UPS
   d. a line filter

9. Define a voltage sag.
   a. An overvoltage condition that lasts for a few milliseconds
   b. An undervoltage condition that lasts for an extended period
   c. An overvoltage condition that lasts for an extended period
   d. An undervoltage condition that lasts for a few milliseconds

10. The most effective grounding system for a microcomputer is _____.
    a. an ESD wrist or ankle strap
    b. the safety ground plug at a commercial AC receptacle
    c. the ground plane of the system board
    d. the chassis ground provided by brass standoffs

A+ OBJECTIVE MAP

CompTIA requires the successful completion of two exams in order to qualify for A+ Certification. The A+ Core Hardware Service Technician exam focuses on hardware and systems integration. The A+ Operating System Technologies exam focuses on software and operating system competencies.

The CompTIA organization has established the following objectives for the A+ Certification exams.

A+ CORE HARDWARE SERVICE TECHNICIAN EXAMINATION (220-301)

The Core Hardware examination measures essential competencies for a microcomputer hardware service technician with six months of on-the-job experience. The student must demonstrate basic knowledge of installing, configuring, upgrading, troubleshooting, and repairing microcomputer systems at the standard defined by this test specification.

Domain 1.0   Installation, Configuration, and Upgrading

The topics covered by this domain are included in approximately 35% of the questions in the A+ Core Hardware exam. This domain requires the knowledge and skills to identify, install, configure, and upgrade microcomputer components and peripherals. The student must be able to follow the established basic procedures for system assembly and disassembly of field replaceable units.

> 1.1 Identify names, purpose, and characteristics of system modules. Recognize these modules by sight or definition.

Examples of concepts and modules are:

- Motherboard - Chapter 2, Lab Procedure 1

- Firmware - Chapter 2, Lab Procedure 3

- Power supply - Chapter 1, Lab Procedure 1

- Processor/CPU - Chapter 2, Lab Procedure 9

- Memory - Chapter 2, Lab Procedure 8

- Storage devices - Chapter 4, Lab Procedure 4

- Display devices - Chapter 1, Lab Procedure 1

- Adapter cards - Chapter 1, Lab Procedure 1

- Ports - Chapter 2, Lab Procedure 1

- Cases - Chapter 1, Lab Procedure 1

- Riser cards - Chapter 1

1.2 Identify basic procedures for adding and removing field replaceable modules for desktop systems. Given a replacement scenario, choose the appropriate sequences.

Desktop components:

- Motherboard - Chapter 2, Lab Procedure 1
- Storage devices - Chapter 1, Lab Procedure 1
    - FDD - Chapter 1, Lab Procedure 1
    - HDD - Chapter 1, Lab Procedure 7
    - CD/CDRW - Chapter 1, Lab Procedure 7
    - DVD/DVDRW - Chapter 1, Lab Procedure 7
    - Tape drive - Chapter 1
    - Removable storage - Chapter 1
- Power supply - Chapter 1, Lab Procedure 1
    - AC adapters - Chapter 7
    - AT/ATX - Chapter 1, Lab Procedure 1
- Cooling systems - Chapter 2, Lab Procedure 9
    - Fans - Chapter 2, Lab Procedure 9
    - Heat sinks - Chapter 2, Lab Procedure 9
    - Liquid cooling - Chapter 2
- Processor/CPU - Chapter 2, Lab Procedure 9
- Memory - Chapter 2, Lab Procedure 8
- Display device - Chapter 3, Lab Procedure 8
- Input devices - Chapter 3, Lab Procedure 8
    - Keyboard - Chapter 3, Lab Procedure 8
    - Mouse/pointer devices - Chapter 3, Lab Procedure 8

- Touch screen - Chapter 3

- Adapters - Chapter 1

  - Network Interface Card (NIC) - Chapter 5, Lab Procedure 1

  - Sound card - Chapter 3

  - Video card - Chapter 1, Lab Procedure 1

  - Modem - Chapter 5, Lab Procedure 1

  - SCSI - Chapter 2

  - IEEE-1394/Firewire - Chapter 3

  - USB - Chapter 3

  - Wireless - Chapter 5

1.3 Identify basic procedures for adding and removing field replaceable modules for portable systems. Given a replacement scenario, choose the appropriate sequences.

Portable components:

- Storage devices - Chapter 7

  - FDD - Chapter 7

  - HDD

  - CD/CDRW - Chapter 7

  - DVD/DVDRW - Chapter 7

  - Removable storage - Chapter 7

- Power sources

  - AC adapter

  - DC adapter - Chapter 7

  - Battery - Chapter 7

- Memory - Chapter 7

- Input devices - Chapter 7

  - Keyboard - Chapter 7

  - Mouse/pointer devices - Chapter 7

  - Touch screen - Chapter 3

- PCMCIA/Mini PCI adapters - Chapter 7

  - Network Interface Card (NIC) - Chapter 7

- Modem - Chapter 7

- SCSI - Chapter 7

- IEEE-1394/Firewire - Chapter 7

- USB - Chapter 7

- Storage (memory and hard drive) - Chapter 7

- Docking station/port replicators - Chapter 7

- LCD panel - Chapter 7

- Wireless - Chapter 5

    - Adapter/controller - Chapter 5

    - Antenna - Chapter 5

1.4 Identify available IRQs, DMAs, I/O addresses, and procedures for altering these settings when installing and configuring devices. Choose the appropriate installation or configuration steps in a given scenario.

Content may include the following:

- Legacy devices (e.g., ISA sound card) - Chapter 3

- Specialized devices (e.g., CAD/CAM) - Chapter 3

- Internal modems - Chapter 5

- Floppy drive controllers - Chapter 3

- Hard drive controllers - Chapter 3

- Multimedia devices - Chapter 3

- NICs - Chapter 3

- I/O Ports - Chapter 3

    - Serial - Chapter 3

    - Parallel - Chapter 3

    - USB ports - Chapter 3

    - IEEE-1394/Firewire - Chapter 3

    - Infrared - Chapter 3

1.5 Identify the names, purposes, and performance characteristics of standardized/common peripheral ports, associated cabling, and their connectors. Recognize ports, cabling, and connectors by sight.

Content might include the following:

- Port types - Chapter 3, Lab Procedure 1

  - Serial - Chapter 3, Lab Procedure 1

  - Parallel - Chapter 3, Lab Procedure 1

  - USB ports - Chapter 3, Lab Procedure 1

  - IEEE-1394/Firewire - Chapter 3

  - Infrared - Chapter 3

- Cable types - Chapter 3

  - Serial (straight through vs. null modem) - Chapter 3

  - Parallel - Chapter 3

  - USB - Chapter 3

- Connector types - Chapter 3

  - Serial - Chapter 3, Lab Procedure 1

    ° DB-9 - Chapter 3, Lab Procedure 1

    ° DB-25 - Chapter 3

    ° RJ-11 - Chapter 3, Lab Procedures 20, 21, 22, & 36

    ° RJ-45 - Chapter 3, Lab Procedures 20, 21, 23, & 36

  - Parallel - Chapter 3, Lab Procedures 23, 24, & 25

    ° DB-25 - Chapter 3

    ° Centronics (mini and 36-pin) - Chapter 3

  - PS2/mini-DIN - Chapter 3, Lab Procedure 1

  - USB - Chapter 3

  - IEEE-1394 - Chapter 3

1.6 Identify proper procedures for installing and configuring common IDE/EIDE devices. Choose the appropriate installation or configuration sequences in given scenarios. Recognize the associated cables.

Content may include the following:

- IDE Interface Types - Chapter 4, Lab Procedure 7
    - EIDE - Chapter 4, Lab Procedure 7
    - ATA/ATAPI - Chapter 4, Lab Procedure 7
    - Serial ATA - Chapter 4
    - PIO - Chapter 4, Lab Procedure 7
- RAID (0,1, and 5) - Chapter 4
- Master/Slave/Cable Select - Chapter 4, Lab Procedure 7
- Devices per channel - Chapter 4, Lab Procedure 7
- Primary/secondary - Chapter 4, Lab Procedure 7
- Cable orientation requirements - Chapter 4

1.7 Identify proper procedures for installing and configuring common SCSI devices. Choose the appropriate installation or configuration sequences in given scenarios.

Content may include the following:

- SCSI Interface Types - Chapter 4
    - Narrow - Chapter 4
    - Fast - Chapter 4
    - Wide - Chapter 4
    - Wide Ultra - Chapter 4
    - LVD - Chapter 4
    - HVD - Chapter 4
- Internal versus external - Chapter 4
- SCSI IDs - Chapter 4
    - Jumper block/DIP switch settings (binary equivalents) - Chapter 4
    - Resolving ID conflicts - Chapter 4
- RAID (0,1, and 5) - Chapter 4
- Cabling - Chapter 4

- Length - Chapter 4

- Type - Chapter 4

- Termination requirements (active, passive, auto) - Chapter 4

1.8 Identify proper procedures for installing and configuring common peripheral devices. Choose the appropriate installation or configuration sequences in given scenarios.

Content may include the following:

- Modems and transceivers (dial-up, cable, DSL, ISDN) - Chapter 5, Lab Procedure 36

- External storage - Chapter 4

- Digital cameras - Chapter 3

- PDAs - Chapter 3

- Wireless access points - Chapter 5

- Infrared devices - Chapter 5

- Printers - Chapter 6 - Chapter 3, Lab Procedures 23, 24, & 25

- UPS (Uninterruptible Power Supply) and suppressors - Chapter 13

- Monitors - Chapter 3

1.9 Identify procedures to optimize PC operations in specific situations. Predict the effects of specific procedures under given scenarios.

Topics may include:

- Cooling systems - Chapter 2, Lab Procedure 9

  - Liquid - Chapter 2

  - Air - Chapter 2, Lab Procedure 9

  - Heat sink - Chapter 2, Lab Procedure 9

  - Thermal compound - Chapter 2

- Disk subsystem enhancements - Chapter 4

  - Hard drives - Chapter 4, Lab Procedure 7

  - Controller cards (RAID, ATA-100, etc.) - Chapter 4

  - Cables - Chapter 4

- NICs - Chapter 5, Lab Procedures 20, 21, & 22

- Specialized video cards - Chapter 3

- Memory - Chapter 1, Lab Procedure 8

- Additional processors - Chapter 2

1.10 Determine the issues that must be considered when upgrading a PC. In a given scenario, determine when and how to upgrade system components.

Issues may include:

- Drivers for legacy devices - Chapter 4

- Bus types and characteristics - Chapter 2

- Cache in relationship to motherboards - Chapter 2

- Memory capacity and characteristics - Chapter 2

- Processor speed and compatibility - Chapter 2

- Hard drive capacity and characteristics - Chapter 4

- System/firmware limitations - Chapter 2

- Power supply output capacity

Components may include the following:

- Motherboards - Chapter 2

- Memory - Chapter 2, Lab Procedure 8

- Hard drives - Chapter 4, Lab Procedure 7

- CPU - Chapter 2, Lab Procedure 9

- BIOS - Chapter 2

- Adapter cards - Chapter 3, Lab Procedures 20, 21, & 22

- Laptop power sources - Chapter 7

  - Lithium ion - Chapter 7

  - NiMH - Chapter 7

  - Fuel cell - Chapter 7

- PCMCIA Type I, II, III cards - Chapter 7

Domain 2.0   Diagnosing and Troubleshooting

The topics covered by this domain are included in approximately 21% of the questions in the A+ Core Hardware exam. This domain requires the ability to apply knowledge relating to diagnosing and troubleshooting common component problems and system malfunctions. This includes symptoms and causes related to common problems.

2.1 Recognize common problems associated with each module and their symptoms, and identify steps to isolate and troubleshoot the problems. Given a problem situation, interpret the symptoms and infer the most likely cause.

Content may include the following:

- I/O ports and cables - Chapter 11
    - Serial - Chapter 11
    - Parallel - Chapter 11
    - USB ports - Chapter 11
    - IEEE-1394/Firewire - Chapter 11
    - Infrared - Chapter 5
    - SCSI - Chapter 11

- Motherboards - Chapter 11, Lab Procedure 8
    - CMOS/ BIOS settings - Chapter 11, Lab Procedure 3
    - POST audible/visual error codes - Chapter 11

- Peripherals - Chapter 11

- Computer case - Chapter 11, Lab Procedure 1
    - Power supply - Chapter 11, Lab Procedure 1
    - Slot covers - Chapter 11
    - Front cover alignment - Chapter 11

- Storage devices and cables - Chapter 11, Lab Procedure 1
    - FDD - Chapter 11, Lab Procedure 1
    - HDD - Chapter 11, Lab Procedures 4 and 7
    - CD/CDRW - Chapter 11, Lab Procedure 7
    - DVD/DVDRW - Chapter 11, Lab Procedure 7
    - Tape drive - Chapter 11
    - Removable storage - Chapter 11

- Cooling systems - Chapter 2
  - Fans - Chapter 2
  - Heat sinks - Chapter 2
  - Liquid cooling - Chapter 2
  - Temperature sensors - Chapter 2
- Processor/CPU - Chapter 11, Lab Procedure 8
- Memory - Chapter 11, Lab Procedure 8
- Display device - Chapter 11, Lab Procedure 8
- Input devices - Chapter 11, Lab Procedure 8
  - Keyboard - Chapter 11, Lab Procedure 8
  - Mouse/pointer devices - Chapter 11, Lab Procedure 8
  - Touch screen - Chapter 3
- Adapters - Chapter 11, Lab Procedure 8
  - Network Interface Card (NIC) - Chapter 11, Lab Procedure 8
  - Sound card - Chapter 11
  - Video card - Chapter 11, Lab Procedure 8
  - Modem - Chapter 11, Lab Procedure 8
  - SCSI - Chapter 11
  - IEEE-1394/Firewire - Chapter 11
  - USB - Chapter 11
- Portable systems - Chapter 7
  - PCMCIA - Chapter 7
  - Batteries - Chapter 7
  - Docking stations/port replicators - Chapter 7
  - Portable unique storage - Chapter 7

2.2 Identify basic troubleshooting procedures and tools, and how to elicit problem symptoms from customers. Justify asking particular questions in a given scenario.

Content may include the following:

- Troubleshooting/isolation/problem determination procedures - Chapter 11, Lab Procedure 8
- Determining whether a hardware or software problem - Chapter 11, Lab Procedure 8

- Gathering information from user - Chapter 11

    - Customer environment - Chapter 11

    - Symptoms/error codes - Chapter 11, Lab Procedure 8

    - Situation when the problem occurred - Chapter 11

Domain 3.0 Preventive Maintenance

The topics covered by this domain are included in approximately 5% of the questions in the A+ Core Hardware exam. This domain requires knowledge of safety and preventive maintenance. Safety includes the potential hazards to personnel and equipment when working with lasers, high-voltage equipment, ESD, and items that require special disposal procedures that comply with environmental guidelines. Preventive maintenance includes knowledge of products, procedures, environmental hazards, and required precautions when working on microcomputer systems.

> 3.1 Identify the various types of preventive maintenance measures, products, and procedures, and when and how to use them.

Content may include the following:

- Liquid cleaning compounds - Chapter 13

- Types of materials to clean contacts and connections - Chapter 13

- Nonstatic vacuums (chassis, power supplies, fans) - Chapter 13

- Cleaning monitors - Chapter 13

- Cleaning removable media devices - Chapter 13

- Ventilation, dust, and moisture control on the PC hardware interior - Chapter 13

- Hard disk maintenance (defragging, scan disk, CHKDSK) - Lab Procedures 27 & 29

- Verifying UPS (Uninterruptible Power Supply) and suppressors - Chapter 13

> 3.2 Identify various safety measures and procedures, and when/how to use them.

Content may include the following:

- ESD (Electrostatic Discharge) precautions and procedures - Chapter 13, Lab Procedure 1

    - What ESD can do, how it may be apparent, or hidden - Chapter 13

    - Common ESD protection devices - Chapter 13, Lab Procedure 1

    - Situations that could present a danger or hazard - Chapter 13

- Potential hazards and proper safety procedures relating to:

    - High-voltage equipment - Chapter 13

    - Power supply - Chapter 13

    - CRTs - Chapter 13

> **3.3 Identify environmental protection measures and procedures, and when/how to use them.**

Content may include the following:

- Special disposal procedures that comply with environmental guidelines. - Chapter 13

    - Batteries - Chapter 13

    - CRTs - Chapter 13

    - Chemical solvents and cans - Chapter 13

    - MSDS (Material Safety Data Sheet) - Chapter 13

Domain 4.0   Motherboard/Processors/Memory

The topics covered by this domain are included in approximately 11% of the questions in the A+ Core Hardware exam. This domain requires knowledge of specific terminology, facts, ways and means of dealing with classifications, categories and principles of motherboards, processors, and memory in microcomputer systems.

> **4.1 Distinguish between the popular CPU chips in terms of their basic characteristics.**

Content may include the following:

- Popular CPU chips (Pentium class compatible) - Chapter 2

- Voltage - Chapter 2

- Speeds (actual vs. advertised) - Chapter 2

- Cache level I, II, III - Chapter 2

- Sockets/slots - Chapter 2

- VRM(s) - Chapter 2

4.2 Identify the types of RAM (Random Access Memory), form factors, and operational characteristics. Determine banking and speed requirements under given scenarios.

Content may include the following:

- Types - Chapter 2
    - EDORAM (Extended Data Output RAM) - Chapter 2
    - DRAM (Dynamic Random Access Memory) - Chapter 2
    - SRAM (Static RAM) - Chapter 2
    - VRAM (Video RAM) - Chapter 2
    - SDRAM (Synchronous Dynamic RAM) - Chapter 2
    - DDR (Double Data Rate) - Chapter 2
    - RAMBUS - Chapter 2
- Form factors (including pin count) - Chapter 2
    - SIMM (Single In-line Memory Module) - Chapter 2
    - DIMM (Dual In-line Memory Module) - Chapter 2, Lab Procedure 8
    - SODIMM (Small Outline DIMM) - Chapter 2
    - MicroDIMM - Chapter 2
    - RIMM (Rambus Inline Memory Module) - Chapter 2
- Operational characteristics - Chapter 2
    - Memory chips (8-bit, 16-bit, and 32-bit) - Chapter 2
    - Parity chips versus non-parity chips - Chapter 2
    - ECC vs. non-ECC - Chapter 2
    - Single-sided vs. double-sided - Chapter 2

4.3 Identify the most popular types of motherboards, their components, and their architecture (bus structures).

Content may include the following:

- Types of motherboards - Chapter 2
    - AT - Chapter 2
    - ATX - Chapter 2, Lab Procedure 1
- Components - Chapter 2, Lab Procedure 1
    - Communication ports - Chapter 2, Lab Procedure 1

- Serial - Chapter 2, Lab Procedure 1

- USB - Chapter 2, Lab Procedure 1

- Parallel - Chapter 2, Lab Procedure 1

- IEEE-1394/Firewire - Chapter 2

- Infrared - Chapter 2

- Memory - Chapter 2, Lab Procedures 1 & 8

  - SIMM - Chapter 2

  - DIMM - Chapter 2, Lab Procedure 8

  - RIMM - Chapter 2

  - SODIMM - Chapter 2

  - MicroDIMM - Chapter 2

- Processor sockets - Chapter 2

  - Slot 1 - Chapter 2

  - Slot 2 - Chapter 2

  - Slot A - Chapter 2

  - Socket A - Chapter 2

  - Socket 7 - Chapter 2

  - Socket 8 - Chapter 2

  - Socket 423 - Chapter 2

  - Socket 478 - Chapter 2

  - Socket 370 - Chapter 2, Lab Procedure 9

- External cache memory (Level 2) - Chapter 2

- Bus architecture - Chapter 2

- ISA - Chapter 2

- PCI - Chapter 2, Lab Procedure 11

  - PCI 32-bit - Chapter 2, Lab Procedure 11

  - PCI 64-bit - Chapter 2

- AGP - Chapter 2, Lab Procedure 1

  - 2X - Chapter 2

  - 4X - Chapter 2

  - 8X (Pro) - Chapter 2

- USB (Universal Serial Bus) - Chapter 2

- AMR (audio modem riser) slots - Chapter 2

- CNR (communication network riser) slots - Chapter 2

- Basic compatibility guidelines - Chapter 2

- IDE (ATA, ATAPI, ULTRA-DMA, EIDE) - Chapter 4, Lab Procedures 4 & 7

- SCSI (Narrow, Wide, Fast, Ultra, HVD, LVD (Low Voltage Differential)) - Chapter 4

- Chipsets - Chapter 2

4.4 Identify the purpose of CMOS (Complementary Metal-Oxide Semiconductor) memory, what it contains, and how and when to change its parameters. Given a scenario involving CMOS, choose the appropriate course of action.

CMOS settings:

- Default settings - Chapter 2, Lab Procedure 3

- CPU settings - Chapter 2, Lab Procedure 3

- Printer parallel port—Unidirectional, bi-directional, disable/enable, ECP, EPP - Chapter 2, Lab Procedure 3

- COM/serial port—memory address, interrupt request, disable - Chapter 2, Lab Procedure 3

- Floppy drive—enable/disable drive or boot, speed, density - Chapter 2, Lab Procedure 3

- Hard drive—size and drive type - Chapter 2, Lab Procedure 3

- Memory—speed, parity, non-parity - Chapter 2, Lab Procedure 3

- Boot sequence - Chapter 2, Lab Procedure 3

- Date/time - Chapter 2, Lab Procedure 3

- Passwords - Chapter 2, Lab Procedure 3

- Plug & Play BIOS - Chapter 2, Lab Procedure 3

- Disabling on-board devices - Chapter 2, Lab Procedure 3

- Disabling virus protection - Chapter 2, Lab Procedure 3

- Power management - Chapter 2, Lab Procedure 3

- Infrared - Chapter 2, Lab Procedure 3

Domain 5.0   Printers

The topics covered by this domain are included in approximately 9% of the questions in the A+ Core Hardware exam. This domain requires knowledge of basic types of printers, basic concepts, printer components, how they work, how they print onto a page, paper path, care and service techniques, and common problems.

> **5.1 Identify printer technologies, interfaces, and options/upgrades.**

Technologies include:

- Laser - Chapter 6

- Ink dispersion - Chapter 6

- Dot matrix - Chapter 6

- Solid ink - Chapter 6

- Thermal - Chapter 6

- Dye sublimation - Chapter 6

Interfaces include:

- Parallel - Chapter 6

- Network - Chapter 6

- SCSI - Chapter 6

- USB - Chapter 6

- Infrared - Chapter 6

- Serial - Chapter 6

- IEEE-1394/Firewire - Chapter 6

- Wireless - Chapter 6

Options/upgrades include:

- Memory - Chapter 6

- Hard drives - Chapter 6

- NICs - Chapter 6

- Trays and feeders - Chapter 6

- Finishers (stapling, etc.) - Chapter 6

- Scanner/fax/copier - Chapter 6

Content may include the following:

- Printer drivers - Chapter 6

- Firmware updates - Chapter 6

- Paper feed and output - Chapter 6

- Calibrations - Chapter 6

- Printing test pages - Chapter 6

- Errors (printed or displayed) - Chapter 6

- Memory - Chapter 6

- Configuration - Chapter 6

- Network connections - Chapter 6

- Connections - Chapter 6

- Paper jam - Chapter 6

- Print quality - Chapter 6

- Safety precautions - Chapter 6

- Preventive maintenance - Chapter 6

- Consumables - Chapter 6

- Environment - Chapter 6

Domain 6.0   Basic Networking

The topics covered by this domain are included in approximately 19% of the questions in the A+ Core Hardware exam. This domain requires knowledge of basic network concepts and terminology, ability to determine whether a computer is networked, knowledge of procedures for swapping and configuring network interface cards, and knowledge of the ramifications of repairs when a computer is networked. The scope of this topic is specific to hardware issues on the desktop and connecting it to a network.

6.1 Identify the common types of network cables, their characteristics, and connectors.

Cable types include:

- Coaxial - Chapter 5

    - RG-6 - Chapter 5

- RG-8 - Chapter 5

- RG-58 - Chapter 5

- RG-59 - Chapter 5

- Plenum/PVC - Chapter 5

- UTP - Chapter 5, Lab Procedures 20, 21, & 22

  - CAT 3 - Chapter 5

  - CAT 5/e - Chapter 5, Lab Procedures 20, 21, & 22

  - CAT 6 - Chapter 5

- STP - Chapter 5

- Fiber - Chapter 5

  - Single-mode - Chapter 5

  - Multimode - Chapter 5

Connector types include:

- BNC - Chapter 5

- RJ-45 - Chapter 5, Lab Procedures 20, 21, & 22

- AUI - Chapter 5

- ST/SC - Chapter 5

- IDC/UDC - Chapter 5

6.2 Identify basic networking concepts including how a network works.

Concepts include:

- Installing and configuring network cards - Chapter 5, Lab Procedures 20, 21, 22, 37, 41, & 42

- Addressing - Chapter 5

- Bandwidth - Chapter 5

- Status indicators - Chapter 5

- Protocols - Chapter 5 - Lab Procedures 37 & 41

  - TCP/IP - Chapter 5, Lab Procedures 37, 38, & 41

  - IPX/SPX (NWLINK) - Chapter 5

  - AppleTalk - Chapter 5

  - NETBEUI/NETBIOS - Chapter 5

- Full-duplex, half-duplex - Chapter 5

- Cabling—twisted pair, coaxial, fiber optic, RS-232 - Chapter 5

- Networking models - Chapter 5

    - Peer-to-peer - Chapter 5, Lab Procedures 37, 41, & 42

    - Client/server - Chapter 5

- Infrared - Chapter 5

- Wireless - Chapter 5

6.3 Identify common technologies available for establishing Internet connectivity and their characteristics.

Technologies include:

- LAN - Chapter 5

- DSL - Chapter 5

- Cable - Chapter 5

- ISDN - Chapter 5

- Dial-up - Chapter 5

- Satellite - Chapter 5

- Wireless - Chapter 5

Characteristics include:

- Definition - Chapter 5

- Speed - Chapter 5

- Connections - Chapter 5

OPERATING SYSTEM TECHNOLOGIES EXAMINATION (220-302)

The OS Technologies examination measures essential operating system competencies for microcomputer hardware service technicians with six months of on-the-job experience. The student must demonstrate basic knowledge of the command-line prompt, Windows 9x/Me, and Windows NT/2000/XP for installing, configuring, upgrading, troubleshooting, and repairing microcomputer systems.

Domain 1.0   Operating System Fundamentals

The topics covered by this domain are included in approximately 28% of the questions in the A+ OS Technologies exam. This domain requires knowledge of the Windows 9x/Me and Windows NT/2000/XP operating systems in terms of their functions and structure for managing files and directories and running programs. It also includes navigating through the operating system from command-line prompts and Windows procedures for accessing and retrieving information.

> 1.1 Identify the major desktop components and interfaces, and their functions. Differentiate the characteristics of Windows 9x/Me, Windows NT 4.0 Workstation, Windows 2000 Professional, and Windows XP.

Content may include the following:

- Contrasts between Windows 9x/Me, Windows NT 4.0 Workstation, Windows 2000 Professional, and Windows XP - Chapters 9 & 10

- Major operating system components

    - Registry - Chapters 9 & 10, Lab Procedure 30

    - Virtual Memory - Chapters 9 & 10, Lab Procedure 17

    - File System - Chapters 9 & 10, Lab Procedures 11, 15, & 18

- Major operating system interfaces

    - Windows Explorer - Chapters 9 & 10, Lab Procedures 11, 15, & 18

    - My Computer - Chapters 9 & 10, Lab Procedures 11, 15, & 18

    - Control Panel - Chapters 9 & 10, Lab Procedures 11, 15, & 18

    - Computer Management console

    - Accessories/System Tools - Chapter 10, Lab Procedure 17

    - Command line - Chapters 9 & 10, Lab Procedure 12

    - Network Neighborhood/My Network Places - Chapters 9 & 10, Lab Procedure 39

- Taskbar/systray - Chapters 9 & 10, Lab Procedures 11, 15, & 18
- Start menu - Chapters 9 & 10, Lab Procedures 11, 15, & 18
- Device Manager - Chapters 9 & 10, Lab Procedures 11, 15, & 18

1.2 Identify the names, locations, purposes, and contents of major system files.

Content may include the following:

- Windows 9x –specific files - Chapter 9
  - IO.SYS - Chapter 9
  - MSDOS.SYS - Chapter 9
  - AUTOEXEC.BAT - Chapter 9
  - COMMAND.COM - Chapter 9
  - CONFIG.SYS - Chapter 9
  - HIMEM.SYS - Chapter 9
  - EMM386.exe - Chapter 9
  - WIN.COM - Chapter 9
  - SYSTEM.INI - Chapter 9
  - WIN.INI - Chapter 9
  - Registry data files - Chapter 9
    - ° SYSTEM.DAT - Chapter 9
    - ° USER.DAT - Chapter 9
- Windows NT –based specific files - Chapter 10
  - BOOT.INI - Chapter 10
  - NTLDR - Chapter 10
  - NTDETECT.COM - Chapter 10
  - NTBOOTDD.SYS - Chapter 10
  - NTUSER.DAT - Chapter 10
  - Registry data files - Chapter 10

Command-line functions and utilities include:

- Command/CMD - Chapter 8
- DIR - Chapter 8
- ATTRIB - Chapter 8
- VER - Chapter 8
- MEM - Chapter 8
- SCANDISK - Chapter 8
- DEFRAG - Chapter 8
- EDIT - Chapter 8
- XCOPY - Chapter 8
- COPY - Chapter 8
- FORMAT - Chapter 8
- FDISK - Chapter 8
- SETVER - Chapter 8
- SCANREG - Chapter 8
- MD/CD/RD - Chapter 8
- Delete/Rename - Chapter 8
- DELTREE - Chapter 8
- TYPE - Chapter 8
- ECHO - Chapter 8
- SET - Chapter 8
- PING - Chapter 8

1.4 Identify basic concepts and procedures for creating, viewing, and managing disks, directories, and files. This includes procedures for changing file attributes and the ramifications of those changes (for example, security issues).

Content may include the following:

- Disks - Chapters 8, 9, & 10

    - Partitions - Chapters 8, 9, & 10

        ° Active partition - Chapter 8

        ° Primary partition - Chapter 8

        ° Extended partition - Chapter 8

        ° Logical partition - Chapter 8

    - File systems

        ° FAT16, FAT32, NTFS4 - Chapters 9 & 10

        ° NTFS5.x - Chapter 10

- Directory Structures (root directory, subdirectories, etc.) - Chapter 8

    - Create folders - Chapters 9 & 10

    - Navigate the directory structure - Chapters 9 & 10

    - Maximum depth - Chapters 9 & 10

- Files - Chapters 8, 9, & 10

    - Creating files - Chapters 8, 9, & 10

    - File naming conventions (most common extensions, 8.3, maximum length) - Chapters 8, 9, & 10

    - File attributes - Read Only, Hidden, System, and Archive attributes - Chapter 8

    - File compression - Chapter 10

    - File encryption - Chapter 10

    - File permissions - Chapter 10

    - File types (text vs. binary file) - Chapter 8

1.5 Identify the major operating system utilities, their purpose, location, and available switches.

- Disk Management Tools

    - DEFRAG.EXE - Chapter 8

    - FDISK.EXE - Chapter 8

- Backup/Restore Utility (MSbackup, NTBackup, etc.) - Chapter 8

- ScanDisk - Chapter 12, Lab Procedure 27

- CHKDSK - Chapter 12

- Disk cleanup - Chapter 8

- Format - Chapter 8

- System Management Tools

  - Device Manager - Chapters 9 & 10

  - System Manager - Chapters 9 & 10

  - Computer Manager - Chapter 10

  - MSCONFIG.EXE - Chapters 9 & 10

  - REGEDIT.EXE (View information/back up Registry) - Chapters 8, 9, & 10, Lab Procedure 30

  - REGEDT32.EXE - Chapter 10, Lab Procedure 30

  - SYSEDIT.EXE - Chapter 8

  - SCANREG - Chapter 9

  - Command/CMD - Chapters 10 & 12

  - Event Viewer - Chapter 12

  - Task Manager - Chapter 12, Lab Procedure 17

- File Management Tools

  - ATTRIB.EXE - Chapter 8, Lab Procedure 12

  - EXTRACT.EXE - Chapter 12

  - Edit.com - Chapter 12

  - Windows Explorer - Chapter 9, Lab Procedure 11

Domain 2.0   Installation, Configuration, and Upgrading

The topics covered by this domain are included in approximately 31% of the questions in the A+ OS Technologies exam. This domain requires knowledge of installing, configuring, and upgrading Windows 9x/Me and Windows NT/2000/XP. This includes knowledge of system boot sequences and minimum hardware requirements.

2.1 Identify the procedures for installing Windows 9x/Me, Windows NT 4.0 Workstation, Windows 2000 Professional, and Windows XP, and bringing the operating system to a basic operational level.

Content may include the following:

- Verify hardware compatibility and minimum requirements - Chapters 9 & 10

- Determine OS installation options - Chapters 9 & 10

  - Installation type (typical, custom, other) - Chapters 9 & 10

  - Network configuration - Chapter 5, Lab Procedures 37, 38, 41, & 42

  - File system type - Chapters 9 & 10

  - Dual boot support - Chapter 10

- Disk preparation order (conceptual disk preparation) - Chapter 8

  - Start the installation - Chapters 9 & 10

  - Partition - Chapter 8

  - Format drive - Chapter 8

- Run appropriate setup utility - Chapters 9 & 10

  - Setup - Chapters 9 & 10

  - Winnt - Chapters 9 & 10

- Installation methods - Chapters 9 & 10

  - Bootable CD - Chapters 9 & 10

  - Boot floppy - Chapters 9 & 10

  - Network installation - Chapters 9 & 10

  - Drive imaging - Chapters 9 & 10

- Device driver configuration - Chapters 9 & 10

  - Load default drivers - Chapters 9 & 10

  - Find updated drivers - Chapters 9 & 10

- Restore user data files (if applicable) - Chapters 9 & 10

- Identify common symptoms and problems - Chapters 10 & 11

2.2 Identify steps to perform an operating system upgrade from Windows 9.x/Me, Windows NT 4.0 Workstation, Windows 2000 Professional, and Windows XP. Given an upgrade scenario, choose the appropriate next steps.

Content may include the following:

- Upgrade paths available - Chapters 9 & 10

- Determine correct upgrade startup utility (e.g., WINNT32 vs. WINNT) - Chapter 10

- Verify hardware compatibility and minimum requirements - Chapters 9 & 10

- Verify application compatibility - Chapters 9 & 10

- Apply OS service packs, patches, and updates - Chapters 9 & 10

- Install additional Windows components - Chapters 9 & 10

2.3 Identify the basic system boot sequences and boot methods, including the steps to create an emergency boot disk with utilities installed for Windows 9x/Me, Windows NT 4.0 Workstation, Windows 2000 Professional, and Windows XP.

Content may include the following:

- Boot sequence - Chapters 9 & 10, Lab Procedure 2
    - Files required to boot - Chapters 9 & 10
    - Boot steps (9.x, NT-based) - Chapters 9 & 10
- Alternative boot methods - Chapters 9 & 10, Lab Procedure 33
    - Using a Startup disk - Chapters 9 & 10
    - Safe/VGA-only mode - Chapters 9 & 10, Lab Procedure 33
    - Last Known Good Configuration - Chapters 9 & 10, Lab Procedure 33
    - Command Prompt mode - Chapters 9 & 10, Lab Procedure 33
    - Booting to a system restore point - Chapters 9 & 10, Lab Procedure 34
    - Recovery Console - Chapter 10
    - Boot.ini switches - Chapter 10
    - Dual boot - Chapter 10
- Creating emergency disks with OS utilities- Chapter 10
- Creating Emergency Repair Disk (ERD) - Chapter 10

2.4 Identify procedures for installing/adding a device, including loading, adding, and configuring device drivers, and required software.

Content may include the following:

- Device driver installation - Chapters 9 & 10
    - Plug-and-Play (PnP) and non-PnP devices - Chapters 9 & 10, Lab Procedures 20, 21, & 22
    - Install and configure device drivers - Chapters 9 & 10, Lab Procedures 20, 21, & 22
    - Install different device drivers - Chapters 9 & 10
    - Manually install a device driver - Chapters 9 & 10

- Search the Internet for updated device drivers - Chapters 9 & 10, Lab Procedures 49, 50, & 51

    - Using unsigned drivers (driver signing) - Chapters 9 & 10

- Install additional Windows components - Chapters 9 & 10

- Determine if permissions are adequate for performing the task - Chapter 10

> 2.5 Identify procedures necessary to optimize the operating system and major operating system subsystems.

Content may include the following:

- Virtual memory management - Chapters 8, 9, & 10

- Disk defragmentation - Chapter 8

- Files and buffers - Chapter 8

- Caches - Chapter 8

- Temporary file management - Chapter 8

Domain 3.0   Diagnosing and Troubleshooting

The topics covered by this domain are included in approximately 25% of the questions in the A+ OS Technologies exam. This domain requires the ability to apply knowledge to diagnose and troubleshoot common problems relating to Windows 9x/Me and Windows NT/2000/XP. This includes understanding normal operation and symptoms relating to common problems.

> 3.1 Recognize and interpret the meaning of common error codes and startup messages from the boot sequence, and identify steps to correct the problems.

Content may include the following:

- Common error messages and codes - Chapter 11

    - Boot failure and errors - Chapter 11

        ° Invalid boot disk - Chapter 11

        ° Inaccessible boot device - Chapter 11

        ° Missing NTLDR - Chapter 12, Lab Procedures 53 & 54

        ° Bad or missing command interpreter - Chapter 12

- Startup messages

    ° Error in CONFIG.SYS line XX - Chapter 12

    ° Himem.sys not loaded - Chapter 12

    ° Missing or corrupt Himem.sys - Chapter 12

    ° Device/service has failed to start - Chapter 12

  - A device referenced in SYSTEM.INI, WIN.INI, Registry is not found - Chapter 12

  - Event Viewer — Event log is full - Chapter 12

  - Failure to start GUI - Chapter 12

  - Windows Protection Error - Chapter 12

  - User-modified settings cause improper operation at startup - Chapter 12

  - Registry corruption - Chapter 12, Lab Procedures 52, 53, & 54

- Using the correct utilities - Chapter 12

  - Dr. Watson - Chapter 12

  - Boot disk - Chapter 12

  - Event Viewer - Chapter 12, Lab Procedure 28

3.2 Recognize when to use common diagnostic utilities and tools. Given a diagnostic scenario involving one of these utilities or tools, select the appropriate steps needed to resolve the problem.

Utilities and tools may include the following:

- Startup disks - Chapters 9, 10, & 11

  - Required files for a boot disk - Chapters 8, 9, & 10

  - Boot disk with CD-ROM support - Chapter 8

- Startup modes - Chapters 9, 10, 11, & 12, Lab Procedure 33

  - Safe Mode - Chapter 12, Lab Procedure 33

  - Safe Mode with command prompt - Chapter 12, Lab Procedure 33

  - Safe Mode with Networking - Chapter 12, Lab Procedure 33

  - Step-by-Step/Single-step mode - Chapter 12, Lab Procedure 33

  - Automatic Skip Driver (ASD.exe) - Chapter 12

- Diagnostic tools, utilities, and resources - Chapter 12, Lab Procedures 27 & 29

  - User/installation manuals - Chapter 11

  - Internet/web resources - Chapters 11 & 12

- Training materials - Chapters 11 & 12

- Task Manager - Chapters 11 & 12

- Dr. Watson - Chapter 12

- Boot disk - Chapter 11

- Event Viewer - Chapters 11 & 12

- Device Manager - Chapter 12

- WinMSD - Chapter 12

- MSD - Chapter 11

- Recovery CD - Chapters 11 & 12

- CONFIGSAFE - Chapter 12

- Eliciting problem symptoms from customers - Chapters 11 & 12

- Having customer reproduce error as part of the diagnostic process - Chapters 11 & 12

- Identifying recent changes to the computer environment from the user - Chapters 11 & 12

3.3 Recognize common operational and usability problems and determine how to resolve them.

Content may include the following:

- Troubleshooting Windows-specific printing problems - Chapter 6

  - Print spool is stalled - Chapter 6

  - Incorrect/incompatible driver for print - Chapter 6

  - Incorrect parameter - Chapters 11 & 12

- Other common problems - Chapter 12

  - General Protection Faults - Chapter 12

  - Blue screen error (BSOD) - Chapter 12

  - Illegal operation - Chapter 12

  - Invalid working directory - Chapter 11

  - System lockup - Chapter 12

  - Option (sound card, modem, input device) will not function - Chapter 12

  - Application will not start or load - Chapter 12

  - Cannot log on to network (option – NIC not functioning) - Chapter 12

  - Applications don't install - Chapter 12

  - Network connection - Chapter 5

- Viruses and virus types - Chapter 13

  - What they are - Chapter 13

  - TSR (Terminate and Stay Resident) programs and virus - Chapter 13

  - Sources (floppy, e-mails, etc.) - Chapter 13

  - How to determine presence - Chapter 13, Lab Procedure 35

Domain 4.0   Networks

The topics covered by this domain are included in approximately 16% of the questions in the A+ OS Technologies exam. This domain requires knowledge of network capabilities of Windows and how to connect to networks on the client side, including what the Internet is about, its capabilities, basic concepts relating to Internet access, and generic procedures for system setup. The scope of this topic is only what is needed on the desktop side to connect to a network.

> 4.1 Identify the networking capabilities of Windows. Given configuration parameters, configure the operating system to connect to a network.

Content may include the following:

- Configure protocols - Chapter 5

  - TCP/IP - Chapter 5, Lab Procedures 37, 41, & 43

    - Gateway - Chapter 5, Lab Procedures 37, 41, & 43

    - Subnet mask - Chapter 5, Lab Procedures 37, 41, & 43

    - DNS (and domain suffix) - Chapter 5, Lab Procedures 37, 41, & 43

    - WINS - Chapter 5, Lab Procedures 37, 41, & 43

    - Static address assignment - Chapter 5, Lab Procedures 37, 41, & 43

    - Automatic address assignment (APIPA, DHCP) - Chapter 5, Lab Procedures 37, 41, & 43

  - IPX/SPX (NWLink) - Chapter 5

  - Appletalk - Chapter 5

  - NetBEUI/ NetBIOS - Chapter 5

- Configure client options - Chapter 5

  - Microsoft - Chapter 5

  - Novell - Chapter 5

- Verify the configuration - Chapter 5

- Understand the use of the following tools - Chapter 5

- IPCONFIG.EXE - Chapter 5

- WINIPCFG.EXE - Chapter 5

- PING - Chapter 5, Lab Procedure 38

- TRACERT.EXE - Chapter 5, Lab Procedure 38

- NSLOOKUP.EXE - Chapter 5, Lab Procedure 38

- Share resources (understand the capabilities/limitations with each OS version) - Chapter 5

- Setting permissions to shared resources - Chapter 5

- Network type and network card - Chapter 5

4.2 Identify the basic Internet protocols and terminologies. Identify procedures for establishing Internet connectivity. In a given scenario, configure the operating system to connect to and use Internet resources.

Content may include the following:

- Protocols and terminologies - Chapter 5

  - ISP - Chapter 5

  - TCP/IP - Chapter 5, Lab Procedures 37, 38, 41, & 43

  - E-mail (POP, SMTP, IMAP) - Chapter 5

  - HTML - Chapter 5

  - HTTP - Chapter 5

  - HTTPS - Chapter 5

  - SSL - Chapter 5

  - Telnet - Chapter 5

  - FTP - Chapter 5

  - DNS - Chapter 5

- Connectivity technologies - Chapter 5

  - Dial-up networking - Chapter 5

  - DSL networking - Chapter 5

  - ISDN networking - Chapter 5

  - Cable - Chapter 5

  - Satellite - Chapter 5

  - Wireless - Chapter 5

  - LAN - Chapter 5

- Installing and configuring browsers - Chapter 5, Lab Procedure 46
  - Enable/disable script support - Chapter 5
  - Configure proxy settings - Chapter 5
  - Configure security settings - Chapter 5
- Firewall protection under Windows XP - Chapter 5

GLOSSARY

An Extended Glossary can be found in the electronic Reference Shelf located on the CD that accompanies this book.

A

Accelerated Graphics Port (AGP) A newer 32-bit video interface specification based on the PCI bus design. Rather than using the PCI bus for video data, the AGP system provides a dedicated point-to-point path between the video graphics controller and system memory. The AGP bus was designed specifically to handle the high data-transfer demands associated with 3D graphic operations.

ACK (ACKnowledge) A data communications code used by the receiver to tell the transmitter it is ready to accept data. During a data transfer this signal is continually used to indicate successful receipt of the last data character or block and to request more.

Active Directory Active Directory (AD) is the central feature of the Windows 2000 architecture. It is a distributed database of user and resource information that describes the makeup of the network (i.e., users and application settings). It is also a method of implementing a distributed authentication process. The Active Directory replaces the domain structure used in Windows NT 4.0. This feature helps to centralize system and user configurations, as well as data backups on the server in the Windows 2000 network.

active partition The disk partition that possesses the system files required to boot the system. This is the logical drive that the system reads at bootup.

adapter A device that permits one system to work with and connect to another. Many I/O device adapters interface with the microcomputer by plugging into the expansion slots on the system board. These specialized circuit boards are often called adapter cards.

Add New Hardware Wizard Windows 9x/2000 applet designed to guide the installation process for non-PnP hardware. When installing Plug-and-Play devices, the Add New Hardware wizard should not be used. Instead, the Windows PnP function should be allowed to detect the new hardware. The new hardware must be installed in the computer before running the wizard.

Add/Remove Programs Wizard Windows 9x/2000 applet designed to guide the installation or removal of application programs. This utility can also be used to install or remove optional Windows components, such as Accessibility options, or to create a Windows Start disk.

Add/Remove Windows components Windows 9x/2000 utilities that can be used to change optional hardware (Add New Hardware) and software (Add/Remove Programs) components installed in the system. These utilities are located in the Windows Control Panel.

address The unique location number of a particular memory storage area, such as a byte of primary memory, a sector of disk memory, or a peripheral device itself.

address bus A unidirectional pathway that carries address data generated by the microprocessor to the various memory and I/O elements of the computer. The size of this bus determines the amount of memory a particular computer can use and, therefore, is a direct indication of the computer's power.

A: drive The commonly understood term designating the first floppy-disk drive in Microsoft's DOS microcomputer operating system.

ASCII (American Standard Code for Information Interchange) The 7-bit binary data code used in all personal computers, many minicomputers, and also in communications services. Of the 128 possible character combinations, the first 32 are used for printing and transmission control. Because of the 8-bit byte used in digital computers, the extra bit can be used either for parity checking, or for the extended ASCII set of characters, which includes foreign language characters and line-draw graphic symbols.

ASIC (Application Specific Integrated Circuit) A very large-scale integration device designed to replace a large block of standardized PC circuitry. Once the parameters of the device have achieved a pseudo standard usage status, IC manufacturers tend to combine all of the circuitry for that function into a large IC custom designed to carry out that function. Examples include integrated VGA controllers, integrated MI/O controllers, and integrated peripheral controllers.

asynchronous transmission A method of serial data transmission in which the receiving system is not synchronized by a common clock signal with the transmitting system.

AT Attachment (ATA) Also known also as IDE. A system-level interface specification that integrates the disk drive controller on the drive itself. The original ATA specification supports one or two hard drives through a 16-bit interface using Programmed IO (PIO) modes. The ATA-2 specification, also known as EIDE or Fast ATA, supports faster PIO and DMA transfer modes, as well as logical block addressing (LBA) strategies.

AT bus Also referred to as the ISA (Industry Standard Architecture) bus. The 16-bit data bus introduced in the AT class personal computer that became the industry standard for 16-bit systems.

ATTRIB The DOS command used to change attributes assigned to files (i.e., system, read-only, and hidden status).

Attributes Properties of DOS files. Special file attributes include system, read-only, and hidden status. These conditions can be altered using the external DOS command ATTRIB.

ATX form factor A newer system board form factor that improves on the previous baby AT form factor standard by reorienting the system board by 90 degrees. This makes for a more efficient design, placing the IDE connectors nearer to the system unit's drive bays and positioning the microprocessor in line with the output of the power supply's cooling fan.

AUTOEXEC.BAT An optional DOS program that the system's command interpreter uses to carry out customized startup commands at bootup.

B

backup An operation normally performed to create backup copies of important information in case the drive crashes, or the disk becomes corrupt. Backup utilities allow the user to quickly create extended copies of files, groups of files, or an entire disk drive.

Backup Domain Controller (BDC) Backup Domain Controllers are servers within the network that are used to hold read-only backup copies of the directory database. A network may contain one or more BCDs. These servers are used to authenticate user logons.

Backup Wizard An automated software routine in Windows 2000 designed to lead users through a step-by-step process of configuring and scheduling a backup job.

BAT file (batch file) A filename extension used to identify a batch file in Microsoft DOS versions. A batch file, created by a word processor, contains a list of DOS commands that are executed as if each were typed and entered one at a time.

baud rate The number of electrical state changes per second on a data communication line. At lower speeds, the baud rate and the bits-per-second rate are identical. At higher speeds, the baud rate is some fraction of the bits-per-second rate.

binary This means base two. In digital computers, all data is processed only after being converted to binary numbers consisting of the two digits 0 and 1.

BIOS (Basic Input Output System) See *ROM BIOS*.

bit (binary digit) One digit of a binary number (0 or 1). Groups of bits are manipulated together by a computer into various storage units called nibbles, bytes, words, or characters.

bit map A term used in computer graphics to describe a memory area containing a video image. One bit in the map represents one pixel on a monochrome screen, while in color or grayscale monitors, several bits in the map may represent one pixel.

Blue Screen A kernel-mode stop that indicates a failure of a core operating system function. Also known as the Blue Screen of Death because the system stops processing and produces a blue screen, rather than risking catastrophic memory and file corruption.

boot To start the computer. It refers to the word bootstrap, since just as straps help in pulling boots on, the bootable disk helps the computer to get its first instructions.

bootable disk A disk that starts the operating system. Normally refers to a floppy disk containing the computer operating system.

Boot Menu The Startup options screen menu displayed during the Windows 2000 bootup process. This menu is produced when the F8 function key is depressed while the "Starting Windows" message is on the screen. This menu is generated by the Boot.ini Boot Loader Menu file. Options in this menu include the variety of operating systems installed on the computer. If no selection is made from this menu after a given time, the default value is selected.

boot partition The disk partition that possesses the system files required to load the operating system into memory. Also referred to as the *active partition*.

boot sector The first sector on a disk (or partition). On bootable disks or partitions, this sector holds the code (called the boot record) that causes the system to move the operating system files into memory and begin executing them.

Boot.ini Boot.ini is a special, hidden boot-loader menu file used by the NTLDR during the bootup process to generate the Boot Loader Menu that is displayed on the screen. If no selection is made from this menu after a given time, the default value is selected.

Bootsect.dos A Windows NT file used to load operating systems other than Windows NT. If an entry from the Boot Loader Menu indicates an operating system other than Windows NT is to be loaded, the NTLDR program loads the BOOTSECT.DOS file from the root directory of the system partition and passes control to it. From this point, the BOOTSECT file is responsible for loading the desired operating system.

bootstrap loader A term used to refer to two different software routines involved in starting a system and loading the operating system. The primary bootstrap loader is a firmware routine that locates the boot record required to load the operating system into memory. The OS loader takes over from the primary bootstrap loader and moves the operating system into memory (known as booting the OS).

bps (bits per second) A term used to measure the speed of data being transferred in a communications system.

bus A parallel collection of conductors that carry data or control signals from one unit to another.

bus master Any class of intelligent devices having the ability to take control of the system buses of a computer.

byte The most common word size used by digital computers. It is an 8-bit pattern consisting of both a high- and a low-order nibble. Computers of any size are frequently described in terms of how many bytes of data can be manipulated in one operation or cycle.

C

cache An area of high-speed memory reserved for improving system performance. Blocks of often-used data are copied into the cache area to permit faster access times. A disk cache memory is an area of RAM used to hold data from a disk drive that the system may logically want to access, thereby speeding up access.

cache controller A highly automated memory controller assigned the specific task of managing a sophisticated cache memory system.

carriage The part in a printer or typewriter that handles the feeding of the paper forms.

cartridge A removable data storage module, containing disks, magnetic tape, or memory chips, and inserted into the slots of disk drives, printers, or computers.

C: drive This is the commonly understood term designating the system or first hard-disk drive in the DOS and OS/2 microcomputer operating systems.

Centronics interface The 36-pin standard for interfacing parallel printers, and other devices, to a computer. The plug, socket, and signals are defined.

certificate A security service used to authenticate the origin of a public key to a user possessing a matching private key.

character printer Any printer that prints one character at a time, such as a dot-matrix printer or a daisy wheel.

chip The common name for an integrated circuit (IC). Preceded by the development of the transistor, ICs can contain from several dozen to several million electronic components (resistors, diodes, transistors, etc.) on a square of silicon approximately 1/16th to 1/2 inch wide and around 1/30th of an inch in thickness. The IC can be packaged in many different styles depending on the specific use for which it is intended.

chipset A group of specifically engineered ICs designed to perform a function interactively.

Chkdsk DOS disk maintenance utility used to recover lost allocation units from a hard drive. These lost units occur when an application terminates unexpectedly. Over a period of time, lost units can pile up and occupy large amounts of disk space.

clients Workstations that operate in conjunction with a master server computer that controls the operation of the network.

client/server network A network in which workstations or clients operate in conjunction with a master server computer to control the network.

clock An internal timing device. Several varieties of clocks are used in computer systems. Among them are the CPU clock, the real-time clock, a timesharing clock, and a communications clock.

cluster Clusters are organizational units used with disk drives to represent one or more sectors of data. These structures constitute the smallest unit of storage space on the disk.

CMOS (Complementary Metal Oxide Semiconductor) A MOS technology used to fabricate IC devices. It is traditionally slower than other IC technologies, but it possesses higher circuit-packing density than other technologies. CMOS ICs are very sensitive to voltage spikes and static discharges and must be protected from static shock.

CMOS setup A software setup program used to provide the system with information about what options are installed. The configuration information is stored in special CMOS registers that are read each time the system boots up. Battery backup prevents the information from being lost when power to the system is removed.

cold boot Booting a computer by turning the power on.

color monitor Also known as an RGB monitor, this display type allows the user to run text and/or color-based applications such as graphics drawing and CAD programs. There are two basic RGB-type monitors: digital (TTL) and analog. Analog RGB monitors allow the use of many more colors than digital RGB monitors.

color printer Any printer capable of printing in color, using thermal-transfer, dot-matrix, electro-photographic, electrostatic, ink-jet, or laser printing techniques.

COM1 The label used in Microsoft DOS versions assigned to serial port #1.

COMMAND.COM COMMAND.COM is the DOS command interpreter that is loaded at the end of the bootup process. It accepts commands issued through the keyboard, or other input devices, and carries them out according to the command's definition. These definitions can be altered by adding switches to the command.

command prompt A screen symbol that indicates to the user that the system is ready for a command. It usually consists of the current drive letter, followed by a colon and a blinking cursor.

compatible A reference to any piece of computer equipment that works like, or looks like a more widely known standard or model. A PC-compatible, or clone, is a PC that, although physically differing somewhat from the IBM-PC, runs software developed for the IBM-PC and accepts its hardware options.

Computer Management Console A Windows 2000 Management Console, that enables the user to track and configure all of the system's hardware and software. It can also be used to configure network options and view system events.

computer name A name created for a computer by a network administrator. This name identifies the computer to other members of the network. It is generally recommended that computer names be 15 characters or less. However, if the computer has the TCP/IP networking protocol installed, its name can range up to 63 characters long but should only contain the numbers 0-9, the letters A-Z and a-z, and hyphens. It is possible to use other characters, but doing so may prevent other users from finding your computer on the network.

CONFIG.SYS A Microsoft operating system configuration file that, upon startup, is used to customize the system's hardware environment. The required peripheral device drivers (with SYS file extensions) are initialized.

configuration A customized computer system or communications network composed of a particular number and type of interrelated components. The configuration varies from system to system, requiring that some means be established to inform the system software about what options are currently installed.

Configuration Manager A component of the Windows Plug-and-Play system that coordinates the configuration process for all devices in the system.

continuous forms Paper sheets that are joined together along perforated edges and used in printers that move them through the printing area with motorized sprockets. Sprockets may fit into holes on both sides of the paper.

control bus A pathway between the microprocessor and the various memory, programmable, and I/O elements of the system. Control bus signals are not necessarily related to each other and can be unidirectional or bi-directional.

control character A special type of character that causes some event to occur on a printer, display, or communications path such as a line feed, a carriage return, or an escape.

Control Panel The Windows component used to customize the operation and appearance of Windows functions. In Windows 9x and Windows NT/2000 the Control Panel can be accessed through the Start button/Settings route, or under the My Computer icon on the desktop.

control protocols Protocols that configure the communication interface to the networking protocols employed by the system. Each network transport supported under Windows 2000 has a corresponding control protocol.

CPU (Central Processing Unit) The part of the computer that does the thinking. It consists of the control unit and the Arithmetic Logic Unit. In personal computers, the CPU is contained on a single chip, whereas on a minicomputer it occupies one or several printed circuit boards. On mainframes, a CPU is contained on many printed circuit boards. Its power comes from the fact that it can execute many millions of instructions in a fraction of a second.

CRC (Cyclic Redundancy Check) The error-checking technique that ensures communications channel integrity by utilizing division to determine a remainder. If the transmitter and receiver do not agree on what the remainder should be, an error is detected.

CRT (Cathode Ray Tube) The vacuum tube that is used as the display screen for both TVs and computer terminals. Sometimes the term is used to mean the terminal itself.

CTS (Clear To Send) An RS-232 handshaking signal sent from the receiver to the transmitter indicating readiness to accept data.

cursor The movable display screen symbol that indicates to the user where the action is taking place. The text cursor is usually a blinking underline or rectangle, whereas the graphics cursor can change into any predetermined shape at different parts of the screen.

cursor keys Special keyboard keys that can be used to move the cursor around the display screen. Enhanced keyboards have two clusters of cursor keys so that the numeric keypad portion of the keyboard can be used separately.

cylinder The combination of all tracks, normally on multiple-platter disk drives, that reside at the same track number location on each surface.

D

data Information assembled in small units of raw facts and figures.

data bus A bi-directional pathway linking the microprocessor to memory and I/O devices, the size of which usually corresponds to the word size of the computer.

data compression Most compression algorithms use complex mathematical formulas to remove redundant bits, such as successive 0s or 1s, from the data stream. When the modified word is played back through the decompression circuitry the formula reinserts the missing bits to return the data stream to its original state.

Data Encryption Standard (DES) A U.S. standard method of encrypting data into a secret code. Down-level clients employ the DES standard to encrypt user passwords.

DCE (Data Communications Equipment) A communications device, usually a modem, that establishes, maintains, and terminates a data transfer session. It also serves as a data converter when interfacing different transmission media.

default The normal action taken, or setting used, by hardware or software when the user does not otherwise specify.

defragmentation Disk maintenance operation performed to optimize the use of disk space by moving scattered file fragments into continuous chains to speed up data retrieval from the drive.

demodulator A device that removes the data from the carrier frequency and converts it to its originally unmodulated form.

DEVICE= CONFIG.SYS commands used to load specified device drivers into memory at bootup (e.g., the statement DEVICE=C:\MOUSE\MOUSE.SYS loads a mouse driver from the MOUSE directory). Used as "DEVICEHIGH=", the command will load the specified device driver into the Upper Memory Blocks, thereby freeing up conventional memory space.

device driver Special memory-resident program that tells the operating system how to communicate with a particular type of I/O device, such as a printer or a mouse.

Device Manager A Windows 95/98/2000 Control Panel utility that provides a graphical representation of devices in the system. It can be used to view resource allocations and set hardware configurations properties for these devices. This utility can also be used to identify and resolve resource conflicts between system devices. The Device Manager is located under the Control Panel's System icon.

diagnostics Software programs specifically designed to test the operational capability of the computer memory, disk drives, and other peripherals. The routines are available on disks or on ROM chips. Errors may be indicated by beep codes or visual reports. They can normally point to a board-level problem, but not down to a particular component, unless the routine has been written for a particular board being used in the system under test. A complete system failure would require a ROM-based diagnostic program as opposed to a disk-based routine.

dial-up networking Methods of accessing the public telephone system to carry on data networking operations. These methods include modem, ISDN, and DSL accesses.

DIMMs Dual in-line memory modules. DIMMs are 168-pin plug-in memory modules similar to SIMMs.

direct I/O An I/O addressing method that uses no address allocations but requires extra control lines.

directory A hierarchical collection of disk files organized under one heading and simulating the concept of a drawer in a file cabinet. In the structure of a disk drive system, the directory is the organizational table that holds information about all files stored under its location. This information includes the file's name, size, time, date of when it was last changed, and its beginning location on the disk.

disk arrays A collection of multiple disk drives operating under the direction of a single controller for the purpose of providing fault tolerance and performance. Data files are written on the disks in ways that improve the performance and reliability of the disk drive subsystem, as well as to provide detection and corrective actions for damaged files. Redundant Array of Inexpensive Disks (RAID) 5 in Windows 2000 is an example.

disk drive The peripheral storage device that reads and writes data to spinning magnetic or optical disks. The drive can either hold removable disks or contain permanent platters.

diskette A term usually applied to a removable, floppy-disk memory storage device.

DMA (Direct Memory Access) The ability of certain intelligent, high-speed I/O devices to perform data transfers themselves, with the help of a special IC device called a DMA controller.

docking station Special platforms designed to work with portable computers to provide additional I/O capacity. The docking station is designed so that the portable computer inserted into it can have access to the docking station's expansion slots, additional storage devices, and other peripheral devices, such as full-size keyboards and monitors. No standards exist for docking stations, so they must be purchased for specific types of portable computers.

domain Collectively, a domain is a group of members that share a common directory database and are organized in levels. Every domain is identified by a unique name and is administered as a single unit having common rules and procedures.

domain name A unique name that identifies a host computer site on the Internet.

Domain Name Service (DNS) A networking service that resolves computer names to IP addresses in a TCP/IP network environment. This service is one of the standard networking services available in the Windows operating systems.

Domain Name System (DNS) A database organizational structure whereby higher-level Internet servers keep track of assigned domain names and their corresponding IP addresses for systems on levels under them. The IP addresses of all the computers attached to the Internet are tracked with this listing system. DNS evolved as a method of organizing the members of the Internet into a hierarchical management structure that consists of various levels of computer groups called domains. Each computer on the Internet is assigned a domain name, which corresponds to an additional domain level.

DOS (Disk Operating System) Can be a generic term, but in most cases it refers to the Microsoft family of computer operating systems (PC-DOS for IBM equipment or MS-DOS for compatibles).

dot-matrix printer A type of printer that forms its images out of one or more columns of dot hammers. Higher resolutions require a greater number of dot hammers to be used.

dot pitch A measurement of the resolution of a dot-matrix. The width of an individual dot in millimeters describes a display's resolution, with the smaller number representing the higher resolution. The number of dots per linear inch describes a printer's resolution, with the higher number representing the higher resolution.

DRAM (Dynamic Random Access Memory) A type of RAM that will lose its data, regardless of power considerations, unless it is refreshed at least once every 2 milliseconds.

drive (1) An electromechanical device that moves disks, discs, or tapes at high speeds so that data can be recorded on the media, or read back from it. (2) In the organizational structure of a DOS system, a drive can be thought of as the equivalent of a file drawer that holds folders and documents. (3) In electronic terms, it is a signal output of a device used to activate the input of another device.

DSR (Data Set Ready) An RS-232 handshaking signal sent from the modem to its own computer indicating its ability to accept data.

DTR (Data Terminal Ready) An RS-232 handshaking signal that is sent to a modem by its own computer to indicate a readiness to accept data.

dual booting A condition that can be established on a hard-disk drive that holds two or more operating systems. A pre-boot option is created that enables the system to be booted from one of the designated operating systems (e.g., Windows 98 or Windows 2000 Professional).

Dynamic Host Configuration Protocol (DHCP) Software protocol that dynamically assigns IP addresses to a server's clients. This software is available in both Windows 9x and Windows NT/2000 and must be *located* on both the server and the client computers (installed on servers and activated on clients). This enables ISPs to provide dynamic IP address assignments for their customers.

Dynamic Link Library (DLL) files Windows library files that contain small pieces of executable code that can be shared between Windows programs. These files are used to minimize redundant programming common to certain types of Windows applications.

E

edge connector The often double-sided row of etched lines on the edge of an adapter card that plugs into one of the computer's expansion slots.

EEPROM (Electrically Erasable Programmable Read Only Memory) A type of nonvolatile semiconductor memory device that allows erasure and reprogramming from within a computer using special circuitry. These devices allow specific memory cells to be manipulated, rather than requiring a complete reprogramming procedure as in the case of EPROM's.

EIA (Electronics Industries Association) An organization, founded in 1924, made up of electronic parts and systems manufacturers. It sets electrical and electronic interface standards such as the RS-232C.

EISA (Extended Industry Standard Architecture) A PC bus standard that extends the AT bus architecture to 32 bits and allows older PC and AT boards to plug into its slot. It was announced in 1988 as an alternative to the IBM Micro Channel.

electron gun The device by which the fine beam of electrons is created that sweeps across the phosphor screen in a CRT.

Electrostatic Discharge (ESD) As it applies to computer systems, a rapid discharge of static electricity from a human to the computer, due to a difference of electrical potential between the two. Such discharges usually involve thousands of volts of energy and can damage the IC circuits used to construct computer and communications equipment.

Emergency Repair Disk A disk created to repair the Windows NT/2000 system when its boot disk fails. The Emergency Repair Disk (ERD) provides another option if Safe Mode and the Recovery Console do not provide a successful solution to a system crash. If you have already created an ERD, you can start the system with the Windows NT/2000 Setup CD or the Setup floppy disks, and then use the ERD to restore core system files.

EMI (ElectroMagnetic Interference) A system-disrupting electronic radiation created by some other electronic device. The FCC sets allowable limits for EMI in Part 5 of its Rules and Regulations. Part A systems are designed for office and plant environments, and Part B systems are designed for home use.

EMM (Expanded Memory Manager) Any software driver that permits and manages the use of expanded memory in 80386 and higher machines.

EMS (Expanded Memory Specification) A method of using memory above one megabyte on computers using DOS. Co-developed by Lotus, Intel, and Microsoft, each upgrade has allowed for more memory to be used. EMS is dictated by the specific application using it. In 286 machines, EMS is installed on an adapter card and managed by an EMS driver. See *EMM*.

Enhanced Cylinder Head Sector (ECHS) format B I O S translation mode used to configure large hard drives (over 504 MB) for operation. This mode is an extended CHS mode and is identical to Large and LBA modes. However, reconfiguring drives to other configration settings risks the prospects of losing data.

Enhanced IDE (EIDE) An improved version of the Integrated Drive Electronics interface standard. The new standard supports data-transfer rates up to four times that of the original IDE standard. It also makes provisions for supporting storage devices of up to 8.4 GB in size, as opposed to the old standard's limit of 528 MB. The new standard is sometimes referred to as Fast ATA or Fast IDE.

enterprise networks Enterprise networks are designed to facilitate business-to-business, or business-to-customer operations. Because monetary transactions and customers' personal information travels across the network in these environments, enterprise networks feature facilities for additional highly protective security functions.

EPROM (Erasable Programmable Read Only Memory) A type of nonvolatile semiconductor memory device that can be programmed more than once. Selected cells are charged using a comparatively high voltage. EPROMs can be erased by exposure to a source of strong ultraviolet light, at which point they must be completely reprogrammed.

ergonomics The study of people-to-machine relationships. A device is considered to be ergonomic when it blends smoothly with a person's body actions.

error checking The act of testing the data transfer in a computer system or network for accuracy.

ESC key (Escape key) This keyboard key is used to cancel an application operation or to exit some routine.

Ethernet A popular network topology that uses Carrier Sense Multiple Access with Collision Detection (CSMA/CD) for collision detection and avoidance. Ethernet can be physically implemented as either a bus, or a star network organization.

Expanded Memory (EMS) A memory management strategy for handling memory beyond the 1 MB of conventional memory. Using this strategy, the additional memory is accessed in 16K pages through a window established in the upper memory area.

expansion slot The receptacle mounted on the system board into which adapter cards are plugged to achieve system expansion. The receptacle interfaces with the I/O channel and system bus, and so the number of slots available determines the expansion potential of the system.

extended memory The memory above one megabyte in Intel 286 and higher computers, and used for RAM disks, disk caching routines, and for locating the operating system files in later versions of Microsoft DOS.

Extended Memory (XMS) A memory management strategy for handling memory beyond the 1 MB of conventional memory. Using this strategy, Windows and Windows-based programs directly access memory above the 1 MB marker. Extended memory requires that the HIMEM.SYS memory manager be loaded in the DOS CONFIG.SYS.

extended partition A secondary partition that can be created after the drive's primary partition has been established. It is the only other partition allowed on a disk once the primary partition has been made using FDISK. However, an extended partition can be subdivided into up to 23 logical drives.

Extended System Configuration Data (ESCD) The portion of CMOS memory that holds PnP configuration information.

F

FAT (File Allocation Table) The part of the DOS file system that keeps track of where specific data is stored on the disk.

FDISK command The disk utility program that performs the partitioning of the hard disk into several independent disks.

file Any program, record, table, or document that is stored under its own filename.

File Allocation Table (FAT) A special table located on a formatted DOS disk that tracks where each file is located on the disk.

File menu A drop-down menu attached to Windows graphical interfaces whose options enable users to Open, Move, Copy, and Delete selected folders, files, or applications.

file system File management system. The organizational structure that operating systems employ to organize and track files. Windows 2000 employs the NTFS5 file system to perform these functions. A file system is a hierarchical directory system that employs directories to organize files into a tree-like structure.

filenames Names assigned to files in a disk-based system. Disk-based systems store and handle related pieces of information in groups called files. The system recognizes and keeps track of the different files in the system through their names. Therefore, each file in the system is required to have a filename that is different from that of any other file in the directory.

Firewire Also known as IEEE-1394, Firewire is a very fast I/O bus standard designed to support the high bandwidth requirements of real time audio/visual equipment. The IEEE-1394 standard employs streaming data transfer techniques to support data-transfer rates up to 400 Mbps. A single Firewire connection can be used to connect up 63 external devices.

firmware A term used to describe the situation in which programs (software) are stored in ROM ICs (hardware) on a permanent basis.

floppy disk Also called a diskette, a removable secondary storage medium for computers, composed of flexible magnetic material and contained in a square envelope or cartridge. A floppy disk can be recorded and erased hundreds of times.

flow control A method of controlling the flow of data between computers. The receiving system signals the sending PC when it can and cannot receive data. Flow control can be implemented through hardware or software protocols. Using the software method, the receiving PC sends special code characters to the sending system to stop or start data flow. Xon/Xoff is an example of a software flow control protocol.

Folder Options Options that enable the user to change the appearance of their desktops and folder content, and to specify how their folders will open. Users can select whether they want a single window to open, as opposed to cascading windows, and they can designate whether folders will open with a single-click or double-click. Folder Options can also be used to turn on the Active Desktop, change the application used to open certain types of files, or make files available when they're not on-line with the network. Changes made in Folder Options apply to the appearance of the contents of Windows Explorer (including My Computer, My Network Places, My Documents, and Control Panel) windows.

folders Icons that represent directories. In Windows 9x/NT/2000, directories and subdirectories are referred to and depicted as folders.

font One set of alphanumeric characters possessing matching design characteristics such as typeface, orientation, spacing, pitch, point size, style, and stroke weight.

forests A group of one or more Active Directory domain trees that trust each other. Unlike directory trees, forests do not share a contiguous namespace. This permits multiple namespaces to be supported within a single forest. In the forest, all domains share a common schema, configuration, and global catalog.

form feed The moving of the next paper form into the proper printing position, accomplished either by pressing the form feed (FF) button on the printer or by sending the printer the ASCII form feed character.

FORMAT command An MS-DOS utility that prepares a disk for use by the system. Track and sector information is placed on the disk while bad areas are marked so that no data will be recorded on them.

formatting The act of preparing a hard or floppy disk for use with an operating system. This operation places operating system–specific data tracking tables on the media and tests its storage locations (sectors or blocks) to make certain they are reliable for holding data.

FQDN Fully Qualified Domain Name. A name that consists of the host name and the domain name, including the top-level domain name (e.g., www.mic-inc.com where www is the host name, mic-inc is the second-level domain name, and com is the top-level domain name).

fragmentation A condition that exists on hard-disk drives after files have been deleted or moved, and areas of free disk space are scattered around the disk. These areas of disk space cause slower performance because the drive's read/write heads have to be moved more often to find the pieces of a single file.

frame (1) A memory widow that applications and the operating system exchange data through, such as the EMS frame in Upper Memory that Expanded Memory managers use to move data between conventional memory and additional memory beyond the 1 MB mark. (2) The construction of a complete package of data with all overhead (headers) for transferring it to another location (e.g., an Ethernet frame). (3) One screen of computer graphics data, or the amount of memory required to store it.

FRU (Field-Replaceable Unit) The components of the system that can be conveniently replaced in the field.

FTP (File Transfer Protocol) An application layer protocol that copies files from one FTP host site to another.

full-duplex A method of data transmission that allows data flow in both directions simultaneously.

function keys A special set of keyboard keys used to give the computer special commands. They are frequently used in combination with other keys, and can have different uses depending on the software application being run.

G

GDI.EXE A Windows core component that is responsible for managing the operating system's/environment's graphical user interface.

General Protection Fault (GPF) A Windows memory usage error that typically occurs when a program attempts to access memory currently in use by another program.

GHz (gigahertz) One billion hertz or cycles per second.

graphics The creation and management of pictures using a computer.

ground (1) Any point from which electrical measurements are referenced. (2) *Earth* ground is considered to be an electrical reference point of absolute zero, and is used as the electrical return path for modern power transmission systems. This ground, often incorporated by electronic devices to guard against fatal shock, is called *chassis* or *protective* ground. (3) An actual conductor in an electronic circuit being used as a return path, also called a *signal* ground.

group The administrative gathering of users that can be administered uniformly. In establishing groups, the administrator can assign permissions or restrictions to the entire body. The value of using groups lies in the time saved by being able to apply common rights to several users instead of applying them one by one.

group policies Administrators use these tools to institute large numbers of detailed settings for users throughout an enterprise, without establishing each setting manually.

Group Policy Editor Utility employed to establish policies in Windows 2000. Administrators use this editor to establish which applications different users have access to, as well as to control applications on the user's desktop.

GUI (Graphical User Interface) A form of operating environment that uses a graphical display to represent procedures and programs that can be executed by the computer.

H

HAL.DLL HAL.DLL is the Hardware Abstraction Layer driver that holds the information specific to the CPU that the system is being used with.

half-duplex communication Communications that occur in both directions, but can occur in only one direction at a time. Most older networking strategies were based on half-duplex operations.

handshaking A system of signal exchanges conducted between the computer system and a peripheral device during the data transfer process. The purpose of these signals is to produce as orderly a flow of data as possible.

hard disk A metal disk that is used for external storage purposes. It is coated with a ferromagnetic coating and is available in both fixed and removable formats.

hardware Any aspect of the computer operation that can be physically touched. This includes IC chips, circuit boards, cables, connectors, and peripherals.

Hardware Abstraction Layer (HAL) The Windows NT HAL is a library of hardware drivers that operate between the actual hardware and the rest of the system. These software routines act to make every architecture look the same to the operating system. The HAL occupies the logical space directly between the system's hardware and the rest of the operating system's Executive Services. In Windows NT 4.0, the HAL enables the operating system to work with different types of microprocessors.

Hardware Compatibility List (HCL) The list of Microsoft-certified compatible hardware devices associated with Windows 2000 Professional and Windows 2000 Server products.

HIMEM.SYS The DOS memory manager that enables Expanded and Extended Memory strategies for memory operations above the 1 MB conventional memory range.

hives The five files that hold the content of the Windows NT Registry. Hives represent the major divisions of all the Registry's keys, subkeys, subtrees, and values. The hives of the Windows NT Registry are the SAM hive, the Security hive, the Software hive, the System hive, and the Default hive. These files are stored in the \Winnt\System32\Config directory along with a backup copy and log file for each hive.

host Any device that communicates over the network using TCP/IP and has an assigned (dedicated) IP address.

I

IC (Integrated Circuit) The technical name for a chip. See *chip*.

icons Graphical symbols that are used to represent commands. These symbols are used to start and manipulate a program without the user having to know where that program is, or how it is configured.

IDE (Integrated Drive Electronics) A method of disk drive manufacturing that locates all the required controller circuitry on the drive itself, rather than on a separate adapter card. Also known as the AT Attachment interface.

impact printer Any printer that produces a character image by hammering onto a combination of embossed character, ribbon, and paper.

Infrared Data Association (IrDA) A data transmission standard for using infrared light. IrDA ports provide wireless data transfers between devices. These ports support data transfer rates roughly equivalent to those of traditional parallel ports. The only down side to using IrDA ports for data communications is that the two devices must be within one or two meters of each other and have a clear line of sight between them.

INI files Windows text files that hold configuration settings that are used to initialize the system for Windows operation. Originally these files formed the basis of the Windows 3.x operating environments. They were mostly replaced in Windows 9x and NT/2000 by the Registry structure. However, some parts of the INI files still exist in these products.

initialization The process of supplying startup information to an intelligent device or peripheral (e.g., the system board's DMA controller, or a modem), or to a software application, or applet.

ink-jet printer A high-resolution printer that produces its image by spraying a specially treated ink onto the paper.

input device Any input-generating peripheral device such as keyboard, mouse, light pen, scanner, or digitizer.

instruction word A class of binary coded data word that tells the computer what operation to perform and where to find any data needed to perform the operation.

intelligent controller Usually an IC, or series of ICs, with built-in microprocessor capabilities dedicated to the controlling of some peripheral unit or process. Single-chip controllers are sometimes referred to as *smart chips*.

interface The joining of dissimilar devices so that they function in a compatible and complementary manner.

interlaced The method of rewriting the monitor screen repeatedly by alternately scanning every other line and then scanning the previously unscanned lines.

Internet This most famous wide area network is actually a network of networks working together. The main communication path is a series of networks established by the U.S. government that has expanded around the world and offers access to computers in every part of the globe.

Internet Printing Protocol (IPP) A protocol included with Windows 2000 that enables users to sort between different printers based on their attributes. This standards-based Internet protocol provides Windows users with the capability of printing across the Internet. With IPP, the user can print to a URL, view the print queue status using an Internet browser, and install print drivers across the Internet.

Internet Protocol (IP) Address A 32-bit network address consisting of four dotted-decimal numbers separated by periods that uniquely identifies a device on the network. Each IP address consists of two parts—the network address and the host address. The network address identifies the entire network, while the host address identifies an intelligent member within the network (a router, a server, or a workstation).

interrupt A signal sent to the microprocessor from the interrupt controller, or generated by a software instruction, which is capable of interrupting the microprocessor during program execution. An interrupt is usually generated when an input or output operation is required.

interrupt controller A special programmable IC responsible for coordinating and prioritizing interrupt requests from I/O devices, and sending the microprocessor the starting addresses of the interrupt service routines so that the microprocessor can service the interrupting device and then continue executing the active program.

intranet An intranet is a network built on the TCP/IP protocol that belongs to a single organization. It is in essence a private Internet. Like the Internet, intranets are designed to share information and are accessible only to the organization's members, with authorization.

I/O (Input/Output) A type of data transfer occurring between a microprocessor and a peripheral device. Whenever any data transfer occurs, output from one device becomes an input to another.

I/O port The external window or connector on a computer, used to create an interface with a peripheral device. The I/O port may appear as either parallel data connections or serial data connections.

IO.SYS A special hidden, read-only bootup file that the bootstrap loader finds and moves into RAM to manage the bootup process. After the bootup has been completed, this file manages the basic input/output routines of the system. This includes communication between the system and I/O devices such as hard disks, printers, floppy-disk drives, and so on.

IP (Internet Protocol) The Network layer protocol where logical addresses are assigned. IP is one of the protocols that make up the TCP/IP stack.

IPCONFIG A TCP/IP networking utility that can be used to determine the IP address of a local machine.

IPX/SPX Internetwork Packet Exchange/Sequential Packet Exchange protocol. A proprietary transport protocol developed by Novell for the NetWare operating system. The IPX portion of the protocol is a connectionless, Network layer protocol, which is responsible for routing. The SPX portion of the protocol is a connection-oriented, Transport layer protocol that manages error checking. These protocols are primarily found on local area networks that include NetWare servers.

IRQ (Interrupt Request) Hardware interrupt request lines in a PC-compatible system. System hardware devices use these lines to request service from the microprocessor as required. The microprocessor responds to the IRQ by stopping what it is doing, storing its environment, jumping to a service routine, servicing the device, and then returning to its original task.

ISA (Industry Standard Architecture) A term that refers to the bus structures used in the IBM PC series of personal computers. The PC and XT use an 8-bit bus, and the AT uses a 16-bit bus.

ISDN (Integrated Services Digital Network) A digital communications standard that can carry digital data over special telephone lines at speeds much higher than those possible with regular analog phone lines.

ISPs (Internet Service Providers) Companies that provide the technical gateway to the Internet. An ISP connects all of the users and individual networks together.

J

joystick A computer input device that offers quick, multidirectional movement of the cursor for CAD systems and video games.

jumper Typically, a 2- or 4-pin BERG connector, located on the system board or an adapter card, which permits the attachment of a wired hardware switch or the placement of a shorting bar to implement a particular hardware function or setting.

K

kernel The Windows 3.x and 95 core files that are responsible for managing Windows resources and running applications.

Kernel Mode The Kernel Mode is the operating mode in which the program has unlimited access to all memory, including those of system hardware, the user mode applications, and other processes (such as I/O operations). The Kernel Mode consists of three major blocks, the Win32k Executive Service module, the Hardware Abstraction Layer, and the Microkernel.

keyboard The most familiar computer input device, incorporating a standard typewriter layout with the addition of other specialized control and function keys.

L

LAN (Local Area Network) A collection of local computers and devices that can share information. A LAN is normally thought of as encompassing a campus setting, a room, or a collection of buildings.

laser printer Any printer that utilizes the electro-photographic method of image transfer. Light dots are transferred to a photosensitive rotating drum, which picks up electrostatically charged toner before transferring it to the paper.

LCD (Liquid Crystal Display) The type of output display created by placing liquid crystal material between two sheets of glass. A set of electrodes is attached to each sheet of glass. The horizontal (row) electrodes are attached to one glass plate, and the vertical (column) electrodes are fitted to the other plate. These electrodes are transparent and let light pass through. A pixel is created in the liquid crystal material at each spot where a row and a column electrode intersect. When the pixel is energized, the liquid crystal material bends and prevents light from passing through the display.

LED (Light Emitting Diode) A particular type of diode that emits light when conducting. It is used in computers and disk drives as active circuit indicator.

legacy devices Adapter cards and devices that do not include plug-and-play capabilities. These are typically older ISA expansion cards that are still being used for some reason.

letter quality Refers to a print quality as good or better than that provided by an electric typewriter.

Logical Block Addressing (LBA) A hard-disk drive organizational strategy that permits the operating system to access larger drive sizes than older BIOS/DOS FAT-management schemes could support.

logon The process of identifying oneself to the network. Normally accomplished by entering a valid user name and password that the system recognizes.

loopback A modem test procedure that allows a transmitted signal to be returned to its source for comparison with the original data.

lost allocation units Also referred to as lost clusters. File segments that do not currently belong to any file in the file allocation table. The DOS command CHKDSK/F can be used to locate and free these segments for future use.

LPT1 The label used in Microsoft DOS versions to refer to parallel port #1, usually reserved for printer operation.

M

magnetic disk The most popular form of secondary data storage for computers. Shaped like a platter and coated with an electromagnetic material, magnetic disks provide direct access to large amounts of stored data, and can be erased and rerecorded many times.

magnetic tape Traditionally, one of the most popular forms of secondary data storage backup for computers. However, Windows 2000 offers a number of other backup capabilities that may render tape an undesirable backup media in the future. Since access to data on tape is sequential in nature, magnetic tape is primarily used to restore a system that has suffered a catastrophic loss of data from its hard disk drive.

mapped drives A technique employed to enable a local system to assign a logical drive letter to the remote disk drive or folder. This is referred to as *mapping the drive letter* to the resource. This will enable applications running on the local computer to use the resource across the network.

Master Boot Record (MBR) Also referred to as the Master Partition Boot Sector. This file is located at the first sector of the disk. It contains a Master Partition Table that describes how the hard disk is organized. This table includes information about the disk's size, as well as the number and locations of all partitions on the disk. The MBR also contains the Master Boot Code that loads the operating system from the disk's active partition.

Master File Table (MFT) The core component of the NTFS system, this table replaces the FAT in an MS-DOS compatible system and contains information about each file stored on the disk.

MEM.EXE The DOS command that can be used to examine the total and used memory of the system.

memory Computer components that store information for future use. In a PC, memory can be divided into two categories: primary and secondary (i.e., semiconductor RAM and ROM and other devices). Primary memory can be divided into ROM, RAM, and cache groups. Likewise, secondary memory contains many types of storage devices—floppy drives, hard-disk drives, CD-ROM drives, DVD drives, tape drives, and so on)

memory management Methodology used in handling a computer's memory resources, including bank switching, memory protection, and virtual memory.

memory map A layout of the memory and/or I/O device addressing scheme used by a particular computer system.

memory-mapped I/O An I/O addressing method where I/O devices are granted a portion of the available address allocations, thus requiring no additional control lines to implement.

menu A screen display of available program options or commands that can be selected through keyboard or mouse action.

MHz (megahertz) One million hertz, or cycles per second.

microcomputer A personal computer, or a computer using a microprocessor as its CPU.

Microsoft Management Console (MMC) A collection of manageability features that accompany Windows 2000. These features exist as "Snap-in" applets that can be added to the operating system through the MMC.

mirroring A RAID fault tolerance method in which an exact copy of all data is written to two separate disks at the same time.

MMX (Multimedia Extensions) technology An advanced Pentium microprocessor that includes specialized circuitry designed to manage multimedia operations. Its additional multimedia instructions speed up high-volume input/output needed for graphics, motion video, animation, and sound.

modem (modulator-demodulator) Also called a DCE device, a modem is used to interface a computer or terminal to the telephone system for the purpose of conducting data communications between computers often located at great distances from each other.

monitor (1) A name for a CRT computer display. (2) Any hardware device, or software program, such as the Windows 95 System Resource Monitor, that checks, reports about, or automatically oversees a running program or system.

MOS (Metal Oxide Semiconductor) A category of logic and memory chip design that derives its name from the use of metal, oxide, and semiconductor layers. Among the various families of MOS devices are PMOS (P-Type semiconductor material), NMOS (N-Type semiconductor material), and CMOS (Complementary/Symmetry MOS material). The first letter of each family denotes the type of construction used to fabricate the chip's circuits. MOS families do not require a highly regulated +5 V dc power supply like TTL devices.

mouse A popular computer I/O device used to point or draw on the video monitor by rolling it along a desktop as the cursor moves on the screen in a corresponding manner.

MSD (Microsoft Diagnostics) Microsoft diagnostic program that can be used from the command prompt to examine different aspects of a system's hardware and software configuration. The MSD utility has been included with MS-DOS 6.x, Windows 3.x, and Windows 9x.

MSDOS.SYS One of the hidden, read-only system files required to boot the system. It is loaded by the IO.SYS file during the bootup process. It handles program and file management functions for MS-DOS systems. In Windows 95, its function is changed to that of providing pathways to other Windows files and supporting selected startup options.

multimedia A term applied to a range of applications that bring together text, graphics, video, audio, and animation to provide interactivity between the computer and its human operator.

multitasking The ability of a computer system to run two or more programs simultaneously.

N

NAK (Negative Acknowledge) A data communications code used by a receiver to tell the transmitter that its last message was not properly received.

NetBEUI (NetBIOS Extended User Interface) The Microsoft networking protocol used with Windows-based systems.

NetBIOS An emulation of IBM's *NETwork Basic Input/Output System*. NetBIOS represents the basic interface between the operating system and the LAN hardware. This function is implemented through ROM ICs located on the network card.

NetWare The Novell client/server network operating system.

Network Connection Wizard Automated setup routine in Windows 2000 that can be invoked to guide the user through the process of creating a network connection.

Network Neighborhood The Windows 95 utility used to browse and connect multiple networks, and to access shared resources on a server without having to map a network drive.

nibble A 4-bit binary pattern, which can easily be converted into a single hexadecimal digit.

NLQ (Near-Letter Quality) A quality of printing nearly as good as that of an electric typewriter. The very best dot-matrix printers can produce NLQ.

NMI (Non-Maskable Interrupt) A type of interrupt that cannot be ignored by the microprocessor during program execution. Three things can cause a non-maskable interrupt to occur: (1) A numeric coprocessor installation error. (2) A RAM parity check error. (3) An I/O channel check error.

non-impact printer Any printer that does not form its characters by using a hammer device to impact the paper, ribbon, or embossed character.

nonvolatile memory Memory that is not lost after the power is turned off, such as ROM.

NT File System (NTFS) The proprietary Windows NT file system. The NTFS structure is designed to provide better data security and to operate more efficiently with larger hard drives than FAT systems do. Its structure employs 64-bit entries to keep track of storage on the disk (as opposed to the 16- and 32-bit entries used in FAT and FAT32 systems).

NTDETECT NTDETECT.COM is the Windows NT hardware detection file. This file is responsible for collecting information about the system's installed hardware devices and passing it to the NTLDR program. This information is later used to upgrade the Windows NT Registry files.

NTLDR NT Loader is the Windows NT bootstrap loader for Intel-based computers running Windows NT. It is the Windows NT equivalent of the DOS IO.SYS file and is responsible for loading the NT operating system into memory. Afterwards, NTLDR passes control of the system over to the Windows NT operating system.

NTOSKRNL NTOSKRNL.EXE is the Windows NT kernel file that contains the Windows NT core and loads its device drivers.

NTSC (National Television Standards Committee) This organization created the television standards in the United States, and is administered by the FCC.

NTUSER.DAT The Windows NT/2000 file that contains the User portion of the Windows NT Registry. This file contains the user-specific settings that have been established for this user. When a user logs onto the system, the User file and System hive portions of the Registry are used to construct the user-specific environment in the system.

null modem cable A cable meeting the RS-232C specification, used to cross-connect two computers through their serial ports by transposing the transmit and receive lines. The computers must be physically located very close to one another, eliminating the need for a modem.

O

odd parity The form of parity checking in which the parity bit is used to make the total number of 1's contained in the character an odd number.

off-hook A condition existing on a telephone line that is capable of initiating an outgoing call, but unable to receive an incoming call.

off-line Any computer system or peripheral device that is not ready to operate, not connected, not turned on, or not properly configured.

on-hook A condition that exists on any telephone line that is capable of receiving an incoming call.

on-line Any computer system or peripheral device that is not only powered up, but also ready to operate.

operating system A special software program, first loaded into a computer at powerup, and responsible for running it. The operating system also serves as the interface between the machine and other software applications.

optical mouse A mouse that emits an infrared light stream to detect motion as it is moved around a special x-y matrix pad.

output device Any peripheral device, such as a monitor, modem, or printer, that accepts computer output.

P

paging file Also known as the swap file. The hidden file located on the hard disk that makes up half of the Windows 2000 virtual memory system. This file holds the programs and data that the operating system's virtual memory manager moves out of RAM memory and stores on the disk as virtual memory.

parallel interface The multi-line channel through which the simultaneous transfer of one or more bytes occurs.

parallel mode The mode of data transfer in which an entire word is transferred at once, from one location to another, by a set of parallel conductors.

parallel port The external connector on a computer that is used to create an interface between the computer and a parallel peripheral such as a printer.

parity bit Used for error checking during the sending and receiving of data within a system and from one system to another. The parity bit's value depends on how many 1 bits are contained in the byte it accompanies.

parity checking A method to check for data transmission errors by using a ninth bit to ensure that each character sent has an even (even parity) or odd (odd parity) number of logic 1's before transfer. The parity bit is checked for each byte sent.

parity error This error occurs when a data transfer cannot be verified for integrity. At least one data bit or the parity bit has been corrupted during the transfer process.

partition A logical section of a hard disk. Partitioning allows a single physical disk to be divided into multiple logical drives that can each hold a different operating system. Most disks contain a single partition that holds a single operating system.

partition boot sector The boot sector of that partition located in the first sector of the active partition. Here the MBR finds the code to begin loading the secondary bootstrap loader from the root directory of the boot drive.

partition table The table present at the start of every hard disk that describes the layout of the disk, including the number and location of all partitions on the disk.

partitioning Partitioning establishes the logical structure of the hard disk in a format that conforms to the operating system being used on the computer. It is a function of the operating system being used. In the case of Microsoft operating systems, the FDISK utility is used to establish and manipulate partitions.

password Unique code pattern associated with a user's logon account that is used to access the resources of a network.

path The location of the file on the disk in reference to the drive's root directory. The file's full path is specified by a logical drive letter and a listing of all directories between the root directory and the file.

PC bus Refers to the bus architectures used in the first IBM PCs, the original 8-bit bus, and the 16-bit bus extension used with the AT.

PCI (Peripheral Component Interconnect) bus A low-cost, high-performance 32-/64-bit local bus developed jointly by IBM, Intel, DEC, NCR, and Compaq.

PCMCIA (Personal Computer Memory Card International Association) card A credit-card-sized adapter card designed for use with portable computers. These cards slide into a PCMCIA slot and are used to implement modems, networks, and CD-ROM drives.

peer-to-peer network A network that does not have a centralized point of management and in which each computer is equal to all the others. In this scenario, all of the members can function as both clients and servers.

peripherals Also called I/O devices, these units include secondary memory devices such as hard-disk drives, floppy-disk drives, magnetic tape drives, modems, monitors, mice, joysticks, light pens, scanners, and even speakers.

permissions Settings that enable security levels to be assigned to files and folders on the disk. These settings provide parameters for activities that users can conduct with the designated file or folder.

Personal Digital Assistant (PDA) Handheld computing devices that typically include telephone, fax, and networking functions. A typical PDA can function as a cell phone, a fax, and a personal organizer. Most are pen-based devices that use a wand for input rather than a keyboard or mouse. PDAs are a member of the palmtop class of computers.

PIFs (Program Information Files) Windows 3.x information files used to identify resources required for DOS-based applications.

pin feed A method of moving continuous forms through the print area of a printer by using mounting pins on each side of a motorized platen to engage the holes on the right and left sides of the paper.

PING Network troubleshooting utility command that is used to verify connections to remote hosts. The PING command sends Internet Control Message Packets to a remote location and then waits for echoed response packets to be returned. The command will wait for up to one second for each packet sent and then display the number of transmitted and received packets. The command can be used to test both the name and IP address of the remote unit. A number of switches can be used to set parameters for the ping operation.

pixel Also called a PEL, or picture element, it is the smallest unit (one dot for monochrome) into which a display image can be divided.

Plug-and-Play (PnP) A specification that requires the BIOS, operating system, and adapter cards to be designed so that the system automatically configures new hardware devices to eliminate system resource conflicts.

pointing device Any input device used for the specific purpose of moving the screen cursor or drawing an image.

Point-to-Point Protocol (PPP) A connection protocol that controls the transmission of data over the wide-area network. PPP is the default protocol for the Microsoft Dial-Up adapter. In a dial-up situation, Internet software communicates with the service provider by embedding the TCP/IP information in a PPP shell for transmission through the modem in analog format. The communications equipment, at the ISP site, converts the signal back to the digital TCP/IP format. PPP has become the standard for remote access.

Point-to-Point Tunneling Protocol (PPTP) The de facto industry standard tunneling protocol first supported in Windows NT 4.0. PPTP is an extension of the Point-to-Point Protocol (PPP) and takes advantage of the authentication, compression, and encryption mechanisms of PPP. PPTP is installed with the Routing and Remote Access service. By default, PPTP is configured for five PPTP ports that can be enabled for inbound remote access and demand-dial routing connections through the Windows 2000 Routing and Remote Access wizard. PPTP and Microsoft Point-to-Point Encryption (MPPE) provide the primary security technology to implement Virtual Private Network services of encapsulation and encryption of private data.

polarizer An optical device that will either block or allow the passage of light through it depending on the polarity of an electrical charge applied to it.

POLEDIT The system policy editor that is used to establish or modify system policies that govern user rights and privileges. The Policy Editor is another tool that can be used to access the information in the Registry. However, unlike the RegEdit utility, Poledit can only access subsets of keys. The Registry editor can access the entire Registry.

policies Network administrative settings that govern the rights and privileges of different users in multi-user operations.

polling A system of initiating data transfer between a computer system and a peripheral in which the status of all the peripherals is examined periodically under software program control by having the microprocessor check the READY line. When it is activated by one of the peripherals, the processor will begin the data transfer using the corresponding I/O port.

POST (Power-On Self-Tests) A group of ROM BIOS-based diagnostic tests that are performed on the system each time it is powered up. These tests check the PC's standard hardware devices including the microprocessor, memory, interrupts, DMA, and video.

power supply The component in the system that converts the AC voltage from the wall outlet to the DC voltage required by the computer circuitry.

preventive maintenance Any regularly scheduled checking and testing of hardware and software with the goal of avoiding future failure or breakdown.

Primary Domain Controller (PDC) Primary Domain Controllers contain the Directory Databases for the network. These databases contain information about User Accounts, Group Accounts, and Computer Accounts. PDCs also are also referred to as Security Accounts Managers.

primary partitions Bootable partitions created from unallocated disk space. Under Windows 2000, up to four primary partitions can be created on a basic disk. The disk can also contain three primary partitions and an extended partition. The primary partition becomes the system's boot volume by being marked as "Active". The free space in the extended partition can be subdivided into up to 23 logical drives.

printer A peripheral device for the printing of computer text or graphics output.

printer font A prescribed character set properly formatted for use by the printer.

profiles Information about each user and group defined in the system that describes the resources and desktop configurations created for them. Settings in the profiles can be used to limit the actions users can perform, such as installing, removing, configuring, adjusting, or copying resources. When users log in, the system checks their profile and adjusts according to their information. This information is stored in the
\WINNT*login_name*\NTUSER.DAT file.

program Any group of instructions designed to command a computer system to perform a specific task. Also called *software*.

programmed I/O A system of initiating data transfer between a computer system and a peripheral in which the microprocessor alerts the specific device by using an address call. The I/O device can signal its readiness to accept the data transfer by using its Busy line. If Busy is active, the microprocessor can perform other tasks until the Busy line is deactivated, at which time the transfer can begin.

prompt A software-supplied message to the user, requiring some specific action or providing some important information. It can also be a very simple symbol, indicating that the program has successfully loaded and is waiting for a command from the user.

protected mode An operational state that allows an 80286 or higher computer to address all of its memory, including memory beyond the 1 MB MS-DOS limit.

protocol A set of rules that govern the transmitting and receiving of data communications.

Q

queue A special and temporary storage (RAM or registers) area for data in printing or internal program execution operations.

quotas Windows 2000 security settings that enable administrators to limit the amount of hard drive space users can have access to.

QWERTY keyboard A keyboard layout that was originally designed to prevent typists from jamming old-style mechanical typewriters, it is still the standard English language keyboard. The name spells out the first six leftmost letters in the first alphabetic row of keys.

R

RAID (Redundant Array of Inexpensive Disks) A set of specifications for configuring multiple hard drives to store data to increase storage capacity and improve performance. Some variations configure the drives in a manner to improve performance, whereas others concentrate on data security.

RAM (Random Access Memory) A type of semiconductor memory device that holds data on a temporary or volatile basis. Any address location in the RAM memory section can be accessed as fast as any other location.

RAM disk An area of memory that has been set aside and assigned a drive letter to simulate the organization of a hard disk drive in RAM memory. Also referred to as a virtual disk.

raster graphics A graphics representation method that uses a dot-matrix to compose the image.

raster scan The display of a video image, line by line, by an electron beam deflection system.

read only (1) A file parameter setting that prevents a file from being altered. (2) Refers to data that is permanently stored on the media or to such a medium itself.

read/write head Usually abbreviated "R/W head," the device by which a disk or tape drive senses and records digital data on the magnetic medium.

real mode A mode of operation in 80286 and higher machines in which the computer functions under the same command and addressing restrictions as an 8086 or 8088.

reboot To restart the computer or to reload the operating system.

refresh A required method of re-energizing a memory cell or display pixel in order for its data to continually be held.

RegEdit The editing utility used to directly edit the contents of the Registry (Regedit.exe and Regedit32.exe). This file is located in the \Winnt\System32 folder.

Registry A multipart, hierarchical database established to hold system and user configuration information in Windows 9x, NT, and 2000.

Registry keys The Registries in Windows 9x, NT, and 2000 are organized into headkeys, subkeys, and values.

RESET A control bus signal, activated by either a soft or a hard switch, which sets the system microprocessor and all programmable system devices to their startup, or initialization, values. This allows the computer to begin operation following the application of the RESET input signal.

resolution A measurement of the sharpness of an image or character, either of a printer or a display monitor. For a monitor, resolution consists of the number of dots per scan line times the number of scans per picture. For a printer, resolution consists of the number of dots present per linear inch of print space.

ROM (Read Only Memory) A type of semiconductor memory device that holds data on a permanent or nonvolatile basis.

ROM BIOS A collection of special programs (native intelligence) permanently stored in one or two ROM ICs installed on the system board. These programs are available to the system as soon as it is powered up, providing for initialization of smart chips, POST tests, and data transfer control.

root directory The main directory of every logical disk. It follows the FAT tables and serves as the starting point for organizing information on the disk. The location of every directory, subdirectory, and file on the disk is recorded in this directory.

RS-232C The most widely used serial interface standard, it calls for a 25-pin D-type connector. Specific pins are designated for data transmission and receiving, as well as a number of handshaking and control lines. Logic voltage levels are also established for the data and the control signals on the pins of the connector.

RS-422 An enhancement to the original RS-232C interface standard and adopted by the EIA, it uses twisted-pair transmission lines and differential line voltage signals, resulting in higher immunity for the transmitted data.

RS-423 Another enhancement to the original RS-232C interface standard and adopted by the EIA, it uses coaxial cable to provide extended transmission distances and higher data-transfer rates.

S

Safe Mode A special Windows 95/98/2000 startup mode that starts the system by loading minimum configuration drivers. This mode is used to allow the correction of system errors when the system does not boot up normally. Safe Mode is entered by pressing F5 or F8 when the "Starting Windows 9x" message is displayed during bootup.

scan rate The total number of times per second that a video raster is horizontally scanned by the CRT's electron beam.

SCSI (Small Computer System Interface) bus A system-level interface standard used to connect different types of peripheral equipment to the system. The standard actually exists as a group of specifications (SCSI, SCSI-2, and SCSI-3) featuring several cabling connector schemes. Even within these three specifications there can exist major variations—Wide SCSI, Fast SCSI, and Fast/Wide SCSI. Apple was the first personal computer maker to select the SCSI interface as the bus standard for peripheral equipment that can provide high-speed data transfer control for up to seven devices, while occupying only one expansion slot. The standard is gaining more widespread support in the PC market, particularly in the area of portable PCs. See *system-level interface*.

sector One of many individual data-holding areas into which each track of a disk is divided during the format process.

serial interface A channel through which serial digital data transfer occurs. Although multiple lines may be used, only one of these will actually carry the data. The most popular serial interface standard is the EIA RS-232C.

serial mode The mode of data transfer in which the word bits are transferred one bit at a time along a single conductor.

serial mouse A type of mouse that plugs into a serial port rather than an adapter card.

serial port The external connector on a computer that is used to create an interface between the computer and a serial device such as a modem. A typical serial port uses a DB-25 or a DB-9 connector.

servers Powerful network computers (or devices) that contain the network operating system and manage network resources for other computers (clients). Some servers take on special management functions for the network. Some of these functions include print servers, web servers, file servers, database servers, and so on.

setup disks Disks created to restart a failed Windows NT/2000 system. These disks are created by the Windows 2000 Backup utility and contain information about the system's current Windows configuration settings.

shadow RAM An area of RAM used for copying the system's BIOS routines from ROM. Making BIOS calls from the RAM area improves the operating speed of the system. Video ROM routines are often stored in shadow RAM also.

shared resource A system resource (device or directory) that has been identified as being available for use by multiple individuals throughout the network environment.

shares Resources, such as printers and folders, which have been made available for use by other network users.

SIMM (Single In-line Memory Module) A circuit board module containing eight (without parity) or nine (with parity) memory chips, and designed to plug into special sockets.

simplex communications Communications that occur in only one direction. An public address system is an example of simplex communications.

SLIP (Serial Line Internet Protocol) Older units running UNIX employ this Internet connection protocol for dial-up services. The protocol wraps the TCP/IP packet in a shell for transmission through the modem in analog format. The communications equipment, at the service provider's site, converts the signal back to the digital TCP/IP format.

SMARTDRV.EXE (SmartDrive) A DOS driver program that establishes a disk cache in an area of extended memory as a storage space for information read from the hard-disk drive. When a program requests more data, the SMARTDRV program redirects the request to check in the cache memory area to see if the requested data is there.

software Any aspect of the computer operation that cannot be physically touched. This includes bits, bytes, words, and programs.

speaker The computer system's audio output device. Measuring 2-1/4 inches in diameter and rated at 8 ohms, 1/2 watts, the speaker is usually used as a system prompt and as an error indicator. It is also capable of producing arcade sounds, speech, and music.

SRAM (Static Random Access Memory) A type of RAM that can store its data indefinitely as long as power to it is not interrupted.

start bit In asynchronous serial data transmission, this bit denotes the beginning of a character and is always a logic low pulse, or space.

static electricity This is often a serious problem in environments of low humidity. It is a stationary charge of electricity usually caused by friction, and potentially very damaging to sensitive electronic components.

stop bit The bit, sent after each character in an asynchronous data communications transmission, that signals the end of a character.

stop errors Errors that occur when Windows 2000 detects a condition that it cannot recover from. The system stops responding, and a screen of information with a blue or black background is displayed. Stop errors are also known as blue screen errors, or the blue screen of death (BSOD).

subnet mask The decimal number 255 is used to hide, or mask, the network portion of the IP address while still showing the host portions of the address. The default subnet mask for Class A IP addresses is 255.0.0.0. Class B is 255.255.0.0, and Class C is 255.255.255.0.

swap file A special file established on the hard drive to provide virtual memory capabilities for the operating system. Windows 3.x can work with temporary or permanent swap files. Windows 95 uses a dynamically assigned, variable-length swap file.

synchronous transmission A method of serial data transmission in which both the transmitter and the receiver are synchronized by a common clock signal.

SYSEDIT.EXE A special Windows text editor utility that can be used to alter ASCII text files such as CONFIG.SYS, AUTOEXEC.BAT, WIN.INI, and SYSTEM.INI.

system board The large printed circuit board (mother board) into which peripheral adapter boards (daughter boards) may plug into, depending on the number of devices working with the system. The system board is populated with 100 or more IC chips, depending on how much on-board memory is installed. Besides RAM chips, the system board contains the microprocessor, BIOS ROM, several programmable controllers, system clock circuitry, switches, and various jumpers. Also, most system boards come with an empty socket into which the user may plug a compatible co-processor chip to give the computer some high-level number crunching capabilities.

system files Files that possess the system attribute. These are normally hidden files used to boot the operating system.

system-level interface An interface that allows the system to directly access the I/O device through an expansion slot without an intermediate interface circuit. The system is isolated from the peripheral device and only sees its logical configuration.

system partition Normally the same as the boot partition. More precisely, the disk partition that contains the hardware-specific files (Ntldr, Osloader, Boot.ini, and Ntdetect) required to load and start Windows 2000.

system software A class of software dedicated to the control and operation of a computer system and its various peripherals.

system unit The main computer cabinet housing containing the primary components of the system. This includes the main logic board (system or mother board), disk drive(s), switching power supply, and the interconnecting wires and cables.

T

tape drive The unit that reads, writes, and holds the tape being used for backup purposes.

task switching The changing of one program or application to another either manually by the user, or under the direction of a multitasking operating system environment.

TCP/IP (Transfer Control Protocol/Internet Protocol) A collection of protocols developed by the U.S. Department of Defense in the early days of the network that became the Internet. It is the standard transport protocol used by many operating systems and the Internet.

telephony In the computer world, this term refers to hardware and software devices that perform functions typically performed by telephone equipment. Microsoft offers the TAPI interface for both clients and servers. See *Telephony API*.

Telephony API (TAPI) Telephony Application Programming Interface. This software interface provides a universal set of drivers that enable modems and COM ports to control and arbitrate telephony operations for data, faxes, and voice. Through this interface, applications can cooperatively share the dial-up connection functions of the system.

toner A form of powdered ink that accepts an electrical charge in laser printers and photocopying machines. It adheres to a rotating drum containing an image that has been given an opposite charge. The image is transferred to the paper during the printing process.

TRACERT A network troubleshooting utility that displays the route and a hop count taken to a given destination. The route taken to a particular address can be set manually using the ROUTE command. The TRACERT utility traces the route taken by ICMP packets sent across the network. Routers along the path return information to the inquiring system, and the utility displays the host name, IP address, and round trip time for each hop in the path.

track A single disk or tape data storage channel, upon which the R/W head places the digital data in a series of flux reversals. On disks, the track is a concentric data circle, whereas on tapes it is a parallel data line.

track ball (1) A pointing device that allows the user to control the position of the cursor on the video display screen by rotating a sphere (track ball). (2) The sphere inside certain types of mice that the mouse rides on. As the mouse moves across a surface, the trackball rolls, creating X-Y movement data.

tractor feed A paper-feeding mechanism for printers that use continuous forms. The left and right edges of the forms contain holes through which the tractor pins pull the paper through the print area.

transmit Although this term usually means to send data between a transmitter and receiver over a specific communications line, it can also describe the transfer of data within the internal buses of a computer or between the computer and its peripheral devices.

Transport Control Protocol (TCP) TCP is a Transport layer protocol used to establish reliable connections between clients and servers.

trees In Active Directory, a collection of objects that share the same DNS name. All of the domains in a tree share a common security context and global catalog.

Troubleshooters A special type of Help utilities available in Windows 9x and 2000. These utilities enable the user to pinpoint problems and identify solutions to those problems by asking a series of questions and then providing detailed troubleshooting information based on the user's responses.

U

UART (Universal Asynchronous Receiver Transmitter) A serial interface IC used to provide for the parallel-to-serial and serial-to-parallel conversions required for asynchronous serial data transmission. It also handles the parallel interface to the computer's bus, as well as the control functions associated with the transmission.

Ultra DMA A burst mode DMA data transfer protocol, used with Ultra ATA IDE devices to support data transfer rates of 33.3 MBps. While the official name of the protocol is Ultra DMA/33, it is also referred to as UDMA, UDMA/33, and DMA mode 33.

Ultra SCSI A series of advanced SCSI specifications that include: (1) Ultra SCSI, which employs an 8-bit bus and supports data rates of 20 MBps; (2) SCSI-3 (also referred to as Wide Ultra SCSI) that widens the bus to 16-bits and supports data rates of 40 MBps; (3) Ultra2 SCSI that uses an 8-bit bus and supports data rates of 40 MBps; and (4) Wide Ultra2 SCSI that supports data rates of 80 MBps across a 16-bit bus.

Uninterruptible Power Supply (UPS) A special power supply unit that includes a battery to maintain power to key equipment in the event of a power failure. A typical UPS is designed to keep a computer operational after a power failure long enough for the user to save their current work and properly shut down the system. Many UPSs include software that provides automatic backup and shutdown procedures when the UPS senses a power problem.

Universal Naming Convention (UNC) A standardized method of specifying a path to a network computer or a device (i.e., \\computername\sharename).

Universal Serial Bus (USB) A specification for a high-speed, serial communication bus that can be used to link various peripheral devices to the system. The standard permits up to 127 USB-compliant devices to be connected to the system in a daisy-chained, or tiered-star configuration.

Upgrading The process of replacing an older piece of hardware or software with a newer version of that hardware or software. Upgrading also serves as an interim solution for bugs discovered in software.

Upper Memory Area (UMA) The area in the DOS memory map between 640 kB and 1 MB. This memory area was referred to as the Reserved Memory Area in older PC and PC-XT systems. It typically contains the EMS Page Frame, as well as any ROM extensions and video display circuitry.

Upper Memory Blocks (UMBs) Special 16 kB blocks of memory established in the upper memory area between the 640 kB and 1 MB marks.

URL (Universal Resource Locator) A unique address on the World Wide Web used to access a web site.

USART (Universal Synchronous Asynchronous Receiver Transmitter) A serial interface IC used to provide for the parallel-to-serial and serial-to-parallel conversions required for both asynchronous and synchronous serial data transmission. It also handles the parallel interface to the computer's bus, as well as the control functions associated with the transmission.

user name The public portion of the user login name that identifies permissions and rights to network resources.

user profiles User profiles are records that permit each user that logs on to a computer to have a unique set of properties associated with them, such as particular desktop or Start menu configurations. In Windows 2000, user profiles are stored in C:\Documents and Settings by default. User profiles are local, meaning that they reside only on that computer. Therefore, users may have different profiles created and stored for them on each computer they log on to.

utility program A term used to describe a program designed to help the user in the operation of the computer.

V

VESA (Video Electronics Standards Association) bus A 64-bit local bus standard developed to provide a local bus connection to a video adapter. Its operation has been defined for use by other adapter types, such as drive controllers, network interfaces, and other hardware.

VGA (Video Graphics Array) Another video standard, developed by IBM, providing medium and high text and graphics resolution. It was originally designed for IBM's high-end PS/2 line, but other vendors have created matching boards for PC and AT machines also, making it the preferred standard at this time. Requiring an analog monitor, it originally provided 16 colors at 640x480 resolution. Third-party vendors have boosted that capability to 256 colors, while adding an even greater 800x600 resolution, calling it Super VGA.

video adapter Sometimes referred to as a display adapter, graphics adapter, or graphics card, it is a plug-in peripheral unit for computers, fitting in one of the system board option slots, and providing the interface between the computer and the display. The adapter usually must match the type of display (digital or analog) it is used with.

View menu A Windows 2000 dialog box drop-down menu that enables the user to toggle screen displays between Large and Small Icons, Details, and Thumbnail views. The dialog boxes can be resized to accommodate as many Thumbnail images as desired.

virtual disk A method of using RAM as if it were a disk.

virtual memory A memory technique that allows several programs to run simultaneously, even though the system does not have enough actual memory installed to do this. The extra memory is simulated using disk space.

Virtual Memory Manager (VMM) The section of the Windows 9x, NT, and 2000 structure that assigns unique memory spaces to every active 32-bit and 16-bit DOS/Windows 3.x application. The VMM works with the environmental subsystems of the User mode to establish special environments for 16-bit applications to run in.

Virtual Private Network (VPN) Virtual Private Networks use message encryption and other security techniques to ensure that only authorized users can access the message as it passes through public transmission media. In particular, VPNs provide secure Internet communications by establishing encrypted data tunnels across the WAN that cannot be penetrated by others.

virus A destructive program designed to replicate itself on any machine that it comes into contact with. Viruses are spread from machine to machine by attaching themselves to (infecting) other files.

VLSI (Very Large-Scale Integration) IC devices containing a very large number of electronic components (from 100,000 to approximately 1,000,000).

volatile memory Memory (RAM) that loses its content as soon as power is discontinued.

volumes Portions of disks signified by single drive designators. In the Microsoft environment, a volume corresponds to a partition.

VOM (Volt Ohm Milliammeter) A basic piece of electronic troubleshooting equipment that provides for circuit measurements of voltage, current, and resistance in logarithmic analog readout form.

W

warm boot Booting a computer that has already been powered up. This can be accomplished by pressing the Reset switch on the front of most computers, or by selecting one of the Restart options from the Windows Exit options dialog box.

web site A location on the World Wide Web. Web sites typically contain a home page that is displayed first when the site is accessed. They usually contain other pages and programs that can be accessed through the home page.

wild cards Characters, such as * or ?, used to represent letters or words. Such characters are typically used to perform operations with multiple files.

Windows A graphical user interface from Microsoft. It uses a graphical display to represent procedures and programs that can be executed by the computer. Multiple programs can run at the same time.

Windows Explorer The Windows 95, Windows 98, and Windows NT/2000 utility that graphically displays the system as drives, folders, and files in a hierarchical tree structure. This enables the user to manipulate all of the system's software using a mouse.

WINNT32 WINNT32.EXE or WINNT.EXE are the programs that can be run to initiate the installation of Windows 2000. The WINNT32.EXE program is designed to run under a 32-bit operating system and will not run from the command line. The WINNT.EXE program is designed to run under a 16-bit operating system and will not run from within a 32-bit operating system such as Windows NT.

WINS A Microsoft-specific naming service that can be used to assign IP addresses to computer domain names within a LAN environment. The LAN must include a Windows NT name server running the WINS server software that maintains the IP address/domain name database for the LAN. Each client in the LAN must contain the WINS client software and be WINS enabled.

wizards Special Windows routines designed to lead users through installation or setup operations using a menu style of selecting options. The wizards carry out these tasks in the proper sequence, requesting information from the user at key points in the process.

word The amount of data that can be held in a computer's registers during a process. It is considered to be the computer's basic storage unit.

workgroups A network control scenario in which all of the nodes may act as servers for some processes and clients for others. In a workgroup environment, each machine maintains its own security and administration databases.

X

x-axis (1) In a two-dimensional matrix, the horizontal row/rows, such as on an oscilloscope screen. (2) The dimension of width in a graphics representation.

Xmodem A very early, and simple, asynchronous data communications protocol developed for personal computers that is capable of detecting some transfer errors, but not all.

Xon-Xoff An asynchronous data communications protocol that provides for synchronization between the receiver and transmitter, requiring the receiver to indicate its ability to accept data by sending either an Xon (transmit on-buffer ready) or Xoff (transmit off-buffer full) signal to the transmitter.

x-y matrix Any two-dimensional form or image, where *x* represents width and *y* represents height.

Y

y-axis (1) In a two-dimensional matrix, the vertical column/columns, such as on an oscilloscope screen. (2) The dimension of height in a graphics representation.

Ymodem An improvement of the Xmodem protocol that increases the data block size from 128 bytes to 1024 bytes. An offshoot known as Ymodem Batch includes filenames in the transmission so that multiple files can be sent in a single transmission. Another variation, labeled Ymodem G, modified the normal Ymodem flow control method to speed up transmissions.

Z

Zmodem This dial-up protocol can be used to transmit both text and binary files (such as .EXE files) across telephone lines (but not the Internet). It employs advanced error checking/correcting schemes and provides Autofile Restart crash recovery techniques.

INDEX

Network+ Certification

Network+ is a CompTIA vendor-neutral certification that measures the technical knowledge of networking professionals with 18-24 months of experience in the IT industry. The test is administered by NCS/VUE and PrometricTM. Discount exam vouchers can be purchased from Marcraft. Earning the Network+ certification indicates that the candidate possesses the knowledge needed to configure and install the TCP/IP client. This exam covers a wide range of vendor and product neutral networking technologies that can also serve as a prerequisite for vendor-specific IT certifications. Network+ has been accepted by the leading networking vendors and included in many of their training curricula. The skills and knowledge measured by the certification examination are derived from industry-wide job task analyses and validated through an industry wide survey. The objectives for the certification examination are divided in two distinct groups, Knowledge of Networking Technology and Knowledge of Networking Practices.

CompTIA seal of approval

i-Net+ Certification

The i-Net+ certification program is designed specifically for any individual interested in demonstrating baseline technical knowledge that would allow him or her to pursue a variety of Internet-related careers. i-Net+ is a vendor-neutral, entry-level Internet certification program that tests baseline technical knowledge of Internet, Intranet, and Extranet technologies, independent of specific Internet-related career roles. Learning objectives and domains examined include: Internet basics, Internet clients, development, networking, security, and business concepts. Certification not only helps individuals enter the Internet industry, but also helps managers determine a prospective employee's knowledge and skill level.

CompTIA seal of approval

The Complete Data Cabling Installers Certification provides the IT industry with an introductory, vendor-neutral certification for skilled personnel that install Category 5 copper data cabling. The Marcraft Complete Data Cabling Installers Certification Training Guide provides students with the knowledge and skills required to pass the Data Cabling Installers Certification exam and become a certified cable installer. The DCIC is recognized nationwide and is the hiring criterion used by major communication companies. Therefore, becoming a certified data cable installer will enhance your job opportunities and career advancement potential.

Server+ Certification

The Server+ certification deals with advanced hardware issues such as RAID, SCSI, multiple CPUs, SANs, and more. This certification is vendor-neutral with a broad range of support, including core support by 3Com, Adaptec, Compaq, Hewlett-Packard, IBM, Intel, EDS Innovations Canada, Innovative Productivity, and Marcraft. This book focuses on complex activities and solving complex problems to ensure servers are functional and applications are available. It provides an in-depth understanding of installing, configuring, and maintaining servers, including knowledge of server-level hardware implementations, data storage subsystems, data recovery, and I/O subsystems.

Fiber Cabling Installers Certification prepares technicians for the growing demand for qualified cable installers who understand and can implement fiber-optic technologies. These technologies cover terminology, techniques, tools, and other products in the fiber-optic industry. This text/lab book covers the basics of fiber-optic design, installations, pulling and prepping cables, terminations, testing, and safety considerations. Labs will cover ST-compatible and SC connector types, both multi- and single-mode cables and connectors. Learn about insertion loss, optical time domain reflectometry, and reflectance. This text covers mechanical and fusion splices and troubleshooting cable systems. This text/lab covers the theory and hands-on skills needed to prepare you for fiber-optic entry-level certification.

Wireless Networking Certification technology is one of the hottest technologies available today, used in electronic devices, such as cell phones and Personal Digital Assistants (PDA), to enable access to e-mail and the Internet. Wireless technology is also utilized in wireless Local Area Networks (LANs). With Marcraft's Wireless Networking Certification, you learn the entire process of designing, building, configuring, and managing a wireless network. This text combines in one place everything needed to successfully design, install, and troubleshoot a simple wireless solution. Keep on the cutting edge of wireless with Marcraft.

Home Technology Integrator+ (HTI+) is an exciting new certification by CompTIA in partnership with Internet Home Alliance (IHA). The HTI+ Certification fills the niche for home technicians as technology in the home environment continues to grow. There is an increasing demand for skilled technicians to install, integrate, and troubleshoot various home sub-systems. This enables consumers to take advantage of and fully enjoy the "Connected Home" sub-systems, such as; home security and surveillance, audio/video, computer networks, control processors, electrical wiring (low andhigh voltage), heating and air conditioning, cable/satellite, access entry control, broadband, telecommunications, systems infrastructure and integration, lighting management, user interface, water control, and commercial wiring. The course is broken into two major certification exam areas, Residential Systems and Systems Infrastructure.

The Complete Introductory Computer Course is an entry level course. It prepares students for the more challenging A+ Certification course. It also provides a careerport™ into the fast-growing IT industry. The MC-2300 is a 45-hour, easy-to-understand exploration of basic computer hardware, software, and troubleshooting. This course helps build students' confidence and basic computer literacy. The fully-illustrated 198-page Theory Text/Lab Guide provides an easy-to understand exploration of the basics of computers: basic computer architecture and operation, step-by-step computer hardware assembly, computer hardware and functions, common software packages, consumer maintenance practices, and troubleshooting a "sick" computer. The reusable MC-2300 Intro Computer Trainer comes with all the necessary hardware, software, and tools to perform over 30 hands-on Lab Explorations.

The Complete Introductory Networking Course is a superbly illustrated theory text and lab guide all in one. It not only provides a great way for students to explore over 45 hours of easy-to-understand basic networking topics, but also develops job skills for starting them on the path towards a new high-tech career!
This manual guides you through such activities as: installation and configuration of local area network hardware, peer-to-peer networking functions, sharing computer resources, mapping to remote resources, and consumer-level network troubleshooting. The Complete Introductory Networking Course provides an excellent starting point for IT Certification including Microsoft's MCSE, Novell's CNA, and Cisco's CCNA.

The Complete Introductory Internet Course takes advantage of the growing demand for qualified Internet technicians. This 45-hour course explores easy-to-understand basic Internet topics and helps develop Internet skills.
This manual guides you through such activities as: configuring e-mail accounts, designing a basic HTML page, setup of a basic firewall for security, and establishing Internet connection slaving. The Complete Introductory Internet Course provides an excellent starting point for IT Certification including CompTIA's i-NET+ and Prosoft's Certified Internet Webmaster (CIW).